Methods in Molecular Biology™

Series Editor
John M. Walker
School of Life Sciences
University of Hertfordshire
Hatfield, Hertfordshire, AL10 9AB, UK

For other titles published in this series, go to
www.springer.com/series/7651

Macrophages and Dendritic Cells

Methods and Protocols

Edited by

Neil E. Reiner

Department of Medicine, Division of Infectious Diseases, Faculties of Medicine and Science, University of British Columbia and Vancouver Coastal Health Research Institute (VCHRI), Vancouver, BC, Canada

Humana Press

Editor
Neil E. Reiner
Department of Medicine
Division of Infectious Diseases
Faculties of Medicine and Science
University of British Columbia
and Vancouver Coastal Health
Research Institute (VCHRI)
Vancouver, BC
Canada

ISSN: 1064-3745 e-ISSN: 1940-6029
ISBN: 978-1-58829-972-7 e-ISBN: 978-1-59745-396-7
DOI: 10.1007/978-1-59745-396-7

Library of Congress Control Number: 2008942272

Printed on acid-free paper

springer.com

Preface

In the face of frequent threats of either exogenous (usually infection) or endogenous (neoplastic transformation) origin, humans and other mammals are endowed with a vigorous and versatile capacity for host defense. This contributes to the maintenance of homeostasis and in the face of millions of years of evolutionary pressure, mammalian species developed two parallel yet highly interdependent systems to protect against infection and malignancy. Thus, the innate and acquired immune systems together perform remarkably well in responding to threats, thereby favoring survival. Not only are these two systems seamlessly integrated, but they also both support and cross-regulate each other at multiple levels. Hence, knowledge of the critical nodes that unite these systems is fundamental to a comprehensive understanding of mammalian host defense. Macrophages and dendritic cells are sentinels and effectors of innate immunity. Far beyond this, however, they are also perhaps more than any other cell type, poised at the interface with the acquired immune system where they critically influence the development of antigen-specific immune responses and long-term memory. The involvement of macrophages and dendritic cells in health and disease is not, however, limited to the realm of classical immunology. Research findings over the past several decades have made it abundantly clear that these cells are also centrally involved in heterogeneous inflammatory conditions and disease processes such as atherosclerosis, neurodegenerative disease, wound healing, and graft-versus-host disease to name only a few. In light of their critical contributions to diverse inflammatory diseases and to immunity and host defense, a contemporaneous understanding of state-of-the-art approaches to investigate the behaviors of macrophages and dendritic cells is useful, and is something this volume seeks to achieve.

An essential starting point to any research concerned with the properties or functions of macrophages and dendritic cells is the availability of adequate numbers of cells representing a highly purified homogeneous population. As such, four chapters are presented that address the isolation and cultures of these cells, including generating growth factor-dependent cell lines, methods for phenotypic characterization, and analysis of ontogeny.

Much of the work of macrophages and dendritic cells is initiated at the level of cell surface receptors that survey the environment for cognate ligands. Recognizing the centrality of receptor ligand interactions to the biology of these cells, two chapters are included that address the identification of novel myeloid cell surface receptors, while two complementary chapters describe approaches aimed at identifying novel ligands.

Phagocytosis is one of the most prominent functional properties of macrophages and to a lesser extent dendritic cells. Consequently, no contemporary volume of research approaches would be complete without addressing this area. Just as whole cell analysis is simplified when adequate quantities of pure starting material are available, this is also one of the challenges facing researchers studying phagosome biology. Furthermore, one of the areas of greatest interest to macrophage biologists is the fate of a phagosome once it is formed or "phagosome maturation." Consequently, chapters are included that address topics including large-scale phagosome isolation, quantitative and real-time analysis of phagosome maturation, and the role of GTPases in regulating phagosome biogenesis.

Macrophages and dendritic cells are inherently resistant to the introduction and expression of foreign genes. This has consistently been a significant obstacle confronting researchers whose aim has been to assign function to individual genes and the proteins they encode. This volume takes advantage of recent advances in the area of genetic manipulation of macrophages and dendritic cells with three chapters addressing this area with a particular emphasis on siRNA approaches.

Macrophages are required to undergo an activation program in order to maximize their effector functions and macrophage activation is an area of intense interest. Controlling cell activation is also critically important to limiting collateral damage resulting from excessive inflammation. In recent years, it has become clear that macrophage activation is not a homogeneous process and that the phenotypic outcome is very much influenced by the local environment, most importantly cytokines, but other factors as well. Currently, two major macrophage activation programs have been described leading to the generation of either M1, proinflammatory, or M2 anti-inflammatory macrophages. Given the importance of this rapidly advancing area of research, three chapters in this volume address the M1 vs. M2 or "classical vs. alternative" paradigm of macrophage activation.

Macrophage activation and for that matter all other stimulus-dependent responses by these cells are brought about through tightly regulated and highly integrated signaling pathways. Cell regulation in these cells has been studied intensively and recently it has become clear that lipid signaling plays an important role in determining phenotype. As such, two chapters address the role of lipid signaling and lipid signaling intermediates in macrophage biology.

Finally, macrophages are endowed with a vast array of degradative enzymes that they use to carry out functional programs and which contribute profoundly to both health and disease. A chapter dealing with the secretion of matrix metalloproteinases by macrophages provides a window into advances in this area and offers a vantage point for future research concerned with how the enzymatic machinery of these cells is linked to tissue inflammation.

It is my hope that readers, both neophytes and seasoned investigators, will find *Macrophages and Dendritic Cells: Methods and Protocols* to be both timely and useful in their research. Most importantly, I thank the authors for valuable time spent in preparing their chapters and for sharing their experience and knowledge. Thanks is also due to John Walker for his editorial advice and Jessica Lin for her critical editorial assistance.

Vancouver, BC ***Neil E. Reiner***

Contents

Contributors

BERENICE ARENDSE • *Institute for Infectious Diseases and Molecular Medicine and Division of Immunology, Health Science Faculty, University of Cape Town, Cape Town, South Africa*

CHRISTIAN BOGDAN • *Institute of Clinical Microbiology, Immunology and Hygiene, University Clinic of Erlangen, Erlangen, Germany*

FRANK BROMBACHER • *Institute for Infectious Diseases and Molecular Medicine and Division of Immunology, Health Science Faculty, University of Cape Town, Cape Town, South Africa*

GORDON D. BROWN • *Institute for Infectious Diseases and Molecular Medicine, Faculty of Health Sciences, University of Cape Town, Cape Town, South Africa*

CECILIA BUCCI • *Dipartimento di Scienze e Tecnologie Biologiche ed Ambientali, Universita degli Studi di Lecce, Lecce, Italy*

ANTONIO CELADA • *Macrophage Biology Group, Institute for Research in Biomedicine, University of Barcelona, Barcelona, Spain*

MAURIZIO CEPPI • *Centre d'Immunologie de Marseille-Luminy, Université de la Méditerranée, Case 906, 13288 Marseille cedex 9, France; INSERM, U631, 13288 Marseille, France; and CNRS, UMR6102, 13288 Marseille, France*

GIN-WEN CHANG • *Sir William Dunn School of Pathology, University of Oxford, Oxford, UK*

STEFANIA CITTERIO • *Department of Biotechnology and Biosciences, University of Milano-Bicocca, Milano, Italy*

ANDREA CLASSEN • *Macrophage Biology Group, Institute for Research in Biomedicine, University of Barcelona, Barcelona, Spain*

ALA-EDDINE DEGHMANE • *Division of Infectious Diseases, Department of Medicine, University of British Columbia and Vancouver Coastal Health Institute, Vancouver, BC, Canada*

MAREIN A.W.P. DE JONG • *Department of Molecular Cell Biology and Immunology, VU University Medical Centre, Amsterdam, The Netherlands*

JEROEN DEN DUNNEN • *Department of Molecular Cell Biology and Immunology, VU University Medical Centre, Amsterdam, The Netherlands*

ALBERT DESCOTEAUX • *INRS-Institut Armand-Frappier, Laval, QC, Canada*

LOT DE WITTE • *Department of Molecular Cell Biology and Immunology, VU University Medical Centre, Amsterdam, The Netherlands*

GREGORY P. DOWNEY • *Departments of Medicine and Pediatrics, and Department of Medicine, National Jewish Medical and Research Centre, and Department of Medicine and Integrated Department of Immunology, University of Colorado Denver Health Sciences Centre, Denver, CO, USA*

JUSTIN P. EDWARDS • *Department of Cell Biology and Molecular Genetics, University of Maryland, College Park, MD, USA*

PAUL T. ELKINGTON • *Department of Infectious Diseases & Immunity, Imperial College London, Hammersmith Campus, London, UK*
MARIA FOTI • *Department of Biotechnology and Biosciences, University of Milano-Bicocca, Milano, Italy*
JON S. FRIEDLAND • *Department of Infectious Diseases & Immunity, Imperial College London, Hammersmith Campus, London, UK*
TEUNIS B.H. GEIJTENBEEK • *Department of Molecular Cell Biology and Immunology, VU University Medical Centre, Amsterdam, The Netherlands*
SIAMON GORDON • *GlaxoWellcome Professor of Cellular Pathology, Sir William Dunn School of Pathology, University of Oxford, Oxford, UK*
FRANCESCA GRANUCCI • *Department of Biotechnology and Biosciences, University of Milano-Bicocca, Milano, Italy*
JUSTIN A. GREEN • *Department of Infectious Diseases & Immunity, Imperial College London, Hammersmith Campus, London, UK*
SERGIO GRINSTEIN • *Cell Biology Program, Hospital for Sick Children, Toronto, ON, Canada; Institute of Medical Science and Department of Biochemistry, University of Toronto, Toronto, ON, Canada*
ALBIN HERMETTER • *Institute of Biochemistry, Graz University of Technology, Graz, Austria*
ZAKARIA HMAMA • *Division of Infectious Diseases, Department of Medicine, University of British Columbia and Vancouver Coastal Health Institute, Vancouver, BC, Canada*
VICTOR W.H. HO • *The Terry Fox Laboratory, BC Cancer Research Centre, Vancouver, BC, Canada*
ALEXANDRA HÖLSCHER • *Division of Infection Immunology, Research Centre Borstel, Borstel, Germany*
CHRISTOPH HÖLSCHER • *Division of Infection Immunology, Research Centre Borstel, Borstel, Germany*
CHENG-CHIH HSIAO • *Department of Microbiology and Immunology, Chang Gung University, Tao-Yuan, Taiwan*
YI-SHU HUANG • *Department of Microbiology and Immunology, Chang Gung University, Tao-Yuan, Taiwan*
SHANKAR S. IYER • *Physiology and Biophysics, and the Graduate Programs in Immunology and Molecular Biology, University of Iowa Carver College of Medicine and Iowa City Veterans Affairs Medical Centre, Iowa City, IA, USA*
STEFFEN JUNG • *Department of Immunology, The Weizmann Institute of Science, Rehovot, Israel*
DAVID J. KUSNER • *Inflammation Program, Division of Infectious Diseases, Department of Internal Medicine, University of Iowa Carver College of Medicine and Iowa City Veterans Affairs Medical Centre, Iowa City, IA, USA*
VIVIAN KWOK • *Division of Respirology, Department of Medicine, University of Toronto and Toronto General Hospital Research Institute of the University Health Network, Toronto, ON, Canada*
LIMOR LANDSMAN • *Department of Immunology, The Weizmann Institute of Science, Rehovot, Israel*

JIMMY S. LEE • *Department of Radiology, Hospital of the University of Pennsylvania, Philadelphia, PA, USA*

HSI-HSIEN LIN • *Department of Microbiology and Immunology, Chang Gung University, Tao-Yuan, Taiwan*

JORGE LLOBERAS • *Macrophage Biology Group, Institute for Research in Biomedicine, University of Barcelona, Barcelona, Spain*

LUISA MARTINEZ-POMARES • *Institute of Infection, Immunity and Inflammation, School of Molecular Medical Sciences, University of Nottingham, Queen's Medical Centre, Nottingham, UK*

ALESSANDRA MORTELLARO • *Singapore Immunology Network (SIgA), Agency for Science, Technology and Research (A*STAR), Singapore*

DAVID M. MOSSER • *Department of Cell Biology and Molecular Genetics, University of Maryland, College Park, MD, USA*

REAGON PETERSON • *Institute for Infectious Diseases and Molecular Medicine and Division of Immunology, Health Science Faculty, University of Cape Town, Cape Town, South Africa*

PHILIPPE PIERRE • *Centre d'Immunologie de Marseille-Luminy, Université de la Méditerranée, Case 906, 13288 Marseille cedex 9, France; INSERM, U631, 13288 Marseille, France; and CNRS, UMR6102, 13288 Marseille, France*

NEIL E. REINER • *Department of Medicine, Division of Infectious Diseases, Faculties of Medicine and Science, University of British Columbia, and Vancouver Coastal Health Research Institute (VCHRI), Vancouver, BC, Canada*

PAOLA RICCIARDI-CASTAGNOLI • *Singapore Immunology Network (SIgA), Agency for Science, Technology and Research (A*STAR), Singapore*

DAVID G. RUSSELL • *Department of Microbiology and Immunology, College of Veterinary Medicine, Cornell University, Ithaca, NY, USA*

GEORGIA SCHÄFER • *Institute for Infectious Diseases and Molecular Medicine, Faculty of Health Sciences, University of Cape Town, Cape Town, South Africa*

ULRIKE SCHLEICHER • *Institute of Clinical Microbiology, Immunology and Hygiene, University Clinic of Erlangen, Erlangen, Germany*

ENRICO SCHMIDT • *Centre d'Immunologie de Marseille-Luminy, Université de la Méditerranée, Case 906, 13288 Marseille cedex 9, France; INSERM, U631, 13288 Marseille, France; and CNRS, UMR6102, 13288 Marseille, France*

LAURA M. SLY • *The Terry Fox Laboratory, BC Cancer Research Centre, Vancouver, BC, Canada*

MARTIN STACEY • *Sir William Dunn School of Pathology, University of Oxford, Oxford, UK*

BENJAMIN E. STEINBERG • *Cell Biology Program, Hospital for Sick Children, Toronto, ON, Canada*

Institute of Medical Science and Department of Biochemistry, University of Toronto, Toronto, ON, Canada

JIM SUN • *Division of Infectious Diseases, Department of Medicine, University of British Columbia and Vancouver Coastal Health Institute, Vancouver, BC, Canada*

MATTIAS SVENSSON • *Centre for Infectious Medicine, Department of Medicine, Karolinska Institutet, Karolinska University Hospital, Huddinge, Stockholm, Sweden*

MATTEO URBANO • *Department of Biotechnology and Biosciences, University of Milano-Bicocca, Milano, Italy*
ERIC VACHON • *Division of Respirology, Department of Medicine, University of Toronto and Toronto General Hospital Research Institute of the University Health Network, Toronto, ON, Canada*
YVETTE VAN KOOYK • *Department of Molecular Cell Biology and Immunology, VU University Medical Centre, Amsterdam, The Netherlands*
CHEN VAROL • *Department of Immunology, The Weizmann Institute of Science, Rehovot, Israel*
ADRIEN F. VINET • *INRS-Institut Armand-Frappier, Laval, QC, Canada*
ROBIN M. YATES • *Department of Microbiology and Immunology, College of Veterinary Medicine, Cornell University, Ithaca, NY, USA*
XIA ZHANG • *Department of Cell Biology and Molecular Genetics, University of Maryland, College Park, MD, USA*

Chapter 1

Generation of Retroviral Macrophage cDNA Expression Libraries and Functional Screening for Surface Receptors

Georgia Schäfer and Gordon D. Brown

Summary

Macrophages, tissue-based phagocytic cells derived from blood monocytes, play important roles in immunity and homeostasis. As professional scavengers, macrophages phagocytose microbes, apoptotic and necrotic cells and take up modified lipoprotein particles. However, many of their complex interactions with other immune cells and/or various ligands are not yet clearly understood. To identify and isolate macrophage cell surface molecules, particularly macrophage receptors, for which ligands are known, a powerful generalized screening method has been established. As discussed in this chapter, this technique based on function has been successfully applied for the identification of dectin-1, the major macrophage receptor involved in the binding and recognition of β-glucans (Nature 413:36–37, 2001).

Key words: cDNA expression cloning, Retroviral cDNA expression library, Functional screening, Surface molecule, Ligand binding, Receptor cloning, Stable transfection, Fluorescent microscopy.

1. Introduction

Cell surface molecules are important for macrophage cell functions. These molecules may be receptors for microorganisms, co-receptors for signal transduction modulating cell response to various stimuli, complement regulatory proteins, or adhesion molecules crucial in cell–cell and cell–matrix interactions *(1)*. Our laboratory mainly focuses on macrophage surface receptors which mediate innate immune recognition as the first and immediate line of defence against microbial invasion. These so-called pattern recognition receptors (PRR) are germ-lined encoded and

Neil E. Reiner (ed.), *Macrophages and Dendritic Cells,* Methods in Molecular Biology, vol. 531

DOI: 10.1007/978-1-59745-396-7_1

recognize highly conserved molecular patterns (PAMPS, pathogen-associated molecular patterns) found only in microorganisms. This is in contrast to the slower but more specific adaptive immune system which uses somatically re-arranged antigen receptors clonally distributed on lymphocytes *(2, 3)*. The recognition of PAMPs by their receptors can directly activate effector mechanisms of innate immunity such as phagocytosis and activation of pro-inflammatory pathways. With the subsequent production of effector cytokines and chemokines and presentation of pathogen-derived peptides on the surface of antigen-presenting cells, the innate immune system is directly linked to the adaptive immune system *(4–6)*. Therefore, activated PRRs determine the type of cellular and immunological response mounted by the host, influencing the outcome of infection.

Although a number of phagocyte receptors have been shown to act as PRRs, their initial identification was for other functions. The mannose receptor, for example, was identified by its ability to bind endogenous self-ligands *(7)*, while CD14 was identified by monoclonal antibodies to human peripheral blood monocytes *(8)*. As no concerted effort had been made to identify these molecules directly, and given their importance in the immune response to infection, a generalized method based on cDNA expression cloning and relying on the inherent ability of PRRs to recognize pathogens was established to isolate these receptors from leucocytes based on their function *(9)*.

cDNA expression cloning using retroviral gene transfer is a powerful method for the isolation and identification of expressed genes that are able to confer a readily identifiable phenotype on specific cell types. Essentially, this method involves the directional cloning of cDNA into a retroviral vector and the generation of pools of stable ecotropic virus-producing cells from this DNA. The cells so derived constitute the library, and the virus they yield can be used to efficiently infect a wide range of cell types, with the foreign DNA stably inserted into the genome, for subsequent functional screening for surface receptors using known ligands *(10)*.

Using this technique, a single receptor that bound to the β-glucan-[1] rich particle zymosan has been isolated from a macrophage cDNA expression library and identified as a previously known molecule, Dectin-1 *(9)*. Further studies involved extensive molecular and functional characterization of this molecule *(11–15)*. The rediscovery of Dectin-1, through its ability to bind β-glucans, demonstrates the power of this screening method to identify receptors based on function. This method can be utilized for the identification for any macrophage cell surface molecule for which a ligand is known, for example receptors involved in host-pathogen interactions using live microorganisms.

[1] Glucose polymers found in the cell walls of plants, fungi and bacteria.

2. Materials

2.1. Cell Culture, Transfection, and Transduction

1. $DMEM_{10}$ (Dulbecco's Modified Eagle's Medium) supplemented with 10% heat-inactivated foetal calf serum (delta bioproducts), 2 mM l-glutamine, 500 U/ml penicillin, and 50 µg/ml streptomycin.
2. $DMEM_0$ (*see* **item 1**, but without serum).
3. Lidocaine hydrochloride dissolved in PBS at 4 mg/ml, supplemented with 10 mM EDTA.
4. G418 at 100 mg/ml; store at 4°C, use at 0.4 mg/ml in $DMEM_{10}$.
5. Hygromycin B at 100 mg/ml; store at 4°C, use at 300 µg/ml in $DMEM_{10}$.
6. Diphtheria toxin at 1 mg/ml; store at 4°C, use at 1 µg/ml in $DMEM_{10}$.
7. FuGENE 6 transfection reagent.
8. 10 mg/ml polybrene.
9. 0.45-µm sterile filters.

2.2 Generation, Expression, and Screening of the Library

1. Trizol® reagent (Invitrogen) for RNA isolation.
2. OligoTEX mRNA Kit (Qiagen).
3. *Denaturing formaldehyde/agarose gel for RNA*. Melt 1 g agarose in 85 ml deionized water, add 10 ml 10× MOPS buffer (0.2 M MOPS; 0.05 M sodium acetate; 0.01 M EDTA, pH 5.5–7.0) and 5.4 ml 37% formaldehyde (caution: formaldehyde is a carcinogen and must be handled with care inside a fume hood). Once the gel is solidified cover with 1× MOPS buffer and load RNA samples resuspended in 2× loading buffer: 50% deionized formamide; 13% formaldehyde; 1× MOPS buffer; 1.5% ethidium bromide; 2% sterile glycerol; 0.5% bromophenol blue (the loading buffer is not stable and should not be used more than 12 h after preparation). Electrophorese the gel at 100 V for approximately 1 h and examine under UV illumination.
4. *Agarose/ethidium bromide gels for DNA*. Melt 1 g agarose in 100 ml 0.5× TBE-buffer (50 mM Tris, 50 mM borate, 1 mM EDTA) and add 3% ethidium bromide. Once the gel is solidified cover with 0.5× TBE-buffer and load DNA samples resuspended in 6× loading buffer. Electrophorese the gel at 100 V for approximately 1 h and examine under UV illumination.
5. Creator™ SMART™ cDNA Library Construction Kit (Clontech).
6. Advantage® 2 PCR Kit (Clontech).

7. *Electroporation system.* Bio-Rad Gene Pulser II.
8. *E .cloni*® 10G SUPREME Electrocompetent Cells (Lucigen® Corporation).
9. *Luria Bertani (LB) broth.* 1% NaCl, 1% bactotrypton, 0.5% yeast extract, pH 7.0, 100 μg/ml ampicillin added after autoclaving and stored at 4°C.
10. *Luria Bertani (LB) agar plates (150 mm and 100 mm).* 1% NaCl, 1% bactotrypton, 0.5% yeast extract, 1.5% agar; pH 7.0, 100 μg/ml ampicillin added after autoclaving when still liquid, poured into plates, and stored at 4°C.
11. PureYield™ Plasmid Midiprep system (Promega).
12. Wizard® Plus SV Miniprep system (Promega).
13. 2× PCR-Mastermix (Fermentas).

2.3. Isolation of Positive Cells

1. Dow Corning High Vacuum Grease.
2. Cloning cylinders, sterile, polystyrene, size: 4.7 mm × 8 mm (Sigma).
3. FITC-labelled zymosan (Molecular Probes).
4. QIAamp® DNA Mini Kit (Qiagen).
5. Advantage® 2 PCR Kit (Clontech).
6. TOPO TA Cloning® Kit for Sequencing (Invitrogen).
7. Wizard® SV Gel and PCR Clean-Up System (Promega).
8. pcDNA™ 3.1 Directional TOPO® Expression Kit (Invitrogen).

3. Methods

3.1. Generation of the Library

The construction of the retroviral cDNA expression library essentially involves the isolation of RNA from macrophages, its reverse transcription into cDNA, and ligation into a suitable vector which allows for subsequent virus production, as discussed in detail in the following.

1. Total RNA from macrophages grown in culture or freshly isolated from the organism/tissue of interest is prepared using the Trizol® reagent (Invitrogen) according to the manufacturer's instruction. This preparation method has been shown to yield high amounts of RNA though it can still contain traces of phenol. To get rid of the phenol and to enrich for mRNA, the total RNA is further purified using the Qiagen OligoTEX mRNA Kit (*see* **Note 1**).
2. For the preparation and cloning of cDNA fragments a commercially available kit is applied with the Creator™ SMART™

cDNA Library Construction Kit (Clontech) preferred in our laboratory. Initially 500 ng mRNA is reverse transcribed into first-strand cDNA using a modified oligo(dT) primer (CDS III/3′ primer) and the SMART IV™ oligonucleotide which serves as a short extended template at the 5 end of the mRNA (*see* **Note 2**). Second-strand DNA synthesis and amplification of the cDNA is then performed by Long-Distance PCR using the Advantage® 2 PCR Kit (Clontech), the CDS III/3′ primer and a 5′ primer complement to the SMART™ anchor. Using 500 ng mRNA as starting material the PCR cycling conditions are as follows: 1 min 95°C; 20× (15 s 95°C; 6 min 68°C). After the amplification the cDNA should be checked on a 1% agarose/ethidium bromide gel and appear as a 0.2–4 kb smear. Following a proteinase K digestion step according to the kit's instruction, the cDNA is digested by the restriction enzyme *Sfi*I for 2 h at 50°C. This enzyme recognizes asymmetrical restriction sites incorporated at the 5′ and 3′ ends of the cDNA fragments by the primers during synthesis and allows for subsequent directional ligation with respect to the transcription initiation site into an *Sfi*I-digested vector containing the same asymmetrical *Sfi*I sites in its MCS (*see* **Note 3**). The *Sfi*I-digested cDNA is size fractionated according to the kit's instruction, and the profile of the fractions is checked on a 1% agarose/ethidium bromide gel. To select for cDNA fragments greater than 500 bp appropriate fractions are collected and pooled accordingly (*see* **Note 4**). The pooled cDNA is then concentrated by precipitation according to the kit's instruction and is then ready for ligation into the *Sfi*I-digested vector.

3. As the cDNA fragments are intended to constitute a retroviral expression library they must be cloned into a suitable vector that allows for their transcription and subsequent packaging of the transcripts into infectious viral particles (*see* **Subheading 3.2**). The vector routinely used in our laboratory is pFBneo (Stratagene) which is derived from the Moloney murine leukaemia virus (MMLV) and can be used to produce high titre viral stocks with MMLV-based packaging cell lines. It contains the bacterial origin of replication and an ampicillin-resistance gene, an extended MMLV-packaging signal (ψ+), a neomycin-resistance gene, and an MCS located between the MMLV 5′ and 3′ long terminal repeat sequences (LTRs) which subsequently provide the retroviral RNA with the requisite *cis*-acting sequences for gene expression. Since pFBneo does not contain the asymmetrical *Sfi*I restriction sites needed for ligation of the cDNA fragments it has to be modified accordingly (*see* **Note 5**).

4. The ligation reaction is then performed under standard conditions. Briefly, approximately 100 ng *Sfi*I-digested pFBneo vector is added to approximately 200 ng *Sfi*I-digested pooled cDNA fragments and incubated at 16°C overnight in the presence of ligation buffer, ATP, and T4 DNA ligase in a total volume of 5 μl as outlined in the kit. The reaction mixture is then purified by precipitation according to the kit's instruction and resuspended in 2 μl sterile H_2O. Electrocompetent *E. coli* cells (*E. cloni*® 10G SUPREME Electrocompetent Cells, Lucigen® Corporation) with a transformation efficiency of approximately 5×10^{10} cfu/μg DNA are transformed with the ligation mixture according to the manufacturer's instructions and plated out completely onto 20–30 150 mm LB-Amp plates. The resultant colonies should add up to about $1–2 \times 10^6$ independent clones with an insert size range of 0.5–6 kb and an average size of 1.5–2 kb (*see* **Note 6**). The plasmid DNA of a representative number of colonies should be isolated using a commercially available kit such as Promega's Wizard® Plus SV Miniprep Kit and sent off for sequencing to check for complete ORFs and enrichment of macrophage-specific cDNAs. Alternatively, a set of macrophage-specific primers could be tested on the library to confirm the presence of macrophage-specific cDNAs.
5. To proceed with the transfection of the library, colonies are scraped from the plates and pooled individually resulting in 20–30 cDNA pools. Plasmid DNA is isolated using a commercially available kit such as Promega's PureYield™ Plasmid Midiprep Kit to obtain high-quality supercoiled DNA for subsequent transfection of the virus-packaging cell line.

3.2. Expression of the Library

Retroviral vectors provide a highly efficient method for gene transfer, particularly for cell types which are often poorly susceptible to transfection methods such as calcium phosphate precipitation or lipid-based transfection agents. Retroviral infection results in the stable integration of one or a few copies of viral DNA into the target genome in a predictable and precise manner which allows subsequent recovery of the insert(s) by PCR. Retroviral vectors are manipulated in DNA form using bacterial plasmids such as pFBneo as described in **Subheading 3.1**, which contain a packaging signal but produce no intact proteins of their own and which are transfected into suitable packaging cells. These cells allow production of replication-defective retrovirus vectors in the absence of helper virus and must encapsidate the plasmid-encoded RNA; provide the viral proteins for infection, reverse transcription, and integration into the genome of target cells; and must produce high titres of virus. A highly transfectable cell line routinely used in our laboratory is the helper-free ecotropic-packaging cell line Phoenix-Eco (G.P. Nolan, Stanford University) which is capable of producing the three major proteins encoded within a retroviral genome: Gag, Pol, and Env, with different non-Moloney promoters for *gag–pol* and *env* to minimize both their recombination potential with introduced retroviral constructs and their inter-recombination potential (*see* **Note 7**). These retroviral structural gene products (*gag*, *pol*, and *env*) are provided in *trans* by separating them from the elements required for packaging retroviral RNA into virions without the concomitant production of replication competent virus, thus creating helper-free retrovirus-packaging cells. Retroviral particles produced in this way can infect target cells and transmit the gene of interest, but not replicate, because genomic information encoding the packaging proteins is not carried in the packaged retroviral particles.

The following transfection/infection procedure describes the optimized conditions for the cell system routinely used in our laboratory. Depending on the particular cell lines to be transfected/infected the following parameters are suggested to be chosen for optimization: method of transfection of packaging cells, time of infection (stage of growth), polybrene concentration, polybrene exposure time, use of deglycosylation agents such as tunicamycin, temperature of infection, spin/non-spin infection *(16)*. It is recommended to test the efficiency of the transfection/infection procedure on the chosen cell system prior to transfection of the library using a plasmid coding for an easily detectable reporter protein (for example GFP, luciferase, or beta-galactosidase).

1. Phoenix-Eco cells are plated out in 6-well plates in 3 ml $DMEM_{10}$ the day before transfection at a density of 1×10^6 cells per well (*see* **Note 8**). The following day the Phoenix-Eco cells are transfected with 1 μg of the cDNA plasmid library per well using FuGENE 6 transfection reagent (Roche Applied Science). Growth medium is replaced by 2 ml of fresh $DMEM_{10}$, while the transfection mixture is prepared according to the manufacturer's instructions. Briefly, 94 μl $DMEM_0$ (serum-free!) and 6 μl FuGENE reagent are mixed and incubated at room temperature for 5 min after which 1 μg plasmid DNA is added and incubated for an additional 15 min at room temperature. 100 μl of the reagent mixture is then added carefully in a dropwise fashion to the Phoenix-Eco cells and incubated for 24 h first at 37°C/5%CO_2 followed by another 24 h incubation, this time at 32°C/5%CO_2 (*see* **Note 9**).

2. The virus-containing supernatant of the Phoenix-Eco cells is harvested after the 48-h culture period and immediately used for infection of the recipient cell line (*see* **Note 10** and **Subheading 3.3** for choice of recipient cell line). For the screening procedure described here, the murine embryonic fibroblast

cell line NIH3T3, which has been plated out on 6-well plates in $DMEM_{10}$ at a cell density of 1×10^5 the previous day (*see* **Note 11**), is used for infection. NIH3T3 culture medium is removed and the viral supernatant (2 ml per well) containing 5 μg/ml polybrene filtered through 0.45-μm filters is directly added onto the NIH3T3 cells (*see* **Note 12**). The plates are then centrifuged at 1250*g* for 90 min at 25°C to increase infectivity, presumably because of virions attached to cellular debris are spun onto cells. The cells are then incubated overnight at 37°C/5%CO_2. The medium is replaced the following day by fresh $DMEM_{10}$ containing 0.4 mg/ml G418 to select for neomycin resistance. The pool of G418-resistant cells now represents the stable library (*see* **Note 13**).

3.3. Screening of the Library

To screen cDNA libraries for cell surface molecules various systems have been developed for the isolation of cDNA clones: cDNA probes *(17)*, antibody capture/panning *(18–20)*, FACS *(21)*, magnetic bead capture *(10)*, or the visual isolation by fluorescent microscopy screening *(9)*, the latter being preferred in our laboratory for the reasons discussed later. Although FACS is a standard method to isolate cells based on specific receptor–ligand interactions it is not sensitive enough to rescue rare cDNAs encoding receptors, and the isolation of false-positives being a major disadvantage. The use of magnetic beads coated with antibodies or ligands for the isolation of cells expressing surface molecules proved to be quick, simple, and effective in screening a cDNA library *(10)* but requires the expression of the cDNA library in a non-adherent cell line. One such cell line, FDC-P1, has been successfully used for retroviral expression system construction previously *(22)* as it proliferates rapidly and is considerably infectable under optimized conditions (*see* **Note 14**). However, the adherent cell line NIH3T3 is routinely and very efficiently used for retroviral transduction with an infection efficiency considerably higher than FDC-P1 cells which is essential for the expression of rare inserts of the library. Using NIH3T3 cells as the expressing cell line allows screening for ligand–receptor binding visualized by fluorescent microscopy. Although very laborious and time consuming this method largely overcomes the problems of insensitivity and isolation of false-positives and provides a means of visual estimation of ligand binding (*see* **Fig. 1c**).

1. Using fluorescent microscopy as the method of choice for screening for surface receptors with a known fluorescently labelled ligand, the background binding must be kept as low as possible. This is essential as the eyes become too easily tired with too many non-specific fluorescent particles being present. For any particular application, the library-expressing cells as well as the incubation conditions for ligand binding (time and

temperature of incubation) have to be tested in preliminary experiments very carefully and optimized accordingly to minimize any non-specific background binding. As a control and to test the screening process it is advisable to express a known receptor in the chosen recipient cell line for which a ligand is available. Also, a macrophage cell line (such as RAW 264.7) should be used to optimize the binding conditions for the particular ligand to be screened with. For example, incubation of NIH3T3 cells with FITC-labelled zymosan as done for the isolation of dectin-1 *(9)* does not lead to non-specific background binding of the fluorescent particles as shown in **Fig. 1a**; therefore, NIH3T3 cells are suitable as the expression cell line for the library. In contrast, RAW 264.7 macrophages which were used for the isolation of mRNA and generation of the library clearly bind zymosan as shown in **Fig. 1b**.

2. When choosing a ligand it must be suitable for, and easily detectable by, fluorescent microscopy. Both fluorescence intensity and particle size should be considered with GFP-expressing microorganisms or FITC-labelled particles/beads coupled to a ligand or antibody being optimal. Particle size should not be smaller than approximately 2 μm.
3. In order to screen NIH3T3 cells stably expressing the cDNA library prepared from RAW 264.7 macrophages for expression of the β-glucan receptor, the cells are transferred to G418-free culture medium with approximately ten FITC-labelled zymosan particles per cell added and incubated for 1h at 37°C/5%CO_2. Cells are washed three times with culture medium $DMEM_{10}$ to wash off all unbound zymosan particles and then incubated in $DMEM_{10}$ containing 0.4 mg/ml G418. The screening is done by fluorescent microscopy searching for FITC-zymosan binding cells by moving the plate on the microscope stage manually. Once a positive cell is detected the spot is marked with a black marker pen for subsequent isolation under sterile conditions. To isolate the cell(s) at the marked spot(s) growth medium is removed and the spot is ringed by a cloning cylinder using Dow Corning High Vacuum grease. Alternatively, the back of a 100-μl (yellow) or 1,000-μl (blue) standard pipette tip dipped carefully into sterile grease can be used to ring the marked spot. It should be checked by microscope that the grease ring is complete to avoid subsequent leakage. A drop of pre-warmed lidocaine/EDTA is added into the ring, incubated for 1–2 min, and cells are recovered from the ring and transferred into fresh 2 ml $DMEM_{10}$ containing 0.4 mg/ml G418 in a well of 6-well plate (*see* **Note 15**). The cells are then expanded in culture for 4–7 days until they reach approximately 80% confluence. The screening and isolation procedure is repeated until the majority of cells are shown to

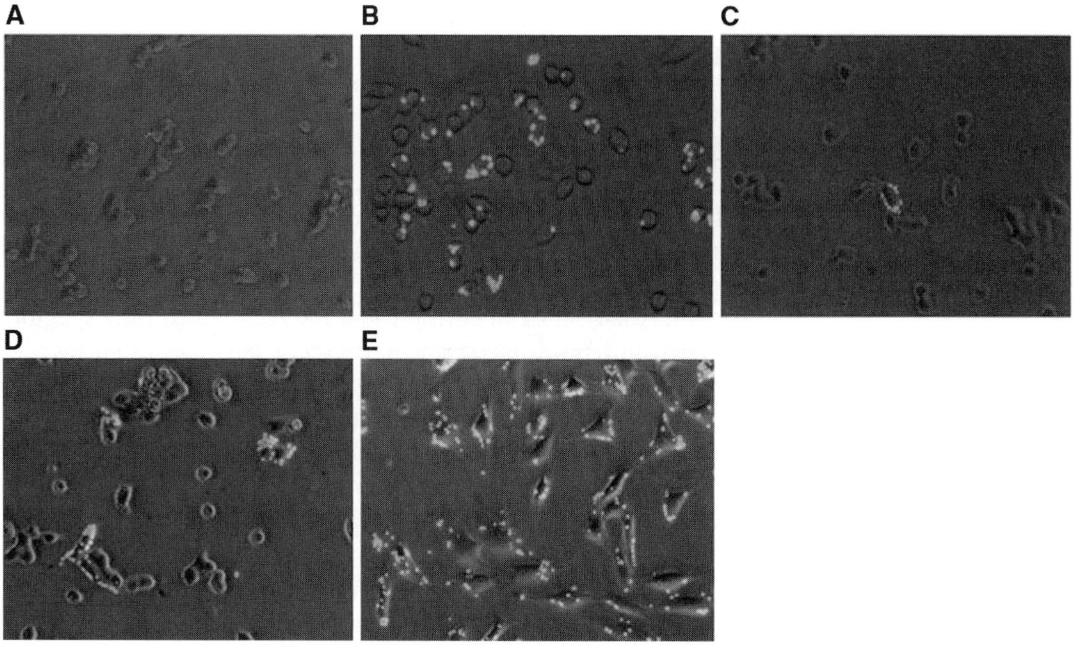

Fig. 1. Binding of FITC-labelled zymosan to negative control cells NIH3T3 (**A**) and positive control cells RAW 264.7 (**B**) using a FITC filter on a Zeiss inverted microscope Axiovert 40 CFL at 20× magnification. **C–E** shows the enrichment of positive FITC-zymosan binding cells during the screening procedure. Starting off with one positive cell (**C**) the following re-screen results in the isolation of a patch of positive cells (**D**) with their subsequent enrichment after a few screening rounds (**E**).

be positive in the functional screen. As shown in **Fig. 1c–e**, a single positive cell which binds FITC-labelled zymosan (**Fig. 1c**) isolated together with many negative cells after the first screening will grow in culture and might give rise to a patch of 5–10 cells seen when re-screened (**Fig. 1d**). Isolation of this cell patch will result in the appearance of many cell patches in the next screen until the cells are finally enriched with the majority binding to the ligand (**Fig. 1e**).

3.4. Identification and Functional Testing of Positive Cell(s)

Once positive ligand-binding cells have been enriched after a couple of screening rounds, genomic DNA is isolated from the cells and conventional PCR is used to recover the proviral cDNA inserts which are stably inserted into the genome.

1. For the genomic DNA isolation approximately 1×10^6 positive cells are plated out the previous day and harvested using a commercially available kit such as the QIAamp® DNA Mini Kit (Qiagen) according to the manufacturer's instructions (*see* **Note 16**). For the subsequent PCR using the primers 5′ Retro and 3′ pFB-Neo (Stratagene) which correspond to the retroviral vector sequences flanking the multiple cloning site and therefore the individual cDNA fragments, 10 ng of genomic

DNA is used along with the Advantage® 2 PCR Kit (Clontech) (*see* **Note 17**). Due to the complexity of the genomic DNA and the high T_m of the primers the PCR cycling parameters have been optimized as follows: 5 min 95°C; 35× (1 min 95°C; 30 s 80°C; 30 s 75°C; 30 s 70°C; 4 min 72°C). Running an aliquot of the PCR reaction on a 1% agarose/ethidium bromide gel one would expect several fragments of different sizes due to the retroviral MOI of approximately 10 under the described conditions (*see* **Note 13**).

2. The PCR reaction is purified using a commercially available kit such as Promega's Wizard® SV Gel and PCR Clean-Up System and directly cloned into the vector pCR®4-TOPO® using the TOPO TA Cloning® Kit for Sequencing (Invitrogen) according to the manufacturer's instructions (*see* **Note 18**).
3. While selected clones are sent off for sequencing of the inserts they can be further cloned into suitable vectors which allow for their functional testing. To test their expression and ligand binding in transient transfections the inserts of selected clones are amplified in a PCR using the primer 3′ pFB-Neo and a modified primer 5′ Retro containing the sequence CACC at its 5′ end which allows directional cloning into the vector pcDNA™3.1D/V5-His-TOPO® using the pcDNA™ 3.1 Directional TOPO® Expression Kit (Invitrogen) according to the manufacturer's instruction (*see* **Note 19**). Alternatively, the recovered proviral cDNA inserts can be recloned into the retroviral vector pFBneo using the unique *Sfi*I restriction sites present in their 5′ and 3′ flanking regions. As outlined earlier, *E. coli* cells are transformed with this recloned cDNA and plasmid DNA isolated to transfect virus-producing cells for subsequent infection of the recipient cells and generation of stable cell lines expressing the various cloned cDNA fragments individually. For validation of successful recloning of the correct cDNA clone, these cells are then functionally analysed for ligand binding as stated earlier.
4. Sequence data are then analysed by accessing available gene bank databases. This might lead to the re-identification of a known receptor as in the case of dectin-1 *(9)*. In case of the identification of an unknown receptor or surface molecule, sequence analysis will provide information of its nature and helps to group the receptor into its relevant receptor class according to its sequence and structural properties. Further molecular and functional characterization of the identified molecule might then include its expression profile in different macrophage populations and tissues, the determination of its ligand specificity, and the investigation of its immunomodulatory effects.

4. Notes

1. The quality and integrity of both the total RNA and the mRNA should be checked on a denaturing formaldehyde/agarose gel before proceeding with the protocol. Total RNA from mammalian sources should appear as a faint smear with two bright bands corresponding to 28S rRNA and 18S rRNA, while intact mammalian mRNA should appear as a smear (usually 0.5–12 kb) with faint 28S and 18S rRNA bands. Also, the concentration of both total RNA and mRNA should be determined by measuring the absorbance at 260 nm (A_{260}) in a spectrophotometer (with $A_{260} = 1$ equivalent to 40 ng/μl RNA) to estimate the mRNA yield – keeping in mind that mRNA accounts for only 1–5% of the total RNA in a typical mammalian cell (although the actual amount depends on the cell type and physiological state) with approximately 12,000 different mRNA species per cell. To ensure highly pure mRNA before proceeding with the library construction the ratio of the readings at 260 nm and 280 nm (A_{260}/A_{280}) should be determined with pure RNA having an A_{260}/A_{280} ratio of 1.9–2.1. Both total RNA and mRNA should be stored at −80°C; repeated freezing and thawing should be avoided.
2. For further information on the underlying SMART™ mechanism please refer to the Clontech User Manual for the Creator™ SMART™ cDNA Library Construction Kit.
3. *Sfi*I sites are extremely rare in mammalian DNA; therefore, *Sfi*I-digested cDNA remains intact.
4. It has been observed regularly in our laboratory that pooling 2–3 fractions before the actual peak fractions (i.e. where the cDNA amount is too low to be detected on the gel) usually contains both large cDNA fragments and cDNA fragments in the medium range. Pooling the peak fractions can result in collecting too many small cDNAs (i.e. smaller than 500 bp).
5. The *Sfi*I-digested control insert contained in the Creator™ SMART™ cDNA Library Construction Kit (Clontech) is ligated into the provided *Sfi*I-digested vector pDNR-LIB and afterwards cut out with the restriction enzymes *Eco*RI and *Xho*I flanking the ligated control insert in the vector. The *Eco*RI/*Xho*I-digested insert in turn is ligated into the *Eco*RI/*Xho*I-digested vector pFBneo allowing its subsequent digestion with *Sfi*I and cloning of the *Sfi*I-digested cDNA fragments.
6. Colonies are picked randomly and checked for insert size distribution by colony PCR using a commercially available PCR

kit such as Fermentas' 2× PCR Mastermix and the pFBneo vector primers 5′ Retro and 3′ pFB-Neo with the following cycling parameters: 5 min 95°C; 30× (1 min 95°C; 1 min 65°C; 4 min 72°C).

7. To monitor *gag–pol* expression on a cell-by-cell basis (i.e. with the help of flow cytometry) an IRES-CD8 surface marker has been introduced downstream of the *gag–pol* reading frame.

8. Phoenix-eco cells are kept in selective medium (1 μg/ml diphtheria toxin; 300 μg/ml hygromycin) constantly except for the transfection experiment. For each pool of the library to be transfected prepare two wells of one 6-well plate. Normally three pools of the library can be handled simultaneously in the subsequent screening.

9. The incubation at 32°C overnight has been shown to be crucial for library infection efficiency since prolonged incubation at 37°C leads to reduced virus titre due to instability of the virus particles.

10. The virus-containing supernatant (filtered and polybrene added) can be stored at –80°C although this might reduce infection efficiency by approximately 50%. For library transduction it is recommended to use fresh virus-containing supernatant for infection.

11. It is important to infect replicating cells with those in exponential phase being most efficiently infected since retroviral infection is largely inhibited in non-replicating cells *(16)*.

12. Polybrene facilitates infection, presumably through its polycationicity, neutralizing negative charges on the surface of target cells and reducing electrostatic repulsion of virions. However, it is toxic to cells and should be kept to a minimum concentration. While the infection of NIH3T3 cells requires 5 μg/ml polybrene, infection of the non-adherent cell line FDC-P1 is generally performed in our laboratory in the presence of 20 μg/ml polybrene. Infection of the murine macrophage cell line RAW 264.7 in the presence of 5 μg/ml polybrene is very low but can be improved by addition of 0.2 μg/ml tunicamycin to the growth medium the day before infection.

13. Under the experimental conditions for the transfection and transduction described here one would expect a MOI of the virus titre of approximately 10, i.e. ten infection events per NIH3T3 cell. Therefore no cell death is expected due to G418. The initial number of 1×10^5 NIH3T3 cells per well might appear low, but the cells will grow for more than 3 days until the start of the screening and should not be confluent then. If the cells are confluent one should consider

splitting them into two or more new wells to avoid them coming off during the screen. Ideally, the cells should be 80–90% confluent on the day of screening.

14. The optimized conditions for infection of the non-adherent cell line FDC-P1 are as follows: 2×10^5 FDC-P1 cells are added to 1.5 ml viral supernatant in a 6-well plate with 20 μg/ml polybrene. Cells are centrifuged for 90 min at 1250*g* at 25°C, agitated by rocking the plate gently back and forth to lift adherent cells and incubated at 37°C/5%CO_2 overnight. The medium is changed the following day and selected for neomycin-resistant cells 48 h post-infection.
15. The incubation with lidocaine/EDTA for more than 5 min has shown to decrease the viability of the cells. Also, trypsin should be avoided since it might stress the cells too much and decreases viability. Special care must be taken at the first screening and isolation with only one positive cell detectable among lots of negative cells. It should be checked by microscope that all cells in the ring have been transferred. Further re-screening and isolation steps will involve enriched positive cells which do not necessarily need to be isolated completely.
16. It is strongly recommended to use a method for the genomic DNA isolation that is not based on phenol/chloroform, since this has shown to limit the sensitivity of the downstream PCR significantly.
17. This PCR kit has performed best in our laboratory compared to several other polymerases tested in terms of amplified fragment sizes. For any PCR problems such as amplification of fragments greater than 3 kb or very rich in GC one should consider to use a specific PCR kit for long-distance PCR or GC-rich PCR, respectively.
18. The cloning system preferentially ligates small fragments of the PCR mixture into the vector. To clone large DNA fragments the PCR mixture could be run on a preparative gel and the desired DNA sizes cut out, purified, and added to the TOPO-cloning mixture.
19. The direct amplification of the cDNA inserts from the genome using the modified primers allowing directional cloning into the expression vector pcDNA™3.1D/V5-His-TOPO® has been shown to be unsuitable due to decreased primer specificity and decreased efficiency with the proofreading polymerases tested.

Acknowledgements

This work was supported by funding from the Deutsche Forschungsgemeinschaft (DFG) to G.S. (grant SCHA 1470/1-1) and the Wellcome Trust to G.D.B.

References

1. Gordon S (1998). The role of the macrophage in immune regulation. *Res Immunol* 149(7–8): 685–688.
2. Medzhitov R and Janeway CA Jr. (1998). Innate immune recognition and control of adaptive immune responses. *Semin Immunol* 10(5): 351–353.
3. Medzhitov R and Janeway CA Jr. (2000). Innate immunity. *N Engl J Med* 343(5): 338–344.
4. Medzhitov R and Janeway CA Jr. (1997). Innate immunity: impact on the adaptive immune response. *Curr Opin Immunol* 9(1): 4–9.
5. Janeway CA Jr. and Medzhitov R (2002). Innate immune recognition. *Annu Rev Immunol* 20: 197–216.
6. Medzhitov R and Janeway CA Jr. (2002). Decoding the patterns of self and nonself by the innate immune system. *Science* 296(5566): 298–300.
7. Pontow SE, Kery V, and Stahl PD (1992). Mannose receptor. *Int Rev Cytol* 137B: 221–244.
8. Kielian TL and Blecha F (1995). CD14 and other recognition molecules for lipopolysaccharide: a review. *Immunopharmacology* 29: 187–205.
9. Brown GD and Gordon S (2001). Immune recognition: A new receptor for beta-glucans. *Nature* 413: 36–37.
10. Zannettino AC, Rayner JR, Ashman LK, Gonda TJ, and Simmons PJ (1996). A powerful new technique for isolating genes encoding cell surface antigens using retroviral expression cloning. *J Immunol* 156: 611–620.
11. Brown GD, Herre J, Williams DL, Willment JA, Marshall AS, and Gordon S (2003). Dectin-1 mediates the biological effects of beta-glucans. *J Exp Med* 197(9): 1119–1124.
12. Herre J, Marshall AS, Caron E, Edwards AD, Williams DL, Schweighoffer E, Tybulewicz V, Reis e Sousa C, Gordon S, and Brown GD (2004). Dectin-1 uses novel mechanisms for yeast phagocytosis in macrophages. *Blood* 104(13): 4038–4045.
13. Brown GD and Gordon S (2003). Fungal beta-glucans and mammalian immunity. *Immunity* 19(3): 311–315.
14. Brown GD and Gordon S (2005). Immune recognition of fungal beta-glucans. *Cell Microbiol* 7(4): 471–479.
15. Brown GD (2006). Dectin-1: a signaling non-TLR pattern-recognition receptor. *Nat Rev Immun* 6: 33–43.
16. Miller AD, Miller DG, Garcia JV and Lynch CM (1993). Use of retroviral vectors for gene transfer and expression. *Methods Enzymol* 217: 581–599.
17. Kavathas P, Sukhatme VP, Herzenberg LA, and Parnes JR (1984). Isolation of the gene encoding the human T-lymphocyte differentiation antigen Leu-2 (T8) by gene transfer and cDNA subtraction. *Proc Natl Acad Sci USA* 81(24): 7688–7692.
18. Wysocki LJ and Sato VL (1978). "Panning" for lymphocytes: a method for cell selection. *Proc Natl Acad Sci USA* 75(6): 2844–2848.
19. Seed B and Aruffo A (1987). Molecular cloning of the CD2 antigen, the T-cell erythrocyte receptor, by a rapid immunoselection procedure. *Proc Natl Acad Sci USA* 84: 3365–3369.
20. Aruffo A and Seed B (1987). Molecular cloning of a CD28 cDNA by a high-efficiency COS cell expression system. *Proc Natl Acad Sci USA* 84: 8573–8577.
21. Kitamura T, Onishi M, Kinoshita S, Shibuya A, Miyajima A and Nolan GP (1995). Efficient screening of retroviral cDNA expression libraries. *Proc Natl Acad Sci USA* 92(20): 9146–9150.
22. Rayner JR and Gonda TJ (1994). A simple and efficient procedure for generating stable expression libraries by cDNA cloning in a retroviral vector. *Mol Cell Biol* 14(2): 880–887.

Chapter 2

Generation of Murine Growth Factor-Dependent Long-Term Dendritic Cell Lines to Investigate Host–Parasite Interactions

Alessandra Mortellaro, Matteo Urbano, Stefania Citterio, Maria Foti, Francesca Granucci, and Paola Ricciardi-Castagnoli

Summary

Substantial progress has been made over the last several years in the development of protocols for the isolation of large numbers of dendritic cells (DCs) from different tissues and their short-term culture. Indeed, several stable DC lines and clones have been established from various tissues of mice and humans, providing useful experimental tools for studying the biology of DCs at both molecular and biochemical levels and for the establishment of new DC-based immunotherapies. In this chapter, we will describe the development of long-term DC lines that maintain the growth factor dependence and their immature functional state, thus providing a unique opportunity to study the mechanisms of the initiation of the immune response to infectious agents.

Key words: Dendritic cell lines, Host–parasite interaction, GM-CSF, Bone marrow, Bacteria, Immune response.

1. Introduction

Dendritic cells (DCs) are distributed especially in tissues that interface with the external environment, such as the skin, the gut, and the lungs *(1–3)*. At these locations, they can perform a sentinel function for incoming pathogens, and have the capacity to recruit and activate cells of the innate immune system upon inflammation *(4–6)*. Uptake of pathogens by DCs induces a state

Neil E. Reiner (ed.), *Macrophages and Dendritic Cells,* Methods in Molecular Biology, vol. 531

DOI: 10.1007/978-1-59745-396-7_2

of activation, which eventually leads to the migration of the antigen-loaded DCs to the lymphoid organs where the cells of the adaptive immune response can be alerted *(7)*.

Until the last decade, the paucity of DCs in most tissues and the lack of specific markers have hampered the study of DC ontogeny, phenotype, and function. Several groups have succeeded in generating large numbers of functional DCs/Langerhans cells in murine or human systems by treating DC precursors with granulocyte-macrophage colony-stimulating factor (GM-CSF) alone or in combination with other growth factors *(8–13)*. However, such DCs could be propagated only for limited periods of time. Growth factor-dependent long-term DC lines from mouse fetal or newborn skin have been established *(14, 15)*. Nevertheless, although these lines possess some properties of DC precursors and maintain an immature phenotype, they cannot be induced to mature in vitro *(14, 15)*.

In recent years, immortalization of DCs from mouse tissues, using retroviral vectors carrying immortalizing oncogenes, has successfully been achieved *(16–18)*. The immortalized DC lines are homogeneous, easily grown, and do not require growth factors for their propagation, being extensively used for functional and biochemical DC characterization. Indeed, the cells exhibited phenotypic and functional features of immature DCs, including the ability to present exogenous antigens on class I and class II molecules and the capacity to induce primary T-cell response in vitro and in vivo *(19–21)*. However, the inability to induce growth factor arrest in these immortal lines has hampered the complete maturation of DCs upon activation.

In the mouse system, we succeeded in generating long-term growth factor-dependent immature DC lines, derived from adult mouse spleen *(22)* or mouse bone marrow. In this system, proliferation and survival are strictly dependent upon the presence of exogenous murineGM-CSF (mGM-CSF) and fibroblast-derived growth factors *(22)*. Long-term DCs preserve an immature phenotype. Activating signals, such as living bacteria, Toll-like receptors agonists and cytokines, promote full maturation of these DC lines, such as the D1 cells, mimicking and recapitulating the whole natural process of DC differentiation that occurs in response to activation by pathogens in vivo.

This chapter focuses on in vitro techniques leading to the establishment of murine long-term DC lines, similar to the D1 cells that have been widely used *(23–26)*. Using a conditioned medium (R1 medium) containing several cytokines, including mGM-CSF produced by GM-CSF-transfected NIH/3T3, we show that DCs can be stimulated to undergo maturation in response to live bacteria, thus allowing investigation of host–pathogen interactions *(22, 27)*.

2. Materials

1. *Iscove's Modified Dulbecco's Medium (complete medium).* IMDM supplemented with 10% heat-inactivated fetal bovine serum (FBS) of Australian origin by Gibco BRL, 2 mM L-glutamine, 100 IU/mL penicillin, 100 μg/mL streptomycin, and 0.05 mM 2β-mercaptoethanol (*see* **Note 1**).
2. *DC-GM medium (R1 medium).* IMDM complete medium supplemented with conditioned medium produced by mGM-CSF-transfected NIH/3T3 fibroblasts (available upon request from P. Ricciardi-Castagnoli) corresponding to 10 ng/mL of mGM-CSF as final concentration. DC medium is stable at 4°C for up to 3 weeks. (For conditioned medium preparation *see* **Subheading 3.1** and **Note 2**).
3. *Phosphate-buffered saline (PBS), pH 7.2–7.4.* 154 mM NaCl, 8.1 mM Na_2HPO_4 ($7H_2O$), 1.9 mM NaH_2PO_4 (H_2O).
4. *Red blood cell (RBC) lysis buffer.* 105 mM NH_4Cl, 10 mM $KHCO_3$, 0.1 mM Na_4EDTA.
5. *PBS-EDTA.* Solution of PBS supplemented with 2 mM EDTA.
6. *Composition of Luria Bertani (LB) medium.* Tryptone 10 g/L, yeast extract 5 g/L, NaCl 10 g/L.

3. Methods

3.1. Production of Conditioned Medium Containing mGM-CSF

1. NIH/3T3 fibroblasts stably transfected with mGM-CSF (1×10^6 in 7 ml) are plated in 100 × 20 mm tissue-cultured-treated petri dish using IMDM medium supplemented with 5% heat-inactivated FBS of Australian origin by Gibco BRL, 2 mM L -glutamine, 100 IU/mL penicillin, 100 μ g/mL streptomycin, and 0.05 mM 2β-mercaptoethanol (*see* **Note 3**).
2. The conditioned medium is collected from culture after 3 days and centrifuged at 270 × *g* for 5 min to pellet floating cells and debris. Then, the supernatant is filtered through a 0.2 μm filter and aliquots stored at –20°C.
3. In order to measure the concentration of mGM-CSF, a specific enzyme-linked immunoabsorbent assay should be performed.

3.2. Preparation of Cell Suspensions from Bone Marrow

1. Mice are euthanized using CO_2 asphyxiation followed by cervical dislocation (*see* **Note 4**).
2. The skin of mouse hind legs is pulled back and the muscles dissected to expose femur and tibia (*see* **Note 5**).

3. Using a scissors and a pair of tweezers, the knee joint is cut, the muscle along the femur is sliced and the bone is severed from the hip joint. Most of the muscle tissues surrounding the bone should be eliminated with the scissors.
4. After removal of both femurs and tibias, all bones are washed twice in PBS and placed in a 60 × 15 mm petri dish containing 5 mL of IMDM complete medium.
5. Cutting both bone edges using scissors exposes the cavity lumen. Then, the BM is flushed out using a 5-mL syringe and 25-G needle filled with IMDM complete medium. Flush the bone cavity until it appears white.
6. To disaggregate clusters of BM cells, the cell suspension is passed through the syringe and filtered using a cell strainer (pores diameter = 70 μm) into a 50-mL tube.
7. Cells are recovered by centrifugation and the pellet resuspended in 10 mL R1 medium.
8. Finally, cells are counted using a Bürker chamber.

3.3. Preparation of Cell Suspensions from Spleen

1. Mice are euthanized using CO_2 asphyxiation followed by cervical dislocation (*see* **Note 4**).
2. Spleens are isolated from mice, placed in a 60 × 15 mm petri dish containing 5 mL of IMDM complete medium, and cut into small pieces. A single cell suspension is obtained by smashing the spleens using a 5 mL-siring plunger until mostly fibrous tissue remains.
3. To avoid cell aggregates, the suspension is filtered through 70-μm cell strainers.
4. The suspension is transferred to a 15-mL tube and centrifuged for 5 min at 400 × *g*.
5. At this stage, the removal of RBC from the spleen cell suspension is necessary. For this purpose, the pellet is resuspended in 1–2 mL of RBC lysis buffer and incubated at 4°C for 9 min. 10 mL IMDM complete medium is added and the aggregates removed by filtration through 70-μm cell strainer. The mononuclear cells are recovered by centrifugation at 270 × *g* for 5 min. The supernatant is discarded and the pellet is resuspended in a suitable volume of R1 medium for counting.

3.4. Generation of Mouse Long-Term Growth Factor-Dependent DC Lines

1. Unfractionated cell populations from BM or spleen are plated at a density of 4×10^5 cells/mL in 100 × 20mm suspension culture dishes in R1 medium and incubated at 37°C with 5% CO_2 (*see* **Note 6**).
2. The culture is fed with fresh R1 medium without the addition of exogenous IL-4 every 3–4 days (*see* **Note 7**).

3. Usually the first passage of DC-enriched culture is performed around day 7, when the cell density is high, using a solution of PBS-EDTA. Then, the cells are counted and replated at a concentration of 2–3 × 10^5 cells/mL (*see* **Note 8**).
4. Once a week, both suspended and weakly adherent cells are collected using PBS, centrifugated at 270 × *g* for 5 min, and seeded at a density of 2–3 × 10^5 cells/mL (*see* **Note 9**).
5. After 3 months of continuous culture, in vitro growing cells can be split every 3–4 days using PBS-EDTA.
6. At this point, long-term growth factor-dependent DC lines are established (*see* **Notes 10** and **11**).
7. The established long-term culture retains a characteristic immature DC phenotype, and the cells can be induced to mature in vitro into terminally differentiated DCs upon activation with a number of stimulatory signals, such as LPS, bacteria, or cytokines. In **Fig. 1,** the phenotypical maturation of BM-derived DC lines induced by LPS is shown.

3.5. Growth of Bacterial Culture

1. A single colony of DH5α *E. coli* bacteria is inoculated into 2 mL of LB medium in a loosely capped 15-mL tube. The culture is incubated for ~8 h at 37°C with vigorous shaking. Using a vessel with a volume of at least four times greater than the volume of medium, the starter culture is diluted 1/500 to 1/1,000 into a larger volume of LB medium and grown with vigorous shaking to saturation (12–16 h, overnight). (*see* **Notes 12** and **13**)
2. The bacterial culture is then diluted 1/10 with LB medium and incubated for ~2.5 h at 37°C with shaking. Growth is monitored every 20–30 min by spectrophotometer and stopped in late-log-phase corresponding to OD_{600} ~0.6.
3. The concentration of the bacterial culture can be calculated using the following formula:

   $y = -29 + 1,191\ (OD_{600}) \times 10^6$ bact/mL (*see* **Note 14**).
4. The bacterial cells are harvested by centrifugation at 6,000 × *g* for 2 min at 4°C.
5. The LB medium is removed by aspiration, leaving the bacterial pellet as dry as possible. Bacteria are resuspended in 1 mL of R1 medium without antibiotics per mL of bacterial culture (*see* **Note 15**).

3.6. Bacterial Infection of DCs

1. The day before the infection, DC lines are harvested using a solution of PBS-EDTA and centrifuged at 250 × *g* for 5 min.
2. After a wash with PBS, DC lines are resuspended in an appropriate amount of R1 medium for counting.

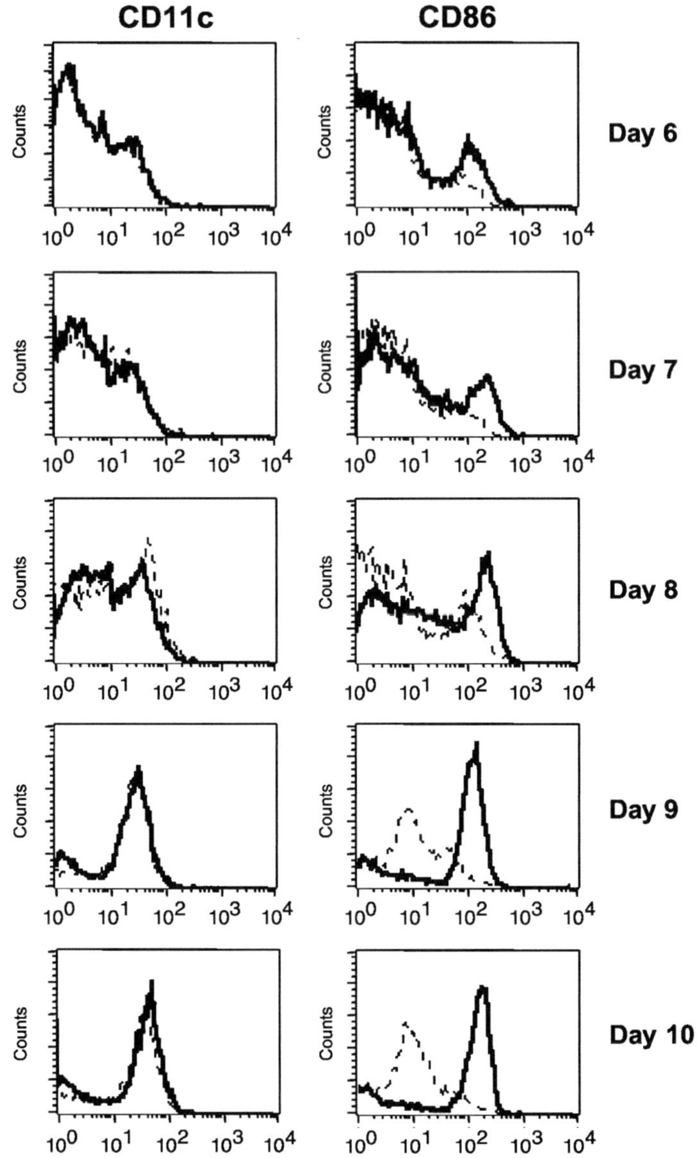

Fig. 1. Analysis of cell surface marker expression in BM-derived DC line cultured in R1 medium. The cells have been harvested at the indicated time and stimulated with LPS (1 μg/mL) for 24 hours. The expression of CD11c and CD86 markers was evaluated by flow cytometry. Dashed histogram: untreated cells; bold histogram: LPS-treated cells.

3. Cells are plated at a concentration of 2–3 × 10^5/mL in suspension petri dishes and incubated at 37°C 5% CO_2 for 16–18 h.
4. The R1 medium is removed and replaced with fresh R1 medium without antibiotics (*see* **Note 16**).
5. DC lines are infected with *E. coli* bacteria at a bacteria:DC ratio of 10:1 and incubated at 37°C 5% CO_2 for 1 h (*see* **Note 17**).

6. At this point, the medium is discarded and the petri dishes washed gently with PBS. Finally, fresh R1 medium supplemented with gentamicin (50 μg/mL) and tetracycline (10 μg/mL) is replated, and the cell culture is incubated at 37°C 5% CO_2 for the desired time.
7. Bacteria are efficient in upregulating the expression of DC maturation surface markers, such as CD80, CD86, MHC class II, and CD40. In **Fig. 2**, the upregulation of costimulatory molecules induced by bacteria in DC lines derived from BM and spleen is shown, as assessed by FACS analysis.

4. Notes

1. To optimize DC growth conditions, different batches of sera should be tested prior to use. In order to avoid phagocytosis of debris by DCs, it is optimal to filter complete medium using 0.2-μm filter.

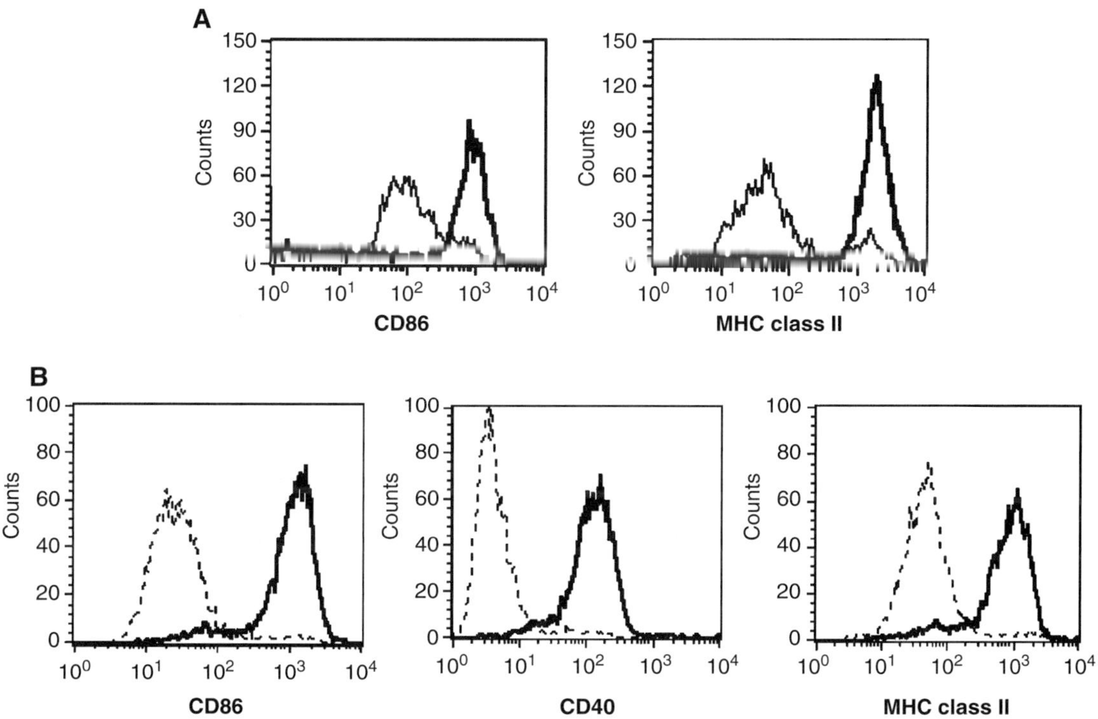

Fig. 2. Phenotypical maturation of BM- and spleen-derived long-term GM-CSF-dependent DCs. BM- (**A**) and spleen-derived (**B**) immature DCs were stimulated with DH5α *E. coli* bacteria (moi: 10) for 1 h, and the expression of CD86, CD40, and I-A MHC class II cell surface markers was measured by flow cytometry. Dashed and bold histograms show untreated cells and cells challenged with DH5α *E. coli* bacteria, respectively.

2. The ideal final concentration of mGM-CSF in the conditioned medium produced by mGM-CSF-transfected NIH/3T3 should be around 30 ng/mL.
3. In order to produce optimal conditioned medium, mGM-SCF-transfected NIH/3T3 fibroblasts should be plated starting from a semiconfluent culture.
4. In general, 8–12 weeks old mice yield sufficient numbers of DCs, precursors, or progenitor cells, and organs of sufficient size to be easily manipulated. Mice younger than 6 weeks may yield fewer cells or to be too small to manipulate easily, and mice older than 12 weeks may be more expensive with no additional gain in cell yield. The use of specific pathogen-free mice is recommended to avoid pathogen-specific effect. To minimize the effect of the anesthetizing or euthanatizing agents that may perturb DC function, CO_2 asphyxiation followed by cervical dislocation is used to kill mice.
5. Both femurs and tibias should be removed to isolate maximal numbers of mononuclear cells from a mouse. Femurs provide 80% of total BM cells.
6. DC lines tend to adhere strongly to plastic. Thus, the use of suspension culture dishes is highly recommended to obtain and culture DC lines.
7. Half of the medium is collected and the floating cells harvested by centrifugation. Then, the cell pellet is resuspended in fresh R1 medium and replated.
8. Cellular growth is monitored daily by microscopy. Proliferating cells are visible in suspension as clusters with veiled morphology.
9. Cell types other that DC precursors also respond to mGM-CSF and grow in R1 medium. For example, macrophages differentiate and strongly attach to the petri dish. These are discarded at each passage by harvesting only cells in suspension. Other major contaminants of nonadherent DCs are granulocytes (especially when starting from BM) visible as clusters of round cells from day 2. However, the majority of granulocyte contaminants tend to die in culture and are absent by the time DCs are harvested. It is often necessary to wash the cell pellet with PBS, to discard debris and dead cells.
10. In order to monitor the differentiation process of DCs, cell surface marker expression is analyzed by flow cytometry. Generally, it is found that the approaches described earlier generate CD11c+ DCs at 80–95% purity.
11. The DC lines once established could be continuously maintained for years but should not kept in culture. As these DC lines are not clonally selected, it is necessary to prepare frozen stocks of the cells kept as a backup storage. The cell

growth is strictly dependent on the presence in the culture medium of mGM-CSF. Indeed, growth factor deprivation leads to cell growth arrest and cell death.

12. Bacterial cultures should always be grown from a single colony picked from a freshly streaked plate. Subculturing directly from glycerol stocks, agar stabs, and liquid cultures is a poor microbiological practice. Inoculation from plates that have been stored for a long time may also lead to liquid culture containing different bacteria. The desired clone should be streaked from a glycerol stock onto a freshly prepared agar plate such that single colonies can be isolated. This procedure should then be repeated to ensure that a single colony is picked.
13. To avoid bacterial death, LB medium should be prewarmed at 37°C before bacteria inoculation. It is often convenient to grow the starter culture during the day and the larger culture overnight for harvesting the following morning.
14. Usually, OD_{600} = 0.6 corresponds to 6.85 × 10^8 bacteria/mL. Because the relationship between the OD_{600} and the number of viable cells per mL varies substantially from strain to strain, it is essential to calibrate the spectrophotometer. This can be achieved by plating serial dilutions of a bacterial culture onto LB agar plates in the absence of antibiotics. The counted colonies are used to calculate the number of bacteria per mL, which is then set in relation to the measured OD_{600} values.
15. The supernatant can be conveniently withdrawn with a disposable pipette tip attached to a vacuum line. Use gentle suction to avoid drawing the pellet into the pipette tip. Any droplets of liquid adherent to the walls of the tube should be removed by vacuum. It is essential to ensure that the bacterial pellet is completely dispersed.
16. It is critically important to remember to not add antibiotics to the R1 medium at this stage to avoid bacterial death.
17. The amount of bacteria used to challenge DC lines can vary depending on the aim of the experiment. It is possible to use lower bacteria:DC ratios and to extend the incubation period to 16–18 h.

Acknowledgments

The authors wish to thank Renato Ostuni for his contribution in the setting up of the protocol of DC differentiation from BM, and Federica Mainoldi and Anna Ranghetti (Sekmed, s.r.l) for technical support.

References

1. Sertl, K., Takemura, T., Tschachler, E., Ferrans, V. J., Kaliner, M. A., and Shevach, E. M. (1986). Dendritic cells with antigen-presenting capability reside in airway epithelium, lung parenchyma, and visceral pleura. *J Exp Med* 163, 436–51.
2. Nestle, F. O., Zheng, X. G., Thompson, C. B., Turka, L. A., and Nickoloff, B. J. (1993). Characterization of dermal dendritic cells obtained from normal human skin reveals phenotypic and functionally distinctive subsets. *J Immunol* 151, 6535–45.
3. Nelson, D. J., McMenamin, C., McWilliam, A. S., Brenan, M., and Holt, P. G. (1994). Development of the airway intraepithelial dendritic cell network in the rat from class II major histocompatibility (Ia)-negative precursors: differential regulation of Ia expression at different levels of the respiratory tract. *J Exp Med* 179, 203–12.
4. Sallusto, F., Schaerli, P., Loetscher, P., Schaniel, C., Lenig, D., Mackay, C. R., Qin, S., and Lanzavecchia, A. (1998) Rapid and coordinated switch in chemokine receptor expression during dendritic cell maturation. *Eur J Immunol* 28, 2760–9.
5. Fernandez, N. C., Lozier, A., Flament, C., Ricciardi-Castagnoli, P., Bellet, D., Suter, M., Perricaudet, M., Tursz, T., Maraskovsky, E., and Zitvogel, L. (1999) Dendritic cells directly trigger NK cell functions: Cross-talk relevant in innate anti-tumor immune responses *in vivo*. *Nat Med* 5, 405–11.
6. Rescigno, M., Granucci, F., Citterio, S., Foti, M., and Ricciardi-Castagnoli, P. (1999) Coordinated events during bacteria-induced DC maturation. *Immunol Today* 20, 200–3.
7. Moll, H., Fuchs, H., Blank, C., and Rollinghoff, M. (1993) Langerhans cells transport *Leishmania major* from the infected skin to the draining lymph node for presentation to antigen-specific T cells. *Eur J Immunol* 23, 1595–601.
8. Scheicher, C., Mehlig, M., Zecher, R., and Reske, K. (1992) An immunoblotting procedure for screening glycophorins and band 3 protein in the same blots: Identification of glycophorin and band 3 variant forms. *J Immunol Methods* 154, 253–64.
9. Inaba, K., Inaba, M., Romani, N., Aya, H., Deguchi, M., Ikehara, S., Muramatsu, S., and Steinman, R. M. (1992). Generation of large numbers of dendritic cells from mouse bone marrow cultures supplemented with granulocyte/macrophage colony-stimulating factor. *J Exp Med* 176, 1693–702.
10. Inaba, K., Steinman, R. M., Pack, M. W., Aya, H., Inaba, M., Sudo, T., Wolpe, S., and Schuler, G. (1992). Proliferating dendritic cell progenitors in human blood. *J Exp Med* 175, 1157–67.
11. Romani, N., Gruner, S., Brang, D., Kampgen, E., Lenz, A., Trockenbacher, B., Konwalinka, G., Fritsch, P. O., Steinman, R. M., and Schuler, G. (1994). Identification of proliferating dendritic cell precursors in mouse blood. *J Exp Med* 180, 83–93.
12. Szabolcs, P., Moore, M. A., and Young, J. W. (1995) Expansion of immunostimulatory dendritic cells among the myeloid progeny of human CD34 + bone marrow precursors cultured with c-kit ligand, granulocyte-macrophage colony-stimulating factor, and TNF-alpha. *J Immunol* 154, 5851–61.
13. Sallusto, F., and Lanzavecchia, A. (1994). Efficient presentation of soluble antigen by cultured human dendritic cells is maintained by granulocyte/macrophage colony-stimulating factor plus interleukin 4 and downregulated by tumor necrosis factor alpha. *J Exp Med* 179, 1109–18.
14. Elbe, A., Schleischitz, S., Strunk, D., and Stingl, G. (1994). Fetal skin-derived MHC class I +, MHC class II- dendritic cells stimulate MHC class I-restricted responses of unprimed CD8 + T cells. *J Immunol* 153, 2878–89.
15. Xu, S., Ariizumi, K., Caceres-Dittmar, G., Edelbaum, D., Hashimoto, K., Bergstresser, P. R., and Takashima, A. (1995). Successive generation of antigen-presenting, dendritic cell lines from murine epidermis. *J Immunol* 154, 2697–705.
16. Sassano, M., Granucci, F., Seveso, M., Marconi, G., Foti, M., and Ricciardi-Castagnoli, P. (1994) Molecular cloning of a recombinant retrovirus carrying a mutated envAKR-mycMH2 fusion gene immortalizing cells of the monocytic-macrophage lineage. *Oncogene* 9, 1473–7.
17. Paglia, P., Girolomoni, G., Robbiati, F., Granucci, F., and Ricciardi-Ca stagnoli, P. (1993). Immortalized dendritic cell line fully competent in antigen presentation initiates primary T cell responses in vivo. *J Exp Med* 178, 1893–901.
18. Girolomoni, G., Lutz, M. B., Pastore, S., Assmann, C. U., Cavani, A., and Ricciardi-Castagnoli, P. (1995) Establishment of a cell line with features of early dendritic cell precursors from fetal mouse skin. *Eur J Immunol* 25, 2163–9.

19. Bachmann, M. F., Lutz, M. B., Layton, G. T., Harris, S. J., Fehr, T., Rescigno, M., and Ricciardi-Castagnoli, P. (1996) Dendritic cells process exogenous viral proteins and virus-like particles for class I presentation to CD8+ cytotoxic T lymphocytes. *Eur J Immunol* 26, 2595–600.
20. Lutz, M. B., Assmann, C. U., Girolomoni, G., and Ricciardi-Castagnoli, P. (1996) Different cytokines regulate antigen uptake and presentation of a precursor dendritic cell line. *Eur J Immunol* 26, 586–94.
21. Lutz, M. B., Rovere, P., Kleijmeer, M. J., Rescigno, M., Assmann, C. U., Oorschot, V. M., Geuze, H. J., Trucy, J., Demandolx, D., Davoust, J., and Ricciardi-Castagnoli, P. (1997). Intracellular routes and selective retention of antigens in mildly acidic cathepsin D/lysosome-associated membrane protein-1/MHC class II- positive vesicles in immature dendritic cells. *J Immunol* 159, 3707–16.
22. Winzler, C., Rovere, P., Rescigno, M., Granucci, F., Penna, G., Adorini, L., Zimmermann, V. S., Davoust, J., and Ricciardi-Castagnoli, P. (1997) Maturation stages of mouse dendritic cells in growth factor-dependent long-term cultures. *J Exp Med* 185, 317–28.
23. Sedlik, C., Orbach, D., Veron, P., Schweighoffer, E., Colucci, F., Gamberale, R., Ioan-Facsinay, A., Verbeek, S., Ricciardi-Castagnoli, P., Bonnerot, C., Tybulewicz, V. L., Di Santo, J., and Amigorena, S. (2003). A critical role for Syk protein tyrosine kinase in Fc receptor-mediated antigen presentation and induction of dendritic cell maturation. *J Immunol* 170, 846–52.
24. Vizzardelli, C., Pavelka, N., Luchini, A., Zanoni, I., Bendickson, L., Pelizzola, M., Beretta, O., Foti, M., Granucci, F., Nilsen-Hamilton, M., and Ricciardi-Castagnoli, P. (2006) Effects of dexamethazone on LPS-induced activation and migration of mouse dendritic cells revealed by a genome-wide transcriptional analysis. *Eur J Immunol* 36, 1504–15.
25. Trottein, F., Pavelka, N., Vizzardelli, C., Angeli, V., Zouain, C. S., Pelizzola, M., Capozzoli, M., Urbano, M., Capron, M., Belardelli, F., Granucci, F., and Ricciardi-Castagnoli, P. (2004) A Type I IFN-dependent pathway induced by *Schistosoma mansoni* eggs in mouse myeloid dendritic cells generates an inflammatory signature. *J Immunol* 172, 3011–7.
26. Granucci, F., Feau, S., Angeli, V., Trottein, F., and Ricciardi-Castagnoli, P. (2003) Early IL-2 production by mouse dendritic cells is the result of microbial-induced priming. *J Immunol* 170, 5075–81.
27. Aebischer, T., Bennett, C. L., Pelizzola, M., Vizzardelli, C., Pavelka, N., Urbano, M., Capozzoli, M., Luchini, A., Ilg, T., Granucci, F., Blackburn, C. C., and Ricciardi-Castagnoli, P. (2005) A critical role for lipophosphoglycan in proinflammatory responses of dendritic cells to *Leishmania mexicana*. *Eur J Immunol* 35, 476–86.

Chapter 3

Macrophage Activation: Classical vs. Alternative

Andrea Classen, Jorge Lloberas, and Antonio Celada

Summary

Macrophages are involved in both innate and adaptative immune responses. Depending on the types of cytokines that macrophages are exposed to, these cells are subjected to classical (Th1) or alternative (Th2) activation. In the first case, macrophages, particularly when activated by interferon gamma (IFN-γ) or by lipopolysaccharide (LPS), have the capacity, through the production of NO and other intermediates, to destroy the remaining microorganisms in the inflammatory loci. In the second case, after exposure to cytokines such as IL-4, IL-10, or IL-13, macrophages produce polyamines and proline, which induce proliferation and collagen production, respectively. Interestingly, in both classical and alternative activation, the essential substrate that drives these pathways is the amino acid arginine. NO synthase 2 (NOS2) is induced by IFN-γ or LPS and degrades arginine into OH-arginine and then into NO. Arginase is induced by Th2-type cytokines, which convert arginine into ornithine and subsequently into polyamines and proline. In this chapter, we present simple and direct methods for analyzing the properties of macrophage populations to determine whether they exhibit either a classical or alternatively activated phenotype.

Key words: Macrophage, Classical activation, Alternative activation, Nitric oxide synthase 2, NO, NOS2, Arginase 1, Cytokines.

1. Introduction

Macrophages play an important role in immune responses, both in innate and in acquired immunity. These cells have multiple functional activities not only in the immune system but also in the regulation of lipid metabolism, iron metabolism, wound healing, etc. When the body is invaded by microorganisms, the first cells that reach the inflammatory loci are neutrophils, which

Neil E. Reiner (ed.), *Macrophages and Dendritic Cells,* Methods in Molecular Biology, vol. 531

DOI: 10.1007/978-1-59745-396-7_3

generate large amounts of damaging products in order to destroy the invading microorganisms. After 24 h, macrophages are transported in blood to the inflammatory tissues, where they remain until the resolution of the inflammatory process. Initially, macrophages are required to kill the microorganisms that have resisted the action of neutrophils. This is the point at which macrophages interact with several molecules, thereby activating these cells. This activation implies that they undergo a series of functional, morphological, and biochemical modifications produced by the regulation of a large number of genes. When macrophages interact with Th1-type cytokines, such as interferon gamma (IFN-γ), or lipopolysaccharide (LPS), they produce a series of products, such as NO and oxygen-free radicals, that destroy microorganisms. This type of activation is known as classical activation or M1. When the inciting stimulus is removed from the inflammatory loci, a period of reconstruction ensues, with the removal of apoptotic cells, production of collagen, etc. During this period macrophages become activated by Th2-type cytokines, such as IL-4, IL-10, or IL-13. This type of activation is called alternative activation or M2 *(1–3)*. Interestingly, although these phenotypes exhibit quite distinct properties, they both involve metabolism of the amino acid arginine through distinct biochemical pathways to yield their ultimate characteristics. IFN-γ or LPS induce macrophage NO synthase 2 (NOS2), which converts arginine into OH-arginine and then into NO (**Fig. 1**). In contrast, when

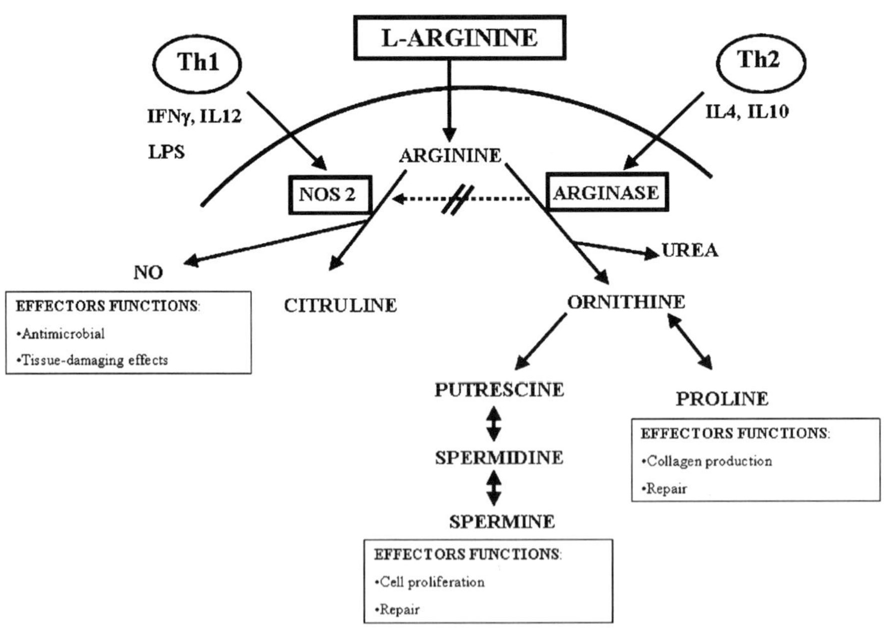

Fig. 1. Catabolism of arginine by macrophages activated by Th1-type cytokines (classical) or by Th2-type cytokines (alternative).

macrophages are activated by IL-4, IL-10 or IL-13, arginase I is induced which degrades arginine into urea and ornithine, which is then subsequently metabolized into proline and polyamines (putrescine, spermidine, and spermine). Proline mediates the production of collagen, while polyamines induce cell proliferation. Thus, alternative activation of macrophages catalyzes the reconstitution of the damaged extracellular matrix, a process that occurs during the final phases of inflammation. Interestingly, the induction of arginase blocks NOS2 at the translational level *(4)*. This observation implies that macrophages are either prepared to destroy by classical activation or to repair by the alternative mode

The entry of arginine to the cell is mediated by specific transporters. We have seen that both classical and alternative activation of macrophages induce the expression of the CAT2 transport system in order to enhance arginine import *(5, 6)*. This transport system limits macrophage activation via either pathway. Arginine is also required for cell proliferation. In this case, it is introduced into the cell by the CAT1 transport system and, once inside it is not degraded but used mainly for new protein synthesis *(7)*.

Investigators are frequently interested to know whether the properties of their particular experimental system favor the generation of M1 vs. M2 macrophages. Here we describe approaches to analyze the properties of macrophage populations including the production of NO and the generation of arginase activity. In addition, we describe a quantitative PCR approach to determine mRNA abundance for both NOS2 and arginase. Finally, we explain how to quantify the amounts of these enzymes by means of Western blots.

2. Materials

2.1. Cell Culture

1. Dulbecco's Modified Eagle's Medium (DMEM).
2. Heat-inactivate Fetal Bovine Serum at 56°C for 30 min; store aliquots at –20°C.
3. Penicillin/Streptomycin.
4. *Stimulating agents*: IFN-γ, LPS, IL-4, IL-10.
5. Cell scrapers.
6. *1× PBS (500 ml)*. 4 g NaCl; 0.1 g KCl; 0.38 g $Na_2HPO_4 \times 2H_2O$; 0.1 g KH$_2$PO4 filled up with ddH$_2$O up to 500 ml.
7. *Buffer for cell lysis*. 1% Triton X-100; 10% Glycerol; 50 mM HEPES, pH 7.5; 150 mM NaCl protease inhibitors: add directly before using aproptinin 1 μg/ml; leupeptin 1 μg/ml; iod-acetamidin 8.6 μg/ml; PMSF 1 mM; phosphatase inhibitors: Na – ortho – vanadate (Na_3VO_4 mM).

2.2. NO Production

1. *100 µM $NaNO_2$*. Dissolve 6.9 mg $NaNO_2$ in 10 ml H_2O; use this stock to prepare a standard curve.
2. H_3PO_4.
3. Sulfanilamide ($H_2NC_6H_4SO_2NH_2$)
4. Naphthyl-Ethylenediamine-di-Hydrochloride ($C_{10}H_7NHCH_2CH_2NH_2 \cdot 2HCl \cdot MeOH$)

2.3. Arginase Activity

1. Eppendorf safe-lock tubes.
2. 0.1% Triton X-100 dissolved in ddH_2O.
3. 50 mM Tris–HCl buffer, pH 7.5.
4. 100 mM $MnCl_2$, for measuring total arginase.
5. 0.5 M Arginine, pH 9.7.
6. H_3PO_4.
7. H_2SO_4.
8. Urea stock solution 600 µg/ml diluted in ddH_2O.
9. Prepare an acid mix containing H_3PO_4, H_2SO_4 and H_2O in a ratio 1/3/7 v/v/v and store it at 4°C.
10. 6% α-isonitrosopropiophenone (α-ISPP) in 100% ethanol; store at 4°C.

2.4. Quantitative Real-Time PCR

1. EZ-RNA Total RNA Isolation Kit.
2. Isopropanol.
3. 75% ethanol absolute diluted in RNase-free H_2O.
4. DNase and RNase-free H_2O.
5. RNase-free 1.5-ml Eppendorf tubes.
6. Sterile filter tips.
7. Quartz glass cuvette, 10 mm.
8. RNase-free 1.5-ml Eppendorf tubes.
9. Sterile pipette tips with filter.
10. M-MLV RT 5× Reaction Buffer, Oligo-(dT) 15 Primer, M-MLV Reverse Transcriptase, dNTP mix. Store these reagents at −20°C.
11. Power SYBR® Green PCR Master Mix.
12. *Primer*. Forward Primer Arginase 1:5′-TTGCGAGACGTAGACCCTGG-3′; T_m = 67.5.
    - Reverse Primer Arginase 1:5′- CAAAGCTCAGGTGAATCGGC-3′; T_m = 66.9.
    - Forward Primer NOS2: 5′-GCCACCAACAATGGCAACA-3′; T_m = 60.
    - Reverse Primer NOS2: 5′-CGTACCGGATGAGCTGTGAATT-3′; T_m = 60.

13. 384-well DNase- and RNase-free PCR plates.
14. PCR ultraclear film.

2.5. Western Blotting

1. Bradford, Protein assay Dye Reagent Concentrate.
2. *Bovine Serum Albumin (BSA)*. Prepare a stock solution of 1 mg/ml.
3. Separating gel buffer 1.5 M Tris–HCl, pH 8.8.
4. Stacking gel buffer 0.5 M Tris–HCl, pH 6.8.
5. 10% Ammonium persulfate (APS).
6. *N,N,N′,N′*-Tetramethylethylenediamine (TEMED).
7. *10× running buffer*. 0.25 M Trizma base; 1.92 M glycin; 1% sodium dodecyl sulfate (SDS); dissolve in H_2O.
8. *5× loading buffer*. For 10 ml: 0.42 ml 0.5 M Tris–HCl, pH 6.8, 2 g 10% SDS, 2.5 ml 0.7% β-mercaptoethanol. 5 ml 10% glycero, 0.5 mg bromophenol-blue-Na-salt, 0.42 ml ddH_2O; store at RT.
9. Prestained SDS-PAGE Standard.
10. *Transfer buffer (for 5 l)*. 15.15 g Trizma base, 72 g glycine, 1 l Methanol; make up to 5 l with water; store at 4°C.
11. Hybond ECL membranes.
12. Whatman paper.
13. *10× TBS (for 1l)*. 60.6 g Trizma base; 87.6 g NaCl; fill with H_2O up to 1 l; adjust pH to 7.5.
14. Tween 20.
15. *Primary antibodies*: Anti-NOS2; anti-Arginase 1; anti-β-Actin.
16. *Secondary antibodies*. Antirabbit-horseradish-peroxidase; antimouse-horseradish-peroxidase.
17. ECL™– Western Blotting Detection reagent.

3. Methods

3.1. Cell Culture (8)

1. Prepare macrophages from bone marrow of Balb/c mice.
2. Kill mice. Remove the legs and separate the femur and tibiae. Cut open the bones and flush with DMEM using an injection needle.
3. Separate cells by pipetting up and down and culture them in DMEM supplemented with 30% M-CSF, 20% FBS, and 1% Penicillin/Streptomycin. The bone marrow extracted from

one mouse is usually divided into four Petri dishes (diameter: 15 cm).

4. Culture cells for 6 days at 37°C in 5% CO_2.
5. After 6 days, detach the adherent cells, an almost homogenous population of macrophages, by scraping. Centrifuge them at 500 g at 4°C for 5 min, and resuspend them in 1 ml DMEM, 10% FBS and 1% Penicillin/Streptomycin.
6. Count cells using a Neubauer cell chamber.
7. Culture cells for 18 h without the macrophage growth factor M-CSF in DMEM 10% FBS and 1% Penicillin/Streptomycin at 37°C in 5% CO_2. Under these conditions macrophages stop proliferating and are arrested in the G0 phase of the cell cycle.

3.2. NO Production (9)

1. Harvest cells. Seed from 100,000 up to 200,000 cells per well in a 96-well culture plate. The total volume per well should be 200 µl. Allow cells to adhere well to the plate at 37°C in 5% CO_2 overnight.
2. The following day, treat cells with the desired stimulating agents. As a positive control, stimulate cells with LPS (100 ng/ml) in combination with IFN-γ (300 units/ml). After adding the stimulating agent, leave cells at 37°C in 5% CO_2 for 24 h.
3. Prepare the working agent before starting the assay because the reagents do not dissolve easily. Add 24.3 ml double-distilled water (ddH_2O) and 735 µl H_3PO_4 to 0.25 g sulfonamide. Wrap the falcon tube in aluminum foil and leave on a roller for 10 min. Afterward, add 0.025 g naphthyl – ethylenediamine – dihydrochloride and allow the components to dissolve while rolling.
4. Meanwhile prepare a standard curve in a new 96-well plate. Prepare sufficient volume for duplicates of each standard value. Prepare the following dilutions:

   0 mM = 100 µl ddH_2O; 5 mM = 5 µl $NaNO_2$ (100 µM) + 95 µl ddH_2O; 10 mM = 10 µl $NaNO_2$ (100 µM) + 90 µl ddH_2O; 25 mM = 25 µl $NaNO_2$

   (100 µM) + 75 µl ddH_2O; 50 mM = 50 µl $NaNO_2$ (100 µM) + 50 µl ddH_2O; 75 mM = 75 µl $NaNO_2$

   (100 µM) + 25 µl ddH_2O; 100 mM = 100 µl $NaNO_2$. Pipette 100 µl of each dilution per well.
5. Transfer 100 µl of the "cell supernatant" per well to the new 96-well plate. From this point on it is not necessary to work in sterile conditions.
6. Add 100 µl of working reagent per well and incubate the reaction for 10 min at RT and protected from light.
7. Measure NO production using an ELISA reader at 540 nm.

8. Generate a standard curve and use this to determine the amounts of NO produced by experimental samples.

3.3. Arginase Activity (9)

1. Harvest cells and count them using a Neubauer cell chamber. Seed 200,000 cells per well in a 96-well culture plate. Culture cells in DMEM 10% FBS and 1% Penicillin/Streptamycin. The total volume per well should be 200 μl. Allow cells to adhere well to the plate at 37°C in 5% CO_2 overnight.
2. The following day treat cells with the stimulating agents of interest. To induce arginase activity in positive control samples, stimulate cells with either IL-4 (10 units/ml) or IL-4/IL-10 (10 units/ml each). Cells are usually incubated for 24 h at 37°C after addition of agonists.
3. The next day, wash cells once with 200 μl 1× PBS and remove PBS by tapping on the plate.
4. Add 100 μl of Triton 0.1% and leave the plate on a rocking platform for 15 min in order to lyse the cells.
5. Add 100 μl of 50 mM Tris–HCl pH 7.5. To measure total arginase, add 10 μl $MnCl_2$. At this point you can stop the reaction and leave the plates wrapped in parafilm at 4°C.
6. Transfer 100 μl per well from the plate in **step 5** to a safe-lock tube (*see* **Note 1**). To measure native arginase, one of the tubes must not contain $MnCl_2$.
7. Incubate the tubes at 56°C for 7 min to activate the enzyme.
8. Add 100 μl of 0.5 M arginine, pH 9.7, and incubate the mixture at 37°C for 2 h. If the stimulus is IL-4, incubate for 1 h; if it is IL-4/IL-10 incubate for only 15 min.
9. Meanwhile prepare the urea standards of the following concentrations:

   0 μg = 100 μl ddH_2O; 7.5 μg = 12.5 μl urea (600 μg/ml) + 87.5 μl ddH_2O; 15 μg = 25 μl urea

   (600 μg/ml) + 75 μl ddH_2O; 30 μg = 50 μl urea

   (600 μg/ml) + 50 μl ddH_2O; 45 μg = 75 μl urea

   (600 μg/ml) + 25 μl ddH_2O; 60 μg = 100 μl urea (600 μg/ml).
10. Stop the reactions from **step 8** by adding 800 μl of an acid mix containing H_3PO_4, H_2SO4, and H_2O in a ratio 1:3:7. Add 900 μl of the same solution to the standards. The reaction can be stopped here and the samples can be left at 4°C for days.
11. Add 40 μl of α-ISPP 6% dissolved in EtOH to all tubes including the standards. Vortex for 5 s (*see* **Note 2**).
12. Incubate all tubes at 95°C for 30 min.
13. Incubate all tubes at 4°C for 30 min.

14. Transfer 200 μl from each tube to a new 96-well cell culture plate.
15. Read the optical density at 540 nm and convert this number using the standard curve in μg urea.
16. Analyze data using the following formula: μg urea/60 (molecular weight of urea) × 50 (dilution factor)/*t* (minutes of incubation with arginine) = units of arginase per 1 × 10^6 cells; 1 unit = amount of enzyme required to hydrolyze 1 μM arginine per minute.

3.4. Determination of mRNA (10)

All reagents and material must be RNase-free. WORK WITH GLOVES!

1. Harvest day 6 bone marrow-derived macrophages as described in **Subheading 3.1** and seed approximately 2 × 10^6 cells per small petri dish (6 cm diameter). Allow cells to adhere and stimulate them the next day.
2. Wash cells once with 2 ml 1× PBS.
3. Add 250 μl of Solution A (EZ-RNA isolation-KIT) per plate and detach cells by scraping (*see* **Note 3**).
4. Transfer the cell suspension to an RNase-free Eppendorf tube and leave the cells for 5 min at RT.
5. Add 250 μl of Solution B (EZ-RNA Total RNA Isolation Kit), invert tubes for 15 s, and incubate the reaction at RT for 10 min.
6. Centrifuge the samples at 12,000 × *g*, 4°C for 15 min.
7. Transfer the upper aqueous phase to a new tube, add 250 μl isopropanol, mix, and incubate for 10 min at RT. You can stop the reaction here and leave the samples at –20°C overnight.
8. Centrifuge the samples at 12,000 × *g* at 4°C for 8 min.
9. Carefully discard the supernatant and add 250 μl 75% EtOH. Mix by tipping the tube.
10. Centrifuge the tubes at 7,500 × *g* at 4°C for 5 min.
11. Discard the supernatant and allow the pellet to dry completely. This might take up to 1 h, but it is important that the pellet is completely dry.
12. Meanwhile prepare a heatblock at 65°C.
13. Dissolve the pellet in approximately 20 μl RNase-free water, depending on the size of the pellet (*see* **Note 4**).
14. Store the samples at –20°C for short-term storage and at –80°C for long-term storage.
15. *Measure RNA*. 1 μl RNA + 400 μl RNase-free H_2O.

16. Measure absorbance at 260 nm using a Quartz cuvette; blank = H_2O; absorbance × 16.04 = µg/µl RNA.
17. For reverse transcription use Rnase-free Eppendorf tubes.
18. Mix 0.1–2 µg RNA with 1 µl Oligo-dT primer mix and fill with ddH_2O to a final volume of 14 µl.
19. Incubate tubes at 65°C for 5 min.
20. Incubate tubes at 4°C for 5 min to prevent the formation of secondary structures.
21. Meanwhile prepare a mastermix: 2.5 µl M-MLV RT 5× Reaction Buffer; 0.625 µl dNTP mix (10 mM each); 0.5 µl M-MLV Reverse Transcriptase; 8.875 µl ddH_2O/per tube.
22. Add 12.5 µl of the mastermix to each tube and spin quickly.
23. Incubate the samples for 2 min at 37°C.
24. Incubate the samples for 50 min at 40°C.
25. Incubate the samples 15 min at 70°C.
26. Spin for a short time and store samples at –20°C.
27. For quantitative Real-Time PCR design primers using the software Primer Express 1.5, Applied Biosystems. The reaction is shown schematically in **Fig. 2**.
28. For normalization, use a gene that is constitutively expressed, like β-Actin or L14.
29. Prepare dilutions of each sample in a ratio 1:4 (sample: H_2O).
30. Prepare a curve using the following dilutions: Dilution 1 *(1)* = 5 µl sample + 15 µl H_2O; Dilution 2 (0.5) = 10 µl of dilution 1 + 10 µl H_2O; Dilution 3 (0.25) = 10 µl of dilution 2 + 10 µl H_2O; Dilution 4 (0.125) = 10 µl of dilution 3 + 10 µl H_2O; Dilution 5 (0.0625) = 10 µl of dilution 4 + 10 µl H_2O. With the values resulting from these dilutions a curve will be made that will allow to evaluate the efficiency of the reaction and will be used to calculate the dilutions of the cycle threshold (CT).
31. Prepare a master mix for each pair of primers:
    - 5.5625 µl SYBR® Green PCR Master Mix
    - 5.5625 µl ddH_2O
    - 0.1875 µl Forward Primer 20 µM
    - 0.1875 µl Reverse Primer 20 µM
    - This is the volume required per well. Calculate for triplicates of each sample and include one well without sample. The standards should be done in duplicate for each gene.
32. Add 11.5 µl master mix and 1 µl sample per well, except the negative control.

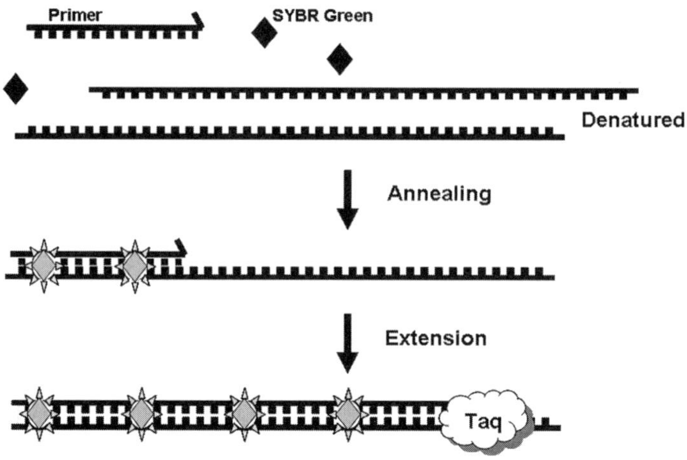

Fig. 2. Schematic representation of real-time PCR with the SYBR® Green I dye. SYBR® Green I dye (DNA nonassociated black diamonds) becomes fluorescent (DNA-bound gray diamonds with spikes) upon binding to double-stranded DNA, thereby providing a direct method for measuring PCR products in real time. (Image provided by Molecular Probes®).

33. Cover the plate with transparent film (*see* **Note 5**).
34. Perform the PCR using the software SDS 2.1. Program the following cycles: 10 min at 95°C; 30 s at 95°C; 30 s at 60°C; 30 s at 72°C. Dissociation stage: 1 min at 95°C during 20 min cooling down to 60°C (1 min); 1 min at 95°C; 35 repeats
35. Analyze data using the software SDS 2.1.

3.5. Determination of Protein Abundance for NOS2 and Arginase 1

All steps should be carried out on ice to avoid protein degradation.

1. Harvest day 6 bone marrow-derived macrophages as described in **Subheading 3.1** and seed approximately 2×10^6 cells per petri dish (diameter: 60 mm). Allow cells to adhere and stimulate the next day.
2. Wash cells once with cold 1× PBS and incubate the plates on ice.
3. Add 150 μl lysis buffer.
4. Detach cells by scraping.
5. Transfer the cells to Eppendorf tubes and leave them rotating at 4°C for 20 min.
6. Centrifuge at 12,000 × *g* at 4°C for 10 min to remove cell wall components.
7. Store the supernatant at –20°C.

Table 1
Recipes for polyacrylamide separating and stacking gels

Reagent	7.5% separating gel	12.5% separating gel	5% stacking gel
30% Acrylamide/0.8% Bis-Acrylamide	2.5 ml	4.2 ml	1.7 ml
1.5M Tris–HCl pH 8.8	2.5 ml	2.5 ml	
0.5 M Tris–HCl pH6.8			2.5 ml
ddH_2O	4.9 ml	3.2 ml	5.7ml
10% Ammonium persulfate	100 μl	100 μl	100 μl
TEMED	4 μl	4 μl	10 μl

8. Dilute Bradford reagent 1:4.
9. Prepare BSA standards of the following volume: 0, 1, 3, 5, 7, 9 μl BSA (1 mg/ml).
10. Add 1 μl of the sample (vortex before) to 1 ml diluted Bradford reagent.
11. Add 1 ml Bradford reagent to the BSA standards.
12. Mix by inverting the tubes.
13. Incubate for 15–30 min at RT.
14. Measure the absorbances of samples and standards at 595 nm using plastic cuvettes.
15. For SDS-PAGE, prepare gels of a thickness of 1.5 mm. For the detection of Arginase1, prepare a 12.5% resolving gel, and for NOS2 a 7.5% resolving gel (**Table 1**).
16. First prepare the separating gel, leaving space for the stacking gel, and overlay with H_2O.
17. As soon as the separating gel is completely polymerized, pour off the water and prepare the stacking gel.
18. Pour in the stacking gel and quickly insert the comb.
19. Prepare the running buffer by diluting 100 ml of the 10× running buffer with 900 ml H_2O.
20. Once the stacking gel is polymerized, remove the comb and assemble the gel unit into the apparatus provided.
21. Fill the tank with 1× running buffer.
22. Prepare the samples by adding 5× loading buffer (dilution 1:4) to approximately 50–100 μg protein (the appropriate volume is determined after quantifying the samples using the Bradford assay).

23. Incubate the samples at 95°C for 6 min and transfer them immediately on ice.
24. Load samples on the gel and include one well for a prestained molecular weight marker.
25. Complete the assembly of the gel unit and connect to a power supply.
26. Run the gel at 80–150 V.
27. When the dye fronts are about to run off the gel, stop the run.
28. For Western Blotting, prepare four Whatman papers and one Hybond-C nitrocellulose membrane (9 cm × 6 cm).
29. Incubate the membrane for 5 min in water.
30. Incubate the membrane and the Whatman papers for 10 min in transfer buffer.
31. Set up the transfer unit as shown schematically in **Fig. 3**.
32. Disconnect the gel unit from the power supply and disassemble it. Separate the two glasses plates. Cut off and discard the stacking gel and transfer the separating gel onto the membrane. Add two Whatman papers and close the transfer cassette.
33. Transfer takes place at 0.8–1.4 mA/cm^2 for 1 h.
34. When the transfer is finished, disassemble the cassette. Use tweezers to move the membrane.
35. From this point on, perform all wash and incubation steps on a rocking platform/shaker.
36. Incubate the membrane for 5 min in 1× TBS 0.1%Tween (TBS-T).
37. Incubate the membrane for 1 h in 50 ml of 1× TBS-T 5% milk to detect NOS2 and for 2 h in 50 ml of TBS-T 10% milk to detect Arginase1.
38. Wash the membrane 2–3 times in TBS-T for 10 min.
39. Incubate the membrane with the first antibody:

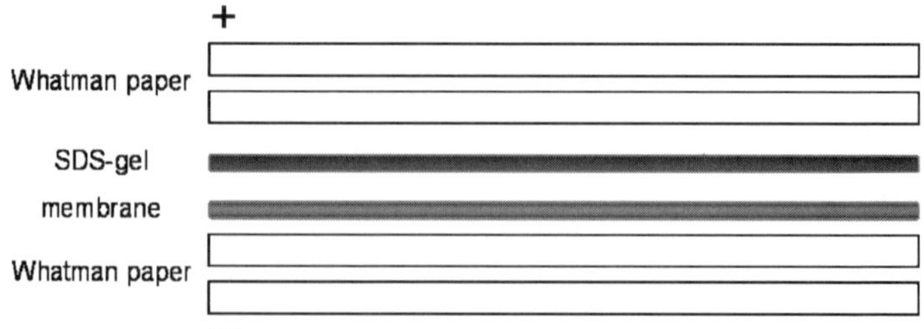

Fig. 3. Schematic representation of the transfer blot.

- *For NOS2.* Anti-NOS2 (1:1000) in TBS-T 0.02% NaN_3.
- *For Arginase 1.* Anti-Arginase 1 (1:10 000) in TBS-T 10% milk 0.02% NaN_3 (*see* **Note 6**).

40. Incubate the membrane with the primary antibody on a roller at 4°C overnight.
41. The next day wash the membrane 2–3 times in TBS-T for 10 min.
42. Incubate the membrane with the secondary antibody. For Arginase1 and for NOS2, you need horseradish-peroxidase-conjugated antirabbit IgG diluted 1:5,000 in TBS-T. Incubate the membrane with this antibody for 1 h at RT on a roller (*see* **Note 7**).
43. Wash the membrane 2–3 times in TBS-T for 10 min.
44. Prepare the ECL solution by mixing both components in the ratio 1:1.
45. Incubate the membrane in ECL solution for approximately 2 min.
46. From this point on, work in the dark using only red light.
47. Dry the membrane carefully and place it between two plastic films located in an X-ray film cassette.
48. Exposure time depends on the intensity of the signal, but usually 1–5 min is sufficient.
49. Once you have achieved a satisfactory result, wash the membrane intensely (put the shaker on max) in TBS-T for 30 min.
50. Incubate the membrane for 1 h with anti-β-Actin (1:5,000) at RT.
51. Wash the membrane 2–3 times in TBS-T for 10 min.
52. Incubate the membranes for 1 h with horseradish-peroxidase-conjugated antimouse IgG (1:5,000) at RT.
53. Wash the membrane 2–3 times in TBS-T for 10 min and repeat the procedure of developing the film after incubating it again in ECL solution.
54. β-Actin serves as a loading control, so you should see a similar intensity of the bands in all lanes.

4. Notes

1. It is important to use safe-lock tubes because later on tubes are incubated at 95°C, which subjects them to high pressure.

2. This step is crucial to avoid a gradient.
3. Ensure that the cell scraper is either new or alternatively incubate it in 0.1M NaOH for 20 min and after that in EtOH for 20 min, before leaving it in 1× PBS.
4. The pellet is normally hardly visible and dissolves very slowly. To shorten the process, incubate the samples at 65°C for 10 min to allow the pellet to dissolve completely.
5. Be careful not to touch the foil except on the edges as this can cause errors in plate reading later on.
6. Primary antibody solutions are prepared in a falcon tube in a total volume of 5 ml. They can be stored at 4°C and be reused for months. Transfer the membrane to the falcon tube using tweezers. The membrane must be rolled carefully to fit in the tube.
7. Secondary antibody solutions should be freshly prepared every time.

Acknowledgments

The authors thank Dr. Manuel Modolell for his help in developing some of the techniques presented here. This work was supported by a grant from the *Ministerio de Ciencia y Tecnología* BFU2004-05725/BMC to A.C. We thank Tanya Yates for editing the manuscript.

References

1. Gordon, S. (2003) Alternative activation of macrophages. *Nat Rev Immunol.* 3, 23–35.
2. Mantovani, A., Sozzani, S., Locati, M., Allavena, P., and Sica, A. (2002) Macrophage polarization: tumor-associated macrophages as a paradigm for polarized M2 mononuclear phagocytes. *Trends Immunol.* 23, 549–55.
3. Noel, W., Raes, G., Hassanzadeh Ghassabeh, G., De Baetselier, P., and Beschin, A. (2004) Alternatively activated macrophages during parasite infections. *Trends Parasitol.* 20, 126–33.
4. Lee, J., Ryu, H., Ferrante, R.J., Morris, S.M. Jr, and Ratan, R.R. (2003) Translational control of inducible nitric oxide synthase expression by arginine can explain the arginine paradox. *Proc Natl Acad Sci U S A.* 100, 4843–8
5. Yeramian, A., Martin, L., Serrat, N., Arpa, L., Soler, C., Bertran, J., McLeod, C., Palacin, M., Modolell, M., Lloberas, J., and Celada A. (2006) Arginine transport via cationic amino acid transporter 2 plays a critical regulatory role in classical or alternative activation of macrophages. *J Immunol.* 176, 5918–24.
6. Martin, L., Comalada, M., Marti, L., Closs, E.I., MacLeod, C.L., Martin del Rio, R., Zorzano, A., Modolell, M., Celada, A., Palacin, M., and Bertran, J. (2006) Granulocyte-macrophage colony stimulating factor increases l-arginine transport through the induction of CAT2 in bone marrow-derived macrophages. *Am J Physiol Cell Physiol.* 290, C1364–72.
7. Yeramian, A., Martin, L., Arpa, L., Bertran, J., Soler, C., McLeod, C., Modolell, M., Palacin, M., Lloberas, J., and Celada, A. (2006) Macrophages require distinct arginine catabolism and transport systems for proliferation and for activation. *Eur J Immunol.* 36, 1516–26.
8. Celada, A., Gray, P.W., Rinderknecht, E., and Schreiber, R.D. (1984) Evidence for

a -interferon receptor that regulates macrophage tumoricidal activity. *J. Exp. Med.* 160, 55–74.

9. Munder, M., Eichmann, K., Moran, J.M., Centeno, F., Soler, G., and Modolell, M. (1999) Th1/Th2-regulated expression of arginase isoforms in murine macrophages and dendritic cells. *J. Immunol.* 163, 3771–3777.

10. Marques, L., Brucet, M., Lloberas, J., and Celada, A. (2004) STAT1 regulates lipopolysaccharide- and TNF--dependent expression of transporter associated with antigen processing 1 and low molecular mass polypeptide 2 genes in macrophages by distinct mechanisms. *J. Immunol.* 173, 1103–1110.

Chapter 4

Analysis of Macrophage Phagocytosis: Quantitative Assays of Phagosome Formation and Maturation Using High-Throughput Fluorescence Microscopy

Benjamin E. Steinberg and Sergio Grinstein

Summary

Phagocytosis of invading pathogens by macrophages represents a fundamental component of the innate immune system. In this chapter, we describe protocols designed for high-throughput analysis of phagosome formation and maturation using latex beads as model phagocytic targets. The method takes advantage of an automated fluorescence microscope platform to investigate Fcγ receptor-mediated particle internalization. First, procedures to opsonize and fluorescently label the model particles are outlined. In combination with the robotic fluorescence microscope, these labeling methods provide for the quantitative high-throughput assessment of phagocytosis. Acidification of the phagosomal lumen can be used as an index of maturation. We describe a fluorimetric procedure to assess phagosomal pH based on the partitioning of a membrane-permeant weak base that accumulates in acidic intracellular compartments. Lastly, a description of the hardware and software components of the robotic high-throughput fluorescence microscope platform is provided.

Key words: Phagocytosis, Acidification, Vacuolar pH, Fcγ receptor, Macrophage.

1. Introduction

A key function of neutrophils and macrophages is to engage and clear invading microorganisms. A variety of receptors present on the plasma membrane of phagocytes mediate interactions with pathogens. These receptors recognize ligands that are either endogenous to the microorganism or are derived from host proteins, such as immunoglobulin G (IgG), components of the complement system or others, that have previously bound (opsonized) the microorganism. IgG molecules that coat the

Neil E. Reiner (ed.), *Macrophages and Dendritic Cells,* Methods in Molecular Biology, vol. 531

DOI: 10.1007/978-1-59745-396-7_4

bacterial surface are recognized by the Fcγ family of receptors, the most highly characterized of phagocytic receptors. Upon engagement with their cognate ligand, Fcγ receptors are thought to cluster at the cell surface, thereby initiating a signaling cascade that brings about active particle internalization into a membrane-bound organelle termed the phagosome. Following its formation, this nascent organelle undergoes an elaborate maturation process whereby both its membrane and luminal composition are modified through a series of coordinated membrane fusion and fission events *(1)*. During its maturation, the phagosome acquires a large armamentarium of antimicrobial components, including proteases and cationic peptides that allow for pathogen clearance and ultimately for the resolution of infection.

A critical element of the maturation process is the gradual acidification of the phagosome lumen to pH values less than 5.5. This acidification is an active process mediated by the proton-pumping vacuolar ATPase (V-ATPase) *(2,3)*. As well as directly affecting bacterial growth, luminal acidification is required for the optimal activity of several bactericidal components. The activity of the various hydrolytic enzymes is exquisitely pH sensitive, requiring acidic conditions. Generation of hydrogen peroxide is also catalyzed by an acidic pH. Moreover, maintenance of an acidic lumen is seemingly required for proper phagosome maturation since dissipation of transmembrane pH gradients with permeant weak bases impairs fusion between phagosomes and lysosomes *(1,4)*.

Phagocytosis can be conceptually divided into two distinct processes: phagosome formation and phagosome maturation. A variety of assays exist to study these two processes independently, often taking advantage of fluorescence microscopy in view of its high sensitivity. Such fluorescence microscopy-based assays rely on the manual acquisition of images, which are subsequently analyzed to discern internalized particles from those that failed to enter the phagocytic cells. To score maturation, multiple fluorescent markers and acquisition channels are sometimes required. When studying multiple time points or conditions, manual data acquisition and analysis can be extremely labor intensive and time consuming. Screening siRNA or small molecule libraries by this approach would be prohibitive.

Automation of both image acquisition and analysis would circumvent these limitations. In this chapter, we describe protocols that make use of a robotic fluorescence microscope along with accompanying digital imaging software to generate high-throughput measurements and analyses of phagocytosis. Phagosome formation is examined by locating cells that have engaged particles and further discriminates between adherent and internalized particles based on a dual-labeling strategy. A method for high-throughput analysis of phagosome maturation is also presented. The method is based on the quantification of luminal acidification using a fluorescent acidotropic dye. Important features of the high-throughput microscopy system and of the ancillary analysis software are also discussed.

2. Materials

1. The assays described in **Subheading 3** can employ either primary cell preparations or established macrophage cells lines, such as the murine RAW 264.7 (ATCC catalog number: TIB-71) or J774 (ATCC catalog number: TIB-67) lines. It is important to note that regardless of cell type, the described procedures entail plating the macrophages on the surface of standard plastic tissue culture plates (*see* **Note 1**). Protocols are given for 24-well plates, but can be readily adapted to smaller well formats (*see* **Note 2**).
2. *Phosphate-buffered saline (PBS).* 140 mM NaCl, 5 mM KCl, 8 mM NaH_2PO_4, and 2 mM KH_2PO_4, adjusted to pH 7.4 with 1 M NaOH.
3. Dulbecco's Modified Eagle's Medium (DMEM) supplemented with 5% fetal bovine serum and 4.5 g/L of glucose, L-glutamine and sodium pyruvate, available commercially.
4. Latex beads are available from a variety of commercial sources.
5. Human IgG and fluorescent secondary antibody conjugates can be purchased commercially (e.g., Sigma-Aldrich or Jackson ImmunoResearch Laboratories), as can Hoechst 33342 and acidotropic fluorescent dyes (available from Molecular Probes and elsewhere).
6. Several commercial high-throughput fluorescence microscope systems are available. The assays described in this chapter make use of the KineticScan HCS Reader and accompanying software modules from Cellomics, Inc. The current state of high-throughput fluorescence microscopy has been the subject of a recent review *(5)*, to which the interested reader is referred.

3. Methods

3.1. Particles

A variety of model particles can be used to carry out phagocytosis assays in macrophages. These include zymosan A, sheep red blood cells, latex beads, and bacteria. We describe protocols employing latex beads as phagocytic targets; nevertheless, other particles can be readily substituted.

3.2. Opsonization

The opsonization of latex beads with IgG simply requires that the particle be incubated with the opsonin (*see* **Note 3**). Other opsonins can be used in a similar manner.

1. Add 40 μL of a 10% suspension of latex beads to 500 μL of PBS and spin for 30 s at 6,000 × *g* in a microcentrifuge, aspirate the supernatant, and resuspend the beads in 500 μL of fresh PBS.
2. Wash twice with PBS. Use 500 μL of PBS and the same centrifugation settings outlined in **step 1** for all subsequent washes.
3. Resuspend beads in 190 μL of PBS and add 10 μL of antihuman IgG (30 mg/mL stock).
4. Incubate for 60 min at room temperature with gentle mixing.
5. Wash three times with PBS to remove excess antibody and resuspend in 500 μL of PBS.

3.3. Fluorescent Labeling

Analysis of phagocytosis by fluorescence microscopy requires that the particles be identifiable. To this end, the opsonized particles can be fluorescently labeled prior to internalization using fluorophore-conjugated secondary antibodies directed against the opsonin (*see* **Note 4**).

1. Add 5 μL of the appropriate fluorophore-conjugated (e.g., Cy3) secondary antibody (1.5 mg/mL stock) to the 500 μL of PBS suspension of opsonized latex beads.
2. Incubate at room temperature for 60 min. The suspension should be kept rotating to prevent the particles from settling and aggregating.
3. Wash four times with PBS and resuspend in 500 μL of PBS. Prior to initiating phagocytosis, the particles can be extruded through a 25-gauge syringe, to disrupt any particle aggregates.

3.4. Particle Presentation and Internalization

3.4.1. Synchronization of Phagocytosis

When assaying multiple conditions for phagocytosis, it is necessary to initiate particle presentation in a temporally defined and homogeneous way. Phagocytosis can be synchronized by rapidly depositing the phagocytic targets onto the cells, but other methods are also available (*see* **Note 5**).

1. Add an aliquot of 15–30 μL of the labeled, opsonized bead suspension (*see* **Subheadings 3.2** and **3.3**) to each well. Ensure that the beads are evenly distributed throughout the bathing medium by briefly shaking the plate.
2. Synchronize phagocytosis by centrifugation at 300 × *g* for 1 min to uniformly settle the beads onto the cells.

3. Incubate the cells at 37°C for 15 min to allow for adequate particle internalization. Different incubation times can be used depending on the experimental objectives and design.

3.4.2. Internal/External Particle Discrimination by Differential Fluorescence Labeling

Once phagocytosis is complete, it is necessary to unambiguously distinguish between those particles that have been internalized from those that remain adherent to the cell membrane but failed to be engulfed. This can be achieved by differentially labeling internalized and external particles using an impermeant fluorophore-conjugated secondary antibody that will stain exclusively the external (exposed) beads. By using an antibody labeled with a fluorophore that is distinct from that used for total bead labeling (*see* **Fig. 1** and **Subheading 3.3**), external beads can be visualized as being dual labeled and differentiated from those that were internalized and are only single labeled (**Fig. 1b**, **c**). The secondary antibody used to identify external beads is similarly directed against the opsonizing IgG.

1. Arrest phagocytosis by placing the cells on ice and washing with cold DMEM to remove beads not associated with the cells.
2. Stain the remaining external, mostly adherent particles by adding 5 μL of a 0.3 mg/mL stock of fluorophore-conjugated (e.g., Cy2) antihuman antibody to the 500 μL solution overlaying each well for 5–7 min in the cold.
3. Wash each well 3–5 times using cold PBS to remove excess secondary antibody.

When assaying for phagosome formation or maturation, proceed to **Subheadings 3.4.3** and **3.5**, respectively.

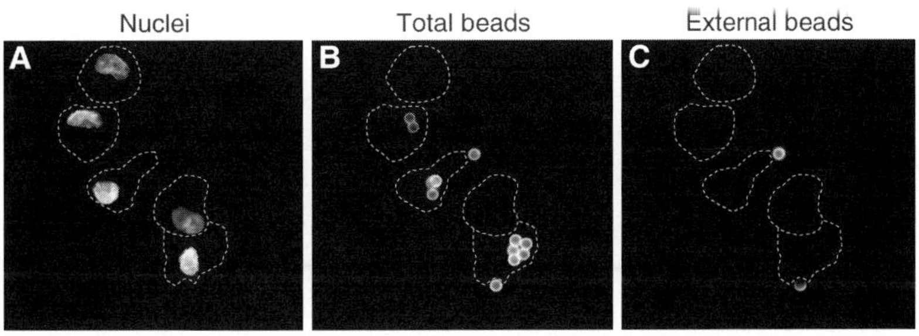

Fig. 1. *Discrimination of internal and external beads by differential fluorescence labeling.* Cy3-labeled, IgG-opsonized latex beads (3.1 μm diameter) were presented to human primary macrophages for 30 min. An image of all the beads associated with the cells after washing is shown in (**B**). External particles were differentially labeled with a Cy2-conjugated secondary antibody and are shown in (**C**). In this way, the external beads can be distinguished by their dual labeling with Cy3 and Cy2, whereas beads that had been successfully engulfed display only the Cy3 label. The cells were fixed and their nuclei stained with Hoechst 33342 prior to imaging. The cell outlines, visualized by differential interference contrast microscopy, are traced by the *dotted lines*, while the fluorescence of the nuclei is shown in (**A**).

3.4.3. Cell Identification by Nuclear Staining

The quantification of phagocytosis requires not only the accurate detection of the internalized particles but also the identification and quantification of the phagocytes themselves. The cells can be seen using either a cytosolic (*see* **Note 6**) or a nuclear stain (**Fig. 1a**) *(6)*.

1. Fix the cells using 4% paraformaldehyde in PBS for 20 min, followed by a wash with 100 mM glycine for at least 10 min, to scavenge excess fixative.
2. Stain the cell nuclei by incubating with the nuclear dye Hoechst 33342 (8 μg/mL) in PBS for 10 min.
3. Wash once and maintain the cells in PBS.

3.4.4. Determination of Phagocytic Index

Subsequent to phagocytosis and external particle labeling, the macrophages are examined using the robotic fluorescence microscope (*see* **Subheading 3.6.1**). Quantification can be performed immediately or digital images can be acquired for subsequent analysis using the image processing software. The efficiency of phagosome formation can be expressed as the phagocytic index (PI), defined as the number of particles internalized per macrophage:

PI = (Total particles − external particles)/total number of macrophages

For each image, the number of internalized beads is simply equal to the difference between the total and external bead numbers. The PI is often normalized per 100 phagocytes.

1. Place the preparation into the microscope chamber, and select the appropriate acquisition protocol.
2. When using dual fluorescent labeling, separately acquire fluorescence images in the channels corresponding to total and external particles, as well as the nuclear stain. Acquire images of multiple fields of view in each well, as needed.
3. Using the object identification software (*see* **Subheading 3.6.2**), identify and count the total number of beads, the total number of external beads, and the total number of macrophages in each field.
4. Compile the data and compute the PI as outlined earlier.

3.5. Phagosome Maturation

Markers of acidification, such as acidotropic fluorescent dyes, can be used to assess phagosome maturation. These compounds are permeant weak bases that are selectively retained in cellular compartments of low pH following their protonation. Acidotropic dyes of assorted colors are commercially available through Molecular Probes and other suppliers, and provide a simple, qualitative evaluation of phagosomal pH (*see* **Note 7**). These dyes can be used according to the manufacturer's instructions. In our protocol, acidic compartments are labeled by incubating the cells with 1 μM LysoTracker® in PBS for 1 min. The cells are washed twice, maintained in cold PBS, and imaged immediately.

3.6. Automated High-Throughput Fluorescence Microscope

The robotic high-throughput fluorescence microscopy provides an integrated system for the automated acquisition and analysis of large populations of cells. High-throughput platforms generally consist of the imaging hardware with either parallel or serial image analysis software modules that can be implemented on- or off-line.

3.6.1. Acquisition

Here we described image acquisition in an automated fashion by the KineticScan HCS Reader. Detailed instructions for its use are provided by the manufacturer. The basic platform consists of a temperature- and CO_2-controlled imaging chamber, outfitted with a mechanical stage that moves the plate across the light path in a predefined trajectory. The general imaging procedure consists of placing the tissue culture plate into the microscope chamber and selecting the appropriate acquisition protocol. Acquisition protocols are defined by three components (the plate, assay, and kinetic protocols), which can be set prior to imaging. Note that for the live cell acidification assays, the chamber is left at room temperature to minimize any further phagosome maturation during the course of image acquisition. Imaging is performed using the XP93 filter set, which allows for recording of DAPI, green, red, and far-red fluorescence channels, with either the 20× or 40× objectives. Autofocus, a feature of the equipment, can be performed at variable intervals, at the discretion of the operator. It is recommended to start by autofocusing every two fields and decreasing the frequency whenever possible (*see* **Note 2**), to increase the acquisition speed.

For phagocytic index assays using dual fluorescent particle labeling, acquire separately fluorescence images in the channels corresponding to the nuclear stain and total and external particles for multiple fields. It is important to acquire the nuclear stain in the first channel, as this is the channel for which the primary object identification will be carried out (*see* **Note 8**). Images of the three channels in a representative field are shown in **Fig. 2a, c, e**. Acidification assays will similarly have three fluorescent channels, corresponding to the total and external bead labels and the acidotropic dye. In this case, the total bead fluorescence should be acquired in the first channel.

3.6.2. Analysis

Image analysis centers upon object identification algorithms. Identification is initially implemented based on user-specified intensity thresholds between adjoining pixels in the first fluorescent channel. Objects within the field can be accepted or rejected for subsequent analyses depending on physical parameters including object area, size, and fluorescent intensity. The accepted objects

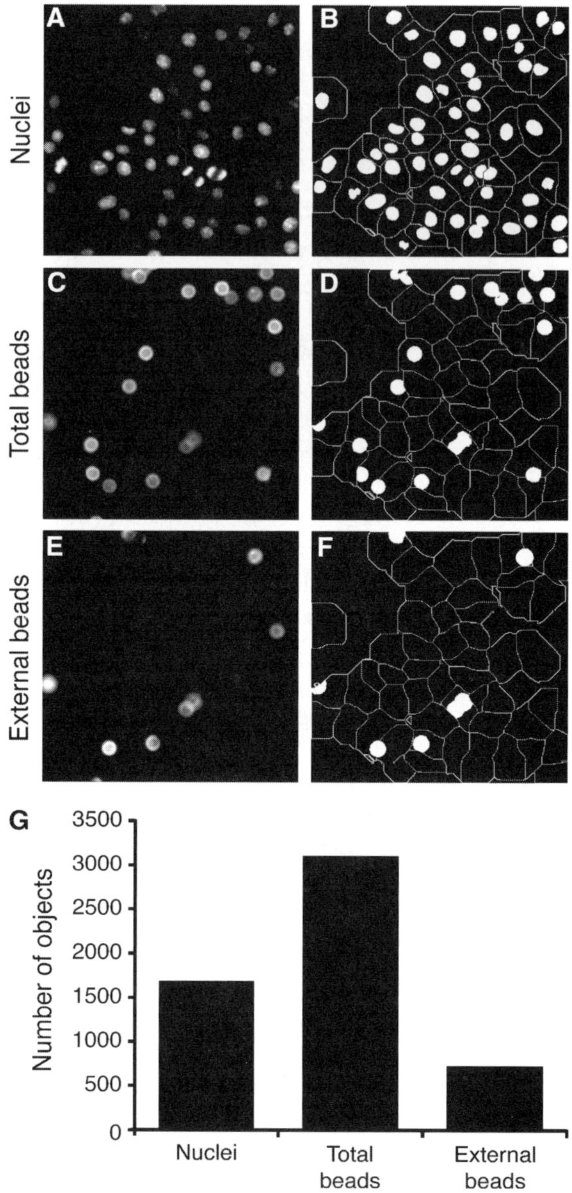

Fig. 2. *Automated quantitation of the phagocytic index.* RAW 264.7 macrophages were allowed to internalize IgG-opsonized, Cy3-labeled 3.1 μm beads as described in the text. Following 15 min of phagocytosis, the remaining external beads were labeled with a Cy2-conjugated antihuman secondary antibody, the cells were fixed, and the nuclei labeled with Hoechst 33342. Imaging was then carried out using the KineticScan HCS Reader. The stained nuclei, used to identify individual cells, are shown in (**A**), all the cell-associated beads (Total beads) are shown in (**C**), while the external beads are displayed in (**E**). The number of objects in each fluorescent channel was quantified using the Spot Detector BioApplication. Objects identified by the software module are shown in for each channel in panels (**B**), (**D**) and (**F**). The cell outlines, defined by the software as an area (a *Circ*) corresponding to 35 pixels beyond the edge of each identified nucleus, are also depicted. These calculated outlines were used to search and quantify objects associated with individual cells. Object counts from a representative experiment are shown in (**G**)

are designated as primary objects, and regions around or within the individual objects are used in the ensuing quantification procedures (*see* **subheading "Regions of Interest"**). Proprietary software modules (termed BioApplications) further refine the analysis of the determined regions of interest. Brief overviews of two such modules are provided as follows, whereas detailed descriptions are available from the manufacturer.

Regions of Interest

Refinement of the image analysis relies heavily on defining appropriate regions of interest. Here we present a summary of the various shapes that can be assigned to such regions. Across the different analysis modules, two different types of regions can be demarcated with reference to the primary object. These are termed the *Circ* and the *Ring*. A *Circ* represents an area similar to, and centered about, that occupied by the primary object. It can be made either smaller or larger than the primary object. In contrast, the *Ring* denotes an annular area defined beyond the edge of the primary object. The user defines the position of the inner and outer perimeters relative to the primary object. In certain applications, individual spots within the regions can be discerned and are termed either *Circ Spots* or *Ring Spots*, depending on the structure of the associated region in which they lie.

Phagocytic Index

The Spot Detector BioApplication is used to calculate the phagocytic index, with the nuclei representing the primary objects (cells). This module offers a generic and adaptable stage for counting well defined cell-associated objects.

1. Following primary object identification, define a region (a *Circ*) delineating approximately 20 μm beyond the edge of each nucleus to fully encompass the cell perimeter. **Figure 2b** illustrates the identified nuclei and the associated regions of interest of a representative field.
2. Determine the number of distinct spots within these regions in both the total and external bead labels. The parameters used for secondary object identification must be appropriately configured. Spot identification is shown for total and external bead channels in **Fig. 2d**, **f**, respectively. Total object numbers in each channel are given in **Fig. 2g**.
3. Compute the PI as defined in **Subheading 3.4.4**.

Phagosome Maturation

The Compartmental Analysis BioApplication is used to quantify individual object fluorescence intensities and thus assess phagosome maturation. In this assay, the total bead label identifies the primary objects. This module offers detailed fluorescence intensity data of individual primary objects and their associated regions in multiple fluorescent channels. Application examples of this protocol to the study of phagosome maturation are available in *(6)*.

1. Following primary object identification, define a region (a *Circ*) delineating approximately 1 μm beyond the edge of each bead. This region represents the area enclosed by the phagosome.
2. Determine the total fluorescence intensity within the region for the acidotropic dye and establish the presence of the external bead label.
3. Establish which objects represent the subpopulation of external particles based on their external-bead label fluorescence. Uninternalized beads will have both the total and external labels, as described earlier. All remaining objects are considered to be contained within phagosomes (*see* **Figs. 1** and **2**).
4. Compute the fluorescence of the acidotropic dye colocalized with the internalized particles as a measure of acidification and thus maturation.

4. Notes

1. Efficient high-throughput acquisition depends on the ability of the microscope to capture accurate (in focus) images with minimal user input. This is accommodated by the autofocusing capabilities (also *see* **Note 2**) of the Cellomics system and of equivalent systems. The ability to autofocus depends on the number of objects on which the algorithm is trying to focus. Should the cells be plated too sparsely, some fields may not contain any identifiable objects. In this case, the system will spend considerable time attempting ineffectively to focus. As this dramatically increases acquisition time, it should be avoided whenever possible. Image analysis requires precise object identification algorithms. When too many objects are captured in the field of view, distinguishing individual particles becomes more difficult. Even with optimal plating conditions, the software will encounter situations where objects will be directly adjacent to each other. To help resolve two adjacent objects, certain software modules include algorithms that discriminate between overlapping particles (termed object segmentation) based on geometry or peak intensities. The geometric method is particularly well suited for resolving adjacent latex beads as they have smooth boundaries and generally uniform size and intensity. While the object segmentation methods provide a valuable tool when imaging at higher object

densities, suitable cell and particle numbers remain crucial for a successful experiment. Ultimately, for efficient imaging, cells should be plated at minimum densities of 40 and 10 cells/mm^2 when using the 40× and 20× objectives, respectively. In fact, we have found that plating densities 10–40 times these minima provide significantly better autofocusing without compromising the object identification algorithms.

2. Imaging is performed through the bottom of the plastic tissue culture plates. As a result, autofocusing is necessary due to the nonuniformity in plate thickness. We empirically found that this problem was minimized using smaller well sizes and recommend that at least 24-well plates be used as they are more easily managed by the autofocus feature of the microscope. Smaller well formats further decrease the need for continual refocusing.
3. A variety of different latex beads are available commercially; however, styrene/divinylbenzene (DVB) copolymer latex beads are, in our experience, preferable. In our hands, beads that do not contain DVB are not efficiently opsonized and are therefore ingested poorly by RAW 264.7 macrophages. Once opsonized, the latex beads can be stored at 4°C for several days. Following prolonged storage, it is advisable to ensure that the beads have maintained the opsonin using a fluorophore-conjugated secondary antihuman antibody.
4. For total particle labeling with a fluorophore-conjugated secondary antibody, it is imperative that the fluorophore display little pH sensitivity. As outlined in **Subheading 1**, the phagosome lumen becomes progressively more acidic, which can severely quench the fluorescence of pH-sensitive dyes, such as fluorescein.
5. Placing the cells on ice and allowing the phagocytic targets to slowly sediment at 1 × *g* can alternatively be used to synchronize phagocytosis. In this way, centrifugation is obviated, yet the particles adhere to the cells without being internalized. The cells are then gently washed and maintained in media prewarmed to 37°C. The protocol is completed as outlined in **Subheading 3.4**.
6. Phagocytosis protocols can similarly be implemented using a cytosolic marker instead of a nuclear stain for cell identification. Cytosol labeling can be accomplished using a variety of dyes, such as the Cell Tracker probes available from Molecular Probes. In this case, the cells are prelabeled with Cell Tracker Green (2 μg/mL) for 30 min at 37°C. The cells are then washed three times with PBS before adding the phagocytic targets. This type of cell labeling is particularly useful when information relating to cell size and shape is required.

7. When using acidotropic dyes, it is important to consider that in some cases dye accumulation is not readily reversible. Even artificial alkalinization using ionophores or a membrane-permeant weak base will not readily disperse the accumulated dye. As a result, treatments that will dissipate the phagosomal pH gradient must be carried out prior to and during application of the acidotropic dye.
8. The automated system does have certain limitations both in terms of its acquisition and analysis that must be considered when designing defined experimental protocols. Some examples are listed here (1) currently, acquisition is limited to five fluorescent channels, with no capacity to acquire a corresponding bright field image; (2) because image acquisition occurs through the tissue culture plate, objectives with suitably long focal distances must be used. The highest possible magnification is currently 40×, which limits the types of structures that can be resolved; (3) primary object identification is carried out on the images acquired in the first channel. The channel number order cannot, at present, be easily modified postacquisition.

Acknowledgments

The authors thank Christopher Fladd for his assistance with the Cellomics KineticScan HSC Reader, as well as the SIDNET facility at the Hospital for Sick Children. B.E.S. is supported by a studentship from the McLaughlin Center for Molecular Medicine. S.G. is the current holder of the Pitblado Chair in Cell Biology.

Research in the authors' laboratory is supported by the Heart and Stroke Foundation of Canada, the Canadian Cystic Fibrosis Foundation, and the Canadian Institutes of Health Research.

References

1. Vieira, O. V., Botelho, R. J., and Grinstein, S. (2002) Phagosome maturation: aging gracefully. *Biochem J* 366, 689–704.
2. Lukacs, G. L., Rotstein, O. D., and Grinstein, S. (1990) Phagosomal acidification is mediated by a vacuolar-type H(±)-ATPase in murine macrophages. *J Biol Chem* 265, 21099–21107.
3. Lukacs, G. L., Rotstein, O. D., and Grinstein, S. (1991) Determinants of the phagosomal pH in macrophages. In situ assessment of vacuolar H(+)-ATPase activity, counterion conductance, and H+ "leak". *J Biol Chem* 266, 24540–24548.
4. Gordon, A. H., Hart, P. D., and Young, M. R. (1980) Ammonia inhibits phagosome–lysosome fusion in macrophages. *Nature* 286, 79–80.
5. Pepperkok, R., and Ellenberg, J. (2006) High-throughput fluorescence microscopy for systems biology. *Nat Rev Mol Cell Biol* 7, 690–696.
6. Steinberg, B. E., Scott, C. C., and Grinstein, S. (2006) High-throughput assays of phagocytosis, phagosome maturation, and bacterial invasion. *Am J Physiol Cell Physiol* 292, C945–C952.

Chapter 5

Detection of Activated Rab7 GTPase with an Immobilized RILP Probe

Jim Sun, Ala-Eddine Deghmane, Cecilia Bucci, and Zakaria Hmama

Summary

The dynamic and coordinated exchange of multiple GTPases between the cytosol and the phagosome membrane represents a critical process during phagosome biogenesis. In particular, acquisition of Rab7 is crucial for progression to the stage where formation of phagolysosomes is observed. Optimal Rab7 effector function requires its conversion to the GTP-bound form where it becomes activated. In light of this regulatory node, the GDP/GTP switch on the Rab7 molecule represents a tractable event to dissect the control of phagosome maturation by intracellular pathogen or their products. Direct measurement of Rab7 activation requires ^{32}P-GTP binding to renatured Rab7 recovered by pull downs and resolved by SDS-Polyacrylamide Gel Electrophoresis (SDS-PAGE) and autoradiography. Here, we describe a novel, alternative, nonradioactive assay to measure Rab7 activity which takes advantage of the specific binding of activated (GTP bound) Rab7 to its effector RILP (Rab7 interacting lysosomal protein). Active Rab7 bound to immobilized recombinant RILP on latex beads can be detected quantitatively by either classical Western blotting or flow cytometry.

Key words: Rab7, RILP, Small GTPase, Flow cytometry, Immunostaining, Immunoblotting.

1. Introduction

Small GTPases function as molecular switches, alternating between inactive GDP- and active GTP-bound states dependent on signals that influence the remodeling of cell membranes *(1, 2)*. Within the Rab GTPase family, Rab7 has been shown to be a major regulator of phagosome fusion with late endosomes and lysosomes *(3–5)*. Rab7 is translocated from the cytosol to phagosome membranes in a GDP-bound (inactive) form, at which point a guanine nucleotide exchange factor (GEF) mediates exchange

Neil E. Reiner (ed.), *Macrophages and Dendritic Cells,* Methods in Molecular Biology, vol. 531

DOI: 10.1007/978-1-59745-396-7_5

of GDP for GTP on membrane-bound Rab7 *(2)*. Subsequent inactivation of GTP-bound Rab7 is catalyzed by GTPase-activating protein (GAP) through GTP hydrolysis. Several studies have shown that the GDP/GTP switch allows direct interaction of Rab7-GTP with RILP (Rab7 interacting lysosomal protein), an essential downstream effector involved in phagosomal fusion with lysosomes *(6–8)*. RILP bridges phagosomes with dynein-dynactin, a microtubule-associated motor complex that drives phagosomes toward lysosomes *(7)*. Therefore, the GDP/GTP switch on Rab7 defines a discrete vesicular trafficking checkpoint that determines in part the ability of phagosomes to fuse with the lysosomal compartment.

Activation state of Rab7 may be assessed with the use of a radioactive nucleotide probe (^{32}P-GTP) to detect active Rab7 in cell lysates resolved by SDS-Polyacrylamide Gel Electrophoresis (SDS-PAGE) and electrotransferred onto PVDF membranes *(6, 9)*. Alternatively, fluorescent chimeric constructs of Rab7 and RILP, in combination with confocal microscopy may be used to define the kinetics of Rab7-RILP association and thus the state of activation of phagosome-associated Rab7 *(10–12)*. With the goal of delineating a less labor-intensive and nonradioactive method for quantification of intracellular active Rab7, we developed RILP-coated latex beads as a specific probe for accurate detection of Rab7-GTP.

This approach could also be applied to other GTPases involved in intracellular trafficking events. For example, Rab5 is an early endosomal marker required for proper vesicle trafficking, and its activation through the GDP/GTP switch allows for interactions with downstream effectors, one of which is EEA1 (early endosomal autoantigen 1) *(13)*. EEA1 is a known cognate binding protein of Rab5, and it could be used in a similar manner as RILP to pull down active Rab5 from cell lysates. This activation assay could also extend to any other small GTPases for which a specific binding effector has been identified.

We highlight the utility of this assay using macrophages infected with *Mycobacterium bovis* BCG. This illustrates how this powerful tool may be used to dissect mechanisms of microbial pathogenesis at the level of the Rab7 GDP/GTP switch contributing to defects in phagosome trafficking.

2. Materials

2.1. Cell Culture and Lysis

1. Murine macrophage cell lines J774A.1 and RAW 264.7.
2. Endotoxin-free Dulbecco's Modified Eagle's Medium (DMEM) supplemented with 10% fetal calf serum (FCS)

and 1% of each of the following supplements: penicillin-streptomycin mixture, nonessential amino acids, and HEPES.

3. Protease inhibitor mixture and PMSF.
4. *Macrophage lysis buffer*. 20 mM Tris buffer, pH 8.0 containing 137 mM NaCl, 1% glycerol, 1% TritonX-100, 1 mM EDTA, 1 mM PMSF, and 100 μg/ml mammalian protease inhibitor mixture.

2.2. Mycobacterial Culture

1. *Mycobacterium bovis* BCG (Pasteur 1173P2 strain) and *M. smegmatis* (mc^2155 strain) were provided by Dr. Richard Stokes (Dept of Pediatrics, University of British Columbia, BC, Canada).
2. *7H9-OADC*. Middlebrook 7H9 supplemented with 10% OADC.

2.3. GST Fusion Protein Expression and Purification

1. *E. coli* strain BL21, RILP-GST plasmid (*see* **Note 1**).
2. Luria–Bertani (LB) media, ampicillin, and chloramphenicol.
3. Glutathione-agarose resin and Isopropyl β-D-1-thiogalactopyranoside (IPTG).
4. *Bacterial lysis buffer*. PBS plus 1 mM DTT, 0.1 mM PMSF, 1 mg/ml lysozyme, and 100 μg/ml of bacterial protease inhibitors.
5. *Elution buffer*. 10 mM reduced glutathione in 50 mM Tris-HCl, pH 9.5 (*see* **Note 2**).

2.4. Cell Transfection

1. OPTI-MEM and HBSS.
2. pEGFP-C1 vector construct expressing wild-type Rab7, Rab7Q67L, or Rab7T22N *(6, 14, 16)*.
3. Lipofectamine 2000.

2.5. Latex Bead Coating

1. Aldehyde/sulfate latex beads (4 μm diameter).
2. 25 mM MES buffer, pH 5.86.
3. *PBS*. 8 g NaCl, 0.2 g KCl, 1.44 g Na_2HPO_4, 0.24 g KH_2PO_4, in 1 L of distilled water, pH 7.4.
4. PBS plus 1% BSA and 0.1% NaN_3 (PBS-BSA-Az).

2.6. Flow Cytometry Analysis

1. Mouse mAb anti-GST and rabbit polyclonal anti-RILP *(6)*.
2. FITC-conjugated goat antimouse and goat antirabbit IgG.
3. *Binding buffer*. HBSS plus 1% FCS and 0.1% NaN_3 (HBSS-FCS-Az).
4. Setting parameters for latex bead analysis (*see* **Fig. 1**).

2.7. SDS-Polyacrylamide Gel Electrophoresis

1. *Separating buffer*. 1.5 M Tris-HCl, pH 8.8, 0.4% SDS. Store at room temperature.

Detector	Voltage	Gain
FSC	E01	2.41
SSC	396	1.00

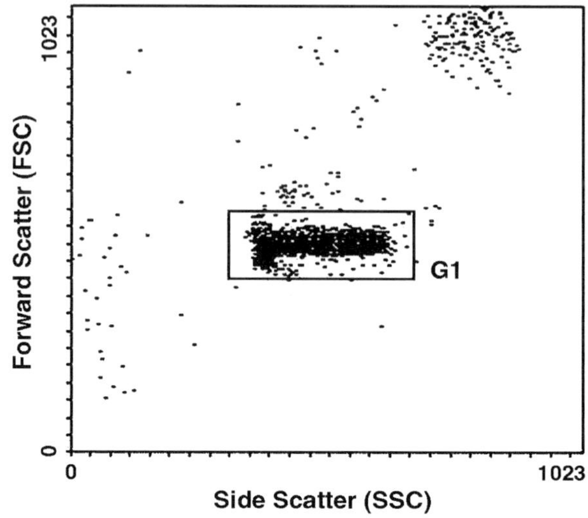

Fig. 1. Setting parameters for FACS analysis of latex beads. RILP-coated 4-μm latex beads (~10^7) were incubated with 500 μg of soluble fraction of cell lysate for 3 h at room temperature. Beads were then washed three times with binding buffer, resuspended in the same buffer, and analyzed by flow cytometry. Beads were localized by plotting forward scatter (FSC) vs. side scatter (SSC) channels on a linear scale using the voltage and gain values indicated. Beads (G1 gate) were readily discriminated from remaining contaminating material in the preparation.

2. *Stacking buffer.* 0.5 M Tris-HCl, pH 6.8, 0.4% SDS. Store at room temperature.
3. Acrylamide/bis-Acrylamide (30% solution). Store at 4°C.
4. *N,N,N,N'*-Tetramethyl-ethylenediamine (TEMED).
5. *Sample buffer.* 62.5 mM Tris-HCl, pH 6.8, 20% glycerol, 2% SDS, 5% β-mercaptoethanol.
6. *Ammonium persulfate.* Prepare 10% solution in water and freeze in single-use (100 μL) aliquots at –20°C.
7. Water-saturated isobutanol. Shake equal volumes of water and isobutanol in a glass bottle and allow separation to occur. Store at room temperature. Use the top layer.
8. *Running buffer.* 25 mM Tris, 192 mM glycine, 0.1% (w/v) SDS, pH 8.3. Store at room temperature.
9. Pageruler prestained protein ladder.

2.8. Immunoblotting

1. Rabbit polyclonal anti-Rab7, mouse mAb anti-GST, and rabbit polyclonal anti-GFP.
2. Horseradish-peroxidase-conjugated antirabbit and antimouse IgG.
3. Nitrocellulose membranes (0.45 μm).
4. *Transfer buffer*. 25 mM Tris, 0.2 M glycine, 20% methanol, 0.04% (w/v) SDS.
5. *TBS-T (wash buffer)*. 100 mM Tris-HCl, pH 7.5, 0.9% (w/v) NaCl, 0.1%–0.5% Tween 20.
6. *Blocking buffer*. TBS-T plus 3% BSA.
7. Enhanced chemiluminescent (ECL) reagents.
8. *Stripping buffer*. 0.5 N NaOH at 37°C.

3. Methods

This assay will allow measurement of the amount of active GTP-bound Rab7 in a prepared cell lysate sample. It utilizes the Rab7 effector, RILP, as a surrogate marker of Rab7 activity. It is important to have highly purified RILP expressed as a fusion protein to GST as well as a GST fusion protein negative control. Purification could be assessed by sample analysis of eluted protein fractions using SDS-PAGE and Coomassie blue staining. The macrophage cell lines, RAW 264.7 and J774, as well as bone marrow-derived mouse macrophages express significant levels of endogenous Rab7. Therefore, there is no need to transfect cells with Rab7 constructs unless the experiment calls for negative mutant (Rab7T22N) or constitutively active (Rab7Q67L) constructs of Rab7. Details for macrophage transfection are provided in materials **Subheading 2.4** and in **Note 3**.

RILP-coated latex beads are used to pull down specifically *active* Rab7 (GTP-bound form) from cell lysate. Bead-associated Rab7 is detected by immunostaining with specific anti-Rab7 antibodies. The extent of Rab7 interaction with its partner molecule RILP is then quantified by flow cytometry. If required, confirmation of the flow cytometry data may be obtained by SDS-PAGE and Western blotting with anti-Rab7 antibodies using equal numbers of beads from various test samples being tested.

To validate this assay, we have transfected cells of the RAW 264.7 macrophage cell line individually with either of three forms of Rab7: wild-type (WT), constitutively active mutant (Q67L), and dominant negative (T22N). Rab7T22N is a GDP-locked mutant and thus unable to interact with RILP. However, the wild-type and constitutively active GTP-bound mutants are competent to associate with RILP-coated beads in vitro and thus function as a readout of Rab7 activity. As described, validation experiments involving FACS quantification (**Fig. 2a**) as well as immunoblotting analysis (**Fig. 2b**) show that Rab7WT and Rab7Q67L but not Rab7T22N bind to immobilized RILP on latex beads.

Active Rab7 is an important regulator of vesicle trafficking and phagosome maturation. Hence, this assay allows rapid and accurate determination of the activation state of Rab7 in cells undergoing active vesicular trafficking. One example of how this novel assay can be exploited to examine the dynamics of phagosome maturation is provided using macrophages infected with

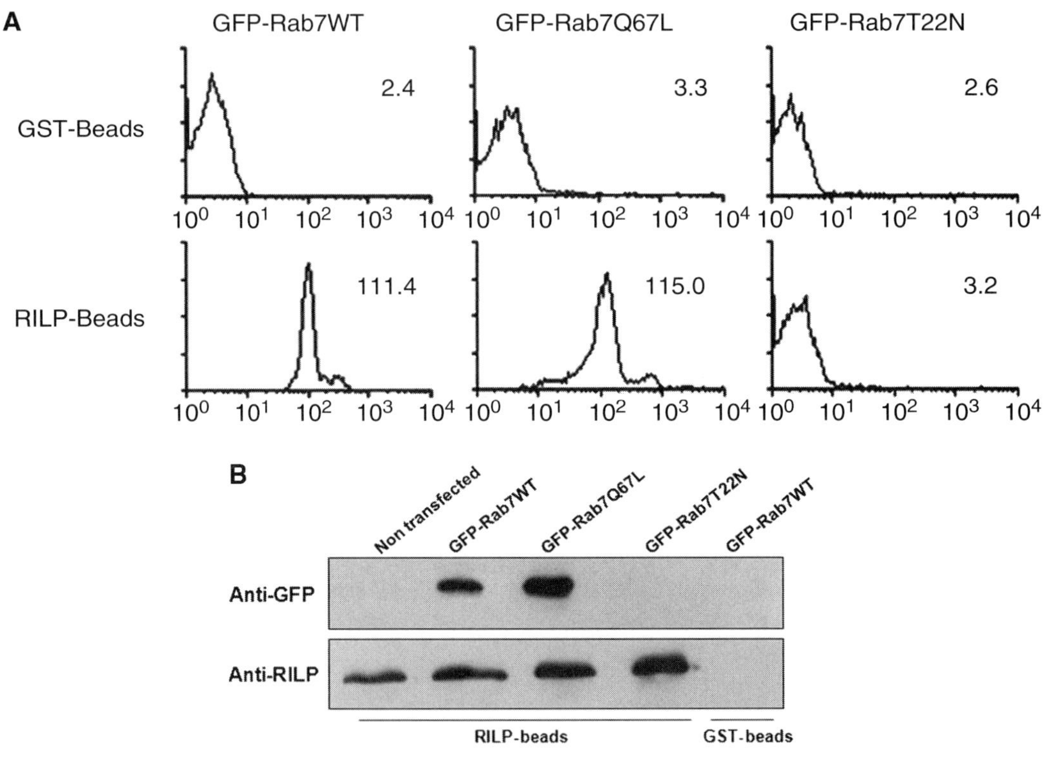

Fig. 2. Validation of Rab7 activation assay. (**A**) adherent RAW cells were transfected with wild-type (GFP-Rab7WT), constitutively active (GFP-Rab7Q67L) or dominant negative (GFP-Rab7T22N) Rab7. Cell lysates were prepared, cleared of insoluble material and then incubated with GST-RILP- or GST (control)-coated latex beads. Beads were then washed and stained with rabbit anti-GFP (1:100 dilution) followed by FITC conjugated to antirabbit (1:50 dilution). Samples were then subjected to analysis by flow cytometry according to parameter sittings shown in **Fig.** 1. Fluorescence signals from 10,000 events were recorded from the G1 gate, and the mean fluorescence intensities were determined (values in top right side of each panel). The shift of fluorescence histogram (binding to GST-RILP-beads relative to binding to GST-beads) shows the extent of Rab7 binding to immobilized RILP. GST-RILP beads were able to pull down GFP-Rab7WT and GFP-Rab7Q67L, but not GFP-Rab7T22N, from cell lysates. (**B**) equal numbers ($\sim 50 \times 10^7$) of latex beads prepared as in (**A**) were subjected to SDS-PAGE and Western blotting with anti-GFP antibodies (*upper panel*). Membranes were stripped and reprobed with rabbit anti-RILP antibodies (lower panel) to control for level of RILP-GST in the reactions. As was observed in the flow cytometry analysis, the dominantly negative form (T22N) of Rab7 was unable to interact with RILP.

pathogenic mycobacteria. The results shown in **Fig.** 3a (FACS analysis) and **Fig.** 3b (Western blotting) indicate that active Rab7 is reduced in cells infected with live *M. bovis* BCG compared to cells exposed to killed BCG or infected with the nonpathogenic species *M. smegmatis*. These findings are consistent with previously published findings showing phagosome maturation arrest in macrophages infected with live BCG but not in cells exposed to either killed BCG or infected with *M. smegmatis (4, 15, 16)*.

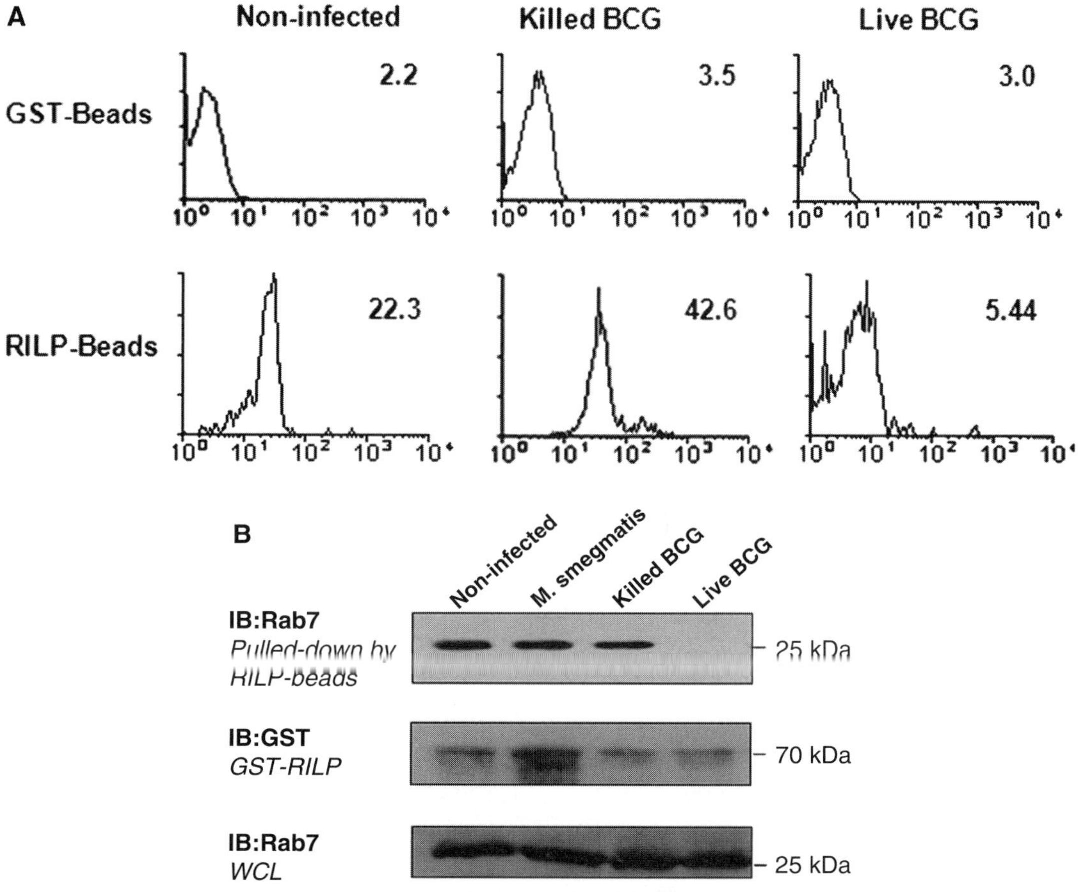

Fig. 3. Live BCG infection disrupts Rab7-RILP interaction in J774 macrophages. (**A**) J774 macrophages were infected with live or killed BCG and cell lysates were prepared at 4 h postphagocytosis. BCG organisms were killed by 2 h treatment with 50 μg/ml gentamycin at 37°C. Lysates were mixed with RILP-GST or GST (control) beads to pull down endogenous active Rab7. Samples were then washed and stained with rabbit anti-Rab7 (1:100 dilution) followed by FITC-conjugated antirabbit (1:50), and subjected to flow-cytometry analysis as described in **Fig. 2a**. The results show that RILP beads failed to pull down Rab7 from lysates of cells infected with live BCG indicating that infection blocked GDP/GTP exchange. (**B**) macrophages were infected with either live or killed BCG or with the nonpathogenic species *M. smegmatis*. Endogenous Rab7 was pulled down as described in (**A**) and equal numbers of beads were subjected to SDS-PAGE and Western blotting with anti-Rab7 antibodies (upper panel). Membranes were stripped and reprobed with rabbit anti-GST antibodies (middle panel) to control for level of RILP-GST in the reactions. Equal amounts of whole-cell lysate (WCL) protein from each treatment sample were subjected to Western blotting with anti-Rab7 antibodies to control for levels of Rab7. Live BCG, unlike either killed BCG or nonpathogenic *M. smegmatis*, blocks the interaction of Rab7 with RILP.

3.1 Cell Culture and Infection

1. Macrophage transfection with Rab7 constructs (*see* **Note 3**).
2. Allow RAW cells to adhere overnight in 6-cm diameter culture dishes: ~10^5/cm^2.
3. Wash cells twice with HBSS and replenish wells with antibiotic-free media.
4. Infect cells with mycobacteria (multiplicity of infection, 20:1) for 2 h at 37°C and 5% CO_2, then wash three times with HBSS and reincubate for an additional 4 h.
5. Wash three times with HBSS and harvest by cell scraper.
6. Lyse cells on ice for 30 min in macrophage lysis buffer.
7. Centrifuge at 13,000 rpm for 10 min at 4°C to remove cell debris. Collect lysate and store at –70°C until ready for incubation with coated latex beads (**Subheading 3.4.1**). This lysate contains the sample of either endogenous Rab7 or transfected GFP-Rab7 for assay of activation state.

3.2. Protein Overexpression and Purification

1. Transform RILP-GST plasmid into *E. coli* strain BL21.
   (a) Mix DNA (1–2 μl) and competent BL21 cells (80–100 μl), then keep on ice for 1–1.5 h.
   (b) Heat shock for 3 min at 42°C, then add 900 μl LB media, and incubate 1 h at 37°C with shaking.
   (c) Plate on LB agar plates containing ampicillin (100 μg/ml) and chloramphenicol (15 μg/ml), then incubate overnight at 37°C.
2. Pick one growing colony and transfer into LB medium containing ampicillin (100 μg/ml) and chloramphenicol (15 μg/ml). Allow the culture to grow to an OD_{600} of 0.6 at 37°C.
3. Induce expression of RILP-GST with 0.2 mM IPTG at 22°C overnight.
4. Spin down bacterial cells (15 min, 5,000 rpm, 4°C), resuspend in bacterial lysis buffer for 30 min, and lyse on ice by sonication for 2–3 min at 30 s intervals.
5. Clarify bacterial lysate (30 min, 15,000 rpm, 4°C), then purify GST fusion protein using glutathione-agarose resin by passing through the column several times (*see* **Note 4.**).
6. Elute the fusion protein using 10 mM reduced glutathione in 50 mM Tris-HCl, pH 9.5.
7. Collect three 1-ml fractions and examine on SDS-PAGE for purity and estimate concentration using Bio-Rad protein concentration assay kit.

3.3. Latex Bead Coating

1. Adjust MES buffer to pH 5.86 (pI of RILP-GST).
2. Transfer 100 μl of aldehyde/sulfate latex beads (about 10^8 beads) into an Eppendorf tube and wash once with 1 ml

MES buffer in a microcentrifuge, 5 min at full speed. Resuspend beads in 50 μl MES buffer.

3. Add purified RILP-GST or GST at a final concentration of 250 μg/ml to the beads in a total volume of 500 μl MES buffer and incubate overnight at room temperature on a shaker.
4. Wash the beads three times with PBS in a microcentrifuge, 5 min at full speed and resuspend in 1 ml of PBS-BSA-Az.
5. In order to confirm proper coating of beads (a) incubate 20 μl sample with mouse anti-GST (1:100 dilution in binding buffer) for 20 min at room temperature. (b) Wash once with binding buffer in a microcentrifuge, 5 min at full speed (c) Stain with FITC-conjugated goat antimouse at 1:50 dilution for 20 min. (d) Wash twice with binding buffer and resuspend in 500 μl binding buffer. Evaluate the coating by FACS analysis by reference to uncoated latex beads stained with the same antibodies as the coated samples.

3.4. Sample Incubation and Washes

1. Incubate each cell lysate sample with 50 μl of RILP-GST bead preparation; where controls are needed, set aside half of the lysate sample to incubate with GST-coated beads (50 μl).
2. Mix on rocker overnight at 4°C or 3–4 h at room temperature (*see* **Note 5**).
3. Wash three times with PBS in a microcentrifuge, 5 min at full speed and resuspend in 100 μl PBS. Split each sample into two equal fractions; set aside one fraction for FACS and another fraction for immunoblot confirmation.

3.5. Flow Cytometry Analysis

1. Stain sample from **Subheading 3.4** with rabbit anti-Rab7 (or rabbit anti-GFP if using transfected Rab7-GFP constructs) diluted 1:100 for 20 min at room temperature.
2. Wash once with 1 ml binding buffer in a microcentrifuge, 5 min at full speed.
3. Stain with FITC-conjugated goat antirabbit IgG at dilution of 1:50 for 20 min.
4. Wash two times with binding buffer and resuspend in 500 μl of the same buffer.
5. Analyze by FACS according to parameter setting shown in **Fig. 1**.

3.6. Immunoblot Confirmation

1. Resuspend beads in sample buffer and heat at 90°C for 10 min.
2. Prepare a 1.5-mm thick, 12% gel by mixing 2.5 ml of separating buffer, 4.0 ml of 30% acrylamide/bis solution, 3.4 ml

distilled water, 50 μl ammonium persulfate solution, and 5 μl TEMED. Pour the gel between the glass plates leaving some room for the stacking gel and overlay with water-saturated isobutanol. It will take about 20–30 min to polymerize.

3. Pour off the isobutanol and rinse the top of gel with water.
4. Prepare the stacking gel by mixing 2.5 ml of stacking buffer with 1.3 ml of acrylamide/bis solution, 6.1 ml water, 50 μl ammonium persulfate solution, and 5 μl TEMED.
5. Pour the stacking gel on top of the separating gel until it overflows. Insert 10- or 15-well comb gently without causing bubbles and overflow more gel mixture. The stacking gel should polymerize within 30 min.
6. Add some running buffer to cover the bottom of tank for the electric current. Carefully place prepared gel into the inner chamber and lock tightly into the electrophoresis tank. Take out comb gently and fill inner chamber with running buffer till it overflows.
7. Load wells with samples leaving one for the prestained molecular weight marker (*see* **Note 6**).
8. Place lid on tank and connect to power supply. The gel can be run at 100 V for about 10 min or until the gel front has reached the separating layer. Then it can be run at 150 V for the remainder of the duration. Stop the gel when the gel front is about to or has just run out of the bottom of the glass plates.

3.7. Immunoblotting Confirmation (Membrane Transfer and Probing)

1. The gel will be transferred to a supported nitrocellulose membrane (NC) elecrophoretically. These directions assume the use of an OWL separation system.
2. To set up the transfer cassette, soak three sheets of Whatman paper in transfer buffer and lay on the cassette surface. Remove bubbles within by rolling over with a stirring rod. Then carefully remove your separating gel from the glass plates and place on top of these three sheets of Whatman paper.
3. Cut a piece of NC membrane slightly larger than size of the gel and soak in transfer buffer for 10 s. Then cut one corner to indicate lane order by marker and lay on top of the gel. Finish by placing three more sheets of soaked Whatman paper on top and chase bubbles with a rod again.
4. Cover with lid of apparatus and set power supply to 200 mA for 20–25 min.
5. Carefully disassemble apparatus after completion and check if the marker has transferred appropriately.

6. Place membrane in shallow container for incubation with 10 ml blocking buffer for 1 h at room temperature on rocker.
7. Remove blocking buffer and add anti-Rab7 or anti-GFP (*see* **Note 7**) at a dilution of 1:1,000 in blocking buffer. Incubate for 1.5–2 h at room temperature with shaking.
8. Recycle the primary antibody and perform three washes of 5 min each with TBS-T and shaking.
9. Prepare fresh secondary antibody (HRPO conjugate) at 1:5,000 dilution in TBS-T. Incubate for 30–40 min at room temperature with shaking.
10. Discard secondary antibody and wash thoroughly four times with TBS-T for 10 min each at room temperature with shaking (*see* **Note 8**).
11. Prepare ECL reagent by mixing 1 ml of each solution and then adding it on top of the membrane to cover it fully. Allow 3–5 min of incubation at room temperature without shaking. Using tweezers, stand membrane on Kimwipe to drain off excess solution.
12. Place membrane on top of a cardboard or glass plate and carefully cover with saran wrap. Make sure to avoid bubbles on the surface of membrane in contact with the wrap.
13. Proceed to dark room to develop the membrane by placing a cut piece of film over the membrane, remembering to cut the corner of the film to align with the membrane. Quickly close the developing cassette and develop for 1 min. Open the cassette and carefully take out the film without moving it around in contact with the membrane, and put into developing solution and shake until bands start to appear. Next, transfer the film to water and quickly rinse and transfer to fixative solution. Shake for 10 s then wash with water again.
14. Dry film and examine by aligning the lanes of the membrane according to marker and analyze for presence of Rab7 at about 24 kDa in the samples that detected positive for active Rab7 by FACS.
15. The bands can be quantified as well by densitometry.
16. The membrane may then be stripped by incubation in stripping buffer for 5 min, 37°C. Then wash the membrane well with distilled water to remove traces of NaOH. Proceed to wash once with TBS-T.
17. Reprobe with mouse anti-GST as described in **step 7** and repeat film exposure and development steps. There is no need to reblock the membrane after stripping. The anti-GST probing should demonstrate equal loading of samples in all the lanes.

4. Notes

1. RILP-GST was prepared using pGEX-4T3 vector as previously described *(6, 16)*.
2. Prepare also a half dilution of the elution buffer for use as wash buffer. At 5 mM reduced glutathione, RILP-GST should not be eluted, but the contaminants will be. It is important to keep small aliquots of the purified protein and perform normal SDS-PAGE with Commassie blue staining to make sure that RILP-GST is free of contaminant bacterial proteins.
3. The transfections used in the experiments described used Lipofectamine 2000 (Invitrogen). According to the manufacturer's instructions, the optimal parameters for transfections should be defined for the cell line chosen. The purity of the plasmids for transfection is critical for the success of transfection. In our laboratory, J774 and RAW 264.7 macrophage cell lines yield optimal transfection rates when transfected at ~90% confluency in 6-cm diameter culture dishes. For RAW cells, ~10 μg DNA in 250 μl Opti-MEM is mixed with equal volume of Opti-MEM containing 12% Lipofectamine. After 20 min incubation at room temperature, 0.5 ml Opti-MEM is added to the preparation and the mixture is added to adherent cells. A similar procedure was used for J774 cells but with lower amount of DNA (~5 μg) in order to reduce toxicity.
4. It is recommended to passage the lysate through the column at least three times if the flow rate is good. Prior to elution, it is also recommended to wash with one column full of the diluted elution buffer to yield better purity, although this step is optional.
5. This experiment was also successful with a shorter incubation period (3–4 h) of macrophage lysate with RILP-beads. So it is not essential for overnight binding if there are time restrictions. However, it is recommended that the 3–4 h incubation be done at room temperature.
6. Prior to loading, quickly spin down the beads in a microfuge, and be careful to pipette only the liquid and not to load beads into the wells. Each well made with a 1.5-mm comb can hold about 50 μl of sample. Be sure to have equal loading in all wells. Only 6–8 μl of the prestained marker is necessary.
7. Anti-Rab7 can be used for cases of endogenous Rab7 or transfected GFP-Rab7. In the case of transfections, using this antibody will produce two bands of Rab7: one at ~52 kDa (GFP-Rab7) and one at ~25 kDa (Rab7 – endogenous). In both cases, only active GTP-bound Rab7 will appear on the membrane.

8. This is the critical step in removing background noise from immunoblotting. The stated times for this step should be followed strictly, and washes that are longer will not be deleterious.

Acknowledgments

This work was supported by operating grants from the Canadian Institutes of Health Research (CIHR) MOP-67232 and the BC Lung Association. Z.H. was supported by scholar awards from MSFHR and the CIHR. Jim Sun was supported by the TBVets Charitable Foundation.

References

1. Garin J, Diez R, Kieffer S, Dermine JF, Duclos S, Gagnon E, et al. (2001). The phagosome proteome: insight into phagosome functions. *J Cell Biol*; 152(1):165–180.
2. Ali BR, Seabra MC (2005). Targeting of Rab GTPases to cellular membranes. *Biochem Soc Trans*; 33(Pt 4):652–656.
3. Desjardins M, Huber LA, Parton RG, Griffiths G (1994). Biogenesis of phagolysosomes proceeds through a sequential series of interactions with the endocytic apparatus. *J Cell Biol*; 124(5):677–688.
4. Via LE, Deretic D, Ulmer RJ, Hibler NS, Huber LA, Deretic V (1997). Arrest of mycobacterial phagosome maturation is caused by a block in vesicle fusion between stages controlled by rab5 and rab7. *J Biol Chem*; 272(20):13326–13331.
5. Buczynski G, Bush J, Zhang L, Rodriguez-Paris J, Cardelli J (1997). Evidence for a recycling role for Rab7 in regulating a late step in endocytosis and in retention of lysosomal enzymes in Dictyostelium discoideum. *Mol Biol Cell*; 8(7):1343–1360.
6. Cantalupo G, Alifano P, Roberti V, Bruni CB, Bucci C (2001). Rab-interacting lysosomal protein (RILP): the Rab7 effector required for transport to lysosomes. *EMBO J*; 20(4):683–693.
7. Jordens I, Fernandez-Borja M, Marsman M, Dusseljee S, Janssen L, Calafat J et al (2001). The Rab7 effector protein RILP controls lysosomal transport by inducing the recruitment of dynein-dynactin motors. *Curr Biol*; 11(21):1680–1685.
8. Harrison RE, Bucci C, Vieira OV, Schroer TA, Grinstein S (2003). Phagosomes fuse with late endosomes and/or lysosomes by extension of membrane protrusions along microtubules: role of Rab7 and RILP. *Mol Cell Biol*; 23(18):6494–6506.
9. Speight P, Silverman M (2005). Diacylglycerol-activated Hmunc13 serves as an effector of the GTPase Rab34. *Traffic*; 6(10):858–865.
10. Wu M, Wang T, Loh E, Hong W, Song H (2005). Structural basis for recruitment of RILP by small GTPase Rab7. *EMBO J*; 24(8):1491–1501.
11. Harrison RE, Brumell JH, Khandani A, Bucci C, Scott CC, Jiang X, et al. (2004). Salmonella impairs RILP recruitment to Rab7 during maturation of invasion vacuoles. *Mol Biol Cell*; 15(7):3146–3154.
12. Vieira OV, Bucci C, Harrison RE, Trimble WS, Lanzetti L, Gruenberg J, et al. (2003). Modulation of Rab5 and Rab7 recruitment to phagosomes by phosphatidylinositol 3-kinase. *Mol Cell Biol*; 23(7):2501–2514.
13. Callaghan J, Nixon S, Bucci C, Toh BH, Stenmark H (1999). Direct interaction of EEA1 with Rab5b. *Eur J Biochem*; 265(1): 361–366.
14. Bucci L, Thomsen P, Nicoziani P, McCarthy J. van Deuvs B (2000). Rab 7: a Key to lysosome biogenesis. *Mol Biol Cell:* 11(2): 467–480.
15. Clemens DL, Lee BY, Horwitz MA (2000). Mycobacterium tuberculosis and Legionella pneumophila phagosomes exhibit arrested maturation despite acquisition of Rab7. *Infect Immun*; 68(9):5154–5166.
16. Vitelli R, Santillo M, Lattero D, Chiariello M, Bifulco M, Bruni CB, et al. (1997). Role of the small GTPase Rab7 in the late endocytic pathway. *J Biol Chem*; 272(7):4391–4397.

Chapter 6

Probing In Vivo Origins of Mononuclear Phagocytes by Conditional Ablation and Reconstitution

Chen Varol, Limor Landsman, and Steffen Jung

Summary

Dendritic cells (DCs) and macrophages (MΦs), collectively termed mononuclear phagocytes (MP), are crucial for homeostatic tissue maintenance as well as the innate and adaptive host defense. These pleiotropic functions are likely to be covered by distinct DC and MΦ subsets, defined by anatomic location and molecular make-up. However, task division within the MP system remains poorly defined. A key to understanding of this issue, which might have important implications for the development of future therapeutic strategies, is the elucidation of the in vivo origins of DCs and MΦs, whose study recently gained striking momentum. Here we present methods to investigate the role of MP progenitors, such as monocytes and MΦ/DC precursors (MDPs), in the replenishment of the peripheral MP system.

Key words: Mononuclear phagocytes, Macrophages, Dendritic cells, Monocytes.

1 Introduction

Mononuclear Phagocytes (MPs) play an important role in homeostasis and the innate and adaptive host defense against pathogens *(1, 2)*. MPs have been divided into two major terminally differentiated subsets: Macrophages (MΦs) and Dendritic cells (DCs). In the organism, both these cell types consist of multiple subpopulations largely defined by distinct anatomic location and phenotypes *(3, 4)*. MΦs include tissue-specific representatives in the serosa, lamina propria (Lp), lung, brain, bone, and liver *(1)*. DCs, on the other hand, have in the mouse been subdivided into epidermal Langerhans cells (LCs), plasmacytoid DCs, and CD11c^{hi} conventional DCs (cDCs) found in the spleen and periphery *(4)*.

Neil E. Reiner (ed.), *Macrophages and Dendritic Cells,* Methods in Molecular Biology, vol. 531

DOI: 10.1007/978-1-59745-396-7_6

Peripheral MP populations are thought to rely on continuous replenishment from BM-resident hematopoetic stem cells (HSCs). The HSC-to-MP differentiation pathway includes a number of BM intermediates, such as common myeloid precursors (CMPs) *(5)*, granulocyte/MΦ precursors (GMPs) *(5)*, and MΦ/DC precursors (MDPs) *(6)*, characterized by progressively limited developmental plasticity arising from asymmetric cell division. MDPs give rise to BM monocytes, which egress to the blood, where they contribute to the inflammatory response and act as circulating precursors of tissue MΦs and DCs *(7–10)*. Notably, some DC and MΦ populations, such as brain microglia, epidermal LCs, and splenic cDCs, arise in the adult steady state from local precursors without monocytic intermediates *(11–13)*.

As in man, murine monocytes comprise two phenotypically distinct subsets characterized as either $Gr1^{hi}CCR2^{+}$ $CD62L^{+}$ CX_3CR1^{int} or $Gr1^{low}CCR2^{-}CD62L^{-}CX_3CR1^{high}$, *(9)*. Under steady-state conditions, $Gr1^{hi}$ monocytes shuttle between the blood and the BM, where they can convert into $Gr1^{low}$ monocytes *(7, 14, 15)*. Inflammation results in rapid CCR2-mediated recruitment of the $Gr1^{hi}$ monocytes to the site of insult *(7, 9, 16)*, whereas the homing pattern of $Gr1^{lo}$ monocytes remains less understood. With regard to differentiation potential, $Gr1^{hi}$ monocytes were shown to give rise to LCs under inflammation *(17)* and to intestinal and lung DCs under noninflammatory conditions *(18, 19)*. Differentiation of $Gr1^{hi}$ monocytes into lung MΦs, however, requires their prior conversion into $Gr1^{low}$ cells *(18)*.

The most direct way to investigate the origin of MPs is by the adoptive transfer of precursor cells into recipient mice and subsequent tracking of graft descendants. Here we present methods that allow studying the potential of MDPs, BM monocytes, and blood monocytes to differentiate in vivo into splenic, intestinal, and pulmonary MPs. In combination with a novel Diphtheria toxin-based conditional in vivo cell ablation strategy *(20)*, this transfer approach allows for efficient in vivo MP reconstitution and sets the stage for future functional studies.

2. Materials

2.1. Animals

Our approaches involve the use of the following mouse strains (*see* **Note 1**):

1. *CD11c*:DTR transgenic mice (B6.FVB-Tg(Itgax-DTR/GFP) 57Lan/J, Jackson laboratory, stock #004509) that carry a human diphtheria toxin receptor (DTR) transgene under the murine CD11c promoter *(20)*.

2. CX_3CR1^{gfp} mutant mice (B6.129P-*Cx3cr1tm1Litt*/J, Jackson laboratory, stock #005582) *(21)* harboring a targeted replacement of the *cx_3cr1* gene by an enhanced green fluorescent protein (EGFP) reporter gene. CX_3CR1 is the receptor of the membrane-tethered chemokine CX_3CL1 (fractalkine (Fkn) *(22)*. In the transfers we generally use heterozygote mutant mice ($CX_3CR1^{gfp/+}$) that show a reduced surface receptor expression, but exhibit no overt phenotype *(21)*. CX_3CR1^{gfp} donor mice have been crossed to mice bearing the CD45.1 allotype (B6.SJL-*Ptprc^a^ Pepc^b^*/BoyJ, Jackson laboratory, stock #002014).

2.2. Conditional In Vivo Ablation of MPs

1. Diphtheria toxin (DTx) is dissolved in PBS at a concentration of 1 mg/ml and stored in 10 μl single-use aliquots at −80°C. Aliquots are diluted in PBS prior to use.
2. *FACS buffer contains.* 1% fetal bovine serum (FBS), 2 mM Na_2EDTA, and 0.05% sodium azide. Fluorochrome-conjugated antibodies used include: CD11c-APC or CD11c-PE (eBioscience, clone N418), MHCII-PE (eBioscience, clone M5/114.15.2), and CD11b-APC (eBioscience, clone M1/70), stored at 4°C. Dilutions are performed in FACS buffer.
3. *FACS-Blocking reagents.* Antimouse CD16/32-FC (FC) block (eBioscience clone #93) or goat IgG (Cat#I5256, Sigma Aldrich, Israel) stored at 4°C.

2.3. Adoptive Transfer of MDPs or Monocytes into MP-Depleted CD11c-DTR transgenic Recipient Mice

1. Ficoll-Paque™ PLUS (Amersham Biosciences AB, Uppsala, Sweden). Ficoll is light sensitive, and therefore should be stored either in the dark or in opaque bottles at RT.
2. *Antibodies.* CD117 (cKit)-PE (BioLegends, clone 2B8), Gr1 APC (eBioscience, clone RB6-8C5), CD11b-PerCP (BD-Pharmingen, clone M1/70), CD115-Biotin (eBioscience, clone AFS98) stored at 4°C.
3. Heparin sodium from bovine intestine is reconstituted at 10,000 units/ml with DDW and stored at 4°C.
4. *Magnetic cell sorting (MACS) buffer contains.* 1% fetal bovine serum and 2 mM Na_2EDTA (*see* **Subheading 2.2.3**) (no Azide!). Five ml of 100 mM EDTA is added to 10 ml of FBS, stored for 10 min at RT, and added to 500 ml of PBS without Ca^{++} and Mg^{++} (PBS−/−), sterile filtered, and degassed.
5. Magnetic Cell Sorting (MACS) instruments and reagents (Miltenyi Biotec, GmbH, Germany): MiniMACS Separator, MS columns, and Streptavidin-Microbeads (cat #130-048-102), which should be stored at 4°C and protected from light are used according to the manufacturer's protocols.

6. Anesthetic: 10% Xylazine (20 mg/ml) and 10% Ketamine (100 mg/ml) in PBS–/–. Mixture volume of 100 μl per 10 g of recipient bodyweight is injected i.p.

2.4. Analysis of Precursor Graft-Derived MPs

1. Collagenase D is dissolved in PBS at a concentration of 200 mg/ml and stored in 20 μl (4 mg) single-use aliquots at –20°C. Aliquots are diluted in PBS with Ca^{+2} and Mg^{+2} (PBS+/+) prior to use, to achieve 1 mg/ml solution.
2. *ACK buffer*. 0.15 M NH_4C, 0.01 M $KHCO_3$) is made by dissolving of 8 g of NH_4Cl and 1 g of $KHCO_3$ in 1 l of DDW. Solution is then divided into 50 ml aliquots and stored at –20°C.
3. A solution of 1 mM DTT is made by dissolving the DTT powder in PBS–/– to a final concentration of 0.1,543 mg/ml.
4. For intestine digestion, collagenase IV (0.5 mg/ml) and DNAse (0.2 mg/ml) are dissolved in PBS+/+.
5. PFA (2%) solution is made by dissolving 10 g of paraformaldehyde in 200 ml of water at 60°C (solution appears milky). NaOH is then added, drop by drop, until solution is cleared. A volume of 50 ml × 10 concentrated PBS is added, and the solution is cooled down. Volume is then completed to a total of 500 ml, and pH is adjusted to 7.4 using HCl.

3. Methods

3.1. Conditional In Vivo MP Ablation

3.1.1. Short-Term In Vivo Ablation of Peripheral MPs

1. Conditional ablation of MP is achieved using a Diphtheria Toxin (DTx)-based cell ablation strategy *(23)*. CD11c-DTR transgenic mice carry a transgene encoding a human Diphtheria Toxin receptor (DTR) fused to the green fluorescent protein (GFP) under the control of the murine CD11c promoter *(20)*. CD11c-expressing MP, including all cDCs and specific Mφ subsets *(23–25)*, are sensitive to DTx and are hence depleted upon toxin injection. In this conditional cell ablation system, targeted cells die by apoptosis and are removed without causing major inflammation *(26)*.
2. For systemic short-term MP depletion, mice are injected once intraperitoneally (i.p) with 4 ng/g body weight DTx *(20)*.
3. After i.p injection, toxin-induced MP depletion in spleen, intestine, BM, and LNs persists for 2 days, after which MP numbers are gradually restored *(20)* (**Fig. 1**). Lung DCs and MΦs, however, are not efficiently depleted by this procedure, but can be targeted by intratracheal (i.t.) DTx application (*see* **subheading 3.1.2**) *(18, 24)*.

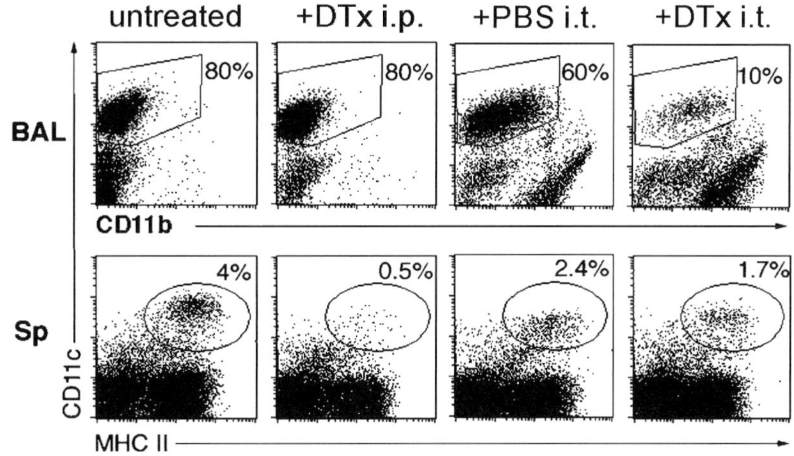

Fig. 1. In vivo depletion of *CD11c*:DTR transgenic CD11c⁺ lung and spleen cells upon intratracheal or intraperitoneal instillation of Diphtheria toxin (DTx), respectively. *CD11c*:DTR mice were treated with DTx either i.p. (4ng/g, + DTx i.p.) or i.t. (100ng, + DTx i.t.). Control littermates were either treated with PBS i.t. (+PBS i.t.) or left untreated. Lungs and spleens were analyzed one day after treatments. Data show FACS analysis of lung cells for CD11c and CD11b expression (*upper panels*) and of spleen cells for CD11c⁺ and MHC class II expression (*lower panels*). Numbers indicate percentage of gated cells from total cells.

4. Recipient mice are DTx treated prior to adoptive transfer of donor cells. I.p injection is usually done one day before, whereas i.t instillation of DTx is performed 3 h before transfer.
5. Transient CD11c^{hi} cell depletion is not associated with signs of illness or long term defects *(20)*. However, repetitive systemic DTx application results in lethality in CD11c-DTR-transgenic mice. For long-term in vivo ablation of peripheral MP see **subheading 3.1.3**.

3.1.2. Short-Term In Vivo Ablation of Pulmonary MPs

1. Mice are lightly anesthetized using an isofluorane inhalator (IMPAC6, VetEquip) and placed in a little suspension rack *(27)* with their thorax placed vertically, suspended by their teeth. The tongue is pulled to the side.
2. Using a micropipette with a long nasal tip 80 μl of a 1.25 μg/ml DTx solution (total of 100 ng) is applied into the larynx, while keeping the tongue pulled out. In this way, the mouse is unable to swallow, and the droplet is aspirated. Gasping of treated mice verifies liquid application to the alveolar space.
3. In our hands, intratracheal installation of toxin is the most efficient way to ablate pulmonary MP, while having no or only limited systemic effects (**Fig. 1**).

3.1.3. Long-Term In Vivo Ablation of Peripheral MPs

1. In contrast to CD11c-DTR transgenic mice, syngeneic [DTR > wt] BM chimeras, generated by reconstitution of lethally irradiated wt recipient mice with CD11c-DTR BM, can be treated with DTx for prolonged periods of time without adverse side effects *(28)*.
2. *BM chimera generation.* C57BL/6 wt mice are exposed to a single lethal total body irradiation of 950 rad, followed by intravenous (i.v.) transfer of 5×10^6 CD11c-DTR transgenic BM cells one day after (*see* **Note 4**). BM cells are isolated according to the procedure described later (*see* **Subheading 3.2.2**). Mice are allowed to rest for 8 weeks before use.
3. For systemic long-term MP depletion [DTR > wt] BM chimeras are injected every other day i.p. with DTx (8 ng/g body weight).

3.1.4. Analysis of Depletion Efficiency by FACS

1. Cells are isolated from the examined tissues (*see* **Subheading 3.3**) and stained with fluorochrome-conjugated monoclonal antibodies (*see* **Notes 2** and **3**).
2. Prior to the staining, cells are incubated with a 1:100 dilution of goat IgG or FC block, for 15 min on ice to block Fc receptors (staining volume ~10 μl/10^6 cells).
3. Cells are then stained for cell-specific markers. We routinely add a 2× concentrated mix of fluorochrome-conjugated CD11c and MHCII or CD11b antibodies and keep the cells 15 min on ice (final staining volume ~20 μl/10^6 cells). All dilutions are done in FACS buffer.
4. Following staining, cells are washed with FACS buffer (~50× staining volume) and centrifuged at 1,200 rpm (290 ×*g*) for 7 min at 4°C.
5. Cells are resuspended in FACS buffer and analyzed by multicolor flow cytometry on a FACSCalibur cytometer (BD Biosciences) using CellQuest Pro software (BD Biosciences) (**Fig. 1**).

3.2. Adoptive Transfer into MP-Depleted CD11c-DTR Recipients

3.2.1. The $CX_3CR1^{gfp/+}$ Transgenic Donor Mice

1. To study in vivo origins of MP, recipient mice are engrafted with $CX_3CR1^{gfp/+}$ MP precursor cells, e.g., MDPs or monocytes. CX_3CR1 is expressed on MDPs *(6)*, as well as BM and blood monocytes *(9, 21)*, which are therefore green fluorescent in CX_3CR1^{gfp} mice.
2. The long half-life of the GFP label allows the detection of adoptively transferred GFP-expressing precursors and their descendants in recipient mice, even if the progeny cease to express CX_3CR1/GFP *(7, 18)*. However, the label can be lost in the CX_3CR1^- cell populations by cell division.

3. In addition to the GFP label, it is advisable to include allotypic markers that identify the grafted cells, such as CD45. We therefore use CD45.1; CX_3CR1^{gfp} mice as donors.

3.2.2. Isolation of Precursor Cells from the Bone Marrow

1. Femura and tibiae of $CX_3CR1^{GFP/+}$ CD45.1 donor mice are isolated, and bone surface is exposed by removing the surrounding soft tissue.
2. Bone is opened at both ends, and using a 27 gauge fitted to a 1-ml syringe filled with 1 ml of cold PBS–/–, the marrow is flushed out of the bone cavity into a 15-ml tube. This step is repeated several times until the bone is empty and becomes white.
3. BM cells are then gently resuspended using 21G1 3-ml syringe until the suspension is homogenous. Cells are washed with 10 ml of PBS–/– by centrifugation at 1,200 rpm (290 × *g*) at 4°C for 7 min.
4. Mononuclear cells are subsequently enriched by granulocyte- and erythrocyte depletion on a Ficoll density gradient: the cell pellet is resuspended in 4 ml of PBS–/– in a 15-ml tube and the cell suspension is gently underlaid with 4 ml of Ficoll. Two layers with sharp interface should be preserved. The cell-containing tube is then centrifuged at 2,200 rpm (974 × *g*) without acceleration and break (!), 22°C (RT), for 15 min. The tube is gently removed from the centrifuge and the cloudy ring at the border between the two layers, which contains the enriched BM mononuclear cells, is isolated using a long Pasteur pipette. Cells are washed from residual Ficoll in 10 ml of PBS–/–, followed by centrifugation at 1,200 rpm (290 × *g*), 4°C for 7 min.
5. Enriched BM mononuclear cells are stained with the following fluorochrome-labeled monoclonal antibodies: CD-17-PE, Gr1-APC, and CD11b-Percp (*see* **Notes 2** and **3**). This staining allows the identification of BM MDP (CX_3CR1/GFP^+ CD117 $(cKit)^+$ $CD11b^-$ $Gr1^-$ *(6)* and BM monocytes (CX_3CR1/GFP^+ $CD11b^+$ $Gr1^{+/-}$) *(7)* (*see* **Note 5**). The staining is performed as described earlier (*see* **Subheading 3.1.4** and **Note 6**).
6. Following immunostaining, cells are purified by high-speed sorting using a FACS Aria (Beckton–Dickinson). Purity is evaluated by flow cytometry prior to the transfer (**Fig. 2a**).
7. Alternatively, a mixed population of BM MDP and monocytes can be isolated on the basis of CD115 expression using magnetic separation (*see* **Subheading 3.2.3**).

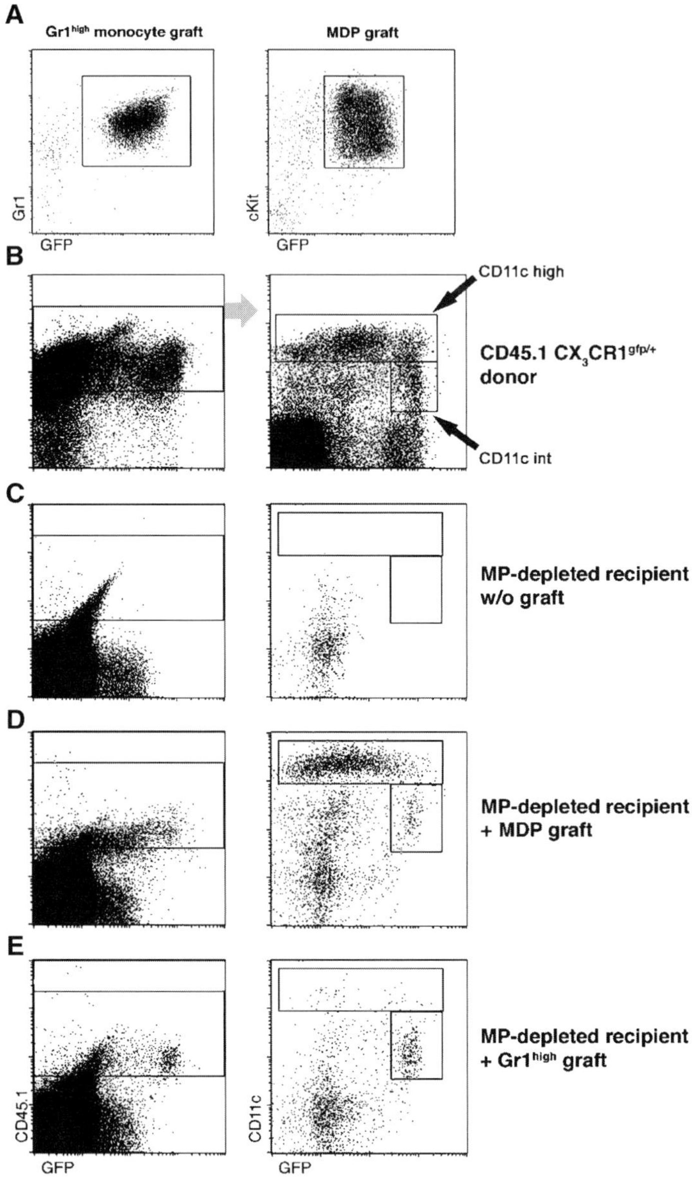

Fig. 2. MΦ/DC precursors (MDP), but not monocytes, replenish splenic conventional CD11c^{high} DCs. MDP and Gr1^{hi} monocytes were isolated from CX$_3$CR1^{gfp} donor mice and adoptively transferred into [DTR > wt] chimeras. Recipients were i.p injected with DTx every 2 days to maintain the state of DC depletion. At day 7 post transfer, recipient mice were killed and spleens were isolated and analyzed by flow cytometry. (**A**) Flow cytometry analysis of Gr1^{high} BM monocyte and cKit$^+$ MDP grafts isolated by high-speed cell sorting. (**B**) Flow cytometry analysis of CX$_3$CR1^{gfp} donor spleen (CD45.1$^+$) showing presence of CD45.1$^+$ CD11c^{high} DC (positive control), (**C**) spleen cells from DTx-treated, MP-depleted mouse without engraftment showing lack of CD11c^{high} DC (negative control), (**D**) spleen cells from MP-depleted mouse that received CX$_3$CR1^{gfp} MDP (CD45.1$^+$) graft (7×10^4 cKit$^+$ CD115$^+$ Gr1$^-$ CD11b$^-$ cells; purity: 96%) showing presence of donor cell-derived CD11c^{high} DC, and (**E**) spleen cells from MP-depleted mouse that received a CX$_3$CR1^{gfp} Gr1^{high} monocyte graft (CD45.1$^+$) (9×10^5 CD115$^+$ Gr1$^+$ CD11b$^+$ cells; purity: 85%). Note lack of graft-derived CD11c^{high} dendritic cells, but presence of CD11c^{low} cells. The *right panels* of (**B–E**) show splenocytes of the respective mice gated for live cells according to scatter. The *left panels* of (**B–E**) show the same splenocytes gated in addition according to CD45.1 expression (as indicated in the *right panels*). Boxes highlight CD11c^{high} DC and CD11c^{low} cells.

3.2.3. Isolation of Monocytes from the Blood

1. For blood monocyte transfers approximately 75 mice are bled from their tail veins to collect 12–15 ml of blood (~200 μl blood/mouse). Alternatively, 20 mice are killed after overdosing with a Xylazine/Ketamine mix (120 μl/10 g bodyweight) and bled to obtain 15–18 ml blood. Heparin is added (50 μl/ml blood) to avoid coagulation.
2. Mononuclear cells are enriched by a Ficoll density gradient, which depletes granulocytes and erythrocytes: in a 15-ml tube, 1 ml PBS–/– is added to 2 ml blood, followed by underlying with 4 ml of Ficoll without interfering with the 3-ml blood layer. Two layers with a sharp interface should be preserved. Continue as described under **Subheading 3.2.2, step 4**.
3. Blood monocytes, defined as CD115 (MCSF-R)-positive cells, are isolated to high purity by magnetic cell sorting.
4. Blood cells are first blocked by incubation with goat IgG, diluted in MACS buffer 1:100, for 15 min.
5. Following Fc receptor blockade, cells are stained for 15 min with biotinylated antimouse CD115 antibody (final dilution of 1:100) (*see* **Notes 2** and **3**).
6. Cells are then washed with MACS buffer and centrifuged at 1,200 rpm (290 × *g*), 4°C for 7 min to remove unbound primary antibody.
7. The supernatant is removed with a pipette and cells are resuspended in 90 μl of MACS buffer (per 10^7 total cells) (*see* **Note 7**).
8. Ten microliter of Streptavidin-Microbeads per 10^7 total cells is added; the tube is mixed and incubated for 15 min at 4–8°C.
9. Cells are then washed with 10 ml of MACS buffer (1,200 rpm (290 × *g*), 4°C for 7 min) and the supernatant is removed with a pipette.
10. Cells (up to 10^8) are resuspended in 500 μl of MACS buffer.
11. For magnetic separation, miniscale (MS) columns are used for up to 10^7 labeled cells (10^8 total cells), and large-scale (LS) are used for up to 10^8 labeled cells (10^9 total cells). Magnetic separation is performed according to the manufacturer's protocols (*see* **Note 8**).
12. After isolation of the column-bound cell fraction, cells are counted and purity is evaluated by staining a small fraction of the positive cells with Streptavidin-fluorochrome, or fluorochrome-conjugated anti-CD115 antibody and analysis by FACS (**Fig. 3a**).

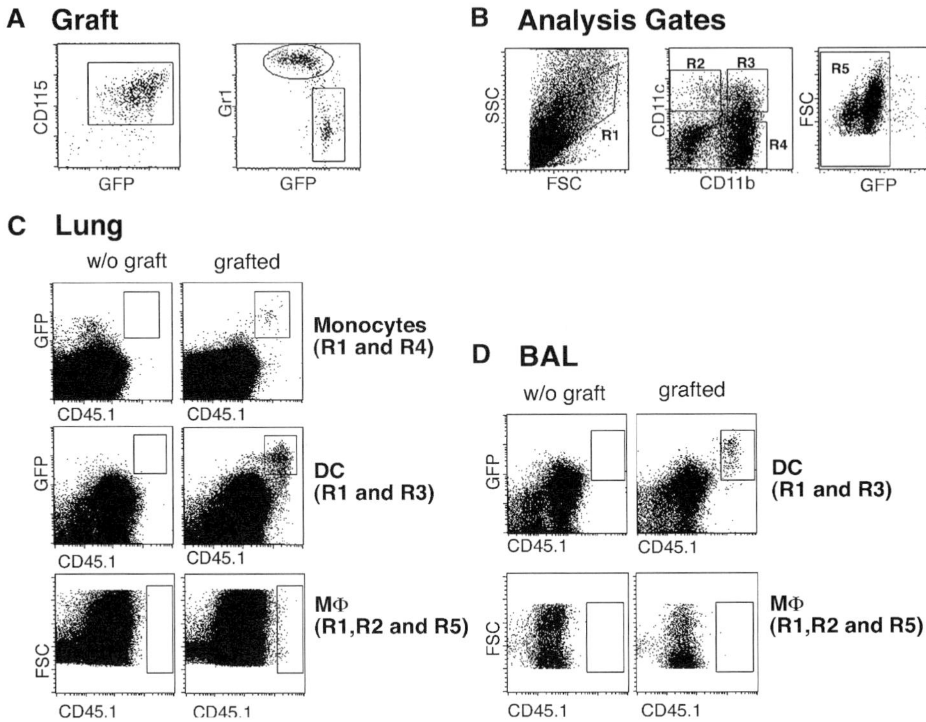

Fig. 3. The fate of adoptively transferred blood monocytes in the lung. Monocytes were isolated from the blood of CX$_3$CR1^{gfp} donor mice and adoptively transferred into DTx-instilled, pulmonary mononuclear phagocyte (MP)-depleted *CD11c*:DTR transgenic mice. At day 7 post transfer, recipient mice were killed and analyzed by flow cytometry. (**A**) Flow cytometric analysis of representative magnetic cell sorting-enriched CD115$^+$ blood monocyte graft isolated from *cx$_3$cr1$^{gfp/+}$*;CD45.1 donor mice. Note presence of both Gr1^{hi}CX$_3$CR1/GFP^{int} and Gr1^{low}CX$_3$CR1/GFP^{hi} monocyte subsets. (**B**) Flow cytometric analysis of lung cells of an untreated *CD11c*:DTR mouse to indicate gates used in (**C**). *Left panel* shows FSC/SSC gates for living cells (R1). *Middle dot* plot shows CD11c/CD11b expression pattern of cells from the R1 gate that were distributed into three secondary mononuclear phagocyte gates (R2–R4) used in the analysis shown in (**C**): (R2, MΦ CD11c$^+$ CD11b$^-$, (R3, DC) CD11c$^+$ CD11b$^+$ and (R4, monocytes), CD11c$^-$ CD11b$^+$. *Right dot* plot shows GFP expression of cells gated in the R1 region and position of R5 gate. This gate is used to further define MΦ which are CX$_3$CR1/GFP-negative (*see* ref. 18). (**c**, **d**) DTx-treated *CD11c*:DTR monocyte-recipient lung, day 4 after transfer. *CD11c*:DTR;CD45.2 mice pretreated i.t. with DTx (100 ng, d.0) either received *cx$_3$cr1$^{gfp/+}$*;CD45.1 CD115$^+$ blood monocyte graft (10^6 cells, grafted) or no graft (w/o graft) 2 h after DTx treatment and were analyzed on day 4. Panel (**C**) shows enclosed in boxes: donor-derived monocytes (R1 and R4), DC (R1 and R3) and MΦ (R1, R2, and R5) found in lung parenchyma. Figure (**D**) shows analysis of bronchoalveolar lavage (BAL): DC (R1 and R3) and MΦ (R1, R2, and R5). Cells were gated as indicated in (**B**). The data show that grafted monocytes give rise to MΦ and DC in the lung parenchyma (**C**) and to DC, but not MΦ in the alveolar space (BAL, **D**).

3.2.4. Adoptive Transfer into the Tail Vein (i.v.)

1. Following their isolation, cells are resuspended in 200 μl of PBS–/–.
2. Recipient mice are moderately heated with an infrared lamp in order to promote vasodilatation, to allow easier injection to the tail vein
3. Cells are injected into recipient mice via the tail vein (*see* **Note 9**).

4. In order to reconstitute the splenic CD11c^{high} conventional DC compartment, BM MDP should be transferred. Monocytes do not give rise to these cells (**Fig. 2**) *(7)*.
5. In order to reconstitute mucosal compartments, such as the intestinal lamina propria (**Fig. 4**) and the lung (**Fig. 3**), MDPs and monocytes can be transferred *(7, 18)*. MDPs differentiate in vivo into monocytes *(7)*.
6. We generally prefer to transfer near physiological numbers, e.g., 2–5 × 10^4 BM MDP and 0.5–1 × 10^6 BM and blood monocytes, respectively *(7, 18)*.

3.2.5. Intrabone Cavity (IBC) Transfer

1. To study precursor differentiation within the marrow, MDPs and monocytes can be transferred directly into the femural bone cavity *(7)*.
2. Mice are anesthetized by i.p injection of Xylazine and Ketamine mixture.
3. The skin covering the knee is incised and the knee is exposed.
4. The knee side of the femur is pierced with a 27G1/2 needle.
5. The cells to be transferred are concentrated in a volume of 5–10 μl sterile PBS–/– and injected into the femural BM cavity using a U-100 insulin syringe (with a 30G needle). The incision is closed (with MikRon Autoclips (Clay Adams Brand, BD, USA) or suture).

3.2.6. Intrasplenic Transfer

1. To directly investigate intrasplenic differentiation pathways (and avoid monocyte differentiation), MDPs can be injected directly into the spleen where they differentiate into splenic conventional CD11c^{high} DCs in situ *(7)*.
2. Mice are anesthetized by i.p injection of Xylazine and Ketamine mixture. A small incision is made in the skin covering the spleen area, to expose the spleen, which is then pulled out gently without damaging blood vessels connected to it.
3. The cells to be transferred are concentrated in a volume of 20 μl and injected slowly into the spleen capsule by using a U-100 insulin syringe (with a 30G needle).
4. A Gel-foam melting sponge (Pfizer Inc, U.S.A) is inserted to prevent bleeding, and the incision is closed (with MikRon Autoclips (Clay Adams Brand, BD, USA) or suture).

3.3. Analysis of Precursors Graft-Derived MPs

The precursor grafts can be expected to seed all organs of the recipient. Here we will focus on the analysis of three tissue compartments of the recipients: the spleen (as representative of a lymphoid tissue), and the lung, and the intestinal terminal ileum (as representatives of mucosal, nonlymphoid tissues).

3.3.1. Analysis of Splenocytes for Graft-Derived MPs

1. Mice are killed and the spleen is removed and placed in PBS in a 5-cm petri dish.
2. The efficient isolation of MPs requires, as opposed to lymphocytes, prior digestion of the tissues with matrix-degrading proteases. To this end the spleen is injected with 1 ml of collagenase D (1 mg/ml in PBS$^{+/+}$) using a 28 G 1/2 needle and incubated for 45 min at 37°C.
3. Following the collagenase D digest, spleen is minced and transferred via passage of an 80-μm mesh strainer into a 15-ml tube.
4. The cell suspension is then washed with 10 ml of PBS–/– and centrifuged at 1,200 rpm (290 × *g*), 4°C for 7 min.
5. Erythrocytes in the suspension are lysed by incubation with 1 ml of hypotonic ACK buffer for 2 min at room temperature (RT). Lysis is stopped by dilution of the ACK buffer with PBS–/– (tenfold volume at least). The suspension is then centrifuged and the pellet is washed.

3.3.2. Analysis of Small Intestinal Lamina Propria MPs

1. Mice are killed and the small intestine is isolated. By choosing proximal, central, or distal portions of the intestine the analysis can be focused on the duodenum, jejunum, and ileum, respectively.
2. Mesenteric tissue (lymph nodes) and fat are removed.
3. The intestine is flushed with PBS–/– to remove all its fecal content.
4. The intestinal tube is flipped inside out and incubated with RPMI for 20 min at 37°C (*see* **Note 10**).
5. The tissue is washed three times with PBS–/– at RT and then incubated for 10 min in 10 ml of 1 mM DTT (in PBS–/–). Following that, the intestine is washed once in PBS–/– (*see* **Note 11**).
6. The intestine is incubated for 10 min in 10 ml of EDTA 30 mM (diluted in PBS–/–) in a 15-ml tube with gently agitation by constant rotation. Incubation is once more repeated, using a fresh EDTA solution. The intestine is then transferred into a fresh 15-ml tube and washed four times with PBS–/– at RT.
7. Collagenase IV digestion is performed with the addition of DNAse, for 1 h at 37°C. (This stage is performed in a dish, with the intestine spread.)
8. The tissue is gently pipetted up and down using 1-ml tips (with their end cut-off) in order to physically release cells from the mucus layer.

9. The cell suspension is then passed through an 80-µm mesh strainer into a 15-ml tube. The dish is washed with PBS–/– in order to collect all released cells.
10. The cells are centrifuged at 1,200 rpm (290 × *g*), 10 min, 4°C (*see* **Note 12**).

3.3.3. Analysis of MPs in the Bronchoalveolar Space and the Lung Parenchyma

1. Mice are killed, their abdomen is opened, and the main artery is cut to allow a maximum blood volume to exit the circulation (*see* **Note 13**).
2. The mouse head is fixed on a Styrofoam board and the neck skin, and salivary glands are removed to expose the trachea.
3. The thin tissue layer covering the trachea is carefully removed using watch-maker forceps and scissors. The trachea rings are now exposed.
4. A 20-cm-long sewing thread is placed beneath the trachea and tied around it in proximity to the mouse head. Holding the string will allow to stretch the trachea for the next stages.
5. Using fine scissors a small hole is cut in the upper side of the trachea, next to, but below, the string.
6. A blunted (cut) 21G butterfly needle is inserted into the hole in trachea, and a 3-ml syringe, filled with 1.5 ml of PBS–/–, is attached to the needle.
7. A volume of 1 ml PBS–/– is slowly inserted into the mouse trachea through the infusion needle, resulting in the filling of the lungs with liquid.
8. The bronchoalveolar lavage (BAL) containing the cells is slowly withdrawn by pulling the syringe plunger.
9. The syringe is then removed from the infusion needle tube, and the BAL is transferred into a 15-ml tube.
10. **Steps 7–9** should be repeated three times.
11. The isolation procedure for MPs from the lung parenchyma is similar to the procedure for the splenic MPs, except that the lung tissue is injected with 1 ml of collagenase D solution at a concentration of 4 mg/ml (in PBS+/+).

3.3.4. Analysis of Graft-Derived MPs by FACS

1. The detection of CX_3CR1^{gfp} graft-derived cells in recipient mice is based on two markers: the expression of EGFP in the grafted cells and their descendants, and the congenic CD45.1 marker. The analysis can rely on either or both the markers (*see* also **Subheading 3.2.1**, **step2**) (**Figs. 2** and **3b**)
2. FACS staining is performed as described earlier (*see* **Subheading 3.1.4**).

3. Additional markers such as CD11c, CD11b, and CD8 can be used to differentiate between DCs and MΦs, as well as different DC subsets derived from the grafted-precursors *(6, 7, 18, 25)*. (*see* **Note 14**).

3.3.5. Analysis of Graft-Derived Lamina Propria DC by Fluorescent Microscopy

1. In CD11c-DTR transgenic mice, the GFP protein is fused to the DTR *(20)* resulting in relatively poor fluorescence intensity. Using conventional fluorescence microscopy, CD11c-DTR transgenic cDCs can therefore not be reliably detected in histology without using an anti-GFP amplification *(29)*. CX_3CR1^{gfp} precursor descendants, on the other hand, harbor an intense GFP label, in particular if they express CX_3CR1 (*see* **Subheading 3.2.1, step 2**). Together, this allows the GFP-based detection of CX_3CR1^{gfp} graft-derived cells in CD11c-DTR transgenic mice *(7, 18)*.
2. In a typical experiment, CX_3CR1^{gfp} graft recipients are killed, and the small intestinal ileum is isolated.
3. Mesenteric material and fat are removed.
4. The ileum is flushed with PBS–/– to remove all content.
5. A longitudinal incision is made along the ileum.
6. The tissue is placed on a microscope slide with its luminal side up.
7. The tissue is examined and imaged with a Zeiss Axioskop II fluorescent microscope using appropriate imaging software, such as Simple PCI.
8. In another approach, a systemic scan and visualization of large areas of the intestine is enabled by using the "Swiss-role" technique.

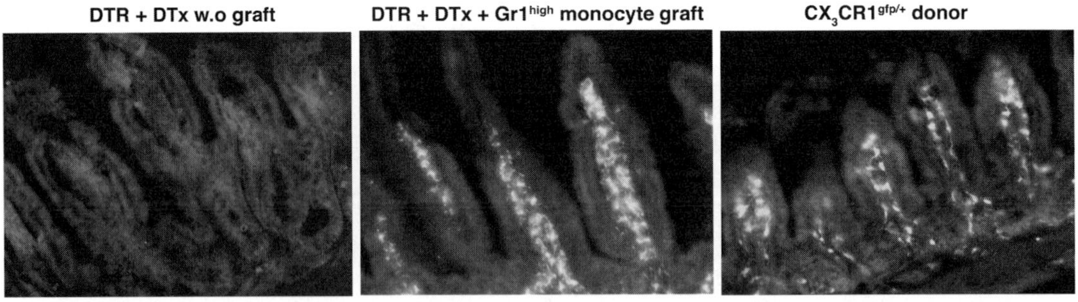

Fig. 4. Monocytes are precursors of intestinal lamina propria (Lp) DC. Fluorescence microscopy analysis of small intestinal villi of CX_3CR1^{gfp} donor mouse (*right-hand panel*) and of mice depleted for LpDC and LpMΦ with (*middle panel*) or without (*left-hand panel*) adoptive transfer of CX_3CR1^{gfp} BM Gr1^{high} monocytes (1×10^6 CD115$^+$ Gr1^{high} CD11b$^+$ cells; purity: 85%). Note presence of graft-derived CX_3CR1/GFP$^+$ LpDC in the fixed cryostat sectioned tissue of BM monocyte recipient (Original magnification, 20×). Graft-derived cells can be identified as DC because of their location, morphology, and functional features (such as the formation of trans-epithelial dendrites *(25)* and migration to the mesenteric LNs (data not shown).

9. Ileum is longitudinally opened along the mesenteric wall, and rolled up, keeping its luminal side out.
10. Rolled tissue is fixed overnight (o.n.) with 2% PFA at RT.
11. Fixed tissue is then incubated o.n. with 15% sucrose at RT.
12. Rolled intestine is embedded in Tissue-Tek O.C.T compound at −20°C.
13. Tissue segments are sectioned into 10-μm segments, using a cryostat, and segments are then imaged with a Zeiss Axioskop II fluorescent microscope (**Fig. 4**).

4. Notes

1. All mice are maintained under Specific Pathogen-Free (SPF) conditions and handled under institutional protocols according to international guidelines.
2. Antibodies are used according to the manufacturer's protocols. All antibodies should be tested and titrated in advance to determine the best staining conditions, before analysis of samples from recipient mice.
3. The suggested total staining volume is 20 μl for up to 1×10^6 cells, 100 μl for 5×10^6 cells. A staining time of 10–15 min on ice is usually sufficient.
4. Irradiated mice receive transiently (for 1 week) an antibiotic (Ciproxin 0.2%) in their drinking water (20 μg/ml) to prevent bacterial infections during the period of immunodeficiency (the water bottle should be either dark or covered with aluminum foil to protect the light-sensitive drug).
5. Both BM MDPs and monocytes are CD115$^+$, which can be used as a marker for identification and isolation of these cells *(7, 18)*.
6. Presorting staining is performed in MACS buffer (instead of FACS buffer) to avoid azide exposure of the cells.
7. When working with less than 10^7 cells, use the indicated volumes. When working with higher cell numbers, scale up all the reagents and total volumes, accordingly.
8. To increase the purity of the magnetically labeled fraction, it can be repassed over a freshly prepared column.
9. Volumes lower than 200 μl can also be injected i.v.
10. The intestine is mounted on a polyethylene tube with a diameter of 2.42 mm. One end of the intestine is tied with a sewing thread, and the rest is flipped on top of this end in order to

invert it. The tissue should be kept wet through the inversion process to avoid ripping. The inversion is a crucial step, as the digestion should be performed on the luminal side.

11. Washing is done by addition of PBS–/– to the tissue in the tube, shaking, and pouring off the fluid.
12. For an updated protocol of small intestinal lamina propria MPs isolation see the reference: Denning et al, Nature immunology, October 2007, vol 8, PP 1086–1094.
13. Blood is absorbed using Kim wipes, in order to prevent blood contamination of BAL fluid at later stages.
14. We suggest that each experiment will include at least two controls: a CD45.1 $CX_3CR1^{gfp/+}$ positive control mouse, and a DTx-treated CD11c-DTR transgenic mouse, that did not receive a graft to evaluate the background.

Acknowledgments

S.J. is the incumbent of the Pauline Recanati Career Development Chair and a Scholar of the Benoziyo Center for Molecular Medicine. This work was supported by the MINERVA Foundation and the EU6 Program for Migration and Inflammation Network (MAIN). We would like to thank F. Geissmann and D.K. Fogg for sharing critical data on the MDPs prior to their publication.

References

1. Gordon, S. 1999. Macrophages and the immune response. In *Fundamental Immunology*. W. E. Paul, ed. Lippincott-Raven, Philadelphia, PA, p. 533–545.
2. Steinman, R. M. 1999. Dendritic cells. In *Fundamental Immunology*, Vol. 1. W. E. Paul, ed. Lippincott-Raven, Philadelphia, PA, p. 547–573.
3. Taylor, P. R., L. Martinez-Pomares, M. Stacey, H. H. Lin, G. D. Brown, and S. Gordon. 2005. Macrophage receptors and immune recognition. *Annu Rev Immunol* 23:901–944.
4. Shortman, K., and Y. J. Liu. 2002. Mouse and human dendritic cell subtypes. *Nat Rev Immunol* 2:151–161.
5. Akashi, K., D. Traver, T. Miyamoto, and I. L. Weissman. 2000. A clonogenic common myeloid progenitor that gives rise to all myeloid lineages. *Nature* 404:193–197.
6. Fogg, D. K., C. Sibon, C. Miled, S. Jung, P. Aucouturier, D. R. Littman, A. Cumano, and F. Geissmann. 2006. A clonogenic bone marrow progenitor specific for macrophages and dendritic cells. *Science* 311:83–87.
7. Varol, C., L. Landsman, D. K. Fogg, L. Greenshtein, B. Gildor, R. Margalit, V. Kalchenko, F. Geissmann, and S. Jung. 2007. Monocytes give rise to mucosal, but not splenic, conventional dendritic cells. *J Exp Med* 204: 171–180.
8. van Furth, R., M. C. Diesselhoff-den Dulk, and H. Mattie. 1973. Quantitative study on the production and kinetics of mononuclear phagocytes during an acute inflammatory reaction. *J Exp Med* 138:1314–1330.
9. Geissmann, F., S. Jung, and D. R. Littman. 2003. Blood monocytes consist of two principal subsets with distinct migratory properties. *Immunity* 19:71–82.
10. Randolph, G. J., K. Inaba, D. F. Robbiani, R. M. Steinman, and W. A. Muller. 1999. Differentiation of phagocytic monocytes into lymph node dendritic cells in vivo. *Immunity* 11:753–761.

11. Naik, S. H., D. Metcalf, A. van Nieuwenhuijze, I. Wicks, L. Wu, M. O'Keeffe, and K. Shortman. 2006. Intrasplenic steady-state dendritic cell precursors that are distinct from monocytes. *Nat Immunol* 7:663–671.
12. Merad, M., M. G. Manz, H. Karsunky, A. Wagers, W. Peters, I. Charo, I. L. Weissman, J. G. Cyster, and E. G. Engleman. 2002. Langerhans cells renew in the skin throughout life under steady-state conditions. *Nat Immunol* 3:1135–1141.
13. Hickey, W. F., K. Vass, and H. Lassmann. 1992. Bone marrow-derived elements in the central nervous system: an immunohistochemical and ultrastructural survey of rat chimeras. *J Neuropathol Exp Neurol* 51:246–256.
14. Sunderkotter, C., T. Nikolic, M. J. Dillon, N. Van Rooijen, M. Stehling, D. A. Drevets, and P. J. Leenen. 2004. Subpopulations of mouse blood monocytes differ in maturation stage and inflammatory response. *J Immunol* 172:4410–4417.
15. Qu, C., E. W. Edwards, F. Tacke, V. Angeli, J. Llodra, G. Sanchez-Schmitz, A. Garin, N. S. Haque, W. Peters, N. van Rooijen, C. Sanchez-Torres, J. Bromberg, I. F. Charo, S. Jung, S. A. Lira, and G. J. Randolph. 2004. Role of CCR8 and other chemokine pathways in the migration of monocyte-derived dendritic cells to lymph nodes. *J Exp Med* 200:1231–1241.
16. Palframan, R. T., S. Jung, G. Cheng, W. Weninger, Y. Luo, M. Dorf, D. R. Littman, B. J. Rollins, H. Zweerink, A. Rot, and U. H. von Andrian. 2001. Inflammatory chemokine transport and presentation in HEV: a remote control mechanism for monocyte recruitment to lymph nodes in inflamed tissues. *J Exp Med* 194:1361–1373.
17. Ginhoux, F., F. Tacke, V. Angeli, M. Bogunovic, M. Loubeau, X. M. Dai, E. R. Stanley, G. J. Randolph, and M. Merad. 2006. Langerhans cells arise from monocytes in vivo. *Nat Immunol* 7(3):265–273.
18. Landsman, L., C. Varol, and S. Jung. 2007. Distinct differentiation potential of blood monocyte subsets in the lung. *J Immunol* 178: 2000–2007.
19. Yrlid, U., C. D. Jenkins, and G. G. Macpherson. 2006. Relationships between distinct blood monocyte subsets and migrating intestinal lymph dendritic cells in vivo under steady-state conditions. *J Immunol* 176:4155–4162.
20. Jung, S., D. Unutmaz, P. Wong, G. Sano, K. De los Santos, T. Sparwasser, S. Wu, S. Vuthoori, K. Ko, F. Zavala, E. G. Pamer, D. R. Littman, and R. A. Lang. 2002. In vivo depletion of CD11c (+) dendritic cells abrogates priming of CD8(+) T cells by exogenous cell-associated antigens. *Immunity* 17: 211–220.
21. Jung, S., J. Aliberti, P. Graemmel, M. J. Sunshine, G. W. Kreutzberg, A. Sher, and D. R. Littman. 2000. Analysis of fractalkine receptor CX(3)CR1 function byl targeted deletion and green fluorescent protein reporter gene insertion. *Mol Cell Biol* 20:4106–4114.
22. Bazan, J. F., K. B. Bacon, G. Hardiman, W. Wang, K. Soo, D. Rossi, D. R. Greaves, A. Zlotnik, and T. J. Schall. 1997. A new class of membrane-bound chemokine with a CX3C motif. *Nature* 385:640–644.
23. Palmiter, R. 2001. Interrogation by toxin. *Nat Biotechnol* 19:731–732.
24. van Rijt, L. S., S. Jung, A. Kleinjan, N. Vos, M. Willart, C. Duez, H. C. Hoogsteden, and B. N. Lambrecht. 2005. In vivo depletion of lung CD11c + dendritic cells during allergen challenge abrogates the characteristic features of asthma. *J Exp Med* 201:981–991.
25. Vallon-Eberhard, A., L. Landsman, N. Yogev, B. Verrier, and S. Jung. 2006. Transepithelial pathogen uptake into the small intestinal lamina propria. *J Immunol* 176:2465–2469.
26. Bennett, C. L., E. van Rijn, S. Jung, K. Inaba, R. M. Steinman, M. L. Kapsenberg, and B. E. Clausen. 2005. Inducible ablation of mouse Langerhans cells diminishes but fails to abrogate contact hypersensitivity. *J Cell Biol* 169:569–576.
27. Ho, W., and A. Furst. 1973. Intratracheal instillation method for mouse lungs. *Oncology* 27:385–393.
28. Zaft, T., A. Sapoznikov, R. Krauthgamer, D. R. Littman, and S. Jung. 2005. CD11chigh dendritic cell ablation impairs lymphopenia-driven proliferation of naive and memory CD8 + T cells. *J Immunol* 175: 6428–6435.
29. Sapoznikov, A., J. A. Fischer, T. Zaft, R. Krauthgamer, A. Dzionek, and S. Jung. 2007. Organ-dependent in vivo priming of naive CD4 + , but not CD8 + , T cells by plasmacytoid dendritic cells. *J Exp Med* 204:1923–1933.

Chapter 7

Multivalent Protein Probes for the Identification and Characterization of Cognate Cellular Ligands for Myeloid Cell Surface Receptors

Hsi-Hsien Lin, Gin-Wen Chang, Yi-Shu Huang, Cheng-Chih Hsiao, Martin Stacey, and Siamon Gordon

Summary

Cell–cell interactions mediated by cell surface receptor–ligand pairs in the immune system are often of low affinity and transient in nature. To begin to study these weak interactions, it is desirable to devise a generally applicable method for screening for and enriching cells expressing low-affinity ligands for specific cell surface receptors. We describe here an experimental strategy that uses a multivalent form of protein as a probe to identify and characterize cognate ligand(s) of myeloid cell surface receptors. Recombinant fusion proteins containing the receptor protein fragment of interest fused to a truncated mouse Fc domain and a unique biotinylation signal are produced, biotinylated, and coupled to (strept) avidin-coated fluorescent or paramagnetic microspheres. These multivalent microparticle probes are then used to screen or capture cells expressing the cognate cellular ligand(s).

Key words: Biotinylation, Cell surface receptor, Fc, Ligand, Low Affinity, Multivalent Protein Probe, Protein–protein Interaction

1. Introduction

Cell surface proteins play an important role in the functions of the immune system and are also critically involved in regulating maturation and differentiation of various immune cells. In addition, cell surface proteins also are one of the major determinants in directing and regulating the effector functions of immune cells *(1–5)*. For example, the interaction of the cell surface proteins

Neil E. Reiner (ed.), *Macrophages and Dendritic Cells,* Methods in Molecular Biology, vol. 531

DOI: 10.1007/978-1-59745-396-7_7

and their ligands can often determine the fate of T_H cells as either T_H1 or T_H2 cells *(6, 7)*.

While certain surface proteins such as cytokine receptors bind their cytokine ligands with relatively high affinity, the majority of the cell surface adhesion molecules show specific but weak and transient interactions with their cellular ligands, which themselves are usually cell surface molecules. A typical example is the E-selectin and E-selectin ligand-1, which have been shown to have a weak association constant of $K_a = \sim 7.4 \times 10^4\ M^{-1}\ S^{-1}$ *(8)*. It is thus essential in order to study the functional properties of the cell surface receptors to be able to characterize and identify their weak interacting cellular ligands.

We have previously demonstrated that the binding of the predominantly leukocyte-restricted CD97 receptor to its cellular ligand, CD55 is of both low affinity (86 μM) and transient (off-rate, 0.6 s^{-1}*9)* *(9)*. During this investigation, we devised an efficient method for characterizing the weak CD97–CD55 interaction. Our method is based on (a) the construction of an expression vector encoding the receptor protein of interest fused to a mouse Fc (mFc)-fragment and a specific C-terminal biotinylation signal sequence (b) the efficient production and purification of mFc-fusion proteins (c) the in vitro biotinylation of the mFc-fusion proteins (d) the generation of multivalent protein probes by coupling the biotinylated mFc-fusion proteins to (strept) avidin-coated fluorescent or paramagnetic microspheres, and (e) detection and selection of ligand-expressing cells by the multivalent protein probes *(10, 11)*. A general methodology that should be applicable to most cell surface proteins is described later using the CD97–CD55 interaction as an example.

2. Materials

2.1. Cell Lines and Cell Culture

1. HEK-293T cells were derived from the human embryonic kidney (HEK) 293 cell line transformed with Ad5. CHO-K1 was derived from Chinese hamster ovary cells. K562 cells were derived from chronic myelogenous leukemia cells. The full details of cell lines used can be obtained from the American Type Culture Collection (http://www.atcc.org/).
2. *Cell culture media*. Ham's F12, RPMI-1640, OPTI-MEM I, and Dulbecco's Modified Eagle's Medium (DMEM).
3. *Media supplements*. 50 IU/ml penicillin, 50 μg/ml streptomycin, 2 mM L-glutamine, and 10% (v/v) heat-inactivated fetal calf serum (FCS).
4. Trypsin–EDTA (10×), liquid.
5. Tissue culture plasticware.

2.2. Construction of Expression Vectors

1. General chemicals are of analytical grade and obtained from Sigma or BDH-Merck, unless otherwise stated.
2. The expression vectors are constructed on the pcDNA3.1 (+) plasmid unless otherwise specified (*see* **Note 1**).
3. Advantage™-HF 2 PCR Kit for the high-fidelity PCR amplification of cDNA fragments (Clontech, Mountain View, CA).
4. UltraPure™ Agarose.
5. QIAquick Gel Extraction Kit (Qiagen, Valencia, CA).
6. 1 Kb Plus DNA Ladder and the PCR®4-Topo TA cloning kit (Invitrogen).
7. Enzymes for the restriction digestion, dephosphorylation, and ligation of DNA (New England Biolabs, Beverly, MA).
8. QIAprep® Spin Miniprep kit and HiSpeed® Plasmid Midi and Maxi kits (Qiagen, Valencia, CA).
9. The murine IgG2b genome DNA for the amplification of the truncated mouse Fc region was kindly provided by Dr. Lisa Gilliland (University of Oxford) *(11, 12)*.
10. *Primers.* XbaBio (5′-AATCTAGAGATCCAAATTCCGGA-3′) and Bio3 (5′-TAGTAGGGGCCCTTAACGATGATT CCACACC-3′) are for the amplification of the biotinylation signal sequence. NotmFc (5′-AGGATCCTGAATTCGCG-GCCGCAGAGCCCAGCGGGCCT-3′) and mFcXba (5′-TTCTCTAGATTTACCCGGAGACCGGGA-3′) are for the mFc fragment. The oligonucleotide primers were produced and purified by Sigma.
11. *6× DNA-loading dye.* 0.05% (w/v) Orange G and 30% (v/v) glycerol
12. *1× TBE buffer (pH8.0).* 0.09 M Tris–base, 0.09 M boric acid, 2 mM EDTA.
13. Ethidium bromide solution.
14. The CD97 full-length cDNA containing the EGF-like motifs 1, 2, and 5 was kindly provided by Dr. Jörg Hamann (University of Amsterdam).

2.3. Large-Scale Calcium Phosphate Transfection of HEK-293T Cells

1. Highly purified expression vector plasmid DNA is prepared using the HiSpeed® Plasmid Maxi kit (Qiagen, Valencia, CA).
2. 14-ml polypropylene round-bottom tubes.
3. *2× HBS.* 1.64% (w/v) NaCl, 1.19% (w/v) HEPES, 0.04% (w/v) Na_2HPO_4, adjusted to pH 7.1 with HCl, filtered through a 0.22-μm filter.
4. Cell-culture-grade dH_2O.
5. 1 M $CaCl_2$, sterile.
6. 1 N HCl, sterile.

2.4. Purification of mFc-Fusion Protein

1. Protein G sepharose™ 4 Fast Flow (GE Healthcare).
2. Glass Econo-Column® Chromatography columns (Bio-Rad, Hercules, CA).
3. *Washing buffer*. 50 mM Tris–HCl, pH 7.5, 10 mM $CaCl_2$, and 150 mM NaCl.
4. *Elution buffer*. 100 mM Glycine, pH 2.9.
5. *Neutralization buffer*. 1 M Tris–base solution, pH 9.0.
6. The BCA™ Protein Assay kit (PIERCE, Rockford, USA).
7. DU 800 spectrophotometer (Beckman Coulter, Fullerton, CA).

2.5. Protein Biotinylation

1. Slide-A-Lyzer® Dialysis Cassettes (PIERCE, Rockford, USA).
2. 10 mM Tris–HCl buffer, pH 8.0.
3. The BirA enzyme and BioMix A and BioMix B buffers (Avidity, Denver, CO).
4. 10 mM Tris–HCl buffer, pH 7.5 containing 100 mM NaCl and 10 mM $CaCl_2$.

2.6. Production of Multivalent Fluorescent and Paramagnetic Protein Probes

1. *Avidin-coated green fluorescent beads*. 0.1% w/v, 5 ml, 0.4–0.6 µm. (Spherotech Inc., Libertyville, IL).
2. Dynabeads® M-280 streptavidin-conjugated paramagnetic polystyrene beads, 2.8 µm in diameter (Dynal A.S., Oslo, Norway).
3. The 6-tube magnet stand, Dynal MPS®-S (Dynal A.S., Oslo, Norway).
4. *Phosphate-buffered saline (PBS)*. Prepare 10× stock with 1.37 M NaCl, 27 mM KCl, 100 mM Na_2HPO_4, 18 mM KH_2PO_4, (adjust to pH 7.4 with HCl). The solution is autoclaved before storage at room temperature. Prepare 1× working solution by adding nine parts dH_2O with one part 10× stock solution.
5. Hanks' balanced salt solution with calcium and magnesium, (HBSS) (1×), liquid.
6. *PBS/BSA*. 10 mg BSA dissolved in 1 ml PBS.
7. *HBSS/BSA*. 5 mg BSA dissolved in 1 ml HBSS.

2.7. Identification and Characterization of Ligand-Expressing Cells

1. 96-well U-bottom tissue culture plates.
2. 10 mM EDTA in PBS, pH 8.0.
3. The sonicator (Heat Systems, Farmingdale, NY).
4. FACSCalibur flow cytometer (BD Biosciences, Franklin Lakes, NJ).

2.8. Enrichment of Ligand-Expressing Cells

1. The 6-tube magnet stand, Dynal MPS®-S (Dynal A.S., Oslo, Norway).
2. Trypan Blue Stain (GIBCO™, Invitrogen).

3. Hemocytometer (Hausser Scientific, Horsham, PA).
4. End-over-end rotator (Digisystem Laboratory Instrument Inc., Taiwan).

3. Methods

It is critical for this application that a large quantity of purified fusion protein is obtained. Care should be taken to optimize the large-scale cell transfection procedure in house. Both HEK-293T and CHO-K1 cells are good protein-producing cells in our experience. We have noticed that an optimal pH is very important for the calcium phosphate precipitation of DNA and hence the transfection efficiency. A good negative control using the fluorescent microspheres or paramagnetic beads alone is also essential and is always included. In addition, we also routinely include a recombinant mFc fragment as a negative protein control *(11)*. Choice of cell types is virtually unlimited, but care must be taken to ensure cell surface or extracellular proteins are not damaged in the cell preparation step *(10, 11)*. An outline of the following experimental procedures described is depicted in **Fig. 1**.

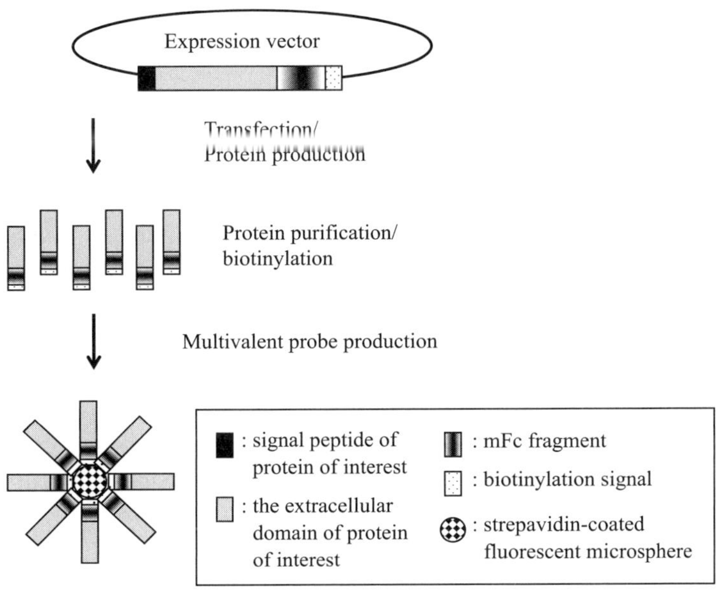

Fig. 1. Schematic diagram showing the experimental procedures for the production of multivalent protein probes. The cDNA of the protein of interest containing its own signal peptide (to ensure secretion) and the extracellular domain is cloned in frame into the mFc-Bio expression vector. The recombinant protein is produced and affinity purified from the conditioned media of transiently transfected cells. Purified proteins are then biotinylated in vitro and coupled to the strepavidin-conjugated fluorescent microspheres to produce the multivalent probes.

3.1. Construction of Expression Vectors

1. The cDNA fragment encoding the peptide sequence DPNSGSLHHILDAQKMVWNHR* (*see* **Note 2**), recognized by the *Escherichia coli* biotin holoenzyme synthetase BirA, is generated using the Advantage™-HF 2 PCR Kit according to the manufacturer's protocol. The XbaB10 and Bio3 primers are used to amplify an HLA-A2 plasmid template, which contains the biotinylation signal peptide sequence *(13)*. The hinge-CH2 and CH3 region of a non-Fc receptor-binding form of murine IgG2b is generated by High-Fidelity PCR using mFcXba and NotmFc primers and a murine IgG2b genomic DNA as a template *(11, 12)*. The cycling parameters used are as follows: the denaturation step (94°C, 30 s), five cycles of 94°C for 30 s and extension at 72°C, five cycles of 94°C for 30 s and extension at 70°C followed by 20–30 cycles of 94°C for 30 s of annealing/extension at 68°C.
2. The amplified DNA fragment is separated by gel electrophoresis in a 1% agarose gel. Agarose gels are prepared in 1× TBE containing 0.2 μg/ml ethidium bromide. DNA samples are mixed in 6× DNA loading dye and run at 50 mA. 1 kb DNA Plus ladder is used as a reference.
3. The amplified DNA band is examined with UV light, excised, and purified from agarose gels using the QIAquick gel extraction kit (*see* **Note 3**).
4. The purified PCR products are individually subcloned into the PCR4-Topo TA cloning vector for subsequent plasmid isolation and DNA sequencing to confirm the integrity of the amplified DNA fragments.
5. The biotinylation peptide signal sequence is cloned into the pcDNA3.1 (+) vector via *Xba* I and *Apa* I sites, while the mFc fragment is cloned subsequently into the resulting construct via the *BamH* I and *Xba* I sites. In general, the vectors are dephosphorylated to prevent religation. The ligation reaction mixture is incubated at 16°C overnight before transformation of competent bacteria.
6. The completed vector, called mFc-Bio/pcDNA3.1, is a pcDNA3.1(+) plasmid containing an mFc fragment followed by a biotinylation signal sequence. To make the final expression vector, the cDNA sequence coding for the protein of interest is inserted in frame immediately before the mFc fragment via appropriate restriction sites. In the case illustrated here, the CD97(EGF 1, 2, 5) fragment coding for the N-terminal EGF motifs 1, 2, and 5 of CD97 is placed in front of the mFc fragment via *Hind* III and *EcoR* I sites to generate the CD97-mFc-Bio expression vector.
7. All expression vectors are purified and subjected to DNA sequencing in both directions to confirm the fidelity of the coding sequence (*see* **Note 4**).

3.2. Large-Scale Cell Transfection by Calcium Phosphate Precipitation of DNA

1. Mock precipitations are first performed to adjust the optimal pH used for the transfection. This is achieved by making *solution I:* mixing 1 ml 2× HBS and different volumes of 1N HCl ranging from 0 to 10 μl in a series of 14-ml polypropylene round-bottom tubes.
2. 1 ml of *solution II*. A mixture of 248 μl of 1 M $CaCl_2$ and 752 μl dH_2O is then slowly added to each tube containing solution I by gradually air bubbling the mixture continuously with a pipette.
3. The tubes are left for 30 min at room temperature for the precipitates to form. The sizes of the precipitates are monitored under a microscope to find the optimal pH condition, i.e., the optimal amounts of 1N HCl for solution I (*see* **Note 5**).
4. When the optimal condition is found, all precipitation is done using the same amount of 1N HCl for solution I. For solution II, 20 μg plasmid DNA and appropriate amount of sterile dH_2O are added to 248 μl of 1 M $CaCl_2$ to a final 1 ml.
5. HEK-293T cells are cultured in DMEM supplemented with 10% (v/v) FCS until they reach about 60–70% confluence. To this was added 4 ml of transfection mixture containing 40 μg DNA which was found to be adequate for one T-175 flask of HEK-293T cells (*see* **Note 6**).
6. Typically, 5 T-175 flasks are used for one expression construct.
7. Cells are fed with fresh medium 1 h before transfection (20 ml/T-175 flask) and the transfection mix was slowly pipetted into the culture medium ensuring an even distribution (*see* **Note 7**).
8. Cells are then left in standard culture conditions for up to 16 h. Afterward, the transfection medium is removed and cells are rinsed carefully with PBS, followed by the addition of 40 ml fresh serum-free OPTI-MEM I medium. Cells can be cultured for up to 7 days (*see* **Note 8**). The conditioned medium is harvested and spun at 2000 *g* for 15 min at 4°C to remove cell debris. The supernatant is then filtered through a 0.45-μm filter and stored at –80°C until protein purification.

3.3. Purification of mFc-Fusion Protein by Protein G Affinity Chromatography

1. Mouse Fc-fusion proteins are purified from conditioned media using protein G sepharose chromatography (*see* **Note 9**). Protein G sepharose (1 ml) was first packed into the chromatography column and equilibrated with 50 ml washing buffer. Conditioned medium is then passed through the column twice under gravity (*see* **Note 10**).
2. The column is washed once with at least 50 ml washing buffer (*see* **Note 11**).
3. The bound mFc-fusion protein is eluted with 100 mM glycine, pH 2.9 elution buffer.

4. ~0.9 ml of eluate/fraction is collected into a 1.5-ml Eppendorf tube containing 100 μl of 1 M Tris–HCl, pH9.0 solution for neutralization. A total of ten fractions are collected (*see* **Note 12**).
5. Eluates are assessed by absorbance at O.D. 280.
6. Fractions containing proteins are combined and dialyzed in a Slide-A-Lyzer® Dialysis Cassette against 10 mM Tris–HCl, pH 8.0 buffer at 4°C overnight.
7. The final protein concentration is measured by the BCA™ protein assay kit according to the manufacturer's protocol, and the purified protein is aliquoted and stored at –80°C.

3.4. Protein Biotinylation

1. The purified mFc-fusion proteins are biotinylated based on the following formula: Eight parts of dialyzed protein are incubated with one part BioMix A buffer, one part BioMix B buffer, and 1 μl BirA enzyme overnight at room temperature *(9, 11)* (*see* **Notes 13** and **14**).
2. Excess biotin is subsequently removed by dialysis against 10 mM Tris–HCl, pH 7.3 buffer containing 10 mM $CaCl_2$ and 100 mM NaCl at 4°C overnight (*see* **Note 15**).
3. The biotinylated mFc-fusion proteins are quantified by dot-blot analysis using myelin basic protein biotin (Avidity, Denver, CO) as standard (*see* **Note 16**).
4. The biotinylated mFc-fusion proteins are then aliquoted and stored at –80°C.

3.5. Production of Multivalent Fluorescent Protein Probes

1. 10 μl of avidin-coated fluorescent microspheres are placed in a 1.5-ml eppendorf tube, spun at 100*g* at 4°C for 5 min, and washed twice with 1 ml PBS.
2. The fluorescent beads are then blocked with 1 mL PBS/BSA at 4°C for 1 h by end-over-end rotation, followed by centrifugation to discard the blocking buffer.
3. The fluorescent beads are then mixed with 1 μg biotinylated fusion proteins in HBSS/BSA in a total volume of 100 μl and incubated at 4°C for 1 h by end-over-end rotation.
4. The fluorescent bead–protein complexes are spun at 100 g at 4°C for 5 min and washed twice with 1 ml HBSS/BSA to remove unbound biotinylated proteins.
5. The fluorescent bead–protein complexes are resuspended in 50 μl HBSS/BSA, placed on ice, and sonicated immediately before use at 20% power for 20 s at 4°C three times with 10-s intervals in between *(9, 11)* (*see* **Note 17**).

3.6. Production of Multivalent Paramagnetic Protein Probes

1. For the magnetic selection of ligand-expressing cells, biotinylated proteins are coated onto streptavidin-conjugated paramagnetic beads *(10)*.

2. 10 μL of paramagnetic beads are placed in a 1.5-ml eppendorf tube next to a magnet for 1 min. The supernatant is discarded carefully not to disturb the beads adhered to the side of the tube.
3. After removal of the tube from the magnet, the beads are blocked with 1 mL HBSS/BSA at 4°C for 1 h.
4. The paramagnetic beads are washed three times with HBSS/BSA and then resuspended in 50 μl HBSS/BSA.
5. The paramagnetic beads are incubated with 2 μg biotinylated proteins at 4°C for 30 min by end-over-end rotation.
6. The tube is then placed next to the magnet for 1 min and the supernatant is carefully discarded to remove unbound biotinylated proteins by magnetic separation.
7. The tube is then removed from the magnet, and the bead–protein complexes are washed three times with 1 ml HBSS/BSA.
8. The paramagnetic bead–protein complexes are then resuspended in 10 μl HBSS/BSA and are ready for use.

3.7. Identification and Characterization of Ligand-Expressing Cells

1. Various cell types can be used to screen for candidate ligands. If adherent cell types such as macrophages or dendritic cells are to be screened, they must be lifted by nonenzymatic dissociation buffer to avoid digestion of the potential cell surface or extracellular matrix ligand(s) *(9–11, 14, 15)* (*see* **Note 18**).
2. To screen for the candidate ligand-expressing cells, the fluorescent bead–protein probes are incubated with the cells to be screened in U-bottom 96-well plates at 1 × 10⁶ cells/50 μl bead–protein probes/well (*see* **Note 19**).
3. The cell–bead mixture is spun at 100 *g* at 4°C for 20 min and incubated for a further 40 min at 4°C in the dark.
4. The cell–bead mixture is resuspended in 200 μl of PBS and placed in a tube for analysis by flow cytometry. Putative ligand-expressing cells will bind the fluorescent probes and give an increased FL-1 signal. In the example illustrated here **(Fig. 2)**, CD55⁺ K562 cells bind the CD97 probe readily and show strong fluorescent signals compared to the negative controls consisting of cells incubated with either fluorescent beads alone or fluorescent beads coupled to only mFc fragment. On the other hand, CHO-K1 cells, which do not express human CD55, show no binding at all and thus no enhanced fluorescent signal (data not shown).
5. Negative controls consisting of either fluorescent beads alone or beads coated with only mFc fragment are always included in each experiment.
6. After the identification of the putative positive ligand-expressing cells, various treatments such as protease digestion and Ab

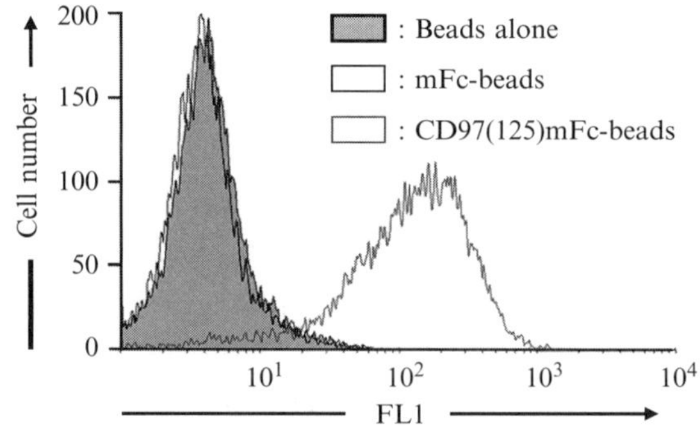

Fig. 2 A typical flow cytometry profile demonstrating the interaction of CD97 fluorescent multivalent probes with CD55 on K562 cells. Negative controls consist of incubating K562 cells with either fluorescent beads alone or fluorescent beads coupled to only mFc fragment.

blocking can be used to confirm the specific receptor–ligand interaction and further characterize the potential cellular ligand(s) *(11)* (*see* **Note 20**).

3.8. Enrichment of the Ligand-Expressing Cells

1. The ligand-expressing cells can be enriched from mixed cell populations such as blood for potential downstream application using the paramagnetic separation *(10)*.
2. Mixed cell populations containing potential ligand-expressing cells are washed with 5 ml PBS/BSA, adjusted to a cell density of 3 × 10^6 cells/ml, and incubated at 4°C with the paramagnetic bead–protein complexes (20 μl bead–protein complexes/ml cell solution/reaction) for 1 h on an end-over-end rotator at 4°C.
3. The cell–bead mixture in 1.5-ml eppendorf tube is then placed next to a magnet for 1 min and the supernatant carefully discarded. The unbound cells are removed by five gentle but thorough washes in 1 ml PBS/BSA coupled with magnetic separation.
4. The remaining cells are separated and isolated from the beads by incubation in HBSS/BSA containing 5 mM EDTA in PBS for 10 min at room temperature followed by magnetic separation (*see* **Note 21**).
5. The total number of recovered cells is determined by counting in a hemocytometer.
6. The isolated ligand-expressing cells are now ready for further analysis such as RNA isolation, protein purification, and immunocytochemistry.
7. Based upon the characteristics of the receptor–ligand interaction, it is possible to molecularly identify the putative cellular ligand(s)

expressed on the isolated ligand-expressing cells. Methods of choice include affinity purification using the multivalent protein probes described here, or expression cloning strategies described elsewhere. We have successfully identified a cellular ligand for myeloid-restricted EMR2 receptor using a panel of mutant cell lines defective in a specific biosynthetic pathway *(11)*.

4. Notes

1. If the mFc fragment is desired as a negative control, an mFc expression vector constructed on the pSecTag2A plasmid (Invitrogen), called pSecTag-mFc, may be used. The pSecTag-mFc construct was made by subcloning the mFc fragment and the biotinylation signal into the pSecTag2 A vector via the same restriction sites described in the text.
2. The biotinylation signal sequence described here is amplified from an HLA-A2 plasmid template. This sequence is recognized and efficiently biotinylated by BirA enzyme purchased from Avidity. However, the BirA enzyme has since been engineered and modified by the company and no longer efficiently works on the sequence listed earlier. The optimal biotinylation signal sequence for the new BirA enzyme is GGGLNDIFEAQKIEWHE*, which can be obtained from a template plasmid from Avidity.
3. Observe the amplified DNA fragments under long-wave UV light if the DNA is to be used for subsequent cloning.
4. HiSpeed® Plasmid Maxi kits are used to obtain large quantities of plasmid DNA for the subsequent large-scale cell transfections. If desired, CsCl banding of plasmid DNA isolation can also be considered.
5. The optimal size of the calcium-phosphate DNA precipitate is approximately the tip of a needle under the microscope at 200× magnification. pH influences the precipitate formation greatly. If no precipitate is seen, it is likely that the pH is too low, whereas if the precipitate is too large, it is likely that the pH is too high. The formation of large precipitates or aggregates affects the ability of cell to take up DNA. This should be avoided and the mock precipitation step should be repeated until an optimal pH condition is found.
6. The amount of solutions I and II is determined by how many flasks of cells are to be transfected. Usually, we prepare the solutions in bulk keeping the amounts of individual components in proportion.

7. HEK-293T cells are only loosely adherent especially when reaching confluence, so care should be taken to minimize disturbing the monolayer when adding reagents or changing medium.
8. Observe the transfected cells daily to check their health in order to decide when to collect the conditioned medium.
9. Can also use protein A sepharose as it binds to the mFc fragment equally well.
10. Care should be taken to make sure the protein G sepharose resin remains in solution and does not dry out.
11. The column should be washed with at least 50× void volume of the sepharose resin.
12. The mFc-fusion proteins usually are eluted in the first 2–4 tubes depending upon the starting amount.
13. Alternatively, the biotinylation reaction can be incubated at 4°C for longer periods or 3–4 h at 30°C.
14. If the protein concentration of starting material is high (>2 mg/ml), use eight parts of protein, one part BioMix A buffer, one part BioMix A buffer, and one part supplemental Biotin.
15. We usually change the dialysis buffer every few hours to facilitate dialysis.
16. A serial dilution of the biotinylated protein is prepared and dot-blotted onto the nitrocellulose filter paper next to the standard biotin-myelin basic protein. After extensive blocking in PBS/BSA, Strepavidin-HRP is applied to react with the biotinylated protein, followed by thorough washes with PBS/BSA and signal detection by ECL reagent (Amersham).
17. Be sure not to overheat the protein–bead complexes.
18. We routinely used 5 mM EDTA/PBS to lift adherent cells from tissue culture plates.
19. The U-bottom plates ensure that the cells interact optimally with the microspheres.
20. Cells can be pretreated with various proteolytic enzymes such as trypsin, α-chymotrypsin, dispase, etc. to compare with untreated cells to determine whether the putative cellular ligand is protease sensitive. Similarly, exogenous chemical reagents such as EGTA can also be included to test whether the ligand-receptor interaction is Ca^{2+} dependent. Finally, blocking Abs can be used to test candidate ligand molecules.
21. In our case, $CD55^{+}$-red blood cells can be efficiently enriched from whole blood cell sample using the CD97-mFc-fusion protein probe on paramagnetic beads.

Acknowledgements

This work was supported by grants from Chang Gung Memorial Hospital (CMRPD33008, CMRPD140131) and the National Science Council, Taiwan (NSC94-2320-B-182-045), to H-H. Lin.

References

1. Butcher, E.C. and Picker, L.J. (1996) Lymphocyte homing and homeostasis. *Science* 272, 60–66.
2. Kunkel, E.J. and Butcher, E.C. (2002) Chemokines and the tissue-specific migration of lymphocytes. *Immunity* 16, 1–4.
3. Pribila, J.T., Quale, A.C., Mueller, K.L. and Shimizu, Y. (2004) Integrins and T cell-mediated immunity. *Annu. Rev. Immunol.* 22, 157–180.
4. Rosen, S.D. (2004) Ligands for l-selectin: homing, inflammation, and beyond. *Annu. Rev. Immunol.* 22, 129–156.
5. Springer, T.A. (1994) Traffic signals for lymphocyte recirculation and leukocyte emigration: the multistep paradigm. *Cell* 76, 301–314.
6. Rothenberg, E.V. and Taghon, T. (2005) Molecular genetics of T cell development. *Annu. Rev. Immunol.* 23, 601–649.
7. Zuniga-Pflucker, J.C. (2004) T-cell development made simple. *Nat. Rev. Immunol.* 4, 67–72.
8. Wild, M.K., Huang, M.C., Schulze-Horsel, U., van der Merwe, P.A. and Vestweber, D. (2001) Affinity, kinetics, and thermodynamics of E-selectin binding to E-selectin ligand-1. *J. Biol. Chem.* 276, 31602–31613.
9. Lin, H.H., Stacey, M., Saxby, C., Knott, V., Chaudhry, Y., Evans, D., Gordon, S., McKnight, A.J., Handford, P. and Lea, S. (2001) Molecular analysis of the epidermal growth factor-like short consensus repeat domain-mediated protein–protein interactions: dissection of the CD97-CD55 complex. *J. Biol. Chem.* 276, 24160–24169.
10. Lin, H.H., Stacey, M., Chang, G.W., Davies, J.Q. and Gordon, S. (2005) Method for selecting and enriching cells expressing low affinity ligands for cell surface receptors. *Biotechniques* 38, 696–698.
11. Stacey, M., Chang, G.W., Davies, J.Q., Kwakkenbos, M.J., Sanderson, R.D., Hamann, J., Gordon, S. and Lin, H.H. (2003) The epidermal growth factor-like domains of the human EMR2 receptor mediate cell attachment through chondroitin sulfate glycosaminoglycans. *Blood* 102, 2916–2924.
12. Martinez-Pomares, L., Hanitsch, L.G., Stillion, R., Keshav, S. and Gordon, S. (2005) Expression of mannose receptor and ligands for its cysteine-rich domain in venous sinuses of human spleen. *Lab. Invest.* 85, 1238–1249.
13. Altman, J.D., Moss, P.A., Goulder, P.J., Barouch, D.H., McHeyzer-Williams, M.G., Bell, J.I., McMichael, A.J. and Davis, M.M. (1996) Phenotypic analysis of antigen-specific T lymphocytes. *Science* 274, 94–96.
14. Stacey, M., Chang, G.W., Sanos, S.L., Chittenden, L.R., Stubbs, L., Gordon, S. and Lin, H.H. (2002) EMR4, a novel epidermal growth factor (EGF)-TM7 molecule up-regulated in activated mouse macrophages, binds to a putative cellular ligand on B lymphoma cell line A20. *J. Biol. Chem.* 277, 29283–29293.
15. Stacey, M., Lin, H.H., Hilyard, K.L., Gordon, S. and McKnight, A.J. (2001) Human epidermal growth factor (EGF) module-containing mucin-like hormone receptor 3 is a new member of the EGF-TM7 family that recognizes a ligand on human macrophages and activated neutrophils. *J. Biol. Chem.* 276, 18863–18870.

Chapter 8

Exploiting Fc Chimaeric Proteins for the Identification of Ligands Specific for the Mannose Receptor

Luisa Martinez-Pomares

Summary

The use of chimaeric molecules bearing tags easily recognised by secondary reagents has facilitated the discovery of protein–protein and protein–carbohydrate interactions using binding assays in situ, in solution and in solid phase. In this chapter we describe our experience in the use of proteins containing selected regions of the mannose receptor fused to the Fc region of human IgG1 or murine IgG2b. Using these reagents we have discovered new and unexpected ligands for the mannose receptor. These ligands were first detected in tissue section using standard histological techniques or ligand blots of whole tissue lysates, identified using affinity chromatography and N-terminal protein sequencing and confirmed using ligand blots or solid-phase-binding assays using purified proteins. These findings have dramatically changed the way we think about this molecule.

Key words: Mannose receptor, Ligands, Carbohydrates, Glycoproteins, Collagens.

1. Introduction

The mannose receptor (MR) is a 175-kDa type I integral membrane receptor. It recognises sulphated carbohydrates terminated in SO_4-4-GalNAc-, SO_4-3-GalNAc-, or SO_4-3-Gal through its cysteine-rich domain (CR) *(1, 2)*, native and denatured collagens through its fibronectin type II domain (FNII) *(3)* and mannose, fucose, and *N*-acetylglucosamine in a Ca^{2+}- and pH-dependent manner, via C-type lectin-like domain (CTLD)-4, with CTLD4-8 providing similar high-affinity binding as the full-length receptor *(4, 5)* (*see* **Fig. 1**). MR is an endocytic receptor that resides in the recycling endocytic compartment; it is expressed by most murine

Neil E. Reiner (ed.), *Macrophages and Dendritic Cells,* Methods in Molecular Biology, vol. 531

DOI: 10.1007/978-1-59745-396-7_8

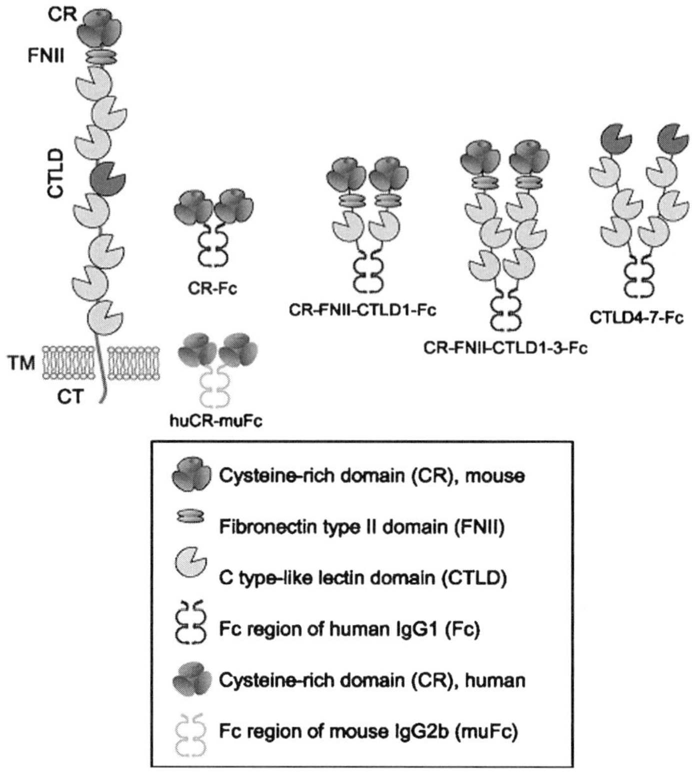

Fig. 1. Schematic representation of the domain structure of MR and Fc proteins used for studying MR-binding properties. *CR* cysteine-rich domain of mouse MR; *FNII* fibronectin-type II domain of mouse MR; *CTLD* C-type lectin-like domain of mouse MR; *TM* transmembrane domain of mouse MR; *CT* cytoplasmic tail of mouse MR; *huCR* cysteine-rich domain of the human MR; *Fc* Fc region of human IgG_1; *muFc* Fc region of murine IgG2b.

macrophage populations, hepatic and lymphatic endothelia, glomerular mesangial cells in the kidneys, tracheal smooth muscle cells, and retinal pigment epithelium. In humans MR has been detected in skin dermis, mucosal lamina propria, and the T-cell areas of tonsil. MR was initially discovered through its involvement in the clearance of endogenous glycoproteins; indeed, MR deficiency does not have a major impact in immunity against *Candida albicans* or *Pneumocystis carinii* but leads to a drastic increase in the circulating levels of multiple lysosomal hydrolases (*see* **ref.** *(6)* for review). MR-derived Fc chimaeric proteins have provided useful information regarding the binding properties of MR. They led to the discovery of cell-associated ligands for the MR domain CR (CR ligands) in lymphoid organs *(7, 8)*, ligands for the CTLD4-7 region in secretory organs *(9)*, one of them being thyroglobulin, and for the FNII region *(3)*. In this chapter we have outlined the methodology used for these studies.

2. Materials

2.1. Detection of Ligands In Situ

2.1.1. Tissue Collection

1. Dissecting tools.
2. Dissecting board.
3. OCT Tissue-Tek compound.
4. Plastic moulds.
5. Iso-pentane.
6. Dry ice.
7. Ice container.
8. Gelatine-coated slides.
9. Charged slides.
10. Cryostat.

2.1.2. Tissue Labelling

1. Fixative: Methanol-free paraformaldehyde (16% solution). To prepare 200 ml of fixative: 25 ml paraformaldehyde, 175 ml dH_2O, 1.8 g NaCl, 0.08 g $CaCl_2$, 1.5 ml 1 M Hepes buffer, pH 7.4.
2. Phosphate-buffered saline (PBS).
3. Lectin-binding buffer: 10 mM Tris–HCl, pH 7.4, 154 mM NaCl, 10 mM $CaCl_2$.
4. Permeabilising solution: 0.1% Triton X-100 in PBS.
5. Quenching solution: add 50 μl of 1 M NaN_3 and 0.09 g glucose to 50 ml of 0.1 M phosphate buffer. Warm to 37°C and add 20 μl glucose oxidase just before use.
6. Avidin/Biotin Blocking Kit.
7. Blocking solution: 5% normal serum in PBS sources of normal sera: donkey, goat, mouse, rabbit or rat. Purified rat IgG.
8. Shandon Sequenza® Slide Rack (Thermo Scientific, 7331017).
9. Shandon Coverplate™ (Thermo Scientific, 72110013).
10. Biotinylated goat anti-human IgG.
11. Peroxidase-conjugated goat anti-Human IgG and peroxidase-conjugated horse anti-mouse IgG.
12. Alkaline phosphatase-conjugated goat anti-Human IgG.
13. Alexa 488-conjugated Goat anti-human IgG.
14. ABC Peroxidase Vector Vectastain Elite Kit.
15. ABC Alkaline Phosphatase Vector Vectastain Elite ABC Kit. For both ABC kits add two drops of solution A to 10 ml PBS and mix well then add two drops of solution B mix well and incubate 30 min at room temperature before using.

16. Cy5-conjugated Streptavidin.
17. Alexa 488-conjugated Streptavidin.
18. 3,3′-Diaminobenzidine tetrahydrochloride (DAB) (5 × 10 mg). To be used with peroxidase-conjugated secondary reagents. DAB is a potential carcinogen and it should be used in a ventilated hood. It is most dangerous in powder form and is not to be removed from the container in this state. Equipment: 20-ml syringe, 22-μm syringe filter, two needles, 0.5- to 10-μl pipette and tip, two beakers, 10 mM imidazole solution (kept at 4°C), hydrogen peroxide. Preparation of developing solution: pour imidazole into beaker and draw 20 ml into syringe. Pour any excess back into the bottle. Push two needles into DAB vial and inject contents of syringe through. Mix. Pipette 6 μl H_2O_2 into beaker. Withdraw DAB solution with syringe and filter into beaker containing H_2O_2. Mix. The solution is now ready for use.
19. Substrate Kit IV BCIP/NBT. To be used with alkaline phosphatase-conjugated secondary reagents. To 5 ml of 100 mM Tris–HCl pH 9.5 buffer add one drop of levamisole (a reagent to quench endogenous alkaline phosphatase activity within tissues) and mix. Add two drops of reagent 1 and mix well. Add two drops of reagent 2 and mix well. Add three drops of reagent 3 and mix well.
20. Methyl green.
21. Histoclear.
22. 4 ,6-Diamidino-2-phenylindole,dilactate. Prepare concentrate stock in PBS (1 mg/ml), aliquot, and store at −20°C. Just before use, dilute in PBS to 400 ng/ml.
23. DPX (VWR, 36125 4D).
24. AquaPerm.
25. Fluorescence-mounting medium.

2.2. Detection of Ligands in Tissue Lysates

2.2.1. Preparation of Tissue Lysates

1. Lysis buffer for preparations of total protein lysates: 10 mM Tris–HCl, pH 8, 2% (v/v) Triton X-100, 10 mM NaN_3, 150 mM NaCl, 2 mM EDTA.
2. Buffer A: 10 mM Tris–HCl, pH 8, 2.5% (v/v) Tween 40, 150 mM NaCl, 10 mM NaN_3, 2 mM EDTA.
3. Buffer B: 10 mM Tris–HCl, pH 8, 10 mM NaN_3, 150 mM NaCl, 2 mM EDTA.
4. Complete Protease Inhibitor Cocktail Tablets.
5. Polytron Homogeniser.
6. Dounce Homogeniser.
7. TC100 centrifuge.

8. Preparative ultracentrifuge.
9. BCA Protein assay kit.

2.2.2. Ligand Blots

1. Non-reducing SDS–PAGE sample buffer: 10 mM Tris–HCl, pH 6.8, 2% (w/v) SDS, 20% (v/v) glycerol, 0.001% (w/v) bromophenol blue.
2. Separating gel (20 ml): 5 ml of 1.5 M Tris–HCl pH 8.8, 0.2 ml of 10% SDS, acrylamide:bis-acrylamide (30%:0.8%) solution (amount depends on % of acrylamide required), MilliQ H_2O to 20 ml, 0.2 ml of 10% (w/v) ammonium persulphate, 30 µl of temed.
3. Stacking gel (10 ml): 2.5 ml of 0.5 M Tris–HCl, pH 6.8, 0.1 ml of 10% SDS, 1.34 ml acrylamide:bis-acrylamide (30%:0.8%) solution, 5.94 ml MilliQ H_2O, 0.1 ml of 10% ammonium persulphate, 20 µl of temed.
4. Running buffer: 25 mM Tris, 192 mM glycine, 0.1% (w/v) SDS, pH 8.3.
5. Rainbow Markers Full Range.
6. Heating block.
7. Western blot transfer buffer: 25 mM Tris, 192 mM glycine, 20% methanol.
8. Western blot apparatus.
9. Hybond-C extra membranes.
10. Blocking buffers: 5% (w/v) non-fat dry milk, 0.1% (v/v) Tween 20 in phosphate-buffered saline or 5% (w/v) non-fat milk, 0.1% (v/v) Tween 20 in 10 mM Tris–HCl, pH 7.4, 154 mM NaCl, 10 mM $CaCl_2$.
11. Washing buffers: 0.1% (v/v) Tween 20 in PBS or 0.1% (v/v) Tween 20 in 10 mM Tris–HCl, pH 7.4, 154 mM NaCl, 10 mM $CaCl_2$.
12. Peroxidase-conjugated secondary Ab against human or mouse IgG.
13. Rotating shaker.
14. ECL Western Blotting Reagents.
15. Hyperfilm ECL.

2.2.3. Detection of Ligands by Enrichment in Solution Using Protein A- or G-Sepharose and Ligand Blot Analysis

1. Lysis buffer for preparations of total protein lysates (*see* **Subheading 2.2.1**).
2. Protease inhibitors.
3. Protein A-sepharose or protein G-sepharose.
4. Rotating wheel.
5. Microcentrifuge.

6. Digoxigenin protein labelling kit.
7. Peroxidase-conjugated anti-Digoxigenin Ab.

2.2.4. Purication of Ligands Using Fc Chimaeric Proteins Directly Conjugated to Protein A- or G-Sepharose

1. PBS.
2. 0.1 M Sodium borate, pH 9.
3. Coupling reagent: dissolve 0.5 g of dimethylpimelimidate in enough 0.1 sodium borate (pH not adjusted) to give a pH of 9. Add 0.1 M sodium borate, pH 9, to give a final volume of 50 ml.
4. Econo Columns.
5. Protein A-sepharose or protein G-sepharose.
6. Lysis buffer for preparations of total protein lysates (*see* **Subheading 2.2.1**).
7. High pH elution buffer (>11): 0.5% (v/v) diethylamine in 0.1% (v/v) Triton X-100.
8. Low pH elution buffer (<3): 0.1 M glycine, pH 2.9 in 0.1% (v/v) Triton X-100.
9. Calcium quelator: EDTA in 0.1% (v/v) Triton X-100.
10. Neutralisation buffer: 1 M Tris–HCl, pH 7.

2.2.5. Assessment of Binding to Candidate Molecule Immunoprecipitated from a Protein Lysate Using a Monoclonal Ab

1. CNBr-activated sepharose or protein A/G-sepharose.
2. Immunoprecipitation washing buffer: A: 10 mM Tris–HCl, pH 8, 500 mM NaCl, 0.5% (w/v) deoxycholate, 0.5% (v/v) Triton X-100, 0.05% (w/v) SDS.
3. Immunoprecipitation washing buffer: B: 10 mM Tris–HCl, pH 8, 150 mM NaCl, 0.5% (w/v) deoxycholate, 0.5% (v/v) Triton X-100, 0.05% (w/v) SDS.
4. Immunoprecipitation washing buffer: C: 10 mM Tris–HCl, pH 8, 0.05% (w/v) SDS.

2.3. Assessment of Binding to Candidate Ligands in Solid Phase Assays

1. MaxiSorp 96-microwell plates.
2. 96-Microwell plates.
3. PBS.
4. Saline (154 mM NaCl).
5. Lectin buffer: 10 mM Tris–HCl, pH 7.5, 10 mM Ca^{2+}, 154 mM NaCl, and 0.05%(w/v) Tween 20.
6. PBS–0.3% bovine serum albumin (BSA).
7. Alkaline phosphatase-conjugated anti-human Fc.
8. Alkaline phosphatase substrate buffer: 100 mM Tris–HCl, 100 mM NaCl, 1 mM $MgCl_2{\cdot}6H_2O$, pH 9.5.
9. Substrate: 4-nitrophenyl phosphate disodium salt hexahydrate 1 mg/ml in substrate buffer.
10. Plate reader with 405-nm filter.

3. Methods

3.1. Detection of Ligands In Situ

1. After collection, tissues are carefully placed in a mould containing OCT-LabTek compound (*see* **Note 1**).
2. Put moulds within a glass beaker containing iso-pentane previously placed on dry ice within an ice container.
3. Once the contents of the mould are frozen, they can be safely placed at –20°C until cutting.
4. Perform cutting in a cryostat at –20°C at 5–6 μm.
5. Sections are collected onto gelatine-coated slides or charged slides (*see* **Note 2**), left for 1 h at room temperature and placed at –20°C in sealed boxes containing silica gel in porous bags.
6. Thaw tissues at room temperature for 30–60 min and place in ice-cold 2% paraformaldehyde solution for 10 min on ice in a Coplin jar (*see* **Note 3**).
7. Rinse three times in PBS, cover slides with a Shandon Coverplate™ (*see* **Note 4**), and place both in the Shandon Sequenza® Slide Rack.
8. Permeabilise the tissues in PBS–0.1% Triton for 10 min (*see* **Note 5**) at room temperature. If using peroxidase-based detection reagents place the slides in quenching solution for 15 min at 37°C.
9. After washing (*see* **Note 6**) block slides with appropriate blocking buffer (*see* **Note 7**) for 30 min. If using a biotin/streptavidin-based detection system, block endogenous biotin with the avidin biotin blocking kit to (*see* **Note 8**)
10. Dilute MR-Fc chimaeric protein of interest in blocking buffer (*see* **Notes 9** and **10**, and **Figs. 1** and **2**) and add to slide.
11. Incubate at room temperature for 90 min (*see* **Note 11**).
12. After washing detection of binding can be performed using techniques outlined in **Table 1**. Washes should be performed in between all steps. *See* **Note 15** for additional information.

3.2. Detection of Ligands in Tissue Lysates

A general overview of the strategies that can be used for the identification of ligands for proteins of interest is described in **Table 2**.

3.2.1. Preparation of Total Tissue Lysates

1. Weigh frozen tissues (*see* **Note 16**) and add ice-cold freshly prepared lysis buffer containing protease inhibitors (approx. 1 ml of buffer/100 mg of sample).
2. Depending of the size of the sample use a polytron homogeniser or a dounce homogeniser to break up the tissue (*see* **Note 17**).

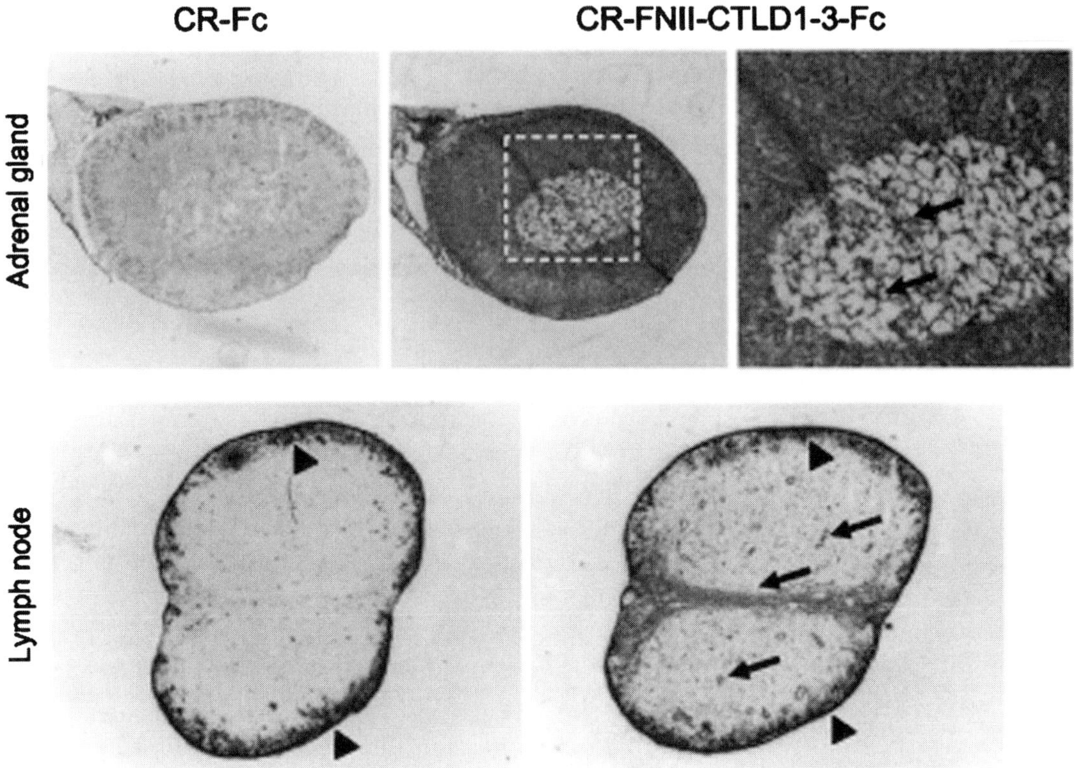

Fig. 2. Detection of MR CR and FNII ligands in situ. Tissues from adult mice were collected, processed, and incubated with cross-linked MR-derived Fc constructs CR-Fc and CR-FNII-CTLD1-3-Fc. Proteins containing FNII bound to structures resembling basement membrane (*arrows*) in the adrenal gland and lymph node. In the lymph node CR-FNII-CTLD1-3-Fc displayed dual binding activity with recognition of ligands (probably sulphated sugars) in the subcapsular sinus (also recognised by CR, *arrow heads*) in addition to basal membrane components in the T-cell region and medulla (*arrows*). Magnification ×10. Area in *inset* has been electronically magnified. Reproduced from *(3)* with permission.

3. After homogenisation, incubate at 4°C for 30–60 min, centrifuge lysate at 1,000 *g* at 4°C for 5 min, transfer the supernatant to another centrifuge tube, and centrifuge at 100,000 × *g* at 4°C for 30 min (*see* **Note 18**).
4. Collect the supernatant, quantify protein using the BCA protein assay kit, aliquot if necessary and store at –20 or –70°C (*see* **Note 19**).

3.2.2. Preparation of Membrane Lysates

This procedure is based on the method described by Williams and Barclay *(10)*.

1. Tissues are homogenised as before using buffer A containing protease inhibitors.
2. Nuclei are removed by centrifugation at 500 × *g* for 15 min at 4°C (*see* **Note 20**), and the supernatant is centrifuged at 35,000 rpm for 60 min at 4°C using a 60.Ti rotor (100,000 × *g*) to pellet the membranes (*see* **Note 21**).

Table 1
Strategies to detect binding of MR-Fc fusion proteins to tissues

	Brightfield		
	Peroxidase[a]	**Alkaline phosphatase**[b]	**Fluorescence**[c]
Two-step procedure	Peroxidase-conjugated anti-Fc (30–45 min)	Alkaline-phosphatase-conjugated anti-Fc (30–45 min)	Fluorochrome-conjugated anti-Fc (30–45 min)
	DAB	BCIP/NBT	
Three-step procedure	Biotin-conjugated anti-Fc (30–45 min)	Biotin-conjugated anti-Fc (30–45 min)	Biotin-conjugated anti-Fc (30–45 min)
	ABC Peroxidase Vector Vectastain Elite Kit (30–45 min)	ABC Alkaline Phosphatase Vector Vectastain Elite Kit (30–45 min)	Fluorochrome-conjugated-streptavidin (30–45 min)
	DAB	BCIP/NBT	
Counterstaining	Methyl green	Not recommended	DAPI
Mounting media	DPX (after dehydration)	AquaPerm	Fluorescence-mounting medium

[a] *See* **Note 12**
[b] *See* **Note 13**
[c] *See* **Note 14**

Table 2
Strategies to characterise ligands in tissue lysates using MR-Fc chimaeric proteins

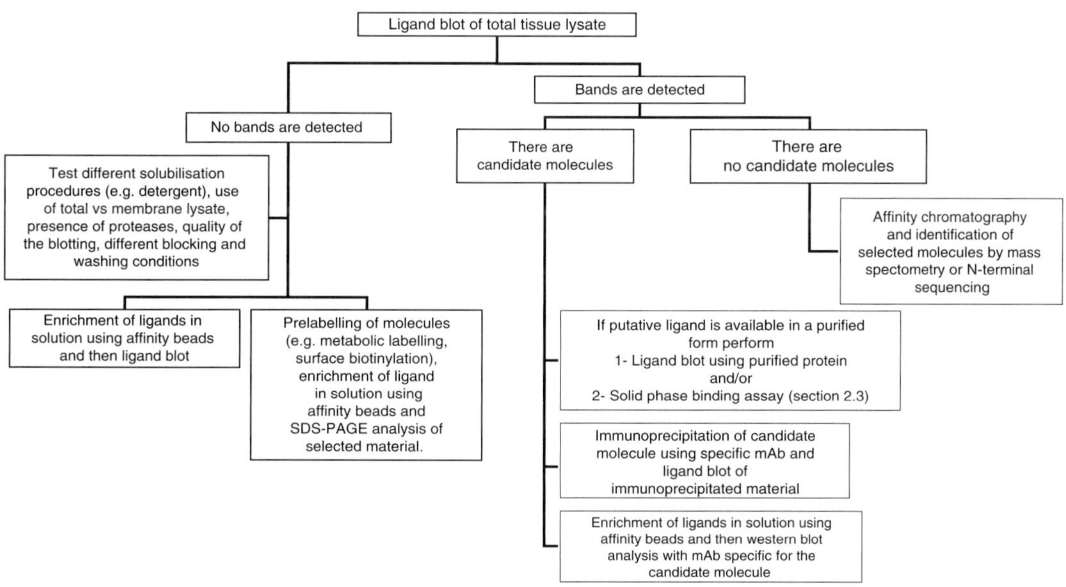

3. The membrane pellet is washed twice in buffer B containing protease inhibitors and proteins are solubilised by incubation in lysis buffer with protease inhibitors. Centrifuge lysate at 100,000 × *g* at 4°C.
4. Collect the supernatant, quantify protein using the BCA protein assay kit, aliquot if necessary and store at –20 or –70°C (*see* **Note 19**).

3.2.3. Ligand Blots

1. Separate proteins prepared in **Subheading 3.2.1** or **3.2.2**, using a non-continuous SDS–PAGE following standard procedures and solutions provided in **Subheading 2.2.2** (*see* **Notes 22** and **23**).
2. Transfer proteins to nitrocellulose filter (*see* **Notes 24** and **25**).
3. Place the filter in blocking buffer on a rotating shaker for 60 min at room temperature.
4. Pour out the blocking solution and add MR-Fc chimaeric proteins in blocking buffer (*see* **Note 26**).
5. Incubate for 60 min in the shaker at room temperature.
6. Wash in appropriate blocking buffer (*see* **Notes 26** and **27**).
7. Add peroxidase-conjugated anti-Fc or muFc secondary Ab diluted in blocking buffer (*see* **Note 28**).
8. Incubate for 60 min at room temperature, wash filter in appropriate washing buffer (*see* **Note 29**).
9. Develop using ECL Western Blotting Reagents (*see* **Note 30**).
10. Expose filter to film (*see* **Note 31**) in the dark and develop.

3.2.4. Detection of Ligands by Enrichment in Solution Using Protein A- or G-Sepharose and Ligand Blot Analysis

Immobilisation of purified recombinant proteins onto beads enables the selection of ligands for these proteins from complex protein solutions such as total or membrane lysates (*see* **Subheadings 3.2.1** and **3.2.2**). In the case of chimaeric proteins bearing the Fc region of human IgG1 (Fc) or mouse IgG2b (muFc), protein A- and/or protein G-sepharose are highly suitable for this purpose as they will readily interact with the Fc region of the recombinant proteins and provide a solid support for the selection for ligands in solution (*see* **Notes 32** and **33**).

1. Thaw protein lysate(s) on ice and examine for the presence of protein aggregates that might have formed during the freezing and thawing process. If present, remove these by centrifugation.
2. To pre-clear lysates of ligands that might bind non-specifically, wash protein A/G-sepharose -that has not been incubated with Fc-fusion proteins- in lysis buffer with protease inhibitors three times.

3. Pellet the sepharose after each wash by centrifugation at 12,000 *g* for 2 min in a microfuge and resuspend in 1 ml of buffer.
4. After the final wash, resuspend the sepharose as a 50% slurry in lysis buffer and add to protein lysate (typically 20–50 μl of slurry/250–1,000 ml lysate) (*see* **Note 34**).
5. Incubate in a rotating wheel at 4°C for 2 h.
6. Centrifuge the lysate to remove sepharose at 12,000 *g* for 5 min in a microfuge and collect the supernatant. This step ensures that compounds that bind to protein A/G-sepharose non-specifically are removed.
7. Add chimaeric protein to pre-cleared lysate (10–20 μg/ml of lysate) together with protein A/G-sepharose washed as before in lysis buffer.
8. Leave in a rotating wheel overnight at 4°C.
9. On the following day, collect the beads by centrifugation and wash in lysis buffer three times.
10. Elute bound proteins by resuspending beads in 1× SDS–PAGE loading buffer and boiling for 5 min.
11. Run sample in a SDS–PAGE, transfer as before, and probe with Fc chimaeric protein labelled with digoxigenin and peroxidase-conjugated anti-digoxigenin Ab.
12. Develop using ECL reagent (*see* **Note 35**).

3.2.5. Purification of Ligands Using Fc Chimaeric Proteins Directly Conjugated to Protein A- or G-Sepharose

Conjugate recombinant Fc fusion protein to protein A/G-sepharose as follows *(11)*:

1. Wash sepharose in PBS by centrifugation and incubate with recombinant protein (2 mg protein/ml of sepharose) in a rotating wheel for 2 h at room temperature.
2. Wash the sepharose with 10–20 volumes of PBS followed by two washes with 10 volumes of 0.1 M sodium borate, pH 9.
3. Prepare the coupling reagent, remove the buffer from the sepharose-Fc protein complex, and add 10 volumes of the coupling reagent.
4. Incubate in a rotating wheel for 30 min at room temperature.
5. Wash the beads with 0.02 methanolamine pH 9 for 10–20 min and then in buffer to be used for the affinity chromatography (*see* **Note 36**).
6. Prepare two columns, one containing the protein A/G-sepharose (pre-clearing column, *see* **Note 37**) and another containing the Fc chimaeric protein coupled to protein A/G-sepharose.

7. Wash both columns with 10 volumes of lysis buffer and then apply the tissue lysate (total or membrane lysate) to the pre-clearing column.
8. Collect the flow through and apply it to the column containing the Fc chimaeric protein (*see* **Note 38**).
9. Wash the column with 50–100 volumes of lysis buffer, PBS, or lectin buffer and elute bound proteins with suitable elution buffer (*see* **Note 39**).
10. Examine eluted proteins by SDS–PAGE (see examples of ligand blot and of ligand enrichment and probing with Ab against candidate molecules in **Fig. 3**).

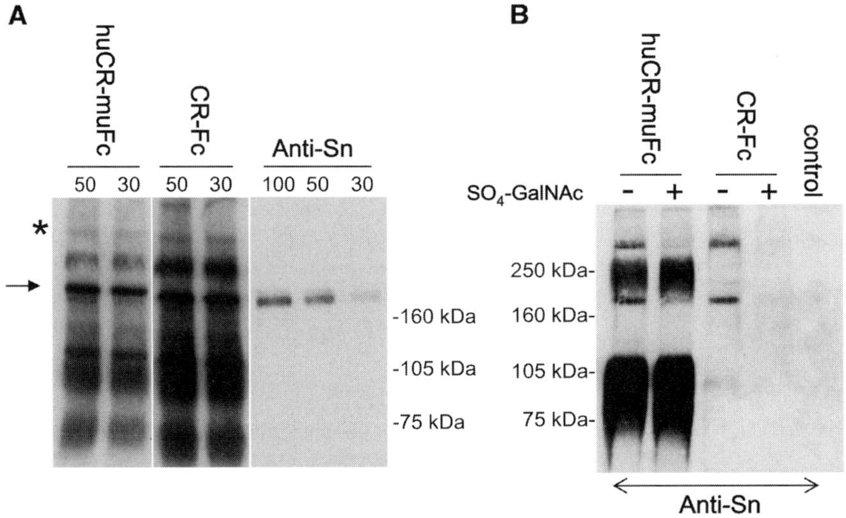

Fig. 3. Analysis of CR ligands in rat spleen lysates. (**A**) Detection of ligands for huCR and CR in rat spleen lysates by ligand blot. Different amounts of protein lysates from rat spleen were separated by SDS–PAGE followed by transfer to nitrocellulose and incubated with huCR-muFc or CR-Fc (50 and 30 μg) or with a monoclonal Ab against the candidate ligand sialoadhesin (Sn) (100, 50, and 30 μg). huCR-muFc and CR-Fc recognised a major band situated between the 160 and 250 kDa MW markers (see *arrow*) that based on size, co-migrated with the Sn band that was recognised by the anti-Sn mAb. Other minor species with rMW above 50 kDa were also detected. The band marked with (asterisk) could correspond to the higher rMW band of Sn that appeared enriched in the preparation of huCR and CR ligands (see band marked with *arrowhead* in **B**). Similar to what was observed previously in murine spleen cells *(7,8)*, a major 250-kDa ligand was detected in rat spleen using this technique. No information regarding the identity of this ligand is available. No binding of the secondary reagent used for detection was observed (data not shown). (**B**) Sn is present in preparations of huCR and CR ligands. HuCR and CR ligands were enriched in the presence (+) or absence (–) of SO_4-4-GalNAc using huCR-muFc or CR-Fc conjugated to protein A-sepharose. Selected proteins were analysed by Western blot using anti-Sn mAb. Two bands immunoreactive with this mAb (marked with *arrow* and *arrowhead*) were detected in the absence of inhibitor. Additional bands present in the preparation of huCR ligands in the presence and absence of inhibitor (first two lanes) may correspond to huCR-muFc eluted from the sepharose as they were recognised by the anti-mouse IgG reagent used for detection (data not shown). The control sample was included to detect proteins that bound non-specifically to protein A-sepharose alone.

3.2.6. Assessment of Binding to Candidate Molecule Immunoprecipitated from a Protein Lysate Using a Monoclonal Ab

This procedure can be used if prior knowledge is available regarding the nature of the ligand; for instance, if the labelling pattern obtained with the Fc chimaeric protein in situ is similar to the distribution of a particular molecule or if the rMW of a ligand detected using ligand blot is characteristic of a putative candidate.

1. Prior to immunoprecipitation, lysates are pre-cleared using protein A-Sepharose for 2 h at 4°C as before.
2. After pre-clearance, lysates are incubated with mAb coupled to sepharose (*see* **Note 40**) overnight at 4°C in a rotating wheel.
3. Beads are collected on the following day and are washed in lysis buffer or in immunoprecipitation washing buffers A, B, and C (3× in A, 2× in B and 1× in C).
4. Proteins are eluted by boiling in 1× SDS-loading buffer and subjected to electrophoresis and transfer as before.
5. Probe membrane with Fc chimaeric protein as described previously (*see* **Note 41**).

3.3. Assessment of Binding to Candidate Ligands in Solid Phase Assays

3.3.1. For the Detection of Binding to Potential Carbohydrate Containing Ligands

1. Coat MaxiSort plates with 50 μl of candidate ligands diluted at 5 μg/ml as follows:
   (a) In the case of purified sugars make dilutions in 0.154 mM NaCl or PBS and incubate at 37°C.
   (b) In the case of PBS-soluble glycoproteins, make dilutions in PBS and incubate at 4°C.
2. Seal plates in parafilm and incubate overnight in a sealed damp box.
3. [illegible] (*see* **Note 42**).
4. Add Fc constructs (2 μg/ml) diluted in lectin buffer (*see* **Note 43**).
5. Incubate for 60–90 min at room temperature.
6. After washes detect binding with alkaline phosphatase-conjugated anti-human IgG Fc-specific (typically diluted 1:1,000 in lectin buffer) (*see* **Note 44**).
7. Wash plates with lectin buffer and then twice with alkaline phosphatase substrate buffer and develop with freshly prepared *p*-nitrophenyl phosphate substrate dissolved in alkaline phosphatase substrate buffer (100 μl/well).
8. Measure absorbance at 405 nm (*see* **Note 45**).

3.3.2. For the Detection of Binding to Ligands in a Carbohydrate-Independent Fashion

1. E.I.A./R.I.A high-binding plates are coated with appropriate candidate proteins diluted at 10 μg/ml (50 μl/well) in PBS (*see* **Note 46**).
2. Incubated overnight at 37°C.

3. Plates are washed three times with PBS–0.3% BSA and blocked with 0.3% BSA in PBS for 60 min at room temperature.
4. Fc chimeric proteins (diluted at 2–10 μg/ml in PBS–0.3% BSA) (*see* **Note 47**) are then added and incubated for 1 h at RT.
5. After three washes in PBS–0.3% BSA, plates are incubated with alkaline phosphatase-conjugated anti-human Fc for 1 h at RT in PBS–0.3% BSA.
6. After washing three times with PBS–0.3% BSA, wells are washed twice with alkaline phosphatase substrate buffer and 100 μl of substrate solution are added to each well.
7. Measure absorbance at 405 nm (*see* **Note 45**).

4. Notes

1. When working with mouse or rat tissues we routinely place several lymphoid organs per block. This does not affect cutting if organs with similar consistency are grouped together.
2. If detecting ligands for proteins able to recognise collagen, such as CR-FNII-CTLD1-Fc and CR-FNII-CTLD1-3-Fc 3 *(12)*, use of charged slides is recommended to avoid binding of the FNII-containing proteins to the gelatine used for coating (*see* **Figs. 1** and **2**).
3. Detection of ligands in specific organs may be fixation sensitive. We have found that fixation with paraformaldehyde is suitable for most of our studies. Alternatives include fixation of fresh frozen tissues with acetone or methanol or the use of perfused tissues *(9)*.
4. The Shandon Sequenza® system enables the labelling of up to 50 slides simultaneously. Assembly needs to be performed with slide and coverplate immersed in buffer and avoiding formation of bubbles. The shape of the coverplate (similar to a funnel) allows the easy application of all the following solutions. For washes, permeabilisation and quenching, the upper reservoir should be filled. In the case of washes, the slide is considered washed once the reservoir has drained. For permeabilisation, quenching and DAPI staining, slides are maintained in the appropriate buffers for specific incubation times.
5. Permeabilisation for 10 min is optimal for most applications. If there is concern about accessibility of the ligands, longer permeabilisation times (30 min) are recommended *(3)*.

6. The buffer to use for washes will depend on the properties of the protein of interest. If binding is expected to take place in the absence of calcium (such as in the case of CR-Fc, huCR-muFc, CR-FNII-CTLD1-Fc and CR-FNII-CTLD1-3-Fc) PBS would be appropriate, but if binding is expected to require calcium (such as in the case of CTLD4-7-Fc), use of the Lectin-binding buffer (10 mM Tris–HCl, pH 7.4, 154 mM NaCl, 10 mM $CaCl_2$) is recommended.
7. The species of origin of the normal serum used for blocking should correspond to that used to raise the secondary Ab used for detection of binding. Absence of ligands in serum should be ensured before using this procedure.
8. New streptavidin-derived proteins with reduced unspecific binding are also available (e.g. NeutrAvidin). The use of these reagents will help to reduce background labelling.
9. We have been successful in detecting ligands for the CR, FNII, and CTLD4-7 regions of the mannose receptor using human IgG1 Fc and mouse IgG2b Fc chimaeric proteins *(3, 8, 9, 13)*. Other examples of the successful use of Fc-derived proteins for detection of ligands in situ are: the lectin macrophage galactose-type C-type lectin 1 and Endo 180 *(12, 14)*.
10. In some instances where recognition of ligands is highly dependent upon protein multimerisation, it is desirable to pre-incubate the chimaeric Fc fusion protein with the anti-Fc reagent use for detection to promote cross-linking of individual molecules. This approach made it possible to observe binding by CR-FNII-CTLD1-Fc and CR-FNII-CTLD1-3-Fc and improve recognition by CR-Fc *(3)* (**Fig. 2**). If using chimaeric proteins with a mutated Fc portion, it is likely that cross-linking would be essential to detect binding *(15)*. The presence of suitable competitors during this incubation will determine the specificity of the interaction. For instance, for CR-Fc we and others have used 10 mM SO_4-4-GalNAc *(2, 13)* and for CTLD4-7-Fc we have used 100 mM mannose *(9)*.
11. In the case of CR-FNII-CTLD1-Fc and CR-FNII-CTLD1-3-Fc in mouse tissues and of huCR-muFc in human spleen we observed binding by incubating overnight incubation at 4°C (*(3, 13)*, and **Fig. 2**).
12. Peroxidase-based detection systems are suitable for strong signals and facilitate location of signal by the use of counter-staining. The use of the ABC kit enhances detection, though it is difficult to quantify. The development step has to be performed using a traditional staining tray.

13. Alkaline phosphatase-based detection systems are suitable for weak signals as the reaction can be developed for longer periods. It provides a less-defined signal and is incompatible with multiple counterstains and DPX. The use of the ABC kit enhances detection. It is difficult to quantify but is very robust. The development step has to be performed using a traditional staining tray.
14. Fluorescence labelling is highly versatile and quantitative. The fluorochrome of choice will depend on the strength of the interaction between the protein and its ligand(s), abundance of the ligand, and the microscope available. For weak signals and fluorescence microscopy, Alexa-488 or FITC and the use of three steps labelling procedures is recommended. The use of Texas red or Cy3 is not suitable for tissues with high levels of autofluorescence if only a fluorescence microscope is available.
15. Combining detection of ligands with Fc chimaeric proteins and labelling with cell type-specific markers will provide information regarding the nature of the cells bearing the ligands and their anatomical location *(15)*.
16. To avoid protein degradation it is recommended that tissues are snap frozen in liquid nitrogen or collected in pre-cooled microfuge tubes maintained on dry ice.
17. Homogenisers have to be washed and rinsed thoroughly and then soaked in lysis buffer with protease inhibitors prior use. Samples must be maintained on ice during the lysis and formation of foam must be avoided. Cutting tissue into smaller fragments with a sterile scalpel in a sterile petri dish and in the presence of lysis buffer with protease inhibitors will facilitate the preparation of lysates using a dounce homogeniser.
18. Centrifugation at 100,000 × *g* will provide a lysate suitable for affinity chromatography, immunoprecipitation, and enrichment of ligand in solution using affinity beads. If lysate is going to be used for ligand blot or Western blot, centrifugation in a refrigerated microfuge at 12,000 *g* for 15 min is also suitable.
19. Avoid repeated freezing and thawing.
20. In some instances, several rounds of centrifugation are required to eliminate all the nuclei.
21. This would depend on the scale of the preparation; for the preparation of small samples (1–5 ml) use a TC100 centrifuge.
22. It is recommended to use non-reducing conditions initially so as not to disturb di-sulphide bonds. The use of 4× concentrated loading buffer will facilitate loading of larger amounts

of protein lysates. Samples should be boiled immediately after preparation. In some instances, boiling could induce aggregation of some proteins; in this case keeping the samples at 65°C for 10–30 min may solve the problem but the risk of protein degradation might increase.

23. The percentage of acrylamide in the gel will depend on the size range that needs to be tested. For initial studies running of gradient gels or a low and a high percentage gel would increase the range of proteins tested.

24. The choice of filter might have major implications for the final results. Hybond C is suitable for most of our studies, but PVDF membranes can also be used as an alternative. These membranes need to be activated prior use.

25. We routinely perform protein transfers overnight at 200 mA using the transfer buffer described in **Subheading 2.2.2**.

26. The blocking buffer to use for incubations and washes will depend on the properties of the protein of interest. If binding is expected to take place in the absence of calcium (such as in the case of CR-Fc and huCR-muFc, *see* **Fig. 1**) 5% (w/v) non-fat dry milk, 0.1% (v/v) Tween 20 in PBS would be appropriate, but if binding is expected to require calcium (such as in the case of CTLD4-7-Fc, *see* **Fig. 1**) use 5% (w/v) non-fat dry milk, 0.1% (v/v) Tween 20 in 10 mM Tris–HCl, pH 7.4, 154 mM NaCl, 10 mM $CaCl_2$. We have never encountered problems using non-fat dry milk as blocking reagent, but if there are concerns, 2–3% bovine serum albumin or casein can be used instead.

27. Washes consist in one rinse in buffer and two 10-min incubations.

28. We have obtained good results using our secondary reagents diluted 1:1,000. A control testing of the binding of the secondary Ab to the lysate should be included, in particular when immunoglobulins might be present in the lysate.

29. The washing buffer to use for the last washes will depend on the properties of the protein of interest. If binding is expected to take place in the absence of calcium (such as in the case of CR-Fc and huCR-muFc) 0.1% (v/v), Tween 20 in PBS would be appropriate, but if binding is expected to require calcium (such as in the case of CTLD4-7-Fc) use 0.1% (v/v) Tween 20 in 10 mM Tris–HCl, pH 7.4, 154 mM NaCl, 10 mM $CaCl_2$.

30. If more sensitivity is required, ECLplus offers a suitable alternative.

31. Avoid direct contact between the film and the filter using cling foil or an acetate sheet.

32. The differences in specificity between protein A and protein G should be taken into consideration when designing the experimental approach.
33. During the preparation of the lysate it should be taken into consideration that the incubation of the protein–bead complex with the lysate has to be done under conditions optimal for binding. For instance, presence of Ca^{2+} is essential for CRD4-7-Fc recognition; therefore, use of EDTA in the lysis buffer would not be recommended unless it is removed at a later stage.
34. To ensure accurate distribution of the sepharose between samples use cut tips for pipetting and vortex between pipettings to maintain the sepharose in suspension.
35. Elution with SDS–PAGE sample buffer will also release the Fc chimaeric protein bound to the protein A/G-sepharose, which will then be loaded into the gel. The use of a digoxigenin-based detection method will ensure that when performing the ligand blot, the Fc protein present in the gel will not be recognised by the reagent used to detect binding of the Fc protein used to probe the filter. This problem can also be avoided by using Fc proteins directly conjugated to protein A/G-sepharose (*see* **Subheading 3.2.5**).
36. Washing the beads with glycine pH 2.9 will remove proteins not covalently bound to the protein A-sepharose.
37. Control Fc protein or purified immunoglobulin coupled to protein A/G-sepharose, prepared as described earlier, can be used as pre-clearing columns.
38. This step can be repeated twice. Pre-cleared lysate can be passed through the column twice to increase recovery of ligands.
39. Choice of elution buffer will depend on the characteristics of the interaction. They can be determined by enriching ligands using Fc protein–protein A/G beads and performing ligand blot analysis on samples eluted using low or high pH, chelating Ca^{2+} or by incubation in 1× SDS-loading buffer. If using high or low pH elution buffers avoid damage of the sample by collecting fractions (500–1,000 μl) in tubes containing 50–100 ml of 1 M Tris–HCl, pH 7.
40. mAb can be coupled to CNBr-activated sepharose (5 mg Ab/ml sepharose) or to protein A/G-sepharose (*see* **Subheading 3.2.5** for suitable protocol).
41. Part of the sample should be probed with the mAb used for the immunoprecipitation using standard western blot procedures to ensure that the procedure worked and as size control.
42. All washes involve three rinses with 250 μl of lectin buffer.
43. To test for specificity, proteins can be pre-incubated with D-mannose, D-galactose, D-fucose at 100 mM for 30 min on

ice with prior to plate application. These steps should be performed in lectin buffer containing 1 M NaCl *(16)*.

44. Soluble MR *(17)* can be used for these assays. Bound soluble MR can be detected by incubation with the anti-MR mAb MR5D3 *(18)* (2 µg/ml) for 120 min at room temperature followed by alkaline phosphatase-conjugated anti-rat IgG (Chemicon).
45. Keep plates in the dark. It is useful to take several readings during the development reaction. The reaction can be stopped with EDTA.
46. Collagen and gelatin (denatured collagen) are diluted at 10 µg/ml in 10 mM acetic acid.
47. Proteins bearing a human Fc region can be pre-incubated or not with alkaline-phosphatase-conjugated anti-human Fc, 1:100–1:200, for 60 min at room temperature in PBS–0.3% BSA. This step is essential to detect binding of CR-FNII-CTLD1-Fc and CR-FNII-CTLD1-3-Fc to collagens *(3)*.

References

1. Liu Y, Chirino AJ, Misulovin Z, et al. (2000). Crystal structure of the cysteine-rich domain of mannose receptor complexed with a sulfated carbohydrate ligand. *The Journal of Experimental Medicine*, 191(7):1105–16.
2. Leteux C, Chai W, Loveless RW, et al. (2000). The cysteine-rich domain of the macrophage mannose receptor is a multispecific lectin that recognizes chondroitin sulfates A and B and sulfated oligosaccharides of blood group Lewis(a) and Lewis(x) types in addition to the sulfated N-glycans of lutropin. *The Journal of Experimental Medicine*, 191(7):1117–26.
3. Martinez-Pomares L, Wienke D, Stillion R, et al. (2006). Carbohydrate-independent recognition of collagens by the macrophage mannose receptor. *European Journal of Immunology*, 36(5):1074–82.
4. Taylor ME, Drickamer K (1993). Structural requirements for high affinity binding of complex ligands by the macrophage mannose receptor. *The Journal of Biological Chemistry*, 268(1):399–404.
5. Taylor ME, Bezouska K, Drickamer K (1992). Contribution to ligand binding by multiple carbohydrate-recognition domains in the macrophage mannose receptor. *The Journal of Biological Chemistry*, 267(3):1719–26.
6. Taylor PR, Gordon S, Martinez-Pomares L (2005). The mannose receptor: linking homeostasis and immunity through sugar recognition. *Trends in Immunology*, 26(2):104–10.
7. Martinez-Pomares L, Crocker PR, Da Silva R, et al. (1999). Cell-specific glycoforms of sialoadhesin and CD45 are counter-receptors for the cysteine-rich domain of the mannose receptor. *The Journal of Biological Chemistry*, 274(49):35211–35218
8. Martinez-Pomares L, Kosco-Vilbois M, Darley E, et al. (1996). Fc chimeric protein containing the cysteine-rich domain of the murine mannose receptor binds to macrophages from splenic marginal zone and lymph node subcapsular sinus and to germinal centers. *The Journal of Experimental Medicine*;184(5):1927–37.
9. Linehan SA, Martinez-Pomares L, da Silva RP, Gordon S (2001). Endogenous ligands of carbohydrate recognition domains of the mannose receptor in murine macrophages, endothelial cells and secretory cells, potential relevance to inflammation and immunity. *European Journal of Immunology*, 31(6):1857–66.
10. Williams AF, Barclay AN. In: Weir DM, ed. Handbook of Experimental Immunology, Oxford: Blackwell; 1986.
11. Simmons DL. In: Hartley DA, ed. Cellular Interactions in Development, Oxford: IRL Press at Oxford University Press; 1993: 93–127.
12. Wienke D, MacFadyen JR, Isacke CM. (2003). Identification and characterization of the endocytic transmembrane glycoprotein Endo180 as a novel collagen receptor. *Molecular Biology of the Cell*, 14(9):3592–604.

13. Martinez-Pomares L, Hanitsch LG, Stillion R, Keshav S, Gordon S. (2005). Expression of mannose receptor and ligands for its cysteine-rich domain in venous sinuses of human spleen. *Laboratory investigation; A Journal of Technical Methods and Pathology*, 85(10):1238–49.

14. Kumamoto Y, Higashi N, Denda-Nagai K, et al. (2004). Identification of sialoadhesin as a dominant lymph node counter-receptor for mouse macrophage galactose-type C-type lectin 1. *The Journal of Biological Chemistry*, 279(47):49274–80.

15. Taylor PR, Zamze S, Stillion RJ, Wong SY, Gordon S, Martinez-Pomares L. (2004). Development of a specific system for targeting protein to metallophilic macrophages. *Proceedings of the National Academy of Sciences of the United States of America*, 101(7):1963–8.

16. Zamze S, Martinez-Pomares L, Jones H, et al. (2002). Recognition of bacterial capsular polysaccharides and lipopolysaccharides by the macrophage mannose receptor. *The Journal of Biological Chemistry*, 277(44):41613–23.

17. Boskovic J, Arnold JN, Stilion R, et al. (2006). Structural model for the mannose receptor family uncovered by electron microscopy of Endo180 and the mannose receptor. *The Journal of Biological Chemistry*, 281(13):8780–7.

18. Martinez-Pomares L, Reid DM, Brown GD, et al. (2003). Analysis of mannose receptor regulation by IL-4, IL-10, and proteolytic processing using novel monoclonal antibodies. *Journal of Leukocyte Biology*, 73(5):604–13.

Chapter 9

The Expression of Exogenous Genes in Macrophages: Obstacles and Opportunities

Xia Zhang, Justin P. Edwards, and David M. Mosser

Summary

Over the past three decades many techniques for expressing exogenous genes in a variety of cells and cell lines have been developed. Exogenous gene expression in macrophages has lagged behind that of other nonhematopioetic cells. There are many reasons for this, but most are due to technical difficulties associated with transfecting macrophages. As professional phagocytes, macrophages are endowed with many potent degradative enzymes that can disrupt nucleic acid integrity and make gene transfer into these cells an inefficient process. This is especially true of activated macrophages which undergo a dramatic change in their physiology following exposure to immune or inflammatory stimuli. Viral transduction of these cells has been hampered because macrophages are end-stage cells that generally do not divide; therefore, some of the vectors that depend on integration into a replicative genome have met with limited success. Furthermore, macrophages are quite responsive to "danger signals," and therefore several of the original viral vectors that were used for gene transfer induced potent anti-viral responses in these cells making these vectors inappropriate for gene delivery. Many of these difficulties have been largely overcome, and relatively high efficiency gene expression in primary human or murine macrophages is becoming more routine. In the present chapter we discuss some of the gene expression techniques that have met with success and review the advantages and disadvantages of each.

Key words: Adenovirus, DEAE-dextran, Electroporation, Lentivirus, Nucleoporation, Transduction, Transfection, Retrovirus, Vector.

1. Introduction

Macrophages are cells that participate in a number of important immunological processes, including phagocytosis, antigen processing and presentation, and the secretion of a wide variety of mediators that can influence host defense. A fundamental property of macrophages is their ability to accumulate in affected tissue

Neil E. Reiner (ed.), *Macrophages and Dendritic Cells,* Methods in Molecular Biology, vol. 531

DOI: 10.1007/978-1-59745-396-7_9

and form an inflammatory focus there. The accumulation of macrophages at inflammatory sites has been associated with many pathogenetic settings, including infectious granulomas, atherosclerosis, rheumatoid arthritis, tumors, etc. Macrophages have great potential as drug delivery vehicles because of their ability to home to inflamed tissue. This potential has led to attempts to design macrophage-specific gene delivery systems that allow the efficient expression of therapeutic genes in macrophages. Thus, the delivery of exogenous gene products using genetically modified macrophages is an area with great therapeutic and/or immunomodulatory potential.

The process of introducing nucleic acid across the host cell membrane by mechanical or physical disruption is termed "transfection." This is distinct from "transduction," a process for delivery of nucleic acid into cells by viral vectors, which we will discuss subsequently. Most of the original transfection techniques enjoyed only limited success with macrophages. This is due to the requirement of fairly high gene copy numbers required to efficiently transfect cells and the relatively high degree of toxicity associated with the process whereby the host cell membrane is made permeable to DNA. However, because nonviral-based gene transfer methods continue to have some conspicuous advantages over viral-based transduction, efforts continue to be devoted to improving these methods. The various transfection methods used to introduce foreign DNA into mammalian cells include: DEAE-dextran, calcium phosphate coprecipitation, cationic lipid vehicles, and physical disruption of the host cell membranes by electroporation or nucleofection. All these approaches have been used with varying degrees of success on macrophages.

In the 1960s, Pagano and his colleagues used DEAE-dextran for nucleic acid transfer into mammalian cells *(1, 2)*. DEAE-dextran is a cationic polymer that can interact with negatively charged nucleic acids. The overall positive charge of the polymer in the nucleic acid/DEAE-dextran complex promotes its interaction with the negatively charged cell membrane, facilitating endocytosis. The calcium phosphate coprecipitation-mediated transfection method was introduced by Graham and van der Eb *(3)*. This method involves mixing the nucleic acid with calcium chloride, dropping this mixture in a controlled fashion into a buffered saline/phosphate solution, and then incubating the final mixture to generate a precipitate. The precipitate is then dispersed onto cells and taken up via endocytosis. This transfection technique gained popularity due to its simplicity and low cost. Another advantage of this technique was the discovery that the concentrations of calcium phosphate used for this technique could inhibit host cell nucleases, protecting exogenous DNA from extensive degradation *(4)*. Although these two methods have been fairly widely used for the transfection of various cultured cell lines, their utility for monocytes and macrophages is limited *(5)*.

Using the macrophage-like cell line RAW264.7, Thompson and colleagues *(6)* made a systematic comparison of different transfection methods and concluded that DEAE-dextran and calcium phosphate coprecipitation had the lowest efficiency and the highest rate of interassay variability.

In 1980, a group led by Papahadjopoulos first reported the successful delivery of DNA into a monkey cell line by using unilamellar phospholipid vesicles *(7)*. Later this technique was refined due to the application of a novel synthetic cationic lipid: *N*-[1-(2,3-dioleyloxy) propyl]-*N*,*N*,*N*-trimethylammonium chloride (DOTMA). In comparison with DEAE-dextran and calcium phosphate coprecipitation, liposome-mediated transfection or "lipofection" had 5-fold to as much as 100-fold greater efficiency of delivery, depending on the cell tested *(8)*. The advantages of lipofection included the simplicity of the methodology and the fact that both transient and stable transfections could be similarly accomplished using this technique. Another conspicuous advantage was that liposome/nucleic acid complexes could be administered in vivo to animals and humans for therapeutic purposes *(9)*.

Liposomes are typically formed by mixing a cationic lipid with a neutral lipid. The positively charged cationic lipid interacts with the negatively charged nucleic acid to form a liposome/nucleic acid complex, which can be taken up by cells via endocytosis. After entering the cells, liposome/nucleic acid complexes appear within endosomes. The endosomes release their contents into cytoplasmic compartments and the nucleus *(10)*. The release of nucleic acids from the endosome is believed to be facilitated by the neutral lipid in the liposome/nucleic acid complex. Some neutral lipids may also assist fusion of the complex with the outer cell membrane to enhance the lipofection efficiency *(11)*. Recent refinements of the liposome technology have led to the development of uniform-sized micelles to deliver DNA with greater efficiency and reproducibility. Many lipid-based reagents are commercially available, including LIPOFECTAMINE2000® from Invitrogen Corporation and the FUGENE® Transfection Reagents from Roche Applied Sciences. Additional components can be added to these basic formulas to more efficiently condense the nucleic acid, or to facilitate their release from endosomes (ExGen® 500 reagent from Fermanta). The FUGENE® reagents have been used to successfully transfect the mouse macrophage-like cell line, RAW264.7 (http://www.roche-applied-science.com), and the human macrophage-line cell line, U937 *(12)*. These methods are quite straightforward and commercially available. Detailed instructions are provided by the manufacturer.

The use of recombinant viruses to infect mammalian cells has emerged as one of the preferred means to deliver exogenous genes to mammalian cells. Adenoviruses, adeno-associated viruses, and retroviruses/lentiviruses have all proven to have utility for gene transfer. All these methods carry the conspicuous advantages of high efficiency gene transfer into mammalian cells, which can result in high expression of the gene product. However, all these systems have some potential disadvantages that must be addressed before they enjoy routine use. The immunogenicity of adenoviruses is a limitation that is being overcome in many of the newer generation viruses. The genotoxicity associated with retroviral integration continues to be an area of concern *(13–15)*. Clinical gene therapy trials with retroviral vectors were dealt a serious blow in 2003 when serious side effects in gene therapy for X-SCID patients were revealed *(14, 16)*. Thus, significant hurdles in vector selection have been cleared but several still remain before large clinical trials can be initiated. Optimization of these viral infection methods to deliver and express genes in hard-to-transfect cells is still in progress, and this is particularly exciting for gene delivery into macrophages.

2. Materials

2.1. Cell Culture

1. RPMI-1640-10: Roswell Park Memorial Institute-1640 (RPMI-1640) (Mediatech, Inc., cellgro.bizatomic.net) supplemented with 10% fetal bovine serum (FBS, HyClone, http://www.HyClone.com), 10 mmol/L glutamine, 100 IU/mL penicillin, and 100 μg/mL streptomycin (penicillin and streptomycin can be replaced by 50 μg/mL gentamicin sulfate). Storage at 4°C.
2. DMEM/F12-10: Dulbecco's Modified Eagle's Medium Nutrient Mixture F-12 (Ham) (1:1) (DMEM/F12) (GIBCO 10565, Invitrogen, Carlsbad, California 92008, http://www.invitrogen.com) supplemented with 10% fetal bovine serum (FBS, HyClone, http://www.HyClone.com), 10 mmol/L glutamine, 100 IU/mL penicillin, and 100 μg/mL streptomycin (penicillin and streptomycin can be replaced by 50 μg/mL gentamicin sulfate). Storage at 4°C.
3. L-929-conditioned medium: L-929 is a murine fibroblast cell line used as a source of M-CSF for culture of bone marrow derived macrophages. L-929 cells (L-929 cells, CCL-1™, ATCC, http://www.atcc.org) are cultured in DMEM/F12-10 until confluent. L-929-conditioned medium is then harvested at confluence. Cells are removed by centrifugation and supernatants are stored at –80°C until use.
4. Cellstripper™ Nonenzymatic cell dissociation solution (Mediatech, Inc., cellgro.bizatomic.net). Storage at room temperature.
5. Falcon® Petri dishes (100 × 15 mm Style) (Becton Dickenson Labware).

6. All mammalian cell lines and primary cells are cultured in their corresponding media in an atmosphere of 5% CO_2 at 37°C.

2.2. Macrophage Cell Lines and Bone Marrow-Derived Macrophages

1. THP-1 (TIB-202™, ATCC, http://www.atcc.org) and U937 (CRL-1593.2™, ATCC, http://www.atcc.org) are cultured in RPMI-1640-10.
2. RAW 264.7 (TIB-71™, ATCC, http://www.atcc.org) and J774A.1 (TIB-67™, ATCC, http://www.atcc.org) are cultured in DMEM/F12-10.
3. Bone marrow-derived macrophages: mouse bone marrow is flushed from the femurs and tibias of mice at 6–10 weeks of age. The cells are plated in petri dishes in DMEM/F12-10 supplemented 20% L-929-conditioned medium. Cells are fed on days 2 and 5. On day 7, cells are removed from petri dishes and cultured on tissue culture dishes in DMEM/F12-10. On the next day, cells are subjected to experiments.

2.3. Electroporation Apparatus

1. BioRad Gene Pulser® II apparatus are obtained from BioRad Laboratory (http://www.biorad.com).
2. Electroporation cuvettes (gap width of 4 mm) can be obtained from numerous vendors including BioRad Laboratory.

2.4. Nucleofection

1. A Nucleofector device is purchased from Amaxa Biosystem (Amaxa GmbH, Cologne, Germany. http://www.amaxa.com).
2. Cell Line Nucleofector™ Kit T (VCA-1002, Amaxa GmbH, Cologne, Germany. http://www.amaxa.com) is used for the transfection of bone marrow-derived murine macrophages as described in **Subheading 3**. Storage conditions are listed in the accompanying manual.

2.5. Adenoviral Transduction

1. A method described by He et al. *(17)* has been widely accepted as a fast and easy alternative to the traditional methods of generating recombinant adenovirus. This system has been improved and commercialized as the AdEasy™ System by many companies including Stratagene® (http://www.stratagene.com), QBiogene® (http://www.qbiogene.com), and the ATCC® (http://www.atcc.org). Storage conditions are listed in the accompanied manual.
2. AdEasy™ vectors are pShuttle, pShuttle-CMV, and pAdEasy-1. The pAdEasy-1 vector is devoid of E1 and E3 regions so that the recombinant virus will not replicate in cells other than complementing cells, such as human embryonic kidney 293 (HEK293).
3. BJ5183 (*rec*A+) (BJ5183-AD1 Electrocompetent Cells, http://www.stratagene.com) is used for in vivo homologous recombination, and DH5a (MAX Efficiency® DH5a™ Chemically Competent Cells, Invitrogen, http://www.invitrogen.com) is used for scale-up production of viral vectors. Storage at –80°C.

4. EndoFree® Plasmid Maxi kit is obtained from QIAGEN (Cat. No.: 12362, QIANGEN, http://www1.qiangen.com). Storage conditions are listed in the accompanied manual.
5. HEK293 cells (CRL-1573™, ATCC, http://www.atcc.org) are used as a host cell to generate recombinant adenovirus and are cultured DMEM/F12-10.
6. Adeno-X™ Rapid Titer Kit is supplied from Takara Bio Company (Cat. No.: 631028, Clontech, http://www.clontech.com). Storage conditions are listed in the accompanied manual.

2.6. Viral Transduction by Retroviruses and Lentiviruses

1. The ViraPower™ Lentiviral Expression System (Invitrogen, Carlsbad, California 92008, http://www.invitrogen.com) is loosely based on the HIV-1 strain NL4-3. This system contains Invitrogen's Directional TOPO and Gateway Lentiviral vectors that can accommodate up to 6 kb of inserted exogenous gene. The packaging mix contains three supercoiled packaging plasmids (gag/pol, rev, and VSV-G envelop) that are needed for helper functions and supplying viral proteins in trans. Also contained in this system are Stbl3 *E. coli* cells for transformation and the 293FT packaging cell line that can facilitate production of high-titer virus. The system also contains EmGFP lentiviral expression vectors for assessment of transfection and transduction efficiency and HT1080 cells for titering viral stock.
2. HT1080 is a human fibrosarcoma cell line (CCL-121™, ATCC, http://www.atcc.org) and culture in DMEM/F12-10.
3. Polybrene® can be obtained from Sigma-Aldrich (Catalog No. H9268, http://www.sigma-aldrich.com).
4. G418 is used to maintain regular culture of 293FT cells and can be obtained from Invitrogen (Geneticin™, Invitrogen, http://www.invitrogen.com).
5. Blasticidin and Zeocin™ can be obtained from InvivoGen (http://www.invivogen.com).
6. Lipofectamine™ 2000 is the product from Invitrogen (http://www.invitrogen.com). Fugene™ 6 transfection reagent is supplied from Roche Applied Science (http://www.roche.com).

3. Methods

3.1. Electroporation

Electroporation is an established technique that has been used in a variety of applications, including but certainly not limited to introducing exogenous nucleic acids into cells. In 1982,

Neumann et al. applied the electroporation technique to introduce DNA into mouse fibroblasts *(18, 19)*. Potter and his colleagues later improved the technique to introduce DNA into a broad range of established cell lines *(20, 21)*. Electroporation has the unique advantage over methods that involve endocytosis and/or phagocytosis since direct uptake of DNA bypasses the lysosomal compartment, limiting the possibility of enzymatic degradation. During the electroporation process, cells are exposed to several electric pulses of varying intensity and duration, creating a trans-membrane potential across the poorly conducting cell membrane. Once this trans-membrane potential reaches a certain threshold, which is proportional to the cell radius and the applied electric field strength, the molecular structure of the membrane will be rearranged to create hydrophilic pores that are permeable to DNA. These pores can be transient in nature and resealed to preserve the integrity of the cell. This process is known as reversible electroporation. An excessive electric field can cause a trans-membrane potential exceeding a tolerable threshold, resulting in pores that cannot be resealed, leading to the destruction of the cell.

Electroporation-based gene transfection into macrophages has received mixed reviews. Since electroporation bypasses lysosomes and causes cell membrane permeabilization that can inhibit phagosomal acidification *(22)*, the potential problems associated with the degradation of DNA by macrophage lysosomal nucleases are minimized. Several groups have successfully used electroporation to introduce exogenous DNA into macrophage-like cell lines. However, the use of electroporation on primary macrophages appears to have been met with more limited success. For example, Stacey et al. found that despite the successful transfection of the macrophage-like RAW264.7 cell line via electroporation, a similar application to primary bone marrow-derived macrophages was much less efficient *(23)*. In many instances, electroporation of primary macrophages results in excessive cell death, regardless of source (synthetic, genomic, or plasmid) or sequence of the DNA.

The following procedures are successfully applied for transfection of macrophage cell lines such as RAW 264.7 cells.

1. Log-phased cells are split 24 h before electroporation to ensure that cells are growing and healthy. Before electroporation, the cells are centrifuged and then resuspended in fresh medium (RPMI-1640) without fetal calf serum or other additives, such as penicillin and streptomycin.
2. Approximately 4×10^6 cells in a 0.25-mL volume are added to the cuvette (4 mm) and then mixed with DNA. The mixture is allowed to stand at room temperature for 10 min (*see* **Note 1**).
3. Gene Pulser® II apparatus is set for 950 μF and the Pulse Controller for 200 Ω. Efficient transfection can be achieved at a voltage of 250 V. Normally by these parameters, a clump of dead cells will be noticeable (*see* **Note 2**).

4. The electroporated cells are removed from the dead cells and transferred into prewarmed complete medium (*see* **Note 3**). The cells are plated in 24 wells of a 48-well plate and allowed to recover overnight.
5. After overnight recovery, the media is removed and replenished with a fresh media, at which time the cells are ready for experimental studies.

3.2. Nucleofection

Nucleofection is a technology developed by Amaxa GmbH (Cologne, Germany). This proprietary technology includes two components: (1) a Nucleofector device that can deliver unique preprogrammed electrical parameters for electroporation, and (2) solutions that are specific for the individual cell types that are targeted for transfection. By varying these combinations, this technology can efficiently deliver DNA into a variety of cell types. The DNA rapidly travels to the nucleus, after which expression of transfected genes can be detected within a short period of time. In 2003, Martinet et al. reported that transfection efficiencies up to 80% without significant cell toxicity could be achieved on human U937 and THP-1 cells *(24)*. Lenz et al. reported similar transfection efficiencies of human monocyte-derived dendritic cells *(25)*. Others have not experienced a similar level of success with nucleofection. For example, nucleofection of DNA into the murine macrophage-like J774A.1 cells resulted in a substantial amount of apoptosis with little exogenous gene expression *(26)*. This group did, however, see up to 75% transfection efficiency when using mRNA rather than DNA.

We have used the following nucleofection procedures to efficiently transfer DNA into primary mouse bone marrow-derived macrophages and RAW264.7 cells *(27, 28)*. Using GFP expression as a readout, we obtained transfection efficiencies of approximately 90% in primary murine macrophages (**Fig. 1**) *(27)*. We have also found this technique to be particularly effective for the delivery of siRNA into primary macrophages. Using siRNA to the MAPKs we were able to achieve a near complete knockdown of ERK mRNA levels (**Fig. 2**) and ERK kinase activity in primary murine macrophages *(28)*.

1. All growth media is warmed to 37°C. Prepare cell culture plates containing growth media and preincubate in a 37°C/5% CO_2 incubator. Bone marrow-derived macrophages are removed from the femurs of mice and grown for 6–7 days in CSF until ready for use. A total of approximately 5×10^6 cells are used per Nucleofection. Cells are centrifuged at $300 \times g$ for 10 min at room temperature and resuspended at a concentration of 5×10^6 cells/mL in PBS. One milliliter of cells is added to 1.5-mL Eppendorf® tubes and centrifuged for 10s at $7{,}000 \times g$ by Eppendorf microcentrifuge.

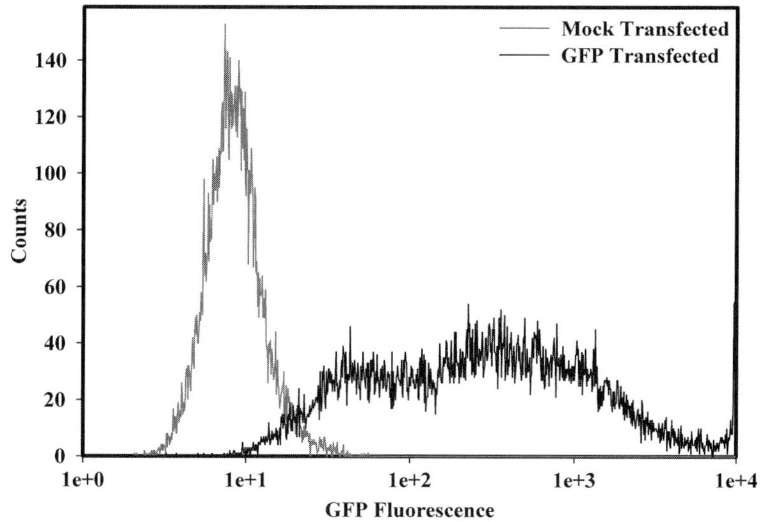

Fig. 1. GFP transfection of bone marrow-derived macrophages (BMMΦ). 5 × 10^6 cells at day 6 (BMMΦ) were subject to nucleofection using program T-20, cell line kit-T, and 3.5 μg of pmaxGFP plasmid (GFP) or no DNA (Mock). GFP expression was assessed by flow cytometry.

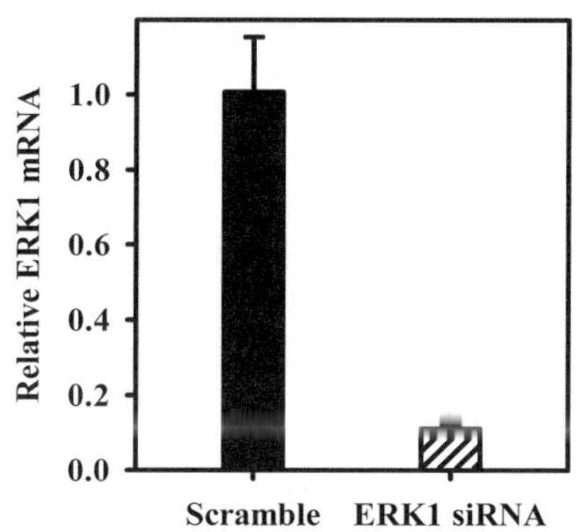

Fig. 2. ERK1 mRNA after nucleofection with ERK1-specfic siRNA. 5 × 10^6 cells at day 6 (BMMΦ) were subject to nucleofection using an ERK1-specific siRNA (*black bar*) or nonspecific scramble dsRNA (*hatched bar*) at a final concentration of 100 nM. ERK1 mRNA levels were assessed 48 h after nucleofection by real-time PCR.

2. PBS is gently aspirated from each tube, and the pellets are resuspended in 100 μL of room temperature Nucleofection media (avoiding bubbles) along with 3–4 μg of plasmid or siRNA at a final concentration of 10–1,000 nM (in 1–2 mL) and gently mixed. The mixture is incubated at room temperature for approximately 5 min.
3. Cells are gently resuspended using plastic pipettes and transferred to a Nucleofection cuvette. It is critical to avoid the formation of bubbles during resuspension and transfer.

4. The cuvette is placed in the Nucleofector and the T-20 program is run. After the program ends, the cuvette is removed and 1 mL of prewarmed growth media is added. The cuvette is recapped and gently tapped to allow cell debris to rise to the top. Cells are gently resuspended using a plastic pipette, being careful to avoid cell debris that has risen to the top.
5. Depending on the application, cells may be counted and directly transferred to preincubated growth media, or if multiple transfections are performed using the same plasmid, cells may be combined, then counted, and then transferred to preincubated growth media.
6. Growth medium is changed the following morning at which time gene expression and/or transfection efficiency may be assessed. After the medium is changed, the transfected cells are cultured for an additional 24 h before gene expression is assessed for either knockdown or gain of function transfections (*see* **Note 4**).

3.3. Adenovirus Transduction

Adenoviruses are virions that have a double-stranded DNA genome with sizes ranging from 26 to 45 kb. Adenoviruses can replicate in either quiescent or dividing cells after infection. A relatively high level of protein expression can be achieved following transduction, and estimates of as high as 35% of total cellular protein have been reported *(29, 30)*. Since transduced genes remain epichromosomal, activation or inactivation of host genes following integration is avoided. Postinfection viability of the host cells remains at nearly 100% for most mammalian cell types; thus, it is well tolerated. For these reasons recombinant adenovirus is the vector of choice for many protein overexpression studies.

Most adenoviruses utilize the ubiquitously expressed coxackie and adenovirus receptor (CAR) for initial attachment and integrin-alpha-V glycoproteins for internalization. The heparan sulfate glycosaminoglycan receptor has also been shown to be involved in the binding of adenoviruses. These features lead to gene delivery in nontarget tissues and make the prospect of systemic gene delivery less plausible. Modifications to refine the specificity in attachment of adenovirus are under development, and these are likely to be especially important for macrophage transduction. Since macrophages do not express the high-affinity adenovirus receptor and only low levels of alpha-V-beta 5 integrin *(31, 32)*; transduction efficiency in these cells is sometimes low. The development of vectors that are targeted to specific receptors on macrophages has begun to address this limitation for in vitro transduction *(33)*. It should be noted, however, that the infection of alveolar macrophages by adenoviruses in vivo appears to proceed reasonably well. This may be due to the presence of surfactant proteins in the lung that may enhance viral uptake *(34, 35)*.

Adenoviruses can be highly immunogenic and induce proinflammatory cytokine production *(36)*. Additionally they induce dendritic cells to become mature antigen-presenting cells *(37)*. In early clinical trials, an Ad5-based gene delivery vector was associated with a fatal systemic inflammatory response *(38)*. Such problems have largely been addressed by engineering nonimmunogenic vectors that are devoid of viral-coding sequences (gutless) and/or engineered viruses that coexpress immunomodulatory molecules *(39)*.

The adeno-associated viruses (AAV) are single-stranded nonpathogenic DNA parvoviruses with a genome of roughly 4.7 kb. AAV needs the presence of an adenovirus or a herpes simplex virus coinfection in order to fulfill its life cycle. In the absence of these helper viruses, AAV integrates into human chromosome 19 via specific AAVS1 site to establish latency *(40)*. This property makes them superior to other viral methods, especially retroviruses, which randomly insert into host chromosomes. There are two open reading frames (ORFs) that encode viral proteins: the left one encodes the proteins essential for replication and the right one encodes the structural proteins for the capsid. Palindromic inverted elements that flank the two ends of the genome are the minimal cis-acting elements necessary for the integration and rescue of the viral genome during the latent stage. These elements are also essential for the replication of the viral genome and packaging into the capsid *(41, 42)*. AAV infection begins with virus binding to the cell surface via its primary receptor, heparan sulfate proteoglycans (HSPG), followed by viral internalization, intracellular trafficking, nuclear entry, and virion disassembly and release of a single-stranded DNA template for second-strand DNA synthesis. Fibroblast growth factor receptor 1 and alpha V beta 5 integrin have been identified as coreceptors for AAV infection *(43)*. In addition, adeno-associated viruses can use O-linked or N-linked sialic acids for cell binding. Different AAV serotypes exhibit different tissue or cell tropisms, which may be exploited for the development of AAV tissue or cell-specific-targeting vectors. The tropism of AAV can also be engineered through modification of the capsid. A chimeric capsid protein containing the variable region of an antibody against CD34 was used to specifically target hematopoietic progenitor cells *(44)*.

McEacher et al. demonstrated a correction of a murine model of Gaucher disease by the intravenous administration of adeno-associated virus vector that contained the human glucocerebrosidase gene *(45)*. Efficient gene knockdown of HIV-1-transactivating region (TAR) in human hematopoietic stem cells by transduction with AAV was demonstrated *(46)*. In this work, antisense RNA resulted in a continuous inhibition of viral replication without selective pressure. Thus, although not covered here in detail, adeno-associated viruses remain a viable alternative for the delivery of exogenous genes into macrophages.

The following procedures are described for adenovirus-mediated transduction of genes into macrophages:

1. The gene of interest is cloned into a shuttle vector. Shuttle vectors that are devoid of a promoter allow the insertion of the gene of interest under control of its own promoter. Alternatively, vectors containing strong constitutive promoters, such as CMV or EF-1 (elongation factor-1) promoter, are available and allow for high level of gene and protein expression (*see* **Note 5**).
2. To achieve homologous recombination of recombinant adenovirus, the shuttle vector containing the gene of interest has to be linearized by *Pme* I and dephosphorylated. One microgram of linearized recombinant transfer vector and 0.1 μg of the pAdEasy-1 vector are then cotransfected into BJ5183 bacterial cells by electroporation. A control transformation lacking the pAdEasy-1 vector should be included.
3. Typical parameters for electroporation of BJ5183 bacterial cells are: 25 μF of capacity, 200 Ω of resistance and 2.5 kV for a Bio-Rad instrument, 5 Ω of resistance, and 2.5 kV with 50 μF capacity for a BTX instrument.
4. After recovery at 37°C for 1 h with 1 mL SOC medium, the electroporated mixture is plated onto three LB plates in the presence of antibiotic for 24 h at 37°C, with 100, 300, and 600 μL on each. Approximately twenty of the smallest colonies are picked up and individually grown in LB medium with antibiotic. Restriction enzyme analysis is performed on mini-prepared plasmid DNA to identify appropriate recombinants.
5. Selected recombinants can be amplified in an electrocompetent *rec*A-strain of *E. coli*, such as DH5α. The procedure is similar to that described earlier for BJ5183. Recombinant plasmid DNA is purified by EndoFree® Plasmid Maxi kit (QIAGEN). Purified plasmid is then linearized by *Pac* I and purified through phenol/chloroform extraction and EtOH precipitation under sterile conditions. Five micrograms of purified linearized recombinant plasmid is used for transfection into HEK293 cells.
6. Approximately 1×10^6 HEK293 cells are plated on a 60-mm-diameter culture dish in DMEM with 5% FBS for 24 h before transfection, by which time they will reach ~70% confluency (*see* **Note 6**). Cells are changed with fresh medium at least 1 h before transfection. Transfection can be accomplished by lipofection or nucleoporation (*see* **Note 7**). The transfected cells are then collected 7–10 days later by scraping cells off the dish and subsequent centrifugation. The pelleted cells are

resuspended in a small volume of media and subject to three freeze/thaw cycles. After centrifugation at maximum speed for 10 min, the supernatants are collected as the original viral stock (*see* **Note 8**). One milliliter of the collected supernatant is generally ready to infect 3 × 10^6 cells to amplify virus (*see* **Note 9**). The remaining original stock solution is stored at –80°C (*see* **Note 10**).

7. To obtain high-titer viral stocks, HEK293 cells are infected at a multiplicity of infection (MOI) of 0.1–1 as determined in 8 and grown for 4 days, at which time virus is collected as described earlier. The process is repeated 1–3 times with a final repeat using a total of 5 × 10^8 HEK293 cells and an MOI of 1–5. Lysis of 50% HEK293 will be found between the third and fifth day following infection. At the fifth day postinfection, the viruses are harvested and purified using a double cesium chloride gradient (*see* **Note 11**), as previously described *(47)*. This is the virus preparation used to transduce macrophages.
8. A viral particle titration should be performed before transduction of the final target macrophages. Protocols used for titration can be divided into two types: physical methods (optical viral unit or viral particle) and biological ones. A fast, easy, and reliable biological assay developed by Bewig and Schmidt *(48)* and commercialized by Clontech Laboratories, Inc. (http://www.clontech.com) as the Adeno-X™ Rapid Titer Kit can be used. Alternatively, other methods can be used to fit the needs of each laboratory.
9. Human macrophages, particularly alveolar macrophages, are known to have low expression levels of the high-affinity coxsackie-adenovirus receptor (CAR). Thus, in addition to keeping cells in optimal condition and using viral titers as high as possible, special steps are needed to facilitate adenovirus infection. Viral particles in prewarmed medium without serum are mixed with cholesterol at 3 μg/mL (Sigma-Aldrich, St. Louis, MO) and incubated at 37°C for 30 min *(49)*. Macrophages are washed and resuspended at 5 × 10^6 cells/mL in complete medium typically with M-CSF (20 ng/mL) and 10% FCS. 5 × 10^5 cells are transferred into a nonadherent tube (Cat. No. 466982, Nunc, Roskilde, Denmark) and infected with the cholesterol/adenovirus mixture at an MOI of 100:1. The mixture is then centrifuged at 2,000 × *g* at 37°C for 2 h. After infection, the cells are washed three times with serum-free medium, and then complete medium is added to the culture *(50)*. After culture for 24–48 h, successful delivery of genes of interest can be examined by methods such as Western blot, flow cytometry, quantitative PCR, etc. as suitable for individual purposes.

3.4. Transduction by Retroviruses and Lentiviruses

Over the past decade, retroviruses have been used as a means to deliver genes into mammalian cells. Retroviruses are named for their ability to reverse-transcribe their RNA genome into DNA after infection. The general limitation associated with retroviral transduction is that they typically integrate only into a dividing genome, and therefore they cannot be used on terminally differentiated, nondividing cells, such as macrophages. The lentiviruses, however, are a subgroup of retroviruses that integrate into the genomes of nondividing cells. Consequently, these viruses have the most potential for macrophage gene delivery. All retroviruses have three coding domains: the *gag* domain that generates the matrix-, capsid-, and nucleoproteins; the *pol* domain that yields the viral protease, reverse transcriptase, and integrase; and the *env* domain that encodes envelope glycoprotein. The life cycle of retroviruses can be simply defined as follows: binding of viruses to their receptors, entry and internalization, reverse transcription, assembly of preintegration complex, nuclear transportation, transcription of integrated virus, translation from spliced mRNA, virion assembly, and exit from the cell.

Lentiviruses (e.g., HIV) are naturally attractive candidates as vectors for gene expression in primary nondividing macrophages. In 1995, a team led by Verma and Trono first detailed the construction of a harmless HIV-derived lentiviral vector that was able to deliver genes into a variety of cells, including human primary macrophages *(51)*. These authors used an HIV-derived lentivirus-based luciferase vector pseudotyped with the VSV G protein to transduce human monocyte-derived primary macrophages. A significant increase in luciferase activity could be detected in an envelope-dependent fashion. The possibility that the vector transduced a small portion of proliferating macrophages was ruled out by mutating Vpr and MA, two virion proteins that are central for HIV infection of primary macrophages. Since then, numerous studies using this or a modified delivery system have been reported. Rossi et al. demonstrated that similar HIV-1-based lentiviral vectors could mediate efficient gene transfer into primary murine macrophages and mature B lymphocytes without the participation of HIV-1 accessory proteins Nef, Vpr, Vif, and Vpu *(52)*. The lentiviral vector-mediated method was used to genetically modify monocytes so that the autocrine and paracrine production of GM-CSF and IL-4 could be used to differentiate human CD14+ monocytes into immature dendritic cells *(53)*.

The subgroup lentivirus includes human immunodeficiency viruses (HIV-1 and HIV-2), simian immunodeficiency viruses, feline immunodeficiency virus (FIV), equine anemia infectious virus, and maedi-visna virus. All these viruses can integrate into the genome of nondividing cells, which makes them attractive delivery vehicles for the expression of exogenous genes or small interfering RNAs. Many optimized lentiviral systems such as the

FIV-based vector have been developed to circumvent safety hurdles for potential application in human subjects. All of them are based on a genetically split gene expression design. The essential viral elements include the minimal LV packaging helper proteins (gag-pol genes), the LV transfer vector RNA containing the transgene expression cassette, and heterologous glycoproteins. The following procedure is based on an HIV-1-based vector system developed by Invitrogen (http://www.invitrogen.com) for academic applications (*see* **Note 12**). The HIV-1-based system is well developed and characterized and been proven to be successful for use on primary macrophages *(51)*.

The procedure can be divided into five basic steps: (a) cloning the gene of interest into the lentiviral vector; (b) transforming *E. coli* and isolating plasmid DNA; (c) testing the construct by transient transfection; (d) harvesting and titering the viral stock; and (e) transducing macrophages with virus.

1. TOPO-technology-based vectors are designed to facilitate PCR-based cloning using a proofreading polymerase. Taq polymerase should not be used due to the inhibitory effect of 3′-A on the D-TOPO reaction. An excess of PCR product inhibits the D-TOPO reaction, thus 1:1 ratio of insert:vector should generally be maintained.

2. All retroviral vectors have two LTRs with 180 bp of repeats; thus, they can recombine in bacteria, easily resulting in smaller products. To reduce the possible occurrence of inappropriate recombination between the LTRs, Stbl3 *E. coli* cells are used for transformation. The choice of LB plates with 100 μg/mL ampicillin also reduces recombination. Only small colonies are picked for subsequent minipreparation, as recombination leads to loss of most of the plasmid, conferring a growth advantage and favoring the formation of the large colonies. EDTA should be included in the miniprep solution to kill Stbl3 *E. coli* cells containing a thermostable periplasmic endonuclease. Phenol/chloroform extraction is added to denature the enzyme. Restriction endonuclease analysis is performed to determine whether unwanted recombinants exist in the preparation.

3. The 293FT cell line is derived from HEK293 cells. Both these cells contain a stably integrated T antigen, but the 293FT cells have the added convenience of rapid growth in culture. Plasmids with an SV40 ori are not appropriate since it can be recognized by T antigen and lead to cell death. Transient transfection of the newly constructed viral vector and packaging vectors (packaging mix) in 293FT cells can be performed by using Lipofectamine 2000™ (Invitrogen) or Fugene™ 6 (Roche). Multinucleated syncytia should be found after transfection since VSV-G glycoproteins (packaging mix) can cause cells to fuse. Cells should be at approximately 90% confluence

by plating 5×10^6 cells per 10 cm^2 1 day before transfection in complete media.

4. Virus-containing supernatants are collected 48–72 h after transfection. Due to the infectious nature of the viruses, BSL-2 guidelines should be followed. The supernatants are centrifuged at 1,800*g* at 4°C for 15 min and then filtered through a 0.45-μm filter. The virus can be kept in the medium used to culture 293 cells (in the absence of G418) in small aliquots at –80°C. The virus can also be concentrated by ultracentrifugation as previously described *(54)*.
5. Viral titering is done on HT1080 cells (human fibrosarcoma cell line from ATCC: http://www.atcc.org). Tenfold serial dilutions of lentiviral stock are prepared and transduced into HT1080 cells in the presence of Polybrene (Sigma, Catalog No. H9268). Twenty-four hours after viral transduction, cells are trypsinized from 6-well culture plates and expanded to 100-mm plates. Twenty-four hours later, 10 μg/mL blasticidin or 100 μg/mL zeocin are added for selection. One week after blasticidin selection or 3 weeks after zeocin, crystal violet staining is carried out to visualize plaques. Cells are washed with PBS, then treated with 1 mL of crystal violet solution (1% crystal violet in 10% ethanol) for 10 min at room temperature, and then washed with PBS twice. The infected plaques are visible to the naked eye for counting to determine the viral titer of the original collected viral supernatant.
6. Cell lines or primary macrophages and monocytes are obtained and maintained as described earlier. One day before transduction, macrophages are plated so that they will be approximately 30% confluent the next day. Virus solutions with a range of MOI from 1 to 100 are prepared in cell culture media with or without Polybrene or DEAE-dextran (*see* **Note 13**). Virus should be kept at a ratio no greater than 1:2 in the final volume of cell culture medium. The final volume in a well of 24-well plates should not exceed 250 μL. The lower the volume, the better. Twenty-four hours after incubation with virus, culture supernantants are removed and fresh culture medium is added. For nonadherent monocytes, on the day of transduction cells are plated at a density so that they will not need to be subcultured for 3 days. The cells are plated in a small volume (100 μL for 24-well plates). Virus solutions with different MOI are added and mixed well with the cells. The final volume should be kept under 200 μL in total. Cells and viruses are mixed every couple of hours at least twice during the daytime and incubated at 37°C for an additional 24 h. Fresh medium (100 μL) is then added, or virus-containing medium is removed by centrifugation and replaced with fresh culture medium. Expression of inserted genes can be monitored beginning at day 2 and continuing until 7 days post-transduction (*see* **Note 14**).

4. Notes

1. Precooling the cuvette and cells before electroporation is not necessary.
2. The BioRad Gene Pulser II apparatus generates exponential pulses by the Pulse Trac™ waveform delivery system for optimal transfection in an electroporation cuvette. Other electroporation devices that generate square wave pulses such as BTX® molecular delivery system (http://www.btxonline.com) have also been well established for the transfection of mammalian cells including human and mouse macrophage cell lines. The parameters are: 260 V and three pulses of 10 ms with a pulse length set to BCM 820 when 4-mm gap cuvette is used. Ten micrograms of DNA in 0.4 mL volume with 5×10^6 cells in total is used. These parameters are also applicable to human THP-1 and U937 cell lines.
3. It is common to lose up to 50% of the cells during the electroporation procedure.
4. We have achieved a transfection efficiency of approximately 90% using this technique on primary bone marrow macrophages (**Fig. 1**).
5. The CMV promoter may not be suitable for the expression of inserted genes in rodent cells due to methylation-dependent downregulation *(55)*. EF-1 (elongation factor-1) promoter or other macrophage-specific promoters are alternative choices.
6. To avoid the occurrence of replication competent adenoviruses (RCAs), passage numbers of HEK293 cells should not be higher than four.
7. Addition of GeneJammer (Stratagene: http://www.stratagene.com) during the adenovirus infection can lead to increases in both the total numbers of infected cells and the level of transgene expression per cell in the absence of CAR *(56)*.
8. In order to avoid the generation of the unwanted recombinants, extraction of recombinant adenovirus plasmid from HEK293 cells should be performed as quickly as possible using the minipreparation procedure for low copy plasmid. Furthermore, a recombinant adenovirus plasmid with a large size insertion is genetically not stable in a *rec*A+ strain such as BJ5183.
9. Good management of the first amplification of viral stock or use of low passage viral stock is critical because they contain the lowest possible ratio of RCA/recombinants. The frequency of RCA occurrence is about one revertant per 10^7 viruses.
10. Nyberg-Hoffman virus storage buffer (Tris 10 mM, pH 8.0, with 2 mM $MgCl_2$ and 4% sucrose) allows the viral particles

to be stored at concentrations up to 1×10^{13} viral particles/mL without precipitation.

11. Cesium chloride purification is essential for in vivo gene delivery because it can remove contaminants that can elicit an immune response in vivo.
12. Other Lentiviral vector-based systems are also available through commercial vendors, such as a series of feline lentiviral vectors supplied by SBI (http://www.sbi.com) and a lenti-siRNA vector from GenScript (http://www.genscript.com). Feline or other nonhuman lentiviral vectors-based gene delivery systems are particularly suitable for gene therapy in human subjects *(57)*.
13. Polybrene (hexadimethrine bromide) is a small positively charged molecule that can enhance transduction by retroviruses because it can reduce repulsion between sialic acid-containing molecules and neutralize surface charge to allow the viral glycoproteins to bind more efficiently to their receptors. However, polybrene must be used with caution, particularly for cells derived from hematopoietic precursors because of its toxicity to T and B cells. DEAE-dextran is an alternative, but both reagents should be titrated before being added to macrophages or monocytes. Titration of polybrene generally begins at 1 μg/mL, and DEAE-dextran at 3 μg/mL. Inclusion of polybrene or DEAE-dextran generally increases transduction efficiency by twofold *(58)*.
14. Because macrophages are particularly adept at sensing 'danger' and migrating to areas of infection or tissue damage, these cells become potential drug delivery vehicles *(63)*. The development of innovative new methods for introducing exogenous macromolecules into macrophages is not only useful for basic bench experimentation, but has also led to the design of new protocols to be applied to clinical gene therapy or drug delivery. Chemical and lipofection methods do not have the concern of the host immune response that is often associated with viral infection. Adenovirus-based gene delivery may have the disadvantage of transient expression of the transduced gene, and it can lead to some side effects in vivo, such as hepatotoxicity *(59)*. Furthermore, the repeated administration of adenovirus will often result in unwanted host immune responses. Lentivirus-based constructs have the advantages of macrophage-specific targeting and continuous expression of the transduced gene due to integration into chromosomal DNA. Thus, lentivirus-based systems are quite promising for both research and clinical application. However, dangers associated with HIV genotoxicity continue to be major limitations for the use of these vectors. Importantly, many new and refined vectors are under development to obviate many of these concerns. New methods, including the use of nanoparticles with cell-specific-targeting moieties,

have been reported *(60)*. Osmotic delivery of small interfering RNA (siRNA) *(61)* and even the use of bacterial ghosts loaded with DNA have been used as methods to efficiently transfer nucleic acids into macrophages *(62)*. The goal is to obtain high transfection efficiency and cell specificity so that genetic manipulation of macrophages will become a routine task.

References

1. McCutchan, J. H. and Pagano, J. S. (1968) Enhancement of the infectivity of simian virus 40 deoxyribonucleic acid with diethylaminoethyl-dextran. *J Natl Cancer Inst* 41, 351–357.
2. Vaheri, A. and Pagano, J. S. (1965) Infectious poliovirus RNA: a sensitive method of assay. *Virology* 27, 434–436.
3. Graham, F. L. and van der Eb, A. J. (1973) A new technique for the assay of infectivity of human adenovirus 5 DNA. *Virology* 52, 456–467.
4. Loyter, A., Scangos, G. A., and Ruddle, F. H. (1982) Mechanisms of DNA uptake by mammalian cells: fate of exogenously added DNA monitored by the use of fluorescent dyes. *Proc Natl Acad Sci U S A* 79, 422–426.
5. Mack, K. D., Wei, R., Elbagarri, A., Abbey, N., and McGrath, M. S. (1998) A novel method for DEAE-dextran mediated transfection of adherent primary cultured human macrophages. *J Immunol Methods* 211, 79–86.
6. Thompson, C. D., Frazier-Jessen, M. R., Rawat, R., Nordan, R. P., and Brown, R. T. (1999) Evaluation of methods for transient transfection of a murine macrophage cell line, RAW 264.7. *Biotechniques* 27, 824–830, 832.
7. Fraley, R., Subramani, S., Berg, P., and Papahadjopoulos, D. (1980) Introduction of liposome-encapsulated SV40 DNA into cells. *J Biol Chem* 255, 10431–10435.
8. Felgner, P. L., Gadek, T. R., Holm, M., Roman, R., Chan, H. W., Wanz, M., et al. (1987) Lipofection: a highly efficient, lipid-mediated DNA-transfection procedure. *Proc Natl Acad Sci U S A* 84, 7413–7417.
9. Glorioso, J. C., Huang, L., Dunbar, C., and Felgner, P. L. (2000) Highlights from the third annual ASGT meeting. American Society of Gene Therapy. *Mol Ther* 2, 96–100.
10. Friend, D. S., Papahadjopoulos, D., and Debs, R. J. (1996) Endocytosis and intracellular processing accompanying transfection mediated by cationic liposomes. *Biochim Biophys Acta* 1278, 41–50.
11. Farhood, H., Serbina, N., and Huang, L. (1995) The role of dioleoyl phosphatidylethanolamine in cationic liposome mediated gene transfer. *Biochim Biophys Acta* 1235, 289–295.
12. Zhang, X., Wang, J. M., Gong, W. H., Mukaida, N., and Young, H. A. (2001) Differential regulation of chemokine gene expression by 15-deoxy-delta 12,14 prostaglandin J2. *J Immunol* 166, 7104–7111.
13. Baum, C., von Kalle, C., Staal, F. J., Li, Z., Fehse, B., Schmidt, M., et al. (2004) Chance or necessity? Insertional mutagenesis in gene therapy and its consequences. *Mol Ther* 9, 5–13.
14. Hacein-Bey-Abina, S., von Kalle, C., Schmidt, M., McCormack, M. P., Wulffraat, N., Leboulch, P., et al. (2003) LMO2-associated clonal T cell proliferation in two patients after gene therapy for SCID-X1. *Science* 302, 415–419.
15. von Kalle, C., Fehse, B., Layh-Schmitt, G., Schmidt, M., Kelly, P., and Baum, C. (2004) Stem cell clonality and genotoxicity in hematopoietic cells: gene activation side effects should be avoidable. [illegible]
16. Engelman, A. (2005) The ups and downs of gene expression and retroviral DNA integration. *Proc Natl Acad Sci U S A* 102, 1275–1276.
17. He, T. C., Zhou, S., da Costa, L. T., Yu, J., Kinzler, K. W., and Vogelstein, B. (1998) A simplified system for generating recombinant adenoviruses. *Proc Natl Acad Sci U S A* 95, 2509–2514.
18. Neumann, E., Schaefer-Ridder, M., Wang, Y., and Hofschneider, P. H. (1982) Gene transfer into mouse lyoma cells by electroporation in high electric fields. *EMBO J* 1, 841–845.
19. Wong, T. K., and Neumann, E. (1982) Electric field mediated gene transfer. *Biochem Biophys Res Commun* 107, 584–587.
20. Potter, H., Weir, L., and Leder, P. (1984) Enhancer-dependent expression of human kappa immunoglobulin genes introduced into mouse pre-B lymphocytes by electroporation. *Proc Natl Acad Sci U S A* 81, 7161–7165.

21. Potter, H. (1988) Electroporation in biology: methods, applications, and instrumentation. *Anal Biochem* 174, 361–373.
22. Lukacs, G. L., Rotstein, O. D., and Grinstein, S. (1990) Phagosomal acidification is mediated by a vacuolar-type H(+)-ATPase in murine macrophages. *J Biol Chem* 265, 21099–21107.
23. Stacey, K. J., Ross, I. L., and Hume, D. A. (1993) Electroporation and DNA-dependent cell death in murine macrophages. *Immunol Cell Biol* 71, 75–85.
24. Martinet, W., Schrijvers, D. M., and Kockx, M. M. (2003) Nucleofection as an efficient nonviral transfection method for human monocytic cells. *Biotechnol Lett* 25, 1025–1029.
25. Lenz, P., Bacot, S. M., Frazier-Jessen, M. R., and Feldman, G. M. (2003) Nucleoporation of dendritic cells: efficient gene transfer by electroporation into human monocyte-derived dendritic cells. *FEBS Lett* 538, 149–154.
26. Van De Parre, T. J., Martinet, W., Schrijvers, D. M., Herman, A. G., and De Meyer, G. R. (2005) mRNA but not plasmid DNA is efficiently transfected in murine J774A.1 macrophages. *Biochem Biophys Res Commun* 327, 356–360.
27. Cao, S., Zhang, X., Edwards, J. P., and Mosser, D. M. (2006) NF-kappaB1 (p50) homodimers differentially regulate pro- and anti-inflammatory cytokines in macrophages. *J Biol Chem* 281, 26041–26050.
28. Lucas, M., Zhang, X., Prasanna, V., and Mosser, D. M. (2005) ERK activation following macrophage FcgammaR ligation leads to chromatin modifications at the IL-10 locus. *J Immunol* 175, 469–477.
29. Garnier, A., Cote, J., Nadeau, I., Kamen, A., and Massie, B. (1994) Scale-up of the adenovirus expression system for the production of recombinant protein in human 293S cells. *Cytotechnology* 15, 145–155.
30. Wurm, F., and Bernard, A. (1999) Large-scale transient expression in mammalian cells for recombinant protein production. *Curr Opin Biotechnol* 10, 156–159.
31. Kaner, R. J., Worgall, S., Leopold, P. L., Stolze, E., Milano, E., Hidaka, C., et al. (1999) Modification of the genetic program of human alveolar macrophages by adenovirus vectors in vitro is feasible but inefficient, limited in part by the low level of expression of the coxsackie/adenovirus receptor. *Am J Respir Cell Mol Biol* 20, 361–370.
32. Huang, S., Endo, R. I., and Nemerow, G. R. (1995) Upregulation of integrins alpha v beta 3 and alpha v beta 5 on human monocytes and T lymphocytes facilitates adenovirus-mediated gene delivery. *J Virol* 69, 2257–2263.
33. De, S. K., Venkateshan, C. N., Seth, P., Gajdusek, D. C., and Gibbs, C. J. (1998) Adenovirus-mediated human immunodeficiency virus-1 Nef expression in human monocytes/macrophages and effect of Nef on downmodulation of Fcgamma receptors and expression of monokines. *Blood* 91, 2108–2117.
34. Harrod, K. S., Trapnell, B. C., Otake, K., Korfhagen, T. R., and Whitsett, J. A. (1999) SP-A enhances viral clearance and inhibits inflammation after pulmonary adenoviral infection. *Am J Physiol* 277(3 Pt 1), L580–L588.
35. Zsengeller, Z., Otake, K., Hossain, S. A., Berclaz, P. Y., and Trapnell, B. C. (2000) Internalization of adenovirus by alveolar macrophages initiates early proinflammatory signaling during acute respiratory tract infection. *J Virol* 74, 9655–9667.
36. Morelli, A. E., Larregina, A. T., Ganster, R. W., Zahorchak, A. F., Plowey, J. M., Takayama, T. et al. (2000) Recombinant adenovirus induces maturation of dendritic cells via an NF-kappaB-dependent pathway. *J Virol* 74, 9617–9628.
37. Philpott, N. J., Nociari, M., Elkon, K. B., and Falck-Pedersen, E. (2004) Adenovirus-induced maturation of dendritic cells through a PI3 kinase-mediated TNF-alpha induction pathway. *Proc Natl Acad Sci U S A* 101, 6200–6205.
38. Stone, D., and Lieber, A. (2006) New serotypes of adenoviral vectors. *Curr Opin Mol Ther* 8, 423–431.
39. Thummala, N. R., Ghosh, S. S., Lee, S. W., Reddy, B., Davidson, A., Horwitz, M. S., et al. (2002) A non-immunogenic adenoviral vector, coexpressing CTLA4Ig and bilirubin-uridine-diphosphoglucuronateglucuronosyltransferase permits long-term, repeatable transgene expression in the Gunn rat model of Crigler–Najjar syndrome. *Gene Ther* 9, 981–990.
40. Kotin, R. M., Linden, R. M., and Berns, K. I. (1992) Characterization of a preferred site on human chromosome 19q for integration of adeno-associated virus DNA by non-homologous recombination. *EMBO J* 11, 5071–5078.
41. Berns, K. I., and Hauswirth, W. W. (1979) Adeno-associated viruses. *Adv Virus Res* 25, 407–449.
42. Muzyczka, N. (1992) Use of adeno-associated virus as a general transduction vector for mammalian cells. *Curr Top Microbiol Immunol* 158, 97–129.
43. Qing, K., Mah, C., Hansen, J., Zhou, S., Dwarki, V., and Srivastava, A. (1999) Human fibroblast growth factor receptor 1 is a co-receptor for infection by adeno-associated virus 2. *Nat Med* 5, 71–77.

44. Yang, Q., Mamounas, M., Yu, G., Kennedy, S., Leaker, B., Merson, J., et al. (1998) Development of novel cell surface CD34-targeted recombinant adenoassociated virus vectors for gene therapy. *Hum Gene Ther* 9, 1929–1937.
45. McEachern, K. A., Nietupski, J. B., Chuang, W. L., Armentano, D., Johnson, J., Hutto, E., et al. (2006) AAV8-mediated expression of glucocerebrosidase ameliorates the storage pathology in the visceral organs of a mouse model of Gaucher disease. *J Gene Med* 8, 719–729.
46. Santat, L., Paz, H., Wong, C., Li, L., Macer, J., Forman, S., et al. (2005) Recombinant AAV2 transduction of primitive human hematopoietic stem cells capable of serial engraftment in immune-deficient mice. *Proc Natl Acad Sci U S A* 102, 11053–11058.
47. Becker, T. C., Noel, R. J., Coats, W. S., Gómez-Foix, A. M., Alam, T., Gerard, R. D., et al. (1994) Use of recombinant adenovirus for metabolic engineering of mammalian cells. *Methods Cell Biol* 43 Pt A, 161–189.
48. Bewig, B., and Schmidt, W. E. (2000) Accelerated titering of adenoviruses. *Biotechniques* 28, 870–873.
49. Worgall, S., Worgall, T. S., Kostarelos, K., Singh, R., Leopold, P. L., Hackett, N. R., et al. (2000) Free cholesterol enhances adenoviral vector gene transfer and expression in CAR-deficient cells. *Mol Ther* 1, 39–48.
50. Mayne, G. C., Borowicz, R. A., Greeneklee, K. V., Finlay-Jones, J. J., Williams, K. A., and Hart, P. H. (2003) Centrifugation facilitates transduction of green fluorescent protein in human monocytes and macrophages by adenovirus at low multiplicity of infection. *J Immunol Methods* 278, 45–56.
51. Naldini, L., Blömer, U., Gallay, P., Ory, D., Mulligan, R., Gage, F. H., et al. (1996) In vivo gene delivery and stable transduction of nondividing cells by a lentiviral vector. *Science* 272, 263–267.
52. Rossi, G. R., Mautino, M. R., and Morgan, R. A. (2003) High-efficiency lentiviral vector-mediated gene transfer into murine macrophages and activated splenic B lymphocytes. *Hum Gene Ther* 14, 385–391.
53. Koya, R. C., Weber, J. S., Kasahara, N., Lau, R., Villacres, M. C., Levine, A. M., et al. (2004) Making dendritic cells from the inside out: lentiviral vector-mediated gene delivery of granulocyte-macrophage colony-stimulating factor and interleukin 4 into CD14+ monocytes generates dendritic cells in vitro. *Hum Gene Ther* 15, 733–748.
54. Reiser, J. (2000) Production and concentration of pseudotyped HIV-1-based gene transfer vectors. *Gene Ther* 7, 910–913.
55. Zarrin, A. A., Malkin, L., Fong, I., Luk, K. D., Ghose, A., and Berinstein, N. L. (1999) Comparison of CMV, RSV, SV40 viral and Vlambda1 cellular promoters in B and T lymphoid and non-lymphoid cell lines. *Biochim Biophys Acta* 1446, 135–139.
56. Fouletier-Dilling, C. M., Bosch, P., Davis, A. R., Shafer, J. A., Stice, S. L., Gugala, Z., et al. (2005) Novel compound enables high-level adenovirus transduction in the absence of an adenovirus-specific receptor. *Hum Gene Ther* 16, 1287–1297.
57. Wang, G., Slepushkin, V., Zabner, J., Keshavjee, S., Johnston, J. C., Sauter, S. L., et al. (1999) Feline immunodeficiency virus vectors persistently transduce nondividing airway epithelia and correct the cystic fibrosis defect. *J Clin Invest* 104, R55–R62.
58. Reiser, J., Harmison, G., Kluepfel-Stahl, S., Brady, R. O., Karlsson, S., and Schubert, M. (1996) Transduction of nondividing cells using pseudotyped defective high-titer HIV type 1 particles. *Proc Natl Acad Sci U S A* 93, 15266–15271.
59. Shayakhmetov, D. M., Gaggar, A., Ni, S., Li, Z. Y., and Lieber, A. (2005) Adenovirus binding to blood factors results in liver cell infection and hepatotoxicity. *J Virol* 79, 7478–7491.
60. Weissleder, R., Kelly, K., Sun, E. Y., Shtatland, T., and Josephson, L. (2005) Cell-specific targeting of nanoparticles by multivalent attachment of small molecules. *Nat Biotechnol* 23, 1418–1423.
61. Aoki, M., Ishii, T., Kanaoka, M., and Kimura, T. (2006) RNA interference in immune cells by use of osmotic delivery of siRNA. *Biochem Biophys Res Commun* 341, 326–333.
62. Paukner, S., Kudela, P., Kohl, G., Schlapp, T., Friedrichs, S., and Lubitz, W. (2005) DNA-loaded bacterial ghosts efficiently mediate reporter gene transfer and expression in macrophages. *Mol Ther* 11, 215–223.
63. Zhang, X., and Mosser, D. M. (2008) Macrophage activation by endogenous danger signals. *J Pathol.* 214, 161–178.

Chapter 10

Genetic Modification of Murine Dendritic Cells by RNA Transfection

Maurizio Ceppi, Enrico Schmidt, and Philippe Pierre

Summary

The ability to manipulate in vitro cultured dendritic cells (DCs) by transfection represents an attractive strategy to load these antigen-presenting cells with genetic material encoding various immunogenic epitopes. The gene transfer approach can also be applied to DCs with the aim of expressing immunologically active molecules such as cytokines, costimulatory molecules, or simply to transiently express proteins to perform cell biology studies. Available gene transfer technologies for DCs include both viral and non-viral vector-based approaches. In this chapter, we describe non-viral strategies of RNA transfection. Special emphasis is given to murine bone-marrow-derived DCs, since gene transfer to human DCs has been extensively described in the literature, especially in the context of cancer immunotherapy and other clinical applications. Methods to deliver small interfering RNA (siRNA) to DCs are described as well. Finally, the potential of exogenously delivered RNA to activate DCs is discussed and some practical advice to avoid DC activation is described.

Key words: Dendritic cells, Mice, Non-viral gene transfer, RNA transfection, RNA electroporation, RNA lipofection, DC activation, Gene expression, Translation.

1. Introduction

Different approaches have been developed to load DCs with antigens *(1)*. Direct use of antigenic peptides is efficient, but is limited to a finite number of MHC-restricted epitopes. DCs can be loaded with recombinant proteins encoding various immunogenic epitopes, but this requires the laborious and expensive production of proteins. These limitations can be overcome through either non-viral or viral gene transfer technologies developed for DC loading *(2)*. Although viral vectors will efficiently transfect

Neil E. Reiner (ed.), *Macrophages and Dendritic Cells,* Methods in Molecular Biology, vol. 531

DOI: 10.1007/978-1-59745-396-7_10

DCs *(3, 4)*, their use is complicated by important safety concerns. Infection of bone-marrow progenitors has also been developed, but the time required for DC differentiation (2–3 days) affects the outcome of the experiments and obviously the conclusions drawn from heterologous gene expression over 48–72 h. Plasmid DNA transfer into DCs does not represent a valid alternative, because of its low transfection efficiency *(5)*. This contrasts profoundly with RNA delivery, with which the efficient strategy of RNA electroporation has recently been described *(6, 7)*. RNA electroporation is by far the most efficient and safest transfection technique for DCs (*see* **Table1**), and is described in detail in this chapter.

Table 1
RNA-transfection procedures, transfection efficiencies, and immunological outcomes measured in dendritic cells

RNA-transfection procedure	DC type	Transfection efficiency	T-cell stimulation/ cytokine secretion	Reference
Passive pulsing				
	Human MoDCs	ND	CTL induction	Nair et al. *(12)*
	Human MoDCs	ND	CTL induction	Heiser et al. *(22)*
	Human MoDCs	ND	CTL induction/IFNγ	Heiser et al. *(21)*
	Porcine MoDCs	1%[a]	ND	Ceppi et al. *(18)*
Lipofection (employed reagent)				
Lipofectin	Human MoDCs	508 pg LUC/10^5 DCs	$CD4^+$ and $CD8^+$ proliferation CTL induction/IFNγ	Weissman et al. *(9)*
DOTAP	Murine BMDCs	ND	CTL induction	Boczkowski et al. *(15)*
DMRIE-C	Human MoDCs	4–8%	CTL induction/IFNγ	Van Tendeloo et al. *(13)*
	Human MoDCs, Murine BMDCs	ND	CTL induction	Boczkowski *(27)*
	Human MoDCs	ND	CTL induction	Thornburg *(28)*
TransFast	Human MoDCs	21%	CTL induction/IFNγ	Strobel et al. *(7)*
	Porcine MoDCs	15–20%	IFN type I induced by RNA lipofection	Ceppi et al. *(10, 18)*
DAC-30	Human MoDCs	14%	ND	Strobel et al. *(7)*

(continued)

Table 1 (continued)

RNA-transfection procedure	DC type	Transfection efficiency	T-cell stimulation/ cytokine secretion	Reference
Electroporation				
	Human MoDCs, CD34⁺ DCs, and LCs	63, 73, and 50%	CTL induction/IFNγ	Van Tendeloo et al. *(6, 13)*
	Human MoDCs	11%	CTL induction/IFNγ	Strobel et al. *(7)*
	Murine BMDCs	70–80%	$CD4^+$ and $CD8^+$ proliferation	Van Meirvenne et al. *(17)*
	Porcine MoDCs	70–80%	CTL induction/IFNγ	Ceppi et al. *(10, 18)*

MoDCs monocyte-derived DCs; *ND* not determined; *CTL* cytotoxic T-lymphocytes; *CD34+* $CD34^+$ progenitor-derived DCs; *LCs* Langerhans cells
[a]% of cells expressing a GFP reporter gene analysed by flow cytometry

RNA transfection of DCs may be advantageous for several reasons. For protein production, the transfected mRNA molecules need to be delivered only into the cytosol of the target cells, while in comparison plasmid DNA also requires entry into the nucleus and subsequent transcription to generate the encoded message *(8)*. This is especially true in non-dividing cells and may partially explain why DNA transfection is so inefficient in DCs *(5)*. In contrast, RNA transfection results in high transfection efficiency (80–90% after electroporation) *(6)* and rapid protein expression (detectable within 2 h of electroporation) *(9)*. Another major advantage of RNA transfection is that several mRNA species can be simultaneously delivered into the target cells leading to the translation of different gene products. In the context of antigen presentation, RNA transfection permits loading of DCs with mRNA encoding multiple antigens, which may then be processed and displayed on the surface of the DCs as defined antigenic peptides, potentially leading to the activation of multiple T cells *(10)*.

Independent of transfection and gene expression, maturing DCs tightly regulate levels of mRNA translation. Cap-mediated translation is considerably inhibited at late time of activation (from 16 to 24 h), thus rendering heterologous protein expression relatively inefficient at these late stages of DC maturation. This inefficiency is illustrated in **Fig. 1**. Here it is evident that the level of luciferase enzymatic activity in mRNA-transfected maturing DCs

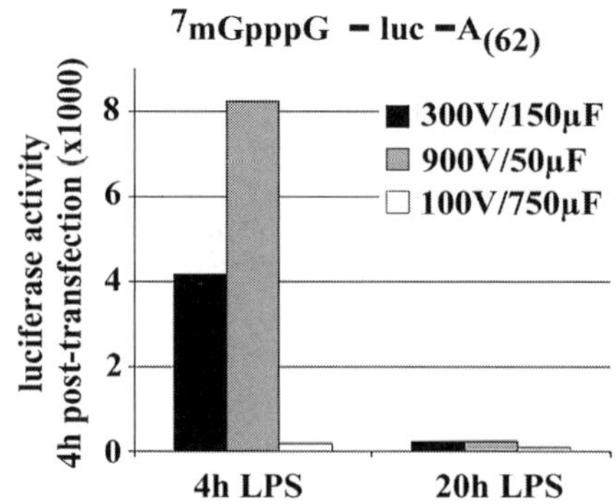

Fig. 1. Immature and LPS-stimulated (16 h) DCs were electroporated with firefly luciferase reporter mRNA applying different voltage (V) and capacitance (μF) as indicated in the figure. DCs were then incubated for further 4 h with fresh complete medium in presence of LPS. Cells were harvested and luciferase activity was measured using a reporter assay system that measures luminescence. The best transfection efficiency is obtained using an electroporation setup of 900 V/50 μF. A different setup may be applied, if the EGFP reporter mRNA is electroporated

is considerably reduced at 20 h of maturation when compared to 4 h, despite the fact that transfected mRNAs were found to be equivalent in the two cell populations *(29)*.

2. Materials

2.1. Cell Culture

1. 7- to 8-Week old male C57-BL6 or Balb/c mice.
2. To isolate bones from mice: gauze, sharp curved tip scissors, and forceps.
3. To isolate bone marrow: petri dishes, 10-ml syringes, 25-gauge needles, and cell strainers.
4. 70% EtOH.
5. RPMI 1640 medium.
6. Red Blood Cells (RBC) lysis buffer: 1.66% NH_4Cl solution.
7. DC Wash Medium (DC-WM): RPMI supplemented with 5% de-complemented foetal bovine serum, 50 μM β-mercaptoethanol, 20 μg/ml gentamicin.
8. DC Growth Medium (DC-GM): DC-WM supplemented with recombinant murine cytokine GM-CSF, produced as a culture supernatant from J558L cells transfected with murine GM-CSF cDNA, as described previously *(11)*.
9. Lipopolysaccharide (LPS).

2.2. Plasmids and In Vitro Transcription of mRNA

1. Several plasmids have been described in the literature for the in vitro transcription of mRNA molecules coding for reporter genes (*see* **Note 1**). In our laboratory, optimal transfection efficiencies of murine and human DCs have been achieved after RNA electroporation of mRNA molecules that had been transcribed in vitro using the following linearized DNA plasmids:
   - *pGEM4Z/GFP/A64* encoding the enhanced green fluorescent protein (EGFP) (*see* **Note 2**). The plasmid can be linearized with the restriction enzyme SpeI, and for in vitro transcription a T7 RNA polymerase should be employed *(7, 12)*.
   - *pSP64/GFP* encoding for EGFP. The plasmid can be linearized with the restriction enzyme EcoRI and for in vitro transcription a SP6 RNA polymerase is used *(13)*.
   - *pT3LUC(pA)* encoding firefly luciferase (LUC). The plasmid can be linearized with the restriction enzyme NotI, and for in vitro transcription a T3 RNA polymerase is used *(14)* (Lelouard et al., in press; Schmidt et al., in press).
2. QIAquick PCR purification system (QIAGEN).
3. mMESSAGE mMACHINE in vitro transcription system (AMBION). The monomethyl guanosine (^{7}mGpppG) cap analogue is provided in the kit.
4. RNeasy Mini RNA purification system (QIAGEN).
5. 1% Denaturing agarose gel.
6. Spectrophotometer.

2.3. RNA Transfection

1. PBS.
2. OptiMEM (Gibco).
3. Gene Pulser II apparatus (Biorad, *see* **Note 3**).
4. 4-mm Gap electroporation cuvette (Biorad, *see* **Note 3**).
5. Lipofection reagent TransFast (Promega, *see* **Note 4**).

2.4. Reporter Gene Expression Analysis

1. Reporter assay system Dual-Luciferase kit (Promega).
2. FACS-staining buffer (FSB): 1% foetal bovine serum in PBS.
3. FACS-fixing buffer (FSB-fix): 2% paraformaldehyde in FSB.
4. Propidium iodide (10 μg/ml).
5. FACScan analytical flow cytometer (Becton Dickinson).

2.5. Antibodies for Immunophenotyping

For the analysis of the surface markers, bone-marrow-derived DCs (BMDCs) should be stained with following fluorochrome-conjugated antibodies:

1. CD11c-FITC or -PE (clone N418, e-Bioscience).
2. CD80-FITC (clone 16-10A1, Miltenyi).
3. CD86-APC (clone GL1, e-Bioscience).

4. CD40-FITC (clone HM40-3, Pharmingen).
5. MHC class I (tested for C57-BL6 mice): H-2K^b – PE or – FITC (clone AF6-88.5, Pharmingen).
6. MHC class II (tested for C57-BL6 mice): IA/IE – PE (clone M5/114.15.2, Pharmingen).

3. Methods

3.1. Generation and Culture of Murine Bone-Marrow Derived DCs

1. Kill the desired number of mice. Typically, 40×10^6 bone-marrow cells can be isolated from one C57-BL6 mouse.
2. Remove femurs and tibias from the mice, and clean off bones from tissue as much as possible using gauze.
3. Transfer the bones in a tube containing RPMI 1640 medium.
4. Remove medium by aspirating and wash bones twice with 70% EtOH.
5. In sterile hood aspirate EtOH and wash bones twice with RPMI 1640 medium. Also sterilize scissors and forceps with EtOH.
6. Place cleaned bones into a Petri dish containing a drop of fresh DC-WM, large enough to wet all bones.
7. Hold the bones with curved forceps and use sharp scissors to snip off both large tips of bones. Put bone tips in a 6-mm dish containing 1–2 ml of medium.
8. Flush the bone marrow out of bone shafts using a 10-ml syringe and a 25-gauge needle.
9. Pipet bone marrow up and down until you have a single-cell suspension.
10. Place a cell strainer (BD Falcon #352350) in a 50-ml Falcon tube. Filter the cell suspension through the strainer to remove extra pieces of bone and connective tissue.
11. Using curved tip scissors, cut bone tips from **step 7** so that marrow is released. Then pipet into a single-cell suspension and pass through the same strainer.
12. Spin cells at 300*g* for 5 min.
13. Resuspend cells in 10 ml of DC-WM (if using ten mice). Add 10 ml of ice-cold RBC lysis buffer.
14. Incubate on ice for 5 min.
15. Fill up the tube with DC-WM. Centrifuge at 1,200 rpm for 5 min. Wash once with medium.

16. Resuspend cell pellet in 10 ml of DC-GM. Pass cell onto a new cell strainer to remove dead cell debris. Wash strainer with extra medium.
17. Count cells.
18. Dilute cell suspension in DC-GM to a cell density of 0.8×10^6 cells/ml. Transfer 5 ml of the cell suspension (4×10^6 cells) into each well of a 6-well plate and incubate at 37°C in a humidified atmosphere supplemented with 5% CO_2.
19. Replace medium every 2 days: remove most of the medium in each well by lifting the plate at 45° and gently aspirating; then gently add 5 ml of fresh pre-warmed DC-GM. Avoid swirling or agitating cells at each manipulation in order to prevent spontaneous maturation.
20. Maturation of BMDCs can be induced by adding 100 ng/ml LPS at day 5.

3.2. mRNA In Vitro Transcription

1. Linearize at least 20 μg of the plasmid DNA template with the recommended restriction enzyme.
2. Purify the linearized plasmid using the QIAquick PCR purification system, following the manufacturer's instruction. Alternatively, an EtOH precipitation step can be performed to purify DNA (*see* **Note 5**).
3. Perform the in vitro transcription reaction on 1 μg purified DNA template choosing the mMESSAGE mMACHINE system having the appropriate RNA polymerase. Follow the manufacturer's instruction. Typical RNA yields from one reaction are 20–30 μg for the T7 and the T3 kits and 15–25 μg for the SP6 kit. If more RNA is needed, the in vitro transcription reaction can be scaled up.
4. Purify the in vitro transcribed RNA with the RNeasy Mini system, following the manufacturer's instructions.
5. Check the integrity of the RNA fragment on a 1% denaturing agarose gel, and measure the OD_{260} with a spectrophotometer to determine RNA concentration.

3.3. mRNA Transfection of DCs

During the whole procedure it is very important to work under sterile and RNase-free conditions. Typically, BMDCs are transfected on day 5 in their immature stage. After careful washing, cells are RNA transfected, either by electroporation or by lipofection. Alternatively, RNA can be 'passively pulsed' to DCs in absence of any transfection reagent *(15)*.

3.3.1. Electroporation

1. Collect cells and wash them twice with ice-cold PBS. Generally $10–15 \times 10^6$ cells can be isolated out of one 6-well plate.
2. Resuspend cells in OptiMEM at a final cell density of 20×10^6 cells/ml.

3. Pre-incubate 200 µl of cell suspension (4 × 10^6 cells) in a 4-mm gap electroporation cuvette (Biorad) for 15 min on ice.
4. If an EGFP mRNA molecule is transfected, add 10–20 µg of in vitro transcribed mRNA (or siRNA, *see* **Note 6**) to the cell suspension and perform the electroporation with a Gene Pulser II apparatus (Biorad), applying a voltage of 300 V and a capacitance of 150 µF (measured pulse times: 5–10 ms). If a LUC mRNA molecule is transfected, add 2.5 µg mRNA to the cells, applying a voltage of 900 V and a capacitance of 50 µF (measured pulse times: 3–4 ms).
5. After electroporation, immediately resuspend cells in 4 ml fresh pre-warmed DC-GM at a final cell density of 10^6 cells/ml. Transfer 2 ml of the transfected cell suspension (2 × 10^6 cells) into 12-well plates and incubate at 37°C in a humidified atmosphere supplemented with 5% CO_2.
6. A maturation signal such as LPS can be added either just after electroporation or between 4 and 24 h after RNA transfection, depending on the experimental goals.

3.3.2. Lipofection

1. Collect cells and wash them twice with ice-cold PBS.
2. Resuspend 2 × 10^6 cells in 500 µl pre-warmed OptiMEM in a 2-ml test tube.
3. Mix 4 µg mRNA (or the synthetic double-stranded RNA poly I:C, *see* **Note 7**) diluted in 500 µl pre-warmed OptiMEM with 12 µl of the lipofection reagent TransFast at a lipid/RNA ratio of 3:1. Incubate the suspension 15 min at RT to allow mRNA/lipid complexes to form.
4. Add the 500 µl lipid/RNA mix to the 500 µl cell suspension and incubate 1 h at 37°C. Gently mix the suspension by inverting the tube 3–4 times during the incubation time.
5. After lipofection, wash cells twice with pre-warmed OptiMEM and resuspend cells in 2 ml fresh pre-warmed DC-GM at a final cell density of 10^6 cells/ml. Transfer cell suspension (2 × 10^6 cells) into 12-well plates and incubate at 37°C in a humidified atmosphere supplemented with 5% CO_2.
6. If needed, add a maturation signal.

3.4. Determination of Transfection Efficiency and Cell Viability of DCs

Transfection efficiency is generally determined following the expression of the reporter gene EGFP qualitatively by microscopy and quantitatively by flow cytometric (FCM) analysis. If the reporter gene LUC is transfected, expression can be measured quantitatively using a reporter assay system which measures luminescence, such as the Dual-Luciferase kit (Promega). Gene expression can be detected as early as 4-h post RNA transfection and it can last for 7 days *(16)*.

The procedure for FCM analysis of EGFP is as follows:

1. Wash cells with FSB.
2. Resuspend cell pellet in 200 μl FSB-fix.
3. Just before FCM analysis, add 10 μl of propidium iodide (10 μg/ml) to a final concentration of 0.5 μg/ml, to access cell viability. Alternatively, ethidium bromide can be used (*see* **Note 8**).
4. Perform FCM analysis by gating on cells (the DCs) exhibiting a large forward scatter (FSC) and side scatter (SSC) profile, in order to allow exclusion of dead cells. Positively transfected $EGFP^+$ cells are detected on FL-1 by 'green signals', whereas dead cells are detected on FL-2 by 'red signals'. Typically, about 80% of viable DCs show high-level EGFP expression after RNA electroporation, while electroporation-related cell mortality on total DC cultures should be around 10% *(13, 17, 18)*. After RNA lipofection 10–20% of DCs should show high-level EGFP expression, while lipofection-related cell mortality should be from 10 to 20% *(6, 7)*.

3.5. Immunophenotyping of DCs

The maturation status of BMDCs should be followed by FCM analysis, before and after RNA transfection, in the absence or presence of the maturation signal LPS. BMDCs should be analysed for the surface markers MHC class I, MHC class II, CD80, CD86, and CD40. FCM analysis should be performed by gating on the CD11c cells (mostly DCs), which under optimal conditions represent 80–90% of the total cell population. mRNA electroporation by itself should not induce DC maturation, while after LPS stimulation mRNA-electroporated DCs should mature like non-transfected DCs *(13, 17, 18)*. In contrast, mRNA lipofection has been reported to induce DC maturation both in murine *(19, 20)* and human *(9, 21, 22)* DCs.

4. Notes

1. Incorporation of the 5′ and 3′ untranslated regions (UTRs) of β-globin mRNA greatly stabilizes RNA molecules transfected into cells and leads to over a 1,000-fold increase in reporter gene expression in transfected cells *(23)*. Lengthening the polyA-tail (e.g. 64 × A) in the mRNA transcript also increases expression of GFP in target cells *(6, 24)*. The impact of different structural modifications of RNA on protein expression in RNA-transfected DCs has been recently reported *(25)*. Holtkamp and colleagues demonstrated that the elements most important for enhancing RNA stability and translational

efficiency are located 3′ of the coding region as was observed for two sequential β-globin 3′ UTR followed by an unmasked poly(A) tail of 120 nucleotides.

2. The 741-bp BamH1–NotI fragment containing the GFP coding region was isolated from pEGFP-N1 (Clontech). This fragment was cloned into the BamH1 and Nar1 sites of pGEM4Z (Promega) along with oligonucleotides containing a Not1 half-site, the pGEM4Z polylinker sequence from BamH1 to EcoRI, 64 A-T bp, a SpeI site, and a Nar1 half-site to create pGEM4Z/GFP/A64. To generate a GFP chimeric protein, the gene of interest can be sub-cloned N-terminal of GFP using the restriction site HindIII, which is located downstream of the T7 RNA polymerase promoter.
3. In our laboratory the Biorad electroporation system has been also successfully used for RNA transfection of human monocyte-derived DCs. However, the best transfection efficiencies for human DCs have been obtained using the Amaxa Nucleofector system in combination with RNA (electroporation program U-002).
4. Few comparative studies have been published for RNA lipofection of DCs, but Strobel et al. *(7)* reported that the strongest expression of a reporter gene mRNA was achieved with the liposomal reagent TransFast (20% GFP^+ cells). Similar results have been reported for the liposomal reagent DMRIE-C *(6)*. Experience with DNA lipofection has taught us that the efficiency of gene transfer is greatly influenced by the choice of the lipid, the concentration versus toxicity of the complexes, and the cell type one desires to transfect *(24)*.
5. EtOH precipitation procedure to purify DNA:
   - Add 0.1 × vol 3 M NaCl and 3 × vol 100% EtOH to the 1 × vol DNA solution
   - Incubate the resulting mix at –20°C for 20 min
   - Centrifuge the mix (30 min, 4°C, 16,000*g*)
   - Wash the DNA pellet with ice-cold 70% EtOH
   - Centrifuge the washed DNA pellet (5 min, 4°C, 14 krpm)
   - Dry the pellet for 20 min
   - Resuspend the DNA pellet in 10 μl TE
6. The Gene Pulser II apparatus (Biorad) can also be used to transfect siRNA molecules into murine BMDCs, to achieve RNAi-mediated gene silencing. The siRNA electroporation should be performed using 4–5 μg of siRNA and a voltage of 900 V and a capacitance of 50 μF.
7. Lipofection of synthetic double-stranded RNA (poly I:C) has been successfully applied to switch non-plasmacytoid dendritic cells into high interferon producers *(26)*. This response is

partially dependent on the cytosolic dsRNA-binding enzyme protein kinase R (PKR).

8. Just before FCM analysis, add ethidium bromide to the fixed cells to a final concentration of 10 μg/ml, to access cell viability.

Acknowledgements

This work is supported by grants to PP from CNRS-INSERM, the Ministère de la Recherche et de la Technologie (ACI), La Ligue Nationale Contre le Cancer, and the Human Frontier of Science Program (HSFP). MC is supported by the Swiss National Science Foundation (SNF) and EKS is supported by the HSFP. The authors would like to thank Dr. Peter Ponsaerts (University of Antwerp, Belgium) for having provided the plasmid *pSP64/GFP*, Professor Eli Gilboa (Duke University, USA) for the plasmid *pGEM4Z/GFP/A64*, and Professor Matthias Hentze (EMBL, Heidelberg, Germany) for the plasmid *pT3LUC(pA)*.

References

1. Zhou Y, Bosch ML, Salgaller ML (2002). Current methods for loading dendritic cells with tumor antigen for the induction of antitumor immunity. *J Immunother*;25(4):289–303.
2. Lundqvist A, Noffz G, Pavlenko M, et al. (2002). Nonviral and viral gene transfer into different subsets of human dendritic cells yield comparable efficiency of transfection. *J Immunother*;25(6):445–51.
3. Jenne L, Schuler G, Steinkasserer A (2001). Viral vectors for dendritic cell-based immunotherapy. *Trends Immunol*;22(2):102–7.
4. Monahan SJ, Salgaller ML (1999). Viral vectors for gene transfer into antigen presenting cells. *Curr Opin Mol Ther*;1(5):558–64.
5. Van Tendeloo VF, Snoeck HW, Lardon F, et al. (1998). Nonviral transfection of distinct types of human dendritic cells: high-efficiency gene transfer by electroporation into hematopoietic progenitor – but not monocyte-derived dendritic cells. *Gene Ther*;5(5):700–7.
6. Van Tendeloo VF, Van Broeckhoven C, Berneman ZN (2001). Gene-based cancer vaccines: an ex vivo approach. *Leukemia*;15(4):545–58.
7. Strobel I, Berchtold S, Gotze A, Schulze U, Schuler G, Steinkasserer A (2000). Human dendritic cells transfected with either RNA or DNA encoding influenza matrix protein M1 differ in their ability to stimulate cytotoxic T lymphocytes. *Gene Ther*;7(23):2028–35.
8. Zabner J, Fasbender AJ, Moninger T, Poellinger KA, Welsh MJ (1995). Cellular and molecular barriers to gene transfer by a cationic lipid. *J Biol Chem*;270(32):18997–9007.
9. Weissman D, Ni H, Scales D, et al. (2000). HIV gag mRNA transfection of dendritic cells (DC) delivers encoded antigen to MHC class I and II molecules, causes DC maturation, and induces a potent human in vitro primary immune response. *J Immunol*;165(8):4710–7.
10. Ceppi M, de Bruin MG, Seuberlich T, et al. (2005). Identification of classical swine fever virus protein E2 as a target for cytotoxic T cells by using mRNA-transfected antigen-presenting cells. *J Gen Virol*;86(Pt 9):2525–34.
11. Lelouard H, Gatti E, Cappello F, Gresser O, Camosseto V, Pierre P (2002). Transient aggregation of ubiquitinated proteins during dendritic cell maturation. *Nature*;417(6885):177–82.
12. Nair SK, Boczkowski D, Morse M, Cumming RI, Lyerly HK, Gilboa E (1998). Induction of primary carcinoembryonic antigen (CEA)-specific cytotoxic T lymphocytes in vitro using human dendritic cells transfected with RNA. *Nat Biotechnol*;16(4):364–9.

13. Van Tendeloo VF, Ponsaerts P, Lardon F, et al. (2001). Highly efficient gene delivery by mRNA electroporation in human hematopoietic cells: superiority to lipofection and passive pulsing of mRNA and to electroporation of plasmid cDNA for tumor antigen loading of dendritic cells. *Blood*;98(1): 49–56.
14. Iizuka N, Najita L, Franzusoff A, Sarnow P (1994). Cap-dependent and cap-independent translation by internal initiation of mRNAs in cell extracts prepared from *Saccharomyces cerevisiae*. *Mol Cell Biol*;14(11):7322–30.
15. Boczkowski D, Nair SK, Snyder D, Gilboa E (1996). Dendritic cells pulsed with RNA are potent antigen-presenting cells in vitro and in vivo. *J Exp Med*;184(2):465–72.
16. Ponsaerts P, Van Tendeloo VF, Berneman ZN (2003). Cancer immunotherapy using RNA-loaded dendritic cells. *Clin Exp Immunol*;134(3):378–84.
17. Van Meirvenne S, Straetman L, Heirman C, et al. (2002). Efficient genetic modification of murine dendritic cells by electroporation with mRNA. *Cancer Gene Ther*;9(9): 787–97.
18. Ceppi M, Ruggli N, Tache V, Gerber H, McCullough KC, Summerfield A (2005). Double-stranded secondary structures on mRNA induce type I interferon (IFN alpha/beta) production and maturation of mRNA-transfected monocyte-derived dendritic cells. *J Gene Med*;7(4):452–65.
19. Bacci A, Montagnoli C, Perruccio K, et al. (2002). Dendritic cells pulsed with fungal RNA induce protective immunity to *Candida albicans* in hematopoietic transplantation. *J Immunol*;168(6):2904–13.
20. Bozza S, Perruccio K, Montagnoli C, et al. (2003). A dendritic cell vaccine against invasive aspergillosis in allogeneic hematopoietic transplantation. *Blood*;102(10):3807–14.
21. Heiser A, Coleman D, Dannull J, et al. (2002). Autologous dendritic cells transfected with prostate-specific antigen RNA stimulate CTL responses against metastatic prostate tumors. *J Clin Invest*;109(3):409–17.
22. Heiser A, Maurice MA, Yancey DR, Coleman DM, Dahm P, Vieweg J (2001). Human dendritic cells transfected with renal tumor RNA stimulate polyclonal T-cell responses against antigens expressed by primary and metastatic tumors. *Cancer Res*;61(8):3388–93.
23. Malone RW, Felgner PL, Verma IM (1989). Cationic liposome-mediated RNA transfection. *Proc Natl Acad Sci U S A*;86(16):6077–81.
24. Mitchell DA, Nair SK (2000). RNA-transfected dendritic cells in cancer immunotherapy. *J Clin Invest*;106(9):1065–9.
25. Holtkamp S, Kreiter S, Selmi A, et al. (2006). Modification of antigen-encoding RNA increa-ses stability, translational efficacy, and T-cell stimulatory capacity of dendritic cells. *Blood*;108(13):4009–17.
26. Diebold SS, Montoya M, Unger H, et al. (2003). Viral infection switches non-plasmacytoid dendritic cells into high interferon producers. *Nature*; 424(6946):324–8.
27. Boczkowski D, Nair SK, Nam JH, Lyerly HK, Gilboa E (2000). Induction of tumor immunity and cytotoxic T lymphocyte responses using dendritic cells transfected with messenger RNA amplified from tumor cells. *Cancer Res* 60:1028–34.
28. Thornburg C, Boczkowski D, Gilboa E, Nair SK (2000). Induction of cytotoxic T lymphocytes with dendritic cells transfected with human papillomavirus E6 and E7 RNA: implications for cervical cancer immunotherapy. *J Immunother* 23:412–8.
29. Lelouard H, Schmidt EK, Camosseto V, Clavarino G, Ceppi M, Hsu HT, Pierre P (2007). Regulation of translation is required for dendritic cell function and survival during activation. *J Cell Biol* 179(7):1427–39.

Chapter 11

Recording Phagosome Maturation Through the Real-Time, Spectrofluorometric Measurement of Hydrolytic Activities

Robin M. Yates, Albin Hermetter, and David G. Russell

Summary

The efficient degradation of internalized particulate matter is a principal objective of the macrophage's phagosome. Assessment of the true hydrolytic capacity within the phagosomal lumen is often difficult as it is subject to many factors beyond recruitment of lysosomal hydrolases. Here we outline three assays that allow quantitative measurements of serine-cysteine protease, triglyceride lipase, and β-galactosidase activities within the phagosomes of macrophages, in real time. The assays utilize ratio fluorometry between particle-associated fluorogenic substrates and calibration fluorochromes to yield internally controlled values that record rates of substrate hydrolysis. The methods described utilize a spectrofluorometer for fluorometric measurements from a population of macrophages. These assays, however, can be expanded to high-throughput or single cell formats. In addition, this approach can be applied to measure a wide variety of phagosomal hydrolytic properties with the design of suitable fluorogenic substrates.

Key words: Phagosome, Lysosome, Phagocytosis, Macrophage, Hydrolase, Lipase, Proteolysis, Lumen.

1. Introduction

The ability of macrophages to efficiently degrade phagocytosed particles is essential to their function as mediators of homeostasis and immunity. While recruitment of individual hydrolases to the phagosome has been documented extensively both biochemically and by immunofluorescence *(1–3)*, the true hydrolytic status of the intralumenal milieu of the phagosome is only now being assessed *(4)*. Delivery of degradative enzymes to the phagosome is a necessary first step for the development of hydrolytic activities within the organelle, but it is the complex interplay with the

Neil E. Reiner (ed.), *Macrophages and Dendritic Cells,* Methods in Molecular Biology, vol. 531

DOI: 10.1007/978-1-59745-396-7_11

physiology of the phagosome that determines the actual hydrolytic activity within. Factors such as pH, ion concentrations, redox potential, activation of proenzymes, and the regulation by cofactors all impact on intraphagosomal hydrolytic activities *(4)*. It is this complexity that precludes an accurate assessment of true phagosomal enzymatic activities based solely on the localization, or even concentration, of recruited hydrolases. In this chapter, approaches that quantify specific hydrolytic activities within the phagosome in real time, in live macrophages, are detailed.

The assays described measure rates of hydrolase activities in real time, exploiting ratio fluorometry of phagocytosed, experimental particles complexed with a fluorogenic substrate and a calibration fluor. Three hydrolytic assays are described that record the degradation of fluorogenic substrates specific for phagosomal cysteine-serine proteases, triglyceride lipases, and β-galactosidases. This approach should not be regarded as limited to the substrates described. Fluorogenic substrates that are pH insensitive and which can be coupled to an experimental particle could readily be used to measure a specific hydrolytic activity of interest. Thus, with the design of suitable substrates, this approach could be used to measure the activities of nucleases, phosphatases, disulfide reductases, and specific cathepsins, to name only a few.

The assays described are population based in design that follow the synchronous uptake of experimental particles by a monolayer of macrophages. This is a convenient and efficient approach as it returns statistically robust data with excellent temporal resolution. In addition, the influence of operator bias is virtually eliminated as minimal qualitative assessment is required. Furthermore, although not documented here, these methodologies could be applied to confocal-based technologies to permit recording of single cell or single phagosome measurements, and thus could assess the variation between individual phagosomes *(5)*. This chapter is intended as a companion to a chapter entitled "Real-Time Spectrofluorometric Assays for the Lumenal Environment of the Maturing Phagosome" published in Humana Press Methods in Molecular Biology series volume 445.

2. Materials

2.1. Cells, Reagents, and Buffers

1. Macrophages: Both bone-marrow-derived murine macrophages (BMMØ) and macrophage-like cell lines have been used (*see* **Note 1**). BMMØs are derived from the bone marrow extracted from the femurs, tibias, and iliums of euthanized mice and maintained in Dulbecco's modified Eagle's medium (DMEM) supplemented with 10% fetal bovine serum (FBS),

5% horse serum, 2 mM L-glutamine, 1 mM sodium pyruvate, and 20% L-cell conditioned media (BMMØ media). RAW 264.7 cells (available from the American Type Culture Collection, Rockville, MD, USA) are maintained in DMEM supplemented with 10% FBS and 1.5 g/ml sodium bicarbonate.

2. Cover slips: Clean 0.13 × 12.5 × 25 mm cover glass (*see* **Note 2**). Sterilize by autoclave.
3. Binding buffer: Tissue-culture-tested PBS pH 7.0 adjusted to contain 1 mM $CaCl_2$, 2.7 mM KCl, 0.5 mM $MgCl_2$, 5 mM dextrose, 10 mM HEPES, and 5% FBS.
4. Cuvette buffer: Tissue-culture-tested PBS pH 7.2 adjusted to contain 1 mM $CaCl_2$, 2.7 mM KCl, 0.5 mM $MgCl_2$, 5 mM dextrose, 10 mM HEPES, and 0.1% calf skin gelatin (*see* **Note 3**).
5. Binding dish: A microbiological Petri dish containing a square piece of parafilm adhered to the lower plate surrounded by a damp Kimwipe® tissue.
6. 0.4% Trypan blue.
7. 3.0 μm Carboxylate-modified silica particles (Si–COOH) 5% suspension (*see* **Note 4**).
8. Streptavidin. Store as desiccate at –20°C.
9. Human IgG. Store as desiccate at 4°C.
10. Cyanamide. Store as desiccate at 4°C.
11. Coupling buffer: 0.1 M sodium borate in ddH_2O. Adjust pH to 8.0 with 10 M NaOH. Filter sterilize through 0.22-μm filter.
12. Quenching buffer: 250 mM glycine in PBS pH 7.2. Filter sterilize through 0.22-μm filter.
13. Sodium azide 2% aqueous solution. Very toxic.
14. Alexa Fluor 594® carboxylic acid, succinimidyl ester (mixed isomers) (Alexa594-SE) (Molecular Probes, Eugene, OR, USA). Dissolve in high-quality anhydrous dimethylsulfoxide (DMSO) at 5 mg/ml before use. Stock solutions can be aliquoted and stored at –20°C. Protect from light and moisture.
15. Biotinylated cysteine-serine protease substrate: (Biotin-LC-Phe-Arg)$_2$-Rhodamine 110. Dissolve in high-quality anhydrous dimethylsulfoxide (DMSO) at 1 mg/ml before use. Stock solutions can be aliquoted and stored at –20°C. Protect from light and moisture.
16. Nucleosil 120-3 C_{18} 3 μm silica core reverse-phase HPLC matrix. 10 mg/ml suspension in chloroform.
17. Triglyceride lipase substrate: 1-trinitrophenyl-amino-dodecanoyl-2-pyrenedecanoyl-3-*O*-hexadecyl-sn-glycerol (donated by Albin Hermetter, Graz University of Technology, Graz, Austria).

Dissolve in 2:1 choloroform:methanol at 1 mg/ml and store at –20°C under nitrogen. Protect from light and moisture.

18. 1-Palmitoyl-2oleoyl-sn-glycero-3-phospho-rac-(1-glycerol). Dissolve in 2:1 choloroform:methanol at 10 mg/ml and store at –20°C under nitrogen.
19. Octadecyl rhodamine B chloride. Dissolve in methanol at 1 mg/ml and store at –20°C under nitrogen.
20. 1,2-Dipalmitoyl-sn-glycero-3-phosphoethanolamine-*N*-(Cap Biotinyl). Dissolve in 2:1 choloroform:methanol at 1 mg/ml and store at –20°C under nitrogen.
21. Cholesterol. Dissolve in 2:1 choloroform:methanol at 1 mg/ml and store at –20°C under nitrogen.
22. Mouse monoclonal (clone BN-34) antibiotin IgG as ascite fluid.
23. β-Galactosidase substrate: 5-dodecanoylaminofluorescein di-β-D-galactopyranoside (C_{12}FDG). Dissolve in 2:1 choloroform:methanol at 10 mg/ml and store at –20°C under nitrogen. Protect from light and moisture.

2.2. Instruments

1. Temperature-controlled spectrofluorometer with variable excitation and emission monochromators. The authors use the QMSE4 model spectrofluorometer from Photon Technologies International (Lawrenceville, NJ, USA) equipped with a thermostat-controlled four chambered turret for simultaneous measurement of four experimental variables. The QMSE4 is interfaced with a PC compatible computer and is managed by Felix32 software (Photon Technologies International, Lawrenceville, NJ, USA).
2. Quartz 10 × 10 × 45 mm cuvettes.
3. Fluorescent microscope with standard FITC and Texas Red filter sets. The authors use the Zeiss Axioskop 2 plus (Carl Zeiss MicroImaging Inc., Thornwood, NY, USA).

3. Methods

3.1. Macrophage Monolayer Preparation and Handling

1. Fully differentiated BMMØ monolayers are grown to confluency in untreated Petri dishes. Growth media is removed and replaced with cold PBS pH 7.2 (without Ca^{2+} and Mg^{2+}), and incubated at 4°C for 10 min to facilitate BMMØ detachment from the plastic. BMMØs are then gently dislodged with a rubber policeman and centrifuged at 230 × *g* at 4°C for 10 min.
2. Sterile, clean 12.5 × 25 mm cover slips are placed in a sterile Petri dish using fine-point forceps that have been dipped in 70% ethanol and flamed (*see* **Note 5**).

3. BMMØs are gently resuspended in 1 ml BMMØ media, counted using a hemocytometer, and diluted appropriately in BMMØ media to achieve ~1.25 × 10^6 macrophages/ml.
4. Ten milliliters of BMMØ suspension is added to the Petri dish and incubated at 37°C for 24 h to allow a monolayer to establish on the cover slips. Care should be exercised to prevent excessive movement of the cover slips in the Petri dish. The BMMØ monolayers covered on cover slips (subsequently referred to as monolayers) are then ready for fluorometric analysis.

3.2. Spectrofluorometer Setup and Operation

1. The spectrofluorometer should be set up according to manufacturer's directions such that optimal measurements can be taken using the desired wavelengths (*see* **Note 6**).
2. Clean quartz cuvettes containing cuvette buffer are inserted into a thermostat-controlled sample holder and warmed to 37°C prior to the loading of the monolayers (*see* **Note 7**).
3. Using fine-point forceps, a monolayer-covered cover slip is grasped at one end (*see* **Note 8**) and dipped 10 times into a sterile 50-ml tube containing binding buffer to remove BMMØ growth media and loosely adhered cells. The cover slip is then placed in the cuvette with a vertical orientation (length of the cover slip parallel to the long axis of the cuvette), on the diagonal (width of the cover slip at 45° to the short axes of the cuvette) and with the cellular side facing the emission slit, as shown in **Fig. 1**.

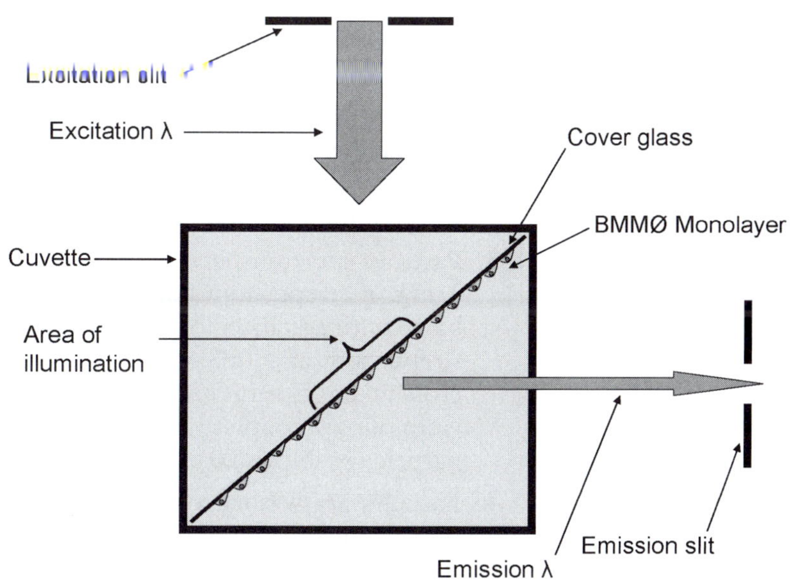

Fig. 1. Orientation of the BMMØ monolayer in the spectrofluorometer. Cover glass is oriented to achieve a 45° incidence with the excitation beam (excitation λ) and with the cells facing the emission slit.

4. At this point, sufficient background measurements of each monolayer are recorded for the wavelengths required.
5. At the conclusion of the background determination, the cover slips are carefully removed from the cuvettes using forceps and placed with the cellular side up, on the parafilm within the binding dish.
6. Eighty-five microliters of a suspension of the appropriate experimental particles is carefully laid over each monolayer. The meniscus should be maintained over the cover slip at room temperature for 3 min (*see* **Note 9**).
7. The cover slips are once again dipped 10 times in binding buffer to remove unbound particles and are placed in the cuvettes with the same orientation.
8. The appropriate successive fluorescent measurements are recorded, alternating between each sample.
9. At the conclusion of the assay, the cover slips are removed by forceps and placed cellular side down onto 30 μl of 0.4% trypan blue on a glass slide and examined with bright-field and fluorescence microscopy. Careful attention should be paid to macrophage viability, optimal bead to BMMØ ratio, and the presence of extracellular experimental particles. This is an extremely important control and must be completed with every sample. Data should be disregarded should there be a decrease in macrophage viability, overloaded macrophages, or the presence of any extracellular particles.

3.3. Kinetic Analysis of Intraphagosomal Cysteine-Serine Protease Activity

3.3.1. Preparation of IgG/Streptavidin-Coupled Particles

1. Fifty micrograms of carboxylate-modified silica particles is washed three times in 1 ml of PBS by brief vortexing and centrifugation in a tabletop microfuge at 2,000 × *g* for 60 s.
2. Particles are resuspended in PBS (pH 7.2) with 25 mg/ml of the heterobifunctional crosslinker cyanamide (freshly made) and incubated at room temperature with agitation for 15 min. Excess cyanamide is removed by washing the particles twice with coupling buffer.
3. Particles are resuspended in 500 μl of coupling buffer with 1 mg of streptavidin and 250 μg of human IgG, and incubated with agitation for 12 h. This step covalently attaches the streptavidin and IgG to the particles through the cyanamide crosslinker. The IgG serves as an opsonin, while the streptavidin allows coupling of the biotinylated substrate onto the particle (*see* **Note 10**).
4. Particles are washed twice with quenching buffer to quench unreacted cyanamide and twice with coupling buffer to remove soluble amine groups.
5. The particles are resuspended in 1 ml of coupling buffer, and 10 μl of the 5 mg/ml stock of the calibration fluor (Alexa Fluor 594®-SE) in DMSO is added (*see* **Note 11**). Incubation at room

temperature with agitation for 1 h allows the particle-bound albumin to be sufficiently labeled with the amine-reactive fluor.

6. The now-fluorescent particles are washed three times with quenching buffer and finally resuspended in 1 ml PBS (*see* **Note 12**). Ten microliters of a 2% solution of the preservative sodium azide can be added for storage at 4°C.

3.3.2. Fluorometric Measurement of Phagosomal Cysteine/Serine Protease Activity

1. 50 μl of IgG/streptavidin particles is washed twice with 500 μl sterile PBS to remove traces of sodium azide and resuspended in 80 μl of PBS.
2. 20 μl of the 1 mg/ml solution of the substrate (Biotin-LC-Phe-Arg)$_2$-Rhodamine 110 in DMSO is added to the washed beads and incubated in the dark, on ice, for 1 h with occasional gentle vortexing.
3. The now-substrate-loaded particles are washed twice with 500 μl sterile PBS to remove unbound substrate and resuspended in an appropriate volume of binding buffer to achieve ~1×10^7 beads/ml (*see* **Note 13**).
4. After 594|620 nm and 490|515 nm (excitation λ|emission λ) background measurements are recorded for BMMØ monolayers alone, 85 μl of the diluted particle suspension is laid onto the monolayers in the binding dish and incubated at room temperature for 3 min (as per **Subheading 3.2**).
5. Unbound particles are washed from the monolayers by dipping in binding buffer and the coverslips are returned to the spectrofluorometer.
6. Both calibration and substrate fluorescent intensities are measured. The fluorescence of the calibration fluor Alexa Fluor 594® (emission at 620 nm with excitation at 594 nm) should remain constant throughout the assay (*see* **Note 14**). The rhodamine 110 fluorescence (emission at 515 nm with excitation at 490 nm) will increase as it is dequenched with sequential cleavage of the amine-linked peptides by cysteine or serine proteases, particularly cathepsin L *(6)*. Typically, an integration time of 1 s per data point is optimal (*see* **Note 15**). Data are collected for at least 60 min or until exhaustion of the substrate (*see* **Note 16**). At the conclusion of the assay, monolayers are examined via microscopy with trypan blue (as per **Subheading 3.2**).
7. Data are exported into a standard spreadsheet application such as Microsoft Excel®.
8. The appropriate background values are deducted (if not already deducted by the acquisition software) and the ratio S_{RT}/C (where S_{RT} is the substrate fluorescence in real time and C is the calibration fluorescence) is plotted against time (**Fig. 2**).

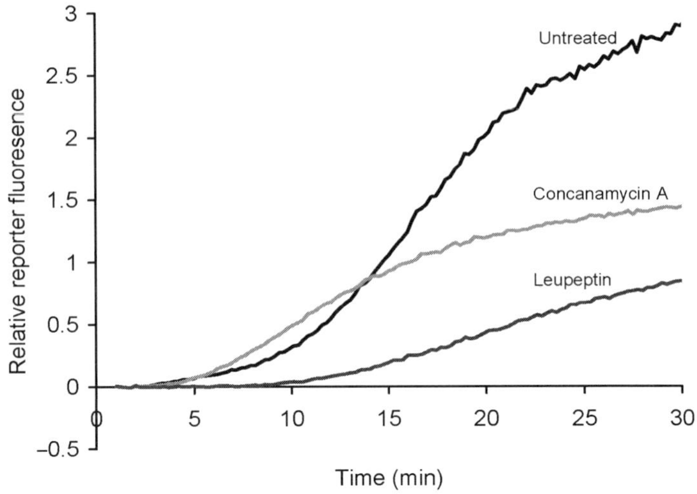

Fig. 2. Phagosomal serine-cysteine protease activity in BMMØs. Serine-cysteine protease activity can be diminished with the serine-cysteine protease inhibitor leupeptin (100 μg/ml) and the V-ATPase inhibitor concanamycin A (100 nm).

9. Gradients of portions of the profiles will give relative values of the cysteine and serine protease activities of the phagosomal population over that period (*see* **Note 17**).

3.4. Kinetic Analysis of Intraphagosomal Triglyceride Lipase Activity

3.4.1. Preparation of Lipase Lipid Monolayer Particles

1. Two hundred microliters of the 10 mg/ml suspension of the Nucleosil 120-3 C_{18} reverse-phase HPLC matrix in chloroform is added to a clean glass test tube along with the following lipids dissolved in 2:1 chloroform:methanol (*see* **Note 18**): 25 μl of the substrate 1-trinitrophenyl-amino-dodecanoyl-2-pyrenedecanoyl-3-*O*-hexadecyl-sn-glycerol (1 mg/ml); 5 μl of the calibration fluor octadecyl rhodamine B chloride (1 mg/ml); 30 μl of the phospholipid 1-palmitoyl-2oleoyl-sn-glycero-3-phospho-rac-(1-glycerol); 5 μl of the biotinylated phospholipid 1,2-dipalmitoyl-sn-glycero-3-phosphoethanolamine-*N*-(CapBiotinyl)(1mg/ml); 5 μl of cholesterol (10 mg/ml) (*see* **Note 19**).
2. The mixture is briefly sonicated in a bath sonicator at 40°C and then dried under nitrogen (*see* **Note 20**).
3. The test tube is transferred to the bath sonicator at 40°C and 500 μl of sterile PBS is added to the tube during sonication. This facilitates the arrangement of the amphipathic lipids to surround the hydrophobic C_{18}-coupled particles, allowing the particles to be miscible in the PBS. The mixture is sonicated until a homogenous suspension is achieved (*see* **Note 21**).
4. The suspension is cooled immediately by placing the test tube on ice. To avoid disruption of the lipid monolayer on the surface of the particles, which results in clumping of the beads,

the suspension must be kept ice cold during subsequent manipulation and not be subjected to excessive shearing or centrifugal forces.

5. Once cooled, the suspension is transferred to 1.5-ml polypropylene tubes and the lipid particles are washed twice with 500 μl ice-cold PBS using gentle centrifugation at 100 × *g* for no more than 30 s.
6. Lipid particles are resuspended in 100 μl PBS to which 5 μl of antibiotin IgG-containing mouse ascite fluid is added. Incubation on ice for 30 min with occasional gentle agitation is sufficient to permit IgG-opsonization of the particles.
7. The opsonized lipid particles are gently washed twice with 500 μl ice-cold PBS to remove excess IgG and finally suspended in 500 μl of PBS (*see* **Note 12**). The particles are stable for 24 h if kept on ice in the dark.

3.4.2. Fluorometric Measurement of Phagosomal Triglyceride Lipase Activity

1. The lipid-coated particles are diluted in an appropriate volume of binding buffer to achieve ~ 1 × 10^7 beads/ml (*see* **Note 13**).
2. After 555|610 nm and 342|400 nm (excitation λ|emission λ) background measurements are recorded for BMMØ monolayers alone, 85 μl of the diluted particle suspension is laid onto the monolayers in the binding dish and incubated at room temperature for 3 min (as per **Subheading 3.2**).
3. Unbound particles are washed from the monolayers by dipping in binding buffer and returned to the spectrofluorometer.
4. Both calibration and substrate fluorescent intensities are measured. The fluorescence of the calibration fluor octadecyl rhodamine B chloride (emission at 610 nm with excitation at 555 nm) should remain constant throughout the assay (*see* **Note 14**). The substrate fluorescence (emission at 400 nm with excitation at 342 nm) will increase with progressive esterolysis of the triglyceride analog as it liberates the fluorescent pyrenedecanoic acid and the quenching trinitrophenylamino acyl residues from the glycerol backbone *(7)*. Typically, an integration time of 1 s per data point is optimal (*see* **Note 15**). Data are collected for at least 60 min or until exhaustion of the substrate. At the conclusion of the assay, monolayers are examined via microscopy with trypan blue (as per **Subheading 3.2**).
5. Data are exported into a standard spreadsheet application such as Microsoft Excel®.
6. The appropriate background values are deducted (if not already deducted by the acquisition software) and the ratio S_{RT}/C (where S_{RT} is the substrate fluorescence in real time and C is the calibration fluorescence) is plotted against time (**Fig. 3**).

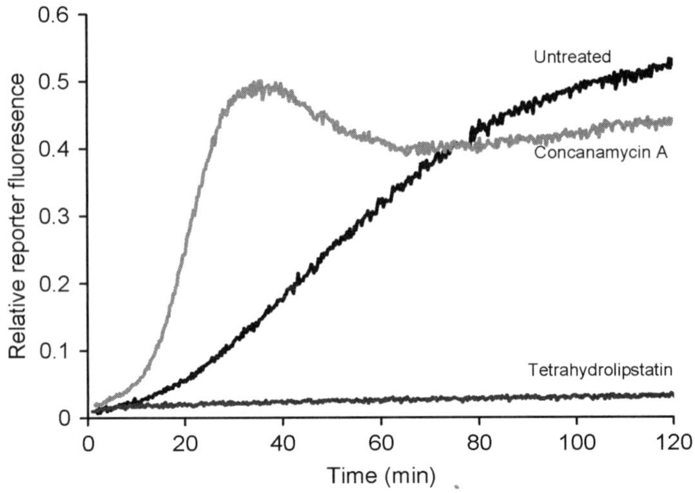

Fig. 3. Phagosomal triglyceride lipase activity in BMMØs. Lipase activity can be diminished with the specific lipase inhibitor tetrahydrolipstatin (50 μg/ml) and is increased in the early phagosome by the V-ATPase inhibitor concanamycin A (100 nm).

7. Gradients of portions of the profiles will give relative values of the triglyceride lipase activity of the phagosomal population over that period (*see* **Note 17**).

3.5. Kinetic Analysis of Intraphagosomal β-Galactosidase Activity

3.5.1. Preparation of β-Galactosidase Lipid Monolayer Particles

1. The lipid monolayer particle is used as the carrier for the β-galactosidase substrate and is essentially prepared as described for the lipase lipid monolayer particles in **Subheading 3.4.1**. However, the lipid composition of the particles is modified to allow for a greater proportion of the β-galactosidase substrate. To 200 μl of the 10 mg/ml suspension of the Nucleosil 120-3 C_{18} reverse-phase HPLC matrix in chloroform the following lipids are added: 10 μl of the substrate 5-dodecanoylaminofluorescein-di-β-D-galactopyranoside (C_{12}FDG) (10 mg/ml); 5 μl of the calibration fluor octadecyl rhodamine B chloride (1 mg/ml); 20 μl of the phospholipid 1-palmitoyl-2oleoyl-sn-glycero-3-phospho-rac-(1-glycerol); 5 μl of the biotinylated phospholipid 1,2-dipalmitoyl-sn-glycero-3-phosphoethanolamine-*N*-(Cap Biotinyl) (1 mg/ml); 5 μl of cholesterol (10 mg/ml) (*see* **Note 19**).
2. The mixture is dried and resuspended in PBS, and particles washed, and IgG opsonized as described in **Subheading 3.4.1**.

3.5.2. Fluorometric Measurement of Phagosomal β-Galactosidase Activity

1. The lipid particles are diluted in an appropriate volume of binding buffer to achieve ~1 × 10^7 beads/ml (*see* **Note 13**).
2. After 555|610 nm and 488|520 nm (excitation λ|emission λ) background measurements are recorded for BMMØ monolayers alone, 85 μl of the diluted particle suspension is laid

onto the monolayers in the binding dish and incubated at room temperature for 3 min (as per **Subheading 3.2**).

3. Unbound particles are washed from the monolayers by dipping in binding buffer and returned to the spectrofluorometer.
4. Both calibration and substrate fluorescent intensities are measured. The fluorescence of the calibration of fluor octadecyl rhodamine B chloride (emission at 610 nm with excitation at 555 nm) should remain constant throughout the assay (*see* **Note 14**). The fluorescent intensity of the fluorescein-based substrate (emission at 515 nm with excitation at 490 nm) will increase as it is dequenched with sequential cleavage of the two galactopyranosides (*see* **Note 22**). Typically, an integration time of 1 s per data point is optimal (*see* **Note 15**). Data are collected for at least 90 min or until exhaustion of the substrate. At the conclusion of the assay, monolayers are examined via microscopy with trypan blue (as per **Subheading 3.2**).
5. Data are exported into a standard spreadsheet application such as Microsoft Excel®.
6. The appropriate background values are deducted (if not already deducted by the acquisition software) and the ratio S_{RT}/C (where S_{RT} is the substrate fluorescence in real time and C is the calibration fluorescence) is plotted against time (**Fig. 4**).
7. Gradients of portions of the profiles will give relative values of the β-galactosidase activity of the phagosomal population over that period (*see* **Note 17**).

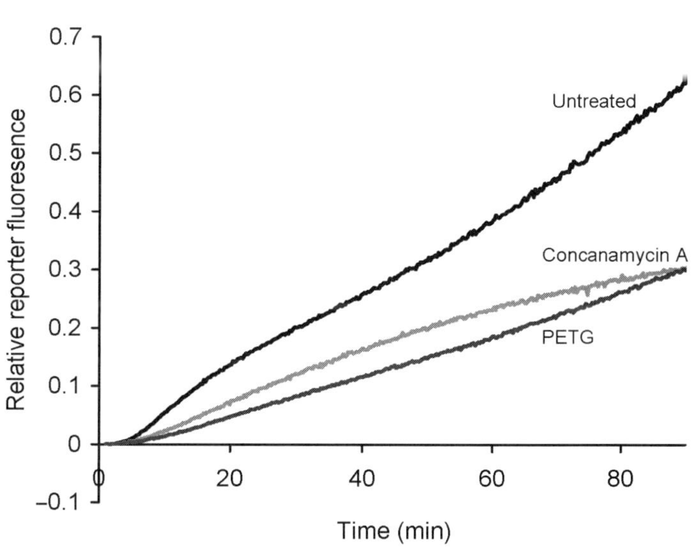

Fig. 4. Phagosomal β-galactosidase activity in BMMØs. β-Galactosidase activity can be diminished with the competitive inhibitor 2-phenylethyl-β-D-thiogalactoside (PETG) (200 μg/ml) and the V-ATPase inhibitor concanamycin A (100 nm).

4. Notes

1. Primary BMMØs are generally preferred for their enhanced phagocytic proficiency and adhesion.
2. 0.13 × 12.5 × 25 mm cover glass is not commercially available. Cover glass can be custom ordered from ProSciTech (Thuringowa, Qld, Australia). Alternatively, 25 × 25 mm cover glass is available from Fisher Scientific (Pittsburgh, PA, USA) and can be cut into half by diamond pencil in house.
3. FBS is substituted for gelatin for spectrofluorometric assays as it has low autofluorescence with excitation wavelengths above 450 nm. If assays are expected to take greater than 6 h, FBS is preferred for sustained macrophage viability.
4. The authors prefer the 3.0-μm –COOH-modified silica particles due to their ease of handling and low autofluorescence; however, polystyrene particles and particles of smaller size can be used successfully. Generally, macrophage-like cell lines do not efficiently phagocytose particles with diameters over 2.0 μm. Therefore particles >2.0 μm are not advised for those cell types.
5. Arrange cover slips so as not to overlap, taking care not to overcrowd them in the Petri dish as cover slips can move after monolayers have been established and damage to BMMØs can occur. Alternatively, cover slips can be separated from each other using partitioned Petri dishes or 6-well plates.
6. Some general considerations are: the focusing of illumination on sample, the addition of long-pass and short-pass filters, and the adjustment of excitation and emission slit width to maximize signal-to-noise ratio and to minimize photobleaching.
7. Cuvette buffer should be of a similar temperature to the cuvettes at addition. This prevents bubble formation that can create unwanted scatter of light.
8. Cover slips should only be grasped by forceps at the uppermost edge to avoid damaging the area of the monolayer that is illuminated in the spectrofluorometer.
9. Binding time may need to be increased if smaller particles or polystyrene beads are used.
10. Particles can be directed through the mannose receptor by substitution of the human IgG with the equivalent amount of α-D-mannosylated-PITC-albumin (Sigma St Louis, MO, USA).
11. Ensure that the fluor/DMSO aliquot is fully thawed and at room temperature before opening to avoid wetting the DMSO.

12. Labeled particles should be microscopically examined initially to ensure adequate fluorescence and absence of clumping.

13. A suitable dilution of beads should be determined for each batch. This should be done by applying the bead suspension to a BMMØ monolayer on cover glass for the desired binding time, washing off unbound beads, and assessing degree of bead adhesion under magnification. For most applications, a target of 1–2 beads/macrophage is desired. Due to their low density, significantly higher concentrations of polystyrene beads are needed to achieve optimal binding to monolayers.

14. It is preferred, but not usually necessary, to record the calibration fluorescence throughout the entire assay. Recording a calibration fluorescence at the beginning and/or conclusion of the assay will increase time resolution of reporter fluor profiles and may allow the use of filter sets that improve signal-to-noise ratios.

15. The integration time is the period over which each fluorescent measurement is taken. The emission value for each measurement is calculated by signal averaging over the integration period performed by the acquisition software. A lower signal noise can be achieved by increasing the integration time. However, as fewer measurements would be taken per minute, the time resolution of the resulting readout will be diminished.

16. The free rhodamine 110 is moderately membrane permeable and thus will leach from the cell over time. This may result in a decrease in fluorescent intensity.

17. The data can be expressed as hydrolase activity which is proportional to the rate of decay of the substrate. Thus it can be calculated over any period of time by determining the linear gradient of the fluorescent ratio plotted against time using line fitting software in Microsoft Excel® or other mathematical software.

18. Warm the stock aliquots to room temperature before opening to ensure that the sample remains anhydrous.

19. The goal of this particle preparation is to create a monolayer of amphipathic lipids that surrounds the particle core. This presents the lipids to the macrophage in an orientation akin to a phospholipid bilayer. As the C_{18}-coupled particles are extremely hydrophobic, a minimum of amphipathic lipid must be included to completely surround the particle allowing it to be miscible in an aqueous environment without clumping. As a general guideline, for complete suspension of the particles, the combined weight of the coating lipids should be greater than 20% of the mass of the particles. The specific lipid composition can be modified to best suit

the needs of the investigator; however; the following points should be considered. The lipid composition itself will affect the nature of the particle, especially when charged or long chain lipid complexes are included. It is usually not feasible to coat the particle entirely with the desired substrate and calibration fluor. Thus, an inert "base" lipid is included to provide the majority of the monolayer structure. We have found that a monounsaturated phosphatidylglycerol such as 1-trinitrophenyl-amino-dodecanoyl-2-pyrenedecanoyl-3-*O*-hexadecyl-sn-glycerol performs well in this role. We have also found that the inclusion of cholesterol to the lipid mixture increases the monolayer's stability on the particles and reduces clumping. Since the monolayer creates a "natural" surface that does not inherently engage scavenger receptors, the incorporation of a phagocytic ligand is usually required to mediate its phagocytosis by the macrophage. We have included the biotinylated phospholipid 1,2-dipalmitoyl-sn-glycero-3-phosphoethanolamine-*N*-(Cap Biotinyl) to provide an incorporated antigen for subsequent IgG opsonization. Other phagocytic ligands such as phosphatidylserine or mannosylated lipids can be incorporated to target specific phagocytic receptors.

20. Gently swirl the test tube while under a gentle stream of nitrogen to dry the material in a film surrounding the bottom of the test tube. This will help in the proper resuspension of the particles in the sonication step.
21. It may be necessary to pipette the suspension up and down to help break the surface tension.
22. The fluorescent properties of fluorescein-based compounds are commonly sensitive to changes in pH and hence unsuitable for real-time measurements within acidifying compartments. However, once incorporated in the lipid monolayer of the experimental particle, the fluorescent intensity of the hydrolyzed C_{12}FDG is less sensitive to changes in pH (data not shown) making it more suitable for phagosomal assays.

References

1. Ullrich, H. J., Beatty, W. L., and Russell, D. G. (1999) Direct delivery of procathepsin D to phagosomes: implications for phagosome biogenesis and parasitism by *Mycobacterium*. *Eur. J. Cell Biol.* 78, 739–748.
2. Garin, J., Diez, R., Kieffer, S., Dermine, J. F., Duclos, S., Gagnon, E., Sadoul, R., Rondeau, C., and Desjardins, M. (2001) The phagosome proteome: insight into phagosome functions. *J. Cell. Biol.* 152, 165–180.
3. Claus, V., Jahraus, A., Tjelle, T., Berg, T., Kirschke, H., Faulstich, H., and Griffiths, G. (1998) Lysosomal enzyme trafficking between phagosomes, endosomes, and lysosomes in J774 macrophages. Enrichment of cathepsin H in early endosomes. *J. Biol. Chem.* 273, 9842–9851.
4. Yates, R. M., Hermetter, A., and Russell, D. G. (2005) The kinetics of phagosome maturation as a function of phagosome/lysosome

fusion and acquisition of hydrolytic activity. *Traffic* 6, 413–420.

5. Henry, R. M., Hoppe, A. D., Joshi, N., and Swanson, J. A. (2004) The uniformity of phagosome maturation in macrophages. *J. Cell. Biol.* 164, 185–194.
6. Assfalg-Machleidt, I., Rothe, G., Klingel, S., Banati, R., Mangel, W. F., Valet, G., and Machleidt, W. (1992) Membrane permeable fluorogenic rhodamine substrates for selective determination of cathepsin L. *Biol. Chem. Hoppe-Seyler* 373, 433–440.
7. Duque, M., Graupner, M., Stutz, H., Wicher, I., Zechner, R., Paltauf, F., and Hermetter, A. (1996) New fluorogenic triacylglycerol analogs as substrates for the determination and chiral discrimination of lipase activities. *J. Lipid Res.* 37, 868–876.

Chapter 12

Derivation and Characterization of Murine Alternatively Activated (M2) Macrophages

Victor W.H. Ho and Laura M. Sly

Summary

Diversity in macrophage responsiveness to inflammatory stimuli has resulted in the description of a new paradigm wherein macrophages are referred to as polarized into one of two distinct phenotypes, classically activated (M1) macrophages and alternatively activated (M2) macrophages. Classically activated, M1 or "killer" macrophages are thought to play a critical role in destroying foreign organisms and tumor cells, while alternatively activated M2 or "healer" macrophages are thought to be important in debris scavenging, wound healing, and angiogenesis. M2 macrophages may also play key roles in chronic infections, tumorigenesis, and tumor metastasis. It is therefore important to establish models of M1 and M2 polarized macrophages to study their characteristics and amenability to manipulation. M1 macrophages are typically derived from myeloid progenitors with murine macrophage-colony-stimulating factor (M-CSF, also known as CSF-1), while M2 macrophages are thought to be derived from mature M1 macrophages by treatment with interleukin-4 (IL-4) or IL-13. M2 macrophages can also be isolated from SH2-containing inositol 5 -phosphatase (SHIP)−/− mice by harvesting macrophages from peritoneal lavage fluids or they can be derived from SHIP−/− bone marrow aspirate cells with addition of 5% human serum. Upon stimulation with lipopolysaccharide (LPS), M1 macrophages produce high levels of proinflammatory cytokines, low levels of anti-inflammatory cytokines, and high levels of inducible nitric oxide synthase (iNOS), which leads to nitric oxide (NO) production. M2 macrophages, on the other hand, express high levels of M2 markers Ym1 and arginase I (ArgI) and, upon stimulation with LPS, produce relatively lower levels of proinflammatory cytokines and NO and higher levels of anti-inflammatory cytokines. In this chapter, we describe methods used in our laboratory to generate and characterize alternatively activated (M2) macrophages.

Key words: Macrophage phenotype, Macrophage polarization, Classically activated macrophage, Alternatively activated macrophage, Arginase, Ym1, SHIP, IL-4.

Neil E. Reiner (ed.), *Macrophages and Dendritic Cells,* Methods in Molecular Biology, vol. 531

DOI: 10.1007/978-1-59745-396-7_12

1. Introduction

Macrophages have been described and characterized that are capable of displaying distinct phenotypes because of exposure to different cytokines and, more recently, because of different genetic backgrounds *(1–3)*. Classically activated (M1) macrophages are critical in fighting infectious agents by both initiating the innate immune response and by directing a subsequent acquired immune response *(4)*. These cells produce large amounts of proinflammatory cytokines such as TNFα, IL-12, and IL-23 *(5, 6)*, low amounts of the anti-inflammatory cytokine IL-10 *(5, 6)*, and large amounts of NO upon activation *(3, 5)*. Alternatively activated (M2) macrophages are important in the resolution of the inflammatory response and serve roles in debris scavenging, tissue remodeling, and angiogenesis *(1, 7, 8)*. In response to inflammatory stimuli, M2 macrophages produce relatively lower levels of proinflammatory cytokines, higher levels of IL-10, and produce little or no NO *(3, 7)*.

Alternatively activated macrophages can be derived from mature M1 macrophages by the addition of IL-4 or IL-13, which acts through STAT6 *(8–10)*. We have recently described the first genetic model of alternatively activated macrophages wherein in vivo differentiated macrophages from the SHIP knockout mouse display an M2 phenotype *(3)*. Furthermore, bone marrow progenitors from the SHIP knockout mouse can be skewed to an M2 phenotype by the addition of human or mouse serum, TGFβ, or IL-10 early during differentiation *(3)*. Additional markers of alternatively activated macrophages have been described and include FIZZ1 and the mammalian chitinase Ym1 *(3, 10–13)*. Arginase I expression and activity are also upregulated in M2 macrophages, and this is part of the critical metabolic switch that occurs in murine macrophages during conversion from an M1 to an M2 phenotype *(3)*. ArgI competes with inducible nitric oxide synthase (iNOS) for their common substrate, L-arginine, thereby dramatically reducing or inhibiting NO production by alternatively activated macrophages despite induction of iNOS *(3)*.

Characteristics of alternative macrophage activation have been described in tumors *(1, 14–16)* and during infection *(11, 15)*. Alternatively activated macrophages have also been found in patients with severe chronic inflammatory disorders, where they have been hypothesized to protect the host from damage by dampening down the innate immune response *(7)* and hence are thought to be beneficial during systemic inflammatory response syndrome (SIRS) and sepsis *(17)*. Further study of these models of alternatively activated macrophages and their amenability to manipulation is critical to understanding their role in human diseases and to harnessing them for therapeutic purposes.

2. Materials

2.1. Cell Culture and Stimulations

1. Iscove's Modified Dulbecco's Medium (IMDM).
2. Fetal bovine serum.
3. Recombinant murine macrophage-colony-stimulating factor (M-CSF also known as CSF-1).
4. Monothioglycerol (MTG).
5. Cell dissociation buffer.
6. Lipopolysaccharide from *Escherichia coli* serotype 0127:B8 (LPS).
7. Recombinant murine interleukin-4 (IL-4).

2.2. SDS–Polyacrylamide Gel Electrophoresis, Adapted from (18)

1. Laemmli's solubilization mix: 75 mM Tris–HCl pH 6.8, 7.5% (w/v) glycerol, 200 mM β-mercaptoethanol, 1.5% (w/v) bromophenol blue.
2. Separating gel mix (4×): 1.5 M Tris–HCl pH 8.8, 0.4% SDS.
3. Stacking gel mix (4×): 0.3 M Tris–HCl pH 6.8, 0.4% SDS.
4. 40% Acrylamide/bisacrylamide solution (37.5:1 with 2.6% C).
5. *N,N,N′,N′*-Tetramethyl-ethylenediamine (TEMED).
6. 10% (w/v) Ammonium persulfate (APS).
7. Pageruler prestained protein ladder.
8. Running buffer (10×): 0.25 M Trizma base, 1.9 M glycine, 1% (w/v) SDS.

2.3. Western Blotting Analyses, Adapted from (19)

1. Transfer buffer (10×): 0.5 M Trizma base, 3.84 M glycine, 1% (w/v) SDS.
2. Immobilon-P membrane 0.45-μm pore polyvinyldifluoride (PVDF).
3. 3-MM chromatography paper.
4. Tris-buffered saline with Tween-20 (TBST): 137 mM NaCl, 2.7 mM KCl, 25 mM Tris–Cl pH 7.4, 0.1% Tween-20.
5. Blocking buffer: 5% (w/v) bovine serum albumin (BSA) fraction V, 0.02% NaN_3 in TBST.
6. Primary antibodies: anti-SHIP, P1C1; anti-GAPDH; anti-ArgI; anti-Ym1. Anti-Ym1 is a rabbit polyclonal antibody and all others are mouse monoclonal antibodies. All antibodies are used at a dilution of 1 in 1,000 in primary antibody buffer.
7. Primary antibody buffer: 2% (w/v) BSA fraction V, 0.008% NaN_3 in TBST.

8. Secondary antibody: antimouse conjugated to horse radish peroxidase (HRP) or antirabbit-HRP diluted 1 in 10,000 in TBST.
9. Western Lightning chemiluminescence reagent plus, enhanced luminal reagent and oxidizing reagent.
10. X-OMAT Blue film.

2.4. ELISAs for Murine TNFα, IL-12p40, IL-10

1. ELISA kits for TNFα, IL-6, IL-12p40, and IL-10.
2. Coating buffer: 0.2 M sodium phosphate pH 6.5 for IL-12p40 and IL-10.
3. Coating buffer: 0.1 M sodium carbonate pH 9.5 for TNFα and IL-6.
4. Assay diluent: 10% heat-inactivated (55°C for 30 min) FBS in Dulbecco's PBS pH 7.4.
5. ELISA substrate: Substrate Reagent A and Substrate Reagent B.
6. Stop solution: 2N H_2SO_4.

2.5. Arginase Assay, Adapted from *(20)*

1. Cell lysis buffer: 0.1% Triton X-100, 25 mM Tris–Cl pH 8.0 + protease inhibitors aprotinin (40 μg/mL), leupeptin (8 μg/mL), PMSF (100 μM).
2. Acid solution: (7:3:1) H_2O: H_2PO_4 44.6N, 85%: H_2SO_4 36N.
3. Colorimetric substrate: 9% (w/v) α-isonitrosopropiophenone (ISPF) in absolute ethanol. Store in the dark.
4. 0.5 M l-Arginine in water pH 9.7.
5. 10 mM $MnCl_2$ in H_2O.
6. Standard stock solution: 50 mM urea in H_2O.

2.6. Griess Assay, Adapted from *(21)*

1. Solution A: 1% (w/v) sulfanilamide in 2.5% H_3PO_4.
2. Solution B: 0.1% (w/v) naphthylethylene diamine dihydrochloride in 2.5% H_3PO_4.
3. 2 mM $NaNO_2$ in IMDM, 10% FBS.

3. Methods

The steadfast hallmark of alternative macrophage polarization in humans and in mice is low expression of proinflammatory cytokines (IL-12) and high expression of anti-inflammatory cytokines (IL-10) in response to toll-like receptor (TLR) activation *(5, 6)*. In addition, L-arginine metabolism via iNOS to NO

(M1) versus ArgI to ornithine and polyamines (M2) provides a key switch in murine macrophage polarization *(3)*. The M1/M2 macrophage polarization paradigm is likely an oversimplification of activated macrophage states that likely reflects a continuum of activation potential from M1 to M2. Alternatively, there may be many subtypes of alternatively activated macrophages. Western blot analyses allow us to examine directly phenotypic markers of M2 macrophages, while the arginase activity assay and Griess assay are quantitative assays of M1/M2 macrophage metabolic function and therefore phenotype severity. Techniques described herein will be valuable in establishing similarities or differences among unique populations of alternatively activated macrophages derived in vitro or in vivo.

3.1. Cell Culture and Stimulations

1. Harvest bone marrow aspirates from femura of 8- to 12-week old SHIP+/+ (wild type) and SHIP−/− mice using a 5-mL syringe and a 26-gauge needle to flush the marrow out with IMDM, 10% FCS (*see* **Note 1**).
2. Suspend bone marrow aspirates in 40 mL IMDM, 10% FCS and allow cells to adhere overnight at 37°C, 5% CO_2 in a 75-cm^2 tissue culture flask.
3. Remove culture supernatant, spin down nonadherent cells, and resuspend at 0.5×10^6 cells/mL (i.e., about 50 mL) in complete bone marrow macrophage medium (IMDM, 10% FCS, 150 μM MTG, 5 ng/mL M-CSF) in a 175-cm^2 filter top tissue culture flask. Replace medium at day 4, spinning down nonadherent cells and returning them to the flask and at day 7, discarding nonadherent cells (*see* **Notes 2** and **3**).
4. Macrophage cultures can be supplemented with 5% human serum on day 0 or 10 ng/mL IL-4 can be added with fresh complete medium at day 10 for three additional days (*see* **Note 4**).
5. Peritoneal macrophages from SHIP+/+ and SHIP−/− mice are isolated by flushing the peritoneal cavity 3 × 5 mL with IMDM, 10% FCS, 150 μM MTG (no M-CSF). An aliquot is counted using a hemocytometer. Macrophages are large and gold in appearance. They can be plated at an appropriate density (0.5×10^6 cells/mL) and become adherent overnight. Adherent cells are washed the next day two times with PBS to remove nonadherent or only loosely adherent cells and can be used in stimulations or can be harvested for SDS–PAGE analysis.
6. At day 10, adherent cells derived from bone marrow aspirate cultures are lifted and replated for stimulations and analyses. Cells are lifted off the tissue culture flask using 5 mL per 75 cm^2 tissue culture flask of Cell Dissociation Buffer. Place buffer on cells for 3 min and then bang the side of the

flask with the heel of your palm firmly several times. Ensure that cells have lifted off of the flask under the microscope, remove resuspended cells, and spin down at 1,200 × g for 5 min. Resuspend cells in a small volume and count viable cells using a hemocytometer. Replate at a concentration of 0.5 × 10^6 cells/mL in IMDM, 10% FCS, 150 μM MTG (no M-CSF).

7. Stimulate peritoneal macrophages the day after plating or the day after replating for bone marrow-derived macrophages by changing the medium to 0.5 volume IMDM, 10% FCS, 150 μM MTG (no M-CSF), and 100 ng/mL LPS.

3.2. SDS–PAGE

1. To harvest cells for SDS–PAGE and Western analyses, remove cell supernatants, wash cells twice with Hank's Balanced Salt Solution, and add 80 μL of LDM to 1 × 10^6 cells in a well. Pipet the cells up and down and transfer to a new Eppendorf tube. The lysed cell suspensions are very viscous. Shear DNA in samples by passing five times through a 26-gauge needle. Boil 1 min. Store samples in the freezer at –20°C until ready to load on SDS–PAGE.
2. SDS–PAGE instructions provided herein are for preparation of a 40-mL separating gel (1.5 mm thick × 14.5 cm wide × 16 cm long) to be used with the Bio-Rad Protean II xi Cell (Bio-Rad Laboratories Inc, Hercules, CA). One long and one short glass plate are cleaned thoroughly with Sparkleen detergent (Fischer Scientific Co., Pittsburgh, PA), rinsed with water and then rinsed with 95% ethanol, and allowed to air dry immediately before use. Spacers and combs are cleaned with 95% ethanol and the pieces are assembled as per manufacturers' instructions (*see* **Note 5**).
3. A 10% separating gel solution is prepared by combining 20 mL distilled water, 10 mL 4× separating buffer, and 10 mL acrylamide solution in a 50-mL Falcon tube and mixing by inversion several times. This mixture is degassed under house vacuum for 10 min. APS (80 μL) and 20 μL TEMED are added and the solution is mixed gently but thoroughly by rocking the Falcon tube back and forth so as to not introduce any air bubbles. Pour the entire 40 mL solution between the glass plates. Using a Pasteur pipet, gently add 5 mL of isopropanol to overlay the top of the gel. Be careful not to cause mixing with the denser gel solution. Allow gel to polymerize about 30 min (*see* **Notes 6** and 7).
4. Pour off the isopropanol overlay. Rinse the gel top two times with distilled water and drain water well (*see* **Note 8**).
5. Prepare the stacking gel mix by combining 9.75 mL water, 1.5 mL acrylamide solution and 3.75 mL 4× stacking gel

buffer, 75 μL APS, and 15 μL TEMED in a 50-mL Falcon tube. Mix by inversion and pipet onto the top of the separating gel. Place the well comb into the top of the gel. Avoid trapping air bubbles below or on the side of the wells. Allow to polymerize for 30 min before removing comb.

6. To load samples into wells, use gel loading tips and apply the sample to the bottom of wells. Prepare 1,400 mL of running buffer by diluting 140 mL of 10× buffer stock solution to 1,400 mL with distilled water. Gently add running buffer to top up the wells with a Pasteur pipet and then fill the upper buffer chamber with running buffer. Pour the remaining running buffer into the bottom buffer reservoir of the gel apparatus.
7. Fill the inner chamber of the gel apparatus with cold water and run gel overnight at 65 V.

3.3. Western Blotting Analyses

1. Instructions provided are for use with the Bio-Rad Trans-Blot Cell (Bio-Rad Laboratories Inc, Hercules, CA). Cut the PVDF membrane and four pieces of 3-MM filter paper to 14.5 cm × 16 cm.
2. In a plastic container, wet PVDF membrane in methanol, pour off the methanol, add 50 mL distilled water, and shake at 23°C on an orbital shaker while preparing for transfer. The membrane is hydrated when water no longer beads or streaks off the membrane surface.
3. Prepare transfer buffer using 400 mL of 10× transfer buffer, 3,200 mL distilled water, and 400 mL methanol (*see* **Note 9**).
4. Disassemble gel apparatus, cut the stacking gel off and discard, and soak the separating gel in transfer buffer along with the PVDF membrane.
5. Assemble the gel sandwich on the clear side of the transfer tank holder wetting each piece generously in transfer buffer as you assemble. The gel sandwich is assembled in the following order: one scotch brite pad, two pieces of 3MM Whatman filter paper, PVDF membrane, gel (from left to right, noting the orientation), two pieces of filter paper, scotch brite pad. Firmly roll out the gel assembly with a disposable 2-mL pipet to remove air bubbles trapped between the transfer layers.
6. Secure the gel sandwich in its holding apparatus and move it into the transfer tank. Fill the transfer tank with transfer buffer. Run cold water through the transfer tank constantly during transfer. Transfer gels for 4 h at 0.6 A. Check occasionally that buffer tank is not getting too warm. If the transfer apparatus feels warm to the touch, place the entire transfer assembly into a secondary plastic container and pack ice around it.

7. Remove and disassemble the gel sandwich. Remove the membranes and mark the molecular weight markers on the membrane with an indelible pen. Place the membrane in 50 mL of blocking solution in a plastic container. Incubate for 1 h at 23°C on an orbital shaker.
8. Incubate the blocked membrane in primary antibody overnight at 4°C on an orbital shaker.
9. Wash the membrane 3 × 10 min in TBST at 23°C with shaking on an orbital shaker.
10. Incubate with secondary antibody for 45 min at 23°C with shaking on an orbital shaker.
11. Wash the membrane 3 × 10 min in TBST at 23°C with shaking.
12. Mix 7.5 mL of ECL reagents A and B together and cover membrane. Gently rock back and forth by hand for 1 min.
13. Place the membrane between two layers of plastic wrap and expose in a dark room to film. Exposure times for these antibodies are very short, typically in the range of 1–5 s for SHIP, Ym1, and GAPDH and 15 s for ArgI. Develop film in a film processor. An example of the results produced is shown in **Fig. 1**.

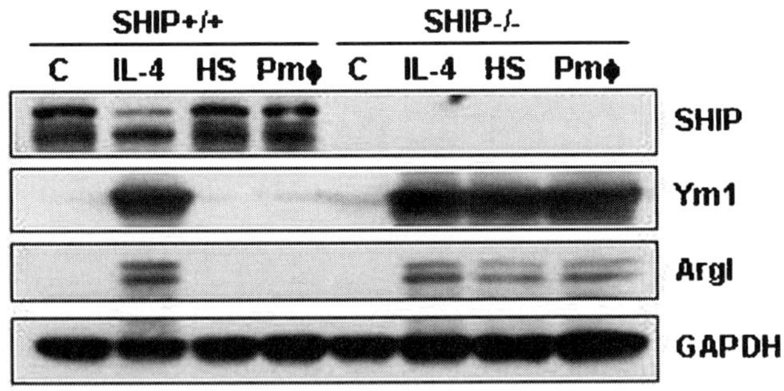

Fig. 1. M2 macrophage marker expression in SHIP+/+ (wild type) and SHIP−/− macrophages. Macrophages (1 × 10^6) were derived in complete medium with 5 ng/mL recombinant murine M-CSF for 10 days (C), were treated with 10 ng/mL IL-4 for an additional 3 days (IL-4), or were derived in complete medium plus 5% human serum (HS) from day "0." Also shown, in vivo differentiated macrophages were harvested from the peritoneal cavity by lavage (Pmϕ). Cells were harvested for SDS–PAGE and Western blotting with antibodies to SHIP (145 and 135 kDa), M2 macrophage markers Ym1 and ArgI (38 and 35 kDa) and GAPDH, as a loading control. IL-4 treatment post differentiation skewed both SHIP+/+ and SHIP−/− macrophages to an M2 phenotype expressing phenotypic markers Ym1 and ArgI. Human serum provided during differentiation skewed only SHIP−/− cells to an M2 phenotype. Peritoneal macrophages develop an M2 phenotype only in the SHIP−/− mice.

3.4. ELISAs

1. To harvest cell supernatants 24 h after stimulation, pipet the supernatant into a 1.5-mL Eppendorf tube. Spin the contents at 1,200 × g to remove any cell debris in the samples. Transfer clarified supernatants to new tubes storing each sample in 0.3- to 0.5-mL aliquots to be thawed individually for assay as needed. Store samples at –80°C until ready to assay.
2. ELISA kits for TNFα, IL-6, IL-12p40, and IL-10 are available from BD Biosciences (Mississauga, ON, Canada), and assays are performed as per manufacturer's instructions (*see* **Note 10**). Cytokine production ± SD from three independent experiments assayed in duplicate is shown in **Fig. 2**.

3.5. Arginase Assay

1. Lyse macrophages (10^6) in 200–400 μL cell lysis buffer.
2. Quantitate protein in cell lysates using Bio-Rad protein quantification assay (Bio-Rad, Hercules, CA).

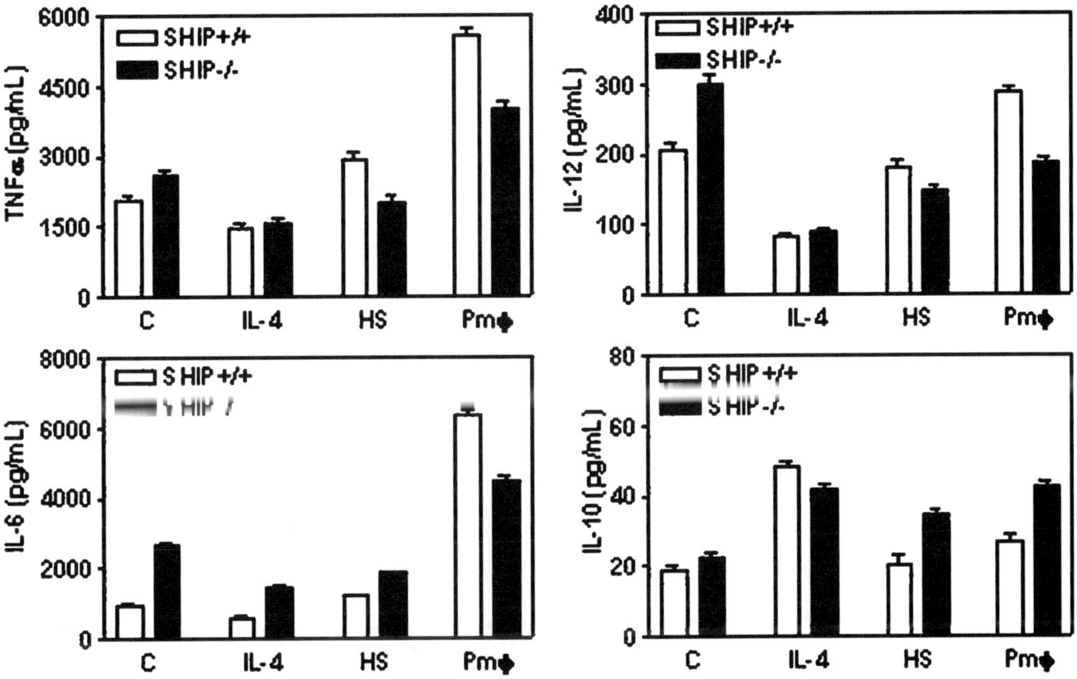

Fig. 2. Proinflammatory (TNFα, IL-12, and IL-6) and anti-inflammatory (IL-10) cytokine production by SHIP+/+ (wild type) and SHIP–/– macrophages in response to LPS stimulation (100 ng/mL for 24 h). Macrophages (1 × 10^6) were derived in complete medium with 5 ng/mL recombinant murine M-CSF for 10 days (C), were treated with 10 ng/mL IL-4 for an additional 3 days (IL-4), or were derived in complete medium plus 5% human serum (HS) from day "0." As well, in vivo differentiated macrophages were harvested from the peritoneal cavity by lavage (Pmϕ). Compared with cells differentiated under control conditions, cells treated with IL-4 showed reduced production of proinflammatory and increased production of anti-inflammatory cytokines in both SHIP+/+ (wild type) and SHIP–/– macrophages. SHIP–/– macrophages differentiated in the presence of human serum, but not their wild-type counterparts, also reduced production of proinflammatory and increased production of anti-inflammatory cytokines in response to LPS. In vivo differentiated SHIP–/– macrophages (Pmϕ) produced less TNFα, IL-6, and IL-12 and more IL-10 than SHIP+/+ (wild type) macrophages (C).

3. Use 5–15 μg protein for each arginase assay, pipetting the desired amount of protein into an Eppendorf tube and topping up the volume to 100 μL with cell lysis buffer.
4. Add 10 μL of 10 mM $MnCl_2$ and heat the samples at 55°C in a water bath for 10 min.
5. Add 100 μL 0.5 M L-arginine into each sample (total volume of 210 μL in each sample), and incubate at 37°C for 1 h (*see* **Note 11**).
6. Add 800 μL acid solution to each sample. Add 40 μL of ISPF solution into each reaction and pipet up and down 3 times (*see* **Note 12**).
7. Prepare serial twofold dilutions of urea stock solution in distilled water to make a standard curve and use distilled water as a blank. Add 100 μL of diluted stocks or distilled water to an Eppendorf tube. Add 400 μL acid solution and then add 25 μL ISPF to each tube.

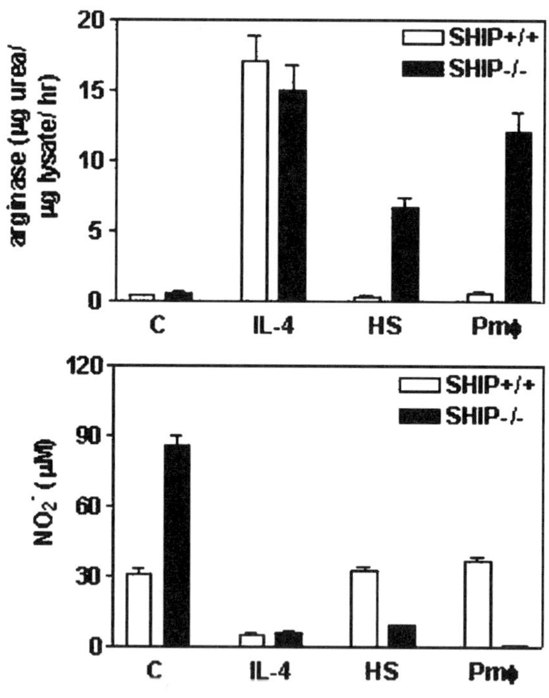

Fig. 3. Arginase activity in cells and NO_2^- in cell culture supernatants of SHIP+/+ (wild type) and SHIP−/− macrophages in response to LPS stimulation (100 ng/mL for 24 h). Macrophages (1 × 10^6) were derived in complete medium with 5 ng/mL recombinant murine M-CSF for 10 days (C), were treated with 10 ng/mL IL-4 for an additional 3 days (IL-4), or were derived in complete medium plus 5% human serum (HS) from day "0." In addition, in vivo differentiated macrophages were harvested from the peritoneal cavity by lavage (Pmϕ). IL-4 treatment resulted in increased arginase activity and decreased nitrite production in both SHIP+/+ (wild type) and SHIP−/− macrophages. Derivation in the presence of human serum and in vivo differentiation resulted in increased arginase activity and decreased nitrite production in SHIP−/− macrophages only.

8. Heat all samples and standards at 100°C for 30 min. Snap-top Eppendorf tube caps must be secured during this step because tubes will pop open. Let samples cool to 23°C in the dark, approximately 10 min (*see* **Note 12**).
9. Read absorbance at 550 nm within 30 min. Arginase-activity-detected ± SD for three independent assays performed in duplicate is shown in **Fig. 3**, upper graph.

3.6. Griess Assay

1. Dilute 2 μM $NaNO_2$ stock to 125 μM in cell culture medium. Make serial twofold dilutions from the 125 μM dilution to prepare a standard curve using cell culture medium as a blank.
2. Aliquot 50 μL of standard from each dilution, blank or 50 μL of culture supernatant into a 96-well flat bottom polystyrene nontissue culture treated plate.
3. Add 50 μL of solution A into each sample or standard.
4. Add 50 μL of solution B into each sample or standard.
5. Incubate the plates for 10 min in the dark. Read the absorbance at 550 nm within 30 min (*see* **Note 13**). Nitrite-detected ± SD for three independent assays performed in duplicate is shown in **Fig. 3**, lower graph.

4. Notes

1. SHIP−/− mice that are 5–8 weeks old show a considerably less profound M2 skewing of their resident peritoneal macrophages, so SHIP−/− mice used to isolate resident M2 macrophages should be 8 weeks of age or older.
2. We have assayed several different sources of L-cell-conditioned media for use as a source of M-CSF and currently use recombinant M-CSF because we have not found a reliable source for M-CSF production. If using L-cell-conditioned media for derivation of bone marrow macrophages, assay M-CSF to ensure that you are providing sufficient growth factor (5 ng/mL) to your cells for differentiation.
3. Macrophages derived as described here are consistently more than 95% positive for macrophage markers, F4/80 and Mac-1.
4. M2 macrophages can also be derived by addition of recombinant murine IL-13 (in place of IL-4) to mature cultures.
5. Check your SDS–PA gel set up to ensure that it will not leak before adding your gel solution by adding distilled water into the assembly while you prepare and degas your gel solution. Ensure that you drain the water thoroughly before adding your gel mix.

6. Unpolymerized acrylamide is a neurotoxin, so care should be taken when handling solutions or gels to avoid exposure.
7. Ammonium persulfate (APS) can be stored in aliquots at –20°C for up to 3 months and once thawed, should be stored at 4°C, used for 1 week and then discarded. Alternatively, APS can be prepared for each use.
8. Do not leave the isopropanol on the top of the running gel for more than the 30 min required to polymerize the gel or the gel will dehydrate, separating from the side spacers.
9. To detect SHIP by Western blotting, wet-gel transfers are required and transfer buffer should contain 10% methanol. Semi-dry transfers and wet transfers performed without methanol are not sufficient to transfer high molecular weight proteins.
10. IL-10 standards can be diluted serially twofold from 250 pg/mL to 3.9 pg/mL. Concentrations above 250 pg/mL are on the plateau of the standard curve and so are of no value. However, because IL-10 levels are typically very low in medium conditioned by stimulated macrophages, the linear range of the standard curve can be extended at the lower range reliably by further diluting the IL-10 standard.
11. The 37°C incubation time for the arginase assay can be lengthened from 1 to 2 h to increase the sensitivity of the assay.
12. ISPF will form a precipitate in the reaction mixture.
13. The Griess assay product is light sensitive, so after performing the assay, samples should be protected from light until the absorbance is read.

Acknowledgments

The authors would like to thank Vivian Lam for technical assistance, and Michael J. Rauh and Dr. Gerald Krystal for their pioneering work establishing the macrophage phenotype from the SHIP knockout mouse as a genetic model of M2 polarized macrophages.

References

1. Gordon, S. (2003) Alternative activation of macrophages. *Nat Rev Immunol* 3, 23–35.
2. Mantovani, A., Schioppa, T., Biswas, S. K., Marchesi, F., Allavena, P., and Sica, A. (2003) Tumor-associated macrophages and dendritic cells as prototypic type II polarized myeloid populations. *Tumori* 89, 459–468.
3. Rauh, M. J., Ho, V., Pereira, C., Sham, A., Sly, L. M., Lam, V., Huxham, L., Minchinton, A. I., Mui, A., and Krystal, G. (2005) SHIP represses the generation of alternatively activated macrophages. *Immunity* 23, 361–374.
4. Fremond, C. M., Yeremeev, V., Nicolle, D. M., Jacobs, M., Quesniaux, V. F., and Ryffel, B.

(2004) Fatal *Mycobacterium tuberculosis* infection despite adaptive immune response in the absence of MyD88. *J Clin Invest* 114, 1790–1799.

5. Mantovani, A., Sica, A., Sozzani, S., Allavena, P., Vecchi, A., and Locati, M. (2004) The chemokine system in diverse forms of macrophage activation and polarization. *Trends Immunol* 25, 677–686.
6. Mantovani, A., Sica, A., and Locati, M. (2005) Macrophage polarization comes of age. *Immunity* 23, 344–346.
7. Mosser, D. M. (2003) The many faces of macrophage activation. *J Leukocyte Biol* 73, 209–212.
8. Stein, M., Keshav, S., Harris, N., and Gordon, S. (1992) Interleukin-4 potently enhances murine macrophage mannose receptor activity: a marker of alternative immunologic macrophage activation. *J Exp Med* 176, 287–292.
9. El-Gayar, S., Thuring-Nahler, H., Pfeilschifter, J., Rollinghoff, M., and Bogdan, C. (2003) Translational control of inducible nitric oxide synthase by IL-13 and arginine availability in inflammatory macrophages. *J Immunol* 171, 4561–4568.
10. Welch, J. S., Escoubert-Lozach, L., Sykes, D. B., Liddiard, K., Greaves, D. R., and Glass, C. K. (2002) TH2 cytokines and allergic challenge induce Yml expression in macrophages by a STAT6-dependent mechanism. *J Biol Chem* 277, 42821–42829.
11. Nair, M. G., Cochrane, D. W., and Allen, J. E. (2003) Macrophages in chronic type 2 inflammation have a novel phenotype characterized by the abundant expression of Yml and Fizzl that can be partly replicated *in vitro*. *Immunol Lett* 85, 173–180.
12. Raes, G., Noel, W., Beschin, A., Brys, L., de Baetselier, P., and Hassanzadeh, G. H. (2002) FIZZ1 and Ym as tools to discriminate between differentially activated macrophages. *Dev Immunol* 9, 151–159.
13. Raes, G., De Baetselier, P., Noel, W., Beschin, A., Brombacher, F., and Hassanzadeh, G. H. (2002) Differential expression of FIZZ1 and Yml in alternatively activated versus classically activated macrophages. *J Leukoc Biol* 71, 597–602.
14. Biswas, S. K., Gangi, L., Paul, S., Schioppa, T., Saccani, A., Sironi, M., Bottazzi, B., Doni, A., Vincenzo, B., Pasqualini, F., Vago, L., Nebuloni, M., Mantovani, A., and Sica, A. (2006) A distinct and unique transcriptional program expressed by tumor-associated macrophages (defective NF-kappaB and enhanced IRF-3/STAT1 activation). *Blood* 107, 2112–2222.
15. Ghassabeh, G. H., De Baetselier, P., Brys, L., Noel, W., Van Ginderachter, J. A., Meerschaut, S., Beschin, A., Brombacher, F., and Raes, G. (2006) Identification of a common gene signature for type II cytokine-associated myeloid cells elicited *in vivo* in different pathologic conditions. *Blood* 108, 575–583.
16. Rodriquez, P. C., Quiceno, D. G., Zabaleta, J., Oritz, B., Zea, A. H., Piazuelo, M. B., Delgado, A., Correa, P., Brayer, J., Sotomayor, E. M., Antonia, S., Ochoa, J. B., and Ochoa, A. C. (2004) Arginase I production in the tumor microenvironment by mature myeloid cells inhibits T-cell receptor expression and antigen-specific T-cell responses. *Cancer Res* 64, 5839–5849.
17. Dal-Pizzol, F. (2004) Alternative activated macrophage: a new key for systemic inflammatory response syndrome and sepsis treatment? *Crit Care Med* 32, 1971–1972.
18. Laemmli, U.K. (1970) Cleavage of structural proteins during the assembly of the bacteriophage T4. *Nature* 227, 680–685.
19. Towbin, H., Staehelin, T., and Gordon, J. (1979) Electrophoretic transfer of proteins from polyacrylamide gels to nitrocellulose sheets: procedure and some applications. *Biotechnology* 24, 145–149.
20. Morrison, A. C., and Correll, P. H. (2002) Activation of the stem cell-derived tyrosine kinase/RON receptor tyrosine kinase by macrophage-stimulating protein results in the induction of arginase activity in murine peritoneal macrophages. *J Immunol* 168, 853–860.
21. Kleinbongard, P., Rassaf, T., Dejam, A., Kerber, S., and Kelm, M. (2002) Griess method for nitrite measurement of aqueous and protein-containing samples. *Methods Enzymol* 359, 158–168.

Chapter 13

Isolation and Culture of Human Hematopoietic Progenitors for Studies of Dendritic Cell Biology

Mattias Svensson

Summary

Understanding the regulation of distinct dendritic cell (DC) function and differentiation pathways is important in many physiological and pathophysiological processes. This includes infectious and neoplastic diseases, vaccination and immunotherapy, allograft rejection, and the pathogenesis of autoimmune diseases. Isolation and culture of human hematopoietic progenitor cells provide a valuable model for studies on DC biology and may help uncover new means to manipulate DC differentiation and function in therapeutic settings. Here, a detailed protocol for the isolation of CD34$^+$ hematopoietic progenitor cells from human cord blood is described. The isolated cell population consists of approximately 85% CD34$^+$ CD45$^+$ hematopoietic progenitor cells that in response to granulocyte-macrophage colony-stimulating factor (GM-CSF) plus tumor necrosis factor (TNF) expand and differentiate into CD11c$^+$ HLA-DR$^+$ DC-expressing CD1a.

Key words: Dendritic cells, Hematopoietic progenitor cells, Cell separation, Flow cytometry, Growth factors, T cell activation.

1. Introduction

DC are a heterogeneous family of cells produced mainly from hematopoietic progenitors in the bone marrow *(1, 2)*. They circulate in the bloodstream and then move into tissues throughout the body. However, several developmental intermediates of DC have been isolated from blood and various tissues, some being more restricted than others in their potential to proliferate and differentiate into distinct subsets of DC with specialized functions *(3–7)*. Research focusing on understanding tissue-specific component interactions with progenitors and DC, that lead to

Neil E. Reiner (ed.), *Macrophages and Dendritic Cells,* Methods in Molecular Biology, vol. 531

DOI: 10.1007/978-1-59745-396-7_13

programming of distinct DC differentiation pathways and functions *(8)*, can help understanding local immunoregulation and the development of new strategies for immune intervention. In vitro studies on human hematopoietic progenitors and DC under specific culture conditions serve as an accessible model aimed at revealing discrete DC developmental pathways and functions.

The existence of human progenitor cells that can generate DC in vitro was first described by Reid et al. *(9)*, and subsequently it was discovered that DC can develop from human $CD34^+$ hematopoietic progenitors cells *(10)*. In response to granulocyte-macrophage colony-stimulating factor (GM-CSF) plus tumor necrosis factor (TNF), $CD34^+$ progenitors expand and differentiate along at least two unrelated developmental pathways generating $CD11c^+$ $HLA\text{-}DR^+$ DC resembling Langerhans cells (expressing CD1a and Langerin) and a subpopulation of DC found in interstitial tissues (expressing CD1a and coagulation factor XIIIa) *(11)*. Human $CD34^+$ hematopoietic progenitors are found at low frequencies in bone marrow and cord blood. These progenitors can be isolated using commercially available magnetic bead cell separation technologies. In this protocol, cord blood progenitor cells are isolated by positive selection using beads coated with antibodies recognizing the CD34 molecule, and this is followed by detachment of the beads from isolated progenitors. Flow cytometry analysis allows determination of purity and phenotypic characteristics of CD34-enriched cells. This also allows verification that enriched cells are devoid of contaminating DC (CD1a, CD1c, CD11c, and CD303), monocytes (CD14), T cells (CD3), B cells (CD19), and NK cells (CD56). DC differentiation potential is confirmed by the capacity of isolated progenitors to develop into immunostimulatory DC in response to GM-CSF plus TNF.

2. Materials

2.1. Isolation of Hematopoietic Progenitor Cells

1. Blood collection tubes containing anticoagulant ethylenediamine tetraacetic acid (EDTA).
2. Cord blood (*see* **Note 1**).
3. Lymphoprep to isolate nucleated cells by gradient centrifugation.
4. Dynabeads M-450 CD34 kit for positive selection of $CD34^+$ progenitor cells and detachment of beads.
5. Dynal Magnetic Particle Concentrator (MPC-L or MPC-15).

6. Phosphate-buffered saline (PBS) pH 7.4: (0.2 g KH_2PO_4, 0.2 g KCl, 1.44 g $Na_2HPO_4 \cdot 2H_2O$, and 8.0 g NaCl, all from Sigma to 1 L).
7. Isolation buffer: PBS with 2 (w/v) % bovine serum albumin (BSA), 0.6 (w/v) % tri-Na-citrate dehydrate, and 100 IU/ml Penicillin and Streptomycin.
8. Washing buffer: PBS with 0.1 (w/v) % BSA.

2.2. Flow Cytometry

1. Flow cytometry buffer: PBS supplemented with 2% fetal bovine serum (FBS), 2.5 mM EDTA, and 0.01% sodium azide.
2. Blocking solution, flow cytometry buffer containing 2 μg/ml of purified immunoglobulins from human serum.
3. Antibodies:
   (a) Alexa fluor 488-conjugated anti-CD11c antibody (clone BU15) (Serotec, Oxford, UK).
   (b) Fluorescein isothiocyanate (FITC)-conjugated anti-CD83 (clone HB15e) (eBioscience, San Diego, CA), anti-CD116 (clone 4H1) (eBioscience), anti-CD1c (clone AD5-8E7) (Miltenyi Biotech, Bergisch Gladbach, Germany), anti-CD14 (clone MEM-18) (ImmunoTools, Friesoythe, Germany), anti-CD3 (clone MEM-57) (ImmunoTools), anti-CD4 (clone MEM-241) (ImmunoTools).
   (c) Phycoerythrin (PE)-conjugated anti-CD1a (clone H148) (eBioscience), anti-CD115 (clone 12-3A3-1B10) (eBioscience), anti-CD56 (clone MEM-188) (ImmunoTools), anti-CD19 (clone LT19) (ImmunoTools), anti-CD14 (clone 61D3) (eBioscience), anti-CD8 (clone MEM-31) (ImmunoTools), anti-CD303 (clone AC144) (Miltenyi Biotech).
   (d) Allophycocyanin (APC)-conjugated anti-CD14 (clone 61D3) (eBioscience), anti-CD11c (clone B-ly6) (BD Biosciences, Mountain View, CA), anti-CD34 (clone 581) (BD Bioscience) San Diego, CA), anti-CD40 (clone 5C3) (BD Bioscience).
   (e) Peridinin Chlorophyll-a protein (PerCp)-conjugated anti-HLA-DR (clone L243) (BD Bioscience).
   (f) Biotinylated anti-CD1c (clone AD5-8E7) (Miltenyi Biotech), anti-CD303 (clone AC144) (Miltenyi Biotech), anti-CD45 (clone H130) (BD Bioscience).
4. Isotype controls and secondary reagents: Labeling with biotinylated antibodies is detected with PerCP-streptavidin and APC-streptavidin, both from BD Biosciences. FITC-conjugated,

PE-conjugated, APC-conjugated, and biotin-conjugated isotype-matched control antibodies all from BD Biosciences.

5. Fix solution: PBS with 4% formaldehyde (freshly made).
6. Flow cytometry analysis: FACSCalibur (BD Biosciences) and the CellQuest software (BD Biosciences).

2.3. Culture of Progenitor Cells to Generate DC

1. Dulbecco's Modified Eagle's Medium (DMEM) is supplemented with 10% FBS, 10 mM Hepes, nonessential amino acids from a 100× stock solution, 100 IU/ml Penicillin and Streptomycin, and 50 μM β-mercaptoethanol (*see* **Note 2**).
2. Growth factors GM-CSF and TNF are dissolved in PBS at 10 μg/ml and stored in single-use aliquots at −20 or −80°C.
3. Lipopolysaccharide is dissolved in PBS at 1 mg/ml and stored at 2 to 8°C.
4. Inverted microscope Nikon Eclipse TS100 and digital camera Nikon CoolPix 4500, both from Nikon, Tokyo, Japan.

2.4. T Cell Isolation and Mixed Leukocyte Reaction

1. Buffy coat (*see* **Note 3**).
2. Pan T cell isolation kit II, CD8 MicroBeads, CD4 MicroBeads, LS columns, and a MidiMACS separator all from Miltenyi Biotech.
3. Buffer for T cell isolation: PBS with 0.5 (w/v) % BSA and 5 mM EDTA.
4. RPMI 1640 with sodium pyruvate is supplemented with 10% heat-inactivated FBS, 2 mM L-glutamine, 10 mM Hepes, 100 IU/ml Penicillin and Streptomycin, and 50 μM β-mercaptoethanol. This is referred to as complete RPMI.
5. For ^{3}H-thymidine incorporation and harvesting of cells: ^{3}H-thymidine, Tomtec harvesting machine, Glass fiber filter, Melt-on scintillation sheet, Sample bags, and 1450 Microbeta counter (Perkin Elmer, Wellesley, MA).

3. Methods

The frequency of CD34$^+$ hematopoietic progenitors in human bone marrow and cord blood is in the range of 0.5–1% and similar techniques can be applied for isolation of progenitors from both specimens. Although bone marrow will be the most suitable source of progenitors for generation of autologous DC in vitro for future use in clinical DC-based therapies, cord blood, when accessible, provides a good and reliable source of progenitor cells for studies on DC differentiation and function under specific culturing conditions. Using this protocol for positive selection of cord blood CD34⁺ hematopoietic progenitor cells, purity of $CD34^+$ $CD45^+$ cells is approximately 85%. If desired, further purification and separation into subpopulations of enriched progenitors can be accomplished by fluorescence-activated cell sorting (FACS).

It is important to confirm that isolated $CD34^+$ progenitors respond to hematopoietic growth factors known to support DC development in vitro, and therefore progenitors are cultured in GM-CSF plus TNF *(11)*. On day 14 of culture a majority of cells are floating and lightly adherent and show a stellar morphology with elongated cytoplasmic projections, typical for DC. Floating and lightly adherent cells are collected and characterized phenotypically and, as determined by flow cytometry analysis, approximately 70% of cells are $CD11c^+$ HLA-DR^+. A majority of $CD11c^+$ HLA-DR^+ cells express the CD1a molecule. Upon generating DC from progenitors using specific culture conditions to explore new function and differentiation pathways it is also important to perform functional assays with these cells, and the DC generated with GM-CSF and TNF can provide a positive control in T cell proliferation assays. In particular, DC stimulated with LPS upregulate their surface expression of HLA-DR and costimulatory molecules including CD40, CD80, and CD83, and thereby become efficient inducers of T cell proliferation in the mixed leukocyte reaction (MLR).

3.1. Isolation of Hematopoietic Progenitor Cells

1. Collect the cord blood in sterile collection tubes containing EDTA. Process the cells within 24 h of collection (*see* **Note 4**).
2. Dilute the cord blood at 1:4 in isolation buffer and then isolate mononuclear leukocytes from the cord blood using Lymphoprep density centrifugation. Transfer up to 35 ml of cell suspension onto 15 ml of Lymphoprep in 50-ml tubes (*see* **Note 5**). Spin down samples for 20 min at 800 × *g*. After centrifugation, transfer cells at the interface to a new 50-ml tube and fill the tube with isolation buffer. Count the number of cells and spin down the cells for 10 min at 300 × *g*. Resuspend the cell pellet in 50 ml of isolation buffer and spin down again. Resuspend the cell pellet at 4×10^7 cells per 900 μl of isolation buffer and then place the cell suspension on ice.
3. Resuspend the Dynabeads thoroughly in the vial and transfer the desired amount (100 μl per 4×10^7 cells) into a 15-ml washing tube. Place the washing tube in the Dynal MPC for 1 min and then aspirate fluid while the tube is still exposed to the magnet. Remove the tube from the magnet and resuspend beads in 2 ml of washing buffer. Repeat the washing step once and then resuspend the Dynabeads in 100 μl of washing buffer and place the suspension on ice.

4. Resuspend the cells and Dynabeads thoroughly, and then mix them together (*see* **Note 6**). Incubate the cell-bead suspension on a rotating wheel at 15 rpm for 30 min at 2–8°C. After incubation, add isolation buffer to the cell-bead suspension to the height of the magnet. Place the tube in the Dynal MPC for 2 min and aspirate the supernatant. Repeat this washing step three times. After the final wash resuspend beads with positively selected cells in 100 μl of isolation buffer per 4×10^7 cells.

5. To detach beads add 100 μl DetachaBead CD34 per 4×10^7 beads. Vortex the tube for 2–3 s and incubate the tube on a rotating wheel at 15 rpm for 15 min at 37°C. After the incubation, add 2 ml of isolation buffer to the bead-cell suspension and vortex for 2–3 s. Place the sample tube in the Dynal MPC for 2 min. Collect the fluid, which contains released cells, to a new tube. Repeat this step three times and add 2 ml of isolation buffer at each time and pool released cells. To remove any residual beads place the tube with released cells in the Dynal MPC for 2 min and transfer the cell suspension into a new tube. Wash the isolated cells twice in 10 ml of isolation buffer and determine the number of cells (*see* **Note 7**). After isolation, resuspend the hematopoietic progenitor cells in complete DMEM and use them in cultures to generate DC or use the isolated cells for flow cytometry analysis and stain cells with anti-CD34, anti-CD45, anti-CD117, anti-CD116, anti-CD115, anti-CD11c, anti-CD1a, anti-CD1c, anti-CD303, anti-CD14, anti-CD56, anti-CD3, and anti-CD19 antibodies (**Figs. 1** and **2**). Most of $CD34^+$ $CD45^+$ progenitor cells stain positive for CD117 (c-kit), whereas cells positive for the growth factor receptors CD115 (M-CSFR) and CD116 (GM-CSFR) are less than 8% (**Fig. 2a**). Together, this demonstrates that a majority of the isolated $CD34^+$ $CD45^+$ hematopoietic progenitor cells probably still have multilineage potential and are not yet committed to either a monocyte or DC differentiation pathway. To confirm that the presence of contaminating, differentiated leukocytes is at a minimum level in the total population of isolated cells CD34 + cells (Rl gate) the cells are stained for several markers indicative of both myeloid and lymphoid cells. This includes staining for various subsets of DC (CD11c, CD1a, CD1c and CD303), monocytes (CD14), NK cells (CD56), T cells (CD3), and B cells (CD19) (**Fig. 2b, c**).

3.2. Flow Cytometry

1. Transfer cells into 5-ml tubes (BD Biosciences) and wash once with flow cytometry buffer (2 ml) (*see* **Note 8**).

2. Resuspend cells in 50–100 μl of blocking solution and incubate for 30 min on ice. If no biotinylated antibodies are used proceed to **step 4**.

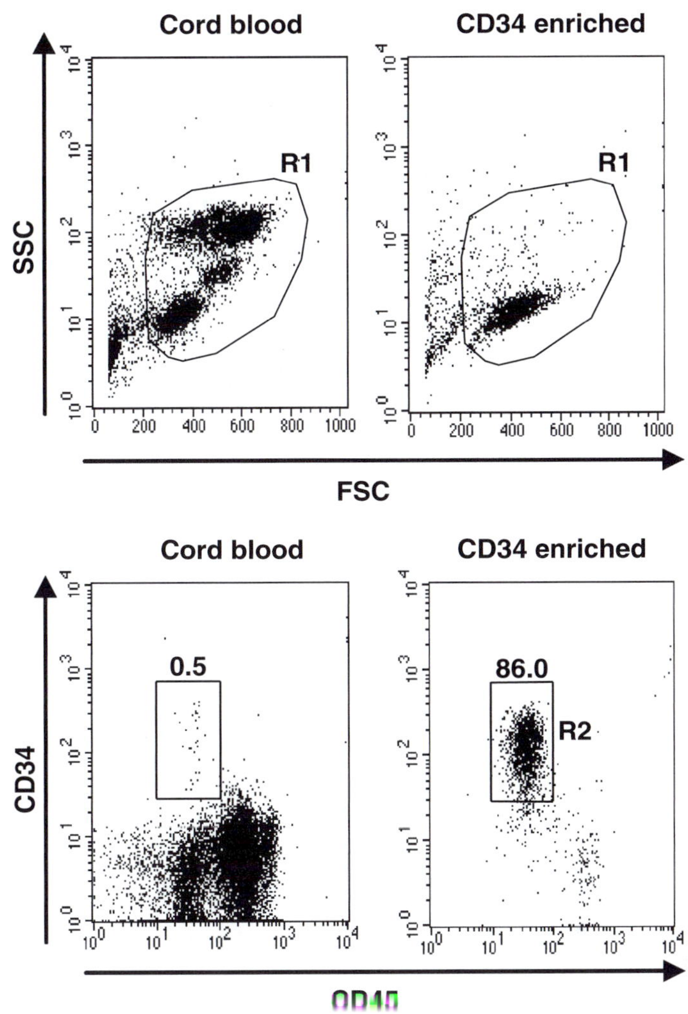

Fig. 1. Frequency of CD34+ CD45+ cells among cells isolated by CD34 enrichment. Whole cord blood or CD34-enriched cells were analyzed by flow cytometry after staining with anti-CD34 and anti-CD45 antibodies. Dot plots show the forward/side scatter size profile and the percentage of cells that are positive for CD34 and CD45. Total cord blood cells and isolated CD34+ progenitors were gated (R1) to include viable cells based on the forward/side scatter profile and hematopoietic progenitor cells were defined as cells expressing CD34 and CD45 (R2).

3. Spin down cells and resuspend in 50–100 µl of flow cytometry buffer containing biotin-conjugated antibodies. Incubate for 45 min on ice and wash cells 2–3 times in flow cytometry buffer.
4. Spin down cells and resuspend cells in 50–100 µl flow cytometry buffer containing fluorochrome-conjugated antibodies and if biotin-conjugated antibodies were added in **step 2** also use fluorochrome-conjugated streptavidin reagents. Incubate

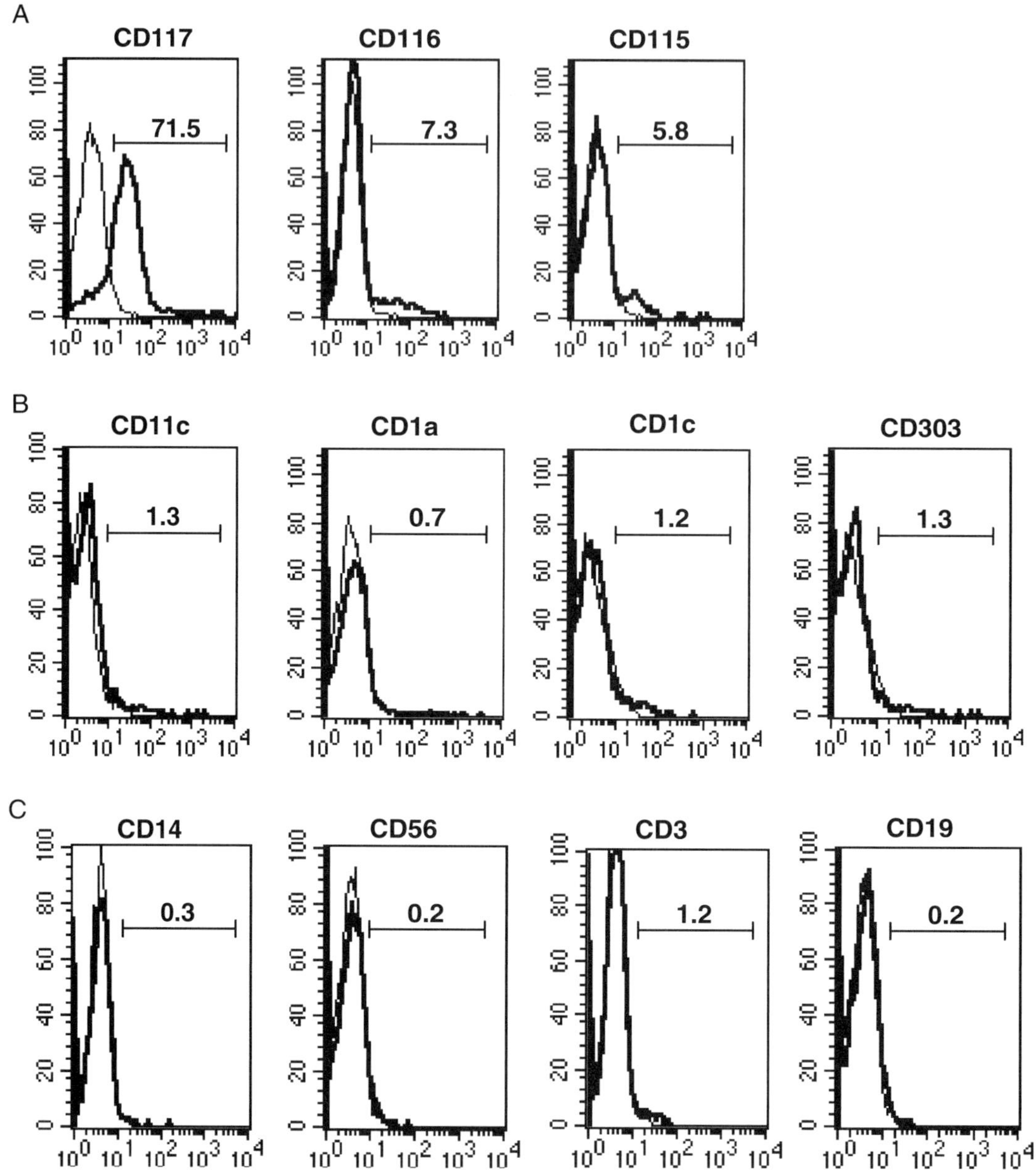

Fig. 2. Surface molecule expression on cells isolated by CD34 enrichment. Isolated CD34+ cells were stained with anti-CD34, anti-CD45, anti-CD117, anti-CD116, anti-CD115, anti-CD11c, anti-CD1a, anti-CD1c, anti-CD303, anti-CD14, anti-CD56, anti-CD3, and anti-CD19. (**A**) Histograms show the surface molecule expression of CD117, CD116, and CD115 (*thick line*) on $CD34^+$ $CD45^+$ cells (gated on R1 and R2, *see* **Fig. 1**). (**B**) Histograms show the surface molecule expression of CD11c, CD1a, CD1c, and CD303 on cells within the R1 gate (total population of isolated CD34+ cells, *see* **Fig. 1**). (**C**) Histograms show the surface expression of CD14, CD56, CD3, and CD19 on cells within the R1 gate (total population of isolated cells, *see* **Fig. 1**). Thin lines represent unstained cells. In (**a**) bars indicate the percentage of positive cells among total $CD34^+$ $CD45^+$ cells and in (**B**, **C**) bars indicate the percentage of positive cells among total cells (*see* **Fig. 1**).

for 45 min on ice and wash cells 2–3 times in flow cytometry buffer.

5. Resuspend cells in fix solution. Incubate for 30 min at room temperature (*see* **Note 9**).
6. Wash cells once in flow cytometry buffer and resuspend in the same buffer prior to acquisition and analysis of the samples using a FACSCalibur (BD Biosciences) and the CellQuest software (BD Biosciences), respectively.

3.3. Culture of Progenitor Cells to Generate DC

1. Wash isolated progenitors in complete DMEM once and resuspend cells at 5×10^4 per ml in complete DMEM containing 50 ng/ml of GM-CSF and 2.5 ng/ml of TNF. Seed 500 μl of cell suspension per well in a 24-well plate (*see* **Note 10**).
2. On day 6 of culture carefully aspirate 400 μl of medium from the wells followed by adding 400 μl of fresh complete DMEM with growth factors. An example of the typical appearance of cultures at day 6 is shown in **Fig. 3a**.
3. On day 12 collect loosely and nonadherent cells. Pool cells and wash once in complete DMEM. Resuspe 3.3 Culture of Progenitor Cells to Generate DC nd cells at 5×10^4 per ml in complete DMEM with GM-CSF and TNF. Seed 2 ml of cell suspension per well in a 12-well plate (*see* **Note 11**). To activate DC add LPS to a final concentration of 1 μg/ml and incubate for 48 h.
4. On day 14 of culture, floating and lightly adherent cells are collected and washed twice in DMEM. An example of the typical appearance of cultures at day 14 is shown in **Fig. 3a**. Use the collected cells for flow cytometry analysis and stain with anti-CD11c, anti-HLA-DR, anti-CD1a, anti CD1c, anti CD14, anti-CD83, anti-CD80, and anti-CD40 antibodies (**Fig. 3b, c**). The detection of CD1a and CD1c on CD11c⁺ HLA-DR⁺ cells demonstrates that the isolated progenitor cells differentiated into DC (**Fig. 3b**). In addition, the lack of CD14 expression on the CD11c⁺ HLA-DR⁺ population confirms that these cells are DC rather than monocytes (**Fig. 3b**). The relatively low surface molecule expression of HLA-DR and costimulatory molecules (CD40, CD80, and CD83), as shown in **Fig. 3c**, is typical for DC that have not yet been activated. However, upon encounter with microbial products, such as LPS, DC are known to respond and undergo a process of cellular activation termed maturation. Upon maturation DC enhance their antigen-presenting capacity by changes to the surface phenotype involving increased expression of HLA-DR and costimulatory molecules. DC generated from progenitor cells also respond to LPS where increased surface expression of HLA-DR and CD40, CD80, and CD83 is evident (**Fig. 3c**) (*see* **Note 12**). The LPS-matured DC can act as efficient inducers of T cell

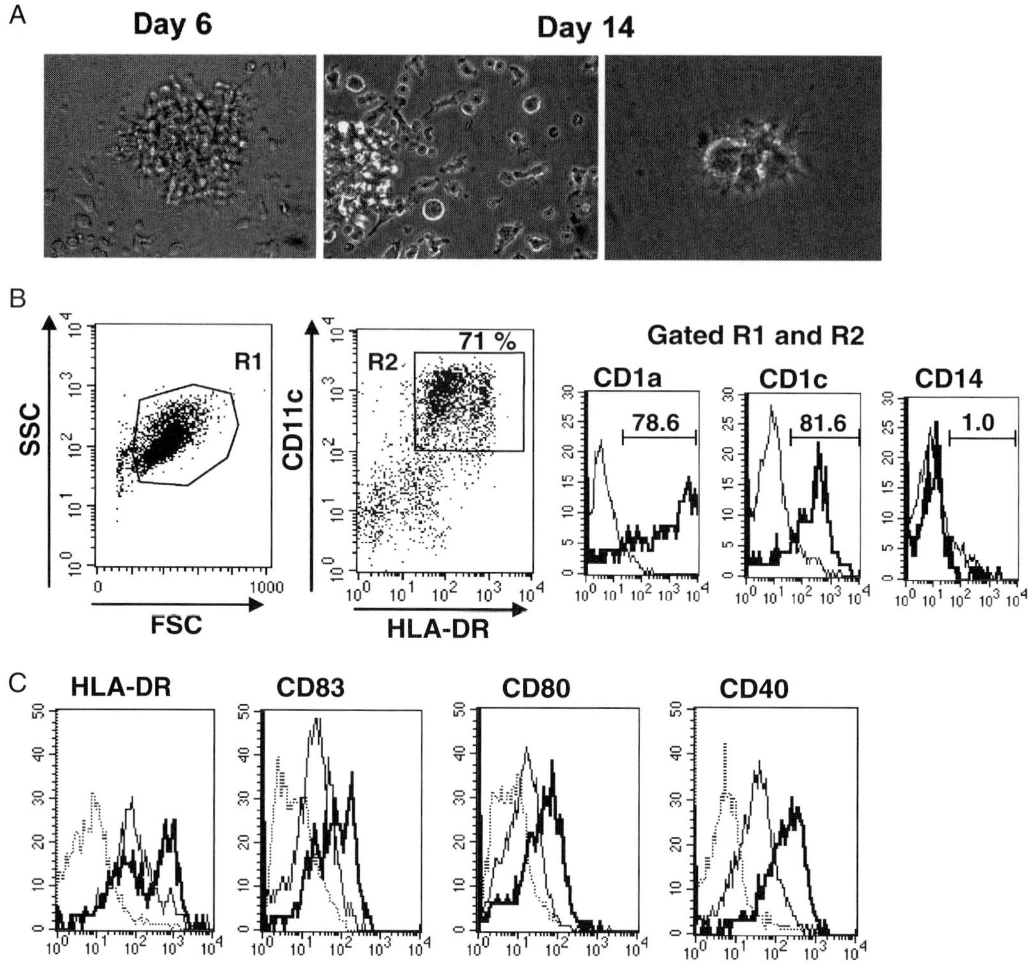

Fig. 3. Morphology and surface molecule expression of DC developing from progenitor cells in response to GM-CSF and TNF. (**A**) The images of day 6 and 14 cell cultures were obtained using an inverted microscope and a digital camera. On day 6 most cells appear in aggregates typical of proliferating hematopoietic cells, and on day 14 cultures contain numerous floating and lightly adherent cells with a DC morphology. (**B**, **C**) Floating and lightly adherent cells were collected on day 14 and analyzed by flow cytometry after staining with antibodies. Cells were stained with anti-CD11c, anti-HLA-DR, anti-CD1a, anti CD1c, anti-CD14, anti-CD83, anti-CD80, anti-CD40, or isotype control antibodies. (**B**) Dot plots show the forward/side scatter size profile and the percentage of cells that are positive for CD11c and HLA-DR. Histograms show the staining of anti-CD1a, anti-CD1c, anti-CD14 (*thick line*), and control antibodies (*thin lines*) on CD11c$^+$ HLA-DR$^+$ cells (gated on R1 and R2). The bars indicate the percentage of positive cells among total CD11c$^+$ HLA-DR$^+$ cells. Together, these results confirm that the isolated progenitor cells differentiated into CD11c$^+$ HLADR$^+$ DC-expressing CD1a and CD1c which is consistent with previous reports *(13)*. (**C**) Histograms show the staining of anti-HLA-DR, anti-CD83, anti-CD80, and anti-CD40 on either nonstimulated (*thin line*) or LPS-stimulated (*thick line*) CD11c$^+$ CD1a$^+$ cells. Dotted lines represent staining with isotype-matched control antibodies on LPS-stimulated cells.

activation and can be used as allogeneic stimulators in the mixed leukocyte reaction (MLR).

3.4. T Cell Isolation and Mixed Leukocyte Reaction

1. Isolate mononuclear leukocytes from samples of normal peripheral blood using Lymphoprep density centrifugation (*see* **Note 13**). Transfer 25 ml of blood cell suspension onto

15 ml of Lymphoprep in 50-ml tubes. Spin samples for 20 min at 800 × *g*. After centrifugation transfer cells at the interface to a new 50-ml tube and fill the tube with PBS. Determine the number of cells and spin down the cells for 10 min at 300 × *g*. Resuspend the cell pellet in 50 ml of PBS and spin down cells again. Resuspend the cell pellet in T cell isolation buffer at 1 × 10^7 cells per 40 μl T cell isolation buffer and place the cell suspension on ice (*see* **Note 14**).

2. Transfer 80 μl of cell suspension into a 15-ml tube and add 20 μl of the Pan T cell biotin-antibody cocktail (*see* **Note 15**). Incubate at 2–8°C for 10 min.
3. Add 60 μl of T cell isolation buffer and 40 μl of beads conjugated with antibiotin MicroBeads. Incubate at 2–8°C for 15 min.
4. Wash the bead-cell suspension by adding 4 ml of T cell isolation buffer and spin down 10 min at 300 × *g*. Repeat this step once.
5. Resuspend cells in 500 μl of T cell isolation buffer. Transfer the cell suspension to an LS column placed in a MidiMACS separator.
6. Apply 3 × 3 ml of T cell isolation buffer to the column and collect the flow through containing the CD3-enriched fraction. Count the cells and take an aliquot to check purity using an anti-CD3 antibody following the protocol for flow cytometry analysis of isolated progenitor cells (**Subheading 3.2**). The purity of isolated cells as determined by their CD3 expression is shown in **Fig. 4a**.
7. Wash CD3-enriched cells once in T cell isolation buffer.
8. Resuspend the cells at 1 × 10^7 cells per 80 μl of T cell isolation buffer and add 20 μl of CD4 or CD8 MicroBeads per 1 × 10^7 cells. Incubate at 2–8°C for 15 min.
9. Add 10 ml of T cell isolation buffer and spin down.
10. Resuspend cells in 500 μl T cell isolation buffer. Transfer the cell suspension to an LS column placed in a MidiMACS separator.
11. Apply 3 × 3 ml of T cell isolation buffer to the column. Remove the column from the separator and place in a new 15-ml tube to collect positively selected cells. Add 3 ml of T cell isolation buffer to the column and immediately flush out the positively selected cells using the plunger supplied with the column.
12. Wash once and count the number of cells. Take an aliquot to check purity using anti-CD3, anti-CD4, anti-CD8 antibodies following the protocol for flow cytometry analysis (**Subheading 3.2**). The purity of isolated CD4 T cells and CD8 T cells

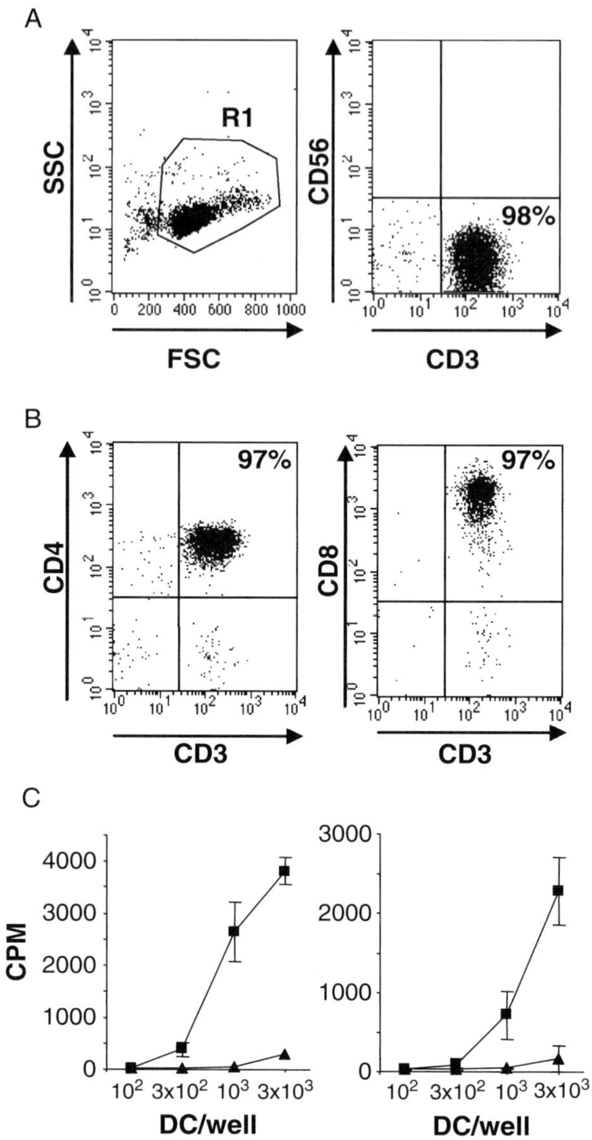

Fig. 4. Isolation of allogeneic T cells and stimulation of T cells in mixed leukocyte reactions using DC derived from progenitor cells. (**A**) CD3-enriched cells were analyzed by flow cytometry after staining with anti-CD3 and anti-CD56 antibodies. Dot plots show the forward/side scatter size profile and the percentage of CD3 single positive cells (gated on R1). (**B**) Positively selected CD4 and CD8 T cells were analyzed by flow cytometry after staining with anti-CD3 and anti-CD4, and anti-CD3 and anti-CD8, respectively. Dot plots show the percentage of cells that are positive for CD3 and CD4 (*left*) and for CD3 and CD8 (*right*) (gated on R1 as in (**A**)). (**C**) Isolated CD4 (*left*) and CD8 (*right*) T cells were used as responder cells in an MLR with DC derived from progenitor cells as stimulators. 1×10^5 responder $CD4^+$ or $CD8^+$ T cells were mixed together with 10^2, 3×10^2, 10^3, or 3×10^3 stimulator DC in triplicate wells. The stimulating activity of DC (*triangles*) or DC stimulated with LPS (1 μg/ml) for 48 h (*squares*) was determined by the degree of [^{3}H]thymidine incorporation in proliferating T cells and is shown as counts per minute (CPM). Wells containing only T cells or irradiated APC incorporated <100 cpm.

is determined by the CD3 and CD4, and CD3 and CD8 surface expression, respectively, and is shown in **Fig. 4b**.

13. Wash cells twice in complete RPMI and then resuspend cells in complete RPMI at 1×10^6 cells per ml.
14. Set up primary mixed leukocyte reactions in flat-bottom 96-well plates with 1×10^5 (100 μl) responder $CD4^+$ or $CD8^+$ T cells per well. In addition, add 10^2, 3×10^2, 10^3, or 3×10^3 day 14 DC derived from progenitor cells as allogeneic stimulator cells in triplicates. Stimulator cells should be irradiated with 2,000 rad prior to mixing with T cells. Incubate the MLR for a total of 96 and 8 h before termination; add 0.5 μCi [^{3}H]thymidine per well (*see* **Note 16**).
15. After pulsing with [^{3}H]thymidine harvest cells onto glass fiber filters and count. Then responses can be reported as mean cpm ± standard deviation (**Fig. 4c**).

4. Notes

1. Cord blood specimens are obtained according to institutional guidelines and approved by the regional ethical review board. Cord blood is collected after cesarean deliveries after clamping and cutting of the cord, and usually 15–20 ml of cord blood can be collected. From this amount of blood the $CD34^+$ selection procedure generates between 0.5×10^6 and 1×10^6 cells.
2. As basal medium DMEM with L-glucose, L-glutamine and pyruvate (Invitrogen) is used. The FBS is heat inactivated at 56°C for 30 min before use. Unless stated otherwise, DMEM with all the supplements is referred to as complete DMEM. All cell cultures are kept at 37°C in humidified, 5% CO_2 incubators.
3. Buffy coats are obtained according to institutional guidelines and approved by the regional ethical review board. From one buffy coat at least 5×10^7 T cells can be isolated.
4. If the cord blood is not processed immediately it can be stored for at least 24 h tilting at room temperature.
5. At the time of doing gradient centrifugations it is critical that all blood, isolation buffer, and the Lymphoprep are adjusted to room temperature. Do the centrifugation at room temperature with low acceleration and no breaks.
6. At the time of adding the 100 μl of Dynabeads M-450 CD34 to the cell suspension it is critical that both solutions have been stored on ice for at least 15 min to prevent nonspecific

attachment of phagocytic cells to the Dynabeads. The final concentration of cells after adding beads is 4×10^7 per ml. After mixing beads and cells, immediately place the tubes on a rotating wheel at 2–8°C. During the washing procedures ensure that the isolation buffer is ice cold. At the steps following addition of DetachaBead CD34 isolation buffer at room temperature is used.

7. Isolated CD34 cells can be cryopreserved in FBS with 10% dimethyl sulfoxide. Also, if necessary isolated cells can be stored in complete DMEM at 2–8°C and used for flow cytomtery analysis the following day.
8. Following this protocol perform all incubations, except fixation, on ice and use ice-cold flow cytometry buffer to wash cells and for dilution of reagents.
9. After fixation cells can be stored in fix solution at 2–8°C for up to 3 days prior to analysis.
10. Starting with 2.5×10^4 per well in a 48-well plate avoids overgrowth of cells during the culture period. The number of cells collected at day 12 is in the range of 5- to 10-fold that of the starting population. Interestingly, addition of stem cell factor (SCF) together with the GM-CSF and TNF in cultures results in an additional 5- to 10-fold increase of the cell yield on day 12 compared to the cultures supplemented with GM-CSF and TNF only. This may be explained by the fact that at least 70% of isolated $CD34^+$ $CD45^+$ cells express CD117 which is the receptor for SCF. In contrast, less than 10% of isolated $CD34^+$ $CD45^+$ cells express the GM-CSF receptor CD116. Importantly, the addition of SCF to progenitor cultures generates more cells in total, but the frequency of $CD11c^+$ $HLA\text{-}DR^+$ $CD1a^+$ cells is decreased.
11. A majority of cells that are collected on day 12 remain $CD11c^+$ $HLA\text{-}DR^+$ $CD1a^+$ and floating also when cultured for 2 days in the presence of complete DMEM with M-CSF (50 ng/ml). This demonstrates that the majority of collected cells are DC rather than monocytes which would develop into adherent macrophages in response to M-CSF.
12. Recently it was demonstrated that Langerhans cells isolated from human skin lack the expression of mRNA for TLR4 and do not respond to LPS ex vivo. Whether the DC that are generated from $CD34^+$ progenitors and resemble Langerhans cells can directly respond to LPS is not yet known. However, the DC population generated from $CD34^+$ progenitors is heterogeneous, and it is possible that the observed response to LPS by DC in these cultures involves both direct and indirect mechanisms *(12)*.

13. Adjust blood and Lymphoprep to room temperature and do the centrifugation at room temperature with low acceleration and no breaks.
14. Always keep the MACS buffer on ice and try to keep cell suspensions on ice as much as possible doing MACS purifications. Also, perform all centrifugation steps at 4°C.
15. Exceeding this number of cells and the corresponding amount of Pan T cell biotin-antibody cocktail per tube may result in poor purity of isolated T cells. It is preferable to isolate $CD4^+$ and $CD8^+$ T cells from the CD3-enriched fraction rather than directly from the mononuclear fraction as this will prevent the copurification of $CD8^+$ NK cells and $CD4^+$ DC present in blood.
16. The stimulating activity of DC is determined by the degree of proliferation in responding T cells according to the amount of [^{3}H]thymidine incorporated into DNA of replicating cells.

Acknowledgments

The author thanks the personnel at the Karolinska University Hospital, Obstetrics Clinic, for collecting the cord blood and Dr. Malin Flodström-Tullberg, Center for Infectious Medicine, Karolinska Institutet, for critical review of the manuscript. Work in the author's laboratory is supported by grants from the Swedish Research Council, the Swedish Foundation for Strategic Research, and the Karolinska Institutet.

References

1. Bruno, L., Seidl, T., and Lanzavecchia, A. (2001) Mouse pre-immunocytes as non-proliferating multipotent precursors of macrophages, interferon-producing cells, CD8α+ and CD8α– dendritic cells. *Eur. J. Immunol.* 31, 3403–3412.
2. Diao, J., Winter, E., Chen, W., Cantin, C., and Cattral, M. S. (2004) Characterization of distinct conventional and plasmacytoid dendritic cell-committed precursors in murine bone marrow. *J. Immunol.* 173, 1826–1833.
3. Bogunovic, M., Ginhoux, F., Wagers, A., Loubeau, M., Isola, L. M., Lubrano, L., Najfeld, V., Phelps, R. G., Grosskreutz, C., Scigliano, E., Frenette, P. S., and Merad, M. (2006) Identification of a radio-resistant and cycling dermal dendritic cell population in mice and men. *J. Exp. Med.* 203, 2627–2638.
4. Naik, S. H., Metcalf, D., van Nieuwenhuijze, A., Wicks, I., Wu, L., O'Keeffe, M., and Shortman, K. (2006) Intrasplenic steady-state dendritic cell precursors that are distinct from monocytes. *Nat. Immunol.* 7, 663–671.
5. O'Keeffe, M., Hochrein, H., Vremec, D., Scott, B., Hertzog, P., Tatarczuch, L., and Shortman, K. (2003) Dendritic cell precursor populations of mouse blood: identification of the murine homologues of human blood plasmacytoid pre-DC2 and $CD11c^+$ DC1 precursors. *Blood* 101, 1453–1459.

6. Siegal, F. P., Kadowaki, N., Shodell, M., Fitzgerald-Bocarsly, P. A., Shah, K., Ho, S., Antonenko, S., and Liu, Y. J. (1999) The nature of the principal type 1 interferon-producing cells in human blood. *Science* 284, 1835–1837.
7. Wakkach, A., Fournier, N., Brun, V., Breittmayer, J. P., Cottrez, F., and Groux, H. (2003) Characterization of dendritic cells that induce tolerance and T regulatory 1 cell differentiation in vivo. *Immunity* 18, 605–617.
8. Svensson, M., and Kaye, P. M. (2006) Stromal-cell regulation of dendritic-cell differentiation and function. *Trends Immunol.* 27, 580–587.
9. Reid, C. D., Fryer, P. R., Clifford, C., Kirk, A., Tikerpae, J., and Knight, S. C. (1990) Identification of hematopoietic progenitors of macrophages and dendritic Langerhans cells (DL-CFU) in human bone marrow and peripheral blood. *Blood* 76, 1139–1149.
10. Caux, C., Dezutter-Dambuyant, C., Schmitt, D., and Banchereau, J. (1992) GM-CSF and TNF-α cooperate in the generation of dendritic Langerhans cells. *Nature* 360, 258–261.
11. Caux, C., Massacrier, C., Vanbervliet, B., Dubois, B., Durand, I., Cella, M., Lanzavecchia, A., and Banchereau, J. (1997) CD34+ hematopoietic progenitors from human cord blood differentiate along two independent dendritic cell pathways in response to granulocyte-macrophage colony-stimulating factor plus tumor necrosis factor α: II. Functional analysis. *Blood* 90, 1458–1470.
12. Flacher, V., Bouschbacher, M., Verronese, E., Massacrier, C., Sisirak, V., Berthier-Vergnes, O., de Saint-Vis, B., Caux, C., Dezutter-Dambuyant, C., Lebecque, S, and Valladeau, J. (2006) Human Langerhans cells express a specific TLR profile and differentially respond to viruses and Gram-positive bacteria. *J. Immunol.* 177, 7959–7967.
13. Caux, C., Vanbervliet, B., Massacrier, C., Durand, I., and Banchereau, J. (1996) Interleukin-3 cooperates with tumor necrosis factor α for the development of human dendritic/Langerhans cells from cord blood CD34+ hematopoietic progenitor cells. *Blood* 87, 2376–2385.

Chapter 14

Generation, Culture and Flow-Cytometric Characterization of Primary Mouse Macrophages

Ulrike Schleicher and Christian Bogdan

Summary

Macrophages are not only host cells for many pathogens, but also fulfill several key functions in the innate and adaptive immune response, including the release of pro- and anti-inflammatory cytokines, the generation of organic and inorganic autacoids, the phagocytosis and killing of intracellular microorganisms or tumor cells, and the degradation and presentation of antigens. Several of these functions are shared by other immune cells, including dendritic cells, granulocytes, NK cells, and/or T lymphocytes. Thus, the analysis of macrophage functions in vitro using primary mouse cell populations requires standardized methods for the generation and culture of macrophages that guarantee high cell purity as well as the absence of stimulatory microbial contaminants. This chapter presents methodology to achieve these aims.

Key words: Macrophages, Bone marrow-derived macrophages, Peritoneal exudate macrophages, Resident peritoneal macrophages, Teflon bags, Flow cytometry, Cell sorting, Cytokines, Interferon-gamma.

1. Introduction

Macrophages (MΦ) are at the center stage of the immune response of mammalian organisms to microbial pathogens and tumor cells and also participate in both the initiation and the effector phases of autoimmune processes. They are potent producers of cytokines, chemokines, and numerous other pro- or anti-inflammatory organic and inorganic mediators such as prostaglandins, enzymes, or nitric oxide (NO); they phagocytose, kill, and degrade viral, bacterial, and protozoan pathogens

Neil E. Reiner (ed.), *Macrophages and Dendritic Cells,* Methods in Molecular Biology, vol. 531

DOI: 10.1007/978-1-59745-396-7_14

as well as apoptotic or necrotic cells in the tissues of the mammalian hosts; and they are capable of presenting exogenous and endogenous antigens in the context of MHC class I or II antigens *(1–4)*. The multiple functions of MΦ are reflected by their reciprocal interactions with other cell types, notably with T lymphocytes ($CD3^+CD4^+NK1.1^-DX5^-$ or $CD3^+CD8^+NK1.1^-DX5^-$), natural killer (NK) cells ($CD3^-NK1.1^+DX5^+$), and NKT cells ($CD3^+NK1.1^+DX5^+$), all of which can confer soluble and/or cell contact-dependent stimulatory signals to MΦ *(5–14)*.

Immunologists frequently use in vitro cultures of primary mouse MΦ to study (a) the activation of signaling cascades of antimicrobial effector mechanisms and of the release of cytokines and other mediators in response to novel microbial or lymphocyte-derived stimuli, and (b) the regulation (activation or suppression) of T lymphocyte functions. In order to avoid false conclusions, these experiments require the use of highly purified MΦ populations, the absence of MΦ-stimulatory contaminants in all reagents during all steps of MΦ preparation, and the application of cell culture conditions that do not lead to a priori activation or suppression of MΦ functions. In this chapter we present methods of MΦ generation, culture, and phenotypic characterization that are specifically designed to fulfill these criteria.

2. Materials

The MΦ discussed here are primary MΦ derived from inbred or outbred mouse strains (e.g., BALB/c, C57BL/6, 129Sv, CD1). It is crucial to use only mice from specific pathogen-free (SPF) facilities, because various mouse pathogens (e.g., mouse hepatitis virus, Sendai virus) have been demonstrated to strongly influence macrophage functions *(15–20)*.

2.1. Peritoneal MΦ

1. Ca^{2+}- and Mg^{2+}-free Dulbecco's phosphate-buffered saline (PBS), prepared from PBS powder and deionized, endotoxin-free water (*see* **Note 1**) or commercially purchased (e.g., from Invitrogen, Karlsruhe, Germany).
2. 4% (w/v) Brewer's thioglycolate broth. The broth is prepared by suspending 40.5 g of the dehydrated Bacto Brewer thioglycolate medium (*see* **Note 2**) in 1 L of endotoxin-free deionized water (*see* **Note 1**), boiling in a microwave oven to dissolve completely, and immediate sterilization in an autoclave (121°C, 15–20 min). Prepare 50- to 100-mL aliquots, which can be stored at room temperature for many months.
3. 0.9% (w/v) NaCl solution containing 5 mM sodium periodate. Prepare fresh immediately before use (*see* **Note 1**).

4. 6% (w/v) Sodium caseinate. The 6% suspension is prepared by suspending 6 g of sodium caseinate in 100 mL of endotoxin-free deionized water or 0.9% (w/v) saline (*see* **Note 1**), stirring with medium heat (ca. 30 min), and immediate sterilization in an autoclave (121°C, 15–20 min). The suspension will look pink. Continue stirring it while still warm until the suspension is uniform. Prepare aliquots (e.g., 5 mL), store at 4°C, and warm to room temperature before use.
5. 1 or 3% (w/v) Proteose peptone. Add 1 or 3% (w/v) proteose peptone to endotoxin-free deionized water (*see* **Note 1**), boil, and autoclave the solution. Prepare aliquots, store up to 3 months at 4°C, and warm to room temperature before use.
6. 1% (w/v) Polyacrylamide beads in sterile saline or PBS (*see* **Note 1**). Prepare freshly before use.
7. 10-mL Sterile, pyrogen-free plastic syringes and needles (20G and 27G), small sterile scissors and forcipes.
8. 70% (v/v) Ethanol.
9. 50-mL Sterile polypropylene tubes.

10 Cell culture medium RPMI1640, supplemented with 2 mM L-glutamine, 23.8 mM $NaHCO_3$, 10 mM HEPES, 50 μM 2-mercaptoethanol, 100 U/mL penicillin/100 μg/mL streptomycin, and varying amounts of fetal calf serum (FCS; 1–5%) (*see* **Note 3**).

11. Styrofoam box with ice.
12. Multicentrifuge 3-SR Sorvall-Heraeus or equivalent.
13. Shandon Cytospin® 4 Cytocentrifuge and accessories (glass slides, filtercards, funnels).
14. Diff-Quick® fixative and staining solutions.
15. 0.04% (w/v) Trypan blue solution.

2.2. Bone Marrow-Derived MΦ (BMMΦ)

2.2.1. Preparation of Teflon bags

1. Biologically inert, transparent, gas-permeable membrane of thermoplastic fluoro-ethylene-propylene copolymer (*see* **Note 4**).
2. Continuous band sealer machine to seal FEP-Teflon® membrane, e.g., Polystar 350/5 DSM.
3. Anprolene® ampoules (containing ethylene oxide) for gas sterilization (*see* **Note 5**).
4. Ethylene oxide indicator tape.
5. Sterilization and aeration cabinet. Alternatively, a commercially available cooling (ice) box (as used in households) will also do, provided it is placed in a fume hood during the entire sterilization and evaporation phase.
6. 70% (v/v) Ethanol.
7. Sterile scalpels.

2.2.2. Generation of BMMΦ

1. Dulbecco's modified Eagle medium (DMEM) containing 3.7 g $NaHCO_3$/L (23 mM), 4.5 g glucose/L (40 mM), 4 mM L-glutamine, and 110 mg/L sodium pyruvate (*see* **Note 1**).
2. FCS (*see* **Note 3**).
3. Horse serum (*see* **Note 3**).
4. 10 mM 2-mercaptoethanol in PBS, sterile filtrated, stored in 5-mL aliquots at –20°C (*see* **Note 1**).
5. Nonessential amino acid solution (100×), store at +4°C (*see* **Note 1**).
6. Penicillin/streptomycin solution (100×; 10,000 U/mL penicillin, 10,000 µg/mL streptomycin; Invitrogen), 5-mL aliquots stored at –20°C (*see* **Note 1**).
7. L929 cell culture supernatant (L929 SN, *see* **Subheadings 2.2.3** and **3.2.3**, stored in aliquots at –20°C).
8. Recombinant murine macrophage-colony-stimulating factor, 10 µg/mL stock solution stored in single-use aliquots at –80°C as recommended by the manufacturer (*see* **Note 1**).
9. Sterile PBS (*see* **Note 1**).
10. 70% (v/v) Ethanol.
11. 0.04% Trypan blue solution.
12. Sterile Teflon® bags, 5 × 30 cm (inner side of the Teflon® bag is hydrophobic).
13. Sterilized pairs of forcipes and scissors for the preparation of mouse femurs (kept in sterile stainless steel box).
14. Sterile, pyrogen-free syringes (10 or 20 mL), i.v. indwelling cannulas (14G), and disposable hypodermic needles (27G).
15. Anatomical clamp (the grooved ends need to be covered with adhesive tape, with the sticky surface facing outward).
16. Plastic closures (normally used for closing dialysis tubings) to lock the Teflon bags after filling.
17. Perforated trays for the incubator.

2.2.3. Preparation of L929 Cell Culture Supernatant (L929 SN)

1. Cell culture medium as described in **Subheading 2.2.2.**
2. Sterile Teflon® bags, 20 × 30 cm (inner side of the Teflon® bag is hydrophilic).
3. L929 fibroblasts, obtained from ATCC.
4. Cell scrapers with thin, flexible, 2-position blades.

2.3. Culture of MΦ for Induction of Cytokine Production and/or Effector Molecules

1. Polystyrene tissue culture plates (e.g., NUNC, Wiesbaden, Germany: 96-well flat-bottomed plates (cat. no. 167008, 0.33 cm^2/well), 24-well plates (cat. no. 142475, 1.9 cm^2/well), small Petri dishes (cat. no. 150288, Ø 5.3 cm, 21.5 cm^2/dish), large Petri dishes (cat. no. 150350, Ø 8.7 cm,

56.7 cm²/dish), 8-well Permanox™ Lab-Tek™ Chamber Slides™ (cat. no. 177445, 0.8 cm²/well).

2. Macrophage cell culture medium (*see* **Subheading 2.1**, **item 10**; **Subheading 2.2.2**, **item 1**; **Subheading 3.2.2**, **step 1**) (*see* **Note 1**).
3. PBS (*see* **Subheading 2.1, item 1**; **Note 1**).
4. rmIFN-γ: 1 mg/mL stock solution in 20 mM Tris–HCl, 0.15 M NaCl, pH 7.5 from Genentech, South San Francisco; stored without loss of activity at 4°C for more than 14 years. Prepare 1-mL aliquots with 10 μg IFN-γ/mL in RPMI1640 plus 5% FCS (long-term storage at −80°C, aliquots for ongoing experiments are stored at 4°C and are stable for at least 4 years if kept sterile; do not refreeze (*see* **Note 1**)).
5. Lipopolysaccharide (LPS), e.g., from *E. coli* O111:B4 (Sigma-Aldrich, Taufkirchen, Germany). Dissolve at 10 mg/mL in deionized water using a sonicating water bath and prepare 50-μL aliquots (stored at −80°C). Working solutions (1 mL) of 10 or 100 μg LPS/mL are prepared in RPMI1640 plus 5% FCS (kept at −80°C; vortex after thawing).
6. rmTNF (R&D Systems, Wiesbaden, Germany: 10 μg/mL stock solution prepared in sterile PBS plus 2.5 mg/mL human serum albumin; store in 20-μL aliquots at −80°C) (*see* **Note 1**).
7. PBS (*see* **Subheading 2.1**, **item 1**) plus 10 mM EDTA (*see* **Note 1**).
8. Accutase™ (PAA Laboratories, Coelbe, Germany), ready-to-use solution, stored in single use aliquots at −20°C
9. Cell scrapers (*see* **Subheading 2.2**, **item 4**).

2.4. Phenotypic Analysis of MΦ by Flow Cytometry

1. PBS (*see* **Subheading 2.1**, **item 1**; **Note 1**).
2. FACS (fluorescence-activated cell sorting) staining buffer: PBS, 2 mM EDTA plus 1% FCS (PAA Laboratories, Coelbe, Germany) (*see* **Note 6**).
3. Propidium iodide (PI) solution. PI (Sigma-Aldrich, cat. no. P4170) is dissolved in PBS. Stock solution (1 mg/mL) is stored in aliquots at −80°C, working aliquot (100 μg/mL) is stored at +4°C in the dark (light sensitive!). PI is potentially mutagenic (DNA-intercalating agent).
4. Purified rat antimouse CD16/CD32 mAb (mouse Fc block) (BD Biosciences, Heidelberg, Germany), stored at +4°C.
5. Fluorochrome-labeled or biotinylated monoclonal antibodies (mAb), fluorochrome-labeled streptavidin, and the respective fluorochrome-labeled isotype control mAbs. Storage as recommended by the manufacturer (mostly at +4°C in the

dark (light-sensitive dyes)). The concentration for optimal staining of the respective macrophage population has to be determined by titration of the mAb.

6. 12 × 75 mm FACS test tubes (polypropylene, not polystyrene!) (e.g., Sarstedt, Nümbrecht, Germany).
7. Accutase (*see* **Subheading 2.3, item 8**).
8. PBS (*see* **Subheading 2.1, item 1**) with 10 mM EDTA (*see* **Note 1**).
9. Cell scrapers (*see* **Subheading 2.2.3, item 4**).
10. 100-μm Nylon mesh (e.g., Fa. Eckert, Waldkirch,Germany).

3. Methods

3.1. Generation of Peritoneal MΦ

3.1.1. General Remarks

1. Resident peritoneal MΦ (RPMΦ) are derived from the peritoneal cavity of naive mice, i.e., they are generated from resident peritoneal cells (PCs). Peritoneal exudate MΦ (PE-MΦ), in contrast, are generated from peritoneal exudate cells (PECs) that are recruited to the peritoneal cavity after intraperitoneal injection of sterile inflammatory agents.
2. The percentage of MΦ within resident PCs is in the range of 40–60%, whereas PECs contain 75–95% MΦ depending on the eliciting agent and the time point of harvesting.
3. Harvesting of peritoneal MΦ does not require a laminar-flow hood as long as the investigator carefully disinfects the mice and wears a gown, facial mask, and disposable gloves.
4. Peritoneal cells should always been evaluated for their cellular composition (% MΦ, lymphocytes, neutrophils, eosinophils, basophils, and mast cells) using cytocentrifugation and Diff-Quick®-staining. An altered cellular composition from what is normally expected may be indicative of an infection in the mouse colony.

3.1.2. Resident Peritoneal Cells

1. Naive mice are euthanized by CO_2 asphyxiation and subsequent cervical dislocation with a large pair of tweezers (*see* **Note 7**). Do not prepare more than 4–5 mice at a time.
2. Fix the dead mice with four pins at the extremities using a Styrofoam™ board.
3. Carefully wet the fur of each of the mice with 70% ethanol, thereby disinfecting the skin and avoiding loose hair which might later contaminate the peritoneal lavage fluid.

4. Make a small incision in the center of the abdominal skin (without damaging the peritoneum!) using sterile scissors. Carefully pull apart the abdominal skin (cranially and caudally) so that the abdominal wall is completely exposed. Do *not* disinfect the abdominal wall, because 70% ethanol will make the peritoneum rigid due to protein denaturation.
5. Using a 10-mL syringe and a 20-G needle inject 10–11 mL sterile PBS (without FCS) into the peritoneal cavity. Insert the needle in the midline of the lower abdomen (between the umbilical area and the bladder) and, while forcefully injecting the PBS (which keeps away the intestine), push the needle slowly toward the right upper quadrant of the peritoneal cavity (where no omental fat will later block the needle during reaspiration). Throughout the procedure the beveled edge of the needle is facing upward.
6. Turn the syringe so that the beveled edge of the needle is facing downward and raise the needle, which will cause tenting of the peritoneal wall (keep the needle strictly parallel to the longitudinal axis of the mouse to avoid perforation of the peritoneum). Withdraw the peritoneal lavage fluid (expected volume ca. 9–10 mL) *slowly* to avoid aspiration of mesenterial tissue. After removal of the needle dispense the lavage fluid into 50-mL polypropylene centrifuge tubes on ice.
7. Repeat **steps 5** and **6** (insert the needle into the previous peritoneal perforation). Pool the lavage fluid from several mice, but discard lavages that contain blood.
8. Centrifuge the cells at 300 × g (8–10 min, 4°C). Resuspend the cell pellet in RPMI1640 cell culture medium (**Subheading 2.1, Item 10**) so that the cell density is at least 5×10^6/mL. For the expected cell yields, *see* **Note 8** and **Table 1**.
9. Remove a 10 (or 20) μL sample, mix it with 90 (or 80) μL trypan blue solution and count the cells (MΦ, lymphocytes, granulocytes) using a hemocytometer (*see* **Note 8** and **Table 1**).
10. Prepare a cytospin slide (using ca. 1×10^5 peritoneal cells in 250 μL PBS) for Diff-Quick® staining, perform a differential cell count, and adjust the peritoneal cell suspension according to the determined macrophage content.

3.1.3. Peritoneal Exudate MΦ

1. Inject the mice intraperitoneally with a defined volume of the elicitating agent (*see* **Note 8** and **Table 1**).
2. At the time point indicated (**Table 1**) harvest the cells from the peritoneal cavity by two sequential peritoneal lavages with serum-free PBS as described earlier (**Subheading 3.1.2 Steps 1–10**) (*see* **Note 8** and **Table 1**).

Table 1
Eliciting agents, expected yields, and cellular composition of peritoneal cells

Type of peritoneal cell population	Volume of i.p. injected inflammatory agent	Hours after i.p. injection when the peritoneal cells are harvested	Expected yield of total peritoneal cells per mouse[a]	% of Macrophages expected prior to adherence (reference)	% of Macrophages expected after adherence (reference)
Resident peritoneal cells	None	n.a.	1–2 × 10^6	ca. 40–60%	83–88% *(30, 42)*
Thioglycolate-elicited PEC	2–3 mL 4% Brewer?s thioglycolate medium	96 h (–120 h)	15–25 × 10^6	>86–95%[b] *(29, 32, 35)*	99% *(29, 30)*
Proteose peptone-elicited PECs	2–3 mL 3% proteose peptone solution	72 h	5–10 × 10^6	75–80%	90–94% *(42)*
Caseinate-elicited PECs	2 mL 6% sodium caseinate solution	72 h	5–10 × 10^6	75–80%	92–96% *(30, 42)*
Sodium periodate-elicited PECs	2 mL 5 mM $NaIO_4$ solution	72 h	5–15 × 10^6	75–80%	78–93% *(30, 42)*
Biogel-elicited PECs	2 mL 1% Biogel P100 bead suspension	120 h	5–15 × 10^6	60%	97% *(24)*

n.a. not applicable

[a]Numbers refer to female CD1 outbred mice (10–12 weeks of age, 20–24 g of weight) (unpublished data of the authors as well as published data)

[b]Thioglycolate-elicited PECs contain numerous vacuoles that are filled with ingested thioglycolate medium *(43)*

[c]Biogel-elicited macrophages do not contain the bead particles, because these are too big to be ingested by the macrophages *(24)*

3.2. Generation of BMMΦ

3.2.1. Preparation of Teflon® Bags

1. The FEB-Teflon® foil is unrolled on a clean surface. The inner side of the Teflon® bag (*see* **Note 9**) is wiped off with 70% ethanol and cut into 30 × 10 cm (BMMΦ) or 30 × 40 cm pieces (L929 cells) using a sterile scalpel. It is recommended to wear unpowdered gloves during the preparation of Teflon® bags.
2. The foil is then folded and sealed so that bags of 30 × 5 cm (BMMΦ) or of 30 × 20 cm (L929) are obtained. One of the

short sides of the bags remains unsealed, but otherwise take care that the sealing seam is tight (indicated by an opaque color).

3. Fifteen to twenty of the BMMΦ Teflon® bags or 10 of the L929 Teflon® bags, all lined up in the same orientation, are wrapped with aluminum foil. The aluminum bags are closed by folding except for the side where the open ends of the Teflon® bags are. A piece of ethylene oxide indicator tape is attached to the outside of the aluminum foil.
4. For sterilization, the aluminum bags, an Anprolene® ampoule (which is enclosed in a gas-permeable plastic bag), and wet paper towels are put together into the so-called liner bag (a gas-impermeable plastic bag) and transferred into the sterilizer container. The wet towels serve to achieve an ambient relative humidity of at least 30% which is required for efficient sterilization. After opening of the Anprolene® ampoule, the sterilizer will be locked and placed in a running fume hood for 24 h. To allow evaporation of residual ethylene oxide at the end of the 24-h sterilization period, the sterilizer container and the liner bag are opened and left in the fume hood for another 24 h. Thereafter, the aluminum bags are placed in a running laminar-flow hood overnight to further aerate the Teflon® bags. Finally, the open side of the aluminum bags is tightly closed by folding over, which allows storage at room temperature until use for cell culture.

3.2.2. Culture of Bone Marrow Cells for the Generation of BMMΦ

1. The following media have to be prepared:
   (a) *Conditioned DMEM medium*: DMEM supplemented with 50 µM 2-ME, 1% nonessential amino acids, 10% FCS, 5% horse serum to inhibit growth of granulocytes, 15% L929 SN as a source of M-CSF (*see* **Subheadings 2.2.3** and **3.2.3**) or 5 ng/mL rmM-CSF (*see* **Note 10**).
   (b) *DMEM medium*: DMEM supplemented with 50 µM 2-ME, 1% nonessential amino acids, 5% FCS, 1% penicillin/streptomycin solution
2. Mice are euthanized and thoroughly disinfected with 70% ethanol. Wear gloves. The skin is peeled from both hind legs by pulling it down over the feet. Without damaging the femurs and tibiae, the muscles are completely removed with forceps and scissors. The bones are stored in cold sterile DMEM medium on ice until the bone marrow is prepared under laminar-flow conditions.
3. The leg bones are severed between the joints, the epiphyses of femur and tibia are opened with sterile scissors, and a 27-G needle (connected to a 10-mL syringe filled with

sterile PBS) is inserted into the bone marrow cavity, which is then flushed until the PBS remains clear and the bones appear white. The washed-out bone marrow is collected in 50-mL polypropylene centrifuge tubes.

4. Bone marrow (BM) cells are centrifuged at 300 × *g*, 5–10 min, 4°C. The total number of nucleated cells (i.e., excluding erythrocytes) is determined using a hemocytometer (*see* **Subheading 3.1.2, item 9**). Depending on the mouse strain expect to recover 30–50 × 10^6 nucleated cells per mouse (two hind femurs and tibiae).
5. 6 × 10^6 Nucleated BM cells are resuspended in 50 mL conditioned DMEM medium.
6. Sterile Teflon® bags are taken from the aluminum foil bag. The open side of the Teflon® bag is stretched between the ends (covered with adhesive tape) of an anatomical clamp. Each bag is filled with 6 × 10^6 BM cells (in 50 mL conditioned DMEM medium) and closed with a clip after removal of air bubbles. Be careful to avoid contaminations especially of the inner side of the Teflon® bag. To allow for sufficient gas exchange the Teflon® bags are incubated at 37°C and 10% (!) CO_2/95% humidified air on perforated trays *(21)* (*see* **Note 11**).
7. After 7–10 days a monolayer of MΦ is present at the bottom of the Teflon® bag. To detach the loosely adherent MΦ from the hydrophobic membrane, the bag is turned over and the medium in the bag is carefully moved back and forth. The Teflon® bag is sprayed with 70% ethanol, which is allowed to evaporate, and the resuspended MΦ are harvested with a 14-G indwelling cannula. Expect to recover ca. 10–20 × 10^6 BMMΦ per bag (*see* **Note 10**).

3.2.3. Culture of L929 Cells for the Generation of L929 Culture Supernatant

1. L929 fibroblasts are grown in DMEM medium (*see* **Subheading 3.2.2, item 1**) in dishes or cell culture flasks and harvested by use of a cell scraper (*see* **Subheading 2.2.3, item 4**).
2. For production of L929 SN, fibroblasts are adjusted to 1 × 10^5/mL in DMEM medium and incubated in Teflon® bags (*see* **Subheading 3.2.1** and **Note 9**) for 7 days at 10% CO_2/95% humidified air, with 250–300 mL per bag. Alternatively, the L929 cell suspension can also be seeded in 175-cm^2 tissue culture flasks, if Teflon® bags are not available.
3. At day 7 (the medium has already turned yellow) bags are sliced at one side, the cell culture supernatant is transferred into 50-mL polypropylene tubes and centrifuged at 300 × *g*, 5–10 min, 4°C.

4. The SN is subjected to sterile filtration (0.2-μm pores) and stored frozen in aliquots at −20°C.

3.3. Culture of MΦ for Induction of Cytokine Production and/or Effector Molecules

This section covers general aspects of macrophage culture and stimulation, but does not provide detailed information on specific questions of macrophage activation.

3.3.1. Culture Medium and Plating of the MΦ

Cell Density

Mouse MΦ are routinely seeded at 2×10^6/mL. As the cell density and the ratio of cell number and culture volume can influence the outcome of certain macrophage functions (e.g., arginine metabolism, uptake of microbes) *(22, 23)*, it is important to apply comparable conditions when using different culture devices (**Table 2**).

Culture Medium

The most commonly used media are RPMI1640 (*see* **Subheading 2.1**, **item 10**) and DMEM (*see* **Subheading 2.2.2**, **item 1** and **Subheading 3.2.2**). The media differ in their composition (notably in their content of arginine and glucose). Although routinely added by many authors including us, neither 2-mercaptoethanol (an antioxidant and SH donor) nor HEPES (a CO_2-independent buffer) are essential for culturing MΦ. Prolonged periods of alkaline pH diminish the responsiveness of MΦ to activating stimuli. It is therefore highly advisable to maintain well-acidified conditions. If prolonged pipetting under laminar-flow conditions (i.e., outside of CO_2 incubator) is necessary, HEPES helps to achieve this goal.

FCS, which is an ill-defined but routinely used source of growth factors, cytokines, hormones, inorganic mediators, and

Table 2
Numbers of MΦ seeded in different tissue culture devices

Cell culture device	Culture area (cm²) (per well)[a]	No. of seeded MΦ	Culture volume (mL)	No. of cells per cm²	No. of cells per mL medium
96-Well flat-bottomed plate	0.33	1×10^5	0.05	3×10^5	2×10^6
24-Well plate	1.9	7×10^5	0.35	3.6×10^5	2×10^6
8-Well LabTek® Chamber Slides®	0.8	4×10^5	0.2	5×10^5	2×10^6
Small Petri dishes (Ø 5.3 cm)	21.5	6×10^6	3	2.8×10^5	2×10^6
Large Petri dishes (Ø 8.7 cm)	56.7	16×10^6	8	2.8×10^5	2×10^6

[a]The numbers given refer to the products from NUNC International. Comparable products with slightly different sizes are available from other suppliers

various other stimulatory or inhibitory compounds, can be readily omitted in macrophage cultures, if necessary. Both inflammatory MΦ and BMMΦ become surface adherent, survive, and respond to various stimuli (e.g., with IFN-γ, TNF, IFN-γ plus LPS) in the absence of FCS *(23, 24)*, although an optimal response to other stimuli (e.g., LPS alone) might require the presence of FCS *(25)*. We did not observe different responses, when we stimulated the MΦ in the presence of 2.5, 5, or 10% FCS.

3.3.2. Adherence

When primary mouse MΦ are seeded into tissue culture plastic plates or dishes, they adhere to the surface within 60 min. After 2 h they are nicely spread out and form a monolayer. MΦ also adhere to glass surfaces and, much less well, to bacteriological (i.e., not surface-treated) Petri dishes. Adherence does not require FCS. Surfaces that impede MΦ adherence are polypropylene *(26)* or hydrophobic Teflon® membranes *(21)*. Adherence or prolonged incubation under adherent conditions prior to stimulation affects various MΦ functions *(23, 27, 28)*.

3.3.3. Washing of the MΦ Monolayer

In order to remove nonadherent cells, MΦ monolayers are washed at least three times with PBS (37°C). The most efficient way to remove the washing fluid is to use a vacuum pump with a sterile 100-μL pipet tip attached to the suction tubing. In the case of PE-MΦ the percentage of contaminating lymphoid cells clearly decreases with an increased number of washing steps. However, lymphoid contaminants remain detectable even after 10 washings (U. Schleicher and C. Bogdan, unpublished observations) *(29)*.

3.3.4. Stimulation of the MΦ Monolayer

1. Standard stimuli for the priming and/or activation of MΦ are IFN-γ (2–20 ng/mL), LPS (1–500 ng/mL), TNF (2–20 ng/mL), and combinations thereof. Production of reactive oxygen intermediates (ROI) by IFN-γ- or TNF-primed MΦ can be triggered by phorbol myristate acetate (PMA). The necessary duration of stimulation depends on the MΦ function under examination (e.g., ROI release: 10–60 min; nitric oxide (NO) release: 24–48 h; TNF release: 8–24 h) *(30–32)*.
2. The various MΦ populations differ in their secretory functions. For example, PE-MΦ are already potent producers of NO in response to IFN-γ alone, whereas resident peritoneal MΦ or BMMΦ usually require combined stimulation with IFN-γ plus LPS or TNF *(30)*. Resident peritoneal MΦ and periodate- or caseinate-elicited PE-MΦ efficiently release ROI after priming with IFN-γ and triggering with PMA, whereas thioglycolate-elicited PE-MΦ fail to do so *(30)*.

3.3.5. Detachment of Adherent MΦ

The detachment of tightly adherent MΦ for subsequent analyses is a challenge, because all procedures can damage the cells (*see* **Note 11**). In our hands, treatment of the MΦ monolayers with Accutase proved to be most effective.

1. The medium is removed and the adherent MΦ are rinsed with sterile PBS (room temperature).
2. Accutase, a mixture of proteolytic and collagenolytic enzymes, is added (10 mL per 75 cm^2 surface).
3. The cultures are returned to the 37°C incubator, incubated for 15–45 min.
4. The detached MΦ are harvested by vigorous washing with PBS. MΦ, which do not lose their adherence, have to be harvested using a cell scraper.

3.3.6. Lysis of Adherent MΦ

For several experimental purposes (e.g., Western blot analysis, immunoprecipitation, electromobility shift assays, preparation of RNA) MΦ have to be lysed. In the case of adherent MΦ the most convenient procedure is to rapidly wash the monolayers with ice-cold PBS (3×) followed by the addition of the respective lysis buffer *(23, 33–35)*. For protein analyses the MΦ are directly scraped in the added volume of lysis puffer (5.3 cm Ø Petri dish: 0.5 mL; 8.7 cm Ø Petri dish: 1 mL). For the preparation of RNA, the added lysis puffer (5.3 cm Ø Petri dish: 2 mL; 8.7 cm Ø Petri dish: 4 mL) is rapidly pipetted up and down until all cells are lysed.

3.4. Phenotypic Analysis of MΦ by Flow Cytometry

In the protocol described later MΦ are stained simultaneously with sets of three differently labeled mAbs (three-color immunofluorescence). Propidium iodide (PI) is added to discriminate viable and dead cells (*see* **Fig. 1**). If the analysis is performed on a flow cytometer with two lasers (blue laser: 488 nm, red laser: 635 nm) (e.g., BD FACS Calibur®) as in this protocol, PI should be detected via the FL3 channel. It is therefore recommended to use fluorescein isothiocyanate (FITC) (FL1 channel)-, phycoerythrin (PE) (FL2 channel)-, and allophycocyanin (APC) (FL4 channel)-labeled mAbs or other suitable fluorochrome conjugates for staining of cell surface markers. Fluorochrome conjugates that are detected via the FL3 channel (e.g., peridinin chlorophyll protein (PerCP)) cannot be used for surface staining in this case. The analysis on a flow cytometer with three lasers (488, 633 nm, and violet laser 405 nm) (e.g., BD FACS Canto II, BD LSR II) allows simultaneous detection of more than three surface markers. In this case the staining protocol and the choice of fluorochrome-conjugates have to be altered accordingly, and it is recommended to use 4 ,6-diamidino-2-phenylindole (DAPI; excited by ultraviolet light) instead of PI for exclusion of dead cells. If biotin-conjugated mAbs are used for staining, a two-step staining procedure is required. As biotin has an extremely strong affinity to avidin, biotin-conjugated mAbs can be detected with fluorochromes (FITC, PE, or APC) coupled to streptavidin.

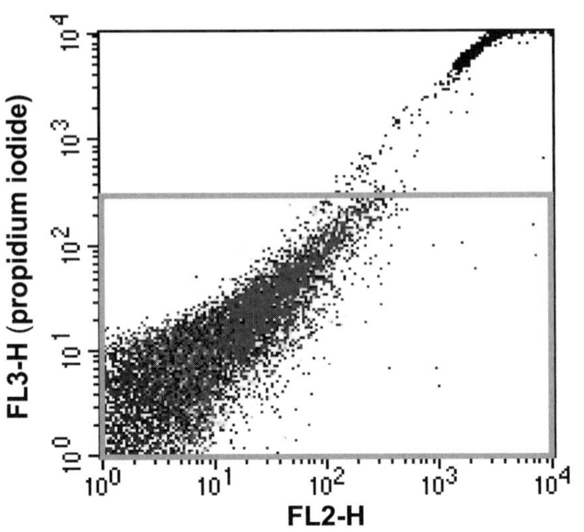

Fig. 1. FACS analysis of viable and dead C57BL/6 thioglycolate-elicited PECs. Prior to flow cytometric analysis PI was added to otherwise unstained PECs. The FL3 channel was used to detect PI fluorescence. PI$^+$ (i.e., dead) PECs are excluded from PI$^-$ cells (located in the *orange gate*) across the entire detection range of FL2 channel. The different colors of the PI$^-$ cells reflect the various subpopulations gated in the forward/side scatter analysis (*see* **Fig. 2b**). (*See Color Plates*)

Therefore, cells are first incubated with biotinylated mAbs, then washed and stained with fluorochrome-labeled streptavidin. It is recommended that only one of the mAbs used for three-color analyses is biotinylated, whereas the other two mAbs are directly conjugated with fluorochromes.

Each FACS analysis requires an unstained control to measure the autofluorescence of the MΦ, appropriate isotype controls for the different mAbs to control for specificity of binding, and individual staining with mAbs representative of each of the fluorochromes that are used to adjust compensation adequately.

1. Prior to staining and FACS analysis single-cell suspensions of MΦ have to be prepared. BMMΦ or PEC can be used directly for staining after harvesting them from Teflon® bags or the peritoneal cavity. Adherent MΦ which have been cultured in plates or dishes are detached from the plastic surface with Accutase (*see* **Subheading 3.3.5**).
2. The harvested MΦ are washed with FACS staining buffer (centrifugation at 300 × *g*, 5–10 min, 4°C) and then resuspended in the same buffer (50 µL per 1 × 10^6 MΦ). Visible clumps of cells have to be removed (e.g., by passing the cells through a nylon mesh (100 µm pore size) into a fresh tube).
3. To prevent nonspecific binding of fluorescence-labeled mAb to the Fc-receptors of MΦ, the suspended MΦ are incubated

with mouse Fc Block (1 μg mAb per 1 × 10^6 cells) for 5–10 min at room temperature. After blocking, the cells are ready for staining without any further washing procedure.

4. During the blocking period prepare all reagents required for staining and label the FACS tubes according to the staining protocol.
5. Dispense 1 × 10^6 MΦ (50 μL) into each tube. During the entire staining procedure MΦ are kept on ice. A cocktail of maximal three different fluorochrome-labeled mAbs or two different fluorochrome-labeled mAbs and one biotinylated mAb per test tube (or the respective controls; see earlier) is added in a volume of 5 μL at the appropriate dilution for efficient staining (*see* **Note 12**). The MΦ suspensions are gently mixed and incubated for 20–30 min in the dark.
6. Cells are washed by adding ca. 2 mL of cold staining buffer to each tube (centrifugation at 300 × *g*, 5–10 min, 4°C). The supernatant is discarded by rapid inversion of the tube.
7. For detection of biotinylated primary mAb the cells have to be stained with fluorochrome-labeled streptavidin followed by a washing step as described earlier.
8. MΦ are resuspended in 200–250 μL cold staining buffer after the last washing step and kept on ice in the dark until analysis by flow cytometry. If clumps of cells have formed, the MΦ suspensions have to be passed again through a 100-μm nylon mesh into a new tube. In order to detect dead cells 1 μL of PI solution is added to each tube prior to analysis (*see* **Note 13**).
9. The samples are analyzed on a BD FACS Calibur® applying the Cell Quest Pro® software. In order to get statistically reliable results for the staining of small subpopulations, at least 100,000 cells per tube should be acquired. Since the granularity of MΦ is very high, we also advise using the log scale for the side scatter. Examples of the forward/side scatter analyses of freshly isolated thioglycolate-elicited PECs or BM MΦ, respectively, are shown in **Figs. 2** and **3**. The gating of viable cells in FL-2 versus FL-3 dot plots is demonstrated with thioglycolate-elicited PECs in **Fig. 1**. The fluorescence parameters of the different stainings should be analyzed after exclusion of the PI positive (i.e., dead) cells (**Fig. 1**, orange gate = gate on viable cells). Both in PECs and BM MΦ different subpopulations (R1, R2, R3) can be defined by forward/side scatter analysis. These subpopulations also differ in the expression of myeloid and lymphoid cell surface markers (Figs. 2 and 3). Typical MΦ are mostly located within region R1, whereas lymphoid cells such as NK or T cells are exclusively found in region R3 *(29)*. Small

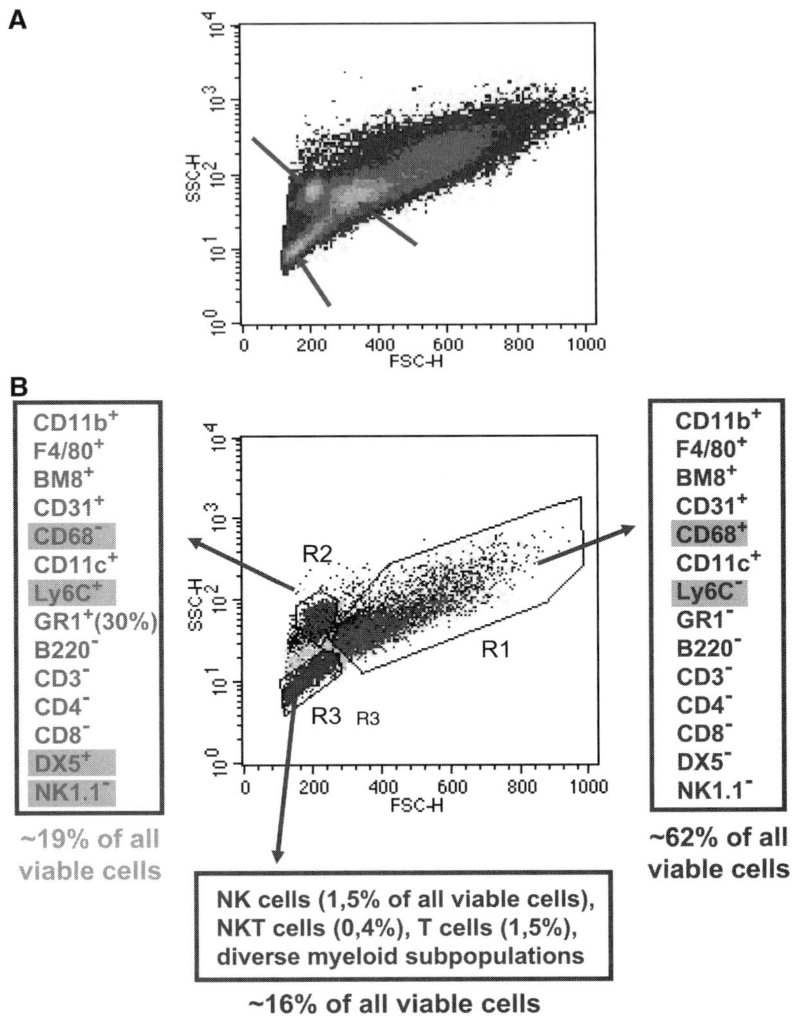

Fig. 2. FACS analysis of C57BL/6 thioglycolate-elicited PECs. (**A**) Forward/side scatter analysis of viable PECs shown as density plot. Three subpopulations within the high density area are distinguishable as indicated by the *red arrows*. (**B**) Forward/side scatter dot plot analysis of viable PECs. The three subpopulations shown in **Fig. 2a** were gated (R1, R2, R3) and analyzed for the expression of multiple myeloid (CD11b, F4/80, BM8, CD31, CD68, CD11c, Ly6C, GR1) and lymphoid (B220, CD3, CD4, CD8, DX5, NK1.1) surface markers. The positive or negative expression of the surface molecules for each subpopulation is listed in *boxes*. Typical MΦ – CD11b$^+$F4/80$^+$BM8$^+$CD68$^+$ – are mostly located within region R1, whereas lymphoid cells such as NK or T cells are found in region R3. (*See Color Plates*)

numbers of contaminant lymphoid cells are present in adherent PE-MΦ, resident peritoneal MΦ, as well as in BMMΦ *(29)*. Due to the high level of autofluorescence typical of MΦ as seen in R1 (*see* **Figs. 1** and **2**, red cells), the staining of contaminating lymphoid cells that are predominantly

Color Plates

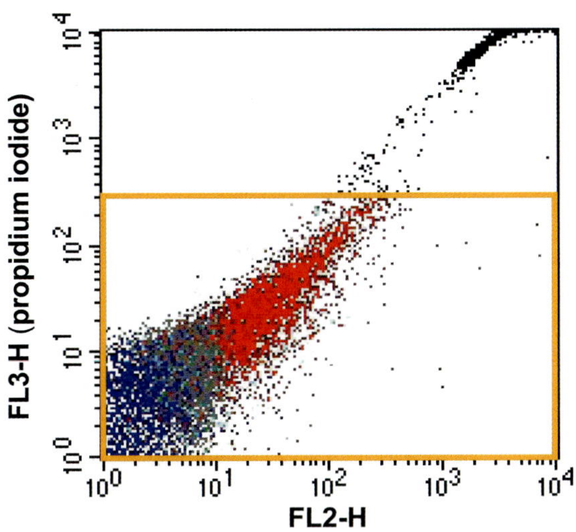

Fig. 1. FACS analysis of viable and dead C57BL/6 thioglycolate-elicited PECs. Prior to flow cytometric analysis PI was added to otherwise unstained PECs. The FL3 channel was used to detect PI fluorescence. PI^+ (i.e., dead) PECs are excluded from PI^- cells (located in the *orange gate*) across the entire detection range of FL2 channel. The different colors of the PI^- cells reflect the various subpopulations gated in the forward/side scatter analysis (*see* **Fig. 2b**).

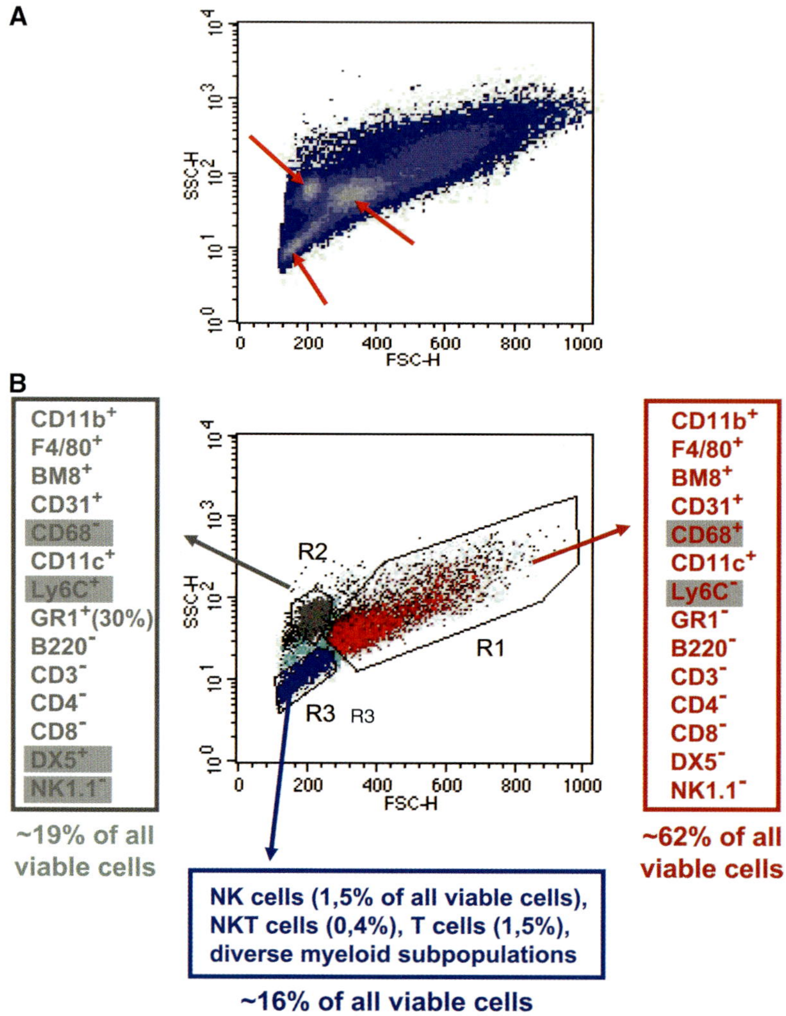

Fig. 2. FACS analysis of C57BL/6 thioglycolate-elicited PECs. (**A**) Forward/side scatter analysis of viable PECs shown as density plot. Three subpopulations within the high density area are distinguishable as indicated by the *red arrows*. (**B**) Forward/side scatter dot plot analysis of viable PECs. The three subpopulations shown in **Fig. 2a** were gated (R1, R2, R3) and analyzed for the expression of multiple myeloid (CD11b, F4/80, BM8, CD31, CD68, CD11c, Ly6C, GR1) and lymphoid (B220, CD3, CD4, CD8, DX5, NK1.1) surface markers. The positive or negative expression of the surface molecules for each subpopulation is listed in *boxes*. Typical MΦ – $CD11b^+F4/80^+BM8^+CD68^+$ – are mostly located within region R1, whereas lymphoid cells such as NK or T cells are found in region R3.

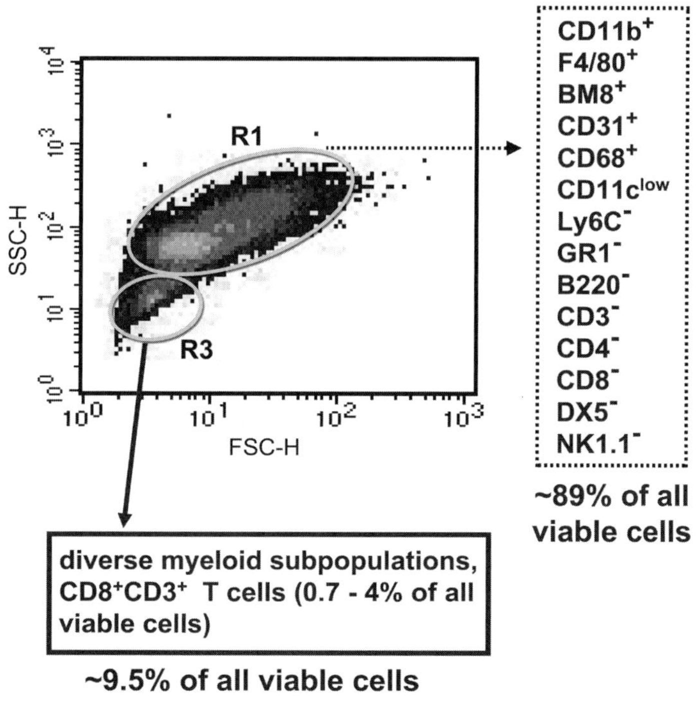

Fig. 3. FACS analysis of C57BL/6 BMMΦ. Forward/side scatter density plot analysis of viable BMMΦ is shown. Two subpopulations were discernible (R1, R3) and analyzed for the expression of multiple myeloid (CD11b, F4/80, BM8, CD31, CD68, CD11c, Ly6C, GR1) and lymphoid (B220, CD3, CD4, CD8, DX5, NK1.1) surface markers. The positive or negative expression of the surface molecules for each subpopulation is listed in *boxes*. Typical MΦ – $CD11b^+F4/80^+BM8^+CD68^+$ – are mostly located within region R1, whereas lymphoid T cells are found in region R3

located within region R3 (*see* **Figs. 1** and **2**, blue cells) may be non visible, if the whole BMM population is analyzed. This is because the small population of positively stained lymphoid cells might shift toward the highly autofluorescent MΦ population. In order to detect any contaminating lymphoid cells, we advise gating of the subpopulations R1, R2, and R3 by forward/side scatter (*see* **Fig. 2**) followed by individual analysis of these gates for their respective stainings.

4. Notes

1. All solutions, buffers, and media that are used for the preparation, culture, or stimulation of MΦ have to be prepared with endotoxin (LPS)-free reagents and deionized water (minimum resistance of 18.2 MΩ × cm, total organic content of less than 5 ppm) and are subjected to sterile filtration

(0.2-μm pores). Alternatively, they are purchased as sterile ready-to-use products certified to be endotoxin-free. The endotoxin-free status of the reagents and the water is verified with the quantitative chromogenic limulus amebocyte lysate endpoint assay (QCL-1000; Lonza Inc., Verviers, Belgium; cat. no. US50-647U), which can be conveniently performed in an ELISA plate and has an exquisite sensitivity (5–10 pg LPS/mL). LPS is not only a potent activator of MΦ, but can also deactivate MΦ (notably at low concentrations) *(36)*.

2. The Bacto™ Brewer Thiogylocate Medium (BTM) from Difco (formula per liter: 500 g infusion from beef, 10 g proteose peptone, 5 g NaCl, 5 g Dextrose, 0.5 sodium thioglycolate, 0.5 g Bacto agar, 0.002 g methylene blue) is no longer available. A product with the same formula can be obtained from Sigma-Aldrich (cat. no. B-2551). The BBL™ Brewer Modified Thioglycolate Medium from BD Biosciences (cat. no. 21-1716; Heidelberg, Germany), in contrast, has a different composition, which has not been tested by us for its inflammatory activity. Independent of the source of the BTM it is strongly recommended to test the 4% (w/v) solution for its content of endotoxin. When thioglycollate medium absorbs oxygen, it will turn green, whereas the oxygen-free medium (autoclaved, stored without shaking) that should be used for injection has a golden-brown appearance.
3. Sera (e.g., FCS) used for the generation and culture of MΦ have to be carefully selected for (a) absent activating or inhibitory effects on MΦ, (b) low endotoxin and low hemoglobin levels (high levels would be a sign of infection of the donors, contamination during serum preparation or for hemolysis, respectively), and for (c) the sufficient support of the differentiation of BM MΦ (we routinely test at least 5–10 different batches from different suppliers). To exclude activating effects we recommend to measure the tumor cytotoxic activity of MΦ (cultured in various batches of sera) against Abelson 8.1 or EL-4 tumor target cells (the effector cell: target cell ratio should be 100:1). Unstimulated MΦ will not show any sign of tumor cell cytotoxicity. Additional tests for activating/inhibitory effects include the culture of MΦ with increasing amounts of FCS (e.g., 0.5–10%) in the absence or presence of suboptimal or optimal concentrations of known MΦ-stimulatory agents (e.g., IFN-γ, LPS, IFN-γ plus LPS); the 24 and 48 h supernatants of these cultures are tested for the accumulation of nitrite and/or MΦ cytokines (e.g., TNF). All sera are heat-inactivated for 30 min at 56°C. Aliquots of 25 or 50 mL are kept at 4°C (for daily use) or stored frozen at –20°C.

4. One side of the FEP-Teflon membrane is chemically etched to become hydrophilic, the other side of the membrane is hydrophobic. During storage the FEP membrane should be tightly packed to avoid contamination of the foil with dust. Teflon® cell culture bags are also commercially available (e.g., Miltenyi, Bergisch-Gladbach, Germany or Süd-Laborbedarf, Gauting, Germany).
5. Anprolene® must be stored in a cool place protected from sunlight (safety cabinet), because it is extremely flammable. Avoid breathing Anprolene® vapor and exposure to liquid Anprolene®, which can cause irritation of the skin and of the respiratory tract, headache, nausea, vomiting, or cardiac irregularities as well as neurotoxicity and mutagenesis during chronic exposure.
6. Fresh preparation of the FACS staining buffer with sterile PBS, FCS and EDTA is recommended for each experiment due to the fast contamination of the buffer. Residual buffer can be stored at 4°C and can be used as long as no bacterial or fungal contamination is visible. Buffer is kept on ice during staining procedures.
7. Cervical dislocation must be performed carefully. Avoid tearing the neck, which will lead to hemorrhages into the peritoneal cavity and subsequent deactivation of the peritoneal MΦ *(37, 38)*.
8. The yield of peritoneal cells increases with the age/size and varies with the mouse strain. Female CD1 outbred mice of 8–12 weeks of age or retired breeders are ideal. Do not use mice younger than 5–6 weeks of age (these mice frequently have an umbilical hernia, which might lead to loss of peritoneal lavage fluid during harvesting of the cells). The cellular composition of PECs depends on the eliciting agent and the length of the time period between i.p. injection and cell harvest. For example, after thioglycolate injection the PECs are neutrophil-rich within the first 18 h (maximum at 5–6 h) *(39)*, lymphocyte-rich at day 2 after injection, and macrophage-rich 4–5 days after injection *(30)*.
9. If the bags are used for the culture of BMMΦ, the hydrophobic side of the Teflon® foil is inside so that the MΦ do not strongly adhere to the membrane. In contrast, the bags that are used for the culture of L929 cells are hydrophilic inside to allow firm adhesion of the fibroblasts to the membrane. The hydrophobic and hydrophilic side of the FEB-Teflon membrane can be identified with the help of a waterproof permanent text marker (e.g., Edding™). It is possible to write on the hydrophilic side of the foil, whereas the textmarker ink fails to stick to the hydrophobic surface.

10. The yield of MΦ per Teflon® bag depends on the number of seeded macrophage precursor cells, the lot of L929 supernatant (SN), and/or the source of rmM-CSF. The concentration of L929 SN in the conditioned medium should be titrated to determine the optimal conditions for generation of BMMΦ. A recovery of more than 50×10^6 viable BMMΦ per bag is not possible, because in this case the nutrient supply in the culture medium would be insufficient and the cells die.

    In general the recovery of BMMΦ is higher with L929 SN compared to rmM-CSF. In our hands the quality of rmM-CSF varies strongly between different commercial sources. Thus, in case the yield of BMMΦ is poor, the testing of other preparations of rmM-CSF is recommended.

11. If self-made Teflon® bags are not available, BMMΦ can also be generated in commercially available bags (*see* **Note 4**) or in cell culture dishes (petriPERM®) with a gas-permeable base made of a hydrophobic plastic foil (bioFolie®) (VivaScience, Hannover, Germany). We do *not* recommend the use of bacteriological Petri dishes or tissue culture flasks for the generation of BMMΦ as described by others *(40)*. BMMΦ strongly attach to the surface of tissue culture plates and can only be detached with a cell scraper (*see* **Subheadings 2.3** and **3.3**), treatment with accutase (*see* **Subheading 3.3.5**), incubation with PBS/10 mM EDTA (10–15 min, 37°C; works poorly in our hands) or combination of these methods. All these methods may damage the cells or modify their activation status *(41)*.

12. If several different MΦ populations are to be stained with the same cocktail of mAbs, one master mix of fluorochrome-labeled mAbs should be prepared.

13. Do not fix the MΦ with paraformaldehyde or commercial FACS fixatives. First, PI can no longer be used for the differentiation of live and dead cells. Second, fixation impairs the separation of distinct subpopulations in the forward and side scatter.

Acknowledgments

The preparation of this chapter as well as part of the experiments reported was supported by grants from the Deutsche Forschungsgemeinschaft (Bo996/3-1 and 3-2, SFB620 A9). We are grateful to Dr. Manuel Modolell and to Dr. Nicole Justies (Max Planck-Institute for Immunobiology, Freiburg, Germany) for introducing us into the "Teflon world" of macrophage culture.

References

1. Bogdan C. Macrophages, Encyclopedia of Life Sciences 2006. Zoiley, New York: DOI; 10, 1038/nPg.els, 0004007.
2. Bogdan C. Reactive oxygen and reactive nitrogen metabolites as effector molecules against infectious pathogens. In: Kaufmann SHE, Medzhitov R, Gordon S, eds. *The Innate Immune Response to Infection*. Washington, DC: ASM; 2004, pp 357–96.
3. Gordon S. Macrophages and the immune response. In: Paul W, ed. *Fundamental Immunology*, 5th edn, Philadelphia: Lippincott Raven; 2003, pp 481–95.
4. Gordon S (2003). Alternative activation of macrophages. *Nat Rev Immunol*;3:23–35.
5. Paulnock DM (1992). Macrophage activation by T cells. *Curr Opin Immunol*;4:344–9.
6. Stout RD, Suttles J, Xu J, Grewal I, Flavell RA (1996). Impaired T cell-mediated macrophage activation in CD40 ligand-deficient mice. *J Immunol*;156:8–11.
7. Andrade RM, Wessendarp M, Gubbels M-J, Striepen B, Subauste CS (2006). CD40 induces macrophage anti-*Toxoplasma gondii* activity by triggering autophagy-dependent fusion of pathogen-containing vacuoles and lysosomes. *J Clin Invest*;116:2366–77.
8. Stout RD. Macrophage activation by T cells: cognate and non-cognate signals (1993). *Curr Opin Immunol*;5:398–403.
9. Warschkau H, Kiderlen AF (1999). A monoclonal antibody directed against the murine macrophage surface molecule F4/80 modulates natural immune response to *Listeria monocytogenes*. *J Immunol*;163:3409–16.
10. Baratin M, Roetynck S, Lepolard C, et al. (2005). Natural killer cell and macrophage cooperation in MyD88-dependent innate responses to *Plasmodium falciparum*. *Proc Natl Acad Sci U S A*;102:14747–52.
11. Welte S, Kuttruff S, Waldhauer I, Steinle A (2006). Mutual activation of natural killer cells and monocytes mediated by NKp80-AICL interaction. *Nat Immunol*;12:1334–42.
12. Tomura M, Yu W-G, Ahn H-J, et al. (1999). A novel function of Vα14⁺ CD4⁺ NKT cells: stimulation of IL-12 production by antigen-presenting cells in the innate immune system. *J Immunol*;163:93–101.
13. Sköld M, Xiong X, Illarionov PA, Besra GS, Behar SM (2005). Interplay of cytokines and microbial signals in regulation of CD1d expression and NKT cell activation. *J Immunol*;175:3584–93.
14. Hegde S, Chen X-H, Keaton JM, Reddington F, Besra GS, Gumperz JE (2007). NKT cells direct monocytes into a DC differentiation pathway. *J Leukoc Biol*;81:1224–35.
15. Mak NK, Leung KN, Ada GL (1982). The generation of cytotoxic macrophages in mice during infection with influenza A or Sendai virus. *Scand J Immunol*;15:553–61.
16. Siren J, Sareneva T, Pirhonen J, et al. (2004). Cytokine and contact-dependent activation of natural killer cells by influenza A or Sendai virus-infected macrophages. *J Gen Virol*;85:2357–64.
17. Boorman GA, Luster MI, Dean JH, et al. (1982). Peritoneal macrophage alterations caused by naturally occurring mouse hepatitis virus. *Am J Pathol*;106:110–7.
18. Lamontagne L, Jolicoeur P (1994). Low-virulent mouse hepatitis viruses exhibiting various tropisms in macrophages, T and B cell subpopulations, and thymic stromal cells. *Lab Anim Sci*;44:17–24.
19. Even C, Rowland RR, Plagemann PG (1995). Mouse hepatitis virus infection of mice causes long-term depletion of lactate dehydrogenase-elevating virus-permissive macrophages and T lymphocyte alterations. *Virus Res*;39:355–64.
20. Flano E, Husain SM, Sample JT, Woodland DL, Blackman MA (2000). Latent murine g-herpesvirus infection is established in activated B cells, dendritic cells and macrophages. *J Immunol*;165:1074–81.
21. Munder PG, Modolell M, Wallach DFH (1971). Cell propagation on films of polymeric fluorocarbon as a means to regulate pericellular pH and pO2 in cultured monolayers. *FEBS Lett*;15:191–6.
22. Rutschman R, Lang R, Hesse M, Ihle JN, Wynn TA, Murray PJ (2001). Stat6-dependent substrate depletion regulates nitric oxide production. *J Immunol*;166:2173–7.
23. El-Gayar S, Thüring-Nahler H, Pfeilschifter J, Röllinghoff M, Bogdan C (2003). Translational control of inducible nitric oxide synthase by IL-13 and arginine availability in inflammatory macrophages. *J Immunol*;171:4561–8.
24. Fauve RM, Jusforgues H, Hevin B (1983). Maintenance of granuloma macrophages in serum-free medium. *J Immunol Methods*;64:345–51.
25. Chen T, Scott E, Morrison DC (1994). Differential effects of serum on lipopolysaccharide receptor-directed macrophage activation for nitric oxide production. *Immunol Lett*;40:179–87.

26. Nacy C, Pappas MG. Destruction of Leishmania. In: Adams DO, ed. *Methods for Studying Mononuclear Phagocytes*. Orlando, FL: Academic; 1981, pp 745–58.
27. Labadia M, Faanes RB, Rothlein R (1990). Role of adherence vs. spreading in the induction of membrane-associated interleukin-1 on mouse peritoneal macrophages. *J Leukoc Biol*;48:420–5.
28. Hodge-Dufour J, Noble PW, Horton MR, et al. (1997). Induction of IL-12 and chemokines by hyaluronan requires adhesion-dependent priming of resident but not elicited macrophages. *J Immunol*;159:2492–500.
29. Schleicher U, Hesse A, Bogdan C (2005). Minute numbers of contaminant $CD8^+$ T cells or $CD11b^+CD11c^+$ NK cells are the source of IFN-g in IL-12/IL-18-stimulated mouse macrophage populations. *Blood*;105:1319–28.
30. Ding AH, Nathan CF, Stuehr DJ (1988). Release of reactive nitrogen intermediates and reactive oxygen intermediates from mouse peritoneal macrophages. Comparison of activating cytokines and evidence for independent production. *J Immunol*;141:2407–12.
31. Bogdan C, Paik J, Vodovotz Y, Nathan C (1992). Contrasting mechanisms for suppression of macrophage cytokine release by transforming growth factor-b and interleukin-10. *J Biol Chem*;267:23301–8.
32. Vodovotz Y, Bogdan C, Paik J, Xie Q-w, Nathan C (1993). Mechanisms of suppression of macrophage nitric oxide release by transforming growth factor-b. *J Exp Med*;178: 605–13.
33. Bogdan C, Thüring H, Dlaska M, Röllinghoff M, Weiss G (1997). Mechanism of suppression of macrophage nitric oxide release by IL-13. *J Immunol*;159:4506–13.
34. Mattner J, Schindler H, Diefenbach A, Röllinghoff M, Gresser I, Bogdan C (2000). Regulation of type 2 NO synthase by type I interferons in macrophages infected with *Leishmania major*. *Eur J Immunol*;30:2257–67.
35. Schindler H, Lutz MB, Röllinghoff M, Bogdan C (2001). The production of IFN-γ by IL-12/IL-18-activated macrophages requires STAT4 signaling and is inhibited by IL-4. *J Immunol*;166:3075–82.
36. Bogdan C, Vodovotz Y, Paik J, Xie Q-w, Nathan C (1993). Traces of bacterial lipopolysaccharide suppress IFN-γ-induced nitric oxide synthase gene expression in primary mouse macrophages. *J Immunol*;151:301–9.
37. Hand WL, King-Thompson NL (1983). Effect of erythrocyte ingestion on macrophage antibacterial function. *Infect Immun*;40:917–23.
38. Hand WL (1984). Inhibition of cell-free oxidative bactericidal activity by erythrocytes and hemoglobin. *Infect Immun*;44:465–8.
39. Baron EJ, Proctor RA (1982). Elicitation of peritoneal polymorphonuclear neutrophils from mice. *J Immunol Methods*;49:305–13.
40. Fortier AH, Falk LA. Isolation of murine macrophages. In: Cooligan AMKea, JE, ed. *Current Protocols in Immunology*. Hoboken, NJ: Wiley; 1995:14.1.1–1.7.
41. Malorny U, Neumann C, Sorg C (1981). Influence of various detachment procedures on the functional state of cultured murine macrophages. *Immunbiology*;159: 327–36.
42. Tsunawaki S, Nathan CF (1984). Enzymatic basis of macrophage activation. Kinetic analysis of superoxide production in lysates of resident and activated mouse peritoneal macrophages and granulocytes. *J Biol Chem*;259:4305–12.
43. Bogdan C, Donhauser N, Döring R, Röllinghoff M, Diefenbach A, Rittig MG (2000). Fibroblasts as host cells in latent leishmaniosis. *J Exp Med*;191:2121–9.

Chapter 15

Analyzing Classical and Alternative Macrophage Activation in Macrophage/Neutrophil-Specific IL-4 Receptor-Alpha-Deficient Mice

Frank Brombacher, Berenice Arendse, Reagon Peterson, Alexandra Hölscher, and Christoph Hölscher

Summary

Macrophage activation can be divided into a classical and an alternative pathway. Interferon-gamma-induced, classically activated macrophages are indispensable for protective effector responses against intracellular pathogens. However, excessive inflammatory immune responses mediated by classical macrophage activation can also be detrimental to the host. In contrast, the IL-4 receptor-alpha-mediated alternative pathway of macrophage activation has been proposed as a mechanism to attenuate excessive inflammation. Indeed, the generation of macrophage/neutrophil-specific IL-4 receptor-alpha-deficient mice (LysM^{cre}IL-4R$\alpha^{-/lox}$) enables us now to evaluate the importance of this type of macrophage activation in vivo. Thus, the analysis of LysM^{cre}IL-4R$\alpha^{-/lox}$ mice and the phenotypic characterization of macrophage activation during inflammatory immune responses become of major importance for inflammation research, and useful markers have been identified that allow classically and alternatively activated macrophages to be distinguished. Inducible nitric oxide synthase and arginase-1 are not only prototypical markers of classical and alternative macrophage activation, but both enzymes are also strongly involved in regulating macrophage effector mechanisms and inflammatory immune responses. In this chapter, we describe the use of LysM^{cre}IL-4R$\alpha^{-/lox}$ mice and present experimental procedures to determine classical versus alternative macrophage activation by analyzing nitric oxide synthase and arginase-1 in vitro and in vivo in this murine model.

Key words: Inflammation, Classical macrophage activation, Interleukin-4 receptor-alpha, Alternative macrophage activation, Inducible nitric oxide synthase, Arginase-1.

Neil E. Reiner (ed.), *Macrophages and Dendritic Cells,* Methods in Molecular Biology, vol. 531

DOI: 10.1007/978-1-59745-396-7_15

1. Introduction

The cell-mediated immune response is known to be critical in host defense against infection with intracellular pathogens such as mycobacteria. Interleukin (IL)-12 promotes the differentiation of T helper (TH)1 cells that play an important role in protective immune responses primarily by the production of interferon-gamma (IFN-γ). IFN-γ in turn stimulates the antimicrobial activity of infected macrophages, allowing intracellular bacterial killing through the production of reactive nitrogen intermediates (RNI), reactive oxygen intermediates, and other effector molecules. This inflammatory reaction causes impairment of tissue function, which is usually reversible following elimination of the invading pathogen. However, persistent chronic infection often leads to hyperinflammation and eventually to pathological tissue destruction. In order to control or terminate inflammation and to prevent uncontrolled release of mediators, multiple regulatory factors are operative in balancing the immune system mainly by modulating inflammatory macrophages.

Myeloid lineage cells such as dendritic cells and macrophages are capable of directing $CD4^+$ T cell polarization toward TH1 or TH2 differentiation *(1–3)*. TH1-dominated immune responses follow recognition of microbial products by innate immune cells that release IL-12 *(2)*. Although less well understood, there is also evidence to support a role for dendritic cells and macrophages in promoting TH2 responses *(1, 3)*. Hence, elucidation of the mechanisms by which this occurs is an area of intense study. Macrophage activation can be distinctly divided into a classical versus alternative pathway dependent on exposure to type 1 or type 2 cytokines, respectively *(1)*. Classically activated macrophages (caMϕ) are induced by IFN-γ and bacterial stimuli such as lipopolysaccharides (LPS). caMϕ produce tumor-necrosis-factor (TNF), IL-12, and RNI and are therefore indispensable effector cells of protective immune responses against intracellular pathogens, such as *Mycobacterium tuberculosis* and *Leishmania major* *(1, 4, 5)*. Despite this beneficial role in host defense, inflammatory immune responses can also be detrimental to host tissue; therefore, an alternative pathway of macrophage activation has been proposed as a mechanism for attenuation of excessive inflammation *(1, 3)*

Alternatively activated macrophages (aaMϕ) are induced by IL-4 and IL-13 via the IL-4 receptor-alpha chain (IL-4Rα), a crucial component that is common to their respective heterodimeric type 1 and type 2 IL-4R receptors. We recently established global (IL-4R$\alpha^{-/-}$) *(6)* and macrophage/neutrophil-specific IL-4Rα-deficient (LysM^{cre}IL-4R$\alpha^{-/lox}$) *(7)* mice as experimental model systems to characterize the phenotypic and functional properties of aaMϕ as well as their potential role in human disease. Examination of these transgenic animal models using *Trypanosoma sp. (8–10)*, *Taenia crassips (11)*, or *Brugia malayi (12)* and subsequent gene expression profiling resulted in the identification of several marker genes for aaMϕ, such as the IL-4Rα, arginase1 (Arg-1), FIZZ1 (RELMα), YM1, the mouse mannose receptor (MMR), macrophage galactose-type C-type lectins (mMGLs), and 12/15 lipoxygenase (12/15-LOX) (**Table 1**). However, little is known about the actual functional role of these markers in aaMϕ. One of these, 12/15-LOX generates bioactive lipid mediators, which serve as ligands for the nuclear hormone receptor PPAR-α, also present on lymphocytes. Binding of aaMϕ-derived lipids to PPAR-α on activated T cells blocks cell proliferation by promoting inhibition of IL-2. This may account for the suppressive function of IL-4/IL-13-activated macrophages in *Taenia* infection by a heterogeneous $CD11b^+$ $Gr\text{-}1^+$ cell population, known as myeloid suppressor cells (MSC) *(11)*. IL-4/IL-13-activated MSC manifest 12/15-LOX activity, thereby secreting molecules that via PPAR-α activation, inhibit proliferation of T cells. Tumor-recruited $CD11b^+$ MSC are also known mediators of tumor-associated

Table 1
Typical markers of caMϕ and aaMϕ and approaches to analysis

Marker	Classical activation	Alternative activation	In vitro analysis	In vivo analysis	References
IL-12	▲	▼	RT-PCR, ELISA	RT-PCR, ELISA	*(7)*
TNF	▲	▼	RT-PCR, ELISA	RT-PCR, ELISA	*(7)*
FIZZ	▼	▲	RT-PCR	RT-PCR	*(28)*
YM-1	▼	▲	RT-PCR	RT-PCR	*(28)*
IL-4Rα	▼	▲	RT-PCR, FACS	RT-PCR, FACS	*(7)*
Mouse mannose receptor (MMR)	▼	▲	RT-PCR, FACS	RT-PCR, FACS, immuno-histo-chemistry (IHC)	*(29)*
12/15 Lipoxygenase (12/15-LOX)	▼	▲	RT-PCR	RT-PCR	*(11)*
Macrophage galactose-type C-type lectins (mMGLs)	▼	▲	RT-PCR, FACS	RT-PCR, FACS	*(9)*
WSX-1	▼	▲	RT-PCR, FACS	RT-PCR, FACS	*(30)*
NOS2	▼	▲	RT-PCR, Griess	RT-PCR, Griess, IHC	*(21)*
ARG-1	▼	▲	RT-PCR, urea	RT-PCR, urea, IHC	*(31)*

immune dysfunction, and recent studies *(12)* demonstrated that IL-4Rα is a marker of these cells. Indeed, IL-4Rα$^+$ CD11b$^+$ cells (but not IL-4Rα$^-$CD11b$^+$ cells) from tumor-bearing mice constitutively released IL-13 and IFN-γ and thereby suppressed the generation of tumor-specific cytotoxic T lymphocytes. This may be explained by a combination of NOS2 and Arg-1 activity resulting in reactive mediators able to suppress cytotoxic T lymphocytes *(12)*, this mechanism that was impaired in LysM^{cre}IL-4Rα$^{-/lox}$ mice, which were able to eject their tumors.

In contrast, *Schistosoma mansoni* infection studies demonstrated a beneficial and crucial role for IL-4Rα-bearing aaMφ in restricting egg-mediated intestinal immunopathology. This prevented the development of sepsis and subsequent mortality during acute schistosomiasis which otherwise was observed to occur in the absence of IL-4Rα-expressing macrophages in infected LysM^{cre}IL-4Rα$^{-/lox}$ mice *(7)*. Moreover, infected, myeloid-cell-specific IL-4Rα deficient LysM^{cre}IL-4Rα$^{-/lox}$ mice showed increased TH1 responses and TH1-dominant liver granuloma formation, but interestingly collagen deposition and fibrosis were present, suggesting that these responses were independent of aaMϕ *(13)*. Conversely, a detrimental role for aaMϕ was observed in *Leishmania major* infection as infected LysM^{cre}IL-4Rα$^{-/lox}$ mice showed strikingly delayed disease progression compared to nonhealer BALB/c mice *(14)*. Interestingly, in both schistosomiasis and in leishmaniasis increased TH1 responses were observed in LysM^{cre}IL-4Rα$^{-/lox}$ mice suggesting that immunomodulatory properties of aaMϕ are in part related to effects on T helper cell dichotomy *(13, 14)*. A similar type1 response was observed during proteoglycan-induced arthritis, which was exacerbated in LysM^{cre}IL-4Rα$^{-/lox}$ mice *(15)*. Together, the investigations of experimental disease models using a myeloid-cell-specific IL-4Rα-deficient mouse have demonstrated the involvement of aaMϕ in immunomodulation, immunosuppression, and immunopathology. These cells were also observed to promote tissue repair, and to influence innate and adaptive immune responses, and their ultimate impact on disease expression was dependent upon the specific model under examination.

Hence, the phenotypic characterization of macrophage activation during inflammatory immune responses is of major importance. As mentioned earlier, numerous markers have been defined that can be used for the experimental determination of classical and alternative macrophage activation in vitro and in vivo. Inducible nitric oxide synthase (NOS2) and Arg-1 are two such prototypic markers of classical and alternative macrophage activation, respectively. Classical macrophage activation plays an important role in combating infection with intracellular pathogens through IFN-γ-induced expression of the NOS2-dependent production of RNI *(16–18)*. However, uncontrolled macrophage activation may also lead to immunopathology *(7)*. Arg-1 is an essential enzyme of the urea cycle and is expressed at high levels in hepatocytes. The enzyme hydrolyzes L-arginine to urea and L-ornithine; therefore, its main function in the liver is the detoxification of ammonia. Because L-ornithine is a necessary metabolite required for the production of prolines which in turn control collagen production, arginase activity is linked to tissue remodeling eventually leading to fibrosis *(19)*. The production of RNI is counter-regulated by IL-4Rα-dependent mechanisms, leading to Arg-1-expressing aaMϕ. Since NOS2 shares L-arginine as a substrate with arginase, substrate depletion by either enzyme is a key regulatory mechanism *(20, 21)*, and differential expression of NOS2 and the Arg-1 is important for regulating macrophage effector functions and immunopathology *(20, 22)* (**Fig. 1**).

As should be clear from the information reviewed earlier, NOS2 and Arg-1 are both prototypical markers of classical and alternative macrophage activation and also centrally involved in regulating inflammatory immune responses. Thus, analysis of both enzymes in vitro and in vivo is an important tool for evaluating differential macrophage activation during inflammatory immune responses. In this chapter, we describe the use of LysM^{cre}IL-4R$\alpha^{-/lox}$ mice and related experimental procedures to examine

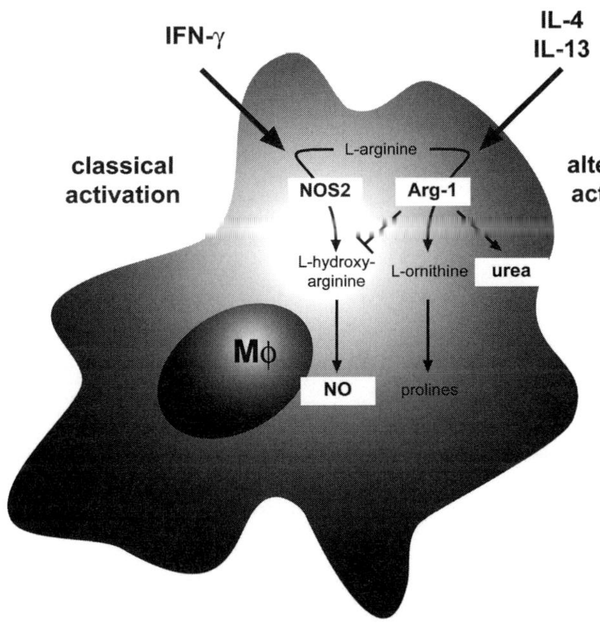

Fig. 1. L-Arginine metabolism in caMϕ and aaMϕ. In IFN-γ-induced caMϕ and IL-4/IL-13-generated aaMϕ, L-arginine is used as a substrate by both NOS2 and Arg-1. NOS2 metabolizes L-arginine to citrulline and NO, which is important for antimicrobial effector mechanisms in macrophages. Arg-1 is an essential enzyme of the urea cycle. The enzyme converts L-arginine to urea and L-ornithine, the latter being a necessary metabolite for the production of prolines which in turn are required for collagen production.

classical versus alternative macrophage activation in vitro and in vivo. Currently, this is the only cell-type specific animal model available to analyze differential macrophage activation in vivo.

2. Materials

2.1. Generation, Breeding Strategy, and Genotyping of Macrophage/Neutrophil-Specific IL-4Rα-Deficient Mice

2.1.1. DNA Extraction from Tail Biopsies

1. Tail lysis buffer: 50 mM Tris–HCl, pH 8, 100 mM EDTA, 100 mM NaCl, 1% (w/v) SDS, proteinase K stock solution (10 mg/mL in ddH_2O; store aliquots at –20°C).
2. We recommend use of commercial double-distilled water (ddH_2O).

2.1.2. PCR

Mice may be genotyped by conventional or real-time PCR the latter also allowing for quantitative analysis of Cre-mediated deletion efficiency. For both methods, we recommend use of commercial ddH_2O and primer pairs at a working concentration of 6.25 μM in ddH_2O (**Table** 2).

Conventional PCR

1. 200 μL PCR strips with lids.
2. Taq polymerase and 10× ThermoPol buffer (5 U/μL).
3. dNTPs (4 × 100 μmol, prepare stocks at 10 mM in ddH_2O).
4. ddH_2O. Appropriate aliquots are stored at –20°C.
5. 10× loading buffer: 1 mM sodium EDTA, 0.4% bromophenol blue, 50% (w/v) glycerol.
6. 10× TBE: 890 mM Tris, 890 mM boric acid, 20 mM EDTA, pH 8.0.
7. 1.6% agarose gel [1.6% (w/w) agarose in 0.5× TBE; microwave, cool to 60°C and add 10 mg/mL ethidium bromide (ETBR) to a final concentration of 0.45 μg/mL (*see* **Note 1**)]. Pour in gel trays and add gel combs.
8. 100-bp DNA ladder.

Real-Time PCR

1. 100 μL PCR tubes with caps.
2. 2× SensiMix DNA kit (50× SYBR Green, 2× Sensimix [reaction buffer, heat-activated Taq polymerase, 6 mM $MgCl_2$, internal reference and stabilizers], 50 mM $MgCl_2$).
3. RotorGene RG-3000A real-time cycler and RotorGene 6 version 6.1 software (Corbett Research).

Table 2
Primer sequences, annealing temperatures, and elongation times for genotyping macrophage/neutrophil-specific LysM^{cre}IL-4R$\alpha^{-/lox}$ mice and quantitative real-time RT-PCR of NOS2 and Arg-1

	Forward primer	Reverse primer	Annealing	Elongation
Conventional PCR			[°C]	[s]
IL-4Rα wild type	TGACCTACAAG-GAACCCAGGC	CTCGGCGCACT-GACCCATCT	58	60
IL-4Rα deleted	GGCTGCTGACCT-GGAATAACC	CCTTTGAGAACT-GCGGGCT	58	60
IL-4Rα lox	CCCTTCCT-GGCCCTGAATTT	GTTTCCTCCTAC-CGCTGATT	60	60
LysMcre	CTTGGGCTGCCA-GAATTTCTC	CCCAGAAAT-GCCAGATTACG	60	60
Real-time PCR			[s] × [°C]	[s]
IL-4Rα wild type	TGACCTACAAG-GAACCCAGGC	CTCGGCGCACT-GACCCATCT	20 × 58	60
IL-4Rα deleted	GGCTGCTGACCT-GGAATAACC	CCTTTGAGAACT-GCGGGCT	20 × 57	30
LysMcre	CTTGGGCTGCCA-GAATTTCTC	CCCAGAAAT-GCCAGATTACG	45 × 57	60
Quantitative real-time RT-PCR			[°C]	[s]
NOS2	AGCTCCTCCCAG-GACCACAC	ACGCTGAGTAC-CTCATTGGC	60	10
ARG-1	CAGAAGAATGGAA-GAGTCAGA	CAGATATGCAG-GGAGTCACC	6[illegible]	10
HPRT	GGCCATGAGGCT-GGATCTC	AACATTTGAATC-CTGCAGCCA	60	10

2.2. Phenotyping Classical/Alternative Macrophage Activation In Vitro

2.2.1. In Vitro Generation of ca/aaMϕ

1. 48-well tissue culture plates, bacterial-grade, and tissue-culture-grade petri dishes.
2. Disposable sterile cell scraper.
3. DMEM: Dulbecco's Modified Eagle's Medium (DMEM, high glucose; supplemented with 10% (v/v) FCS, 2 mM L-glutamine, 100 U/mL penicillin/100 μg/mL streptomycin, 1 mM sodium–pyruvate, 50 μM 2-mercaptoethanol.
4. PLUZNIK medium: DMEM (high glucose) supplemented with 10% (v/v) FCS, 5% (v/v) horse serum, 30% macrophage-colony-stimulating factor (M-CSF)-containing L929

supernatant (*see* **Note 2**), 2 mM L-glutamine, 100 U/mL penicillin/100 µg/mL streptomycin, 1 mM sodium–pyruvate, 50 µM 2-mercaptoethanol. Accutase.

5. For tissue culture purposes, we recommend use of commercial PBS w/o Mg^{2+} and Ca^{2+} (PAA).
6. Recombinant murine IFN-γ, IL-4, IL-13, and LPS are diluted in DMEM at the indicated final concentrations.

2.2.2. Gene Expression Analysis of ca/aaMϕ

11. RNAse-free 1.5-mL microtubes.
12. Lightcycler capillaries and adapters.
13. We recommend use of commercial PBS and double-distilled water (ddH_2O).
14. Primer pairs at a working concentration of 6.25 µM in ddH_2O (**Table** 2).
15. RNA extraction:
    (a) Trifast.
    (b) 1-brom-3-chlorpropane.
    (c) GenElute linear polyacrylamide.
    (d) Isopropanol, 75% (v/v) ethanol in diethylpyrocarbonate water (*see* **Note 3**).
6. Reverse transcription (RT):
    (a) Oligo $p(dT)_{12-18}$ (25 U in 750 µL DEPC water).
    (b) dNTPs (100 µmol each, prepare stocks at 10 mM in DEPC water).
    (c) Ribolock ribonuclease inhibitor (40 U/µL).
    (d) Revertaid H minus M-muLV reverse transcriptase including 5× reaction buffer (10,000 U).
7. Quantitative real-time PCR:
    (a) $MgCl_2$ (50 mM $MgCl_2 \times 6H_2O$, autoclave).
    (b) 10× PCR buffer (200 mM Tris, 500 mM KCl, pH 8.4, sterile filtrate).
    (c) dNTPs (4 × 100 µmol, prepare stocks at 10 mM in ddH_2O).
    (d) 100× bovine serum albumin.
    (e) SYBR Green (dilute 1:1,000 in DMSO).
    (f) Taq polymerase (5 U/µL). Appropriate aliquots are stored at −20°C.

2.2.3. Metabolic Analysis of ca/aaMϕ In Vitro

1. Flat-bottomed 96-well microtiter plates.
2. We recommend use of commercial PBS w/o Mg^{2+} and Ca^{2+} and ddH_2O. For serial dilutions of the nitrite standard, DMEM is (*see* **Subheading 2.2.1**) used.

3. Griess reaction (detection of NO_2): 2 mM $NaNO_2$, 2.5% (v/v) H_3PO_4, Griess reagent #1 (1% sulfanilamide in 2.5% H_3PO_4), Griess reagent #2 (0.1% N-(1-naphthyl) ethylenediamine dihydrochloride in 2.5% H_3PO_4). All solutions are stored at 4 C in the dark.
4. Urea assay (detection of arginase activity): 0.1% (v/v) Triton X-100 in ddH_2O supplemented with protease inhibitor cocktail, 25 mM Tris–HCl (pH 7.5), 10 mM $MnCl_2$, 0.5 M L-arginine (pH 9.7), 20 mg/mL urea, stop solution (1:3:7 [v/v/v] 96% H_2SO_4, 85% H_3PO_4 (ddH_2O), freshly prepared 9% (w/v) α-isonitrosopropiophenone (ISPF) dissolved in 100% ethanol.

2.3. Functional Analysis of Classical/Alternative Macrophage Activation n Vivo

2.3.1. Histopathological and Immunohistochemical Analysis of ca/aaMϕ

General Buffers and Chemicals

1. Xylol.
2. Different concentrations (100%, 70%, 40% [v/v]) of acetone in ddH_2O.
3. TBS (150 mM M NaCl, 10 mM Tris, pH 7.4).
4. 1% (v/v) H_2O_2 in TBS.
5. 3,3′-Diaminobenzidine (DAB) Sigma FAST Tablet set.
6. Kaiser's glycerol gelatin.
7. Gill's hematoxylin (20 mM hematoxylin, 3 mM sodiumiodate, 155 mM aluminum sulfate, 250 mL 25% (v/v) ethylene glycol, 6% (v/v) conc. acetic acid in tap water) (*see* **Note 4**).

NOS2 Staining

1. For antigen-retrieval, any pressure cooker could be used.
2. 10 mM citric acid monohydrate (pH 6.0).
3. 10% (v/v) FCS in TBS.
4. Rabbit antimouse NOS2 monoclonal antibody.
5. Mouse serum.
6. Goat antirabbit IgG peroxidase.
7. Rabbit antigoat IgG peroxidase.

Arg-1 Staining

1. 1% (w/v) SDS in TBS.
2. Avidin/Biotin-Blocking kit containing avidin D and biotin.
3. M.O.M. (*mouse on mouse*) Immunodetection kit containing mouse immunoglobulin (Ig)-blocking reagent.
4. M.O.M. protein concentrate.
5. M.O.M. biotinylated antimouse IgG reagent.
6. Vectastain ABC reagent A and reagent B.
7. Mouse antimouse Arg-1.

2.3.2. Metabolic Analysis of ca/aaMϕ In Vivo

1. Proteinase inhibitor cocktail (complete Mini EDTA-free tablets).
2. Nitrate determination:
   (a) Serum separator tubes.
   (b) Micron YM-30 centrifugal filter units.
   (c) Cayman Nitrate/Nitrite Colorimetric Assay kit containing nitrate reductase, enzyme cofactors, nitrate standard, nitrite standard.
   (d) Griess reagents #1 and #2.
   (e) 96-well microtiter plates.
3. Arginase activity:
   (a) Tissue homogenizator (e.g., Potter Elvehjem homogenizator).
   (b) For further material *see* also **Subheading 2.2.3**.

3. Methods

3.1. Generation, Breeding Strategy, and Genotyping of Macrophage/ Neutrophil-Specific IL-4Rα-Deficient Mice

Functional studies on the role of aaMϕ in experimental mouse models for human diseases have been aided by the use of macrophage/neutrophil-specific IL-4Rα-deficient mice. These mice are created using homologous recombination in embryonic stem cells in combination with the Cre/loxP recombinase system. Gene targeting in BALB/c embryonic stem (ES) cells and Cre/loxP-specific site-specific recombination was performed to generate so called floxed IL-4Rα$^{lox/lox}$ BALB/c mice, flanking exon 7–9 of *IL4Rα (7)*. This results in a silent mutation of the IL-4Rα gene. Mice that specifically express the Cre recombinase in macrophages/neutrophils under control of the lysozyme M promoter (LysM^{cre} mice) were generated by a ***knock-in*** approach *(23)*. LysM^{cre} mice were first backcrossed to BALB/c for nine generations and then intercrossed with global IL-4Rα$^{-/-}$ BALB/c mice *(6)* to establish double transgenic LysM^{cre}IL-4Rα$^{-/-}$ BALB/c mice. These mice were further intercrossed with IL-4Rα$^{lox/lox}$ BALB/c mice to generate cell-type-specific LysM^{cre}IL-4Rα$^{-/lox}$ BALB/c mice *(7)* (**Fig.** 2). Efficient deletion of the IL-4Rα gene and subsequent impairment of IL-4Rα responsiveness in macrophages and neutrophils only was demonstrated *(7)*. In experiments, transgene negative littermates IL-4Rα$^{-/flox}$ are used as controls. This breeding strategy has the advantage of avoiding potential aberrant Cre expression. IL-4Rα hemizygosity ($^{-/lox}$) increases the probability of Cre-mediated deletion of the "floxed" allele *(7)*

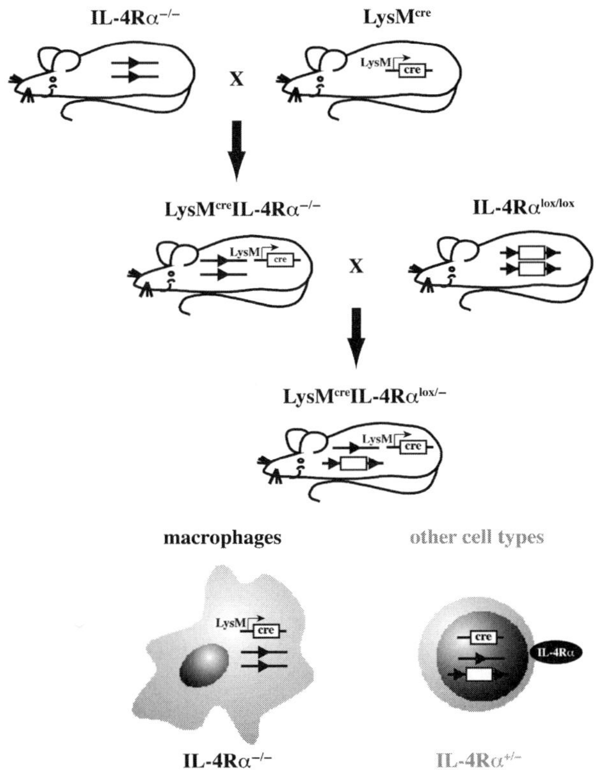

Fig. 2. Principle of macrophage/granulocyte specific deletion of the IL-4Rα. Conditional IL-4Rα$^{lox/-}$ mice are generated by homologous recombination. In these mice, exons of the IL-4Rα are flanked by two loxP sites (*triangles*) that are recognized by the Cre recombinase. Mice that specifically express the Cre recombinase in macrophages/neutrophils under control of the lysozyme M promoter (LysM^{cre} mice) were first intercrossed with global IL-4Rα$^{-/-}$ mice to avoid non-Mendelian inheritance due to early and aberrant Cre activity (unpublished observation). To facilitate efficient Cre-mediated recombination, LysM^{cre} IL-4Rα$^{-/-}$ mice were crossed with conditional IL-4Rα$^{lox/lox}$ mice. Because the Cre recombinase is only expressed in macrophages and neutrophils of hemizygote LysM^{cre} IL-4Rα$^{lox/-}$ offspring, loxP-flanked exons of the IL-4Rα locus on one allele are deleted only in these cell types. Hemizygote mice are used to reduce the substrate for the enzyme and to increase efficiency of Cre-mediated deletion in macrophages/neutrophils. In other cell types, the enzyme is not active and a functional IL-4Rα is still expressed. In experiments, Cre-negative IL-4Rα$^{lox/-}$ littermates serve as controls for macrophage/neutrophil-specific LysM^{cre} IL-4Rα$^{lox/-}$ mice.

Control and cell-type-specific LysM^{cre}IL-4Rα$^{-/lox}$ mice are routinely genotyped by either conventional or real-time PCR (**Fig. 3**). By real-time PCR, Cre-mediated deletion efficiency in cell-type-specific LysM^{cre}IL-4Rα$^{-/lox}$ mice was examined in purified macrophage cell suspensions. Nonmyeloid cells from cell-type-specific LysM^{cre}IL-4Rα$^{-/lox}$ mice may also serve as wild-type controls.

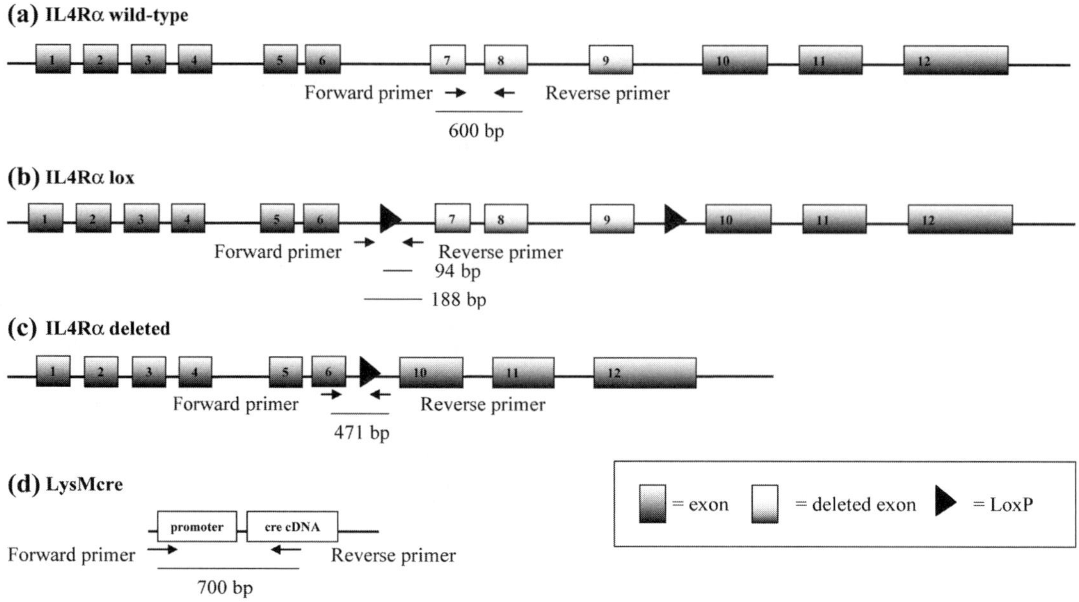

Fig. 3. Primer binding sites for genotyping of macrophage/granulocyte-specific LysM^{cre}IL-4Rα$^{lox/-}$ mice. IL-4Rα locus maps with primer binding sites for (**A**) IL-4Rα wild-type allele, the forward primer binds in exon 7 and the reverse primer in exon 8 resulting in the amplification of a 600-bp band. (**B**) IL4Rα lox PCR, the forward and reverse primer binds in intron 6 (3 of exon 6 and 5 of exon 10), flanking the lox p site, resulting in an amplified product of 188 bp (lox p specific) or 94 bp (wild type). **(C)** IL-4Rα deleted PCR, gene targeting, and Cre-mediated site-specific recombination at intron 6 and intron 9 results in the deletion of exons 7, 8, and 9 in the conditional IL4Rα$^{lox/-}$ mouse. The forward primer binds in exon 6 and the reverse primer in the intron 5′of exon 10 resulting in an amplification product of 471 bp. (**D**) LysM^{cre} PCR, the forward primer binds upstream, within the *knocked-in* transgene, to the lysozyme M promoter and the reverse primer binds within the cre cDNA yielding an amplification product of 700 bp.

3.1.1. DNA Extraction from Tail Biopsies

1. Use a robust pair of surgical scissors to perform the tail biopsies.
2. Add 500 μL of lysis buffer containing 0.5 mg/mL proteinase K to a 1-cm mouse tail in a 1.5-mL microtube and incubate overnight at 56°C with rotation.
3. After lysis, agitate tube to make sure that digest is complete and centrifuge samples at 1,400 × *g* for 10 min.
4. Remove supernatant and add to 500 μL isopropanol in a fresh 1.5-mL microtube. Mix well to precipitate DNA and centrifuge at 14,000 × *g* for 10 min.
5. Carefully remove supernatant, leaving the DNA pellet. Wash pellet with 70% ethanol at 14,000 × *g* for 2 min.
6. Remove ethanol and allow excess ethanol to dry at room temperature. Add 500 μL ddH2O and dissolve pellet well. Use 2 μL per PCR reaction for mouse genotyping.

3.1.2. PCR

Conventional PCR

1. Keep all reagents and samples on ice. The Taq enzyme should be kept in a *cooling block* on the bench.
2. For preparation of PCR master mix, calculate the final amount of following components based on the number of sample plus 2. Per sample add 5 μL 10× PCR buffer, 4 μL dNTPs, 2 μL 6.25 μM forward primer, and 2 μL 6.25 μM reverse primer, 0.05 μL 5 U/μL Taq polymerase, 34.95 μL ddH_2O.
3. Aliquot 48 μL of master mix to each PCR tube, add 2 μL of sample DNA and firmly close tubes.
4. Set up the PCR program. The following parameters are the same for the different primer sets: 40 cycles of 94°C denaturation for 30 s, annealing (annealing temperature; **Table 2**) for 20 s, and extension at 72°C (for extension time see **Table 2**). There is usually an initial 60-s denaturation at 94°C for all primer sets.
5. After PCR, add 10 μL 6× loading buffer to 50 μL of the amplified product. Run 30 μL on a 1.6% agarose gel to which ETBR is added at 0.45 μg/mL using 0.5× TBE as running buffer (*see* **Note 1**). Use a DNA ladder to size products.
6. After gel electrophoresis, genotypes are evaluated according to the resulting band sizes (**Fig. 3**, **Table 3**).

Real-Time PCR

1. Keep all reagents and samples on ice.
2. For preparation of the PCR master mix, it is advisable to make up at least two extra volumes of the reaction mix. Calculate the final volume of the following components based

Table 3
Genotyping of macrophage/neutrophil-specific LysM^{cre}IL-4Rα$^{-/lox}$ mice

	+/+	+/−	−/−
Conventional PCR	Band size [bp]		
IL-4Rα wild type	600	600	–
IL-4Rα deleted	–	471	471
IL-4Rα lox	188	188/94	94
LysMcre	–	700	700
Real-time PCR	Melting curve range [°C]		
IL-4Rα wild type	84.5–86.5	84.5–86.5	–
IL-4Rα deleted	–	86–88	86–88
LysMcre	–	85–87	85–87

on the number of sample plus the extra volume. Per sample add 10 μL 2× Sensimix, 0.5 μL 6.25 μM forward primer, and 0.5 μL 6.25 μM reverse primer, 0.4 μL 50× SYBR green, 6.6 μL ddH_2O.

3. Aliquot 18 μL of master mix to each PCR tube, add 2 μL of sample DNA, and firmly close tubes.
4. Set up the PCR program. The following parameters are the same for the different primer sets: 40 cycles of 94°C denaturation for 30 s, annealing at (annealing temperature; **Table 2**) for (annealing time; **Table** 2), and extension at 72°C for (extension time; **Table 2**). There is usually an initial 60-s denaturation at 94°C for all primer sets.
5. A melting range of 72–95°C is set up for all primer pairs, with an initial 45 s hold at the first temperature increment of 0.5°C, and a 5-s hold for each temperature increment thereafter.
6. On completion of the PCR reaction, genotypes can be evaluated according to the resulting melting curve range obtained for each primer pair (**Fig. 3**, **Table 3**).

3.2. Phenotyping Classical/Alternative Macrophage Activation In Vitro

caMϕ are induced by IFN-γ/LPS whereas alternative macrophage activation is mediated by IL-4 and IL-13. The generation of both types of macrophages is observed in the presence of the respective stimuli.

3.2.1. In Vitro Generation of ca/aaMϕ

To analyze macrophage activation in vitro, different types of primary macrophages may be used. Here we describe the in vitro generation of macrophages from bone marrow precursor cells (BMMϕ) *(24)*.

Generation of BMMϕ

1. Euthanize mouse and fix the body on a cork board on a clean bench. Peel skin from the top of each hind leg and down over the foot. Remove excess muscle from legs by holding end of bone with forceps using scissors to push muscle downward away from forceps. Sever leg bones between joints and prepare femur and tibia.
2. Attach 10-mL syringe to 26-G needle and fill with DMEM. Insert needle into bone marrow cavity of femur and tibia. Flush bone cavities with DMEM medium until bones appear white. Collect flushed medium in a sterile 50-mL conical tube on ice.
3. Centrifuge cells at 320 × *g* for 10 min at 4 C. Resuspend cell pellet in 10 mL PLUZNIK medium per mouse and transfer to a tissue-culture-grade petri dish.
4. Incubate cells at 37°C and 5% CO_2 in a humidified incubator overnight.

5. Transfer nonadherent cells to 50-mL sterile conical tube and centrifuge cell suspension at 320 × *g* for 10 min at 4°C. Resuspend cell pellet in PLUZNIK medium and count cells.
6. Adjust concentration to 1.5×10^6 cells per mL and distribute every 10 mL of cell suspension to bacterial-grade petri dish (1.5×10^7 cells). Incubate cells for 4 days at 37°C and 5% CO_2 in a humidified incubator (*see* **Note 5**).
7. Take off supernatant and add 10 mL fresh medium. Continue incubation for another 3 days.
8. Remove and discard culture supernatant. Wash remaining adherent cells with 15 mL prewarmed PBS.
9. Discard PBS wash and add 5 mL accutase to detach cells and incubate dishes 10 min at 37°C.
10. Gently remove cells by unidirectional scraping dish with a disposable sterile cell scraper (*see* **Note 6**).
11. Add 10 mL DMEM to dish and harvest detached cells. Wash remaining cells in dish with 10 mL DMEM, collect washes in 50-mL conical tubes, and centrifuge cell suspension at 320 × *g* for 10 min at 4°C. Resuspend cell pellet in DMEM and count cells.

Induction of caMϕ and aaMϕ by Stimulation of BMMϕ with IFN-γ/LPS or IL-4/IL-13

Classical or alternative activation of macrophages is facilitated by the presence of microbial stimuli or different cytokines. Whereas LPS and IFN-γ mediate the development of caMϕ, IL-4 and IL-13 induce aaMϕ. Hence, incubation of in vitro generated BMMϕ with either IFN-γ/LPS or IL-4/IL-13 will lead to classical or alternative activation, respectively *(7, 25)*.

1. Adjust cell concentration to 1.0×10^6 per μL in DMEM. Place 500 μL cell suspensions into wells of 48 well plates. Prepare enough samples for duplicate or triplicate sets to be processed under the following conditions:
   (a) Resting cells alone.
   (b) Cells treated with IFN-γ/LPS.
   (c) Cells treated with IL-4.
   (d) Cells treated with IL-13.
2. Incubate cells 4 h to allow macrophages to adhere, then gently wash wells two times with 500 μL DMEM.
3. To appropriate samples add:
   (a) DMEM.
   (b) IFN-γ/LPS to 10 U/mL and 10 ng/mL respectively, final concentrations.
   (c) IL-4 to 50 U/mL final concentration.
   (d) IL-13 to 500 U/mL final concentration.

4. Incubate cells for 24–72 h at 37°C and 5% CO_2 in a humidified incubator.
5. Supernatants and cell lysates are taken at 24, 48, and 72 h to analyze the expression of markers for classical and alternative macrophage activation (**Subheadings 3.2.2** and **3.2.3**).

3.2.2. Gene Expression Analysis of ca/aaMϕ In Vitro

We routinely perform quantitative analysis of NOS2 and Arg-1 gene expression in activated BMMϕ and tissue using a Light Cycler (Roche) *(4)* (*see* **Note 7**).

RNA Isolation

1. For each individual sample, prepare RNAse-free 1.5-mL microtubes and add 83 μL PBS to each.
2. After collecting culture supernatants for further analysis (*see* **Subheading 3.2.3 "NOS2 Activity (Griess Reaction in Supernatants)", step 2**), add 250 μL Trifast to each well and resuspend cells. Check for efficient cell lysis under a microscope. Remove lysates and add to microtubes containing prealiquotted PBS and incubate for 10 min at room temperature (*see* **Note 8**).
3. Add 100 μL 1-brom-3-chlorpropane (BCP) per tube, shake well, and incubate at room temperature for 15 min.
4. For each individual sample, prepare fresh RNAse-free 1.5-mL microtubes and add 1 μL linear polyacrylamide (LPA). After centrifugation of samples at 14,000 × *g* for 20 min at 4°C, carefully transfer the upper aqueous phase to the tubes containing LPA. Add 250 μL isopropanol, mix by carefully turning tubes and incubate for 10 min at room temperature.
5. Centrifuge for 10 min at 14,000 × *g* at 4°C. Carefully remove supernatants, add 1 mL 75% ethanol, and vortex.
6. Centrifuge for 5 min at 9,000 × *g* at 4°C. Carefully remove supernatants, air dry pellet, and add 50 μL DEPC water. Store samples at −80°C.

Reverse Transcription

1. Unfreeze RNA on ice and preheat thermoblocks.
2. For each individual sample, prepare RNAse-free 1.5-mL microtubes and add 2 μL oligo dT.
3. Add 8 μL total RNA from samples to oligo dT-containing tubes, vortex, and incubate for 10 min at 65°C.
4. In the meantime, prepare RT master mix. Calculate the final amount of the following components based on the number of samples to be run plus 2. Per sample add 2 μL ddH_2O, 4 μL 5× reaction buffer, 2 μL dNTPs, 1 μL ribonuclease inhibitor, 1 μL reverse transcriptase to a single microtube and vortex.
5. After incubation, spin tubes briefly and place on ice. Add 10 μL RT master mix to each sample, vortex, and incubate for 90 min at 37°C. Stop transcription by increasing the temperature to 95°C and incubate for 2 min.

6. Quickly place samples on ice. After the samples are cooled, add 180 μL ddH_2O. Samples can be stored at 4°C. For long-term storage freeze samples at −80°C.

Quantitative Real-Time PCR of NOS2 and Arg-1

1. Set up the PCR program. The following parameters are the same for the different primer sets: 95°C denaturation for 3 s, annealing at (annealing temperature; **Table** 2) for 5 s, and extension at 72°C for (extension time; **Table** 2). There is usually an initial 30-s denaturation at 95°C for all primer sets.
2. Place Lightcycler capillaries in centrifuge adaptors and cool at 4°C.
3. Prepare dilutions of samples and standards (start with 3.73 ng/mL [1 × 10^6 copies/μL], make up five dilutions 1:10 down to 10 copies/μL) in ddH_2O. Keep dilutions on ice.
4. For preparation of PCR master mix, calculate the final amount of following components based on the number of samples to be run plus 2. Per sample add 4.75 μL ddH_2O, 0.7 μL 50 mM $MgCl_2$, 1.0 μL 10× PCR buffer, 0.5 μL 10 mM dNTPs, 0.6 μL BSA, 0.4 μL 6.25 μM forward primer, and 0.4 μL 6.25 μM reverse primer. Before aliquotting master mix into capillaries, add 0.2 μL SYBR green and 0.1 μL 5 U/μL Taq polymerase.
5. Vortex master mix and add 9 μL to each capillary. Add 1 μL of each sample to capillaries and carefully place the cap on the capillary by gently applying firm pressure from directly above using the tip of a finger. Put cooled centrifuge adaptors with light cycler capillaries into the centrifuge. Quick spin at 380 × *g*. Remove capillaries and keep in cooling block until they are placed in the carousel of the light cycler (*see* **Note 9**).
6. [illegible] Press down firmly using pressure from directly above the capillary and place the carousel into the Lightcycler.
7. Start the PCR program by clicking on the *RUN* button. When the run is finished the Lightcycler will automatically exit the *Running Screen* and display the collected data on the Lightcycler *Data Analysis* (*LCDA*) front screen. Select the *Melting Curve* program by clicking on the *Melting Curve* button. Check that the water controls are clear and that the product melting peaks are defined.
8. Use the Lightcycler Software to calculate the amount of target from the standard curve. You may use either the *Fit Points* or *Second Derivative Maximum* methods. Use both the *Comparative Threshold Cycle* (*CT*) *Method* and *Standard Curve Method* to compare the fold difference between samples.

3.2.3. Metabolic Analysis of ca/aaMϕ

To analyze enzyme activity of NOS2 and Arg-1 in in vitro cultivated macrophages, specific metabolites of both enzymes are measured in either culture supernatants (NOS2) or cell lysates

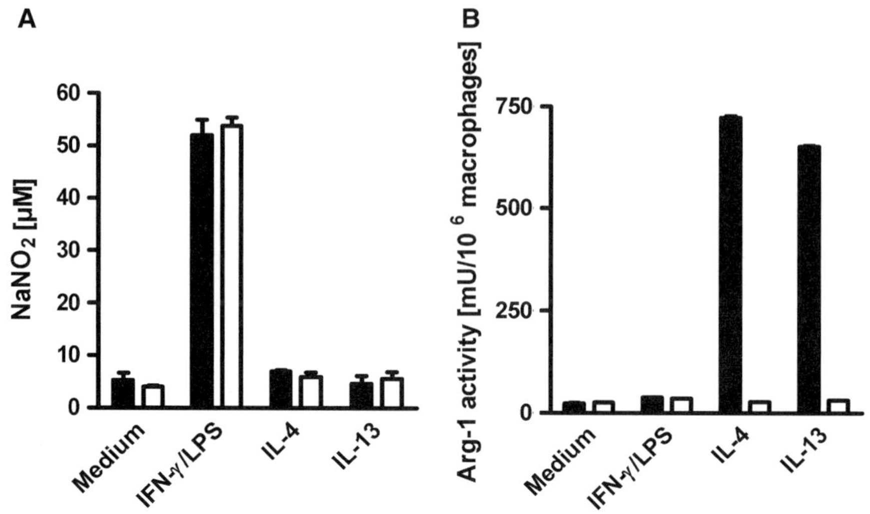

Fig. 4. Nitric oxide and urea production of caMϕ and aaMϕ in vitro. BMMϕ from control (*black bars*) and macrophage/neutrophil-specific LysM^{cre}IL-4R$\alpha^{-/lox}$ mice (*white bars*) were stimulated with medium, IFN-γ/LPS, IL-4, or IL-13. After 72 h, (**A**) $NaNO_2$ production in supernatants and (**B**) Arg-1 activity were measured using the Griess reaction and urea production, respectively. Whereas IFN-γ/LPS promote enzymatic activity of NOS2 and production of NO (classical activation), IL-4 and IL-13 induce Arg-1 expression and the release of urea (alternative macrophage activation).

(Arg-1) *(14)*. Whereas the Griess reaction measures the NOS2-mediated production of nitrite (**Fig. 4a**), the urea assay measures the Arg-1-dependent production of urea (**Fig. 4b**).

NOS2 Activity (Griess Reaction in Supernatants)

Nitric oxide undergoes a series of reactions with several molecules present in biological fluids. In supernatants of activated macrophages, the vast majority of NO is converted nitrite (NO_2^-). The amount of nitrite may be quantified using the Griess reaction, in which nitrite is converted into a deep purple azo compound. Photometric measurement of the absorbance due to this azo chromophore accurately determines nitrite concentration.

1. Add 50 μL of macrophage supernatants that have been collected after 24, 48, and 72 h of stimulation to wells of a 96-well microtiter plate (*see* **Note 10**).
2. In this plate, set up twofold serial dilutions in DMEM of nitrite solution (1 mM to 1 μM final concentration) in a final volume of 50 μL.
3. First, add 50 μL of Griess reagent #1 to nitrite standard and samples. Then add 50 μL Griess reagent #2 (*see* **Note 11**).
4. Measure absorbance at 550 nm in a microtiter plate reader (*see* **Note 12**).

Arginase Activity (Urea Assay)

Urea is synthesized from l-arginine by Arg-1. To analyze enzyme activity in macrophages in vitro, exogenous L-arginine is added to cell lysates and urea turnover is measured *(14, 26)*.

1. Samples, controls, and urea standard are required for this assay as follows:
   (a) Cell lysates with exogenous arginine.
   (b) Cell lysates without exogenous arginine.
   (c) All reagents without cell lysates.
   (d) Serial dilutions of urea as standard.
2. Wash cells two times with 500 µL PBS (*see* **Note 13**).
3. Add 100 µL of 0.1% Triton X-100 containing a protease inhibitor cocktail to cells and incubate on a shaker for 30 min (*see* **Note 14**).
4. Add 100 µL of 25 mM Tris–HCl and place 100 µL of each lysates into two fresh 1.5-mL microtubes (a) and (b), add 10 µL of 10 mM $MnCl_2$ and activate Arg-1 activity by heating for 10 min at 56°C. Place also 100 µL of 0.1% Triton X-100 with protease inhibitor cocktail and 100 µL of 25 mM Tris–HCl in a separate tube (c).
5. Add to one lysate 100 µL of 0.5 M L-arginine (a), add 100 µL ddH_2O to control lysates (b). Incubate lysates at 37°C for 15–20 min to conduct arginine hydrolysis (*see* **Note 15**).
6. In the meantime, set up 200 µL twofold serial dilutions of urea standard (1 mg/mL to 1 µg/mL final concentration in ddH_2O) (d).
7. Add 800 µL of stop solution to all tubes and add 40 µL α-isonitrosopropiophenone solution; vortex tubes thoroughly until phases are mixed, and heat at 95°C for 30 min (*see* **Note 16**).
8. Add 200 µL of samples (a), controls (b, c), and urea standard (d) to wells of a 96-well microtiter plate and measure the urea concentration at 540 nm in a microtiter plate reader (*see* **Note 17**).

3.3. Functional Analysis of Classical/Alternative Macrophage Activation In Vivo

Classical and alternative macrophage activation may also be analyzed in murine tissue and serum, e.g., after infection with various pathogens *(7, 14, 26)*. In contrast to in vitro studies of pure macrophage cultures, it is difficult to correlate markers of caMϕ and aaMϕ such as the production of RNI or urea, respectively, in vivo to a single cell type because these metabolites are also produced by other cells. In contrast, flow cytometric analysis, e.g., of MMR or IL-4Rα expression on gated macrophages can identify aaMϕ in vivo. Alternatively, immunohistochemical analysis of NOS2 and Arg-1 expression may also be used to identify caMϕ and aaMϕ, respectively. Gene expression analysis or determination of enzymatic activity of NOS2 and Arg-1 in whole tissue may also classify classical and alternative macrophage activation. Here we present immunohistochemical and enzymatic methods to detect NOS2 and Arg-1 in murine tissue or serum.

3.3.1. Histopathological and Immunohistochemical Analysis of ca/aaMϕ

Both enzymes can be detected in formalin-fixed and paraffin-embedded tissue *(7, 27)*.

Tissue Processing

After removing organs from mice, tissue specimens are fixed and placed in 10% neutral buffered formalin. The purpose of fixation is to preserve tissues permanently in as life-like a state as possible. Fixation should be carried out as soon as possible after removal of the tissues to prevent autolysis. Once the tissue has been fixed, it has to be dehydrated and infiltrated with paraffin. The tissue, placed in cassettes, is processed using an automated tissue processor. The automation process, used to cope with large volumes of routine samples, moves the tissues through the various reagents on a preset time frame. Once processed, the tissue is removed from the cassettes manually and placed in a block over which molten paraffin is poured. This *embedding* process is very important, as the tissue must be aligned, or oriented, correctly in the block of paraffin. Once the tissues have been embedded, they are cut into 2–10 μm sections using a microtome. The cut sections are floated on a warm water bath that helps to remove "wrinkles" in the section and thereafter picked up on a coated glass microscopic slide. The glass slides are placed on a warm plate for approximately 3 h to facilitate drying and adherence of the section to the slide.

1. The embedding process must be reversed in order to get the paraffin wax out of the tissue and allow water soluble dyes to penetrate the sections. Therefore, before any staining can be done, the slides are "deparaffinized" by running them through xylol to acetone to water. Once placed in a slide rack, slides can be easily transferred to different staining dishes. By this means, slides are deparaffinized by consecutive incubation steps for 10 min each in xylol, 100% acetone, 70% acetone, 40% acetone. Slides are then rinsed with ddH_2O.
2. Place slides three times in different trays filled with TBS. Before staining, leave slides in TBS.

Formalin or other aldehyde fixation forms protein crosslinks that mask the antigenic sites in tissue specimens, thereby giving weak or false negative staining for immunohistochemical detection of certain proteins such as NOS2 and Arg-1. Depending on the antigen, different antigen retrieval methods have to be evaluated to obtain optimal staining results.

NOS2 Expression

1. For immunohistochemical staining of NOS2 (**Fig. 5a, b**), a citrate-based buffer is used for antigen retrieval to break the protein crosslinks, thereby unmasking the epitope in the formalin-fixed and paraffin-embedded tissue sections. This enhances staining intensity of the anti-NOS2 antibodies. Boil citrate buffer in a pressure cooker, add rack with tissue

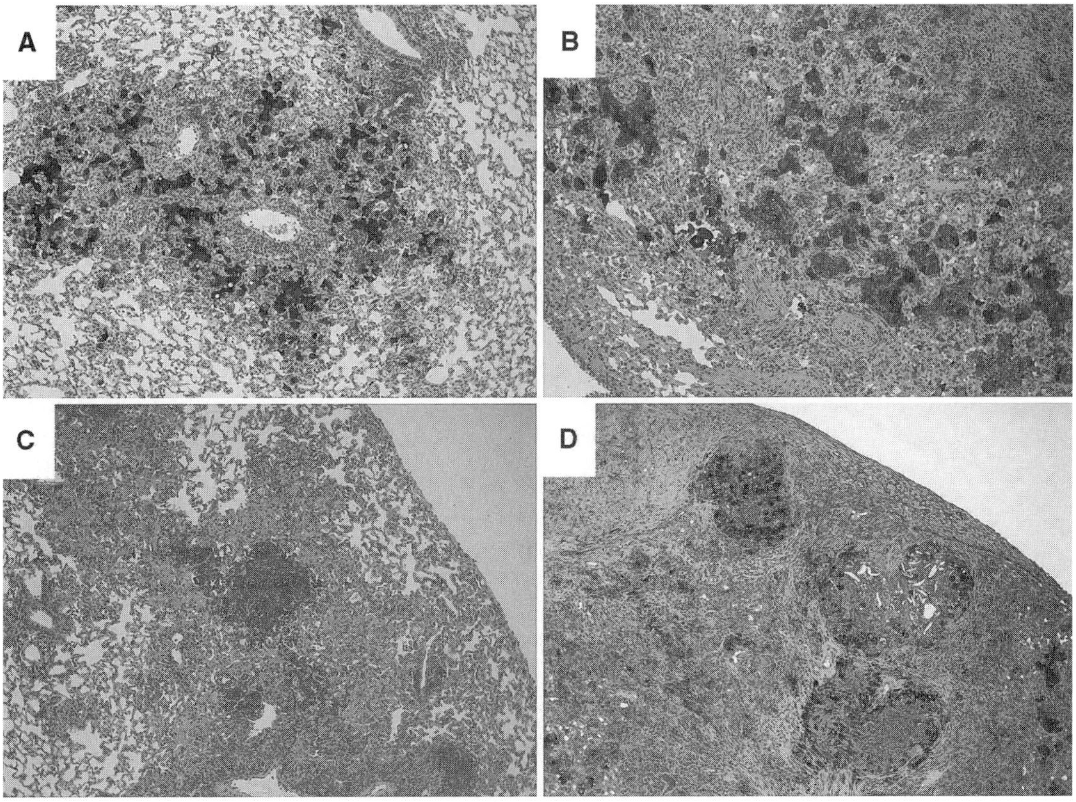

Fig. 5. NOS2 and Arg-1 expression in murine tissue in vivo. (**A**, **C**) C57BL/6 and (**B**, **D**) IL-13-transgenic mice were infected with 100 CFU of M. tuberculosis via the aerosol route. After 63 days, the expression of (**A**, **B**) NOS2 and (**C**, **D**) Arg-1 was determined in formalin-fixed and paraffin-embedded lung tissue by immunohistochemistry (notice brown stainings). Whereas IFN-γ production in both *M. tuberculosis*-infected C57BL/6 and IL-13-transgenic mice leads to NOS2 expression (classical macrophage activation), overexpression of IL-13 also induces and is required for Arg-1 expression (alternative activation).

sections, and heat slides for another 2 min. Afterward, rinse slides three times in different staining dishes filled with TBS. Block endogenous peroxidase by incubating slides in freshly prepared 1% H_2O_2/TBS for 20 min in the dark. Wash slides three times in TBS.

2. Drain slides and wipe excess buffer. For staining, add 200 μL rabbit anti-NOS antibody diluted 1:800 in TBS/10% FCS and place cover slips on slides to evenly disperse solution. Incubate slides in a humid chamber for 45 min at room temperature.
3. Discard cover slips and wash slides three times with TBS. Drain slides and wipe excess buffer. Add 200 μL secondary antibody solution containing goat antirabbit IgG peroxidase conjugate (1:30 in TBS/10% FCS) and mouse serum (1:10 in TBS/10% FCS). Place cover slips on slides and incubate in a humid chamber for 45 min at room temperature.

4. Discard cover slips and wash slides three times with TBS. Drain slides and wipe excess buffer. Add 200 μL rabbit antigoat IgG peroxidase conjugate diluted 1:50 in TBS/10% FCS. Place cover slips on slide and incubate in a humid chamber for 45 min at room temperature.
5. Fifteen minutes before incubation is finished, prepare DAB substrate solution by mixing 1 DAB and 1 urea tablet in 5 mL ddH_2O.
6. Discard cover slips and wash slides three times with TBS. Drain slides and wipe excess buffer. Add 200 μL DAB solution and incubate without cover slip for 5 min in the dark. Staining should be controlled under the microscope. Stop enzymatic reaction by washing slides with TBS.
7. Counterstain in Gill's hematoxylin for 3 min. Wash in running tap water for 10 min until nuclei are blue.
8. Mount slides in 70 μL Kaiser's glycerol gelatin that has been prewarmed at 37°C.

Arg-1 Expression

1. For immunohistochemical staining of Arg-1 (**Fig. 5c, d**), SDS is used for antigen retrieval to increase the staining intensity by Arg-1 immunohistochemistry. Place tissue section in a staining dish containing 1% SDS in TBS and incubate for 5 min at room temperature. Afterward, rinse slides three times in different staining dishes filled with TBS. Quench endogenous peroxidase by incubating slides in freshly prepared 1% H_2O_2/TBS for 20 min in the dark. Wash slides three times in TBS. Drain slides and wipe excess buffer.
2. To block endogenous biotin, add 200 μL avidin D-blocking reagent, add cover slips to evenly disperse the solution, and incubate in a humid chamber for 15 min at room temperature. Remove cover slip after incubation and discard. Rinse slides three times with TBS, drain, and wipe excess buffer. Add 200 μL biotin-blocking reagent. Add cover slips and incubate for 15 min in humid chamber at room temperature.
3. Remove cover slip and discard. Rinse slides three times for 2 min each with TBS, drain, and wipe excess buffer. Add 200 μL M.O.M. Ig-blocking reagent (two drops of reagent in 2.5 mL TBS) to block unspecific binding of endogenous immunoglobulins. Add cover slips and incubate in humid chamber for 1 h at room temperature. Remove cover slip after incubation and discard. Rinse slides three times with TBS for 2 min each, drain, and wipe excess buffer. Add 200 μL M.O.M. diluent (600 μL protein concentrate in 7.5 mL TBS) and incubate in humid chamber for 5 min at room temperature. Drip off excess M.O.M. diluent after incubation (*see* **Note 18**).

4. For staining of Arg-1, add 200 μL mouse anti-Arg-1 antibody diluted 1:250 in M.O.M. diluent to slides. Add cover slips on slides and incubate in a humid chamber for 45 min at room temperature.
5. Remove cover slip after incubation and discard. Rinse slides three times for 2 min each with TBS, drain, and wipe excess buffer. Add 200 μL biotinylated antimouse IgG reagent in M.O.M. (10 μL antibody solution in 2.5 mL M.O.M. diluent). Add cover slips and incubate in a humid chamber for 10 min at room temperature.
6. In the meantime, prepare Vectastain ABC reagent (add two drops of reagent A in 2.5 mL TBS and mix; add two drops of reagent B to this solution and mix; ABC reagent should be prepared 15 min before use).
7. Remove cover slip after incubation and discard. Rinse slides three times for 2 min each with TBS, drain, and wipe excess buffer. Add 200 μL Vectastain ABC reagent. Add cover slips and incubate in a humid chamber for 5 min at room temperature.
8. Rinse slides three times for 5 min each with TBS, drain, and wipe excess buffer. Add 200 μL DAB solution and incubate without cover slip for 5 min in the dark. Staining should be monitored microscopically. After sufficient staining (**Fig. 5**), stop enzymatic reaction by washing slides with TBS.
9. Counterstain in Gill's hematoxylin for 3 min. Wash in running tap water for 10 min until nuclei are blue.
10. Mount slides in 70 μL Kaiser's glycerol gelatin that has been prewarmed at 37°C.

3.3.2 Metabolic Analysis of ca/aaMϕ

Determination of Nitrate

The final products of NO in vivo are both nitrite and nitrate (NO_3^-). Because nitrate is not detected in the Griess reaction, it has to be reduced to nitrite first. To measure NO production in murine tissue or serum, the first step is the conversion of nitrate to nitrite utilizing the nitrate reductase. This conversion can be measured using the Griess reaction as described in **Subheading 3.2.3 "NOS2 Activity (Griess Reaction in supernatants)"**. However, to facilitate the conversion of nitrate to nitrite we utilize a commercial nitrate/nitrite colorimetric assay. To obtain reasonable results, samples taken from murine tissue have to be deproteinized first.

1. For determination of nitrate in murine tissue, prepare pieces of organs of approximately 1 cm². Determine tissue weight (*see* **Note 19**) and place pieces in 1.5-mL microtubes containing 1 mL of a proteinase inhibitor cocktail in PBS. Homogenize organs and centrifuge at 14,000 × *g* for 20 min at 4°C. Transfer supernatants into fresh 1.5-mL microtube.

2. Place YM-30 filters into these new 1.5-mL microtubes. Equilibrate filters by adding 100 μL ddH_2O and centrifuge at 14,000 × *g* for 5 min at 4°C. Discard filtrate and place washed filters in new tubes (*see* **Note 20**).
3. Transfer 300 μl homogenate supernatants into washed filters. Centrifuge at 14,000 × *g* for 20 min at 4°C, discard filter, and use filtrate for assay (*see* **Note 21**).
4. For determination of nitrate in serum, add freshly isolated murine blood to serum separator tubes on ice. Centrifuge at 4,000 × *g* for 10 min at 4°C. Use supernatant for assay (*see* **Note 22**).
5. To prepare a nitrate standard, place 0.9 mL assay buffer in a 1.5-mL microtube. Add 0.1 mL of reconstituted nitrate and vortex. The concentration of this stock is 200 μM. In a 96-well microtiter plate, set up twofold serial dilutions of this nitrate stock solution (100 μM to 0.8 μM final concentration) in a final volume of 80 μL.
6. Samples containing nitrate are assayed by the addition of up to 80 μL of sample per well to the plate. When using less than 80 μL of sample, the volume must be adjusted to 80 μL by addition of the appropriate volume assay buffer. When necessary, dilution of samples should be done using the assay buffer. Serum should be diluted 1:2 in assay buffer.
7. Add 200 μL of water or assay buffer to the microtiter plate as blank. Do not add any other reagents to these wells.
8. Add 10 μL of the enzyme cofactor mixture to each well. Add 10 μL of the nitrate reductase mixture to each well. Seal the plate and incubate at room temperature for 3 h.
9. Add 50 μL of Griess reagent #1 to each well. Immediately, add 50 μL of Griess reagent #2 to each well. Allow the color to develop for 10 min at room temperature.
10. Measure absorbance at 550 nm in a microtiter plate reader (*see* **Note 23**).

Arg-1 Activity

To analyze enzyme activity of Arg-1 in murine tissue ex vivo, exogenous L-arginine is added to tissue homogenates and urea turnover is measured as described in **Subheading 3.2.3 "Arginase Activity (Urea Assay)"** *(7, 26)*

1. To determine arginase activity in murine tissue, weighed pieces of organs are placed in 1.5-mL microtubes. Add 100 μL of 0.1% Triton X-100 containing a protease inhibitor cocktail. Homogenize organs and determine arginase activity ex vivo using 1–100 μL of homogenates following the method described in **Subheading 3.2.3 "Arginase Activity (Urea Assay)"** (*see* **Note 24**).

4. Notes

1. Protective gloves must be worn at all times when handling ETBR as well as eye and skin protection. ETBR and ETBR-contaminated debris should be treated as hazardous waste.
2. M-CSF-containing supernatants are produced using L929 fibroblasts (ATCC [CCL-1], Rockville, MD USA). In numerous 175-cm^2 tissue culture flasks (Nunc), 2×10^7 cells are cultured at 37°C and 10% CO_2 in 100 mL DMEM medium (Biochrom) supplemented with 10% (v/v) FCS (Biochrom), 2 mM L-glutamine (PAA), 100 U/mL/100 μg/mL streptomycin (Biochrom). After 7 days, collect supernatants and centrifuge at 2,000 × *g* for 10 min at room temperature. Pool supernatants and store aliquots at –80°C.
3. DEPC inactivates RNAses. To prepare RNAse-inactivated DEPC water, dilute DEPC (Sigma) 1: 1,000 in ddH_2O (B. Braun). Shake well until no more bubbles rise, leave for 24 h, and autoclave.
4. Dissolve all the solids in tap water first. Then add ethylene glycol and acetic acid. Stir at least for 3 h and filter solution before use.
5. The yield of bone marrow cells obtained per mouse varies with the strain. However, a yield of 3–10 × 10^6 cells per mouse can be expected.
6. Use of a cell scraper limits destruction of cells. To limit damage further, scrape in one direction only.
7. Gene expression of caMϕ and aaMϕ could also be determined in vivo in murine tissue.
8. After this step aliquots may be stored at –80°C.
9. Be careful when handling the capillaries as they break easily. Do not centrifuge capillaries with speeds higher than 500 × *g*.
10. NO_2^- synthesis begins 4–6 h after treatment with IFN-γ and LPS and is linear for up to 72 h.
11. For optimal results, add sulfanilamide before naphthylenethylenediamine.
12. Production of nitrite can be expressed as total concentration of NO_2^- in μM or calculated as moles NO_2^- on the basis of cell number. The results of the standard dilution should give a standard curve that is linear between 0 and 125 μM nitrite. The detection threshold for this method is about 1 μM NO_2^-.
13. It is important to wash macrophages in PBS so as to deplete the cells of arginine-containing medium.

14. At this step, plates can be stored at –80°C.
15. Depending on the amount of Arg-1, incubation time can vary between 15 and 120 min.
16. Secure caps on microtubes to ensure caps do not pop at this high temperature (e.g., by placing a weight on the tubes once in the heating block)
17. One unit of enzyme activity is defined as the amount of enzyme that catalyzes the formation of 1 µmol urea/min; arginase activity of macrophages is calculated as units of enzyme activity on the basis of cell number.
18. After addition of M.O.M. diluent, do not add cover slip. After incubation do not wash with TBS; only dip off excess buffer.
19. Concentration of nitrate/nitrate and arginase activity in murine tissue will be calculated on the basis of tissue weight.
20. Turbidity and proteins in tissue homogenates could interfere with absorbance readings. Therefore, samples are filtrated before the assay.
21. Samples could be stored at –80° until further use.
22. Serum could be stored in separator tubes at –80°C. For assay, use only samples that are not hemolytic.
23. Production of nitrite and nitrate can be expressed as total concentration of NO_2^- and NO_3^- in µM or calculated as moles NO_2^- and NO_3^- on the basis of weight tissue. The absorbance of the samples should be between 0.05 and 1.2 absorbance units. Higher absorbance values imply higher nitrate levels. Under these conditions, however, there may be incomplete conversion of nitrate to nitrite. The detection limit of the assay is approximately 1 µM NO_2^-.
24. One unit of enzyme activity is defined as the amount of enzyme that catalyzes the formation of 1 µmol urea/min. Arginase activity in organ homogenates is calculated as units of enzyme activity on the basis of weight tissue.

Acknowledgments

Related projects are supported by grants to FB (The Wellcome Trust and Royal Society, UK; German Research Foundation, Germany; National Research Foundation and Medical Research Council, ZA) and CH (University of Lübeck, Germany, Research Focus "Host Defense against Infectious Diseases", Project B2

"Arginase-1 mediated modulation of granuloma necrosis and immune defense against mycobacterial infections"; Nation-wide Collaborative Grant: "Pulmonary Tuberculosis – host and pathogen determinants of resistance and disease progression." Work-packages E (Animal models).

References

1. Gordon, S. (2003) Alternative activation of macrophages. *Nat. Rev. Immunol.* 3, 23–35
2. Holscher, C. (2004) The power of combinatorial immunology: IL-12 and IL-12-related dimeric cytokines in infectious diseases. *Med. Microbiol. Immunol. (Berl)* 193, 1–17
3. Goerdt, S. and Orfanos, C. E. (1999) Other functions, other genes: alternative activation of antigen-presenting cells. *Immunity* 10, 137–142
4. Holscher, C., Atkinson, R. A., Arendse, B., Brown, N., Myburgh, E., Alber, G., and Brombacher, F. (2001) A protective and agonistic function of IL-12p40 in mycobacterial infection. *J. Immunol.* 167, 6957–6966
5. Louis, J., Himmelrich, H., Parra-Lopez, C., Tacchini-Cottier, F., and Launois, P. (1998) Regulation of protective immunity against *Leishmania major* in mice. *Curr. Opin. Immunol.* 10, 459–464
6. Mohrs, M., Ledermann, B., Kohler, G., Dorfmuller, A., Gessner, A., and Brombacher, F. (1999) Differences between IL-4- and IL-4 receptor alpha-deficient mice in chronic leishmaniasis reveal a protective role for IL 13 receptor signaling. *J. Immunol.* 162, 7302–7308
7. Herbert, D. R., Holscher, C., Mohrs, M., Arendse, B., Schwegmann, A., Radwanska, M., Leeto, M., Kirsch, R., Hall, P., Mossmann, H., Claussen, B., Forster, I., and Brombacher, F. (2004) Alternative macrophage activation is essential for survival during schistosomiasis and down modulates T helper 1 responses and immunopathology. *Immunity* 20, 623–635
8. Noel, W., Hassanzadeh, G., Raes, G., Namangala, B., Daems, I., Brys, L., Brombacher, F., Baetselier, P. D., and Beschin, A. (2002) Infection stage-dependent modulation of macrophage activation in Trypanosoma congolense-resistant and -susceptible mice. *Infect. Immun.* 70, 6180–6187
9. Raes, G., Brys, L., Dahal, B. K., Brandt, J., Grooten, J., Brombacher, F., Vanham, G., Noel, W., Bogaert, P., Boonefaes, T., Kindt, A., Van den, B. R., Leenen, P. J., De Baetselier, P., and Ghassabeh, G. H. (2005) Macrophage galactose-type C-type lectins as novel markers for alternatively activated macrophages elicited by parasitic infections and allergic airway inflammation. *J. Leukoc. Biol.* 77, 321–327
10. Ghassabeh, G. H., De Baetselier, P., Brys, L., Noel, W., Van Ginderachter, J. A., Meerschaut, S., Beschin, A., Brombacher, F., and Raes, G. (2006) Identification of a common gene signature for type II cytokine-associated myeloid cells elicited in vivo in different pathologic conditions. *Blood* 108, 575–583
11. Byrs, L., Beschin, A., Raes, G. G., Hassanzadeh, G. G., Noel, W., Brandt, J., Brombacher, F., and de Baetselier, P. (2005) Reactive Oxygen Species and 12/15-lipoxygenase contribute to the anti-proliferative capacity of alternatively activated myeloid cells elicited during helminth infection. *J. Immunol.* 174, 6095–6104
12. Gallina, G., Dolcetti, L., Serafini, P., De Santo, C., Marigo, I., Colombo, M. P., Basso, G., Brombacher, F., Borrello, I., Zanovello, P., Bicciato, S., and Bronte, V. (2006) Tumors induce a subset of inflammatory monocytes with immunosuppressive activity on CD8 + T cells. *J. Clin. Invest* 116, 2777–2790
13. Leeto, M., Herbert, D. R., Marillier, R., Schwegmann, A., Fick, L., and Brombacher, F. (2006) TH1-dominant granulomatous pathology does not inhibit fibrosis or cause lethality during murine schistosomiasis. *Am. J. Pathol.* 169, 1701–1712
14. Holscher, C., Arendse, B., Schwegmann, A., Myburgh, E., and Brombacher, F. (2006) Impairment of alternative macrophage activation delays cutaneous leishmaniasis in nonhealing BALB/c mice. *J. Immunol.* 176, 1115–1121
15. Cao, Y., Brombacher, F., Tunyogi-Csapo, M., Glant, T. T., and Finnegan, A. (2007) Interleukin-4 regulates proteoglycan-induced arthritis by specifically suppressing the innate immune respose. *Arthritis Rheum.* 56, 861–870
16. Green, S. J., Mellouk, S., Hoffman, S. L., Meltzer, M. S., and Nacy, C. A. (1990)

Cellular mechanisms of nonspecific immunity to intracellular infection: cytokine-induced synthesis of toxic nitrogen oxides from L-arginine by macrophages and hepatocytes. *Immunol. Lett.* 25, 15–19

17. Liew, F. Y., Millott, S., Parkinson, C., Palmer, R. M., and Moncada, S. (1990) Macrophage killing of Leishmania parasite in vivo is mediated by nitric oxide from l-arginine. *J. Immunol.* 144, 4794–4797
18. Diefenbach, A., Schindler, H., Rollinghoff, M., Yokoyama, W. M., and Bogdan, C. (1999) Requirement for type 2 NO synthase for IL-12 signaling in innate immunity. *Science* 284, 951–955
19. Ehlers, S. and Holscher, C. DTH-associated pathology. In: Kaufmann, S. H. E. 705–730. 2005. London, Arnold Publishing. Microbiology and microbial infections. Topley and Wilson
20. Rutschman, R., Lang, R., Hesse, M., Ihle, J. N., Wynn, T. A., and Murray, P. J. (2001) Cutting edge: Stat6-dependent substrate depletion regulates nitric oxide production. *J. Immunol.* 166, 2173–2177
21. El Gayar, S., Thuring-Nahler, H., Pfeilschifter, J., Rollinghoff, M., and Bogdan, C. (2003) Translational control of inducible nitric oxide synthase by IL-13 and arginine availability in inflammatory macrophages. *J. Immunol.* 171, 4561–4568
22. Munder, M., Eichmann, K., and Modolell, M. (1998) Alternative metabolic states in murine macrophages reflected by the nitric oxide synthase/arginase balance: competitive regulation by CD4 + T cells correlates with Th1/Th2 phenotype. *J. Immunol.* 160, 5347–5354
23. Clausen, B. E., Burkhardt, C., Reith, W., Renkawitz, R., and Forster, I. (1999) Conditional gene targeting in macrophages and granulocytes using LysMcre mice. *Transgenic Res.* 8, 265–277
24. Holscher, C., Kohler, G., Muller, U., Mossmann, H., Schaub, G. A., and Brombacher, F. (1998) Defective nitric oxide effector functions lead to extreme susceptibility of *Trypanosoma cruzi*-infected mice deficient in gamma interferon receptor or inducible nitric oxide synthase. *Infect. Immun.* 66, 1208–1215
25. Munder, M., Eichmann, K., Moran, J. M., Centeno, F., Soler, G., and Modolell, M. (1999) Th1/Th2-regulated expression of arginase isoforms in murine macrophages and dendritic cells. *J. Immunol.* 163, 3771–3777
26. Kropf, P., Fuentes, J. M., Fahnrich, E., Arpa, L., Herath, S., Weber, V., Soler, G., Celada, A., Modolell, M., and Muller, I. (2005) Arginase and polyamine synthesis are key factors in the regulation of experimental leishmaniasis in vivo. *FASEB J.* 19, 1000–1002
27. Reiling, N., Holscher, C., Fehrenbach, A., Kroger, S., Kirschning, C. J., Goyert, S., and Ehlers, S. (2002) Cutting edge: Toll-like receptor (TLR)2- and TLR4-mediated pathogen recognition in resistance to airborne infection with *Mycobacterium tuberculosis*. *J. Immunol.* 169, 3480–3484
28. Raes, G., De, B. P., Noel, W., Beschin, A., Brombacher, F., and Hassanzadeh, G. G. (2002) Differential expression of FIZZ1 and Ym1 in alternatively versus classically activated macrophages. *J. Leukoc. Biol.* 71, 597–602
29. Martinez-Pomares, L., Reid, D. M., Brown, G. D., Taylor, P. R., Stillion, R. J., Linehan, S. A., Zamze, S., Gordon, S., and Wong, S. Y. (2003) Analysis of mannose receptor regulation by IL-4, IL-10, and proteolytic processing using novel monoclonal antibodies. *J. Leukoc. Biol.* 73, 604–613
30. Ruckerl, D., Hessmann, M., Yoshimoto, T., Ehlers, S., and Holscher, C. (2006) Alternatively activated macrophages express the IL-27 receptor alpha chain WSX-1. *Immunobiology* 211, 427–436
31. Hesse, M., Modolell, M., La Flamme, A. C., Schito, M., Fuentes, J. M., Cheever, A. W., Pearce, E. J., and Wynn, T. A. (2001) Differential regulation of nitric oxide synthase-2 and arginase-1 by type 1/type 2 cytokines in vivo: granulomatous pathology is shaped by the pattern of l-arginine metabolism. *J. Immunol.* 167, 6533–6544

Chapter 16

Analysis of Matrix Metalloproteinase Secretion by Macrophages

Paul T. Elkington, Justin A. Green, and Jon S. Friedland

Summary

Matrix metalloproteinases (MMPs) are zinc-dependent proteases whose physiological roles include control of leukocyte migration. They are implicated in tissue destruction in inflammatory and infectious diseases. MMPs are not only capable of degrading all components of the extracellular matrix, but they also can modulate the immune response by cleaving cytokines and chemokines to alter their activity. Macrophages secrete a broad range of MMPs and represent a key source of MMPs in inflammatory lesions such as granulomas. Zymography is substrate-based gel electrophoresis that allows direct visualization of MMP activity. Here we describe measurement of MMP secretion from macrophages focusing on quantitative zymography. We also discuss complementary methods that should be used in parallel with zymography. The ability to analyze and quantify MMP secretion by macrophages offers an additional window through which to understand the contributions of macrophages to a wide variety of infectious, inflammatory, and immunologic disorders.

Key words: Macrophage, Matrix metalloproteinase, Extracellular matrix, Zymography.

1. Introduction

Inflammatory diseases are frequently characterized by excessive degradation of the extracellular matrix (ECM). Matrix metalloproteinases (MMPs) are zinc-dependent proteases that collectively can degrade all components of the ECM *(1)*. They also perform an immunomodulatory role by cleaving cytokines and chemokines to either enhance or reduce their activity *(2)*. Excess MMP activity has been implicated in diverse diseases including atherosclerosis, emphysema, inflammatory arthritis, cancer progression, and, more recently, infectious diseases *(3, 4)*. MMP

Neil E. Reiner (ed.), *Macrophages and Dendritic Cells,* Methods in Molecular Biology, vol. 531

DOI: 10.1007/978-1-59745-396-7_16

activity is tightly regulated at the level of gene transcription, by secretion as proenzymes that require proteolytic cleavage for activation, by compartmentalization and the secretion of specific tissue inhibitors of metalloproteinases (TIMPs) *(5)*.

Macrophages, as central effector cells of the innate immune response, secrete a broad array of MMPs. The number and the quantity of MMPs secreted by macrophages increase during differentiation from monocytes *(6)*. Zymography is a functional assay that involves electrophoretic separation of proteins followed by degradation of enzyme substrate embedded into the gel, and therefore identifies MMPs with potential functional activity secreted by cells *(7)*. The benefits of the technique include being able to identify multiple MMPs with the same substrate specificity on a single gel, the possibility of identifying both the proenzyme and active form (i.e., MMPs with functional activity secreted by cells), as well as a relative lack of expense. However, zymography is not adequate in isolation, and it is often useful to identify total immunoreactive MMP concentrations. Therefore, in this chapter we shall also briefly consider additional approaches to analysis of MMP secretion which complement zymography. Complex functional and migration assays (which do not usually distinguish between specific MMPs) are beyond the scope of this chapter.

2. Materials

Source of materials is shown but where no specific reference is made, supplies are readily obtainable from Sigma.

2.1. Cell Culture

1. RPMI supplemented with 200 mM glutamine, ±10% fetal bovine serum. Antibiotics can be added if required.
2. Macrophage-colony-stimulating factor (M-CSF). Reconstitute to a final concentration of 10 mg/mL and store in 250 mL aliquots at –80°C.
3. Ficoll Paque. Store in the dark.

2.2. Gelatin Zymography

1. Gelatin solution: Make a 1.2% (w/v) solution by dissolving 1.2 g gelatin in 100 mL water in a water bath set at 65°C for 10 min. Make 5 mL aliquots and store at 4°C.
2. MMP-9 standard. Make aliquots to a final concentration of 1 ng/mL in buffer of 60 mM Tris, 15 mM $CaCl_2$, 80 mM NaCl, and 0.1% (w/v) bovine serum albumin (BSA) and store at –20°C.
3. 5× sample loading buffer: 0.25 M Tris–HCl, pH 6.8, 50% (w/v) glycerol, 5% (w/v) sodium dodecyl sulfate (SDS), 0.01 g bromophenol blue. Make 10 mL and store in 1 mL aliquots at room temperature.

4. 40% acrylamide (29:1 acrylamide:bis-acrylamide ratio) and 1.44 M Tris–HCl, 0.384% SDS, pH 8.8 running gel buffer. For stacking gel buffer use 0.5 M Tris–HCl, 0.4% SDS, pH 6.8.
5. 10% (w/v) ammonium persulfate: 0.1 g in 1 mL ddH$_2$O, make up fresh on each occasion.
6. *N,N,N,N*-Tetramethylethylenediamine (TEMED).
7. Running buffer: 25 mM Tris base, 190 mM glycine, 0.1% (w/v) SDS. Make up 10× stock by dissolving 30.3 g Tris base and 144.1 g glycine in 1 L ddH$_2$O. Store at room temperature. Make working solution by adding 100 mL 10× stock and 10 mL 10% (w/v) SDS and ddH$_2$O up to a final volume of 1 L.
8. 2.5% (v/v) Triton X-100: 25 mL Triton X-100 in 1 L ddH$_2$O, prepare in advance on stirrer since Triton-X takes time to dissolve. Store at room temperature.
9. Low-salt collagenase buffer: 55 mM Tris–HCl, 200 mM sodium chloride, 5 mM calcium chloride, 0.02% Brij, pH 7.6. Dissolve 60.6 g Tris, 117 g NaCl, and 5.5 g CaCl$_2$ in 900 mL ddH$_2$O, adjust pH to 7.6 with concentrated HCl, make up to 1 L, and store at 4°C. To make 1× working solution, make 100 mL 10× stock up to 1 L with ddH$_2$O, add 670 mL Brij-35, then recheck pH and correct to 7.6 if necessary.
10. 0.2% Coomassie blue stock solution: Dissolve one tablet PhastGel-Blue (Pharmacia, Sweden) in 80 mL ddH$_2$O and stir for 10 min. Add 120 mL methanol; then filter at 4°C through Whatman number 1 filter paper. Store at 4°C.
11. Destain solution: 200 mL glacial acetic acid, 600 mL methanol, 1,200 mL ddH$_2$O to give proportion 1:3:6. Store at room temperature.
12. Single-step stain–destain solution: 5 mL 0.2% Coomassie blue stock with 95 mL destain solution per gel.

2.3. Casein Zymography

1. Novex precast 12% Casein gels (Invitrogen, Paisley, UK). These need to be run using the X-Cell *Surelock* Minigel system (Invitrogen).
2. MMP-1 standard. Aliquot 1 μL neat MMP-1, store at –20°C.
3. MMP-1 standard buffer: 50 mM Tris base, 5 mM CaCl$_2$, 0.05% (v/v) Brij 35. 0.6 g Tris base, 0.55 g CaCl$_2$ with 0.05 mL Brij 35 made up to 100 mL, freeze in 0.5 mL aliquots at –20°C.
4. Running buffers, sample loading buffer, low-salt collagenase buffer and destain solutions are as for gelatin zymography (**Subheading 3, item 2**).

5. 0.1% stain solution: 20 mL stock 0.2% Coomassie blue (see earlier), 16 mL ddH_2O, 4 mL acetic acid.

3. Methods

3.1. Cell Culture

MMP secretion increases with monocyte maturation into monocyte-derived macrophages (MDMs). However, the precise conditions of maturation will influence the MMP secretion phenotype. For example MDMs matured in granulocyte-macrophage-colony-stimulating factor (GM-CSF) are likely to have a reduced inflammatory secretion profile producing less MMPs when compared with MDMs matured in M-CSF. We briefly outline our macrophage maturation protocol below, highlighting the key steps with regard to analysis of MMP secretion.

1. Obtain leukocytes either by venesection using a 50-mL syringe or by obtaining buffy coat (leukocyte-rich) residues from blood transfusion services if available. 50 mL human blood will provide ~1×10^7 monocytes which will coat a 24-well plate at 250,000 cells/cm^2. A buffy coat from 500 mL donated blood will usually produce 1×10^8 monocytes, sufficient to plate a total of 400 cm^2 of tissue culture plastic.

2. Isolate monocytes by density centrifugation through Ficoll-Paque in 50-mL falcon tubes followed by five wash steps by resuspending the PBMC layer in HBSS and centrifuging at 308RCF.

3. Accurate quantification of monocyte numbers prior to adhesion is critical in generating a confluent monolayer that will secrete sufficient MMPs for detection by zymography. Take 20 μL from the 50-mL cell suspension and place in a Neubauer counting chamber. If a buffy coat from 500 mL blood is being used, a 1 in 25 dilution is necessary. Place the counting chamber in a tissue culture incubator at 37°C for 5 min while performing penultimate wash. When final wash has started, remove the counting chamber and examine under phase II of an inverted light microscope. Monocytes will have adhered to the counting chamber, appear gray, and show pseudopodia. Lymphocytes will not adhere and appear brighter, rounder, and smaller.

4. After the final wash step, resuspend the cells in warmed RPMI, with no FCS, since this reduces cell adhesion. Plate the cells at 250,000 monocytes per cm^2 and incubate for 1 h at 37°C. During cell adhesion, prepare the RPMI with FCS and M-CSF.

5. After adhesion, wash monolayer three times with HBSS to remove nonadherent cells. Finally add RPMI with FCS and M-CSF 100 ng/ml and incubate for 4 days at 37°C in a 5% CO_2 tissue culture incubator.
6. On day 4 (after 96 h in M-CSF) aspirate the RPMI/FCS/M-CSF cell culture supernatant and replace with RPMI/FCS only. Then rest the cells for 24 h.
7. On day 5, the cells are ready for stimulation; this is experiment day 0. Prior to commencing the experiment, the RPMI with FCS is aspirated, cells are washed once more with warmed HBSS, then stimulated in serum-free RPMI.

3.2. Gelatin Zymography

MMPs are secreted as proenzymes that, in vivo, require proteolytic cleavage by the release of the cysteine switch *(8)*. Zymography activates proenzyme MMPs by releasing the cysteine switch in a nonproteolytic manner, so that substrate degradation allows the detection of both proenzymes and active cleaved forms of each MMP being analyzed. Consequently, zymography provides data on all the potentially active MMP present. The molecular weight of each band will give an indication of which MMP is causing proteolysis in the gel, but the exact identification needs to be confirmed by running a recombinant MMP standard, performing ethylenediamine tetraacetic acid (EDTA) inhibition (see later) and by a second method such as Western blotting.

This protocol can be applied to any gel system. Our routine practice is to use the Hoeffer full-size plates (15 × 18 cm) since larger plates gives more crisp resolution of the gelatinolytic bands. However, this protocol could easily be amended for minigel systems.

1. Set up plates for gel pouring.
2. Melt gelatin in water bath at 65°C for 10 min (*see* Note 1).
3. Prepare 11% polyacrylamide gel by mixing 22 mL 40% acrylamide, 20 mL running gel buffer, 30 mL ddH_2O, 8 mL 1.2% gelatin stock, 160 mL TEMED, and 320 mL APS. This volume is sufficient for two full-size plates. Pour gel using a 25-mL disposable serological pipette to level approximately 5 mm below where the comb will be and then overlay with 1 mL isopropanol.
4. Once gel has set (approximately 20 min), pour off the isopropanol, insert combs, and pour stacking gel. Remove combs once the stacking gel has set. Once made up, gelatin gels can be stored overnight at 4°C.
5. Prepare samples and standards by mixing each sample with 5× sample loading buffer to make a final volume of 20 mL (4 mL loading buffer with 16 mL sample). Standards should be diluted to a final concentration of 0.1 ng/mL (e.g., 56 mL

MMP-9 standard buffer, 16 mL sample loading buffer, 8 mL standard at a concentration of 1 ng/mL). Load 20 mL of standard into lane one on each gel and 20 mL of each sample into subsequent wells (*see* **Note 2**).

6. Run gel at 180 V until marker dye reaches bottom of plate, usually 3–4 h (*see* **Note 3**).
7. Once the gel has run, dismantle the electrophoresis tank. Remove the spacers from each side of the gel and lift the upper plate off carefully. Use a gel cutter to remove the stacking gel and then cut a triangle off the gel in the top left hand corner for orientation.
8. Place the gel over a plastic container containing 200 mL 2.5% Triton-X 100. Gently lever off the gel with a spatula so that it falls into the Triton. The gels are fairly robust, but tears have been known to occur at this stage. Incubate gel in Triton for one hour with gentle shaking at 30 rpm on a rocker, thus washing the SDS off the gels.
9. Pour off the Triton, rinse gel in 150 mL of collagenase buffer twice, and then add 200 mL collagenase buffer for incubation (*see* **Note 4**). Place in incubator at 37°C overnight. Minimum incubation time should be 16 h; we routinely incubate for between 16 and 20 h.
10. Pour off collagenase buffer and rinse gel briefly in ddH_2O.
11. Add 100 mL single-step stain–destain solution to container. Bands of gelatinolytic activity will be visible within about 2 min, but the optimal length of staining is for 1 h. Gels can be left staining for up to 4 h, though this does not improve resolution further. Use standard band as an indication of when to stop staining.
12. Rinse off stain solution and wash gel once with water. Place on transparency film and wrap in cling-film. Acquire image using a light box with digital camera.
13. For densitometric analysis, we use Scion Image software, which can be downloaded free of charge from http://www.sciocorp.com/pages/scion_image_windows.htm. This was designed for the analysis of black on white bands, such as western blots, and so we invert the image using Adobe Photoshop before analysis. This analysis gives a linear standard curve between 10 and 500 pg MMP-9 (**Fig. 1**).
14. For comparison between different gels, in particular if they have been run on different days, each sample must be standardized by dividing the densitometric value generated by that of the MMP-9 standard. This controls for gel-to-gel variability in proteolysis.

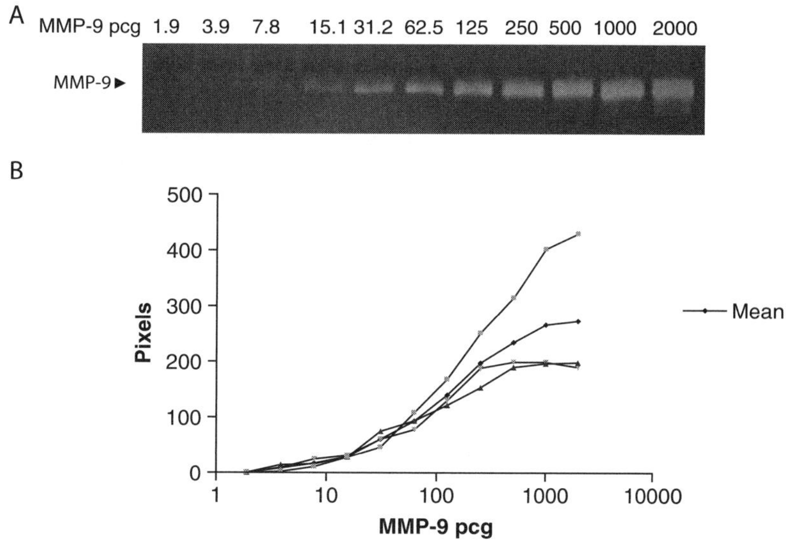

Fig. 1. (**A**) Recombinant MMP-9 was serially diluted to generate a standard curve and analyzed by gelatin zymography. (**B**) Densitometry of three separate gelatin zymograms demonstrating relationship between pixels versus pg MMP-9 loaded per lane, analyzed by NIH Image. Black squares indicate mean of three values.

3.3. Casein Zymography

The technique of casein zymography has many similarities to gelatin zymography, though there are subtle differences that affect sensitivity which are highlighted later. MMP-9 can degrade casein, though not as rapidly as gelatin, and so a band of proteolysis at 90 kDa is seen. However, MMP-1, the major human collagenase, degrades casein relatively slowly, and so prolonged incubation of the gel is needed (*see* **Note 5**). Serial dilutions of recombinant MMP-1 analyzed by casein zymography demonstrate that the lower level of detection is 0.1 ng MMP-1 (**Fig. 2**). Therefore casein zymography is approximately 2 log units less sensitive for MMP-1 than gelatin zymography is for MMP-9. MMP-3 is not usually secreted by cells of the monocyte lineage in sufficient quantities to be detected by casein zymography, but since MMP-3 has a similar molecular weight to MMP-1, the identity of bands must be confirmed by Western blotting for MMP-1 and -3.

MMP-7 also degrades casein, and so a third band of proteolysis occurs at 28 kDa, caused by pro-MMP-7 (**Fig. 3A**). If active MMP-7 is present, further bands representing proteolytically cleaved components of the enzyme may be visualized, though this may require concentration by lyophilization (**Fig. 3B**). Therefore, casein zymography can give multiple readouts identifying several MMPs secreted by macrophages.

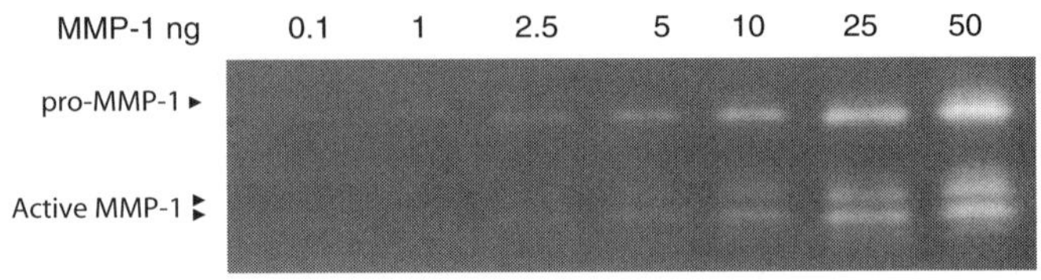

Fig. 2. Recombinant MMP-1 was serially diluted and analyzed by casein zymography.

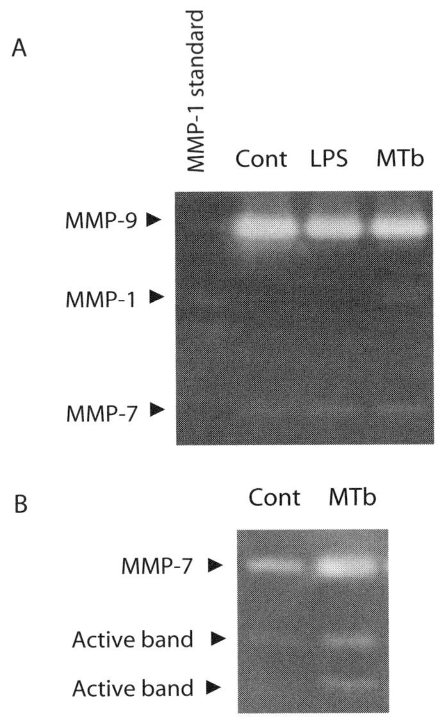

Fig. 3. (**A**) Identification of multiple MMPs on casein zymography. MDMs were left unstimulated or stimulated with LPS or by infection with live *M. tuberculosis* (MTb). Supernatants were harvested at 24 h, sterile filtered, and then analyzed by casein zymography. MMP-9 activity is detected at 92 kDa, MMP-1 at 50 kDa -only in MTb infected cells- and MMP-7 activity at 28 kDa. (**B**) MDMs were infected with live MTb or unstimulated. MMP activity was analyzed in cell culture medium at 72 h after tenfold concentration by lyophilization followed by casein zymography.

1. Remove casein gels from plastic packet and rinse each well three times with 100 μL running buffer (*see* **Note 6**).
2. Assemble minigel tank and fill with running buffer.
3. Prepare standards and samples. 5 ng MMP-1 standard should be loaded. For example, if undiluted standard is 48 μg/mL, 0.52 μL standard mixed with 80 μL MMP-1 standard buffer and 20 μL loading buffer, will give 5 ng standard per well. Add 16 μL of each sample to 4 μL loading buffer.

4. Load 20 μL standard or sample per well and run at 125 V until blue marker reaches end of gel. 2.5 h is usually sufficient (*see* **Note 7**).
5. When gel has run, pour off running buffer, and remove the gels. Extracting the gel from the casing can easily cause tears, so this should be done with care. First, using a metal palette (which is provided with the X-cell Electophoresis module), crack open all three sides of the casing, with the front of the gel casing downward (*see* **Note 8**). A quick, sharp movement is most effective. Then, lift off the back of the casing, ensuring that the gel remains adhered on the front part of the case. Use the palette to cut around the gel, removing the comb indent and freeing the bottom of the gel, and cut a triangle off the top left side for orientation.
6. Place the gel over a plastic container measuring approximately 9 × 15 cm (we use large pipette tip box lids) containing 100 mL 2.5% Triton-X 100. Gently lever the gel off with a spatula so that the gel falls into the Triton. The gel is fragile and so care is needed. Incubate at room temperature for 1 h with gentle agitation.
7. Pour off the Triton and rinse the gel once in 75 mL low-salt collagenase buffer, then incubate in 75 mL low-salt collagenase buffer for 30 min at room temperature with agitation.
8. Place the gel in 100 mL fresh collagenase buffer, cover lid with cling film, and incubate the gel for ~40 h (two nights) at 37°C (*see* **Note 5**).
9. Pour off collagenase buffer and rinse gel briefly with ddH_2O. Stain gel with 0.1% Coomassie blue solution for one hour with agitation.

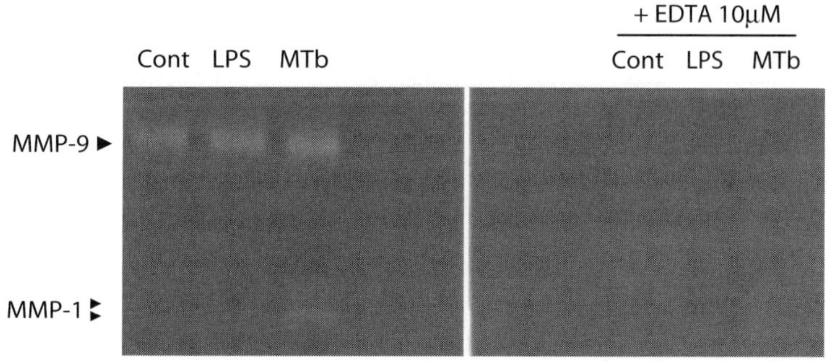

Fig. 4. Cell culture medium from control, LPS-treated, or MTb-infected MDMs was run in duplicate on a casein zymogram. The gel was cut into half and one half developed in collagenase buffer containing 10 mM EDTA. Proteolysis was completely inhibited by divalent cation sequestration, confirming that the bands are caused by MMPs.

10. Pour off stain solution, rinse briefly in water, and then add 100 mL destain solution. Incubate at room temperature with agitation.
11. Usually 30–45 min destain is sufficient. Since this is not a single-step stain–destain solution, the timing of stopping destaining is more critical than for gelatin zymography (*see* **Note 9**).
12. When sufficient destaining has occurred (judged by watching the standard), pour off destain solution and rinse briefly with ddH_2O. Place on transparency film, wrap in cling film and acquire image using a lightbox with digital camera.
13. As with MMP-9, standardize between gels by dividing value for samples by MMP-1 standard. MMP-1 appears as a couplet at 50 kDa, while the MMP-1 standard appears as a single band at 50 kDa, with two bands at MW of ~40 kDa (*see* **Note 10**).
14. The identity of proteolytic bands as MMPs should be confirmed by EDTA inhibition (*see* **Note 11** and **Fig. 4**).

3.4. Measuring Immunoreactive MMP and TIMP Concentrations; Western Analysis, ELISAs and Luminex Bead Assays

Zymography is an important method for analysis of MMP secretion since it identifies proteolytic activity, although it may be limited in sensitivity as described earlier. Therefore, we also employ complementary techniques to confirm the identity of the proteolytic bands and to improve sensitivity for MMPs that are secreted at a low level. These complementary approaches involve antibody detection of MMPs and therefore will detect all the immunoreactive MMP being studied, irrespective of whether it has proteolytic potential.

3.4.1. Western Blotting

This is relatively straightforward, but the sensitivity for MMP-9 is significantly less than for gelatin zymography. Western analysis of MMP-1 has an equivalent sensitivity to casein zymography. A full description of Western analysis may be found in any major methods textbook.

3.4.2. Elisa

Several commercially produced ELISAs for MMP analysis are available. Although some paired antibody kits are available, many only come as individual precoated plates and therefore are relatively expensive for the analysis of numerous samples.

3.4.3. Multiplexing

More recently, multiplex analysis of MMPs by bead array technology has become available. This requires a Luminex machine and commercial MMP kits. The technique is straightforward and allows analysis of multiple MMPs in a single 50-μL sample. It is particularly useful for the analysis of precious clinical specimens and low volumes from animal experiments. However, it is less useful for the analysis of single MMPs when the cost means that it offers no advantage over a single ELISA plate. Some success has been achieved by conjugating antibody to prepurchased beads, which can reduce costs somewhat, but needs quality control. It is not possible to purchase labeled beads for flow cytometric multiplex analysis as are available for cytokine measurements. We understand that some companies are in the process of optimizing this methodology for MMP analysis.

3.4.4. Sample Sterilization

MMPs are implicated in the immunopathology of many infectious diseases, and therefore the sterilization of samples to remove pathogens may be necessary. Filtration through a 0.2-μM filter will remove bacteria, but the choice of filter membrane is critical if MMP concentrations in the filtrate are to be analyzed. We have found that MMPs bind to the Anopore membrane, and therefore MMPs are only detectable in the filtrate if present in very high concentrations in the original sample *(9)*. Similarly, polypropylene membranes remove MMPs from the filtrate, which may lead to false negative results. At present, such artifacts in the analysis of MMP activity in infectious diseases models are frequently not recognized. Currently, we use the Durapore 0.2-μM membrane for filtration of *Mycobacterium tuberculosis*-infected samples, as we have found that this membrane displays minimal MMP binding. We recommend that any candidate filtration membrane first be checked for MMP binding activity in a specific pathogen-based culture system before use in sterilizing samples for MMP analysis.

4. Notes

1. Melting gelatin without overheating improves reliability of gelatin zymography. Though gelatin can be melted in a microwave, we find that warming in a water bath at 65°C for 10 min produces more consistent results.
2. Macrophages secrete very high quantities of MMP-9. For gelatin zymography, dilution of cell culture supernatant by 1 in 100 is needed, so that the gelatinolytic activity is not above the linear part of the standard curve. In contrast, it is not normally necessary to dilute monocyte supernatants.
3. Since the gelatinases MMP-9 and MMP-2 have MWs of 90 kDa and 72 kDa, respectively, a longer running time is acceptable and may be useful if attempting to separate pro- and active forms of MMPs.
4. The pH of the collagenase buffer is critical for sensitive zymography.

5. The sensitivity of casein zymography can be increased by prolonged incubation in collagenase buffer. However, this leads to less precise bands of proteolysis due to diffusion of MMPs within the gel and if a sample has high levels of either MMP-9 or MMP-7, these may cause widespread proteolysis which may affect other bands that are less intense. This can be circumvented by excising the upper and lower thirds of the gel, leaving only the area of 50 kDa around MMP-1 remaining. If MMP-7 is being analyzed and is present at high concentrations, incubation for 16 h may be optimal to prevent excessive caseinolysis.
6. We have attempted to make casein zymograms "in house" but have never been successful in making gels with equivalent sensitivity to those commercially available from Invitrogen. However, these commercially available gels do go off with time, and their sensitivity falls as they approach their sell by date. Therefore it is advisable to try to perform zymography in batches using fresh gels.
7. Excessive electrophoresis time may lead to MMP-7 running off the end of the gel.
8. The precast gels have an opening at the front about 1 cm from the bottom of the gel, where the gel emerges. We refer to this side as the front, while the side without the opening is described as the back.
9. Experience is needed to decide when sufficient destaining has been done, but often a slightly longer destain improves sensitivity. One approach we have used for training is to remove the gel after half an hour, take a digital image, and then destain further, repeat image acquisition, and compare the results, continuing until the gel is excessively destained.
10. The two bands of MMP-1 at 50 kDa represent glycosylated and nonglycosylated forms of pro-MMP-1. The recombinant MMP-1 standard does not have a glycosylated form, but has two characteristic bands at a lower MW due to autoactivation and proteolytic cleavage of the pro-MMP-1.
11. To confirm that a band of proteolysis is caused by MMPs, divalent cations can be chelated by adding 10 mM EDTA to the collagenase buffer. Samples should be loaded in duplicate on either side of a zymography gel, and after it has been run, the gel should be divided down the middle. One half is developed normally, while the other is developed in collagenase buffer containing 10 mM EDTA. The disappearance of bands in the presence of EDTA confirms that they are caused by a metalloproteinase (**Fig. 4**).
12. MMP activity is stable through at least nine freeze–thaw cycles (unpublished data).

Acknowledgments

Some of the work described was supported by the Wellcome Trust (PE) and the MRC UK (JG)

References

1. Nagase, H., R. Visse, and G. Murphy. (2006). Structure and function of matrix metalloproteinases and TIMPs. *Cardiovasc Res.* 69: 562–573
2. Parks, W. C., C. L. Wilson, and Y. S. Lopez-Boado. (2004). Matrix metalloproteinases as modulators of inflammation and innate immunity. *Nat Rev Immunol* 4: 617–629
3. Brinckerhoff, C. E., and L. M. Matrisian. (2002). Matrix metalloproteinases: a tail of a frog that became a prince. *Nat Rev Mol Cell Biol* 3: 207–214
4. Elkington, P. T., M. O'Kane C, and J. S. Friedland. (2005).The paradox of matrix metalloproteinases in infectious disease. *Clin Exp Immunol* 142: 12–20
5. Brew, K., D. Dinakarpandian, and H. Nagase (2000). Tissue inhibitors of metalloproteinases: evolution, structure and function. *Biochim Biophys Acta* 1477: 267–283
6. Campbell, E. J., J. D. Cury, S. D. Shapiro, G. I. Goldberg, and H. G. Welgus. (1991). Neutral proteinases of human mononuclear phagocytes. Cellular differentiation markedly alters cell phenotype for serine proteinases, metalloproteinases, and tissue inhibitor of metalloproteinases. *J Immunol* 146: 1286–1293
7. Leber, T. M., and F. R. Balkwill. (1997). Zymography: a single-step staining method for quantitation of proteolytic activity on substrate gels. *Anal Biochem* 249: 24–28
8. Van Wart, H. E., and H. Birkedal-Hansen. (1990).The cysteine switch: a principle of regulation of metalloproteinase activity with potential applicability to the entire matrix metalloproteinase gene family. *Proc Natl Acad Sci U S A* 87: 5578–5582
9. Elkington, P. T., J. A. Green, and J. S. Friedland. (2006). Filter sterilization of highly infectious samples to prevent false negative analysis of matrix metalloproteinase activity. *J Immunol Methods* 309: 115–119

Chapter 17

Identification of Pathogen Receptors on Dendritic Cells to Understand Their Function and to Identify New Drug Targets

Lot de Witte*, Marein A.W.P. de Jong*, Jeroen den Dunnen, Yvette van Kooyk, and Teunis B.H. Geijtenbeek

Summary

Dendritic cells (DCs) are crucial in the defence against invading pathogens. These professional antigen-presenting cells express a diversity of pattern recognition receptors to recognize pathogens and to induce adaptive immune responses. However, pathogens have also developed several mechanisms to suppress or modulate DC function through specific receptors, thereby ensuring pathogen survival and dissemination. In this chapter, we will discuss techniques to identify and functionally characterize pathogen receptors on DCs and to determine whether DCs elicit protective immune responses or whether pathogens subvert these responses to escape immunity.

Key words: Pathogens, Dendritic cells, C-type lectins, Binding, Transmission.

1. Introduction

Defining molecular mechanisms involved in pathogen recognition is important in order to understand elicited immune responses against pathogens and to eventually develop new antimicrobial therapies. With their unique function of forming a bridge between pathogen invasion and initiation of adaptive immune responses, dendritic cells (DCs) are targets for pathogens (**Fig. 1**). Extensive research on interactions of DCs with pathogens has revealed that DCs can contribute to both immunity and disease, depending on the nature of the specific pathogen interactions *(1, 2)*.

Neil E. Reiner (ed.), *Macrophages and Dendritic Cells,* Methods in Molecular Biology, vol. 531

DOI: 10.1007/978-1-59745-396-7_17

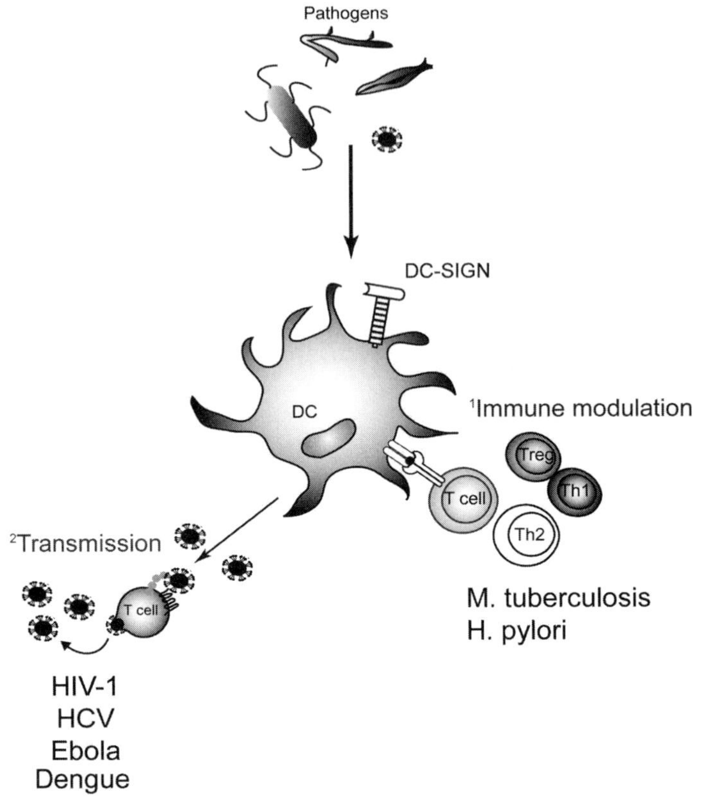

Fig. 1. Pathogens interfere with DC functions to infect the host. DCs interact with different pathogens such as viruses and bacteria. Some of these pathogens have evolved to suppress DC function to escape immune surveillance[1], or subvert DC function for infection and dissemination[2].

Here, we discuss a variety of approaches that are available in DC research to identify pathogen receptors. First, we will briefly review the current concepts in the field, and subsequently we will discuss different DC models and techniques, which can be used to identify novel pathogen receptors and to characterize DC–pathogen interactions.

1.1. Dendritic Cells Express Receptors for Antigen Uptake

Immature DCs express specialized pathogen receptors on their cell–surface that facilitate pathogen capture. Binding of a pathogen to these receptors activates processes required for antigen presentation, which include pathogen binding, internalization, degradation, and MHC class I and II antigen presentation *(3)*. Moreover, triggering of these receptors by the pathogen is necessary for DC maturation, which results in morphological changes, up-regulation of co-stimulatory molecules, migration, and production of pro- and anti-inflammatory cytokines (**Table 1**). The transformation of a resting immature DC into a mature DC is a

Table 1
A basic overview of DC activation and methods to test different parameters

DC function	Immature state	Mature state	Method to measure maturation
Antigen capture	High	Low	Down-regulation pathogen receptors Decreased pathogen binding
Antigen uptake	High	Low	Uptake ligands (e.g. Dextran-FITC)
Morphology	Small dendrites	Large dendrites, cell clustering	Light microscopy Increased side scatter in flow cytometry
Migration	Low	High	Migration assay Up-regulation chemokine receptors
Co-stimulatory molecules	Low	High	Up-regulation CD80,CD83,CD86, HLA-DR
Cytokine production	Low	High	Up-regulation cytokine protein or mRNA levels
T-cell activation	Low	High	Mixed Leucocyte reaction (MLR) Specific T-cell stimulation
T-cell differentiation	T reg	TH1/TH2/TH17	T-cell stimulation assays

complex multi-step process that must be carefully controlled to avoid auto-immunity and allergy *(4)*.

1.2. Dendritic Cells Express Pattern Recognition Receptors

DCs express different classes of pathogen receptors (**Table 2**), including the specialized pathogen recognizing receptors, which are called pattern recognition receptors (PRRs). PRRs recognize pathogen-associated molecular patterns (PAMPs) *(5)*. Main families of cell-surface PRRs are the Toll-like receptors (TLRs), the C-type lectins, and the scavenger receptors (SRs). PRRs recognize pathogenic structures that are shared between different pathogens, such as the bacterial cell wall component LPS. The best known PRRs are the TLRs that signal via conserved pathways to induce the activation of several transcription factors, of which nuclear factor-κB (NF-κB) appears pivotal to DC maturation as well as cytokine production. C-type lectins recognize carbohydrate structures on pathogens, which facilitate pathogen capture and internalization *(6)*. This receptor family is not only important in antigen presentation, but it is now becoming evident

Table 2
Different pathogen receptors expressed by DCs

Receptor	Ligands	Examples	Mediates
Toll-like receptors (TLRs)	For example, CpG, LPS, LTA	TLR1 to 11	DC activation and antigen processing
C-type lectins	Carbohydrates	DC-SIGN, Mannose receptor, Dectin	Pathogen-binding, uptake, DC activation
Scavenger receptors (SRs)	Polyanionic ligands, low-density lipoproteins	Marco, SR-A	Pathogen binding and uptake
Pathogen-specific receptors	Proteins, carbohydrates, lipids	CD4/CCR5; CD150; syndecans	Pathogen binding, entry, internalization, activation

that these receptors can induce DC activation *(7, 8)*. In addition to PRRs, other specific cell-surface molecules act as receptors for pathogens to either facilitate or mediate infection of DCs, such as HIV-1 receptor CD4, measles virus receptor CD150, and heparan sulphates that serve as attachment receptor for several viruses, such as herpes simplex virus. These receptors do not function as PRRs, but have other cellular functions and are subverted by viruses to infect the host.

1.3. Pathogens Bind Specific Receptors to Subvert Dendritic Cell Function

Within the host, there is a constant battle between the host's immune system and invading pathogens. Pathogens have developed a variety of immune evasive strategies to enable survival and replication in the host (**Fig. 1**). DCs are crucial in the initiation of adaptive immune responses, and it is becoming evident that pathogens can subvert the function of DCs. For example, the C-type lectin DC-SIGN is an important receptor on DCs that functions as an adhesion receptor mediating early DC–T cell interaction and DC migration *(9)*. Besides recognizing cellular proteins, DC-SIGN also functions as a broad-spectrum pathogen receptor. It recognizes a great variety of pathogens, including viruses, mycobacteria, bacteria, and parasites *(8)*. Strikingly, the immune responses initiated by the interaction of DC-SIGN with these various pathogens differ between pathogens. Viruses target DC-SIGN for viral transmission, whereas DC-SIGN interactions with mycobacteria and bacteria may result in either DC activation or inactivation and in the case of the latter ultimately immune suppression *(10, 11)*. Thus, various pathogens have evolved different strategies to subvert DC function, and most of the underlying mechanisms remain to be elucidated. These mechanisms can be important or even essential for pathogen dissemination and survival. Therefore, DCs are promising targets for developing preventive or curative treatments.

2. Materials

2.1. Pathogen-Binding Assay Using FITC Labelling

1. DCs: Culture monocyte-derived DCs as described by Sallusto et al. *(12)*. Use the cells between day 5 and 7 (*see* **Note 1**).
2. Phosphate-buffered saline (PBS) (10×) 1.37 M NaCl, 27 mM KCl, 100 mM Na_2HPO_4, 18 mM KH_2PO_4, pH 7.4, autoclave before storage at room temperature. Prepare a fresh 1× working solution by 1:10 dilution in MilliQ water.
3. Pathogen: Yeast or bacteria stocks in PBS (store in freezer or fridge).
4. Fresh FITC solution: Dissolve FITC (Fluorescein 5′-IsoThio-Cyanate isomer I $C_{21}H_{11}NO_5S$) in DMSO (Dimethyl sulphoxide) at a concentration of 10 mg/mL and protect the solution from light.
5. TSM buffer (10×) 200 mM Tris–HCl, 1,500 mM NaCl, 10 mM $CaCl_2$, 20 mM $MgCl_2$, pH 7.4, autoclave before storage at room temperature. Prepare a fresh 1× working solution by a 1:10 dilution in MilliQ water.
6. Bovine serum albumin (BSA).
7. TSA: Prepare a solution of 1× TSM containing 0.5% BSA, prepare fresh.
8. V-bottom 96-well plate.
9. Flow cytometer.

2.2. Bead Adhesion Assay

1. Fluorescent Beads: transfluorospheres 488/645; 1 μm; 2% solids in water containing 2 mM sodium azide, store at 4°C, protected from light.
2. MES buffer: 50 mM MES, pH 6.0, store at 4°C.
3. Streptavidin stock: Dissolve streptavidin at a concentration of 5.0 mg/mL in MES buffer, snap freeze aliquots in Eppendorf tubes, and store at –80°C.
4. EDAC solution: Dissolve EDAC (1-ethyl-3-(3-dimethylaminopropyl)-carbodiimide, store stock at –20°C) in MES buffer at a concentration of 1.33 mg/mL, do not re-use the EDAC after opening the vial.
5. Glycine buffer: 1.1 M glycine.
6. PBA: Prepare a solution of PBS, containing 0.5% BSA and 0.02% Sodium azide (use gloves, very toxic); store at 4°C.

7. Biotinylated antibody: Biotin-SP-Affinipure F(ab′)$_2$ fragment goat anti-human or -mouse IgG Fc (gamma) fragment; prepare a stock at 0.5 mg/mL; store in aliquots at –20°C.
8. V-bottom 96-well plate.
9. Streptavidin-coated beads: store at 4°C, protected from light.
10. TSA: Prepare a solution of TSM containing 0.5% BSA, prepare fresh for every experiment.
11. 0.5 M EDTA stock store at 4°C.
12. Mannan stock 50 mg/mL; store at –20°C.
13. Blocking antibodies, store as recommended.
14. Blocking reagent, working dilution: Prepare a 4× blocking solution in TSA (*see* **Note 4**).
15. Flow cytometer.

2.3. Generation of Hybridomas

1. BALB/c mice.
2. Complete and incomplete Freund's adjuvant.
3. Dulbecco's Modified Eagle's Medium (DMEM).
4. Foetal calf serum (FCS).
5. Penicillin, streptomycin, and glutamine 100× stock solution.
6. Complete DMEM: DMEM supplemented with 10% FCS heat-inactivated, 100 units/mL penicillin, and 100 mg/mL streptomycin; store at 4°C.
7. Hybridoma medium: DMEM supplemented with 15% FCS not heat-inactivated, 5% Hybridoma Cloning Factor, 1× HAT medium (hypoxanthine/aminopterin/thymidine), 100 units/mL penicillin, and 100 mg/mL streptomycin; store at 4°C.
8. SP2/0 cells cultured in complete DMEM.
9. 100-μm cell strainer and syringe plunger.
10. Polyethylene Glycol (PEG), store at 4°C.
11. 96-well flat-bottom plates.

2.4. Detection of DC Maturation and Cytokine Secretion

1. Plates: 96-well round-bottom plate (*see* **Note 15**), 96-well V-bottom plate.
2. DC culture medium: RPMI-1640 supplemented with 10% FCS heat-inactivated, 100 units/mL penicillin, 100 mg/mL streptomycin and 2 mM glutamine, 500 units/mL IL-4, and 800 units/mL GM-CSF.
3. Cytokine ELISA kits.
4. Antibodies against DC maturation markers: anti-CD83, anti-CD80, and anti-CD86; store at 4°C.
5. PBA (*see* **Subheading 2.2**).

2.5. Viral Infection of DCs and Transmission to T Cells

1. Plates: 96-well round-bottom plate, 96-well V-bottom plate (*see* **Note 15**).
2. DC culture medium (*see* **Subheading 2.4**)
3. RPMI complete: RPMI-1640 supplemented with 10% FCS heat-inactivated, 100 units/mL penicillin, 100 μg/mL streptomycin, and 2 mM glutamine.
4. Blocking antibody or blocking reagent: Prepare a fresh 10× dilution in DC medium, and if necessary sterilize the solution using a spin filter and centrifugation.
5. Virus and Mock control preparations (stocks stored at −80°C): Prepare your virus dilutions in DC culture medium on ice, just before adding it to your cells.
6. Activated CD4$^+$ T cells: Stimulate peripheral blood mononuclear cells (PBMCs) with phytohaemagglutinin (PHA) 2 μg/mL in RPMI complete for 3 days. Isolate the CD4$^+$ T cells using the CD4$^+$ T-cell isolation kit (MACS) according to the manufacturer's protocol. Culture the isolated CD4$^+$ T cells in RPMI complete, supplemented with IL-2 (100 units/mL) and use the cells after 2–5 days.
7. Antibodies against T-cell or DC marker: anti-CD3, anti-HLA-DR, respectively.

3. Methods

3.1. Pathogen Binding Assays

In order to identify a pathogen receptor, it is essential to develop and validate a pathogen-binding assay, which can be either a cellular method or a molecular method. Particular conditions will depend upon the type of pathogen and the research question. For cellular-binding methods, it is necessary to label the pathogen in order to measure binding of the pathogen by either flow cytometry or microscopy. Cellular methods have the advantage that binding is measured on a single cell basis. Moreover, using flow cytometry the binding is quickly quantified. Here we will describe two cellular methods that are suitable to demonstrate that C-type lectins such as DC-SIGN are receptors for viruses and mycobacteria.

3.1.1. FITC Labelling of Bacteria, Yeast, or Parasites

This binding method is simple and broadly applicable to characterize binding of both bacteria and yeast to cells. A drawback of this method is that the FITC-labelling method can interfere with the binding, since it might alter the structure of the bacterial surface proteins. In that case, other labelling techniques such as recombinant GFP expressing bacteria are preferable.

1. Harvest the pathogen in an Eppendorf tube, wash with PBS, and resuspend in PBS at a concentration between 1×10^8 and 1×10^{10}/mL. This depends on the size of the pathogen; larger pathogens should be at lower concentrations.
2. Prepare the FITC solution, and incubate the pathogen with 1% FITC/DMSO (final concentration: 0.1 mg/mL FITC) at room temperature for 1 h, gently shaking. Protect all FITC-labelled solutions from light.
3. To remove all free FITC, wash 3–6 times extensively with PBS using centrifugation between 2,000 and 4,000 rpm (depending on the size of the pathogen) for 5 min (*see* **Note 2**), and subsequently incubate with PBS/4%BSA to crosslink any free FITC to BSA for 15 min at room temperature.
4. Wash extensively with PBS as described in **step 3** and store up to 2 weeks at 4°C (*see* **Note 3**) or proceed with adhesion assay.
5. Add 50.000 DCs per well in a 96-well V-bottom plate. Wash DCs by centrifuging for 2 min at 450 g and discard supernatant.
6. Resuspend the cells in TSA (*see* **Note 4**).
7. Optional: add blocking reagent to block receptors at 37°C for 30 min (*see* **Note 5**).
8. Determine the concentration of the FITC-labelled pathogen, since the multiple washing steps will result in a decreased concentration.
9. Add different concentration of FITC-labelled pathogens at 37°C for 45 min in a total volume of 40 μL (*see* **Note 6**).
10. Wash cells two times by centrifuging 2 min at 450 g with 100 μL TSA. Resuspend in 100 μL TSA and measure the binding using flow cytometry. Use cells without the addition of FITC labelled pathogen as negative control.

3.1.2. Fluorescent Bead Adhesion Assay

The fluorescent bead adhesion assay is very effective to measure binding of purified glycoproteins, virus-like particles *(13)*, or proteins derived from bacteria and parasites *(8, 14)* to cells (**Fig. 2**). Fluorescent beads are coated with streptavidin and subsequently with biotin-labelled antibodies specific for the protein or carbohydrate *(15, 16)*. These antibody-coated beads are used to capture protein or glycoprotein of interest for particle coating. Moreover, it is possible to coat beads with proteins present in a crude lysate by incubating the lysate with antibody-coated beads. The assay has the advantage that the size of the beads prevents internalization, and therefore the interaction of beads with cells is a direct reflection of ligand binding to the DC surface (**Fig. 2**).

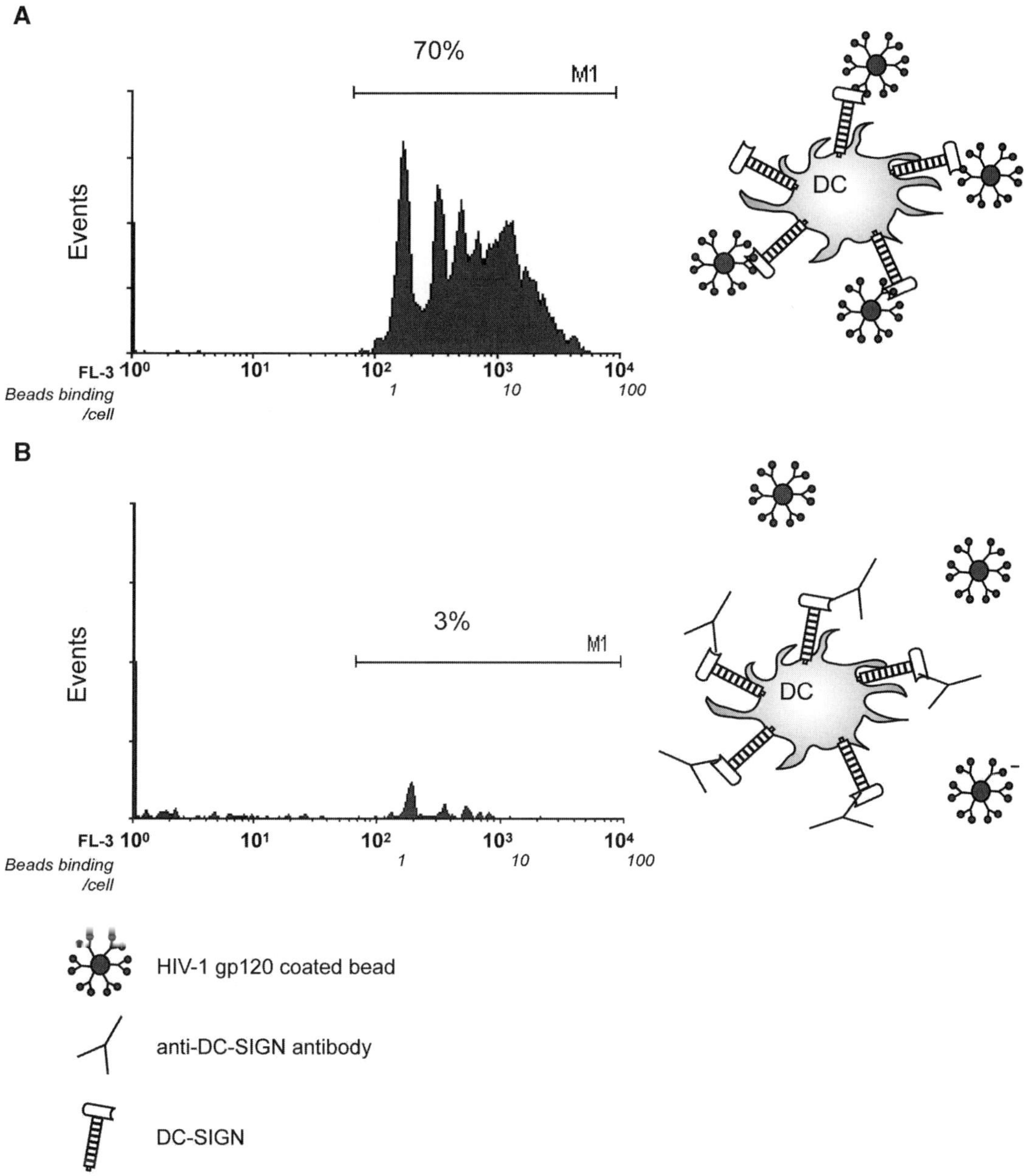

Fig. 2. The fluorescent bead adhesion assay is useful to determine pathogen binding to host cells. (**A**) DCs interact with HIV-1 gp120-coated fluorescent beads. DCs are incubated with gp120-coated fluorescent beads for 30 min at 37°C, washed and the binding is determined by flow cytometry. (**B**) Pre-incubation of the DCs with blocking antibodies against DC-SIGN abrogate the bead binding.

1. Covalent coupling of streptavidin: Incubate 50 μL beads with 20 μL streptavidin (5.0 mg/mL in MES buffer) in an Eppendorf tube at room temperature for 15 min.

2. Dissolve EDAC in MES Buffer (1.33 mg/mL), and incubate beads with 30 μL fresh EDAC solution, adjust pH to 6.5, and incubate for 2 h at room temperature while shaking.
3. Stop reaction using 10 μL 1.1 M glycine and incubate for 30 min at room temperature.
4. Wash beads extensively with PBS by centrifuging in an Eppendorf centrifuge for 2 min at 12,000 g. Remove the supernatant using a 1-mL pipette, resuspend the pellet in 100 μL of PBS by pipetting up and down, and add 900 μL PBS. Repeat the washing steps two times using PBS and one time using PBA.
5. Resuspend beads in 150 μL PBA (*see* **Note 7**). Store the beads at 4°C or proceed with the coupling of monoclonal antibodies.
6. Incubate 15 μL streptavidin-coated beads with 20 μL biotinylated antibody (0.5 mg/mL) at 37°C for 3 h in a shaker at 450 g.
7. Wash extensively using PBA by centrifuging at 12,000 g for 2 min, and incubate with the specific antibody (5 μg in 300 μL PBA) for 48 h at 4°C while shaking.
8. Wash extensively as described in **step 7**; resuspend beads in 100 μL PBA and store at 4°C (*see* **Note 8**) or proceed with the adhesion assay.
9. Wash 50.000 DCs per well in TSA by centrifuging 2 min at 450 g in a V-bottom 96-well plate. Resuspend the cells in 20 μL TSA (*see* **Note 4**).
10. Optional: Add blocking antibody or blocking reagents for 30 min at 37°C (*see* **Note 5**).
11. Add 2 μL beads per well in a total volume of 40 μL TSA and incubate 45 min at 37°C. Different concentrations beads can be used to optimize the assay dependent on ligand–receptor interaction.
12. Wash cells with 100 μL TSA and measure fluorescence at 645 nm by flow cytometry. Beads without cells should be used to determine the optimal settings for the fluorescent beads. The setting we use most is when one bead has a mean fluorescence of 100 in a 10^0–10^4 range.

3.2. Receptor Identification Using Hybridoma Screening

After the development of a binding assay, specific approaches can be used to identify the DC receptor(s) responsible for binding to either the pathogen or the pathogen ligand. The first and easiest approach to identify the receptor is to use specific inhibitors to known receptors on DCs and to measure the ability of these inhibitors to reduce the signal in the binding assays.

Different inhibitors can be used, either blocking antibodies against specific receptors or high concentrations of a competitive ligand (*see* **Note 5**).

A potential problem with receptor-specific antibodies is that not all of these will function as blocking antibodies and thus do not interfere with ligand binding. Moreover, it is possible that a receptor that interacts with a pathogen is unknown. The hybridoma antibody screening method can be used to generate antibodies that inhibit pathogen–cell interaction and are directed against receptors involved *(10)*. Although this method is time consuming, it has the great advantage of directly isolating a receptor-specific antibody that blocks the interaction. These antibodies are extremely useful in identifying unknown receptors through immune precipitation, but they are also indispensable in functional assays.

3.2.1. Immunization

1. Day 1: Immunization of BALB/c mice with DC lysate (5×10^6 cells) in complete Freund's adjuvant (CFA) intraperitoneally (*see* **Note 9**, **10**).
2. Day 21/35/49 booster: (5×10^6 DCs) in incomplete Freund's adjuvant (IFA) (0.1 mL) subcutaneously.
3. Day 52: Test serum for the presence of antibodies against DCs by flow cytometry. If yes, continue with fusion.

3.2.2. Fusion and Screening

4. Day –2: Split SP2/0 cells 1:4, make >10 T-175 flasks (*see* **Note 11**).
5. Day 0: sacrify mouse, isolate spleen. Generate a single cell suspension of the spleen using a 100-µm cell strainer and a syringe plunger.Wash the SP2/0 and spleen cells three times with plain DMEM (*see* **Note 12**).
6. Count the spleen cells and mix them 1:1 with SP2/0 cells.
7. Wash once in plain DMEM (10 min at 130 g).
8. Dispose the supernatant using a pipette and loosen the palette gently.
9. Add 1.5 mL Polyethylene Glycol (PEG) during 1 min (one drop at the time).
10. Shake the tube gently in the 37°C water bath for 1.5 min.
11. Add plain DMEM with the following interval, 1 mL in 30 s, 4 mL in 1 min, 15 mL in 1 min.
12. Incubate mixture for 1 h in 37°C water bath, shake gently every 15 min.
13. Centrifuge cells for 10 min at 130 g.
14. Dispose the supernatant using a pipette and loosen the palette gently.

15. Resuspend the cells in Hybridoma medium.
16. Plate: 5 × 10^6 spleen cells per 96-well plate; 200 μL per well in a 96-well flat-bottom plate (*see* **Note 13**).
17. When medium turns yellow harvest supernatants (usually after 10–15 days).
18. Pre-incubate the DCs with 50 μL supernatant for 30 min.
19. Measure the binding using your specific pathogen-binding assay as described in the previous section.

3.3. DC Activation by Pathogens

The effect of a pathogen on DC maturation can be determined by measuring the cell-surface expression of co-stimulatory molecules and MHC Class I and II by flow cytometry. Most notable maturation markers are CD83 and the co-stimulatory molecules CD80 and CD86, which are expressed at low levels on immature and high levels on mature DCs. In addition, MHC class I and II expressions are also upregulated on mature DCs (**Table1**). Pathogen receptors such as C-type lectins and scavenger receptors are usually down-regulated upon maturation *(15, 17)*.

In addition to analysis of maturation markers, which only determines immune activation of DCs, analysis of cytokine production also gives insight into the type of immune response that occurs, such as pro- or anti-inflammatory immune responses. Moreover, the DC cytokine profile is indicative of what can be expected in terms of driving T-cell differentiation. For example, IL-12 and IL-23 are inducers of a T-helper 1 response, whereas IL-4 drives the T-cell response towards T-helper 2 *(18)*. In addition, the anti-inflammatory cytokine IL-10 can be involved in suppression of the immune response. However, DC cytokine response profiles are only a guide, and it is essential to investigate directly the type of T-cell response that ensues. Cytokine production can be determined by using the supernatant of the stimulated DCs in an ELISA.

1. Plate 100.000 DCs in a round-bottom 96-well plate in 100 μL DC medium.
2. Add pathogen to DCs in a total volume of 200 μL of DC medium (*see* **Note 14**, **15**).
3. After 24 h, transfer to a V-bottom 96-well plate and centrifuge for 2 min at 450 g. Collect supernatant for cytokine ELISA and analyse cells for expression of maturation markers by flow cytometry. Store supernatant at –20°C until analysis.
4. For the analysis of maturation markers, pipette 50.000 DCs in a V-bottom 96-well plate.
5. Wash DCs in PBA by centrifuging 2 min at 450 g. Vortex briefly afterwards.
6. Add 10 μg/mL primary antibody at 4°C for 30 min in a total volume of 25 μL.

7. Wash cells once with 100 μL PBA.
8. Incubate with secondary antibody at 4°C for 30 min in a total volume of 25 μL.
9. Wash cells once with 100 μL PBA.
10. Determine expression of maturation markers by flow cytometry (*see* **Note 16**).

3.4. Identification of an Entry Receptor

Pathogens can also use immune cells for replication to produce progeny or as a vehicle to reach their target cell (**Fig. 3**). To investigate whether a receptor is involved in infection of DCs, blocking antibodies can be used. When the receptor is involved in infection, these blocking antibodies prevent or decrease infection. Read-out of infection is dependent on the pathogen being studied, but may include measuring pathogen proteins by flow cytometry or specific CFU assays. This method is especially suitable for viruses, since they can replicate intracellular, and host cells will display viral glycoproteins on their surface that can be detected by flow cytometry. This method can also be used for intracellular bacteria, such as *Mycobacteria tuberculosis.* However, since extracellular pathogens do not infect DCs, they will primarily affect DCs on the level of immune modulation as described in the previous section. Therefore, for these extracellular pathogens, identification of binding receptors and immune modulation are of greater importance.

It is important to keep in mind that although a pathogen may bind to a specific receptor, this may not be essential for infection of DCs. Strikingly, some receptors do not function as entry receptors but are able to facilitate attachment of pathogen to the target cell. These receptors facilitate infection in cis *(19)* (**Fig. 3**). This process is dependent on the first interaction of pathogen with the attachment receptors, and the second step involves interaction of

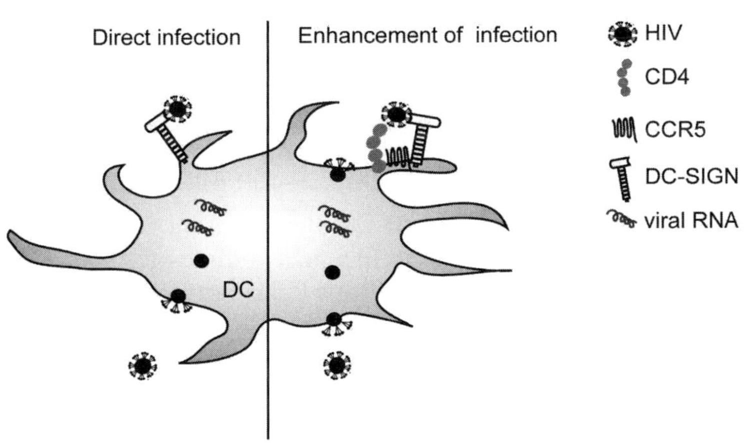

Fig. 3. Viruses interact with receptors to infect DCs. DCs express receptors that are involved in viral infection or enhance infection in cis.

the pathogen with the actual entry receptors. For example, receptor A may capture a pathogen. This will not lead to infection of the DCs, but instead it facilitates the interaction of a pathogen with receptor B. Receptor B, in turn, is an entry receptor and binding of the pathogen to receptor B will lead to infection of the DCs. This is an example in which receptor A facilitates infection in cis, while receptor B acts as an entry receptor.

When binding to either receptor A or receptor B is inhibited by using blocking antibodies, a decrease in infection will be observed. Thus care must be taken to not conclude from inhibition experiments that a receptor is an actual entry receptor.

1. Add 100.000 DCs per well in 100 μL 96-well round-bottom plate in DC medium.
2. Optional: Pre-incubate DCs with a blocking antibody (20 μg/mL) or blocking reagent for 1 h at 37°C.
3. Add virus and mock in different concentrations (*see* **Note 17, 18**).
4. After different time point, harvest cells or supernatant and read out virus infection by flow cytometry or ELISA (*see* **Note 19**).

3.5. Identification of Receptors Involved in Viral Transmission

In case of viral transmission, pathogens use immune cells as a vehicle to increase viral dissemination. Several studies have demonstrated that DCs capture virus, but that the virus is protected and efficiently transmitted to other target cells *(10, 20, 21)*. Viral transmission can be independent of viral infection of DCs, although it is possible that viral infection also facilitates transmission *(21)*. Here we describe HIV-1 transmission to $CD4^+$ T cells.

1. Seed 50.000 DCs in a 96-well V-bottom plate in 50 μL DC medium.
2. Optional: pre-incubate DCs with blocking antibody (20 μg/mL) for 1 h at 37°C to determine receptor involvement.
3. Add different concentrations of HIV-1 (e.g. Tissue Culture Inflammatory Dose 50 ($TCID_{50}$) 10 and 100) in 50 μL of DC medium.
4. Incubate for 2 h at 37°C.
5. Wash three times with 200 μL warm DC medium, centrifuge for 2 min at 450 g.
6. Add DCs in different ratios to PHA/IL2-activated CD4 T cells in a final volume of 200 μL (e.g. 1:10–1:200 DC-T cells) in a 96-well flat-bottom plate (*see* **Note 20**).

3.5.1. Detection of Infection by ELISA

7. Harvest 100 μL supernatant and refresh with 120 μL DC medium (to compensate for evaporation) every 2 or 3 days, store supernatant for HIV-1 p24 capsid ELISA at –20°C. Follow infection for 14 days.
8. Test supernatant for HIV-1 p24 content by ELISA.

3.5.2. Detection of Infection by Flow Cytometry

9. Harvest cell samples every 2 or 3 days.
10. Fix and permeabilize cells. Stain for intracellular HIV-1 p24.
11. Double stain using a T-cell and DC marker (e.g. CD3 or HLA-DR, respectively).
12. Follow infection for 14 days.

3.6. Identification of Receptors Involved in Enhancement of Viral Infection

The formation of the infectious synapse between DCs and T cells provides a scaffold that enhances interaction of virus with T-cell surface and presumably the receptors involved in infection. This process facilitates entry of virus in the target cell and thus DCs enhance infection. Using a similar assay as the transmission assay, it is possible to determine whether DCs are able to enhance infection of target cells. In this assay, HIV-1 infection of T cells is examined in the presence and absence of DCs. This assay is subtly different from the transmission assay since sub-optimal virus concentrations are used as well as the absence of a washing step to remove virus. In every condition, the amount of virus is the same and independent of the amount captured by DCs. Thus, the ability of DCs to enhance infection is determined, and the involvement of a specific receptor on DCs can be investigated using blocking antibodies.

3.6.1. HIV-1 Enhancement Assay

1. Seed 50.000 DCs in a 96-well flat-bottom plate.
2. Optional: pre-incubate DCs with blocking antibody (20 μg/mL) for 1 h at 37°C to determine receptor involvement.
3. Add different concentrations of virus (HIV-1 TCID 0.5, 1, 10, and 100).
4. Incubate for 2 h at 37°C.
5. Importantly, do not wash! Add 100,000 PHA/IL-2-activated $CD4^+$ T cells to DCs in a final volume of 200 μL.
6. Follow infection for 14 days as described for the HIV-1 transmission assay, by either flow cytometry or ELISA on different days (*see* **Note 21**).

3.7. Concluding Remarks

Protection against pathogens is a major challenge for the immune system and DCs are a vital component of this ingenious system. DCs operate at the interface of innate and acquired immunity by detecting pathogens, which are internalized, processed, and presented on MHC class I and II molecules to T cells to initiate pathogen-specific immune responses. The efficacy of DCs in activating and directing immune responses is attributed to their particular array of receptors that mediate pathogen recognition and induce appropriate immune responses. However, many pathogens target the same receptors to escape immune surveillance and to persist within the host. Identification and functional characterization of these pathogen receptors is therefore of vital importance in understanding the role of DCs in these infections.

In this chapter, we have described a number of strategies that can be used to characterize pathogen receptors on DCs. These included a novel approach to functionally identify receptors involved in pathogen recognition, using an unbiased, rapid, and high-throughput screen of antibody libraries to isolate antibodies that inhibit defined DC-pathogen interactions. These inhibitory antibodies are pivotal not only in the identification of receptors, but also in the characterization of receptor function. Together with soluble inhibitors, these antibodies enable to examine the role of DC receptors in the generation of immune responses to pathogens. Importantly, they are useful tools to determine whether DCs elicit protective immune responses or whether their functions are subverted by the pathogen to escape immunity.

Besides studying DCs cultured in vitro, it is essential to investigate pathogen interactions with DC subsets isolated directly ex vivo, which will provide insight into the complex functions of DC subsets in pathogen recognition in vivo. The in vivo role of DC subsets and pathogen receptors can be further determined by investigating the localization, receptor-expression, and infection of DC subsets in infected human tissues.

4. Notes

1. Always analyse the phenotype of the immature monocyte-derived DCs. Microscopically one can observe that the DCs are in suspension and have an irregular cell-membrane-containing dendrites. Moreover, the immature DCs should express CD80, CD86, HLA-DR, and DC-SIGN, and low levels of CD83, which can be analysed by flow cytometry.
2. All free FITC should be carefully washed away; check the supernatant of your last washing for free FITC by incubating the same volume of supernatant as pathogens with the cells.
3. Check your labelling efficiency using fluorescence microscopy or flow cytometry. Optimize your labelling efficiency by varying pathogen concentration, FITC concentration, and labelling time. Labelled pathogens should be kept away from light since this will strongly diminish the fluorescence.
4. Always use a buffer or medium that contains calcium, since C-type lectins require calcium for their function.
5. For competitive blocking, DCs should be pre-incubated with inhibitors before the addition of the ligand (without washing). C-type lectins interact with pathogens through recognition of carbohydrate structures *(17)*. Therefore, carbohydrates are often used at high concentrations as

competitive inhibitors of C-type lectins *(22)*. For blocking antibodies use a final concentration between 10 and 50 μg/mL, and for competitive ligands, such as the carbohydrate mannan concentrations between 50 μg/mL and 1 mg/mL. EDTA is a calcium and magnesium chelator and can be used as a blocking reagent for receptors that are calcium and magnesium dependent (for example C-type lectins). Standard concentration for blocking is 10 mM.

6. A typical range of the amount of pathogens per well to start the first experiment is: 5×10^4 (MOI 1), 1.5×10^5 (MOI3), 5×10^5 (MOI 10), 1.5×10^6 (MOI 30), 5×10^6 (MOI 100).
7. The fluorescent beads should be kept away from light at all times; beads should be stored at 4°C and not be frozen.
8. Here a streptavidin–biotin step is included; however, the ligand can also be coated onto the beads directly.
9. The best results are obtained using primary cells.
10. If possible, immunize two mice and choose the best responder at day 52.
11. Cells must be in log phase of growth.
12. After the generation of a single cell suspension spleen cells are very vulnerable, discard the supernatant carefully. Centrifuge at low speed (200 g, 15 min). Resuspend the cells gently by using a pipette.
13. Many cells (non-fused cells) should die during the first night.
14. Make sure lab safety levels are taken into consideration when live pathogens are used. To avoid this, heat killed or otherwise inactivated pathogens can be used.
15. DCs are in optimal conditions when they have contact with each other, and therefore functional DC experiments are carried out in 96-well round-bottom plates. However, for washing 96-well V-bottom plates are recommended to minimize loss of cells during multiple washing steps.
16. Cytokine secretion can be measured using cytokine specific kits according to the manufacturer's instructions.
17. An optimal concentration needs to be determined for each virus.
18. After 2 h of incubation virus can also be washed away by using three centrifugation steps (2 min 450 g in a 96-well V-bottom plate) in warm medium to remove dead and unbound virus.
19. An optimal time to read out infection needs to be determined for each virus.

20. To infect T cells efficiently, the cells should be in log phase. Ideally, the cells should be cultured at a concentration between 1 and 2 million cells/mL.
21. Enhancement of infection will have occurred when the T cells in the DC/T cell co-culture are efficiently infected at the sub-optimal virus concentration that is not enough to cause infection of T cells alone.

Acknowledgements

This work was supported by the Dutch Scientific Organization (NWO), grants 91746367 (LdW/MdJ) and 91204025 (JdD/MdJ).

References

1. van Kooyk Y, Appelmelk B, Geijtenbeek TB. (2003) A fatal attraction: Mycobacterium tuberculosis and HIV-1 target DC-SIGN to escape immune surveillance. *Trends Mol Med*; 9(4):153–159
2. Palucka K, Banchereau J. (2002). How dendritic cells and microbes interact to elicit or subvert protective immune responses. *Curr Opin Immunol*; 14(4):420–431
3. Banchereau J, Steinman RM. (1988). Dendritic cells and the control of immunity. *Nature*; 392(6673):245–252
4. Bonifaz L, Bonnyay D, Mahnke K, Rivera M, Nussenzweig MC, Steinman RM. (2002). Efficient targeting of protein antigen to the dendritic cell receptor DEC-205 in the steady state leads to antigen presentation on major histocompatibility complex class I products and peripheral CD8+ T cell tolerance. *J Exp Med*; 196(12):1627–1638
5. Janeway CA, Medzhitov R. (2002). Innate immune recognition. *Annu Rev Immunol*; 20:197–216
6. Geijtenbeek TB, van Vliet SJ, Engering A, 't hart BA, van Kooyk Y. (2004). Self- and nonself-recognition by C-type lectins on dendritic cells. *Annu Rev Immunol*; 22:33–54
7. Rogers NC, Slack EC, Edwards AD et al. (2005). Syk-dependent cytokine induction by Dectin-1 reveals a novel pattern recognition pathway for C type lectins. *Immunity*; 22(4):507–517
8. Geijtenbeek TB, van Vliet SJ, Koppel EA et al. (2003). Mycobacteria target DC-SIGN to suppress dendritic cell function. *J Exp Med*; 197(1):7–17
9. Geijtenbeek TB, Engering A, van Kooyk Y. (2002). DC-SIGN, a C-type lectin on dendritic cells that unveils many aspects of dendritic cell biology. *J Leukoc Biol*; 71(6):921–931
10. Geijtenbeek TBH, Kwon DS, Torensma R et al. (2000). DC-SIGN, a dendritic cell-specific HIV-1-binding protein that enhances trans-infection of T cells. *Cell*; 100(5):587–597
11. de Witte L., Abt M, Schneider-Schaulies S, van Kooyk, Y., Geijtenbeek TB. (2006). Measles virus targets DC-SIGN to enhance dendritic cell infection. *J Virol*; 80(7):3477–3486
12. Sallusto F, Lanzavecchia A. (1994). Efficient presentation of soluble antigen by cultured human dendritic cells is maintained by granulocyte/macrophage colony-stimulating factor plus interleukin 4 and downregulated by tumor necrosis factor alpha. *J Exp Med*; 179(4):1109–1118
13. Ludwig IS, Lekkerkerker AN, Depla E et al. (2004). Hepatitis C virus targets DC-SIGN and L-SIGN to escape lysosomal degradation. *J Virol*; 78(15):8322–8332
14. Bergman MP, Engering A, Smits HH et al. (2004). *Helicobacter pylori* modulates the T helper cell 1/T helper cell 2 balance through phase-variable interaction between lipopolysaccharide and DC-SIGN. *J Exp Med*; 200(8):979–990
15. Geijtenbeek TBH, Torensma R, van Vliet SJ et al. (2000). Identification of DC-SIGN, a novel dendritic cell-specific ICAM-3 receptor

that supports primary immune responses. *Cell*; 100(5):575–585

16. Geijtenbeek TBH, van Kooyk Y, van Vliet SJ, Renes MH, Raymakers RA, Figdor CG. (1999). High frequency of adhesion defects in B-lineage acute lymphoblastic leukemia. *Blood*; 94(2):754–764
17. Drickamer K. (1999). C-type lectin-like domains. *Curr Opin Struct Biol*; 9(5):585–90
18. Sallusto F, Lanzavecchia A. (1999). Mobilizing dendritic cells for tolerance, priming, and chronic inflammation. *J Exp Med*; 189(4):611–614
19. Lee B, Leslie G, Soilleux E et al. (2001). cis Expression of DC-SIGN allows for more efficient entry of human and simian immunodeficiency viruses via CD4 and a coreceptor. *J Virol*; 75(24):12028–12038
20. Pope M, Betjes MG, Romani N et al. (1994). Conjugates of dendritic cells and memory T lymphocytes from skin facilitate productive infection with HIV-1. *Cell*; 78(3):389–398
21. Turville SG, Santos JJ, Frank I et al. (2004). Immunodeficiency virus uptake, turnover, and 2-phase transfer in human dendritic cells. *Blood*; 103(6):2170–2179
22. Curtis BM, Scharnowske S, Watson AJ. (1992). Sequence and expression of a membrane-associated C-type lectin that exhibits CD4-independent binding of human immunodeficiency virus envelope glycoprotein gp120. *Proc Natl Acad Sci U S A*; 89(17):8356–8360

Chapter 18

Stable Lentiviral Vector-Mediated Gene Silencing in Human Monocytic Cell Lines

Jimmy S. Lee and Neil E. Reiner

Summary

A major obstacle in studying monocyte cell biology has been the resistance of these cells to genetic manipulation, particularly when using nonviral methods. In the approach outlined in this chapter, we describe a strategy for stable gene silencing of monocytic cells. Using a vesicular stomatitis virus (VSV)-pseudotyped lentiviral vector expressing short hairpin RNA (shRNA), stable silencing of the p110α isoform of PI3-kinase in the human monocytic cell lines THP-1 and U-937 was achieved.

Key words: Monocyte, PI3-kinase, Lentiviral vector, Transduction, siRNA, shRNA, RNAi.

1. Introduction

Studying mononuclear phagocyte cell biology through genetic manipulation by nonviral transfection methods has been challenging due to the dual problems of low transfection efficiency and the difficulty in obtaining stable transfection. To overcome this problem, we developed a system for mediating RNA interference (RNAi) in monocytic cells. The p110α isoform of phosphoinositide 3-kinases (PI3K) was silenced using a lentiviral vector expressing short hairpin RNA (shRNA). This resulted in the generation of stable THP-1 and U-937 monocytic cell lines deficient in p110α.

RNA interference is a sequence-specific, post-transcriptional gene silencing mechanism initiated by the introduction of double-stranded RNA (dsRNA) into target cells through either viral infection or experimental manipulation *(1)*. The RNAi pathway begins by processing dsRNA into short (<30 bp) dsRNA

Neil E. Reiner (ed.), *Macrophages and Dendritic Cells,* Methods in Molecular Biology, vol. 531

DOI: 10.1007/978-1-59745-396-7_18

duplexes, termed small-interfering RNA (siRNA), by a host RNAse Dicer. The siRNA then becomes incorporated into a multicomponent nuclease complex called the RNA-induced silencing complex (RISC). RISC then uses the siRNA sequence as a guide to recognize cognate mRNAs for degradation.

Delivery of siRNAs into mammalian cells by transfection of siRNA or DNA vectors expressing shRNA has been shown to mediate RNAi successfully *(2–5)*. Transfection of siRNA is transient, lasting only for a week or so *(6)*, although DNA-based vectors may last longer with drug selection *(4)*. In contrast, viral vectors have also been used to deliver siRNA successfully, and these methods tend to provide more stable gene silencing *(7–10)*.

This chapter describes how human monocytic cell lines can be effectively transduced using a lentiviral vector to stably silence an endogenous lipid kinase, PI3K. This involves three major steps: construction of shRNA sequences targeting the gene of interest, production of viral vectors using packaging cells, and transduction of monocytic cells.

2. Materials

2.1. Reagents and Antibodies

RPMI 1640, Dulbecco's Modified Eagle Medium (DMEM), Hanks' balanced salt solution (HBSS), penicillin/streptomycin and 1 M HEPES solution, fetal bovine serum (FBS).

1. Polybrene, cell dissociation solution, and poly-L-lysine (Sigma-Aldrich, Oakville, ON).
2. Antibodies to human p110δ (Calbiochem, San Diego, CA). Antibody to human p110α (clone 19) (BD Biosciences, Mississauga, ON). Antibodies to human p110β and actin (Santa Cruz Biotechnology, Santa Cruz, CA). Anti-p85-N-SH3 antibody (Upstate Biotechnology, Lake Placid, NY).

2.2. Cell Culture

The promonocytic cell lines THP-1 and U-937 were cultured in RPMI 1640 supplemented with 10% FBS, 2 mM L-glutamine, penicillin (100 U/mL), and streptomycin (100 μg/mL). Cultures were maintained without exceeding 0.5×10^6 cells/mL. 293T human embryonic kidney (HEK) cells were also from ATCC and were cultured in DMEM, supplemented with 10% FBS, 2 mM L-glutamine, penicillin (100 U/mL), and streptomycin (100 μg/mL), and 20 mM HEPES.

2.3. Lentiviral Vector Construction and Transduction of Monocytic Cells

1. *Constructs* – The U6 promoter vector pSHAG-1 (**Fig. 1A**) was a gift from Dr. G.J. Hannon (Cold Spring Harbor Laboratory, Cold Spring Harbor, NY) *(3)*. pSHAG-1 contains the *att*L1/L2 transposition elements that are compatible with Gateway Cloning Technology (Invitrogen Canada Inc., Burlington, ON).

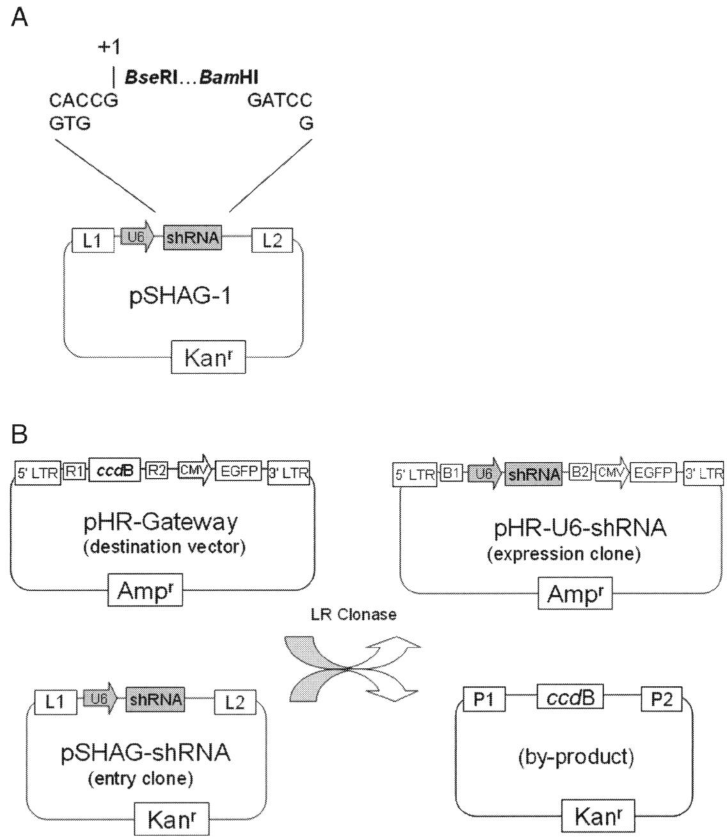

Fig. 1. pSHAG-1 plasmid and LR Clonase-mediated transposition. (**A**) pSHAG-1 vector. Schematic diagram of pSHAG-1 showing U6 promoter, the *att*L1/L2 transposition elements that are compatible with Gateway Cloning Technology, and directional insertion sites for shRNA encoding fragment, generated by double digestion with *Bse*RI and *Bam*HI. (**B**) Generation of pHR-U6-shRNA vector. The Gateway LR Clonase enzyme mix (Invitrogen) catalyzes the *in vitro* recombination between an entry clone (containing a gene of interest flanked by *att*L sites) and a destination vector (containing *att*R sites) to generate an expression clone. The resulting transposition elements are labeled *att*P1/P2, and *att*B1/B2. The pSHAG vector containing the shRNA sequence serves as the entry clone, while the pHR-Gateway is the destination vector. The expression clone is selected on LB plates containing ampicillin.

2. Antisense to p110α mRNA was targeted to two nucleotide segments: 5′-ATATACATTCCTGATCTTCCTCGTGCTG-3′ (nucleotide positions 1171–1198, referred to as α3) and 5′-CAAGACCATCATCAGGTGAACTGTGGG-3′ (nucleotide positions 8–35, referred to as α1). The hairpin-containing sequence was created as described *(8)*, using a protocol available at http://katahdin.cshl.org:9331/homepage/portal/scripts/main2.pl (*see* **Note 1**).
3. Oligonucleotides p110α1 and p110α3 listed in **Table 1** were synthesized by Qiagen Inc. (Valencia, CA). All the sequences contained a *Hind* III site in the hairpin region, a site that is not

Table 1
Short hairpin RNA encoding sequences targeting human p110α mRNA

Construct	5′-Antisense sequence (28 nt) haripin loop (8 nt) Sense sequence (28 nt) Termination (6 T's)-3′
p110α1	CCCCACAGTTCACCTGATGATGGTCTTG-*GAAGCTTG*CGAGACCGTCATCGGGTGAGCT-GTGGGGCATTTTTT GATC AAAAAAATGCCCCACAGCTCACCCGAT-GACGGTCTCG *CAAGCTTC* CAAGACCATCAT-CAGGTGAACTGTGGGG CG
p110α3	CAGCACGAGGAAGATCAGGAATGTATAT-*GAAGCTTG* ATATGCATTCCTGGTCTTCTTCGT-GTTGCTCTTTTTT *GATC* AAAAAAGAGCAACACGAAGAAGACCAG-GAATGCATAT *CAAGCTTC* ATATACATTCCT-GATCTTCCTCGTGCTG CG

nt nucleotide(s)
Hairpin sequences are shown with the *Hind*III site underlined and italicized. For each construct, the two strands of DNA were annealed and ligated into the pSHAG-1 vector. The first strand is an example of "oligo A," while the second strand is "oligo B" (*see* **Note 1**). The underlined sequences at the 5′ and 3′ ends are for directional cloning into pSHAG-1, which was cut with *Bse*RI and *Bam*H1 (reproduced from **ref.** *10* with permissions from American Society for Biochemistry and Molecular Biology)

present in the native pSHAG-1 vector, and *Bam*HI and *Bse*RI ends to enable directional cloning. Competent DH5α *E. coli* (Invitrogen) were transformed with pSHAG-1 containing the sequences of interest and clones were screened by *Hind*III digestion.

4. Construction of the lentiviral transducing plasmid, pHR-CMV-EGFP (9401 bp), the packaging vector pCMV R8.2 (13.4 kb), and the VSV envelope vector pMD.G (6.01 kb) (*see* **Note 2**) has been described elsewhere *(11, 12)*, and the vectors were obtained from Dr. Alice Mui (Department of Surgery, Faculty of Medicine, University of British Columbia). All three vectors contain an ampicillin resistance gene. Purified pSHAG-1, pSHAG-p110α1, and pSHAG-p110α3 served as entry clones. The lentiviral transducing vector pHR-CMV-EGFP was modified by inserting the Gateway vector conversion cassette (Invitrogen) into the *Cla*I site, that is located downstream of the 5′LTR, but upstream of the CMV promoter (**Fig. 1b**). The resulting pHR-Gateway served as a destination vector since it contained *att*R1/2 sites (*see* **Note 3**). pHR-Gateway was also obtained from Dr. Alice Mui

(Department of Surgery, University of British Columbia). The various entry clones were transposed to the pHR-Gateway by Gateway LR Clonase Enzyme Mix (Invitrogen). Positive clones were then isolated and the plasmids (pHR-U6, pHR-p110α1, pHR-p110α3) purified. All plasmid purifications were carried out using Qiagen Endofree Plasmid kits.

2.4. Flow Cytometry Analysis

1. Binding buffer: HBSS, 1% FCS, and 0.1% NaN_3. Also prepare another binding buffer stock with 1.85% paraformaldehyde prior to use.
2. HRPO conjugated antirabbit, antimouse, and antigoat secondary antibodies.

3. Methods

3.1. Construction of VSV-Pseudotyped Lentiviral Vector Expressing shRNA (see Note 1*)*

1. Reconstitute the synthesized sense and antisense oligonucleotides encoding the shRNA (**Table 1**) in TE buffer at 100 μM.
2. Anneal the oligonucleotide pairs at 1:1 by heating the mixture in a heating block at 94°C for 15 min, followed by cooling at room temperature for 40 min. Use 5 μL of each oligonucleotide, plus 90 μL nuclease-free water. The mixture will give 5 μM of duplex DNA in 100 μL total volume.
3. Ligate the duplex into pSHAG-1 via the *Bam*HI/*Bse*RI site using ligase at 16°C overnight. Use a 3:1 insert to vector ratio, 1 μL ligase, and add appropriate volumes of 5× buffer and water to make up a total reaction volume of 10 μL.
4. Transform competent *E. coli* and plate overnight without selection.
5. Select several colonies from each plate, and add each to a 4-mL LB broth plus kanamycin (50 μg/mL). Incubate overnight on a shaker at 37°C.
6. Purify plasmids using a Miniprep kit (Qiagen) (*see* **Note 4**). Plasmids containing an insert will be cleaved by *Hind*III digestion and will migrate slower (~2,500–3,000 bp band) on 1% agarose in TAE when compared to pSHAG-1 without insert which will not be digested.
7. Purify the positive clones and transpose the U6-shRNA element into the viral vector pHR-Gateway (**Fig. 1B**) using Invitrogen LR Clonase kit (a mix of lambda recombination proteins that mediate the *att*L × *att*R recombination reaction); carefully following instructions provided with the kit. The resulting plasmid – pHR-U6-shRNA – is then ready for

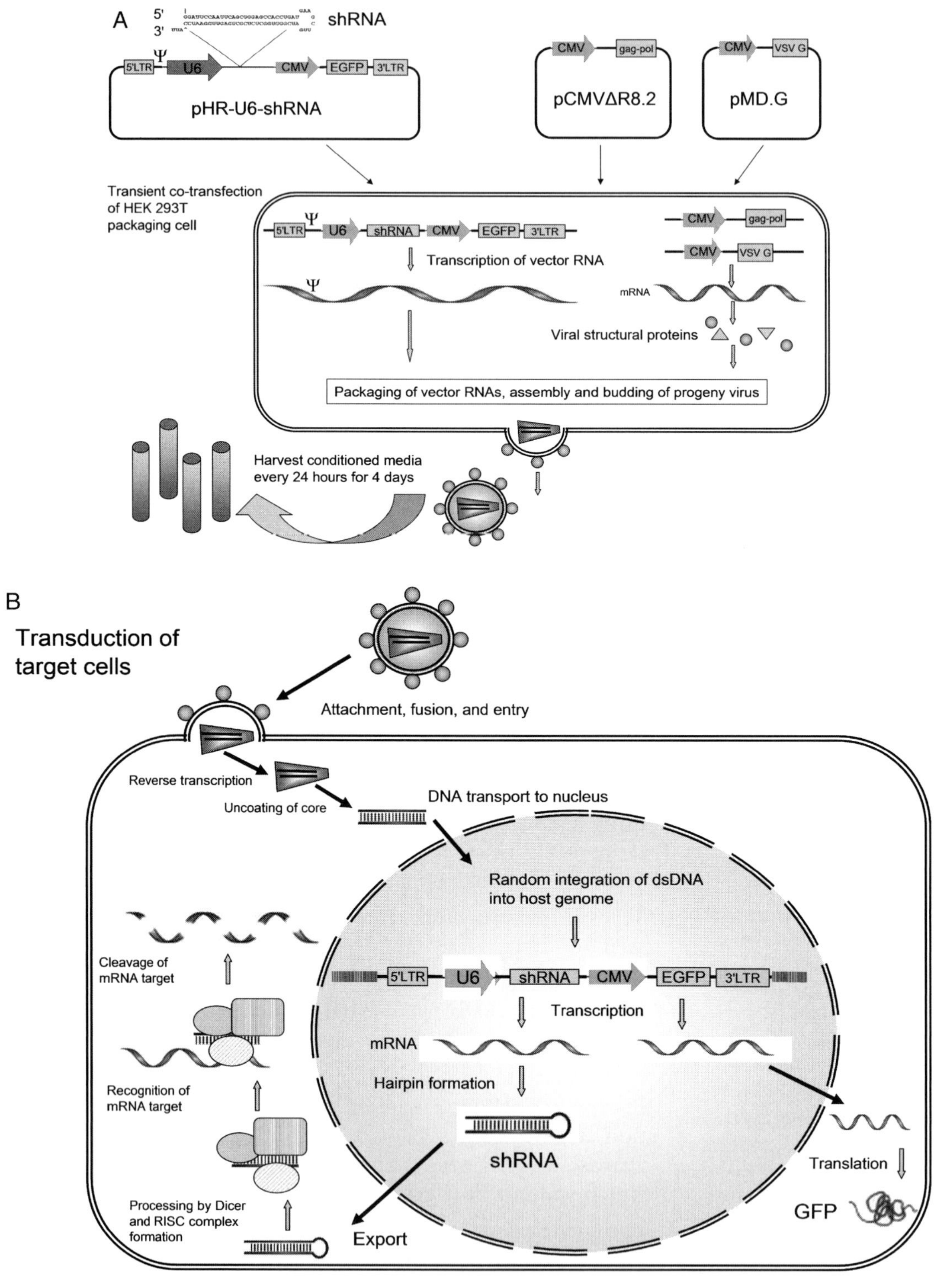

Fig. 2. Construction of a lentiviral vector for transduction of shRNA into target cells. (**A**) To produce the recombinant lentiviral vectors, the packaging cell line HEK 293T was cotransfected by the vector plasmid (pHR-U6-shRNA), helper

use for transient transfection of the packaging cell line HEK 293T (**Fig. 2A**).

3.2. Transient Transfection of HEK 293T Packaging Cells

1. The three vectors pHR-U6-shRNA (hairpin vector), pCMVΔR8.2 (helper plasmid), and pMD.G (envelop plasmid) should all be prepared using an endotoxin-free plasmid purification kit (e.g., Qiagen Endofree Maxi kit). Concentration and purity should be checked by both OD reading and gel electrophoresis. Purified plasmids should be dissolved in endotoxin-free TE buffer.
2. The day before transfection, coat 10 cm cell culture plates with poly-L-lysine (*see* **Note 5**) by adding 3 mL of a 0.01% solution to one plate. Then remove and transfer to the next plate, making sure that each plate is completely coated before transferring to the next. Keep repeating the procedure until all the plates are coated. Then seed 1.6 × 10^6 HEK 293T cells per plate, in complete DMEM. Incubate in a 5% CO_2 incubator at 37°C for 12 h overnight.
3. On the next day, add the necessary volumes of the three plasmids to Opti-MEM I Reduced Serum Media in an Eppendorf tube, final volume 1.5 mL. Label this "mix A." The amounts of plasmids to use are: 10 μg pHR-U6-shRNA, 7.5 μg of pCMVΔR8.2, and 2.5 μg of pMD.G (*see* **Note 5**). In another vial, labeled "mix B," add 60 μL of Lipofectamine 2000 with 1.5 mL Opti-MEM for 5 min at room temperature. Then combine "mix A" and "mix B" and incubate for 20 min at

Fig. 2. (continued) plasmid (pCMVΔR8.2), and envelope plasmid (pMD.G). The [illegible] viral vector-delivered siRNA is to segregate the *trans*-acting sequences that encode for viral proteins from the *cis*-acting sequences (nonencoding regions recognized by viral proteins) involved in the transfer of vector sequences encoding the shRNA [reviewed in **ref.** 15]. The vector plasmid contained a U6 promoter-driven shRNA coding sequence, followed by a CMV-driven enhanced green fluorescent protein (EGFP) reporter. The shRNA nucleotide sequence shown is not specific and is only intended to illustrate a generic shRNA. These elements were flanked by long terminal repeats (LTR), and also contained *cis*-acting sequences that allowed the vector RNA to be packaged and subsequently, to be reverse transcribed and integrated in the target cell. The packaging sequence (Ψ) was only present in the vector plasmid, and not in the other two plasmids. Following transfection, the plasmids pCMVΔR8.2 and pMD.G were transcribed downstream of CMV promoters, and they provided the viral structural proteins in *trans.* These included viral integrase, protease, reverse transcriptase, capsid and matrix proteins, and vesicular stomatitis virus G protein. Together, these proteins act to *trans*-complement the vector by assembling the progeny viral particles, which are limited to a single round of infection. Vector proteins were produced as well, so transfected cells were GFP positive. Conditioned medium was then harvested, concentrated by ultracentrifugation, and stored at –70°C. (**B**) Transduction of target cells was done at a MOI of 10:1. Virions attach at the cell surface via VSV G proteins, fuse with the cell membrane, and release the viral core. Reverse transcription and uncoating of the viral core occurs in the cytoplasm. The dsDNA is then transported into the nucleus where it integrates randomly into the target cell genome. Following integration, the U6 and CMV promoters transcribe their respective genes, and this results in shRNA production and mRNA for the GFP reporter. The shRNA and mRNAs are exported to the cytoplasm. GFP is then translated, and the shRNA is processed by Dicer and then incorporated into the RNA-induced silencing complex (RISC) [reviewed in **ref.** 8]. RISC then targets and degrades cognate mRNAs (reproduced from **ref.** *10* with permissions from American Society for Biochemistry and Molecular Biology).

room temperature. The total amount of mix A + B required will be determined by the number of plates of 293T cells to be transfected.

4. Remove the media from the plates containing 293T cells and replace with 15 mL of fresh complete DMEM.
5. Add the 3 mL of combined mix A + B solution to each plate, to give a final volume of 18 mL per plate. Swirl plate gently, and incubate overnight at 37°C.
6. On the next day, remove the media and add 6 mL of complete DMEM to each plate (*see* **Note 6**). Plates can be checked for transfection by examining by fluorescent microscopy. Most of the cells should be strongly GFP positive at this time point. Incubate overnight again at 37°C.
7. Roughly 48 h post-transfection, begin the first supernatant collection. Collect the entire 6 mL from each plate and replace with 6 mL of fresh complete DMEM.
8. The collected conditioned media is cleared of debris by low-speed centrifugation (2,500 × g for 5 min, 4°C) and filtered through a 0.45 μm (*see* **Note 7**) filter. Label this tube "Day 1," and store the filtered collection at –70°C immediately.
9. Repeat this collection procedure every 12 or 24 h, daily for three more days (*see* **Note 8**).
10. Thaw the conditioned media from the four individual collections on ice (*see* **Note 9**), and pool these setting aside 500 μL for titering purposes. Label this 500 μL "Before concentration." Ultracentrifuge the remainder at 100,000 × *g*, at 4°C for 2 h.
11. Aspirate the supernatant carefully without disturbing the pellet, and keep 2 mL for titering purposes (see later). Label this 2 mL "Undiluted supernatant." Resuspend the pellet in 500 μL of complete DMEM (chilled on ice), and place on a nutator or flat bed shaker at 4°C overnight. Pipette the resuspended pellet a few times while it is shaking.
12. After shaking the resuspended virus, transfer it to a microcentrifuge tube and spin at 3,000 rpm for 10 min to remove any remaining debris. Remove 6 μL for titering purposes (see later) and label this sample "Concentrated." Store the 6 μL and the remainder in aliquots (25–200 μL) at –70°C (*see* **Note 10**).
13. Prepare the dilutions shown in **Table 2** for titering purposes (*see* **Note 11**).
14. Add 1 mL of each diluted sample plus 20 μL polybrene (8 μg/mL final) to 1 × 10^5 HEK 293T cells plated the night before in a 6-well plate (*see* **Note 12**). Plate an additional three wells to count at the time of titration to get an average cell number per well. Incubate overnight at 37°C.

Table 2
Volumes and dilutions for titering virus concentrations on HEK 293T cells

Sample	Dilution	Volumes to use
Before concentration	10	222.2 μL supernatant + 2 mL complete DMEM
	100	222.2 μL of 1/10 dilution + 2 mL complete DMEM
	1,000	222.2 μL of 1/100 dilution + 2 mL complete DMEM
After concentration	Undiluted supernatant	Use 1 mL undiluted supernatant
	10	222.2 μL of supernatant + 2 mL complete DMEM
	100	222.2 μL of 1/10 dilution + 2 mL complete DMEM
Concentrated	500	4.01 μL concentrated supernatant + 2 mL complete DMEM
	5,000	222.2 μL of 1/500 dilution + 2 mL complete DMEM
	50,000	222.2 μL of 1/5,000 dilution + 2 mL complete DMEM

15. Change the medium the next day, and incubate overnight once again.
16. Remove medium and rinse the wells with PBS. Remove cells with cell dissociation solution and spin down the cells. Wash once with binding buffer (HBSS, 1% FCS, and 0.1% NaN_3) and spin the cells down once again. Resuspended in 1 mL of binding buffer containing 1.85% paraformaldehyde. Analyze at least 10,000 cells in flow cytometer and measure the percent GFP positive cells using nontransduced cells as controls. Calculate the titer by the following formula: transduction units/mL = (average cell number at the time of titration × % of GFP positive cells)/100 × dilution factor. Example: 30% positive at 1:100 dilution of 8×10^5 cells = $0.30 \times 100 \times 8 \times 10^5 = 2.4 \times 10^7$ transduction units/mL. Expect 1×10^8 to 1×10^9 transduction units/mL in the concentrated samples.

3.3. Transduction of Human Monocytic Cell Lines

1. Seed fresh cultures of 1×10^5 THP-1 or U-937 cells in each well of a 12-well plate in 500 μL of complete RPMI.
2. Based on the viral titer calculations, add enough lentiviral vectors for a multiplicity of infection of 10:1 (*see* **Note 13**). Transduction should be carried out in the presence of polybrene (8 μg/mL). Premix the viral stock with polybrene before adding to the cells.

3. Incubate the transduced cells at 37°C for 6 days. On day 3–4, cells may be examined by immunofluorescent microscopy to monitor GFP expression. If cells proliferate rapidly during the 6 days, add enough complete medium to keep the cells from exhausting the medium.
4. Analyze the transduced cells by flow cytometry after 6 days for % GFP positive. Expect greater than 90% GFP positivity (**Fig. 3A**).
5. Allow cells to proliferate under optimal conditions (do not exceed 1×10^6 cells/mL) until enough cells are obtained for Western blot analysis and storage in liquid nitrogen.
6. Western blot analysis of the targeted protein should reveal marked reduction relative to appropriate controls (**Fig. 3B, C**).
7. Freeze positive clones and control cells in liquid nitrogen for future use (*see* **Note 14**).

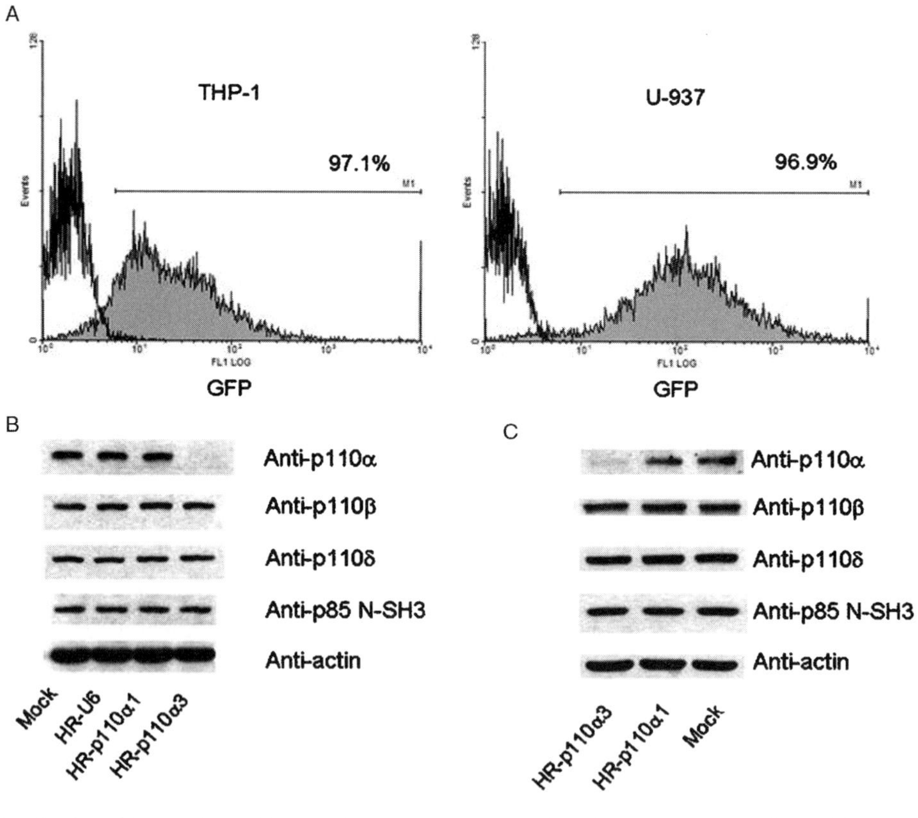

Fig. 3. Transduction of monocytic cell lines by lentiviral vectors is efficient and generates stable cell lines deficient in p110α. (**A**) Flow cytometry analysis of transduced (solid histogram) or mock transduced cells (clear histogram) was performed 6 days after viral transduction. 10,000 cells were analyzed, and GFP fluorescence intensity was measured on the FL1 channel. Approximately 97% of the THP-1 and U-937 cells were GFP positive. The mean fluorescence intensity (MFI) for mock-infected cells was 8.5 for THP-1 and 6.6 for U-937. Transduced cells had MFIs of 38.3 for THP-1 and 132.3 for U-937. (**B**) and (**C**) Western blot analysis of class IA PI3K p110 catalytic subunit isoforms (α, β, and δ), and p85 regulatory subunit in THP-1 cells and U-937 cells. Actin was used as protein loading control (reproduced from **ref.** *10* with permissions from American Society for Biochemistry and Molecular Biology).

4. Notes

1. The protocol for designing oligonucleotides for insertion into *Bse*RI *Bam*HI cut pSHAG-1 vector is as follows (from Dr. G. Hannon, Cold Spring Harbor Laboratory):

Note that N1, N2…N30, N31 are numbered positions for any nucleotide, N.

(a) Using the sense coding sequence for the gene of interest to be targeted, find 5′-N1 NNNNN….NNNNNNNNNN C N30 N31–3′ such that the oligo must end in a "C" so that pol III, which initiates at a "G" in the U6 promoter, will initiate precisely at the first base of the antisense strand.

(b) Get the reverse complement of the sequence in step (a) which is:

5′- N31′ N30′ G N′N′N′N′N′N′…..N′N′N′N′N′N′ N′N′N′N1′-3′

Note that N31′ N30′…N1′ are complementary to N31, N30…N1, respectively.

(c) Remove N30′ N31′ from sequence in step (b) to get *5′- G* N′N′N′N′N′N′N′N′…..N′N′N′N′N′N′N′N1′-3′

(d) Add 5′-GAAGCTTG-3′ to 3′END of the sequence in step (c) to get 5′- G N′N′N′N′N′N′N′N′N′… ..N′N′N′N′N′N′N1′*GAAGCTTG -3′*

(e) Optional (to reduce hairpin formation by DNA oligonucleotides prior to ligation)

From sequence in step (a), in positions N2 through N28 convert every third base possible from A to G or from C to T such that:

- Adjacent bases are not changed
- More than four bases are not changed
- Homopolymeric runs greater than six bases in length do not result

(f) To the 3′END of the sequence in step (d), add the sequence in step (e) to get

5′- G N′N′N′N′N′N′N′N′N′….N′N′N′N′N′N′N1′GAAGC TTG *N1 NNNNNNN…..NNNNNNNN C N30 N31*

(g) Add pol III terminator TTTTTT to the sequence in step (f) to get

5′- G N′N′N′N′N′N′N′N′N′….N′N′N′N′N′N′N1′GAAGCTTG N1

NNNNNNN…..NNNNNNNN C N30 N31 *TTTTTT*

The inclusion of the HindIII site allows for rapid identification of clones containing a hairpin.

(h) Drop the 5′- G in the sequence in step (g) to get

5′-*N*′N′N′N′N′N′N′N′N′....N′N′N′N′N′N′N1′GAAGC TTG N1

NNNNNNNN....NNNNNNN C N30 N31 TTTTTT

This sequence is now herein after referred to as "oligo A."

(i) Get reverse complement of the sequence in step (h).

(j) To the sequence in step (i), Add GATC to 5′ end.

(k) To the sequence in step (j), add CG to 3′ end.

This yields what is herein after referred to as "oligo B."

Examples of oligo A and B are shown in **Table 1**. Note that with the exception of the criteria stated in step (a), the target sequences chosen are randomly selected. Check the uniqueness of the sequences using GenBank. Prepare at least three target sequences. More sophisticated methods are now available through commercial venders or through free web sites such as: http://katahdin.cshl.org:9331/homepage/siRNA/RNAi.cgi?type=siRNA. See **ref.** *13* for more information on rationale siRNA design. Scrambled sequences may be used for control purposes. On the other hand, editorial boards of certain journals have explicit guidelines for the types of controls required for RNAi gene silencing experiments and authors are urged to consult the journals for specific details.

2. The vesicular stomatitis virus (VSV) glycoprotein G is a substitute for the lentiviral gp120/gp41 as the viral coat protein since it broadens the range of cell types that can be infected by the virus and also helps to stabilize the virion, yielding higher titers of the virus *(11)*. Furthermore, by stabilizing the virion, VSV G protein also allows the viral particles to be concentrated by ultracentrifugation, thereby providing higher titers for transduction *(11, 14)*.

3. DB3.1-competent cells are required to propagate the destination pHR-Gateway vector because these cells are resistant to the effects of the *ccd*B gene product produced by the Gateway conversion cassette, which is also present on the pHR-Gateway. The *ccd*B gene encodes a protein that interferes with *E. coli* DNA gyrase. When recombination occurs between the destination vector (e.g., pHR-Gateway) and an entry clone (e.g., pSHAG-shRNA), the *ccdB* gene on the destination vector is replaced by the U6-shRNA element from the pSHAG-shRNA. Cells that take up unreacted pHR-Gateway will fail to grow in non-DB3.1 cells.

4. A different commercial kit will suffice. Follow the manufacturer's instructions for optimal results.

5. Use early passage HEK 293T cells for transfection to get better results. Poly-L-lysine enhances adherence of the cells to the plate during the transfection protocol. The 4:3:1 ratio for pHR-shRNA, pCMV R8.2, and pMD.G, respectively, may be varied to achieve optimal viral production.

6. Lentiviral vectors should be prepared in a BSL-2 facility at a minimum. Check with your local authorities if in doubt.

7. A 0.2-µm filter maybe used without losing any viral particles. However, some clogging may occur. You may need to filter through a 0.8-µm and a 0.45-µm filter first.
8. 12-h collection yields the most virus, but collections can be done at 24 h intervals for convenience.
9. Keep everything on ice to maximize viral recovery. Using clear centrifuge bottles will facilitate pellet identification.
10. As an optional step, viral stocks can also be assayed for the p24 core antigen using commercial HIV-1 Antigen ELISA kits. This will give an approximation of how many viral particles are present; however, it does not directly indicate how many effective virions were made. This may be a helpful step for troubleshooting when viral titers are low.
11. All the samples used for titering should be frozen to –70°C and thawed at least once before titering. This will result in a more accurate estimation of effective transduction units after thawing the viral stocks for use in monocyte transduction. The three different samples allow for troubleshooting if viral yield is low in the "Concentrated" sample. The undiluted supernatant from the "After concentration" sample should not contain many transduction units, if at all. If it does, it indicates that the ultracentrifugation step or removable of the supernatant, was not performed optimally.
12. Polybrene acts as a transduction adjuvant to promote viral attachment to cells.
13. The multiplicity of infection may be varied to achieve optimal silencing. It is recommended that the minimal amount of virus to achieve silencing should be used in order to minimize the chance of nonspecific effects from random integration events.
14. When cells are thawed, perform FACS analysis to verify that the percent GFP positivity of the transduced cells is above 85–90%. Since there is no drug selection, FACS sorting maybe performed to enrich GFP positive cells. Always do Western blot analysis on the targeted protein of interest to verify silencing prior to experimentation.

Acknowledgments

The authors acknowledge Dr. Alice Mui for construction of the pHR-Gateway vector and for help with technical development. We also thank Dr. Greg Hannon for the gift of the pSHAG-1 vector. Work in the authors' laboratory was supported by Canadian Institutes of Health Research (CIHR) operating grant MOP-8633 (NR).

References

1. Shi Y. (2003). Mammalian RNAi for the masses. Trends Genet;19:9–12
2. Elbashir SM, Harborth J, Lendeckel W, Yalcin A, Weber K, Tuschl T. (2001) Duplexes of 21-nucleotide RNAs mediate RNA interference in cultured mammalian cells. Nature;411:494–498
3. Paddison PJ, Caudy AA, Bernstein E, Hannon GJ, Conklin DS. (2002). Short hairpin RNAs (shRNAs) induce sequence-specific silencing in mammalian cells. Genes Dev;16:948–958
4. Brummelkamp TR, Bernards R, Agami R. (2002). A system for stable expression of short interfering RNAs in mammalian cells. *Science*;296:550–553
5. Sui G, Soohoo C, Affar el B et al. (2002). A DNA vector-based RNAi technology to suppress gene expression in mammalian cells. *Proc Natl Acad Sci U S A*;99:5515–5520
6. Hannon GJ. (2002). RNA interference. *Nature*;418:244–251
7. Xia H, Mao Q, Paulson HL, Davidson BL. (2002). siRNA-mediated gene silencing in vitro and in vivo. *Nat Biotechnol*;20:1006–1010
8. Paddison PJ, Hannon GJ. (2002). RNA interference: the new somatic cell genetics? *Cancer Cell*;2:17–23
9. Tiscornia G, Singer O, Ikawa M, Verma IM. (2003). A general method for gene knockdown in mice by using lentiviral vectors expressing small interfering RNA. *Proc Natl Acad Sci U S A*;100:1844–1848
10. Lee JS, Hmama Z, Mui A, Reiner NE. (2004). Stable gene silencing in human monocytic cell lines using lentiviral-delivered small interference RNA. Silencing of the p110alpha isoform of phosphoinositide 3-kinase reveals differential regulation of adherence induced by 1alpha,25-dihydroxycholecalciferol and bacterial lipopolysaccharide. *J Biol Chem*;279:9379–9388
11. Naldini L, Blomer U, Gallay P et al. (1996). In vivo gene delivery and stable transduction of nondividing cells by a lentiviral vector. *Science*;272:263–267
12. Naldini L, Blomer U, Gage FH, Trono D, Verma IM. (1996). Efficient transfer, integration, and sustained long-term expression of the transgene in adult rat brains injected with a lentiviral vector. *Proc Natl Acad Sci U S A*;93:11382–11388
13. Reynolds A, Leake D, Boese Q, Scaringe S, Marshall WS, Khvorova A. (2004). Rational siRNA design for RNA interference. *Nat Biotechnol*;22:326–330
14. Follenzi A, Naldini L. (2002). HIV-based vectors. Preparation and use. *Methods Mol Med*;69:259–274
15. Buchschacher GL, Jr., Wong-Staal F. (2000). Development of lentiviral vectors for gene therapy for human diseases. *Blood*;95:2499–2504

Chapter 19

Use of Fluorescent Probes to Detect Lipid Signaling Intermediates in Macrophages

Vivian Kwok, Eric Vachon, and Gregory P. Downey

Summary

To fulfill their function in host defense, professional phagocytes such as neutrophils and macrophages exhibit the ability to ingest (phagocytose), kill, and dispose of pathogenic microorganisms. Recent studies have provided strong evidence for the importance of membrane lipids such as polyphosphoinositides in these processes. In turn, reversible phosphorylation events, involving protein and lipid kinases and phosphatases, regulate signaling pathways involving metabolism of membrane lipids. Our ability to study lipid signaling events has been greatly facilitated by the development of fluorescent molecular imaging techniques. In particular, the expression of recombinant fusions of derivatives of the jellyfish-derived green fluorescent proteins (GFP) coupled to reporter molecules enables real-time monitoring of signaling events in live cells. Here, we discuss methods to monitor alterations in membrane polyphosphoinositides involved in signaling events regulating phagocytosis. To illustrate the use of this technology, we will focus on the role of protein tyrosine phosphatase MEG2 in phagocytosis and its modulation by phosphatidylinositol-3,4,5-triphosphate (PIP_3). This approach enables investigators to ascertain the involvement of lipid intermediates in diverse signaling pathways.

Key words: Fluorescent probes, Green fluorescent protein (GFP), Macrophages, Phagocytosis, Lipids, Phosphoinositides, Protein tyrosine phosphatase (PTP), Signal transduction, Confocal microscopy.

1. Introduction

Alterations in membrane lipids are integral to diverse cellular processes such as proliferation and programmed cell death (apoptosis), motility, and uptake of fluid (endocytosis) and particles (phagocytosis). The latter is a process by which cells engulf large (>3 µm diameter) particles. In unicellular eukaryotes, phagocytosis is crucial for nutrition. In higher eukaryotes including mammals, phagocytosis is pivotal in innate and adaptive immune responses

Neil E. Reiner (ed.), *Macrophages and Dendritic Cells,* Methods in Molecular Biology, vol. 531

DOI: 10.1007/978-1-59745-396-7_19

and in clearance of dead cells and debris *(1, 2)*. Phagocytosis is initiated by the binding of ligands displayed on the particle surface to specific receptors such as the Fcγ and complement (CR3) receptors on the surface of the phagocyte. This triggers signaling pathways that lead to rearrangement of the actin cytoskeleton and membrane fusion events that facilitate closure and maturation of the phagosome *(3, 4)*. Among many signaling intermediaries, protein and lipid kinases and phosphatases and their substrates appear to be particularly important in regulating phagocytosis. In this chapter, we focus on a subset of these reactions involving reversible tyrosine phosphorylation-dependent events regulated by the reciprocal actions of protein tyrosine kinases (PTK) and protein tyrosine phosphatases (PTP) *(5–9)*.

PTP-MEG2, first identified in megakarocytes and endothelial cells *(10)*, has recently been reported to interact specifically with polyphosphoinositides PIP_2 and PIP_3 through its N-terminal lipid-binding domain *(11, 12)*. Dynamic alterations in PIP_2 and PIP_3 occur at the phagocytic cup, and these are believed to play central roles in recruiting actin-associated proteins enabling phagocytosis to proceed *(13–15)*. Given the presence of PTP-MEG2 in the phagosome and its affinity to bind PIP_3 in vitro *(11, 12)*, we considered the possibility that regulation of PTP-MEG2 during phagocytosis is modulated by these interactions. We have recently shown that PIP_3 colocalizes with PTP-MEG2 during phagocytosis *(16)*, possibly triggering downstream signaling pathways regulating phagocytosis.

Fluorescent probes are widely used as reporters to monitor dynamic processes in living cells. Fluorescent tags can be engineered to fuse to signaling proteins thus allowing subcellular localization of these proteins and enabling researchers to track their movement and dynamic interactions in response to different agonists or other stimuli in live cells *(17)*. Transfection of fluorescently tagged molecules that bind specifically and with high affinity to specific lipids enables real-time visualization of dynamic alterations in lipid intermediates using confocal fluorescence microscopy. For example, the pleckstrin homology (PH) domain of Akt (Akt-PH) binds specifically to PIP_3, the primary product of phosphoinositide-3 kinase (PI3K) while the C2 domain of PKCδ binds to PIP_2. In the case of phagocytosis, fluorescent particles (e.g., beads, bacteria) coated with immunoglobulins serve as phagocytic prey and can be visualized simultaneously by fluorescence microscopy. Additionally, the use of paramagnetic beads enables isolation of phagosomal components -including lipids and proteins- by magnetic sorting (MACS) which can then be identified by biochemical techniques such as western blotting.

To illustrate the utility of these approaches, we describe their use to study the role of PTP-MEG2 in the dynamic turnover of membrane lipids during phagocytosis. These imaging techniques can be combined with molecular techniques to generate point mutant and/or truncated recombinant MEG2 proteins that allow characterization of the functional importance of the various domains of PTP-MEG2. Finally, the ability to reconstitute some membrane events in vitro using mixed liposomes, the composition of which can be varied, enables the study of the role of specific lipids in regulation of PTP-MEG2.

2. Materials

2.1. Cell Culture and Lysis

1. High Glucose Dulbecco's Modified Eagle's Medium (High Glucose DMEM) supplemented with 10% fetal bovine serum (FBS), 100 units/mL penicillin, and 100 μg/mL streptomycin (*see* **Note 1**).
2. Sterile Polyethylene Cell Lifters.
3. Phosphate-buffered saline (PBS). Autoclave before storage at 4°C.
4. Sterile Polyethylene Cell Scrapers.
5. SDS lysis buffer: For a 40 mL aliquot, combine 5 mL of 0.5 M Tris–HCl pH 6.8, 8 mL 100% SDS, 4 mL 100% glycerol, and QS with water. For every 4.875 mL of SDS lysis buffer, add 125 μL of 1 M Dithiothreitol (DTT) before use (*see* **Notes 2** and **3**).
6. 10× Laemmli sample buffer for cell lysis: 60 mM Tris–HCl, pH 6.8, 100 mM DTT, 2% (w/v) SDS, 10% (v/v) glycerol, 0.001% (w/v) bromophenol blue. Store in aliquots at –20°C.

2.2. Cell Transfection

1. Plasmid DNA. The following plasmid constructions were used for transfection. Green fluorescent protein-tagged pleckstrin homology domain of AKT (Akt-PH). The recombinant fusions of PTP-MEG2 were generated using either restriction digests or site-directed mutagenesis (using the Quick-Change™ site-directed mutagenesis kit, Stratagene, La Jolla, CA) were cloned into pcDNA3.0. Full length wild-type PTP-MEG2; the N-terminal domain of PTP-MEG2 fused to 6 histidine (polyHis) epitope tags; the catalytically inactive mutant of PTP-MEG2 (C515S MEG2); and lipid-binding domain mutants (K55M, K184M, and K55M/K184M MEG2). For clarification of the lipid-binding domain mutants, lysines at positions 55 and 184 in MEG2, K^{55} and K^{184}, were mutated individually or in combination to methionine residues (M), giving rise to K55M, K184M single mutants and the K55M/K184M double mutant. Mutations were confirmed by DNA sequencing. A schematic diagram of all the PTP-MEG2 recombinant DNAs utilized is illustrated in **Fig. 1**.
2. Plasmid DNA is diluted to a concentration of 1 μg/μL such that accurate amounts can be used for transfection. Freeze at –80°C for long-term storage to avoid degradation (*see* **Note 4**).

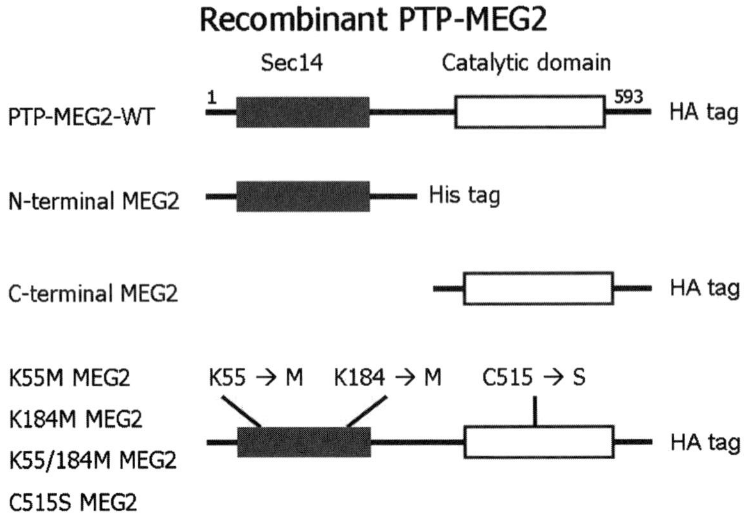

Fig. 1. Schematic diagrams of recombinant PTP-MEG2 proteins. Open and solid bars represent the catalytic domain and the Sec14-like lipid-binding domain of PTP-MEG2, respectively. PTP-MEG2 wild type is referred to as PTP-MEG2-WT. The N-terminal MEG2 has a poly His-tag and all other constructs are tagged with hemagglutinin (HA). Point mutations in the Sec14 domain (K55M, K184M, and K55/184M MEG2) all impair the ability of MEG2 to bind lipids. Lysines at positions 55 and 184 in MEG2, K^{55} and K^{184}, were mutated individually or in combination to methionine residues (M), giving rise to K55M, K184M, and the K55M/K184M double mutant. The catalytically inactive domain mutant and the C-terminal domain are referred to as C515S MEG2 and C-terminal MEG2, respectively (reproduced from **ref.** *16*).

3. SuperFect Transfection Reagent (*see* **Note 5**).
4. Sterile serum-free DMEM. Prewarm DMEM at 37°C and equilibrate with 5% CO_2 before use for cell culture (*see* **Note 6**).
5. Phosphate-buffered saline (PBS): 1× solution. Prewarm at 37°C before use.
6. 12-well polystyrene cell culture plates.
7. 18-mm-diameter circular glass microscope coverslips, 0.25 mm thick.

2.3. Confocal Immunofluorescence for PTP-MEG2

1. 18-mm-diameter circular microscope glass coverslips, 0.25 mm thick.
2. Microscope slides.
3. Phosphate-buffered saline (PBS): 1× solution at room temperature.
4. 16% Paraformaldehyde Solution (PFA): Prepare 4% (v/v) solution in PBS fresh for each experiment. (PFA is a rapid fixative. Avoid contact with the body. Wear protective clothing. PFA is also flammable. Do not breathe vapors) (*see* **Note 7**).
5. Permeabilization solution: 0.1% (v/v) Triton X-100 in PBS.
6. Blocking and antibody dilution buffer: 5% (v/v) goat serum and 3% (w/v) BSA in PBS.

7. Primary antibodies: Rabbit polyclonal anti-HA or mouse monoclonal anti-KDEL. Anti-HA antibody stains for recombinant HA-tagged PTP-MEG2. KDEL is a motif located at the carboxy terminal of endoplasmic reticulum luminal proteins; it enables precise sorting of these proteins along the secretory pathway. KDEL serves as an endoplasmic reticulum (ER)-specific marker *(18)*.
8. Secondary antibodies: donkey-antirabbit FITC or donkey-antimouse Texas Red.
9. Mounting medium: DAKO.

2.4. Liposome Preparation

1. Lipids: phosphatidylinositol-4,5-bisphosphate (PIP_2), phosphatidylinositol-3,4,5-triphosphate (PIP_3), and phosphatidylserine (PS). Keep under inert gas (e.g., argon) and seal to avoid oxidation.
2. Chloroform (Chloroform evaporates easily into the air. Breathing chloroform may cause dizziness, fatigue, headache, and loss of consciousness. Work in a well-ventilated hood to avoid unnecessary exposure to chloroform. Chloroform is difficult to pipette because it leaks from the tip after aspirating. Do not use plastic containers for chloroform. It must be stored and handled in glass containers).
3. Dioleoyl-phosphatidylcholine (DOPC).
4. Rotary evaporator and vials.
5. Liposome buffer: 30 mM Hepes, pH 7.2, 100 mM NaCl, and 1 mL EDTA.
6. 22-gauge and 27-gauge needles.
7. Ethanol and dry ice. (To perform freeze–thaw cycles).
8. Extruding chamber with 100 nm filter.

2.5. Phosphatase Assays

1. Recombinant bacterially expressed PTP-MEG2 (30 μg/mL) proteins were synthesized from recombinant PTP-MEG2 DNAs as described in **Subheading 2.2.1** the PTP-MEG2 recombinant DNAs used are summarized in **Fig.** 1. Briefly, full length wild-type and mutant PTP-MEG2 were subcloned into the prokaryotic expression vector pGEX-4T-1 (PTP-MEG2-WT, C515S MEG2, C and N-terminal) or pGEX-6T-1 for lipid-binding domain mutants (K55M, K184M, and K55/184M MEG2). Fusion proteins were expressed in *Escherichia coli* and purified using glutathione-sepharose beads *(12)*. The glutathione-S-transferase (GST) was removed by cleavage with thrombin (Sigma-Aldrich Ltd).
2. Phosphatase buffer: 40 mM Hepes pH 7.2, 100 mM NaCl, 1 mM EDTA, 10 mM DTT, 0.025% Triton X-100, and 0.02% Nonidet P-40.
3. 10 mg/mL *p*-nitrophenyl phosphate (*p*NPP) and 10 mM DTT. *p*NPP is a phosphate ester used as a substrate for protein

phosphatases. When it interacts with phosphatases, it is hydrolyzed yielding a soluble end product that is yellow in color and can be quantified by absorbance at 405 nm. The intensity of the yellow color corresponds to the catalytic activity of a particular phosphatase. Dithiothreitol (DTT) protects the proteins with cysteine residues such as PTP from oxidative modification that can compromise their catalytic activity.

4. Microplate reader.

2.6. Phagocytosis

1. Three micrometer latex beads in 0.2% solution. Vortex well before use.
2. Purified lyophilized human IgG. Human IgG is utilized to coat the latex beads for Fcγ receptor (FcγR)-specific phagocytosis.
3. Prewarmed complete DMEM.
4. Phosphate-buffered saline (PBS): 1× solution. Keep one aliquot at 4°C and another at room temperature.
5. Ice.

2.7. Confocal Immunofluorescence for Localization of PTP-MEG2 and Akt-PH During Phagocytosis

1. The materials and reagents required for confocal immunofluorescence are the same as described earlier (*see* **Subheading 2.3**). Primary and secondary antibodies used are listed as follows.
2. Primary antibodies: Rabbit polyclonal anti-HA.
3. Secondary antibody: donkey-antirabbit Texas Red.

2.8. Confocal Immunofluorescence of PTP-MEG2 at Nascent Phagosomes

1. Materials and reagents required for confocal immunofluorescence and phagocytosis are described earlier (*see* **Subheadings 2.3** and **2.6**
2. TRITC conjugated goat-antihuman IgG. TRITC conjugated antihuman IgG antibody is used to stain noninternalized portion of the prey.

2.9. Phagosome Isolation

1. Polystyrene and sterile tissue culture dish, 60 × 15 mm.
2. Three micrometer magnetic beads. These beads serve as the particles to be ingested by the phagocytic cells. The beads containing phagosomal elements can be easily retrieved using a magnet.
3. Purified human IgG is utilized to opsonize the magnetic beads to facilitate the uptake of particles via Fcγ receptors.
4. Latrunculin B and Wortmannin. Latrunculin B is an actin polymerization inhibitor and Wortmannin is a phosphatidyl inositol 3 kinase inhibitor. They are used to block phagocytosis and these samples serve as negative controls.
5. Phosphate-buffered saline (PBS): 1× solution. Keep one aliquot at 4°C and another at room temperature.

6. Hanks Balanced Salt Solution (HBSS++) with 0.5 mM of Ca^{2+} and 0.5 mM of Mg^{2+}.
7. Ice.
8. Sterile Polyethylene Cell Scrapers.
9. Cytoskeletal Extraction Buffer (CSKB): 0.5% Triton X-100, 50 mM NaCl, 300 mM sucrose, 3 mM $MgCl_2$, 10 mM PIPES, 20 μg/mL aprotinin, 1 μg/mL pepstatin, 1 mM PMSF. Aprotinin, pepstatin, and PMSF are protease inhibitors; they should be added just before the buffer is used. The buffer without the protease inhibitors can be prepared ahead of time and stored at 4°C. Buffer should be chilled.
10. Protease inhibitor cocktail tablet. The tablet contains a mixture of protease inhibitors that inhibit many proteases including serine-cysteine- and metalloproteases. When dissolved in aqueous solution, the tablet offers extensive protection of the proteins in cell lysates.
11. Potter homogenizer and sonicator. These instruments are used briefly to break down the cell membranes, allowing the recovery of components within the cells.
12. Capture-Tec™ stand (Invitrogen Canada Inc.). The stand facilitates the isolation and recovery of the magnetic beads within the cell lysates solution. Prechill the stand on ice before use.

2.10. SDS–Polyacrylamide Gel Electrophoresis (SDS–PAGE)

1. 0.5 M Tris–HCl, pH 6.8, for stacking gel. Store at 4°C.
2. 1.5 M Tris–HCl, pH 8.8, for separating gel. Store at 4°C.
3. 30% acrylamide/bis solution (37.5:1 with 2.6% C) (This is a neurotoxin and it may cause cancer and heritable genetic damage. Avoid exposure by wearing lab coat, goggles, and gloves).
4. Sodium dodecyl (lauryl) sulfate (SDS): prepare 10% solution in water and store room temperature (*see* **Notes 8** and **9**).
5. 1,2-Di-(Dimethylamino)Ethane (TEMED) (TEMED is highly flammable in liquid and vapor. It should be used and stored away from any heat source) (*see* **Note 10**).
6. Ammonium persulfate: prepare 10% solution in water and immediately freeze in 500 μL aliquots at −20°C (*see* **Note 11**).
7. Sterile water.
8. Water-saturated isobutanol. Shake equal volumes of water and isobutanol in a glass bottle and allow to separate. Use the top layer only. Store at room temperature.
9. Running buffer: For 1 L, prepare 10× stock by combining 30.3 g Tris, 144 g glycine, and 100 mL 10% SDS. QS with water. Mix thoroughly (do not adjust pH). Store at 4°C. Dilute 100 mL 10× running buffer stock with 900 mL water for use.

10. Prestained molecular weight marker: PageRuler Prestained Protein Ladder Plus (Fermentas, EU) (*see* **Note 12**).

2.11. Western Blotting for Phagosomal Proteins

1. Transfer buffer (10×): For 1 L, prepare 10× stock by combining 30.3 g Tris, 144 g glycine. QS with water. Mix and store at 4°C (1×: 25 mM Tris, 192 mM glycine, 20%, v/v methanol).
2. Mix 100 mL 10×transfer buffer, 200 mL methanol, and 700 mL water for use. Store at 4°C. Prepare buffer in advance and refrigerate. It is important that buffer temperature is 4°C at the start of transfer. Buffer preparation is extremely important. Do not adjust transfer buffer pH by addition of acid or base unless indicated in the instructions. Improperly made buffer will cause excess heat generation and potential safety hazards.
3. Nitrocellulose membrane and Whatman blotting paper. Cut them so they are slightly larger than the gel.
4. Fill Bio-Ice cooling unit with water and store it in –20°C in advance. The ice block serves as a heat sink for the heat generated during an electrophoretic transfer.
5. Tris-buffered saline with Tween (TBS-T): Prepare 1.5 L of 10× stock by mixing 36.3 g Tris and 120 g NaCl in water. Dilute 100 mL 10× stock with 900 mL water and add in 1 mL of Tween-20. Mix well before use.
6. Blocking buffer: 5% (w/v) nonfat dry milk in TBS-T.
7. Ponceau S solution (0.1% Ponceau S w/v in 5% acetic acid (v/v): (*see* **Note 13**) Dilute 5 mL Ponceau S with 45 mL water. Store at room temperature in dark container.
8. Primary antibody dilution buffer: TBS-T supplemented with 5% (w/v) albumin bovine serum fraction V (BSA). Store at 4°C.
9. Primary antibody: rabbit anti-PTP-MEG2.
10. Secondary antibodies: ECL™ antimouse IgG, horse radish peroxidase linked whole antibody (from sheep) or ECL™ antirabbit IgG, horse radish peroxidase linked whole antibody (from donkey). Dilute in 5% (w/v) milk in 1× TBS-T.
11. Enhanced chemiluminescence (ECL) reagents. Mix equal parts of Luminol and Oxidizing Reagent together and store in tinted container at 4°C until use.
12. Bioflex Econo Film.

2.12. Stripping and Reprobing

1. Stripping buffer: 64 mM Tris–HCl pH 6.8, 2% (w/v) SDS. For every 10 mL stripping buffer, add 79.7 µL of mercaptoethanol and mix well before use (*see* **Note 14**).
2. Water bath at 50°C.
3. Wash buffer: 1× TBS-T.

4. Primary antibodies: mouse antilysosome-associated-membrane-protein 1 (LAMP1), rabbit anticytochrome C.
5. Secondary antibodies: ECL™ antimouse IgG, horse radish peroxidase linked whole antibody (from sheep) or ECL™ antirabbit IgG, horse radish peroxidase linked whole antibody (from donkey). Dilute in 5% (w/v) milk in 1× TBS-T.

3. Methods

To determine the subcellular localization of PTP-MEG2, wild-type PTP-MEG2 cDNA was introduced by transfection into RAW264.7 murine macrophages and visualized using immunofluorescence microscopy and antibodies to the epitope tag (hemagglutinin; HA). The distribution of PTP-MEG2 was compared to that of known organelle markers to assist in determination of its localization to specific intracellular compartments. Demonstrated previously to bind to phosphoinositides PIP_2 and PIP_3 *(12)*, regulation of PTP-MEG2 phosphatase activity by these purified lipids in liposomes was tested using recombinant PTP-MEG2. A colorimetric phosphatase assay using *p*NPP *(19)* was used to determine if the different lipids were able to modulate the catalytic activity of PTP-MEG2. The domain responsible for this lipid-mediated regulation can be identified and confirmed by in vitro assays using bacterially expressed recombinant mutants of PTP-MEG2.

To ascertain the role of PTP-MEG2 in phagocytosis, fluorescently tagged PTP-MEG2 was transfected into RAW264.7 macrophages along with the pleckstrin homology domain of Akt that binds specifically to PIP_3 *(20)*. IgG-coated beads were then fed to the macrophages as prey to initiate Fc receptor-specific phagocytosis *(21)*. The subsequent recruitment of these fluorescent proteins to the nascent phagosome was tracked using confocal fluorescence microscopy. Recruitment of these molecules to the phagosome was verified by magnetic phagosome isolation *(22)* and western blot analyses of the phagosome-associated proteins.

3.1. Cell Culture

1. Murine macrophages RAW 264.7 are cultured in complete DMEM. When at 80% confluence, cells are removed from the surface of the flask by gentle scraping with a cell lifter.
2. The cells are kept under exponential growth conditions at 37°C with 5% CO_2.

3.2. Cell Transfection

1. All the transfections are performed according to the general protocols given later. Specific details for transfection for each

experiment, including the types of plasmid DNAs utilized are highlighted in the subsequent subheadings.

2. One day prior to transfection, 2.5×10^5 cells are seeded on each 18-mm-diameter glass coverslip in a 12-well plate (in 1 mL complete DMEM).
3. For transfection the following day, combine 1.5 μg of plasmid DNA with 7.5 μg of SuperFect Reagent in a final volume of 75 μL of serum-free DMEM in a labeled tube (*see* **Note 4**).
4. Mix by pipetting up and down five times or by vortexing for 10 s.
5. Incubate the samples at room temperature for 20 min to allow transfection-complex formation.
6. While complex formation takes place, gently aspirate growth medium from the plate and wash cells once with 1 mL PBS.
7. Add complete DMEM to the transfection mixture to a total volume of 1 mL.
8. Immediately transfer the total volume to cells adhered on coverslips in 12-well plate (*see* **Note 15**).
9. Incubate cells with transfection complex for at least 6 h under normal growth conditions (*see* **Note 16**).
10. Double transfections can be performed using the same procedures, except 1.5 μg of each vector and 15 μL of SuperFect Reagent are used per transfection.

3.3. Confocal Immunofluorescence for PTP-MEG2

1. Transfection of RAW cells with HA-tagged PTP-MEG2-WT is performed according to the procedures described in **Subheading 3.2.** As illustrated in **Fig. 1**, PTP-MEG2-WT consists of an N-terminal lipid-binding domain homologous to yeast Sec14, *(23)*, as well as a catalytic domain at its C-terminus.
2. Post-transfection (6–24 h), fix cells with 1 mL of 4% paraformaldehyde for 20 min at room temperature (*see* **Note 17**). Remove fixative by washing cells twice with PBS. Leaving samples in fixative for long periods of time ("overfixation") will lead to degradation of the immunofluorescence signal likely due to epitope modification.
3. Permeabilize cell membranes with 1 mL of 0.1% Triton X-100 in PBS at room temperature for 20 min. Rinse cells twice with PBS after permeabilization.
4. Block nonspecific binding sites by incubating samples at room temperature with blocking buffer (5% goat serum and 3% BSA) for 30 min.

5. Dilute primary antibodies in blocking buffer: rabbit anti-HA (1:500) or mouse anti-KDEL (1:250). These antibodies can be prepared ahead of time and stored at 4°C until use. For cotransfected samples, combine each antibody at the appropriate dilution.
6. Carefully aspirate the blocking buffer from the wells and coverslips (*see* **Note 18**).
7. Add 250 μL of primary antibody solution to the sample of interest. Ensure that the glass coverslip is evenly covered with the antibody. Incubate samples with antibody for 1 h at room temperature.
8. Remove primary antibody by two washes with PBS.
9. Prepare secondary antibodies in blocking buffer at the following dilutions: donkey antirabbit FITC (1:500), and/or donkey antimouse Texas Red (1:500). Dispense 200–250 μL of secondary antibody solution in the same way as for primary antibody. Incubate samples for 1 h at room temperature.
10. Discard secondary antibody by rinsing cells twice with PBS for 20 min. Samples are ready to be mounted on slides.
11. Dispense a drop of mounting medium on a labeled microscope slide. Using a pair of forceps with fine tips, carefully lift and invert coverslips on microscope slide making certain that there are no bubbles (these can be removed by gently tapping the slide with the forceps) (*see* **Note 19**).
12. Store and dry slides flat in the dark at room temperature overnight (in slide box or covered with aluminum foil).
13. Samples can be viewed with a microscope when the mounting medium is completely dry. Slides can be stored flat in the dark temporary at 4°C or long-term at –20°C.
14. Fluorescent images are captured with a confocal microscope (ZEISS LSM510) or with a conventional fluorescence microscope (Leica DMRA2) equipped with a cooled CCD camera (QImaging). Excitation at 484 nm induces the FITC (green emission 515 nm) for HA-tagged PTP-MEG2-WT, while excitation at 568 nm induces Texas Red (red emission) to detect endogenous KDEL. Fluorescent images can be overlayed using imaging software (OpenLab by Improvision or Adobe Photoshop). Examples of fluorescent images demonstrating the distribution of PTP-MEG2 and its colocalization with an ER marker, KDEL, are shown in **Fig. 2**.

3.4. Liposome Preparation

1. Each lyophilized lipid is dissolved in chloroform at a concentration of approximately 1 mg/mL and transferred to glass tubes or vials. Seal tubes with parafilm.

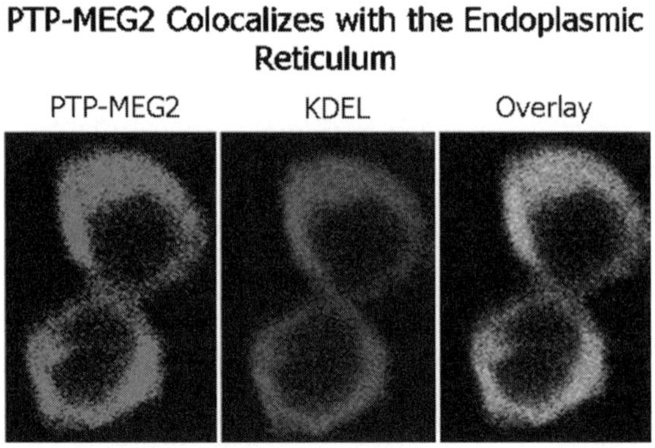

Fig. 2. PTP-MEG2 wild type colocalizes with the endoplasmic reticulum in resting macrophages. RAW264.7 murine macrophages grown on glass coverslips were transfected with PTP-MEG2-WT. Cells were fixed, permeabilized, and stained with anti-HA and anti-KDEL as described in methods. (a) PTP-MEG2-WT is shown in green, (b) the endoplasmic reticulum-specific marker is in red, and (c) colocalization of PTP-MEG2-WT in endoplasmic reticulum appears in yellow (overlay) (reproduced from **ref.** *16)*.

2. In a rotary-evaporator vial, mix DOPC solution with test lipid solution in a 19:1 ratio to form mixed liposomes. The bottom of the vial is immersed in a 37°C water bath, while the top of the vial is connected to a rotary evaporator.
3. The rotary evaporator rotates the vial in the water bath and applies suction that facilitates evaporation of the chloroform. The remaining lipid mixture will appear as a film on the side of the vial. When completely evaporated, there should be no residual odor of chloroform.
4. Dissolve lipid film in buffer to a final concentration of 1 mM. Resuspend lipid by tapping the vial and by pipetting up and down through a needle (first use a 22-gauge and then a 27-gauge needle).
5. Transfer the sample to a plastic microfuge tube and warm to 37°C. Plastic can be used from this point on because there is no chloroform remaining.
6. Subject the solution to three cycles of freeze–thawing to disrupt very large vesicles and generate a suspension of more uniform size. For each cycle, samples are frozen in a container of ethanol and dry ice for 5 min and then warm to 37°C for 5 min.
7. Incubate the samples at room temperature for 20 min and then vortex gently. Pass samples through an extruding chamber containing a 400-nm filter. Collect the filtered samples in the same plastic tubes and keep at 37°C until all samples have been prepared. Samples may then be stored at 4°C until use.

3.5. Phosphatase Assays

1. Incubate 30 μg/mL of recombinant PTP-MEG2 protein for 40 min at 37°C with or without liposomes (300 μM) in phosphatase buffer.
2. Following the incubation, add 40 μL of phosphatase buffer containing 10 mg/mL para-nitrophenylphosphate (*p*NPP) and 10 mM DTT to each sample.
3. Incubate samples for an additional 40 min at 37°C with agitation. Measure absorbance at 405 nm on a microplate reader. **Table 1** summarizes the absorbance readings obtained from the recombinant PTP-MEG2 proteins in both the presence and the absence of the various test lipids; the values shown represent the means ± standard deviation (SD) and the 95% confidence interval of six experiments. Test lipids were considered "present" in liposomes containing 5% PIP_2, PIP_3, or PS (in addition to 95% DOPC) and "absent" in liposomes containing only DOPC. DOPC is regarded as a vehicle control in these experiments. The phosphatase activities of the recombinant PTP-MEG2 proteins, in the absence of any test lipids (i.e., only DOPC was present), are shown in **Fig. 3A**. Percentage of phosphatase activity is expressed

Table 1
Phosphatase activity of recombinant PTP-MEG2 is modulated by lipids. The phosphatase activity of PTP-MEG2-WT is modulated by PIP_3 and PIP_2, but not by PS. The N-terminal mutants (K55M, K184M, K55/184M) with impaired lipid-binding ability displayed much less phosphatase activity compared to that of the PTP-MEG2-WT/DOPC activity. Other PTP-MEG2 constructs are not affected significantly by lipids. We speculate that the enhancement in MEG2 phosphatase activity may occur by a conformational change in the molecule that unfolds the lipid-binding domain from the catalytic domain, leading to enhanced activity. Values represent the means ± SD and the 95% confidence interval of $n = 6$ experiments (reproduced from ref. *16*)

Means ± SD CI [95%]	PTP MEG2-WT	C-truncated MEG2	K55M MEG2	K184M MEG2	K55/184M MEG2	C515S MEG2	N-truncated MEG2
DOPC	100	146 ± 101	17 ± 20	23 ± 20	9 ± 10	0 ± 0	0 ± 0
		[67–227]	[1–33]	[7–39]	[1–17]		
PIP_2	136 ± 29	123 ± 112	20 ± 15	37 ± 24	12 ± 11	0 ± 0	0 ± 0
	[112–160]	[32–213]	[8–32]	[17–57]	[4–20]		
PIP_3	158 ± 37	138 ± 103	26 ± 20	40 ± 20	13 ± 15	0 ± 0	0 ± 0
	[125–191]	[56–220]	[0–54]	[24–56]	[1–25]		
PS	95 ± 42	93 ± 79	30 ± 28	50 ± 38	18 ± 26	0 ± 0	0 ± 0
	[54–136]	[17–169]	[3–57]	[23–77]	[0–43]		

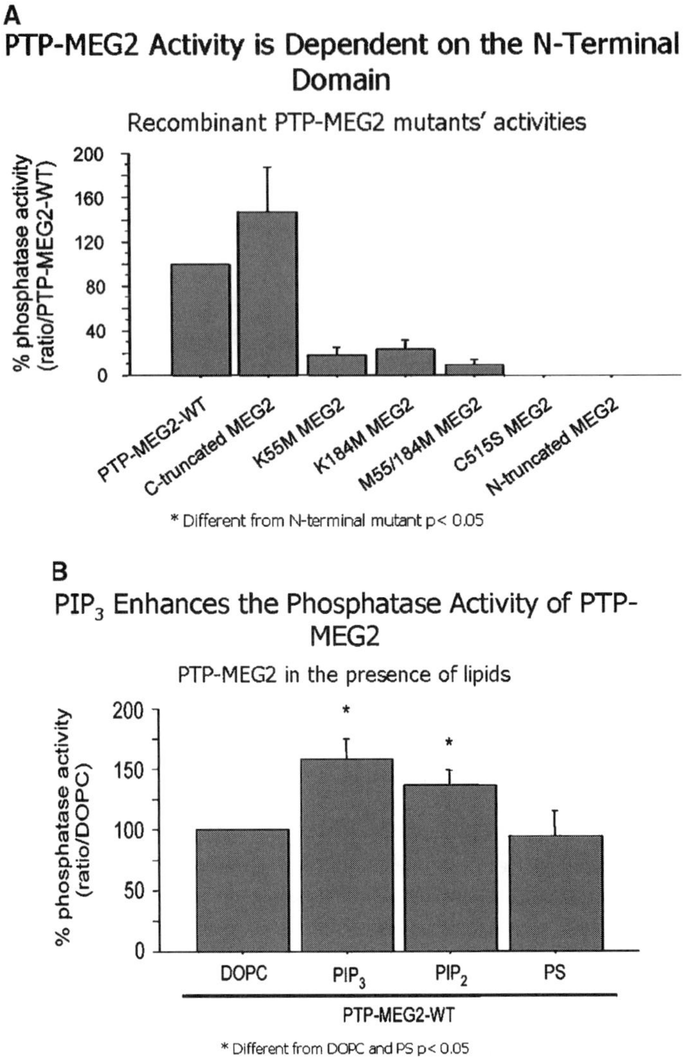

Fig. 3. The phosphatase activity of recombinant PTP-MEG2 is dependent on the integrity of its N-domain. (**A**) Recombinant proteins were mixed with liposomes containing only DOPC for 40 min. followed by addition of the substrate, *p*NPP substrate. Samples were incubated for 40 min at 37°C and absorbance was measured at 405 nm. The phosphatase activity is reported as percentage of PTP-MEG2-WT activity. Values represent the means ± SD and the 95% confidence interval of six experiments. In the presence of only DOPC, the C-terminal domain of MEG2 (i.e., N terminal truncated) has the highest phosphatase activity, compared to the full length PTP-MEG2-WT (100%). C515S MEG2 and N-terminal MEG2 possessed no phosphatase activity due to loss of a key cysteine residue and lack of the phosphatase domain, respectively. The lipid-binding mutants (K55M, K184M, and K55/184M) which retain their C-terminal catalytic domain had much lower phosphatase activity compared to PTP-MEG2-WT. These findings imply that the lysine-to-methionine point mutations of the N-terminal Sec14 homology domain affect the phosphatase activity of PTP-MEG2. This suggests an intact Sec14 domain may serve as a regulatory domain that controls the magnitude and extent of PTP-MEG2 activation, and it may be dependent upon its ability to associate with certain lipids in determining the tertiary structure of the molecule (reproduced from **ref.** *16*). (**B**) Phosphatase activity of recombinant PTP-MEG2 wild type is modulated by lipids. The recombinant protein was mixed with various test lipid-containing liposomes for 40 min at 37°C followed by addition of *p*NPP Samples were incubated for an additional 40 min at 37°C. Absorbance was measured at 405 nm. Phosphatase activities were reported as a percentage of PTP-MEG2-WT/DOPC activity. Values represent the means ± SD and the 95% confidence interval of six experiments. The asterisk (*) represents significant difference from PS, P 0.05. Mixed liposomes containing 5% PIP_3 enhanced the phosphatase activity of PTP-MEG2-WT, compared to DOPC alone (100%). PIP_2 also increased the phosphatase activity of PTP-MEG2, but the effect was of a smaller magnitude (reproduced from **ref.** *16*).

relative to PTP-MEG2-WT (PTP-MEG2 WT as 100%). The phosphatase activities of PTP-MEG2-WT in the presence of different test lipids are illustrated in **Fig. 3b**. These data suggest that the N-terminal domain exerts a negative regulatory influence on MEG2 catalytic activity because when it is deleted, the activity increases. However, the catalytic activity of the Sec14 domain point mutants is dramatically decreased compared to WT control. One possible explanation for these observations is that the mutations in these residues result in a conformational change in the molecule that prevents access of the substrate to the enzymatic site. The percent phosphatase activity is calculated relative to the value obtained from DOPC which was set at 100%.

3.6. Phagocytosis

1. Double transfections of HA-tagged PTP-MEG2-WT and GFP-AKT-PH into RAW macrophages are performed according to the procedures outlined in **Subheading 3.2.**
2. Proceed with the phagocytosis assay the following day.
3. Sediment 100 μL latex beads by brief centrifugation at 2,000 g in a microfuge.
4. Wash beads twice with 1 mL PBS. Carefully aspirate PBS to avoid loss of beads.
5. Coat beads with 1 mg/mL human IgG in PBS for 1 h at 37°C with slow rotation.
6. Centrifuge beads briefly and wash twice with 1 mL PBS. Keep on ice until use.
7. Following DNA transfection, wash cells once with 1 mL chilled PBS. Cool cells by placing culture plate on ice.
8. For each sample, add 1 mL human IgG-coated latex beads solution to cells (*see* **Note 20**).
9. Incubate the samples 20 min on ice. During this period, the beads will settle and bind to the cells. Phagocytosis of the beads by the cells is restrained by the low temperature. This enables the onset of the phagocytic process to be accurately timed and synchronized. Contact of the cells and beads can be hastened by brief centrifugation at 800 g for 1 min at 4°C.
10. Remove excess unbound beads by washing coverslips once with 1 mL cold PBS. Check and note the extent of bead binding to the cells. Aspirate all the PBS from wells.
11. Initiate phagocytosis by adding 1 mL prewarmed (37°C) complete DMEM to each sample. Incubate cells at 37°C for 5 min with 5% CO_2.
12. Wash cells twice with chilled PBS to terminate the process of phagocytosis. Samples are ready to be examined by immunofluorescence.

3.7. Confocal Immunofluorescence for Localization of PTP-MEG2 and Akt-PH During Phagocytosis

1. The procedures for immunofluorescence are outlined in **Subheading 3.3, steps 1–4**.
2. Dilute primary antibody in blocking buffer: rabbit anti-HA (1:500). 250 μL of primary antibody solution is added carefully and evenly to each sample. Incubate samples with antibody for 1 h at room temperature.
3. Remove primary antibody by two washes of PBS.
4. Secondary antibody is prepared with blocking buffer: donkey antirabbit Texas Red (1:500). Dispense 200–250 μL of secondary antibody solution in the same way as with primary antibody. Incubate samples for 1 h at room temperature.
5. Wash and mount coverslips onto microscope slides as described in **Subheading 3.3, steps 10–13**.
6. Fluorescent images are captured with a confocal microscope (ZEISS LSM510) or with a conventional fluorescence microscope (Leica DMRA2) equipped with a cooled CCD camera (QIImaging). Excitation at 484 nm induces the FITC (green emission: 515 nm) for GFP-AKT-PH domain, while excitation at 568 nm induces Texas Red (red emission) to detect HA-tagged PTP-MEG2. Fluorescent images can be overlaid using imaging software (OpenLab by Improvision or Adobe Photoshop). **Fig. 4a, b** are examples of the fluorescent images of GFP-AKT-PH and PTP-MEG2-HA. It is evident that during phagocytosis, these two molecules are recruited to the nascent phagosome enclosing the IgG-opsonized latex bead within. **Fig. 4c** represents a western blot of phagosome-associated proteins illustrating recruitment of the phagosomal protein LAMP1 along with PTP-MEG2 to the phagosome. Cytochrome C is a cytosolic protein included as a negative control.

Fig. 4 . (**A**) PTP-MEG2-WT colocalizes with Akt-PH domain in nascent phagosomes. RAW cells grown on glass coverslips were cotransfected with PTP-MEG2-WT and GFP-Akt-PH domains. Cells were fed human IgG-coated latex beads on ice for 20 min and rewarmed for 5 min to allow phagocytosis to proceed. Cells were then fixed and immunostained with the anti-HA antibody. PTP-MEG2-WT is shown in red and GFP-Akt-PH in green. Colocalization of PTP-MEG2 and Akt-PH domain appears in yellow (overlay). Images were acquired using a confocal microscope (reproduced from **ref.** *16*). (**B**) PTP-MEG2 is recruited at early times to the phagosome. RAW macrophages cultured on glass coverslips were transfected with PTP-MEG2-WT. Cells were incubated with human IgG-coated latex beads on ice for 20 min and rewarmed for 5 min to allow phagocytosis to proceed. Cells were then fixed for immunofluorescence with anti-HA antibody. The external part of the beads was labeled in red with TRITC conjugated anti-IgG antibody prior to permeabilization. PTP-MEG2-WT appears in green. Images were captured using a confocal microscope as described in the methods (reproduced from ref. *16*)(**C**) PTP-MEG2 is recruited to the nascent phagosome. RAW macrophages grown on 60 × 15 mm tissue culture plates were fed with IgG-coated magnetic beads (3 μm) for incubation times ranging from 0 min to 2 h. Following phagocytosis, phagosomes were isolated by MACS and separated by SDS–PAGE. Western analysis of phagosome-associated proteins showed maximal accumulation of MEG2 1 h after phagocytosis was initiated. Treatment of RAW macrophages with phagocytosis inhibitors wortmannin or latrunculin B as well as LAMP1 and cytochrome C immunoblotting confirmed the efficiency and specificity of the phagosome isolation technique (reproduced from **ref.** *16*).

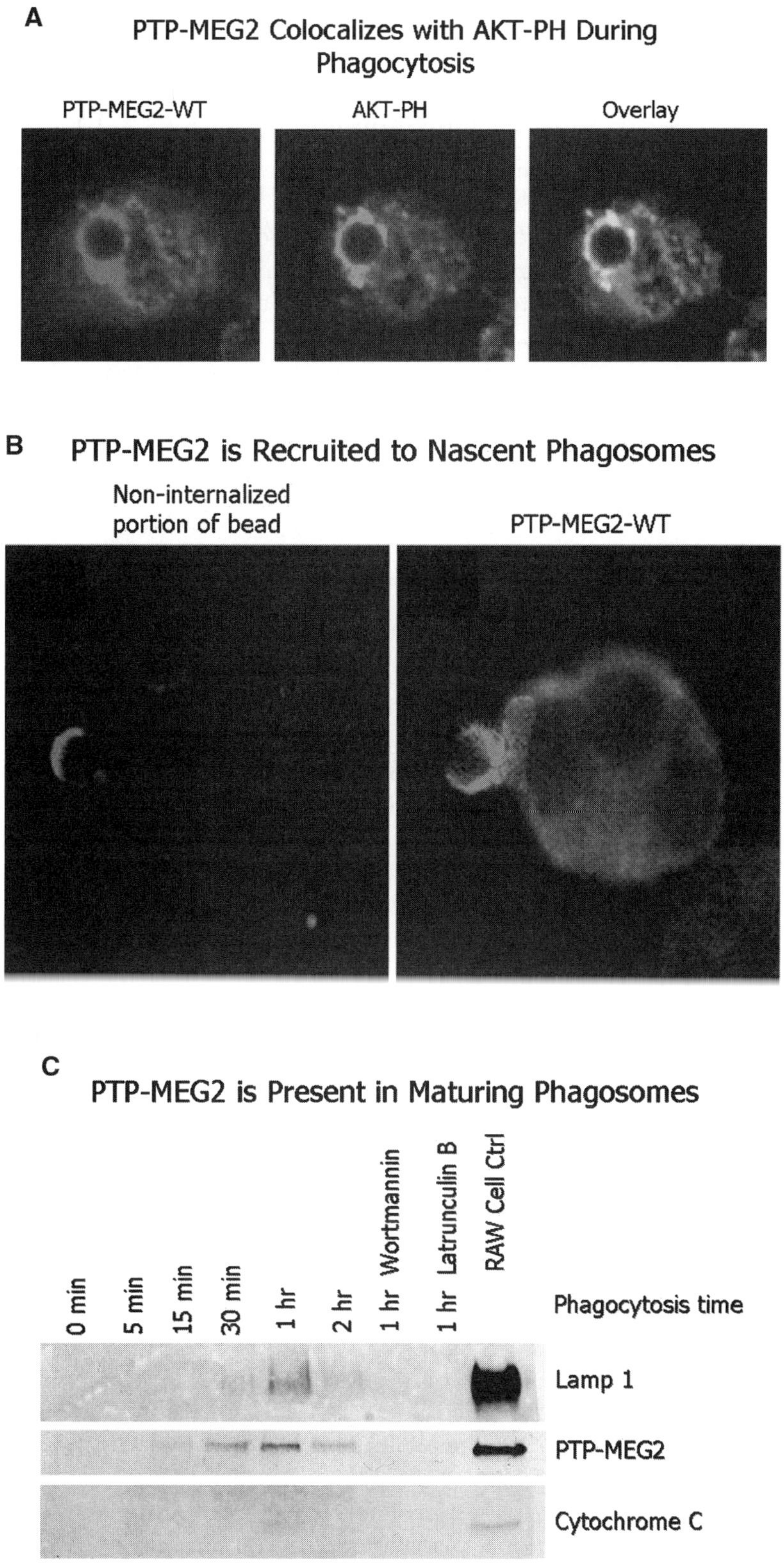
A
PTP-MEG2 Colocalizes with AKT-PH During Phagocytosis
PTP-MEG2-WT
AKT-PH
Overlay
B
PTP-MEG2 is Recruited to Nascent Phagosomes
Non-internalized portion of bead
PTP-MEG2-WT
C
PTP-MEG2 is Present in Maturing Phagosomes
0 min
5 min
15 min
30 min
1 hr
2 hr
1 hr Wortmannin
1 hr Latrunculin B
RAW Cell Ctrl
Phagocytosis time
Lamp 1
PTP-MEG2
Cytochrome C

3.8. Confocal Immunofluorescence of PTP-MEG2 at Nascent Phagosome

1. Transfection of RAW cells with HA-tagged PTP-MEG2-WT is same as before (*see* **Subheading 3.2**).
2. Next day post-transfection, proceed with phagocytosis assay as outlined in **Subheading 3.3, steps 3–12**.
3. Continue on to the immunofluorescence procedures in **steps 1–4, Subheading 3.3.** In addition, prior to permeabilization, stain the noningested portion of the bead first with TRITC-conjugated goat-antihuman IgG (1:500) to delineate the noninternalized portion of the prey.
4. Prepare primary antibody in blocking buffer: rabbit anti-HA (1:500). 250 μL of primary antibody solution is added to each sample. Incubate samples with antibody at room temperature for 1 h. Wash samples twice with PBS to remove primary antibody afterward.
5. Dilute secondary antibody in blocking buffer: donkey anti-rabbit FITC (1:500). Dispense 200–250 μL of secondary antibody solution in the same way as for primary antibody. Incubate samples for 1 h at room temperature.
6. Proceed to washing and mounting coverslips onto microscope slides as described in **Subheading 3.3, steps 10–13**.
7. Fluorescent images are captured and overlaid as earlier (*see* **Subheading 3.3**, **step 14** and **Subheading 3.7**, **step 6**). Excitation at 484 nm induces the FITC for HA-tagged PTP-MEG2-WT, and excitation at 568 nm induces Texas Red to detect the noninternalized portion of the latex bead that is opsonized with human IgG. Examples of the fluorescent images demonstrating the recruitment and enrichment of PTP-MEG2 to the nascent phagosome are illustrated in **Fig. 4A, B**.

3.9. Phagosome Isolation

1. To determine the recruitment of various proteins to the nascent phagosome, the duration of phagocytosis can be set at different time points: 0, 5, 15, 30, 60, and 120 min. For negative control purposes, cells are pretreated for 1 h at 37°C 5% CO_2 with either 1 μM latrunculin B or 100 nm wortmannin (pharmacological agents that prevent phagocytosis from proceeding). Always collect a sample of total cell lysate for analysis by SDS–PAGE and Western blotting to confirm the Mr of the particular protein to be studied.
2. Plate RAW267.4 macrophages (phagocytes) in a total volume of 4 mL of complete DMEM on each of nine 60 × 15 mm cell culture plates. Culture cells at 37°C with 5% CO_2 until near confluence. Each plate is used for one time point for phagocytosis or control condition. For control purposes, prepare an additional plate under the same conditions for collection of total cell lysates.

3. Coat 1 mL of the 3-μm magnetic beads (i.e., phagocytic prey) with 50 μg/mL human IgG for 30 min rotating at 37°C (in PBS/HBSS). After incubation, wash the beads twice with PBS. Resuspend beads to a total volume of 1 mL. Sonicate beads for 10 s with a probe sonicator to minimize clumping.
4. Aspirate the culture medium from the macrophages and dispense 4 mL of HBSS++ buffer for each plate. The phagocytic assay will be conducted in HBSS++ buffer.
5. Add 100 μL of the human IgG-coated beads to each sample of macrophages. Swirl gently to distribute beads evenly.
6. Incubate cells on ice for 20 min. Beads will sediment and bind to the cells without being ingested because the low temperature inhibits phagocytosis. In this manner, the duration of phagocytosis can be accurately timed and synchronized among all the samples (*see* **Note 20**).
7. After incubation on ice, place the dishes in a 37-C incubator with 5% CO_2 to initiate phagocytosis. Allow phagocytosis to proceed for different time periods (from 0 min to 2 h). Incubate cells with beads for 1 h with latrunculin B or wortmannin as negative controls.
8. Following phagocytosis, place the samples immediately on ice to stop phagocytosis. Wash cells three times with cold PBS to remove unbound beads.
9. Dissolve one tablet of protease inhibitor cocktail tablet in 10 mL of chilled CSKB buffer. Mix thoroughly before dispensing. Place CSKB buffer on ice.
10. Collect cells using a cell scraper from each dish in 1 mL CSKB containing protease inhibitors. Put samples into labeled tubes on ice.
11. With samples submerged in ice, disrupt the cells using a Potter homogenizer (20 strokes) and sonicator (10 s). Phagosomes containing internalized magnetic beads are released during this process and can be retrieved.
12. Place the tubes into the prechilled Capture-Tec™ stand for the magnetic isolation of the phagosomes containing the magnetic beads. The magnetic beads will be sedimented by the magnet.
13. With the tubes remaining in the stand, carefully aspirate the excess CSKB buffer without disturbing the magnetic beads. Wash the beads 2–3 more times with 1 mL CSKB. Sediment the beads using the magnetic stand and aspirate the CSKB.
14. To each sample of phagosomes containing magnetic beads, add 30–100 μL of 10× Laemmli sample buffer to elute the phagosomal proteins from the beads. The amount of Laemmli

sample buffer to be used depends primarily on the amount of phagosomal components retrieved (i.e., internalized beads) (*see* **Note 21**).

15. For control purposes, lyse the macrophages in the additional plate prepared in 1 ml SDS lysis buffer using a cell scraper (*see* **Subheading 3.9, step 2,** and **Note 22**). Collect total cell lysates in a labeled tube and add in 100 μL 10× Laemmli sample buffer.
16. Close tubes tightly and secure lids with plastic guards. Boil samples for 10 min; then vortex briefly and centrifuge at 2,000 g for 30 s in a microfuge to sediment the magnetic beads.
17. Samples are ready for separation by SDS–PAGE once they cool to room temperature. Avoid loading of the magnetic beads.
18. Store the leftover phagosome lysates at –20°C for further analyses. Boil, vortex, and centrifuge before use.

3.10. SDS–Polyacrylamide Gel Electrophoresis (SDS–PAGE)

1. The following directions are for the use of Bio-Rad Mini-Protean 3 Cell System. The system consists of a gel casting stand and glass plates with built-in spacers to eliminate leaking during hand casting.
2. The spacer plate is the taller glass plate with gel spacers permanently set. Various thicknesses of the spacer plates and combs are available: 1.5-mm thick spacer plates and a 15-well comb are used in this SDS–PAGE protocol.
3. Before use, wash spacer plate, short plate, and comb with detergent and rinse extensively with distilled water. Dry with Kim-Wipe and remove residual moisture with 70% ethanol.
4. Align spacer and short plates, with short plate facing front. Slide them into the casting frame. Make certain that both plates are perpendicular to the level surface to avoid leaking. Lock the pressure cams to secure the glass plates in place. This forms the gel cassette assembly.
5. Engage the spring-loaded lever and place cassette assembly on the gray casting stand. The lever pushes the spacer plate down against the gray rubber gaskets.
6. Prepare a 10% separating gel by mixing together 3.3 mL 30% acrylamide, 2.5 mL 1.5 M Tris–HCl of pH 8.8, 4.1 mL of water, 100 μL 10% SDS solution, 5 μL TEMED, and 50 μL 10% ammonium persulfate solution.
7. With a transfer pipette, transfer the solution into the space between the spacer and short plates, leaving about 2 cm of space for the stacking gel. Overlay with water-saturated isobutanol to prevent evaporation and bubble formation. The separating gel should polymerize in about 30 min (*see* **Note 23**).

8. Pour off isobutanol and rinse the top of the gel with water until there is no residual odor of isobutanol.
9. Prepare 4% stacking gel by mixing together 1.3 mL 30% acrylamide, 2.5 mL 0.5 M Tris–HCl of pH 6.8, 6.1 mL of water, 100 μL 10% SDS solution, 20 μL TEMED, and 100 μL 10% ammonium persulfate solution.
10. Pour the 4% gel on top of the polymerized separating gel. Avoid bubbles. Insert the comb in between the two glass plates. The stacking gel should polymerize within 10 min. When the stacking gel is set, remove the gel cassette sandwich from the casting frame (*see* **Notes 24** and **25**).
11. Place the gel cassette sandwich into the slot at the bottom of each side of the electrode assembly with short plate facing inward toward the notches of the U-shaped gaskets. If only one gel is to be run, use the one-piece molded buffer dam for the other side of the electrode assembly. The electrode assembly houses the sealing gasket, upper and lower electrodes, and the connecting banana plugs.
12. Slide the gel cassette sandwiches and electrode assembly into the clamping frame. Press down the electrode assembly while closing the two cam levers of the clamping frame. This holds the gel cassette sandwiches and electrode assembly in place and insures a proper seal of the Short Plate against the notch on the U-shape gasket. This forms the inner buffer chamber.
13. Lower the inner chamber into the mini tank.
14. Prepare 1× running buffer from 10× stock with water. Remove comb from gel cassette sandwiches and carefully pour approximately 125 mL 1× running buffer into the inner chamber. Excess buffer will cause siphoning of buffer into the lower chamber which can result in buffer loss and interruption of electrophoresis.
15. Add approximately 200 mL of 1× running buffer to mini tank (lower buffer chamber).
16. With a gel-loading tip, wash wells with running buffer.
17. Load 20 μL of each sample in a well. Load samples slowly to allow them to settle evenly on the bottom of the well. Be careful not to puncture the well bottom with pipette tip. Reserve one well for prestained molecular weight markers.
18. Place the lid on the mini tank. Make sure color-coded banana plugs and jacks are correctly oriented and insert properly into the power supply. The anode is red and the cathode is black.
19. The gel is first run at 75 V for 15 min or until dye front is through the stacking gel, and the voltage is then increased to 150 V through the separating gel. Depending on the Mr of the proteins of interest, the dye front can be run off the

gel to maximize protein separation to study large molecular weight proteins. Alternatively, the electrophoresis can be stopped early to enable detection of low molecular weight proteins.

3.11. Western Blotting for Phagosomal Proteins

1. The samples separated by SDS–PAGE are transferred to nitrocellulose membranes electrophoretically. These instructions are for the use of the Mini Trans-Blot Electrophoretic Transfer Cell from Bio-Rad.
2. To avoid membrane contamination with human skin proteins, always handle nitrocellulose membrane with forceps or wear gloves.
3. Label the membrane with a permanent marker to identify the gel and orientation. In separate trays, soak the membrane, six precut pieces of Whatman blotting paper and two fiber pads in cold 1× transfer buffer for 30 min before use. Complete wetting of all these components is important for proper binding. Insufficient wetting can cause entrapment of air bubbles in the matrix and block transfer of protein molecules.
4. Following electrophoresis, remove gel carefully from spacer and short plates. Cut away the stacking gel with a sharp spatula. Rinse gel in 1× transfer buffer prior to blotting to remove running buffer salts and detergents. If salts are not removed, they will increase the conductivity of the transfer buffer and the heat generated during the transfer.
5. Slide and lift the latch to open gel holder cassette. One panel of the cassette is clear and the other is gray. The clear panel is the anode (+) and the gray is the cathode (−). For the electrode module, the cathode is the black electrode panel and the anode is the red panel located in the center of the buffer tank. Insert the gel cassette such that the gray plastic faces the black plastic of the cathode electrode.
6. Lay the gray panel side of the cassette flat down on a surface. Place a presoaked fiber pad on top of the gray panel. All components should be centered such that they do not extend past the edge of the cassette. Otherwise, they will catch on the guide rails and distort the blot-gel contact and transfer pattern.
7. Place three pieces of soaked blotting paper on top of fiber pad and then the rinsed gel on top. Make sure the gel is aligned at the center of the cassette and make certain that there are no air bubbles trapped between the gel and the blotting papers.
8. Hold membrane at opposite ends, allow center portion to contact gel first, and gradually lower the ends. Place another three pieces of soaked blotting paper on top of the membrane.

9. With a plastic pipette or test tube, roll over gel and membrane sandwich with steady pressure to exclude all bubbles and ensure good gel and membrane contact. Finish the assembly by placing another piece of saturated fiber pad on top of the blotting paper.
10. Close the cassette by holding it firmly and secure the latch. Place it into the buffer tank so that the gray panel of the holder is facing the black cathode electrode panel. This orientation is crucial; otherwise, the proteins will be lost from the gel into the blotting paper rather than transferred to the membrane.
11. Place a magnetic stir bar at the bottom of the tank. Place in Bio-Ice cooling unit. Fill the tank with 1× transfer buffer just above the level of the gel holder cassette. Set tank on top of magnetic stirrer and secure the lid in place (*see* **Note 26**).
12. Ensure that the electrode wires on the lid are attached to the appropriate pins of the electrode module (i.e., black wire to cathode and red wire to anode). Connect transfer unit to power supply. Turn on power supply and magnetic stirrer to initiate transfer and circulating bath.
13. The transfer is usually run at 100 V for 2 h. To maintain the temperature of the transfer buffer around 10–15°C, the Bio-Ice cooling unit should be changed every 30 min to avoid overheating and protein degradation.
14. When the transfer is complete, carefully take out gel holder cassette and disassemble the gel-blot sandwich. Remove the first layer of fiber pad and blotting papers. Slowly peel the membrane off the gel and rinse it briefly with water. The membrane should be kept moist at all times.
15. Decant water and stain the membrane with diluted Ponceau S solution for 2–3 min on rocking platform at room temperature. Ponceau S solution stains the protein bands transferred from gel to membrane red. Decant the Ponceau S solution and wash the membrane with 1× TBS-T until bands are visible. The transfer pattern and quantification of proteins can be quickly noted and, if necessary, an image captured. Excess membrane can be trimmed away at this time.
16. Reverse Ponceau S stain with several TBS-T washes on rocking platform. When all the dye is removed, block the membrane with 10–15 mL of blocking buffer for 1 h at room temperature on a rocking platform (*see* **Note 27**).
17. Discard the blocking buffer and quickly rinse the membrane once with TBS-T prior to addition of 1:2,000 dilution of rabbit anti-PTP-MEG2 antibody. Incubate the membrane with antibody overnight at 4°C on rocking platform.

18. Remove the primary antibody and wash the membrane three times for 15 min with TBS-T (*see* **Note 28**).
19. Prepare secondary antibody fresh for every experiment at the recommended (e.g., 1:10,000-fold) dilution in blocking buffer. Add to membrane for 40 min at room temperature on a rocking platform. Prolonged incubation with the secondary antibody will result in a high background.
20. Pour off the secondary antibody solution and wash the membrane three times for 20 min with TBS-T. Incubate the blot with premixed ECL solution on shaker for 1 min. Line the X-ray film cassette in advance with an acetate sheet protector. Place the blot between the leaves of the acetate sheet. In a darkroom, expose the film for a suitable amount of time, usually ranging from 30 s to 2 min. **Fig. 4C** is an example demonstrating the increased presence of PTP-MEG2 as phagosomes mature.

3.12. Stripping and Reprobing

1. When a suitable exposure for the first protein to be detected is obtained, the membrane is ready to be stripped to remove the first antibody and can then be reprobed with another antibody that recognizes another protein of interest. For example, PTP-MEG2 can be visualized first and after stripping; other proteins such as lysosome-associated-protein 1 (LAMP1; a phagosomal protein)) or cytochrome C (a cytosolic protein) can be visualized **(Fig. 4C)**.
2. Prior to stripping, wash membrane with TBS-T for 10 min to remove the ECL solution.
3. In a container with a lid, add to the blot 10 mL of stripping buffer with mercaptoethanol. Close the lid tightly and incubate blot in a 50°C water bath for 30 min with agitation.
4. When blot is stripped, wash it three times with a large volume of TBS-T; each wash is for 15 min. Block blot again in blocking buffer.
5. Reprobe the blot with mouse anti-LAMP1 (1:1,000 in TBS-T/5% BSA) with washes, antimouse secondary antibody, and ECL detection as discussed earlier. Lysosome-associated-membrane-protein 1, LAMP-1, is a well-established marker that is recruited to phagosomes as they fuse with the lysosomes during the maturation process. This provides them with the degradative properties required to destroy ingested materials *(24)*. The purpose of LAMP-1 immunoblotting is to demonstrate the specificity of the phagosome isolation, to show kinetics of phagosome maturation, and to validate the isolation techniques. An example of the result produced is shown in **(Fig. 4C)**.

6. Repeat stripping and reprobing steps for detection of cytochrome C (1:500 in TBS-T/5% BSA). Cytochrome C immunoblotting serves as a negative control marker as it is found exclusively in the mitochondria of healthy cells *(25)*. Therefore, no detection of cytochrome C is expected from the samples containing only the purified phagosomal isolates (**Fig. 4c**).
7. If needed for further analyses, freeze blot at −20°C.
8. Primary antibody is removed from the blot during the stripping procedure; however, some target proteins are dislodged from the blot as well. Hence, avoid excessive stripping of the blot and consider running identical samples in two gels so that two blots can be utilized simultaneously.

4. Notes

1. Medium prepared with all these components is referred as the "complete DMEM" or "complete medium."
2. Unless stated otherwise, all solutions should be prepared using Milli Q water that has a resistivity of 18.2 MΩ-cm and total organic content of less than five parts per billion. It is by this standard that "water" is referred to in this text.
3. Dithiothreitol (DTT) is widely used for disruption of protein disulfide bonds in SDS–PAGE. It is not stable in solution. Make 1 M DTT solution and immediately freeze 500 μL aliquots at −20°C. Thaw and add appropriate amount of DTT to [illegible] lysis [illegible] just [illegible]
4. Plasmid DNA is usually diluted in water or TE buffer. When the dilution is done with cell growth medium, ensure that the medium does not contain any serum, proteins, or antibiotics. Serum and antibiotics present will interfere with complex formation and will significantly decrease transfection efficiency.
5. For every new plasmid and/or new cell line used, the amount of plasmid DNA needed for transfection should be adjusted to optimize transfection efficiency and protein expression levels. Some factors to consider are the transfection reagent/ DNA ratio, cell density, growth phase, and optimal time to measurement of reporter gene activity.
6. Save aliquots of sterile serum-free culture medium when preparing for the complete medium. It is useful for transfection.
7. Store unused 4 or 16% paraformaldehyde solution at 4°C in a shaded container (no longer than 1 week). To avoid oxidation, displace oxygen in the container with nitrogen or argon gas.

8. Fine powder of SDS is irritating to eyes, respiratory system, and skin. Wear suitable protective clothing when handling SDS and measure in a hood.
9. Do not put SDS on ice; it will precipitate.
10. Buy small bottle of TEMED as it may degrade after opening and as a result it will take longer for gels to polymerize.
11. Add APS last when making gels as it will cause gels to polymerize rapidly.
12. We have found that the PageRuler Prestained Protein Ladder transfers completely from gel to nitrocellulose membrane. It contains two orange reference bands so that proper orientation can be easily identified.
13. Ponceau S solution is a light-sensitive reagent. Stock and diluted Ponceau S solution should be store in shaded containers. Ponceau S solution can stain protein bands on nitrocellulose membrane. Its red color makes it easy to quantify protein loading and transfer efficiency. Staining is reversible by washing the nitrocellulose membrane in TBS-T. Proceed to the blocking step once the red stain is removed.
14. Mercaptoethanol gives off an extremely unpleasant odor (rotten eggs). When membranes need to be stripped, mix and dispense stripping buffer in a well-ventilated hood and use containers with tight-fitting lids.
15. In contrast to many liposomal transfection reagents, the presence of serum and antibiotics during transfection with SuperFect Reagent enhances transfection efficiency. Use complete medium with serum that the cells have adapted in normal culture condition during incubations with transfection complexes afterward to optimize expression of the transgene. However, it is not recommended to use serum during complex formation between SuperFect Reagent and plasmid DNA because it inhibits complex formation.
16. If the plasmid DNA is conjugated with a fluorescent reporter, the samples can be viewed under the fluorescent microscope with the appropriate filter to ascertain expression of the introduced gene and percentage of cells transfected.
17. If proteins expressed are fluorescently labeled, cover sample with aluminum foil to prevent unnecessary bleaching of the signal.
18. Before primary antibody incubation, use a Pasteur glass pipette to aspirate all PBS, especially around the rim of the coverslips. This prevents spilling of the antibody when it is added on top of the coverslips. By this method, less antibody is used for economy. If the antibody is very scarce, consider chamber slides. Avoid touching or scratching the surface of the coverslips.

19. To minimize bubbles, first tilt the coverslip at an angle and carefully lay it down onto microscope slide. Avoid using excess mounting medium.
20. Usually excess phagocytic prey is added to the phagocytes. The usual ratio of prey to phagocyte ranges between 5:1 and 20:1.
21. Adjust the volume of 10× Laemmli sample buffer for the samples accordingly. Determine the amount needed for gel loading and always prepare extra for future analyses. Do not overdilute the samples.
22. The cell lysate will be very viscous at this stage because of the release of DNA. It is very hard to pipette. Cut pipette tips to increase the size of the opening; autoclave pipette tips before use to collect lysate. The viscosity of cell lysates will reduce during boiling due to the destruction of DNA.
23. Keep leftover gel mixture and use it as an indicator of gel polymerization. Do not disturb cast gel. It will distort the boundary between stacking and separating gels and affect running pattern.
24. Be careful with splashing of unpolymerized gel mix, especially during the insertion of the comb. Wear protective gloves, lab coat, and goggles. Ensure comb thickness corresponds to thickness of the Spacer Plate. Stacking gel polymerizes much faster than separating gel.
25. It is best to prepare the gel 1 day prior to use for SDS–PAGE. Remove Gel Cassette Sandwich from Casting Frame. Wrap it with a moist paper towel and plastic wrap. Store the gel with combs at 4°C. This makes the gel compact and firm such that it can be handled without tearing or fracturing.
26. Transfer buffer at 1× working concentration can be reused for up to five transfers as long as constant voltage is maintained for each run (the current will increase each time). To prevent heat-induced damage to the apparatus and the experimental samples, ensure that the buffer is cooled by using a refrigerated/circulating bath with ice.
27. Ensure 5% milk solution is not spoiled before use for blocking.
28. Primary antibody in 5% BSA solution may be saved for other experiments and can be frozen at –20°C for long-term storage. Thaw antibody in a 37°C water bath. This is especially useful when primary antibody is scarce. Antibodies will be depleted over many usages, so the length of exposure and type of film (normal vs. sensitive) may need to be adjusted.

Acknowledgments

We would like to acknowledge the advice and technical expertise of Drs. Vera Cherepanov and Hong Ouyang. This work was funded by an operating grant from the Canadian Institutes of Health Research to GD. VK was supported by a research fellowship from the CIHR training program in Regenerative Medicine.

References

1. Aderem, A. and D.M. Underhill. (1999). *Mechanisms of phagocytosis in macrophages. Annu Rev Immunol.* 17: 593–623
2. Greenberg, S. (2001). *Diversity in phagocytic signalling. J Cell Sci.* 114(Pt 6): 1039–1040
3. May, R.C. (2001). *Phagocytosis in C. elegans: CED-1 reveals its secrets. Trends Cell Biol.* 11(4): 150
4. May, R.C. and L.M. (2001). Machesky, *Phagocytosis and the actin cytoskeleton. J Cell Sci.* 114(Pt 6): 1061–1077
5. Gaudry, M., et al. (1992). *Evidence for the involvement of tyrosine kinases in the locomotory responses of human neutrophils. J Leukoc Biol.* 51(2): 103–108
6. Grinstein, S. and W. Furuya. (1991). *Tyrosine phosphorylation and oxygen consumption induced by G proteins in neutrophils. Am J Physiol.* 260(5 Pt 1): C1019–C1027
7. Hunter, T. (1995). *Protein kinases and phosphatases: the yin and yang of protein phosphorylation and signaling. Cell.* 80(2): 225–236
8. Kruger, J., et al. (2000). *Deficiency of Src homology 2-containing phosphatase 1 results in abnormalities in murine neutrophil function: studies in motheaten mice. J Immunol.* 165(10): 5847–5859
9. Tonks, N.K. and B.G. (1996). Neel, *From form to function: signaling by protein tyrosine phosphatases. Cell.* 87(3): 365–368
10. Gu, M., I. Warshawsky, and P.W. Majerus. (1992). *Cloning and expression of a cytosolic megakaryocyte protein-tyrosine-phosphatase with sequence homology to retinaldehyde-binding protein and yeast SEC14p. Proc Natl Acad Sci U S A.* 89(7): 2980–2984
11. Huynh, H., et al. (2003). *Homotypic secretory vesicle fusion induced by the protein tyrosine phosphatase MEG2 depends on polyphosphoinositides in T cells. J Immunol.* 171(12): 6661–6671
12. Kruger, J.M., et al. (2002). *Protein-tyrosine phosphatase MEG2 is expressed by human neutrophils. Localization to the phagosome and activation by polyphosphoinositides. J Biol Chem.* 277(4): 2620–2628
13. Botelho, R.J., et al. (2000). *Localized biphasic changes in phosphatidylinositol-4,5-bisphosphate at sites of phagocytosis. J Cell Biol.* 151(7): 1353–1368
14. Sechi, A.S. and J. Wehland. (2000). *The actin cytoskeleton and plasma membrane connection: PtdIns(4,5)P(2) influences cytoskeletal protein activity at the plasma membrane. J Cell Sci.* 113 Pt 21: 3685–3695
15. Vieira, O.V., et al. (2001). *Distinct roles of class I and class III phosphatidylinositol 3-kinases in phagosome formation and maturation. J Cell Biol.* 155(1): 19–25
16. Vachon, E., Kwok, V., et al. *Protein-tyrosine-phosphatase-MEG2 regulation by phosphatidylinositol-3,4,5-trisphosphate and recruitment to nascent phagosomes* (unpublished data)
17. Gerdes, H.H. and C. Kaether. (1996). *Green fluorescent protein: applications in cell biology. FEBS Lett.* 389(1): 44–47
18. Pelham, H.R. (1996). *The dynamic organisation of the secretory pathway. Cell Struct Funct.* 21(5): 413–419
19. Montalibet, J., K.I. Skorey, and B.P. Kennedy. (2005). *Protein tyrosine phosphatase: enzymatic assays. Methods.* 35(1): 2–8
20. Shirai, T., et al. (1998). *Specific detection of phosphatidylinositol 3,4,5-trisphosphate binding proteins by the PIP3 analogue beads: an application for rapid purification of the PIP3 binding proteins. Biochim Biophys Acta.* 1402(3): 292–302
21. Vachon, E., et al. (2006). *CD44 is a phagocytic receptor. Blood.* 107(10): 4149–4158
22. Lutz, D.A., X.M. Chen, and B.J. McLaughlin. (1993). *Isolation of the phagocytic compartment from macrophages using a paramagnetic, particulate ligand. Anal Biochem.* 214(1): 205–211
23. Saito, K., L. Tautz, and T. Mustelin. (2007). *The lipid-binding SEC14 domain. Biochim Biophys Acta.* 1771(6): 719–726
24. Huynh, K.K., et al. (2007). *LAMP proteins are required for fusion of lysosomes with phagosomes. EMBO J.* 26(2): 313–324
25. Garrido, C., et al. (2006). *Mechanisms of cytochrome c release from mitochondria. Cell Death Differ.* 13(9): 1423–1433

Chapter 20

Large-Scale Phagosome Preparation

Adrien F. Vinet and Albert Descoteaux

Summary

Phagocytosis is the process by which cells engulf and destroy large particles such as pathogens or apoptotic cells. In this way, macrophages play a pivotal role in the resolution of microbial infections. However, many microorganisms have evolved efficient strategies to preempt the weaponry of macrophages. A better understanding of the components engaged in the phagosome formation and maturation is necessary to devise novel approaches aimed at counteracting these microbial strategies. Recently, large-scale approaches have been used to improve our understanding of phagosome functional properties by the identification of hundreds of proteins and by studying each of them.

Presently, purification of pathogen-containing phagosomes presents several technical challenges, whereas the use of latex beads to isolate phagosomes presents many advantages because this system can mimic host–pathogen interactions during phagocytosis. This system thus remains the best approach to advance our knowledge of phagosome biology, notably when used in conjunction with functional approaches. In this chapter, we outline an approach for the isolation of large-scale phagosome preparations with high degrees of purity.

Key words: Phagosome, Phagocytosis, Proteome, Isolation.

1. Introduction

Phagocytosis by specialized cells is an efficient process for the uptake and degradation of particles larger than 0.5 μm. Newly formed phagosomes, whose membranes originate from the plasma membrane and from internal vesicles *(1–3)*, undergo compositional modifications through a maturation process. Acquisition of microbicidal properties by maturing phagosomes requires highly regulated sequential interactions with endosomes and lysosomes, allowing for the recruitment of molecules conferring new functions to these maturing phagosomes *(4, 5)*. Despite recent major

Neil E. Reiner (ed.), *Macrophages and Dendritic Cells,* Methods in Molecular Biology, vol. 531

DOI: 10.1007/978-1-59745-396-7_20

advances in the identification of phagosomal proteins, many remain to be identified and their roles remain largely unknown.

To study recruitment kinetics to phagosomes of specific effectors, a method for isolation of phagosomes was needed. A method introduced by Wetzel and Korn *(6)* and "re-discovered" by Desjardins and colleagues allowed new advances in phagosome biology. Thus latex-bead-containing phagosomes can be isolated by taking advantage of the low density of the beads, thereby permitting subsequent immunochemistry or biochemical assays. These phagosome preparations, which are devoid of major contaminants from other organelles *(7, 8)*, possess several of the functional properties required to generate a microbicidal phagolysosome *(8, 9)*, as they mature into phagolysosomes *(10)* and display degradative molecules such as hydrolases *(11)*, reflecting the high level of complexity of the cellular processes involved in phagolysosome biogenesis *(7, 8)*.

Using this approach, we previously showed that PKC-α plays a role during phagosome maturation by regulating the acquisition of molecules associated with microbicidal properties *(12)*. Phagosome preparations can be used to identify new proteins not previously known to be associated with these organelles and to demonstrate their role in regulating phagosome biology *(12, 13)*. Multiprotein complexes can also be isolated by immunoprecipitation and analyzed subsequently by 2D-gel electrophoresis. Ultimately, data obtained with these approaches need to be validated by current immunochemical or biochemical methods such as western blot or confocal immunofluorescence. In this chapter, we describe methods for the large-scale isolation of phagosome preparations with high degrees of purity.

2. Materials

2.1. Cell Culture

1. Dulbecco's modified Eagle's medium with glutamine (DMEM).
2. DMEM is supplemented with 10% heat-inactivated (56°C, 30 min) fetal bovine serum.
3. 1% Streptamycin/penicillin from Invitrogen and 10% 10 mM HEPES, pH 7.3, from Bioshop are added.
4. Cells are grown in 100 × 15 mm dishes in a 37-°C incubator with 5% CO_2.

2.2. Phagosome Isolation and Immunoprecipitation

1. Deionized, distilled water should be used throughout these protocols (ddH_2O).
2. Tissue culture dishes of 150 × 20 mm.

3. Latex beads: 0.8 μm diameter, 10% suspension, blue dyed.
4. Protease Inhibitor Cocktail Tablets. Prepare a 25× solution by dissolving one tablet in 2 mL ddH_2O. Store at –20°C.
5. Sucrose solutions: 8.55%, 10%, 25%, 35%, and 62% (w/v), add Imidazol to each solution at a final concentration of 3 mM and 1× protease inhibitor solution. Solutions can be heated to dissolve sucrose crystals. Adjust pH to 7.4 and filter on Millipor 0.45 μm (except the 62% sucrose solution). Store at 4°C.
6. 1% NP-40 lysis buffer: 150 mM NaCl, 20 mM Tris–HCl, EDTA 10 mM, 1% (v/v) NP-40 and without protease and phosphatase inhibitors. Complete with ddH_2O and adjust pH to 7.5.
7. 1% NP-40 lysis buffer containing protease and phosphatase inhibitors: NP-40 lysis buffer with the same composition as in **item 6** but with the addition of 50 mM NaF, 10 mM $Na_4P_2O_7$, 1 mM Na_3VO_4, 1.5 mM EGTA, and 1× protease inhibitor.
8. 0.1% NP-40 lysis buffer without protease and phosphatase inhibitors: Tris–HCl, EDTA 10 mM, 0.1% (v/v) NP-40. Complete with ddH_2O and adjust pH to 7.5.
9. Immobilized Protein A IPA300.

2.3. SDS–Polyacrylamide Gel Electrophoresis (SDS–PAGE)

1. 30.8% acrylamide/bis solution: 30% (w/v) acrylamide, 0.8% (w/v) bisacrylamide, adjust with ddH_2O. Store at 4°C.
2. 10% (w/v) SDS in ddH_2O.
3. Separating gel solution (4×): Tris–HCl 1.5 M, pH 8.8, 0.4% SDS. Complete with ddH_2O. Store at room temperature.
4. Stacking buffer (4×): 0.5 Tris–HCl M, pH 6.8, 0.4% SDS. Complete with ddH_2O. Store at room temperature.
5. Ammonium persulfate: prepare 10% (w/v) solution in ddH_2O aliquot, and freeze at –20°C. APS can be stored at 4°C several weeks.
6. N,N,N,N′-Tetramethyl-ethylenediamine (TEMED).
7. Running buffer (5×): 1.5% (w/v) Tris base, 7.2% (w/v) glycine, 0.5% SDS. Complete with ddH_2O. Store at room temperature.
8. 2× SDS-loading buffer: 60 mM Tris–HCl, pH 7.5, 2 mM EDTA, 0.2 M DTT, 20% glycerol (v/v), 2% SDS (v/v from a 10% SDS stock w/v in ddH_2O), and 0.1 mg/mL bromophenol blue (The dye allows the investigator to track the progress of the electrophoresis). Complete with ddH_2O.

2.4. Western Blotting

1. Transfer buffer: 25 mM Tris, 250 mM glycine, 20% methanol. Complete with ddH_2O. Store at room temperature.

2. Nitrocellulose membrane, 3-MM paper.
3. Ponceau S solution: 0.5% (v/v) Ponceau S, 1% (v/v) acetic acid, adjusts with ddH_2O. Store at room temperature.
4. Phosphate-buffered saline (PBS) 10×: 1.37 mM NaCl, 27 mM KCl, 100 mM Na_2HPO_4, 15 mM KH_2PO_4 (adjust to pH 7.4 if necessary). Autoclave before storage at room temperature. Working solution is prepared by diluting one part with nine parts ddH_2O.
5. Enhanced chemiluminescence (ECL) reagents.

2.5. Two-Dimension Gels

1. Rehydration/lysis buffer: 8 M urea, 2 M thiourea, 4% (w/v) CHAPS, 40 mM DTE, 20 mM Tris, 2% (v/v) IPG buffer, 0.0025% bromophenol blue, complete with ddH_2O.
2. Agarose solution 1%: 0.188 M Tris–HCl, pH 8.8, 0.1% (w/v) SDS, 9% (v/v) glycerol, 1% (w/v) agarose, 0.005% (v/v) bromophenol blue, complete with ddH2O.
3. Equilibration buffer: 6 M urea, 2% (w/v) SDS, 30% (v/v) glycerol, and 0.1 M Tris–HCl, pH 8.8.
4. Equilibration buffer I: Equilibration buffer, 13 mM DTE.
5. Equilibration buffer II: Equilibration buffer, 2.5% (w/v) iodoacetamide.
6. After silver staining, the gel is scanned, and the protein pattern is analyzed with the Image Master 2D software (Amersham–Pharmacia Biotech).

2.6. Synchronized Phagocytosis

1. Microscope coverslips (Circles No. 1 – 0.13–0.17 mm thick; Size: 12 mm) and microscope slides (25 × 75 × 1 mm).
2. 3 μm polybeads dyed microparticles. Prepare a diluted solution by adding 0.5 mL of the stock solution in 4.5 mL of cold PBS, NaN3 0.1%. Particle number can be counted to determine concentration. Store at 4°C for several months.
3. Zymosan. Prepare a diluted solution by adding 4 mL of the stock solution in 36 mL of cold PBS 0.1% NaN3. Particle number can be counted to determine concentration. Store at 4°C during several month.
4. Sheep Red Blood Cells. Store at 4°C during 1 month. Prepare a diluted solution by adding 1 mL of the stock solution in 9 mL of cold PBS. Particle concentration should be determined. Store at 4°C up to several days.

2.7. Confocal Immunofluorescence

1. Paraformaldehyde: prepare a fresh 2% (v/v) solution in PBS for each experiment. Store at room temperature before use.
2. Blocking/permeabilization solution: 0.1% (v/v) Triton X-100, 1% (w/v) BSA, and 20% (v/v) normal goat serum,

6% (w/v) milk, 50% (v/v) fetal bovine serum. This solution must be freshly prepared for each experiment.

3. Anti-mouse or Anti-rabbit AlexaFluor 488 or 568. DRAQ-5 5 mM.
4. Fluoromount-G.
5. Detailed analysis of protein localization on phagosomes is performed using an oil immersion Nikon Plan Apo 100X (N.A. 1.4) objective mounted on a Nikon Eclipse E800 microscope equipped with a Bio-Rad Radiance 2000 confocal imaging system.
6. Fluorochrome excitation is achieved using a 10-mW Argon-Krypton laser for 488 nm (Alexa488) and 568 nm (Alexa568), and a 10-mW diode laser for 638 nm (Alexa647). Images are obtained using appropriate filters, through the sequential scanning mode of the LaserSharp software (Bio-Rad Laboratories) with a Kalman filter of at least 4, and converted using MRCtoM 1.9.3 and AdobePhotoshop 6.0.

3. Methods

A simple technique can be used to isolate pure preparations of phagosomes from macrophage cell lines such as RAW264.7 or J774 cells (**Fig. 1**). Enrichment of specific phagosome components associated with the microbicidal activity of phagosomes, such as hydrolases (e.g., cathepsin D and S) or LAMP-1, can easily be assessed by Western blot (Fig. 2). Phagosome isolation has been used to identify new phagosome-associated proteins as well as to study protein modifications during phagosome maturation *(14)*. After phagosome isolation and lysis, components can be separated by two-dimension gel electrophoresis, enabling the identification of proteins according to their isoelectric point on immobilized pH gradients 4–7 and their molecular weight (standard SDS–PAGE).

A global view of the compositional changes that occur during phagolysosome biogenesis can be obtained by comparing proteomic patterns of samples from phagosomes isolated at various time points. More specific studies on protein complex formation can be achieved by immunoprecipitation of a known component of the phagosome proteome. Obviously, these methods are not sufficient to clearly demonstrate the presence of these newly identified components, and other methods (e.g., Western blotting and confocal microscopy) must be used to confirm and validate the proteomic data. Ultimately, it is important to

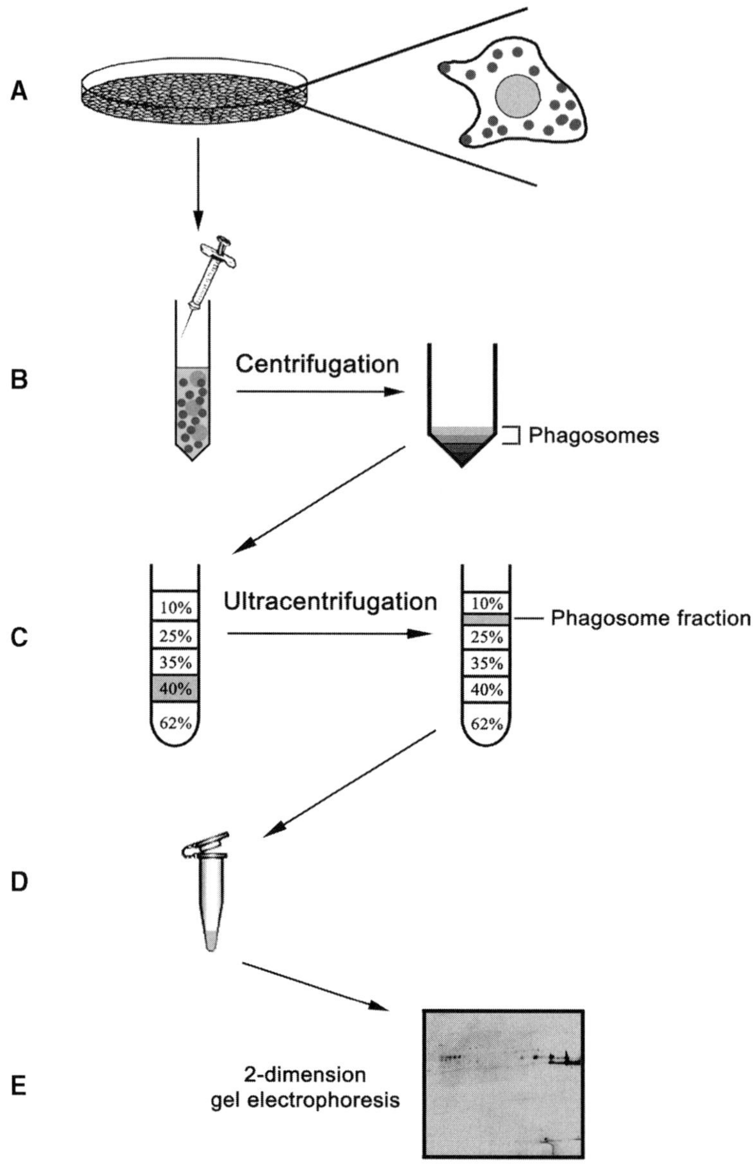

Fig. 1. Scheme of phagosome purification. (**A**) *Phagocytosis*. Macrophages are allowed to internalize a large amount of latex beads. (**B**) *Homogenization*. Cells are scrapped in PBS and homogenized by vigorously ejecting the cell suspension through a needle on the wall of the tube. After centrifugation, the phagosome layer corresponding to the two clearer phases is mixed with 62% sucrose solution in order to obtain a 40% sucrose solution containing phagosomes. (**C**) *Purification*. The 40% sucrose solution containing phagosomes is laid down on a 62% sucrose solution and covered up by the sucrose solutions as shown. Ultracentrifugation allows purification of latex-beads-containing phagosomes by migration according to beads density, at the interface between the 10 and the 25% sucrose solution. (**D**) *Lysis*. Phagosome solution is then mixed with PBS and ultracentrifugation allows phagosome precipitation at the bottom of the tube. Phagosomes can be lysed. (**E**) *Analysis*. Immunoprecipitation of a protein known to be involved in complex formation is possible on phagosome lysates and separation of protein complexes can be realized by two-dimension gel electrophoresis.

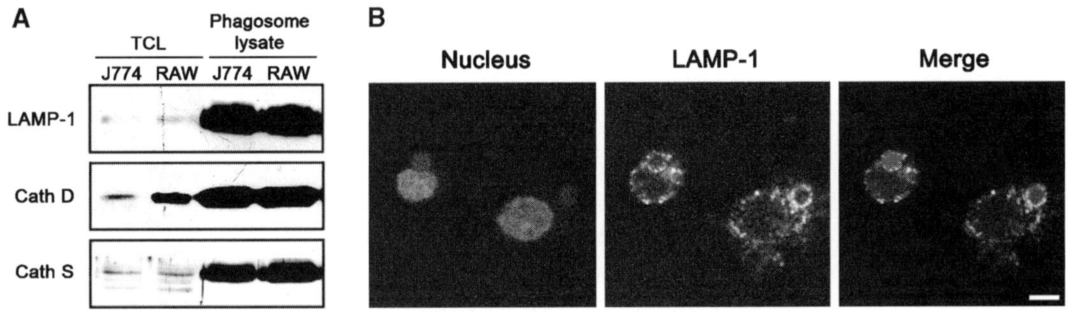

Fig. 2. Enrichment of proteins in the phagosomal compartment. The lysosomal marker LAMP-1 and the hydrolases Cathepsin D and S are massively acquired during the late steps of phagosomal maturation. (**A**) Phagosomes were obtained after a 90-min phagocytosis. 15 μg of total cell lysate (TCL) and 30 μg of phagosome lysate from RAW264.7 and J774 cell lines were loaded on a 10% acrylamide gel, transferred, and blotted with an anti-LAMP-1, an anti-Cath D, and an anti-Cath S antibody. (**B**) Immunofluorescence analysis by confocal microscopy shows recruitment of LAMP-1 on phagosomes. RAW264.7 cells were allowed to internalize fluorescent latex beads for 90 min before fixation. Cells were stained with an anti-LAMP-1 antibody and an anti-rat coupled with a 488 fluorochrome (Molecular Probes). Nuclei were stained using DRAQ-5 reagent (Biostatus, Leicestershire). Bar, 3 μm.

determine the functions of these components during phagocytosis and phagolysosome biogenesis.

3.1. Phagosome Isolation

1. Adherent macrophages (5×10^7 per 150 × 20 mm tissue culture dish) are incubated 24 h, reaching confluence between 70 and 80%.
2. Vortex latex beads vigorously before use to disrupt aggregates. Prior to initiating internalization, medium is gently removed and cells are incubated at 4°C for 10 min in the presence of 0.8 μm-diameter latex beads diluted 1:50 in 10 mL of complete medium, to allow beads to make contact with the cell monolayer. Cells and beads are then transferred to 37°C and incubated for 90 min to allow internalization to take place (*see* **Note 1**).
3. Gently wash cells three times with warm medium to remove non-internalized beads. During washes, dishes are put on a shaker. After this step, cells can be observed by light microscopy to verify the presence of a high number of bead containing phagosomes (black points in cells).
4. To obtain mature phagolysosomes, cells are further incubated for a chase period of 60 min in fresh medium at 37°C. Cells are then washed (3 × 5 min) in PBS at 4°C on a shaker, scraped with a rubber policeman in 4 mL of ice-cold PBS, and transferred to a 15-mL Falcon tube (one Falcon tube can accommodate cells from two dishes).
5. Cells are washed twice in 8 mL ice-cold PBS (centrifugation at 1,500 rpm for 3 min) to remove noninternalized beads.

A third wash is performed in 2 mL of homogenization buffer (8.5% sucrose).

6. Cells are pelleted in 1 mL homogenization buffer and homogenized on ice with a 1 mL syringe using a 22-G needle (12–15 strokes) in the 15-mL Falcon tube.
7. Homogenization is carried out until about 90% of cells are broken without major breakage of nuclei, as monitored by light microscopy.
8. Cell extracts are pelleted in a 15-mL Falcon tube at 2,000 rpm for 5 min at 4°C. The supernatant (about 1 mL) contains the phagosomes (**Fig.** 1). The phagosome suspension is carefully removed and is brought to 40% sucrose by adding an equal volume of a 62% sucrose solution in a 2-mL microfuge tube. Mix thoroughly with a pipet.
9. This 40% sucrose phagosome suspension is gently loaded on top of a 3-mL cushion of 62% sucrose, followed by the addition of solutions of 2 mL of 35% sucrose, 2 mL of 25% sucrose, and 2 mL of 10% sucrose.
10. Centrifugation is performed at 4°C in a swinging bucket rotor (SW41; Beckman Instruments) for 1 h at 100,000 × *g*.
11. Phagosomes (a band colored in blue) are carefully collected at the interface of the 10% and 25% sucrose layers and resuspended in 12 mL cold PBS containing 1× protease inhibitors. Phagosomes from two tubes can be pooled for the next centrifugation.
12. The phagosomes are pelleted at 4°C by a 15-min centrifugation at 40,000 × *g* in an SW41 rotor.
13. Supernatant is removed and the phagosome pellet is resuspended in 40–50 μL of ice-cold 1% NP-40 lysis buffer containing protease and phosphatase inhibitors (*see* **Note 2**). It is important to dry out the wall of the tube before adding lysis buffer to remove PBS 1×. Place on ice for 10 min and store at –20°C. The protein concentration of the phagosome preparations can be determined using the Pierce BCA protein assay reagent or any other standardized protein assay system.

3.2. Immunoprecipitation

1. Aliquot 50 μL of immobilized Protein A into four separate 1.5-mL microfuge tubes (tubes 1, 2, 3, and 4) and equilibrate three times with 500 μL 1% NP-40 lysis buffer without protease and phosphatase inhibitors (i.e., add lysis buffer; mix gently, spin down, and remove supernatant).
2. Tubes 1 and 2 are used for antibody binding: add 500 μL of 1% NP-40 lysis buffer without protease and phosphatase inhibitors and 5 μg of the antibody. Incubate for 3–4 h at 4°C in a rotary shaker.

3. Tubes 3 and 4 are used for preclearing phagosome extracts: add 700 μg per tube of phagosome extract in 0.5 mL total (adjust with 1% NP-40 lysis buffer with protease and phosphatase inhibitors if necessary) to equilibrate beads and incubate for 1 h at 4°C in a rotary shaker in order to eliminate non-specific binding.
4. After incubation with the antibody, beads from tubes 1 and 2 are washed three times in 500 μL of 1% NP-40 lysis buffer without protease and phosphatase inhibitors by mixing gently, spinning down, and removing supernatant.
5. Transfer precleared phagosome extracts from tubes 3 and 4 into tubes 1 and 2 containing antibody linked to beads. Incubate overnight at 4°C in a rotary shaker.
6. Spin tubes 1 and 2 down and remove supernatants; wash the beads twice with 1% NP-40 lysis buffer without protease and phosphatase inhibitors and twice with lysis buffer 0.1% NP-40 without protease and phosphatase inhibitors.
7. Resuspend the beads in a small volume of rehydration/lysis buffer (cf. **Subheading 2.5**, **step 1**), pool the contents of the two microfuge tubes, spin down and resuspend beads in 450 μL of rehydration/lysis buffer.
8. Vortex 1 h at room temperature before loading the samples for two-dimensional gel electrophoresis.

3.3. Two-Dimensional Gel Electrophoresis

1. Proteins are first separated according to their isoelectric points on 24-cm linear immobilized pH-gradient strips. Remove a dry strip of pH 4–7 from −20°C and allow to equilibrate at room temperature for 15 min.
2. Load the sample into the rehydration tray, leave about 1 cm at each end.
3. Note the basic end of the strip and position it at the left side of the tray.
4. Place the IPG strip gel-side down on the top of the sample; verify that there are no bubbles.
5. Completely overlay with mineral oil, cover the tray with lid, and leave at room temperature overnight.
6. Cut two electrode papers of 1.5 cm and wet with ddH_2O. Mop up until the papers become semi-dry.
7. Take out IPG strip and lay it down on the filter paper gel-side at top to remove oil excess.
8. Place the IPG strip in a strip holder gel-side on top and the acid side (+) at the positive side. The strip must be placed between the electrodes.
9. Lay down electrode papers lengthwise at 0.5 cm of the gel end for both sides, and gently lay down electrodes on the last

0.5 cm of the electrode paper in order that they are aligned properly.

10. Place strip holder cover and close the apparatus to test the voltage for 500 V. If voltage fails, verify that electrode papers are on the strip and that the electrode papers are not too dry.
11. Remove cap and completely cover the strip with mineral oil.
12. First dimension separation according to the isoelectric point.
13. Replace strip holder cover, close the apparatus, and proceed with the migration. At this step, voltage time volt-hours (Vh) will total approximately 106,000 Vh according to the following program:

500 V	15 min
1,000 V	30 min
2,000 V	30 min
3,000 V	30 min
4,000 V	30 min
5,000 V	60 min
6,000 V	60 min
8,000 V	Overnight

14. The strip is then rapidly taken out and after excess oil is drained out on filter paper, is placed in a glass tube containing Equilibration Buffer I. Incubate 10 min on a shaker at room temperature.
15. Remove the strip and place it in a glass tube containing Equilibration buffer II for 5 min at room temperature on a shaker. During this step, melt agarose solution which can be stored in a boiling hot beaker to keep it liquid.
16. Second dimension separation according to molecular weight: Prepare a 10% SDS–polyacrylamide gel (cf. **Subheading 3.5**) before the equilibration steps so that it can polymerize during the equilibration steps. Mix 7.9 mL H_2O, 6.7 mL 30.8% acrylamide/bis, 5 mL 1.5 M Tris–HCl, pH 8.8, 200 μL 10% SDS, 200 μL 10% ammonium persulfate, and 10 μL TEMED. Leave about 1.5 cm from the top for the strip.
17. Overlay with 0.1% SDS to avoid the drying of the gel and the gel should polymerize in about 20–30 min.
18. Remove the 0.1% SDS solution and rinse the top of the gel twice with ddH_2O. Mop up remaining water with a filter paper.
19. Place the strip on the top of the gel, leaving space for agarose. Place the acid side on the left. Add two small filter papers saturated with molecular weight marker at both ends of the gel.

20. Add the agarose solution and with care, quickly push the strip in until it touches the polyacrylamide separation gel. Make sure that the plastic-side of the gel remains pressed on the glass. Avoid bubbles between the strip and the separation gel. Let the agarose solidify.
21. Add running buffer and proceed with the migration by running the gel at 200 V. This step takes several hours.
22. Stop the migration as soon as the colorimetric marker leaves the gel. Disassemble the migration system, remove the agarose and the strip, take the gel out, and identify the pH by piercing at both ends.

3.4. Coomassie Blue Coloration, Nonfixing Silver Stain, and Protein Extraction

3.4.1. Coomassie Blue (see Note 3)

1. Wash the gel three times with ddH_2O (5 min each).
2. Proceed as described for the Colloidal Blue Staining Kit.
3. Non-fixing silver stain.
4. Always use freshly prepared solutions and perform all steps at room temperature with constant gentle agitation. Place the polyacrylamide gel in a plastic container.
5. Incubate the gel for 30 min in fixation solution consisting of 125 mL ethanol, 12.5 mL glacial acetic acid, and 112.5 mL ddH_2O. For a double fixation, repeat this step for an additional 30 min.
6. Pour out fixing solution and wash the gel for 10 min in a mixed solution of 125 mL ethanol and 125 mL ddH_2O. Then wash twice with ddH_2O (10 min each wash).
7. Incubate the gel for 5 min in a sensitizing solution: 0.02 g sodium thiosulfate in 250 mL ddH_2O.
8. Pour out sensitizing solution and wash the gel three times with ddH_2O (5 min each wash).
9. For the silver reaction, incubate the gel for 30 min in silver solution: 0.25 g silver nitrate and ddH_2O to a volume of 250 mL.
10. Pour out silver solution and wash the gel once with ddH_2O for 1 min.
11. Incubate the gel in developing solution: 5 g sodium carbonate, 0.25 mL formaldehyde (37% w/v) and ddH_2O until 250 mL. Do not allow the gel to overstain, and once the gel spots become visible, stop the reaction.
12. Briefly wash the gel in ddH_2O and stop the reaction by incubating the gel in a solution of 12.5 mL acetic acid and 237.5 mL ddH_2O for 5 min. The gel can be stored in a solution of 2.5 mL acetic acid and 247.5 mL ddH_2O for several days.
13. Extraction of protein spots. For the following steps, it is absolutely necessary to work with latex gloves, bonnet, mask,

and any additional protection to prevent keratin contamination of the samples. Wash all components with ethanol.

14. Put the gel between two acetate sheets wetted with ultrapure water.
15. Scan the gel and number the protein spots.
16. Lay down the gel between acetate sheets on a plexiglass tray.
17. Add ultrapure water on the gel.
18. Extract each protein spot with a scalpel. Wash the scalpel between each extraction with ethanol and ultrapure H_2O. Place pieces of gel containing proteins in wells of a 96-well plate. The plate should be prepared beforehand by filling wells with 0.2 mL of ultrapure H_2O, 1% acetic acid.
19. Cover and seal the plate with parafilm. Samples can be stored at 4°C for several days.
20. The samples are now suitable to be analyzed by matrix-assisted laser desorption/ionization-time-of-flight mass spectrometry.

3.5. SDS–Polyacrylamide Mini-Gel Electrophoresis (SDS–PAGE)

1. Prepare a 10% separating gel by mixing 4 mL H_2O, 3.3 mL 30.8% acrylamide/bis, 2.5 mL 4× separating gel solution, 100 μL 10% ammonium persulfate, and 5 μL TEMED. Let about 1.5 cm from the top for the stacking gel.
2. Overlay with 0.1% SDS to avoid the drying of the gel which should polymerize in 20–30 min.
3. Remove the 0.1% SDS solution and rinse the top of the gel twice with ddH_2O.
4. Prepare the stacking gel by mixing 3 mL H_2O, 650 μL 30.8% acrylamide/bis, 1.25 mL 4× Tris stacking buffer, 25 μL 10% ammonium persulfate, and 5 μL TEMED. Rinse the top of the separating gel a final time with 0.5 mL of the stacking gel solution, then add the stacking solution over the separating gel, and insert the comb. The gel should polymerize in about 20–30 min.
5. Prepare the running buffer by diluting 160 mL of the 5× running buffer with 640 mL H_2O and mix.
6. When the stacking gel has set, remove the comb and assemble the gel unit.
7. Add running buffer. It is important to carefully wash twice the wells with running buffer by using a 25-G needle before loading the samples.
8. The protein concentration of each sample has to be known and adjusted to have the same amount of protein in all samples. Adjustment may be done by adding lysis buffer. Be careful not to add too much lysis buffer because the protein

sample is subsequently diluted 1:1 (v/v) with 2× SDS-loading buffer, and the final volume should not exceed 15 μL for loading.

9. Incubate samples for 5 min at 100°C, perform a quick spin, mix and load 15 μL of each sample in a well. One well must include molecular weight markers prepared according to the supplier's instructions.
10. Complete the assembly of the gel unit and connect to a power supply. The gel can be run at 100 V.
11. When the dye front reaches the bottom of the gel, transfer to the nitrocellulose membrane may be carried out (the dye fronts can be run off the gel if desired).

3.6. Western Blotting

1. Make sure that all parts of the apparatus are clean.
2. Cut three pieces of Whatman 3-MM filter paper barely larger than the gel and pre-wet with transfer buffer. Lay down the three pieces on the transfer apparatus. A sheet of the nitrocellulose barely larger than the separating gel size is laid on the surface of the 3-MM paper to wet the membrane. Pour transfer buffer onto the membrane and remove any air bubbles.
3. After the samples have been separated by SDS–PAGE, the gel unit is disassembled. The stacking gel is removed and one corner of the separating gel is cut to track its orientation. The separating gel is then laid on the top of the nitrocellulose membrane and the gel surface is moistened with transfer buffer.
4. Three additional pieces of 3-MM paper of the appropriate size are submerged in the transfer buffer and carefully laid on top of the gel. It is also extremely important to make sure of the proper orientation of the resulting sandwich, or proteins will be lost into the buffer (components must be placed in the following order: three pieces of 3-MM paper, nitrocellulose membrane, polyacrylamide gel, and finally three other pieces of 3-MM paper. Remove any bubbles after each step). Close the transfer system.
5. Set the power supply at 15 V for 30 min.
6. After the transfer, the gel and the membrane are disassembled from the apparatus and the membrane is promptly rinsed with ddH_2O.
7. The membrane is then stained with Ponceau S for 1 min at room temperature to visualize the sample proteins and to assess the efficiency of the transfer. Red protein bands should become visible after removing excess dye with ddH_2O. The positions of the lanes and the markers are marked by gently pricking the membrane with the point of a needle.

8. Destain the membrane completely by rinsing in PBS on a shaker for about 10 min (*see* **Note 4**).
9. Block with blocking buffer (PBS-0.1% Tween, 5% BSA) for 2 h at room temperature or overnight at 4°C on a shaker (*see* **Note 5**).
10. Wash with PBS-0.1% Tween four times for 15 min each on a shaker.
11. Incubate the membrane with primary antibody diluted in 15 mL PBS + 5%BSA for 3 h at room temperature on a shaker or overnight at 4°C.
12. Wash with PBS-0.1% Tween four times for 15 min each on a shaker.
13. Incubate the membrane with the secondary antibody diluted in 15 mL PBS + 5% BSA for 45 min at room temperature on a shaker.
14. Wash with PBS-0.1% Tween four times for 15 min each on a shaker.
15. Following the instructions provided with the ECL kit, mix 5 mL Solution 1 and 5 mL Solution 2 immediately before use and incubate the blot for exactly 1 min (two blots can successively be developed with the same solution) which is rotated by hand to ensure the entire coverage of the membrane (*see* **Note 6**).
16. The blot is placed on an acetate sheet and promptly covered up with Saran wrap to avoid drying of the membrane. Keep out of light.
17. In the darkroom, the acetate-containing membrane is placed immediately in an autoradiography cassette with a medical film for a suitable exposure time (start from 30-s exposures to 45 min).

3.7. Preparation of Samples for Immunofluorescence

3.7.1. Synchronized Phagocytosis

1. Place round coverslips into wells of a 24-well tissue culture plate. The coverslips are sterilized or kept in alcohol until required. Coverslips kept in alcohol are dried in a sterile environment and dropped into each well with sterile forceps.
2. Harvest and resuspend macrophages in complete DMEM at 1–4 × 10^5 cells/mL. Seed 0.5 mL into each well of the 24-well plate and incubate at least 2 h or overnight at 37°C in 5% CO2 to allow cells to adhere to the coverslip.
3. During cell adherence, particles to be internalized are opsonized if necessary. Usually, the particle-to-cell ratio is 10:1 or 20:1.
4. Zymosan particles are laid down in a microfuge tube, spun 1 min at 14,000 × *g*, and resuspended in cold, sterile PBS 1× solution twice for washing (aspirate the supernatant carefully

using a 26-G needle). Particles can be opsonized in 150 μL of pure mouse serum or in 0.3–0.5 mL of diluted mouse serum in sterile PBS 1× solution. Do not dilute the serum to less than 10%. Incubate 40 min to 1 h at 37°C for complement opsonization. The tube is shaken by inversion three or four times during incubation to allow optimal particle opsonization.

5. For IgG opsonization, sheep red blood cells (SRBC) or beads can be used.
6. SRBC are laid down in a 15-mL Falcon tube and centrifugated at 200 × *g* for 5 min at 4°C and resuspended twice in cold sterile PBS for washing. After the last wash, SRBC are suspended in 7 mL sterile cold PBS and 7 μL of SRBC-specific IgG at 1 μg/μL (from mouse or rabbit) is added. Incubate SRBC 30 min in a rotary shaker at 4°C.
7. Beads are added to a microfuge tube, centrifugated 1 min at 14,000 × *g*, and resuspended in sterile cold PBS twice for washing (aspirate the supernatant carefully with a 26-G needle). After the last wash, beads are suspended in 1 mL 50 mM Tris–HCl, pH 9, and 1 μl of IgG at 1 μg/μL (from mouse or rabbit) is added. Incubate beads for 40 min in a rotary shaker at 4°C.
8. After opsonization, wash three times with cold sterile PBS 1× solution. For SRBC, gently shake the tube after centrifugation to avoid cell lysis. For zymosan and latex beads, particles can be vigorously shaken after centrifugation to avoid aggregate formation. Resuspend particles in an appropriate volume of complete DMEM and keep at 4°C until phagocytosis (keeping in mind that a volume of 300 μL will be added to each well for phagocytosis).
9. Once macrophages are ready for phagocytosis, remove the medium by gently aspirating the contents of each well. Wash cells twice with 0.5 mL cold DMEM. Keep plates at 4°C for 5 min before adding particles.
10. Remove medium and gently add 300 μL of the cold particle suspension. Keep the plates at 4°C during 10 min to allow particle deposition and their binding to the cells.
11. Remove unbound particles by three washes with cold DMEM and incubate cells at 37°C for 90 min for internalization.
12. Coverslips are then washed three times with PBS to eliminate non-internalized particles and cells are fixed in PBS 1×+2% paraformaldehyde for 10 min at room temperature.
13. Wash coverslips twice with PBS 1× and incubate at room temperature for 10 min before a final wash (see **Note 8**).

14. Plates containing coverslips can be stored at 4°C for 1 month before immunofluorescence staining. Be careful that coverslips are always covered with cold PBS.

3.7.2. Confocal Immunofluorescence

1. For each subsequent step involving incubation of coverslips containing adherent cells (i.e., blocking/permeabilization, first and second antibody incubation), place a piece of parafilm in the bottom of a 150 × 20 mm dish. The outside of the dish (both top and bottom) must be fully covered beforehand with aluminium foil. Place 50–80 μL of the incubation solution (e.g., blocking/permeabilization solution, first antibody solution, or second antibody solution) into the dish, and using forceps gently place each coverslip with the cells face down in the desired solution. Do not press on coverslips. After incubation, carefully remove coverslips with forceps, and immerse them in wells containing PBS 1× solution. Keep the cell-side face up.
2. To permeabilize cells and block nonspecific surface Fcγ-receptors, promptly drain excess PBS 1× and incubate in the blocking/permeabilization buffer at room temperature for 15–20 min.
3. Coverslips are then dipped in PBS 1× and washed three times. Washes have to be gentle to maintain cell attachment.
4. Excess PBS is promptly drained from the coverslips, and the primary antibody solution (usually at a dilution of 1/1,000 to 1/100 in PBS) is added for 1 h at room temperature.
5. Cells are gently washed three times in PBS 1×.
6. Coverslips are promptly drained for excess PBS and incubated with a solution containing the secondary antibody (1/500 dilution) coupled to an Alexa fluorochrome (Alexa 488, 568, or 647 for example) for 30 min at room temperature. A nuclear stain such as DRAQ 5 can be used and is diluted at 1/400 in the secondary antibody solution. From this step, be careful to protect samples from direct light to avoid bleaching.
7. Samples are gently washed three times and are ready to be mounted.
8. Coverslips are promptly drained for excess PBS and are mounted on glass slides with Fluoromount-G. Drops of Fluoromount-G are placed on glass slides and coverslips are laid down cell-face in contact with fluoromount. Excess fluoromount is removed and slides are then sealed with nail polish on the edges of coverslips.
9. Freshly mounted slides must be dried at room temperature and protected from light for 24 h before use. Slides can be stored for up to a month at 4°C in the dark.

4. Notes

1. Depending on the experiments, various internalization time points are possible during phagosome isolation, and the chase period must be adapted to the protein component of interest, which may be recruited to phagosomes at early or later time points after initiation of phagocytosis. Internalization between 30 and 120 min is often used, and the chase period can cover a period from 30 min to more than 2 h. For example, to observe the early recruitment of a specific protein on phagosomes, cells and medium containing beads can be kept at 4°C for 20 min and then placed at 37°C for 30 min before phagosome isolation.
2. Phagosomes can be resuspended in ice-cold lysis buffer containing 150 mM NaCl, 20 mM Tris–HCl, pH 7.5, and 1% NP-40, but 1% Triton X-100 can be used instead of NP-40.
3. Coomassie blue staining is preferable if proteins are visible on acrylamide gel before sample isolation and mass spectrometry identification.
4. TBS can be used instead of PBS according to the manufacturer providing the first antibody.
5. Nitrocellulose membranes can be blocked with blocking buffer containing milk (PBS 0.1% Tween, 5% (w/v) milk) for 2 h at room temperature or overnight at 4°C on a shaker.
6. If the signal is too strong during exposure, the ECL solutions can be diluted (from 1/2 to 1/20) in ddH_2O as long as solutions 1 and 2 remain at the ratio of 1:1.
7. If the silver stain is not sufficient, the gel can be incubated in the silver solution overnight at room temperature with agitation.
8. During preparation of coverslips for immunofluorescence, observation by light microscopy after washing is advised in order to verify that cells have not detached during washing. Do not expose samples to light after incubation with the secondary antibody.

Acknowledgments

We are grateful to John Derek Ng Yan Hing for developing phagosome isolation procedures in our laboratory. This work was supported by the Canadian Institutes for Health Research. AD is the holder of a Canada Research Chair. AFV was partly supported by a fellowship from the Fondation Armand-Frappier.

References

1. Bajno L, Peng XR, Schreiber AD, Moore HP, Trimble WS, Grinstein S. (2000). Focal exocytosis of VAMP3-containing vesicles at sites of phagosome formation. *J Cell Biol*; 149(3):697–706
2. Braun V, Fraisier V, Raposo G, et al. (2004). TI-VAMP/VAMP7 is required for optimal phagocytosis of opsonised particles in macrophages. *EMBO J*; 23(21):4166–4176
3. Gagnon E, Duclos S, Rondeau C, et al. (2002). Endoplasmic reticulum-mediated phagocytosis is a mechanism of entry into macrophages. *Cell*; 110(1):119–131
4. Jahraus A, Tjelle TE, Berg T, et al. (1998). In vitro fusion of phagosomes with different endocytic organelles from J774 macrophages. *J Biol Chem*; 273(46):30379–30390
5. Vieira OV, Botelho RJ, Grinstein S. (2002). Phagosome maturation: aging gracefully. *Biochem J*; 366(Pt 3):689–704
6. Wetzel MG, Korn ED. (1969). Phagocytosis of latex beads by *Acahamoeba castellanii* (Neff). 3. Isolation of the phagocytic vesicles and their membranes. *J Cell Biol*; 43(1):90–104
7. Desjardins M, Huber L, Parton R, Griffiths G. (1994) Biogenesis of phagolysosomes proceeds through a sequential series of interactions with the endocytic apparatus. *J Cell Biol*; 124(5):677–688
8. Desjardins M, Celis J, van Meer G, et al. (1994). Molecular characterization of phagosomes. *J Biol Chem*; 269(51):32194–32200
9. Desjardins M, Nzala N, Corsini R, Rondeau C. (1997) Maturation of phagosomes is accompanied by changes in their fusion properties and size-selective acquisition of solute materials from endosomes. *J Cell Sci*; 110(18):2303–2314
10. Desjardins M. Biogenesis of phagolysosomes: the 'kiss and run' hypothesis. (1995). *Trends Cell Biol*; 5(5):183–186
11. Claus V, Jahraus A, Tjelle T, et al. (1998). Lysosomal enzyme trafficking between phagosomes, endosomes, and lysosomes in J774 macrophages. Enrichment of cathepsin H in early endosomes. *J Biol Chem*; 273(16):9842–9851
12. Ng Yan Hing JD, Desjardins M, Descoteaux A. (2004) Proteomic analysis reveals a role for protein kinase C-alpha in phagosome maturation. *Biochem Biophys Res Commun*; 319(3):810–816
13. Garin J, Diez R, Kieffer S, et al. (2001). The phagosome proteome: insight into phagosome functions. *J Cell Biol*; 152(1):165–180
14. Defacque H, Bos E, Garvalov B, et al. (2002). Phosphoinositides regulate membrane-dependent actin assembly by latex bead phagosomes. *Mol Biol Cell*; 13(4):1190–1202

Chapter 21

Coordinate Regulation of Sphingosine Kinase and Actin Dynamics

Shankar S. Iyer and David J. Kusner

Summary

The activation of lipid-modifying enzymes generally involves a physical change in their interactions with the membrane substrate. For sphingosine kinase, a predominantly cytosolic enzyme in resting cells, activation is accompanied by translocation to specific subsets of cellular membranes where catalysis occurs. As all eukaryotic membranes have a tightly associated filamentous actin skeleton, we investigated potential regulatory interactions between sphingosine kinase and actin. Sphingosine kinase 1 (SK1) exhibited constitutive- and stimulus-enhanced association with actin filaments and F-actin-enriched membrane fractions in both intact macrophages and an in vitro reconstitution assay, whereas SK1 bound G-actin only under stimulated conditions. Actin inhibitors disrupted SK1 localization and increased its enzymatic activity. Both the localization and the activity of SK1 were coordinately regulated with the actin cytoskeleton. The association of enzymes with the actin cytoskeleton and how this regulates their activities and functions are subjects of intense interest. Here, we describe the approach we used to investigate regulation of SK1. This provides general methods that can be used to examine the role of actin in regulating enzyme activity in macrophages and other myeloid cells.

Key words: Enzyme, Lipid, Signal transduction, Cytoskeleton, Phosphorylation.

1. Introduction

Sphingosine kinases (SK), constitute an evolutionarily conserved enzyme family that regulate critical cellular functions, including motility, proliferation, and differentiation *(1–6)*. The two mammalian isoforms, SK1 and SK2, exhibit approximately 45% identity and 80% similarity *(7)*. SK activity is stimulated by cytokines, growth factors, immune complexes, complement components, and phorbol esters *(6, 8)*. SK catalyzes the phosphorylation of sphingosine to sphingosine-1-phosphate (S1P), and its critical

Neil E. Reiner (ed.), *Macrophages and Dendritic Cells,* Methods in Molecular Biology, vol. 531

DOI: 10.1007/978-1-59745-396-7_21

roles in health and disease are due to the dynamic interconversion of these two signaling lipids *(6, 8)*. S1P transduces biologic signals both extracellularly as well as intracellularly. The broad responsiveness of diverse cell types to S1P argues for precise spatiotemporal regulation of SK1 activity. Furthermore, since agonists induce only modest increases (1.5- to 3-fold) in the specific activity of SK1, localization must be critical to its regulation. As the majority of SK activity is localized to the cytosol *(3, 5, 6, 8–10)* stimulation involves translocation to the lipid substrate of the membrane.

Several lipid-modifying enzymes, including phospholipases C and D, are known to interact with the membrane-associated actin cytoskeleton *(11–16)*. These physical interactions have important bidirectional functional effects, including modulation of lipase activity as well as actin dynamics. In the case of SK, binding to actin may serve as a determinant of its localization to specific cellular membranes. In addition, actin is critical to several cellular functions to which SK has been linked, including motility *(17–20)*, vesicle trafficking *(21–23)*, and secretion *(21, 24)*. To characterize the physical interactions between SK and the actin cytoskeleton, it is necessary to consider both monomeric G-actin and filamentous, polymeric F-actin. Confocal microscopy is a valuable method for assessing the association of proteins with actin filaments. Biochemical methods serve as complementary approaches to define binding interactions and to characterize regulatory factors. In terms of functional effects, both the enzymatic activity of SK and its subcellular localization are modulated by interactions with actin. The approach described later to investigate the regulation of SK1 based upon its association with actin, provides general methods that may be applied to study actin-dependent regulation of enzyme activity in macrophages and other myeloid cells.

2. Materials

1. H/K^{++} buffer: 25 mM HEPES, pH 7.4, 100 mM KCl, 3 mM NaCl, 5 mM $MgCl_2$, 1 mM EGTA.
2. 2 mM leupeptin, 0.5 mM phenylmethylsulfonylfluoride (PMSF), 1 mM dithiothreitol (DTT).
3. Sphingosine Kinase (SK) Assay Buffer: 0.2 M Tris, pH 7.4; 0.9 mM $CaCl_2$, 1 mM EGTA, 40 mM β-glycerophosphate, 0.5 mM deoxypyridoxine, 15 mM NaF, 1 mM sodium vanadate, 10 μg/mL each of the protease inhibitors leupeptin, aprotinin, and soybean trypsin inhibitor, 1 mM PMSF, 10% glycerol, and 0.01% 2- mercaptoethanol.

4. PMA: 1 mM stock in DMSO; store at –20°C.
5. Phalloidin: 10 mM stock in methanol, store at –20°C.
6. Zymosan.
7. Triton X-100.
8. PVDF membrane.
9. Polystyrene beads: 3 μm diameter.
10. EZ View Protein G-agarose.
11. DNase 1, bovine pancreas.
12. Polyclonal rabbit anti-SK1 antibody was a gift from Dr. Lina Obeid, MUSC, South Carolina.
13. Polyclonal rabbit anti-SK1 antibody.
14. Murine antiactin monoclonal antibody (Ab-1).

3. Methods

Characterization of the physical interactions between SK1 and actin involves microscopic definition of the enzyme's association with actin filaments and biochemical evaluation of the binding of SK1 to both F- and G-actin. Examination of the functional effects of these physical interactions requires assay of lipid kinase activity and microscopic and biochemical assessment of actin cytoskeletal dynamics.

3.1 Characterization of the Association of SK1 and Actin Filaments by Confocal Microscopy

1. The RAW 264.7 murine macrophage cell line and human THP-1 promonocytic leukemia cells were cultured in RPMI containing 10% fetal bovine serum and 1% penicillin/streptomycin (P/S).
2. Plasmids encoding enhanced green fluorescent protein (EGFP) fusion proteins of wild-type SK1, catalytically inactive $SK1^{G82D}$ *(25–27)*, phosphorylation-defective $SK1^{S225A}$ *(28)*, and/or red fluorescent protein (RFP)-actin *(29, 30)* were transfected into RAW 264.7 or THP-1 cells using FuGENE6. Cells were loaded onto 25-mm glass coverslips and allowed to adhere. The next day, cells were transfected with 1 μg of plasmid DNA. Confocal microscopy was performed 24 h after transfection.
3. Primary human monocyte-derived macrophages (MDM) were isolated from venous blood from healthy adult volunteers in accordance with the human subjects' guidelines approved by the University of Iowa Institutional Review Board *(31)*. Blood was diluted 1:1 with sterile 0.9 M NaCl, layered over Ficoll-Hypaque density gradient medium, and

centrifuged at 300 × *g* for 45 min at 25°C. The peripheral blood mononuclear cells (PBMC) were removed and cultured in RPMI containing 20% autologous serum in Teflon wells for 5 days at 37°C, 5% CO_2 to enable differentiation of monocytes to macrophages. MDM were purified by adherence to glass chamber slides for 2 h at 37°C in RPMI, 20 mM HEPES, pH 7.4, 10% autologous serum. MDM monolayers were washed three times and then incubated in RPMI containing 1% bovine serum albumin, without antibiotics, for use in experiments (*see* **Note 1**).

4. Preparation of phagocytic particles. IgG-coated polystyrene beads and complement-opsonized zymosan (COZ) were used as model phagocytic particles. IgG-coated beads: latex beads (3 μm diameter) were rotated overnight in 2% bovine serum albumin (BSA) at room temperature and opsonized by incubating with 1:200 dilution of rabbit anti-BSA IgG for 2 h at 37°C *(32)*. Beads were then washed and resuspended in RPMI containing 1% bovine serum albumin. IgG opsonization was verified by indirect immunofluorescence utilizing Oregon Green-conjugated antirabbit IgG. COZ: zymosan A was boiled for 15 min at 100°C, washed with PBS, and opsonized in 50% fresh human serum for 30 min at 37°C *(33)*. COZ was then washed three times with PBS and stored on ice until used (*see* **Note 2**).
5. Confocal microscopy – For fixed cell imaging, MDM or RAW 264.7 macrophages were adhered in 8-chamber glass culture slides at approximately 50% confluence and incubated with appropriate stimuli for the indicated times. Cells were fixed in 3.75% paraformaldehyde for 15 min and permeabilized in ice-cold methanol: acetone (1:1) or acetone alone (for experiments using phalloidin) (*see* **Note 3**) *(34)*. Samples were sequentially incubated with blocking buffer (PBS, 5% BSA, 10% horse serum), Texas Red-phalloidin (0.17 μM), rabbit polyclonal anti-SK1 Ab (1:100 dilution), and Oregon Green-conjugated goat antirabbit IgG 2° Ab, all for 1 h at 25°C. In select experiments, cells were preincubated with 100 nM PMA (in 0.1% DMSO) for 5–30 min. The 0.1% DMSO solvent control exhibited no differences in viability or SK1 localization, compared to cells incubated in buffer alone. Analysis was performed using a Zeiss 510 laser scanning confocal microscope. Fifty cells were analyzed per sample and duplicate samples were run for each experimental condition.
6. For live-cell confocal imaging, RAW 264.7 cells were cultured and transfected as described earlier. On the day of analysis, the coverslips were placed in a heated stage at 37°C, and analyzed at rest, during phagocytosis of model particles,

or after incubation with various pharmacologic agents, using the Zeiss 510 laser scanning microscope and the associated LSM time series imaging software. Z-series confocal images were acquired every 30–45 s for 45 min. Loss of fluorescence at later time points due to photobleaching was compensated for by increasing the gain of the photomultiplier tube. Quantification of differences in fluorescent staining between samples, including the degree of colocalization, was performed using ImageJ software.

3.2. Definition of the Interaction of SK1 with Actin-Enriched Membrane Fractions of Intact Cells

To further define the interaction of SK1 with actin filaments, we characterized the detergent solubility of SK1 in resting and stimulated macrophages. For this purpose we utilized the murine macrophage cell line RAW 264.7.

1. RAW cells were cultured in RPMI 1640 with 10% FBS and 1% P/S. Freshly cultured cells adherent to tissue culture flasks were scraped, washed, and resuspended in H/K^{++} buffer at 3×10^7 cells/2 mL. A 2 mL aliquot of the cell suspension was used as control cells. Another 2 mL aliquot was stimulated with 2 μM PMA (*see* **Note 4**) for 30 min at 37°C. Poststimulation, the cells were washed and resuspended in 2 mL of buffer.
2. Control and PMA-stimulated cells were disrupted by nitrogen cavitation (450 psi, 25 min, 4°C) (*see* **Note 5**). The undisrupted cells and nuclei were removed by centrifugation at 900 × *g* for 8 min at 4°C to yield the postnuclear supernatant. Membranes and cytosol were isolated a second time by ultracentrifugation at 150,000 × *g* for 60 min at 4°C. Membranes were washed with H/K^{++} and the cytosol clarified by [illegible] centrifugation at [illegible]. Washed [illegible] were suspended in 2 mL H/K^{++} buffer and homogenized with a Tenbroeck tissue grinder.
3. Membranes from control and PMA-treated cells were subjected to detergent extraction by incubating them in 1% Triton X-100 in H/K buffer for 60 min on ice. The detergent-soluble (TxS) and detergent-insoluble pellets (TxI) were separated by centrifugation at 14,000 × *g* for 15 min at 4°C. The insoluble pellets (TxI) were washed twice in H/K buffer with 1% Triton X-100 and resuspended in H/K buffer without detergent.
4. The TxS and TxI fractions obtained by extraction of membranes from control and PMA-treated cells were subjected to 9% SDS–PAGE using the Laemmli buffer and transferred to polyvinylidene difluoride (PVDF) membrane.
5. The PVDF membrane was blocked with 5% nonfat dry milk and probed with a polyclonal rabbit antibody to sphingosine

kinase 1 (anti-SK1, 1:100 dilution) followed by immunodetection using horseradish-peroxidase-coupled secondary antibody and enhanced chemiluminescence (ECL).

6. The majority of SK1 in membranes from resting macrophages were detected in the Triton X-100 insoluble fraction (**Fig. 1A,** major protein doublet at ~43 kDa). The additional protein bands at higher molecular weights likely represent post-translational modifications of SK1.

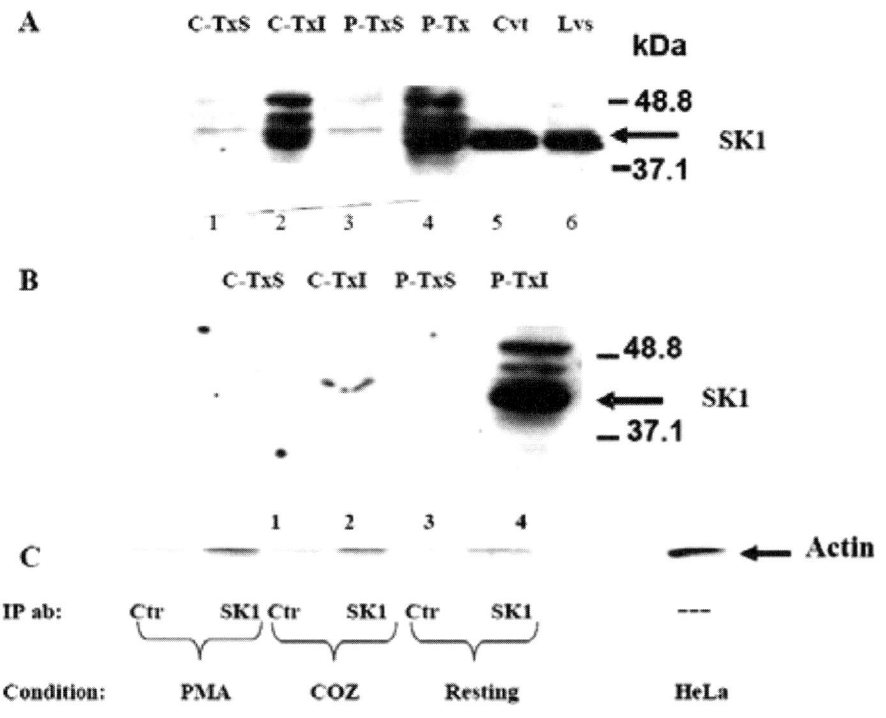

Fig. 1. SK1 exhibits constitutive and PMA-stimulated association with detergent-resistant membrane domains. (**A**) RAW 264.7 cells were incubated in the presence of PMA (2 μM) or buffer for 30 min at 37°C. Cells were disrupted by nitrogen cavitation and membrane, and cytosol fractions were separated by differential centrifugation. Membranes were extracted with lysis buffer containing 1% Triton X-100, and the detergent-insoluble membrane fraction was reisolated and washed. Membrane-derived fractions were subjected to SDS–PAGE followed by immunoblotting for SK1. Lanes are as follows: (1) control, Triton X-100 soluble (C-TxS); (2) control, Triton X-100 insoluble (C-TxI); (3) PMA-stimulated, Triton X-100 soluble (P-TxS); (4) PMA-stimulated, Triton X-100 insoluble (P-TxI). Positive controls included: (5) cytosol from U937 cells, and (6) HeLa cell lysate. (**B**) Cell-free assay: Membrane and cytosol fractions from resting RAW 264.7 cells were incubated with PMA (2 μM) or buffer for 15 min at 37°C. The membrane fraction was reisolated by centrifugation, washed, and extracted with 1% Triton X-100 in lysis buffer. Detergent-soluble and -insoluble fractions were subjected to SDS–PAGE followed by immunoblotting for SK1. Lane designations are as follows: (1) control, Triton X-100 soluble (C-TxS); (2) control, Triton X-100 insoluble (C-TxI); (3) PMA-stimulated, Triton X-100 soluble (P-TxS); (4) PMA-stimulated, Triton X-100 insoluble (P-TxI). (**C**) Coimmunoprecipitation assay: Lysates from resting, PMA-stimulated or COZ-stimulated RAW 264.7 cells were prepared by nitrogen cavitation. These were precleared and then immunoprecipitated using anti-SK1 or control rabbit IgG. Immunoprecipitates were washed extensively in a RIPA-like lysis buffer and subjected to SDS–PAGE followed by Western blotting with an antiactin antibody. HeLa lysate was used as a control. Reprinted with permission from **ref.** *35.*

7. In membranes isolated from cells after PMA stimulation, there was increased detection of SK1 in the Triton X-100-insoluble fraction. The level of SK-1 in the Triton X-100 soluble fractions was low and did not change significantly after PMA stimulation.

3.3. Characterization of the Association of SK1 with Actin Filaments in a Reconstituted Cell-Free Assay System

Cell-free assay systems have contributed significant insights into the interactions between actin filaments and phospholipases, sphingomyelinases, and lipid kinases/phosphatases. Our working model is that activation of SK1 leads to its stable association with actin filaments, rendering SK1 detergent insoluble. We hypothesized that these SK1-actin interactions could be mimicked in a broken cell preparation.

1. Membranes and cytosol from resting RAW 264.7 cells were prepared essentially as detailed earlier (*see* **Subheading 3.2.2**). For the assay, a volume corresponding to 3×10^6 cell equivalents of membranes was incubated with a volume corresponding to 1×10^6 cell equivalents of cytosol in an H/K^{++} buffer, in the absence and presence of 2 μM PMA for 15 min at 37°C. Membranes were isolated a second time by centrifugation (150,000 × *g*, 60 min, 4°C), washed with buffer, and extracted with 1% Triton X-100 for 60 min on ice. The detergent-soluble and -insoluble fractions were separated and washed as described earlier (*see* **Subheading 3.2.3**) and subjected to SDS–PAGE and Western blotting.
2. Control membranes, derived from incubation with cytosol in buffer, contained very low level of SK1 in the Triton X-100-insoluble fraction (**Fig. 1B**). Likewise, there was no detectable SK1 in the detergent-soluble fraction.
3. On the other hand, the Triton X-100-insoluble fraction derived from activated membranes, prepared by incubating membranes with cytosol in the presence of PMA, contained approximately 56-fold greater level of SK1 than the corresponding control (**Fig. 1B**). Again, there was no detectable SK1 in the detergent-soluble fraction.

3.4. Coimmunoprecipitation of SK1 and Actin

To directly evaluate the proposed physical interaction of SK1 with actin, a coimmunoprecipitation assay was undertaken.

1. RAW cells were stimulated with 500 nM PMA, COZ (particle:cell ratio of 10:1), or buffer control for 20 min at 37°C and then washed in RPMI. Cells were scraped, pelleted, and resuspended in a RIPA-like lysis buffer (H/K buffer containing 1% Triton X- 100, 1% octylglucoside, 1% deoxycholate, 0.05% SDS with protease inhibitors), passed through an 18-gauge needle 10 times, and incubated on ice for 60 min.
2. Insoluble material was removed by centrifugation at 14,000 × *g* for 15 min at 4°C.

3. The lysates were precleared by incubation with a 50-μL aliquot of a 50% suspension of EZ View Protein G-agarose (Sigma) for 2 h at 4°C.
4. Control antirabbit IgG or anti-SK1 IgG were preadsorbed to the Protein G-agarose by incubating with the beads for 2 h at 4°C. The beads were extensively washed with lysis buffer to remove unadsorbed IgG.
5. Precleared lysates were incubated with the preadsorbed control IgG or anti-SK1 IgG by incubation for 3 h at 4°C. The immunoprecipitates were washed extensively with lysis buffer and then boiled in SDS sample buffer and subjected to 9% SDS–PAGE.
6. After transfer to PVDF membrane, blots were blocked in 5% nonfat dry milk, washed, and probed for actin by incubating overnight in antiactin antibody (monoclonal IgM) at 4°C. Detection involved the use of horseradish-peroxidase-coupled secondary antibody and ECL.
7. No actin was detected in immunoprecipitates (IPs) obtained with control, irrelevant antibody (**Fig. 1C**). In contrast, each of the anti-SK1 IPs contained actin, and the level of immunoprecipitated actin was greater in PMA- and COZ-treated samples (**Fig. 1c**) compared with buffer-treated controls.

3.5. Determination of the Binding of SK1 to Actin Filaments by Velocity Sedimentation Density Gradient Centrifugation

Velocity sedimentation density gradient centrifugation is a useful method to examine the physical form of actin and to analyze actin-associated proteins. An advantage of this technique over differential centrifugation is that it avoids artifactual copelleting in a centrifugal field. The method can be used to identify microfilament-associated proteins in the presence of the actin filament-stabilizing bicyclic peptide toxin, phalloidin (*see* **Note 6**). Stabilization of microfilaments by phalloidin increases the size of microfilament cores, hence shifting the filament peak in velocity sedimentation density gradient centrifugation to fractions of greater density. This is referred to as the characteristic "phalloidin-shift."

1. Membranes and cytosol were freshly isolated from RAW cells as described earlier (**Subheading 3.2.2**).
2. For the experiment, membranes and cytosol from 2×10^8 cells were incubated with PMA (100 nM) for 30 min at 37°C. In select samples, phalloidin was added at 10 μM for the final 15 min of the incubation.
3. Post incubation, membranes were reisolated by centrifugation at 17,500 × *g* for 30 min at 4°C and washed in H/K^{++} buffer.
4. Washed membranes were solubilized in 500 μL of TEB (1% Triton X-100 in H/K buffer) for 60 min on ice and loaded

on top of a 4-mL linear sucrose gradient (20–55%) prepared in TEB. A 0.5-mL sucrose cushion (80%) was placed at the bottom of each tube.

5. Samples were centrifuged at 150,000 × *g* for 16 h at 8°C using an Optima XL ultracentrifuge (Beckman) with an SW55Ti rotor. Fractions (400 μL) were collected from the top of the gradient.
6. Fractions were subjected to 9% SDS–PAGE and after transfer to PVDF membrane; blots were blocked in 5% nonfat dry milk, washed, and probed for actin by incubating overnight in antiactin antibody (monoclonal IgM) at 4°C. The blots were also probed for SK1 using the anti-SK1 rabbit polyclonal antibody. Detection utilized horseradish-peroxidase-coupled secondary antibody and ECL.
7. In the absence of phalloidin, SK1 was detected primarily in fractions 4–6 (**Fig. 2A**). These fractions also contained a significant amount of actin.
8. In the presence of phalloidin, however, SK1 exhibited a "density shift" and became localized to more dense fractions, 7–9 (**Fig. 2A**). There was a similar shift in the localization of actin to fractions of greater density.

3.6. Analysis of SK1 Binding to Actin Filaments by Cosedimentation

A second method to biochemically assess the binding of SK1 to actin filaments involves cosedimentation. Cytosolic G-actin can be efficiently converted to F-actin by the addition of GTPγS. The GTPγS-induced polymerization of G-actin is stabilized by the addition of jasplakinolide. After polymerization and/or stabilization, actin filaments were sedimented in a low centrifugal field and washed. Proteins that are physically associated with F-actin cosediment with the actin filaments.

1. Cytosol isolated from murine macrophages (RAW cells) or the human promonocytic line (THP-1 cells) as described earlier (**Subheading 3.2.2**) was precleared by ultracentrifugation (150,000 × *g*, 30 min at 4°C).
2. Aliquots of cytosol (100 μg) in H/K buffer were incubated with GTPγS (100 μM) to induce actin polymerization, in the absence or presence of jasplakinolide, added at a final concentration of 1 μM to stabilize the formed actin filaments.
3. Actin filaments were pelleted by centrifugation at 17,500 × *g* for 30 min at 4°C and the supernatants saved. Pellets were washed extensively in H/K buffer.
4. One-tenth aliquots of the supernatants and all the pellets were analyzed on 9% SDS–PAGE gels and probed for SK1 and actin as noted earlier. Results obtained with the pellet fractions are shown in **Fig. 2B**.

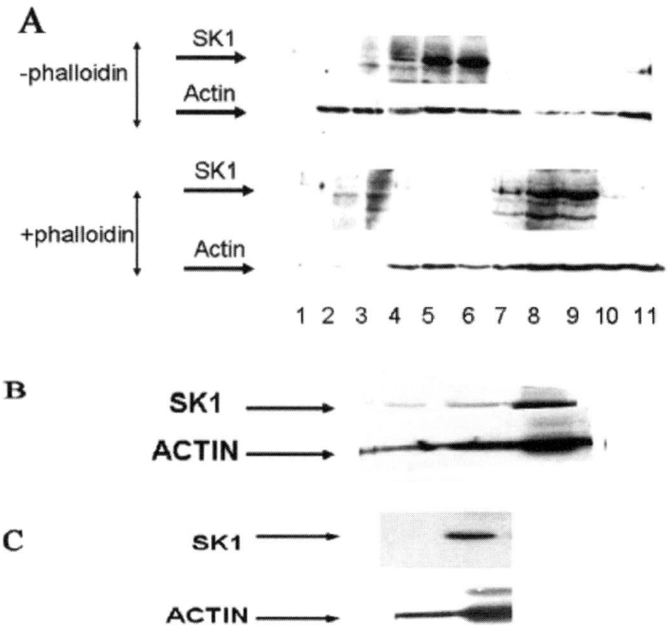

Fig. 2. SK1 binds to actin filaments and G-actin. (**A**) Effect of phalloidin on velocity sedimentation on sucrose gradients. Membranes and cytosol from RAW 264.7 (or THP-1) cells were incubated with PMA (100 nM) at 37°C for 30 min. Membranes were then reisolated by centrifugation at 17,500 × *g*, washed, and phalloidin (10 μM) was added to select samples for the final 15 min of the incubation. Membranes were washed and solubilized in 1% Triton X-100 buffer and then loaded on top of a 4-mL linear gradient of sucrose (20–55%). Samples were centrifuged at 150,000 × *g* for 16 h at 8°C, and fractions (400 μL) collected from the top of gradient were subjected to SDS–PAGE followed by Western blotting for SK1 and actin. (**B**) Cosedimentation assay. Cytosol from 10^8 THP-1 cells was precleared by ultracentrifugation (150,000 × *g*, 30 min, 4°C). Aliquots (100 μg) were incubated with GTPγS (100 μM) (*lanes 2 and 3*) to induce actin polymerization, and jasplakinolide was added at a final concentration of 1 μM (*lane 3*) to stabilize actin filaments. Actin filaments were pelleted by centrifugation at 17,500 × *g* for 30 min at 4°C, washed extensively, and the pellet fractions analyzed by 10% SDS–PAGE gels and probed for SK1 and actin by immunoblotting. (**C**) Coisolation of SK1 with G-actin by binding to immobilized DNase1. Cytosol from 10^8 THP-1 cells was dialyzed extensively against actin monomer buffer (AMB), precleared by centrifugation, and then incubated with (*lane 2*) or without (*lane 1*) PMA (100 nM) for 30 min at 37°C. An equal aliquot of immobilized DNase1 was added to each fraction and incubated for 4 h at 4°C. The DNase-bound material was pelleted and washed extensively with AMB before being subjected to SDS–PAGE and immunoblotting for SK1 and actin. Reprinted with permission from **ref.** *35*.

5. Incubation with GTPγS alone resulted in the recovery of low amount of SK1 in the pellet (**Fig. 2B**). Addition of jasplakinolide resulted in a much greater recovery of both actin and SK1 in the pellet fraction (*see* **Note 7**).
6. The results of the velocity sedimentation and cosedimentation assays confirm the coimmunoprecipitation and confocal

microscopy studies to support the hypothesis that SK1 associates with actin filaments and/or globular G-actin.

3.7. Determination of SK1 Binding to G-Actin by Coisolation with DNase 1

DNase 1 is a well-characterized G-actin binding protein that forms a stable 1:1 complex with G-actin. We utilized immobilized DNase 1 to pull down G-actin and, in the process, hypothesized that any other protein associated with G-actin would also be coisolated.

1. Cytosol from RAW or THP-1 cells was isolated as described earlier (**Subheading 3.2.2**) and dialyzed extensively against actin monomer buffer (AMB, 5 mM Tris–HCl, pH 8.0, 0.2 mM $CaCl_2$ with 0.2 mM ATP, 0.5 mM dithiothreitol) and then precleared by ultracentrifugation.
2. Aliquots of clarified cytosol (100 μg) were incubated with or without PMA (100 nM) for 30 min at 37°C.
3. Immobilized DNase 1 (*see* **Note 8**) was added to each fraction and incubated for 4 h at 4°C.
4. The DNase 1-bound material was pelleted at low speed (2000 × *g*, 5 min at 4°C) and washed extensively with AMB buffer.
5. The pelleted agarose beads were subjected to 9% SDS–PAGE after addition of SDS sample buffer and heating for 5 min at 90°C.
6. The proteins were transferred to PVDF membrane; blots were blocked in 5% nonfat dry milk, washed, and probed for actin by incubating overnight in antiactin antibody (monoclonal IgM) at 4°C. The blots were also probed for SK1 using the anti-SK1 rabbit polyclonal antibody. Detection utilized horseradish-peroxidase-coupled secondary antibody and ECL.
7. In the absence of PMA, no SK1 was detected in the G-actin–DNase 1 complex (*lane 1*, **Fig. 2C**). However, in the presence of PMA (*lane 2*, **Fig. 2C**), SK1 was detected in association with the DNase1 pellet, supporting the hypothesis that SK1 binds G-actin under stimulated, but not basal, conditions.

3.8. Assessment of the Effects of Modulation of Actin Polymerization on SK1 Activity

We evaluated whether modulation of actin dynamics would affect the enzymatic activity of SK1. Sphingosine kinase activity was determined in control RAW cells and cells preincubated with the known actin cytoskeleton modifiers, jasplakinolide and latrunculin B. Jasplakinolide promotes actin polymerization by increasing the rate of monomer nucleation and via stabilization of actin filaments *(35)*. Latrunculin B binds G-actin monomers with high affinity resulting in progressive depolymerization of actin filaments.

1. RAW 264.7 cells were incubated with jasplakinolide (1 μM, 15 min), latrunculin B (20 μg/mL, 10 min), or buffer control at 37°C.

2. PMA (100 nM, final concentration) was added to select samples and incubated for 30 min.
3. Cells were washed once with ice-cold phosphate-buffered saline and scraped into ice-cold SK Assay Buffer.
4. Cells were disrupted by sonication on ice and assessed for cell lysis by microscopy.
5. Aliquots of each whole cell lysate were used for determination of enzymatic activity by incubation with the substrate, sphingosine (1 mM sphingosine prepared in 5% Triton X-100, final concentrations: 0.25% Triton X-100, 50 μM sphingosine). The reaction was started by the addition of [γ-^{32}P]ATP (0.025 μCi/sample) and was terminated after 10 min at 37°C.
6. ^{32}P-labeled sphingosine 1-phosphate formed during the reaction was isolated by thin layer chromatography using the solvent system, 80 butanol: 20 ethanol: 10 acetic acid: 20 water.
7. The radioactivity in the sphingosine 1-phosphate band was quantified using the Typhoon PhosphorImager (GE Healthcare).
8. SK activity of the samples was expressed as the percent of control cells incubated in buffer alone (mean ± range).
9. The positive control, PMA, increased SK activity by 77% (range: 66–88%, $p < 0.02$, $n = 5$). Jasplakinolide caused an 85% increase in SK activity, compared to buffer-treated control cells (range: 79–91%, $p < 0.01$). Latrunculin B resulted in a modest 38% increase in SK activity (range: 25–51%, $p < 0.02$). The fact that both jasplakinolide, which increases actin polymerization, and latrunculin, which decreases polymerization, have similar positive effects on SK activity suggests that it is their common physiologic effect – that of decreasing the concentration of G-actin – which is responsible for enhancement of SK activity. In this model, G-actin inhibits SK activity, and effectors which decrease the concentration of G-actin cause an increase in the activity of SK.
10. These results are consistent with the hypothesis that the enzymatic activity of SK1 is modulated by changes in actin dynamics and/or the state of actin polymerization.

4. Notes

1. Effects of experimental manipulations on MDM viability were assessed by exclusion of trypan blue, and monolayer density was determined by nuclei counting with naphthol blue-black

stain *(33)*. Purity and viability of MDMs were >95% by Wright staining and trypan blue exclusion, respectively.

2. COZ contains the complement component, C3bi, as its active surface ligand. Since serum contains factors which degrade C3bi, it is imperative that COZ be washed carefully to remove traces of serum. Maintaining COZ on ice will prolong its stability.
3. For experiments in which phalloidin is used to image actin filaments, methanol is omitted from the permeabilization media due to its interference with phalloidin.
4. PMA is the commonly used phorbol ester. Phorbol 12-myristate 13-acetate is a potent tumor promoter. Stock solution (10 mM) was prepared in absolute ethanol or DMSO and stored at –20°C.
5. N_2 cavitation: Cell disruption is performed by the nitrogen decompression method in the Parr Cell Disruption Bomb precooled at 4°C. The cells are pressurized with N_2 and left on ice for equilibration with the gas. The N_2 pressure and the duration of equilibration depend on the cell type and the number of cells. Efficiency of cell disruption can be evaluated by monitoring release of cytosolic constituents, such as lactate dehydrogenase, or by microscopic examination. Controlled cell disruption occurs when the pressure in the chamber is released by opening the discharge valve and collecting the homogenate.
6. Phalloidin is a bicyclic toxin from the mushroom *Amanita phalloides*. Care must be exercised in its handling. Stock solution at 10 mg/mL is prepared in anhydrous methanol and stored at –20°C.
7. Because intact cytosol was utilized, the cosedimentation of SK1 with actin does not indicate direct binding to F-actin. The association of SK1 with actin filaments may be indirect, via actin-binding proteins.
8. Immobilized deoxyribonuclease 1 (DNase 1) was prepared essentially according to published protocol *(36)*. 200 mg of DNase 1 (Bovine pancreas) was dissolved in 10 mL of coupling buffer (100 mM HEPES, pH 7.2, 80 mM $CaCl_2$. 1 mM PMSF) and dialyzed overnight against the same buffer at 4°C. It was mixed with 10 mL of washed Affi-Gel 10 matrix and incubated for 4 h at 4°C. Excess reactive sites were blocked with 10 mM ethanolamine (pH 7.0) for 1 h at 4°C. Coupling efficiency was determined from protein amounts before and after coupling. For column chromatography, we coupled DNase 1 to HiTrap-NHS- activated matrix (GE Healthcare Biosciences, NJ) following the manufacturer's protocol.

Acknowledgments

The authors would like to thank their colleagues in the Inflammation Program at the University of Iowa for their support and Randy Nessler of the Central Microscopy Research Facility for assistance with the confocal microscopy. This work was supported by National Institutes of Health RO1 grants GM62302 and AI055916, P01 grant, AI44642–08, and VA Merit Review to DJK.

References

1. Spiegel S, Milstien S. (2002). Sphingosine 1-phosphate, a key cell signaling molecule. *J. Biol. Chem.* 277:25851–25854
2. Taha TA, Hannun YA, Obeid LM. (2006). Sphingosine kinase: biochemical and cellular regulation and role in disease. *J. Biochem. Mol. Biol.* 39:113–131
3. Liu H, Chakravarty D, Maceyka M, Milstien S, Spiegel S. (2002). Sphingosine kinases: a novel family of lipid kinases. *Prog. Nucleic Acid Res. Mol. Biol.* 71:493–511
4. Pyne S, Long JS, Ktistakis NT, Pyne NJ. (2005). Lipid phosphate phosphatases and lipid phosphate signalling. *Biochem. Soc. Trans.* 33:1370–1374
5. Maceyka M, Milstien S, Spiegel S. (2005). Sphingosine kinases, sphingosine-1-phosphate and sphingolipidomics. *Prostaglandins Other Lipid Mediat.* 77:15–22
6. Wattenberg BW, Pitson SM, Raben DM. (2006). The sphingosine- and diacylglycerol-kinase superfamily of signaling kinases. Localization as a key to signaling function. *J. Lipid Res.* 47:1128–1139
7. Liu H, Sugiura M, Nava VE, Edsall LC, Kono K, Poulton S, Milstien S, Kohama T, Spiegel S. (2000). Molecular cloning and functional characterization of a novel mammalian sphingosine kinase type 2 isoform. *J. Biol. Chem.* 275:19513–19520
8. Luna EJ. (1998). F-actin blot overlays. *Methods Enzymol.* 298:32–42
9. Kohama T, Olivera A, Edsall L, Nagiec MM, Dickson R, Spiegel S. (1998). Molecular cloning and functional characterization of murine sphingosine kinase. *J. Biol. Chem.* 273:23722–23728
10. Nava VE, Lacana E, Poulton S, Liu H, Sugiura M, Kono K, Milstien S, Kohama T, Spiegel S. (2000). Functional characterization of human sphingosine kinase-1. *FEBS Lett.* 473:81–84
11. Panebra A, Ma SX, Zhai LW, Wang XT, Rhee SG, Khurana S. (2001). Regulation of phospholipase C-gamma 1 by the actin-regulatory protein villin. *Am. J. Physiol. Cell Physiol.* 281:C1046–C1058
12. Papakonstanti EA, Emmanouel DS, Gravanis A, Stournaras C. (2000). PLC-gamma 1 signaling pathway and villin activation are involved in actin cytoskeleton reorganization induced by Na^{+}/Pi cotransport up-regulation. *Mol. Med.* 6:303–318
13. Pei Z, Yang L, Williamson JR. (1996). Phospholipase C-gamma 1 binds to actin-cytoskeleton via its C-terminal SH2 domain in vitro. *Biochem. Biophys. Res. Commun.* 228:802–806
14. Iyer SS, Kusner DJ. (1999). Association of phospholipase D activity with the detergent-insoluble cytoskeleton of U937 promonocytic leukocytes. *J. Biol. Chem.* 274:2350–2359
15. Kusner DJ, Barton JA. (2001). ATP stimulates human macrophages to kill intracellular virulent *Mycobacterium tuberculosis* via calcium-dependent phagosome–lysosome fusion. *J. Immunol.* 167:3308–3315
16. Kusner DJ, Barton JA, Qin C, WangX, Iyer SS. (2003). Evolutionary conservation of physical and functional interactions between phospholipase D and actin. *Arch. Biochem. Biophys.* 412:231–241
17. Hobson JP, Rosenfeldt HM, Barak LS, Olivera A, Poulton S, Caron MG, Milstien S, Spiegel S. (2001). Role of the sphingosine-1-phosphate receptor EDG-1 in PDGF-induced cell motility. *Science.* 291:1800–1803
18. Kee TH, Vit P, Melendez AJ. (2005). Sphingosine kinase signalling in immune cells. *Clin. Exp. Pharmacol. Physiol.* 32:153–161

19. Kaneider NC, Kaser A, Dunzendorfer S, Tilg H, Wiedermann CJ. (2003). Sphingosine kinase-dependent migration of immature dendritic cells in response to neurotoxic prion protein fragment. *J. Virol.* 77:5535–5539

20. Kaneider N, Djanani A, Fischer C, Wiedermann C. (2002). Sphingosine kinase-dependent directional migration of leukocytes in response to phorbol ester. *Biochem. Biophys. Res. Commun.* 297:806–810

21. Bader MF, Doussau F, Chasserot-Golaz S, Vitale N, Gasman S. (2004). Coupling actin and membrane dynamics during calcium-regulated exocytosis: a role for Rho and ARF GTPases. *Biochim. Biophys. Acta.* 1742:37–49

22. Eitzen G. (2003). Actin remodeling to facilitate membrane fusion. *Biochim. Biophys. Acta.*1641:175–181

23. Qualmann B, Kessels MM, Kelly RB. (2000). Molecular links between endocytosis and the actin cytoskeleton. *J. Cell Biol.* 150:111–116

24. Yadav M, Clark L, Schorey JS. (2006). Macrophage's proinflammatory response to a mycobacterial infection is dependent on sphingosine kinase-mediated activation of phosphatidylinositol phospholipase C, protein kinase C, ERK1/2, and phosphatidylinositol 3-kinase. *J. Immunol.* 176:5494–5503

25. Pitson SM, Moretti PAB, Zebol JR, Xia P, Gamble JR, Vadas MA, D'Andrea RJ, Wattenberg BW. (2000). Expression of a catalytically inactive sphingosine kinase mutant blocks agonist-induced sphingosine kinase activation. A dominant negative sphingosine kinase. *J. Biol. Chem.* 275:33945–33950

26. Johnson KR, Becker KP, Facchinetti MM, Hannun YA, Obeid LM. (2002). PKC dependent activation of sphingosine kinase 1 and translocation to the plasma membrane. Extracellular release of sphingosine-1-phosphate induced by PMA. *J. Biol. Chem.* 277:35257–35262

27. Pitson SM, Moretti PAB, Zebol JR, Zareie R, Cerian CK, Darrow AL, Qi J, D'Andrea RJ, Bagley CJ, Vadas MA, Wattenberg BW. (2002). The nucleotide-binding site of human sphingosine kinase 1. *J. Biol. Chem.* 277:49545–49553

28. Pitson SM, Moretti PAB, Zebol JR, Lynn HE, Xia P, Vadas MA, Wattenberg BW. (2003). Activation of sphingosine kinase 1 by ERK1/2-mediated phosphorylation. *EMBO J.* 22:5491–5500

29. Kodama A, Lechler T, Fuchs E. (2004). Coordinating cytoskeletal tracks to polarize cellular movements. *J. Cell. Biol.* 167:203–207

30. Kodama A, Karakesisoglou I, Wong E, Vaezi A, Fuchs E. (2003). ACF7: an essential integrator of microtubule dynamics. *Cell.* 115:343–354

31. Thompson CR, Iyer SS, Melrose N, VanOosten R, Johnson K, Pitson SM, Obeid LM, Kusner DJ. (2005). Sphingosine kinase 1 (SK1) is recruited to nascent phagosomes in human macrophages: Inhibition of SK1 translocation by *Mycobacterium tuberculosis.* *J. Immunol.* 174:3551–3561

32. Lorenzi R, Brickell PM, Katz DR, Kinnon C, Thrasher AJ. (2000). Wiskott-Aldrich syndrome protein is necessary for efficient IgG-mediated phagocytosis. *Blood.* 95:2943–2946

33. Malik ZA, Thompson CR, Hashimi S, Porter B, Iyer SS, Kusner DJ. (2003). Cutting Edge: *Mycobacterium tuberculosis* blocks Ca^{2+} signaling and phagosome maturation in human macrophages via specific inhibition of sphingosine kinase. *J. Immunol.* 170:2811–2815

34. Malik ZA, Iyer SS, Kusner DJ. (2001). *Mycobacterium tuberculosis* phagosomes exhibit altered calmodulin-dependent signal transduction: Contribution to inhibition of phagosome–lysosome fusion and intracellular survival in human macrophages. *J. Immunol.* 166:3392–3401

35. Kusner DJ, Thompson CR, Melrose NA, Pitson SM, Obeid LM, Iyer SS. (2007). The localization and activity of sphingosine kinase 1 are coordinately regulated with actin cytoskeletal dynamics in macrophages. *J. Biol. Chem.* 282:23147–23162

36. Kron SJ, Drubin DG, Botstein D, Spudich JA. (1992). Yeast actin filaments display ATP-dependent over surfaces coated with rabbit muscle myosin. *Proc Natl. Acad. Sci. U.S.A.* 89, 4466–4470

INDEX

R

S

T

U

W

Z

PassKey
Learning Systems

EA Review

Part 1: Individuals

Enrolled Agent Study Guide

May 1, 2021-February 28, 2022 Testing Cycle

Joel Busch, CPA, JD
Christy Pinheiro, EA, ABA®
Kolleen Wells, EA
Thomas A. Gorczynski, EA, USTCP

Executive Editor: Joel Busch, CPA, JD

This study guide is designed for exam candidates who will take their exams in the May 1, 2021, to February 28, 2022 testing cycle.

Title: PassKey Learning Systems EA Review Part 1 Individuals; Enrolled Agent Study Guide, May 1, 2021-February 28, 2022 Testing Cycle

ISBN: 978-1-935664-73-4

First Printing, March 2021.

PassKey EA Review®, PassKey Learning Systems® are U.S. Registered Trademarks.

Cover image licensed with permission. ©Janpietruszka at Dreamstime.com

Official website: www.PassKeyonline.com

Study Note: Prometric will NOT TEST on any legislation or court decisions passed after December 31, 2020. For exams taken between May 1, 2021, to February 28, 2022, all references on the examination are to the Internal Revenue Code, forms and publications, as amended through December 31, 2020. Also, unless otherwise stated, all questions relate to the calendar year 2020. Questions that contain the term 'current tax year' refer to the calendar year 2020.

This page intentionally left blank.

Table of Contents

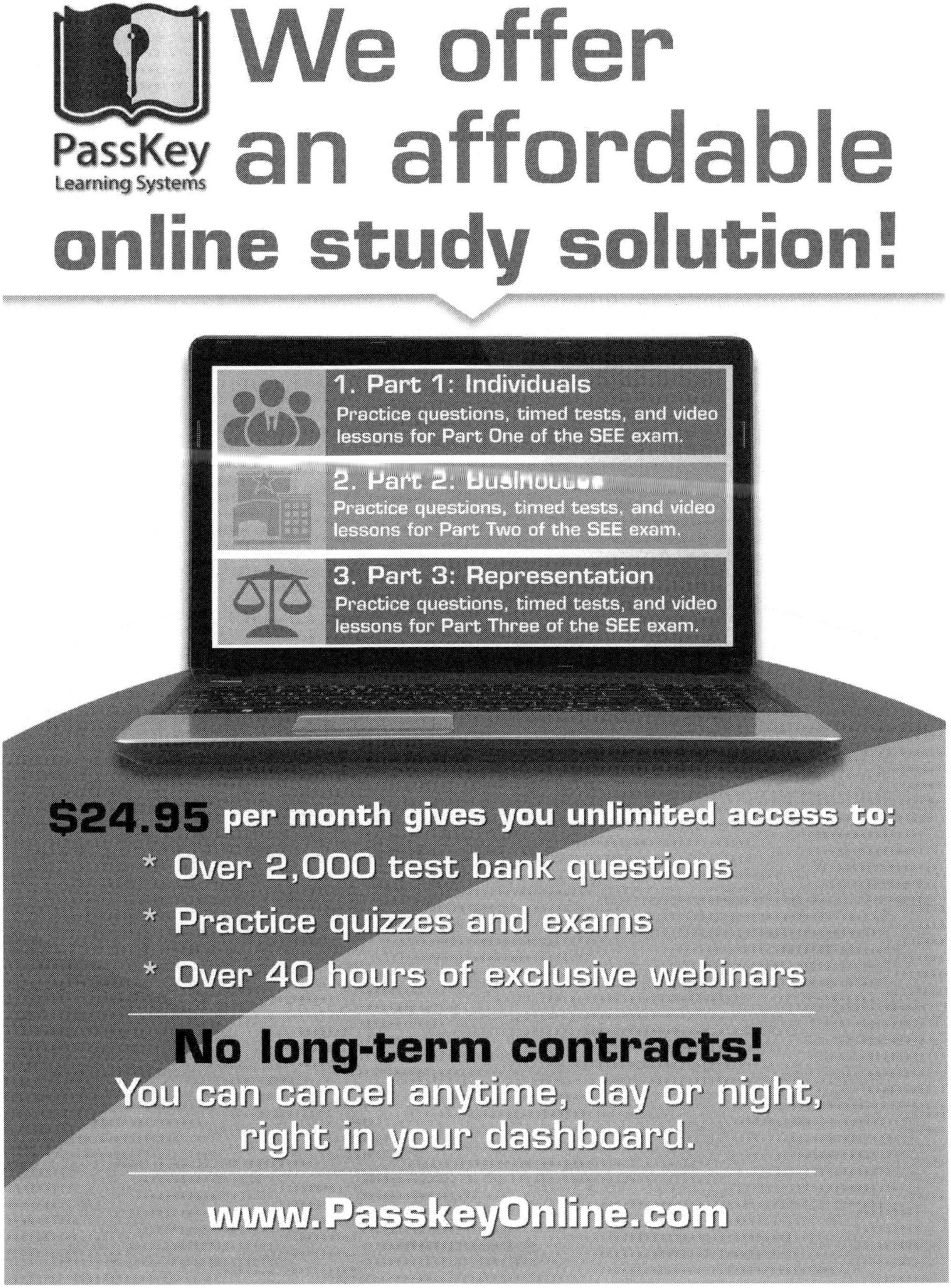
PassKey
Learning Systems
We offer
an affordable
online study solution!
1. Part 1: Individuals
Practice questions, timed tests, and video lessons for Part One of the SEE exam.
2. Part 2:
Practice questions, timed tests, and video lessons for Part Two of the SEE exam.
3. Part 3: Representation
Practice questions, timed tests, and video lessons for Part Three of the SEE exam.
$24.95 per month gives you unlimited access to:
* Over 2,000 test bank questions
* Practice quizzes and exams
* Over 40 hours of exclusive webinars
No long-term contracts!
You can cancel anytime, day or night, right in your dashboard.
www.PasskeyOnline.com

Recent Praise for the PassKey EA Review Series

(Real customers, real names, public testimonials)

Passed on First Try
Jake Bavaro
I recently passed the first part of the EA exam using just the textbook and separate practice test workbook. The textbook is very easy to read and understand. Although I have a background in accounting and tax, someone with little or no knowledge of either should be able to grasp all of the various topics covered in the book. I really do believe that it is a superior preparation resource.

I Highly recommend these materials
Tosha H. Knelangeon
Using only the [PassKey] study guide and the workbook, I passed all three EA exams on my first try. I highly recommend these materials. As long as you put in the time to read and study all the information provided, you should be well-prepared.

You can pass using just this book.
Vishnu Kali Osirion
I really rushed studying for this section. These authors make tax law relevant to your day-to-day experiences and understandable. You can pass the exam with just this as a resource. I do recommend purchasing the workbook as well, just for question exposure. The questions in the book and in the workbook are pretty indicative of what's on the exam. This is a must-buy. Cheers.

Suika Yutaka
I prefer self-study over any other type of course, and I loved this book. I have a very demanding job, and this made me greatly appreciate the concise and to-the-point style of this book. Also, note that this is the most reasonably priced full review (i.e., covering all three parts of the exam) I know of. Greatest praise!

PassKey was the only study aid that I used
Stephen J Woodard, CFP, CLU, ChFC
The guides were an invaluable resource. They were concise and covered the subject matter succinctly with spot-on end-of-chapter questions that were very similar to what I encountered on the exams.

100% Success!
Shreejith Nair
Very easy to understand with very good examples on each topic. I cleared [the exam] on my first attempt. I would highly recommend PassKey to all folks. Best of luck.

Worked like a charm.
Brian Lang (New York, New York)
I passed on my first try.

Very useful, I passed my exams by reading only PassKey!
Shixiong Feng
Very useful, I passed the 1st and 2nd exams by only reading the PassKey EA Review. If you are willing to spend some time to read the whole book thoroughly, then this book is the only thing you need to pass the EA exams.

Amazing!
Sopio Svanishvilion
PassKey helped me pass all three parts of the Enrolled Agent exam. They are a "must-have" if you want to pass your EA exams.

A great EA review book
William Highfield (Lafayette, Colorado)
I used the Complete EA Review book as a study guide and passed all my tests the first time. Don't get the idea the tests were easy, but the book was so well-organized and inclusive that the memorization and familiarization processes went very well.

This review is the best on the market.
Yaw Asiante-Asamoah
I passed on all three parts on one attempt. The questions in the EA Review and Workbook are similar to the real exams. I got a big raise, and my bonus went up at my seasonal job. It's worth the money, trust me.

Excellent explanations!
Janet Briggs
The best thing about these books is that each answer has a comprehensive explanation about why the answer is correct. I passed all three EA exams on the first attempt.

This book is worth the money.
Bridgette Holzapple
I passed Part 2 on my first try. The questions on the test were very similar to the problems in the workbook. You will pass, no doubt!

I passed all three parts on my first attempt.
Michelle D. Stroschen
I passed all three parts on my first attempt. I would definitely recommend it! These books are reasonably priced and have up-to-date information.

Introduction

Congratulations on taking the first step toward becoming an enrolled agent, a widely respected professional tax designation. The Internal Revenue Service licenses enrolled agents, known as EAs, after candidates pass a competency exam testing their knowledge of federal tax law. As an enrolled agent, you will have the same representation rights as a CPA, with the ability to represent taxpayers in IRS audits and appeals—an EA's rights are unlimited before all levels and offices of the IRS.

The PassKey study guide series is designed to help you study for the EA exam, which is formally called the *IRS Special Enrollment Examination* or *"SEE."*

EA Exam Basics

The EA exam consists of three parts, which candidates may schedule separately and take in any order they wish. The computerized exam covers all aspects of federal tax law, with Part 1 testing the taxation of individuals; Part 2 testing the taxation of businesses; and Part 3 testing representation, practice, and procedures.

Each part of the EA exam features 100 multiple choice questions, with no written answers required. The exam will include some experimental questions that are not scored. You will not know which of the questions count toward your score and which do not.

Computerized EA Exam Format

Part 1: Individual Taxation–100 questions

Part 2: Business Taxation–100 questions

Part 3: Representation, Practice, and Procedures–100 questions

You will have 3.5 hours to complete each part of the exam. The actual seat time is four hours, which allows time for a pre-exam tutorial and a post-exam survey. An on-screen timer counts down the amount of time you have to finish.

Note: Beginning May 1, 2020, the Special Enrollment Exam (SEE) will include one scheduled 15-minute break. Once you have answered questions 1-50, completed your review of your answers, and acknowledged you have completed section one, the test timer will stop for up to 15 minutes. After acknowledging that you have completed the first section of the exam, you will no longer be able to access the first section of the test content, including making changes to your answers. You may choose to decline the scheduled break and continue testing.

The testing company Prometric exclusively administers the EA exam at thousands of testing centers across the United States and in certain other countries. You can find valuable information and register online at ***https:/www.prometric.com/IRS***.

Prometric Testing Center Procedures

The testing center is designed to be a secure environment. The following are procedures you will need to follow on test day:

1. Check in about a half-hour before your appointment time and bring a current, government-issued ID with a photo and signature. If you do not have a valid ID, you will be turned away and will have to pay for a new exam appointment. Refunds will not be issued by Prometric if you forget to bring a proper ID with you.
2. The EA exam is a closed-book test, so you are not allowed to bring any notes or reference materials into the testing room. The center supplies sound-blocking headphones if you want to use them.
3. No food, water, or other beverages are allowed in the testing room.
4. You will be given scratch paper and a pencil to use, which will be collected after the exam.
5. You will be able to use an on-screen calculator during the exam, or Prometric will provide you with a handheld calculator. You cannot bring your own calculator into the examination room.
6. Before entering the testing room, you will be scanned with a metal detector wand.
7. You will need to sign in and out every time you leave the testing room. Beginning May 1, 2020, the Special Enrollment Exam (SEE) will include one scheduled 15-minute break. Additional breaks are permitted, but the test timer will continue to count down.
8. You are not allowed to talk or communicate with other test-takers in the exam room. Prometric continuously monitors the testing via video, physical walk-throughs, and an observation window.

Important Note: Violation of any of these procedures may result in the disqualification of your exam. In cases of cheating, the IRS says candidates are subject to consequences that include civil and criminal penalties.

Exam-takers who require special accommodations under the Americans with Disabilities Act (ADA) must contact Prometric directly to obtain an accommodation request. The test is administered in English; a language barrier is not considered a disability.

Exam Content

Each year, using questions based on the prior calendar year's tax law, the IRS introduces multiple new versions of each part of the EA exam. If you fail a particular part of the exam and need to retake it, do not expect to see identical questions the next time.

Prometric's website includes broad content outlines for each exam part. When you study, make sure you are familiar with the items listed, which are covered in detail in your PassKey guides. Questions from older exams are available on the IRS website for review. Be aware that tax law changes every year, so be familiar with recent updates and do not rely too heavily on these earlier questions and answers.

Your PassKey study guides present an overview of all the major areas of federal taxation that enrolled agents typically encounter in their practices and are likely to appear on the exam. Although our guides are designed to be comprehensive, we suggest you also review IRS

publications and try to learn as much as you can about tax law in general, so you are well-equipped to take the exam.

In addition to this study guide, we highly recommend that all exam candidates read:

- Publication 17, *Your Federal Income Tax* (for Part 1 of the exam), and
- Circular 230, *Regulations Governing the Practice of Attorneys, Certified Public Accountants, Enrolled Agents, Enrolled Actuaries, and Appraisers before the Internal Revenue Service* (for Part 3 of the exam)

You may download these publications for free from the IRS website.

Note: Some exam candidates take *Part 3: Representation, Practice, and Procedures* first rather than taking the tests in order, since the material in Part 3 is considered less complicated. However, test-takers should know that several questions pertaining to taxation of *Individuals* (Part 1) and *Businesses* (Part 2) are often included on the Part 3 exam.

Exam Strategy

Each multiple-choice question has four answer choices. There are several different question formats, and examples of each format are featured in your PassKey study guides. During the exam, you should read each question thoroughly to understand precisely what is being asked. Be particularly careful when the problem uses language such as "not" or "except."

Format One–Direct Question

Which of the following entities are required to file Form 709, *United States Gift Tax Return*?

A. An individual
B. An estate or trust
C. A corporation
D. All of the above

Format Two–Incomplete Sentence

Supplemental wages do not include payments for:

A. Accumulated sick leave
B. Nondeductible moving expenses
C. Vacation pay
D. Travel reimbursements paid at the federal government's per diem rate

Format Three–All of the Following Except

Five tests must be met for you to claim an exemption for a dependent. Which of the following is not a requirement?

A. Citizen or Resident Test
B. Member of Household or Relationship Test
C. Disability Test
D. Joint Return Test

If you are unsure of an answer, you may mark it for review and return to it later. Try to eliminate clearly wrong answers from the four possible choices to narrow your odds of selecting the right answer. But be sure to answer every question, even if you have to guess, because all answers left incomplete will be marked as incorrect. Each question is weighted equally.

There may also be a limited number of questions that have four choices, with three incorrect statements or facts and only one with a correct statement or fact, which you would select as the right answer.

With 3.5 hours allotted for each part of the exam, you have slightly more than two minutes per question. Try to answer the questions you are sure about quickly, so you can devote more time to those that include calculations or that you are unsure about. Remember, the clock does not stop for bathroom breaks, so allocate your time wisely.

To familiarize yourself with the computerized testing format, you may take a tutorial on the Prometric website. However, the tutorial only illustrates what the test screens look like; it does not allow you to revisit questions you have left open or marked for review, as you can do during the actual exam.

Scoring Methods

The EA exam is not graded on a curve, and the IRS does not reveal either a percentage of correct answers needed to pass or a predetermined pass rate. Each question on the exam is worth one point. The IRS determines scaled scores by calculating the number of questions answered correctly from the total number of questions in the exam and converting to a scale that ranges from 40 to 130. The IRS has set the scaled passing score at 105, which corresponds to the minimum level of knowledge deemed acceptable for EAs.

After you finish your exam and submit your answers, you will exit the testing room, and a Prometric staff member will print results showing whether you passed or failed. Test results are automatically shared with the IRS, so you do not need to submit them yourself. Test scores are confidential and will be revealed only to you and the IRS. If you pass, your printed results will show a passing designation but not your actual score. The printout also will not indicate which specific questions you answered correctly or incorrectly.

If you fail, you will receive a scaled score, so you will be able to see how close you are to the minimum score of 105. You will also receive the following diagnostic information to help you know which subject areas to concentrate on when studying to retake the exam:

- *Level 1: Area of weakness where additional study is necessary. You need to focus on this domain as you prepare to retake the test. You may want to consider taking a course or participating actively in a study group on this topic.*
- *Level 2: Might need additional study.*
- *Level 3: Clearly demonstrated an understanding of the subject area.*

These diagnostic indicators correspond to various sections of each part of the exam.

If necessary, you may take each part of the exam up to four times during the current testing window. You will need to re-register with Prometric and pay fees each new time you take an

exam part. In general, exam-takers may carry over passing scores for individual parts of the exam up to two years from the date they take them. However, due to the global pandemic, the IRS extended the two-year period to three years.

This new carryover rule applies to any examination parts that had not expired as of February 29, 2020, and any examination parts passed on June 1, 2020, and later. For example, assume a candidate passed Part 1 on November 15, 2019. Subsequently, the candidate passed Part 2 on February 15, 2020. That candidate has until November 15, 2022, to pass the remaining part.

Applying for Enrollment

Once you have passed all three parts of the EA exam, you can apply to become an enrolled agent. The process includes an IRS review of your tax compliance history. Failure to timely file or pay personal income taxes can be grounds for denial of enrollment. The Return Preparer Office will review the circumstances of each case and make determinations on an individual basis. You may not practice as an EA until the IRS approves your application and issues you an enrollment card, a process that takes up to 60 days or more.

Successfully passing the EA exam can launch you into a fulfilling and lucrative new career. The exam requires intense preparation and diligence, but with the help of PassKey's comprehensive *EA Review*, you will have the tools you need to learn how to become an enrolled agent.

We wish you much success.

This page intentionally left blank.

Ten Steps for the EA Exam

STEP 1: Learn

Learn more about the enrolled agent designation, and explore the career opportunities that await you after passing your EA exam. In addition to preparing income tax returns for clients, EAs can represent individuals and businesses before the IRS, just as attorneys and CPAs do. A college degree or professional tax background is not required to take the EA exam. Many people who use the PassKey study guides have had no prior experience preparing tax returns, but go on to rewarding new professional careers.

STEP 2: Gather Information

Gather more information before you launch into your studies. The IRS publishes necessary information on its website *(www.irs.gov/Tax-Professionals/Enrolled-Agents)*.

You will also find valuable information about the exam itself on the Prometric testing website at www.prometric.com/IRS. Be sure to download the official Candidate Information Bulletin, which takes you step-by-step through the registration and testing process.

STEP 3: Obtain a PTIN

PTIN stands for "Preparer Tax Identification Number." Before you can register for your EA exam, you must obtain a PTIN from the IRS. The PTIN sign-up system can be found at ***www.irs.gov/ptin.*** You will need to create an account and provide personal information. Foreign-based candidates without a Social Security number are also required to have a PTIN in order to register to take the exam; they will need to submit additional paperwork with their Form W-12 (PTIN Application and Renewal).

STEP 4: Register with Prometric

Once you have your PTIN, you may register for your exam on the Prometric website by creating an account to set up your user ID and password. You must also complete Form 2587, Application for Special Enrollment Examination.

STEP 5: Schedule Your Test

After creating an account, you can complete the registration process by clicking on "Scheduling." Your exam appointment must be scheduled within one year from the date of registration. You can choose a test site, time, and date that are convenient for you. Prometric has test centers in most major metropolitan areas of the United States, as well as in many other countries.

You may schedule as little as two days in advance—space permitting—through the website or by calling Prometric directly Monday through Friday. Be aware that the website and the phone line show different available times and dates, so you may want to check both for your preferred testing dates. The testing fee is nonrefundable. Once you've scheduled, you'll receive a confirmation number. Keep it for your records because you will need it to reschedule, cancel, or change your appointment.

STEP 6: Adopt a Study Plan

Focus on one exam part at a time, and adopt a study plan that covers each unit of your PassKey guides. You'll need to develop your own individualized study program. The period of time you'll need to prepare for each exam is truly unique to you, based on how much prior tax preparation experience you have and your current level of tax knowledge, how well you understand and retain the information you read, and how much time you have to study for each test.

For those without prior tax experience, a good rule of thumb is to study *at least* 60 hours for each of the three exam sections. Part 2: Businesses may require additional study preparation, as evidenced by the lower pass rates. One thing is true for all candidates: for each of the tests, start studying well in advance of your scheduled exam date.

STEP 7: Get Plenty of Rest and Good Nutrition

Get plenty of rest, exercise, and good nutrition prior to the EA exam. You'll want to be at your best on exam day.

STEP 8: Test Day

Be sure to arrive early at the test site. Prometric advises arriving at least 30 minutes before your scheduled exam time. If you miss your appointment and are not allowed to take the test, you'll forfeit your fee and have to pay for a new appointment. Remember to bring a government-issued ID with your name, photo, and signature. Your first and last name must exactly match the first and last name you used to register for the exam.

STEP 9: During the Exam

This is when your hard work finally pays off. Focus and don't worry if you don't know the answer to every question, but make sure you use your time well. Give your best answer to every question. All questions left blank will be marked as wrong.

STEP 10: Congratulations. You Passed!

After celebrating your success, you need to apply for your EA designation. The quickest way is by filling out Form 23, Application for Enrollment to Practice Before the Internal Revenue Service, on the IRS website. You may also pay online. Once your application is approved, you'll be issued an enrollment card, and you'll officially be a brand-new enrolled agent!

Essential Tax Law Figures for Individuals

Here is a quick summary of some of the essential tax figures for the enrolled agent exam cycle that runs from May 1, 2021, to February 28, 2022:

Note: The *American Rescue Plan Act (ARPA)* was signed into law on March 11, 2021. This bill includes many retroactive provisions that impact 2020 and 2021 tax returns. However, because these are retroactive changes passed after December 31, 2020, they will not be tested in the current EA exam testing cycle. We have added some relevant footnotes to the text, but the provisions in the ARPA will not be covered.

Important Legislation for the 2020 Tax Year (in order of enactment):

1. The *Setting Every Community Up for Retirement (SECURE) Act* was signed into law on December 20, 2019. Most of the provisions in the act became effective on January 1, 2020, and apply to the 2020 tax year.

2. The *Families First Coronavirus Response Act (FFCRA)* was passed on March 18, 2020, and became effective on April 1, 2020. This was one of the federal government's first responses to the COVID-19 crisis. The *FFCRA* required certain employers to provide their employees with paid sick leave or expanded family and medical leave for specified reasons related to COVID-19.

3. *The Coronavirus Aid, Relief, and Economic Security (CARES) Act* became law on March 27, 2020. This $2.2 trillion economic stimulus bill included a host of new tax credits and retroactive provisions to provide COVID-19 relief to individuals and businesses.

4. The Consolidated Appropriations Act, 2021 (CAA 2021) was signed into law on December 27, 2020, by President Donald Trump. This legislation extends and modifies many provisions of the FFCRA and the *CARES Act.* The *Consolidated Appropriations Act* included a second round of stimulus payments and numerous tax extenders.

Individual Income Tax Return Filing Deadline: April 15, 2021 (extended due date: October 15, 2021).

FBAR Due Date: The official due date for the FBAR (FinCen 114) coincides with the filing of the federal tax return (April 15). However, an automatic extension is allowed until October 15.[1]

2020 Standard Deduction Amounts (by Filing Status):

- MFJ or Qualifying Widow(er) $24,800
- Single or MFS: $12,400
- HOH: $18,650

[1] FBAR refers to Form 114, Report of Foreign Bank and Financial Accounts, that must be filed with the Financial Crimes Enforcement Network (FinCEN), which is a bureau of the Treasury Department. Although the FBAR is not filed directly with the IRS, the IRS is responsible for FBAR enforcement. After a misworded posting caused confusion about the 2020 deadline to file FBARs, the Treasury's Financial Crimes Enforcement Network (FinCEN) extended the 2019 deadline to Oct. 31, 2020.

- Additional Standard Deduction for Age 65 and Over and/or Blindness
    - MFJ, QW or MFS: $1,300
    - Single or HOH: $1,650
- Dependent of another taxpayer; the lesser of:
    - The greater of: $1,100 or Earned Income + $350, or
    - $12,400

2020 Gross Income Filing Thresholds for U.S. Citizens and U.S. Residents:

- Single: $12,400
- Head of household: $18,650
- Married filing jointly: $24,800
- Married filing separately (of any age): $5 (this is not a typo; it really is $5)
- Qualifying widow(er) with dependent child: $24,800
- Dependent standard deduction: the lesser of:(1) $1,100, or (2) earned income plus $350 (but the total cannot be more than the standard deduction for their filing status).
- The filing thresholds above are increased for taxpayers who are 65 and older by the following:
    - $1,650 for Single or Head of Household
    - $1,300 for married taxpayers or Qualifying Widow(er)

2020 Estate and Trust *Exemption* Amounts[2]

- Estate Exemption Amount: $600
- Simple Trust: $300
- Complex Trust: $100
- Qualified disability trusts: $4,300

2020 Estate and Gift Tax *Exclusion* Amounts

- 2020 Annual Exclusion for Gifts: $15,000
- Lifetime *noncitizen* marital threshold for gift tax: $157,000[3]
- Estate and Gift Tax Unified Credit: $11,580,000[4]
- Generation-Skipping Transfer Tax Exemption: $11,580,000
- The basic credit amount for 2020 is $4,577,800.
- Highest estate and gift tax rate: 40%

2020 Tax Rates and Brackets: The following seven tax brackets apply for individuals in 2020: 10%, 12%, 22%, 24%, 32%, 35% and 37%.

2020 Foreign Earned Income Exclusion: $107,600[5]

---

[2] For estates and trusts, the exemption amount is not allowed in the entity's final tax year (the year of dissolution).

[3] There is no limit on the amount that a U.S. citizen can transfer to another U.S. citizen spouse in a calendar year. This limitation only applies to noncitizen spouses.

[4] A deceased spouse's unused credit (DSUE) amount is portable to a surviving spouse in 2020.

[5] For tax year 2020, the Internal Revenue Service provided a waiver related to the minimum time requirements for the foreign earned income exclusion. This waiver will be covered in more detail later.

2020 "Kiddie Tax" Threshold: The "Kiddie Tax" age limit is for those under 18 and certain dependents under 24. The unearned income threshold is $2,200.

- Unearned income is taxed at the rates of the child's parents.[6]
- However, earned income is taxed at single tax bracket rates.

2020 Retirement Plan Contribution Limits:

- Roth and traditional IRAs: $6,000 (additional catch-up contribution of $1,000 for taxpayers age 50 or older)[7]
- Roth IRA contribution limit phaseout (MAGI):
    - $196,000–$206,000: MFJ/QW
    - $124,000–$139,000: Single and HOH
    - $0 to $10,000: MFS[8]
- SIMPLE IRA elective deferral limits
    - Under age 50: $13,500
    - Age 50 and over: $16,500
- Profit Sharing/SEP-IRA contribution limits (employee + employer):
    - Up to 25% of compensation, up to a maximum of $57,000
    - Age 50 and over $63,500

- Qualified plan contribution Limits
    - 401(k)/403(b) plan deferral limits: $19,500 (50 and over $26,000)
    - Defined contribution plan limits (employee + employer):
    - Up to $57,000, if age 50 or older: $63,500
    - Employee compensation limit for calculating contributions: $285,000
    - Total contributions cannot exceed 100% of compensation.
    - Defined Benefit Plan Limits:[9]
        - Annual compensation maximum limit: $285,000
        - Normal maximum annual retirement benefit limit: Lesser of (1) $230,000, or (2) the average of the three highest years of compensation
    - Key employee threshold for nondiscrimination testing: $185,000
    - Highly compensated employee threshold for nondiscrimination testing: $130,000

2020 Long-Term Care Premiums: Maximum Deduction (Per Person): The maximum amount of qualified long-term care premiums includible as medical expenses has increased. The

---

[6] When the kiddie tax applies, the tax is reported on Form 8615, which is attached to the child's Form 1040. Alternatively, parents can elect to include the child's unearned income directly on their own return, using Form 8814, if certain requirements are met.

[7] The 2020 Traditional and Roth IRA Contribution Deadline is April 15, 2021.

[8] With regards to the Roth contribution limit, if the taxpayer is "married filing separately" but did not live with their spouse at any time during the year, the taxpayer may use the higher phaseout threshold for single taxpayers.

[9] A defined benefit plan is also called a "traditional pension" and these retirement plans are typically funded solely or primarily by the employer, not the employee. Actuarial assumptions and computations are required to figure these employer contributions.

limit on the deduction for premiums is for *each* person (not per tax return). Long-term-care premiums up to the amounts shown below can be included as medical expenses on Schedule A.

- Age 40 or under: $430
- Age 41 to 50: $810
- Age 51 to 60: $1,630
- Age 61 to 70: $4,350
- Age 71 or over: $5,430

2020 Maximum Compensation Subject to FICA

- OASDI[10] maximum wage base: $137,700
- Social Security Tax Rate:
    - Employee: 6.2%
    - Self-employed: 12.4%
- Maximum Social Security Tax
    - Employee: $8,537.40
    - Self-employed: $17,074.80
    - Medicare: No limit (2.9% for self-employed, 1.45% for employees)
    - Self-employed tax rate: 15.3%
- *Additional* Medicare Tax: 0.9% on earned income exceeding the following thresholds:
    - Married filing jointly: $250,000[11]
    - Married filing separately: $125,000
    - Single: $200,000
    - Head of household: $200,000
    - Qualifying widow(er) with dependent child: $200,000

2020 AMT Alternative Minimum Tax Exemptions: The AMT exemption amount has increased to $72,900 ($113,400 if MFJ or QW; $56,700 if MFS). The income levels at which the AMT exemption begins to phase out have increased to $518,400 ($1,036,800 if MFJ or QW).

2020 Net Investment Income Tax (NIIT): The tax is the *lesser* of: 3.8% of net investment income or the amount of modified adjusted gross income (MAGI) over the following thresholds:

- Married filing jointly: $250,000,
- Married filing separately: $125,000,
- Single or head of household: $200,000
- Qualifying widow(er) with a child: $250,000
- Estates and trusts: the NIIT is 3.8 percent on the *lesser* of:
    - The undistributed net investment income, or

10 "OASDI" is the official name for Social Security in the United States, and the terms are often used interchangeably. The acronym stands for "Old-Age, Survivors, and Disability Insurance."

11 Earned income of spouses is combined towards this Additional Medicare Tax threshold for MFJ returns. Employers must withhold this tax from wages or compensation when they pay employees more than $200,000 in a calendar year, regardless of the employee's filing status.

- The excess of the adjusted gross income over the dollar amount at which the highest tax bracket begins for an estate or trust for the tax year. For estates and trusts, the 2020 threshold is $12,950.

2020 Credits and Exclusions

- **Child Tax Credit (CTC):** $2,000 per qualifying child.
- **Additional Child Tax Credit (ACTC):** Maximum refundable portion: $1,400.
    - CTC/ACTC phaseout begins ($50 for every $1,000 of MAGI) over:
    - Married filing jointly: $400,000
    - All other filers: $200,000
- **Adoption Credit:** $14,300 (AGI phaseout range: $214,521–$254,520). The exclusion for employer-paid adoption reimbursement also $14,300.[12]
- **Other Dependent Credit (ODC):** $500. There is no refundable portion.
- **Credit for Child and Dependent Care Expenses:** $3,000 maximum qualifying expenses (one child); $6,000 (two or more children)
- **Earned Income Tax Credit (EITC):**[13] The maximum amount of the EITC for the year is:
    - $6,660 with three or more qualifying children
    - $5,920 with two qualifying children
    - $3,584 with one qualifying child
    - $538 with no qualifying children
    - Investment income must also be $3,650 or less for the year to be eligible for EITC.

Children Claimed	Maximum AGI (Single, HOH, QW)	Maximum AGI (MFJ)
Zero	$15,820	$21,710
One	$41,756	$47,646
Two	$47,440	$53,330
Three or more	$50,594	$56,844

2020 Capital Gains and Long-Term Dividends:[14]

Short-term capital gains and ordinary dividends are taxed at ordinary income rates. The top rates for qualified dividends and long-term capital gains are as follows:[15]

Marginal Rate	Single	HOH	MFJ/ QW	MFS	Estates and trusts
0%	$0–$40,000	$0–$53,600	$0–$80,000	$0 - $40,000	$0 - $2,650
15%	$40,001–$441,450	$53,601 - $469,050	$80,001 - $496,600	$40,001 - $248,300	$2,651 - $13,150
20%	Over $441,450	Over $469,050	Over $496,600	Over $248,300	Over $13,150

[12] Unlike most other credits, the adoption credit has the same phaseout range for all filing statuses.
[13] The IRS cannot issue refunds claiming the Earned Income Tax Credit (EITC) and the Additional Child Tax Credit (ACTC) before February 15, 2021. This is a congressional provision in the *Protecting Americans from Tax Hikes (PATH) Act*.
[14] The individual tax rates on long-term capital gains and the 3.8% net investment income tax (NIIT) are unchanged in 2020.
[15] A maximum 28% capital gain tax applies specifically to collectibles in 2020.

2020 Section 179 Expense:

- Maximum deduction amount: $1,040,000.
- Beginning phaseout limitation: $2,590,000.
- Heavy SUV Limit: $25,900

Note: One of the most significant differences between Section 179 and bonus depreciation is that Section 179 is limited by taxable business income, while bonus depreciation can create a business loss. We cover this topic more extensively in *PassKey Book 2, Businesses.*

2020 Bonus Depreciation: The 100% bonus depreciation amount remains in effect through December 31, 2022 (the deduction starts to phase down in 2023). Bonus depreciation also applies to used property. Assets that qualify for bonus depreciation include:

- MACRS property with a recovery period of 20 years or less
- Computer software
- Water utility property
- Qualified film or television production (excluding pornographic films)
- Qualified live theatrical production, as defined in section 181(e)
- Fruit and nut-bearing trees[16]

2020 QBI deduction Limits: In 2020, the qualified business income (QBI) deduction is up to 20% of QBI from a pass-through entity conducting a trade or business in the U.S. It also includes up to 20% of qualified real estate investment trust (REIT) dividends and qualified publicly traded partnership (PTP)income. Certain limitations may reduce or eliminate the deduction amount. The Section 199A limitation phase-in ranges are as follows and are based on taxable income:

- Married filing jointly: $326,600-$426,600
- Head of Household/QW/Single: $163,300-$213,300
- Married filing Separately: $163,300-$213,300

2020 Standard Mileage Rates:

- Business: 57.5¢ per mile[17]
- Charitable purposes: 14¢ per mile
- Medical and moving: 17¢ per mile[18]

---

16 This includes grapevines, orange trees, almonds and olive orchards, etc. In the past, fruit and nut bearing trees would not be "placed in service" for several years, because the trees would not be "placed in service" until they bear fruit. Now, farmers are allowed to take bonus depreciation at the time of planting. This is an election for bonus depreciation only. These plants and trees would not be eligible for Section 179 in their pre-productive period. A farmer may also choose to wait, and when the trees begin bearing fruit or nuts, then the farmer may claim section 179 or regular MACRS depreciation.

17 Business mileage is no longer deductible as an unreimbursed employee business expense, except for U.S. armed forces reservists, state or local government officials paid on a fee basis, and certain performing artists.

18 Moving mileage is deductible *only* by U.S. armed forces members on active duty who move pursuant to a military order and incident to a permanent change of station.

2020 HSA and HDHP Limits: To qualify to contribute to a health savings account, the taxpayer must have a high-deductible health insurance policy. The plan must also have an annual limit on out-of-pocket expenses (not including premiums).[19]

HSA contribution limits	Self-only: $3,550 Family: $7,100
HSA catch-up contributions (age 55 or older)	$1,000
HDHP minimum deductible	Self-only: $1,400 Family: $2,800
HDHP maximum out-of-pocket amounts (not including insurance premiums)	Self-only: $6,900 Family: $13,800

2020 QSEHRA Limits (Maximum payments and reimbursements through the QSEHRA)

- Self-only: $5,250
- Family: $10,600

2020 FSA Limits:

- Health Care FSA: $2,750.
- Dependent Care FSA (DCFSA): $5,000 ($2,500 if MFS).

Note: As part of the disaster relief provisions implemented by the CAA 2021, employers may allow participants to carryover unused benefits or contributions remaining in an FSA from 2020 to 2021. If a dependent aged out during the pandemic, the use of dependent FSA (DCFSA) funds is permitted up to age 14 rather than the usual age of 13. Employers can also allow employees to change their FSA contribution elections outside of open enrollment for plan years ending in 2021.

2020 Retirement Savings Contributions Credit (Saver's Credit):[20] The credit is 10% – 50% of eligible contributions to IRAs and retirement plans up to a maximum credit of $1,000 ($2,000 MFJ). The Saver's Credit can be taken for contributions to an ABLE account if the taxpayer is the designated beneficiary of the ABLE account. The income limitations are as follows:

Credit Rate	MFJ	HOH	Single, QW, MFS
50% of the contribution	AGI not more than $39,000	AGI not more than $29,250	AGI not more than $19,500
20% of the contribution	$39,001 - $42,500	$29,251 - $31,875	$19,501 - $21,250
10% of the contribution	$42,501 - $65,000	$31,876 - $48,750	$21,251 - $32,500

[19] An HSA can be combined with a qualified high-deductible health plan and offers the opportunity to save for health care on a pre-tax basis. Another name for an HDHP is an "HSA-Eligible" Plan.

[20] The IRS uses two different names for this particular credit: the "Saver's Credit" and the "Retirement Savings Contribution Credit." However, they are the same credit.

2020 Education-Related Credits and Deductions

American Opportunity Credit: The credit is up to $2,500 per student for the first four years of higher education expenses paid. The credit phases out for unmarried taxpayers with MAGIs between $80,000 and $90,000 ($160,000 and $180,000 for MFJ).

Lifetime Learning Credit: 20% of tuition paid up to a credit of $2,000 per return. The credit phases out between $118,000–$138,000 of MAGI for MFJ filers and $59,000–$69,000 for unmarried filers (Single, HOH, QW).

Coverdell Education Savings Accounts (Also called an "Education IRA"): The contribution limit is $2,000 in 2020. The income limit for making a maximum contribution to a Coverdell is $190,000-$220,000 of MAGI for MFJ tax returns. For any taxpayers not filing a joint return, the contribution limit range is $95,000-$110,000 of AGI (same as the previous year).

Section 529 Plans (Qualified Tuition Programs or QTP): 529 plans now allow *distributions* of up to $10,000 for educational expenses in connection with the enrollment at a public, private, or religious elementary or secondary school. The IRS does not specify a specific dollar amount for annual contribution limits to 529 college savings plans, but contributions are considered gifts for tax purposes and subject to the gift tax limits.

Tuition and fees deduction: This is an above-the-line exclusion from income for up to $4,000 in tuition and fees. The final year for this deduction is on 2020 tax returns. Phaseout limits:

- MFJ: $130,000-$160,000
- Single, HOH, QW: $65,000-$80,000
- MFS filers cannot take the deduction.

Student loan interest deduction: Student loan interest includes both required and voluntarily pre-paid interest payments. The maximum amount per return is $2,500, regardless of filing status. Phaseouts limits:

- MFJ: $140,000-$170,000
- Single, HOH, QW $70,000-$85,000
- MFS filers cannot take the deduction.

Educational Savings Bond Expense Exclusion: The savings bond education tax exclusion allows taxpayers to exclude interest income upon the redemption of eligible Series EE and I Bonds when the bond owner pays qualified higher education expenses at an eligible institution. This exclusion is subject to the following income limitations. Modified adjusted gross income phaseout range:

- MFJ and QW: $123,550 – $153,550
- Single and HOH: $82,350 – $97,350
- MFS filers cannot take the deduction.

Educator Expense deduction: Also called the "teacher credit," this deduction remains $250 in 2020; however, teachers may now apply the cost of Personal Protective Equipment (PPE) supplies (such as disinfectant or masks) used to prevent the spread of COVID-19 in their classrooms if the costs were paid or incurred after March 12, 2020.

2020 Personal and Dependency Exemptions: The personal exemption was eliminated through the 2025 tax year by the *Tax Cuts and Jobs Act.* Although the current exemption amount is zero, the ability to claim an exemption may make taxpayers eligible for other tax benefits. For 2020 tax year filings, the gross income limitation for a qualifying relative is $4,300.[21]

2020 "Nanny Tax" on Household Employees: The nanny tax threshold is $2,200 in 2020. A household employer is normally obligated to withhold and pay federal FICA (Social Security and Medicare) taxes for any household employee they paid $2,200 or more during the year. A household employer is required to pay FUTA taxes if they paid a household employee $1,000 or more in a calendar quarter in the current or prior year. These thresholds are on a *per-employee* basis.

2020 Repayment Caps for APTC: Although the individual Shared Responsibility Payment (also known as the "healthcare penalty" or "ACA penalty") has been reduced to zero, most of the other provisions of the ACA remain in force. The Advanced Premium Tax Credit (APTC) and the Premium Tax Credit (PTC)still exist, and if a taxpayer receives a Marketplace subsidy and their income subsequently changes, they may have to pay back APTC.[22]

Income (% of the federal poverty line)	**Taxpayers Filing Single**	**All other filing statuses**
Under 200%	$325	$650
200%-299%	$800	$1,600
300%-399%	$1,350	$2,700
400% and above	No cap (full repayment)	No cap (full repayment)

[21] In 2020, a "deemed personal exemption" amount of $4,300 is used for purposes of determining who is a "qualifying relative" under IRC Sec. 152(d)(1)(B). This exemption amount still applies to Qualified Disability Trusts, which were not subject to an exemption repeal under the TCJA.

[22] The American Rescue Plan Act (ARPA), passed on March 11, 2021, waived the payback for the advanced premium tax credit (APTC) in 2020, since this was a retroactive change passed after December 31, 2020, the APTC repayment is still covered in the book.

SECURE Act of 2019

The following tax law changes in the *SECURE Act* apply to the 2020 tax year:[23]

Taxable fellowship and stipends: For 2020, taxable fellowship and stipend payments may be treated as "qualifying compensation" for the purpose of IRA contributions. Compensation will include any amount included in gross income and paid to aid in the individual's pursuit of graduate or postdoctoral study.

Repeal of maximum age for traditional IRA contributions: Starting in 2020, the SECURE Act eliminated the 70½ age limit for making contributions to traditional IRAs.[24] As a result, people over age 70½ who are still working or running a business can now choose to contribute to a traditional IRA beginning in 2020.

Qualified charitable distributions: QCD can be made by a taxpayer who is age 70 ½ or older (unchanged from the previous year). However, the excludable portion of current and future QCDs is reduced by the total traditional IRA deductions taken with respect to post-age 70 ½ traditional IRA contributions.

Penalty-free withdrawals from retirement plans for birth or adoption: Beginning in 2020, an IRA owner or a participant in a workplace defined contribution plan (401(k) or 403(b) plan) can withdraw up to $5,000 within one year of the birth or adoption[25] of a child without incurring the 10% penalty on early distributions.

Required Minimum Distribution (RMD): The *SECURE Act* raised the required minimum distribution (RMD) age from 70 ½ to 72 for taxpayers turning 70 ½ after December 31, 2019. This is a permanent change. On March 27, 2020, the *CARES Act* waived the RMD requirement for the 2020 tax year. [26]

Required distribution rules for designated beneficiaries: QCD can be made by a taxpayer who is age 70 ½ or older (unchanged from the previous year). However, the excludable portion of current and future QCDs is reduced by the total traditional IRA deductions taken with respect to post-age 70 ½ traditional IRA contributions. "Stretch IRAs"[27] have been eliminated, and the beneficiary is not required to take RMDs from an inherited IRA. Instead, the entire balance must be distributed by the end of the 10th year after death. Certain eligible designated beneficiaries can continue to use the traditional "stretch IRA" rules.

---

[23] Source: https://apps.irs.gov/app/vita/content/globalmedia/4491_whats_new.pdf.

[24] This provision only applies to traditional IRAs, because there is no age limit for contributions to a Roth IRA.

[25] An "eligible adoptee" means any individual (other than a child of the taxpayer's spouse) who has not attained age 18 or is physically or mentally incapable of self-support.

[26] This also includes April 1, 2020 RMDs for taxpayers who turned 70½ in 2019. Anyone who took a required minimum distribution (RMD) in 2020 also had the opportunity to recontribute those funds back into their retirement account by August 31, 2020. This repayment is not subject to the one rollover per 12-month period limitation.

[27]A "stretch IRA" allowed non-spousal beneficiaries to withdraw assets of inherited accounts over their lifetimes. Now, those who inherit an IRA have 10 years to withdraw the IRA funds, or choose to be taxed on the money all at once. Exceptions to this rule include spouses, disabled beneficiaries, and minor children. This law is not retroactive, so inherited accounts of individuals who died before 2020 are not affected.

Difficulty-of-care payments: Taxpayers can elect to treat non-taxable difficulty-of-care payments (sometimes called "Medicare waiver payments) as "compensation" for the purposes of IRA contributions (either a traditional or a Roth IRA). The contributions are non-deductible and create basis in a traditional IRA.

Expansion of Section 529 plans (QTP): More expenses now qualify for tax-free and penalty-free withdrawals from a qualified tuition program.[28]

- **Student loan payments:** Withdrawals can be used to pay principal or interest on a designated beneficiary's or their siblings'[29] student loan. The amount of distributions for loan repayments of any individual is limited to $10,000 lifetime. Interest paid with these funds does not qualify for the student loan interest deduction.
- **Apprenticeship programs:** A 529 plan can now be used to pay qualifying expenses for a designated beneficiary to participate in an apprenticeship program that is registered and certified by the U.S. Department of Labor. "Qualifying expenses" include expenses for required fees, books, supplies, and equipment.

Families First Coronavirus Response Act (FFCRA)

The *Families First Coronavirus Response Act (FFCRA)* was signed into law on March 18, 2020, by President Trump. This bill provides small and midsize employers refundable tax credits that reimburse them, dollar-for-dollar, for the cost of providing paid sick and family leave wages to their employees for leave related to COVID-19.

FFCRA Sick and Medical Leave: Required certain employers to provide employees with paid sick leave[30] or expanded family and medical leave[31] for specified reasons related to COVID-19. This is also sometimes called "FFCRA paid leave" or "COVID-19 sick leave."

FFCRA Self-Employed Credits: The FFCRA extended equivalent refundable credits to self-employed individuals and household employers (taxpayers who file Schedule H). Form 7202 is used by self-employed taxpayers to figure the amount to claim for qualified sick and family leave equivalent credits.

Extended, but not mandatory: The *mandatory* FFCRA leave requirements expired on December 31, 2020, but were modified and extended by the *Consolidated Appropriations Act, 2021*. Employers can choose to provide FFCRA leave on a voluntary basis after December 31, 2020, and continue to take available tax credits through March 31, 2021.[32]

---

[28] These changes apply to 2020 and are also retroactive to 2019, so any distributions during 2019 that meet these guidelines also qualify for tax-free and penalty-free treatment.

[29] In this case, the term "sibling" includes sister, brother, or step-sister or step-brother.

[30] "Paid sick leave" – means paid leave under the Emergency Paid Sick Leave Act.

[31] "Expanded family and medical leave" – means paid leave under the Emergency Family and Medical Leave Expansion Act. See full definitions at: https://www.dol.gov/agencies/whd/pandemic/ffcra-questions.

[32] The paid sick and family leave refundable tax credits enacted as part of the FFCRA were extended through March 31, 2021, however, employers are no longer required to provide *mandatory* FFCRA leave after December 31, 2020. The reconciliation bill pending would extend this to September 2021.

Coronavirus Aid, Relief, and Economic Security (CARES) Act

The *CARES Act* was passed on March 27, 2020, and made many tax law changes that apply to the 2020 tax year.

Tax relief for social security tax: The *CARES Act* permits businesses, self-employed individuals, and household employers to defer the employer portion of social security tax imposed for the period beginning on March 27, 2020, and ending December 31, 2020.[33]

Paycheck Protection Plan (PPP) loans: Taxpayers may exclude from gross income any covered loan forgiveness. Congress expanded the Paycheck Protection Program (PPP) and clarified that debt forgiven under the PPP is not includible in gross income, but increases basis for partnership and S corporation owners. Business expenses paid with forgiven PPP funds are tax-deductible. Congress authorized a second round of PPP funding at the end of 2020. The IRS refers to first-round PPP Loans as "First Draw PPP Loans" and the second round as "Second Draw PPP Loans."

Coronavirus-related Retirement Withdrawals: The CARES Act authorized eligible retirement plans to offer a new type of distribution, a *Coronavirus-Related Distribution* (CRD) up to $100,000 from IRAs or workplace retirement plans without a 10% early withdrawal penalty before December 31, 2020. The distributions can be reported over three years and may be recontributed and treated as a rollover contribution. CRD distributions are claimed on the new Form 8915-E, *Qualified 2020 Disaster Retirement Plan Distributions and Repayments.*

Above-the-line deduction for charitable gifts: Taxpayers who do not itemize may qualify to take a deduction for charitable contributions of up to $300 ($150 if MFS) as an AGI adjustment in 2020. The gifts must be made in cash (gifts of property do not qualify).[34]

AGI Limits on Cash Contributions: For tax year 2020, qualified cash contributions are not subject to the 60%-of-AGI limit. Individuals who itemize are allowed to elect to claim a charitable income tax deduction up to 100% of adjusted gross income (AGI) for cash contributions.[35]

Health care spending: Qualified medical expenses for an HSA, MSA, FSA, and HRA now include OTC medications without a prescription as well as menstrual products. The 2020 CARES Act changed this requirement, making it possible for medical savings accounts to cover OTC products without a prescription as well as menstrual products. The change is retroactive to January 1, 2020, meaning that individuals can seek reimbursement for eligible purchases made at the beginning of the year.

Exclusion for certain employer payments of student loans: Employers may provide a student loan repayment benefit to employees on a tax-free basis. An employer may contribute up to $5,250 annually toward an employee's student loans, and such payment would be excluded

---

[33] The CAA 2021 extended the repayment period for these deferred payroll taxes. If an employer or self-employed individual voluntarily deferred payment of Social Security taxes between September 1, 2020 and December 31, 2020, they now have until December 31, 2021 to have affected employees repay these amounts. Penalties and interest will not begin to accrue on the deferred amounts until January 1, 2022.

[34] For 2020, this deduction is limited to $300 per tax return ($150 if filing MFS). Starting in 2021, a married couple filing jointly will be eligible for a $600 if they make qualifying gifts to charity.

[35] The Consolidated Appropriations Act of 2021 extends this benefit to 2021 as well.

from the employee's income. The $5,250 cap applies to both the new student loan repayment benefit as well as other educational assistance (e.g., tuition, fees, books).[36]

Higher education emergency financial aid grants: Emergency financial aid grants under the CARES Act for expenses related to the disruption of college campus operations due to the COVID-19 pandemic are not taxable.

Economic Impact Payments (EIP-1 and EIP-2) and Recovery Rebate Credits: Economic Impact Payments (EIP-1 and EIP-2) and the Recovery Rebate Credit are authorized by the *Coronavirus Aid, Relief, and Economic Security (CARES) Act* and the *COVID-related Tax Relief Act.* Economic Impact Payments are an *advance* payment of the Recovery Rebate Credit. These are commonly called "stimulus payments."[37] Eligible individuals include any individual taxpayer *except* for: nonresident aliens, dependents, an Estate or Trust, and deceased taxpayers. By the end of 2020, most eligible taxpayers had already received their first EIP (EIP-1).

Recovery Rebate Credit: This is a tax credit against the taxpayer's 2020 income tax. This credit is figured like both of the EIPs, except the amounts are based on tax year 2020 figures, instead of tax year 2019, and in some circumstances for EIP-1, 2018. The maximum credit is: (1) $1,200 ($2,400 if married filing jointly) plus $500 for each qualifying child (for EIP-1), and (2) $600 ($1,200 if married filing jointly) plus $600 for each qualifying child. A child born in 2020 also entitles the parent to the additional credit for a qualifying child, subject to the phase-out of the credit.

Consolidated Appropriations Act, 2021 (CAA 2021)

The CAA 2021 implements numerous COVID-19 relief provisions and expands or corrects many of the earlier tax provisions in the CARES Act. The CAA-2021 included a number of smaller bills, including the *COVID-Related Tax Relief Act of 2020 (COVIDTRA);* The *Coronavirus Response and Relief Supplemental Appropriations (CRRSA) Act*; and *The Taxpayer Certainty and Disaster Tax Relief Act (TCDTR).*

Additional Recovery Rebates (EIP-2): The *CAA 2021* authorizes a *second* round of economic stimulus payments for individuals as well as a second round of PPP loans.

- **Second Stimulus (EIP-2):** The bill includes a second wave of direct stimulus payments, up to $600 for eligible individuals, $1,200 for joint taxpayers, and an additional $600 for each dependent child under 17. A taxpayer who received an EIP based on 2019 income will not have to repay the credit (or recognize income) if their 2020 income exceeds the phaseout limitation.
- **Paycheck Protection Program Loans (Second round):** The CAA 2021 authorizes a second round of PPP loans. Previously, the IRS indicated that the expenses covered by PPP loans that were forgiven would not be deductible. The CAA 2021 clarifies that

---

[36] This provision was set to expire but was extended through December 31, 2025 by the CAA 2021.

[37] These advanced payments of the Recovery Rebate Credit are referred to as the "first EIP" and "second EIP." Economic impact payments are not taxable for federal income tax purposes but will reduce a taxpayer's Recovery Rebate Credit. The only offset that applies to the EIP is unpaid child support. Taxpayers must have an SSN that is valid for employment purposes.

these expenses may be deducted, even if the PPP loan is forgiven. The CAA 2021 provides a simplified forgiveness procedure for PPP loans up to $150,000.

Economic Injury Disaster Assistance (EIDL) Loans and Advances: The Act allows Economic Injury Disaster Assistance (EIDL) Advances provided as emergency grants under the CARES Act to be excluded from gross income while the corresponding expenses would remain deductible. Additionally, loan forgiveness granted to an EIDL loan recipient under discretionary powers provided by the CARES Act does not result in gross income or a denial of deductions for allocable expenses.[38]

Disaster Tax Relief

As part of the CAA 2021, the *Taxpayer Certainty and Disaster Tax Relief Act (TCDTR)* also implemented special disaster relief provisions for disasters other than COVID-19,[39] also called "Qualified Disasters."

Qualified Disaster Area Distributions (non-COVID related): Residents of qualified disaster areas may take qualified distributions of up to $100,000 from a retirement plan or an IRA without penalty. The tax on the withdrawals may be paid over a three-year period, or the amounts may be recontributed to the plan.

Disaster-related plan loans: The CAA 2021 allows retirement plan sponsors to increase their retirement plan's loan limits to allow participants to receive disaster-related plan loans in amounts up to $100,000 or 100% of the present value of their vested account balance.

Return of Withdrawals for Home Purchase/Construction: Taxpayers who withdrew retirement funds in order to purchase a home are also allowed to recontribute the funds back into their retirement accounts, if those funds were not used due to a Qualified Disaster.

Qualified disaster-related personal casualty losses: Individuals who have a net disaster loss may increase their standard deduction amount by the amount of the net disaster loss. This means that the loss will be allowed *in addition* to the standard deduction, subject to $500 per casualty floor (up from $100 from the prior year). Additionally, the amounts are exempt from the 10% AGI limit in 2020.

Employee Retention Credit for Employers Affected by Qualified Disasters (other than COVID-19): This is a tax credit of 40% of wages (up to $6,000 per employee) to employers in FEMA disaster zones (other than COVID-19). This provision specifically denies businesses' use of the same wages in qualifying for the ERC under the CARES Act or other potential credits (no double-dipping).

[38] The CAA 2021 repeals Section 1110(e)(6) of the CARES Act that required PPP loan forgiveness to be reduced by any EIDL advances (up to $10,000). This retroactive provision will allow any PPP borrowers who had forgiveness reduced by EIDL advances to have it forgiven.

[39] In this case, "qualified disaster zones" does not refer to any area that was declared a disaster zone only because of the effect of COVID-19. In other words, this relief is for *other* presidentially declared disasters.

Other Important Tax Changes

Medical Expense Deduction Floor: The new legislation permanently reduces the AGI threshold to 7.5%for all taxpayers.

Lookback for the EITC and the CTC: In 2020, a special temporary rule allows lower-income individuals to use their earned income from tax year 2019 to determine the Earned Income Tax Credit and the Additional Child Tax Credit for the 2020 tax year. However, taxpayers can only make this election if their 2019 earned income was greater than their earned income in 2020.

Discharge of Qualified Principal Residence Indebtedness: The exclusion from gross income for discharge of qualified principal residence indebtedness was extended through 2025. In 2020, a taxpayer can exclude up to $2 million ($1 million for MFS filers) of discharge-of-debt income if qualified principal residence debt is discharged.[40]

Private mortgage insurance (PMI) deduction: The deduction for PMI has been extended for 2020 and 2021. The deduction begins to phase out at $100,000, and phases out completely once AGI reaches $109,000 (if MFS, the phaseout begins at $50,000 and phases out completely at $54,500).

Individual Taxpayer Identification Numbers (ITINs): ITINs with middle digits "88" will expire December 31, 2020, as well as ITINs that were not used at least once in the last three consecutive years. Taxpayers with these ITINs need to take action to renew the number will be included on a U.S. federal tax return.

Estimated Tax Payments: Estimated tax payments for 2020, normally due on April 15, 2020, and June 15, 2020, were treated as timely if made by July 15, 2020.

Cryptocurrency and virtual currency: The 2020 Form 1040 includes an inquiry about transacting in cryptocurrency during tax year 2020. The question is now on page 1 of Form 1040 or 1040-SR (last year, it was on Schedule 1).

Residential Energy-Efficient Property Credit (REEP): This personal tax credit was extended. The credit is for expenditures of qualified solar electric property, qualified solar water heating property, qualified fuel cell property, qualified small wind energy property, and qualified geothermal heat pump property.

Identity Protection PIN Opt-In Program: The IRS has extended the availability of IP PINs to all taxpayers. This is a voluntary program, and each IP PIN is valid for one calendar year. Taxpayers who are confirmed identity theft victims or who have filed an identity theft affidavit will automatically receive an IP PIN via mail once their cases are resolved.

Employee Retention Tax Credit (ERTC): The employee retention tax credit is a broad-based refundable tax credit designed to encourage employers to keep employees on their payroll. For eligible 2020 quarters, the credit is 50% of up to $10,000 in wages paid by an employer whose

[40] The CAA-2021 extends this exclusion through the end of 2025, but lowers the amount of debt that can be discharged tax-free to $750,000 ($375,000 for MFS) starting with tax year 2021.

business is fully or partially suspended because of COVID-19 or whose gross receipts decline by more than 50%.[41]

Net Operating Losses (NOLs): The TCJA eliminated the net operating loss (NOL) carryback for most businesses, starting in 2018. Under the TCJA, NOL carrybacks were not allowable, except for farmers and casualty insurance companies, who were allowed a two-year carryback. The CARES Act temporarily repealed the NOL carryback prohibition rules and made other changes:

- **NOL under the CARES Act:** The CARES Act created a default 5-year carryback for losses in 2018, 2019, and 2020.[42] This means that an NOL that arose in 2020 can be carried back to 2015. The taxpayer may also elect out of the carryback period.
- **NOL 80% Limit Repealed:** For tax years 2018-2020, the CARES Act repeals the 80% limitation on the deductibility of NOL carryovers, making the limitation equal to 100% of taxable income before the NOL deduction.
- **NOLS for Farmers:** The CAA-2021 allows farmers who elected a two-year NOL carryback to retain the two-year carryback rather than claim the five-year carryback provided in the CARES Act. Farmers who previously waived an election to carry back an NOL may also revoke the waiver.

Student Loan Discharges: On January 15, 2020, the IRS released Revenue Procedure 2020-11, providing relief when the federal loans are discharged by the Department of Education under the Closed School or Defense to Repayment discharge process, or where the private loans are discharged based on settlements of certain types of legal causes of action against nonprofit or other for-profit schools and certain private lenders. The procedure includes federal student loans to finance attendance at a school owned by Corinthian College, Inc. (CCI) or American Career Institutes, Inc. (ACI), respectively, and whose loans were discharged by ED under the "Closed School" or "Defense to Repayment" discharge process.

[41] Source, U.S. Treasury Dept: https://home.treasury.gov/system/files/136/Employee-Retention-Tax-Credit.pdf.

[42] Revenue Procedure 2020-24 provides guidance to taxpayers with net operating losses that are carried back under the CARES Act.

New IRS Forms and Form Changes

New Form 1099-NEC, Nonemployee Compensation: The IRS revived the previously-retired Form 1099-NEC in 2020. Nonemployee compensation will now be reported on Form 1099-NEC instead of Form 1099-MISC

Form 1040, U.S. Individual Income Tax Return: Now has additional lines to accommodate charitable contributions, federal income tax withholding from Form W-2, Form 1099, and other forms, and the recovery rebate credit.

Electronic submission of Form 1040-X: Starting in 2020, preparers were able to file Form 1040-X electronically. At this time, only 2019 tax year Forms 1040 and 1040-SR can be amended electronically. Taxpayers still have the option to submit a paper version of Form 1040-X.

New Form 1040-NR: Form 1040-NR has been revised to more closely follow the format of Forms 1040. Beginning in 2020, Form 1040-NR will use Schedules 1, 2, and 3. Form 1040-NR-EZ is no longer available.

Form 1040 (SP) in Spanish: Form 1040 and Form 1040-SR will be available in Spanish for the first time, as well as the instructions for Forms 1040 and 1040-SR and Schedules 1, 2, and 3.

Form 1040, Schedule SE, Self-Employment Tax: The form is no longer available in a "short" version. Each taxpayer with taxable net self-employment earnings must use a separate Schedule SE, including joint filers.

New Form 9000, Request for Alternative Format or Language: This form can be used by taxpayers with disabilities to elect to receive notices from the IRS in an accessible format and, when available, in a language other than English.

Schedule LEP, *Request for Change in Language Preference:* Schedule LEP is a new form that allows taxpayers to receive written communications from the IRS in a language other than English. It is filed along with the taxpayer's Form 1040.

Form 1098-T: Form 1098-T, *Tuition Statement* has changed for the 2020 tax year. The amount billed (box 2) is no longer fillable; in other words, educational institutions will only report the amounts actually paid by the student in box 1.

This page intentionally left blank.

Unit 1: Preliminary Work with Taxpayer Data

More Reading:
Publication 5307, *Tax Reform: Basics for Individuals and Families*
Publication 17, *Your Federal Income Tax*
Publication 971, *Innocent Spouse Relief*

For Part 1 of the enrolled agent exam, you will be expected to know a broad range of information about preparing tax returns for individual taxpayers. This information includes the basics of filing status, requirements, and due dates; taxable and nontaxable income; deductions, credits, adjustments to income; determining the basis of property; figuring capital gains and losses; rental income; retirement income; estate and gift taxes, and much more. We begin with the preliminary work that tax return preparers are expected to do to prepare accurate tax returns for their individual clients.

For the current exam cycle, Part 1 of the exam is broken down into the following sections and corresponding percentages of questions:

1. Preliminary Work with Taxpayer Data – 14 questions
2. Income and Assets – 17 questions
3. Deductions and Credits – 17 questions
4. Taxation and Advice – 15 questions
5. Specialized Returns for Individuals – 11 questions[43]

We will cover preliminary work with taxpayer data, as well as the importance of a taxpayer's biographical information in this unit.

Use of Prior Year Returns

When tax professionals prepare tax returns for clients, they are expected to perform due diligence in collecting, verifying, and gathering taxpayer data. A preparer is also expected to review prior-year tax returns for compliance, accuracy, and completeness.

A preparer is required by law to notify a taxpayer of an error or omission if discovered on a prior-year tax return, and the consequences of not correcting the error or omission. However, a preparer is not required to correct the mistake. The use of prior year returns can help prevent major mathematical errors and alert a preparer to specific issues that might affect the taxpayer.

In reviewing prior-year tax returns, a preparer needs to determine whether there are items that affect the current year's return, including the following:

- Carryovers,
- Net operating losses,
- Credit for prior year minimum tax (Form 8801, *Credit for Prior Year Minimum Tax-Individuals, Estates, and Trusts*),
- Prior-year depreciation and asset basis.

[43] The current exam specifications are listed in the official *Enrolled Agent Special Enrollment Examination Candidate Information Bulletin,* which is available for download on the official Prometric website.

Taxpayer Biographical Information

When filing tax returns, certain biographical information of the client is required. A tax professional must collect this information from each taxpayer to prepare an accurate tax return:

- Legal name, date of birth, and marital status
- Residency status and/or citizenship
- Dependents
- Taxpayer identification number (SSN, ITIN, or ATIN)

To prevent filing returns with stolen identities, a tax preparer should ask taxpayers to provide identification (picture IDs are preferable) that includes the taxpayer's name and current address. Also, seeing Social Security cards, ITIN letters, and other documents avoids including incorrect TINs for taxpayers, spouses, and dependents on returns. Tax preparers should take care to ensure that they transcribe all TINs correctly.[44]

A taxpayer can request an identity protection personal identification number (IP PIN) that must be entered into software for the IRS to accept an electronically filed tax return. Starting in 2021, the IRS expanded the Identity Protection PIN Opt-In Program to all taxpayers. This means that anyone can now request an IP PIN, whether they have been a victim of identity theft or not (IR-2021-09).

The IRS requires each individual listed on a federal income tax return to have a valid taxpayer identification number (TIN). That includes the taxpayer, his or her spouse (if married), and any dependents listed on the return. The types of TINs are:

- **Social Security number (SSN)**
- **Individual taxpayer identification number (ITIN)**
- **Adoption taxpayer identification number (ATIN)**[45]

> **Note:** A taxpayer's personal information is considered highly sensitive and confidential. A preparer who wrongfully discloses a taxpayer's information could face civil and criminal charges.

A taxpayer who cannot obtain an SSN must apply for an ITIN or an ATIN in order to file a U.S. tax return. Generally, only U.S. citizens and lawfully admitted noncitizens authorized to work in the United States are eligible for a Social Security number.

Nonresident aliens with a U.S. tax liability generally have ITINs, although not always. For example, an ITIN would be required when a U.S. soldier marries a foreign spouse and wishes to file jointly. To file a joint return, the couple would need to request an ITIN for the alien spouse. People who do not have lawful status in the United States may obtain an ITIN for tax reporting purposes only. The issuance of an ITIN does not affect an individual's immigration status or give the taxpayer the right to work in the United States.

---

[44] These are guidelines from Publication 4491, VITA/TCE Training Guide. Incorrect taxpayer identification numbers are one of the most common causes of rejected tax returns. Due diligence requirements with regards to taxpayer data are covered more extensively in the EA review for Part 3, *Representation.*

[45] A special form is used for ATIN requests; Form W-7A, *Application for Taxpayer Identification Number for Pending U.S. Adoptions.* This form is used to apply for an ATIN for a child who is placed in the taxpayer's home for legal adoption.

A taxpayer with an ITIN is not eligible to receive Social Security benefits or the Child Tax Credit or Earned Income Tax Credit. ITINs are for federal tax reporting only and are not intended to serve any other purpose.

Example: Umberto is an Italian citizen who has never been to the United States. On January 20, 2020, he inherited a rental property from his deceased aunt, Giuseppina, who was a green-card holder living in the U.S. On the advice of his accountant, Umberto decides to keep the rental property. He hires a management company to receive the rents and manage the property in his absence. Umberto requests an ITIN for tax reporting purposes. He will report his U.S. rental income on Form 1040-NR. He will not be taxed on his worldwide income, only his income from U.S. sources.

Example: Kristal is a U.S. citizen living in Norway. In 2020, she met and married Trond, a Norwegian citizen. The couple plans to live in Norway. Kristal and Trond make the election to file jointly and treat Trond as a U.S. resident alien by attaching a statement to their joint return. To make this election, Trond must request an ITIN.

Individual Taxpayer Identification Number (ITIN) application process

To request an ITIN, taxpayers must file Form W-7, Application for IRS Individual Taxpayer Identification Number, and supply documentation that establishes their foreign status and true identity.[46] There are three ways to apply for an ITIN.

- Using Form W-7
- Using an IRS-authorized Certified Acceptance Agent (CAA) or
- In-person at a designated IRS Taxpayer Assistance Center

All ITINs now expire, unless they are renewed. ITIN procedures now include:

- Enhanced documentation for new Individual Taxpayer Identification Numbers (ITINs)
- Older ITINs will expire if not renewed.
- Newer ITINs will expire if not used within three years.
- The IRS will no longer accept passports of dependents as stand-alone documents that lack a date of entry into the United States.

A taxpayer can also employ the services of a CAA, or Certified Acceptance Agent, to request an ITIN. CAAs can authenticate a passport and/or birth certificate for taxpayers who want to request an ITIN, but do not wish to mail their original documents to the IRS.

Example: Adriana is a U.S. citizen with a Social Security number. Adriana lives and works in Mexico for an international accounting firm. Later in the year, she marries Carlos, a citizen of Mexico, who has a daughter from a prior marriage. Adriana decides to file jointly with her new husband, Carlos, and claim her stepdaughter as a dependent. In order to do so, they must request ITINs for Carlos and his daughter.

---

[46] When a taxpayer applies for an ITIN, his Form W-7 must include original documentation such as: an original passport, birth certificate, or certified copies of these documents from the issuing agency. Notarized copies are no longer accepted.

Adoption Taxpayer Identification Number (ATIN)

ATINs are designed explicitly for adopted children who are not yet eligible for a Social Security number. An ATIN is requested using Form W-7A, *Application for Taxpayer Identification Number for Pending U.S. Adoptions.* For an adopted child who does not have an SSN, a taxpayer may request an ATIN if:

- The child is placed in the taxpayer's home for legal adoption.
- The adoption is a domestic adoption, or the adoption is a foreign legal adoption, and the child has a permanent resident alien card or certificate of citizenship.
- The taxpayer cannot obtain the child's existing SSN, even though he has made a reasonable attempt to obtain it from the birth parents, the placement agency, and other persons.
- The taxpayer cannot obtain an SSN for other reasons, such as the adoption not yet being final.

An ATIN issued for an adoptive child will expire after 2 years from the date it is issued, although an extension can be requested. An ATIN cannot be used to obtain the Earned Income Tax Credit, the Child Tax Credit, or the American Opportunity Tax Credit.

Exception: Special Rules for a Deceased Child

If a child is born and dies within the same tax year and is not granted an SSN, the taxpayer may still claim that child as a dependent.

Example: Morganna gave birth to a son on November 1, 2020. The baby had health problems and died a week later. He was issued a birth certificate and a death certificate, but not an SSN. Morganna can claim her son as a qualifying child in 2020. She must paper-file her return to claim her deceased child as a dependent. Her son will be considered a "qualifying child" for tax purposes, even though the child only lived a short time.

The tax return must be filed on paper with a copy of the birth certificate or a hospital medical record attached. The birth certificate must show that the child was born alive; a stillborn infant does not qualify. The taxpayer would enter "DIED" in the space for the dependent's Social Security number on the tax return.

Recordkeeping Requirements for Individuals

Whether a paid tax return preparer is involved or not, a taxpayer is responsible for keeping copies of tax returns and maintaining other records for as long as they may be needed for the administration of any provision of federal tax law. Generally, a taxpayer should keep copies of tax returns and supporting documentation for at least three years from the date the returns were filed or the date they were due, whichever is later.

The IRS does not require taxpayers to keep records in any particular way, but it says individuals need good records for the following purposes:

- **Identify sources of income:** Taxpayers receive money or property from a variety of sources. Individuals need this information to separate business from nonbusiness income and taxable from nontaxable income.

- **Keep track of expenses:** Tracking expenses as they occur helps taxpayers identify expenses that can be used to claim deductions.
- **Keep track of the basis of property:** Taxpayers need to retain records showing the original cost or other basis of property they own and any improvements made to them.
- **Support items reported on tax returns:** If the IRS has questions about items on a return, a taxpayer should have records to substantiate those items. In an IRS audit, the burden of proof is on the taxpayer to prove their expenses in order to deduct them.[47]
- **Prepare tax returns:** Good records help taxpayers (and their preparers) file accurate returns more quickly.

> **Note:** Even if a tax professional prepares and signs an individual's tax return, the taxpayer is ultimately responsible for the accuracy of its contents.

The IRS allows taxpayers to maintain records in any way that will help determine the correct tax. Electronic records are acceptable as long as a taxpayer can reproduce the records in a legible and readable format. Necessary records that all taxpayers should keep include items related to:

- **Income:** Forms W-2, Forms 1099, bank statements, pay stubs, brokerage statements, Schedules K-1
- **Expenses:** Sales slips, invoices, receipts, credit card statements, canceled checks or other proof of payments, written communications from qualified charities, Forms 1098 to support mortgage interest and potentially real estate taxes paid (if the taxes are paid through an impound account)
- **Home purchase and sale:** Closing statements, HUD statements, purchase and sales invoices, proof of payment, insurance records, receipts for improvement costs
- **Investments:** Brokerage statements, mutual fund statements, Forms 1099-DIV

Basic Tax Forms for Individuals

Form 1040: A redesigned Form 1040 was released for the 2020 tax year. The redesigned Form 1040 still uses a "building block" approach. The three numbered schedules that remain[48] are the following:

- **Schedule 1:** ***Additional Income and Adjustments to Gross Income***
- **Schedule 2,** ***Additional Taxes***
- **Schedule 3,** ***Additional Credits and Payments***

Form 1040-SR: This form is specifically for use by seniors who are age 65 or older. The new tax form is essentially the same as the standard Form 1040 but is designed to be easier to read with a bigger font.

Form 1040-NR: Form 1040-NR is used by nonresident aliens to report their U.S. source income. Beginning in 2020, Form 1040-NR will use Schedules 1, 2, and 3, just like Form 1040. The 1040NR is *never* used by U.S. citizens or U.S. residents. The IRS defines an "alien" as any

[47] The responsibility to prove entries, deductions, and statements made on a taxpayer's tax return is known as the "burden of proof. Generally, taxpayers must meet their burden of proof by having the information and receipts (where needed) for the expenses and deductions claimed on their return. However, in tax-related criminal cases and civil fraud cases, the burden of proof is on the government.

[48] Schedules 4, 5, and 6 have been permanently eliminated.

individual who is not a U.S. citizen or U.S. national. A *nonresident* alien is an alien who has not passed the green card test or the substantial presence test. Form 1040NR is used by investors overseas, as well as nonresident taxpayers who earn money while in the U.S.

Example: Reynaldo is a worldwide boxing champion and a legal citizen of the Philippines. Reynaldo receives a nonimmigrant visa to fight in a boxing match in the U.S., where he earns $500,000 for the fight. He only remains in the U.S. for six days. After his boxing appearance, he returns to the Philippines. Reynaldo is not eligible for an SSN and must request an ITIN to report his U.S. income. Without the ITIN, he would be subject to automatic backup withholding on his U.S. earnings. Reynaldo's tax accountant correctly reports his income and tax on Form 1040-NR. Reynaldo does not have to report his worldwide income on his Form 1040-NR, only the income he earned in the United States.

Form 1040-X, *Amended U.S. Individual Income Tax Return*: This form is used to correct errors in a previously filed Form 1040, Form 1040SR, or 1040-NR. Starting in 2020, Form 1040-X can be filed electronically. At the time of this book's printing, only 2019 tax year Forms 1040 and 1040-SR can be amended electronically.

Federal Income Tax Rates

An individual's federal taxable income is taxed at progressive rates in the United States. The more taxable income a taxpayer has, the higher the percentage of that income he pays in taxes. The IRS groups individuals by ranges of their taxable income level, or *brackets*, and applies increasing tax rates at each successive level.

For tax year 2020 there are still seven tax brackets for individuals: 10%, 12%, 22%, 24%, 32%, 35%, and 37%. For example, a single taxpayer with $30,000 of taxable income would be in the 12% tax bracket in 2020. If the taxpayer had $90,000 of taxable income, he would be in the 24% tax bracket, while a taxpayer with more than $518,401 of taxable income would be in the highest tax bracket of 37%. The bottom rate remains at 10%.

The applicable tax rate for each successive bracket that is applicable to the taxpayer applies only to the additional amounts of taxable income that fall *within* that particular bracket.

2020 Federal Income Tax Brackets and Rates

Tax Rate	Single	MFJ/QW	MFS	HOH
10%	Up to $9,875	Up to $19,750	Up to $9,875	Up to $14,100
12%	$9,876 to $40,125	$19,751 to $80,250	$9,876 to $40,125	$14,101 to $53,700
22%	$40,126 to $85,525	$80,251 to $171,050	$40,126 to $85,525	$53,701 to $85,500
24%	$85,526 to $163,300	$171,051 to $326,600	$85,526 to $163,300	$85,501 to $163,300
32%	$163,301 to $207,350	$326,601 to $414,700	$163,301 to $207,350	$163,301 to $207,350
35%	$207,351 to $518,400	$414,701 to $622,050	$207,351 to $311,025	$207,351 to $518,400
37%	Over $518,400	Over $622,050	Over $311,025	Over $518,400

In addition to the regular tax in the United States, there is a parallel tax called the alternative minimum tax (AMT). A taxpayer must pay *either* the regular tax or the AMT, depending on whichever amounts to the greater tax. The AMT is covered in detail later.

Tax Return Due Dates and Extensions

The normal due date for individual tax returns is April 15. If April 15 falls on a Saturday, Sunday, or legal holiday, the due date is extended until the next business day. The IRS will accept a postmark as proof of a timely filed return. For example, if a tax return is postmarked on April 15, but does not arrive at an IRS service center until April 30, the IRS will accept the tax return as having been filed on time. In cases where a tax return is filed close to the deadline, it is advisable for a taxpayer to pay for proof of mailing or certified mail. This is also called the "mailbox rule." E-filed tax returns are given an "electronic postmark" to indicate the day they are accepted and transmitted to the IRS.

Example: Seraphina is an enrolled agent. Her client, Watson, is a single father with one child, a 14-year old daughter named Tiffany. Watson has sole custody of Tiffany and provides all his daughter's financial support. On April 15, 2021, Seraphina attempted to efile Watson's 2020 tax return, but the return was rejected because the dependent on his return has already been claimed by another person. Watson believes that his estranged ex-wife may have tried to claim Tiffany, but he cannot be sure, and has no way to contact his ex-wife to confirm. Seraphina recommends filing on paper because she does not believe that the e-file rejection can be resolved. She prints out the paper return for Watson, who signs it with an original signature, and mails it certified mail before the post office closes on April 15. The return is considered timely and goes through regular processing. Watson receives his full refund about 45 days later.

If a taxpayer cannot file his tax return by the due date, he may also request an extension by filing Form 4868, *Application for Automatic Extension of Time to File*, which may be filed electronically. The extension must be filed by the original due date. An extension grants an additional six months to file a tax return.

Note: Although an extension gives a taxpayer extra time to *file* his return, it does not extend the time to *pay* any tax due. Taxpayers are expected to estimate and pay the amount of tax due by the original filing deadline.

Filing Deadline Exceptions

Federal Disaster Areas: Taxpayers in federally declared disaster areas (FEMA disasters) are granted extensions to file and pay their income taxes and to make estimated tax payments. The IRS may also abate interest and any late filing or late payment penalties that apply to taxpayers in these disaster areas.[49] This type of tax relief generally includes:

- Individuals and businesses located in a disaster area,
- Those whose tax records are located in a disaster area, and
- Relief workers who are working in the disaster area.

[49] The *Consolidated Appropriations Act of 2021* includes the COVID-Related Tax Relief Act of 2020 (COVIDTRA) and The Taxpayer Certainty and Disaster Tax Relief Act of 2020 (TCDTR), both of which provide numerous disaster-related provisions to impact individual taxpayers. We will cover specific provisions in more detail later.

A taxpayer does not have to be *physically* located in a federally declared disaster area to qualify as an "affected taxpayer." Taxpayers are also considered "affected" if the records necessary to meet a filing or payment deadline postponed during the relief period are located in a covered disaster area. Therefore, disaster relief also applies to tax preparers (and their clients) who are unable to file returns or make payments on behalf of their clients because of a disaster.

Example: Declan owns a 30% interest in a partnership that is located in a federally declared disaster area. However, Declan himself does not live in the disaster zone. Since he must rely on the information (Schedule K-1) from the partnership to file his individual tax return, he qualifies as an "affected taxpayer" for purposes of receiving filing and payment relief. Declan's filing and payment deadlines are suspended until the end of the postponement period, just like the affected partnership.

June 15 Deadlines (Automatic Two-Month Extension)

Three groups of taxpayers are granted an automatic two-month extension to file:

- Nonresident aliens who do not have wage income subject to U.S. withholding,
- U.S. citizens or legal U.S. residents who are living outside the United States or Puerto Rico, and their main place of business is outside the U.S. or Puerto Rico,
- Taxpayers on active military service duty outside the U.S.

A citizen or resident alien living abroad must attach a statement to his tax return, explaining which situation qualifies him for the special two-month extension. Even if allowed an extension, the taxpayer will have to pay interest on any tax not paid by the regular tax deadline of April 15.

Taxpayers Who Live Abroad: A taxpayer who is out of the country can request an additional discretionary two-month extension of time to file his tax return beyond the regular six-month extension of October 15. For calendar-year taxpayers, the "additional" extension date would be December 15.[50] Unless the extension request is denied, the taxpayer will not receive a response from the IRS.

Special Exception for Combat Zones: The deadline for filing a tax return, claim for a refund, and the deadline for payment of tax owed, is automatically extended for any service member, Red Cross personnel, accredited correspondent, or contracted civilian serving in a combat zone. These taxpayers have their tax deadlines suspended from the day they started serving in the combat zone until 180 days after they leave the combat zone. These deadline extensions also apply to the spouses of armed service members serving in combat zones.

Example: Ramon is a U.S. Marine who has served in a combat zone since March 1, so he is entitled to extra time to file and pay his taxes. The 46 days between the date he entered the combat zone and the April 15 filing deadline are added to the normal extension period of 180 days, so he has a 226-day extension period *after* he leaves the combat zone. IRS deadlines for assessment and collection are also suspended during any period that a U.S. service member is in a combat zone.

---

[50] In addition to the normal 6-month extension, taxpayers who are out of the country can request a discretionary 2-month additional extension of time to file their returns (to December 15). To request this extension, you must send the IRS a letter explaining the reasons why you need the additional 2 months (see Publication 54 for complete instructions on how to request this extension).

Penalties and Interest

The IRS can assess a penalty on individual taxpayers who fail to file, fail to pay, or both. The failure-to-file penalty is greater than the failure-to-pay penalty. If someone is unable to pay all the taxes he owes, he is better off filing on time and paying as much as he can. The IRS will consider payment options to individual taxpayers. These penalties can be abated if the taxpayer can establish that there was a reasonable cause for not paying or filing on time. Common penalties include:

- **Failure-to-file**: When a taxpayer does not file their tax return by the return due date, (or extended due date, if an extension to file is requested and approved).
- **Failure-to-pay**: When a taxpayer does not pay the taxes reported on their return in full by the due date, April 15. An extension to file does not extend the time to pay.
- **Failure to pay proper estimated tax**: When a taxpayer does not pay enough taxes due for the year with their quarterly estimated tax payments (or through withholding), when required.
- **Interest on the amount due:** In addition to filing penalties, the taxpayer will also be charged interest on the amount due.

Failure-to-File Penalty: The penalty for filing Form 1040 late is usually 5% of the unpaid taxes for each month or part of a month that a return is late. The penalty is based on the tax that is not paid by the due date. The penalty will not exceed 25% of a taxpayer's unpaid taxes.

If both the failure-to-file penalty and the failure-to-pay penalty apply in any month, the 5% failure-to-file penalty is reduced by the failure-to-pay penalty. For the tax year 2020 (for returns filed in 2021), the failure-to-file penalty is as follows:

- 5% of the unpaid balance per month (or part of a month) for a maximum penalty of 25% of the unpaid tax. However, if the failure to file on time is determined to be fraudulent, the penalty is 15% of the unpaid balance per month (or part of a month) for a maximum penalty of 75% of the unpaid tax.
- For returns filed more than 60 days late, the smaller of $435 or 100% of the tax due on the return.
- The failure-to-file penalty is reduced by failure-to-pay penalty if both penalties apply.
- No penalty will be assessed if the taxpayer is due a refund.

Failure-to-Pay Penalty: If a taxpayer does not pay his taxes by the original due date (determined without regards to any extension), he could be subject to a failure-to-pay penalty of ½ of 1% (0.5%) of unpaid taxes for each month, or part of a month, after the due date that the taxes are not paid.

This penalty can be as much as 25% of a taxpayer's unpaid taxes. The failure-to-pay penalty rate increases to a full 1% per month for any tax that remains unpaid the day after a demand for immediate payment is issued, or ten days after notice of intent to levy certain assets is issued.

Note: A taxpayer may request penalty abatement due to "reasonable cause." Acceptable reasons for abatement include: fire, casualty, natural disaster or other disturbances, inability to obtain records due to a casualty or a disaster, death, serious illness, incapacitation, or unavoidable absence of the taxpayer or a member of the taxpayer's immediate family.

Interest on the Amount Due: In addition to filing penalties, the taxpayer will also be charged interest on the amount due. Generally, interest accrues on any unpaid tax from the due date of the return until the date of payment in full. The interest rate is determined quarterly and is the federal short-term rate plus 3%. Interest compounds daily. Unlike late penalties, interest cannot be reduced or abated for reasonable cause.[51]

Example: Nicoletta died two years ago. She had a filing requirement when she passed away. However, Nicoletta died without a will, and an executor was not named by the court until November 10, 2020. Nicoletta's brother, Ezequiel, was named the executor. Ezequiel filed two years of delinquent tax returns on behalf of his deceased sister, and also requested a penalty abatement for filing Nicoletta's final tax returns late. The IRS granted the penalty abatement, although the interest on the amount due was not abated and still had to be paid by the executor.

Note: These are the penalties that apply to individual taxpayers only. Different penalty amounts apply to business entities, which are covered in detail in *Book 2, Businesses.*

Estimated Taxes for Individuals

The federal income tax is a "pay-as-you-go" tax, meaning a taxpayer must pay taxes as he earns or receives income throughout the year. If a taxpayer earns income that is not subject to withholding, such as self-employment income, interest, or rents, or if his taxes withheld are insufficient to cover his tax liability, he may be required to make quarterly estimated tax payments. Estimated tax is used to pay income tax as well as self-employment tax and alternative minimum tax.

Safe Harbor Rule: Taxpayers can avoid making estimated tax payments by ensuring they have enough tax withheld from their income. A taxpayer must generally make estimated tax payments if:

- He expects to owe at least $1,000 in tax (after subtracting withholding and tax credits)
- He expects the total amount of withholding and tax credits to be less than the *smaller* of:
  - 100% of the tax liability on his prior year return
  - 90% of the tax liability on his current year return

A taxpayer will not face an underpayment penalty if the total tax liability on his return (minus the amounts of tax credits or paid through withholding) is under $1,000.

Example: Mariana is a full-time secretary. She also earns money part-time as a self-employed manicurist. In 2020, she did not make any estimated payments. However, Mariana made sure to increase her withholding at her regular job to cover any amounts that she would have to pay on her self-employment earnings. When she files her tax return, she discovers that she still owes $750. Although she is responsible for paying the additional tax that is owed, she will not owe an underpayment penalty because her total tax liability, after withholding, is still less than $1,000.

---

[51] Taxpayers may request abatement of interest by filing Form 843, *Claim for Refund and Request for Abatement,* or by submitting a request by letter. Interest will only be abated in extremely unusual circumstances, such as in the case of a mathematical error made by the IRS.

Example: Jomar earned $95,000 during 2020 and paid $8,200 in tax, which was enough to cover his tax liability for the year. Although he expects his income to increase in 2021, he will not be assessed a penalty for underpayment of estimated taxes, provided he pays at least $8,200 in estimated tax during the year (100% of the tax liability on his prior year return).

A U.S. citizen or U.S. resident is not required to make estimated tax payments if he had zero tax liability in the prior year.

Example: Orlando, age twenty-five and single, earned $2,700 before he was laid off in the prior year. He received $3,500 in unemployment compensation after the layoff. He did not file a return or pay any income tax that year because his gross income was less than the annual filing requirement. In 2020, Orlando began working as a self-employed programmer but made no estimated tax payments during the year. Even though he owed $5,000 for the 2020 tax year, Orlando does not owe an underpayment penalty because he had zero tax liability in the prior year.

If a taxpayer wishes to change his withholding amounts from his wages, he must use Form W-4, *Employee's Withholding Certificate*, and submits the form to his employer. The Form W-4 is not submitted to the IRS.

Safe Harbor Rule for Higher-Income Taxpayers: If the taxpayer's adjusted gross income was more than $150,000 ($75,000 if MFS), the taxpayer must pay the *smaller of* 90% of their expected tax liability for the current year or *110%* (instead of the normal 100%) of the tax shown on their prior-year return to avoid an estimated tax penalty.

Example: Massimo earned $205,000 in 2020. After applying all of his credits, he had a $30,000 tax liability for the year. In 2021, he expects to earn closer to $450,000. As long as he pays at least 110% of his tax liability for the prior year (110% x $30,000 =$33,000), he will not owe an estimated tax penalty, regardless of how much he owes when he files his 2021 return.

Estimated Tax Due Dates for Most Individuals

The year is divided into four payment periods for estimated taxes, each with a specific payment due date. If the due date falls on a Saturday, Sunday, or legal holiday, the due date is the next business day. A taxpayer must complete Form 1040-ES, *Estimated Tax for Individuals*, to pay his estimated tax. If a payment is mailed, the date of the U.S. postmark is considered the date of payment.[52]

First Payment Due: April 15

Second Payment Due: June 15

Third Payment Due: September 15

Fourth Payment Due: January 15 (of the following year)

Estimated Taxes for Farmers and Fishermen

Special rules apply to the payment of estimated tax by qualified farmers and fishermen (those who file on Schedule F). If at least two-thirds of the taxpayer's gross income in the current year

[52] For tax year 2020, the estimated tax payments normally due on April 15, 2020 and June 15, 2020 were treated as timely if paid by July 15, 2020.

comes from (or in the prior year came from) farming or fishing activities, the following rules apply:

- The taxpayer does not have to pay estimated tax if he files his return and pays all tax owed by the first day of the third month after the end of his tax year (generally, this is March 1).
- The taxpayer does not have to pay estimated tax if his current year income tax withholding is at least two-thirds (⅔ or .6667) of the total tax liability on his current tax return or 100% of the total tax liability on his prior-year return.
- If the taxpayer must pay estimated tax, he is required to make only one estimated tax payment (called the "required annual payment") by the fifteenth day after the end of his tax year (for individuals, this is usually January 15).

For this special tax treatment, qualified farming income includes gross farming income on Schedule F, gross farming rental income, gains from the sale of livestock, and crop shares for the use of a farmer's land. This rule also applies to qualified fishermen.

Example: Nicholas is a self-employed owner of a commercial fishing vessel. He reports his income and loss on Schedule F. All of his income is from commercial fishing, so he is not required to pay quarterly estimated taxes. Nicholas's records are incomplete, so he asks his tax accountant to file an extension on his behalf. Since Nicholas will be unable to file his 2020 tax return by March 1, 2021, his accountant notifies Nicholas that he is required to make a single payment of estimated taxes by January 15, 2021.

Note: If a qualified farmer (or fisherman) files their 2020 Form 1040 by March 1, 2021, and pays all the tax they owe at that time, they do not need to make any estimated tax payments during the year. This rule does not apply to *any other type* of business activity—it only applies to farmers and fishermen.

Example: Naomi earns 100% of her income from growing organic strawberries. She is a qualified farmer and reports all her business income on Schedule F. She is not required to pay quarterly estimated taxes. Naomi filed her 2020 tax return on February 20, 2021, and enclosed a check for her entire balance of $4,900. Since she filed before the March 1, 2021 deadline, she will not be subject to any estimated tax penalties.

Example: Xavier is a flower farmer who grows rare hothouse orchids to florists in his community and online. He makes a tidy profit selling the flowers every year. Xavier also earns a considerable sum as a professional bookkeeper. In 2020, his net income from farming is $47,000. His net income from his bookkeeping business is $33,000. Since two-thirds of his income is not from farming activities, Xavier is not eligible for the special rule for estimated payments. He is required to pay quarterly estimates throughout the year, just like every other business.

Note: This special estimated tax rule also applies to a person's share of gross income from partnerships, where the majority of its income is derived from farming or fishing. This safe harbor for estimated payments does *not* apply to C corporations; however, regardless of the business activity.[53]

[53] See a more extensive explanation on these special rules on the IRS website here: https://www.irs.gov/businesses/small-businesses-self-employed/estimated-taxes-for-fishermen

Backup Withholding

There are times an entity is required to withhold certain amounts from a payment and remit the amounts to the IRS. For example, the IRS requires backup withholding if a taxpayer's name and Social Security number on Form W-9, *Request for Taxpayer Identification Number and Certification*, does not match its records.

The IRS will sometimes require backup withholding if a taxpayer has a delinquent tax debt, or if he fails to report all his interest, dividends, and other income. Payments that are subject to backup withholding may include wages, interest, dividends, rents, royalties, and payments to independent contractors.

Backup withholding also applies, following notification by the IRS, where a taxpayer underreported interest or dividend income on their federal income tax return. To *stop* backup withholding, the payee must correct any issues that caused it. They may need to give the correct TIN to the payer, resolve the underreported income and pay the amount owed, or file a missing return.

Note: The current backup withholding rate in 2020 is 24% for all U.S. citizens and legal U.S. residents. Generally, backup withholding applies only to U.S. citizens, resident aliens, and not to nonresident aliens. However, a nonresident alien may be subject to withholding, as well. Nonresident aliens are subject to U.S. tax withholding on "fixed or determinable, annual, or periodic" (FDAP) income. Most types of U.S. source income received by a foreign person are subject to withholding of 30% (unless an exemption or tax treaty applies).

Example: Randy is a U.S. citizen. He owns several investments through ABC Financial Advisors, Inc. In 2020, the IRS notifies ABC Financial Advisors that Randy's Social Security number is incorrect. ABC Financial Advisors informs Randy by mail that the company needs his correct Social Security number, or it will have to start backup withholding on his investment income. Randy ignores the notice and never bothers to update his SSN. ABC Financial Advisors must begin backup withholding on Randy's investment income.

Example: Federico is a citizen of Spain. He does not live in the U.S., but he owns several U.S. investments, including stock in several U.S. companies and U.S. Treasury bonds. He is required to provide an ITIN to his investment firm. If he does not provide a tax identification number, the investment firm will be required to automatically withhold taxes from his U.S.-source income.

Under the current backup withholding rules, a business, financial institution, or bank *must* withhold taxes from a payment if:

- The individual did not provide the payor with a valid taxpayer identification number;
- The IRS notified the payer that the TIN or SSN is incorrect;
- The IRS notified the payor to start withholding on interest and dividends because the payee failed to report income in prior years; or
- The payee failed to certify that he was not subject to backup withholding for underreporting of interest and dividends

Relief from Joint Tax Liability

In some instances, a spouse can be relieved of the tax, interest, and penalties on a joint return. When spouses file a joint return, they are both legally responsible for the entire tax liability. However, a taxpayer can file a claim for spousal relief under three different grounds:

- **Innocent Spouse Relief**
- **Separation of Liability Relief**
- **Equitable Relief**

Innocent Spouse Relief: This is when a joint return has understated tax liability due to "erroneous items" attributable to a taxpayer's spouse or former spouse. Erroneous items include income received by a spouse that is omitted from the return. Deductions, credits, and property basis are also "erroneous items" if they are incorrectly reported on the joint return. To be considered an "innocent" spouse, the taxpayer must establish that he or she did not know (or have reason to know) that there was an understated tax liability at the time of signing the joint return. In other words, a taxpayer could seek innocent spouse relief from the IRS if they later become aware of a tax liability and they believe that it is not theirs.

Example: Emery and Barton filed joint returns during their marriage. On February 20, 2020, Emery leaves Barton and files for divorce. Their divorce was final on December 20, 2020. Emery later receives an IRS notice for a prior-year joint return, indicating that $25,000 in gambling income was not reported. Emery finds out that Barton was hiding a gambling problem, and he had won that money during their marriage and failed to report it. Emery had no knowledge of the gambling winnings because Barton hid the money in a separate bank account and never told her about it. Emery immediately files for innocent spouse relief by filing Form 8857, *Request for Innocent Spouse Relief.*

The taxpayer must request relief within two years after the date on which the IRS begins collection activity. In most cases, innocent spouse relief is limited to taxpayers who are no longer married, including when one spouse is deceased.

Separation of Liability Relief: The above restrictions also apply to separation of liability relief. In this case, however, the taxpayer must no longer be married to, or must be legally separated from, his or her spouse, or must be widowed or have lived apart for at least twelve months from the spouse with whom the joint return was filed. The understated tax, plus interest and penalties, would be allocated to the taxpayer based on the amount for which he or she is responsible. In order to qualify for separation of liability relief, one spouse has to be guilty of doing something that the other spouse was unaware of.

Example: Athena and Roman have always filed joint returns. In 2018, they filed a joint return reporting Roman's wages of $42,000 and Athena's self-employment income of $10,000. On March 1, 2020, Athena and Roman file for divorce and begin living in separate homes. The IRS later audits their 2018 return and finds that Athena underreported $20,000 of self-employment income. This resulted in understated tax, plus interest and penalties for the 2018 tax year. Since Roman is now legally separated from Athena, he can file Form 8857 to request separation of liability relief. Roman must be able to prove that he didn't know about the $20,000 of underreported income at the time he signed the joint return.

Equitable Relief: If a taxpayer does not qualify for the first two types of relief, he or she may be eligible for equitable relief. The IRS will review the facts and circumstances of the taxpayer's case and determine whether it would be unfair to hold the taxpayer liable for the understated tax. Unlike the other two forms of relief, equitable relief may also be granted for an underpaid tax, meaning it was properly reported on a tax return but not paid. Further, in some cases, the spouse requesting relief may have known about the understated or underpaid tax but did not challenge the treatment for fear of his or her spouse's retaliation.

Example: Margot is a victim of domestic violence who now lives apart from her husband. When she signed her joint return, she knew her husband was underreporting income from his business but was afraid of what would happen if she refused to sign. After the IRS discovered the understated tax, Margot filed for equitable relief and was able to document her history of spousal abuse using affidavits from family members and other legal proof. The IRS granted her request for relief of her portion of the understated tax, penalties, and interest.

If the tax was paid, the taxpayer has until the expiration of the refund statute of limitations to request equitable relief. If the tax is unpaid, the taxpayer has until the expiration of the collection statute of limitations (ten years) to seek equitable relief. The same form, Form 8857, *Request for Innocent Spouse Relief*, is used to request all three types of relief. [54]

Injured Spouse Claims

An "injured spouse" claim and "innocent spouse" relief have similar-sounding names, but they are entirely different. To be considered an injured spouse, a taxpayer must meet all of the following criteria:

- Have filed a joint return
- Have paid federal income tax or claimed a refundable tax credit
- All or part of the taxpayer's refund was, or is expected to be, applied to his or her spouse's past financial obligations, and
- Not be responsible for the debt

A spouse who believes that he is entitled to a portion of the refund on a joint return can file Form 8379, *Injured Spouse Allocation.*

Example: Gerard filed a joint return with his wife, Kimberly, who has delinquent student loan debt. Kimberly incurred the student loan debt before she was married. Gerard files Form 8379 to request his portion of their tax refund as an injured spouse. The IRS will retain Kimberly's share of the couple's tax refund to offset her debt but will allow Gerard to obtain his portion of the refund.

Refund Claims and Amended Returns

To claim a refund, a taxpayer must generally file an amended tax return (Form 1040-X) within three years from the date the return was filed, or two years from the date the tax was paid, whichever is later.[55] If a taxpayer wants a refund of withholding or estimated tax payments

[54] The examples in this section are modified from examples in Publication 971, Innocent Spouse Relief.

[55] If the taxpayer had an extension to file (for example, until October 15), but the taxpayer filed earlier and the IRS received it July 1, the return is considered *filed on* July 1 (Form 1040-X instructions).

made, then the amended return must be filed within three years of the due date in order to preserve the right to those amounts.

If a claim is not filed within the applicable period, a taxpayer generally will not be entitled to a refund. However, if the taxpayer files an extension and files his original return prior to the October 15 extension deadline, the three-year period begins on the date that the taxpayer originally filed his return.

Starting in 2020, amended returns Form 1040-X can be filed electronically. At this time, only 2019 tax year Forms 1040 and 1040-SR can be amended electronically. Taxpayers still have the option to submit a paper version of Form 1040-X.

Example: Jenny prepared her own 2016 tax return and filed it after the deadline, on November 1, 2017. She did not request an extension, so the return was delinquent when she filed it. She later discovered that she had forgotten to claim the Earned Income Tax Credit. Approximately three years later, she files an amended return on October 5, 2020. Jenny's refund claim is denied because she filed her original return past the filing date without a valid extension. Therefore, since her amended return was not filed timely, her refund is forfeited.

Example: Myles e-filed his 2016 Form 1040 early, on March 29, 2017. He later discovered that he failed to claim a credit on his return that would result in a refund. Myles mailed an amended return on April 15, 2020. Since returns filed before the due date are considered filed on the due date of the return, his amended return was filed within the three-year statute period. He will receive a refund.

Example: Jiao has not filed a tax return for a long time, and now he wants to file several years of delinquent tax returns as well as his current year return: 2015 through 2020. Jiao files the returns and realizes that he was entitled to refunds for every year. If he files all the back tax returns and the current-year return by April 15, 2021, he will receive refunds for his 2017-2020 tax returns. His refunds for 2015 and 2016, however, have expired. He will not receive a refund for those years unless an exception applies.

Extended Statute for Filing Late and Claiming Refunds

In some cases, a late-filed tax return and claiming a tax refund beyond the deadline will be honored. The IRS will consider many sound reasons with reasonable cause for failing to file a tax return, make a deposit, or pay tax when due. Sound reasons, if established, include:

- Fire, casualty, natural disaster, or other disturbances
- Inability to obtain records
- Death, serious illness, incapacitation, or unavoidable absence of the taxpayer or a member of the taxpayer's immediate family

Several unique scenarios allow a taxpayer to request a refund beyond the "normal" deadline. These unique scenarios involve:

- A bad debt from worthless securities (up to seven years prior)
- A payment or accrual of foreign tax (up to ten years prior)
- A net operating loss carryback
- A carryback of certain tax credits

- Exceptions for military personnel
- Taxpayers in federally declared disaster areas
- Taxpayers who have been affected by a terroristic or military action

Example: Asher has been helping his elderly mother, Evita, file her tax returns for the last several years. Over time, she has become forgetful of things. In 2020, Renaldo discovers a large file in his mother's home filled with old brokerage statements. Several of the brokerage statements show losses from worthless securities, dating back many years. Evita had been putting the statements away because she believed that they were unimportant. Evita's Form 1099-B from 2014 shows a significant loss from worthless stock (over $18,000 in losses that were never reported). Even though the brokerage statement is six years old, Evita is still allowed to amend her 2014 tax return to claim the stock losses. That is because the IRS allows up to seven years to amend a tax return for losses from worthless securities. Evita can file a Form 1040-X to claim the losses and still receive a refund under this extended statute of limitations.

Time periods for claiming a refund are also extended when a taxpayer is "financially disabled." This usually requires that the taxpayer be mentally or physically disabled to the point that he is unable to manage his financial affairs. For a joint income tax return, only one spouse has to be financially disabled for the time period to be suspended.

Example: Samantha timely-filed her tax return for 2017 on April 15, 2018. Her preparer later finds an error on the return. The last date for Samantha to file a refund claim under the statute of limitations for the 2017 taxable year would normally be April 15, 2021. Before she can file an amended return, on March 15, 2021, Samantha was in a terrible car accident. The doctor did not expect her to survive, and she was in a coma for nine months (until December 15, 2021). If Samantha shows that she meets the qualifications to be considered financially disabled, the statute of limitations for filing a refund claim would be extended by the nine-month duration of her disability.[56]

Note: A lack of funds, in and of itself, is not considered "reasonable cause" for failure to file or pay taxes on time.

The Statute of Limitations for IRS Assessment and Collection

The IRS is generally required to assess tax within three years after the return is filed or, if filed early, the due date of the return. If a taxpayer files pursuant to an extension, or files his tax return late, then IRS has three years from the actual filing date.

If a taxpayer *never* files a return, or a return is fraudulent, then there is no statute of limitations for an assessment of tax. The IRS has six years to assess tax on a return if a "substantial understatement" is identified, meaning that gross income was understated by more than 25%. The statute of limitations for IRS collection is ten years from the date tax is assessed. This is also called the Collection Statute Expiration Date (CSED).

[56] To claim financial disability, the taxpayer (or their representative) must complete the appropriate income tax return or amended income tax return and also submit a statement of proof of the financial disability. For full instructions, read the section on financial disability in Publication 17.

This ten-year period begins to run on the date of the tax assessment, not on the date of filing. So, for example, if the taxpayer owes when they file their tax return, the IRS will send a bill. The bill date is the assessment date. The IRS can attempt to collect unpaid taxes for up to ten years from the date the taxes are *assessed*.

The IRS assigns a collection statute expiration date or "CSED" to every delinquent taxpayer account. Once the CSED expires, the IRS loses its right to seize assets or make payment demands. Certain events can extend the amount of time the IRS has to collect.

Example: Franco has always filed his tax returns on time. Five years ago, Franco was self-employed and did not understand how to manage his money or pay estimated taxes. He had a large tax bill from that year. Franco still filed his tax return on time and correctly reported the amount due, intending to make monthly payments. The IRS issued its assessment and sent Franco a bill for $24,000 (the amount that Franco owes, including penalties and interest). Franco requested an installment agreement and began making monthly payments toward his tax debt. Shortly thereafter, Franco had a car accident and became disabled. He no longer has the means to work or pay the bill. The IRS has five years left to collect on the debt, and after that, the statute for collection expires. Although the interest and penalties will continue to accrue, if Franco does not have any assets or any means to pay the bill, the debt will likely be deemed "uncollectible."

Example: Dalila filed her 2017 tax return on February 27, 2018. Since she filed her return before the actual due date, the three-year statute period for audit began April 15, 2018, and ends on April 15, 2021. After that date, the IRS must be able to prove fraud or a substantial understatement of gross income to assess additional tax on Dalila's tax return.

Unit 1: Study Questions

(Test yourself first, then check the correct answers at the end of this quiz.)

1. The 2020 backup withholding rate for U.S. taxpayers is:

A. 10%
B. 24%
C. 25%
D. 30%

2. Julissa and Albert file a joint return. Their tax refund will be applied toward Albert's unpaid child support obligations from an earlier relationship. To request her portion of their refund, Julissa should file:

A. As an innocent spouse.
B. As a damaged spouse.
C. As an injured spouse.
D. For equitable relief.

3. Tatiana is 41 years old and divorced. She files as head of household and has two dependent children. Tatiana is a citizen of Canada and a legal U.S. resident (a green card holder). She lived in Canada for the entire tax year and earned all her income working in Canada. She earned $63,000 in 2020 and plans to itemize her deductions. Which tax form should Tatiana use to report her income?

A. Form 1040
B. Form 1040-NR
C. Form 1040-X
D. Form 1040-SR

4. What is the statute of limitations for an IRS assessment on a tax return from which more than 25% of the taxpayer's gross income was omitted?

A. There is no statute of limitations on a return in which 25% of gross income was omitted.
B. Three years from the date the return was filed, or the return was due, whichever is later.
C. Six years from the date the return was filed.
D. Ten years from the date the return was filed.

5. Isabella files as single and has no refundable credits. She is not self-employed. Based on the figures below, is she required to pay estimated taxes in the current year?

AGI for prior tax year	$73,700
Total tax on prior-year return	$9,224
Anticipated AGI for the current year	$82,800
Total current year estimated tax liability	$11,270
Tax expected to be withheld in the current year	$10,250

A. Yes, she is required to make estimated tax payments.
B. No, she is not required to make estimated tax payments.
C. She is not required to make estimated tax payments because she does not have self-employment income.
D. None of the above is correct.

6. Generally, how long should taxpayers keep the supporting documentation for their tax returns?

A. Four years from the date the return was filed, or the return was due, whichever is later.
B. Three years from the date the return was filed, or the return was due, whichever is later.
C. Two years from the date the return was filed, or the return was due, whichever is later.
D. Ten years from the date the return was filed, or the return was due, whichever is later.

7. Which of the following taxpayers is required to have an individual taxpayer identification number (ITIN)?

A. A nonresident alien with a Social Security number who moves outside the U.S.
B. Anyone who does not have a Social Security number.
C. A nonresident alien who must file a U.S. tax return and is not eligible for a valid Social Security number.
D. All nonresident aliens and resident aliens that are physically present in the U.S. for more than six calendar months.

8. Abdiel's 2017 tax return was due April 15, 2018. He managed to file the return before the deadline, on March 30, 2018. Later, Abdiel discovered that he is eligible for an education credit that will result in a refund. He neglected to take this credit on his 2017 return. What is the *latest date* that Abdiel can amend his 2017 tax return in order to receive a refund?

A. March 30, 2020.
B. April 15, 2020.
C. April 15, 2021.
D. October 15, 2021.

9. Cristiano is single and earned $350,000 as a self-employed website developer during the current year. Under the estimated tax safe harbor rules for high-income taxpayers, he can avoid an underpayment penalty if he pays what percentage of his prior-year tax liability?

A. 50%
B. 90%
C. 100%
D. 110%

10. Rochelle is a U.S. citizen who lives and works in England the entire tax year. She owes $4,700 of U.S. income tax in 2020. Which of the following statements is correct regarding her filing and payment requirements?

A. She must file and pay her taxes by April 15.
B. She must remit her taxes by April 15, but she does not have to file until October 15.
C. She is allowed an automatic two-month extension to file and pay her taxes, but she must attach a statement to her return, explaining why she qualifies for the extension.
D. Since she is an ex-pat, she will not owe any additional interest on her tax liability.

11. Which of the following is not an acceptable reason for extending the statute of limitations for claiming a refund past the normal filing deadline?

A. A bad debt from worthless securities.
B. Living in a federally declared disaster area.
C. Exceptions for military personnel.
D. Living outside the country for three years.

12. If a taxpayer files his tax return more than 60 days after the due date or extended due date, what is the minimum penalty he will face?

A. A minimum of 25% of his unpaid taxes.
B. A minimum of 5% of his unpaid taxes.
C. The smaller of $210 or 100% of the unpaid tax.
D. The lesser of $435 or 100% of the unpaid tax.

13. Which of the following documents will be accepted as a valid means of identification for a taxpayer applying for an ITIN?

A. Notarized copies of birth certificates and passports.
B. Color copies of birth certificates and passports.
C. Original or certified copies of birth certificates and passports.
D. Photocopies of birth certificates and passports.

14. Ricky files his 2020 tax return on February 25, 2021. He has a balance due of $800 on the return. How long can he wait to pay the amount owed and not incur a late payment penalty?

A. He will owe a late payment penalty unless he pays his tax liability when he files his return.
B. He has until the due date of the return (not including extensions) to pay the amount owed and not owe a penalty.
C. He has until the due date of the return (including extensions) to pay the amount owed and not owe a penalty.
D. He does not have to pay the amount due by a certain date because it is less than the safe harbor amount of $1,000.

15. Coralys is a legal U.S. resident who paid estimated tax in 2020 totaling $2,560. In 2021, she closed her business as a self-employed translator and is now unemployed. Coralys expects to have zero tax liability in 2021. Which of the following statements is correct?

A. She is still required to make estimated tax payments in 2021.
B. She is not required to make any estimated tax payments in 2021.
C. She must pay a minimum of $2,560 in estimated tax payments in 2021, or she will be subject to a failure-to-pay penalty.
D. She must make a minimum of $1,000 in estimated tax payments in 2021, or she will be subject to an underpayment penalty.

16. Catherine files an extension request (Form 4868), which allows her an additional six months to file her tax return. When she finally prepares her return on October 10, she realizes that she owes a substantial amount of tax. She pays the tax when she files the return, which she does before the extended due date. Which penalties, if any, will Catherine be likely to owe?

A. She will owe interest on the amount owed and a late payment penalty.
B. She will owe interest on the amount owed and a late filing penalty.
C. She will owe interest on the amount owed, a late payment penalty, and a late filing penalty.
D. She will not owe any penalties because she filed before the extended due date and paid the taxes owed with the return.

Unit 1: Quiz Answers

1. The answer is B. The 2020 backup withholding rate is 24%. The IRS may require backup withholding if a taxpayer has a delinquent tax debt; if he fails to report all his interest, dividends, and other income, or if his Social Security number does not match records provided to the IRS.

2. The answer is C. Julissa should file a claim as an injured spouse to request her portion of their tax refund. She would do so by filing Form 8379, Injured Spouse Allocation. If the request is granted, the IRS will retain her husband's portion of their tax refund to offset his unpaid child support but will allow Julissa to obtain her portion of the refund. In contrast, innocent spouse relief is when tax has been incorrectly reported on a joint return, and one spouse is relieved of the obligation to pay the other spouse's portion of the tax liability.

3. The answer is A. Since Tatiana plans to itemize her deductions, she must file Form 1040. Form 1040-NR is only for nonresident taxpayers, and Form 1040-SR is for seniors that are 65 years of age or older. With few exceptions, green card holders are taxed as U.S. citizens and do not file Form 1040-NR, regardless of where they live.

4. The answer is C. If a taxpayer omitted more than 25% of his gross income on his return, the IRS has up to six years to assess a deficiency.

5. The answer is B. Isabella does not need to pay estimated tax because she expects her income tax withholding in the current year ($10,250) to be greater than both—90% of the tax to be shown on her current year return ($11,270 × 90% = $10,143) and 100% of her prior-year tax liability ($9,224). Therefore, Isabella qualifies for the safe harbor rule and is not required to make estimated tax payments. A taxpayer is not required to pay estimated tax if:

- The taxpayer was a U.S. citizen or resident alien and had no tax liability in the prior year, and
- The prior tax year covered a twelve-month period.

A taxpayer also does not have to pay estimated tax if she pays enough through withholding so that the tax due on the return is less than $1,000. In most cases, a taxpayer must pay estimated tax if she expects withholding (plus any refundable credits) to be less than the smaller of:

- 90% of the tax to be shown on the current year tax return, or
- 100% of the tax shown on the prior-year tax return.

6. The answer is B. Taxpayers should keep the supporting documentation for their tax returns for at least three years from the date the return was filed, or three years from the date the return was due, whichever is later. This includes applicable worksheets, receipts, and other forms.

7. The answer is C. If a taxpayer must file a U.S. tax return or is listed on a tax return as a spouse or dependent and is not eligible for a Social Security number, he must apply for an ITIN.

8. The answer is C. If Abdiel has his amended 2017 return postmarked on or before April 15, 2021, it will be within the three-year limit, and the return will be accepted. If the amended return is postmarked after that date, it will fall outside the three-year statute of limitations, and he will not

receive a refund. To claim a refund on withholding or estimated tax payment amounts, the amended return must be filed no later than three years from the date the return was due.

9. The answer is D. To avoid an underpayment penalty, Cristiano must pay the smaller of:

- 110% of his prior-year tax liability or
- 90% of his expected tax for the current year.

This estimated tax safe harbor rule applies to higher-income taxpayers with an adjusted gross income of more than $150,000 ($75,000 if filing an MFS return).

10. The answer is C. Rochelle is allowed an automatic two-month extension to file and pay her taxes, but she must attach a statement to her tax return, explaining why she qualifies for the extension. A U.S. citizen or resident alien living outside the United States has an automatic two-month extension to file and pay her taxes. The same is true for members of the military who are serving outside the United States. She will still owe interest on the tax that was due before the regular filing deadline, if she does not pay the amount due by that date.

11. The answer is D. Living outside the country is not a valid reason to extend the statute of limitations for claiming a refund. In some cases, a request for a tax refund will be honored past the normal three-year deadline. Exceptions exist for military personnel, individuals who are financially disabled, taxpayers who live in federally-declared disaster areas, and taxpayers who have bad debts from worthless securities.

12. The answer is D. For the tax year 2020, the failure-to-file penalty has increased to $435 or 100% of the unpaid tax (whichever is less) for a taxpayer who files his return more than 60 days late.

13. The answer is C. Only original documents of birth certificates and passports are accepted (or documents that have been "certified" by the original issuing agency). Notarized copies are no longer accepted.

14. The answer is B. Ricky has until the original due date of the return (not including extensions) to pay the amount owed and not incur a late payment penalty. Taxpayers should submit their payment of taxes due on or before April 15 (or the next business day if April 15 falls on a Saturday, a Sunday, or a legal holiday). For the 2020 tax year, Ricky has until April 15, 2021, to pay the amount he owes.

15. The answer is B. Coralys is not required to pay estimated tax if she expects to have zero tax liability for the current tax year.

16. The answer is A. Even though she files Form 4868, Catherine may owe interest and a late payment penalty on the amount owed if she does not pay the tax due by the regular due date. However, she will not be assessed a late filing penalty (failure-to-file) because she filed her tax return before the extended due date.

Unit 2: Determining Filing Status and Residency

For additional information, read:
Publication 17, *Your Federal Income Tax*
Publication 501, *Dependents, Standard Deduction, and Filing Information*
Publication 54, *Tax Guide for U.S. Citizens and Resident Aliens Abroad*
Publication 519, *U.S. Tax Guide for Aliens*

The IRS uses a taxpayer's filing status to determine filing requirements, standard deductions, eligibility for certain credits, and the amounts of tax owed. There are five filing statuses, with rules governing each, including special rules for annulled marriages and widow(er)s with dependent children. Some taxpayers are eligible to use more than one filing status. Usually, the taxpayer will choose the filing status with the lowest tax rate.

In general, a taxpayer's marital status on the last day of the year (December 31) determines their marital status for the entire year. For federal tax purposes, "marriage" was traditionally defined as a legal union between a man and a woman as husband and wife.

For tax years 2013 and beyond, a marriage between same-sex spouses is also recognized as a legal union, as long as the marriage was performed in a domestic or foreign jurisdiction that recognizes the validity of same-sex marriage.[57]

Note: Federal law does not allow Registered Domestic Partners to file a joint return. This rule also applies to civil unions.[58] However, the IRS *does* recognize common-law marriages. Currently, the only states that recognize common law marriage are the District of Columbia, Colorado, Iowa, Kansas, Montana, Oklahoma, Rhode Island, South Carolina, Texas, and Utah. Common-law marriage laws vary from state to state, and cohabitation alone does not constitute a common-law marriage. Several states now recognize same-sex common-law marriages. You must be familiar with the laws of your state in order to correctly determine filing status.

Example: Tavor and Natasha legally divorced on December 28, 2020. They do not have any dependents. They each must file as "single" for 2020. It doesn't matter that they were legally married for almost the entire year. The fact that the divorce became final at the end of the year means that they are *unmarried* for tax purposes.

Example: Stephanie and Paola are a same-sex couple living in California. They are registered domestic partners (RDPs). Under California law, they are considered "married" and must file a joint *California* return. However, for federal tax purposes, they are not considered "married." They must file "Single" federal returns. If Stephanie and Paola want to file a joint federal return, they must get legally married.

---

[57] On September 2, 2016, the IRS issued final regulations (T.D. 9785) to reflect the holdings of the landmark Supreme Court cases Obergefell v. Hodges and United States v. Windsor. The final regulations defined (for federal tax purposes) that a marriage of two individuals would be recognized if the marriage is recognized by the state, possession, or territory of the United States in which the marriage is entered into, regardless of the married couple's place of domicile. Legal marriages performed in foreign countries are also recognized.

[58] See Revenue Ruling 2013-17. Although RDPs are legally treated in the same manner as marriages in the state of California, for federal tax law purposes, they are not. On the EA exam, you will not be tested on the particular marriage laws of any particular state, but you must know that only a legal marriage is recognized for IRS purposes, and not any other type of civil union or registered domestic partnership.

Example: Bart and Alvis are a same-sex couple living in Maine. Both are U.S. citizens. On May 10, 2020, they took a one-month trip to Canada and got married. The United States recognizes foreign marriages performed in Canada, so Bart and Alvis are now legally married for federal tax law purposes. They may file either MFJ or MFS for the tax year. Neither one can file "Single."

Example: Dwight and Charlotte live together in Texas, which is a common-law state. Although Dwight and Charlotte never applied for a marriage license or went through a formal marriage ceremony, they tell their family and friends that they are married, they use the same last name, own a house together, and have three children together. In the state of Texas, their conduct rises to the level of "holding oneself out to the public" as a married couple. Therefore, they are considered "married" under the common-law statutes and can file a joint federal return together.

Single

Marital status is generally determined on the last day of the year. A taxpayer is considered single for the entire tax year if, on the last day of the tax year, he or she was:

- Unmarried,
- Legally separated under a decree of divorce or separate maintenance,
- Legally divorced.

Example: Alastair and Bernardine separated on July 3, 2020. The same day, Alastair filed for divorce. Their divorce was final on December 30, 2020. Neither Alastair nor Bernardine have any children or dependents. Since their divorce was final before the end of the year, they are considered "single" for tax purposes. This will be their filing status on their 2020 tax returns.

Married Filing Jointly (MFJ)

The "married filing jointly" status typically provides more tax benefits than filing a separate return. On a joint return, spouses report all of their combined income, allowable expenses, exemptions, and deductions. Spouses can file a joint return even if only one spouse had income.

This filing status is an election, not the default. This is because *both* spouses must agree to sign a joint return, and *both* are responsible for any tax owed, even if all the income was earned by only one spouse. If one spouse does not wish to file jointly, then both spouses must default to MFS, (unless one qualifies for a different filing status).[59] A subsequent divorce usually does not relieve either spouse of the liability associated with the original joint return, although there are exceptions for innocent spouse relief, in some cases. Taxpayers can file jointly if they are married as of December 31 and:

- Live together as married spouses, or
- Live together in a common-law marriage recognized in the state where they now reside or in the state where the common law marriage began,
- Live apart but are not legally separated or divorced,[60] or
- Are separated under an interlocutory (not final) divorce decree.

---

59 Both spouses must sign the income tax return. However, special rules apply when a spouse cannot sign the tax return because of death, illness, or temporary absence.

60 State law governs whether a taxpayer is married or legally separated under a divorce or separate maintenance decree. Single filing status generally applies if the taxpayer is not married, divorced, or legally separated according to state law.

In addition, a widowed taxpayer may use the married filing jointly status and file jointly with their deceased spouse, if the taxpayer's spouse died during the year and the taxpayer has not remarried as of the end of the year.

Nonresident Alien Spouses: Special rules apply to nonresident alien spouses. A U.S. resident or U.S. citizen who is married to a nonresident alien can elect to file a joint return as long as *both* spouses agree to be taxed on their worldwide income. An election statement must be attached to the joint return.[61]

Example: Patricia is a U.S. citizen living in Indonesia. She is married to Vikal, a nonresident alien and citizen of Indonesia. The spouses elect to treat Vikal as a U.S. resident (for tax purposes). Patricia and Vikal must request an ITIN for Vikal and report their worldwide income for the year they make the choice, and for all later years unless the election is ended or suspended. Although Patricia and Vikal must file a joint return for the year they make the election, as long as one spouse is a U.S. citizen or U.S. resident, they can file either joint or separate returns for later years.

Married Filing Separately (MFS)

The MFS status is for taxpayers who are married and either:

- Choose to file separate returns, or
- Do not agree to file a joint return.

If one spouse chooses to file MFS, the other is forced to do the same, since a joint return must be signed by both spouses. The MFS filing status means the two spouses report their own income, exemptions, credits, and deductions on separate returns, even if one spouse had no income. This filing status may benefit a taxpayer who wants to be responsible only for his own tax, or if it results in less tax than filing a joint return.[62] Typically, a married couple will pay more tax on a combined basis when filing separately, than they would by filing jointly.

Example: Arush and Namita have always filed jointly in the past. However, Namita has chosen to separate her finances from her husband this year, even though they are still living together. Arush wants to file jointly with Namita, but she has refused. Namita files her tax return using married filing separately as her filing status; therefore, Arush is forced to file MFS, as well.

Specific features of the MFS filing status include the following:

- The tax rates are generally higher at the same levels of taxable income than those applicable to MFJ.
- The exemption amount for the alternative minimum tax is half that which is allowed on a joint return.
- Various credits, including the Earned Income Tax Credit, the Premium Tax Credit, and those for child care, are either not allowed or are more limited than on a joint return.
- The capital loss deduction is limited to $1,500, half of what is allowable on a joint return.
- The standard deduction is half the amount allowed on a joint return and cannot be claimed if the taxpayer's spouse itemizes deductions.
- Neither spouse can deduct student loan interest on an MFS return.

---

[61] This is called a "§6013(g) election," and a required election statement must be attached to the return.
[62] Special rules apply for community property states.

Example: Harrison and Regina keep their finances separate and choose to file MFS. Harrison plans to itemize his deductions this year, so Regina is forced to either itemize her deductions or claim a standard deduction of zero.

Married taxpayers sometimes choose to file separate returns when one spouse does not want to be responsible for the other spouse's tax obligations, or because filing separately may result in a lower total tax. For example, if one spouse has high medical expenses or a large casualty loss, separate returns may result in a lower total tax liability because a lower adjusted gross income allows more expenses or losses to be deducted.

Another common reason a taxpayer may choose the MFS filing status is to avoid a refund offset against the other spouse's outstanding prior debt. This might include delinquent child support or student loans, or a tax liability one spouse incurred before the marriage.

Example: Phillip and Imelda were married in 2020. Imelda owes several years of back taxes as well as delinquent student loans. Phillip chooses to file separately from Imelda, so his refund will not be offset by her overdue tax debts. If they were to file jointly, their entire refund might be retained in order to pay the debt.

Amending Filing Status from MFS

There are rules for when married taxpayers are allowed to change their filing status. Although it is possible to amend a person's filing status, there are strict rules for doing so.

Taxpayers generally cannot change from a joint return to a separate return *after the due date* of the return. For example, if a married couple files a joint 2020 return on February 1, 2021, and subsequently decide they wanted to file separately instead, they would have only until April 15, 2021 (the due date of the original return) to file amended returns using the MFS filing status.

Example: Alvin and Darla are married and live in Florida. They file their 2020 tax return jointly, on March 1, 2021. Later, Darla discovers that Alvin may not be reporting all the income from his business, and she is afraid of being audited in the future. Darla decides to quickly amend her joint return to a separate return by filing Form 1040-X on March 15, 2021. Since she filed her amended return before the filing deadline, the IRS will process the return, and her filing status will be adjusted to MFS, making her responsible only for her own tax liability.[63]

A notable exception to this rule allows a personal representative for a deceased taxpayer to change from a joint return, elected by the surviving spouse, to a separate return for the decedent for up to a year after the filing deadline.

Example: Purvis and Bianca have always filed jointly. Bianca dies suddenly in 2020, and her last will and testament names Laura, her daughter from a previous marriage, as the executor of her estate. Purvis files a joint return with Bianca for the tax year 2020, but Laura, as the executor, decides that it would be better for her deceased mother's estate if Bianca's final tax return were filed as MFS. Laura files an amended return claiming MFS status for Bianca and signs the return as the executor. Laura has a full year after the filing deadline to submit the amended return.

[63] The Internal Revenue Manual outlines the procedure for returns that are amended from MFJ to MFS (IRM 21.6.1.5.6). The IRS creates a "substitute" MFS return for the other spouse for return processing, and then that SFR can be amended by the second spouse if desired.

To change from separate returns to a joint return (MFS to MFJ), taxpayers must file an amended return using Form 1040-X, and may do so at any time within three years from the due date of the separate returns (not including extensions).

Head of Household (HOH)

A taxpayer who qualifies to file as head of household will usually have a lower tax rate than a single or MFS taxpayer and will receive a higher standard deduction. The head of household status is available to taxpayers who meet all of the following requirements:

- The taxpayer must be single, divorced, legally separated, or "considered unmarried" on the last day of the year.
- The taxpayer must have paid more than half the cost of keeping up a home for the year.
- The taxpayer must have had a qualifying person living in his home for more than half the year. There are exceptions for temporary absences,[64] as well as for a qualifying parent, who does not have to live with the taxpayer. This would include hospitalization and stays in a nursing home.

Example: Rhonda is unmarried. Her son, Nathaniel, was eighteen years old at the end of the year. Nathaniel lived away from his mother all year because he was going to college. He lived in the campus dorms and returned home only on holidays. Nathaniel does not work and does not provide any of his own support. Since his time away from home to attend school is considered a "temporary absence," Rhonda may claim head of household filing status, and claim Nathaniel as her dependent.

"Considered Unmarried" for HOH Status

There are some instances where a taxpayer can be "considered unmarried" for tax purposes only. To be "considered unmarried" on the last day of the tax year, a taxpayer must meet all of the following conditions:

- File a separate return from the other spouse.
- Pay more than half the cost of keeping up a home for the tax year, and maintain the home as the main residence of a qualifying child, stepchild, or foster child for more than half the year.
- Not live with a spouse in the home during the last six months of the tax year.
- Be able to claim an exemption for the child (although there is an exception for divorced parents, explained later).

For the purpose of determining head of household filing status, valid household expenses used to calculate whether a taxpayer is paying more than half the cost of maintaining a home include:

- Rent, mortgage interest, property taxes
- Home insurance, repairs, utilities
- Food eaten in the home

---

[64] For IRS purposes, "temporary absences" include time away from home going to college, vacation, business, medical care, hospitalization, military service, summer camp, and detention in a juvenile facility.

Valid expenses do *not* include clothing, education, medical treatment, vacations, life insurance, or transportation. Welfare payments are not considered amounts that the taxpayer provides to maintain a home. The qualifying person for HOH filing status must generally be related to the taxpayer either by blood, adoption, or marriage. However, a foster child also qualifies if the child was legally placed in the home by a government agency. For purposes of the head of household status, a "qualifying person" is defined as:

- A qualifying child,
- A married child who can be claimed as a dependent, or
- A dependent parent,
- A qualifying relative that meets certain relationship tests

A taxpayer's qualifying person may include: a child or stepchild, sibling or step-sibling, or a descendant of any of these. For example, a niece or nephew, stepbrother or stepsister, or grandchild may all be eligible as qualifying persons for the HOH filing status.[65]

Example: Rodger's grandchild, Marie, lived with him the entire year. Marie turned 26 at the end of the year. She does not have a job, did not provide any of her own support, and cannot be claimed as a dependent by anyone else. She is not disabled. Although she is not a qualifying child, (because of her age), she is a qualifying relative. As a result, Rodger may use the HOH filing status.

Example: Asmara is unmarried and age 52. Asmara's 27-year-old son, Ziyad, lives with her all year long. He has a small part-time job and earns $5,800 in wages during the year. He is not disabled or a student, so he does not meet the age test for a qualifying child. Since he made over the "deemed exemption" amount, he is also not a qualifying relative. As a result, Asmara cannot file as head of household because her son is not a dependent (he does not qualify under the rules for a "qualifying child" or for a "qualifying relative"). Asmara is forced to file as Single.

An unrelated individual may still be considered a "qualifying relative" for dependency purposes but will not be a qualifying person for the HOH filing status.[66]

Example: Sergey is unmarried and age 54. He earns wages of $46,000 for the year. His old Army buddy, Emmet, lives with Sergey all year long. Emmet does not work, because he is disabled. Emmet and Sergey are not related, but they are best friends. Sergey pays for all the household costs as well as food and utilities for both of them. As a result, Sergey can claim Emmet as a "qualifying relative" dependent, but Sergey cannot file as "head of household" because Emmet is not a qualifying person for HOH filing status (i.e., he is not related to Sergey by blood, marriage, or adoption).

Divorced and Noncustodial Parents: A taxpayer can qualify as HOH, even though they may not claim a qualifying child as their dependent. This happens most often with divorced parents. This is because the head of household filing status applies to the taxpayer who maintains the main home of a qualifying child. However, a custodial parent may choose to *release* the dependency exemption to a noncustodial parent. In this scenario, the custodial parent would

---

[65] A taxpayer cannot file HOH if their only dependent is a Registered Domestic Partner. To see a full list of these rules, see: https://apps.irs.gov/app/vita/content/globalmedia/head_of_household_qualifying_person_4012.pdf

[66] The rules for qualifying children and qualifying relatives will be covered in detail in the next unit, Personal and Dependency Exemptions.

claim head of household filing status, while the noncustodial parent would claim the dependency exemption.

Example: Nicolas and Vivian have been divorced for five years. They have a twelve-year-old daughter named Cristina, who lives with her mother during the week and only sees her father on weekends. Therefore, Vivian is considered the custodial parent. The parents agree, however, to allow Nicolas to claim the dependency exemption for Cristina on his tax return. In 2020, Nicolas correctly files as "Single" and claims Cristina as his dependent. This entitles him to the Child Tax Credit. Vivian may still file as HOH if she otherwise qualifies, but she will not claim the dependency exemption for Cristina.

The "considered unmarried" rules apply in determining who can claim a child for dependency and HOH purposes. A couple, even if not formally separated or divorced, must live apart for *more than half the year* for either spouse to claim HOH status.

Example: Darya and Craig physically separated on August 10, 2020, but had not filed for divorce by the end of the year. They have one minor child, Krissy, age eight. Even though Darya lived with Krissy and supported her for the remainder of the year, Darya does not qualify for HOH filing status because she and Craig did not live apart for the last six months of the year.

Example: Austin and Cayla physically separated on February 10, 2020, and lived apart for the remainder of the year. They do not have a written separation agreement and have not filed for divorce. Their six-year-old daughter, Brigid, lived with her father all year, and Austin paid more than half the cost of keeping up the home. Austin claims Brigid as his dependent because he is the custodial parent. Austin can claim head of household status. Although Austin is still legally married, he can file as HOH because he meets all the requirements to be "considered unmarried."

Death or Birth during the Year: A taxpayer may still file as head of household if the qualifying child is born or dies during the year. The taxpayer must have provided more than half of the cost of keeping up a home that was the child's main home while he was alive.

Example: Eleonore gives birth to a son on September 1, 2020, who dies within one week of his birth. She can claim him on her tax return as a qualifying child even though he only lived a short while. Assuming she qualifies, the child would be a qualifying child for the Child Tax Credit and the Earned Income Tax Credit. This is true even if she was unable to obtain a Social Security number for the child.[67]

Dependent Parents: If a taxpayer's qualifying person is a dependent parent, the taxpayer can file as HOH even if the parent does not live with the taxpayer. The taxpayer must pay more than half the cost of keeping up a home that was the parent's main home for the entire year. This rule also applies to a parent in a rest home. A qualifying "parent" may be a stepparent, in-law, or grandparent who is related to the taxpayer by blood, marriage, or adoption.

Example: Janie is single and fully financially supports her mother, Leona, who lives in her own apartment. Leona dies suddenly on May 2, 2020. Janie can claim her mother as a dependent and file as HOH for 2020, even though Leona was not alive for the whole year.

[67] If a child was born and died in the same year and was not issued an SSN, the taxpayer may enter "DIED" on the Form 1040, and attach a copy of the child's birth certificate. The tax return must be filed on paper.

Example: Greta is 54 years old and single. She pays the monthly bill for Shasta Pines Nursing Home, where her 80-year-old mother lives. Greta's mother has lived at Shasta Pines for two years and has no income. Since Greta pays more than half of the cost of her mother's living expenses, Greta qualifies for head of household filing status, even though her mother lives in a retirement home.

Nonresident Alien Spouses: Special Rules

A taxpayer who is married to a nonresident alien spouse may elect to file as HOH by "disregarding" the nonresident alien spouse. This is a *unique* rule that only applies to taxpayers who are married to nonresident aliens.

This is true even if both spouses lived together throughout the year. The taxpayer must not elect to treat the spouse as a resident, and the taxpayer must have a qualifying child (or another qualifying dependent, such as a parent) to qualify for the HOH status. The taxpayer's nonresident alien spouse is not a qualifying person for head of household purposes. The taxpayer must have another qualifying person and meet the other tests to be eligible to file as a head of household.

Example: Two years ago, Wharton, a U.S. citizen, met and married Paloma, a nonresident alien who is a citizen of Greenland. The couple lived together in Greenland while Wharton was on sabbatical from his university teaching position. They had a son, who was born on January 18, 2020. Paloma does not wish to file jointly with Wharton and does not wish to make the election to be treated as a U.S. resident, because she does not want to pay tax on her worldwide income, as she would be required to do if she filed jointly with Wharton. Wharton can file as head of household and claim his son as a dependent, even though he and Paloma lived together all year, because Paloma is a nonresident alien.

Qualifying Widow(er) With a Dependent Child

Qualifying widow(er) with a dependent child is the least common filing status. A qualifying widow(er) receives the same standard deduction as married taxpayers who file jointly. In the year of the spouse's death, a taxpayer can generally file a joint return. However, if a surviving spouse remarries before the end of the year, the married filing separately status must be used for the decedent's final return.

Example: Dauphine and her husband, Vince, have a 12-year-old son. Vince dies suddenly of a heart attack on February 1, 2020. Dauphine remarries on December 20, 2020. Since she remarried in the same year her late husband died, she no longer qualifies for the joint return filing status with her deceased husband. However, Dauphine does qualify to file jointly with her new husband. Therefore, Vince's filing status for his final tax return must be MFS. The executor of Vince's estate would be responsible for filing his final tax return.

For each of the two years following the year of the spouse's death, the surviving spouse can use the qualifying widow(er) filing status if he has a qualifying dependent and does not remarry. After two years, the taxpayer's filing status converts to single or HOH, depending upon which status applies. For example, if a taxpayer's spouse died in 2019 and he did not remarry, the taxpayer could use the qualifying widow(er) filing status for tax year 2020 *and* 2021 if he has a qualifying dependent.

Example: Sampson's wife died on July 3, 2020. Sampson has one dependent child who is ten years old. Sampson has not remarried. Therefore, Sampson's filing status for 2020 is MFJ (the last year his wife was alive). For 2021 and 2022, he can file as a "qualifying widow with a dependent child," which is a more favorable filing status than single or HOH. For 2023, he would file as HOH, assuming he remains single and does not remarry.

Filing Status After the Death of a Spouse (with Dependent Child)	
Tax Year	**Filing Status**
Year of death	MFJ or MFS
1st year after death	Qualifying widow(er) with dependent child*
2nd year after death	Qualifying widow(er) with dependent child*
3rd and subsequent years after death	Head of household or single

To be eligible for the qualifying widow(er) filing status, the taxpayer normally must:

- Not have remarried before the end of the year.
- Have been eligible to file a joint return in the year the spouse died; (it does not matter if a joint return was actually filed).
- Have a qualifying child for the year. A qualifying child can be a child, adopted child, or a stepchild, but does *not* include a foster child for the purposes of this filing status.
- Have furnished over half the cost of keeping up the child's home for the entire year.

Note: The federal requirements for the Qualifying Widow(er) filing status recently changed. While the taxpayer still needs a qualifying child that meets certain qualifications, the child *does not* have to be claimed as a dependent on the tax return. The taxpayer must only provide the child's name on the return.

Annulments

Annulment is a legal procedure for declaring a marriage null and void. If a taxpayer obtains a court decree of annulment that holds no valid marriage ever existed, the couple is considered *unmarried* even if they filed joint returns for earlier years. Unlike divorce, an annulment is retroactive.

Taxpayers who have annulled their marriage must file amended returns (Form 1040-X), claiming single (or head of household status, if applicable) for all the tax years affected by the annulment that are not closed by the statute of limitations.

Example: Nora and Enzo were granted an annulment on October 31, 2020. They were married for two years. Enzo has sole custody of one son from a prior relationship. For 2020, Nora must file as single and must amend the prior two years' tax returns to single as well. Enzo must also amend his joint returns. If he otherwise qualifies, Enzo can amend his returns to head of household filing status, claiming his son as a dependent.

Determining Residency for Tax Purposes

To file an accurate tax return, a taxpayer must determine whether he is considered a *resident* or a *nonresident*. For IRS purposes, an "alien" is an individual who is not a U.S. citizen. Aliens are further classified as "nonresident" aliens and "resident" aliens. Residency status is important because these taxpayers are taxed in different ways:

- **Resident aliens** are generally taxed on their worldwide income, the same as U.S. citizens.
- **Nonresident aliens** are taxed only on their income from sources within the United States and on certain income connected with the conduct of a trade or business in the U.S.
- **Dual-status aliens** are those that are both nonresident and resident aliens during the same tax year. Different rules apply for the part of the year a taxpayer is a U.S. resident and the part of the year he is a nonresident.

Residency for IRS purposes is not the same as legal immigration status. An individual may be considered a U.S. resident for tax purposes, based upon the time he spends in the United States, regardless of immigration status. A nonresident alien could be someone who lives outside the U.S., and simply invests in U.S. property or stocks, and is therefore required to file a tax return to correctly report his earnings.

Tax Residency Tests

Certain rules exist for determining the residency for aliens. If a taxpayer is an alien (not a U.S. citizen), he is considered a nonresident alien for tax purposes unless he meets at least one of two tests: the *green card* test or the *substantial presence* test.

Green Card Test: An alien taxpayer is automatically considered a U.S. resident if he is a "lawful permanent resident" of the United States at any time during the tax year. A taxpayer generally has this status if he is a lawful immigrant and has been issued an alien registration card, also known as a "green card."[68] An alien who has been present in the U.S. any time during a calendar year as a lawful permanent resident may opt to be treated as a resident alien for the entire calendar year.

Example: Masha is a citizen of Russia. She arrived in the United States on January 4, 2020, as a student on an F-1 visa. On June 1, 2020, she marries Sammy, a U.S. citizen. Masha immediately petitioned USCIS for a change in immigration status to that of a lawful permanent resident based upon her marriage to Sammy. USCIS approved her petition to become a lawful permanent resident of the United States, and issues Masha a green card on November 1, 2020. Masha passes the Green Card Test on November 1, 2020. Although she is not required to do so, Masha could also *elect* to be taxed as a U.S. resident for the entire tax year by filing jointly with her U.S. citizen spouse, Sammy.

Substantial Presence Test: An alien taxpayer without a green card is considered a U.S. resident for tax purposes only if he meets the substantial presence test for the calendar year. To meet this test, he must be physically present in the United States for at least:

- 31 days during the current tax year (2020), and

---

[68] Image provided by Department of Homeland Security, U.S. Citizenship and Immigration Services Verification Division.

- 183 days during the three-year period, which includes the current year (2020) and the two years immediately preceding the current year (2019 and 2018).

For purposes of the 183-day requirement, all the days present in the current year are counted, along with:

- 1/3 of the days present in the previous year (i.e., 2019), and
- 1/6 of the days present in the second year before the current year (i.e., 2018).

Example: Vienna is a citizen of Brazil. She obtains a visitor's visa and was physically present in the U.S. for 120 days in each of the years 2018, 2019, and 2020. To determine if she meets the substantial presence test for 2020, she must count the full 120 days of presence in 2020, 40 days in 2019 (1/3 of 120), and 20 days in 2018 (1/6 of 120). Since the total for the 3-year period is 180 days (and therefore under the 183-day requirement for the substantial presence test), Vienna is not considered a resident under the substantial presence test for 2020.

If an individual meets the requirements of the "substantial presence" test, the taxpayer is considered for federal tax purposes a resident alien of the United States, even though he or she may not have legal residency in the United States.

Study Tip: You should memorize details of the substantial presence test for the EA exam, including the 183-day requirement and exceptions to the rule.

Tax Residency through Marriage

A nonresident alien who does not meet the substantial presence test and does not have a green card, may still elect to be treated as a resident for tax purposes if he or she is married to a U.S. citizen or resident. This election can be made only if:

- At the end of the year, one spouse is a nonresident alien, and the other is a U.S. citizen or resident, and
- Both spouses agree to file a joint return and treat the nonresident alien as a resident alien for the entire tax year.

Example: Veronica and Sergio are married, and both are nonresident aliens at the beginning of the year. On February 1, 2020, Sergio becomes a legal U.S. resident alien and obtains a green card and a Social Security number. Veronica and Sergio may both choose to be treated as resident aliens for tax purposes by attaching a statement to their joint return. Veronica is not eligible for a Social Security number yet, so she must apply for an ITIN if she wants to file jointly with her husband. Veronica and Sergio must file a joint return for the year they make the election, but they can file either joint or separate returns for later years.

Exempt Individuals

Numerous exceptions are considered when counting days for the substantial presence test. Days in the United States are not counted if the alien taxpayer:

- Regularly commutes to work in the U.S. from a residence in Canada or Mexico, generally more than 75% of the workdays during the applicable working period (this is deemed a "closer connection to home country"),
- Is present in the U.S. as a crew member of a foreign vessel,

- Is unable to leave because of a medical condition that arose while in the United States,
- Is a professional athlete in the U.S. to compete in a charitable sports event. These athletes exclude only the days in which they actually competed in the sports event, but do not exclude days used for practice, travel, or promotional events;
- Is an exempt individual. Exempt individuals include aliens who are:
    - Foreign government-related individuals in the U.S. temporarily[69] under an "A" or "G" visa (such as foreign ambassadors and other diplomats);
    - Teachers on temporary visas;
    - Visiting Scholars or researchers (scholars are exempt from the substantial presence test for two years;
    - Students on temporary visas who do not intend to reside permanently in the U.S. (students are exempt from the substantial presence test for five years).

If the taxpayer does not meet either the green card test or the substantial presence test, he is considered a nonresident alien for tax purposes and is subject to U.S. income tax only on his U.S. source income. A foreign alien who cannot satisfy these two tests is considered a nonresident alien.

Example: Marisela is a Portuguese citizen and a translator who was physically present in the United States as a visitor for fifteen days in each of the years 2018, 2019, and 2020. She is not a green card holder. Marisela earned $32,000 in 2020 as a translator for a famous musician who was traveling to the U.S. to perform a concert. Since the total days she was present in the U.S. for the three-year period do not meet the substantial presence test, Marisela is not considered a U.S. resident for tax purposes for 2020, and her earnings are taxed as a nonresident. Marisela is required to file Form 1040-NR, *U.S. Nonresident Alien Income Tax Return.*

Example: Susanna is a folk singer and a popular recording artist in her home country of Australia. Susanna comes to the U.S. on tour, playing a variety of different venues during the month of April. Afterward, she returns to her home country. Susanna is not a U.S. resident for tax purposes, although she entered the U.S. legally on a P-2 Visa.[70] She is required to report her U.S. source income. Susanna's accountant files a Form 1040-NR to report the income that she earned while she was touring in the U.S. She will only report and be taxed on her U.S. source income.

International Students and Scholars

Most international students and scholars fall under the status of nonresident aliens. An international student is anyone who is temporarily in the U.S. on an F, J, M, or Q visa. Immediate family members of a student, including spouses and unmarried children under age twenty-one who reside with the student, are also considered students for tax purposes. International students holding specific visas are exempt from the substantial presence test for the first five calendar years they are in the U.S.

The five calendar years need not be consecutive. Any part of a calendar year in which the student is present in the U.S. counts as a full year.

---

[69] A foreign government-related individual is considered "temporarily" present in the United States regardless of the actual amount of time present in the United States.

[70] This is a type of temporary visa issued to individual performers, artists or entertainers.

Example: Myung-soon, a citizen of South Korea, is in the U.S. as a graduate student on F-1 visa status, enrolled in a doctoral degree program at Stanford University. She has resided in the U.S. since arriving on February 15, 2015, going back to her home country only for short visits between semesters. She was in the U.S. continuously all of 2020. Because international students are exempt from the substantial presence test for five years, Myung-soon became a U.S. resident alien for federal income tax purposes in 2020. Myung-soon is married to Quim, who lives in South Korea and is a nonresident alien. Beginning in the 2020 tax year, Myung-soon and Quim can both elect to be treated as U.S. residents for tax purposes on a jointly filed return.

Example: The first time Shaniya came to the U.S. was in 2013, when she arrived as a foreign student on an F-1 student visa from her home country of India. She studied at Purdue University in the U.S. until the end of 2015 and then returned home. She re-entered the U.S. on a J-1 student visa in 2020 to attend graduate school. She is allowed to legally work for the university as a graduate teaching assistant on a J-1 student visa. For federal income tax purposes, Shaniya is still taxed as a nonresident alien because she has been in the U.S. for less than five years as a student. She will report her earnings from her on-campus job by filing Form 1040-NR. This is true even if she remains in the U.S. the entire year.

Dual Status Aliens: A taxpayer is considered a dual-status alien when he has been both a resident alien and a nonresident alien in the same tax year. The most common dual-status tax years are the years of arrival and departure to and from the U.S.

A taxpayer's status on the last day of the year determines whether he is a resident alien or a nonresident alien for the tax year. For the part of each year the taxpayer is a *nonresident* alien, he is taxed only on his U.S.-source income. For the part of each year the taxpayer is a *U.S. resident alien*, he is taxed on his worldwide income. This applies even if the income was earned earlier in the year while the taxpayer was a nonresident alien but was received after he became a resident for tax purposes.

Example: Ismael became a legal U.S. resident for tax purposes on January 5, 2020. On January 30, 2020, he received $2,000 of income for some contract work he did during the previous tax year. Even though the income was *earned* while he was a nonresident alien, it was received *after* he became a U.S. resident. This income must be reported and taxed on Form 1040, not on Form 1040-NR.

Tax Treaties

The United States has income tax treaties with many foreign countries. Under these treaties, residents of foreign countries may be taxed at reduced rates or be exempt from U.S. income taxes on certain items of income they receive from U.S. source income. These reduced rates and exemptions vary among countries and specific items of income. Treaty provisions are generally reciprocal.

Therefore, a U.S. citizen or resident who receives income from a treaty country and who is subject to taxes imposed by foreign countries may be entitled to certain credits, deductions, exemptions, and reductions in the rate of taxes of those foreign countries. However, it is important to note that many tax treaties contain a "saving clause" that limits the ability of U.S. citizens and residents to use treaty provisions to mitigate their U.S. tax liability.

Income received by a nonresident alien that is effectively connected with a trade or business in the United States is, after allowable deductions, taxed at the rates that apply to U.S. citizens and residents. Withholding would be made at the highest applicable rate.

Note: For nonresident aliens, income or gains from U.S. sources is generally subject to backup **withholding at 30%**, unless a lower treaty rate applies. The normal backup withholding rate for U.S. citizens and U.S. residents in 2020 is a flat 24% rate.

2020 Gross Income Filing Thresholds

Not every person is required to file a tax return. Whether a taxpayer is required to file a federal income tax return depends on several factors, but a taxpayer's filing status and gross income generally determine whether a taxpayer has to file a tax return. The IRS defines "gross income" as *all income* a taxpayer received in the form of money, goods, property, and services that are not exempt from tax. The 2020 filing requirement thresholds, expressed as levels of gross income, are as follows:

- Single: $12,400 (65 or older: $14,050)
- Head of household: $18,650 (65 or older: $20,300)
- Married filing jointly: $24,800
    - 65 or older (one spouse): $26,100
    - 65 or older (both spouses): $27,400
- Married filing separately (of any age): $5 (this is not a typo; it really is $5)
- Qualifying widow(er) with dependent child: $24,800 (65 or older $26,100)

Note: "Earned income" includes all the taxable income a taxpayer receives from working, such as wages, salaries, tips, and other employee compensation. Earned income also includes self-employment earnings that a taxpayer earns by owning a business or farm. Most other types of income are considered **unearned income**, including interest income, dividends, capital gains, retirement income, gambling income, and prizes.

Example: Fauvette and Kipling are married and file jointly. Fauvette is 66 and had gross income of $12,225 for the year. Kipling is 68 and had gross income of $7,500 for the year. Since their combined gross income was $19,725, they are not required to file a tax return in 2020. The filing requirement threshold for joint filers when both spouses are 65 or older is $27,400 in 2020.

Example: Emeline is 70, married, and had $1,500 of wage income in 2020. Her husband, Ricardo, also 70, had $22,700 in wage income. They have no dependents. Normally, Ricardo and Emeline would not have a filing requirement because their gross income is under the filing threshold for joint filers age 65 and over. However, Emeline wants to file separately from her husband. She is therefore required to file a tax return because the filing threshold for MFS taxpayers of any age is $5 in 2020. Ricardo must also file a tax return because his filing status is MFS by default. Ricardo cannot choose to file jointly with his wife unless she agrees, since both spouses are required to sign a joint return.

Filing Requirements for Dependents

Sometimes dependent children are also required to file their own tax returns. The filing thresholds are different depending on whether the child has "earned income" or "unearned income." The filing threshold is much lower for those with "unearned" income. *Earned* income includes wages, tips, self-employment income, and taxable scholarships. *Unearned* income includes interest, dividends, and capital gain distributions. A dependent under 65 must file a return if *any* of the following apply:

- Their "unearned" income was over $1,100 in 2020;
- Their earned income was over $12,400; or
- Their gross income was the larger of (1) $1,100, or (2) their earned income plus $350 (but the total cannot be more than the basic standard deduction for their filing status).

Example: Barrett is 19, single, and a full-time college student. Barrett's mother claims him on her tax return. He received $200 of dividend income and earned $5,650 of wages from a part-time job. Barrett's total income is below the gross income filing threshold for dependents. His investment income is also below the filing requirement. Barrett is not required to file a tax return in 2020, and his mother can claim him as a dependent on her tax return. Even if Barrett isn't required to file a tax return, he may still choose to file in order to receive a refund of the taxes he had withheld from his wages.

Example: Javier is a 16-year-old high school student who is claimed as a dependent on his parents' tax return. He worked as a pizza delivery driver 5 hours a week and earned $3,200 of wages in 2020. He also had $1,250 of interest income from a certificate of deposit that his grandmother gave him last Christmas. Javier is required to file a tax return because his unearned income exceeded $1,100 in 2020. If Javier did not have any interest income, he would not be required to file a return. The investment income is what triggers his filing requirement.

Example: Nadya is 18 and is claimed as a dependent on her parent's tax return. Working part-time at an ice cream parlor during the school year, Nadya earned a total of $12,850 in wages in 2020. She had no other income, and her parents provide more than one-half of her total support, as well as pay for her college tuition and her housing. Nadya must file a tax return because her total earned income is more than $12,400, but her parents can still claim her as a dependent.

Filing Requirements for Self-Employed Taxpayers

There are different requirements for self-employed taxpayers. Generally, a taxpayer is required to file a tax return if he has net self-employment earnings of $400 or more.

Example: Zoe is 27 and earns $8,000 in wages during the year. Normally, she would not have a filing requirement, but she also has $575 in self-employment income for a modeling gig that she did at the beginning of the year. She had a profit motive in the modeling activity and hopes to pick up more modeling gigs in the future. Although she did not receive a 1099-NEC for the contract work, any taxpayer that has $400 or more in self-employment income during the year is required to file a return. Therefore, Zoe must file a Form 1040. She will report her wages, and she must also attach a Schedule C to report her self-employment income.

Do not confuse the filing threshold amount for self-employed taxpayers with the filing requirement for information returns (most notably, Form 1099-NEC and 1099-MISC).[71]

Starting in 2020, the Form-NEC is used to report payments to an independent contractor who is paid at least $600 during the year. This $600 "reporting threshold" has nothing to do with the income tax filing requirement for a self-employed person. Form 1099-MISC is still used to report other types of payments, such as rents, royalties, prizes, and awards.

Additional Filing Requirements

Sometimes a taxpayer is required to file a tax return even if the gross income threshold is not met, such as in the previous example, when a taxpayer has self-employment earnings of $400 or more. Other examples include the following:

- A taxpayer who earned $108.28 or more as a church employee. For the purposes of this rule, a "church employee" is an employee of a church or religious organization that has a certificate electing an exemption from employer social security and Medicare taxes.[72]
- If the taxpayer owes Social Security tax or Medicare tax on tips not reported to his employer.
- If the taxpayer must pay the alternative minimum tax.
- If the taxpayer owes additional tax in connection with a retirement plan, such as an IRA, a health savings account, or another tax-favored health plan.
- If the taxpayer received a Medicare Advantage MSA, Archer MSA, or health savings account (HSA) distribution.
- If the taxpayer owes household employment taxes for a household worker, such as a nanny. If a taxpayer is filing a return only because they owe this tax, the taxpayer can file Schedule H by itself.
- If the taxpayer must recapture an education credit, investment credit, or other credit.
- If the taxpayer received advance payments of the Premium Tax Credit for himself, his spouse, or a dependent who enrolled in coverage through the Health Insurance Marketplace. The taxpayer should receive Forms 1095-A showing the amount of the advance payments, if any.
- Any taxpayer who received payments of the health coverage tax credit. The taxer should receive Form 1099-H showing the amount of the advance payments.
- Any taxpayer receives taxable income under section 965 or is paying in installments under section 965(h) or deferred by making an election under section 965(i).

Example: Calhoun is 28 and single. In 2020, he was unemployed for half of the year. He only earned $9,000 in wages during the year. Normally, he would not have a filing requirement. However, he withdrew $1,200 from his traditional IRA account at the beginning of the year to pay his bills. The IRA withdrawal triggers a filing requirement for Calhoun. He must file a tax return and report the distribution, even though his income is less than the filing threshold for single filers.

[71] For tax year 2020, the IRS reinstated the Form 1099-NEC, *Nonemployee Compensation*, which will be used in to report payments to contractors starting in 2020. The Form 1099-NEC is the revival of an older form that was last used in 1982.
[72] For the purposes of this rule, a "church employee" does not include an ordained minister, a member of a religious order (such as a nun or a monk), or a Christian Science practitioner.

Even if a taxpayer is not legally required to file a tax return, the taxpayer should do so if he or she is eligible to receive a refund. A taxpayer should file a tax return if:

- Had income tax withheld from his pay,
- Made estimated tax payments or had prior year overpayments,
- Qualifies for the Earned Income Tax Credit, or
- Qualifies for any other refundable tax credits.

Example: Susie is single, has a 9-year-old son, and qualifies for HOH filing status. She can claim her son as a dependent. In 2020, she earns $12,100 of wages and $900 of self-employment income from cleaning houses on the weekends. Although Susie makes less than the filing threshold for her filing status, she must file a tax return because her earnings from self-employment exceed $400. Even if Susie did not have self-employment earnings, she should still file a tax return, because she likely qualifies for the Earned Income Tax Credit as well as the Child Tax Credit. The EITC is a refundable credit that could give Susie a sizable refund.

Unit 2: Study Questions

(Test yourself first, then check the correct answers at the end of this quiz.)

1. Reyna, age 22, is single and a full-time college student who is claimed as a dependent on her father's tax return. Her father provides the majority of his daughter's support and pays for all her college tuition and books. In 2020, Reyna earned $13,000 in wages from her part-time job as a waitress. She had no other income. Is she required to file a tax return?

A. Yes.
B. No.
C. Reyna is only required to file a tax return if she is a full-time student.
D. Reyna should file a return because she will receive a refund, but she is not required to file.

2. Janella, age 65, and Marcello, age 66, are married and file jointly. Janella's income was $17,600 in wages, and Marcello's net earnings from self-employment was $520, and he also had $4,000 in Social Security income. Neither had any other income during the year. Based on this information, which of the following statements is correct?

A. Janella and Marcello are not required to file tax returns.
B. Janella and Marcello are both required to file tax returns.
C. Only Janella is required to file a tax return.
D. Only Marcello is required to file a tax return.

3. Taxpayers are considered to be "married" for the entire year if:

A. One spouse dies during the year, and the surviving spouse does not remarry.
B. The spouses are legally separated under a separate maintenance decree.
C. The spouses are divorced on December 31 of the tax year.
D. The spouses had their marriage annulled during the tax year.

4. Ezequiel and Candra are married, but they choose to file separate returns for 2020 because the IRS is auditing Ezequiel for a previous tax issue. Ezequiel and Candra file their MFS returns on time. A few months after filing their separate returns, the audit is over, and Ezequiel's previous tax issue has been resolved. He then wishes to file amended returns and file jointly with his wife to claim the Earned Income Tax Credit (EITC). Which of the following statements is correct?

A. Taxpayers are prohibited from changing their filing status to claim the EITC.
B. Ezequiel and Candra can amend their MFS tax returns to MFJ in order to claim EITC.
C. Ezequiel and Candra can amend their MFS tax returns to MFJ, but they cannot claim the EITC on an amended return.
D. Candra cannot file jointly with Ezequiel after she has already filed a separate tax return.

5. Tania's divorce became final on October 1, 2020. She has sole custody of her two children, who lived with her the entire year. The children are under the age of 17. She provided more than half of the cost of keeping up the home. What filing status should she use?

A. Single.
B. Married Filing Separately.
C. Head of Household.
D. Qualifying Widow(er).

6. Yolanda's husband died on November 14, 2020. She has one dependent son, who is eight years old. She did not remarry during the year. What is the most beneficial filing status for Yolanda to use?

A. Married filing jointly.
B. Single.
C. Qualifying widow(er).
D. Head of household.

7. Madison and Pierre are not married and do not live together, but they have a two-year-old daughter named Ivette. Madison and her daughter lived together all year while Pierre lived alone in his own apartment. Pierre cares for his daughter two days a week. Madison earned $13,000 working as a grocery store bagger. Pierre earned $48,000 managing a hardware store. Pierre paid over half the cost of Madison's apartment for rent and utilities, where his daughter Ivette lives. He also gave Madison child support and extra money for groceries. Pierre does not support any other family member. Which of the following statements is correct?

A. Pierre can file as head of household.
B. Madison can file as head of household.
C. Pierre and Madison can file jointly.
D. Neither Pierre nor Madison can claim head of household filing status.

8. When may a taxpayer amend a joint tax return from "married filing jointly" to "married filing separately" after the original filing deadline?

A. Never.
B. Only within the statute of limitations for filing amended returns.
C. Only when a marriage has been annulled.
D. An estate's personal representative may amend a joint return elected by the surviving spouse to a separate return for the decedent.

9. Rosemarie, age 65, and Domenico, age 72, were married on December 26, 2020. They have no dependents. Rosemarie had wages of $2,000, and Domenico had Social Security income of $19,000 for the year. Domenico wants to file jointly, but Rosemarie wants to file separately. Which of the following statements is correct?

A. Domenico is required to file a tax return using the MFS status. Rosemarie is not required to file a return.
B. Domenico may claim Rosemarie as a dependent, as long as she does not file her own separate return.
C. Domenico and Rosemarie are both required to file tax returns, and they must both file MFS.
D. Domenico and Rosemarie may both file as single since they were married for less than one month during the taxable year.

10. In 2020, Clarence took legal and physical custody of his ten-year-old grandson, Bobby. Bobby's parents were both incarcerated all year and do not have the right to claim Bobby as a dependent. How long must Bobby live in Clarence's home for Clarence to qualify for head of household status?

A. At least three months.
B. More than half the year.
C. The entire year.
D. More than twelve months.

11. A U.S. citizen who is married to a nonresident alien can file a joint return as long as both spouses:

A. Sign the return and agree to be taxed on their worldwide income.
B. Are living overseas and do not plan to reside in the United States.
C. Have valid Social Security numbers.
D. Are physically present in the United States.

12. Victor is 39 years old and has lived apart from his wife, Eleanor, since February 1, 2020. Their divorce was not yet final at the end of the year, and they were not legally separated under a separate maintenance decree. They have two children, a son, age fifteen, and a daughter, age nine. After Victor and Eleanor split up, their son lived with Victor. Their daughter chose to live with Eleanor. Victor provides all of the support for the minor child living with him. Eleanor refuses to file jointly with Victor in 2020. The most beneficial filing status that Victor qualifies for is:

A. Married filing separately.
B. Single.
C. Head of household.
D. Married filing jointly.

13. Which of the following statements is correct regarding the HOH filing status?

A. The taxpayer must be unmarried to qualify for the head of household filing status.
B. The taxpayer's spouse must live in the home during the tax year.
C. The taxpayer's dependent parent does not have to live with the taxpayer to qualify for head of household filing status.
D. The taxpayer must have paid roughly half of the cost of keeping up the house for the entire year.

14. The married filing separately (MFS) status is for taxpayers who:

A. Are legally divorced on the last day of the year.
B. Are married and choose to file separate returns.
C. Are unmarried but engaged to be married.
D. Are unmarried but have a dependent child.

15. Huang is an international student temporarily in the U.S. on an F-1 Visa. Huang arrived in the U.S. on January 1, 2020, and was present in the U.S. all year. How long is he exempt from the substantial presence test?

A. One year.
B. Three years.
C. Five years.
D. There is no exemption to the substantial presence test.

16. Liza and Stuart were married for nine years. Stuart died on April 3, 2018. Liza did not remarry after her husband's death. Liza has one dependent child, age 5. Which filing status should Liza use for her 2020 tax return?

A. Single.
B. Married filing jointly.
C. Head of household.
D. Qualifying widow with a dependent child.

17. Adrienne and Troy are married and lived together all year. Adrienne earned $1,900 in wages during the year, and Troy earned $72,000. Adrienne wants to file a joint return, but Troy refuses to file with Adrienne and instead files a separate return on his own. Which of the following statements is correct?

A. Adrienne can file a joint tax return and e-file it if Troy refuses to provide his signature.
B. Adrienne and Troy must both file separate returns.
C. Adrienne can file as single because Troy refuses to sign a joint return.
D. Adrienne does not have a filing requirement because her income is below the filing threshold.

18. Which dependent relative may qualify a taxpayer for head of household filing status?

A. An adult stepdaughter who lives in her own apartment who is supported by the taxpayer.
B. A cousin who lives with the taxpayer all year.
C. A parent who lives in his own home and not with the taxpayer.
D. An adopted child who lived with the taxpayer for five months of the tax year.

19. All of the following individuals are required to file an income tax return except:

A. A taxpayer who owes household employment tax for a nanny.
B. A church employee who is exempt from FICA taxes, who earned $104 of wages in 2020.
C. A 67-year-old qualifying widower who is blind and earned $47,500 in 2020.
D. A single taxpayer who earned $6,500 in 2020 and owes excise tax on withdrawals from a traditional IRA account.

20. Lauren is an 18-year-old high school senior in her last year of high school. She worked as a grocery store bagger on weekends and earned $1,400 in wages during 2020. She also received $3,400 for a winning scratch-off lottery ticket. Her parents claim Lauren as a dependent on their joint tax return. Does Lauren have to file her own return?

A. Yes, because of the amount of her unearned income.
B. Yes, because of the combined amount of her unearned and earned income.
C. No, because her earned income is below the threshold for a dependent.
D. No, because it is illegal for a high school student to play the lottery.

21. Which of the following dependency relationships would not qualify a taxpayer to claim qualifying widow(er) as their filing status after the death of a spouse?

A. A biological child.
B. A foster child.
C. An adopted child.
D. A stepchild.

22. Louisa legally separated from her husband in 2020. They share custody of a 13-year-old son. Which of the following facts would prevent Louisa from filing as head of household?

A. Louisa has maintained a separate residence from her husband since February 1, 2020.
B. Her son's principal home is with Louisa.
C. Louisa's parents assisted her with 40% of her household costs.
D. Louisa's son lived with her for four months. He lived with his father for the rest of the year.

23. Elisabete and Sirius were married in 2016. They have no children or other dependents. They split up two years ago but never officially filed for divorce. Although they lived apart all of 2020, they are neither divorced nor legally separated. Which of the following filing statuses can they use?

A. Single or married filing separately.
B. Married filing jointly or married filing separately.
C. Married filing separately or head of household.
D. Single or qualifying widow(er).

24. Alexandra's younger brother, Sebastian, is 18 and a full-time student. Sebastian lived with a friend from January through February of 2020. From March through July, Sebastian lived with his sister, Alexandra. On August 1, 2020, Sebastian moved back in with his friends and stayed with them for the rest of the year. However, since Sebastian did not have a job, Alexandra gave him money every month and provided the majority of his financial support for the entire year. Alexandra has no other dependents. Which of the following statements is correct?

A. Alexandra can file as head of household.
B. Alexandra can file jointly with Sebastian.
C. Alexandra cannot file as head of household.
D. Sebastian can file as head of household.

25. Leslie's marriage was annulled on February 25, 2020. She filed jointly with her husband in the previous two years. She has not yet filed her 2020 tax return. Leslie has no dependents. Which of the following statements is correct?

A. She must file amended returns, claiming single filing status for all open years affected by the annulment. She will file as single for 2020.
B. She is not required to file amended returns. She can file jointly with her husband because she was still married to him for part of the year.
C. She is not required to amend returns for any prior years. She must file as married filing separately in 2020.
D. She is not required to amend returns for any prior years. She must file as single in 2020.

Unit 2: Quiz Answers

1. The answer is A. A single dependent whose earned income was more than $12,400 in 2020 must file a return. Her father may still claim Reyna as a dependent and a qualifying child because she is a full-time student and under age 24 at the end of the year, and did not provide more than one-half of her own support.

2. The answer is B. Janella and Marcello must both file tax returns. Normally, Janella and Marcello would not be required to file because their combined gross income was less than the filing requirement, and they are both over 65 (this threshold applies if both spouses are 65 or over and they are filing jointly). However, because Marcello's net earnings from self-employment exceeds $400, he is required to file a return, including Schedules C and SE. Further, if Janella did not wish to file a joint return with Marcello, she would nevertheless be required to file separately because her income exceeds the applicable threshold of $5 for MFS filers in 2020. Whether they choose to file jointly or separately, both are required to file tax returns for 2020.

3. The answer is A. Taxpayers are considered "married" for the entire year if:

- They were married on the last day of the tax year, or
- One spouse died during the year, and the surviving spouse has not remarried as of the end of the year.

4. The answer is B. Ezequiel and Candra are allowed to amend their separate returns to a joint return in order to claim the credit. If a taxpayer files a separate return, he may elect to amend the filing status to married filing jointly at any time within three years from the due date of the original return (not including any extensions). However, the same does not hold true in reverse. Once a taxpayer files a joint return, he cannot choose to file a separate return for that year after the due date of the return (with a rare exception for deceased taxpayers).

5. The answer is C. Because she is legally divorced, Tania could file as Single. However, because she has children and meets the requirements for Head of Household, she should use this as her filing status because it will result in a lower tax.

6. The answer is A. If a taxpayer's spouse died during the year, the taxpayer is considered married for the whole year and can file as MFJ. Therefore, Yolanda should file a joint return for 2020.

7. The answer is D. Although Pierre provided over half the cost of maintaining a home for Madison and Ivette, he cannot file as head of household since Ivette (his daughter) did not live with him for more than half the year. Madison cannot file as HOH either because she did not provide more than one-half the cost of keeping up the home for her daughter. However, either Pierre or Madison may still claim Ivette as a dependent and file as "Single." Generally, a child is the qualifying child of the custodial parent, so Madison would have the primary right to claim Ivette. But Madison may also choose to release the dependency exemption to Pierre (who is the noncustodial parent) by using Form 8332.

8. The answer is D. An executor for a deceased taxpayer can amend a joint return to an MFS return up to one year after the filing deadline. This is the only exception to a rule that generally prevents a taxpayer from amending a joint return to a separate return past the filing deadline. Answer "C" is incorrect because if a marriage has been annulled, the filing status would be amended to "single" rather than "MFS" because an annulment invalidates the original marriage contract.

9. The answer is C. Since Domenico and Rosemarie are married, they can file either jointly or separately. If Rosemarie does not agree to file jointly with Domenico, both taxpayers must file MFS. The filing requirement threshold for married filing separately in 2020 is $5, so both spouses have a filing requirement.

10. The answer is B. Bobby must live with his grandfather for more than half the year (over six months) in order to qualify as his qualifying child. There are exceptions for temporary absences.

11. The answer is A. A U.S. citizen (or U.S. resident), who is married to a nonresident alien, can elect to file a joint return as long as both spouses sign the return and agree to be taxed on their worldwide income. A Social Security number is not required for the nonresident spouse because a nonresident spouse that is ineligible for an SSN may request an ITIN to file jointly with a U.S. resident spouse. An election statement must be attached to the return.

12. The answer is C. Victor qualifies for head of household filing status because he can be "considered unmarried" for tax purposes. His son lived with him for more than six months, he did not live with his spouse the last half of the year, and he paid more than half the cost of keeping up a home for the year for a qualifying child. Couples who are living apart but not yet divorced or legally separated are allowed to file jointly, but both spouses must agree to do so. Therefore, if Eleanor refuses to file jointly with Victor, the most beneficial filing status for Victor is head of household.

13. The answer is C. A dependent parent does not have to live with a taxpayer for the taxpayer to elect the head of household filing status. This special rule applies to parents who are related to the taxpayer by blood, marriage, or adoption if the taxpayer pays more than half of the qualifying parent's household costs. Answer "A" is incorrect because a married person can still qualify for head of household if they are "considered unmarried" for tax purposes. A married person can be "considered unmarried" in certain circumstances if they live apart from their spouse and can file as head of household.

14. The answer is B. The married filing separately (MFS) status is for taxpayers who are married and either:

- Choose to file separate returns, or
- Do not agree to file a joint return.

15. The answer is C. Huang is exempt from the substantial presence test for five years. In determining residency status for tax purposes, students temporarily in the U.S. on an F, J, M, or Q visa are exempt from the substantial presence test for five years. In addition, an individual who is in either of the following categories is temporarily exempt from counting days toward the substantial presence test:

- **Teacher or trainee:** This includes any nonimmigrant temporarily present in the U.S. on a J or Q visa who is not a student. The definition includes physicians, au pairs, short-term scholars, summer camp workers, and cultural exchange visitors temporarily present in the U.S.
- **Closer connection to home country:** This includes individuals who have a tax home in a foreign country and a closer connection to that country than they do to the U.S.

16. The answer is D. In 2020, Liza is eligible for "qualifying widow(er) with dependent child" filing status. Liza and Stuart qualified to file MFJ in the year he died, with Liza signing the tax return as a surviving spouse. The year of death is the last year for which a taxpayer can file MFJ. For each of the *two years* following the year of the spouse's death, the surviving spouse can use the qualifying widow status, if she has a qualifying dependent and does not remarry.

17. The answer is B. Married couples must agree to file jointly. If one spouse does not agree to file jointly, they are individually subject to the MFS filing threshold. In this case, Adrienne and Troy are both required to file separate tax returns because both are above the applicable earnings threshold for MFS.

18. The answer is C. A parent is the only dependent relative who does not have to live with the taxpayer for the taxpayer to claim "head of household" status. In order to file for head of household, the "qualifying person" must be one of the following: a birth child, adopted child, grandchild, stepchild, foster child, brother, sister, half-brother, half-sister, stepbrother, stepsister, or a descendant of any of those. The qualifying person must also live with the taxpayer (unless the absence is temporary). The only exception to the residency test is a parent, who does not have to live with the taxpayer. A cousin does not qualify because they do not meet the relationship test. The adopted child in answer "D" does not qualify because the child lived with the taxpayer for less than one-half of the year.

19. The answer is B. Church employees who are exempt from Social Security and Medicare taxes and have wages of $108.28 or more for the year are required to file a tax return. In answer B, the church employee's wages are below that threshold. In all of the other answers, the taxpayer would be required to file a return.

20. The answer is A. Lauren has to file a tax return because of the amount of her unearned income: i.e., the $3,400 lottery prize. Her earned income—$1,400 in wages—was not high enough to trigger a filing requirement, but the lottery winnings (unearned income) do trigger a filing requirement. Answer "D" is incorrect because most U.S. states allow 18-year-olds to play the state lottery because they are legal adults. Despite the fact that Lauren has to file her own return, her parents can still claim her as a qualifying child.

21. The answer is B. To be eligible for the qualifying widow(er) filing status, the taxpayer normally must have a dependent child. For the purposes of this filing status, a qualifying child can be an adopted child, biological child, or stepchild, but does *not* include a foster child. This special rule for dependents that excludes foster children only pertains to the qualifying widow(er) filing status.[73]

---

[73] Note that this is a very unique rule that applies to the qualifying widower filing status ONLY. For a qualifying widower (a taxpayer whose spouse has died) a "qualifying child" does not include a foster child. Please be aware that qualifying

Answer "C" is incorrect because legally adopted children are always treated the same as biological children for federal tax law purposes.

22. The answer is D. For Louisa to file as head of household, her home must have been the main home of her qualifying child for more than half the tax year (i.e., over six months). Since her son lived with her for only four months, he would not have been in the household sufficient time to qualify her for this filing status.

23. The answer is B. As long as they are married and are neither divorced nor legally separated, Elisabete and Sirius can file a joint return or file separately. They cannot file as single.

24. The answer is C. Alexandra cannot claim head of household status because Sebastian lived with her for only five months, which is less than half the year.

25. The answer is A. Leslie must file amended tax returns for the previous two years. She cannot file jointly with her former husband in 2020. If a couple obtains a court decree of annulment, the taxpayer must file amended returns (Form 1040-X), claiming single or head of household status for all tax years affected by the annulment that are not closed by the statute of limitations for filing an amended tax return.

---

widower filing status is very rare and a scenario where you would have a surviving spouse with a foster child would be even more so. It is unlikely that you would ever see this scenario in actual practice, but we briefly cover it here, because on the EA exam the IRS does test on exceptions, in addition to the general rules..

Unit 3: Dependency Relationships

For additional information, read:
Publication 501, *Dependents, Standard Deduction, and Filing Information*
Publication 504, *Divorced or Separated Individuals*

Personal and dependency exemptions are suspended (reduced to $0) until tax year 2025. However, the ability to *claim* a dependent can make taxpayers eligible for other tax benefits. For example, the following tax benefits are all associated with a dependent:

- Child Tax Credit (CTC) and the Additional Child Tax Credit (ACTC),
- Earned Income Tax Credit (EITC),
- Child and Dependent Care Credit,
- Head of household filing status (HOH),
- Credit for Other Dependents (ODC) and other tax benefits.

Although the Tax Cuts and Jobs Act eliminated the benefit of the dependency exemption itself, the law remains unchanged on who qualifies as a dependent for tax purposes. For 2020 tax year filings, taxpayers can determine a dependent's eligibility by using the "deemed exemption" amount of $4,300.[74] Dependents are either a "qualifying child" or a "qualifying relative" of the taxpayer. Examples of dependents include a child, stepchild, brother, sister, or parent.

Primary Tests for Dependency

Identifying and determining the correct number of dependents is a critical component of completing a taxpayer's return. In order to determine if a taxpayer can claim a dependent, there are three primary tests:

- **Dependent taxpayer test**
- **Joint return test**
- **Citizenship or residency test**

Test #1: Dependent Taxpayer Test

A taxpayer (or taxpayer's spouse, if filing a joint return) who may be claimed as a dependent by another taxpayer may not claim anyone as a dependent on his or her own tax return. In other words, the dependent taxpayer test specifies that any taxpayer who can be claimed as a dependent cannot claim a dependent themselves.

Example: Jayne is an 18-year-old single mother who has an infant son who is three months old. Jayne lives with her parents and has a part-time job, but she does not make enough money to support herself or her infant son. Jayne is claimed as a dependent by her parents, so she is prohibited from claiming her infant son as a dependent on her own tax return.

Sometimes an individual meets the rules to be a qualifying dependent of more than one person. Regardless, only one person can claim an individual as a dependent on his tax return.

---

[74] In 2020, the gross income limitation for a qualifying relative is $4,300. This amount is used for purposes of determining a qualifying relative under IRC Sec. 152(d)(1)(B).

Example: Pearce and Annika are unmarried and live together with their daughter, Juliana. Juliana is a qualifying child for both Pearce and Annika, but only one of them can claim Juliana as a dependent on their tax return. Although only one parent can claim Juliana as a dependent, the two parents can agree on which parent should claim the child to achieve the best tax outcome.

Test #2: Joint Return Test

If a married person files a joint return, that individual normally cannot be claimed as a dependent by another taxpayer. Even if the other dependency tests are met, a taxpayer is generally not allowed to claim a dependent if that person files a joint return with his or her spouse.

Example: Irina is 18 years old and had no income in 2020. Irina lived with her father for the whole year. Irina got married on December 31, 2020, to Xander, who is 24 years old. Irina's new husband earned $28,700 during 2020, and they file jointly. Irina's father supported her the entire year and even paid for her wedding. However, her father cannot claim Irina as his dependent in 2020 because she is filing jointly with her new husband, Xander.

There is only one narrow exception to this test. The joint return test *does not apply* if the joint return is filed by the dependent only to claim a refund, and neither spouse would have a tax liability, even if they filed separate returns.

Example: Robbie and Rosalie are both 18 years old and recently married. They both live with Rosalie's mother, Sylvia. In 2020, Robbie earned $1,950 from a part-time job. That was the only income that Robbie and his wife earned all year. Neither Robbie nor Rosalie are required to file a tax return, but they decide to file a joint return to obtain a refund of the taxes that were withheld from Robbie's wages. Robbie and Rosalie correctly check the box next to "Can anyone claim you as a dependent?" on their joint tax return. As the exception to the joint return test applies, Sylvia can claim both Robbie and Rosalie on her tax return, if all the other tests for dependency are met.

Test #3: Citizenship or Residency Test

A dependent must be a citizen or resident of the United States or a citizen or resident of Canada or Mexico (with an exception for foreign-born adopted children).[75] If a U.S. citizen or U.S. national legally adopts a child who is not a U.S. citizen, U.S. resident alien, or U.S. national,[76] this test is met as long as the child lives with the taxpayer as a member of the household all year. If all other dependency tests are met, the child can be claimed as a dependent. This also applies if the child was lawfully placed with the taxpayer for legal adoption.

Example: Carmella, who is a U.S. citizen, adopted an infant boy from China who lived with her for the entire tax year. Even though Carmella's child is not yet a U.S. citizen, he meets the "citizen or resident test" because he was a member of Carmella's household for the entire year.

---

[75] Foreign exchange students generally are not U.S. residents and do not meet the citizen or resident test, so they cannot be claimed as dependents, even if they live in the taxpayer's home all year.

[76] A "U.S. national" is an individual who, although not a U.S. citizen, owes his or her allegiance to the United States. U.S. nationals include American Samoans and Northern Mariana Islanders who chose to become U.S. nationals instead of U.S. citizens.

Dependency Relationships

A dependent may be either a **"qualifying child"** or a **"qualifying relative."** Both types of dependents have unique rules, but some requirements are the same for both. Remember, a person must meet the requirements of either a qualifying child or a qualifying relative to be claimed as a dependent. There are very specific tests to identify the difference between the two.

> **Note:** Both "qualifying children" and "qualifying relatives" must *first* meet all of the primary dependency requirements already specified: the dependent taxpayer, joint return, and citizenship or residency tests. If these three tests are met, the person is a dependent. A taxpayer's spouse cannot be claimed as a dependent; however, a taxpayer's registered domestic partner *may* qualify as a dependent, assuming all the tests for dependency are met. A taxpayer cannot file as head of household if the taxpayer's only dependent is his or her registered domestic partner.

Rules for a Qualifying Child

The tests for a "qualifying child" are more stringent than the tests for a "qualifying relative." Having a qualifying child entitles a taxpayer to claim refundable tax credits, including the Earned Income Tax Credit and the Additional Child Tax Credit. Having a qualifying relative, on the other hand, does not qualify a taxpayer for these special credits. There are five tests for a qualifying *child*:

- **Relationship Test**
- **Age Test**
- **Residency Test**
- **Support Test**
- **Tiebreaker Test (for a qualifying child of more than one person)**

Test #1: The Relationship Test

The qualifying child must be related to the taxpayer by blood, marriage, or legal adoption. Qualifying children include:

- A child, stepchild, or adopted child. An adopted child also includes a child who was lawfully placed with a person for legal adoption, even if the adoption is not yet final.
- A sibling, half-sibling, or stepsibling (includes; half-brother, half-sister, stepbrother, stepsister, etc.)
- A descendant of one of the above (such as a grandchild, niece, or nephew)
- A foster child

For the purposes of this test, an adopted child is always treated the same as a natural child.

Test #2: The Age Test

In order to be a qualifying child, the dependent must be:

- Under the age of 19 at the end of the tax year, or

- Under the age of 24 at the end of the tax year and a full-time student,[77] or
- Permanently and totally disabled at any time during the year, regardless of age.

A child who is claimed as a dependent must be *younger* than the taxpayer who is claiming him, except in the case of dependents who are disabled. For taxpayers filing jointly, the child must be younger than one spouse listed on the return but does not have to be younger than both spouses.

Example: Gordon and Denise are both 23 years old, married, and file jointly. Denise's 24-year-old stepbrother, Casey, is a full-time student and lives with Gordon and Denise, who provide all of his financial support while he is going to college. Casey is not disabled. Gordon and Denise are both younger than Casey. Therefore, Casey is not their qualifying child, even though he is a full-time student.

Example: Stavros, age 31, and Audrey, age 22, are married and file jointly. Audrey's 23-year-old brother, Brayden, is a full-time college student, is single, and lives with Stavros and Audrey. They provide all of Brayden's support. In this case, Stavros and Audrey can claim Brayden as a qualifying child on their joint tax return because he is a full-time student and is *younger* than Stavros.

Example: Arnold is 55 years old and mentally disabled with Down syndrome. Crystal, his 38-year-old sister, provides all of Arnold's support and cares for him in her home, where he lives with her full-time. Despite Arnold's age, he is considered a qualifying child and a dependent for tax purposes because he is disabled. Crystal can claim Arnold as her qualifying child, and she can also file as head of household.

Test #3: The Residency Test

A qualifying child must live with the taxpayer for more than half the tax year (over six months). The taxpayer's home is any location where they regularly live; it does not need to be a traditional home. For example, a child who lived with the taxpayer for over half the year in a homeless shelter meets the residency test.[78]

In most cases, because of the residency test, a child is automatically the qualifying child of the custodial parent. However, exceptions to the residency test apply for children of divorced parents, kidnapped children, children who were born or died during the year,[79] and temporary absences (such as for summer camp or a missionary trip).

A "temporary absence" includes illness, college, vacation, military service, institutionalized care for a child who is permanently and totally disabled and incarceration in a juvenile facility. It must be reasonable to assume that the child will return to the home after the temporary absence.

---

[77] To qualify as a "full-time" student, the child must be enrolled in the number of hours or courses the school considers full-time during some part of at least five months of the year. See Publication 17 for additional details.

[78] See IRS Publication 596, *Earned Income Credit*, for similar examples and scenarios.

[79] A taxpayer cannot claim a stillborn child as a dependent. The child must be born alive, even if he or she lived only for a short time.

Example: Martino is unmarried and lives with his 10-year-old son, Kevin. Martino provides all of his son's financial support. In 2020, Kevin was diagnosed with a rare form of pediatric cancer and was hospitalized for eleven months. Kevin is still considered Martino's qualifying child because the hospitalization counts as a temporary absence from home. Martino can claim Kevin as his qualifying child, and he can also file as head of household.

Example: Cesare, age 22, is a full-time college student and lived in the dorms at his university for the entire year. Cesare worked part-time, but did not pay over half of his total support. Instead, his mother, Kamille, supported him and paid most of his tuition and living expenses. Cesare's time spent in the dorms counts as a "temporary absence." Therefore, Kamille can claim Cesare on her tax return as a qualifying child, because he meets the relationship, age, residency, and support tests.

Example: Ramona's 16-year-old granddaughter, Korine, lives with her for five months of the year, with her mother for three months, and with her aunt for four months. Korine is not Ramona's qualifying child because the residency test is not met. However, she may be Ramona's qualifying relative if other tests are met.

Test #4: The Support Test

A qualifying child cannot provide more than one-half of his own support. This test is different from the support test for a qualifying relative, and should not be confused as such. State benefits provided to a person in need, such as welfare, food stamps, or subsidized housing, are generally considered support provided by the state.

However, if a child receives Social Security benefits, and uses them for his or her own support, the benefits are considered to be provided by the child. A full-time student does not take scholarships (whether taxable or nontaxable) into account when calculating the support test.[80]

Example: Stuart and Vanessa file jointly. They have one daughter named Edith, age 27. Edith earned $4,000 in wages before she was laid off in March and moved back in with her parents. Stuart and Vanessa provided the majority of Edith's support for the rest of the year. Edith got a new job in December and moved out. She is not a qualifying child for federal tax purposes. Although Edith meets the support test as well as the residency test, she does not meet the age test.

Example: Ernesto has a 19-year-old daughter named Gladys. Ernesto provided $6,000 toward his daughter's support for the year. Gladys has a part-time job as a waitress and provided $15,000 of her own support. Therefore, Gladys provided over half of her own support for the year. Gladys does not pass the support test, and consequently, she is not Ernesto's qualifying child. Gladys can file her own tax return as Single.

80 A scholarship received by a child who is a student isn't taken into account in determining whether the child provided more than half of his or her own support (Publication 501).

Example: Anton is a single parent with one 23-year old daughter named Catia, who lives with him. Catia is a full-time college student at the University of Nevada. Anton contributes $12,000 to his daughter's support. Catia receives a $9,000 scholarship during the year, but has no other income. Since the scholarship is not counted for the support test, then Catia can be claimed as Anton's qualifying child.

Note: The definition of "**support**" includes only income that is actually used for living expenses. A person's own funds are not "support" unless they are *actually spent* for support. For example, if a child earns income that is saved in a bank account rather than spent on the child's living expenses, the amounts saved are not included in the support test.

Example: Mikhail, age 12, had a small role in a television series. He earned $45,000 as a child actor, but his parents put all the money in a trust fund for him. Mikhail lived at home with his parents all year. Mikhail meets the support test since none of his earnings were used for his own support. He meets the tests for a qualifying child, so he can be claimed as a dependent by his parents. Mikhail must file his own return to report his wages, but he is still treated as a "qualifying child" for tax purposes.

Foster parents may be eligible to claim a foster child, provided the child is legally placed in their home by the courts or a government agency. Payments received from a child placement agency for the support of a foster child are considered "support" provided by the agency, rather than support provided by the child.

Example: Hilda is a foster parent who provided $3,500 toward her 7-year-old foster son's support for the year. The state of Nevada provided $6,000, which was considered support provided by the state, not by the child. Hilda's foster child did not provide more than half of his own support for the year. Therefore, Hilda can claim her foster son as a qualifying child.

Test #5: Tie-breaker Test

Only one person can claim a qualifying child, even if the child qualifies for more than one person. If more than one taxpayer *attempts* to claim the same child under the dependency rules, the tiebreaker rules apply in the following sequence:

- By the child's parents, if they file a joint return.
- By the parent, if only one of the taxpayers is the child's parent.
- By the parent with whom the child lived the longest during the year.
- By the parent with the highest AGI, if the child lived with each parent for the same length of time during the tax year.
- By the taxpayer with the highest AGI, if neither of the child's parents can claim the child as a qualifying child.
- By a taxpayer with a higher AGI than either of the child's parents who can also claim the child as a qualifying child, but does not.

Example: Isabel is single and has a three-year-old son named Jeffrey. They live with Isabel's father, Robert (the child's grandfather). Robert made $65,000 in wages during the year. Isabel made $19,000 in wages during the year, and she has a filing requirement. As the child's mother, Isabel has the primary right to claim Jeffrey as her qualifying child, which means the child may not be the qualifying child of Robert, the grandfather.

Example: Rosita and her sister, Evita, live together. Their seven-year-old nephew, Quinn, lived with his aunts all year while Quinn's mother was incarcerated in a maximum-security prison. Rosita's AGI is $18,600. Evita's AGI is $29,000. Quinn is a qualifying child of both Rosita and Evita because he meets the relationship, age, residency, and support tests for both of his aunts. However, Evita has the primary right to claim Quinn as her qualifying child because her AGI is higher than Rosita's.

Note: Remember, the tiebreaker test only applies when two people attempt to claim the same child. In cases where the parents are in agreement, there is no tiebreaker test.

Rules for a Qualifying Relative

A person who is not a qualifying child may still qualify as a dependent under the rules for qualifying relatives. Even an individual who is not a family member can be a qualifying relative. Unlike a qualifying child, a qualifying relative can be any age. The tests for a qualifying relative are applied only when the tests for a qualifying child are not met. To be claimed as a qualifying relative, the dependent must meet the following four tests:

- **Not a qualifying child test**
- **Member of household or relationship test**
- **Gross income test**
- **Support test**

Test #1: "Not a Qualifying Child" Test

If a child is already a qualifying *child* for any taxpayer, he cannot also be a qualifying *relative* of another taxpayer. A taxpayer cannot claim an individual who can be claimed as a dependent on another tax return.

Example: Nigel lives with his girlfriend Madeline, and her 3-year-old daughter, Farrah, who lived with Nigel all year in his home. Nigel pays the majority of the costs for keeping up the home, but he is not the father of the child. Nigel earned $56,000 in wages, while Madeline earned $14,200 in wages during the year. Madeline has a filing requirement, so she files Single (not HOH) and claims her daughter, Farrah. She also claims the Earned Income Tax Credit on her return. Madeline's daughter is *her* qualifying *child*, so Nigel cannot claim Farrah as his qualifying *relative*.

Test #2: "Member of Household" or "Relationship" Test

A dependent that is not related to the taxpayer must have lived with the taxpayer the *entire tax year* in order to meet the member of household or relationship test. However, a family member who is related to the taxpayer in any of the following ways does not have to live with the taxpayer to meet this test:

- A child, stepchild, foster child, or descendant of any of them (for example, a grandchild)
- A sibling, stepsibling, or half-sibling
- A parent, grandparent, stepparent, or another direct ancestor (but not a foster parent)
- A niece or nephew, son-in-law, daughter-in-law, father-in-law, mother-in-law, brother-in-law, or sister-in-law

Example: Erick is 45 and single. Erick's 12-year-old nephew, Chilton, lived with him for four months in 2020. For the remainder of the year, Chilton lived with his mother, Inga, in another state. Inga is Erick's 32-year-old sister. Inga did not have a job during the year and does not have any taxable income. Even though Erick and Inga do not live together, Erick still provided all of Inga and Chilton's financial support. Chilton is not Erick's qualifying child because he did not live with his uncle for more than half the year and therefore, does not meet the residency test. However, both Chilton and Inga would meet the requirements to be Erick's qualifying *relatives*.

For the relationship test, "family members" do not include cousins, who are treated as unrelated persons for tax purposes. A cousin must live with the taxpayer for the entire year and also meet the gross income test to qualify as a dependent, and even then, a cousin cannot be a qualifying child—only a qualifying relative.

Also, a taxpayer may not claim a housekeeper or other household employee as a dependent, even if the employee lives with the taxpayer all year.

Example: Marianna is 20 years old and works as a live-in nanny for Henry. Marianna lives with Henry all year and takes care of his two toddlers. Henry cannot claim Marianna on his tax return as a dependent, because a qualifying relative cannot be a household employee.

Example: Theodore is 32 and single. Theodore has lived with his first cousin, Melanie, the entire year. Melanie is 24 and has no taxable income. She is not required to file a tax return. Theodore provided all the household support for Melanie. Therefore, Melanie passes the "not a qualifying child test" to be Theodore's dependent. If Theodore meets all other tests, Melanie may be claimed on Theodore's tax return as a qualifying relative.

Any relationship that is established by marriage does not end as a result of death or divorce.[81] For example, if a taxpayer supports his mother-in-law, he can continue to claim her as a dependent even if he and his ex-spouse are divorced or if he becomes widowed.

Example: Evangelista lived all year with her boyfriend, Oscar, and his two children in her home. Evangelista is not the mother of the children. Oscar was unemployed for the entire tax year and has no taxable income and no filing requirement. Oscar and his two children are not related to Evangelista as family members, but they may be qualifying relatives if they meet all the other tests. If Evangelista and Oscar were later to marry, then Evangelista would be able to claim Oscar's children as her stepchildren, and they would be qualifying *children*, instead of qualifying *relatives*.

Example: Celeste and Giancarlo have always financially supported Celeste's elderly mother, Lucinda, and claimed her as their dependent on their jointly filed returns. In 2018, Celeste died, and Giancarlo became a widower. Giancarlo remarries in 2020, but he has continued to support his late wife's mother. Giancarlo can continue to claim his late wife's mother, Lucinda, as a qualifying relative, even though he has remarried.

[81] Treasury Regulation section 1.152-2(d) currently provides that "the relationship of affinity once existing will not terminate by divorce or death of spouse."

Test #3: Gross Income Test

To meet the gross income test, the dependent's gross income for the tax year must be less than the threshold amount. A qualifying relative cannot earn more than the "deemed exemption" amount, which is $4,300 in 2020. For the purposes of this test, "gross income" includes all income in the form of money, property, and services that are not exempt from tax.[82]

Example: Beatrice is 56 and earned $67,000 in wages for 2020. She financially supported her nephew, Jacob, who is 28 and a full-time college student. Jacob is not disabled. Jacob has a small part-time job, and he earned $5,990 in 2020. Although Beatrice financially supported Jacob, she cannot claim him as a dependent because Jacob does not meet the age test for a qualifying child. Jacob also does not meet the test for a qualifying relative because his income exceeds the gross income test.

Note: Remember that there is no "gross income test" for a qualifying child—only for a qualifying relative! A person may be a qualifying child if they are permanently and totally disabled at any time during the year, regardless of age.[83]

Example: Keegan is 31 and has lived on his own for many years. He earns $13,000 in wages until February 16, 2020, when he is involved in a horrible car accident, rendering him permanently disabled. Keegan moves in with his mother, Annika, on May 3, 2020, after he gets out of the hospital. Keegan's mother cares for him in her home and hires a home-health aide to care for Keegan when she is working. Keegan continues to live with his mother until the end of the year, with his mother providing the majority of his financial support. Annika earns $45,000 in wages in 2020. Although Keegan was not a dependent in prior years, he is now Annika's qualifying child; because he lived with his mother for more than six months in 2020, he does not provide his own support, and he is permanently disabled. He is Annika's qualifying child in 2020.

Test #4: Support Test

To claim an individual as a qualifying relative, the taxpayer must provide *more than half* of the dependent's total support during the year. Support includes: food, clothing, shelter, education, medical and dental care. It also includes amounts from Social Security and welfare payments, even if that support is nontaxable.

Support can include the fair market value of housing. Note that this "support test" is very different from the one for a qualifying child.

Example: Alexi, 26, is a full-time graduate student and lives with his parents. He is not disabled. He worked part-time, earning $4,100. He did not pay over half of his total support. Alexi meets the relationship, residency, and support tests for a qualifying *child*, but he does not meet the *age* test. Alexi can be claimed as a qualifying *relative* by his parents.

---

[82] For purposes of this test, the gross income of an individual who is permanently disabled does not include income from a sheltered workshop.

[83] See the dependency requirements on the IRS' "Tax Tutorial" page: https://apps.irs.gov/app/understandingTaxes/hows/tax_tutorials/mod04/tt_mod04_03.jsp.

Example: Cherise supports her elderly father, Albert, who lives with her. Cherise earns $56,000 in wages during the year. Albert received $2,800 from Social Security during the year. He spent only $700 for his own support and put the rest in a savings account. Cherise spent $6,600 of her own income for Albert's support, so she has provided over half of her father's support for the year. Cherise can claim Albert as her qualifying relative and also file as head of household.

Example: Angela's son, Darwin, is 22 years old. Darwin is not a full-time student or disabled. Angela provides the majority of her son's support. Darwin's gross income is $3,500 for the year. Darwin is not Angela's "qualifying child" because he fails the age test and he is not a full-time student. However, he is still Angela's dependent because he is a qualifying relative. Darwin meets the relationship test because he is Angela's child, and he meets the gross income test because his income is under the exemption amount for the year ($4,300 for 2020), and he meets the support test because Angela provides the majority of his support.

Special Rules for Divorced and Separated Parents

Generally, to claim a child as a dependent, the child must live with the taxpayer for more than half the year. However, special rules apply if the dependent is supported by parents who are divorced, separated, or live apart. In most cases, the child is the qualifying child of the custodial parent. However, a custodial parent may permit the noncustodial parent to claim the child. The noncustodial parent must attach Form 8332, *Release/Revocation of Release of Claim to Exemption for Child by Custodial Parent*, to his or her tax return. A child may be treated as the qualifying child of the noncustodial parent if *all* the following conditions apply:

- The parents are divorced or legally separated, or if they lived apart at all times during the last six months of the year.
- The child received over half of his or her support for the year from the parents.
- The child is in the custody of one (or both) parents.
- The custodial parent signs Form 8332 (or a similar statement) and the noncustodial parent attaches this declaration to their return.

This rule is an exception to the normal residency test for a qualifying child. It does not apply to the determination of head of household filing status or to eligibility for the Earned Income Tax Credit. The EITC and HOH filing status can be claimed only by the custodial parent, even if the noncustodial parent claims the child.

If a divorce decree does not specify which parent is the custodial parent or which parent is allowed to claim the child, the dependent should be claimed by the parent who has physical custody for the majority of the year.

Example: Johan and Penelope are legally divorced and live in separate homes. They share custody of their 8-year-old son, Lucas. During the year, Lucas stayed with Johan for 195 nights and with Penelope for 170 nights. Therefore, for federal tax purposes, Johan is considered the custodial parent and has the right to claim Lucas as his qualifying child.

Example: Anders and Wilma are divorced and have one child. Wilma is the custodial parent, but she allows Anders to claim the child by signing Form 8332. Anders correctly files as "single" and claims his son as his dependent. Wilma may still file as head of household, even though she does not claim her son as a dependent, because she maintained the home where the child lived for most of the year.

If the child lived with each parent for an equal number of nights during the year, the custodial parent is deemed to be the parent with the higher adjusted gross income.

The custodial parent can also revoke the release by using Form 8332. A copy of the revocation must be attached to the tax return for each year the child is claimed after the revocation. The custodial parent must also provide the noncustodial parent with a copy of the revocation or make a reasonable effort to provide the noncustodial parent with a copy of the revocation. The earliest the revocation will apply is the year following the year the revocation was provided (or a reasonable effort was made to provide) to the noncustodial parent. The custodial parent must keep a copy of the revocation and evidence of delivery of the notice to the noncustodial parent, or of reasonable efforts to provide actual notice.

Multiple Support Agreements

A *multiple support agreement* is when two or more people jointly provide for a person's support. This happens commonly when adult children are taking care of their parents. Under a multiple support agreement, family members together must pay *more* than half of the person's total support, but no one member individually may pay more than half. Taxpayers use Form 2120, *Multiple Support Declaration,* to report a multiple support arrangement. When a taxpayer uses this form, they are acknowledging that they do not pay more than half the cost of supporting a dependent, but that the other individuals that share the costs are allowing the taxpayer to claim that person as a dependent.

In addition, the taxpayer who claims the dependent must provide more than 10% of the person's support. Only one family member can claim a dependent in a single year, but different qualifying family members can agree to claim the dependent in other years.

Example: Altair, Valentin, and Yesenia are siblings who support their disabled mother, Leanne. Leanne is 83 years old and lives in a nursing home. In 2020, Leanne receives 20% of her financial support from Social Security, 40% from Valentin, 30% from Altair, and only 10% from Yesenia. Under the IRS rules for multiple support agreements, either Valentin or Altair can claim their mother as a dependent if the other signs a statement agreeing not to do so. Yesenia cannot claim her mother as a dependent, because she does not provide more than 10% of the support for Leanne during the year.

Example: Bohdana and Elinor are sisters who help financially support their 66-year-old father, Josef. Each pays approximately 20% of his care in a residential facility for elderly people. The remaining 60% is paid for by a wealthy friend who is not related to Josef. Because more than half of Josef's support is provided by someone unrelated to him, no one can claim Josef as a dependent.

Unit 3: Study Questions

(Test yourself first, then check the correct answers at the end of this quiz.)

1. Urion is 23 years old, single, and a full-time graduate student. He studied on a student exchange program in Costa Rica during the year. He did not live at home with his parents a single day during the tax year. Urion's parents provided the majority of his financial support and want to claim him as a dependent. Which of the following is true?

A. His parents may claim Urion as a qualifying child.
B. His parents may claim Urion as a qualifying relative.
C. His parents may not claim Urion as a dependent.
D. Urion should file his own tax return.

2. A taxpayer cannot claim a qualifying child as a dependent if that child provides more than _______ of their own support.

A. 25%
B. 33%
C. 50%
D. 75%

3. Greta is 80 years old. She has three children: Luther, Silas, and Caprice. Each child contributes financially towards her support. Luther and Silas each provide 45%, and Caprice provides 10%. Which taxpayer would be eligible to claim Greta as a dependent parent under a multiple support agreement?

A. Luther or Silas.
B. Caprice or Silas.
C. Luther, Silas, or Caprice.
D. No one is eligible to claim Greta.

4. Khristina lives with Fyodor, her 17-year-old son. She provided $5,100 toward her son's support for the year. Fyodor also has a part-time job and provided $12,900 toward his own support. Can Khristina claim her son as a dependent?

A. Yes, she can claim her son as a qualifying child.
B. Yes, she can claim Fyodor as a qualifying relative.
C. No; Fyodor provided more than half of his own support for the year. Therefore, he is neither Khristina's qualifying child nor her qualifying relative.
D. None of the above.

5. Kingston provides the sole support for his mother. To claim her as a dependent on his Form 1040, Kingston's mother must be a resident or citizen of which of the following countries?

A. The United States.
B. Mexico.
C. Canada.
D. Any of the above.

6. All of the following statements are correct about the rules of dependents except:

A. One spouse is never considered the dependent of the other spouse.
B. A taxpayer may not claim a stillborn child as a dependent.
C. A taxpayer may claim a nanny as a dependent, as long as the nanny lives with the taxpayer all year.
D. A child is considered to have lived with the taxpayer during periods when the child is temporarily absent.

7. Astrid and Sergey divorced years ago. They have six-year-old twins who live with Astrid. Her AGI is $41,000, and Sergey's AGI is $48,000. Although Astrid is the custodial parent, their divorce decree states that Sergey can claim the children on his tax return. However, Astrid refuses to sign Form 8332. Which of the following statements is correct?

A. Sergey can claim one child as a dependent, and Astrid can claim the other.
B. Sergey and Astrid can each claim the children as dependents on their respective tax returns.
C. Sergey cannot claim either child.
D. Neither Astrid nor Sergey can claim the children as dependents.

8. Joseph, 52, is a single father who lives with his son Wyatt, who has Down syndrome. Wyatt is 32 years old and permanently disabled. Wyatt had $800 of interest income and $5,000 of wages from a part-time job. Joseph provided $25,000 toward Wyatt's support. Which of the following statements is correct?

A. Joseph can file as head of household, with Wyatt as his qualifying child.
B. Joseph does not qualify for head of household, but he could still claim Wyatt as his qualifying relative because Wyatt does not meet the age test for a qualifying child.
C. Joseph can file as head of household, with Wyatt as his qualifying relative.
D. Joseph must file as single, and he cannot claim Wyatt because of the amount of Wyatt's income.

9. Cheryl is 46 and unmarried. Her nephew, Bradley, lived with her all year and turned 18 years old on December 28, 2020. Bradley is not a full-time student and did not provide more than one-half of his own support. He had $4,200 of income from wages and $1,000 of investment income. Which of the following statements is correct?

A. Bradley is Cheryl's qualifying child.
B. Bradley is not a qualifying child; however, Cheryl can claim him as a qualifying relative.
C. Bradley is not a qualifying child or qualifying relative.
D. Cheryl can claim Bradley only if he goes back to college.

10. Rebekah is 22 and a full-time college student. During the year, she lived at home with her parents for four months and lived in the college dorms for the remainder of the year. She worked part-time and earned $6,000, but that income did not amount to half of her total support. Can Rebekah's parents claim her as a dependent?

A. No, because Rebekah earned more than the gross income threshold.
B. No, Rebekah did not live with her parents for more than half the year, and she does not meet the age test.
C. Yes, her parents can claim her as a qualifying child.
D. Yes, her parents can claim her as a dependent, but only as a qualifying relative.

11. Ursula and her son live together. Kayden is 27 years old, not disabled, and has a part-time job. Ursula provides more than half of Kayden's support. Ursula can claim Kayden as a qualifying relative, as long as he does not earn _____ or more in 2020.

A. $1,100
B. $3,500
C. $4,300
D. $12,400

12. Ingrid and Wesley file for divorce. Ingrid has one teenage son from a prior relationship named Asher, age 17. After the divorce is final, Ingrid develops a drug problem and disappears. In 2020, Asher lives for nine months with his (former) stepfather, Wesley, who provides all of Asher's support. Which of the following statements is correct?

A. Wesley can claim Asher as his qualifying child.
B. Wesley can claim Asher as his dependent but not as a qualifying child because the divorce dissolved any legal relationship between them.
C. Wesley cannot claim Asher as his dependent because they are not related persons.
D. Only Ingrid can claim Asher as her dependent.

Unit 3: Quiz Answers

1. The answer is A. His parents may claim Urion as a qualifying child. He was a full-time student, and temporary absences for education are allowed and do not count as time living away from home.

2. The answer is C. A taxpayer cannot claim another person as a dependent if that person provided more than half of their own support (more than 50%).

3. The answer is A. Only Luther or Silas are eligible to claim Greta under a multiple support agreement. Caprice is not eligible because she does not provide more than 10% of her mother's support. Either Luther or Silas may use Form 2120, Multiple Support Declaration, to report their multiple support arrangement.

4. The answer is C. Fyodor provided more than half of his own support for the year, so he is not Khristina's qualifying child or her qualifying relative. To meet the support test, the child cannot have provided more than half of his own support for the year.

5. The answer is D. A dependent must be a citizen or resident alien of the United States, Canada, or Mexico.

6. The answer is C. A taxpayer may not claim a housekeeper or other household employee as a dependent, regardless of whether or not the employee lived with the taxpayer.

7. The answer is C. Since Astrid is the custodial parent and refuses to sign Form 8332, Sergey cannot claim either child. Without Form 8332, *Release/Revocation of Release of Claim to Exemption for Child by Custodial Parent,* signed and attached to the return, Sergey does not have the primary right to claim the children, since he is not the custodial parent.

8. The answer is A. Even though Wyatt is over the normal age threshold for a qualifying child, he is considered a qualifying child. This is because Wyatt is permanently disabled, and Joseph provides the majority of his financial support and care. The normal age thresholds for "qualifying children" do not apply in the case of permanently disabled individuals.

9. The answer is A. Bradley is Cheryl's qualifying child because he meets the age test, support test, and relationship test. Also, because Bradley is single, he is a qualifying person for Cheryl to claim head of household filing status. Bradley is not required to be a full-time student because any child under the age of 19 at the end of the tax year will be treated as a qualifying child if all the other tests are met. Bradley is only 18 years old and therefore passes the age test.

10. The answer is C. Rebekah meets all the qualifying child tests: the relationship test, the age test (because she is under 24 and a full-time student), the residency test (because the time spent at college is a legitimate temporary absence), and the support test (because she did not provide over half of her own support). Therefore, her parents can claim Rebekah as a qualifying child.

11. The answer is C. Kayden cannot be a qualifying child for Ursula because he does not meet the age test, but he can be claimed as a qualifying relative. The 2020 limit for gross income for qualifying relatives is $4,300. Therefore, if Kayden earns less than this amount during the year, his mother can claim him as a "qualifying relative" dependent on her tax return.

12. The answer is A. A qualifying child must be related to the taxpayer by blood, marriage, or legal adoption. A "step" relationship formed by marriage is not dissolved by divorce or death for federal tax purposes. Since Asher did not live with his mother, but *did* live with his stepfather, Wesley, for more than half the year, Wesley is considered the custodial parent for tax purposes, and he can claim his stepson as a qualifying child.

Unit 4: Taxable and Nontaxable Income

For additional information, read:
Publication 525, *Taxable and Nontaxable Income*
Publication 15-B, *Employer's Tax Guide to Fringe Benefits*
Publication 3, *Armed Forces' Tax Guide*

The Internal Revenue Code (IRC) describes types of income that are taxable and nontaxable. Throughout the next few units, we will cover the most common types of both. In this unit, we focus on various forms of employee compensation, but we start with a look at broader concepts regarding the taxability of income.

Federal tax law sets forth that all income is taxable unless it is specifically excluded. An *exclusion* is not the same as a *deduction*, and it is important to understand the distinction because some deductions and credits are phased out as a taxpayer's gross income increases. Excluded income, on the other hand, retains its character without regard to the amount of the taxpayer's gross income. Most types of excluded income do not have to be reported on a tax return, although there are some notable exceptions, like municipal bond interest.[84]

Example: Lance is a popular recording artist who earned more than $1 million of taxable income during the year. Because of his high income, many tax deductions and credits are phased out for Lance. However, on July 1, 2020, Lance is involved in an auto accident and sustains major injuries. Lance sues the other driver and receives an insurance settlement of $95,000 related to his injuries resulting from the accident. The settlement is excluded from his gross income because compensation for physical injuries is not taxable to the recipient, regardless of his taxable income level. Lance does not even have to report the injury settlement on his tax return.

Calculating Taxable Income

For a taxpayer to figure out how much tax he owes, he first needs to determine his **gross income**. **Gross income** is all income a taxpayer receives in the form of money, goods, property, and services that are not exempt from tax. In addition to wages, salaries, commissions, tips, and self-employment income, gross income includes other forms of compensation, such as interest, dividends, capital gains, taxable fringe benefits, and stock options.

Next, the taxpayer calculates his **adjusted gross income (AGI)** by subtracting from gross income certain specific deductions or adjustments. Examples of some of these "for AGI" (commonly referred to as "above the line") deductions include certain IRA contributions, certain expenses for self-employed individuals, deductible alimony payments[85], and moving expenses.[86] The amount of a taxpayer's AGI is important because it helps determine eligibility for certain deductions and credits.

---

84 Municipal bonds are debt securities issued by state, city, and local governments. Municipal bond interest is tax-free at the federal level but can be taxable at state or local income tax levels.

85 Alimony payments are no longer deductible for divorces entered into after 2018. In addition, alimony payments may potentially be non-deductible for pre-2018 divorces under certain circumstances (to be discussed in Unit 11).

86 Moving expenses are no longer deductible for most taxpayers. However, an exception exists for members of the armed forces on active duty who move pursuant to a military order and incident to a permanent change of station.

Finally, the taxpayer calculates his **taxable income** by subtracting additional deductions (standard or itemized) from AGI. The table below is a simplified example of how to calculate income tax.

How to Calculate Taxable Income and Tax Liability for Most Individuals

Start with gross income

Subtract adjustments to income ("above the line" deductions)

= Adjusted gross income (AGI)

Subtract greater of itemized deductions or the standard deduction

= Taxable income

× Tax rate

= Gross tax liability

Subtract credits

= Net tax liability or refund receivable (based on the amount of prepaid tax, if any)

Earned Income vs. Unearned Income

Earned income such as wages, salaries, tips, professional fees, or self-employment income is received for services performed. *Unearned income* includes interest, dividends, retirement income, taxable alimony, and disability benefits. Earned income is generally subject to Social Security and Medicare taxes (also called FICA taxes).

Investment income and other unearned income are generally not subject to FICA taxes. The amount of taxable income is used to determine the taxpayer's gross income tax liability before applicable credits.

Constructive Receipt of Income

The doctrine of constructive receipt requires that cash-basis taxpayers be taxed on income when it becomes available and is not subject to substantial limitations or restrictions, regardless of whether it is actually in their physical possession. Income received by an agent for a taxpayer is constructively received in the year the agent receives it.

Example: Logan is a landlord who owns several rental properties. On December 30, 2020, a tenant delivers a $750 rent check to Logan's payment lockbox. Logan does not collect the rental deposits in the lockbox on December 30 and instead leaves town later that day to celebrate New Year's Eve. Logan does not actually take physical possession of the check until January 5, 2021, the same day he deposits the check in his bank account. He is considered to have constructive receipt in 2020 and must include the $750 of gross income on his 2020 tax return because the check was available to Logan at that time without any substantial limitations or restrictions.

Note: Most individuals are cash-basis taxpayers who report income when it is actually or constructively received during the tax year. This concept of constructive receipt would not apply to accrual-basis taxpayers who recognize income when it is earned rather than when it is received. We will cover accrual-basis taxpayers in Book 2, Businesses.

If there are significant restrictions on the income, or if the income is not accessible to the taxpayer, it is not considered to have been constructively received. According to the IRS,

constructive receipt requires that an amount credited to an individual's account be subject to "unqualified demand."

Example: Raakel owns a large plot of land in Chicago, IL. On January 2, 2020, the county filed a condemnation action to acquire Raakel's land in order to build a public highway. Raakel does not want to sell her land and decides to fight the condemnation. On May 1, 2020, the county deposited $800,000 as "probable compensation" for the property with the IL state treasurer. Raakel could have withdrawn the funds, but to do so would have jeopardized her ability to sue. On June 4, 2020, Raakel files a lawsuit against the county, challenging the government's right to take her property. Raakel eventually settles the lawsuit, but not until the following year, when she and the county agree to a settlement. Raakel finally accepts the condemnation award for her property on March 31, 2021. In this case, constructive receipt occurred in 2021.[87]

Income is also not considered to have been "constructively received" if a taxpayer declines to accept an item, such as a prize or an award. When determining the value of a prize or an award, the IRS defines **fair market value** (FMV) in this way: the price at which a property would change hands between a buyer and a seller when both have reasonable knowledge of all the necessary facts and neither is being forced to buy or sell.

If parties with adverse interests place a value on property in an arms-length transaction, that is strong evidence of FMV. If there is a stated price for services, this price is treated as the FMV unless there is evidence to the contrary.

Example: Lucia won front-row concert tickets valued at $1,200 from a local radio station. The value of the tickets is clearly printed on the tickets. Lucia would be required to pay taxes based on the fair market value of the tickets. However, on the day of the concert, the radio station does not receive the tickets in time from the promoter, and Lucia is not able to attend the concert. Since she never received the tickets, the prize is not taxable to her because she never had constructive receipt of it.

The "Claim of Right" Doctrine

Under the "claim of right" doctrine, income received without restriction (over which the taxpayer has complete control) must be reported in the year received, even if there is a possibility it may have to be repaid in a later year.

The tax treatment of the repayment differs based on the type of income. If the taxpayer is self-employed, and if in the prior year it had been included as self-employment income, the repayment is deducted on Schedule C by reducing income in the year the amounts were repaid.

Example: In 2020, Marilyn sells a painting in her art gallery for $28,000. She properly includes $28,000 in her gross income and pays taxes on the income. On February 2, 2021, the customer discovers the painting is a forgery and returns the painting, demanding a full refund of $28,000. Marilyn promptly refunds the customer. Since Marilyn pays back the $28,000 in 2021, she is entitled to deduct the amount from her gross income in 2021. She does not have to amend her prior-year tax return.

---

[87] This example is based directly on Private Letter Ruling 200944012, where the IRS concluded that a taxpayer was not in constructive receipt of condemnation proceeds that had been deposited with the state treasurer during the time the taxpayer was contesting the condemnation in a legal action.

However, if the income was previously reported as wages, taxable unemployment compensation, Social Security, or other nonbusiness income, the tax treatment is different.

If there is a dispute and income is later repaid, the repayment is not deductible in the year repaid unless the repayment is over $3,000.[88] A taxpayer should not amend his or her reported gross income for the earlier year.

Example: Rosalie filed for unemployment on February 1, 2019, and started receiving unemployment benefits. Rosalie received a Form 1099-G for unemployment compensation that she received during the year and properly reports the amounts as taxable income on her 2019 return. Her former employer appealed the decision, claiming that Rosalie made false statements on her unemployment application. The state later determines that Rosalie was not eligible for unemployment and forces her to repay the amounts in 2020. Rosalie is forced to pay back $5,000 in unemployment benefits in 2020. Since the amount exceeds $3,000, she can take a deduction for the repaid amounts.[89]

Example: Webster is age 64. He retired from his teaching job several years ago and started receiving pension payments. In 2020, Webster receives a letter from his pension administrator informing him that the administrator made a mistake and overpaid his pension benefits by $2,300 in 2019 (the prior year). The administrator requests that Webster repays the overpayment by writing a check back to the pension plan. Webster writes a check for the full amount and remits it to his pension administrator on September 1, 2020. Since the amount Webster repaid was less than $3,000, he cannot deduct the repayment.

Self-Employed Taxpayers

Self-employment income is earned by taxpayers who work for themselves. A taxpayer who has self-employment income of $400 or more in a year must file a tax return and report the earnings to the IRS. Starting in 2020, taxpayers who are independent contractors usually receive Form 1099-NEC from their business customers showing the income they were paid for the year (if $600 or more). The amounts reported on Forms 1099-NEC,[90] along with any other business income, are reported by most self-employed individuals on Schedule C, *Profit or Loss from Business*, of Form 1040.

Self-employed farmers or fishermen report their earnings on Schedule F, *Profit or Loss from Farming*, of Form 1040. Self-employment income also includes:

- Income of ministers, priests, and rabbis for the performance of services such as baptisms and marriages.
- The distributive share of trade or business income allocated by a partnership to its general partners or, in certain circumstances, by a limited liability company to its

---

[88] Per Publication 525, the repayment is deducted on the same form or schedule on which it was previously included. If it had been included as self-employment income on Schedule C, Profit or Loss from Business, it is deducted on Schedule C. If it had been included as capital gain on Schedule D, Capital Gains and Losses, it is deducted on Schedule D. If it was reported as wages, taxable unemployment compensation, or other non-business ordinary income, it is deducted on Schedule A, Itemized Deductions (but only if over $3,000).

[89] If the amount repaid was $3,000 or less, Claim of Right under IRC Section 1341 does not apply. See IRS Publication 525, under *Repayments Under Claim of Right.*

[90] For 2020 the IRS reinstated the Form 1099-NEC, *Nonemployee Compensation*, which is used to report certain payments to contractors starting in 2020.

members. The income is reported to the individual partners on Schedule K-1 (Form 1065).

A taxpayer does not have to conduct regular full-time business activities to be considered self-employed. A taxpayer may have a side business in addition to a regular job, and this is also considered self-employment.

Example: Nelson earned $48,000 as a full-time employee for Royal Roofing, Inc. He also advertises general handyman services online and performs household repair services for various local customers. During the year, Nelson did several handyman side-jobs on the weekends for private clients. Nelson received payments of $9,000 from several different individuals for his handyman work. He did not receive Forms 1099-NEC for the $9,000 (because they were individuals who are not required to issue Forms 1099-NEC), but he must report the payments as self-employment income on Schedule C.

Example: Colleen operates a popular taco truck with her brother, Orlando. They both split profits and losses equally, and they operate their business as a partnership. They correctly file Form 1065, *U.S. Return of Partnership Income*, to report the gross income from the taco stand. Colleen and Orlando both receive a Schedule K-1 from the partnership every year. Colleen and Orlando must each report their distributive share of income from the taco stand on their respective Forms 1040, Schedule E (Part 2). The income is considered self-employment income and is subject to self-employment tax.

FICA Tax (Payroll Taxes)

The Federal Insurance Contributions Act (FICA) tax includes two separate taxes: one is Social Security tax, and the other is Medicare tax. The current rate for Social Security is 6.2% for the employer and 6.2% for the employee, or 12.4% total. The current rate for Medicare is 1.45% for the employer and 1.45% for the employee, or 2.9% total.

The combined FICA tax rate for 2020 is 15.3% and applies up to $137,700 of a taxpayer's combined earned income, including wages, tips, and net earnings from self-employment. If the taxpayer's combined earned income exceeds $137,700 in 2020, a rate of 2.9%, representing only the Medicare portion, applies to any excess earnings over the earned income threshold.

There is no cap on earnings subject to the 2.9% Medicare tax. For certain high-income individuals, an *additional* Medicare surtax of 0.9% is applied to wages and self-employment income above certain thresholds.[91]

Example: Bernadetta is a registered nurse who works for a medical office. To calculate her FICA tax contribution as an employee, her payroll department multiplies Bernadetta's gross pay by the current Social Security and Medicare tax rates. Bernadetta's taxable wages are $80,000 in 2020, so all of her wages would be subject to FICA tax. Bernadetta's social security contribution would be: $80,000 x 6.2%, or $4,960, which is credited to her Social Security account. Her Medicare contribution would be: $80,000 x 1.45%, or $1,160. These are also the amounts her employer would pay.

[91] The Additional Medicare Tax applies to wages, railroad retirement (RRTA) compensation, and self-employment income over certain thresholds. This tax will be covered in more detail later.

Note: The 7.65% FICA tax rate is the *combined* rate for Social Security and Medicare. The Social Security portion (also called "OASDI") is 6.2% on earnings up to the applicable taxable maximum amount ($137,700 in 2020). *Remember:* the Medicare portion is 1.45% on *all* earned income. There is no yearly maximum for Medicare tax.

Note: If a taxpayer works for more than one employer and his total compensation is over the $137,700 Social Security base limit for 2020, too much Social Security tax may have been withheld. In this case, a taxpayer can claim the excess as a credit against his income tax. This is officially called the "Credit for Excess Social Security and RRTA Tax Withheld" and is fully refundable on a taxpayer's individual return.

Self-Employment Tax

Self-employment tax (SE tax) is imposed on self-employed individuals in a manner similar to the Social Security and Medicare taxes that apply to wage earners. Self-employed individuals are responsible for paying the entire amount of Social Security and Medicare taxes applicable to their net earnings from self-employment. Self-employment tax is calculated on IRS Schedule SE, Self-Employment Tax. If a taxpayer has wages in addition to self-employment earnings, the Social Security tax on the wages is paid first. There are two adjustments related to the self-employment tax that reduce overall taxes for a taxpayer with self-employment income.

- First, the taxpayer's net earnings from self-employment are reduced by 7.65%. Just as the employer's share of Social Security tax is not considered wages to the employee, this reduction removes a corresponding amount from the net earnings before the SE tax is calculated.
- Second, the taxpayer can deduct the employer-equivalent portion of his self-employment tax in determining his adjusted gross income.

More Than One Business: If a taxpayer owns more than one business, he must net the profit or loss from each business to determine the total earnings subject to SE tax. However, married taxpayers cannot combine their income or loss from self-employment to determine their individual earnings subject to SE tax.

Example: Brian is a sole proprietor who owns a barbershop. He has $49,000 of net income from the business in 2020. His wife, Ellen, has a candle-making business, which has overall losses of ($12,000) in 2020. Brian must pay self-employment tax on $49,000, regardless of how he and Ellen choose to file. That is because married couples cannot offset each other's income from self-employment, even if they file jointly, for self-employment tax purposes. The income of each business is allocated to each individual.

Example: Rocco is a married taxpayer who is a sole-proprietor of two small businesses, a computer repair shop and a car wash business that he runs only during the summer months. Rocco's wife is a homemaker and does not work in either business. Rocco's computer business has net income of $50,000, while the car wash has a net loss of ($23,000) for the year. Rocco only has to pay self-employment tax on $27,000 ($50,000 - $23,000) of income because he may net the income and losses from both his businesses.

Employee Compensation and Worker Classification

Wages, salaries, bonuses, tips, and commissions are compensation received by employees for services performed. Employee compensation is taxable income to the employee and a deductible expense for the employer.

For federal tax purposes, the IRS classifies "workers" in two broad categories: employees or independent contractors. These workers are taxed in different ways, and businesses must identify the correct classification for each individual to whom it makes payments for services.

In general, a business must withhold and remit income taxes, Social Security and Medicare taxes (payroll taxes), and pay unemployment tax on salaries and wages paid to an employee. Employers are required by January 31 to issue Forms W-2, which shows the amounts of wages paid to employees for the previous year.

A business generally does not have to withhold or pay taxes on payments to independent contractors, because the earnings of a person working as an independent contractor are subject to self-employment tax.

The general rule is that an individual is an independent contractor if the payer has the right to control or direct only the result of the work, not what will be done and how it will be done. If a worker receives a Form 1099-NEC, but believes that they are an employee and should have received a Form W-2 instead, they can file Form SS-8, *Determination of Worker Status for Purposes of Federal Employment Taxes and Income Tax Withholding* with the IRS, and if a determination is made that they are an employee, they will file Form 8919, *Uncollected Social Security and Medicare Tax on Wages*, with their tax return.

Example: Kristin got hired to work as a file clerk for a small car wash company in 2020. The business classified Kristin as an independent contractor in order to avoid having to pay payroll taxes. Kristin worked in the office every day from 9-5, under the full control of the company, and was clearly an employee. The business issued Kristin a 1099-NEC at the end of the year. Kristin disagrees with her classification, so she fills out Form SS-8 and files it with the IRS. The IRS will investigate the classification issue, and if they determine that she was an employee, they will make sure that her employer pays the payroll taxes that were their responsibility, and Kristin will be liable for the income tax on the amount that she earned, just as she would have been, had she been classified correctly. She would file Form 8919 with her tax return to account and pay for her share of Social Security and Medicare taxes on her wages.

Example: Terrence works for a company as a delivery driver. At the end of the year, Terrence's employer issues him a Form 1099-NEC instead of a Form W-2. Terrence believes he was misclassified as an independent contractor. While he completed and files Form SS-8 with the IRS, he has not yet received a response from the IRS by the tax return due date. Therefore, he files Form 8919, *Uncollected Social Security and Medicare Tax on Wages* with his tax return. Terrence lists the name of the employer, provides the employer's Federal Employer Identification Number, the reason he is filing, and his total alleged wages with unreported Social Security and Medicare taxes.

Worker classification is considered a "hot-button" issue for the IRS and is covered in more detail in *Book 2, Businesses.*

Advance Wages: If an employee receives advance wages, commissions, or other earnings, he must recognize the income in the year it is actually or constructively received, regardless of whether he has earned the income. If the employee is later required to pay back a portion of the earnings, the amount would be deducted from his taxable wages at that time.

Example: Damian requests a modest salary advance of $1,200 on December 1, 2020, so he can take a two-week Christmas vacation. His employer gives him the check on December 20, 2020. Damian must recognize the income on his 2020 tax return, even though he will not actually "earn" the money until 2021, when he returns from his vacation.

Supplemental Wages

Supplemental wages are compensation paid to an employee in addition to his regular pay. These amounts are listed on the employee's Form W-2 and are taxable, just like regular wages, even if the pay is not actually for work performed. Vacation pay and sick pay are examples of supplemental wages that are taxable just like any other wage income, even though the employee has not technically "worked" for the income. Supplemental wages may also include:

- Bonuses, commissions, prizes
- Severance pay, back pay, and holiday pay
- Payment for nondeductible moving expenses

Garnished Wages

An employee may have his wages garnished for various reasons, such as when he owes child support, back taxes, or other debts. Regardless of the amounts garnished from the employee's paycheck, the full amount of his gross wages must be included in his taxable wages at year-end.

Example: Joseph's employer garnishes part of his salary for back child support. Since this amount would have normally been included in Joseph's paycheck, he must recognize the income as if he had received it himself.

Property or Services "in Lieu" of Wages

Wages paid in any form other than cash are measured by their fair market value. An employee who receives property for services performed must generally recognize the fair market value of the property when it is received as taxable income. However, if an employee receives stock or other property that is restricted, the property is not included in income until it is available to the employee without restriction.

Example: Leonard's company gives him 500 shares of stock, valued at $9,000. He cannot sell or otherwise use the shares for five years. If Leonard quits his job, he forfeits the shares. He does not have to recognize the stock as income in the year he receives it because the stock is subject to substantial restrictions. Leonard will report it as taxable income when the restrictions lapse, and he gains complete control over the stock.

Another common arrangement is when colleges offer tuition reduction and/or free on-campus housing in lieu of wages to student teachers. Any portion of a grant or scholarship that is compensation for services is taxable as wages.

Example: Adelaide is a doctoral student attending Northwestern University. Adelaide received a grant of $32,500 to pay her tuition and on-campus housing. As a condition for receiving the scholarship, Adelaide must serve as a part-time teaching assistant. Of the $32,500 scholarship, $11,000 represents payment for teaching. The University gives Adelaide a Form W-2 showing $11,000 as wages. All the money was used to offset her tuition and course-related expenses. Assuming that all other conditions are met, $21,500 of her grant is tax-free. However, the $11,000 Adelaide received for teaching is taxable as wages, because it was for services that she performed.

Tip Income

Tips received by food servers, baggage handlers, hairdressers, and others for performing services are taxable income. An individual who receives $20 or more per month in tips must report the tip income to his employer. An employee who receives less than $20 per month in tips while working one job does not have to report the tip income to his employer. Tips of less than $20 per month are exempt from Social Security and Medicare taxes, but are still subject to federal income tax.

Example: Sherrie works two jobs: as an administrative assistant during the week and as a bartender on the weekends. She reports her tip income from the bartending job of $3,000 to her employer. Her W-2 Forms show wage income of $31,000 (administrative assistant) and $8,250 (bartender). Sherrie must report $39,250, the total amount earned at both jobs, on her Form 1040. Since she reported the tip income to her employer, her bartending tips are already included on her Form W-2 for that job.

An employee who does not report all of his tips to his employer generally must report the tips and related Social Security and Medicare taxes on his Form 1040. Form 4137, *Social Security and Medicare Tax on Unreported Tip Income,* is used to compute the additional tax. Noncash tips (for example, concert tickets, or other items) do not have to be reported to the employer, but they must be reported and included in the taxpayer's income at their fair market value. Taxpayers who are self-employed and receive tips must include their tip income in gross receipts on Schedule C.

Example: Matthew is a licensed barber who works for a popular salon franchise, Super-Duper Cuts. He is an employee of the franchise and receives minimum wage as well as tips. He must report these tips to his employer. Matthew also cuts hair in the evenings in his garage, offering his barbering services to friends and family. All the income he earns cutting hair at home (including tips) is treated as self-employment income and must be reported on Schedule C.

Taxable Fringe Benefits for Employees

Employers often offer fringe benefits to employees; common fringe benefits include health insurance, retirement plans, and parking passes. Although most employee fringe benefits are nontaxable, some benefits must be reported on the employee's Form W-2 and included in his taxable income. Most entertainment expenses are no longer deductible. Therefore, the cost of entertainment provided to an employee is no longer a non-taxable fringe benefit.[92]

---

[92] There is a narrow exception for entertainment expenses that are directly for the benefit of employees, other than highly compensated employees, (i.e., office parties or company picnics that include lower-paid staff).

This means that an employer can no longer provide occasional sporting event tickets as a nontaxable benefit to employees. Examples of taxable fringe benefits include:

- Off-site athletic facilities and health club memberships,
- Concert and athletic event tickets,
- The value of employer-provided life insurance over $50,000,
- Any cash benefit or benefits in the form of a credit card or gift card (an exception applies for occasional meal money or transportation fare to allow an employee to work beyond normal hours),
- Transportation benefits, if the value of a benefit for any month is more than a specified nontaxable limit,[93]
- Employer-provided vehicles, if they are used for personal purposes.

Example: Great National Bank pays for country club memberships for all its top executives. Membership costs $8,000 a year per person. Bank executives use the club to entertain prospective clients and investors. Even though the club membership is used frequently for business purposes, this type of fringe benefit is taxable compensation to the employees. Great National Bank must include the full amount of the club membership ($8,000) in the employee's wages, subject to income tax and payroll taxes.

Example: Mayan Travel, Inc. is a travel agency that owns a timeshare on the Mayan Riviera that its employees may use free of charge. Lester, an employee of Mayan Travel, visits the resort with his family for 5 days in 2020. The fair market value of the stay is $2,000. Even though Lester paid nothing for the trip, the $2,000 FMV of the vacation must be included in his taxable wages.

Nontaxable Fringe Benefits for Employees

Most fringe benefits are not taxable and may be excluded from an employee's income. For example, the value of accident or health plan coverage provided by an employer is not included in an employee's income. The following sections cover the rules for some common types of nontaxable employee fringe benefits.

Retirement Plans

Employer contributions on behalf of their employees' qualified retirement plans are not taxable to the employees when they are made. However, when an employee receives distributions from a retirement plan, the amounts received are taxable income. Retirement plans may also allow employees to contribute part of their pre-tax compensation to the plan.

This type of contribution is called an elective deferral and is excluded from taxable compensation for income tax purposes but subject to Social Security and Medicare taxes.[94]

---

[93] The nontaxable benefit for both mass transit and parking is $270 for 2020, although the amounts are no longer deductible by the employer, they are still non-taxable to the employee if the employer continues to provide the benefit. Any expense over that amount is included in the employee's taxable income as wages. An employee can receive both parking and transit benefits in the same month.

[94] The tax provisions of retirement plans are covered in detail later.

Cafeteria Plans

A cafeteria plan provides employees an opportunity to receive certain benefits on a pretax basis. Participants in a cafeteria plan must be permitted to choose from at least one taxable benefit (such as cash) and one qualified (nontaxable) benefit. Qualified benefits include:

- Accident, dental, vision, and medical benefits (but not Archer medical savings accounts or long-term care insurance)
- Flexible Spending Accounts (health FSA and dependent care FSA),[95]
- Adoption assistance and dependent care assistance

Employee contributions are usually deducted based upon salary reduction agreements (i.e., the money is withheld directly from the employee's paycheck and deposited into an account). Salary reduction contributions are not considered actually or constructively received by the employee and therefore are not treated as taxable wages, and not subject to employment taxes.[96] An employer may choose to make benefits available to employees, their spouses, and dependents.

Flexible Spending Arrangements (FSAs)

An FSA is a form of cafeteria plan benefit that reimburses employees for expenses incurred for certain qualified benefits, such as health care and daycare expenses. In 2020, employee salary reduction contributions to a health-care FSA are capped at $2,750. Separate from the health-care FSA is the Dependent Care FSA (also known as Dependent Care Assistance Plan), which is used to pay for the care of dependents. The limit for the Dependent Care FSA remains at $5,000 in 2020. Both employer and employee may contribute to an employee's health-care FSA, but contributions from all sources combined must not exceed the annual maximum.

The benefits are subject to annual maximum limits and are typically subject to an annual "use-it-or-lose-it" rule, with a short (two-and-a-half-months) grace period after year-end to use any remaining balance, although last-minute legislation changed these rules for 2020 and 2021.

Note: As part of the disaster relief provisions implemented by the *Consolidated Appropriations Act of 2021,* employers may allow employees to carryover unused benefits or contributions remaining in an FSA from 2020 to 2021. If a dependent "aged out" during the pandemic, the use of dependent FSA (DCFSA) funds is permitted up to age 14 rather than the usual age 13. Employers can also allow employees to change their FSA contribution elections outside of open enrollment for plan years ending in 2021.

If a taxpayer *overcontributes* to their health-care FSA, the taxpayer must pay income tax, plus a 6% excise tax, on any excess contributions and related earnings for each tax year the excess contributions remain in the account. In order to avoid the excise tax on excess contributions, the

---

[95] An FSA is *not the same* thing as an HSA. A health savings account is always paired with a high deductible health plan, and it is an account that a taxpayer may establish and fund on his own. An FSA, on the other hand, is always offered by an employer as part of a cafeteria plan.

[96] Generally, qualified benefits under a cafeteria plan are not subject to FICA, FUTA, Medicare tax, or income tax withholding. However, group-term life insurance that exceeds $50,000 of coverage is subject to social security and Medicare taxes, but not FUTA tax or income tax withholding. Adoption assistance benefits provided in a cafeteria plan are subject to social security, Medicare, and FUTA taxes, but not income tax withholding. If an employee elects to receive cash instead of any qualified benefit, it is treated as wages subject to all employment taxes.

taxpayer must remove the year's excess contributions and related investment earnings before the last day to file federal income taxes for the pertinent tax year, generally April 15.

Example: Max has a health care FSA at his current job. In 2020, he contributes the maximum to his account. In late November, he switches jobs and mistakenly contributes to the HSA that his new employer offers him. At the end of 2020, Max has contributed a total of $5,500 to both accounts. He has an excess contribution for the year. If Max does not withdraw the excess contribution by the filing deadline (April 15, 2021), he will be subject to a 6% excise tax, as well as income tax, on the excess contribution and any related investment earnings. These penalties will continue to accrue until the excess contribution is corrected.

However, in 2020, and 2021 employers are permitted, but not required, to allow employees to "rollover" unused amounts in their FSA accounts.[97]

Adoption Assistance in a "Cafeteria Plan": An employee can exclude amounts paid or reimbursed by an employer under a qualified adoption assistance program ($14,300 for 2020).

Dependent Care Assistance Program: This is also sometimes called a Dependent Care FSA, or Dependent Care Flexible Spending Account (DCFSA). An employee can exclude up to $5,000 in 2020 ($2,500 if MFS) of benefits received under a qualified dependent care assistance program each year. The amounts can be used to pay for eligible daycare services, before or after school programs, and adult daycare for disabled dependents. Amounts paid directly to the taxpayer or to a daycare provider qualify for the exclusion.

Example: Jennifer has a six-year-old son. Jennifer participates in her employer's dependent care FSA. She fills out a form that directs the payroll department to set aside $400 each month from her paycheck. This amount is deposited into her dependent care FSA. At the end of each month, her daycare provider gives Jennifer a receipt, which she submits to her employer for reimbursement. Jennifer's employer then reimburses the funds directly from her FSA account. The money she contributes to her Dependent Care FSA is not subject to payroll tax or income tax, so she will end up paying less in taxes when she files her annual tax return.

Highly Compensated Employees (HCEs) and Key Employees

A cafeteria plan cannot have rules that favor eligibility for highly compensated employees to participate, contribute, or benefit from a cafeteria plan. If a benefit plan favors HCEs, the value of their benefits may become taxable. This is to discourage companies from offering excellent tax-free benefits to their top executives while ignoring the needs of lower-paid employees. Per Publication 15-B, an HCE is normally any of the following:

- A company officer.
- A shareholder who owns more than 5% of the voting power or value of all classes of the employer's stock.
- An employee who is highly compensated based on the facts and circumstances.
- A spouse or dependent of an officer or shareholder described above.

[97] Typically, up to $500 of unused FSA money may be carried over to the following year. An employer must choose between either a grace period (where the period to use the FSA funds from one year extends into the following year) or the "carryover" option. 2020 and 2021 are unusual because participants are allowed, if permitted by their employer, to roll over unused amounts in (FSAs) from 2020 to 2021 and from 2021 to 2022.

The IRS uses a process called "family attribution" in order to make the determination of who qualifies as an HCE, which means that an employee can be determined to be an HCE merely by familial relationship.

An employee who is a spouse, child, grandparent, or parent of someone who is a 5% (or greater) owner of the business, is also automatically considered an "owner" under the family attribution rules.[98] HCEs hired in the middle of the year will not receive HCE status until the start of the *following* year, when they are eligible to collect the entirety of their salary. For example, an HCE hired in April 2020 does not qualify as an HCE until January 1, 2021, regardless of their salary level.[99]

Example: Nolan is an employee-shareholder with 3% stock ownership in USA Rentals, Inc. His wife, Maddison, also works for USA Rentals and owns 4% of the stock ownership in the company. Nolan and Maddison are both considered HCEs under the family attribution rules, because their combined stock ownership exceeds 5% (their combined total interest in the company is 7%).

"Highly Compensated" Employees and "Key Employees" have similar-sounding names, but the rules for defining Key Employees are slightly different. Employer-provided benefits also cannot favor "key employees." Publication 15-B defines "Key Employees" as any of the following:

- A company officer having annual pay of more than $185,000 in 2020 (the officer does not have to be an owner of the company).
- An employee who is either of the following:
    - A 5% owner of the business, or;
    - A 1% owner of the business whose annual pay is more than $150,000 in 2020.

Although the compensation threshold is *lower* for HCEs than Key Employees, an employee can be classified as a "key employee" without having any ownership in the company at all.

Example: Colton is the vice-president of Grainger, Inc., a plastics manufacturing firm. Colton is not an owner of the company, and he is not related to any of the owners. His salary is $250,000 in 2020, and was $198,000 in the previous year. Colton is classified as a "key employee," even though he does not have an ownership stake in the company.

A plan is considered to have improperly "favored" HCEs and key employees if more than 25% of all the benefits are given to those employees.

If a cafeteria plan or a retirement plan fails to pass IRS non-discrimination testing, highly compensated employees and key employees may lose the tax benefits of participating in the plan. If this happens, then the plans can lose their tax-favored status, and the HCEs or key employees must include the value of these benefits as taxable compensation. These types of "corrections" often take the form of taxable distributions to plan participants.

---

[98] In this case, family members include the spouse, parents, children, and grandparents. Family members for this purpose do not include grandchildren, siblings, aunts, uncles, or in-laws.

[99] Corporate executives often receive extraordinary fringe benefits that are not provided to other corporate employees. Any property or service that an executive receives in lieu of or in addition to regular taxable wages is a fringe benefit that may be subject to taxation. This is such an important issue to the IRS that they have developed an Audit Technique Guide about the subject (Executive Compensation-Fringe Benefits Audit Techniques Guide).

Example: McGovern Energy, Inc. is a C corporation with 300 employees, twenty-five of whom are considered highly compensated employees. McGovern Energy's cafeteria plan and its benefits are available to all full-time employees, and the benefits offered are the same for everyone, regardless of the employee's level of pay. Everyone is treated equally under the plan. Therefore, the discrimination rules do not apply, and the employees' benefits are not taxable, and fully deductible by the employer as a business expense.

Example: Dixie Motorsports is a small corporation with forty-five employees. The sole shareholder of the company, Randall, sets up a cafeteria plan as well as a 401(k) retirement plan. However, he only allows his wife and his two sons to participate in the plans. The rest of the employees are not offered any type of benefits, and in fact, are never told about the plans. Later, Dixie Motorsports goes through a plan audit, and the company fails discrimination testing. Randall is forced to recognize the value of his pretax benefits as taxable income. Randall's spouse and his two sons are also considered HCEs because they are Randall's family members, so they are also forced to recognize their benefits as taxable income, as well. They will be required to amend the business' tax returns as well as their individual returns to include the additional compensation.

Other Types of Employee Fringe Benefits

Educational Assistance: An employer can offer employees educational assistance for the cost of tuition, fees, books, supplies, and equipment. The payments may be for either undergraduate or graduate-level courses, and do not have to be work-related.

In 2020, up to $5,250 in educational assistance may be excluded per year per employee. If an employer pays more than $5,250, the excess is generally taxed as wages to the employee.[100] The *CARES Act* expanded this provision for qualified educational expenses to include student loan repayments. An employer may contribute up to $5,250 annually toward educational expenses, student loans, or a combination of both. The Consolidated Appropriations Act of 2021 extended this provision through tax year 2025. The cost of courses involving sports, games, or hobbies is not covered unless they are related to the business or are required as part of a degree program. The cost of lodging, meals, and transportation is also not included.

Tuition Reduction Benefits: A college or other educational institution can exclude the value of a qualified undergraduate tuition reduction to an employee, his spouse, or a dependent child. A tuition reduction is "qualified" only if the taxpayer receives it from, and uses it at, an eligible educational institution. Graduate education only qualifies if it is for the education of a graduate student who performs teaching or research activities for the educational organization.

Example: Mayra is a graduate teaching assistant at Louisiana State University. As part of her employment agreement with the college, Mayra is offered a 50% tuition waiver, reducing the cost of her own graduate tuition at the school. The normal graduate tuition cost is $14,800 per year. Because of the tuition waiver, Mayra only pays $7,400. The tuition reduction is not taxable to Mayra, but any wages that she receives as compensation for student teaching would be taxable.

[100] There is an exception for job-related education. If the education is directly job related, amounts in excess of the $5,250 limit may qualify for exclusion as a working condition fringe benefit. For example, an accounting firm pays for a staff accountant to attend courses directly related to the preparation of business returns. Those amounts would be fully deductible by the business and not taxable to the employee, even if the cost exceeded the annual limit.

Employer-Provided Meals and Lodging: An employer may exclude the value of meals and lodging provided to employees if they are provided:

- On the employer's business premises, and
- For the employer's convenience.

For lodging, there is an additional rule: it must be required as a condition of employment. Lodging can be provided for the taxpayer, the taxpayer's spouse, and the taxpayer's dependents and still not be taxable to the employee. The exclusion from taxation does not apply if the employee can choose to receive additional pay instead of lodging.

Example: Patrick is a project supervisor for Birchwood Construction. He is provided free lodging at remote job sites in an RV, where he is required to stay on-site for several months while the timber is cleared and the grounds are prepared for construction projects. The value of the lodging and his meals are excluded from his income because it is primarily for the employer's security and convenience.

Meals may be provided to employees for the convenience of the employer on the employer's business premises for several reasons, such as when:

- Police officers and firefighters need to be on call for emergencies during the meal period.
- The nature of the business requires short meal periods.
- Eating facilities are not available in areas near the workplace, such as in the case of remote or dangerous locations.
- Meals are furnished immediately after working hours because the employee's duties prevented him from obtaining a meal during working hours.

Meals furnished to restaurant employees before, during, or after work hours are also considered furnished for the employer's convenience and are not taxable to the employee.

Example: Paramedic Transport, Inc. regularly provides meals to employees during working hours so that paramedics are available for emergency calls during the meal. The employees are not permitted to take regular lunches or eat off-site because of the nature of their employment. The value of the free meals is therefore excludable from the employees' wages, and the employer is allowed to deduct the cost of the meals as a business expense, subject to the 50% limit.

Transportation Fringe Benefits

Employers may provide transportation benefits to their employees up to certain amounts without having to include the benefits in the employees' taxable income. Qualified transportation benefits include transit passes, paid parking, and a ride in a commuter highway vehicle between the employee's home and workplace.

Due to the TCJA, transportation benefits are no longer deductible by the employer, but transportation benefits are still non-taxable to the employee if the employer continues to provide the benefit (with the notable exception of bicycle commuting benefits, which became taxable to the employee under the TCJA).

Any expense over the threshold amount ($270 per month in 2020 for transit and parking benefits) is included in the employee's taxable income as wages. An employee can receive both parking and transit benefits in the same month. The use of a company car for commuting

purposes or other personal use is generally a taxable benefit. Therefore, the value of the vehicle's use for either of these purposes is considered taxable wages to the employee.

There is an exception in IRS regulations that exempts the personal-use of certain types of vehicles. Qualified nonpersonal use vehicles, such as police or fire vehicles, school buses, and ambulances, are exempt from fringe benefit reporting, even if the vehicles are used for commuting purposes, as long as the employer requires their use for the employees to do their jobs.

Example: Sienna was offered a lucrative new job in New York City as a computer programmer. As part of her employment contract, she negotiates a parking space for her car. Her new employer agrees to pay the cost of the space at the garage across the street from her work. Monthly parking is quite expensive in New York City, and the monthly parking fee at the garage is $550. Since this amount exceeds the allowable limit for parking fringe benefits, a portion of the parking costs will be taxable to Sienna as wages. In 2020, the allowable transportation benefit for parking is $270. Therefore, an additional $280 ($550-$270 limit) would be taxable to Sienna each month as wages.

Example: Dominic is employed by a lumber company. He drives an employer-provided pickup truck, hauling equipment on job sites and delivering lumber to customers. He also gets to take the truck home in the evenings. In 2020, Dominic drives the truck 20,000 miles, of which 4,000, or 20%, are personal miles (4,000/20,000 = 20%). The truck has an annual lease value of $4,100. Personal use is therefore valued at $820 and is included in Dominic's taxable wages, subject to all payroll taxes.

Cell Phones: The value of the business use of an employer-provided cell phone may be excluded from an employee's income to the extent that, if the employee paid for its use, the payment would be deductible. There must be substantial "noncompensatory" reasons for the use of a phone that relate to the employer's business.

Legitimate reasons include the employer's need to contact the employee in the event of work-related emergencies, and the employee's need to be available to speak with clients when away from the office. If a cell phone is provided simply to promote goodwill, to boost an employee's morale, or to attract a prospective employee, the value of the cell phone must be added to the employee's wages.

Group-Term Life Insurance Coverage: Up to $50,000 of life insurance coverage may be provided as a nontaxable benefit to an employee. The cost of insurance coverage on policies that exceed $50,000 is a taxable benefit.

If an employer provides more than $50,000 of coverage, the amount included in the taxpayer's income is reported as part of their taxable wages on their Form W-2. The taxable amount is shown separately with a "code C" in box 12 of their Form W-2.

Work-Related Moving Expense Reimbursements: Moving expenses are no longer deductible for most taxpayers, except for certain members of the armed forces. Therefore, moving expenses that are reimbursed or paid by an employer must be included in the employee's taxable income as wages.

Example: Margaret was offered a new job in another state on November 1, 2020. Her new employer offered to reimburse her moving expenses as a condition of her employment. She accepted the position and moved on December 16, 2020. Margaret submits the paperwork, and her employer reimburses her moving expenses on December 30, 2020. Even though she submitted receipts for reimbursement, all of the amounts would be taxable to Margaret as wages. The employer may deduct the amounts as employee compensation, and all the normal payroll taxes that are applicable to regular wages would apply.

No-Additional-Cost Services: Nontaxable fringe benefits also include services provided to employees that do not impose any substantial additional cost to the employer because the employer already offers those services in the ordinary course of doing business. Employees do not need to include these no-additional-cost services in their income. Typically, no-additional-cost services are excess capacity services, such as unused airline seat tickets for airline employees or open hotel rooms for hotel employees.

Example: Dalilah is a flight attendant with Starlight Airlines. She is allowed to fly for free on standby flights when there is an extra seat. This fringe benefit is allowed at no additional cost to the employer and is therefore nontaxable to Dalilah.

If an employee is provided with free or low-cost use of a health club on the employer's premises, the value is not included in the employee's compensation. The gym must be used primarily by employees, their spouses, and their dependent children. However, if the employer pays for a fitness program or use of a facility at an *off-site* location, the value of the program is included in the employee's compensation.

Employee Achievement Awards: Employers may generally exclude from an employee's taxable wages the value of awards given for length-of-service or safety achievement. The tax-free amount is limited to the following:

- $400 for awards that are not qualified plan awards. A qualified plan award is one that does not discriminate in favor of highly compensated employees, and that is established under a written plan.
- $1,600 for qualified plan awards.

Example: Wallace has worked for Financial Corp. for ten years. Financial Corp. makes a qualifying length-of-service award to Wallace in the form of an engraved gold watch. The cost of the watch was $395. The watch was presented to Wallace during a meaningful presentation. All the company employees are eligible to receive length-of-service awards based on their tenure with the company. The watch is deductible to Financial Corp. as a business expense, and the value of the watch is not taxable to Wallace.

The exclusion for employee awards does not apply to awards of cash, gift cards, lodging, stocks, bonds, or tickets to sporting events.

De Minimis (Minimal) Benefits: This is a property or service an employer provides that has so little value that accounting for it would be impractical. Examples of de minimis benefits include the following:

- Occasional personal use of a company copying machine.
- Holiday gifts with a low fair market value (such as a holiday turkey or a gift basket)

- Beverages and snacks, such as coffee or doughnuts for employees
- Cash and gift cards are not excludable as de minimis benefits unless they are for occasional meal money or transportation fare.

In order to be non-taxable, the benefit must also be provided so that an employee can work an unusual, extended schedule.

Example: Wayne works for Sunrise Dairy Farms as a farmhand. One day, there was an emergency on the farm where several dairy cows accidentally ingested tainted feed. The cows began to have seizures, and all the employees were forced to work overtime to stabilize the livestock and administer medicine. Sunrise Dairy Farms gives Wayne $20 in cash to purchase a meal during this unusual overtime shift. The cash can be excluded as a *de minimis* benefit because it is for the benefit of his employer that Wayne is working overtime, and it is an unusual and infrequent situation.

Example: Bennett owns Greenhaven Farms. He has 10 employees. On August 22, 2020, severe storms struck the area, and all of the company's crops were at risk. Bennett asks all his employees to work overtime in order to bring in crops and secure the farm buildings and fencing. During this emergency situation, Bennett gives his employees $25 in cash to purchase their lunch and dinner at a nearby deli. The amounts would be excluded from the employees' wages as a *de minimis* benefit, because the storm is an unusual and infrequent occurrence.

Employee Discounts: Employers may exclude the value of employee discounts from wages up to the following limits:

- For services, a 20% discount of the price charged to nonemployee customers.
- For merchandise, the company's gross profit percentage multiplied by the price nonemployee customers pay.

Reimbursement of Employee-Business Expenses

When a business *reimburses* its employees for certain business expenses, such as meals and travel, reimbursements are not taxable income if employees meet all of the following requirements of an accountable plan:

- Have incurred the expenses while performing services as employees.
- Adequately account for travel, meals, and lodging.
- Provide evidence of their employee business expenses, such as receipts or other records.
- Return any excess reimbursement within a reasonable time.

Under an accountable plan, a business may advance money to employees. The cash advance must be reasonably calculated to equal the anticipated expenses, and it must be advanced within a reasonable period of time. If any expenses reimbursed under this arrangement are not substantiated, they are considered taxable income for the employee.

Qualifying expenses for travel are excludable from an employee's income if they are incurred for temporary travel on business away from the area of the employee's tax home. Travel expenses paid in connection with an indefinite work assignment cannot be excluded from income. Any work assignment in excess of one year is considered "indefinite."

Travel expense reimbursements include:

- Costs of travel to and from the business destination (such as flights and mileage reimbursements).
- Transportation costs while at the business destination (such as taxi fares and shuttles).
- Lodging, meals, and incidental expenses.
- Cleaning, laundry, and other miscellaneous expenses while away from home on assignment.

Example: Craig works for a travel agency in Seattle. He flies to Detroit for a business conference that lasts an entire week. His employer pays the cost of the flight to and from Detroit, as well as lodging and meals while there. The reimbursements for substantiated travel expenses are excluded from Craig's income.

Example: Miriam runs a tax preparation business as a sole-proprietor. She advances $250 to her only employee, Nasser, so that he can become a registered notary. Nasser spends $90 on an online notary course and then another $100 to take the notary exam. Nasser returns the unused funds ($60), as well as copies of his receipts to Miriam. The expenses are qualified expenses under an accountable plan, so the amounts paid are not taxable income for Nasser, and still deductible as business expenses by Miriam.

Taxation of Clergy Members

There are special rules regarding the taxation of clergy members, defined as individuals who are ordained, commissioned, or licensed by a religious body or church denomination. A clergy member's salary is reported on Form W-2 and is taxable. Offerings and fees received for performing marriages, baptisms, and funerals must also be reported as self-employment income on Schedule C.

Housing Allowance for Clergy: A clergy member who receives a housing allowance may exclude the allowance from gross income to the extent it is used to pay the expenses of providing a home. The exclusion for housing is limited to the lesser of:

- Fair market rental value (including utilities), or
- The actual cost to provide the home.

The housing allowance cannot exceed reasonable pay and must be used for housing in the year it is received. Salary, other fees, and housing allowances must be included in income for purposes of determining self-employment tax.

Even if a minister is considered an employee, churches cannot withhold Social Security and Medicare taxes from his wages. They are treated as self-employed for the purposes of these taxes.

Example: Garrison is an ordained pastor. His church allows him to use a cottage that has a rental value of $8,000. He is paid a salary of $22,000, and his church does not withhold Social Security or Medicare taxes. Garrison's income for self-employment tax purposes is $30,000 ($22,000 + $8,000 housing).

Example: Emanuel is an ordained minister who receives $32,000 in salary from his church. He receives an additional $4,000 for performing marriages and baptisms. His housing allowance is $500 per month, for a total of $6,000 per year, and is excluded from his gross income. Emanuel must report the $32,000 as salary and the $4,000 as self-employment income. The $6,000 housing allowance is subject to self-employment tax, but not to income tax.

A clergy member may apply for an exemption from self-employment tax if he is conscientiously opposed to public insurance because of religious principles. For a clergy member or a minister to claim an exemption from SE tax, the minister must file IRS Form 4029, *Application for Exemption from Social Security and Medicare Taxes and Waiver of Benefits.*

The sect or religious order must also complete part of the form. The exemption does not apply to federal income tax, only to self-employment tax. If the exemption is granted, the clergy member will not pay Social Security or Medicare taxes on his earnings, and he will not receive credit toward those benefits in retirement.

If a clergy member is a member of a religious order that has taken a vow of poverty, he is exempt from paying SE tax on his earnings for qualified services. The earnings are tax-free because they are considered the income of the religious order, rather than of the individual clergy member.

Combat Pay and Veterans' Benefits

Wages earned by military personnel are generally taxable. However, there are several special rules for military personnel regarding taxable income. Combat zone wages (combat pay) are not taxable income.

Hazardous duty pay is also excludable for certain military personnel. Enlisted personnel who serve in a combat zone for any part of a month may exclude their pay from tax. For officers, the pay is excluded up to a certain amount, depending on the branch of service.

Example: Yakov is an Air Force pilot who served in a combat zone from January 1, 2020, to November 3, 2020. He is only required to report his income for December, because all of the other income is excluded from taxation as combat-zone pay. Even though Yakov only served three days in November in a combat zone, his income for the entire month of November is excluded.

Similarly, veterans' benefits paid by the Department of Veterans Affairs to a veteran or his family are not taxable if they are for education (the GI Bill), training, disability compensation, work therapy, dependent care assistance, or other benefits or pension payments given to the veteran because of disability.

Medicare Waiver Payments

Medicare waiver payments are also called "difficulty-of-care" payments.[101] Payments to a taxpayer for home-care services provided to a disabled individual living in the same residence

[101] Per IRS Notice 2014-7, the IRS has determined that payments made through state Medicaid and Medicare Personal Care programs for the provision of in-home supportive care to eligible recipients will be treated as "difficulty of care payments". The payments are excludable from the gross income of the provider under section 131 of the tax Code. See full FAQs here: https://www.irs.gov/individuals/certain-medicaid-waiver-payments-may-be-excludable-from-income.

may be excluded from gross income. The exemption applies to individuals who provide care in their home, regardless of who owns the home. The taxpayer does not have to be related to the disabled individual, although generally this is the case.

Note: Qualified Medicare waiver payments may be excluded from income *only* when the care provider and the care recipient reside in the same home. When the care provider and the care recipient do *not* live together in the same home, the Medicare waiver payments may not be excluded from gross income.

Example: Alina moved into her elderly mother's home to care for her. Alina begins to receive $575 monthly payments under a state Medicare Home and Community-Based Services waiver program for supportive home care. The payments are not taxable to Alina.

Example: Timothy cares for his elderly uncle five days a week. Timothy eats all his meals at his uncle's home and sleeps there occasionally. Most evenings and weekends, Timothy leaves work at 6PM and goes home to his wife and family in their separate home. Timothy receives monthly Medicare waiver payments for his uncle's care. Since Timothy has a separate home, the Medicare waiver payments are taxable to Timothy.

Taxpayers who receive these payments may choose to include them in their income for purposes of the earned income credit (EITC) or the additional child tax credit (ACTC).[102] In addition, under the SECURE Act, taxpayers can use them to fund an IRA, but since the contributions come from amounts excluded from tax, they are treated as nondeductible contributions.

Disability Payments

There are several types of disability payments, and the taxability of the income depends on several factors. Some types of disability-related payments are given to workers that are not taxable at all. Worker's compensation is one such example.

Worker's compensation should not be confused with disability insurance, sick pay, or unemployment compensation; it is a type of benefit that only pays workers who are injured on the job. Worker's compensation is paid to a taxpayer under a worker's compensation act or another state statute. The amounts are always exempt from tax.

Example: Hudson is a construction worker. In 2020, he is struck by falling concrete on a construction site. The concrete crushes his pelvis, causing catastrophic injuries and a long hospital stay. Worker's compensation covers Hudson's medical costs as well as a portion of his lost wages while he is recovering from the injury. The amounts are not taxable to Hudson and do not need to be reported on his tax return.

Workers' compensation is a type of mandatory business insurance, meaning most large and mid-sized employers are required to have coverage for their employees.

[102] See a reference here: https://www.irs.gov/pub/irs-utl/vta-2020-03.pdf.

Disability Insurance Benefits

A taxpayer may also receive long-term disability payments as a result of an insurance policy. As a general rule, long-term disability payments from an insurance policy are excluded from income if the *taxpayer* pays the premiums for the policy. If an *employer* pays the insurance premiums, the employee must report the payments as taxable income.

Disability Insurance Premiums	Taxability of Benefits
The employer pays 100%	100% taxable
The employer pays a portion, and the employee pays the balance with post-tax dollars	Partially taxable; the taxable percentage is based on the premiums paid by the employer
The employer pays a portion, and the employee pays the balance with pretax dollars	100% taxable
The employee pays 100% with post-tax dollars	Not taxable
The employee pays 100% with pre-tax dollars	100% taxable

If both an employee and his employer have paid premiums for a disability policy, only the employer's portion of the disability payments would be reported as taxable income.

Example: Robyn became disabled in 2020 and began to receive a long-term disability benefit of \$4,200 a month. The original insurance policy was paid for by both her employer and herself. Before Robyn became disabled, her employer paid 80% of the disability insurance premiums. Robyn paid the remaining premium amount (20%) with post-tax dollars. In this case, because the employer paid 80% of the policy premiums, 80% of the benefits received would be taxable to Robyn. This means that \$3,360 (\$4,200 x 80%) would be taxable. The remaining benefits of \$840 (20% x \$4,200) would not be taxable since Robyn paid that portion of the insurance premium with her own post-tax dollars.

Disability Retirement Benefits

Disability *retirement* benefits are taxable as **<u>wages</u>** if a taxpayer retired on disability *before* reaching the minimum retirement age. The benefit is usually based on the employee's final average earnings and their years of actual service.

Once the taxpayer reaches retirement age (usually, this is age 62), the payments are no longer taxable as wages. They are taxable as pension income.

This type of disability retirement benefit is offered to most Federal government workers and U.S. Postal Service employees and is often called "FERS disability" because the disability retirement benefits are offered under the Federal Employees Retirement System (FERS).[103] To apply for this benefit, the employee's disability generally must have caused them to discontinue working.

[103] Social Security Disability Insurance (SSDI) benefits is a separate benefit from disability retirement benefits that are offered to federal and postal service employees. Supplemental Security Income (SSI) is also different from SSDI. SSI is a non-taxable needs-based federal benefit.

Example: Sloan is a U.S. Postal Service employee. She is 50 years old and has worked for the postal service for over sixteen years, but she is still many years away from official retirement age. On January 10, 2020, Sloan sustains a life-altering spinal injury and becomes permanently disabled. She immediately applies for disability retirement under the Federal Employees Retirement System, or FERS, and is awarded disability retirement benefits. Her disability retirement benefits will be taxable as wages until she reaches retirement age (usually 62 years of age). After she reaches retirement age, the benefits will be taxable as pension income instead of wages.

Veteran's Disability Benefits

Veteran's *disability* benefits (also called *VA Disability Compensation*) are a type of disability benefit paid specifically to a veteran for disabilities that are service-connected, which means the injury or disease linked to their military service. Veteran's disability benefits are exempt from taxation if the veteran was terminated through separation or discharged under honorable conditions. The VA typically does not issue Form W-2, Form 1099-R, or any other tax-related document for veterans' disability benefits.

Example: Phoebe is a Navy veteran who was discharged after she sustained a serious injury in Iraq. She lost vision in one eye and the use of one hand due to an explosion. Since Phoebe's discharge from the Armed Forces, she has received $1,950 per month in Veteran's disability benefits. She now has a civilian job working in a factory, where she earns regular wages as an employee. Her wages are taxable, but the disability compensation remains non-taxable to Phoebe. Her veteran's disability benefits do not need to be reported on her tax return.

Note: Do not confuse sick pay with disability pay or disability benefits. Sick pay, or sick leave, is always taxable as wages, just like vacation pay and holiday pay.

Life Insurance Payments

Life insurance payouts generally are not taxable to a beneficiary if the payment was the result of the death of the insured. This is true even if the proceeds were paid under an accident or health insurance policy. However, interest income received as a result of life insurance proceeds is usually taxable. Further, if a taxpayer surrenders a life insurance policy for cash, he must generally include in income any proceeds that are more than the cost of the policy. However, an exception exists for when a terminally ill person receives a viatical settlement.[104] In this case, the funds are tax-free.

Sometimes, a taxpayer will choose to receive life insurance proceeds in installments rather than as a lump sum. In this case, part of the installment generally includes interest income.

If a taxpayer receives life insurance proceeds in installments (also called a life insurance annuity), he can exclude part of each installment from his income. To determine the excluded part, the amount held by the insurance company (generally the total lump sum payable at the

104 A "viatical settlement" when the policyholder is deemed to be terminally or chronically ill and executes a "deemed sale" of their life insurance policy. As long as the taxpayer has proof from a physician that they have a life expectancy of 24 months or less, the sale of their life insurance policy is treated as a viatical settlement and is tax-free.

death of the insured person) is divided by the number of installments to be paid. The taxpayer would include any amount over this excluded portion as taxable interest income.

Example: Molly's brother died in 2020, and she is the sole beneficiary of his life insurance. The face amount of the policy is $75,000. Rather than take a lump sum payment, Molly chooses to receive 120 monthly installments of $1,000 each. The excluded part of each installment is $625 ($75,000 ÷ 120), or $7,500 for an entire year. The rest of each payment, $375 a month (or $4,500 for an entire year), is taxable interest income to Molly.

Unit 4: Study Questions

(Test yourself first, then check the correct answers at the end of this quiz.)

1. Paxton is a flight attendant who earned wages of $61,000 in 2020. The airline provided free transportation on standby from his home in Little Rock to the airline's hub in Charlotte, NC. The fair market value of the commuting flights was $5,000. Paxton also received advances under an accountable plan of $9,000 for overnight travel, but only spent $6,000. He returned the excess ($3,000) to his employer. Paxton was injured on the job and received worker's compensation of $4,100. What amount must he include in gross income on his individual tax return?

A. $61,000
B. $64,000
C. $65,000
D. $71,000

2. Income was constructively received in 2020 in each of the following situations *except*:

A. Wages were deposited in the taxpayer's bank account on December 26, 2020, but were not withdrawn by the taxpayer until January 8, 2021.
B. A taxpayer was informed his check for services was available on December 15, 2020. The taxpayer did not pick up the check until January 30, 2021.
C. A taxpayer received a check on December 31, 2020, but did not deposit the check until January 5, 2021.
D. A taxpayer's vacation property was sold on December 28, 2020. The payment was not received by the taxpayer until January 2, 2021, when the escrow company released the funds.

3. Chandra received the following income and fringe benefits in 2020:

Wages	$30,000
End-of-the-year bonus	$2,000
Parking pass per month	$90
Employer contributions to her 401(k) plan	$900
Occasional free use of a copier on the employer's premises	$15

How much income must Chandra report on her tax return?

A. $30,000
B. $32,000
C. $32,500
D. $34,480

4. Which of the following tip income, if any, is exempt from federal income tax?

A. Tips of less than $20 per month.
B. Noncash tips.
C. Tips not reported to the employer.
D. None of the above - all tips are taxable.

5. Bartholomew is a naval officer who was injured while serving in a combat zone. He was later awarded Veterans Affairs (VA) disability benefits. How are these payments reported on Bartholomew's tax return?

A. 100% of the disability benefits may be excluded from income.
B. Up to 50% of the disability benefits may be excluded from income.
C. 100% of the disability benefits may be excluded from income for enlisted personnel, but not for officers.
D. The disability benefits are all taxable as pension income.

6. Which of the following fringe benefits is taxable (or partially taxable) to the employee?

A. Health insurance covered 100% by the employer.
B. An employer-provided company car that is used for commuting.
C. Group-term life insurance coverage of $50,000.
D. Employer contributions to an employee's 401(k) plan.

7. Flavian owns a restaurant. He furnishes his daytime waitress, Alida, two meals during each workday. Flavian encourages (but does not require) Alida to have her breakfast on the business premises before starting work so she can help him answer phones. She is required to have her lunch on the premises. How should Flavian treat this fringe benefit to Alida?

A. None of Alida's meals at the restaurant are taxable.
B. All of Alida's meals at the restaurant are taxable.
C. Alida's lunch is not taxable, but her breakfast is.
D. Alida's meals are taxed at a flat rate of 15%.

8. What is "adjusted gross income"?

A. The sum of all sources of taxable income that the taxpayer receives during the year, minus any allowable credits.
B. The amount of earned income a taxpayer receives during the year.
C. Another term for taxable income.
D. Gross income minus certain allowable adjustments, calculated before the standard deduction or itemized deductions are taken.

9. Self-employment income does not include:

A. The income of ministers for the performance of services such as baptisms and marriages.
B. Ordinary partnership income allocated to general partners on Schedule K-1.
C. Wages earned by a temporary employee.
D. Payments to independent contractors.

10. Orrin is an ordained minister in the Evangelical Church of Savannah. He owns his home, and his monthly house payment is $900. His monthly utilities total $150. The fair rental value in his neighborhood is $1,000. Orrin receives a housing allowance from his church in the amount of $950 per month. What portion of his monthly housing allowance would he include in his gross income for income tax purposes?

A. $0
B. $100
C. $150
D. $950

11. Which of the following types of fringe benefits are deductible by an employer, but not taxable to the employee?

A. De minimis fringe benefit.
B. Use of an employer's apartment, vacation home, or boat.
C. Membership in a country club or athletic facility.
D. A gift card.

12. Salvador is an enlisted soldier in the U.S. Army who served in a combat zone from January 30, 2020, to September 2, 2020. He returned to the United States and received his regular duty pay for the remainder of the year. How many months of his income are taxable in 2020?

A. Zero. All the income is tax-free.
B. Three months of wages are subject to tax.
C. Four months of wages are subject to tax.
D. Twelve months of wages are subject to tax.

13. Which of the following fringe benefits provided by the employer will result in taxable income to the employee?

A. A cell phone used by a salesperson to talk to clients while on the road.
B. Reimbursements paid by the employers for qualified business travel expenses.
C. Use of a company van for daily commuting.
D. Occasional personal use of an office copy machine.

14. Rasheed is employed as a staff accountant by a large CPA firm. When he travels for his audit work, he submits his travel receipts for reimbursement by his firm, which has an accountable plan for its employees. Which of the following statements is correct about accountable plans?

A. The reimbursed amounts are not taxable to Rasheed.
B. Rasheed may deduct his travel expenses on his personal tax return.
C. His employer cannot deduct the travel expenses as a business expense, even though Rasheed was reimbursed in full.
D. Reimbursed expenses are taxable to the employee.

15. Of the following items, only ___________ is not taxable income to an employee:

A. A holiday bonus.
B. Overtime pay.
C. Vacation pay.
D. A mileage reimbursement under an accountable plan.

16. Debby broke her leg in a car accident and was unable to work for three months. She received an accident settlement of $13,000 from her insurance company. During this time, she also received $7,500 of sick pay from her employer. In addition, she received $5,000 from an accident policy she had purchased herself. How much of this income is taxable to Debby?

A. $5,000
B. $7,500
C. $12,500
D. $18,000

17. Alphonse was the sole beneficiary of his mother's life insurance policy. His mother died on June 1, 2020. Alphonse received the following payments on December 31, 2020:

- $360,000 lump-sum death benefit from his mother's life insurance policy.
- $175 of interest income on the life insurance proceeds.

What is the proper treatment of these payments?

A. The life insurance proceeds are taxable in 2020. The interest is not taxable.
B. The life insurance proceeds and interest income are both taxable to Alphonse in 2020.
C. Only the $175 of interest income is taxable in 2020. The life insurance proceeds are not taxable.
D. None of these payments are taxable to Alphonse. Instead, they are taxable to his mother's estate.

18. Orval and Rainelle are married, and both are self-employed with their own businesses. Orval owns a business that has a $9,750 net profit during the year. His wife, Rainelle, has an overall business loss of ($11,100). They both file Schedules C to report their self-employment income. Which of the following statements is correct?

A. On their joint return, they will not have to pay self-employment tax, because the losses from Rainelle's business will offset Orval's income.
B. Orval must pay self-employment tax on $9,750, regardless of his wife's income or losses.
C. They can file MFS and offset each other's self-employment tax.
D. If they choose to file separate returns, they may split the profits and losses equally between their two businesses.

19. Anastasia is a sales rep who sells pharmaceutical drugs to doctor's offices on commission (she is an employee). On December 25, 2020, Anastasia receives $12,000 of income from commissions, plus an advance of $1,000 for future commissions. She also receives a $200 check for expense reimbursements from her employer after turning in her receipts as part of an accountable plan. How much taxable income should Anastasia report on her 2020 tax return?

A. $11,800
B. $12,000
C. $13,000
D. $13,200

Unit 4: Quiz Answers

1. The answer is A. Paxton only has to include his wages on his tax return ($61,000). The free flights offered on standby to airline personnel are considered no-additional-cost services and are not taxable to the employee. Reimbursements under an accountable plan and amounts paid for workers' compensation are nontaxable. Since Paxton returned the unspent amounts to his employer, the travel reimbursements qualify under an accountable plan, and the amounts spent are not taxable to him.

2. The answer is D. A taxpayer does not need physical possession of income to have constructive receipt. However, income is not considered constructively received if the taxpayer cannot access the funds because of restrictions. Since the taxpayer's control of the receipt of the funds in the escrow account was substantially limited until the transaction had closed, the taxpayer did not constructively receive the income until the following year.

3. The answer is B. Only the wages and the bonus are taxable ($30,000 + $2,000). The parking pass is a nontaxable transportation benefit, and the employer contributions are not taxable until Chandra withdraws the money from her retirement account. Chandra does not have to report the use of the copier, because it is considered a *de minimis* fringe benefit.

4. The answer is D. All tip income is subject to federal income tax, whether cash or noncash. An individual who receives less than $20 per month of tips while working one job does not have to report the tip income to his employer, but the income is still subject to federal income tax and must be reported on the taxpayer's Form 1040.

5. The answer is A. All of the disability benefits can be excluded from Bartholomew's taxable income. VA disability compensation is exempt from taxation if the veteran was terminated through separation or discharged under honorable conditions. The VA does not issue Form W-2, Form 1099-R, or any other tax-related document for veterans' disability benefits.

6. The answer is B. An employer-provided company car would be partially taxable if it was used for personal driving. The value of the personal use of the automobile must be added to the employee's wages. These valuation rules are covered in IRS Publication 15-B, *Employer's Tax Guide to Fringe Benefits.*

7. The answer is A. Meals furnished to Alida are not taxable because they are for the convenience of the employer. Meals that employers furnish to a restaurant employee during, immediately before or after the employee's working hours are considered furnished for the employer's convenience. Since Alida is a waitress who works during the normal breakfast and lunch periods, Flavian can exclude from her wages the value of those meals. If Flavian allowed Alida to have meals without charge on her days off, the value of those meals would be included in her wages.

8. The answer is D. Adjusted gross income (AGI) is gross income (the sum of all income subject to taxation that the taxpayer receives during the year) minus certain allowable deductions or adjustments. AGI is calculated before the standard deduction, or itemized deductions are taken.

9. The answer is C. Wage income is never considered self-employment income. The other examples listed are all types of self-employment income and subject to self-employment tax on Form 1040.

10. The answer is A. Clergy members may exclude from gross income for income tax purposes, but not for self-employment tax purposes, the rental value of a home, or a rental allowance to the extent the allowance is used to provide a home, even if deductions are taken for home expenses paid with the allowance.

11. The answer is A. A *de minimis* fringe benefit is deductible by the employer but is not taxable to the employee. The IRS defines a de minimis benefit in this way: a benefit that, considering its value and the frequency with which it is provided, is so small as to make accounting for it unreasonable or impractical. For example, a de minimis fringe benefit might include occasional snacks, coffee, or doughnuts provided in a company's break room. The items in the other choices would be taxable to the employee.

12. The answer is B. If a taxpayer serves in a combat zone as an enlisted person for *any part* of a month, all of his pay received for military service that month is excluded from gross income. Since Salvador served for a few days in September, as well as January, all the income for those months is excluded as combat pay. Only October through December would be taxable.

13. The answer is C. Use of a company vehicle for commuting is not a qualified fringe benefit. Commuting expenses are not deductible. The use of a company van after normal working hours is personal use and not business use, so it would result in taxable income to the employee. The cell phone, reimbursements for business travel, and the occasional personal use of an office copy machine are noncash fringe benefits that are not taxable.

14. The answer is A. The reimbursed amounts are not taxable to Rasheed. Under an accountable plan, employee reimbursements are not included in the employee's income. In this scenario, the travel expenses incurred by the employee would be deductible by Rasheed's employer as an ordinary business expense.

15. The answer is D. Mileage reimbursements, if paid through an accountable plan, are not included in an employee's wages.

16. The answer is B. Only Debby's sick pay is taxable, because sick pay from an employer is always taxable as wages and is therefore included in Debby's gross income. Settlements for personal injuries from an accident are not taxable. If a taxpayer pays the full cost of an accident insurance plan, the benefits for personal injury or illness are not included in income. If the employer pays the cost of an accident insurance plan, the amounts are taxable to the employee.

17. The answer is C. Alphonse must report the interest income in the year he receives it. Only the $175 of interest income is taxable. Life insurance proceeds are not taxable to the recipient. However, any interest earned on life insurance proceeds is taxable.

18. The answer is B. Orval must pay self-employment tax on his earnings, regardless of how he and Rainelle choose to file. Taxpayers cannot combine both spouses' income or loss to determine their earnings subject to SE tax. However, if a taxpayer has more than one business, he must combine the net profit or loss from each to determine the total earnings subject to SE tax.

19. The answer is C. Anastasia's commissions must be included in gross income, as well as advance payments in anticipation of future services ($12,000 + $1,000 = $13,000). The expense reimbursements from an accountable plan ($200) would not be included in her taxable income.

Unit 5: Investment Income and Expenses

For additional information, read:
Publication 550, *Investment Income and Expenses*
Instructions for Schedule B

The Tax Cuts and Jobs Act (TCJA) brought several important changes regarding the treatment of investment income and expenses. The TCJA did not change the rates on interest and dividends for most taxpayers, but it did change the treatment of investment income that is earned by minor children (i.e., the "kiddie tax"). This particular change significantly increased the tax rates that applied to the taxable portion of scholarships and to military survivor benefits of U.S. veterans. The SECURE Act *repealed* the TCJA's changes in the kiddie tax and is effective for tax year 2020 and beyond. We will go over the kiddie tax in more detail in a later chapter.

This unit also covers interest and dividend income. Taxpayers who deposit cash or invest in securities such as stocks, bonds, and mutual funds may earn income from interest, dividends, and capital appreciation. Other types of income from investments, such as capital gains resulting from sales, are covered later.

Interest Income

Interest is a form of income that may be earned from deposits, such as in bank and money market accounts, notes receivable, and investments in instruments such as bonds. Some interest income is taxable, and some is not.

Certain distributions, commonly referred to as dividends, are actually reported as taxable interest. These include "dividends" on deposits or share accounts in cooperative banks, credit unions, domestic savings and loan associations, and mutual savings banks. A taxpayer can also have taxable interest from certificates of deposits (CDs) and other deferred interest accounts.

Interest income is generally reported to the taxpayer on Form 1099-INT by the financial institution or another payor if the amount of interest is $10 or more for the year. Even if a taxpayer does not receive Form 1099-INT from a payor, all taxable interest income must be reported. If taxable interest income exceeds $1,500, the taxpayer must report the interest on Schedule B, *Interest and Ordinary Dividends*.

Gift for Opening a Bank Account: If a taxpayer receives noncash gifts or services for making deposits or for opening an account in a savings institution, the value of the gift may have to be reported as interest. For deposits of less than $5,000, gifts or services valued at more than $10 must be reported as interest. For deposits of $5,000 or more, gifts or services valued at more than $20 must be reported as interest. The value of the gift is determined by the financial institution.

A cash bonus for opening a new checking or credit card account is also taxable interest. However, rewards earned on credit and debit card purchases are generally not taxable interest income. The IRS generally views credit card rewards as "rebates" and not income.

They are generally not taxable, and the same is true for customer loyalty programs like grocery store discount cards, punch cards that provide a price reduction after a number of purchases, and discounts for opening a store credit card.[105]

Example: Trixie has three savings accounts in different banks. The total amount of interest earned from all her accounts is $1,950. Trixie will receive three Forms 1099-INT. She must list each payor and the amount of interest she receives from each bank on Schedule B and file it with her tax return.

Example: Matthew applies for a new credit card on January 1, 2020, through Express Airlines Visa. The card company offers a 20,000 in frequent flyer miles for spending $10,000 in the first six months. Matthew makes over $10,000 in purchases between January and April, and receives 20,000 bonus miles. The value of the bonus miles are not taxable to Matthew.

Example: Kisana earns $33,000 in wages during the year. She also earns some interest from her two savings accounts. In 2020, Kisana earns $9 in interest from the first savings account and $8 in interest from the second account. Because the amounts are below the reporting threshold, she does not receive a Form 1099-INT from either bank. The interest is still taxable and must be reported on her return. She can report the interest directly on page 1 of her Form 1040. She does not have to file a Schedule B, since the amount of interest is less than $1,500.

Interest Earned on a Certificate of Deposit

Interest earned on a certificate of deposit (CD) is generally taxable when the taxpayer receives it or is entitled to receive it without paying a penalty.

The interest a taxpayer pays on funds borrowed from a financial institution to meet the minimum deposit required for a CD, and the interest a taxpayer earns on the CD are two separate items. The taxpayer must include the total interest earned on the CD in income. If the taxpayer itemizes deductions, he can deduct the interest paid as investment interest, up to the amount of net investment income by using Form 4952, *Investment Interest Expense Deduction*.[106]

Example: Tiffany wanted to invest in a $50,000 six-month CD. She deposited $40,000 of her own money in a CD with a bank and borrowed an additional $10,000 from the same bank to make up the minimum deposit required to buy the six-month CD. The certificate of deposit earned $575 at maturity in 2020, but Tiffany actually received a net amount of $265 for the year after taking into account the $310 of interest paid to the bank. This represented the $575 Tiffany earned on the CD, minus $310 interest charged on the $10,000 loan. The bank gives Tiffany a Form 1099-INT showing the $575 interest she earned. The bank also gives Tiffany a statement showing that she paid $310 in investment interest during the year. Tiffany must include the total interest amount that she earned, $575, in her gross income for the year. She can deduct the interest expense of $310 only if she itemizes deductions on Schedule A.

---

105 IRS Announcement 2002-18 addresses frequent flyer miles and promotional card benefits.

106 The TCJA temporarily suspends miscellaneous itemized deductions subject to 2%-of-AGI, which includes the deduction for investment expenses. Other examples include: safe deposit fees, trustee fees, and investment advisor fees. However, the TCJA did *not* repeal the deduction for investment interest expense. Investment *interest* expense is any interest incurred on loans used to purchase taxable investments.

Tax-Exempt Interest

Interest earned on debt obligations of state and local governments (also commonly called *muni bonds* or *municipal bonds*) is generally exempt from federal income tax but may be subject to income taxes by state and local governments. However, interest on federally guaranteed state and local obligations is generally taxable.

Also, even if interest on an obligation is nontaxable, the taxpayer may need to report a capital gain or loss when the investment is sold. The taxpayer's Form(s) 1099-INT may include both taxable and tax-exempt interest. Tax-exempt interest must be reported on Form 1040, even though it is not taxable.

Example: Tacitus is a software programmer who earns $109,000 in wages during the year. He also received $2,950 in municipal bond interest. The bond interest was reported to him on Form 1099-INT. Tacitus must report his wages as well as the full amount of the bond interest on his tax return, but the interest is not taxable.

Interest on U.S. Treasury Bills, Notes, and Bonds

Interest on U.S. obligations, such as U.S. Treasury bills, notes, and bonds issued by any agency of the United States, is normally taxable for federal income tax purposes. The **Series EE bond** is the most common type of U.S. savings bond. These bonds are issued at a discount, and the difference between the purchase price and the amount received when the bonds are later redeemed (or "cashed in") is interest income.

Series I bonds are issued at face value with a maturity period of thirty years. The face value and accrued interest are payable at maturity. Individual taxpayers can generally report interest income from a Series EE or Series I savings bond either:

- When the bond matures or is redeemed (whichever occurs first), or
- Each year as the bond's redemption value increases.

However, a taxpayer must use the same reporting method for all the Series EE and Series I bonds he owns. When a taxpayer redeems savings bonds, he should receive a Form 1099-INT from the bank or another payor.

The Education Savings Bond Program

A taxpayer may be able to exclude interest from income all or part of the interest they receive on the redemption of qualified U.S. savings bonds during the year if they pay qualified higher-education expenses during the same year. The expenses must be for the taxpayer, a spouse, or dependents. This exclusion is known as the *Education Savings Bond Program.*

The taxpayer must use both the principal *and* interest to pay for qualified education expenses. If the amount of savings bonds cashed during the year exceeds the amount of qualified educational expenses paid during the year, the amount of excludable interest is reduced.

To exclude interest earnings on Series EE and Series I bonds, a taxpayer must be at least twenty-four years old before the bond's issue date. Certain rules must be followed for the educational exclusion to qualify:

- The bonds must be purchased by the owner. They cannot be a gift, although the bond proceeds can be used to pay the tuition expenses of a dependent child.
- Qualified higher-education expenses must be reduced by certain tax-free benefits received and by expenses used to claim the American Opportunity and Lifetime Learning credits.
- The total interest received may be excluded only if the combined amounts of the principal and the interest received do not exceed the taxpayer's qualified higher education expenses.

Example: Sonya is 29 and a full-time college student. She redeemed several education savings bonds in 2020 to pay for her college expenses. The total bond proceeds were $10,000 ($8,000 principal and $2,000 in bond interest). Sonya's qualified educational expenses were only $8,000. She used the remaining $2,000 to make a down payment on a new car. Therefore, since Sonya used only 80% of the bond proceeds for qualified expenses, she can only exclude 80% of the bond interest. The excludable portion would equal $1,600 (80% x $2,000 bond interest = $1,600). She would pay tax on the remaining $400 of bond interest.

Married taxpayers who file separately (MFS) do not qualify for the education savings bond interest exclusion. If a taxpayer cashes an education savings bond during the year and then files MFS, all the interest would be taxable, regardless of whether or not the taxpayer had qualifying education expenses.

Example: Isaiah is married but files separately from his wife. In 2020, Isaiah cashed out qualified Series EE U.S. savings bonds. He received proceeds of $7,520, representing principal of $5,000, and interest income of $2,520. Isaiah paid $11,000 of college tuition for his graduate program using the bond proceeds. Normally, Isaiah would be able to exclude all the bond interest from his taxable income. However, since he is filing MFS, all the interest is taxable.

For the purposes of this exclusion, qualified educational expenses include:

- College tuition and fees (such as lab fees and other required course expenses), except for expenses for any course or other education program involving sports, games, or hobbies that are not part of a degree program.
- Expenses paid for any course required as part of a degree or certificate program.

Note: The costs of room and board, as well as required textbooks, are *not* eligible expenses for the savings bond interest exclusion. However, the cost of required textbooks *is* a qualified educational expense for the purposes of the Lifetime Learning Credit and the American Opportunity Credit.

The amount of qualified expenses is reduced by the amount of any scholarships, fellowships, employer-provided educational assistance, and other forms of tuition reduction. The exclusion is calculated and reported on Form 8815, *Exclusion of Interest from Series EE and I U.S. Savings Bonds Issued After 1989.*

Dividend Income

A dividend is a distribution of cash, stock, or other property from a corporation or a mutual fund. Most corporations pay dividends in cash. The payor will generally use Form 1099-DIV to

report dividend income to taxpayers. If a taxpayer does not receive Form 1099-DIV from a payor, the taxpayer must still report all taxable dividend income. Generally, if a taxpayer's total dividend income is more than $1,500, it must be reported on Schedule B, *Interest and Ordinary Dividends.* Otherwise, it can be reported directly on Form 1040.

Dividends are not subject to employment taxes. In 2020, the top rate on long-term capital gains[107] and qualified dividends of 20% remains in effect. This means that the maximum tax rate for qualified dividends is 20%, regardless of the taxpayer's individual tax bracket. However, many higher-income taxpayers may also be subject to the Net Investment Income Tax on long-term capital gains and qualified dividends (the NIIT is covered in detail later).

Example: Aiden earned $590,000 in wages in 2020. This puts him in the highest marginal tax bracket, at 37%. Aiden also earned $120,000 in qualified dividends from various investments. The dividends will be taxed at 20%, a much lower rate, and the dividends are also not subject to employment taxes. However, Aiden will be subject to the Net Investment Income Tax (NIIT) on a portion of his income because his gross income is over the threshold amount

Ordinary Dividends: Ordinary dividends are corporate distributions in cash (as opposed to property or stock shares) that are paid to shareholders out of earnings and profits. Unless they are qualified dividends, they are taxed at ordinary income tax rates rather than at lower long-term capital gain rates. Ordinary dividends are reported in Box 1a of Form 1099-DIV.

Qualified Dividends: Whereas ordinary dividends are taxable as ordinary income, qualified dividends that meet certain requirements are taxed at lower capital gain rates if specific criteria are met. Short-term capital gains and ordinary dividends are taxed at ordinary income rates. The top rates for qualified dividends and long-term capital gains are as follows:[108]

Marginal Rate	Single	HOH	MFJ/ QW	MFS	Estates and trusts
0%	$0–$40,000	$0–$53,600	$0–$80,000	$0 - $40,000	$0 - $2,650
15%	$40,001– $441,450	$53,601 - $469,050	$80,001 - $496,600	$40,001 - $248,300	$2,651 - $13,150
20%	Over $441,450	Over $469,050	Over $496,600	Over $248,300	Over $13,150

Qualified dividends are reported to the taxpayer in Box 1b of Form 1099-DIV. In order for the dividends to qualify for these preferred tax rates, the following are the two most common requirements that must be met:

- The dividends must be paid by a U.S. corporation or qualified foreign corporation,[109] and
- The taxpayer generally must have held the stock for *more than sixty days* during the 121-day period that begins sixty days before the ex-dividend date.

---

[107] Note that *short-term* capital gains, which are generated by the sale of investments held for one year or less, are taxed at the individual taxpayer's ordinary income rate. This is why the holding period is so important. We will discuss the holding period in more detail later.

[108] A maximum 28% capital gain tax applies specifically to collectibles in 2020.

[109] A "qualified foreign corporation" for the purposes of this rule is generally a foreign corporation whose stock is traded on a U.S. stock exchange or if a tax treaty between the U.S. and the foreign country of the corporation allows for qualified dividend status.

When figuring the holding period for qualified dividends, the taxpayer may count the number of days he held the stock, with the first day being the day after the stock was acquired (the date the taxpayer acquires the stock is not included in the holding period), and include the day he disposed of the stock.

A longer holding period may apply for dividends paid on preferred stock. The "ex-dividend date" is the date a shareholder will no longer be entitled to receive the most recently declared dividend (typically the day following the record date).[110]

Nondividend Distributions: Distributions that are not paid out of earnings and profits are nondividend distributions. They are considered a recovery or return of capital and therefore are generally not taxable. However, these distributions reduce the taxpayer's basis in the stock of the corporation. Once the basis is reduced to zero, any additional distributions are capital gains and are taxed as such. Nondividend distributions are reported in Box 3 of Form 1099-DIV.

Money market funds: Money market funds pay dividends and are offered by nonbank financial institutions, such as mutual funds and stock brokerage houses. Generally, amounts received from money market funds should be reported as dividends, not as interest.

Stock Dividends and Stock Distributions

A stock dividend is a distribution of stock, rather than money, by a corporation to its own shareholders. A stock dividend is generally not a taxable event and does not affect the shareholder's income in the year of distribution because he is not actually receiving any money, and all shareholders increase their total number of shares pro-rata. When a stock dividend is granted, the total basis of the shareholder's stock is not affected, but the basis of individual shares is adjusted by the inclusion of the newly-issued shares.

Example: Dragon Corporation declares a year-end stock dividend. Sharon is a shareholder in Dragon, and prior to the stock dividend, she owns 100 shares. Her basis in the shares is $5,000, or $50 per share. Sharon receives a stock dividend of 100 additional shares. After the dividend, Sharon owns 200 shares. Her overall basis in the shares does not change (it is still $5,000), but her new basis in each individual share is $25 per share ($5,000/200 = $25 per share). Sharon does not have any taxable income as a result of the stock dividend.

If a shareholder has the option to receive cash *instead* of stock, the stock dividend is taxable in the year it is distributed. The recipient of the stock must include the FMV of the newly issued stock in his gross income, and that same amount is the basis of the shares received.

Example: The Pacific Corporation declares a year-end stock dividend and gives its shareholders the option of receiving cash instead of stock. Therefore, the stock dividend becomes a taxable event. Before the dividend, Danton owns 1,000 shares in Pacific Corp., and his basis in the shares is $10,000, or $10 per share. Danton decides to take the stock instead of cash and receives an additional 100 shares. The FMV of the stock at the time of the distribution is $15 per share. Danton must recognize $1,500 of income ($15 FMV × 100 shares = $1,500), which also is his basis in the new shares.

[110] The "ex-dividend date" is the day on which a corporation's shares that are bought and sold no longer come attached with the right to receive the most recently declared dividend. This is important, because if a taxpayer purchases stock *after* its ex-dividend date, the taxpayer who bought the shares will not receive the next dividend payment. Instead, the seller of the stock receives the dividend.

Dividend Reinvestment Plans (DRIP)

A dividend reinvestment plan allows a taxpayer to use their dividends to purchase more shares of stock in a corporation instead of receiving dividends in cash. If the taxpayer uses his dividends to buy more stock at a price equal to its fair market value, he must still report the dividends as income.

Some plans also allow taxpayers to invest cash to buy shares of stock at a price less than fair market value. In this case, the taxpayer must report as dividend income the difference between the cash he invests and the FMV of the stock he purchases.

Example: Francesca owns 100 shares of Diamond Corporation, which is currently trading at $50 a share on the open market. Through Diamond's dividend reinvestment plan, Francesca buys 50 additional shares at $40 per share. She must report $500 as dividend income ($10 per share difference between FMV and purchase price multiplied by 50 shares).

Mutual Fund Distributions

A mutual fund is an investment strategy that allows investors to pool their money to invest in stocks, bonds, and other securities. The combined holdings of stocks, bonds, or other assets the fund owns are known as its "portfolio." Mutual funds are professionally managed by a portfolio manager. Mutual funds generally distribute all of their ordinary income to shareholders by the end of the year to obtain favorable tax treatment.

A taxpayer who receives mutual fund distributions during the year will also receive Form 1099-DIV, identifying the types of distributions received.

Mutual fund distributions are reported based upon the character of the income source and may include ordinary dividends, qualified dividends, capital gain distributions, exempt-interest dividends, and nondividend distributions. Ordinary dividends are the most common type of distribution from a mutual fund; these dividends are taxable as ordinary income.

Capital gain distributions from a mutual fund are always treated as long-term, regardless of the actual period the mutual fund investment is held. Distributions from a mutual fund investing in tax-exempt securities are tax-exempt interest and retain their tax-exempt character for the payee. Even so, the taxpayer must report them on his tax return.

If a mutual fund or Real Estate Investment Trust (REIT) declares a dividend payable to shareholders in October, November, or December, but actually pays the dividend during January of the following year, the shareholder is considered to have received the dividend on December 31 of the prior tax year and must report the dividend in the year it was declared.

Example: Alessandro has money invested in Great Shares Mutual Fund. The fund declared a $230 dividend on December 27, 2020. Alessandro did not actually receive the dividend until the following year, on January 6, 2021. Alessandro must report the dividend in 2020. The dividend is taxable in the year *declared*, regardless of whether Alessandro withdraws the dividends or reinvests them.

Constructive Distributions/Dividends

Certain transactions between a corporation and its shareholders may be regarded as constructive distributions. In general, constructive distributions (also called "constructive dividends") are assessed under audit, and they can have very negative consequences for the company as well as to the shareholder. They may be considered dividends and therefore taxable to the shareholders and non-deductible to the corporation. Examples of constructive distributions include:

- **Payment of personal expenses:** If a corporation pays personal expenses on behalf of an employee-shareholder, the amounts should be classified as a distribution, rather than expenses of the corporation.
- **Unreasonable compensation:** If a corporation pays an employee-shareholder an unreasonably high salary considering the services actually performed, the excessive part of the salary may be treated as a distribution.
- **Unreasonable rents:** If a corporation rents property from a shareholder and the rent is unreasonably higher than the shareholder would charge an unrelated party for the use of the property, the excessive part of the rent may be treated as a distribution. Conversely, if a corporation rents property to a shareholder and the rent is unreasonably low, the discounted portion of the rent could be treated as a distribution as well.
- **Cancellation of a shareholder's debt:** If a corporation cancels a shareholder's debt without repayment by the shareholder, the amount canceled may be treated as a distribution.
- **Property transfers for less than FMV:** If a corporation transfers or sells property to a shareholder for less than its FMV, the excess may be treated as a distribution.
- **Below market or interest-free loans**: If a corporation gives a loan to a shareholder on an interest-free basis or at a rate below the applicable federal rate, the uncharged interest may be treated as a distribution.

Example: Erika's father owns 95% of Spitfire Motorsports, Inc., and she and her siblings own the remaining 5%. Erika performs administrative assistant duties on a part-time basis for the corporation and is paid a salary of $700,000 a year. The corporation also pays for various personal expenses Erika incurs, such as monthly payments on the car she uses to commute to work. The IRS would likely consider Erika's salary as unreasonably high based on the nature of her duties, meaning that a portion of the salary and the personal expenses would be reclassified as constructive distributions. If that happens, then the constructive distribution becomes taxable to Erika as a taxable dividend, and the amounts are no longer deductible by the corporation as a business expense.

Unit 5: Study Questions

(Test yourself first, then check the correct answers at the end of this quiz.)

1. Constance is using educational savings bonds to help pay her college expenses. Which of the following is a "qualified expense" for the educational savings bond exclusion?

A. College tuition.
B. Room and board.
C. Required textbooks.
D. Student health fees.

2. Which of the following dividends should be reported as interest income on a taxpayer's return?

A. Stock dividends.
B. Preferred dividends.
C. Dividends earned on deposits in credit unions.
D. Qualified dividends.

3. Six years ago, Derrick bought a U.S. Series EE savings bond and decided to report the interest earned each year until maturity. This year, he bought *another* Series EE savings bond. How should Derrick report the interest on this new bond?

A. He must wait until the second bond matures to report all the interest earned at that time.
B. He must report the interest earned each year until maturity.
C. He can use either method to report interest earned, as long as he makes the election on a timely filed return.
D. This type of interest is now exempt from federal income tax.

4. Bastien received a Form 1099-DIV from his brokerage firm, showing that he earned $1,200 of ordinary dividends in 2020. He received no other dividends during the year. How should this income be handled on Bastien's tax return?

A. He must report the dividend income on Schedule B, but it is not taxable.
B. He must report the dividend income on Schedule D.
C. He can report the dividend income on page one of his Form 1040, taxable as ordinary income.
D. He does not have to report the dividend income until he sells the stock from the corporations that distributed the dividends.

5. Nondividend distributions are:

A. Considered a return of capital.
B. Never taxable.
C. Always taxable as ordinary income.
D. Always taxable as passive income.

6. A taxpayer must generally have held stock for ________ in order for his dividend income to be considered "qualified dividends."

A. More than 30 days during the 121-day period that begins 60 days before the ex-dividend date.
B. More than 60 days during the 121-day period that begins 60 days before the ex-dividend date.
C. More than 120 days.
D. More than one year.

7. Delbert is a 5% shareholder of a family-owned C corporation, Archetype Builders, Inc., where he works as a full-time architect. Archetype Builders, Inc. pays for many expenses for the benefit of Delbert. Which of the following would the IRS likely classify as a constructive distribution?

A. Use of a company copy machine for making occasional personal copies.
B. Payment of licenses, dues, and memberships directly related to his job.
C. Dental insurance premiums paid by the corporation through a cafeteria plan.
D. Payment of Delbert's monthly gym membership by the corporation.

8. All of the following statements about dividends are correct *except*:

A. A taxpayer will pay a higher tax rate on an ordinary dividend than on a qualified dividend.
B. A taxpayer will pay a higher tax rate on a qualified dividend than on an ordinary dividend.
C. The ex-dividend date is the date a shareholder will no longer be entitled to receive the most recently declared dividend (normally right after the record date).
D. When figuring the holding period for qualified dividends, the taxpayer may count the number of days he held the stock (starting the day after the stock was acquired) and include the day he disposed of the stock.

9. All of the following statements about stock dividends are correct except:

A. When a stock dividend is distributed, the basis of the stockholder's existing shares is adjusted to reflect the issuance of the new shares.
B. A stock dividend occurs when a corporation distributes stock to its own shareholders.
C. A taxpayer generally recognizes income only when he sells the stock received in a stock dividend distribution.
D. A stock dividend is never taxable, even if a taxpayer has the choice to receive cash instead of stock.

10. Araceli received $500 of interest from municipal bonds issued by the state of New Jersey. How should she report this on her Form 1040?

A. It must be reported on her tax return, but it is not taxable income.
B. It must be reported as interest income, and it is 100% taxable.
C. She does not have to report the bond interest.
D. She must report the interest on her state tax return, but it does not have to be reported on her federal return.

11. Miguel deposited $4,000 of his own funds and also borrowed $12,000 from the bank to buy a nine-month certificate of deposit for $16,000. The certificate earned $375 at maturity in 2020, and Miguel received $175, which represented the $375 he earned minus $200 of interest charged on the $12,000 loan. The bank gives Miguel a Form 1099-INT showing the $375 interest he earned. The bank also gives him a statement showing that he paid $200 of interest. How should Miguel report these amounts on his tax return?

A. He should report $175 of interest income.
B. He should report $375 of interest income. The $200 of interest he paid to the bank is not deductible.
C. He should report $375 of interest income and can deduct $200 on his Schedule A, subject to the net investment income limit.
D. He does not have to report any income from this transaction.

12. Leonardo invested in a mutual fund during the year. The fund declared a dividend on December 20, 2020, and Leonardo received the $19 dividend distribution on January 2, 2021. He did not receive a Form 1099-DIV for the amount, and he did not withdraw the money from his mutual fund. Leonardo sold his investment in the mutual fund on January 19, 2021. Which of the following statements is correct?

A. The dividend is not reportable in 2020 because Leonardo did not withdraw the earnings.
B. The dividend is not reportable in 2020 because Leonardo did not receive a 1099-DIV.
C. The dividend is taxable and must be reported in 2020.
D. The dividend is taxable but does not have to be reported until 2021.

13. Marcelo opened a savings account at his local bank and deposited $800. The account earned $20 interest during the year. On his credit card account, Marcelo received $100 worth of reward points for charging $10,000 of purchases, which he used to pay a portion of his credit card bill. How much interest income must Marcelo report on his Form 1040?

A. $20
B. $75
C. $120
D. $900

Unit 5: Quiz Answers

1. The answer is A. Constance can use the amounts to pay her college tuition, but none of the other expenses are eligible for the savings bond exclusion. The savings bond education tax exclusion permits qualified taxpayers to exclude from their gross income all or part of the interest paid upon the redemption of eligible Series EE and I Bonds. Eligible educational expenses include tuition and required fees. The costs of room and board, as well as required textbooks, are *not* eligible expenses for the educational savings bond exclusion.

2 The answer is C. The dividends earned on deposits in credit unions are reported as interest income rather than dividend income.

3. The answer is B. Derrick must report the interest earned each year until maturity. Savings bond owners must use the same interest-reporting method for all the Series EE and Series I bonds they own.

4. The answer is C. Ordinary dividends are taxable as ordinary income in the year they are earned. Only amounts over $1,500 must be reported on Schedule B, so Bastien can report the $1,200 of dividend income directly on page one of his Form 1040.

5. The answer is A. Nondividend distributions are not paid out of a corporation's earnings and profits. They are considered a recovery or return of capital and therefore are generally not taxable. However, these distributions reduce the taxpayer's basis in the stock of the corporation. Once the basis in the stock is reduced to zero, any additional nondividend distributions are taxed as capital gains.

6. The answer is B. A taxpayer must generally have held stock for more than 60 days during the 121-day period that begins 60 days before the ex-dividend date. The ex-dividend date is the date a shareholder will no longer be entitled to receive the most recently declared dividend. When figuring the holding period for qualified dividends, the taxpayer may count the number of days he held the stock and include the day he disposed of the stock. The date the taxpayer acquires the stock is not included in the holding period. A longer holding period may apply for dividends paid on preferred stock.

7. The answer is D. The payment of personal expenses on behalf of an employee-shareholder is treated as a constructive distribution. In this case, the payment of his monthly gym membership is likely to be reclassified as a taxable dividend to Delbert or a nondividend distribution, depending upon whether the corporation has earnings and profits. Choice C is incorrect because dental and medical benefits paid by an employer are an allowable employee benefit. Answer A is incorrect because the use of a company copier is an allowable de minimis fringe benefit. See Publication 5137, *Fringe Benefit Guide,* for more information.

8. The answer is B. Ordinary dividends are taxed at higher ordinary income rates than qualified dividends. If certain conditions are met, qualified dividends are given preferred tax treatment.

Qualified dividends must have been paid by a U.S. corporation or a qualified foreign corporation, and the taxpayer generally must have held the stock for more than sixty days during the 121-day period that begins sixty days before the ex-dividend date.

9. The answer is D. If a taxpayer is given a choice between receiving cash or stock, a stock dividend is taxable in the year it is distributed.

10. The answer is A. Although the interest is not taxable, Araceli must still report the income on her federal return. Interest earned on state and local bonds (municipal bonds or "muni" bonds) are generally tax-exempt at the federal level. Note that these bonds may be taxable at the state and local level, even if they are not taxable at the federal level.

11. The answer is C. Miguel must include the total amount of interest earned, $375, in his income. If he itemizes deductions on Schedule A, he can deduct $200 of interest expense, subject to the net investment income limit. He may not report the investment income and expenses on a net basis (i.e., the taxable interest income less the allowable deduction).

12. The answer is C. Leonardo is deemed to have earned the dividends in 2020, and whether or not he received a 1099-DIV is irrelevant. Mutual fund dividends are taxable regardless of whether the taxpayer withdraws the dividends or reinvests them. Furthermore, if dividends from a mutual fund (or REIT) are declared in October, November, or December and paid no later than January of the following year, the dividends are taxable in the year declared, even though they are not paid until the following year, so Leonardo must report the earnings in 2020.

13. The answer is A. If no other interest is credited to Marcelo during the year, the Form 1099-INT he receives will show $20 of interest for the year. The IRS does not count reward points or cashback from a credit card as taxable interest income, (it is treated as a rebate), so Marcelo does not have to report the $100 in rewards points or pay any tax on it.

Unit 6: Calculating the Basis of Assets

For additional information, read:
Publication 551, *Basis of Assets*
Publication 544, *Sales and Other Dispositions of Assets*

Much of tax law deals with the taxation of assets. In order to calculate gains and losses from the sale or other disposition of an asset, you need to be able to properly *classify* the asset first. There are two main types of assets: real property and personal property.

"Real property" is real estate. Real property includes land and anything permanently attached to it. Examples include: buildings, farmland, personal homes, commercial buildings, residential rentals, and subsurface mineral rights.

"Personal property" is *anything other* than real estate. Personal property includes: furniture, equipment, vehicles, household goods, collectibles, and even livestock. It also includes intangible assets, such as corporate stock, trademarks, cryptocurrency,[111] and copyrights. The tax treatment of an asset also varies based on whether the asset is personal-use, business property, or investment property.

Note: Do not get the term "personal property" confused with "personal-use property." The term "personal property" is an accounting and legal term which describes all movable assets, whether they are used in a business or not. "Personal-use" property refers to any property that is used *personally* by the taxpayer and *not* used in a trade, business, or for investment.

Basis in General

To correctly calculate gains and losses, you must also understand the concept of "basis." The initial basis of an asset is usually its cost. However, there are instances in which basis is determined based upon the fair market value of the asset when acquired by the taxpayer, rather than its cost, typically when property is acquired by inheritance and sometimes by gift. The basis of an asset may include:

- Sales taxes charged during the purchase
- Freight-in charges and shipping fees
- Installation costs and testing fees
- Delinquent real estate taxes that are paid by the buyer of a property
- The cost of any major improvements to the property
- Legal and accounting fees for transferring an asset
- Legal fees for obtaining title to a property

All of these costs will *increase* an asset's basis. The result of these adjustments to the basis is the "adjusted" basis.

[111] As of 2020, the IRS views cryptocurrency, or virtual currency, as "property" and not as currency. The IRS deems cryptocurrency to be a capital asset in most situations, and gains or losses on the sale of cryptocurrency are normally capital in nature.

Example: Patrick paid $7,800 for an attorney's services in a title dispute for a parcel of farmland that he purchased earlier in the year. The farmland originally cost $45,000. The legal fees are added to the farmland's basis. Therefore, Patrick's adjusted basis in the farmland is $52,800 ($45,000 cost + $7,800 legal fees).

Example: Edwin purchases a new car for $15,000. The sales tax on the vehicle is $1,200. He also pays a delivery charge to have the car shipped from a dealership in another state to his home. The delivery charge is $210. Therefore, Edwin's basis in the vehicle is $16,410 ($15,000 + $1,200 + $210).

Example: Della is a self-employed writer. She purchases a new printer for her home office. The printer costs $540 with an additional $34 for sales tax. Therefore, Della's basis in the printer is $574 ($540 + $34).

Example: Calix buys a house for $120,000. Four months after he closes the sale, he paves the driveway, which costs $6,000. Calix's adjusted basis in the home is now $126,000 ($120,000 original cost + $6,000 for major improvements).

Study Note: Understanding basis and how it is applied to various types of property is critical to your success in passing Part 1 *and* Part 2 of the EA exam. You may be expected to calculate basis in multiple scenarios.

Depreciation Deduction

Depreciation is an income tax deduction that allows a business to recover the cost or basis of property used in the business over time. Depreciation *decreases* the basis of an asset, usually over several years.

Depreciation is an annual allowance for the wear and tear, deterioration, or obsolescence of assets. The amount allowed as an annual depreciation deduction is intended to roughly approximate the reduction in the value of assets as they age. Property ceases to be depreciable when the business has fully recovered the property's tax basis, or when the taxpayer sells or retires it from service, whichever happens first.

Some types of property, such as land, cannot be depreciated. Most other types of tangible property, such as buildings, machinery, vehicles, furniture, and equipment, are depreciable.

Study Note: Depreciation is an important accounting concept, so it is tested most often on *Part 2: Businesses* of the EA exam. For Part 1 of the EA exam, test-takers must understand depreciation primarily in the context of residential rental property.

Holding Period

An asset's holding period determines whether a gain or loss will be long-term or short-term. An asset's holding period begins on the day after it is purchased or acquired and ends on the day of its sale or disposition. When an asset is sold, the difference between the asset's basis and the selling price may be a taxable gain or loss. Sometimes, when an asset is disposed of or sold, no gain or loss is recognized until a later date.

In order to correctly report a taxable gain or loss related to the disposition of an asset, a taxpayer needs to identify:

- Whether the asset is personal-use or used for business or investment;
- The asset's basis or adjusted basis:
    - As described above, the initial basis of an asset is usually its purchase cost, including certain ancillary charges.
    - Adjusted basis includes the original basis plus any increases or decreases resulting from events, transactions, or tax benefits that occur after the original purchase or acquisition by the taxpayer (such as subsequent improvements, depreciation deductions, casualty losses, rebates, and insurance reimbursements).
- The asset's holding period:
    - *Short-term* property is held for one year or less.
    - *Long-term* property is held for more than one year (at least a year, plus one day).[112]
- The proceeds from the sale.

Basis of Real Property (Real Estate)

The basis of real estate usually includes a number of costs in addition to the purchase price. If a taxpayer purchases real property (such as land or a building), certain fees and other expenses are automatically included in the cost basis. The transaction might include real estate taxes the *seller* owed at the time of the purchase. If delinquent real estate taxes are paid by the buyer, those amounts must be added to the property's basis.

Example: Solange sells Anthony a home for $125,000. She had fallen behind on her property tax payments, so Anthony agrees to pay $3,500 of delinquent real estate taxes as a condition of the sale. Because a taxpayer is not allowed to deduct property taxes that are not his legal responsibility, Anthony must add the property taxes paid to his basis. Anthony's basis in the home is $128,500 ($125,000 + $3,500).

If a property is constructed rather than purchased, the basis of the property includes all the expenses of construction. This includes the cost of payments to contractors, building materials, and inspection fees. Demolition costs and other costs related to the *preparation* of land prior to construction must be added to the basis of the land, rather than to any buildings constructed on it later.

Example: Dianne pays $50,000 for an empty lot where she plans to build her home. She also pays $2,800 for the removal of tree stumps and $6,700 to demolish an existing concrete foundation on the lot. These costs must be added to the basis of the land, not to the basis of the future house. Therefore, Dianne's basis in the land is $59,500 ($50,000 + $2,800 + $6,700).

If raw land is purchased on its own, the basis includes the purchase price plus any legal and recording fees, abstract fees, and land survey costs.

---

[112] Long-term capital gains are given more favorable tax treatment. Although most assets have to be held for over one year in order to be treated as "long term" an exception applies to assets acquired through inheritance, which we will cover later.

Settlement Costs: Generally, a taxpayer must include settlement costs for the purchase of property in his basis. The following fees are some of the closing costs that can be included in a property's basis:

- Abstract fees
- Charges for installing utilities
- Legal fees (including title search and preparation of the deed)
- Recording fees and land surveys
- Transfer taxes
- Owner's title insurance

Also included in a property's basis are any other amounts the seller legally owes that the buyer agrees to pay, such as recording or mortgage fees, charges for improvements or repairs, and sales commissions. However, a taxpayer cannot include fees incidental to getting a loan in the basis of the property financed with proceeds from the loan.

Settlement costs do not include any amounts placed in escrow for the future payment of items such as taxes and insurance.

Basis of Securities

A taxpayer's basis in securities (such as stocks or bonds) is usually the purchase price plus any additional costs (e.g., brokers' commissions, settlement fees).

When a taxpayer sells securities, his investment broker should provide the taxpayer with Form 1099-B, *Proceeds from Broker and Barter Exchange Transactions,* showing the proceeds of the sale. The IRS also receives a copy of Form 1099-B.

If Form 1099-B does not identify a taxpayer's basis in the sold securities, the taxpayer must provide this information from his own records. If a taxpayer cannot provide evidence of his basis in an asset sold, the IRS may deem the basis to be zero.

A taxpayer may own more than one block of shares in a particular company's stock. Each block may differ from the others in its holding period (long-term or short-term), its basis, or both. When directing a broker to sell stock, a taxpayer may specify which block, or part of a block, to sell; this is called *specific identification*. The specific identification method requires good recordkeeping. However, it simplifies the determination of the holding period, and the basis of stock sold and gives the taxpayer better control over the recognition of gains and/or losses when selling part of an investment. If the taxpayer cannot identify a specific block at the time of sale, shares sold are treated as coming from the earliest block purchased. This method is called First In, First Out (FIFO).

Example: Sharleen buys two blocks of 400 shares of stock (800 shares total). She buys 400 shares on May 1, 2014, for $11,200 and an additional 400 shares two months later for $11,600. On September 10, 2020, she sells 400 shares for $11,500 without specifying which block of shares she is selling. The sold shares are therefore treated as coming from the *earliest* block purchased (those purchased in May 2014). Since the basis and holding period defaults to the *original* block of shares, Sharleen realizes a long-term capital gain of $300 ($11,500 - $11,200).

Note: The IRS requires stockbrokers and mutual fund companies to report the basis for most stock sold. The reporting is made to investors and to the IRS. You must understand how to calculate the basis of securities because this subject is frequently tested on Part 1 of the exam.

Events that occur after the purchase of stock can require adjustments (increases or decreases) to the basis per individual share.

For example, the original basis per share can be changed by events such as stock dividends and stock splits. Stock dividends and stock splits usually are not taxable events. However, a stock dividend may be taxable when shareholders have the option to receive cash or other property instead of stock.

- **Stock dividends** are additional shares a company grants to its shareholders in lieu of paying cash dividends and are often nontaxable. When nontaxable, these additional shares increase the number of shares owned by an individual shareholder, so his original basis is spread over more shares, which decreases the basis per individual share. The total basis of all the shares remains the same.
- A **stock split** is similar to a stock dividend and occurs when a company issues additional shares of stock for every existing share an investor holds. Stock splits are a way for a company to lower the market price of its stock. The stock's market capitalization, however, remains the same. For example, in a 2-for-1 stock split, a corporation issues one share of stock for every share outstanding. This decreases a shareholder's basis per individual share by half. An original basis of $200 for 100 shares becomes $200 for 200 shares in a 2-for-1 stock split. However, the total basis in the stock remains the same even though the basis per share decreases.

Example: Leticia pays $1,050 for 100 shares of stock, plus a broker's commission of $50. Her basis in the 100 shares is $1,100 ($1,050 original cost + $50 broker's commission), or $11 per share ($1,100/100). Leticia later receives 10 additional shares of stock as a nontaxable stock dividend. Her $1,100 basis must be spread over 110 shares (100 original shares plus the ten-share stock dividend). Her basis per share decreases to $10 ($1,100/110).

Example: Irwin buys 100 shares of Cortex, Inc. for $50 per share. His cost basis is $50 × 100 shares or $5,000. Six months later, Cortex, Inc. declares a 2-for-1 stock split, and Irwin receives 100 additional shares of stock. Therefore, his new basis in each individual stock is $25 = ($5,000 ÷ [100 + 100]). His total basis in the shares remains $5,000.

Stock Options

A taxpayer may purchase *options* to buy or sell securities (such as stocks or commodities) through an exchange or in the open market. He may realize a gain or loss from the sale or trade of an option itself, or he may exercise the option to buy or sell the underlying securities and realize a gain or loss from the disposition of those securities.

Companies may also grant options to their employees, as compensation for their service and as an incentive that allows them to purchase the company's stock at a later date. Companies like to offer stock options to their employees, because the options can be offered as part of an equity

compensation plan. Stock options can be used to motivate employees and generate loyalty, as well as reduce employee turnover.

If an employee receives stock options, he may have income when the options are granted, when he exercises them (to buy the company's stock), or when he sells or otherwise disposes of the options or the stock. In general, there are two types of stock options:

- Options granted under an employee stock purchase plan (ESPP) or an incentive stock option (ISO) plan are **statutory stock options.**
- Stock options that are granted neither under an employee stock purchase plan or an ISO plan are **nonstatutory stock options.**[113]

The nature, timing, and amount of income that needs to be reported by the taxpayer depends on whether the options are considered to be *statutory* or *nonstatutory* options.

The tax advantage of a *statutory* stock option is that income is not reported when the option is granted or when it is exercised. Income is only reported once the stock is ultimately sold.

Note: For Part 1 of the EA Exam, you must understand the concept of stock options from the perspective of the individual taxpayer *receiving* the options. For Part 2 of the EA Exam, you must understand stock options from the point of view of the corporation *issuing* the stock options.

Statutory Stock Options

If an employer grants an employee a statutory stock option, the employee generally does not include any amount in their gross income when they receive or exercise the option. However, a taxpayer may be subject to alternative minimum tax in the year they exercise an ISO. The employee will either have taxable income (or a deductible loss) when the employee eventually sells the stock they bought by exercising the option. The amount is treated as a capital gain or loss.

However, if the taxpayer does not meet special holding period requirements,[114] the taxpayer will have to treat income from the sale of the stock as ordinary income.

Incentive Stock Option (ISO)-After exercising an ISO, the taxpayer will receive a Form 3921, *Exercise of an Incentive Stock Option*, from their employer. This form will report important dates and values needed to determine the correct amount of capital and ordinary income (if applicable) to be reported on the employee's individual tax return.

Employee Stock Purchase Plan (ESPP) - After the employee sells stock acquired by exercising an option granted under an employee stock purchase plan, the employee will receive Form 3922, *Transfer of Stock Acquired Through an Employee Stock Purchase Plan*, from their employer.

This form will report important dates and values needed to determine the correct amount of capital and ordinary income to be reported on the employee's individual tax return.

---

[113] Refer to Publication 525, *Taxable and Nontaxable Income* for more information on the treatment of statutory or nonstatutory stock options.

[114] If the taxpayer held the stock or option for less than one year, the sale will result in a short-term gain or loss, which will be taxed as ordinary income. Options sold after *a one year or longer* holding period are considered long-term capital gains or losses.

Example: Muscle Fitness, Inc. has an employee stock purchase plan (ESPP). The plan allows employees to purchase company stock at a discounted price. The "option price" is the lower of the stock price at the time the option is granted, or at the time the option is exercised. Marla is an employee of Muscle Fitness, and she decides to take advantage of the ESPP that her employer provides. Muscle Fitness deducts $5 from Marla's pay every week for 48 weeks (total = $240 [$5 × 48]). The value of the stock when the option was granted was $25. When Marla exercises her options, the FMV of the stock is $20. Marla receives 12 shares of Muscle Fitness stock ($240 ÷ $20). Her holding period for all 12 shares begins the day *after* the option is exercised, even though the money used to purchase the shares was deducted from her pay on many different days. Marla's basis in each share is $20. (based on an example in Publication 525).

Basis Other Than Cost

The following are examples of situations in which an asset's basis is determined by something other than the purchase cost.

Property in Exchange for Services: If a taxpayer receives property in payment for services, he must include the property's FMV in income, and this becomes his basis in the property. If two people agree on a cost for services beforehand, the agreed-upon cost may be used to establish the amount included as income and as the asset's basis.

Example: Jeremy is a CPA who prepares tax returns for a long-time client named Maryanne. Maryanne loses her job and cannot pay Jeremy's bill, which totals $400. Maryanne offers Jeremy an antique vase instead of paying her invoice. The fair market value of the vase is approximately $525. Jeremy agrees to accept the vase as full payment on Maryanne's delinquent invoice. Jeremy's basis in the vase is $400, the amount of the invoice that was agreed upon by both parties before the barter.

Basis After Casualty Loss: If a taxpayer has a casualty loss, he increases the basis in the property by the amount spent on repairs that restore the property to its pre-casualty condition. However, he must also decrease the basis of the property by any related insurance proceeds.

Example: Duke paid $5,000 for a work truck several years ago. His truck was damaged in a severe hailstorm, so he spends $3,000 to repair it. He does not have flood insurance on the vehicle. Therefore, his new basis in the truck is $8,000 ($5,000 + $3,000).

Basis After Mortgage Assumption: If a taxpayer buys a property and assumes an existing mortgage on it, the taxpayer's basis includes the amount paid for the property plus the amount owed on the mortgage. The basis also includes the settlement fees and closing costs paid to buy the property. However, fees and costs for obtaining a loan on the property (points) are not included in a property's basis.

Example: Sabeen buys an office building for $220,000 cash, and she also assumes an existing mortgage of $800,000 on the property. Therefore, Sabeen's basis in the building is $1,020,000 ($220,000 cash + $800,000 mortgage assumption).

Basis of Property Transfers Incident to Divorce

The basis of property transferred by a spouse (or former spouse if the transfer is due to divorce) is the same as the spouse's adjusted basis. Generally, there is no gain or loss recognized on the transfer of property between spouses (or between former spouses if the transfer is because of divorce).

For property transfers related to a divorce, the transfer generally must occur within one year after the date the marriage ends. This nonrecognition rule applies even if the transfer was in exchange for cash, the release of marital rights, the assumption of liabilities, or other financial considerations.[115]

Example: Quinton and Adrienne finalized their divorce on January 23, 2020. Quinton owns a vacation home in Hawaii with a current adjusted basis of $285,000 and a fair market value of $550,000. Pursuant to their divorce agreement, Quinton agrees to transfer his ownership in the home to Adrienne. He transferred the property to Adrienne on December 1, 2020. Since the transfer was made within a year after their divorce was made final, there is no gain or loss recognized by either spouse, and no tax reporting is required. Adrienne's basis in the property is the same as Quinton's basis before the transfer: $285,000.

Example: Adelynn and Graham jointly owned an antique collector Porsche that had a basis of $50,000 and an FMV of $150,000. When they divorced in 2020, Adelynn transferred her entire interest in the automobile to Graham as part of their property settlement. Graham's basis in the vehicle is the same as their original joint basis of $50,000.

The Basis of Gifted Property

The basis of property received as a gift is determined differently than property that is purchased or inherited. The taxpayer must know the donor's adjusted basis in the property when it was gifted, its fair market value on the date of the gift, and the amount of gift tax the donor paid on it (if any). The concept of "fair market value" is important when calculating any capital gains tax liability on a gift, so it's important to know how the basis and FMV is determined.

Generally, the basis of gifted property for the donee is equal to the donor's adjusted basis. This is called a "transferred basis." For example, if a father gives his son a car and the father's basis in the car is $2,000, the basis of the vehicle remains $2,000 for the son. The holding period of the gift would also transfer to the donee.

Example: Shira's father gives her 50 shares of IBM stock that he purchased ten years ago. Her father has an adjusted basis in the stock of $1,800. Shira's basis in the stock, for purposes of determining gain on any future sale, is also $1,800 (this is a "transferred basis"). Shira is also considered to have "held" the stock for ten years, the same amount of time that her father held the stock.

However, in situations where the fair market value of the property on the date of the gift is *less* than the transferred basis, the donee's basis for *gain* is the transferred basis. However, if the donee reports a *loss* on the sale of gifted property where the fair market value of the property on

[115] A divorce, for this purpose, includes the end of a marriage by annulment or due to violations of state laws, such as bigamy.

the date of the gift is less than the transferred basis, his basis is the FMV of gifted property on the date of the gift.

The sale of gifted property can also result in no gain or loss. This happens when the sale proceeds are greater than the gift's FMV but less than the transferred basis in situations where the fair market value of the property on the date of the gift is less than the transferred basis.

Example: Orrick's aunt, Fatima, bought 100 shares of Airways Group Inc. stock when it was at $92 per share. Fatima's basis for the 100 shares is $9,200. Fatima gives the stock to Orrick when it is selling at $70 and has an FMV of $7,000 (it has lowered in value). In this case, Orrick has a "dual basis" in the stock. He has one basis for purposes of determining gain, and a different basis for determining a loss. Here are three separate scenarios that help illustrate how the gain or loss would be calculated when Orrick sells the gifted stock:

Scenario #1: If Orrick sells the stock for *more* than his aunt's basis, he will use her basis to determine his amount of gain. For example, if he sells the stock for $11,000, he will report a gain of $1,800 ($11,000 - $9,200).

Scenario #2: If Orrick sells the stock for *less* than the FMV of the stock at the time of the gift ($7,000 in the example), he will use as his basis the FMV at the time of the gift to determine the amount of his loss. For example, if the stock continues to decline, and Orrick eventually sells it for $4,500, he can report a loss of $2,500 ($7,000 - $4,500).

Scenario #3: If Orrick sells the stock for an amount *in between* the FMV and the donor's basis, no gain or loss will be recognized. For example, if Orrick sells the stock for $8,000, there will be no gain or loss on the transaction (his basis will be deemed to be $8,000, the same as his sales price).

The Basis of Inherited Property

The basis of inherited property is treated very differently for tax purposes. In most cases, the basis is the FMV of the property on the date of the decedent's death, regardless of what the deceased person paid for the property or the adjusted basis of the property right before death. In addition, when inherited property is sold by the beneficiary, it is deemed to have a long-term holding period, regardless of how long the beneficiary held it.

When inherited property is sold by a beneficiary, the gain will be calculated based on the change in value from the date of death. This usually results in a beneficial tax situation for anyone who inherits property because the taxpayer generally gets an increased or "stepped-up" basis.

Example: Rosanne's uncle bought 300 shares of stock many years ago for $850. Rosanne inherited the stock when her uncle died. On the date of his death, the stock was valued at $9,000, so Rosanne's basis is also $9,000. This is a "stepped up" basis. Roseanne later sells the stock for $11,000. She has a capital gain of $2,000 ($11,000 - $9,000).

However, there are cases in which this rule can work against taxpayers. Although the value of most property such as stocks, collectibles, and bonds generally increases over time, there are also instances in which a property's value drops. This creates a "stepped-down" basis.

Example: Norbert purchased a home with cash in Connecticut for $240,000. His neighborhood becomes riddled with crime, and Norbert's home declines in value. On February 3, 2020, Norbert dies. On the date of his death, the home's FMV was only $185,000. Norbert's daughter, Jayleen, inherits the home. Her basis in the home is $185,000. This is a "stepped-down" basis.

Example: Anson bought 100 shares of stock many years ago for $10,000. In 2020, Anson dies, and his daughter, Haley, inherits her father's stock. On the date of Anson's death, the value of the stock had plummeted to $5,000, meaning Haley's basis in the stock is "stepped down" for tax purposes to $5,000. The stock continues to decline, so six months later, she sells the stock for $4,000. Haley has a capital loss of $1,000 ($5,000 -$4,000), the difference between her inherited basis and the selling price.

Although the basis of an estate for estate tax purposes is usually determined on the date of death, a special rule allows the personal representative of the estate to elect a different valuation date of six months after the date of death. This is known as the alternate valuation date.

To elect the alternate valuation date, the estate's value and related estate tax must be *less* than they would have been on the date of the taxpayer's death. If the alternate valuation date has been elected for the estate, the basis for inherited assets is normally the fair market value of the assets six months after the date of death.

However, if any assets are received from the estate less than six months after the date of death, the basis in these inherited assets is the fair market value as of the date the asset was distributed to the heir.

If a federal estate tax return (Form 706) is not filed for the deceased taxpayer, the basis in the beneficiary's inherited property is the FMV value at the date of death, and the alternate valuation date does not apply.

Unit 6: Study Questions

(Test yourself first, then check the correct answers at the end of this quiz.)

1. Stephen purchases a truck for $15,000 to use in his carpentry business. He pays $5,000 in cash and finances the remaining $10,000 with a five-year loan. He also pays taxes and delivery costs of $1,300 and $250 to install a protective bedliner. What is Stephen's basis for depreciation of the truck?

A. $6,550
B. $10,000
C. $16,300
D. $16,550

2. Which of the following is *not* added to the basis of property?

A. Legal and accounting fees for transferring the title.
B. Points on a loan.
C. Sales tax.
D. Freight-in charges.

3. Esteban installs artificial turf at a client's home and bills the client $1,500 for his services. After the installation, his client, Alice, receives a foreclosure notice and is unable to pay Esteban's bill. Alice has a pedigreed Golden Retriever show dog that just had puppies. The FMV of each puppy is $1,800. Esteban loves animals and decides to take one of the puppies as full payment on Alice's delinquent bill. What is Esteban's basis in his new dog?

A. $0
B. $300
C. $1,500
D. $1,800

4. Mackenzie purchases an empty lot at auction for $50,000. She pays $15,000 in cash and finances the remaining $35,000 with a bank loan. The lot has a $4,000 tax lien against it for unpaid property taxes, which she also agrees to pay as a condition of the sale. What is Mackenzie's basis in the lot??

A. $19,000
B. $46,000
C. $50,000
D. $54,000

5. On February 27, 2020, Henry bought 1,000 shares of Pharma Technology, Inc. stock for $4 per share and paid an additional $70 for his broker's commission. What is Henry's overall basis in the stock?

A. $1,000
B. $3,930
C. $4,000
D. $4,070

6. The basis of inherited property is generally:

A. The adjusted basis to the decedent.
B. The fair market value of the property on the date of the decedent's death.
C. The purchase price that the decedent paid.
D. Determined nine months after the death of the decedent.

7. On January 13, 2020, Brigit purchased 1,000 shares of Arrow Energy, Inc. stock at the cost of $5,100, including the broker's commission. On August 14, 2020, she sold 500 shares for $3,300. What is the adjusted basis of the stock she *sold?*

A. $2,550
B. $3,255
C. $3,300
D. $5,100

8. Which statement is *correct* about the basis of assets?

A. The basis of an asset is always equal to its cost.
B. Depreciation increases the basis of an asset.
C. The basis rules are the same for assets received through inheritance as those obtained by gift.
D. The cost basis of an asset generally includes sales tax and other expenses connected with the original purchase.

9. Four years ago, Arnold paid $1,050 for 100 shares of Kirkner Corporation stock, including a broker's commission of $50. In 2020, Arnold received ten additional shares of Kirkner stock as a nontaxable stock dividend. What is the adjusted basis of Arnold's stock at the end of the year?

A. $9 per share.
B. $10 per share.
C. $11 per share.
D. $25 per share.

10. Julian owned one share of common stock that he bought for $45. The corporation distributed two new shares of common stock for each share held. Julian then had three shares of common stock. What is Julian's basis for each share?

A. $5
B. $15
C. $45
D. $135

11. If a taxpayer cannot determine his basis in a property and the property is sold, the IRS will deem the basis to be:

A. Zero.
B. Fair market value.
C. Actual cost.
D. Average cost.

12. During the year, Clementine bought 52 total shares of GRE Corporation stock for $624. That cost included a $40 broker commission. Two months later, GRE Corporation issued a 2-for-1 stock split. What is her basis per share after the split?

A. $6 per share.
B. $12 per share.
C. $24 per share.
D. $26 per share.

13. Which of the following must be added to the basis of a property, rather than deducted, as a current expense on a taxpayer's return?

A. Casualty loss.
B. The cost of demolishing a building.
C. Personal property tax based on the value of a car.
D. Investment interest expense.

14. Vladimir wishes to sell a home that he inherited from his mother in 2020. His mother paid $45,000 for the home ten years ago. She put a new roof on the property two years ago at a cost of $10,500. The fair market value of the home on the date of his mother's death was $120,000. An estate tax return was not required for his mother's estate, and the alternate valuation date was not elected. What is Vladimir's basis in the inherited home?

A. $34,500
B. $45,000
C. $55,500
D. $120,000

15. Yoshiko owns two shares of common stock in Kirby Toys, Inc. She bought one share for $30 in 2017 and the other for $45 in 2018. In 2020, the corporation distributed two additional shares of common stock for each share held (a 3-for-1 stock split). Yoshiko owns six shares after the stock split. How is Yoshiko's basis allocated between these six shares?

A. All six shares now have a basis of $12.50.
B. Three shares have a basis of $10 each, and three have a basis of $15 each.
C. The shares are all valued at $45 each.
D. Three shares have a basis of zero, and three shares have a basis of $30.

16. Which of the following does not *decrease* the basis of an asset?

A. Depreciation.
B. Manufacturers' rebates.
C. Theft losses.
D. Assessments for local improvements.

17. Moria owns a piece of farmland that she purchased several years ago for $250,000. The land is now worth $750,000. During the year, she borrows $500,000 from the bank to improve the property. She uses $260,000 of the loan to demolish two existing buildings on the property and clear the land for construction of a stockyard and horse stable, which will begin next year. What is Moria's basis in the land after the demolition is completed?

A. $250,000
B. $460,000
C. $510,000
D. $750,000

18. Flora gifted her grandson, Clifford, a residential rental property. She had purchased the property ten years ago for $120,000 and has claimed $18,000 in depreciation. The fair market value of the rental house on the day of transfer was $144,000. Assuming no gift tax was paid, what is Clifford's basis in the property?

A. $102,000
B. $120,000
C. $126,000
D. $144,000

Unit 6: Quiz Answers

1. The answer is D. Stephen's basis in the truck includes the cost of acquiring the property (including any taxes associated with the purchase and delivery charges) and preparing it for use (in this case, installing the bedliner). Therefore, his basis is as follows: ($15,000 + $1,300 + $250) = $16,550. Any funds that are borrowed to pay for an asset are included in the basis.

2. The answer is B. Points related to a loan used to acquire property may be deductible in the year they are paid or amortizable over the term of the loan. Points are a type of mortgage interest. They are not added to the basis of the property.

3. The answer is C. Esteban's basis in the animal is $1,500. If a taxpayer receives property as payment for services, he must include the property's FMV in income, and this becomes his basis in the property. However, if the two parties agree on a cost beforehand, the IRS will usually accept the agreed-upon cost as the asset's basis.

4. The answer is D. Mackenzie's basis is determined as follows: ($50,000 + $4,000 = $54,000). She cannot deduct the delinquent property taxes on her Schedule A. Any obligations of the seller assumed by the buyer increase the basis of the asset and are not currently deductible. Since Mackenzie did not owe the property taxes, but she still agreed to pay them, she must add the property tax to the basis of the property.

5. The answer is D. Henry's basis in the Pharma Technology, Inc. stock is $4,070 ([1,000 × $4] = $4,000 + $70).

6. The answer is B. The basis of inherited property is generally the FMV of the property on the date of the decedent's death, regardless of what the deceased person paid for the property or the tax basis in the property in the hands of the decedent right before death.

7. The answer is A. Brigit's original basis in the total stock was $5,100, which is $5.10 per share, so her basis in the 500 shares she sold is 500 × $5.10, or $2,550.

8. The answer is D. The cost basis of an asset includes sales tax and other expenses connected with the purchase. In most situations, the basis of an asset is its cost, including any sales tax, installation costs, or brokers' commissions paid. However, there are many other times when cost cannot be used to determine basis, such as when an asset is inherited or received as a gift. None of the other answers are correct.

9. The answer is B. Arnold's original basis per share was $11 ([$1,050 + $50 broker's commission = $1,100] ÷ 100). After the stock dividend, his $1,100 basis must be spread over 110 shares (100 original shares plus the additional 10 shares). Therefore, if Arnold's basis in the stock was $1,100 for 100 shares, the ten additional shares mean Arnold's basis per share decreased to $10 per share ($1,100 ÷ 110).

10. The answer is B. Julian's basis in each share is $15 ($45 ÷ 3). If a taxpayer receives a nontaxable stock dividend, he divides the adjusted basis of the stock by the total number of shares of stock (old and new). The result is the taxpayer's basis for each share of stock.

11. The answer is A. To compute gain or loss on a sale, a taxpayer must determine his basis in the property sold. If he cannot determine his basis in the property, the IRS will deem the basis to be zero.

12. The answer is A. Clementine's stock is $6 per share after the stock split. Figure the answer as follows: Initial purchase:

- 52 shares = $624 (the $40 broker commission is already included in the basis)
- 2-for-1 stock split doubles the shares to 104 total shares,
- so, $624 (original basis) ÷ 104 shares = **$6 per share.**

13. The answer is B. Demolition costs are not deductible. They must be added to the basis of the land on which the building was located. The costs increase the basis of the land, and not the basis of any subsequent building that may be constructed on the property at a later date.

14. The answer is D. Vladimir's basis in the home is $120,000, the FMV on the date of his mother's death. Heirs can generally use a stepped-up basis for inherited property, regardless of what the deceased person actually paid for the asset. The basis of inherited property is generally the FMV of the property on the date of the decedent's death. When the property is ultimately sold, the beneficiary's gain or loss will be calculated based on the change in value from the date of death.

15. The answer is B. Yoshiko's shares are now valued as follows: three with a basis of $10 each ($30 ÷ 3), and three with a basis of $15 each ($45 ÷ 3). If a taxpayer receives a nontaxable stock dividend, she must divide the adjusted basis of the old stock by the number of shares of old and new stock. The result is the taxpayer's basis for each share of stock. The basis per share after the 3-for-1 stock split is calculated by dividing the original price by 3.

16. The answer is D. The basis of property must be *increased* for tax assessments the taxpayer is required to pay to finance local improvements, such as paving roads, installing pedestrian sidewalks, and building ditches. Basis is decreased for depreciation deductions and manufacturers' rebates received, and when the taxpayer incurs theft or other casualty losses.

17. The answer is C. Moria's basis in the land is calculated as follows: $250,000 (cost basis) + $260,000 (demolition costs) = $510,000. The loan amount is irrelevant because the act of borrowing alone does not increase basis; the amount spent on the improvement of the property increases its basis.

18. The answer is A. Clifford's basis is $102,000. The basis of gifted property for the donee is generally equal to the donor's adjusted basis, which is called a "transferred basis," when its FMV exceeds the donor's basis ($120,000 minus $18,000 depreciation = $102,000) at the time of the gift. While not the case here, if the fair market value of the property on the date of the gift is *less* than the transferred basis, the donee's basis for gain is the transferred basis. However, if the donee reports a loss on the sale of gifted property when the fair market value of the property on the date of the gift is less than the transferred basis, his basis is the lower of: the transferred basis *or* the FMV of the property on the date of the gift.

Unit 7: Capital Gains and Losses

For additional information, read:
Publication 550, *Investment Income and Expenses*
Publication 523, *Selling Your Home*
Publication 544, *Sales and Other Dispositions of Assets*

Capital Assets

In the previous chapter, we discussed assets in general. In this chapter, we will discuss capital gains and losses, which occur when a taxpayer sells or disposes of a capital asset.

Many of the items a taxpayer owns and uses for personal or investment purposes are classified as "capital assets." This means that the net gains that result from their sale or disposition may be subject to tax at favorable capital gains tax rates. Examples of capital assets owned by an individual include:

- A main home or vacation home
- Furniture, a car, or a boat
- Antiques and collectibles[116]
- Stocks, bonds, and mutual funds (except when held for sale by a professional securities dealer)
- Cryptocurrency or virtual currency[117]

Note: Losses from the sale of personal-use property, such as a main home, a vacation home, personal-use furniture, or jewelry, are not deductible. However, *gains* from the sale of personal-use assets usually are taxable, subject to certain exclusions.

Example: Sanjay owns a station wagon that he uses to commute to work, run errands, and take on weekend ski trips. He purchased the car four years ago for $21,000. During the current year, he sells the car for $13,000. Sanjay cannot claim a loss from the sale of the car since it is his personal-use vehicle.

Example: Judith collects antique coins as a hobby. She is not a professional coin dealer. Two years ago, Judith purchased an antique Roman coin at an estate sale for $50. In 2020, she was offered $6,000 for the coin, and she promptly sells it. Judith has a taxable capital gain of $5,950 that she must report on her tax return. Since she held the coin for more than one year, she may be eligible for favorable capital gains rates if her applicable tax rate on other income happens to be greater than 28%.

Example: Vishnu sold his personal laptop computer to his friend for $456. He paid $1,980 for the computer five years ago. Vishnu used the computer to play games, surf the internet, and pay bills online. He did not use the computer for business. Vishnu cannot deduct a loss on the sale of his personal computer.

---

116 Antiques and collectibles (such as artwork and coin collections), while normally capital assets for nondealers, have special tax rates applicable if they are sold at a gain and held greater than a year prior to sale. The tax rate on long-term capital gains on antiques and collectibles is taxed at the individual's ordinary tax rate, but at a maximum rate of 28%.

117 IRS Notice 2014-21 states that, for federal tax purposes, virtual currency is treated as property.

The applicable capital gains tax rate depends on the holding period, the type of asset, and the taxpayer's ordinary income tax bracket.

Noncapital Assets

Assets held for business-use or created by a taxpayer for purposes of earning revenue (copyrights, inventory, etc.) are considered *noncapital* assets. Gains and losses from the sale of business property are reported on Form 4797, *Sales of Business Property*, and in the case of individual taxpayers, the amounts flow through to Form 1040, Schedule D, *Capital Gains and Losses.* The following assets are *noncapital* assets:

- Inventory or any similar property held for sale to customers
- Depreciable property used in a business, even if it is fully depreciated
- Real property used in a trade or business, such as a commercial building or a residential rental
- *Self-produced* copyrights, transcripts, manuscripts, drawings, photographs, or artistic compositions
- Accounts receivable or notes receivable acquired by a business
- Stocks and bonds held by professional securities dealers
- Business supplies
- Commodities and derivative financial instruments

Unlike capital assets, the costs of many noncapital assets may be deducted as business expenses when they are sold, and losses are generally fully deductible.

Example: Olen is the sole proprietor of a fitness club. In 2020, he sells several used treadmills in order to make room for new gym equipment. Since the used equipment was business property, Olen reports the sales on Form 4797**.** Also, during the year, Olen sells some stock at a substantial profit. He has a capital gain on the stock that he must report on Schedule D.

Example: Shawn is a self-employed fisherman who reports his income and expenses on Schedule F. In 2020, he sells some of his commercial fishing equipment. The fishing equipment is a noncapital asset, and the sale must be reported on Form 4797**,** *Sales of Business Property.* Also, during the year, Shawn sells his vacation home at a substantial loss. Unlike the fishing equipment, the vacation home is a capital asset, but since it is also personal-use property, he cannot deduct the loss.

Holding Period (Short-Term or Long-Term)

When a taxpayer disposes of investment property, his holding period affects the tax treatment of his capital gain or loss. This is important because long-term capital gains are taxed at lower rates than short-term gains. If a taxpayer holds investment property for more than one year, any capital gain or loss is long-term capital gain or loss. If a taxpayer holds investment property for one year or less, any capital gain or loss is short-term capital gain or loss.

Long-term = more than one year (at least a year and a day)

Short-term = one year or less

To determine how long a taxpayer has held an investment property, he must begin counting on the date after the day he acquires the property. The day the taxpayer disposes of the property is part of the holding period.

Example: Chloris bought 50 shares of stock on February 2, 2020, for $10,000. She sells all the shares on February 2, 2021, for $20,500. She held the stock for exactly one year. Since Chloris's holding period is not more than one year, she has a *short-term* capital gain of $10,500. The short-term gain is taxed at ordinary income tax rates. If Chloris had waited just one more day, she would have received long-term capital gain treatment on her gain and been taxed at a lower rate.

Example: Zoran bought 100 shares of stock on January 1, 2020, for $1,200. To determine his holding period, Zoran must start counting his holding period on January 2, 2020 (the day *after* the purchase). He sells all the stock on January 10, 2021, for $2,850. Zoran's holding period has been more than one year, and therefore, he will recognize a long-term capital gain of $1,650 in 2021, the year in which the stock was actually sold ($2,850 - $1,200).

Stock shares acquired as a result of a nontaxable stock dividend or stock-split have the same holding period as the original shares owned.

Example: Five years ago, Cagney bought 500 shares of Stellar, Inc. stock for $1,500, including a broker's commission. On June 6, 2020, Stellar, Inc. distributed a 2% nontaxable stock dividend (10 additional shares). Three days later, Cagney sells all his Stellar, Inc. stock for $2,030. Although Cagney owned the 10 shares he received as a nontaxable stock dividend for only three days, a long-term holding period applies to all of his shares in the stock. Because he bought the stock for $1,500 and then sold it for $2,030 more than a year later, Cagney has a long-term capital gain of $530 on the sale of the 510 shares.

The holding period for a gift is treated differently than the holding period for purchased property. If a taxpayer receives a gift of property, his holding period normally includes the donor's holding period. This concept is known as "tacking on" the holding period.

Example: Eugenia gives her nephew, Dustin, an acre of land. At the time of the gift, the land had an FMV of $23,000. Eugenia's adjusted basis in the land was $22,500. Gena only held the property for six months prior to making the gift. Dustin holds the land for another seven months. Neither held the property for over a year. Regardless, Dustin may "tack on" his holding period to his aunt's holding period. Therefore, if Dustin were to sell the property, he would have a long-term capital gain or loss, because jointly they held the property for 13 months, or more than one year.

Inherited property is always considered long-term property. In other words, assets acquired from a decedent automatically receive long-term holding period treatment when sold by a beneficiary. This is true, regardless of how long the beneficiary actually holds it.

Example: Nella inherited a vacation home from her father, who died on February 10, 2020. The FMV of the house is $210,000 on the date of her father's death. Nella immediately decides to sell the house. On April 30, 2020, the house is sold for $215,000. Nella has a long-term capital gain of $5,000 on the sale. All the gain is treated as long-term, even though she held the property for only a few months, because inherited property is always treated as long-term.

Determining Capital Gain or Loss

A taxpayer determines gain or loss on a sale or trade of stock or property by comparing the amount realized with the adjusted basis of the property.

Example: Andros receives Form 1099-B showing a net sales price of $1,200 on the sale of 600 shares of Centrex, Inc. He bought the stock six years ago and sold it on September 25, 2020. His basis in Centrex, Inc., including commissions paid, is $1,455. Andros will report a $255 loss on Schedule D.

A disposition of stock and the related income or loss must always be reported in the year of the sale, regardless of when the taxpayer receives the proceeds. Capital losses are *netted* against any capital gains that may be generated in the same year. A taxpayer can deduct up to $3,000 ($1,500 for MFS) of *net* capital losses against ordinary income in a tax year. Unused losses above this limit are carried over to later years.

Example: Hubert purchased stock three years ago for $16,000. The stock declines in value, and he sells it in 2020 for $12,000. Hubert has a $4,000 long-term capital loss on the stock sale. He also has $60,000 of wages in 2020. He can claim $3,000 of his long-term capital loss against his ordinary income, thereby lowering his gross income to $57,000 ($60,000 - $3,000). The remainder of the long-term capital loss ($1,000) must be carried forward to the following tax year.

Married taxpayers are at a disadvantage when deducting capital losses. On a joint return, the net capital loss deduction limit is $3,000, which is the same limit for single taxpayers. MFS filers only get half of that (a $1,500 capital loss limit).

Example: Kandi and Jerrod are married and file separate returns (MFS). In 2020, Kandi sells some stock that she owns and incurs a $5,000 capital loss. Jerrod also sells some stock and has a $12,500 capital gain. Kandi can only claim $1,500 of her loss on her tax return because she is filing MFS. Jerrod must pay tax on the entire gain on his separate tax return. If they had filed *jointly*, then their capital losses would have "offset" each other, which would have reduced the amount of their taxable gain to $7,500 ($12,500 Jerrod's capital gain - $5,000 Kandi's capital loss).

Example: Ariana purchased 100 shares of BMC, Inc. stock two years ago for $6,800. The stock declines in value, and she sells all her BMC shares on December 20, 2020, for $4,000, resulting in a $2,800 capital loss. She is married, but files separately from her husband. She has $52,000 in wages for the year. Since she is filing MFS, Ariana can only claim $1,500 of her long-term capital loss against her ordinary income, thereby lowering her gross income to $50,500 ($52,000 - $1,500). The remainder of the long-term capital loss ($1,300) must be carried forward to the following tax year.

The carryover losses are combined with gains and losses that occur in the next year. Cryptocurrencies (such as Bitcoin) are treated like other capital assets for income tax purposes.

Example: On April 30, 2020, Hayden sells Bitcoin for a total of $6,300. The Bitcoin was purchased on November 2, 2016, for $780. Hayden has a long-term capital gain of $5,520 on the sale. Also, on May 10, 2020, Hayden sells Litecoin for $382. He had purchased Litecoin (another type of cryptocurrency) on February 2, 2020, for $966 (purchased and sold in the same year). Hayden, therefore, has a $584 short-term capital loss on the sale. His losses and gains are "netted" for the year. Hayden will report a net long-term capital gain in 2020 of $4,936.

Virtual Currency	Basis	Sale Price	Gain or (Loss)
Bitcoin	$780	$6,300	Long-term gain: $5,520
Litecoin	$966	$382	Short-term loss: $584
Hayden's Net Capital Gain:			**$4,936**

In a tax year, a taxpayer first nets short-term capital gains and losses (including carryover losses) against each other, and then long-term capital gains and losses (including carryover losses) against each other. The results are then netted against each other, if applicable.

Any net capital losses carried over retain their character as either long-term or short-term and are reported on Schedule D. Thus, a long-term capital loss carried over to the next tax year will reduce that year's long-term capital gains before it reduces that year's short-term capital gains.

Example: Angelina is single. She purchased 50 shares of Formosa, Inc. stock five years ago for $19,000. Two years ago, she purchased 750 shares of Inertia, Inc. stock for $8,200. In 2020, Angelina sells all her stock in both corporations. Her Formosa stock sells for $2,000, and her Inertia stock sells for $13,000. Angelina's gain and loss are both long-term because she held both stocks for more than one year. Her long-term losses and long-term gains are netted against each other, resulting in a net long-term capital loss, as follows:

Stock	Basis	Sale Price	Gain or (Loss)
Formosa Inc.	$19,000	$2,000	($17,000)
Inertia Inc.	$8,200	$13,000	$4,800
Angelina's net long-term capital loss: ($12,200)			

Angelina also earned $55,000 in wages during the year. Angelina may deduct $3,000 of her net $12,200 capital loss against her wage income in the current year. The remaining capital losses must be "carried over" to the next tax year, where they can reduce her taxable income in future years.

A net capital loss can be carried over indefinitely during the taxpayer's life. However, once a taxpayer dies, the capital losses not used on the final return cannot be carried over to a beneficiary or an heir. Capital losses always belong to the decedent. Any capital loss carryovers that are not used on the taxpayer's final return are lost forever.

Example: Ethan has $15,000 of capital losses from the sale of cryptocurrency in 2020. On December 20, 2020, Ethan dies. His executor may claim the capital losses on Ethan's final individual tax return, up to the allowable limit. However, any unused capital losses cannot be carried over to a future year, because Ethan is dead. The losses do not transfer to Ethan's estate or to his heirs.

Capital Gains from Mutual Funds

A mutual fund is a regulated investment company generally created by pooling funds of investors to allow them to take advantage of a diversity of investments and professional management. Two different types of transactions may result in taxable capital gains reporting by a taxpayer who invests in mutual funds.

First, profits resulting from investments made by the fund itself are reported to its own shareholders as capital gain distributions on Form 1099-DIV. The capital gain distributions are always taxed at long-term capital gains tax rates, without regard to how long a taxpayer has owned shares in the mutual fund.

In addition, if a taxpayer disposes of shares that represent all or a portion of his investment in the mutual fund itself, Form 1099-B will be issued. The taxable gain or loss that results from the sale or exchange of the taxpayer's shares in the mutual fund is reported on Form 1040, Schedule D. Brokers are now required to include the basis of mutual funds on Form 1099-B.

Wash Sales

A "wash sale" occurs when an investor sells a security to claim a capital loss, only to repurchase it again very soon thereafter. A taxpayer cannot deduct a loss on the sale of an investment if a substantially identical investment is purchased within 30 days before or after the sale. A wash sale is considered to have occurred when a taxpayer sells a security at a loss and, within 30 days:

- Buys the identical security,
- Acquires a "substantially identical" security in a taxable trade, or
- Acquires a contract or option to buy the identical security.

If a taxpayer's loss is disallowed because of the wash sale rules, he must add the disallowed loss to the basis of the new stock or securities. The result is an increase in the taxpayer's basis in the new stock or securities. This adjustment postpones the loss deduction until the later disposition of the new stock or securities.[118] It is considered a wash sale if a taxpayer sells stock and his spouse then repurchases identical stock within 30 days, even if the spouses file separate tax returns.

Example: Yakov sells 800 shares of Quanta Corporation stock on December 4, 2020, resulting in a loss of $3,200. He regrets selling the stock, so on January 2, 2021, he repurchases 800 shares of Quanta stock on the open market. Because of the IRS wash sale rules, all of the $3,200 loss is disallowed, and he must add the disallowed loss to the basis of the newly purchased shares. He cannot take the loss until he finally sells the repurchased shares at some later time.

[118] Wash sale rules do not apply to trades of commodity futures contracts and foreign currencies. The rules also do not apply to professional securities dealers of stocks or securities.

In situations where only a portion of the stock is repurchased during the applicable wash sale period, only the percentage of the shares repurchased will be used to determine the amount of the disallowed loss.

Example: Ayami sells 1,000 shares of Zaxxon Corporation stock on July 4, 2020, resulting in a loss of $5,000. On August 1, 2020, she repurchases 200 shares of Zaxxon stock on the open market. Because of the IRS wash sale rules, 20% of the $5,000 realized loss, $1,000, is disallowed, but the remaining $4,000 loss is recognized.

For purposes of the wash sale rules, securities of one corporation are not considered identical to securities of another corporation. This means that a person can sell shares in one corporation and then purchase shares in a different corporation, and this will not trigger a wash sale. Similarly, preferred stock of a corporation is not considered identical to the common stock of the same corporation.

Home Sale Gain or Loss

The tax rules for the sale of a primary residence are advantageous for taxpayers. Most of the time, a home sale does not trigger a taxable gain. There are special rules regarding the sale of a taxpayer's primary residence. We will go over those rules later, in the chapter dedicated to nonrecognition property transactions. In this unit, we will only cover how to determine the basis of a home. The following are used to determine basis and figure the gain (or loss) on the sale of a home:

- Selling price
- Amount realized
- Basis
- Adjusted basis

Selling Price: The selling price is the total amount the taxpayer received for his main home. The "selling price" includes more than just cash. It includes all money, notes, mortgages, or other debts taken over by the buyer as part of the sale, and the fair market value of any other property or services that the seller received. Real estate sales proceeds are reported on Form 1099-S, *Proceeds from Real Estate Transactions*. If a taxpayer does not receive a Form 1099-S, he must rely upon sale documents and other records.

Amount Realized: The "amount realized" is the selling price minus selling expenses, which include commissions, advertising fees, legal fees, and loan charges paid by the seller, such as points.

Basis in a Home: The basis in a home is determined by how the taxpayer obtained the home. For example, if a taxpayer purchases a home, the basis is the cost of the home. If a taxpayer builds a home, the basis is the building cost plus the cost of land. If the taxpayer inherited the home, the basis is generally its FMV on the date of the decedent's death, or the later alternate valuation date chosen by the representative for the estate.

If a taxpayer receives a home as a gift, the basis is normally the donor's adjusted basis at the time of the gift.

Example: Misty is single. She sells her home for $350,000. She purchased the home 15 years ago for $50,000 and had lived in it continuously since then. She pays $4,000 in seller's fees to sell the home. Her amount realized in the sale is $346,000 ($350,000 - $4,000 = $346,000). Her basis is subtracted from her amount realized to figure her gain: ($346,000 - $50,000 basis) = $296,000.

Adjusted Basis: The adjusted basis is the taxpayer's basis in the home increased or decreased by certain amounts. Increases include additions or improvements to the home that have a useful life of more than one year. Repairs that simply maintain a home in good condition are not considered improvements and should not be added to the basis of the property. Decreases to basis include deductible casualty losses, credits, and product rebates.

Depreciation reduces the basis of business. assets, such as rental property. Depreciation is never taken on personal-use property, such as a primary residence

The formula for figuring adjusted basis:

Basis + Increases - Decreases = Adjusted Basis

Example: Raphael purchased his home ten years ago for $125,000. In 2020, he added another bathroom to the property at the cost of $25,000. Raphael's adjusted basis in the home is therefore $150,000 ($125,000 purchase price + $25,000 addition).

If the amount realized on the sale of a home is less than the adjusted basis, the difference is a loss. A loss on the sale of a primary residence (like other personal-use property) can never be deducted.

If the amount realized is more than the adjusted basis of the property, the difference is a gain (but not always a *taxable* gain). As described in detail later, the taxpayer may be able to exclude all or part of the gain. If not excluded and the taxpayer owns a home for one year or less, the gain is reported as a short-term capital gain. If the taxpayer owns the home for more than one year, the gain is reported as a long-term capital gain.

Related Party Transaction Rules

Special rules apply to related party transactions, which are between two parties who are joined by a special relationship. If a taxpayer sells an asset to a close family member or to a business entity that the taxpayer controls, he may not receive all the benefits of the capital gains tax rates, and he may not be able to deduct his losses. The rules were made to prevent related persons and entities from shuffling assets back and forth and taking improper losses.

More Than "50% Control" Rule: If a taxpayer controls *more than* 50% of a corporation, partnership, or other business entity, any property transactions between the taxpayer and the majority-owned business are subject to related party transaction rules.

In general, a loss on the sale of property between related parties is not deductible. When the property is later sold to an unrelated party by the original party buyer, a *gain* is recognized by the related party buyer only to the extent it is more than the disallowed loss to the original party seller. However, if the property is later sold at a *loss* by the original party buyer, the loss that was disallowed to the related party cannot be recognized.

If a taxpayer sells or trades property at a loss (other than in the complete liquidation of a corporation), the loss is not deductible if the transaction is between the taxpayer and the following related parties:

- Members of an immediate family, including a spouse, siblings, half-siblings, direct ancestors (e.g., parents, grandparents) and lineal descendants of those persons (i.e., grandchildren.)
- A partnership, corporation, or other business entity that the taxpayer controls. A taxpayer "controls" an entity when he has more than 50% ownership in it. This also includes partial ownership by other family members.
- A tax-exempt or charitable organization controlled by the taxpayer or a member of his family
- Losses on sales between certain closely related trusts or business entities controlled by the same owners

Note: For purposes of this rule, the following are *not* considered related parties: uncles, aunts, nephews, nieces, cousins, step-children, step-parents, in-laws, and ex-spouses.

Example: On February 2, 2020, Roxie purchases stock from her father, Eugene, for $8,600. Eugene's basis in the stock is $11,000. He sold the stock to his daughter at a loss, but he cannot claim that loss on his tax return. The stock continues to decline in value, and Roxie sells the stock on the open market for $6,900 on December 10, 2020. Her recognized loss is $1,700 (her $8,600 basis minus the $6,900 sales price). Roxie cannot deduct the loss that was disallowed to her father.

Example: Selma buys 300 shares of stock from her brother, Nolan, for $7,600. Nolan's cost basis in the stock is $10,000. Nolan cannot deduct the loss of $2,400 because of the related party transaction rules. Later, Selma sells the same stock on the open market for $10,500, realizing a gain of $2,900. Selma's reportable gain is $500 (the $2,900 gain minus the $2,400 loss that was not previously allowed to her brother).

Example: Irene sells 100 shares of stock to her step-brother, Saul. She recognizes a $3,000 capital loss on the transaction. Since her stepbrother is not considered a "related party" for IRS purposes, she is allowed to take the full amount of the loss on her tax return.

In the case of a related party transaction, if a taxpayer sells multiple pieces of property and some are at a gain while others are at a loss, the gains will generally be taxable while the losses cannot be used to offset the gains.

Installment Sales

An installment sale is a sale of property in which at least one payment is expected to be received after the tax year in which the sale occurs. If a taxpayer sells a property and receives payments over multiple years, he may use the installment method to defer tax by only reporting a portion of his gain as each installment is received.

A taxpayer's gain, or gross profit, is the amount by which the selling price exceeds the adjusted basis in the property sold. A gross profit percentage is calculated by dividing the gross profit from the sale by the selling price.[119]

Study Note: Test-takers may be required to determine gross profit percentage on an installment sale for either Part 1 or Part 2 of the EA exam.

Note: The installment sale rules do NOT apply to property that is sold at a loss or to the sale of inventory.

Each payment received on an installment sale typically consists of the following three parts:

- Interest income
- Return of the adjusted basis in the property
- Gain on the sale (determined by applying the gross profit percentage to the amount of the payment received minus the interest portion)

Each year the taxpayer receives a payment, he must report the interest income and the portion of the payments that relate to his gain on the sale. The taxpayer does not include in income the part that is the return of his basis in the property.

Example: In 2020, Sheri sells an empty lot with a basis of $40,000 for $100,000 in a private-party sale. Sheri agrees to carry the buyer's note. Her gross profit is $60,000 ($100,000 - $40,000) for a gross profit percentage of 60%. She receives a $20,000 down payment and the buyer's note for $80,000 at the time of the sale. In 2020, Sheri must report a $12,000 gain allocated from the down payment she received. The note provides for four annual payments of $20,000 each, plus 8% interest, starting in 2021. Exclusive of the interest income, she must report $12,000 of her installment gain for each $20,000 payment received ($20,000 × .60 = $12,000). [Based on an example in Publication 537, *Installment Sales*]

The selling price includes the cash and any other property to be received from the buyer, any existing mortgage or debt the buyer pays or assumes, and any selling expenses the buyer pays.

However, if the buyer assumes or pays off a mortgage or other debt on the property sold, the calculation of gross profit percentage is affected. The mortgage assumption is considered a recovery of basis in the year of sale and is subtracted before calculating the gross profit percentage, except to the extent that it exceeds the adjusted basis of the property for installment sale purposes.

In contrast, if the property is sold to a buyer who holds a mortgage on it and the mortgage is canceled rather than assumed, the cancellation is treated as a payment received in the year of the sale and is not subtracted in calculating the gross profit percentage.

Example: Sylvester sells property in an installment sale for $6,000. His gross profit is $1,500. The gross profit percentage on the sale is 25% ($1,500 ÷ $6,000). After subtracting interest, Sylvester reports 25% of each payment, including the down payment, as installment sale income in the year received. The remainder of each payment is the tax-free return of the property's basis.

[119] For more information on installment sales and more extended examples, see Publication 537, *Installment Sales.*

If installment payments are made according to a schedule other than what was originally agreed, income is recognized according to the actual payments received. However, if the parties subsequently agree to adjust the selling price, the gross profit percentage must be recalculated, and income from future installments must be recognized based upon the adjusted gross profit.

The installment method is the default method when at least one payment is expected to be received after the tax year in which the sale occurs. If a taxpayer elects out of the installment method, he must report all the gain in the year of the sale. In addition, any depreciation recapture must be recognized in full in the year of the sale.

The installment method cannot be used for publicly traded securities, such as stocks and bonds. A taxpayer must report the gain on the sale of securities in the year of the sale, regardless of whether the proceeds are received in the following year.

Example: Wilmer owns 500 shares of stock, which he sells at a gain on December 29, 2020, through his online brokerage account. The sales proceeds weren't deposited into his bank account until January 3, 2021. Wilmer is required to report the capital gain on the sale of the stock on his 2020 tax return, *not* his 2021 return. He cannot delay reporting the gain, and the sale is not considered an installment sale.

Installment sales to related persons are generally allowed. However, if a taxpayer sells a property to a related person who then sells or disposes of the property within two years of the original sale, the taxpayer will lose the benefit of installment sale reporting.

Installment sales are reported on Form 6252, *Installment Sale Income,* which is attached to Form 1040. A taxpayer may also be required to complete Schedule D or Form 4797.

Example: Dimitri sells a plot of land to his daughter, Zahara. The sale price is $25,000, and Dimitri realizes a profit on the sale of $10,000. Tamara agrees to pay in five installments of $5,000. A year later, Zahara decides she no longer wants the property, and she sells the land to another person. Dimitri must report the entire profit of $10,000 on the sale, even though he may not have received all the installment payments. The installment sale method is disallowed on the related-party sale because the property was disposed of during the two-year holding period.

How to Report the Sale of Capital Assets

An individual usually owns many assets, including investments, like stocks and bonds. The gain or loss on each asset is figured separately, and the tax treatment depends on the type of asset that is sold. In the case of capital assets,[120] the gains and losses are typically reported on these two forms:

- Schedule D, *Capital Gains and Losses*, and
- Form 8949, *Sales and Other Dispositions of Capital Assets.*

Schedule D is used to report gain or loss on the sale of investment property and most capital gain (or loss) transactions. However, before the taxpayer can calculate their net gain or loss on

[120] Capital assets include homes, stocks, and even collectibles. In the case of individuals, a "capital asset" is typically anything the taxpayer owns for personal or investment purposes.

Schedule D, he may also have to complete Form 8949, *Sales and Other Dispositions of Capital Assets.*

Form 8949 reports the details about each stock trade the taxpayer makes during the year. There are two parts to Form 8949. The first is for short-term assets, and the second part is for long-term assets. Form 8949 is used to report the following:

- The sale or exchange of capital assets
- Gains from involuntary conversions (other than from casualty or theft)
- Nonbusiness bad debts and
- Worthless securities

Some transactions can be reported directly on Schedule D without needing to report them on Form 8949. A taxpayer can skip filing Form 8949 if <u>both</u> of the following are true:

- He received a Form 1099-B that shows basis was reported to the IRS and does not show a nondeductible wash sale loss in box 1g, and
- He does not need to make any adjustments to the basis or type of gain or loss (short-term or long-term) reported on Form 1099-B, or to his gain or loss.

The information reported on Form 8949 describes all sales and exchanges of capital assets, including stocks, bonds, and mutual funds. This form must be filed along with Schedule D, which contains the summary of all capital gains and losses.

Reporting Worthless Securities

A taxpayer may choose to "abandon" a security that has lost its entire value in order to take advantage of the loss for tax purposes rather than retaining ownership. Stocks, stock rights, and bonds (other than those held for sale by a securities dealer) that became worthless during the tax year are treated as though they were sold for zero dollars on the last day of the tax year.

A loss from worthless securities receives special tax treatment. Unlike other losses, a taxpayer is allowed to amend a tax return for up to seven years in order to claim a loss from worthless securities. This is more than double the usual three-year statute of limitations for amending returns.

To abandon a worthless security, a taxpayer must permanently surrender all rights to it and receive no consideration in exchange. Taxpayers should report worthless securities on Form 8949 and indicate as a worthless security deduction by writing "WORTHLESS" in the applicable column of Form 8949.

Example: Leandro owned 500 shares of Crossroad Corporation stock. The company files for bankruptcy, and the bankruptcy court extinguishes all rights of the former shareholders. Leandro learns of the bankruptcy court's decision on December 20, 2020. Rather than wait for a formal notice from the court, he chooses to abandon all his Crossroad securities, knowing that his shares are essentially worthless. He takes a capital loss on his 2020 tax return, reflecting the value of his worthless shares as "zero."

Example: Gerri owns 2,000 shares of Boathouse Makers, Inc. She purchased the stock five years ago for $7,500. In 2020, the company files for bankruptcy, and Gerri's stock becomes worthless. She chooses to abandon the securities to take a tax deduction in 2020. Then she reports the valueless stock on Form 8949 and treats the abandonment as a sale. For the sale date, she puts December 31, 2020, and she lists her proceeds as $0. She now has a long-term capital loss of ($7,500) that she can use to offset other taxable income.

Note: Once a corporation has been delisted from a stock exchange as a result of bankruptcy, the stockholder will often have to fill out a worthless securities processing request. Some brokerage firms will purchase worthless stock for a nominal amount (such as a penny), to provide closure and an official sale date to the customer on their brokerage statement.[121]

121 "Worthless securities" are stocks or bonds that have a market value of zero. A taxpayer may treat worthless securities as though they were sold or exchanged on the last day of the tax year.

Unit 7: Study Questions

(Test yourself first, then check the correct answers at the end of this quiz.)

1. Simeon owns 100% of the stock in TOP Corporation. Gerald owns 100% of the stock in DAB Corporation. In 2020, TOP Corporation sold used manufacturing equipment to DAB Corporation at a $52,000 loss. Simeon and Gerald are stepbrothers. Concerning the related party transaction loss rules, how should this transaction between Simeon and Gerald be handled?

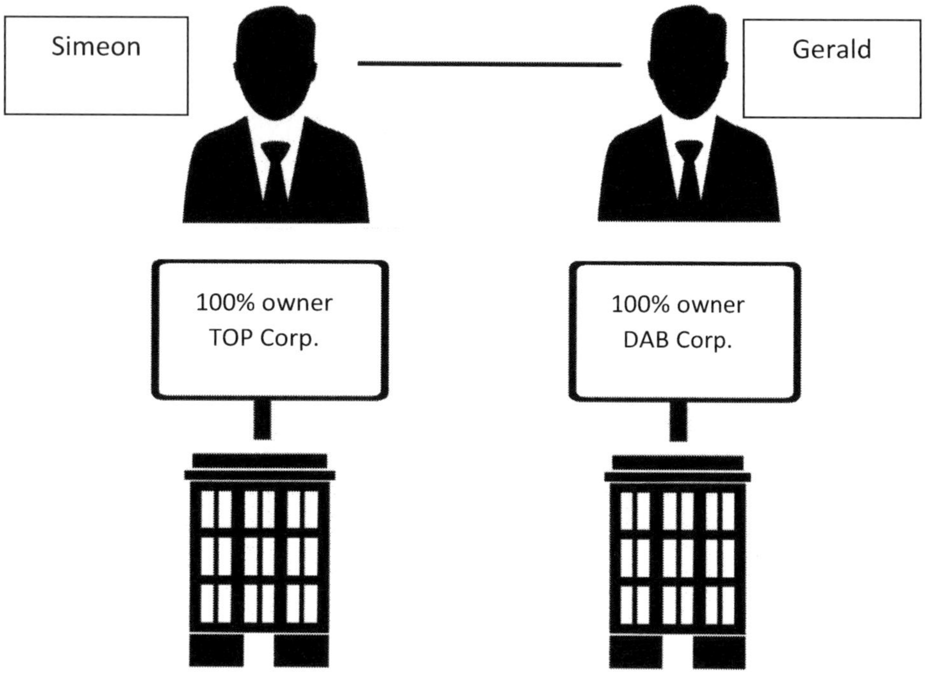

A. Any losses on the sale of property between the corporations would be disallowed, and the transaction would be treated as a constructive dividend to Simeon.
B. The related party transaction rules do not apply to their corporations, but they would apply individually to Simeon and Gerald, resulting in taxable income to each of them.
C. The related party transaction rules apply individually to Simeon and Gerald, but not to their corporations.
D. The related party transaction rules do not apply in this scenario.

2. When trying to determine the holding period for an investment property, which of the following is important?

A. The cost of the property.
B. In the case of gifted property, the amount of the gift.
C. The date of acquisition.
D. The amount realized in the transaction.

3. Consuela is unmarried and files as "single." She purchased 1,000 shares of Hometown Mutual Fund on February 15, 2015, for $15 per share. On April 30, 2020, she sold all her shares for $3.75 per share. She also earned $49,000 of wages in 2020. She has no other transactions during the year. How should this transaction be reported on her tax return?

A. She has a capital loss of $11,250 that she can deduct against her wage income.
B. She must carry over the losses to a future tax year and offset future capital gains.
C. She can deduct a $3,000 capital loss on her tax return, and the remainder of the losses will carry forward to subsequent years.
D. She can deduct a $1,500 capital loss on her tax return, and the remainder of the losses will carry forward to subsequent years.

4. Noah bought two blocks (each of 400 shares) of Acme Corporation stock. He purchased the first block on May 30, 2015, for $1,200 and the second block on March 8, 2020, for $1,600. In June of 2020, he needed money to fix his car, so he sold 400 shares for $1,500 but did not specify which block of stocks he sold. Noah's stock sale results in a:

A. Long-term loss of $100.
B. Long-term gain of $300.
C. Short-term loss of $100.
D. Short-term gain of $300.

5. What is the maximum number of years a taxpayer can carry over an unused capital loss?

A. One year.
B. Two years.
C. Five years.
D. Indefinitely.

6. Which of the following losses is deductible?

A. A loss on the sale of a primary residence.
B. A loss on the sale of a vacation home.
C. A loss on the sale of rental property.
D. A loss on the sale of a personal-use mobile home.

7. Nikhil's adjusted basis in 500 shares of Edico Corporation was $2,550. He owned the shares for only three months. If he sells all 500 shares for $3,300, what is the resulting gain or loss?

A. $750 short-term gain.
B. $700 short-term gain.
C. $750 long-term gain.
D. $750 long-term loss.

8. Ruben bought 100 shares of stock on February 1, 2019, when the share price was $26. He sold the stock for $20 a share on February 1, 2020 (exactly one year later). How should this trade be reported, and what is the nature of Ruben's gain or loss?

A. A long-term capital loss of $600.
B. A short-term capital loss of $500.
C. A short-term capital loss of $600.
D. This is a wash sale, and there is no gain or loss.

9. Five years ago, Marsha bought 100 shares of stock. Her sale date was February 10, 2020. Marsha's original cost for the stock was $10,110, plus an additional $35 of broker's fees. When she sold the stock, she received gross proceeds of $8,859. What is the net gain or loss from this transaction?

A. $1,286 long-term capital loss.
B. $1,286 short-term capital loss.
C. $1,251 long-term capital loss.
D. $1,251 long-term capital gain.

10. Salazar bought ten shares of Griffon Corporation stock on May 2, 2019. He sold them for a $7,000 loss on May 2, 2020. He has no other capital gains or losses. He also has $20,000 of wage income during the year. How must Salazar treat this transaction on his tax return?

A. He can deduct the $7,000 as a long-term capital loss on his return.
B. He can deduct the $7,000 as a short-term capital loss on his return.
C. He can deduct $3,000 as a short-term capital loss to offset his wage income on his return. The remaining amount, $4,000, must be carried over to future tax years.
D. He cannot deduct any of the capital loss; it must be carried over to future tax years.

11. Salome sells an empty lot with an adjusted basis of $20,000. Her buyer assumes an existing mortgage on the property of $15,000 and agrees to pay Salome $10,000, with a cash down payment of $2,000 and then $2,000 every year (plus 12% interest) in each of the next four years. What is Salome's gross <u>profit</u> and gross profit <u>percentage</u> on the installment sale?

A. The gross profit is $5,000, and the gross profit percentage is 20%.
B. The gross profit is $10,000, and the gross profit percentage is 100%.
C. The gross profit is $15,000, and the gross profit percentage is 20%.
D. The gross profit is $5,000, and the gross profit percentage is 50%.

12. Mario purchased his main home five years ago for $150,000. He sold it at a loss, for $115,000 in 2020. Which of the following statements is correct?

A. If he itemizes deductions, Mario can claim a loss of $35,000 on his tax return.
B. Mario can claim a loss of $3,000 but must carry over the remainder to future years until the loss is completely deducted.
C. Mario can claim a loss of $35,000 because the home sale was an involuntary conversion.
D. Mario cannot claim a loss for the sale of his home.

13. Tahir purchased 100 shares in Foresthill Mutual Fund On June 1, 2020, for $750. He received a capital gain distribution of $120 in 2020, but he did not sell his shares in the mutual fund during the year. The $120 was reported to him on Form 1099-DIV. How should this be reported on his tax return?

A. He must reduce his stock's basis by $120.
B. He must report the $120 as interest income.
C. He must report the $120 as a long-term capital gain.
D. He must report the $120 as a short-term capital gain.

14. Melissa purchased 1,000 shares of Sunshine Foods, Inc. stock five years ago at $10 per share. She sold 900 shares on January 15, 2020, at $9 per share, resulting in a $900 loss. Melissa's husband, Alex, purchased 900 shares of Sunshine Foods Inc. stock on February 10, 2020. Alex and Melissa keep their finances separate and will file MFS. Which of the following statements is correct?

A. Melissa can deduct the $900 capital loss on her tax return.
B. Melissa has a wash sale, and her loss is not deductible.
C. Alex can deduct the loss on his separate tax return.
D. None of the above.

15. Ammon and Tetyana owned a vacation home for 14 months before selling it for $254,000. Their adjusted basis in the home was $232,000, and they incurred $12,500 of selling expenses. Prior to the sale, they did not rent the home. What is the nature and amount of their gain?

A. $22,000 long-term capital gain.
B. $9,500 long-term capital gain.
C. $9,500 short-term capital gain.
D. $34,500 long-term capital gain.

16. Colin purchased 100 shares of Entertainment Media, Inc. stock for $1,000 on January 3, 2020. He sold these shares for $750 on December 22, 2020. Colin has seller's remorse, and on January 19, 2021, he repurchases 100 shares of Entertainment Media for $800. Which of the following statements is correct?

A. Colin can report a $250 capital loss in 2020.
B. Colin can report a taxable loss in 2021.
C. Colin cannot deduct his stock loss of $250 and must add the disallowed loss to his basis.
D. Colin can deduct the loss as an adjustment to income in 2020.

17. Francoise bought 1 share in the Vanest Mutual Fund four years ago for $8. Since then, she received the following nondividend distributions:

- 2017: $2 per share
- 2018: $2 per share
- 2019: $3 per share
- 2020: $3 per share

What is Francoise's remaining basis in the 1 share, and what amount of gain (if any) must she report in 2020?

A. $0 basis; $6 gain.
B. $14 basis; $0 gain.
C. $0 basis; $2 gain.
D. $8 basis; $3 gain.

Unit 7: Quiz Answers

1. The answer is D. The related party transaction rules do not apply in this scenario. Related party transaction rules are designed to prevent improper deductions between two parties joined by a special relationship. However, the related party transaction rules do not apply to stepsiblings, so there are no related party issues between Simeon and Gerald or their corporations. Related party transaction rules do not apply to uncles, aunts, nieces, nephews, cousins, stepchildren, stepsiblings, stepparents, or in-laws.

2. The answer is C. To determine the holding period, a taxpayer must begin counting on the day *after* the acquisition date. If a taxpayer's holding period is not more than one year, the taxpayer will have a short-term gain or loss. The amount realized in the transaction has no bearing on the holding period.

3. The answer is C. Consuela cannot deduct all her stock losses in the current year. However, she is allowed to claim a $3,000 capital loss on her 2020 tax return. The remainder of the losses will carry forward indefinitely to subsequent years.

4. The answer is B. Noah realized a long-term gain of $300 because the basis and holding period would automatically default to the oldest block of shares, which he purchased years ago. The "FIFO method" is used if the taxpayer cannot or does not specifically identify the shares sold.

5. The answer is D. Unused capital losses may be carried over indefinitely until they are utilized. There is no limit to how many years an individual taxpayer can claim the losses. However, capital losses do not transfer to an estate or surviving spouse after the taxpayer has died.

6. The answer is C. Losses on the sale of personal-use property, including a loss on the sale of a primary residence or a vacation home, are not deductible. Only losses associated with business property and investment property (such as stocks and bonds or rental property) are deductible.

7. The answer is A. The sales price is $750 more than the adjusted basis of the shares. The gain is short-term since Nikhil did not own the shares for more than one year.

8. The answer is C. Ruben has a short-term capital loss of $600 = (100 shares × $26) - (100 shares × $20) that would be reported in the year of sale. Ruben's holding period was not more than one year, which means that the loss must be treated as short-term. To determine the holding period, you must begin counting on the day *after* the date the taxpayer acquires the property.

9. The answer is A. The answer is calculated as follows: The original basis is increased by the broker's commission. Therefore, Marsha's adjusted basis is $10,145 ($10,110 + $35). The gross proceeds from the sale are $8,859, which is subtracted from the basis, resulting in a long-term capital loss of $1,286 ($8,859 - $10,145) because she held the stock for more than one year.

10. The answer is C. Salazar has a short-term capital loss because he did not hold the stock for more than one year. He can deduct $3,000 of the loss, netting it against his wage income. The remaining

amount, $4,000, must be carried over to future tax years. A capital loss carryover retains its character as either long-term or short-term.

11. The answer is D. Salome's gross profit is $5,000, and the gross profit percentage is 50%. Her selling price is $25,000 ($2,000 down payment + $8,000 to be paid over four years + $15,000 for buyer's assumption of mortgage). Therefore, Salome's gross profit is $5,000 ($25,000 – $20,000 adjusted basis). If the entire selling price were payable in cash, her gross profit percentage would have been 20% ($5,000/$25,000). However, if a buyer assumes or pays off a mortgage or other debt on a property, the calculation of the installment sale gross profit percentage is affected. The mortgage assumption is subtracted before calculating the gross profit percentage, except to the extent that it exceeds the adjusted basis of the property for installment sale purposes, to derive what the IRS calls "contract price" rather than selling price. The mortgage assumption is considered a recovery of the seller's basis in the year of sale. Although the mortgage assumption is considered a payment, none of the gross profit is recognized in connection with the assumption. Instead, in this case, the contract price is considered to be $10,000 ($25,000 selling price - $15,000 mortgage assumption). Therefore, Salome's gross profit percentage is 50% ($5,000 ÷ $10,000). Salome must report half of each payment received as gain from the sale. She must also report all interest received as ordinary income.

12. The answer is D. Mario cannot claim a loss for the sale of his home. Losses on the sale of personal-use property, including a personal residence, are never deductible. If the house had been a rental property, however, the loss would have been deductible and reported on Form 4797 and potentially Schedule D as well.

13. The answer is C. Tahir must report the $120 as a long-term capital gain. Mutual funds frequently distribute capital gains to shareholders. Capital gain distributions for mutual funds are always taxed as long-term capital gains, no matter how long a taxpayer has actually held the mutual fund shares.

14. The answer is B. The loss is disallowed. Melissa has a wash sale because her spouse repurchased identical securities within 30 days. It does not matter if they file separate returns. If a taxpayer sells the stock and her spouse then repurchases identical stock within 30 days, the taxpayer has a wash sale. The fact that the taxpayers file MFS is irrelevant—the wash sale rules still apply, even if the taxpayers file separate returns.

15. The answer is B. The sale of a second home is a taxable event in the event of a gain. Since Ammon and Tetyana owned the property for longer than one year, their gain is long-term. The gain is calculated as follows:

Sale price	$254,000
Minus selling expenses	(12,500)
Net proceeds	241,500
Minus adjusted basis in the property	(232,000)
Taxable gain on the sale	**$9,500**

16. The answer is C. Because Colin bought shares in the same corporation within 30 days of its sale at a loss, this is considered a "wash sale," and he cannot deduct his loss of $250 on the sale. Instead,

he must add the disallowed loss to the cost of the new stock to obtain his adjusted basis in the new stock. It would be treated as if he had never sold the shares in the first place.

17. The answer is C. The first $8 of nondividend distributions per share reduces Francoise's basis to zero. In 2020, the final $2 of nondividend distribution must be reported as a capital gain.

Unit 8: Nonrecognition Property Transactions

For additional information, read:
Publication 544, *Sales and Other Dispositions of Assets*
Publication 523, *Selling Your Home*

For some transactions in which a taxpayer sells or exchanges property, gains may be nontaxable, partially taxable, or deferred. Three of the most common types of nonrecognition transactions involve:

- **Sale of a main home** (section 121, excluded gain)
- **Like-kind exchanges** (section 1031 nontaxable/deferred exchange)
- **Involuntary conversions** (section 1033 exchange)

Note: For Part 1 of the EA Exam, you will be tested primarily on the sale of a main home, involuntary conversions of personal-use property, and like-kind exchanges of residential rental property (Form 1040, Schedule E). For Part 2 of the EA exam, you will be tested on nonrecognition property transactions, but exclusively with business or rental property.

Sale of Main Home (Section 121 Exclusion)

In many cases, a taxpayer may exclude the gain from the sale of a main home. Up to $250,000 of gain may be excluded by single filers and up to $500,000 by joint filers. Generally, if the taxpayer can exclude all of the gain, it is not even necessary to report the sale, unless the taxpayer receives Form 1099-S for the sale proceeds. However, if part of the gain is taxable, the sale must be reported on Form 8949. Gain from the sale of a residence that is not the taxpayer's main home must be reported as taxable income.

The section 121 exclusion applies only to a "main home" and not to rental properties, vacation homes, or second homes. A taxpayer's main home is the residence where he lives most of the time. It does not have to be a traditional house. The main home can be a house, houseboat, mobile home, cooperative apartment, or condominium. To qualify as a home, it must have sleeping, kitchen, and bathroom facilities.

Example: Parker owns and lives in a house in Phoenix, Arizona. He also owns a lake cottage in Lake Tahoe, Nevada, which he uses only during the summer. The house in Phoenix is his main home; the lake cottage is not. Parker sells the cottage and has $220,000 of capital gain on the sale. The gain cannot be excluded because the cottage is not his main home. He must pay tax on the entire gain.

Example: Mickie lives in one-half of a duplex she owns and lets her brother live in the other unit of the duplex rent-free. She purchased the duplex ten years ago for $200,000. In 2020, Mickie sells the duplex for $340,000, a gain of $140,000. Since only half of the duplex counts as her main home, Mickie may exclude only half of the gain ($70,000). She must report the other $70,000 as a long-term capital gain on Schedule D (Form 1040).

If the home was used for business purposes or as a rental property, the gain is reported on Form 4797, *Sales of Business Property.* If a taxpayer took depreciation deductions because he used his home as a rental or for other business purposes, he cannot exclude the part of the gain

equal to any deductible depreciation. Section 121 applies only to the nonbusiness portion of a home.

Eligibility Requirements for Section 121

To be eligible for the section 121 exclusion, a taxpayer must:

- Have sold his main home
- Meet "ownership and use" tests
- Not have excluded gain in the two years prior to the current sale of a home

Ownership Test and Use Test

The IRS figures the ownership and use tests *separately*, and the time periods do not have to be continuous. During the five-year period ending on the date of the sale, the taxpayer must have:

- Owned the home for at least two years (the ownership test), and
- Lived in the home as his main home for at least two years (the use test).

Example: Briella is 25 years old and single. Since she was born, Briella has lived with her parents in the home her parents owned. On January 6, 2020, she bought her childhood home from her parents. Her parents moved out of the home and purchased a home in another state. Briella continued to live in the home until December 11, 2020, when she sold it because she decided that she wanted a bigger house. Briella does not meet the requirements for exclusion. Although she *lived* in the property as her main home for more than two years, she did not *own* it for the required two years. Therefore, she does not meet both the ownership and use tests. She must report and pay tax on all her gain from the sale.

A taxpayer meets both tests if he *owned* and *lived* in the property as his main home for either 24 full months or 730 days (365 × 2) during the five-year period. The required two years of ownership and use do not have to be continuous. Further, ownership and use tests can be met during different two-year periods.

Example: Mabel bought a house on September 1, 2015. After living there for ten months, she moved in with her boyfriend and left her house vacant. They later broke up, and Mabel moved back into her own house in 2018. She lived there for an additional 16 months until she sold it on September 1, 2020. Mabel meets the ownership and use tests because, during the five-year period ending on the date of sale, she owned the house for five years and lived in the house a total of 26 months - both more than the required 24-month (2-year) requirements.

Example: Germaine owns and uses a house as her principal residence from 2011 to the end of 2016. On December 30, 2016, Germaine moves overseas to live in Australia. Germaine's daughter, Tamera, moves into the house in March 2017 and uses it as her residence until it is sold on July 1, 2020. Germaine may not exclude any of the gain from the sale under section 121 because she did not use the property as her principal residence for at least 2 years out of the 5 years preceding the sale. The gain would be taxed as a long-term capital gain to Germaine.

Short, temporary absences, even if the property is rented during those absences, are still counted as periods of use. Short absences include vacations and seasonal absences. Longer breaks, such as a one-year sabbatical, are not included.

Example: Alannah is a college professor who teaches Medieval history. She purchases and moves into her home on April 1, 2018. On August 1, 2019, she moves abroad for a one-year sabbatical to study ancient manuscripts in Germany. On August 1, 2020, she returns to the U.S. from her sabbatical, and on September 1, 2020, she sells the house, because she wants to move into a smaller apartment. Even though she *owned* the home for over two years, the year-long sabbatical is not considered a short, temporary absence. She is not entitled to take the section 121 exclusion because she did not satisfy the "*use* requirement."

Example: Juanita bought her home on February 1, 2016. Each year, she left her home for a three-month vacation in Ecuador. Juanita sold the house on March 1, 2020. She may exclude up to $250,000 of gain. Her vacations are considered short temporary absences and are counted toward her periods of use.

Remember, the periods of "use" and the periods of "ownership" do not need to be concurrent.

Example: In 2011, Lionel began living in an apartment he rented from a landlord. The apartment complex was later converted to condominiums. Lionel purchased his unit on December 1, 2017. Lionel later becomes seriously ill, and on April 14, 2020, he moves into his daughter's home. After several months, he did not recover from his illness, so he decided to remain living in his daughter's home. He did not return to his condo, and on July 10, 2020, while still living in his daughter's home, Lionel sells his condo. He can exclude all the gain on the sale because he meets the ownership and use tests. His five-year "lookback" period is from July 11, 2015, to July 10, 2020 (five years *before* the date he actually sold the condo). He *owned* the condo from December 1, 2017, until July 10, 2020 (more than two years). He *lived* there from 2011 until April 14, 2020 (more than two years), so he would qualify to exclude all the gain, even though his ownership and use periods do not always overlap.

Different Rules for Married Homeowners

The ownership and use tests are applied differently to married homeowners. Married homeowners can exclude gain of up to $500,000 if they meet all of the following conditions:

- They file a joint return.
- Either spouse meets the ownership test (only one is required to own the home).
- Both spouses meet the use test.
- Neither spouse has excluded gain in the two years before the current sale of the home.

If they do not satisfy these requirements, the couple cannot claim the maximum $500,000 exclusion for married couples. However, one spouse may figure his or her exclusion separately, if only one spouse qualifies.

Example: Irene owns her home and has lived in it continuously for the last seven years. She meets Julien and marries him in September 2020. They move in together, but Julien doesn't like Irene's house, and he convinces her to sell it a few months later. Irene sells the home on December 10, 2020, and has $350,000 of gain. Irene meets the ownership and use tests, but Julien does not meet the use test because he only lived in the house for a few months. Irene can exclude up to $250,000 of gain on her 2020 tax return, whether she files MFJ or MFS. The $500,000 exclusion for joint returns does not apply.

Example: Hubert owns a home that he has lived in continuously for a decade. On June 1, 2016, he marries Jasmine, she moves into the home, and they both live in the house together until December 1, 2020, when the house is sold. Hubert meets the ownership test and the use test. Jasmine does not own the home because Hubert is listed as the sole owner of the property and the only one listed on the deed. However, she meets the "use test" because she lived in the home for at least two years. Therefore, on a jointly filed return, they can claim the maximum $500,000 exclusion.

Legally married spouses are eligible for the maximum $500,000 exclusion from gain on their jointly filed returns. If an unmarried couple owns and lives in a house together, and later gets married, the $500,000 exclusion applies if they file a joint return. If the couples file separate returns, each spouse would figure their exclusion separately on their own return.

Example: Paige and Halden were legally married in California a year ago. In 2020, they sell the house they had co-owned and lived in together for fifteen years. They are both listed as co-owners on the deed, even though they were not married when they bought the home. They purchased the house for $210,000 and sold it for $785,000, which means they have a profit of $575,000. Paige and Halden may claim the maximum $500,000 exclusion for married couples when they file jointly in 2020. If they chose to file separate returns, each one would be eligible for a $250,000 exclusion on their own, separate returns. The remaining $75,000 of gain ($575,000 profit -$500,000 exclusion) is taxable as a long-term capital gain. They would have to recognize the gain whether they file jointly or separately.

A special rule for the holding period also applies to a home that is transferred by a spouse in a divorce.[122] The receiving spouse is considered to have owned the home during any period of time that the transferor owned it.

Example: Vidal buys a home for $400,000 on January 1, 2015. Two years later, Vidal meets Wanda, and they get married. Wanda moved in with Vidal, but the home's ownership remains in Vidal's name only. They start having marital difficulties, and Wanda moves out on June 1, 2020. Three months later, they get divorced. As part of their divorce settlement, Vidal transfers ownership of the house to Wanda. The home reminds Wanda of unhappy times, so on December 25, 2020, she sells the home for $475,000, making a $75,000 profit on the sale. She is entitled to the Section 121 exclusion, because IRS regulations treat Wanda as having owned the home during the time it was owned by Vidal. She may exclude the entire $75,000 gain on her tax return.

Unrelated Individuals: An unmarried couple or other taxpayers who own a home and live together may take the $250,000 exclusion individually on their separate returns if they meet the use and ownership tests.

Example: Salma and Carolyn are sisters. They are both widowed in 2020 and decided to purchase a home and live together. If they later sell the home, the ownership and use tests would apply to them individually. Each could claim an exclusion of up to $250,000 for her portion of the sale on her individual return.

---

122 This is a tax-free transfer of property "incident to a divorce." If a taxpayer obtains property from a former spouse in a divorce, the period that the taxpayer owns the property will include the period that the former spouse owned the property.

Deceased Spouses: When a taxpayer's spouse dies, the taxpayer is considered to have owned and lived in a home during any period of time that the spouse owned and lived in it as a main home (provided that the taxpayer did not remarry before the date of sale). In effect, the holding period of the deceased spouse is "tacked on" for surviving spouses. As a result, the surviving spouse may exclude up to $500,000 of gain even if he sells the home within two years from the date of death of the deceased spouse.

Example: Harmony owned and lived in her home for seven years. She married Gerard on January 10, 2020, and he moved into the home with her. Harmony died six months later, and Gerard inherited the property. He did not remarry. Gerard decides to sell the home on December 1, 2020. Even though he did not own or live in the house for two years, he meets the test requirements because his period of ownership and use includes the period that Harmony owned and used the property before her death. Gerard may exclude up to $500,000 of the gain under the special rule that applies to deceased spouses.

Military Personnel Exception: Members of the armed forces are often required to move and might have difficulty meeting the tests for ownership and use within the five-year period prior to the sale of a home. The five-year period can be suspended for up to ten years for U.S. military[123] as well as for Foreign Service personnel, Peace Corps workers, and intelligence officers that are on official extended duty. This provides the taxpayer a better opportunity to meet the two-year use test even if he and/or his spouse did not actually live in the home during the normal five-year period required of other taxpayers.

Example: Ensign Smith is a U.S. naval officer. He is single and owns his own home. Ensign Smith bought and moved into his home on January 2, 2012. He lived in it as his main home for 2½ years. For the following 6 years, he didn't live in the home because he was on qualified official extended duty with the U.S. Navy. He did not return to the home during that time and lived overseas. Ensign Smith sold his home for a $125,000 gain on December 26, 2020. To meet the use test, he may suspend the normal 5-year test period for the time he was on qualifying official extended duty. This means that Ensign Smith can disregard the 6 years that he lived abroad when he is calculating his period of "ownership and use." He meets the "ownership and use" tests because he owned and lived in the home for at least 2 years. Ensign Smith may exclude all the gain from the sale on his individual tax return.

Disability Exception: There is an exception to the use test if, during the five-year period before the sale of the home, a taxpayer becomes physically or mentally unable to care for himself, but he has owned and lived in the home for at least one year. The taxpayer is considered to have lived in the home during any time that he is forced to live in a licensed facility, including a nursing home. The taxpayer must still meet the two-year ownership test.

Rules for Reduced Exclusions

A taxpayer who owned and used a home for less than two years (and therefore does not meet the ownership and use tests) or who has used the home sale exclusion within the prior two-year period may be able to claim a reduced exclusion under certain conditions.

[123] This includes members of the U.S. Army, Navy, Air Force, Marine Corps, etc.

This may apply if a home sale has occurred primarily because of "unforeseen circumstances" during the taxpayer's period of use and ownership. Unforeseen circumstances include the following:

- Death, divorce, or legal separation;
- Certain health reasons related to care for the taxpayer, a spouse, a child, or certain other related persons. The related person does not have to be a dependent for the reduced exclusion to apply;
- Unemployment or a job change: the job-change exclusion applies if a new job is at least 50 miles farther from the old home than was the former place of employment. If there was no former place of employment, the distance between the new place of employment and the old home must be at least 50 miles;
- Multiple births resulting from the same pregnancy;
- Damage to the residence resulting from a disaster, an act of war, or terrorism; and
- Involuntary conversion of the property.

The circumstances may involve the taxpayer, his spouse, a co-owner, or a member of the taxpayer's household. The IRS also has the discretion to deem other circumstances as "unforeseen."

Example: Farrell purchased his new home in Mississippi on January 10, 2020, but he lost his job shortly after he moved in. He found a new job in Alaska and sold his house on November 30, 2020, generating a small profit of $6,000 on the sale. Because the distance between Farrell's new place of employment and his former home is at least 50 miles, the sale satisfies the distance requirement. Farrell's sale of his home is due to a change in place of employment, and he is entitled to claim a reduced exclusion on his gain from the sale of his home.

The reduced exclusion amount equals the full $250,000 (or $500,000 for married couples filing jointly) multiplied by a fraction. The numerator is the *shorter* of:

- The period the taxpayer owned and used the home as a principal residence during the five-year period ending on the sale date, or
- The period between the last sale for which the taxpayer claimed the exclusion and the sale date for the home currently being sold.

The denominator is two years or the equivalent in months or days. Thus, the amount of the reduced exclusion is figured by multiplying the full exclusion amount by the number of days or months the taxpayer owned and used the property and dividing by either 730 days or 24 months.

Example: Elena, an unmarried taxpayer, lived in her principal residence in San Francisco for one full year (365 days) before selling it. The sale generated a $260,000 gain. Even though she only lived in the house for a year, she qualifies for the reduced exclusion because she recently gave birth to twins (multiple births exclusion). Elena can exclude $125,000 of gain ($250,000 × [365 ÷ 730]).

Example: On January 5, 2020, Jareth, who is single, purchases his home and uses it as his principal residence. On July 5, 2020, (six months later), Jareth is forced to sell his home because his employer transfers his job to another state. He may exclude up to a maximum of $62,500 ($250,000 maximum exclusion X 6/24 months) of the gain on the sale. If his gain on the sale is *less* than $62,500, then he will not have a taxable gain.

Land Sales: If a taxpayer sells the land on which his main home is located but not the house itself, he cannot exclude the gain. Similarly, the sale of a vacant plot of land with no house on it does not qualify for the section 121 exclusion.

Example: Bernarda purchased an empty lot three years ago for $90,000, planning to build her dream home. Construction was delayed, and her house was never completed. In December 2020, Bernarda sells the land for $150,000. She owned the property for more than a year, so she has $60,000 of long-term capital gain. None of the gain can be excluded from income because there is no residence on the property. Section 121 only applies to actual homes, not to an empty lot.

If a taxpayer sells a vacant lot that is directly adjacent to his main home, he may be able to exclude the gain from the sale under some (rare) circumstances. Gain from the sale of vacant land that was used *in connection* with a principal residence may be excluded if the land sale occurs within two years before or after the sale of the home.

The land must have been adjacent to the land on which the home was located, and the taxpayer must have owned and used the land as part of their home and not for any business purpose. The sale of the land and the sale of the home are treated as one sale for purposes of the exclusion.

Gains from Depreciation Recapture or Unrecaptured §1250 Gain

In situations where depreciation has been taken on real property (such as buildings), Section 1250 depreciation recapture can potentially apply on sales at a gain, but only if the amount of depreciation taken up to the time of sale exceeds straight-line depreciation, which is not common. A common scenario of sales of depreciable real estate at a gain is when a taxpayer has a small business home office.

The amount of straight-line depreciation claimed in prior years is considered as "unrecaptured §1250 gain" up to the amount of recognized gain. This is only applicable to the sale of depreciable real estate. "Unrecaptured §1250 gain" is *technically* long-term capital gain, with a special maximum rate of 25%.

Example: Tania is an attorney that works out of her home. She has a qualified home office for which she deducts all relevant expenses, including straight-line depreciation, for five years. In 2020, Tania sells her home at a gain. Since the home is her primary residence, the sale qualifies for the section 121 exclusion, but the depreciation that she claimed on her home office is subject to unrecaptured section 1250 gain, and will be taxed using ordinary tax rates, with a maximum capital gains rate of 25%.

Like-Kind Exchanges (Section 1031 Exchange)

A section 1031 like-kind exchange occurs when a taxpayer exchanges qualifying real property for other qualifying real property. Gain is *deferred*, (but not forgiven), in a like-kind exchange. The simplest type of Section 1031 exchange is a simultaneous swap of one property for another (also called a "simultaneous swap").

Deferred exchanges are more complex but allow more flexibility. A deferred exchange allows a taxpayer to dispose of property and subsequently acquire one or more other like-kind replacement properties at a later date.

As like-kind exchanges only apply to exchanges of qualifying real estate, any "exchange" of personal property will be treated as a non-cash sale and will not qualify for nonrecognition treatment under Section 1031. The IRS issued regulations defining real property for Section 1031 purposes:

- Land and improvements to land (such as buildings, concrete parking lots, foundations),
- Unsevered natural products of land,
- Water and air space superjacent to land,
- Certain intangible interests in real property (such as leaseholds and options), and
- Property that is real property under state or local law.

If the exchange qualifies under section 1031, and if no other property (other than the like-kind real estate) is given or received, the taxpayer does not recognize any resulting gain and cannot deduct any losses until he later disposes of the property received. To qualify for nonrecognition treatment, the exchange must meet all of the following conditions:

- The property must be held for investment or for productive use in a business. Property held for personal use, such as a personal residence, does not qualify.
- The property must NOT be "held primarily for sale" (such as real estate held as inventory by a real estate dealer).
- There must be an actual exchange of two or more assets or properties (the exchange of *property* strictly for cash is always treated as a sale, not as an exchange).
- For instances in which a property is transferred in exchange for like-kind property to be received later (known as a deferred exchange), the property to be received must be identified in writing (or actually received) within 45 days[124] after the date of transfer of the property given up.
- In general, a "qualified intermediary" must be procured to facilitate the exchange using escrow accounts. This type of qualified intermediary (sometimes also known as an exchange accommodator or facilitator) promises to return the proceeds of the exchange to the transferor of the property.[125]

---

[124] For tax year 2020 only, the IRS extended time-sensitive deadlines for section 1031 exchanges. IRS Notice 2020-23 expanded on prior COVID-19 tax deadline extensions to include time-sensitive actions, including deadlines for actions to be taken in 1031 exchanges. If a deadline under a 1031 exchange transaction fell between March 31, 2020 and before July 15, 2020 the deadline to complete such time-sensitive action was extended until July 15, 2020.

[125] Only in a "simultaneous" 1031 exchange (a two-party swap) is a qualified intermediary not needed. That occurs only when the exchange is processed on the same day and there is no delayed exchange.

Further, the replacement property in a section 1031 exchange must be received by the earlier of:

- The 180th day after the date on which the property was given up was transferred, or
- The due date, including extensions, of the tax return for the year in which the transfer of that property occurs. The IRS is very strict about these deadlines.

Taxpayers report like-kind exchanges on Form 8824, *Like-Kind Exchanges*. The taxpayer must calculate and keep track of their basis in the new property they acquired in an exchange. The most common type of section 1031 exchange is a simultaneous swap of one residential rental property for another. However, taxpayers may exchange different types of real property, including buildings, farmland, timberland, even undeveloped land.

In general, any exchange of any real property generally qualifies as like-kind, regardless of how each property is used or whether each property is improved or unimproved. For instance, the exchange of an office building for farmland would qualify, as would the exchange of an apartment complex for an office building.

Nonqualifying Exchanges: Personal-use realty is not eligible for a like-kind exchange. So, the exchange of a personal residence for another personal residence does not qualify, nor would an exchange of a personal residence for an apartment building. The exchange of property within the United States for similar property *outside* the United States also would not be a qualifying exchange. Foreign real estate is not eligible for nonrecognition treatment. And remember, inventory is *never* eligible for like-kind treatment.

Example: Lawrence is a professional real estate developer. Lawrence purchases large tracts of land and then markets and sells the subdivided lots for later development. All of the lots he purchases are available for sale to customers. In this case, the land lots are not capital assets, because Lawrence is a professional real estate dealer: to him, the land is inventory. Lawrence cannot use section 1031 to escape recognition of gain on the transfer or sale of his land lots.

Example: Madalynn is a full-time house-flipper. She buys distressed properties at auction, fixes them up, and then re-sells them, usually within six months of purchase. She does not rent them out or live in the properties while they are being rehabbed. In 2020, she has five houses that are in the process of being flipped. Once the current restorations are complete, Madalynn intends to re-sell the homes to future buyers. The properties are treated as inventory, rather than capital assets. Therefore, none of the properties would be eligible for a section 1031 exchange.

Example: Cassidy exchanges a residential rental in Hawaii with an adjusted basis of $100,000 with a vacation property in Cancun, Mexico. The Cancun property has a fair market value of $145,000. The exchange of foreign realty for real property in the United States does not qualify for section 1031 treatment. Instead, the transaction is treated as a sale. Since the exchange does not qualify for nonrecognition treatment, Cassidy must recognize $45,000 of taxable income on the transaction. Her basis in the Cancun property is $145,000, which would be the same treatment if the property had been purchased with cash.

Taxable Exchanges: If a taxpayer receives property in exchange for other property that does not meet the like-kind exchange rules, he may need to recognize gain if the fair market value of the property received is greater than the adjusted basis of the property given up. His basis in the property received is generally its FMV at the time of the exchange.

Cash Boot and Mortgage Boot

Although the Internal Revenue Code itself does not use the term "boot," it is frequently used to describe cash or other property added to an exchange to compensate for a difference in the values of properties traded. A taxpayer must generally not receive "boot" in an exchange, in order for the exchange to be completely tax-free.

This doesn't mean that the exchange is not valid, but the taxpayer who receives boot may have to recognize taxable gain to the extent of the cash and the FMV of unlike property received, but the recognized gain when boot is received is still limited to the realized gain on the exchange. The amount considered boot would also be reduced by any qualified costs paid in connection with the transaction.

Example: Glenn exchanges a residential rental property for a parcel of farmland in a section 1031 exchange. The relinquished rental property has an FMV of $60,000 and an adjusted basis of $30,000. The farmland Glenn receives has an FMV of $50,000, and he also receives $10,000 of cash as part of the exchange. Glenn, therefore, has a realized gain of $30,000 on the exchange (combined value of $60,000 received minus his basis of $30,000 in the rental he exchanged). He is required to pay tax and recognize gain on only $10,000, the cash (boot) received in the exchange. The rest of his gain is deferred until he disposes of the farmland at a later date.

Example: Kaden exchanges an office building for a large commercial warehouse. The office building has a fair market value of $190,000 and an adjusted basis of $150,000. The warehouse has a fair market value of $200,000. As part of the exchange, Kaden also receives a forklift valued at $21,000. Kaden does not recognize gain on the exchange of the real estate because it qualifies as a nontaxable exchange. However, he must recognize the value of the forklift on his return because it is "unlike" property (i.e., not real estate).[126]

In situations when there is a realized loss on a section 1031 exchange, and the taxpayer receives boot, none of the loss is recognized. However, the deferred loss is added to the basis of the contributed like-kind property given to the other party to determine the basis of the like-kind property received.

Boot can be given, as well as received, in a like-kind exchange. If cash is given to the other party in a like-kind exchange, none of the realized gain (or loss) will be recognized. However, if non-cash boot is given to the other party, then gain (or loss) will be recognized based on the difference between the non-cash boot's fair market value and adjusted basis at the time of the exchange.

When an exchange involves property that is subject to a liability (such as an existing mortgage), the assumption of the liability is treated as if it was a transfer of cash and thus considered boot by the party who is relieved of the liability. Sometimes this is called "mortgage boot" or "debt reduction boot." On the other hand, if a party assumes a mortgage from the other

[126] Scenarios based on examples illustrated in Publication 544, *Sales and Other Dispositions of Assets.*

party, it is treated as cash boot given to the other party. If each property in an exchange is transferred subject to a liability, a taxpayer is treated as having received boot only if he is relieved of a greater liability than the liability he assumes. When there is mortgage boot and cash boot in the same transaction, the mortgage boot paid does not offset any "cash boot" received. Net cash boot received is *always* taxable if there is a realized gain on the exchange.

Example: Marjorie exchanges an apartment building with a FMV of $700,000 and an existing mortgage of $100,000 for a commercial factory building with a FMV of $650,000 and an existing mortgage of $150,000. Marjorie assumes the mortgage on the factory building, and also receives cash boot of $60,000 in the exchange. Marjorie may offset the mortgages, which means that she has paid $50,000 in "mortgage boot" in the transaction. She is not allowed to deduct the mortgage boot paid from the cash boot received, however. Therefore, her potential taxable boot in this transaction (up to the amount of realized gain on the exchange) is $60,000, which is the amount of cash that she received.

The Basis of Property Received in a Like-Kind Exchange

The basis of property acquired in a straight Section 1031 exchange is the basis of the property given up with some adjustments. Gain is deferred, but not forgiven, in a like-kind exchange.

Example: Evianna owns a residential rental property with a FMV of $350,000 an adjusted basis of $270,000. In 2020, she trades her rental property for a commercial parking lot with an FMV of $360,000. No cash was exchanged, and it was a straight exchange of properties. Evianna's basis in the parking lot is $270,000, equal to the adjusted basis of the rental property she exchanged. The fair market value of the properties is irrelevant in this case.

If a taxpayer trades property and also pays money as part of the exchange, the basis of the property received is the basis of the property given up, increased by any additional money paid.

Example: Gavin trades a parking lot with an adjusted basis of $30,000 for a parcel of farmland in another state with an FMV of $70,500. He pays an additional $4,000 of cash to complete the transaction. Gavin's basis in the new farmland is $34,000—his $30,000 basis in the old parking lot *plus* the additional $4,000 cash he paid.

If a taxpayer receives boot in connection with an exchange and recognizes gain, the basis of the property received is equal to the basis of the property given up *plus* the amount of gain recognized. The taxpayer may reduce the amount of recognized gain by any exchange expenses (closing costs) paid.

Example: Joshua exchanges a tract of farmland with an adjusted basis of $80,000 for a plot of timberland with an FMV of $100,000. He receives cash of $10,000 in connection with the exchange and must recognize gain to the extent of the boot received. However, he also pays $5,000 in exchange expenses and other related closing costs to his attorney in order to complete the exchange. Joshua's recognized (taxable) gain is only $5,000, figured as follows: (cash boot received $10,000 - $5,000 exchange expenses paid = $5,000 in recognized gain).[127]

[127] Example based on scenario in Publication 544, Sales and Other Dispositions of Assets.

Example: Geri owns a plot of timberland with a basis of $500,000 and a FMV of 750,000. Rowan owns an office complex with a FMV of $900,000. Geri and Rowan agree to exchange properties. Since Rowan's property is worth more, Geri pays $150,000 in cash to complete the exchange, which is the difference in the property's fair market values. Once the 1031 exchange is complete, Geri's basis in the office complex would be $650,000 ($150,000 cash she paid, plus the $500,000 adjusted basis in her old property).[128]

Related Party Like-Kind Exchanges

Like-kind exchanges are permitted between related parties. However, if either party disposes of the property within two years after a 1031 exchange, the exchange is disqualified from nonrecognition treatment; any gain or loss that was deferred in the original transaction must be recognized in the year the disposition occurs.

For purposes of this rule, a related person includes a close family member (such as a spouse, sibling, parent, or child). It also includes a corporation or partnership in which a taxpayer holds ownership or interests of more than 50%. The two-year holding period rule does not apply:

- If one of the parties involved in the exchange subsequently dies;
- If the property is subsequently converted in an involuntary exchange (such as a fire);
- If it can be established to the satisfaction of the IRS that the exchange and subsequent disposition were not done mainly for tax avoidance purposes.

The IRS gives close scrutiny to exchanges between related parties because they can be used by taxpayers to evade taxes on gains.

Involuntary Conversions (Section 1033 Exchanges)

An involuntary conversion occurs when a taxpayer's property is lost, damaged, or destroyed, and the taxpayer receives an award, insurance money, or some other type of payment, as a result of:

- Casualty, disaster, or theft,
- The loss of a property due to an exercise of eminent domain, or
- Condemnation (or threat of condemnation).

Involuntary conversions are also called "involuntary exchanges." Involuntary conversions can occur with business property as well as personal-use property, but the rules differ for each. Sometimes, a taxpayer will have a taxable gain from an involuntary conversion. This usually happens when a taxpayer's insurance reimbursement exceeds their basis in the property. Gain or loss from an involuntary conversion is usually recognized for tax purposes unless the property is a main home (covered later).

A taxpayer reports the gain or deducts the loss in the year the gain or loss is realized. This does not mean that an involuntary conversion is a taxable event, even when an insurance reimbursement exceeds the taxpayer's basis.

[128] Example based on scenario in Publication 551, Basis of Assets.

Example: Parker owns an office building. A fire destroyed his building on January 3, 2020. He purchased the building several years ago for $150,000. The depreciation deductions he had taken were $78,000, so the building had an adjusted basis of $72,000. Parker received a $120,000 insurance payout on May 1, 2020, realizing a gain of $48,000 ($120,000 payout - adjusted basis of $72,000). Parker immediately spends $100,000 of the insurance payment to purchase a replacement property. He uses the rest of the insurance money to go on vacation to Hawaii. Since $100,000 of the $120,000 insurance payment was used to buy replacement property, his taxable gain under the rules for involuntary conversions is limited to the remaining $20,000 insurance payment. His taxable gain is limited to $20,000.[129]

Under section 1033, a taxpayer can elect to *defer* reporting the gain on an involuntary conversion if he receives proceeds from insurance or another source and reinvests in property that is similar to the converted property. In other words, the gain on an involuntary conversion can be deferred until (a later) taxable sale or exchange occurs. Unlike a section 1031 exchange, in general, replacement property cannot be purchased from a "related" party for an involuntary conversion to qualify for nonrecognition treatment.

Longer Replacement Period: While a section 1031 exchange only has a 180-day exchange period, a section 1033 exchange has a much longer time for completion. The replacement period for an involuntary conversion generally ends two years after the end of the first tax year in which any part of the gain is realized. There is no requirement under Section 1033 that a qualified intermediary be employed to hold the escrow funds or conversion proceeds.

Property Type	Replacement Period
Most property except those noted below; the two-year replacement period also includes personal homes.	Two years
Real property (real estate) that is held for investment or business use, such as residential rentals and office buildings	Three years
Sale of livestock due to weather-related conditions	Four years
Main home in a federally declared disaster area	Four to five years, depending on IRS guidance

Real property that is held for investment or used in a trade or business is allowed a three-year replacement period. The replacement period is four years for livestock that is involuntarily converted because of weather-related conditions.

Example: Stanford owns a drywall repair business. On September 1, 2020, a flood destroyed his warehouse, which was filled with his tools and construction supplies. Stanford's insurance company reimburses him for the loss on October 26, 2020. He has until December 31, 2022 (the end of the second year after the gain was realized in 2020) to replace the shed and supplies using the insurance proceeds. Stanford is not required to report the insurance proceeds on his 2020 tax return if he reinvests all the proceeds in a replacement property.

If a taxpayer's main home is damaged or destroyed and is in a federally declared disaster area, the replacement period is extended to four years. A five-year replacement period has been applied to certain extreme disaster areas, but only if the replacement property is purchased in

[129] Example based directly on a scenario in Publication 544, *Like-Kind Exchanges and Involuntary Conversions.*

the same area. If a taxpayer reinvests in replacement property similar to the converted property, the replacement property's basis is the same as the converted property's basis on the date of the conversion, subject to the following adjustments: The basis is **decreased** by the following:

- Any loss a taxpayer recognizes on the involuntary conversion
- Any money a taxpayer receives that he does not spend on similar property

The basis is **increased** by the following:

- Any gain a taxpayer recognizes on the involuntary conversion
- Any additional costs of acquiring the replacement property

Example: Xerxes owns an apartment fourplex in Texas with a basis of $250,000. He receives an insurance settlement of $400,000 after the building is destroyed by a tornado. Two years later, Xerxes purchases another apartment building in Wisconsin for $380,000. His realized gain on the involuntary conversion is $150,000 ($400,000 - $250,000 basis). He must recognize $20,000 of gain because he received an insurance payment of $400,000 but only spent $380,000 on the replacement property ($400,000 - $380,000). His basis in the new property is $250,000, which is calculated as the cost of the new property in Wisconsin minus the deferred gain ($380,000 - $130,000 = $250,000). If Xerxes had used all the insurance proceeds and reinvested it in the new property, he would not have to report any taxable gain.

Example: A hurricane destroys Theresa's rental condo that had an adjusted basis of $49,000. The insurance company gives Theresa a check for $175,000, which is the FMV of the condo on the date that it was destroyed. Theresa buys a replacement rental property six months later for $175,000. Her gain on the involuntary conversion is $126,000 ($175,000 insurance settlement minus her $49,000 basis). However, Theresa does not have to recognize any taxable gain because she reinvested all the insurance proceeds in another, similar property under a qualified 1033 exchange. In this scenario, the basis of her replacement property is the same as the property that was destroyed: $49,000.

Condemnations and Eminent Domain

A "condemnation" is a specific type of involuntary conversion. If a building is dangerous to public health and safety, the property may also be legally condemned. Condemnation is also a legal process by which private property is taken from its owner for public use. Sometimes this process is called "eminent domain." A condemnation is a type of "forced sale," or forced disposition, with the owner being the seller and the government or other third party being the buyer.

Eminent domain allows the government to take private property in exchange for compensation. A property may be condemned by a state or local government or by a private organization that has the legal power to seize it.

The owner generally receives a condemnation award (money or property) in exchange for the property that is taken.

Example: A local government informs Louis that his farmland is being condemned to create a public highway. Although Louis does not want to sell his land, the government forces the sale and issues a condemnation award to Louis, paying him the property's fair market value of $400,000. Louis's original basis in the farmland was $80,000. Louis is frustrated by his government and decides not to purchase replacement farmland. Therefore, he has a taxable event, and he must recognize $320,000 as income ($400,000 - $80,000 = $320,000). However, if Louis were to purchase replacement property with the condemnation award, he would have a nontaxable section 1033 exchange. He has up to three years to decide if he wants to reinvest the proceeds.

Amounts taken out of a condemnation award to pay debts on the property are considered paid to the taxpayer and are included in the amount of the award.

Example: The state condemned Kenton's property to build a light rail system. The court award was set at $200,000. The state paid him only $148,000 because it paid $50,000 to his mortgage company and $2,000 in accrued real estate taxes that were delinquent on the property. Kenton is considered to have received the entire $200,000 as a condemnation award.

The time period for replacing condemned property is the same as other qualified section 1033 exchanges, two years after the end of the first tax year in which any part of the gain on the condemnation is realized. For real property held for business use or investment, the replacement period is three years instead of two.

Example: Hammond owns a strip mall. On March 12, 2020, the building is condemned by the county in order to build a public skatepark. Hammond decides not to fight the condemnation, and the strip mall is torn down a few months later, and he receives his condemnation award from the government on November 30, 2020. Since the strip mall is business-related real estate, Hammond has three full years to reinvest the proceeds in a similar property. He has until December 31, 2023, to replace the condemned strip mall with a similar building (three years from the *end* of the year in which he received the condemnation award). As long as he buys a similar business property within the next three years with the proceeds, he will not have to recognize any of the gain or report it on his return.

Condemnation or Destruction of a Main Home

If a taxpayer has a gain because his main home is condemned or destroyed, he can generally exclude the gain as if he had sold the home under the section 121 exclusion. This includes homes that are seized or disposed of under the "threat of condemnation." In the case of a condemnation, the property owner must be aware of the threat and must reasonably believe that a condemnation is likely to occur.

If the taxpayer's main home is eligible for a section 121 exclusion, single filers can exclude up to $250,000 of the gain and joint filers up to $500,000. Any *excess* gains above these amounts may be potentially deferred under section 1033 if the taxpayer reinvests all the proceeds in another, similar property (see examples, next).

Example: Janice has owned and lived in her home continuously for seven years. On January 3, 2020, a local government informed Janice that it wished to acquire her home and surrounding land in order to create a public highway. This is a condemnation of private property for public use. After the local government took legal action to condemn her property, Janice went to court to keep her home. The court decided in favor of the government. The governmental agency takes possession of Janice's home. Janice receives a $355,000 condemnation award from the government on December 27, 2020. Her basis in the home is $153,000. Even if she decides not to reinvest the proceeds of the condemnation award, Janice will not have a taxable gain, because the gain would have been excludable under section 121 if she had voluntarily sold the home ($355,000 award - $153,000 basis = $202,000 non-taxable capital gain).

Example: On February 8, 2020, a fire destroys Claudia's main home. She bought the home ten years ago for $80,000. Claudia's insurance company pays Claudia $400,000 for the house, which was the fair market value of the home when it was destroyed. Claudia realizes a gain of $320,000 ($400,000 insurance proceeds - $80,000 basis). Claudia decides to downsize, and on August 27, 2020, she purchases a smaller condo at the cost of $100,000. Because the destruction of her old house is treated as a "sale" for purposes of section 121, Claudia may exclude $250,000 of the realized gain from her gross income. For purposes of section 1033, the amount "realized" is then treated as being $150,000 ($400,000 insurance proceeds - $250,000 section 121 exclusion) and the gain realized is $70,000 ($150,000 amount realized - $80,000 basis). Claudia elects under section 1033 to recognize only $50,000 of the gain ($150,000 amount realized - $100,000 cost of new house). The remaining $20,000 of gain is deferred and Claudia's basis in the new house is $80,000 ($100,000 cost - $20,000 gain not recognized).[130]

[130] The examples in this section are modified from IRS Final Regulations, *Exclusion of Gain from Sale or Exchange of a Principal Residence,* [TD 9030]. RIN 1545-AX28. https://www.irs.gov/pub/irs-regs/td9030.pdf.

Unit 8: Study Questions

(Test yourself first, then check the correct answers at the end of this quiz.)

1. Grady exchanges his residential rental property with an adjusted basis of $50,000 and an FMV of $80,000 for 10 acres of undeveloped land with an FMV of $70,000. He plans to hold the land as an investment. What is Grady's basis in the land after this Section 1031 exchange?

A. $50,000
B. $70,000
C. $80,000
D. This is not a qualifying like-kind exchange.

2. Alistair and Gabrielle are married and file jointly. They sold their primary residence in Los Angeles after living in it for 292 days because Gabrielle gave birth to triplets, and they needed a larger home. They bought the home for $585,000 and sold it for $845,000. The total gain on the sale of their home is $260,000. Since they lived there for less than two years but meet one of the exceptions, what is the actual amount of their *reduced* exclusion? (Two years = 730 days.)

A. $60,000
B. $200,000
C. $260,000
D. $500,000

3. Heather is single and bought her first home ten years ago for $350,000. She lived continuously in the house until she sold it in 2020 for $620,000. Which of the following statements is correct?

A. She may exclude $250,000 of the gain and report the remaining amount as a long-term capital gain.
B. She may exclude the entire gain. No amount needs to be reported.
C. She may not exclude any of the gain.
D. She may exclude $250,000 of gain. The remaining amount must be reported as ordinary income.

4. Which of the following would not be an acceptable "unforeseen circumstance" for a taxpayer to take a reduced exclusion on the sale of his primary residence?

A. The home is condemned by the city.
B. A legal separation that will lead to a divorce.
C. The birth of twin girls.
D. Moving to another state to be closer to grown children.

5. Chrystal exchanged a retail building with an adjusted basis of $160,000 for a warehouse. The fair market value of the warehouse she received was $200,000. She also received $10,000 of cash and paid $5,000 of exchange expenses to complete the exchange. What is her recognized (taxable) gain on the transaction, if any?

A. $0
B. $5,000
C. $10,000
D. $45,000

6. Clayton trades a commercial building with an adjusted basis of $84,000 for an industrial tractor with a fair market value of $97,000. Clayton plans to use the tractor in his farming business. What is the basis of the tractor, and how much taxable gain, if any, must Clayton report?

A. $0 gain; $97,000 basis.
B. $0 gain; $13,000 basis.
C. $13,000 gain; $84,000 basis.
D. $13,000 gain; $97,000 basis.

7. A fire destroyed Bryant's main home on July 15, 2020. On November 23, 2020, he received an insurance reimbursement, which exceeds his basis in the home. Rather than recognizing any gain, Bryant wants to replace the home, but he hasn't found a property that he likes yet. What is the latest date that Bryant can purchase replacement property to defer all the gain from his insurance reimbursement?

A. July 15, 2021
B. August 23, 2022
C. December 31, 2022
D. July 15, 2023

8. Uriah exchanges a residential rental property in Las Vegas with a basis of $100,000 for an investment property in Miami Beach valued at $220,000. Uriah also received $15,000 of cash boot in the exchange. What is Uriah's taxable gain on the exchange, if any, and what is his basis in the new property in Miami Beach?

A. Taxable gain: $15,000; basis: $115,000.
B. Taxable gain: $0; basis: $235,000.
C. Taxable gain: $15,000; basis: $135,000.
D. Taxable gain: $15,000; basis: $220,000.

9. Which of the following transactions does *not* qualify for a section 1031 like-kind exchange?

A. An exchange of a building in Chicago for empty farmland in Nebraska.
B. An exchange of an apartment building in Delaware for a factory building in Alaska.
C. An exchange of a residential rental for an undeveloped lot of land.
D. An exchange of a developer's land inventory for a house flipper's housing inventory.

10. Geoff is a self-employed tax preparer. He sold his main home in 2020 at a $29,000 gain. He meets the "ownership and use" tests to exclude the gain from his income. However, he used one bedroom of the home as a business office for the last two years. His records show he claimed $3,000 of depreciation for a qualified home office, taking the deduction on his Schedule C. What is Geoff's taxable gain on the sale, if any?

A. $0
B. $1,000
C. $2,000
D. $3,000

11. Jonah exchanged farmland that he held for investment for an office building. The original cost of the farmland was $16,000, and he made $10,000 of land improvements (such as permanent fencing) prior to the exchange. The fair market value of the office building at the time of the exchange was $66,000. Jonah did not receive or pay any cash in the exchange. What is his basis in the office building?

A. $16,000
B. $26,000
C. $40,000
D. $66,000

12. Mitchell and Kaylie are married and file jointly. They owned and used their house as their main home for 15 months. Mitchell got a new job in another state, so they sold their home. What is the maximum amount they can exclude from income under the rules regarding a reduced exclusion?

A. $156,250
B. $250,000
C. $312,500
D. $500,000

13. Mackenna is a farmer. He trades a plot of pastureland (adjusted basis $300,000, FMV $700,000) for agricultural land with an existing almond orchard (FMV $725,000), and in addition, he pays $60,000 of cash to complete the exchange. What is his basis in the orchard property?

A. $325,000
B. $360,000
C. $690,000
D. $725,000

14. Elvis bought a house for $189,000 on July 1, 2017. He lived there continuously for 13 months and then moved in with his girlfriend. They later separated, and Elvis moved back into his own house and lived there for an additional 12 months until he sold it on July 30, 2020, for $220,000. What is the amount and nature of his gain?

A. $0.
B. $31,000 long-term capital gain.
C. $31,000 short-term capital gain.
D. $30,000 long-term capital gain.

15. Isaiah has lived in and owned his home for 15 months when he decides to move in with his girlfriend, so he sells his home for $285,000. His adjusted basis in the home is $160,000. What is the amount and nature of his taxable gain on the sale?

A. $0
B. $35,000 long-term capital gain.
C. $125,000 long-term capital gain.
D. $125,000 short-term capital gain.

16. Annalise sold her primary residence in Utah and moved to Iowa. She had purchased the house in 2010 for $200,000, and she sold it in 2020 for $550,000, net of selling expenses. During the time she lived in the house, she paid $25,000 for major improvements and $15,000 for general repairs. Assuming that Annalise utilizes the maximum available exclusion, what amount would she report as a taxable capital gain?

A. $0
B. $60,000
C. $75,000
D. $100,000

17. Magnus and Grace were married on January 12, 2011. They purchased their first home together on March 30, 2011, for $150,000. On February 2, 2020, Magnus and Grace legally separate, and the court granted Grace ownership of the home as part of the divorce settlement. The divorce became final on November 10, 2020, and the fair market value of the home was $370,000 when ownership was transferred to Grace. She sells the house on December 23, 2020, for $480,000. What is Grace's taxable gain in this transaction?

A. $0
B. $80,000
C. $120,000
D. $210,000

Unit 8: Quiz Answers

1. The answer is A. This is a qualifying 1031 exchange, so Grady's basis in the land is the same as the basis of the property given up: $50,000. IRC Section 1031 does not limit "like-kind" property to certain types of real estate. Any real property held for productive use in a trade or business *or* for investment can be considered "like-kind" property.

2. The answer is B. Alistair and Gabrielle are allowed to claim a *reduced* exclusion of $200,000 (292/730 multiplied by the $500,000 maximum exclusion available for married taxpayers). The remaining $60,000 would be considered taxable capital gain income and would be reported on Schedule D. This move qualifies for the reduced exclusion because multiple births from the same pregnancy are considered an unforeseen circumstance.

3. The answer is A. As a single taxpayer, Heather may exclude a maximum gain amount of $250,000 from the sale of her home. Her gain is $270,000 ($620,000 - $350,000). Her taxable gain is $20,000 ($270,000 gain - $250,000 exclusion), which must be reported as a long-term capital gain.

4. The answer is D. The move to be closer to grown children would not qualify. All of the following events would be qualifying events to claim a reduced exclusion from a premature sale:

- A divorce or legal separation.
- A pregnancy resulting in multiple births or serious health issues.
- The home is sold after being seized or condemned.
- A move due to a new job or new employment.

If any of these exceptions apply, the taxpayer may figure a reduced exclusion based on the number of days he owned and lived in the residence.

5. The answer is B. Although Chrystal's total gain on the transaction is $45,000, the recognized gain is only $5,000. The answer is calculated as follows:

FMV of like-kind property received (i.e., the warehouse)	$200,000
Cash boot received	10,000
Total received	210,000
Subtract: Exchange expenses paid	(5,000)
Amount realized	205,000
Subtract: Adjusted basis of the retail building (the property transferred)	(160,000)
Realized Gain	$45,000
Cash received (boot)	$10,000
Subtract: Exchange expenses paid	(5,000)
Recognized (taxable) gain	**$5,000**

6. The answer is D. This is not an acceptable like-kind exchange, so the entire transaction is treated as a sale. This is a taxable exchange of property that is not similar, or "unlike" property. Therefore, the entire $13,000 gain ($97,000-$84,000) is taxable and Clayton's basis in the tractor is $97,000.

7. The answer is C. This is an involuntary conversion. Bryant must acquire qualifying replacement property by December 31, 2022 (*two* years from the *end* of the tax year during which any part of the gain is realized.) Since Bryant received the reimbursement check in 2020, he has two years from December 31, 2020, to acquire replacement property. Different types of property have different replacement periods. For example, if Bryant's main home had been destroyed in a federally declared disaster area, he may have had four years to replace the property.

8. The answer is A. Uriah's total gain on the exchange is $135,000 ($220,000 value of new property + $15,000 cash - $100,000 basis in the old property). However, only the cash boot received is taxable in this transaction. Uriah's basis in the new building is $115,000 (the original basis in the property he gave up plus the gain recognized as a result of the boot received).

9. The answer is D. Inventory never qualifies for like-kind exchange treatment, regardless of whether it is real property or not. The property in a section 1031 exchange must NOT be held "primarily for sale." Generally, real property exchanges will qualify for like-kind treatment, even though the properties themselves might be dissimilar, so all the other exchanges would be allowable.

10. The answer is D. Geoff can exclude $26,000 ($29,000 - $3,000) of his gain. He has a taxable gain of $3,000. He must report the prior depreciation as unrecaptured §1250 gain (taxed at a maximum 25% capital gains rate). If a taxpayer took depreciation deductions because he used his home for business purposes or as a rental property, he cannot exclude the part of the gain equal to any depreciation allowed as a deduction.

11. The answer is B. Jonah's basis in the new building is the same as his basis in the farmland that he originally exchanged. The $10,000 spent on improvements is added to the $16,000 cost, so the adjusted basis of the relinquished farmland was $26,000. Therefore, this is his basis in the new property, as well. The fair market value of the new property is irrelevant in this calculation.

12. The answer is C. A reduced exclusion is available, even though the taxpayers did not live in the home for two full years. They qualify for a reduced exclusion because they are moving for a change in Mitchell's employment. Their maximum reduced exclusion is $312,500 ($500,000 × [15 months/24 months]). The reduced exclusion applies when the premature sale is primarily due to a move for employment in a new location.

13. The answer is B. Mackenna's basis in the orchard property is $360,000: the $300,000 basis of the relinquished pastureland plus the $60,000 cash he paid. The fair market value of the property has no bearing on Mackenna's basis in the new property.

14. The answer is A. Elvis has no taxable gain because the sale qualifies for the section 121 exclusion. This sale qualifies for section 121 treatment. Elvis meets the "ownership and use" tests because, during the five-year period ending on the date of sale, he owned the house for three years and lived in it for a total of 25 months (over two years). The gain is not taxable and does not need to be reported.

15. The answer is C. Isaiah's gain is $125,000, the result of subtracting the adjusted basis in the home from the amount realized ($285,000 - $160,000 = $125,000). Since he does not meet the ownership or use tests or qualify for a reduced exclusion, he cannot exclude any of his gains under section 121, (because he hasn't lived in the house for two out of the last five years). He owned the property for more than a year, so the gain is taxed as a long-term capital gain.

16. The answer is C. Annalise's adjusted basis in the house would be the total of her original purchase price of $200,000 and the $25,000 cost of improvements. The cost of repairs would not be considered in determining her adjusted basis. Therefore, her gain on the sale would be $325,000, or the excess of her net proceeds over her adjusted basis. Since she met the requirements for ownership and use of the house as her primary residence, she qualifies for the maximum exclusion of $250,000 available to a single taxpayer, and the taxable portion of her gain would be $75,000.

The purchase price of the house	$200,000
Cost of improvements	25,000
Adjusted basis	225,000
Net proceeds of the sale	**$550,000**
Gain on sale	325,000
Exclusion for a single taxpayer	(250,000)
Taxable gain	**$75,000**

17. The answer is B. Grace meets the ownership and use tests, and the basis in the property remains the same. Property transfers related to a divorce are generally nontaxable, and the FMV of the property at the time of the divorce has no bearing on the taxable outcome. Since she owned the property for longer than one year, the taxable portion of Grace's gain would be reported as a long-term capital gain. The gain is calculated as follows:

Original cost	$150,000
Sale price	480,000
Total realized gain	330,000
Section 121 exclusion	(250,000)
Long-Term Capital Gain (taxable)	**$80,000**

Unit 9: Rental and Royalty Income

For additional information, read:
Publication 527, *Residential Rental Property (Including Rental of Vacation Homes)*
Publication 946, *How to Depreciate Property*
Publication 525, *Taxable and Nontaxable Income*

Rental income is any payment received for the use or occupation of a property. Taxpayers must include amounts received as rent in their gross income. Royalty income is also a type of income received for the use of someone's property. Royalty income includes any payments received from a patent, a copyright, or some natural or mineral resource (such as forestland, oil and gas wells, or a copper mine).

Example: Augustus owns a residential duplex. He has two tenants, one on each side of the duplex. He is not a real estate professional. He manages the rental property himself and does many of the repairs and general maintenance. The rental income he receives from his tenants is taxable and would be reported on Schedule E, *Supplemental Income and Loss.*

Example: Madeline owns 200 acres of forestland that she inherited from her grandfather. She leases the forestland to a lumber company that harvests and processes the timber. Madeline receives quarterly payments under a contract agreement with the timber company based on the value of the timber taken from the property during the year. At the end of the year, the timber company provides Madeline with a Form 1099-MISC reporting the payments as "Royalties" in Box 2. Madeline reports the royalty payments received as royalty income on Schedule E, *Supplemental Income and Loss.*

Rental Income Defined

Property owners can deduct the expenses of managing, conserving, and maintaining their rental properties. Common rental expenses include:

- Mortgage interest and property taxes
- Maintenance, repairs, and cleaning fees
- Advertising for new tenants
- Utilities, if paid by the homeowner
- Homeowner's insurance, liability insurance, and natural disaster insurance
- Depreciation

A taxpayer can deduct the expenses paid by a tenant if they are deductible rental expenses. The owner of the property would then include the fair market value of the property or services received (or amounts paid by the tenant) in their rental income, and deduct that same amount as a rental expense.

Advance Rent: Taxpayers must report rental income when it is actively or constructively (i.e., available without restrictions) received. This includes advance rent, which is any amount received before the period that it covers. Thus, a taxpayer must include advance rent in income in the year he receives it, regardless of the period covered or the accounting method used, unless the amounts are subject to restrictions.

Example: Amos rents out a duplex. On December 20, 2020, his tenant Cynthia pays two months of rent in advance for January 2021 and February 2021 because she is leaving town on an extended vacation. Amos cannot delay reporting the income. He must report all the advance rent as taxable income in 2020 (when he received it).

Example: Calvin owns a residential rental property. His tenant, Angelique, is planning to go overseas for four months at the end of the year. She gives Calvin five checks for the rent for January through April of 2021, but she post-dates all the checks. Since the post-dated checks are dated for a future date, Calvin cannot deposit them until 2021. Since the checks are subject to "substantial restriction," he does not have constructive receipt of the income until he actually deposits the checks in the months in which they are payable. He does not have to recognize the advance rental payments until 2021, when he can legally deposit the checks.

Lease Cancellation: If a tenant pays to cancel a lease, the amount received for the cancellation is rental income. The payment is included in the year received regardless of the taxpayer's accounting method.

Refundable Security Deposits: A security deposit is not considered income upon initial receipt, if the deposit is refundable to the tenant at the end of the lease. However, if the taxpayer keeps some or all of the security deposit because the tenant did not live up to the terms of the lease or because he damaged property, then the deposit amount retained is recognized as income in the year it is forfeited by the tenant.

Example: Ahmad signs a lease to rent his residential rental. He receives $750 for the first month's rent and a $500 refundable security deposit from his new tenant. Ahmad must include $750 in his rental income, but the refundable security deposit would not be reported, unless it was later forfeited by the tenant on account of damages to the property.

Insurance Premiums Paid in Advance: If a cash-basis taxpayer pays an insurance premium for a policy period of more than one year, he can deduct only the part of the premium payment that applies to that year. He cannot deduct the total premium in the year he pays it.

Local Benefit Taxes: In most cases, a taxpayer cannot deduct charges for local taxes that increase the value of a rental property, such as assessments for streets, sidewalks, or water and sewer systems. These charges are non-depreciable capital expenditures that must be added to the basis of the property. Only taxes to maintain or repair such infrastructure, or to pay interest charges related to financing its construction, can be deducted.

Property or Services in Lieu of Rent: If a taxpayer receives property or services as payment for rent instead of cash, the fair market value must be recognized as rental income. If the tenant and landlord agree in advance to a price, the agreed-upon price is deemed the fair market value unless there is evidence to the contrary.

Example: Loretta owns an apartment complex with five units. One of Loretta's tenants, Maloney, is a professional chimney sweep. Maloney offers to clean all of Loretta's chimneys in her apartment building instead of paying three months' rent in cash. Loretta accepts Maloney's offer. Loretta must recognize income for the amount Maloney would have paid for three months' rent. However, Loretta can deduct that same amount as a business expense for the maintenance of the property.

If a tenant pays expenses on behalf of the landlord, the landlord must recognize the payments as rental income. However, the property owner can deduct the expenses as rental expenses.

Example: Elizabeth owns an apartment building. While she is out of town on vacation, the furnace in the apartment building breaks down. Diego, Elizabeth's tenant, pays for the emergency repairs out-of-pocket and deducts the furnace repair bill from his rent payment. Elizabeth must recognize as rental income both the actual amount of rent received in cash from Diego and the amount he paid for the repairs. Elizabeth can deduct the cost of the furnace repair as a rental expense.

Vacant Rental Property

A taxpayer cannot deduct any loss of rental income for the period a property is vacant. However, if the taxpayer is actively *trying* to rent the property, he can deduct ordinary and necessary expenses as soon as the property is "made available" for rent, even if the taxpayer doesn't find a tenant right away.

In other words, if the house is available for rent, the taxpayer can write off expenses, including depreciation, even when it's empty.

Example: Finnegan purchased a rental property and made the property available for rent on March 1, 2020, by advertising it in the local newspaper. He found a tenant who moved in on July 1, 2020. Even though the rental was unoccupied from March through July, Finnegan can still deduct the mortgage interest and other expenses related to the property during that period, because the property was available and advertised to rent.

Sometimes a rental property will stand vacant for other reasons. For example, if a landlord must make repairs after a tenant moves out, the owner may still depreciate the rental property during the time it isn't available for rent. This is assuming the rental property had already been placed in service as a rental.[131]

Example: Sarek owns a residential rental that he has rented continuously for over a decade. In January 2020, he is forced to evict his tenant for non-payment. His tenant vandalizes the property before leaving in the middle of the night. When Sarek finally visits the property, he discovers that it will need extensive repairs, which may take over six months to fix. The home will be uninhabitable until the repairs are completed. Sarek may continue to claim the expenses on the property, including depreciation, while the repairs are being made. This is considered "idle property."

The rules are different, however, if the owner makes rental property repairs *before* actually placing the property into service. In this case, the repairs must be capitalized and included in the property's basis. The owner can only deduct expenses once the property is placed into service for the production of rental income.[132]

[131] See IRS Publication 527, *Residential Rental Property*, under the subheading "Idle Property."

[132] In order to deduct costs as expenses rather than having to capitalize them, the rental unit must be placed into service, i.e., it must be ready and available for rent. (IRS Reg. § 1.263(a)-2(d)(1)).

Example: Janessa purchased a rental property in Montana on November 1, 2020. The cost of the home was $145,000. She spends another $12,000 on repairs before actually placing the property into service on January 2, 2021, when she begins advertising it for rent. She cannot deduct any of the expenses in 2020, including any mortgage interest or repairs in 2020, because the rental was not placed into service until the following year. Instead, those costs would be added to her basis. She can begin depreciating the property in 2021, the year in which she actually placed the property into service.

Depreciation of Rental Property

A taxpayer begins to claim deductions for depreciation of a rental property when he places it in service for the production of income. Rental property is considered "placed in service" when it is ready and available for rent. Depreciation ends when a taxpayer has either fully recovered his cost (or other basis), or when the property is retired from service, whichever happens first. Three basic factors determine how much depreciation a taxpayer can deduct:

- The property's basis,
- The recovery period for the property,
- The depreciation method used, including certain conventions.

The cost of land is never depreciated because land does not wear out, become obsolete, or get used up. Most residential rental buildings are depreciated over 27.5 years. For example, a residential rental home with a cost basis of $137,500 would generate depreciation of $5,000 per year ($137,500/27.5 years) over most of the years of its depreciable life. Nonresidential buildings are generally depreciated over 39 years, with a half-month's worth of depreciation allowed for the first and last month of the depreciable life of the property (i.e., the mid-month convention). An example of a nonresidential rental would be an office complex, where the offices are rented to business tenants, but nobody actually lives or sleeps in the building.

Converting a Home to Rental Use: Sometimes, taxpayers will convert their personal residence to a rental property. For a personal home that is later converted to rental property, the depreciable basis is the lower of:

- The taxpayer's adjusted basis in the property, or
- The fair market value of the property at the time of conversion.

If a taxpayer changes a main home or second home to rental use at any time other than the beginning of a tax year, he must divide his expenses between rental use and personal use. He can deduct as rental expenses only the portion that is for the part of the year the property was used or held for rental purposes.

Example: Mason purchased a rental tri-plex on January 1, 2020, for $395,000. The assessed value of the building is $275,000. The assessed value of the land is $120,000. For tax purposes, a MACRS class life[133] of 27.5 years is used. Using straight-line depreciation, the yearly depreciation amount is calculated as follows: $275,000/27.5 years = $10,000 depreciation expense per year.

---

133 Under MACRS, fixed assets are assigned to a specific asset class, which has a designated depreciation period associated with it. Residential rental property has a 27.5-year class life.

Example: In 2020, Bernice buys a rental property for $200,000 and immediately places it into service as a rental. The most recent property tax assessment made by the county assessor's office places the value of the home at only $160,000, (which is less than what she actually paid). On the property tax statement, $136,000 is allocated to the house, and $24,000 to the land. In order to figure out her basis for depreciation, Bernice can allocate 85% ($136,000 ÷ $160,000) of the purchase price to the house and 15% ($24,000 ÷ $160,000) of the purchase price to the land. Therefore, the basis of the house is $170,000 (85% of $200,000) and her basis in the land is $30,000 (15% of $200,000). Bernice may use $170,000 as her basis for depreciation on the property.

For property that is converted to rental use, the property is treated as being "placed in service" on the conversion date. Also, when a taxpayer converts property held for personal use to rental use, the basis for depreciation will be the <u>*lesser*</u> of fair market value or his adjusted basis on the date of conversion.

Example: Five years ago, Albert purchased a home for $180,000. On the date of purchase, the assessed value of the land was $30,000, and the value of the home was $150,000. After living in the home for five years, Albert converted it to a rental property on January 30, 2020. The real estate values in Albert's neighborhood have decreased significantly, and in 2020, the county assessor's office assigned the property a FMV of $130,000, of which $20,000 was for the land value, and $110,000 for the house. The basis for depreciation of the house is the FMV on the date of conversion ($110,000) because it is *less* than Albert's allocated cost when he purchased the property ($150,000). Albert must use $110,000 as his basis to calculate depreciation on the converted rental, which is reported on Schedule E, *Supplemental Income and Loss* (since land is not depreciable, Albert includes only the cost of the house when calculating his basis for depreciation).

Section 179 Rules for Certain Types of Rental Property

In 2020, the maximum Section 179 deduction is $1,040,000. Section 179 is now adjusted for inflation. In prior years, a taxpayer could not claim the section 179 deduction for any property that was used to produce rental income. The prohibition included *any* rental assets (such as furniture and appliances) as well as capital improvements, such as building additions and HVAC systems.

The TCJA expanded the section 179 deduction to certain types of tangible personal property that is used predominantly to furnish lodging. This new provision includes some types of lodging facilities, such as dormitories, hostels, or any other facility where sleeping accommodations are provided. As always, Section 179 is elective and can be taken on new or used property. It also includes personal property used in apartment complexes and other residential properties that are rented out to tenants.

The TCJA also expanded the definition of "eligible property" to include certain expenditures for nonresidential buildings: including roofs, heating, ventilating, and air conditioning (HVAC) equipment, fire protection and alarm systems, and security systems. Nonresidential commercial property includes office buildings, medical centers, hotels, and malls.

Example: Isaac owns a medical office building that he rents out exclusively to medical and dental professionals. During the year, Isaac spends $17,525 on a new HVAC system for the building. He also installs a new alarm system, which cost $16,750. Isaac may deduct the entire cost of the equipment by taking the section 179 election on his tax return. He does not need to depreciate the HVAC system or the alarm system over their useful life.

All these properties produce rental revenue for their owners, although the tax treatment of the revenue varies on several different factors.

Under current IRS rules, if 80% or more of the annual gross rental income from the mixed-use building is generated from the residential rental apartments, the entire building and its structural components will qualify as a residential rental property.[134]

Example: Benny purchases a building in historic downtown Sacramento in 2020. He renovates the building into a mixed-use development consisting of two distinct sections. The upstairs contains 4 residential rental apartments, and the bottom of the building is a retail space rented out to two commercial tenants: a coffee shop and a clothing retailer. 30% of the rental income generated is from the residential apartments. The remaining 70% of the revenue comes from the commercial tenants (the coffee shop and clothing store). In this scenario, the entire building would be treated as nonresidential (commercial) property. Benny would depreciate the building over 39 years. Later in the year, Benny spends $14,000 to install sprinklers and a new fire protection system. Since the building is treated as nonresidential commercial property, he may use Section 179 to expense the entire cost of the upgrades.

Repairs vs. Improvements to Rental Property

A taxpayer can currently deduct the cost of repairs to rental property but cannot currently deduct the cost of substantial improvements.[135] Instead, the taxpayer must recover the cost of an improvement by taking depreciation deductions over its applicable recovery period. A repair generally keeps an asset or property in good working condition but does not add to the value of the asset or substantially prolong its life. Repainting, fixing leaks, and replacing broken windows are examples of repairs.

The IRS' tangible property regulations are a highly complex set of rules governing repairs and capitalization that affect all taxpayers who use tangible property in their businesses. These rules change the way businesses treat expenditures for tangible property.

For the EA exam, most of the specific details of these regulations will likely not be tested. However, you should have a general understanding of the concept that a business may recover the costs of property either through current deductions or through periodic depreciation deductions for items required to be capitalized. An "improvement" is anything that results in the betterment of a property, restoration of a property, or adaptation of a property to a new or different use.

---

134 This rule for mixed-use properties includes any real property that is a rental building or structure for which 80% or more of the gross rental income for the tax year is from dwelling units. It does *not* include a unit in a hotel, motel, inn, or other establishment where more than half of the units are used on a transient or short-term basis.

135 Sometimes, the IRS will use the different terms to mean the same thing, such as "betterment of a property" instead of "improvement." These are keywords that the IRS may use interchangeably on the exam.

Examples of *improvements* include:

- Additions of an extra bedroom, bathroom, deck, or garage
- The installation of a new roof
- Installation of central air conditioning, new plumbing, wall-to-wall carpeting, or upgraded wiring
- Construction of a retaining wall, fence, or swimming pool

Example: Odette owns a residential rental property. In 2020, she spent $18,000 to replace the plumbing, $9,540 to re-pave the driveway, and $175 to repair a couple of broken gutters. Only the gutter repair ($175) can be expensed on her 2020 tax return. The costs of the new plumbing and the new driveway must be capitalized and depreciated over time.

The capitalized cost of an improvement is depreciated separately from the original cost of the asset or property that is being improved.

Example #1: Quaid owns a rental home. A baseball broke a window, so he replaced it with an upgraded model, an insulated double-pane window that helps control heating and cooling costs. Even though this window is a substantial upgrade from the previous one, it is still considered a repair, because the old window was broken and needed to be replaced. If Quaid were to replace all the windows in the house, the upgrade would be considered an "improvement," rather than a repair, and he would be required to capitalize the cost and claim depreciation deductions over a period of years.

Example #2: Later in the same year, Quaid also replaces the house's septic tank at the cost of $17,500. This is considered a substantial improvement, and the cost of the septic tank must be depreciated over time rather than deducted against current income.

Under the de minimis safe harbor rule of the tangible property regulations,[136] the taxpayer can elect to expense tangible property costing no more than $2,500[137] per invoice or item in the year they are used or consumed.

Example: Kenneth owns a residential rental property. During the year, Kenneth replaces the linoleum flooring in the bathroom and the kitchen. His friend is the installer, and gives him a discount on the price. The total cost for installation and materials is $1,900 and is clearly listed on the invoice. Kenneth may deduct this cost as a repair or as supplies, because the total invoice amount is less than $2,500, which is under the safe harbor rule. Kenneth should attach a statement titled "Section 1.263(a)-1(f) de minimis safe harbor election" to his timely filed federal tax return.

Deductible Rental Losses

The tax treatment of rental income, expenses, and losses depends on several factors: whether a taxpayer is a real estate professional or actively participates in managing a property; whether there is any personal use of the rental property, and if so, whether the dwelling is considered a

---

136 The tangible property regulations are covered in greater detail in Book 2, *Businesses*. For Part 1 of the exam, you may have to know how these new regulations apply to rental property.

137 The Internal Revenue Service, in Notice 2015-82, increased the *de minimis* safe harbor threshold from $500 to $2,500 per invoice or item for taxpayers without applicable financial statements ($5,000 for taxpayers with applicable financial statements).

home; and whether the rental activity is for "carried on" for profit. We will briefly review the rules related to each of these situations next.

The deductibility of losses from passive activities is limited, and a taxpayer usually cannot deduct losses from passive activities to offset his nonpassive income (such as wages). In general, a trade or business activity is considered a passive activity if the taxpayer does not *materially participate* in it; however, rental activities are generally considered passive activities regardless of the participation of the owners.

A taxpayer "materially participates" in an activity if he is involved in the operation of that activity on a regular, continuous, and substantial basis.

Rental activities that provide substantial services along with the rental property may be classified as business activities, rather than passive rental activities. An example of this would be a hotel owner, or the owner of a bed-and-breakfast. In this case, the rental income and expenses, including interest and taxes, would be reported on Schedule C as a non-passive activity[138] subject to self-employment tax (motel and hotel owners are covered in more detail later in the chapter).

Generally, losses from passive activities that exceed income from passive activities in the same year are disallowed. The disallowed losses are carried forward to the next taxable year and can be used to offset future income from passive activities. There is a special "$25,000 exception" to this rule, however, for rental real estate activities.

Special $25,000 "Loss Allowance" for Real Estate Rental Activities

When a taxpayer *actively participates* in a rental real estate activity, he may be able to deduct up to $25,000 of losses against his nonpassive income. It should be noted that *active* participation is a different and less stringent standard than *material* participation.

Note: "Active participation" is not the same standard as "material participation." Material participation is a much higher standard. For example, the owner of a rental property will generally be treated as *actively* participating if he makes management decisions such as approving new tenants, deciding rental contracts, approving repairs, and other similar management decisions.

To be considered "actively participating" in a rental activity, a taxpayer must own at least 10% of the rental property and must make management decisions in a significant and bona fide way, such as approving new tenants and establishing the rental terms. In this case, active participation can also include participation by the taxpayer's spouse.

Example: Clement owns a residential rental property in San Diego, California. He lives in San Diego and has a regular job that he works full-time. Clement actively manages his rental by choosing his own tenants, hiring workers to do any required repairs, and personally collecting the rent. Clement is *actively* participating in this rental activity.

The full $25,000 loss allowance is available for taxpayers, whether single or MFJ, whose modified adjusted gross income (MAGI) is $100,000 or less.

138 For tax purposes, "substantial services" include such regular cleaning, changing linen and towels, or daily maid service, such as a person might receive at a hotel.

If a taxpayer is married and files a separate return, but lived apart from his spouse for the entire tax year, the taxpayer's special allowance for rental losses cannot exceed $12,500; this full allowance would be available if his MAGI is $50,000 or less. However, if the taxpayer *lived* with his spouse at any time during the year and is filing MFS, the taxpayer cannot use any of his passive rental losses to offset nonpassive income. Only rental activities qualify for this "special loss allowance," and certain taxpayers do not qualify. The following taxpayers are not allowed to claim the special loss allowance:

- A limited partner in an activity,
- A taxpayer who has less than 10% ownership in a rental activity,
- A trust or corporation (The $25,000 special allowance is available only to natural persons, although grantor trusts are permitted.)

Rental losses that cannot be deducted due to the limitations described above can be carried forward indefinitely and used in subsequent years, subject to the same limitations.

Note: If the IRS determines a taxpayer has not actively participated, rental losses are not currently deductible, and he is not eligible for the special $25,000 loss allowance.

Example: Joaquin works as a store manager and makes $80,000 in wages per year. He also owns two residential rental properties and provides basic services to his tenants. He manages the property and personally collects the rents. Whenever repairs are needed, he hires the contractors to complete them. He also has a full-time job as a restaurant manager. He is not a real estate professional. Joaquin should report his rental income and losses on Schedule E. His rental income is considered passive activity income, and it is not subject to self-employment tax. He is also eligible for the $25,000 loss allowance, if his rentals have losses for the year.

Example: Corina owns a rental condo in Hawaii. She lives and works in Nevada. Corina hired a management company to manage the property and screen new tenants. The management company handles all the repairs and collects the rent. The management company charges a fee for its services and then remits the net proceeds to Corina monthly. It has been several years since Corina has even visited the property. Corina is not actively participating in this rental activity. In 2020, she has $43,000 in rental income from the property, but her expenses are $51,000, which means she had a net rental loss of ($8,000). Since she is not actively participating in the rental activity, she is not eligible for the special loss allowance. In 2020, she has $75,000 in wages and no other income. Since she does not have any other passive income to offset, she must carry over her $8,000 passive loss to a future tax year.

Example: Delton and Emeline are married. They own a residential rental property that they manage themselves. In 2020, they have combined wages of $98,000 and a rental loss of $26,800. Because they meet both the active participation and the MAGI tests, they are allowed to deduct $25,000 of the rental loss as an offset to their nonpassive income (wages). The remaining amount over the $25,000 limit ($1,800) that cannot be deducted in the current year is carried forward and may potentially be used in the following year.

For every $2 by which a taxpayer's MAGI exceeds $100,000, the allowance is reduced by $1. If a taxpayer's MAGI is $150,000 or more (or $75,000 or more if married filing separately), the $25,000 allowance is fully phased out, and all the losses must be carried forward.

Example: Ernesto and Fabiola file jointly and have MAGI of $140,000. They have $25,000 of losses from the residential rental property that they actively manage. Because they actively manage the property, they potentially qualify to deduct up to $25,000 of losses against their nonpassive income. However, because their joint income is over $100,000, they are subject to the phaseout. Therefore, Ernesto and Fabiola's deduction for rental losses is reduced by $20,000 (0.5 × [$140,000 - $100,000]). They can deduct $5,000 ($25,000 - $20,000) against their nonpassive income. The additional $20,000 of losses is carried forward to the following year.

Example: Jerold owns a rental property in San Francisco. He actively participates in the rental activity and manages the property himself. In the previous tax year, he incurred ($9,000) in losses on his rental. Jerold's modified adjusted gross income was $175,000 for the year. Because of his income threshold, Jerold's rental losses are suspended, and he is not allowed to deduct any rental losses. The following year, Jerold had $5,000 in losses from his rental activity. However, he also changed jobs in the middle of the year, and now his AGI is much lower. In 2020, Jerold's AGI is $85,000, so his rental losses are now allowable. His suspended rental losses from the prior year ($9,000) and his current year losses ($5,000) will be allowed on his 2020 tax return, for a total deduction of ($14,000).

Definition. MAGI is a taxpayer's adjusted gross income with certain deductions added back in. These may include IRA contributions, rental losses, student loan interest, and qualified tuition expenses, among others. A taxpayer's MAGI is used as a basis for determining whether he qualifies for certain tax deductions.

Renting Only Part of Property

A taxpayer who rents only part of a property must divide certain expenses between the part of the property used for rental purposes and the part used for personal purposes, as though there were actually two separate pieces of property. Expenses related to the part of the property used for rental purposes can be deducted as rental expenses on Schedule E. This includes a portion of expenses that normally are nondeductible personal expenses, such as painting the outside of a house. If an expense applies to both rental use and personal use, such as a heating bill for the entire house, the taxpayer must divide the expense between the two. The two most common methods for dividing such expenses are based on:

- The number of rooms in the house, and
- The square footage of the house.

Example: Lucius rents out a single bedroom in his house. The room is 12 × 15 feet or 180 square feet. Lucius' entire house is 1,800 square feet. Lucius can deduct as a rental expense 10% of any expense that must be divided between rental use and personal use. Any expense that is allocatable *only* to the rental portion can be fully deducted. In 2020, Lucius replaces the torn wallpaper in the rental bedroom at a cost of $525. He does not replace the wallpaper in the rest of the house. He can fully deduct the $525 cost, because it was allocatable to the rental portion. Lucius' heating bills for the *entire* house totaled $600, and therefore $60 ($600 × .10) can be considered a deductible rental expense. The balance, $540, is a personal expense that Lucius cannot deduct.

Another common situation involves a duplex in which the property owner lives in one side of the building and rents out the other. Certain expenses, like mortgage interest and real estate taxes, apply to the entire property and must be split to determine rental and personal expenses.

Example: Marisa owns a duplex with two units of the same size. She lives in one side and rents out the other. In 2020, Marisa paid $12,000 of mortgage interest and $4,000 of real estate taxes for the entire property. Marisa can deduct $6,000 of mortgage interest and $2,000 of real estate taxes on Schedule E. She can claim the other $6,000 of mortgage interest and $2,000 of real estate taxes attributable to her personal use on Schedule A as itemized deductions.

If a taxpayer owns a partial interest in a rental property, he can deduct expenses paid according to the percentage of ownership.

Personal Use of Dwelling Unit

When a taxpayer has a residence (whether a main home or a second home) that is used personally at certain times and rented out at other times, he must divide his expenses between rental use and personal use.

Rental expenses generally will be no more than a taxpayer's total expenses multiplied by the following fraction: the denominator is the total number of days the dwelling is used, and the numerator is the total number of days actually rented at a fair rental price. Any day the unit is rented at a fair rental price is a day of rental use. Any day the unit is available for rent but not actually rented is not a day of rental use.

Example: Gwyneth owns a vacation home in Miami, Florida, that she rented for 90 days in January, February, and March. She can deduct the rental expenses, including mortgage interest and real estate taxes on Schedule E only for those 90 days. However, she can deduct expenses the mortgage interest and real estate taxes for the other 275 days of the year on her Schedule A.

Partial Rental Activity (with a Profit Motive)

If a taxpayer uses a property for both rental and personal purposes, the tax treatment of expenses depends on whether his personal use is considered to be usage as a "residence." It is considered "a residence" if the taxpayer uses the property for personal purposes during the year for more than the greater of <u>fourteen days</u>, or 10% of the total days it is rented at a fair rental price. Days of personal use are counted when:

- A member of the taxpayer's family uses the property without paying a fair rental price (this is treated as personal use of the property),
- Anyone uses the property at less than the fair rental price,
- Use of the property is donated to a charitable organization.

However, any day the taxpayer spends working on repairs and maintaining the property is not counted as personal use, even if his family is also staying there. If a taxpayer's rental expenses are more than his rental income, he cannot use the excess expenses to offset income from other sources. However, excess deductions may be carried forward to the next year and treated as rental expenses for the same property, subject to the same limits.

Example: Travis owns a condominium in the U.S. Virgin Islands. He uses it as a personal residence for five months out of each year, and rents it out to tenants for the rest of the year. He has a profit motive in the rental activity. Travis' rental income is $8,000 in 2020, and his rental expenses are $10,000 (during the time it was available for rent). Travis cannot deduct the full $10,000 of rental expenses, because the condominium is not strictly a rental. It is also a personal home. Travis can carry over the remaining ($2,000) in unused losses and deduct that amount from future rental income on the condominium.

Example: William owns a mountain cabin at Lake Tahoe that was used as follows in 2020: He rented it for 60 days during the ski season, spent a week at the cabin cleaning and making repairs before the rental period began, and donated a week of rental use to a local charity. In apportioning expenses:

1. Days used by the charity (7/67 days) would be treated as personal use; expenses such as mortgage interest and property taxes would be deductible in this ratio on his Schedule A.
2. The remaining 60/67 days would be treated as rental use, and this fraction of total expenses incurred would be deductible on Schedule E.
3. The seven days of cleaning and making repairs would not count as either personal or rental use for purposes of allocating expenses.

William's cabin is not considered a "residence" because his personal use was less than 14 days and less than 10% of the total days it was rented for fair market value. His losses are not limited.

Not-For-Profit Rentals and Below-Market Rentals

If a taxpayer does *not* rent the property with the intent to make a profit, the taxpayer cannot deduct any rental expenses that exceed the taxpayer's rental income. The presumption is made of whether a rental is for profit is when rental income exceeds rental expenses for three out of five years. In the case of a "not-for-profit" rental, the rental income is not reported on Schedule E, and the taxpayer cannot deduct a loss. Any unused expenses on a "not-for-profit" rental cannot be carried forward to the next year.

When a taxpayer rents below fair market price, such as rental to a close family member, the taxpayer would be considered to be renting "not-for-profit." Below-market rentals to a family member or another related party is the most common type of "not-for-profit" rental.

Example: Sandra rents her second home to her grandson for $500 per month, which is much less than fair market value. There is no profit on the rental, because Sandra's rental expenses exceed the income generated by the property. Since the rental activity does not have a profit motive, Sandra should report the rental income on Form 1040 as "other income." The rental expenses (such as mortgage interest and property taxes)[139] are deductible on Schedule A, just like they would be for any other second home. She would not use Schedule E to deduct the losses or claim any deductions.

---

[139] Because of changes in the Tax Cuts and Jobs Act, property taxes (along with other state and local taxes) for non-business and non-rental activities are generally subject to an overall deduction limit of $10,000 ($5,000 for those that file MFS). This will be covered in more detail in Unit 12.

Not-for-profit rental income is reported on Form 1040 as "other income." If the taxpayer itemizes deductions, he can include mortgage interest and real estate taxes on the appropriate lines of Schedule A (Form 1040).

Minimal Rental Use (15-Day Rule)

If a taxpayer rents a main home or vacation home that is considered a "residence" for fewer than 15 days, he does not have to recognize any of the income as taxable. However, he cannot deduct any rental expenses. This is called the "15-day rule," or "minimal rental use."

Example: Estelle owns a condo on the Gulf Coast, which is her personal residence. While she was away on vacation, she rented her condo for 11 days, charging $100 per day for a total of $1,100. She also had $320 of rental expenses during that time, because her renters broke a bathroom window that she had to get replaced. Estelle does not report any of the income or expenses based on the exception for minimal rental use.

Example: Stephen lives in Arlington, Texas. In 2020, the World Series was held in Arlington, and Stephen's home is within walking distance of the ballpark. Stephen took this opportunity to rent his home during the series in order to make some extra cash. He offered his home for rent online and rented the home during the World Series. During that time, he slept on his friend's couch in a neighboring city. He rented his personal home for 7 days, charging $350 per night, for a total of $2,450 in rental income. Since the rental period is fewer than 15 days, it is considered minimal rental use. He does not have to report any of the income. He also cannot deduct any expenses related to the rental.

Exception for Real Estate Professionals

If a taxpayer qualifies as a real estate professional, losses from rental real estate activities in which he materially participates are not considered passive and are fully deductible.[140] If the tests for material participation are not met, rental losses are considered passive and are normally deductible only up to $25,000, based upon the passive activity rules outlined previously.

To be classified as a real estate professional, a taxpayer must provide more than one-half of his total personal services in real property trades or businesses in which he materially participates and perform more than 750 hours of services during the tax year in real property business activities, which includes property development, redevelopment, construction, reconstruction, acquisition, conversion, rental, operation, management, leasing, or brokerage services.

In most instances, if a property owner provides only basic services to tenants, such as trash collection, he reports rental income and expenses on Schedule E, Form 1040. It is not subject to self-employment tax.

---

140 The determination of whether someone is a "real estate professional" is based on a number of factors. In general, a taxpayer qualifies as a real estate professional if (1) he performs more than 750 hours of services during the taxable year in real property trades or businesses in which he materially participates, and (2) more than one-half of the total personal services performed in trades or businesses by the taxpayer during the year are performed in real property trades or businesses in which the taxpayer materially participates.

Example: Hoshi spends 800 hours a year repairing, maintaining, and dealing with tenants at her five apartment complexes, which she owns. Every spring, she also works part-time in her father's accounting firm, to help him through the busy season. She works 500 hours total at her father's accounting firm. Because Hoshi (1) spends more than 750 hours materially participating in real estate, and (2) the 800 hours of real estate services is more than half of the 1,300 hours of total time she spends on both real estate and accounting services for the year, she is classified as a real estate professional. As such, if she generates a tax loss in her rentals for the year, she will be able to deduct the losses on her return without any limitations.

Example: Juniper, who is single, is a full-time self-employed real estate agent and owns four rental properties. She also materially participates in each of the rental activities, as she is generally the only one doing any work for them. She works more than 2,000 hours per year (40 hours a week), working in her real estate business and managing the properties that she owns. As she meets both hours tests for real estate professional status and can deduct any losses from the rentals against non-passive income.

In contrast, owners of property who provide substantial services to the renter, such as maid cleaning and housekeeping services, are generally required to report revenue and expenses related to the property on Schedule C, *Profit or Loss from Business*, and any net profit is subject to self-employment tax. The most common examples of taxpayers who report their rental activities on Schedule C, instead of on Schedule E, are hotel owners and motel operators.

Hotels, Motels, and Bed & Breakfasts

Operators of hotels, boarding houses, and bed and breakfasts must report their income on Schedule C, not Schedule E. If the property is rented only for short periods and if the taxpayer provides "substantial services" to the tenant, such as daily maid service, laundry service, or regular breakfast service, the taxpayer should report the rental income and expenses on Schedule C (Form 1040), *Profit or Loss from Business*, rather than Schedule E.

Example: Stephanie owns a motel in downtown Cincinnati. Stephanie does not offer long-term rentals. The hotel offers full maid service, cleaning, and breakfast daily. Since she provides "significant services" as a motel owner, the income would be reported on her Schedule C.

In some cases, renting out all or part of a house can be classified for tax purposes as the equivalent of running a bed-and-breakfast. The facts and circumstances of each situation must be taken into account to determine if the taxpayer is providing "substantial services" to a tenant.

Example: Moriah lives in a popular tourist area in Palm Springs, CA. She has a small granny cottage behind her home. Moriah listed her granny cottage on a popular website for vacation rentals, Airweb. She used Airweb to rent her cottage 140 days last year to several different tenants. She provided cleaning service, daily breakfast service, and fresh towels and linens, just like a hotel would. Even though she is not a real estate professional, Moriah would report the rental income and related expenses on Schedule C, not Schedule E, because she is providing a short-term rental and "substantial services" to her tenants.

Royalty Income

Like rental income, royalty income is reported on Schedule E. Royalties from copyrights, patents, and oil, gas, and mineral properties are taxable as ordinary income, but the amounts are generally not subject to self-employment tax. Royalty payments are always reported to the taxpayer on Form 1099-MISC. A business is required to issue Form 1099-MISC, *Miscellaneous Income,* to each person to whom he has paid at least $10 of royalties for the year.

Example: William owns 150 acres of farmland. In 2020, natural gas deposits were discovered on his property. William negotiates a contract with an energy company that wishes to extract the natural gas from his land. The contract stipulates that he will receive 12% of the revenue generated by the gas extracted from his property. In 2020, William receives $98,000 in royalties from the energy company. The amounts were reported as royalties to William on Form 1099-MISC, and he will report this income on his Schedule E, Form 1040.

In many cases, a taxpayer reports details of royalties on Schedule E, *Supplemental Income and Loss*. However, self-employed writers, musicians, and inventors report income on Schedule C, *Profit or Loss from Business,* and are subject to self-employment tax.

Royalties from copyrights on literary, musical, or artistic works, or from patents on inventions, are usually paid to a taxpayer for the right to use his work over a specified period of time. Royalties can also be based on the number of units sold, such as the number of books, tickets to a performance, or machines sold.

Example: Lorelai is a professional photographer. In 2020, she takes several photos of celebrities and sells them on a popular online stock photo website. Her celebrity photographs are licensed by several media outlets and she earns $52,000 in royalties. Since she is self-employed, and the photographs were self-created, she must report these royalties as business income on Schedule C, not Schedule E.

Example: In 2020, Orel's brother died. Orel inherited a copyright from his brother, who had written a bestselling instruction manual on woodworking. Orel then leased the copyrighted material to schools and colleges for their use. Since he had not created the copyright himself, Orel will report the royalty income on Schedule E. The income is subject to income tax, but not self-employment tax.

Example: Nellie is the self-employed writer of a popular series of books for young children. She receives royalties from her publisher based on the number of books she has sold over a certain period of time. Nellie must report these royalties as taxable business income on her Schedule C.

Unit 9: Study Questions

(Test yourself first, then check the correct answers at the end of this quiz.)

1. Treyton signs a three-year lease from a business tenant who wishes to rent a building he owns. He offers a substantial discount to the tenant if payment is made in advance. The tenant agrees, and in December 2020, Treyton receives $12,000 for the entire first year's rent and $12,000 as rent for the last year of the lease. He also receives a $1,500 security deposit that is refundable at the end of the lease. How much rental income must Treyton include in his 2020 tax return?

A. $1,500
B. $12,000
C. $24,000
D. $25,500

2. Kenia is single and has $40,000 of wages and $2,000 of passive activity income from a limited partnership. These are her only sources of income for the year. She also has a $3,500 passive activity *losses* from a rental real estate activity in which she actively participated. Which of the following statements is correct?

A. The first $2,000 of her $3,500 passive loss offsets her passive income. She can deduct the remaining $1,500 loss to reduce taxation of her wages.
B. She cannot deduct the passive loss to reduce taxation of her wages.
C. She cannot offset the rental loss against the passive income from the partnership because it is not the same type of passive activity.
D. She must carry over her loss to the subsequent tax year.

3. Which of the following costs related to rental property should be classified as a capital improvement and depreciated rather than being expensed currently?

A. Replacing an entire outdoor deck.
B. Repairing a broken toilet.
C. Painting the family room.
D. Patching a hole in the wall.

4. Pamela ordered an HVAC unit for her rental property on November 15, 2020. It was delivered on December 28, 2020, and was installed and ready for use on January 2, 2021. She paid for the unit using a credit card and paid off the card on February 3, 2021. On which date would the HVAC unit be considered "placed in service" for depreciation purposes?

A. November 15, 2020.
B. December 28, 2020.
C. January 2, 2021.
D. February 3, 2021.

5. Annika converted her primary residence to rental use during the year. Her original cost was $189,000, of which $13,200 was allocated to the land, and $175,800 was to the house. The property's value has gone down since its purchase, and on the date of the conversion to a rental property, the property had a fair market value of $158,000, of which $11,000 was allocable to the land and $147,000 to the house. What is Annika's basis for depreciation on Schedule E?

A. $147,000
B. $158,000
C. $175,800
D. $189,000

6. Asher decides to convert his primary residence into a rental property. He moves out of his home on May 1, 2020, and starts renting it on June 1, 2020. He has $12,000 of mortgage interest for the year. How should Asher report his mortgage interest expense?

A. Report the entire $12,000 on Schedule E.
B. Report the entire $12,000 on Schedule A.
C. Report $7,000 on Schedule E as interest expense and $5,000 on Schedule A as mortgage interest.
D. Report $8,000 on Schedule E as interest expense and $4,000 on Schedule A as mortgage interest.

7. Rosemary's home is used exclusively as her residence all year, except for 13 days. During this time, Rosemary rents her home to alumni while the local college has its homecoming celebration. She made $3,000 of rental income and had $500 of rental expenses during this 13-day period. Which of the following statements is correct?

A. Rosemary must recognize all $3,000 of rental income, and deduct the $500 in rental expenses on Schedule E.
B. Rosemary can exclude only $2,500 of the rental income.
C. Rosemary can deduct her expenses when she reports her rental income on Schedule E.
D. All of the rental income may be excluded.

8. Kyung-Hu owns a residential rental house. Last year, she paid $968 to repair a broken window. The cost of the labor was $468, and the cost of the replacement window was $500. She replaced the broken window with a premium energy-saving window. What is the correct treatment of this expense?

A. She cannot deduct the cost since it was an improvement; she must add it to the basis of the property.
B. She can deduct $468 as a rental expense on Schedule E (the labor cost). The cost of the actual window ($500) must be capitalized and depreciated.
C. She can deduct the entire $968 as a rental expense on Schedule E.
D. She can deduct $968 on Schedule A as an itemized deduction.

9. Matthew and Diane are legally separated and have lived apart for three years. They file separate tax returns (MFS). They own a rental property jointly; actively participate in the rental activity, and share income and losses equally. The rental property had $30,000 of losses during the year. Matthew has wage income of $48,000. He has no other items of income or loss. What is the maximum amount of rental losses that Matthew can claim on his *separate* return?

A. $0
B. $12,500
C. $15,000
D. $25,000

10. Which of the following describes depreciation?

A. A business expense that applies only to rental properties.
B. An improvement to an asset that must be capitalized.
C. A common type of accounting method used by most partnerships.
D. A tax deduction that allows a business to recover the cost basis of an asset over time.

11. In 2020, Travis and Brittany moved to Florida. They decided to rent their old house in California instead of selling it. They had purchased the home five years ago for $500,000 and had paid $80,000 for various major improvements over the years. The purchase price of $500,000 was attributable to fair market values of $100,000 for the land and $400,000 for the house. Their new tenant paid a refundable security deposit of $6,000 and moved in on July 1, 2020. The FMV of the property on July 1 was $525,000, comprised of $105,000 for the land and $420,000 for the house. The tenant then paid rent of $3,000 each month from July through December of 2020. Travis and Brittany incurred the following expenses in 2020 related to the house:

- **Mortgage interest:** $10,000
- **Property taxes:** $10,000
- **Casualty insurance:** $1,000

In addition, they paid $500 for repairs during December. Exclusive of depreciation expense, what was Travis and Brittany's taxable rental income?

A. $1,500
B. $7,000
C. $7,250
D. $13,000

Unit 9: Quiz Answers

1. The answer is C. Treyton must include $24,000 in his income in the first year. He must recognize all the advance rent as income in the year of receipt. The security deposit does not have to be recognized as income because it is refundable to the tenant.

2. The answer is A. Kenia can use $2,000 of her rental loss to offset the passive activity income from the limited partnership. The remaining $1,500 loss can be offset against her $40,000 of wages. A taxpayer can deduct up to $25,000 per year of losses for rental real estate activities in which she actively participates, as long as their modified AGI does not exceed a certain amount. This special allowance is an exception to the general rule disallowing losses in excess of income from passive activities against nonpassive income.

3. The answer is A. The replacement of the deck would be considered a depreciable improvement. The other choices are repairs and may be deducted as current expenses.

4. The answer is C. Depreciation begins on the placed-in-service date when an asset becomes ready and available for first use. Typically, the placed-in-service date and the purchase date are the same, but that is not always the case. Since Pamela did not have the HVAC unit installed and ready for use until January 2, 2021, she must wait until 2021 to begin depreciating the unit. The fact that the unit was paid for with a credit card is irrelevant (it is treated the same as if it was paid by check or cash).

5. The answer is A. Annika's basis for depreciation on the house is its fair market value on the date of the conversion ($147,000) because the FMV on the date of conversion is less than the amount of her original cost that was allocable to the house ($175,800). When a taxpayer converts property held for personal use to rental use (for example, the rental of a former home), the basis for depreciation will be the *lesser* of fair market value or the adjusted basis on the date of conversion.

6. The answer is C. Asher must allocate his expenses between personal use and rental use. He can deduct as rental expenses seven-twelfths (7 months/12 months) of annual expenses, such as taxes and insurance. Starting in June, he can deduct as rental expenses the amounts he paid for items generally billed monthly, such as utilities. When figuring his allowable depreciation, he should treat the property as placed in service on June 1.

7. The answer is D. All the rental income may be excluded under the "15-day rule." Rosemary's home is primarily for personal use, and a rental period of fewer than 15 days is disregarded, which means the IRS does not consider it a rental. The rental income is not taxable, but the rental expenses (such as utilities or maintenance costs) are also not deductible.

8. The answer is C. Kyung-Hu may deduct the entire $968 as a rental expense on Schedule E. Generally, the expenses of renting a property, such as maintenance, insurance, taxes, and interest, can be deducted from rental income. This cost is a repair, not an improvement, because the window was already broken. If *all* the windows had been replaced with energy-efficient windows, the cost would have been considered an improvement and added to the property's basis.

9. The answer is B. Matthew is allowed to claim a maximum of $12,500 of losses on his separately filed return. If a taxpayer actively participated in a passive rental real estate activity that produced a loss, he can deduct the loss to offset his nonpassive income, up to $25,000. However, married persons filing separate returns who lived apart during the year are each allowed a maximum of $12,500 for losses from passive real estate activities. Married persons who file separate returns but lived together during the year are not allowed to take losses on rental real estate activity. Instead, the losses are suspended and must be carried over until the property produces income, or the property is disposed of.

10. The answer is D. Depreciation is an income tax deduction that allows a business to recover the cost or basis of property it uses over time. It is an annual allowance for the wear and tear, deterioration, or obsolescence of assets.

11. The answer is B. Travis and Brittany must report six months of rental income at $3,000 per month, or $18,000, but the refundable security deposit of $6,000 is not recognized as income in 2020. They can deduct 6/12 of the amounts incurred for mortgage interest, property taxes, and casualty insurance, or $10,500, plus the $500 cost of repairs while the house was rented. Thus, their reportable net rental income before considering depreciation would be $7,000. The calculations are as follows:

Taxable rental income:	
Six months of rent (at $3,000 per month)	$18,000
Minus deductible expenses:	
Mortgage interest (for six months)	5,000
Property taxes (for six months)	5,000
Casualty insurance (for six months)	500
Repair cost	500
Expenses before depreciation	(11,000)
Rental income before depreciation	**$7,000**

Unit 10: Other Taxable Income

For additional information, read:
Publication 525, *Taxable and Nontaxable Income*
Publication 4681, *Canceled Debts, Foreclosures, Repossessions, and Abandonments*
Publication 504, *Divorced or Separated Individuals*

In this unit, we discuss several other types of taxable income that must be reported on Form 1040. The TCJA made many significant changes to the treatment of alimony, hobby income, gambling income and losses, and the tax treatment of some types of court awards.

Taxable Recoveries

A "recovery" is a return of an amount a taxpayer deducted or took a credit for in an earlier year. The most common recoveries are refunds, reimbursements, and rebates of deductions itemized on Schedule A. A taxpayer must include a recovery in income in the year he receives it, to the extent the deduction or credit reduced his tax in the earlier year.

State and local income tax refunds are reported as taxable income in the year received only if (1) the taxpayer itemized deductions in the prior year in which those taxes were overpaid and (2) the amounts paid in the prior year reduced his tax liability in that year (i.e., provided a tax benefit). The payer of the tax refunds should send Form 1099-G, *Certain Government Payments*, to the taxpayer by January 31, and also send a copy to the IRS.

Example: Kadam claimed the standard deduction on his prior-year federal tax return. In 2020, he received a refund of $600 for state income taxes he paid during the prior year. The state tax refund is not taxable in 2020, as Kadam received no federal tax benefit from his state tax payments because he did not itemize deductions in the previous year.

Refunds of federal income taxes are not included in a taxpayer's income because they are never allowed as a deduction.

Alimony Received

The Tax Cuts and Jobs Act changed the treatment of alimony starting in 2019, making it nondeductible to the payor and nontaxable to the recipient. Divorce and separation agreements entered into before 2019 are "grandfathered," so there will continue to be alimony deductions and taxable alimony income for individuals with divorce agreements that were finalized prior to 2019. However, if a "grandfathered" agreement is later modified, and expressly invokes the new treatment, then the alimony receives the new treatment. The payor does not have to itemize to deduct alimony payments made (for divorce decrees that are grandfathered).

Example: Ivan and Patsy divorced in 2015. As a result, their divorce decree is "grandfathered," and the pre-TCJA rules apply. Their divorce decree requires Ivan to pay Patsy $200 per month as child support and $150 per month as alimony. Ivan makes all of his child support and alimony payments on time. Therefore, in 2020, he can deduct $1,800 ($150 × 12 months) as alimony paid, and Patsy must report $1,800 as alimony received as taxable income. The amount paid as child support, $2,400 ($200 × 12) is not deductible by Ivan and is not reported as income by Patsy.

Example: Taylah and Canute finalized their divorce on March 20, 2020. As a condition of the divorce decree, Canute is required to pay alimony of $1,000 per month. These amounts are not deductible by Canute and are not reportable as income by Taylah.

In contrast, child support is never taxable income to the receiver and not deductible by the payer because it is viewed as a payment a parent makes simply to support his or her own child.

If a divorce agreement specifies payments of both alimony and child support and only partial payments are made by the payer, the partial payments are considered child support until that obligation is fully paid. Any additional amounts paid are then treated as alimony.

Example: Dayna and Clemente legally divorced in 2016. Their divorce decree is "grandfathered," and the pre-TCJA rules apply. Their divorce decree requires Clemente pay Dayna $2,000 a month ($24,000 [$2,000 × 12] a year) as child support and $1,500 a month ($18,000 [$1,500 × 12] a year) as alimony. Clemente falls behind on his payments and pays only $36,000 during the year. In this case, the first $24,000 paid is considered child support and only the remaining amount of $12,000 ($36,000 - $24,000) is considered alimony. Clemente can deduct $12,000 as alimony paid. Dayna must report $12,000 as alimony income received.

If an alimony payment is subject to reduction based on a contingency relating to a child (e.g., attaining a certain age, marrying, or going to college), the amount subject to reduction is treated as child support for tax purposes. This is regardless of whether or not the contingency is likely to occur.

Example: Khalil and Reema's divorce was final in 2017. Khalil agrees to pay Reema $4,000 a month ($48,000 per year), but the divorce agreement specifies that the payments will be reduced to $3,000 a month once their only child, Taavi, reaches the age of 18. Since this is clearly a contingency related to a child, only $1,000 of the monthly payments are actually considered "alimony" for federal tax purposes. In 2020, Reema pays a tax attorney to review her divorce decree, and he notifies her about the contingency in her decree. Reema decides to report only $12,000 as taxable alimony ($1,000 x 12 months) in 2020. Khalil, on the other hand, reports the full $48,000 as alimony paid. Both of their returns are subsequently audited. Reema shows the IRS auditor the contingency in her divorce decree, and the auditor agrees with her. Reema will only be taxed on $12,000 of alimony, and Khalil will have his return adjusted by the IRS, reducing the amount of alimony paid that he is allowed to deduct.

If alimony payments continue after the receiving spouse dies, they will not be considered alimony. For a payment to qualify as alimony:

- The divorce agreement may not include a clause indicating that the payment is something else (such as child support or repayment of a loan).
- The payor must have no liability to make any payment after the death of the former spouse.

Not all payments that are made to an ex-spouse qualify as taxable alimony. Alimony does *not* include:

- Payments that are a former spouse's share of income from community property
- Payments to keep up the payer's property
- Free use of the payer's property

- Noncash property settlements
- Any payment made other than in cash
- Any payments made to an ex-spouse when the divorce was finalized in 2019 or later years.

Note: Property settlements are simply a division of property and are not treated as alimony. In general, property transferred to an ex-spouse as part of a divorce proceeding is not a taxable event.

Example: Brooklynn and Galvin divorce in 2020. As part of their divorce agreement, Brooklynn must transfer a portion of her 401(k) account to Galvin. The transfer is properly outlined in their divorce settlement agreement, and a QDRO[141] is issued by the court. On October 1, 2020, their divorce becomes final. Two days later, the retirement plan transfer is completed, and $105,000 is transferred directly from Brooklynn's 401(k) to Galvin's retirement account. The transfer is considered a division of marital assets. The transfer is also not subject to an early withdrawal penalty.

Payments made to a third party can be considered alimony in some cases. For example, if, under the terms of a divorce agreement, a spouse pays the medical bills of his ex-wife, a cash payment to the hospital can count as alimony.

For a jointly owned home, half of the mortgage payments and real estate taxes may be deducted as alimony, assuming the divorce decree or separation agreement requires a taxpayer to pay these expenses for his ex-spouse. The ex-spouse must include the payments as alimony received.

Government Benefits

Most government welfare benefits, including food stamps, heating assistance programs, and nonfederal assistance benefits from states or local agencies are exempt from federal taxation. Worker's compensation, which provides wage replacement and medical benefits to injured workers, is not taxable income. In contrast, unemployment compensation is taxable.[142]

Example: Haima was laid off from her job in 2020. She received $300 a week of unemployment compensation for 26 weeks. When she was unable to find another job, she began receiving benefits from her state's WIC program, which provided vouchers for food for her and her toddler. The unemployment compensation would be taxable income, but the welfare (WIC) benefits would not be taxable income.

Social Security Income

Social Security income is reported to the taxpayer on Form SSA-1099, *Social Security Benefit Statement,* and these benefits are taxable in certain cases, depending upon a taxpayer's income

[141] A QDRO (Qualified Domestic Relations Order) is a judgment, decree or court order that is used to assign company provided benefits to an alternate payee, typically as part of divorce or marital separation proceedings. An ex-spouse (or spouse, if legally separated and not yet divorced) may roll over tax-free all or part of a distribution from a qualified retirement plan that he or she received under a QDRO.

[142] The American Rescue Plan Act (ARPA), passed on March 11,2021, included a retroactive provision making the first $10,200 ($20,400 for MFJ filers) unemployment compensation nontaxable for tax year 2020, for households earning less than $150,000. Since this is a retroactive change, it will not be tested during the current exam cycle.

and the amount of benefits received for the year. To determine if any percentage of his Social Security benefits is taxable, a taxpayer must compare the base threshold amount for his filing status with the total of:

- One-half of his benefits, plus
- All of the taxpayer's other income, including tax-exempt interest.

If the sum is less than the base amount for his filing status, none of the Social Security is taxable. If the sum is more than the base amount for his filing status, a percentage of the Social Security is taxable.

Base Amounts for Calculating Taxability of Social Security

MFJ: $32,000

Single, HOH, QW, or MFS (and lived apart from his/her spouse all year): $25,000

MFS (if lived with spouse at any time during the year): $0

The taxpayer calculates the taxable portion on a worksheet in the *Instructions for Form 1040*, or Publication 915, *Social Security and Equivalent Railroad Retirement Benefits.* The taxable portion of Social Security benefits is never more than 85% and, in most cases, is less than 50%.

Spouses who file jointly must combine their incomes and Social Security benefits when figuring the taxable portion of their benefits, even if one spouse did not receive any benefits.

Example: George and Mabel are both over 65. They file jointly, and both received Social Security benefits during 2020. At the end of the year, George received a Form SSA-1099 showing net benefits of $7,500. Mabel received a Form SSA-1099 showing net benefits of $3,500. George also received wages of $20,000 and taxable interest income of $500. He did not have any tax-exempt interest.

1. Total Social Security benefits	$11,000
2. Enter one-half of Social Security (X 50%)	$5,500
3. Enter taxable interest and wages	$20,500
4. Sum ($5,500 + $20,500)	**$26,000**

George and Mabel's benefits are not taxable because the total above is not more than the base amount ($32,000) for married filing jointly.

Other Income

"Other income" includes items that do not have separately identified lines on Form 1040. In 2020, other income is reported directly on Schedule 1, Form 1040. Examples of "other income," which we cover in detail next, include:

- Gambling winnings
- Cancellation of debt income
- Hobby income
- Certain types of court awards
- Prizes and awards

- Taxable distributions from a Coverdell education savings account or a qualified tuition program if they are more than the qualified higher education expenses for a designated beneficiary

Note: Remember, taxpayers are required to report all taxable income, whether or not the taxpayer receives a document from the payor reporting the amount paid.

Gambling Winnings

Gambling income may include winnings from lotteries, raffles, horse races, and casinos. Gambling winnings will be reported to a taxpayer on Form W-2G if he wins:

- $600 or more from regular gambling (i.e., horse racing, card tables, etc.)
- $1,200 or more from bingo or slot machines
- $1,500 or more from keno
- Any amounts subject to federal income tax withholding

A taxpayer must report and pay tax on all gambling winnings, regardless of whether he receives a Form W-2G. In 2020, gambling losses are deductible on Schedule A as a miscellaneous itemized deduction, but the deduction is limited to the amount of gambling winnings.

Example: Janette had $11,000 of gambling winnings and $23,000 of gambling losses during the taxable year. Her deduction for gambling losses cannot exceed $11,000, the amount of her gambling winnings. To claim the deduction for her losses, Janette must itemize and list her gambling losses on Schedule A, Form 1040. If Janette does not itemize, she will not be able to deduct any of her gambling losses.

Note: The TCJA expanded the definition of "gambling losses." In prior years, professional gamblers who filed on Schedule C were able to generate an NOL from their wagering activities. The TCJA modified the limit on gambling losses so that all the deductions for expenses incurred in carrying out gambling activities, not just direct gambling losses, are limited to the extent of gambling winnings. For example, an individual who is a professional gambler can include expenses traveling to and from a casino as gambling losses as an offset against any gambling winnings, but cannot use the expenses to generate a loss on Schedule C.[143]

The taxpayer must keep an accurate diary or similar record of gambling winnings and losses, along with tickets, receipts, canceled checks, and other documentation. He is not required to include these supporting records with his tax return, but they should be retained in case of an audit.

Cancellation of Debt Income

Generally, if a taxpayer's debt is canceled or forgiven, the taxpayer must include the debt forgiveness in his gross income. If a lender cancels a debt and issues Form 1099-C, the lender will indicate on the form if the borrower was personally liable for repayment of the debt. The tax impact depends on the type of debt and whether the loan is recourse or nonrecourse.

A recourse debt holds the borrower personally liable. All other debt is considered nonrecourse. Cancellation of debt may include any indebtedness for which a taxpayer is

[143] The TCJA modified IRC Sect. 165(d) to provide that all deductions for expenses incurred in carrying out gambling and wagering activities are limited to the extent of gambling winnings.

personally liable, or which attaches to the taxpayer's property, such as an auto loan, credit card debt, mortgage, or home equity loan.[144]

Note: A "nonrecourse" loan does not allow the lender to pursue anything other than the collateral to collect the debt. For example, if a borrower defaults on a nonrecourse home loan, the bank can only foreclose on the home. The bank cannot take further legal action to collect the money owed on the debt. Whether a debt is recourse or nonrecourse may vary from state to state, depending on state law. If a lender forecloses on property subject to a recourse debt and cancels the portion of the debt in excess of the FMV of the property, the canceled portion is treated as ordinary income. This amount must be included in gross income unless it qualifies for an exception or exclusion.

Most home mortgages are "nonrecourse loans." This means that if the borrower defaults, the lender can seize the home, but cannot seek out the borrower for any further compensation, even if the FMV of the home does not cover the remaining loan balance. If the taxpayer abandons property that secures a debt for which the taxpayer is not personally liable (a nonrecourse loan), the abandonment is treated as a sale or exchange.

If a loan is nonrecourse and the borrower does not retain the asset (such as through a foreclosure of the property by the lender), the borrower does not have to recognize cancellation of debt income. However, there is a deemed sales price based on the amount of the nonrecourse loan at the time of the abandonment, foreclosure or short sale.

A taxpayer may question the taxability of canceled debt because it can apply in a tax year in which cash is not received. In a situation where a property is surrendered or repossessed, such as a foreclosure, the taxpayer may feel that by giving up the property, he should be relieved from any further obligation.

Example: Linus lost his home to foreclosure because he lost his job and could no longer make his mortgage payments. At the time of the foreclosure, Linus owed a balance of $170,000 to his mortgage lender, and the fair market value of the home was $140,000. The mortgage is a nonrecourse loan. Linus moves out, abandoning the property, and the bank forecloses on the home. Linus is not personally liable for the debt (since it is a nonrecourse loan). The abandonment is treated as a sale (for tax purposes), and the "selling price" would be $170,000, which is the balance of the loan.

Example: Lisa borrows $10,000 from her bank in order to take a vacation. She defaults on the loan after paying back only $2,000. She has the ability to pay back the loan, but chooses not to. The lender writes off the remaining balance of the loan instead of pursuing Lisa for the loan balance. Therefore, there is a cancellation of debt of $8,000, which is taxable income to Lisa.

If the original debt is a nonbusiness debt, the canceled debt amount is reported as "other income" on Schedule 1, Form 1040. The taxpayer must generally report two transactions: (1) the cancellation of debt income, and (2) gain or loss on the sale or repossession, generally equal to the difference between the FMV of the property at the time of the foreclosure and the taxpayer's adjusted basis in the property.

---

144 There is no taxable income from a canceled debt if it is intended as a gift (for example, if a taxpayer owes his parents money, but they choose to forgive the debt).

If a personal asset such as a vehicle is repossessed, the repossession is treated as a sale for tax purposes, and a gain or loss must be computed. A loss related to a personal asset would be nondeductible.

Example: Zeus lost his yacht to repossession because he could no longer afford to make his payments. At the time of the repossession, he owed a balance of $170,000 to the lender, and the FMV of the yacht was $140,000. Zeus is personally liable for the debt (recourse loan), so the repossession is treated as a sale. The "selling price" from the repossession is $140,000, and Zeus must recognize $30,000 in debt forgiveness income ($170,000 outstanding debt - $140,000 FMV).

Example: Larissa bought a new car for $15,000. She made a $2,000 down payment and borrowed the remaining $13,000 from her bank. Larissa is personally liable for the car loan (recourse debt). The bank repossessed her car because she stopped making payments. The balance due on the car loan at the time of the repossession was $10,000. The FMV of the car when it was repossessed was only $9,000. Since repossession is treated as a sale for tax purposes, the gain or loss must be computed. Larissa compares the amount realized ($9,000) with her adjusted basis ($15,000) to determine that she has a $6,000 nondeductible loss. She also has ordinary income from the cancellation of debt. That income is $1,000 ($10,000 canceled debt – $9,000 FMV). Larissa must report the canceled debt as income.

Definition: A **nonrecourse debt** is a type of loan that is secured by collateral in which the borrower does not have personal liability for the loan. The most common type of nonrecourse debt is a home mortgage.

Nontaxable Canceled Debt

There are several circumstances in which canceled debt is not taxable. The law provides several exceptions in which the canceled debt is excludable from income or nontaxable due to the nature of the debt.

Insolvency: A taxpayer is insolvent when his total debts are more than the FMV of his total assets immediately prior to the discharge of the debt. If a taxpayer is insolvent when the debt is canceled, the canceled debt is not taxable, but only to the extent of the insolvency (i.e., by how much his debts exceed his assets).

For this purpose, the taxpayer's assets include the value of everything he owns, including pensions and retirement accounts.

Example: In 2020, Marnie had $5,000 of credit card debt, which she could not afford to pay. The bank decided to cancel the entire $5,000 credit card balance. She received a Form 1099-C from her credit card company showing canceled debt of $5,000. Immediately before the cancellation, Marnie's total liabilities were $15,000, and the FMV of her total assets was $7,000. Therefore, at the time the debt was canceled, Marnie was insolvent to the extent of $8,000 ($15,000 total liabilities minus $7,000 FMV of her total assets). Marnie can exclude the entire $5,000 canceled debt from income. Even if the amount is not taxable, Marnie must report the amount of debt forgiven on her return by completing Form 982, *Reduction of Tax Attributes Due to Discharge of Indebtedness.*

Bankruptcy: Debts discharged through bankruptcy court in a Title 11 bankruptcy case (generally Chapters 7 and 13) are not considered taxable income. The taxpayer must attach Form 982, *Reduction of Tax Attributes Due to Discharge of Indebtedness,* to his federal income tax return to report debt canceled in bankruptcy.

Home Mortgage Debt Cancellations

Normally, when a bank forecloses on a home and sells it for less than the borrower's outstanding mortgage, the bank forgives the unpaid mortgage debt, and the canceled debt is taxable income to the homeowner. However, a taxpayer may exclude income realized as a result of loan modification or foreclosure of a taxpayer's principal residence.

Under the *Mortgage Forgiveness Debt Relief Act*, mortgage debt on a primary residence that was forgiven was excluded from taxable income. This provision had expired, but was extended until 2025 by the *Consolidated Appropriations Act of 2021.*

Note: In 2020, a taxpayer can exclude up to $2 million ($1 million for MFS filers) of discharge-of-debt income if "qualified principal residence debt" is discharged in 2020.[145]

"Qualified principal residence indebtedness" or QPRI, is a mortgage secured by a taxpayer's principal residence that was taken out to buy, build, or substantially improve that residence and may also include debt from refinancing. Debt reduced through mortgage restructuring as well as mortgage debt forgiven in connection with a foreclosure may qualify for the exclusion. This exclusion *only* applies to a main home: it does *not* apply to second homes, rental properties, or vacation homes.[146]

Example: Anakin purchased a vacation home for $175,000, with a mortgage of $150,000. Anakin was unable to make the payments and he defaults on the loan. The home later sold in a short sale for $130,000. The lender forgives the remaining balance of the mortgage. Anakin was not insolvent or in bankruptcy. The forgiven debt is not eligible for the qualified principal residence indebtedness exclusion because it is a vacation home. Anakin must report the canceled debt as taxable income.

QPRI cannot be more than the cost of the home (plus improvements). The maximum amount that can be treated as QPRI in 2020 is $2 million ($1 million if MFS). The taxpayer must report the amount of debt forgiven on his return by completing Form 982, *Reduction of Tax Attributes Due to Discharge of Indebtedness.*

Example: Adam's primary residence is subject to a $320,000 recourse mortgage. Adam's mortgage lender forecloses on the home on January 10, 2020. The residence is later sold by the bank for $280,000 on May 1, 2020. Adam has $40,000 of canceled debt income from the discharge of indebtedness. All of the mortgage debt was *qualified principal residence indebtedness*. Therefore, he can claim the qualified principal residence *exclusion* by filing Form 982 with his 2020 tax return.

---

145 After 2020, the CAA-2021 lowers the amount of qualified principal residence debt that can be discharged tax-free to $750,000 ($375,000 for married individuals filing separately).

146 The lender is usually required to report the amount of the canceled debt to the taxpayer a Form 1099-C, Cancellation of Debt.

Example: Valentino incurred a mortgage debt of $800,000 when he purchased his main home for $880,000. He made a down payment of $80,000 and financed the rest through his bank. When the FMV of the property was $1 million, Valentino refinanced the debt for $850,000. At the time of the refinancing, the balance of the original loan was $740,000. Valentino used the $110,000 he obtained from the refinancing ($850,000 minus $740,000) to take a three-month-long luxury vacation in the Bahamas. A year after the refinancing, Valentino lost his job and stops making payments on the loan. Valentino's home had declined in value to $750,000. The lender agreed to a short sale of the property for $735,000, and cancellation of the remaining $115,000 of the $850,000 debt. Valentino can exclude only $5,000 of the canceled debt from his income using the exclusion for canceled QPRI ($115,000 canceled debt minus the $110,000 amount of the debt that was not QPRI, which was the amount he used to take a luxury vacation). Valentino is not insolvent and did not file for bankruptcy, so he must include the remaining $110,000 of canceled debt in income.

Even if the canceled debt does not qualify under the *qualified principal residence indebtedness* exclusion, canceled mortgage debt does not have to be included in taxable income if the debt was canceled in a bankruptcy case or while the taxpayer was insolvent (up to the amount of the insolvency of the taxpayer right before the debt cancellation).

Example: Alejandro's vacation home is subject to a $320,000 recourse mortgage. He stops making payments on the loan. Alejandro's mortgage lender forecloses on the home in January 2020, when the fair market value of the home was $280,000. The residence is later auctioned off by the bank for $280,000. Alejandro has $40,000 of canceled debt from the discharge of indebtedness because the mortgage was $40,000 more than the property's fair market value at the time of the foreclosure. The home was not his main home, so the canceled debt is not "qualified principal residence indebtedness." However, right before the foreclosure, Alejandro was insolvent – with the amount of all his debts (including this mortgage) equaling $400,000 and the value of all of his assets being $350,000 at that time – resulting in an insolvency amount of $50,000. Since the $40,000 canceled debt is less than the $50,000 extent of his insolvency, the forgiven debt is not taxable. Alejandro must report the amount of debt forgiven on his return by completing Form 982, *Reduction of Tax Attributes Due to Discharge of Indebtedness*, and marking the box to report his insolvency.

Cancellation of Student Loans

Certain student loans contain a provision that all or part of the debt incurred to attend a qualified educational institution will be canceled if the student later works for a specified period of time in certain professions. The canceled debt does not have to be recognized as income on a taxpayer's return.

Example: Paula is a medical student completing her residency. In return for forgiveness of her student loans, she agrees to work for four years as a pediatrician in a state program in Minnesota that serves rural and poor communities. The canceled debt does not have to be recognized as income.

Discharges of student loans (including private student loans) will not be taxable when the discharge is on account of death or permanent disability. It also excludes forgiveness in the event

of death, even if there is a cosigner on the loan. This provision covers eligible student loans until December 31, 2025.

Example: Aurelius takes out a student loan of $32,500 and uses it to pay his college tuition and textbooks. He is personally responsible for the loan. On November 1, 2020, Aurelius dies in a car accident. The student loan is forgiven by the lender. The forgiven debt is not taxable to Aurelius on his final tax return, and the liability does not transfer to his estate or his heirs.

On January 15, 2020, the IRS also released Revenue Procedure 2020-11,[147] which establishes a safe harbor extending relief to taxpayers who took out federal or private student loans to finance attendance at a nonprofit or for-profit school that closed because of certain illegal business practices. Students who took out federal or private student loans to finance their attendance at several nonprofit or for-profit schools now qualify for safe harbor with regard to cancellation of debt income for these discharged student loans.

Example: Habiba took out a student loan to finance attendance at a for-profit Corinthian College. The college was investigated for widespread fraud by the federal government and other authorities. After federal investigations, Corinthian College filed for Chapter 11 bankruptcy and was forced to shut down. Habiba had cancellation of debt income from her student loans associated with her attendance at this college. The canceled debt is not taxable to Habiba and does not have to be reported on her tax return, according to Revenue Procedure 2020-11.

Qualified Farm Indebtedness: If a taxpayer incurred the canceled debt in a farming business, it is generally not considered taxable income.

Canceled Debt that is Otherwise Deductible: If a taxpayer uses the cash method of accounting, he should not recognize canceled debt income if payment of the debt would have otherwise been a deductible expense.

Example: Raima is a self-employed interior designer. A CPA firm agrees to file her business tax return and bill her at a later date. Raima receives $2,200 of tax preparation and bookkeeping services for her business on credit. Later, Raima loses a major design account and has trouble paying her debts, so her CPA forgives the amount she owes. Raima does not include the canceled debt in her gross income because payment of the debt would have been deductible as a business expense had it been paid.

Hobby Income

A "hobby" is an activity typically undertaken primarily for pleasure. Even though it may produce income, a hobby is not considered a business because it is not carried on to make a profit. Gross income from a hobby is taxable and reported on Form 1040, Schedule 1. Hobby income is not subject to self-employment tax.

The IRS presumes that an activity is "carried on for a profit" if it makes a profit during at least three of the last five tax years, including the current year. However, that presumption can be

[147] This Revenue Procedure provides relief when the federal loans are discharged by the Department of Education under the Closed School or Defense to Repayment discharge process, or where the private loans are discharged based on settlements of certain types of legal causes of action against nonprofit or other for-profit schools and certain private lenders. The procedure includes federal student loans to finance attendance at a school owned by Corinthian College, Inc. (CCI) or American Career Institutes, Inc. (ACI), respectively, and whose loans were discharged by the Department of Education under the "Closed School" or "Defense to Repayment" discharge process.

rebutted by considering a number of factors as outlined in Treasury regulations, including an analysis of the following:

- Does the effort put into the activity indicate an intention to make a profit?
- Does the taxpayer depend on income from the activity?
- If there are losses, are they due to circumstances beyond the taxpayer's control, or did they occur in the start-up phase of the business?
- Has the taxpayer changed methods of operation to improve profitability?
- Does the taxpayer have the knowledge needed to carry on the activity as a successful business?
- Has the taxpayer made a profit in similar activities in the past?
- Does the activity make a profit in some years?
- Can the taxpayer expect to make a profit in the future from the appreciation of assets used in the activity?
- Is there an element of personal pleasure or recreation?

Note: The use of hobby expenses to offset hobby-related income is no longer permitted. The Tax Cuts and Jobs Act repealed most miscellaneous itemized deductions, including the deduction for hobby-related expenses on Schedule A. A taxpayer with hobby income is still allowed to deduct cost of goods sold (COGS), if it applies, in order to arrive at taxable income.[148]

Example: Stefan buys and breeds aquarium fish as a hobby. Twice a year, he goes to an Exotic Fish convention and sells some of his fish. Although he makes money on occasion, he mainly does this activity for pleasure and not for profit. Stefan plans to continue attending the conventions, whether he makes money or not. Therefore, the income is hobby income. His expenses are not deductible, and his income is taxable. Stefan is allowed to deduct the cost of goods sold (i.e., the cost of the fish he sells to customers) to calculate his hobby-related income.

Court Awards and Damages

Court awards for compensation for lost wages or profits are generally taxable as ordinary income, as are punitive damages. Interest payments on any settlement award are also taxable. Compensatory damages for personal physical injury or physical sickness are not taxable income, whether they are from a settlement or an actual court award.

Damages received for emotional distress due to "physical injury or sickness" are treated the same way as damages for physical injury or sickness, so they are not included in income. However, if the plaintiff's emotional distress is *not* due to a physical injury (for example, an employment lawsuit in which a taxpayer suffers emotional distress for injury to reputation), the proceeds are taxable, except for any damages received for medical care that are directly related to that emotional distress.

"Emotional distress" can include physical symptoms such as headaches, depression, insomnia, and stomach disorders.

[148] Treasury Regulation Section 1.183-1(e) states that a taxpayer may determine gross income from <u>any activity</u> by subtracting the cost of goods sold (COGS) from the gross receipts so long as he consistently does so and follows generally accepted methods of accounting in determining such gross income.

Example: Sheila won a court award for emotional distress caused by unlawful discrimination. The emotional distress resulted in her hospitalization for a nervous breakdown. The court awarded Sheila damages of $100,000, including $20,000 to refund the cost of her medical care for the nervous breakdown. In this case, $80,000 ($100,000 - $20,000) would be considered a taxable court award. The $20,000 of damages for her medical care would not be taxable.

Example: Terrill was injured in a car accident. Both his legs were broken, and he suffered other serious physical injuries. He received an insurance settlement for his injuries totaling $950,000. The settlement is nontaxable because it is payment for a physical injury. He does not have to report the amounts on his tax return.

Punitive damages are *always taxable,* even if the punitive damages were received in a settlement for personal physical injuries or physical sickness. Punitive damages are legal damages assessed in order to "punish" the defendant for outrageous or malicious conduct. Punitive damages should be reported as "Other Income" on Schedule 1 (Form 1040).

Example: Morgana purchases a new car; a sporty sedan called the "Flinto." She enjoys the vehicle and drives it to and from work every day. After about six months of ownership, she has a small fender-bender on a residential street. During the accident, her car's gas tank mysteriously explodes. Morgana manages to escape the burning vehicle, but she experiences third-degree burns on her right arm and leg from the blast. Morgana later discovers that the "Flinto" has a serious design flaw, and the manufacturer of the car knew about it, but refused to issue a recall. She decides to sue the manufacturer of the car in a civil action. The case goes to trial, and the jury awards Morgana $2 million in compensatory damages for her injuries, but also an additional $15 million in punitive damages, which was designed to punish the manufacturer for its conduct. The $2 million in compensatory damages would not be taxable to Morgana, as it was payment for her physical injuries. The $15 million in punitive damages would be taxable as "other income" on Schedule 1 of her Form 1040.

Civil damages, restitution, or other monetary awards that the taxpayer received as compensation for wrongful incarceration are not taxable.

Example: Ryan was wrongfully convicted of murder and later released after spending almost 15 years in prison. Ryan was awarded $50,000 per year of wrongful imprisonment. None of the award is taxable income to Ryan.

No tax deduction is allowed for any settlement, payout, or attorney fees related to sexual harassment or sexual abuse if the payments are subject to a nondisclosure agreement.

Example: Santiago is a self-employed therapist who files on Schedule C. Santiago has several employees who work in his office. On January 4, 2020, Santiago's full-time secretary, Keira, sues him for sexual harassment. Rather than risk a public lawsuit that might damage his reputation, Santiago settles with Keira, coming to a confidential settlement with Keira and her attorney. The settlement was $25,000, and their settlement agreement was subject to a nondisclosure clause. Santiago also incurred $5,000 in legal fees for his attorney to negotiate the settlement. Santiago cannot deduct the settlement or his legal fees as a business expense. However, Keira is required to report the full amount of the settlement as taxable income on her individual return.

Prizes and Awards

Prizes and awards are taxable and are reported as "other income" on Form 1040, Schedule 1. If the prize or award is in the form of property rather than cash, the fair market value of the property is treated as the taxable amount. The winner may avoid taxation of the award by rejecting the prize. The taxpayer may also avoid taxation by having the payer directly transfer the prize to a charity or other nonprofit organization.

Example: A national education association chooses Paulo, a college instructor, as its teacher of the year. He is awarded $3,000, but he does not accept the prize. Paulo directs the association to give all his winnings to a college scholarship fund, instead. Paulo never receives a check or has control over the funds; therefore, the award is not taxable to him.

Example: Wendy purchased a $1 ticket for a raffle conducted by her church, which is a qualified charitable organization. On October 31, 2020, a drawing was held and Wendy wins $900. The church must file Form W-2G with the IRS and give a copy of Form W-2G to Wendy. The prize is fully taxable as "other income" to Wendy.[149]

Employee awards for safety, length-of-service, or achievements are generally not taxable to the employee unless they exceed specified limits.[150]

Educational Assistance

Many types of educational assistance are tax-free if they meet certain requirements. Tax-free educational assistance includes scholarships, Pell Grants, and employer-provided educational assistance.

Qualifying educational assistance plans (Qualified EAPs) provided under an employer's qualified educational assistance program, now include the payments of tuition and fees, as well as *student loans,* up to an annual maximum of $5,250.[151] The CAA-2021 extends the exclusion for eligible student loan repayments through the end of 2025.

Example: Deloot Accounting, Inc. is a multinational accounting firm. The company offers an educational assistance program to its employees as a fringe benefit. As part of the plan, the company reimburses costs for tuition, fees, and books for college and university classes. Gregory is a junior auditor working for Deloot Accounting. In 2020, he incurs $6,300 in educational expenses. He submits copies of his tuition statements and receipts for his books to his employer. The company reimburses Gregory for $5,250 worth of his expenses (the annual maximum). The reimbursed amounts are not taxable to Gregory, and fully deductible by the company. However, if Gregory is eligible for an education credit, he must reduce the amounts of his qualified educational expenses by the amounts that were reimbursed.

---

[149] Based on an example in this IRS news release: https://www.irs.gov/pub/irs-tege/notice_1340.pdf

[150] Employee awards are covered in greater detail in Book 2, *Businesses*, because they are a common employee fringe benefit. Fringe benefits are generally tested on Part 2 of the EA exam.

[151] The Coronavirus Aid, Relief, and Economic Security Act (CARES Act) added student loan repayments to the types of payments that are eligible for this exclusion, if they are made after March 27, 2020, and before January 1, 2021. The CAA-2021 then extended this CARES Act provision to 2025.

Scholarships and Fellowships: A scholarship is an amount paid to an undergraduate or graduate student to pursue a college degree. A fellowship is an amount paid to an individual to pursue research. A scholarship or fellowship is excluded from income only if:

- The taxpayer is a degree candidate at an eligible educational institution
- The amounts do not exceed qualified educational expenses.
- It is not designated for other purposes, such as room and board.
- It does not represent payment for teaching, research, or other services.

Qualified educational expenses include: tuition, required fees, and course-related expenses such as books. An athletic scholarship is tax-free only if it meets the requirements described above.

Example: Marybeth is a graduate student at a private university who received a scholarship of $30,000. Under its terms, she must serve as a part-time teaching assistant. From the $30,000 scholarship, she receives $12,500 for teaching, which is listed as income on her Form W-2. She had expenses of more than $18,000 for tuition and course-related books. Marybeth may exclude $17,500 of the scholarship funds from income, but the $12,500 she earned as a teaching assistant is taxable and must be included on her individual tax return.

Pell Grants: A Pell Grant is a need-based grant that is treated as a scholarship for tax purposes. It is tax-free to the extent it is used for qualified educational expenses during the specified grant period.

Payment to Service Academy Cadets or Midshipmen: An appointment to a United States military academy is not a scholarship or fellowship. Cadets and midshipmen receive free tuition and room and board, which is nontaxable. However, they also receive government pay while at the military academy; these amounts are taxable income.

Veterans' Educational Benefits: Veterans' benefits for education are tax-free if administered by the Department of Veterans Affairs.

Example: Laurence served in Afghanistan and has since returned to college. He receives two education benefits under the GI bill: a $1,534 monthly basic housing allowance and $3,840 tuition paid directly to his college. Neither of these benefits is taxable to Laurence, and he is not required to report them on his tax return.

Qualified Tuition Programs

QTPs, also known as Section 529 plans, are established and maintained by states or educational institutions. These plans allow a taxpayer to either prepay a student's qualified educational expenses at an eligible educational institution or contribute to an account that will be used to pay future expenses. A Section 529 functions somewhat like a Roth IRA account: the amounts contributed to a Section 529 plan are not deductible for federal tax purposes,[152] but the earnings grow tax-free.

---

152 Although there is no federal tax deduction for contributions to a 529 plan, some states do allow a deduction for contributions. This can be a factor when taxpayers are deciding between different types of educational savings accounts.

Contributions to a Section 529 are treated as gifts for tax purposes, which means that a donor can contribute up to $15,000 in 2020, per beneficiary, without incurring any gift tax. The amounts contributed to a 529 are removed from the calculation of a donor's gross estate (this is why 529 plans are commonly used for estate planning purposes).

Unlike a Coverdell ESA, (covered in the next section), a 529 plan does not impose age limits or income limits to contribute. Distributions from a 529 plan are reported to the taxpayer on Form 1099-Q. The part of a distribution representing the amount paid or contributed to the plan (the taxpayer's basis) is not included in income.

The beneficiary also generally does not have to include in taxable income any earnings distributed from a 529 plan if the total distribution is less than or equal to a student's qualified education expenses (after reduction of the latter by other tax-free education assistance received during the year). The definition of "qualified higher education expenses" for distributions from 529 accounts also includes the purchases of computer equipment and technology.

"Qualified expenses" include tuition, fees, books, computer equipment, and software, and room and board for any time the beneficiary is enrolled in school. A beneficiary may be anyone the taxpayer designates: himself, a child, a grandchild, or an unrelated person.

Eligible institutions include virtually all accredited colleges, universities, vocational schools, and postsecondary educational institutions. The TCJA modified Section 529 plans to allow distributions (not exceeding $10,000 per year) for tuition expenses incurred in connection with the enrollment or attendance at any public, private or religious elementary or secondary (K-12) school. This means that Section 529 plans can be used for private elementary schools, middle schools, and high schools.

The SECURE Act expanded Section 529 plans even further to permit tax-free distributions to pay for fees, books, supplies and equipment required for a qualifying apprenticeship[153] program, or to pay the principal or interest (up to $10,000) on a qualified education loan of the designated beneficiary, or a sibling of the designated beneficiary.

If the total distribution is greater than a student's adjusted qualified expenses, an allocable portion of the earnings is taxable. In this type of taxable distribution, an additional excise tax of 10% generally applies to the amount included in income.

Any amount distributed from a 529 plan is not taxable if it is rolled over to another 529 plan for the use of the same beneficiary or for a member of the beneficiary's family. The amount must be rolled over to another educational account within 60 days after the date of distribution.

Example: Bernardo still had $3,000 left in his 529 plan after he graduated from college. He wanted to help his younger sister, who was still in high school. Within 60 days after the distribution of the remaining portion of his 529 plan, he contributed the money to his sister's 529 plan, so the distribution was not taxable to him or his sister. Instead of taking a distribution, Bernardo could also have instructed the trustee of his 529 account to simply change the name of the beneficiary on his account to his sister.

---

[153] Qualifying apprenticeship programs must first be registered and certified by the U.S. Secretary of Labor. Acceptable programs are varied and can include: electricians, dental assistants, welders, and pipefitters.

Coverdell Education Savings Accounts (ESA)

Formerly called "Education IRAs," these plans were renamed in 2002, after the late Senator Paul Coverdell, who was their primary backer. A Coverdell ESA is a tax-advantaged investment account for higher education. A Coverdell is generally structured as a trust or custodial account set up to pay qualified elementary, secondary, or higher education expenses for a designated beneficiary. The funds in a Coverdell can be withdrawn tax-free when used for educational purposes.

Coverdell ESAs have income and age limits, but under certain conditions, they can offer more flexibility in investing. Coverdell accounts are self-directed, which means that there are a variety of investment options available, whereas 529 plans are limited to the state's selected investment options. In order to contribute fully to a Coverdell ESA, the contributor's MAGI in 2020 must be below $190,000- $220,000 (for joint filers) or $95,000-$110,000 (for all other filing statuses). All contributions must be in cash (not property or stock) and must be made by the due date of the contributor's tax return (not including extensions). So, for example, if a taxpayer wanted to set up a Coverdell account for his child in 2020, he would have until April 15, 2021, to set up the account and fund it.

Contributions to a Coverdell must be made before the beneficiary reaches age 18, and the use of the account must be made by age 30, unless the beneficiary is special-needs. If there is a balance in the ESA when the beneficiary reaches age 30, it must be distributed within 30 days of turning 30 (or within 30 days after the death, if before age 30 of the beneficiary). The beneficiary can also choose to transfer the ESA to another beneficiary (such as a younger sibling or another family member) to avoid the tax.

Example: Akim earned a full scholarship to Stanford University. He enrolled when he was 19 and had a Coverdell ESA with a balance of $52,000 that was set up by his parents when he was a child. Since his tuition was already paid by his scholarship, Akim only used the ESA for books and required lab fees. Akim graduated from college 4 years later and had only used a total of $29,000 from his ESA. Rather than withdrawing the money and paying the 10% tax, Akim transferred the Coverdell account to his younger sister, who is 17 and still in high school. His sister can use the remaining amounts in the Coverdell for her own future college expenses. His sister will have until age 30 to use the funds for her college expenses.

If the beneficiary is special-needs, the Coverdell account can continue in existence (without transfer to another beneficiary) after the beneficiary turns 30. Contributions to a Coverdell ESA are not tax-deductible, but amounts deposited in the account grow tax-free until they are later distributed.

There is no limit to the *number* of Coverdell accounts that can be established for a beneficiary; however, the total contribution to all accounts on behalf of a beneficiary cannot exceed $2,000 per year, no matter how many accounts are established. However, if a taxpayer wants to do some year-end tax planning, they can set up a Coverdell as late as the filing deadline, and contribute $2,000 for 2020 and another $2,000 for 2021 up until April 15, 2021, the individual filing deadline.

All contributions that exceed $2,000 for a single beneficiary in a taxable year will be treated as excess contributions. There will be a 6% excise tax if the excess contributions and earnings on

them are not withdrawn from the child's accounts before June 1 of the following tax year. This tax will apply to each year that the excess remains in the account. Any earnings withdrawn as part of a corrective distribution are taxable in the year of the excess contribution, even if the corrective distribution occurs in the following year.

The penalty for excess contributions is imposed on the beneficiary of the account (usually a minor child), and not on the person who overcontributed to the account. The excise tax must be reported on the child's income tax return, using IRS Form 5329, *Additional Taxes on Qualified Plans (Including IRAs) and Other Tax-Favored Accounts.* This rule seems contrary to common sense, but the penalty is imposed on the child, not the child's parents, or the contributor of the excess funds. An additional penalty tax of 10% applies to distributions that are not used for qualifying educational expenses.

Example: Three Coverdell ESAs were set up for Kendra when she was born: one by her parents, one by her grandparents, and one by her great-uncle. In 2020, her grandparents contribute $1,500 to Kendra's account. The most her parents and great uncle can contribute is a combined $500, because the maximum contribution per year for a single beneficiary is $2,000.

The beneficiary of a Coverdell account can receive distributions to pay qualified education expenses that are tax-free if the amount of the distributions does not exceed the beneficiary's adjusted qualified education expenses. If a distribution does exceed the beneficiary's qualified education expenses, a portion of the earnings is taxable and is reported as "other income" on Schedule 1 of Form 1040.

There is no law that prevents a taxpayer from contributing to both a Coverdell and a 529 for the same beneficiary, so a taxpayer could potentially set up a Coverdell and a Section 529 for the same child, and the earnings would grow tax-free in both accounts.

If a beneficiary receives distributions from both a 529 plan and a Coverdell ESA in the same year, and the total distributions exceed the beneficiary's adjusted qualified education expenses for that year, the expenses must be allocated between the distributions from each account.

The total expenses must also be reduced by any amounts used in claiming an American Opportunity or Lifetime Learning Credit for that year.

Miscellaneous Other Income

Other types of income that are taxable to the recipient and reported on line 8 of Schedule 1 include the following (this list is not exhaustive):

- Strike benefits,
- Jury duty pay (when it is not turned over to the employee's employer and deducted as an adjustment to income),
- Fees paid by an estate to a personal representative/executor,[154]
- Gifts or gratuities received by a host or hostess of a party or event where sales are made.

[154] Executor fees are considered taxable income to the recipient. Executors of an estate will typically receive some type of compensation for their work on the estate. Some states follow the Uniform Probate Code, including the section on how to compensate the executor of a will. Most U.S. states have a specific flat percentage listed in their probate codes. We will cover estates more extensively in a later unit.

Example: Shirley is 72 years old and retired. She supports herself primarily with her Social Security income. In 2020, she receives a jury duty summons. She is chosen for the jury, and she is paid $40 a day for serving ten days on a jury trial. Shirley was also reimbursed by the court for reasonable transportation expenses and parking fees. The $400 she earned for jury duty is taxable and must be reported on her Form 1040. The reimbursement for transportation and parking fees is not taxable and does not have to be reported on her return.

Example: Johanna hosts a cooking party for 15 friends, which includes a live demonstration by a Pampered Chef consultant. At the end of the evening, the women order $2,000 worth of Pampered Chef cookware and other merchandise from the consultant. Johanna receives a gift of $115 of products for hosting the party, which she must report as income at its fair market value.

Example: Hulderick is the executor of his grandmother's estate. His grandmother died on January 29, 2020. Her estate includes several rental properties that must be managed after her death. Hulderick is not an attorney or professional executor, but he did agree to manage his grandmother's estate. Hulderick pays bills, hires an accountant to file the estate's tax returns, and manages his late grandmother's rental properties. His grandmother's final will stipulates that the executor should receive 4% of the income generated by the estate, as well as reimbursement for all estate-related business expenses. In 2020, Hulderick receives $9,500 in executor fees, which he reports as other income on his Form 1040 (Schedule 1).

Table: Taxable vs. Nontaxable Income

Taxable Income	Nontaxable Income (or Variable)
Wages, salaries, tips, bonuses, vacation pay, severance pay, commissions	Most employer-provided fringe benefits
Interest on bank and money market accounts; CDs; dividends; Treasury bonds	Interest on most state and local bonds
Gains from sales of property, stocks and bonds, stock options, etc.	Life insurance proceeds paid on the death of the insured
Fees paid to an estate's executor	Gifts and inheritances
Alimony (pre-2019 divorce decrees)	Alimony (post-2019 divorces) and child support
Social Security benefits (above the base amount and limited to 85% of benefits)	Welfare payments, food stamps, other forms of public assistance
Court awards for punitive damages, sexual harassment claims, and lost wages	Compensation or court awards for physical injury or illness, and awards for wrongful incarceration
Unemployment compensation; strike benefits	Worker's compensation
Barter and hobby income	Combat pay and certain veteran's benefits
Certain distributions from Coverdell savings accounts or qualified tuition programs	Scholarships, Pell grants, employer-provided educational assistance
Cancellation of debt income (unless excludable)	Canceled qualified principal residence indebtedness, canceled debt while in bankruptcy, or insolvency, canceled student loans after death or permanent disability.
Gambling winnings; most prizes and awards	Certain employee awards for safety, achievement, or service

Unit 10: Study Questions

(Test yourself first, then check the correct answers at the end of this quiz.)

1. Lucian, age 70, experiences age-related discrimination on his job and sues his company. After he files the lawsuit, he is physically attacked by the company owner, who breaks Lucian's arm. The court awards Lucian the following amounts:

- $4,000 for emotional distress attributable to the age discrimination lawsuit.
- $10,000 for loss of wages.
- $35,000 for physical injury related to the assault.
- $16,000 reimbursement for medical expenses.

How much of this award is taxable to Lucian?

A. $4,000
B. $10,000
C. $14,000
D. $49,000

2. Jafar and Samantha filed jointly and received the following income during the year. How much income should be reported on their joint return?

- W-2 income for Samantha for wages of $40,000.
- 1099-MISC for Samantha for $2,000, the value of a prize trip she won to the Bahamas. She is planning to take the trip in the following year.
- Court settlement of $10,000 paid to Jafar from a car accident for serious injuries he suffered.
- $4,000 child support for Samantha's son from a previous marriage.

A. $40,000
B. $42,000
C. $46,000
D. $52,000

3. Karly is trying to get her finances in order. During the year, she negotiated a settlement with her credit card company, to which she owed a delinquent debt. She owed $10,000 on her credit card. As part of the negotiation, the credit card company agreed to accept a $2,500 settlement as payment in full. Karly was not insolvent and not in bankruptcy when the debt was canceled. What amount should be reported as "other income" on Karly's Form 1040 (Schedule 1)?

A. $0
B. $2,500
C. $7,500
D. $10,000

4. In which of the following instances is canceled debt not excluded from income in 2020?

A. Mortgage debt of a vacation home where the borrower is not insolvent or in bankruptcy.
B. Qualified farm indebtedness.
C. Medical debt discharged in bankruptcy.
D. Student loans discharged after death.

5. Lakshmi had $9,000 of gambling winnings during the year. She also incurred $15,000 of gambling losses. How should these transactions be reported on her tax return?

A. The $9,000 of winnings are reported as income, and the $15,000 of losses are reported as an adjustment to income on Schedule 1.
B. The $9,000 of winnings are reported as income, and the $15,000 of losses are reported as an itemized deduction on Schedule A.
C. The $9,000 of winnings are reported as income, and $9,000 of losses are reported as an itemized deduction on Schedule A.
D. The $9,000 of winnings are reported as income, but the gambling losses are not deductible.

6. Sven, age 64, is single and retired. He earned the following income in 2020. To determine if any of his Social Security is taxable, Sven should compare how much of his income to the $25,000 base amount?

Part-time job	$8,000
Bank interest	5,000
Social Security	11,000
Taxable pension	6,000
Total	**$30,000**

A. $11,000
B. $24,500
C. $25,000
D. $30,000

7. Marcello received $32,000 of wages in 2020. He also won a prize from his homeowner's association for developing a new water conservation plan. The prize was free landscaping service for a year, valued at $600. Marcello also received $7,000 in child support and $2,000 in alimony from his ex-wife, whom he divorced in 2017. Marcello has sole custody of his children. What is Marcello's gross income (before deductions and adjustments) for 2020?

A. $32,000
B. $32,600
C. $34,600
D. $39,600

8. Hank received Social Security in 2020 totaling $11,720. Hank also liquidated all of his stock and moved into senior housing during the year. He received $350,500 of taxable income from the stock sale. What is the maximum *taxable* amount of Hank's Social Security benefits?

A. $0
B. $5,860
C. $9,962
D. $11,720

9. Rosemary was discharged from her liability to repay $9,000 of credit card debt. The lender reported the discharged debt on Form 1099-C. Immediately prior to the debt cancellation, Rosemary had liabilities of $15,000, and the fair market value of her assets was $2,000. What portion of the canceled debt must Rosemary include in income?

A. $0
B. $3,000
C. $7,000
D. $9,000

10. Latrice and Jackson's divorce decree requires Jackson to pay Latrice $250 per month of child support and $1,500 per month of alimony. Their divorce was final on January 13, 2020. Jackson makes all of his child support and alimony payments on time during the year. How much of these payments is Latrice required to report as taxable income on her 2020 return?

A. $0
B. $1,500
C. $18,000
D. $21,000

11. Archer is a former National Football League cornerback. In 2020, he is awarded a sizable settlement in a class-action lawsuit for concussion injuries for physical pain and suffering. The settlement will be paid in installments over a period of ten years. How should Archer report the damages he is awarded on his income tax return?

A. He must include the entire amount of his settlement in gross income for the year.
B. He must include in his gross income only the portion of the settlement paid to him each year when it is received.
C. He must report the settlement on his tax return, but it is not taxable income.
D. He may exclude the payments from his gross income.

12. Ginny had the following income and losses in 2020:

Source	**Amounts**
Wages	$14,000
Interest income	125
Gambling winnings	1,000
Gambling losses	(2,000)
Discrimination lawsuit settlement	10,000
Child support payments	9,000
Food stamp benefits	5,000

How much gross income must Ginny report on her tax return?

A. $14,125
B. $15,125
C. $25,125
D. $39,000

13. Which of the following is not taxable income to the recipient?

A. Long-term disability payments from a policy paid by the recipient's employer.
B. Bartering income.
C. Gains from the sale of stock.
D. $25,000 of group-term life insurance coverage provided by an employer.

14. Jean divorced from her husband in 2017. In 2020, she received the following income (listed below). What amount of her income is taxable?

Source	**Amounts**
Wages	$13,000
Interest income	15
Child support	6,000
Taxable alimony	2,000
Inheritance	10,000
Worker's compensation	1,000
Lottery winnings	5,000

A. $13,015
B. $16,015
C. $20,015
D. $30,015

15. Armando had a $15,000 loan from his credit union but stopped making payments. The credit union determined that the legal fees to collect might be higher than the amount Armando owed, so it canceled the remaining amount of $5,000 due on the loan. Armando did not file for bankruptcy, nor is he insolvent. How much income must he include from the debt cancellation?

A. $0
B. $5,000
C. $10,000
D. $15,000

16. Sabra is 16 years old. She has two Coverdell accounts. One was set up by her grandparents, and the other was set up by her mother. Sabra received $3,200 in total contributions in her Coverdell accounts in 2020. Which of the following statements is true?

A. The contributions are deductible and can remain in the accounts until Sabra reaches 30 years of age.
B. Sabra has an excess contribution of $1,200. The excess contribution must be withdrawn, or it will be subject to an excise tax.
C. Sabra may withdraw the funds penalty-free and invest the amounts in a Roth IRA.
D. Sabra has an excess contribution of $200. She can transfer this excess contribution to an IRA account.

17. Which of the following would be considered taxable income to the recipient?

A. Life insurance proceeds paid to a beneficiary.
B. Adoption expense reimbursements.
C. Unemployment compensation.
D. Welfare benefits.

Unit 10: Quiz Answers

1. The answer is C. Lucian must report $14,000 in taxable income. The amounts for loss of wages and emotional distress are taxable as ordinary income ($4,000 + $10,000 = $14,000). Damages for emotional distress that is not due to physical injury or sickness are usually taxable (as in this case where the distress was attributed to the job discrimination and lawsuit). The damages awarded for physical injury are not taxable.

2. The answer is B. The answer is $42,000 ($40,000 wages + $2,000 prize). Samantha must recognize the prize even though she has not taken the trip because she had constructive receipt of the winnings. The accident settlement and child support payments are not taxable.

3. The answer is C. Karly would report $7,500 in canceled debt income ($10,000 - $2,500) on her Form 1040 (Schedule 1).

4. The answer is A. Foreclosure of a vacation property does not qualify for the exclusion of canceled debt income. Canceled mortgage debt related to second homes and vacation homes does not qualify, (unless the taxpayer has filed bankruptcy or is insolvent).

5. The answer is C. Lakshmi must report $9,000 of her winnings as taxable income, and $9,000 of the losses are reported on Schedule A as an itemized deduction. The amount of losses deducted may not exceed gambling winnings.

6. The answer is B. Sven does not have to pay tax on his Social Security. In order to figure out the taxable portion of Social Security, the taxpayer's total income, including tax-exempt interest, must be compared to the base amount for his filing status, which is $25,000. The amount of income that should be compared to the $25,000 base amount is calculated as follows:

Part-time job	$8,000
Interest	5,000
½ of Social Security	5,500
Taxable pension	6,000
Total	$24,500

His income plus one-half of Social Security is less than the applicable base amount ($25,000). However, he is still required to file a tax return, because his overall income exceeds the minimum filing requirement.

7. The answer is C. The wages and the prize are both reportable as taxable income. Child support is not taxable to the receiver, nor deductible by the payer. The alimony is taxable to Marcello and deductible by his ex-wife, since the divorce decree was finalized *before* 2019, when the TCJA alimony changes took effect. The answer is calculated as follows: ($32,000 + $600 + $2,000) = $34,600.

8. The answer is C. The maximum amount that is ever taxable on net Social Security benefits is 85%, which in Hank's case is (11,720 x 85% = 9,962).

9. The answer is A. Rosemary does not have any taxable canceled debt. The amount of Rosemary's assets immediately prior to the debt cancellation exceeded the amount of debt that was discharged. The entire amount of the debt cancellation can be excluded from income, due to her insolvency. She should still report the canceled debt by filing Form 982, and checking the box for "insolvency." The canceled debt will not be taxable.

Liabilities	$15,000
The fair market value of assets	(2,000)
Amount of insolvency	13,000
Amount of debt cancellation	**$9,000**

10. The answer is A. Since the divorce decree was finalized in 2020, none of the alimony is deductible by Jackson, and the alimony is not reported as income by Latrice.

11. The answer is D. Gross income does not include damages received due to physical injuries or sickness, regardless of whether the damages are paid as lump sums or as periodic payments. Archer may exclude all the payments from gross income.

12. The answer is C. The wages, interest income, gambling income, and settlement from a discrimination lawsuit must all be reported ($14,000 + $125 + $1,000 + $10,000 = $25,125). The child support payments and the food stamp benefits are not taxable. The gambling losses do not affect the inclusion of the gambling income within gross income. However, if Ginny chooses to itemize deductions, her gambling losses may be deducted on Schedule A to the extent of her gambling income. If Ginny does not itemize, the gambling losses are not deductible.

13. The answer is D. An employer may provide up to $50,000 of life insurance coverage as a nontaxable benefit to an employee. The value of any insurance coverage that exceeds $50,000 is a taxable benefit. All of the other items are taxable.

14. The answer is C. Jean must report $20,015 in taxable income. The wages, interest, alimony, and lottery winnings are taxable income ($13,000 + $15 + $2,000 + $5,000 = $20,015). Child support, inheritances, and worker's compensation are non-taxable income.

Note: Do *not* confuse worker's compensation with unemployment compensation. Worker's compensation is NOT taxable, while unemployment compensation is fully taxable.

15. The answer is B. Armando's inability to pay his debt is not a result of bankruptcy or insolvency, so he must include the full amount of the canceled debt ($5,000) in his gross income.

16. The answer is B. Sabra has an excess contribution of $1,200. The excess contribution must be withdrawn by June 1 of the next tax year, or it will be subject to an excise tax of 6%, plus an additional 6% on any interest or profits derived from the excess contribution. This tax will apply to each year that the excess remains in the account. The maximum contribution to a Coverdell is $2,000 per year per beneficiary, regardless of how many accounts the beneficiary has. Any *earnings* withdrawn as

part of a corrective distribution are taxable in the year of the excess contribution, even if the corrective distribution occurs in the following year (note that the rules for excess contributions do not apply to 529 plans, there is no limit that can be contributed to a 529, although there may be gift tax considerations if the amounts contributed exceed annual gift limits).

17. The answer is C. Unemployment compensation is taxable income. None of the other amounts would be taxable to the recipient.

Unit 11: Adjustments to Gross Income

For additional information, read:
Publication 504, *Divorced or Separated Individuals*
Publication 970, *Tax Benefits for Education*
Publication 590-A, *Contributions to Individual Retirement Arrangements*

An "adjustment to income" reduces taxable income and thus the amount of tax owed. The *Consolidated Appropriations Act of 2021* made several significant changes to adjustments to gross income. Congress passed several new provisions, including an above-the-line deduction for charitable gifts. The tuition and fees deduction was also extended for one more year. We will cover these tax law changes in this chapter.

Adjustments to income are reported on Form 1040, Schedule 1, *Additional Income and Adjustments to Income.* Adjustments are subtracted from gross income to arrive at adjusted gross income (AGI), whereas itemized deductions and the standard deduction are subtracted from AGI. Because adjustments are taken before AGI is calculated, they are designated as "above-the-line" deductions. *Adjustments* are beneficial because they not only reduce taxable income, but a lower AGI may increase a taxpayer's eligibility for certain credits and deductions and the amounts that he can claim. Unlike "below-the-line" deductions, adjustments are not added back when calculating the alternative minimum tax.

Common Adjustments to Gross Income

There are many types of adjustments to gross income, and we will cover the most common ones in this unit. These are the adjustments listed in the order they are reported on *Schedule 1,* Form 1040:

- Line 10: Qualified educator expenses
- Line 11: Certain business expenses of Armed Forces reservists, performing artists, and fee-basis government officials.[155]
- Line 12: Health savings account deduction (HSA deduction).
- Line 13: Moving expenses for members of the Armed Forces.
- Line 14: Deductible part of self-employment tax.
- Line 15: Self-employed SEP-IRA, SIMPLE, and qualified plans
- Line 16: Self-employed health insurance deduction
- Line 17: Penalty for early withdrawal of savings
- Line 18: Alimony paid (the form requires the amount paid, recipient's SSN, and the date of the original divorce or separation agreement)
- Line 19: Traditional IRA deduction
- Line 20: Student loan interest deduction
- Line 21: Tuition and fees deduction
- Line 22: Miscellaneous write-in adjustments

[155] Although most employee-related business expenses are now disallowed, business expenses for reservists, performing artists, and fee-basis government officials are still allowed. An employee with impairment-related work expenses is also still allowed to deduct those expenses. Form 2106 is used to calculate the Employee Business Expenses.

Charitable Deduction for Non-Itemizers

In addition to the adjustments listed on Schedule 1, starting in 2020, there is a special adjustment for charitable contributions on Form 1040, page 1. This new deduction permits taxpayers who do not itemize deductions to deduct up to $300 ($150 if MFS) of cash contributions to charitable organizations. The deduction lowers both adjusted gross income and taxable income.

Qualified charitable contributions include contributions to public charities, private operating foundations, and federal, state, and local governments. Gifts made directly to individuals or donor-advised funds do not count. The gifts must be made in cash in order to take this deduction, gifts of property are not eligible.

Line 10: Qualified educator expenses

This is sometimes called the "Teacher Credit" or the "Educator Expense Deduction." An eligible educator is allowed to deduct up to $250 of unreimbursed expenses for books, supplies, computer equipment (including related software and services), other equipment, and supplementary materials used in the classroom. Professional development expenses are also allowed.

Note: The *COVID-Related Tax Relief Act of 2020 (COVIDTRA)*, passed as part of the *CAA-2021*, provides an expansion of qualified educator expenses to include personal protective equipment (PPE), such as face masks, disinfectant, and other sanitation supplies purchased after March 12, 2020 used for the prevention of the spread of COVID-19.

Since this is an adjustment to income, teachers can deduct these expenses even if they do not itemize deductions. For courses in health and physical education, expenses are deductible only if they are related to athletics. Nonathletic supplies for physical education and expenses related to health courses do not qualify. Materials used for homeschooling cannot be deducted.

An eligible educator must work at least 900 hours a school year in a school that provides elementary or secondary education (K-12). College instructors do not qualify. For the purposes of this credit, an "educator" includes a:

- Teacher
- Counselor
- Principal
- Teacher's aide
- School coach

Example: Donnie is a part-time math teacher at an elementary school. He spent $185 on qualified expenses for his students. During the tax year, he worked 550 hours at the school. Because Donnie does not have enough hours of documented employment as an educator during the tax year, he cannot deduct any of his unreimbursed educator expenses. The required minimum is 900 hours during the school year.

Example: Gayle is a third-grade teacher who worked 1,600 hours during the tax year. She spent $262 on supplies for her students. Of that amount, $212 was for educational software. The other $50 was for supplies for a unit she teaches on reproductive health. Only the $212 is a qualified expense that she can deduct.

On a joint tax return, if both taxpayers are eligible, they each may take the deduction, up to a maximum of $500. In 2020, any educator expenses that exceed the $250 adjustment to income deduction cannot be deducted as unreimbursed employee business expenses on Schedule A.

Line 11: Certain business expenses of reservists, performing artists, and fee-basis government officials

Certain employees are allowed to claim specified work-related expenses as an adjustment to income. Although most employee-related business expenses are no longer deductible, business expenses for reservists, performing artists, and fee-basis government officials are still allowed.[156] However, no deduction is allowed for certain entertainment expenses, membership dues, and facilities used in connection with these activities for amounts paid or incurred in 2020.

Form 2106, *Employee Business Expenses*, is used to calculate the deduction. This adjustment applies only to reservists[157] (members of the reserve component of the Armed Forces of the United States, National Guard, or the Reserve Corps of the Public Health Service), qualified performing artists; and state or local government officials who are compensated on a fee basis.

Armed Forces Reservists are able to claim a deduction for amounts attributable to travel more than 100 miles away from their home. The travel must be reserve-related.

Example: Anthony is an Army reservist. He also has a regular full-time job in addition to his job as a reservist. Anthony's drill location is 200 miles away from his home, where he normally reports for reserve drills and official meetings. He trains one weekend a month plus an additional two weeks per year. Anthony is allowed to deduct the mileage and other travel expenses related to his reservist duties on Form 2106. The amounts are then transferred to Schedule 1, Form 1040, and claimed as an adjustment to income.

Line 12: Health savings account deduction

A high deductible health plan (HDHP) can be combined with a health savings account (HSA), allowing the taxpayer to pay for medical expenses on a tax-preferred basis. The HSA contributions are deductible as an adjustment to income on Form 1040.

Before a taxpayer can contribute to an HSA, the taxpayer must *first* be enrolled in a high-deductible health plan (HDHP). Once the HSA is set up, the taxpayer can take tax-free withdrawals from the HSA to pay for his qualifying medical expenses. An HSA must be established *exclusively* to pay medical expenses for the taxpayer, his spouse, and his dependents. HSA accounts are usually set up with a bank, an insurance company, or through an employer. To qualify for an HSA, the taxpayer:

- Must not be enrolled in Medicare,

---

[156] An employee with impairment-related work expenses is also still allowed to deduct employee business expenses, if the expenses are directly related to his or her work and disability.

[157] These deductions for travel-related expenses are not available for active duty service members, only reservists.

- Cannot be claimed as a dependent on anyone else's tax return,
- Must be covered under a high deductible health plan and have no other health coverage, other than for a specific disease or illness; a fixed amount for a certain time period of hospitalization; or liabilities incurred under worker's compensation laws or tort liabilities.

An employee and his employer are both allowed to contribute to the employee's HSA in the same year. If an employer makes an HSA contribution on behalf of an employee, it is excluded from the employee's income and is not subject to income or payroll taxes.

2020 HSA contribution limits and HDHP guidelines	
HSA contribution limit	Self-only: $3,550
	Family coverage: $7,100
HSA catch-up contributions (55 and older)	$1,000
HDHP minimum deductibles	Self-only: $1,400
	Family coverage: $2,800
HDHP maximum out-of-pocket amounts	Self-only: $6,900
	Family: $13,800

HSA holders who are age 55 and older get to contribute an extra $1,000, beyond the regular limits (as detailed in the chart), as a catch-up contribution. Any excess contributions over these limits are subject to a 6% penalty. Any amount the employer puts into the employee's HSA counts toward the employee's contribution maximum for the year.

Example: Octavian is 32 years old and married with three children. His employer provides a health care HSA paired with a high-deductible health plan that covers Octavian's entire family. Octavian's employer adds $500 to his HSA account during 2020. Octavian may contribute up to $6,600 more to his HSA account in 2020 if he wishes. The amounts that Octavian contributes to his own HSA would be deductible as an adjustment to income, and he is able to withdraw the amounts tax-free, to pay for qualified medical expenses.

Allowable medical expenses are those that would generally qualify for purposes of the deduction for medical expense deduction. However, starting in 2020, Qualified medical expenses for an HSA, MSA, FSA and HRA now include telehealth services, over-the-counter medications without a prescription, as well as menstrual products.[158] Although an account holder can withdraw funds from an HSA at any time, withdrawals that are not used for qualifying medical expenses are generally subject to income tax. They may also be subject to a 20% penalty, except in the following instances:

- When a taxpayer turns age 65 or older
- When a taxpayer becomes disabled
- When a taxpayer dies

[158] The 2020 CARES Act changed this requirement, making it possible for FSAs and HSAs to cover OTC products without a prescription as well as menstrual products. The change is retroactive to January 1, 2020, meaning that individuals can seek reimbursement for eligible purchases made at the beginning of the year.

Example: Frederic is 67, single, and has an HSA through his employer. In 2020, his car breaks down, and he doesn't have the funds to repair it. Frederic withdraws $2,000 from his HSA to pay for the car repairs. Since he did not use the funds to pay for qualifying medical expenses, the entire withdrawal is subject to income tax. However, Frederic avoids the 20% additional penalty tax because he is over 65.

A taxpayer will receive Form 5498-SA from the HSA trustee showing the amount of contributions for the year. The deduction for an HSA is reported on Form 8889, *Health Savings Accounts*. To claim the HSA deduction for a particular year, the HSA contributions must be made on or before that year's tax filing date (without extensions). For 2020, HSA contributions must be made on or before the tax year filing deadline (before April 15, 2021).

Note: Do *not* confuse an HSA (Health Savings Account) with a health-care FSA (Flexible Spending Arrangement). The two are *not the same thing*. Although both types of accounts are used to pay medical expenses on a pre-tax basis, there are significant differences between an HSA and a health-care FSA. An HSA is *always* paired with a high-deductible health plan. Self-employed individuals can set up and contribute to an HSA, (but not to an FSA). And unlike an FSA, funds in an HSA do not expire from year-to-year.

Line 13: Moving expenses for members of the Armed Forces

The Tax Cuts and Jobs Act eliminated the moving expense deduction for most taxpayers, with the exception of Armed Forces personnel moving pursuant to military orders or a permanent change of station. An employee of the armed forces is also allowed to deduct the costs of moving a spouse, dependents, and household goods or pets. A "permanent change of station" includes:

- A move from home to their first post of active duty,
- A move from one permanent post of duty to another, and
- A move from their last post of duty to a home or to a nearer point in the United States.

For 2020, the standard mileage rate for moving expenses is 17 cents a mile. A service member cannot deduct any amounts that were already reimbursed by the government. Form 3903, *Moving Expenses*, is used to calculate the qualifying moving expenses of Armed Forces personnel.

Example: Catarina is a U.S. Army medic. In 2020, she is transferred from Fort Rucker Army Base in Alabama to Tripler Army Medical Center in Hawaii. She is offered a relocation reimbursement by the Army that covers the majority of her moving expenses. The only costs that the Army would not cover were the transport costs for her pets. She pays $900 to a pet relocation service in Hawaii to process the transportation of her pets on a private airline, as well as to board her pets for the quarantine period required by the state of Hawaii. The cost of transporting pets is a deductible moving expense, and Catarina is eligible to deduct any out-of-pocket moving expenses because she is an employee of the U.S. Armed Forces. She files Form 3903, *Moving Expenses*, and correctly deducts the $900 that she paid to transport her pets as a moving expense.

If a taxpayer is not a U.S. service member, and an employer reimburses their moving expenses, the reimbursement is taxable to the employee. Employers who reimburse employees for their moving expenses must now include the reimbursements on the employee's Form W-2, and the entire amount is taxable as wages.

Example: Cedric was offered a job at Highland Engineering, Inc. on February 2, 2020. He agreed to accept the offer if the company paid all his moving expenses. The cost of his professional movers was $9,600, which the company paid. Highland Engineering also reimbursed Cedric $7,500 for temporary storage fees and other travel expenses. The total reimbursement was $17,100. Because moving expenses are no longer a deductible expense, the entire $17,100 is taxable as wages, and must be included on Cedric's Form W-2. The amount is deductible to Highland Engineering, but it is categorized as a wage expense and therefore subject to payroll tax.

Line 14: Deductible part of self-employment tax.

A self-employed taxpayer can subtract from income 50% of their self-employment tax, equal to the amount of Social Security and Medicare taxes that an employer normally pays for an employee, which is excluded from an employee's income. The deduction is figured on Schedule SE. A self-employed taxpayer cannot deduct one-half of the Additional Medicare Tax on earned income.[159]

Example: Archie is a self-employed house painter. His Schedule C shows a profit of $10,500. His self-employment tax is $1,484; this amount is comprised of $1,202 in Social Security tax and $281 in Medicare tax. The tax-deductible portion is $742 ($1,484 x 50%), which can be deducted as an adjustment to income on Form 1040.

Line 15: Self-employed SEP, SIMPLE, and qualified plans

When a taxpayer is self-employed, they have access to some of the same kinds of retirement plans that are utilized by larger employers. Self-employed individuals can deduct contributions to the following types of retirement plans:

- **Simplified Employee Pension (SEP) plans**
- **Savings Incentive Match Plan for Employees (SIMPLE) plans**
- **Qualified plans**

A taxpayer must have self-employment income to contribute to his own plan.[160] However, a self-employed taxpayer does not need to show a profit on Schedule C to contribute to an *employee's* retirement plan.

Example: Ricardo is a self-employed kickboxing instructor. He has a full-time receptionist named Dayanara that works in his training gym. In 2020, Ricardo makes a large fitness equipment purchase for his training gym. The fitness equipment qualifies for Section 179 or bonus depreciation. Ricardo claims bonus depreciation on the equipment and reduces his taxable income to zero for the year. He cannot contribute to his own retirement plan because he has no taxable income on his Schedule C. However, Ricardo is still allowed to contribute to Dayanara's retirement plan. This is true even if it generates a loss on his Schedule C.

[159] The Additional Medicare Tax and other provisions of the Affordable Care Act are covered later.
[160] SEP, SIMPLE, and qualified retirement plans are primarily tested on the businesses section of the EA exam (Part 2), so they are covered primarily in Book 2, Businesses.

Line 16: Self-employed health insurance deduction

A self-employed taxpayer may be able to deduct up to 100% of his health insurance premiums as an adjustment to income. Premiums paid by the taxpayer for his spouse and dependents under age 27 at the end of the year are also deductible. However, the deduction is limited to the net profit or other earned income from the business under which the health coverage is arranged. The taxpayer must either:

- Be self-employed and have a net profit for the year,[161]
- Be a partner in a partnership with net earnings from self-employment, or
- Have received wages from an S corporation in which he was a more-than-2% shareholder.

A self-employed taxpayer may not take the deduction if either he or his spouse (if MFJ) is eligible to participate in an employer-sponsored and subsidized health insurance plan, even if they decline coverage.

Example: Paige and Ludwig are married. Ludwig is self-employed and pays for his own individual insurance policy. Paige works for a grocery store as a cashier. Ludwig was eligible to participate in a subsidized health plan through Paige's employer, but Ludwig declined the coverage because he didn't want to switch doctors. Ludwig cannot take an adjustment for the health insurance premiums that he paid because he declined to participate in his wife's employer-sponsored coverage.

Long-term care insurance and Medicare premiums are also considered health insurance for purposes of this deduction.

Line 17: Penalty for early withdrawal of savings

If a taxpayer withdraws money from a certificate of deposit (CD) or other time-deposit savings account prior to maturity, he usually incurs a penalty for early withdrawal. This penalty is charged by the bank or other financial institution and withheld from a taxpayer's proceeds.

Taxpayers can take an adjustment to income for early withdrawal penalties. The penalties are reported on a taxpayer's Form 1099-INT, *Interest Income*, or on Form 1099-OID, *Original Issue Discount*, which lists interest income as well as the penalty amount.

Example: Early in 2020, Nikita invested in a $15,000 one-year certificate of deposit. In November, she had an unexpected medical expense and had to liquidate the CD. She paid a penalty of three months' interest, which totaled $150. Nikita can claim the penalty ($150) as an adjustment to income.

Note: Don't be confused by this concept! It is frequently tested. Only the penalty for early withdrawal from a timed deposit (a certificate of deposit) is tax-deductible. The penalty for early withdrawal from an IRA or a retirement plan is never deductible.

[161] For self-employed individuals filling a Schedule C or F, a health insurance policy can be either in the name of the business or in the name of the individual.

Line 18: Alimony paid

By definition, alimony is a payment to a former spouse under a divorce or separation instrument. The payments do not have to be made directly to the ex-spouse. For example, payments made on behalf of the ex-spouse for expenses such as medical bills, housing costs, and other expenses can also qualify as alimony.

In order to deduct alimony paid, the payor's Form 1040 requires the amount paid, recipient's SSN, and the date of the original divorce or separation agreement. If the divorce decree was finalized *before* 2019, alimony paid is normally an adjustment to income for the payor. Alimony *received* is generally treated as the mirror image, and is taxable income to the payee, which is claimed on Schedule 1 (Line 2a) of Form 1040.[162]

Example: Farrah and Weaver were legally divorced on November 10, 2017. Their divorce settlement requires that Farrah must pay her ex-husband $28,000 a year in alimony. Since their divorce was finalized before 2019, it is considered "grandfathered," and the alimony is deductible by Farrah and taxable to Weaver.

Example: Elizabeth and Archibald's divorce decree was finalized on April 3, 2020. The divorce settlement requires that Archibald must pay his ex-wife $16,000 a year. Per the divorce agreement, he also must pay her ongoing medical expenses. Archibald cannot deduct any of these expenses as alimony, because their divorce was finalized in 2020.

Voluntary payments that are not required by a divorce decree or separation instrument do not qualify as alimony.

Example: Finn and Rita legally divorced in 2018. Under the terms of their divorce, Finn must pay his ex-wife $12,600 per year ($1,050 per month). Finn also pays $10,000 a year for Rita's medical insurance, because that is required as part of their divorce decree. As a personal favor, he also makes $2,400 in auto loan payments on her car, so she can keep steady employment. Since his divorce was final before 2019, Finn can claim $22,600 ($12,600 +$10,000) as alimony paid, and claim the amounts as an adjustment to income on his Form 1040. However, Finn cannot deduct the auto payments as alimony because they were not required by the divorce agreement.

Line 19: Traditional IRA deduction

An individual retirement arrangement (IRA) offers tax advantages for setting aside money for retirement. Some taxpayers can claim a deduction for the amounts contributed to a traditional IRA as an adjustment to gross income. Only amounts contributed to a *traditional* IRA are deductible. Amounts that do *not* qualify for deduction include:

- Contributions to a Roth IRA,
- Contributions to a traditional IRA that are nondeductible because the taxpayer and/or spouse is covered by an employer-sponsored retirement plan and modified adjusted gross income (MAGI) exceeds certain limits,
- Contributions that apply to the previous tax year,
- Rollover contributions.

---

[162] Due to the TCJA, alimony paid will no longer be deductible by the payor, effective for divorce agreements executed in 2019 or future tax years. Divorces executed *prior* to 2019 are "grandfathered" and the prior treatment of alimony will apply.

Deductions are allowed in full for contributions to a traditional IRA by a taxpayer (and spouse, if married) who is not covered by a retirement plan at work. If the taxpayer (and/or spouse) is covered by a retirement plan at work, deductions are phased out at certain income levels.[163]

Line 20: Student loan interest deduction

Generally, personal interest (other than mortgage interest) is not deductible. However, interest on a qualified student loan is deductible. A qualified student loan is a loan used solely to pay qualified higher-education expenses for the taxpayer, his spouse, or his dependents. A taxpayer can claim the deduction for 2020 if:

- He paid interest on a qualified student loan on which he was legally obligated,
- His filing status is not married filing separately,
- Neither he (nor his spouse, if filing jointly) can be claimed as a dependent on someone else's return.

In order for student loan interest to qualify, the student must have been enrolled in a higher education program leading to a degree, certificate, or other recognized educational credential. A student who used the loan to take classes for other purposes does not qualify. The maximum deduction for student loan interest in 2020 is $2,500. The student loan interest deduction limit is per return, not per student. For example, if a taxpayer has three children and pays $2,000 in student loan interest for each of them, the maximum deduction is still only $2,500.

A phaseout applies to higher-income taxpayers. This deduction is subject to income limitations, and begins to phase out for taxpayers with MAGI between $70,000 – $85,000 ($140,000 – $170,000 for joint filers) in 2020. Taxpayers who file MFS are not allowed to take a deduction for student loan interest.

Example: Tasha is an unmarried physician with a modified adjusted gross income of $249,000. She paid $4,400 of student loan interest in 2020. Due to her high income, she cannot deduct any of her student loan interest as an adjustment to income.

Example: Rudy graduated from a technical college where he was enrolled full-time in a certificate program for automotive repair. Rudy is single and earned $48,000 in wages during the year. He had no other income. Rudy paid $1,250 in student loan interest in 2020. He may take the student loan interest deduction and deduct all the interest that he paid as an adjustment to income.

A student loan is not eligible if it is from certain related persons (such as family members or certain corporations, partnerships, or trusts). Loans from an employer plan also do not qualify. Qualified higher-education expenses are the costs of attending an eligible educational institution, including graduate schools, such as:

- Tuition and fees,
- Room and board,
- Books, supplies, and required equipment, and other necessary school-related expenses.

[163] The rules regarding IRA contributions, distributions (withdrawals), and rollovers are covered in detail later, in a dedicated unit for retirement plans.

Qualified expenses must be reduced by the amounts of tax-free items used to pay them, such as the following:

- Employer-provided educational assistance benefits,
- Tax-free withdrawals from a Coverdell Education Savings Account or 529 plan,
- U.S. savings bond interest already excluded from income,
- Tax-free scholarships and fellowships,
- Veterans' educational assistance benefits,
- Any other nontaxable payments (except gifts or inheritances) received for educational expenses.

Example: Rhonda is an Army veteran receiving the GI Bill. Rhonda's college tuition expenses are $7,200. She also receives a gift of $2,000 from her aunt and $1,000 of her veterans' GI Bill. Therefore, Ronda's qualified higher education expenses are $6,200 because veterans' assistance benefits must be subtracted. The gift from her aunt does not have to be subtracted.

Lenders are required to send the taxpayer Form 1098-E, *Student Loan Interest*, when the amount of interest paid is at least $600 or more.

Line 21: Tuition and fees

The above-the-line Tuition and Fees deduction has been reinstated and extended retroactively for 2020.

Taxpayers can deduct qualified tuition and related higher education expenses paid for academic periods beginning in 2020 and the first three months of 2021. For example, if a taxpayer paid $1,500 in December 2020 for qualified tuition for the spring semester that begins in January 2021, the taxpayer would be able to deduct that $1,500 on their 2020 return.

The Tuition and Fees Deduction is subject to income phaseouts. The deduction could be either as high as $4,000 or $2,000, depending on the taxpayer's MAGI. The deduction ceiling is $4,000 for taxpayers with MAGI of $65,000 or less ($130,000 for MFJ). The deduction ceiling is $2,000 for taxpayers with MAGI between $65,001 and $80,000 ($131,001 and $160,000 for MFJ). A taxpayer whose modified adjusted gross income is greater than $80,000 ($160,000 for joint filers) cannot claim the tuition and fees deduction.

Qualified education expenses include: tuition, fees, and other *required* course materials (textbooks and equipment are only deductible if they are *required*). Qualified expenses do *not* include:

- Room and board, any medical expenses (including student health fees, even if they are required by the college), transportation, or other personal expenses,
- Any optional course-related books, supplies, equipment, and nonacademic activities and fees,
- Any course or other education involving sports, games, or hobbies, or any noncredit course, unless the course is required by the student's degree program.

A taxpayer cannot claim the tuition and fees deduction based on expenses that have already been paid with a tax-free scholarship, fellowship, grant, or education savings account.

Note: The expenses that qualify for the tuition and fees deduction are more limited than the expenses that qualify for the student loan interest deduction. Generally, for the tuition and fees deduction, qualified education expenses are only amounts paid for tuition expenses and required books at an eligible college or vocational institution.

A taxpayer filing MFS cannot take the tuition and fees deduction. If a taxpayer is claimed as a dependent on someone else's return, he cannot take the deduction for himself. Nonresident aliens also do not qualify for this deduction.

A taxpayer cannot claim the tuition and fees deduction and an education credit for the same student. A taxpayer who is eligible to claim the American Opportunity Credit or Lifetime Learning Credit is allowed to figure his return both ways and choose the deduction resulting in the lowest tax.

Example: Montgomery has two daughters in college. In 2020, he pays $3,900 in tuition and fees for his youngest daughter, Nigella, who is 18 years old and a college freshman. He also pays an additional $5,700 for his eldest daughter, Geneva, who is 23 years old and a full-time graduate student. Both of his daughters will be claimed as dependents on his tax return. Montgomery earns $64,000 in wages in 2020 and has no other taxable income. He can claim the American Opportunity Credit for Nigella, and the tuition and fees deduction for Geneva if he wishes.

A taxpayer must have received a Form 1098-T, *Tuition Statement,* from an eligible educational institution in order to claim the Tuition and Fees Deduction.

Line 22: Miscellaneous write-in adjustments

The last line of Schedule 1, Form 1040 (line 22) is used as both the total for all adjustments to income as well as for writing-in more obscure deductions. This line on the form allows the taxpayer to manually indicate what type of adjustment is being taken. Some of the miscellaneous adjustments that may be entered on line 22 include deductions to an Archer MSA, jury duty pay remitted to an employer, and repayment of unemployment benefits.

Although these deductions are not frequently seen, they are still available. A taxpayer does not need to itemize in order to deduct these amounts. These "other adjustments" are listed in the instructions for Form 1040.

- Archer MSA deduction (see Form 8853),
- Jury duty pay remitted to an employer,
- Deductible expenses related to the rental of personal property engaged in for-profit (this would be income from the rental of personal property (such as equipment or vehicles), when the taxpayer was not "in the business" of renting personal property),
- Nontaxable amount of the value of Olympic and Paralympic medals and USOC prize money,
- Reforestation amortization and expenses,
- Repayment of supplemental unemployment benefits,
- Contributions to section 501(c)(18)(D) pension plans,
- Contributions by certain chaplains to section 403(b) plans,
- Attorney fees and court costs for actions involving certain unlawful discrimination claims, but only to the extent of gross income from such actions.

- Attorney fees and court costs paid in connection with an award from the IRS for information provided that helped the IRS detect tax law violations, up to the amount of the award includible in the taxpayer's gross income. These awards are called "whistleblower awards,"
- Excess deductions of section 67(e) expenses from Schedule K-1 (Form 1041). These are deductions that are passed through to the beneficiary on the final return of an estate or trust.

An example of one of these "uncommon" adjustments is the deduction for court costs from unlawful discrimination claims. A taxpayer may deduct, as an adjustment to income on Schedule 1 (Form 1040), attorney fees, and court costs for legal claims or litigation involving a claim of unlawful discrimination. This includes job-related discrimination on account of race, sex, religion, age, or disability.

However, the amount the taxpayer can deduct is limited to the amount of the judgment or settlement the taxpayer includes in income for the tax year. The deductible fees will be reported as "UDC" in the Adjusted Gross Income section.

Example: Francine, age 52, sues her employer for age discrimination after she discovers an incriminating email from her supervisor, stating that the company was planning to fire Francine because she was "too old" and they could hire a younger worker for less money. She makes a copy of the email and gives it to her lawyer, who immediately files suit. Rather than face an expensive trial, Francine's employer agrees to settle the suit. The total settlement amount is $800,000, and Francine's employment lawyer charges a 40% contingency fee, which is typical for her type of legal claim. Francine must report the full amount of the settlement as income, but she is allowed to take a deduction for the legal fees she paid to her attorney, which are $320,000 ($800,000 X 40%).

Unit 11: Study Questions

(Test yourself first, then check the correct answers at the end of this quiz.)

1. Graciela, age 41, had an HSA account set up with her employer that had $4,000 in the account at the end of the year. She then quit her job in late May and withdrew all the funds from her HSA. She did not use the $4,000 for qualifying medical expenses. Instead, she used the funds to buy a used car. What is the consequence of this action?

A. Nothing; taxpayers are allowed to withdraw from their HSA accounts at any time.
B. Her withdrawal is prohibited and will result in a forfeiture of the funds.
C. Graciela must pay income tax and a 20% penalty on the withdrawal.
D. Graciela must pay income tax and a 6% penalty on the withdrawal.

2. Deborah was a self-employed poultry farmer in 2020. She files Schedule F to report her income and loss. She had total self-employment tax of $4,896 on her Schedule SE. Which of the following statements is correct?

A. She can deduct 100% of the self-employment tax as an adjustment to income on Form 1040.
B. She can deduct 50% of the self-employment tax as an adjustment to income on Form 1040.
C. She can deduct 50% of the self-employment tax as a business expense on Schedule F.
D. She cannot deduct the self-employment tax.

3. Theodore and Keyah have MAGI of $75,000. They are married and file a joint return. Four years ago, they took out a loan so their daughter, Miranda, could earn an associate's degree at a local junior college. Miranda is 23 and their dependent. In 2020, they paid $3,000 of student loan interest on Miranda's student loan. How much student loan interest can Jermaine and Keyah deduct on their tax return?

A. $0
B. $1,000
C. $2,500
D. $3,000

4. All of the following statements are correct about the qualified educator expense deduction except:

A. A school counselor may qualify.
B. A part-time teacher may qualify.
C. A school principal may qualify.
D. A college instructor may qualify.

5. Rick and Linda's divorce was finalized in 2017. Under the terms of his divorce decree, Rick must pay the medical expenses of his former spouse, Linda. In January 2020, Rick sends a check totaling $4,000 directly to Mercy General Hospital to pay for Linda's emergency surgery. Which of the following statements is correct?

A. This payment qualifies as alimony, and Linda must include the $4,000 as taxable alimony on her individual tax return.
B. This payment does not qualify as alimony, but Rick can claim a deduction for the medical expenses on his return.
C. Linda must include the $4,000 as income on her return, but Rick cannot deduct the expense as alimony because it was paid to a third party.
D. None of the above

6. Chuck and Mallory are married and file jointly. Chuck is self-employed, and his net profit from his Schedule C business was $50,000 in 2020. They pay $700 per month for Chuck's health insurance coverage. Mallory was a homemaker until she started working for a construction company in early February. Mallory and Chuck became eligible to participate in her employer's subsidized health plan on March 1, 2020, but they did not want to switch insurance providers, so Mallory declined her employer's coverage. Which of the following statements is correct?

A. They can deduct $700 for both January and February, and $350 per month for each of the last ten months of the year, as self-employed health insurance premiums on Chuck's Schedule C.
B. They can deduct $1,400 in self-employed health insurance premiums, which is for January and February, the two months they were not eligible to participate in an employer plan.
C. They can deduct 100% of their health insurance premiums because they declined the employer coverage.
D. They can deduct 50% of their health insurance premiums on Chuck's Schedule C.

7. Cleveland is 26 and has an HSA. He becomes permanently disabled during the year due to a serious accident. He withdraws all his money from his HSA, but does not use the funds for medical expenses in 2020. Which of the following statements is correct?

A. He may withdraw money from his HSA for nonmedical expenses, but the withdrawals will be subject to income tax and also an additional penalty of 20%.
B. He may withdraw money from his HSA for nonmedical expenses. The withdrawals will be subject to income tax but will not be subject to a penalty.
C. He may not take nonmedical distributions from his account.
D. He must be at least 65 to take nonmedical distributions from an HSA.

8. Two full-time teachers who are married and file jointly can deduct a maximum of ____ in qualified educator expenses:

A. $100
B. $250
C. $500
D. $750

9. Marshall lost his job last year and withdrew money from a number of bank and investment accounts. He paid the following penalties:

The penalty for early withdrawal from a CD	$140
The penalty for early withdrawal from a traditional IRA	200
A late penalty for not paying his credit card on time	50

What amount can Marshall deduct as an adjustment to income on his Form 1040?

A. $0
B. $140
C. $200
D. $250

10. Bruce makes an excess contribution to his HSA by accidentally contributing over the maximum allowable amount. What is the *penalty* on excess contributions if Bruce does not withdraw the overcontribution?

A. No penalty.
B. 6% penalty.
C. 10% penalty.
D. 20% penalty.

11. An adjustment to income is considered the most beneficial type of deduction because:

A. It favors taxpayers who choose to itemize their deductions.
B. It is simpler to figure out qualifying expenses for adjustments to income than it is other deductions.
C. It lowers a taxpayer's adjusted gross income and thus can affect the amounts of certain credits and deductions he may be able to claim.
D. There is no significant difference between an adjustment to income and other tax deductions.

12. Obadiah paid $14,000 of alimony to his ex-wife in 2020. His divorce became final in 2016. Which of the following statements is correct?

A. He can deduct alimony paid as an adjustment to income.
B. The deduction for alimony is entered on Schedule B.
C. He can deduct alimony only if he itemizes deductions on his tax return.
D. He cannot deduct the alimony.

13. Gael is a college instructor at Nevada State University. In 2020, he paid $300 for materials that he used in the classroom. He also paid $210 in parking fees to park across the street from the university when the faculty lot was full. What amount of qualifying expenses does he have for purposes of the educator expense deduction?

A. $0
B. $250
C. $300
D. $510

14. Georgina was offered a management position in another city on March 31, 2020. Her new employer reimburses her $4,550 for her moving expenses. Georgina submitted all the proper receipts to her new employer. How should this reimbursement be treated for tax purposes?

A. The employer can reimburse Georgina on a pre-tax basis.
B. The expense is nontaxable as long as Georgina's employer gives her a gift card.
C. The reimbursement is tax-exempt because it is a qualified moving expense.
D. Because this is a reimbursement of a nondeductible expense, it is treated as taxable wages and must be included on Georgina's Form W-2.

15. Jasmine is a part-time art teacher at an elementary school. She spends $350 on qualified expenses for her art students and $75 on materials for a health course that she also teaches. She worked 440 hours as an educator during the tax year. How much can she deduct in educator expenses as an adjustment to income?

A. $0
B. $250
C. $350
D. $425

Unit 11: Quiz Answers

1. The answer is C. Graciela must pay income tax and a 20% penalty on the withdrawal. Withdrawals from an HSA for non-eligible expenses are allowed, but the withdrawal is subject to a 20% penalty, in addition to regular income tax.

2. The answer is B. Deborah can deduct 50% of the self-employment tax she paid as an adjustment to income on Schedule 1 of her Form 1040.

3. The answer is C. Theodore and Kayah's maximum deduction for student loan interest is $2,500. The deduction is limited to the lesser of $2,500 or the amount of interest actually paid. It doesn't matter how many qualifying student loans there are; the maximum is $2,500 per tax return (not per taxpayer).

4. The answer is D. College instructors do not qualify. An eligible educator must work 900 hours a year in a school that provides elementary or secondary education (K-12). Part-time teachers qualify if they meet the yearly teachers' requirement for hours worked. The term educator includes instructors, counselors, principals, and aides.

5. The answer is A. This payment qualifies as alimony, and Linda must include the $4,000 as taxable alimony income on her return as the divorce was finalized prior to 2019. The payment may be treated as alimony for tax purposes because the payments of Linda's medical expenses are a condition of the divorce agreement. Payments to a third party on behalf of an ex-spouse under the terms of a divorce instrument can be alimony, if they qualify. These include payments for a spouse's medical expenses, housing costs (rent and utilities), taxes, and tuition. The payments are treated by the ex-spouse as if they were received directly and included as income.

6. The answer is B. Chuck and Mallory can deduct only $1,400 ($700 x two months) of self-employed health insurance for the months that they were ineligible to participate in an employer plan. No deduction is allowed for self-employed health insurance for any month that the taxpayer has the *option* to participate in an employer-sponsored and subsidized plan. This is true even if the taxpayer declines the coverage. A self-employed taxpayer can deduct 100% of health insurance premiums as an adjustment to income, but only if neither he nor his spouse was eligible to participate in an employer's health plan.

7. The answer is B. Withdrawals for nonmedical expenses from an HSA are allowed but are subject to income tax. Nonmedical distributions are also subject to an additional penalty tax of 20%, except when the taxpayer has turned 65, become disabled, or died. Cleveland has become permanently disabled, in which case his HSA withdrawals are not subject to penalty, but the withdrawals will still be subject to income tax.

8. The answer is C. On a jointly filed tax return, if both taxpayers are teachers, they both may take the qualified educator expense deduction, up to a maximum of $500 ($250 each).

9. The answer is B. Marshall can only deduct the $140 early withdrawal penalty from the CD. Early withdrawal penalties are deductible if made from a time deposit account, such as a certificate of deposit. The other types of penalties are not deductible.

10. The answer is B. Bruce will have to pay a 6% excise penalty if he does not correct the overcontribution. A 6% penalty applies to excess contributions to a health savings account.

11. The answer is C. Adjustments are deducted from gross income to derive adjusted gross income (AGI), and itemized and standard deductions are subtracted from AGI. The amount of a taxpayer's AGI is important, as it can affect his eligibility for certain deductions and the amounts that he can claim. For example, certain items are phased out at specified levels of AGI, and some itemized deductions must exceed specified percentages of AGI to be deductible. In addition, itemized deductions may be subject to the alternative minimum tax or may total less than the taxpayer's applicable standard deduction.

12. The answer is A. Obadiah can deduct alimony paid as an adjustment to income, because his divorce was final before the 2019 tax year and is therefore considered "grandfathered." He does not need to itemize his deductions in order to take the deduction. He must file Form 1040 and enter the amount of alimony paid as an adjustment to income on Schedule 1.

13. The answer is A. Gael cannot deduct any of his expenses. The educator expense deduction is only available for K-12 educators. College instructors do not qualify.

14. The answer is D. The moving expense reimbursement must be reported as wages on Georgina's Form W-2. If an employer pays or reimburses moving expenses, the amounts are treated as taxable compensation. The only exception to this rule is for moving expenses reimbursed by the government on behalf of U.S. Armed Forces personnel.

15. The answer is A. Because Jasmine worked only 440 hours as an educator during the tax year, she cannot deduct her educator expenses as an adjustment to income. An educator must have at least 900 hours of qualified employment during the school year to take this deduction as an adjustment to income.

Unit 12: Standard Deduction & Itemized Deductions

For additional information, read:
Publication 502, *Medical and Dental Expenses*
Publication 600, *State and Local General Sales Taxes*
Publication 936, *Home Mortgage Interest Deduction*
Publication 526, *Charitable Contributions*
Publication 561, *Determining the Value of Donated Property*

The Tax Cuts and Jobs Act (TCJA) made sweeping changes to the standard deduction and itemized deductions. The standard deduction nearly doubled after the enactment of the TCJA. As a result, fewer taxpayers are forced to itemize.

Many itemized deductions have been eliminated or restricted through 2025. The TCJA also temporarily removed the so-called "Pease limitation" on itemized deductions, which means that itemized deductions will no longer be phased out at higher income levels.

A taxpayer generally may choose either to claim a standard deduction amount or to itemize deductions. Depending on the option selected, either the applicable standard deduction amount or the taxpayer's total itemized deductions is subtracted from his adjusted gross income. The choice should be based on which option results in a lower tax liability.

The Standard Deduction

The standard deduction is a specific dollar amount that reduces the amount of income on which a taxpayer is taxed. Using the standard deduction eliminates the need for a taxpayer to itemize his actual allowable deductions, such as medical expenses, charitable contributions, or state and local taxes. The standard deduction amounts are based on a taxpayer's filing status and are adjusted every year for inflation. The standard deduction amounts for the 2020 tax year are as follows:

Filing Status	2020 Standard Deduction
Single or MFS	$12,400
Head of Household	$18,650
Married Filing Jointly or QW	$24,800
Dependent Standard Deduction[164]	$1,100

Additional Standard Deduction

An *additional* standard deduction is available to taxpayers who, at the end of the year, are:

- 65 or older, and/or
- Blind or partially blind.

The standard deduction is $1,300 higher for joint filers who are over 65 and/or blind, and $1,650 higher for unmarried taxpayers (Single and head of household). A taxpayer who is *both*

[164] Alternatively, if higher, the standard deduction for dependents is $350 plus their earned income for the year, up to (for most dependents) $12,400 in 2020.

blind and 65 or older may take the basic standard deduction, as well as additional standard deduction amounts for both age and blindness.

For filing purposes, a taxpayer is considered to be age 65 in the tax year 2020 if they were 65 on December 31, 2020, or if they turned 65 on January 1, 2021.

Additional Standard Deduction Amounts-2020	
Taxpayers who are age 65 and/or blind	
Filing Status	**Additional Amount Allowable**
Single, HOH	$1,650
MFS, MFJ, QW	$1,300

The additional amount for blindness is allowed if the taxpayer is blind on the last day of the tax year, even if he was not blind the rest of the year. A taxpayer must obtain a statement from an eye doctor indicating that:

- The taxpayer cannot see better than **20/200**, even when corrected with eyeglasses, or
- The taxpayer's field of vision is not more than 20 degrees (the taxpayer has disabled peripheral vision).

Example: Thane, a single taxpayer, is age 50 and legally blind. He would be entitled to a basic standard deduction and an *additional* standard deduction for his blindness. This means that his total standard deduction amount would be $14,050 in 2020 ($12,400 + $1,650).

Example: Wardell, 46, and Tamara, 33, file jointly. Neither is blind. They decide not to itemize their deductions. Their standard deduction is $24,800 in 2020.

Example: Upton, age 63, and Priscilla, age 66, are married and do not itemize deductions. Because they file jointly, their base standard deduction is $24,800 in 2020. Priscilla is over 65, so she can claim an *additional* standard deduction amount of $1,300. Therefore, the total standard deduction of their joint return is $26,100 ($24,800 + $1,300).

Example: Riggs is 83 years old and unmarried. Riggs is entitled to the regular standard deduction for single filers ($12,400) plus an additional standard deduction amount for being older than 65 ($1,650). In 2020, his standard deduction is $14,050 ($12,400 + $1,650).

The standard deduction for a deceased taxpayer is the same as if the taxpayer had lived the entire year, with one exception: If the taxpayer died *before* his actual 65th birthday, the higher standard deduction for being 65 does not apply.

Example: Octavio is single and died on November 1, 2020. He would have been 65 if he had reached his birthday on December 18, 2020. He does not qualify for a higher standard deduction because he died before his 65th birthday, even though it would have happened during the tax year. His standard deduction is $12,400 on his final income tax return, which must be filed by his executor on or before April 15, 2021.

Standard Deduction for Certain Dependents

In 2020, the standard deduction for a dependent which can be claimed on another person's return is limited to the greater of:

- $1,100, or
- The dependent's earned income (such as wages) plus $350, but not more than the regular standard deduction amount. For a single person, this is generally $12,400 in 2020. However, the standard deduction amount can be higher if the dependent is 65 or older and/or blind.

Example: Tessa is single, 22, and a full-time college student with a part-time job. Her parents provide the majority of her support, so they claim her as a dependent on their joint tax return. Tessa files a return and takes the standard deduction, which she is entitled to do, even though her parents are claiming her as a dependent. She has wages of $7,800 from her part-time job. Her standard deduction is $8,150 ($7,800 wages + $350).

Itemized Deductions

Itemized deductions may normally be taken *in lieu* of the standard deduction; they allow taxpayers to reduce their taxable income based on specific personal expenses. If a taxpayer's total itemized deductions are greater than his applicable standard deduction amount, they will normally result in lower taxable income and a lower tax liability. In most cases, a taxpayer may choose whether to claim itemized deductions or the standard deduction, depending on which is more beneficial. However, taxpayers are *required* to itemize in the following cases:

- If the taxpayer is filing MFS, and one spouse itemizes, the other spouse also must itemize. In this case, the taxpayer's standard deduction is zero, and they are both forced to itemize any deductions, even if the spouses do not have enough itemized deductions to exceed the standard deduction.[165]
- If the taxpayer is a nonresident alien or dual-status alien (who is not married to a U.S. citizen or U.S. resident)
- If the taxpayer files a tax return for a period of less than twelve months due to a change in accounting methods (this scenario would be *extremely rare* for an individual taxpayer)

If a taxpayer itemizes deductions, he must complete and file Schedule A along with his Form 1040. We will review the specific requirements for various itemized deductions next.

Medical and Dental Expenses

Medical and dental expenses (other than self-employed health insurance premiums) are deductible only if a taxpayer itemizes deductions. Qualifying medical expenses include the costs of diagnosis, cure, mitigation, treatment, or prevention of disease, and the costs of medical (but not cosmetic) treatments. The IRS defined qualifying costs as:

- Medically necessary equipment, supplies, and diagnostic devices,
- Dental and vision care,

---

165 This rule only applies when *both* spouses are filing MFS. If one spouse is MFS, but the other spouse qualifies for HOH filing status (Head of Household), then the spouses are not forced to itemize, and they may choose the standard deduction if they wish.

- Transportation to obtain medical care,
- Qualified health insurance and long-term care insurance.

Deductible medical expenses include:

- Fees paid to doctors, dentists, surgeons, chiropractors, psychiatrists, psychologists, and nontraditional medical practitioners,
- In-patient hospital care or nursing home services, including the cost of meals and lodging charged by the hospital or nursing home,
- Acupuncture treatments,
- Lactation supplies (breastfeeding supplies),
- Treatment at centers for alcohol or drug addiction, participation in smoking-cessation programs, and prescription drugs to alleviate nicotine withdrawal,
- Weight-loss programs prescribed by a physician (but not diet food items)
- Insulin and prescription drugs (but prescription drugs brought in or shipped from a different country are generally not deductible),
- Admission and transportation to a medical conference relating to a chronic disease (but the costs of meals and lodging while attending the conference are not deductible),
- Veterinary care when it relates to the care of animals trained to assist persons who are visually impaired, hearing-impaired, or disabled.

Example: Carnell is a Gulf War Veteran. Carnell is recovering from severe Post-Traumatic Stress Disorder. He also has frequent seizures related to a head injury sustained during combat. Carnell's physician recommends that he obtain a service dog to help him with his recovery. The doctor gives Carnell a written physician's statement explaining the recommendation. With the help of a Veteran's support group, Carnell obtains a trained service dog. The dog's veterinary costs are deductible medical expenses on Carnell's individual tax return.

A taxpayer may only deduct medical expenses they *paid* during the year, regardless of when the services were provided.[166] Qualified medical expenses include expenses paid for:

- The taxpayer or the taxpayer's spouse
- Dependents (the individual must have been a dependent at the time the medical services were provided or at the time the expenses were paid). However, there is an exception to this rule for children of divorced or separated parents.

Medical expenses must be primarily to alleviate or prevent a physical or mental defect or illness. Medical expenses do not include expenses that are merely beneficial to general health, such as vitamins, spa treatments, gym memberships, or vacations.

A taxpayer can deduct medical expenses paid on behalf of an adopted child, even before the adoption is final. A taxpayer can also deduct medical expenses paid for a dependent parent. All the standard rules for a dependency exemption apply, so the dependent parent does not have to live with the taxpayer to qualify.

[166] An exception to this rule exists for deceased taxpayers (covered later).

Example: Bianca, age 50, pays all the medical expenses for her father, Fred, age 86. Fred is her dependent, but does not live with her. The medical expenses are deductible on Bianca's tax return as an itemized deduction to the extent they exceed the 7.5% threshold.

Note: If a child of divorced or separated parents is claimed as a dependent on either parent's return, each parent can deduct medical expenses they individually paid for the child. This is true even if the other parent claims the child's dependency exemption. Basically, it doesn't matter which parent claims the child—the medical expenses are deductible for the parent that pays them.

Example: Bernard and Cindy are divorced. Their son, Michael, lives primarily with Cindy, who claims him as a dependent on her tax return. Cindy also deducts Michael's annual medical and dental bills, including orthodontia expenses for his braces. However, in September, Michael falls on the playground and fractures his arm. The out-of-pocket expenses for Michael's broken arm are $5,500. Michael's father, Bernard, pays for the emergency room visit and the expenses related to the injury. Therefore, Bernard can deduct the expenses on Schedule A, even though he does not claim his son as a dependent.

Taxpayers can deduct only the amount of unreimbursed medical expenses that exceed 7.5% of adjusted gross income (AGI).

Example: Hattie, age 53, had unreimbursed medical expenses totaling $2,500 in 2020. Her AGI was $40,000. Hattie cannot deduct any of her medical expenses on Schedule A because they are not more than 7.5% of her AGI ($40,000 × 7.5% = $3,000).

Example: Garrison, age 46, paid $12,000 in out-of-pocket expenses for knee surgery in 2020. His AGI was $100,000. The amount of medical expenses in excess of $7,500 (AGI of $100,000 × 7.5%), or $4,500, is allowed as an itemized deduction on Schedule A.

Example: Florinda had medical expenses of $8,000 in 2020. Her AGI was $70,000. She can deduct the amount in excess of the 7.5% AGI floor ($70,000 × 7.5% = $5,250). This means that she will have a deduction of $2,750 on Schedule A ($8,000 medical expenses - $5,250 AGI floor).

Medical Insurance: If a taxpayer receives insurance reimbursement for medical care expenses, those amounts are not deductible. Qualifying medical expenses include medical insurance and long-term care insurance premiums that the taxpayer paid with after-tax dollars.

Note: The cost of an employee's annual health care coverage is typically reported on Form W-2. The amount includes the portions paid by both the employer and the employee. Although this amount is reported on Form W-2, it does not mean the amount is taxable; it is for informational purposes only.

Payments for medical expenses reimbursed out of a health savings account (HSA) are not deductible, but contributions to HSAs may be deducted as an adjustment to gross income, and withdrawals from an HSA are tax-free as long as they are used to pay for qualifying medical costs.

Long-Term Care Premiums: A taxpayer may include amounts paid for qualified long-term care services and insurance premiums in his medical expense deductions. Long-term care services include necessary diagnostic, preventive, therapeutic, rehabilitative, maintenance, and

personal care services that are required by a chronically ill individual and provided under a plan of care by a licensed doctor.

The deductibility of costs of qualified long-term care premiums is limited by the age of the taxpayer. The expenses generally cannot include costs that would be reimbursed under Medicare. The limits on deductible long-term care premiums are per individual, not per tax return.

2020 Limits-Long Term Care Premiums	
Age	**Maximum deduction**
Age 40 or under	$430
Over 40 but not more than 50	$810
Over 50 but not more than 60	$1,630
Over 60 but not more than 70	$4,350
Over 70 years of age	$5,430

Other Medical Expenses: If a taxpayer or a dependent is in a nursing home, and the primary reason for being there is medically-related, the entire cost, including meals and lodging, is a medical expense. A taxpayer can deduct any legal fees necessary to authorize treatment for mental illness. However, legal fees for the management of a guardianship estate or for conducting the affairs of a person being treated are not deductible as medical expenses.

Medical Expenses of Deceased Taxpayers: In addition to expenses paid before a taxpayer's death, a deceased taxpayer's executor (or personal representative) can elect to treat medical expenses paid by the estate within one year after his death as if the taxpayer had paid when the medical services were provided. In other words, an executor can elect to treat medical expenses as if they were paid at the time they were incurred, even if the expenses are paid the year *after* the taxpayer's death.[167]

Example: Brody had heart surgery on November 1, 2020 and incurred over $20,000 of medical bills. The surgery did not go well, and when he died on December 20, 2020, his medical bills had not yet been paid. The executor of Brody's estate is his adult son, Damon. Damon pays his late father's outstanding medical bills on March 3, 2021. As the executor, Damon may elect to deduct Brody's final medical expenses on his 2020 individual return (Brody's final tax return), even though the medical expenses were not paid until 2021. This special election *only* applies to deceased taxpayers.

Cosmetic Surgery: Cosmetic surgery is only deductible if it is used to correct a defect or disease. A cosmetic procedure simply for the enhancement of someone's physical appearance is not a deductible medical expense.

Example: Delia undergoes a mastectomy to remove her breasts as part of treatment for breast cancer. A cosmetic surgeon later reconstructs her breasts to correct the deformity that is directly related to cancer. The cost of her cosmetic surgery is deductible as a medical expense because the surgery corrects an earlier defect or disease.

---

[167] If this election is made by the executor, the medical expenses cannot be claimed as a deduction for Federal estate tax purposes as well.

Medically Related Transportation, Meals, and Lodging: Vehicle mileage may be deducted if transportation is for medical reasons, such as trips to and from doctors' appointments. If a taxpayer uses his own car for medical transportation, he can deduct actual out-of-pocket expenses for gas and other expenses, or he can deduct the standard mileage rate for medical expenses, which is 17 cents per mile in 2020. A taxpayer can also deduct the costs of taxis, buses, trains, planes, or ambulances, as well as tolls and parking fees.

A taxpayer can deduct the cost of meals and lodging at a hospital or similar institution if the principal reason for being there is to receive medical care. The amount for lodging cannot be more than $50 for each night for each person, although the taxpayer can include lodging for a person traveling with the person receiving the medical care, up to $100. The cost of meals are not included.

Example: Andrew is 12 years old and has severe allergies. Andrew's father, Harlan, accompanies his son to a treatment facility in a neighboring state so he can receive treatment from an allergy specialist. Harlan books a hotel room across the street from the hospital, where they stay for one week while Andrew is receiving outpatient medical treatment and blood tests. The cost of lodging at the hotel is $110 per night. Harlan may deduct up to $100 per night as a medical expense.[168]

Capital Improvements for Medical Reasons: Capital improvements such as home improvements are usually not deductible. However, a home improvement may qualify as a deductible expense if its main purpose is to provide medical care to the taxpayer (or to family members).

The deduction for capital improvements is limited to the excess, of the actual cost of the improvements, over the related increase in the fair market value of the home. Home improvements that qualify as deductible medical expenses may include:

- Wheelchair ramps
- Lowering of kitchen cabinets
- Railings and support bars
- Elevators
- Special lift equipment

Tenants can deduct the entire cost of disability-related improvements, even if they are not the owners of the property.

Example: Elliott, age 61, has a heart condition. He cannot easily climb stairs or get into a bathtub. On his doctor's advice, he pays for the installation of a special sit-in bathtub and a stairlift in his rented house. The landlord did not pay any of the costs. Elliott can deduct the entire amount as a medical expense, subject to the 7.5% threshold.

State and Local Income Taxes

The Tax Cuts and Jobs Act instituted a cap on State and Local taxes (also called the "SALT cap"). The deduction for state and local income, sales or property taxes (on a combined basis) is capped at $10,000 ($5,000 for MFS filers).

---

[168] Based on an example in Publication 502, Medical and Dental Expenses.

Taxpayers can deduct certain taxes if they itemize deductions. To be deductible, a tax must have been imposed on the taxpayer and paid by the taxpayer during the tax year. Deductible taxes include:

- State, local, and foreign income taxes,[169]
- State and local sales taxes,
- Real estate taxes (but not for foreign real estate),
- Personal property taxes (such as DMV fees).

State and Local Taxes: Taxpayers are allowed to deduct either *sales/use* taxes or state and local *income* taxes, depending on which provides the larger deduction, but not both. Income taxes paid include taxes withheld from salaries and wages, amounts paid for prior years, and estimated tax payments.

Real Estate Taxes: State and local real estate taxes, based on the assessed value of the taxpayer's real property (such as a house or land), are deductible. If the taxes are paid from a mortgage escrow account, the taxpayer can deduct only the amount actually paid out of the escrow account during the year to the taxing authority.

Some real estate taxes are not deductible, including taxes imposed to finance improvements of property, such as assessments for streets, sidewalks, and sewer lines. In addition, itemized charges for services and homeowner's association fees are not deductible.

Example: Ernestine makes the following payments in 2020: state income tax, $2,000; real estate taxes on her personal residence, $900; local benefit tax for maintaining the sewer system, $75; and homeowner's association fees on her personal residence of $250. Her total deductible taxes are $2,900 ($2,000 + $900 = $2,900). The $75 local benefit tax and the $250 homeowner's association fee are not deductible.

If a property is sold, the real estate taxes are prorated between the buyer and the seller, according to the number of days that each owned the property, and adjustments are charged or credited on the settlement statement depending upon which party is responsible for paying the taxing authority.

Escrow accounts: If a portion of the taxpayer's monthly mortgage payment goes into an escrow account, and periodically the lender pays the real estate taxes out of the account to the local government, the taxpayer is only allowed to deduct the amount that was actually paid out of the escrow account during the year to the taxing authority.

Personal Property Taxes (DMV Fees): Personal property taxes for individuals are deductible if they are:

- Charged on personal property, including cars, motorcycles and boats;
- Based on the value of the property; and
- Charged on a yearly basis, even if collected more or less than once a year.

---

[169] Foreign income taxes are not subject to the "SALT" cap. These taxes are still deductible in full. Also, taxes incurred in a trade or business, or for the production of income, (on Schedules C, E, and/or F), are not subject to the cap.

Example: Debbie receives an annual registration notice for her automobile from the California Department of Motor Vehicles. The bill is broken down as follows:

- Registration: $25
- Vehicle license fee: $58
- Weight fee: $32
- County fee: $13
- Owner responsibility fee: $15

The notice states that the vehicle license fee is based on the car's value. Only the vehicle license fee is tax deductible on Schedule A.

Note: The Tax Cuts and Jobs Act eliminated the deduction for foreign real estate taxes. These taxes are no longer deductible on Schedule A as an itemized deduction. Foreign *income* taxes are still deductible, however. Foreign income taxes are *not subject* to the SALT cap. State and local taxes are reported on lines 5a, 5b, and 5c of Schedule A. Foreign Income tax is listed on line 6, "Other Taxes."

Example: Zahra lives and works in New York, which has a high cost of living. She earns $195,000 in wages per year. Zahra paid $11,000 in property taxes on her NY condo and $11,900 in NY state income taxes. The state income tax was automatically withheld from her wages. She also owned a vacation home in Rio de Janeiro, Brazil. She paid $4,000 in foreign real estate taxes on her vacation home. The foreign real estate taxes are not deductible at all, and the other taxes are limited because of the SALT cap. The maximum deduction that she can take for the taxes she paid on Schedule A is $10,000.

Example: Hideo is a U.S. citizen who lives and works in Japan. He earns $178,000 in wages during the year working for a Japanese company. He owns a home in Japan which is his primary residence. During the year, he pays $3,600 in foreign property taxes on his home. These amounts are not deductible, because the home is considered foreign real estate. Hideo also pays $24,000 in foreign income taxes to Japan. The foreign income taxes are fully deductible on Schedule A and not subject to the SALT cap.

Foreign Income Taxes: Generally, a taxpayer can choose between claiming the Foreign Tax Credit or claiming an itemized deduction on Schedule A for income taxes paid to a foreign country, depending on which option results in the lowest tax. The rules regarding which foreign taxes qualify for either the credit or the deduction are covered later. Foreign income taxes are not subject to the "SALT cap."

Deductible Interest

Taxpayers are allowed to deduct certain types of interest. Qualified interest payments are deductible as itemized deductions on Form 1040, Schedule A. Deductible interest includes:

- Home mortgage interest,
- Late fees on a mortgage loan,
- Points on a mortgage loan,

- PMI, or private mortgage insurance premiums are treated as mortgage interest for tax purposes,
- Investment interest expense.

Home Mortgage Interest

Home mortgage interest is paid on a loan secured by a taxpayer's home. The loan may be a mortgage, a second mortgage, a home equity loan, or a line of credit. A taxpayer is allowed to deduct the interest related to a primary residence and a second home. The maximum amount of qualified acquisition Indebtedness secured by a qualified primary or secondary residence to allow a full deduction for home mortgage interest is $750,000 in 2020 ($375,000 for MFS).[170]

Interest paid on home equity debt related to a main home and a second home is deductible only if the loan proceeds were used to acquire, build, or substantially improve the primary residence that secures the loan. Remember, the deductibility of mortgage interest on an equity loan depends primarily on what the loan is used for.

Example: Harrison owns his own home. He decides to borrow a $45,000 home equity line to consolidate his credit card debt and buy a new car. None of the interest is deductible as mortgage interest in 2020.

An empty lot does not qualify for the mortgage interest deduction. If a taxpayer builds a house that becomes a qualified home when ready for occupancy, he can deduct mortgage interest for a period of up to 24 months from when construction begins. A taxpayer can deduct late fees on a mortgage loan as mortgage interest.

Example: Fergus owns his home and pays his mortgage on a monthly basis. During the year, he falls behind on his mortgage payments and sends in his payment late on two occasions. The mortgage company charges Fergus a $35 fee for each late payment. The late fees are deductible as mortgage interest on Schedule A.

A second home can include any other residence a taxpayer owns and treats as a home, but the taxpayer does not have to actually use the second home during the year to deduct the mortgage interest paid on the related loan.

Note: Although a taxpayer can potentially deduct real estate taxes on more than two properties, he cannot deduct mortgage interest on more than two personal homes.

Example: Ellery owns three homes. None of the homes are rental properties. He has a $150,000 mortgage on his main home in Boise, ID, where he lives most of the time. He also has a $75,000 mortgage on a beach cottage in North Carolina and a $90,000 mortgage on a ski condo in Utah. Ellery can deduct the mortgage interest on his main home and on the ski condo, but he cannot deduct the mortgage interest on the beach cottage because the deduction is limited to two homes. He is allowed to deduct the property taxes on all three homes. However, those amounts are subject to the $10,000 SALT cap.

[170] If the qualified acquisition indebtedness was incurred on or before December 15, 2017, then the grandfathered limit of $1 million ($500,000 MFS) applies.

Mortgage Insurance Premiums (PMI)

In 2020, a taxpayer can deduct private mortgage insurance premiums (also called "PMI") for insurance coverage related to their home mortgage. The deduction is available for payments for a principal residence and one other home, like a vacation home.[171] The deduction for mortgage insurance premiums is phased out for higher-income taxpayers. The deduction begins to phase out at $100,000, and phases out completely once AGI reaches $109,000 (if MFS, the phaseout begins at $50,000 and phases out completely at $54,500).

Mortgage insurance premiums paid during the year are reported to the taxpayer on Form 1098, *Mortgage Interest Statement,* by the bank or financial institution that received the payments. A taxpayer can deduct the interest on home equity debt only if the home equity line is used to acquire, construct, or substantially improve the home, and the loan amounts do not add up to more than the $750,000 ($375,000 for MFS) mortgage limit.

For example, if a taxpayer borrows $250,000 in a home equity line of credit, and all of the loan proceeds are used to substantially improve the home, then the entire amount would be considered a qualifying loan for the mortgage interest deduction.

Example: Brandy has a mortgage of $500,000 against her primary residence. In 2020, she takes out a home equity line of credit of $45,000 in order to add a sunroom and a patio. Since the home equity loan was taken out to "substantially improve" the home, then the interest on the loan is deductible.

Example: Jackie takes out a $30,000 home equity loan in 2020 to pay for her daughter's college tuition. This home equity line is secured by her residence, but the interest is not deductible, because the home equity loan was not used to "acquire, build, or substantially improve" her primary residence.

Example: Jeannette is single and owns her home. She has an existing mortgage on the property totaling $475,000. Jeannette applies for a home equity line of credit to finance the improvements. She decides to add an extra bedroom, a new bathroom, and she installs a new pool. The new bedroom addition cost $66,000, the new bathroom cost $22,000, and the new pool cost $29,000, for a total cost of $117,000. Since the home equity loan was used entirely to improve the property, and her total acquisition debt does not exceed $750,000, all of the interest is deductible as mortgage interest.

Points and Prepaid Mortgage Interest

Points are interest charges a borrower pays up-front to obtain a loan. Points generally represent prepaid interest a borrower pays at closing to obtain a lower interest rate. Points may also be called loan origination fees, including VA and FHA fees, maximum loan charges, premium charges, loan discount points, or prepaid interest.

Loan fees paid for specific services, such as home appraisal fees, document preparation fees, or notary fees are not interest and are not deductible.

---

[171]The deduction for PMI has been retroactively reinstated for tax years 2020 and 202 as part of the Taxpayer Certainty and Disaster Relief Tax Act of 2020 (P.L. 116-260).

In order to deduct points, the following requirements must be met:

- The mortgage must be secured by the taxpayer's main home, and the mortgage must have been used to buy, build, or improve the home.
- The points must not be an excessive or unusual amount for the local area.
- The points paid must not be more than the amount of unborrowed funds.
- The points must be computed as a percentage of the loan principal, and they must be listed on the settlement statement.

If all these requirements are met, the taxpayer can deduct points in connection with the acquisition or construction of the home either in the year paid or over the life of the loan. Tax law treats "purchase" mortgage points differently from "refinance" mortgage points.

Points paid to refinance a mortgage are generally not fully deductible in the year paid and must be deducted over the life of the loan unless the proceeds are used to improve a main home. A second home or vacation home would not qualify for this exception.

Example: Tammy refinanced her home on January 19, 2020 in order to get a lower interest rate. She paid $1,500 in points for a 15-year refinance of her existing home mortgage. She is entitled to deduct only $100 per year on her Schedule A ($1,500 ÷ 15 years, the life of the loan).

Investment Interest Expense

The TCJA suspended all the miscellaneous itemized deductions subject to the 2%-of-AGI floor, which includes the deduction for investment expenses, (for example, safe deposit fees, trustee fees, and investment advisor fees). However, the TCJA did *not* repeal the deduction for investment *interest* expense. Investment *interest* expense is any interest incurred on loans used to purchase taxable investments.

A common type of investment interest expense is margin interest. One way investors borrow funds from brokerage houses is through margin accounts. The investor uses the loan to purchase stocks and bonds without having to invest the full amount in cash.

Example: Anton likes to invest in stocks using his online brokerage account. He applies for a margin-approved brokerage account in order to buy more stock. At the beginning of the year, Anton has $100,000 in cash and stocks in his existing brokerage account. His brokerage firm approves him for a 20% margin loan. This means that Anton can purchase an additional $20,000 worth of marginable stock. The extra $20,000 is granted to him in the form of a margin loan, for which he will have to pay interest. The interest would be potentially deductible on Schedule A as a miscellaneous itemized deduction (subject to limitations, as detailed below).

When a taxpayer borrows money to buy property held for investment, the interest he pays on that borrowed money is *investment interest expense* and may be deductible. The amount of investment interest expense a taxpayer can deduct each year is limited to the amount of net investment income earned. However, he can carry forward any disallowed investment interest expense to the next year.

Example: Maritza borrows money from a bank to buy $3,000 worth of short-term corporate bonds. The bonds mature during the year, and Maritza makes $400 of investment interest income. She also has $210 in investment interest expense, which she paid on the loan originally taken out to buy the bonds. Maritza must report the full amount of $400 as investment interest income. She can deduct the $210 of investment interest expense on Schedule A.

Example: Randolph borrows money from a bank to buy $8,500 worth of U.S. gold coins as an investment. During the year, the coins lose value, and he has no investment income. Randolph paid $326 of investment interest expense on the loan he used to buy the coins. He may not take a deduction for the investment interest expense because he has no investment income, but he may carry over to the next tax year the investment interest expense he could not deduct.

The deductible amount of investment interest expense and any disallowed amount that may be carried over to the following year are calculated on Form 4952, *Investment Interest Expense Deduction.* A taxpayer cannot deduct interest related to passive activities or incurred to produce tax-exempt income (such as state and local bonds that generate tax-exempt interest income) as investment interest expense.

Example: Melvin borrowed $15,000 to purchase municipal bonds in 2020. The tax-free municipal bonds yield 5% in interest income, and Melvin paid 3% in investment interest expense on the loan. Since muni bond interest is exempt from federal tax, Melvin cannot deduct any of the interest he paid on the loan.

Nondeductible Interest and Investment Expenses: The following expenses cannot be deducted as investment interest:

- Interest on personal loans, such as car loans
- Fees for credit cards and finance charges for nonbusiness credit card purchases
- Loan fees for services needed to get a loan
- Interest on debt the taxpayer is not legally obligated to pay
- Service charges
- Interest to purchase or carry tax-exempt securities
- Late payment charges paid to a public utility
- Expenses relating to stockholders' meetings or investment-related seminars
- Interest expenses from single-premium life insurance and annuity contracts
- Interest incurred from borrowing against an insurance policy
- Short-sale expenses
- Fines and penalties paid to any government entity for violations of the law

Example: Noah and Magdalena file a joint return. During the year, they paid:

1. $3,180 of home mortgage interest reported to them on Form 1098
2. $400 of credit card interest
3. $1,500 for an appraisal fee on their personal residence
4. $2,000 of interest on a personal car loan

Noah and Magdalena can deduct only their home mortgage interest ($3,180). None of the other charges are allowable as a tax deduction.

Charitable Contributions

Taxpayers who itemize deductions can deduct certain charitable contributions to qualified organizations. Congress made significant changes to the treatment of charitable contributions in 2020. For tax year 2020, individuals who itemize are allowed to elect to claim a charitable income tax deduction up to 100% of adjusted gross income (AGI) for cash contributions to charity. Different AGI limits apply to contributions of property (covered next).

A taxpayer can only deduct a charitable contribution in the year it is actually made. A donation charged to a credit card before the end of 2020 counts for 2020, even if the credit card bill is not paid until the following year. A donation made by check counts for 2020 if the donor mails it in 2020, even if the charity cashes the check in the following year.

Note: In 2020, taxpayers who do not itemize may qualify to take a deduction for charitable contributions of up to $300 ($150 if MFS) as an adjustment to income in 2020. In order to qualify for this special deduction, the gifts must be made in cash. Gifts of property do not qualify.

Contribution Limits

In 2020, a taxpayer cannot deduct aggregate charitable contributions that exceed 100% of his adjusted gross income. This means that if a taxpayer had $100,000 of adjusted gross income in 2020, the maximum charitable contributions he could deduct would be $100,000. Charitable contributions cannot generate a net operating loss. Excess contributions that exceed a taxpayer's AGI may be carried over and deducted over a 5-year period. Carryovers are subject to the same percentage limits in the year to which they are carried.

The 100%-of-AGI limit applies to *cash contributions only*—not real estate, not stocks, not furniture, or any other types of noncash donations.[172] The taxpayer's deduction may be further limited to 50%, 30%, or 20% of AGI, depending on the type of property donated and the type of organization the donor gives it to. In 2020, there are four major AGI limits:

- **The 100% limit**: In 2020, this limit applies only to cash contributions to a public charity, specifically, 501(c)3 organizations.
- **The 50% limit:** this limit applies to most noncash contributions to public charities. Examples of noncash contributions include furniture, clothing, and housewares. This limit also applies to gifts of inventory and depreciable property.
- **The 30% limit**: this limit applies to donations of *appreciated* property, such as stock, land, or real estate that has appreciated in value.
- **The 20% limit**: this limit applies specifically to gifts of appreciated property to certain to non-public charities.

Any amounts disallowed as a result of these AGI limits can be carried forward to future years. Be aware that the 50% limit applies to most *noncash* charitable contributions, only *cash donations* are subject to the higher, 100%-of-AGI limit. The 100%-of-AGI contribution limit applies to cash contributions made to:

- Churches, synagogues, and similar religious organizations,
- Hospitals,

---

172 Cash contributions include those paid by cash, check, electronic funds transfer, debit card, credit card, payroll deduction, or a transfer of a gift card redeemable for cash.

- Most schools and colleges,
- State or federal government entities,
- Nonprofits organized solely for charitable, religious, educational, scientific, or literary purposes or for the prevention of cruelty to children or animals,
- Organizations that foster youth sports, or national or international amateur sports competition (examples include: Little League Baseball and Softball, the Olympics, Special Olympics, and the Paralympic Games).

A taxpayer's deductible contributions to certain other types of nonprofit organizations are limited to either 30% or 20% of his AGI. The **30% limit** applies to organizations that include the following:

- Certain private nonoperating foundations,[173]
- Veterans organizations and fraternal benefit societies (such as the Knights of Columbus, the Freemasons, and the Shriners),
- Nonprofit cemeteries.

In addition, a **separate 30% limit** applies in the following cases:

- Gifts for use by the charitable organization (such as the donation of a vehicle the [illegible]),
- Gifts of appreciated property (also called capital gain property).

The **20% limit** applies to contributions of capital gain property to organizations subject to the 30% limit.

Example: Maguire's adjusted gross income is $40,000. During the year, he donated 100 shares appreciated stock with an FMV of $11,000 to the Knights of Columbus, a fraternal benefit society, which is a 30% limit organization. The gift of stock is appreciated property, so it is subject to an additional restriction—the 20%-of-AGI limit applies based on the nature of the organization. Maguire's allowable deduction is $8,000 (20% x $40,000 = $8,000). The remainder will have to be carried over to a future year ($11,000 FMV of the stock - $8,000 allowable deduction= $3,000 carryover).

Charitable Contribution Carryovers

To the extent a taxpayer's deductions for contributions are limited; they may be carried over to subsequent years. However, the carryover period is generally limited to five years. Any carryover amounts that cannot be deducted within five years due to AGI limits are lost. Any contributions made by the taxpayer and carried over to future years retain their original character. For example, contributions made to a 30% organization continue to be subject to the 30%-of-AGI limit in future years.

Qualified Charitable Gifts

In order to claim deductions for noncash donations, the donated items must be in good condition. In most cases, the taxpayer will be able to claim a deduction for the fair market value of the contribution (generally, what someone would be willing to pay at a garage sale or thrift

173 A private nonoperating foundation grants money to other charitable organizations. Private foundations usually established with funds from a single source, such as single wealthy family or corporate money.

store). No deduction is allowed for items that are in poor or unusable condition. Deductible contributions may include:

- Unreimbursed expenses that relate directly to the services the taxpayer provided for the organization.
- The amount of a contribution in excess of the fair market value of items received, such as merchandise and tickets to a charity ball.
- Transportation expenses, including bus fare, parking fees, tolls, and either the actual cost of gas and oil or a standard mileage deduction of 14 cents per mile in 2020.

Volunteer Expenses: A taxpayer cannot deduct a monetary value for hours he spends volunteering. However, taxpayers are allowed to deduct out-of-pocket costs related to their volunteer work for qualifying organizations.

A taxpayer can deduct expenses incurred while traveling to perform services for a charitable organization only if there is no significant element of personal pleasure in the travel. However, a deduction will not be denied simply because the taxpayer enjoys providing the services. The taxpayer can take a charitable contribution deduction for the expenses if he is on duty in a genuine and substantial way throughout the trip.

Example: Louisa is an attorney who donates time to her local homeless shelter for its legal needs. In 2020, she spent ten hours drafting legal documents for the shelter, which is a qualified charitable organization. She also had $200 of out-of-pocket expenses because she purchased a new printer for the shelter. The printer was delivered directly to the shelter for its use. Louisa can take a charitable deduction for $200, the amount she spent on behalf of the shelter. She cannot deduct the value of her time.

Example: Odessa regularly volunteers at her local animal shelter, a qualified animal rescue organization. She uses her own car to travel to and from the shelter. She is not reimbursed for mileage. Odessa also fosters kittens on behalf of the shelter. She pays for cat food for the foster kittens and other supplies out-of-pocket. She receives an annual statement from the animal shelter substantiating her donations. Odessa can deduct her mileage and her unreimbursed expenses as a charitable contribution but cannot deduct the value of her time.

Qualified Charitable Distributions

Donors age 70½ or older may also donate up to $100,000 per tax year directly from a traditional IRA, in lieu of taking an annual required minimum distribution (RMD). This is called a "Qualified Charitable Distribution" or QCD.

Note: The *SECURE Act,* passed in December 2019, raised the age to start taking required minimum distributions from 70½ to age 72. Then the *CARES Act,* passed in March 2020, waived the RMD requirement for everyone in 2020. Even though the CARES Act waived the RMD requirement for the year, taxpayers are still allowed to make a Qualified Charitable Distribution from their IRA accounts if they choose.

If a taxpayer takes a QCD, the amount of the distribution from a traditional IRA will not be included in taxable income. However, the taxpayer will not be able to claim a charitable deduction for the amounts given via the QCD to a qualified charity.

Nonqualifying Organizations and Donations

Not all nonprofit organizations qualify as charitable organizations for purposes of donors being able to claim tax deductions. An organization may qualify for nonprofit status so that its own activities are not subject to income tax, but this designation does not automatically provide qualification for purposes of deductible contributions. The following are examples of items that do not qualify as deductible charitable contributions:

- Gifts to civic leagues, social and sports clubs, and Chambers of Commerce,
- Gifts to groups run for personal profit,
- Gifts to political groups, candidates, or political organizations,
- Gifts to homeowner's associations,
- Donations made directly to individuals,
- The cost of raffle, bingo, or lottery tickets, even if the raffle is part of a qualified organization's fundraiser,
- Dues paid to country clubs or similar groups,
- Gifts and dues to labor unions,
- Blood donated to a blood bank or to the Red Cross (although the mileage incurred to donate blood may be deductible),
- Any part of a contribution that benefits the taxpayer, such as the FMV of a meal eaten at a charity dinner,
- Donors who purchase items at a charity auction may claim a charitable contribution deduction only for the excess of the purchase price paid for an item over its fair market value.

Example: Timothy goes to a church fundraiser that includes a bingo game. Timothy spends $200 on bingo cards but does not win anything. Even though the $200 went directly to the church, the cost of the bingo game is not considered a charitable gift (because it is a wagering activity) and is therefore not deductible.

Example: Tonya participates in a charity auction for her church. All the auction proceeds go to the church. She bids on a $100 gift certificate to a popular restaurant in town. She pays $135 for the gift certificate. The FMV for the gift certificate is $100, so her qualifying donation is $35 ($135 amount paid - $100 FMV of the certificate).

Example: Scarlett paid the Chamber of Commerce a $30 entry fee to run in a 10K race it was sponsoring on behalf of a cancer-related charity. The Chamber is not a qualifying charitable organization, so none of Scarlett's entry fee is tax-deductible as a charitable contribution. If the race had been organized by the charity itself, part of her entry fee might have been deductible.

Substantiation Requirements for Charitable Gifts

There are strict recordkeeping requirements for taxpayers who claim deductions for charitable contributions, depending upon the nature of the donation and the dollar amounts. The IRS imposes recordkeeping and substantiation rules on donors as well as disclosure requirements on the charities themselves. Here are the basic rules for ALL charitable gifts:

- At a minimum, the donor must have at least a bank record **<u>or</u>** a written receipt (or written acknowledgment) from a charity for **<u>any</u>** cash contribution before the donor can claim a charitable deduction.
- The *donor* is responsible for obtaining a written receipt from a charity for any single contribution of $250 or more before he can claim a charitable deduction.

Rules for Cash Donations

Cash Donations of <u>LESS</u> than $250: Cash contributions include those paid by cash, check, debit card, credit card, or payroll deduction. If the value of an individual donation is *less* than $250, the taxpayer must keep a reliable written record, such as the following:

- A bank, credit union, or credit card statement that shows the name of the qualified organization, the date of the contribution, and the amount of the contribution
- A receipt (or a letter or other written communication) from the qualified organization showing its name, the date of the contribution, and the amount of the contribution
- For payroll deductions, a pay stub or Form W-2, plus a pledge card or other document showing the name of the qualified organization
- For text donations, a telephone bill, as long as it shows the name of the qualified organization, the date of the contribution, and the amount given

A donor should not attach the acknowledgment or receipt to his tax return but must retain it to substantiate the contribution.

Example: Rodger donates $25 per month to the Humane Society. Rodger always pays by check, and he keeps the canceled check as a record of his contribution. This is a valid method of recordkeeping for donations under $250. He does not need to have an additional receipt from the organization to substantiate his deduction.

Cash Donations of $250 or <u>MORE</u>: For cash donations of $250 or more, the taxpayer must have a receipt or a written acknowledgment from the organization that includes:

- The amount of cash the taxpayer contributed,
- The date of the contribution,
- Whether the qualified organization gave any goods or services as a result of the contribution (other than certain token items and membership benefits). The absence of this simple statement by a charity has led to court cases in which major cash contributions have been challenged, and in some cases, disallowed.
- If applicable, a description and a good faith estimate of the value of goods or services provided by the organization as a result of the contribution (if applicable).

A single annual statement from the charitable organization may be used to substantiate multiple contributions of $250 or more. These are also commonly called "donor acknowledgment letters." There is no specific IRS form for the acknowledgment.

Example: Trudy donates $100 a month to her local Little League, which is a qualified 501(c)3 charity. She does not keep a record of her individual gifts, but at the end of the year, the Little League mails out an annual donor acknowledgment letter, listing her total donations and listing the specific amounts she contributed during the year. The annual statement will suffice to substantiate her deduction.

Rules for Noncash Donations (Gifts of Property)

Noncash Contributions of Less than $250: For each contribution of less than $250, the taxpayer must obtain a receipt from the receiving organization and keep a list of the items donated.

Example: Grant donated ten dress shirts to Goodwill during the year. He made a list of the items he donated and received a receipt from the organization when he dropped off his donation. In Grant's town, Goodwill sells dress shirts in their thrift shops for about $5 each. Based on the thrift store's valuation of his donation, Grant has made a charitable donation of $50 (10 shirts x $5 FMV each).

Noncash Donations between $250 and $500: For each contribution of at least $250, but not exceeding $500, the taxpayer must have the same documentation as described above, for noncash contributions less than $250. In addition, the organization's written acknowledgment must state whether the taxpayer received any goods or services in return and included a description and a good faith estimate of the fair market value of any such items.

Noncash Donations Over $500: If a taxpayer's total deduction for all noncash contributions for the year is more than $500, he must also file Form 8283, *Noncash Charitable Contributions.*

Noncash Donations Over $5,000: If any single donation or a group of similar items is valued at more than $5,000, a qualified appraiser is required to make a written appraisal of the donated property. The taxpayer must also complete Form 8283, Section B, and attach the form to his tax return. The taxpayer generally does not have to attach the appraisal itself but must retain a copy for his records. For donations of artwork valued at more than $20,000, or property valued at more than $500,000, the appraisal itself must be included with the tax return.[174]

Example: Michelle has AGI of $125,000 in 2020. She decides to donate a plot of land to her church, a qualified 501(c)(3) organization. The land is worth over $5,000, so Michelle hires a qualified appraiser to give her a written appraisal for the property before she donates it. The appraiser values the land at $18,000. She also requests a receipt for the donation from her church. When she files her tax return, she claims a charitable deduction of $18,000 on her Schedule A. She also attaches Form 8283 to her return. She is not required to attach the actual appraisal, but she must keep a copy of it for her records. Michelle has complied with all of the IRS' recordkeeping requirements for her property donation.

Example: Ratcliffe is a wealthy industrialist that likes to donate to many different causes. In 2020, he donates 100,000 shares of Ford Motor Co. to a qualifying charity. The value of the stock on the date of the donation is $1,150,000. Since the stock is from a publicly-traded company, Ratcliffe does not need to obtain a qualified appraisal. He will still be required to obtain an acknowledgment letter from the organization, as well as file Form 8283 with his tax return.

---

[174] Per Publication 526, a qualified appraisal is not required for contributions of certain inventory, publicly traded securities, or certain intellectual property. See Regulations section 1.170A-16(e)(2). Also, if the taxpayer is required to obtain a qualified appraisal, they cannot take a deduction for the cost of the appraisal itself (per Publication 526).

Special Rules for Donated Vehicles

Special rules apply to any donation of vehicles, including boats and airplanes. If the taxpayer claims a deduction of more than $500, he can only deduct the *smaller* of:

- The gross proceeds from the sale of the item by the charity, or
- The fair market value on the date of the contribution.

The charitable organization should provide Form 1098-C, *Contributions of Motor Vehicles, Boats, and Airplanes*, which shows the gross proceeds from the sale of the vehicle donated. If the taxpayer does not attach Form 1098-C, the maximum deduction that can be taken for the donation is $500.

Example: Porter donates his used motorcycle to his church fundraiser. According to Blue Book values, the FMV of the motorcycle is $2,500 on the date he makes his donation. The church sells the motorcycle 60 days later at a fundraising auction for $1,700 and sends Porter a Form 1098-C. He can deduct only $1,700 on his Schedule A (the smaller of the FMV or the gross proceeds from the sale) and must attach a copy of Form 1098-C to his tax return.

Two exceptions apply to the rules regarding vehicle donations:

- If the charity keeps the vehicle for its own use, the taxpayer can generally deduct the vehicle's FMV.
- If the charity gives the vehicle directly to a needy person, the taxpayer can generally deduct the vehicle's FMV.

Example: Theodore owns a used minivan that is still in good working condition. He donates the minivan to Meals-on-Wheels, a 501(c)3 charity that delivers hot meals to disabled people and homebound seniors. The organization uses the minivan to deliver meals to needy individuals. The FMV of the minivan is $3,900 on the date of Theodore's donation. Since the vehicle was put into use by the charity, Theodore may deduct the FMV of the vehicle, as long as he obtains a contemporaneous written acknowledgment that the charity kept the vehicle for its own use. The deduction is subject to a 30%-of-AGI limit, and Theodore will be required to attach Form 8283 to his return.

Special Rules for Conservation Easements

Conservation easements are used for land conservation purposes by restricting the future use of the land in order to protect its conservation values. There are unique rules that apply to charitable gifts of this type. [175] A taxpayer can potentially claim a charitable contribution deduction by permanently restricting the use of their real estate for conservation purposes. Unlike other capital gain property, if the real property has appreciated in value, the charitable deduction is not limited to 30% of adjusted gross income. The charitable deduction allowed for conservation property (including easements) is generally limited to 50% of adjusted gross

[175] Per Publication 526, Charitable Contributions, for qualified farmers and ranchers, the charitable deduction allowed for conservation easements is limited to 100% of adjusted gross income, minus the deduction for all other charitable contributions. The PATH Act made the enhanced conservation easement donation deduction permanent. Conservation easements are also known as a "conservation restriction" or "conservation agreement..

income, minus the deduction for all other charitable contributions, regardless of whether or not the property has appreciated.

Also, the carryforward period for a donor to take tax deductions for a conservation agreement is fifteen years, rather than the usual five years for other types of charitable gifts.

Example: Kamden decides to give a permanent easement of his property to The Nature Conservancy. The property is 500 acres of wetlands and the easement is given with the intent to preserve the area for fishing and wildlife in perpetuity. Kamden purchased the land twenty years ago for $1,000,000. The land has appreciated in value. Kamden obtains a qualified appraisal of the easement, stating that the easement has a current fair market value of $1,400,000. In 2020, Kamden's AGI is $400,000. Because of the special threshold that applies to conservation easements, Kamden will be able to take a charitable deduction of up to 50% of his $400,000 AGI. Therefore, his $1,400,000 gift permits a deduction of $200,000 ($400,000 AGI x 50% = $200,000) in 2020 and has a charitable carryforward of $1,200,000 that he can use in future years to offset his taxable income. The carryforward is valid for fifteen years, rather than the usual five.

Personal Casualty and Theft Losses

The Tax Cuts and Jobs Act suspended the itemized deduction for most personal (i.e., non-business, non-production of income) casualty and theft losses through tax year 2025. Only losses derived from federally declared disaster areas are deductible in 2020. Taxpayers in a federal disaster area who incur disaster-related casualty losses can deduct their unreimbursed losses for the year in which the loss occurred, or if elected, in the year *prior* to the year of the loss.[176] This special rule about being able to potentially claim a casualty loss in the prior tax year allows taxpayers in a presidentially-declared disaster area to quickly obtain the tax benefits associated with the deduction without having to wait (up to) a year from the casualty event before their tax return for the year of the event can be filed.

In 2020, individuals who have qualified disaster-related personal casualty losses may increase their standard deduction amount by the amount of the net disaster loss. This means that the loss will be allowed in addition to the standard deduction, subject to $500 per casualty floor (up from $100 from the prior year). Additionally, the deduction is not limited by the normal 10% AGI floor in 2020.

Example: Reese lives in Mississippi. On October 28, 2020, a hurricane hit the state, and the resulting storms and flooding destroyed Reese's home and his car. The area where Reese lived was designated a federal disaster area. Reese immediately files a claim with his insurance company. Reese assumed that his insurance would recover the full amount of his losses. His insurance claim was finally settled on March 1, 2021, but Reese's insurance company reimbursed him for only half of his losses. The IRS deems the "disaster year" to be 2021 (not 2020 when the actual hurricane occurred), because that's when it became certain that he would not be fully reimbursed for his loss. Reese can either deduct the unreimbursed loss in 2021, or make an election to deduct the unreimbursed loss on his 2020 tax return.[177]

176IRC section 165(i)

177 Scenario modified directly from an example in IRS Instructions for Form 4684, Casualties and Thefts.

The casualty loss deduction on a personal-use asset is the *lesser* of (1) the decrease in the fair market value of the property (before and after the casualty event) or (2) the taxpayer's adjusted basis in the property at the time of the casualty event.

In tax year 2020 only, the casualty loss deduction is further limited to a $500 limit per casualty. The limitation only applies to personal casualty losses (losses of nonbusiness property). Casualty losses of business property and rental property are 100% deductible, but those losses are not reported on Schedule A. Business casualty losses are covered in more detail in Part 2, *Businesses.*

Example: On September 7, 2020, Kelsey's mobile home was completely destroyed in the Oregon wildfires. Her county was later declared a federal disaster area by the president. Kelsey did not have insurance on her mobile home, so she did not receive any insurance reimbursement. The fair market value of the mobile home before the wildfire was $80,000. It was completely destroyed, so its FMV was $0 afterward. Her basis in the home was $13,800 at the time of the fire. As such, her loss on the home is limited to $13,800. Her AGI was $25,000 for the year. Kelsey would figure her deductible casualty loss as follows:

Loss on the mobile home	$13,800
Subtract $500	($500)
Allowable casualty loss deduction on Schedule A	**$13,300**

Miscellaneous Itemized Deductions

The Tax Cuts and Jobs Act suspended miscellaneous itemized deductions subject to the 2%-of-AGI floor through 2025, including most unreimbursed employee business expenses. There are still some miscellaneous itemized deductions that a taxpayer can deduct on Schedule A. These are less commonly seen, but some of them are still tested on the EA exam. Miscellaneous itemized deductions that are still allowable in 2020 include:

- The amortizable premium on taxable bonds,
- Casualty and theft losses from "income-producing" property,
- Federal estate tax on income "in respect of a decedent" (IRD),
- Gambling losses to the extent of gambling winnings,
- Impairment-related work expenses of persons with disabilities,
- Losses from Ponzi-type investment schemes,
- Excess deductions of an estate or trust in the entity's final tax year,
- Repayments of more than $3,000 under a claim of right,
- Unrecovered investment in an annuity.

The amortizable premium on taxable bonds: If the amount a taxpayer pays for a bond is greater than its stated principal amount, the excess is called a bond premium. Annual amortization of the premium is treated as a miscellaneous itemized deduction.

Casualty or theft losses from "income-producing" property: A taxpayer can deduct a casualty or theft loss as a miscellaneous itemized deduction if the damaged or stolen property was income-producing property (meaning property held for investment, such as gold coins,

silver coins, artwork, and vacant lots). The taxpayer must report the loss on Form 4684, *Casualties and Thefts,* Section B.

Gambling losses to the extent of gambling winnings: The full amount of a taxpayer's gambling winnings must be reported on Form 1040. Gambling *losses* are deducted on Schedule A, up to the total amount of gambling winnings. Taxpayers must have kept a written record of their losses. Gambling losses in excess of winnings are not deductible.

Example: Akeem likes to gamble at the blackjack tables at his local casino. In 2020, he wins $6,200 playing blackjack but has $9,500 in gambling losses. He is required to report the full amount of the winnings on Form 1040. His deduction for gambling losses is limited to $6,200 on Schedule A. He cannot write off the remaining $3,300 in losses. He also cannot carry the losses forward to future years. If Akeem chooses not to itemize his deductions, then none of his gambling losses would be deductible.

Work-related expenses for individuals with a disability: These are expenses that enable a disabled person to work, such as special equipment or attendant care services at his workplace. Impairment-related work expenses must be incurred in connection with the taxpayer's place of work, or necessary for the taxpayer to be able to work.

Example: Fareeda has a serious visual disability, macular degeneration. She requires a large screen magnifier to see well enough to perform her work. Fareeda purchased her screen magnifier for $550. Her employer did not reimburse the cost. She can deduct its cost as an itemized deduction. This means she is able to deduct the full cost of the magnifier on Schedule A without any income limitations.

Estate tax on income in respect of a decedent: Income in respect of a decedent (IRD) is income owed to a decedent at the time he died. If a decedent's estate has paid federal estate taxes on IRD assets, a beneficiary may be able to claim an IRD tax deduction. IRD is covered more extensively later, in the chapter that covers estate tax.

Repayments of more than $3,000 under a claim of right: On occasion, a taxpayer may have to repay income that was included on a previous year's tax return because at the time the taxpayer received it, they thought they had an unrestricted right to it. One example could be when a taxpayer has to repay the unemployment benefits that they received.

Example: Katie lost her job and promptly applied for unemployment. She received unemployment all year. Katie's former employer appealed to the state, and it was determined that Katie made false statements and held back important information on her unemployment claim. Katie is now required to repay the benefits she received earlier. Katie will be forced to repay $8,000 in unemployment benefits. She is allowed to take an itemized deduction for these repayments on her Schedule A, because the amount of the repayment exceeds $3,000.

Losses from Ponzi-type investment schemes: Victims of fraudulent investment schemes can claim a theft loss deduction if certain conditions apply. Under IRS rules, an investor who is a victim of a Ponzi scheme is entitled to deduct Ponzi losses as a *theft* loss, instead of a *capital* loss

from an investment. Ponzi scheme losses are not limited to the $3,000 annual limit that applies to other capital losses.[178]

Example: Alanna is a potential investor. She is looking for a financial advisor to help her invest. Bernie holds himself out to the public as an investment advisor and securities broker. In 2020, Alanna is persuaded to invest with Bernie. She opens an investment account with Bernie and contributed $100,000 to the account and provided Bernie with a power of attorney to use the funds to purchase and sell securities on her behalf. Unbeknownst to Alanna, Bernie only invests a small amount of her funds and embezzles the rest into his own personal accounts. Later, it is discovered that Bernie's purported investment advisory and brokerage activity was, in fact, a fraudulent investment arrangement known as a "Ponzi" scheme. Bernie is convicted of securities fraud and sentenced to prison. Alanna is only able to recover $5,000 of her original $100,000 investment. Therefore, Alanna has a $95,000 deductible theft loss. She would report the loss on Schedule A as an itemized deduction, and the losses are not limited.

Excess Deductions of an Estate or Trust: Generally, if an estate or trust has an excess deduction resulting from total deductions being greater than its gross income, in the entity's final tax year, the beneficiary can deduct the excess deductions, depending on its character. The excess deductions retain their character as an adjustment to gross income on Schedule 1 (Form 1040), as a non-miscellaneous itemized deduction reported on Schedule A (Form 1040), or as a miscellaneous itemized deduction.

Deductions for Nonresident Aliens

Specific limitations on deductions apply to nonresident aliens who are required to file Form 1040-NR. Nonresident aliens cannot claim the standard deduction. Further, except for certain allowable itemized deductions, they can claim deductions only to the extent they are connected with income related to their U.S. trade or business. The following itemized deductions are allowed:

- State and local income taxes,
- Qualifying charitable contributions to U.S. nonprofit organizations (not foreign nonprofits),
- Casualty and theft losses in a presidentially declared disaster area,
- Some miscellaneous itemized deductions.

Itemized deductions related to mortgage interest are not allowed. There are special exceptions in the law for tax treaty partners, but the IRS will not test on any specific tax treaties with other nations.

Nondeductible Expenses

The IRS has a lengthy list of expenses that individual taxpayers cannot deduct.[179] These are just a sample of personal expenses the IRS lists as nondeductible:

- Lunch with coworkers or meals while working late
- Country club dues, athletic club fees, and gym memberships

---

[178] A "Ponzi scheme" is a type of criminal fraud or embezzlement. For more guidance on the IRS' official position regarding Ponzi schemes, see IRS Revenue Ruling 2009-9 and Revenue Procedure 2009-20.

[179] A basic rule is that most personal, living, or family expenses are not deductible.

- Home repairs, insurance, and rent
- Losses from the sale of a home, furniture, or a personal car
- Brokers' commissions
- Burial or funeral expenses, including the cost of cemetery lots
- Fees and licenses, such as car license or registration costs (except certain portions that may be considered deductible property taxes), marriage licenses, and dog tags
- Fines and penalties for breaking the law, such as parking tickets
- Life and disability insurance premiums
- Investment-related seminars
- Lost or misplaced cash or property
- Political contributions
- Expenses of attending stockholders' meetings
- Voluntary unemployment benefit fund contributions
- Adoption expenses (although a taxpayer may be able to claim an adoption credit)
- Travel expenses for another individual
- Interest on a personal credit card
- Expenses of earning or collecting tax-exempt income

Unit 12: Study Questions

(Please test yourself first, then check the correct answers at the end of this quiz.)

1. Connor is deaf. He purchased a special device to use at his workplace so he can identify when his phone rings. He paid for the device out-of-pocket, and his employer did not reimburse him. How should Connor report this on his tax return?

A. Connor can claim the purchase as an itemized deduction on Schedule A.
B. Connor can deduct the purchase as an adjustment to income.
C. Connor cannot deduct the purchase because he is not totally disabled.
D. Connor cannot deduct the purchase because he is not self-employed.

2. Christopher and Ariel file a joint return. During the year, they paid:

Mortgage interest on their main home (on an original mortgage of $300,000)	$5,000
Credit card interest	600
Auto loan interest	4,000
Loan interest on an empty lot that was purchased to build a second home	3,000

What amount can they report as deductible mortgage interest?

A. $0
B. $5,000
C. $8,000
D. $8,600

3. Which of the following taxes can taxpayers potentially deduct on Schedule A?

A. Federal income tax.
B. Real estate taxes on a U.S. property.
C. Taxes on alcohol and tobacco.
D. Foreign real estate taxes.

4. Which of the following taxpayers must either itemize deductions or claim zero as their standard deduction?

A. Mindy, who files a joint return with her husband.
B. Leslie, who is single, claims two dependents, and files Form 1040.
C. Pearl, whose itemized deductions are more than the standard deduction.
D. Gabriel, whose wife files a separate return and itemizes her deductions.

5. Clemens owns three homes and has an AGI of $128,000 in 2020. His primary residence is in Chicago. He also owns a mountain cabin in Lake Tahoe and a small condo in Las Vegas, which he uses several times a year. In 2020, Clemens did not use the mountain cabin, and it sat empty all year. He pays property tax and mortgage interest on all three properties.

Home Location	Mortgage Interest	Property Tax
Main home in Chicago	$18,500	$7,500
Cabin in Tahoe	$5,200	$2,800
Condo in Las Vegas	$4,500	$1,950

All of the mortgage debt is qualifying acquisition debt. Based on the information above, which of the following statements is correct?

A. Clemens may claim a mortgage interest deduction of $18,500 and a property tax deduction of $7,500 on Schedule A.
B. Clemens may claim a mortgage interest deduction of $23,700 and a property tax deduction of $10,300 on Schedule E.
C. Clemens may claim a mortgage interest deduction of $28,200 and a property tax deduction of $12,250 on Schedule A
D. Clemens may claim an allowable mortgage interest deduction of $23,700 and a property tax deduction of $10,000 on Schedule A.

6. Emelie donates $430 in cash to her church. Which of the following is required on the receipt to substantiate the donation correctly for IRS recordkeeping requirements?

A. The reason for the contribution.
B. Emelie's home address.
C. The amount of the donation.
D. Emelie's method of payment.

7. Julio is a volunteer delegate for the United Methodist Church. He spent three days attending his church's annual conference. He spent $250 on a plane ticket to the meeting and $25 on materials for the meeting. In the evening, Julio went to the theater with two other meeting attendees. He spent $50 on theater tickets. The church did not reimburse Julio for any of his costs. How much can he deduct as a charitable expense?

A. $0
B. $125
C. $250
D. $275

8. Which of the following home improvements cannot be deducted as an itemized medical expense?

A. The cost of installing stairlifts for a disabled individual.
B. The cost of lowering cabinets to accommodate a disability.
C. The cost of making doorways wider to accommodate a wheelchair.
D. An elevator that costs $14,000 and adds $15,000 to the FMV of the home.

9. Which of the following taxes can taxpayers deduct on Schedule A?

A. Local sales taxes.
B. Fines for speeding.
C. Social Security taxes.
D. Homeowners' association fees.

10. Which of the following taxpayers is required to itemize deductions and cannot take the standard deduction?

A. Sophie, who has one dependent child.
B. Andrea, who wants to deduct the alimony she paid to her ex-husband.
C. Leslie, whose itemized deductions are more than the standard deduction.
D. Qiang, who is a nonresident alien.

11. Alejandra had the following medical expenses in 2020:

- Botox injections for wrinkles: $6,000.
- Treatment of a broken leg: $9,000 (of which $8,000 was reimbursed by insurance).
- Doctor-prescribed back brace: $1,900.
- Child care while in the hospital: $200.

What is her medical expense deduction *before* the limitation based on the 7.5%-of-AGI threshold?

A. $1,900
B. $2,900
C. $7,900
D. $8,900

12. For a tax to be deductible in 2020, all of the following must be correct except:

A. The tax must be imposed during the tax year.
B. The taxpayer must be legally liable for the tax.
C. The tax must be paid during the tax year.
D. The tax must be paid by the taxpayer.

13. Rochelle is single and has the following income and expenses:

Wages	$70,000
Interest income from a CD	3,000
Mortgage interest paid on her primary residence (on an original mortgage of $400,000)	(24,000)
Investment interest expense	(5,000)
Personal credit card interest	(3,400)
Car loan interest on her personal vehicle	(1,200)
Late fees incurred on her mortgage	(50)

She plans to itemize this year. What is her total allowable deduction for interest expense on her Schedule A?

A. $24,000
B. $27,000
C. $27,050
D. $32,400

14. All of the following factors determine the amount of a taxpayer's standard deduction *except:*

A. The taxpayer's filing status.
B. The taxpayer's adjusted gross income.
C. Whether the taxpayer is 65 or older, or blind.
D. Whether the taxpayer can be claimed as a dependent.

15. Oscar donated a leather coat to a thrift store operated by his church. He paid $450 for the coat three years ago. Similar coats in the thrift store sell for $50. What is Oscar's charitable deduction?

A. $0
B. $50
C. $400
D. $450

16. Herschel and Angeline will file separate tax returns in 2020. Herschel plans to itemize his medical expenses; therefore, what must Angeline do?

A. They will have to file jointly.
B. Angeline must take the standard deduction.
C. Angeline must either itemize her deductions or claim zero as her standard deduction.
D. Angeline may choose to itemize or take the standard deduction.

17. Kiara bought her car seven years ago for $15,000. A used car guide shows the FMV for her model and make of car is currently $5,000. Kiara's friend, Buck, offered her $4,500 for the car a week ago, but she declined to sell it to him. Instead, she decides to donate her used car to a qualified charity. She receives Form 1098-C from the charity showing the car was sold at auction for $1,900. How much is Kiara's charitable deduction?

A. $1,900
B. $4,500
C. $5,000
D. $15,000

18. Leandra's adjusted gross income was $75,000 in 2020. She incurred the following expenses:

Homeowners' association dues	$1,000
Fine from homeowner's association for violation of bylaws	100
Mortgage interest on her main home	9,000
Property taxes on her main home	2,800
Political contributions to the Democratic Party	250
Unreimbursed orthodontic fees for a tooth extraction	1,200
Private mortgage insurance (PMI) on her main home	450

Based on the information provided, what is the amount of expenses they can deduct as an itemized deduction on Schedule A?

A. $11,800
B. $12,250
C. $13,450
D. $14,450

19. Which of the following taxes is not deductible on Schedule A?

A. Property taxes paid on a vacation home located in Hawaii.
B. State income taxes.
C. Property taxes based on a vehicle's value (DMV fees).
D. Property taxes paid on a home in Mexico.

20. All of the following miscellaneous itemized deductions are allowable in 2020 except:

A. Union dues.
B. Impairment-related work expenses of persons with disabilities.
C. Federal estate tax on income in respect of a decedent.
D. Gambling losses to the extent of gambling winnings.

21. Bowen donated to all of the following nonprofit organizations in 2020. What is his allowable deduction for charitable gifts on Schedule A?

Organization	**Amount**
Methodist church	$100
County animal shelter	120
Salvation Army	75
American Red Cross	25
Republican party	50
Chamber of Commerce	300
Total contributions	**$670**

A. $220
B. $320
C. $520
D. $670

22. Lamar donates to his church multiple times during the year. Which one of the donations listed below will require a qualified appraisal before the contribution can be deducted on his return?

A. A cash donation of $12,000.
B. A donation of antique furniture valued at $6,500.
C. A donation of appreciated stock with a fair market value of $12,500.
D. A donation of an old motorcycle valued at $450.

23. Angie and Sheldon, both age 41, file a joint return and claim their two children as dependents. They have adjusted gross income of $125,000. In 2020, the family accumulated $12,120 of unreimbursed medical and dental expenses that included the following:

Prescription medications filled in the U.S.	$6,500
Prescription medications ordered and shipped from another country	1,320
Prescription contact lenses for Angie	500
Teeth whitening procedure by Angie's dentist and custom bleach trays	2,600
Prescribed smoking cessation program for Sheldon	1,200

What amount can they deduct for their medical expenses?

A. $0
B. $6,500
C. $8,200
D. $9,375

24. Isaac's main home was damaged by a hurricane, and his county was later deemed a federal disaster area. He incurred $90,000 worth of flood damage to his home, but $80,000 was reimbursed by his homeowner's insurance. His basis in the home was $200,000 at the time of the hurricane. Isaac's employer had a disaster relief fund for its employees. Isaac received $4,000 from the fund and spent the entire amount on repairs to his home. What is Isaac's casualty loss (before the calculation of any limitations)?

A. $0
B. $4,000
C. $6,000
D. $10,000

25. Gonzalo is a visiting professor from Spain who is teaching at a U.S. university on a J-1 visa. He is classified as a nonresident alien for tax purposes and will file Form 1040-NR. Which of the following is Gonzalo potentially allowed to claim on his income tax return?

A. Disability insurance premiums.
B. A charitable gift of $150 to the American Cancer Society.
C. Mortgage interest on his main home.
D. The standard deduction.

Unit 12: Quiz Answers

1. The answer is A. Connor can claim the expenses for the special device as an impairment-related work expense. If a taxpayer has a physical or mental disability that limits employment, he can deduct the expense as a miscellaneous itemized deduction.

2. The answer is B. Only their home mortgage interest ($5,000) is potentially deductible as interest on Schedule A. The other types of interest are all personal interest, which is not deductible. Interest paid on a plot of land is not deductible as mortgage interest, even if the taxpayer later decides to build a home on the property. Only the interest secured by an actual home (not land) is deductible as mortgage interest.

3. The answer is B. Only the real estate taxes incurred on a U.S. property are deductible. Taxpayers can deduct real estate tax on Schedule A as an itemized deduction.

4. The answer is D. Gabriel is not permitted to utilize the standard deduction. A married taxpayer who files separately and whose spouse itemizes deductions must either itemize his deductions or claim zero as his deduction.

5. The answer is D. The mortgage interest and property tax on both his main home in Chicago and the mountain cabin are deductible (assuming the ceiling on qualifying mortgage debt is not an issue). The mortgage interest on the third home is not deductible. The property tax on all the homes is *potentially* deductible, but the deduction is limited to $10,000 by the SALT cap in 2020. The mortgage interest on a second home is deductible, even if the taxpayer did not use the home during the year. A taxpayer may deduct mortgage interest on up to two homes. The answer is calculated as follows:

Home Location	Mortgage Interest	Property Tax
Main home in Chicago	$18,500	$7,500
Cabin in Tahoe	5,200	2,800
Condo in Las Vegas	3rd home Not Deductible	1,950
Totals before limitations	**$23,700**	**$12,250**
Allowable deduction	**$23,700**	**$10,000 SALT limit**

6. The answer is C. Emelie can claim a deduction for a contribution of $250 or more only if she has a receipt or acknowledgment from a qualified organization. The receipt must include:

- The amount of cash contributed.
- Whether the qualified organization gave the taxpayer any goods or services in return.
- If applicable, a description and good faith estimate of the value of any goods or services provided in return by the organization.

A receipt must also show the date of the donation and the name of the organization that was paid.

7. The answer is D. Julio's charitable contribution is $275 ($250 plane ticket + $25 materials = $275). He can claim his travel and meeting expenses as charitable contributions because they are directly related to his charitable activities. However, he cannot claim the cost of the evening at the theater, as that is a personal entertainment expense.

8. The answer is D. The deduction for capital improvements is limited to the excess of the actual cost of the improvements over the increase in the fair market value of the home. Since the increase in the fair market value of the home exceeds the cost of the elevator, none of the costs can be deducted as a medical expense.

9. The answer is A. A taxpayer has the option of claiming sales taxes as an itemized deduction on Schedule A instead of claiming state and local income taxes. A taxpayer cannot claim both. The other expenses listed are not deductible on Schedule A.

10. The answer is D. A nonresident or dual-status alien (who is not married to a U.S. citizen or resident) must itemize deductions. Qiang cannot use the standard deduction. The other taxpayers listed are not required to itemize their deductions but may elect to do so if they wish.

11. The answer is B. Alejandra's medical expense deduction (before any AGI limitations) is $2,900 ($1,900 + $1,000). The childcare cost is not deductible, even though it was incurred while she was obtaining medical care. The amount reimbursed by insurance is not deductible. Most cosmetic procedures are not deductible, unless they are specifically to correct a disease or defect, so the Botox injections for wrinkles are not deductible.

12. The answer is A. Taxpayers can deduct taxes imposed during a *prior* year, as long as the taxes were *paid* during the current tax year.

13. The answer is C. Rochelle's allowable deduction is $27,050. The answer is calculated as follows: $24,000 + $3,000 + $50 = $27,050. The deduction for investment interest expense is *limited* to her net investment income of $3,000. The excess amount of interest expense of $2,000 ($5,000 - $3,000) must be carried over to the next tax year and may be used to offset investment income in future tax years. Late fees paid on a qualifying home mortgage are deductible as mortgage interest on Schedule A. The credit card interest and car loan interest are not deductible.

14. The answer is B. The standard deduction amount is based on the taxpayer's filing and dependent status, and whether the taxpayer is blind or at least 65 years old. It is not based on a taxpayer's income.

15. The answer is B. Oscar's donation is limited to $50. Generally, the FMV of used clothing and household goods is far less than the original cost. For used clothing, a taxpayer should claim as the value the price that a buyer typically would pay in a thrift shop or at a garage sale.

16. The answer is C. Since they are both filing MFS, Angeline is forced to either itemize her deductions or claim "zero" as her standard deduction. A taxpayer whose spouse itemizes deductions must either itemize deductions or claim zero as the standard deduction. This only applies in situations when both taxpayers are filing MFS. If one spouse qualifies for Head of Household filing status, then neither spouse would be forced to itemize.

17. The answer is A. Kiara can deduct $1,900 for her donation. She is allowed to take the lesser of the car's FMV or the amount for which the charity was able to sell the car. Since the charity sold the

car for only $1,900, that is the amount of her allowable deduction, regardless of any other estimates of its value.

18. The answer is B. Only the mortgage interest and property taxes are deductible. Neither the homeowner's association dues, nor the fine, or political contribution are deductible. Although the orthodontic fees for the tooth extraction are a qualified medical expense, the amounts are less than 7.5% of her AGI, so she cannot deduct her medical costs, either. The answer is figured as follows:

Homeowners' association dues	NO
Fine from homeowner's association for violation of bylaws	NO
Mortgage interest on her main home	9,000
Property taxes on her main home	2,800
Political contributions to the Democratic Party	NO
Unreimbursed orthodontic fees for a tooth extraction	NO
Private mortgage insurance (PMI) on her main home	450
Total allowable deductions on Schedule A	$12,250

19. The answer is D. Property taxes paid on a home in Mexico are not deductible. The deduction for foreign real property taxes is no longer allowed.

20. The answer is A. The union dues are not deductible as a miscellaneous itemized deduction. All of the other expenses would be deductible on Schedule A.

21. The answer is B. The contributions to the political organization and the Chamber of Commerce are not deductible on Schedule A. Bowen's allowable deduction is calculated as follows: $100 + $120 + $75 + $25 = $320.

22. The answer is B. The antique furniture donation would require an appraisal. Lamar must also complete Form 8283 and attach it to his tax return. The IRS requires a taxpayer to obtain a written appraisal by a qualified appraiser for any *noncash* contribution of more than $5,000. The antique furniture would require a qualified written appraisal before the taxpayer could deduct the donation on his tax return. Lamar must retain a copy of the appraisal for his own records, but in most cases, he does not have to attach the appraisal to his tax return. Answer A is incorrect because a cash donation does not require an appraisal. Answer C is incorrect because the donation of stock or other securities does not require an appraisal. A donation of a vehicle valued at less than $500 does not require an appraisal or any other type of documentation beyond a written acknowledgment from the organization.

23. The answer is A. Angie and Sheldon cannot deduct any of their medical expenses. In 2020, only the medical expenses that exceed 7.5% of the taxpayer's AGI are deductible. The total of Angie and Sheldon's *qualifying* medical expenses, $8,200, is less than $9,375 ($125,000 × 7.5%). Of the items listed, only the smoking cessation program, the contact lenses, and the prescription medications filled in the United States are qualified medical expenses. Prescription medications shipped from other countries are ineligible. The teeth whitening procedure would be considered a cosmetic enhancement and would not be a qualified medical expense, whether performed by a dentist or not.

24. The answer is C. Isaac's casualty loss is $6,000. Isaac must reduce his loss ($90,000) by the $80,000 insurance proceeds and the $4,000 he received from his employer.

25. The answer is B. Gonzalo is allowed to deduct the charitable gift to a U.S. charity on his Form 1040-NR. Nonresident aliens are limited as to the types of itemized deductions they can claim. Among other restrictions, they are not allowed to claim the deduction for mortgage interest. Answer "D" is incorrect because nonresident aliens cannot claim the standard deduction.

Unit 13: Individual Tax Credits

For additional information, read:
Publication 972, *Child Tax Credit*
Publication 503, *Child and Dependent Care Expenses*
Publication 596, *Earned Income Credit*
Publication 970, *Tax Benefits for Education*

A tax credit directly reduces a taxpayer's liability on a dollar-for-dollar basis, which means it is usually more valuable than a tax deduction of the same dollar amount that only reduces the amount of taxable income. Various types of tax credits are either *refundable* or *nonrefundable.*

Nonrefundable Tax Credits

A *nonrefundable* tax credit reduces a taxpayer's liability for the year to zero but not beyond that, so any remaining credit is not refunded to the taxpayer. The most common nonrefundable tax credits are:

- Foreign Tax Credit (covered later)
- Child and Dependent Care Credit
- Child Tax Credit (CTC)
- Adoption Credit
- American Opportunity Tax Credit (also has a refundable component)
- Lifetime Learning Credit
- Retirement Savings Contributions Credit or, the "Saver's Credit"
- The Credit for Other Dependents (ODC)

Refundable Tax Credits

A *refundable* tax credit can reduce a taxpayer's liability to zero and also generate a refund to the taxpayer for the amount by which the credit exceeds the amount of tax he would otherwise owe. Refundable tax credits include the following:

- Additional Child Tax Credit (ACTC)
- Earned Income Tax Credit (EITC)
- Premium Tax Credit (related to the Affordable Care Act, covered later in chapter 14)
- American Opportunity Tax Credit (AOTC, partially refundable)
- Credit for excess Social Security and RRTA tax withheld
- 2020 Recovery Rebate Credit

Stringent diligence requirements apply to Tax Preparers who prepare returns claiming the Earned Income Tax Credit (EITC), the Child Tax Credit (CTC), and the American Opportunity Tax Credit (AOTC). Also, the IRS prohibits retroactive claims of the Earned Income Tax Credit, the Child Tax Credit, and the American Opportunity Credit for any individual that did not have a valid tax identification number for the taxable year. In the past, a taxpayer was allowed to amend their return to claim these credits retroactively after a valid taxpayer identification number was issued, but this is no longer permitted. Due diligence requirements also apply to the determination of Head of Household filing status. Tax preparers must complete Form 8867, *Paid*

Preparer's Due Diligence Checklist, for each EITC, CTC/ACTC, or AOTC claim they prepare. This requirement is covered in more detail in Book 3, Representation.

Child and Dependent Care Credit

The Child and Dependent Care Credit allows a taxpayer a credit for a percentage of child care expenses for children under age 13 and for disabled dependents of any age. This is a nonrefundable credit for child care expenses that allow taxpayers to work or to seek work. The credit offsets regular tax and the alternative minimum tax. The credit ranges from 20% to 35% of qualifying expenses, depending on a taxpayer's income.

For 2020, the limit on qualifying expenses is $3,000 for one child and $6,000 for two or more children. If a taxpayer receives a reimbursement under a flexible spending account, the amount is treated as being pretax, and the taxpayer must deduct the reimbursed amount from his qualified expenses to determine the credit. A taxpayer must pass five eligibility tests to qualify for the Credit for Child and Dependent Care Expenses:

- **Qualifying person test**
- **Earned income test**
- **Work-related expense test**
- **Joint return test**
- **Provider identification test**

Test #1: Qualifying Person Test

For purposes of the Child and Dependent Care Credit, a "qualifying person" is:

- A dependent child *under* the age of 13 (at the time the care was provided),
- A spouse who is physically or mentally unable to care for himself,
- Any other disabled person who is unable to care for himself and that the taxpayer either claims as a dependent.

Example: Conrad paid someone to care for his disabled wife, Dacia, so he could work. Dacia is disabled and requires a full time, in-home care aide. Conrad also paid to have someone prepare meals and babysit his 11-year-old daughter, Tammy. Both Dacia and Tammy are qualifying persons for the Child and Dependent Care Credit.

Test #2: Earned Income Test

Both the taxpayer and his spouse, if married, must have "earned income" during the year to qualify for this credit. This generally means both spouses must work (if filing a joint return). The credit is not available to MFS filers. In the event one spouse does not have earned income, for purposes of this test the taxpayer's spouse is treated as having earned income for any month he is:

- A full-time student, or
- Disabled.

For any month that a spouse has no actual earned income, but has "deemed earned income" because they were a full-time student or disabled, the amount of deemed earned income by that

nonworking spouse is $250 per month if the couple has a qualifying individual for this credit, or $500 per month if the taxpayer has two or more dependents.

Example: Teriza and Jordan are married and have one 5 year old son named Timmy. Timmy is in daycare. Jordan works full-time for an accounting firm. Teriza attended college full-time from January 1 to June 30. She was unemployed during the summer and did not attend school for the rest of the year. Teriza is treated as having "earned income" for the six months she attended school full-time. In other words, they are allowed to take the dependent care credit in the months that Teriza was attending school. The daycare expenses that were incurred when Teriza was not in school or working would not be qualifying expenses for the purposes of the credit.

The amount of work-related expenses to figure the credit cannot be more than:

- The taxpayer's earned income for the year, if he is single at the end of the year, or
- The smaller of his or his spouse's earned income for the year if he is married at the end of the year.

Test #3: Work-Related Expense Test

Child and dependent care expenses must be "work-related" to qualify for this credit, meaning a taxpayer must be working (or actively searching for work). There are exceptions for a spouse who is disabled or a full-time student. Expenses incurred so that a spouse may do volunteer work or take care of personal business, or so that a married couple can go on a "date night" do not qualify.

Example: Nikita is a stay-at-home mom who volunteers several hours a week for a local suicide hotline. Her husband works full-time as a custodian. They pay a babysitter to stay with their daughter during the hours Nikita volunteers. The couple does not qualify for the credit because the babysitting expense is not "work-related." Since Nikita does not have a job, is not disabled, and is not a full-time student, their child care expenses are ineligible for the credit.

Example: Cheng and Jingyi are married and file jointly. Cheng works full time. His wife, Jingyi, is permanently disabled. They have one 7 year old daughter, who is in elementary school. Cheng pays for after-school care for his daughter, and picks her up at school when he is finished with his workday. The cost of the after-school care would be a qualifying expense for the Child and Daycare credit, even though Cheng's wife is not working, because Jingyi is disabled.

Example: Maureen's four-year-old son attends a daycare center while she works three days a week. The daycare charges $150 for three days a week and $250 for five days a week. Sometimes Maureen pays the extra money so she can run errands or go to the doctor on her days off. This extra charge is not a qualifying expense. Maureen's deductible expenses are limited to $150 a week, the amount of her work-related daycare expense.

The following kinds of expenses qualify for the credit:

- **Preschool education:** Preschool or other programs *below* the level of kindergarten;
- **After-school care:** Daycare that is after-school care (or before school) for a child in kindergarten or above,

- **Disabled care:** Adult daycare or supportive care for a disabled dependent or spouse (of any age, there is no age limit when the person is disabled),
- **Transportation costs:** Costs incurred for a care provider to take a qualifying person to or from a place where care is provided,
- **Fees and Deposits:** Any fees and deposits paid to a daycare or preschool to acquire child care,
- **Household services:** if they are at least partly for the well-being and protection of a qualifying person (such as the services of a full-time nanny or in-home care aide).

Example: Marina is single and her elderly mother, Luella, is her dependent. Luella is completely disabled and must be in an adult daycare. Marina pays $8,000 per year for Luella to be in an adult daycare. Marina may claim the Child and Dependent Care Credit because Luella is her dependent, and she is disabled and incapable of self-care.

Examples of child care expenses that do *not* qualify for the credit include:

- Tuition costs for children in kindergarten and above (like private school costs for an elementary school),
- Summer school or tutoring programs,
- The cost of sending a child to an overnight camp or a long-term camp (but *day camps* generally do qualify),
- The cost of transportation not provided by a daycare provider,
- A forfeited deposit to a daycare center (since it is not for care and therefore not a work-related expense).

Example: Zhuang's 9-year-old son attends a private elementary school. In addition to paying for tuition, Zhuang pays an extra fee for before and after-school care so he can be at work during his scheduled hours. Zhuang can count the cost of the before and after-school daycare program when figuring the credit, but cannot count the cost of private school tuition.

Example: Lorie is divorced and has custody of her 12-year-old daughter, Jani, who takes care of herself after school. In August, Lorie spends $2,000 to send Jani to an overnight camp for two weeks. She also sends Jani to a Girl Scout day camp for a week in July. The cost of the Girl Scout camp is $750. Lorie may only count the $750 toward the credit because the cost of sending a child to an overnight camp is not considered a qualifying child care expense. Next summer, when Jani turns 13, she will no longer be a qualifying child under the rules for this credit.

Care expenses do not include amounts paid for food, clothing, education, or entertainment. Small amounts paid for these items, however, can be included if they are incidental and cannot be separated from the cost of care.

Example: Irma takes her three-year-old child to a nursery school that provides lunch and activities as part of its program. The meals are included in the overall cost of care, and they are not itemized on her bill. Irma can count the total cost when she figures the credit.

Payments for child care will not qualify for the credit if made to a family member who is either:

- The taxpayer's own child under age 19,
- Any other dependent listed on the taxpayer's tax return.

Example: Garrison, age 30, pays his 60-year old mother, Bettie, $400 per month to watch his 5 year old son. Bettie watches her grandson while Garrison is at work. Normally, the $400 Garrison pays his mother would be a qualifying childcare expense. However, in 2020, Garrison claims his mother as a dependent on his tax return, along with his son. Since Garrison is claiming his mother as a dependent, then the payments made to her for childcare are not qualifying expenses for the purposes of the Child and Dependent Care Credit.

Taxpayers may combine costs for multiple dependents. For example, if a taxpayer pays daycare expenses for three qualifying children, the $6,000 limit on qualifying expenses does not need to be divided equally among them.

Example: Darby has three children, all under the age of 13. His qualifying daycare expenses are $2,300 for his first child; $2,800 for his second child; and $900 for his third child. Darby can use the total amount, $6,000, when figuring his credit.

Example: Gilles and Francine both work and have three children. They have $2,000 of daycare expenses for their first child, $3,000 for their second child, and $4,000 for their third child. Although their total child care expenses are $9,000, they may use only the first $6,000 as their basis for the credit.

Example: Elyse is a single mother with a 6-year-old son. She takes him to daycare five days per week so she can work. Elyse makes $46,000 of wages and spends $5,200 per year on daycare. The maximum amount of qualifying expenses she can claim for the credit is $3,000 since she only has one qualifying child, even though her actual expenses exceed that amount.

Test #4: Joint Return Test

The joint return test specifies that married couples who wish to take the credit must file jointly. However, a married taxpayer can be "considered unmarried" for tax purposes if he qualifies for head of household filing status. With divorced or separated taxpayers, only the custodial parent is allowed to claim the Child and Dependent Care Credit.

Test #5: Provider Identification Test

This test requires that taxpayers provide the name, address, and taxpayer identification number of the person or organization who provided the care for the child or dependent. If a daycare provider refuses to supply its taxpayer identification information, the taxpayer may still claim the credit. If the provider refuses to provide a tax ID, the taxpayer must report whatever information he has (such as the provider's name and address) and attach a statement to Form 2441, *Child and Dependent Care Expenses,* explaining the provider's refusal to supply the information. There is also an exception for foreign providers, who are not required to have a U.S. tax ID.

Example: Zedong is a U.S. defense contractor working temporarily overseas in Saudi Arabia. Zedong has sole custody of his 11-year old daughter, Ping. Zedong pays a full-time nanny to watch his daughter while he is working. Since the care was provided in a foreign country, the nanny is not required to have a U.S. tax ID, and Zedong is still allowed to claim the full amount of the Child and Dependent Care Credit.

The Child Tax Credit and Additional Child Tax Credit

This credit is totally separate from the child and dependent care credit. The TCJA made the following changes to the Child Tax Credit (CTC) and the Additional Child Tax Credit (ACTC) for tax years through 2025:

- The *nonrefundable* Child Tax Credit (CTC) is $2,000 per qualifying child
- The Additional Child Tax Credit (ACTC) is a maximum of $1,400 per qualifying child.
- The AGI phaseout for the Child Tax Credit is $200,000 ($400,000 for MFJ). If income exceeds the limit, the credit will decrease by $50 for every $1,000 that the AGI exceeds the limit.
- The child must have a valid Social Security number to qualify for the $2,000 Child Tax Credit. ITINs and ATINs are not sufficient.

Taxpayers with income below the AGI threshold can claim the Child Tax Credit for each qualifying child *under* the age of 17. A taxpayer whose tax liability is zero cannot take the Child Tax Credit because there is no tax to reduce. In addition, the Child Tax Credit is limited to the amounts of regular income tax and any alternative minimum tax owed.

However, a taxpayer with zero tax liability may be able to take the Additional Child Tax Credit, which is a refundable credit. In order to qualify for the Additional Child Tax Credit, the taxpayer must have "earned income," such as wages or income from self-employment.

Example: Eduardo files as head of household and has two children, ages 6 and 7. Both children qualify for the Child Tax Credit. His MAGI is $54,000, and his tax liability is $4,680. Eduardo is eligible to take the full credit of $2,000 per child ($2,000 X 2 children = $4,000) because his MAGI is less than $200,000 and his tax liability is greater than $4,000.

Example: Mendel and Jada file jointly and have two children who qualify for the Child Tax Credit. Their MAGI is $36,000, and their tax liability is $954. They can offset the $954 in tax using the Child Tax Credit, reducing their tax to zero. Since their tax liability is zero, Mendel and Jada cannot claim the maximum Child Tax Credit of $2,000 per child, but they may be eligible for the Additional Child Tax Credit, which is a refundable credit.

Example: Joshua and Anika are married and file jointly. Joshua has wages of $195,000. Anika does not work, but she has various profitable investments. Anika has rental income of $50,000 and dividend income of $250,000. They have one 11-year old child. Their joint AGI is $495,000. They are not eligible to take the Child Tax Credit, because their joint AGI is above the phaseout threshold for joint filers ($400,000 is the phaseout for joint filers)

Note: Unlike the Earned Income Tax Credit, disability has no effect on the eligibility for this credit. The child's age is the primary determining factor.

Definition of a Qualifying Child for the Child Tax Credit: To be eligible to claim the Child Tax Credit, the taxpayer must have at least one qualifying child. To qualify, the child must meet the following tests:

- **Age Test:** The child must have been *younger* than 17 on December 31, 2020.
- **Relationship Test:** The child must be the taxpayer's son, daughter, stepchild, foster child, brother, sister, stepbrother, stepsister, half-brother, half-sister or a descendant of any of

them. For example, a qualifying child could include grandchildren, nieces, and nephews. Adopted children always qualify as the taxpayer's own child.

- **Support Test:** The child must not provide more than half of their own support for the year.
- **Dependency Test:** The child must be a dependent claimed on the tax return. A noncustodial parent may claim the child tax credit for his or her child if he or she is allowed to claim the child as a dependent and otherwise qualifies to claim the child tax credit.
- **Joint Return Test:** The child cannot file a joint return for the year unless the only reason they are filing is to claim a refund, and otherwise the child would not have a tax liability.
- **Citizenship Test:** The child must be a U.S. citizen, U.S. national, or U.S. resident alien with a valid Social Security Number. An ITIN or ATIN is no longer acceptable. Citizens or residents of Mexico and Canada do not qualify for this credit.
- **Residency Test:** In most cases, the child must have lived with the taxpayer for more than half of the year (over six months). Exceptions exist for temporary absences[180] and children who are born or die within the year.[181]

Example: Lissette's adopted son, Myron, is 14. His adoption was finalized on November 1, 2020, but before that date, he lived with Lisette all year as her foster child. Myron is a U.S. citizen. Lissette provided all of her son's support. Myron is a qualifying child for the Child Tax Credit because he was under age 17 at the end of the tax year; he meets the relationship requirement; he lived with Lissette for more than six months of the year, and he didn't provide his own support.

Example: Alfonso and Yolanda file jointly and have four dependent children under the age of 17. Alfonso is a green card holder and has a valid SSN. Yolanda and the children have Individual Taxpayer Identification Numbers (ITINs). They cannot claim the Child Tax Credit.

Example: Isaiah's son, Timothy, turned 17 on the last day of the year: December 31, 2020. He is a U.S. citizen and has a valid Social Security number. According to the Child Tax Credit rules, Timothy is not a qualifying child for the Child Tax Credit because he was not *under* age 17 at the end of the year.

Example: Jennifer gave birth to a son on December 30, 2020. The baby stayed at the hospital for several days after his birth, receiving treatment for jaundice. Jennifer was finally able to take her son home on January 10, 2021. Even though the baby did not technically live with Jennifer for a single day in 2020, the child meets the residency requirement, because hospitalization is considered a temporary absence. The baby is a qualifying child for the purposes of the Child Tax Credit.

---

180 Temporary absences include: school, vacation, medical care, military service, or incarceration in a juvenile facility. These absences count as time lived at home. The same is true if the child lived with the taxpayer more than half the year except for any required hospital stay following birth.

181 There are special rules for children of divorced or separated parents, as well as children of parents who never married. In some cases, the noncustodial parent may be entitled to claim the child as a dependent and thus the Child Tax Credit and Additional Child Tax Credit. In addition, there is an exception for an infant who is born during the tax year and has not lived long enough to meet the six-month requirement.

Additional Child Tax Credit (ACTC)

The Additional Child Tax Credit is available for certain individuals who do not qualify for the full amount of the nonrefundable Child Tax Credit. In order to claim the Additional Child Tax Credit, a taxpayer must be able to claim the Child Tax Credit, even if he does not qualify for the full amount.

Since the Additional Child Tax Credit is refundable, it can produce a refund even if the taxpayer does not owe any tax. The additional child tax credit allows eligible taxpayers to claim up to $1,400 for each qualifying child. The credit is based on the *lesser* of:

- 15% of the taxpayer's taxable earned income that is over $2,500 or
- The amount of unused child tax credit (caused when the tax liability is less than the allowed Child Tax Credit)

Note: In 2020, a special temporary rule allows lower-income individuals to use their earned income from the previous tax year (2019) to determine the Earned Income Tax Credit and the Additional Child Tax Credit for the 2020 tax year (the taxpayer can only make this election if their 2019 earned income was higher than their income in 2020).[182]

Schedule 8812, *Child Tax Credit,* is used to report both the Child Tax Credit and the refundable Additional Child Tax Credit. Although most of the rules for claiming the Child Tax Credit and the Additional Child Tax Credit are identical, there is one notable difference between the two. A taxpayer cannot claim the *refundable* Additional Child Tax Credit if he or she files Form 2555, *Foreign Earned Income Exclusion.*

Example: Liliana is a U.S. citizen who lives and works overseas in Italy. She has one child named Nicole, who is 9 years old. Liliana qualifies for the Foreign Earned Income Exclusion and files Form 2555 with her tax return. After calculating all her deductions, her remaining tax liability is $1,300. She is eligible to take the Child Tax Credit for Nicole, but her credit is limited to $1,300, the amount of her tax liability. She will not receive the *refundable* Additional Child Tax Credit, because she filed Form 2555 with her return.

Other Dependent Credit (ODC)

The $500 "Other Dependent Credit" (also called the "Credit for Other Dependents" or "ODC") applies to dependents who do not qualify for the $2,000 Child Tax Credit, such as children who are over the age of 17 or other dependents (such as elderly parents). Taxpayers cannot claim the ODC credit for themselves or a spouse; in other words, the credit is only available for dependents who are listed on the return.

The dependent must be a U.S citizen, U.S. national, or U.S. resident.[183] The AGI phaseout for the Credit for Other Dependents is the same as the phaseout for the Child Tax Credit ($200,000 for unmarried taxpayers in 2020 and $400,000 for joint filers).

---

182 This temporary rule is provided through the *Taxpayer Certainty and Disaster Tax Relief Act of 2020 (TCDTR),* which was passed as part of the *Consolidated Appropriations Act of 2021.*

183 Dependents who are residents of Canada or Mexico do not qualify for either the Child Tax Credit or the Credit for Other Dependents.

Example: Robert and Hazel file a joint return and they both have valid SSNs. Their tax liability is $2,000. They have three qualifying dependents. Amber is their 20-year-old daughter, has an SSN, and meets the qualifying child test. Jiang is their 11-year-old adopted child, has an ATIN, and meets the qualifying child test. Robert's mother, Esther, is 75 years old, has a valid SSN, and meets the "qualifying relative" test. They are all U.S. residents for IRS tax purposes. Amber, Jiang, and Esther are not qualifying dependents for the Child Tax Credit, but they are *all* qualifying dependents for the Credit for Other Dependents, or ODC.

To claim the Credit for Other Dependents, the dependent must have a valid identification number (ATIN, ITIN, or SSN) by the due date of the return (including extensions).

Adoption Credit

In 2020, a nonrefundable credit of up to $14,300 per child can be taken for qualified expenses paid to adopt a child. An eligible child is:

- Under 18 years of age, or
- Physically or mentally disabled, regardless of age.

For a special-needs child, the maximum credit amount is allowed even if the taxpayer does not have any adoption expenses. If an employee receives employer-provided adoption benefits that are excluded from income, the employee may still be able to take the Adoption Credit. However, the exclusion and the credit cannot be claimed for the same expenses, and any allowable exclusion must be claimed before any allowable credit (i.e. no double-dipping allowed).

Unlike most other tax credits, the adoption credit has the same phaseout range for all filing statuses. The MAGI phaseout range in 2020 starts at $214,521 and ends at $254,520. If a taxpayer's MAGI is higher than $254,520 in 2020, they cannot claim the credit. Taxpayers who file MFS cannot claim the Adoption Credit.

Although the Adoption Credit is nonrefundable, any unused credit may be carried forward for up to five years. Qualified adoption expenses must be directly related to the adoption of the child. Qualifying expenses may include:

- Adoption fees and court costs,
- Attorney fees,
- Travel expenses related to the adoption, including meals and lodging,
- Costs of an unsuccessful adoption of a U.S. citizen or U.S. national,
- Re-adoption expenses to adopt a foreign child.

Qualified expenses do *not* include: any illegal adoption expenses, any surrogate parenting arrangement, or the adoption of a spouse's child.[184]

[184] Although a taxpayer cannot deduct adoption expenses to adopt a spouses' child, qualified adoption expenses include expenses paid by a registered domestic partner to adopt his or her partner's child, as long as those expenses otherwise qualify for the credit.

Example: Theodora and Edison are married and file jointly. During the year, Theodora legally adopts Edison's 16-year old daughter, Layla, who is his child from his first marriage. The legal fees for the adoption total $5,600. None of these costs are deductible, and the amounts are not eligible for an adoption credit, because the costs associated with the adoption of a spouse's child are not qualifying costs for the purposes of the Adoption Credit.

Special-Needs Adoptions

A taxpayer can claim the full credit for a special-needs child regardless of actual expenses paid or incurred. For the purposes of this rule, a special-needs child must be a United States citizen or U.S. resident when the adoption begins.[185] Further, one of the following must apply:

- The state has determined the child cannot (or should not) be returned to the parents' home, or,
- The state has determined the child will not be adopted unless assistance is provided to the adoptive parents.

In making the determination about special needs, a state may take into account the following factors: a child's ethnic background and age; whether he is a member of a minority or sibling group; and whether he or she has a physical, mental, or emotional handicap. The child does not have to be disabled in order for the child to qualify as "special needs."

Example: Olympia adopts two special-needs children from the U.S. foster care system in 2020. She incurs only $2,100 in adoption expenses; however, because both children are considered special-needs, Olympia is allowed an adoption credit of $28,600 ($14,300 x 2). This credit may be used to offset income tax on her return.

Example: Roman and Marylou adopt a special needs child, and the adoption is finalized in 2020. Their actual adoption expenses are $7,500. They are allowed to claim the full $14,300 credit because they adopted a special needs child. Their income tax liability is $8,000 so the adoption credit will reduce their tax liability in 2020 to zero. They can carry forward any unused adoption credit for up to five years.

Unsuccessful Adoptions: A taxpayer who has attempted to adopt a child in the U.S. and been unsuccessful is still eligible for the credit. Eligible expenses may include those related to unsuccessful attempts to adopt as well as an adoption attempt that is ultimately successful. However, if the eligible child is from a foreign country, the taxpayer cannot take the credit or exclusion unless the adoption becomes final. A foreign child is defined as a child who was not a citizen or resident of the United States at the time the adoption effort began.

The Timing of Payment: Adoption expenses are generally deductible in the year the adoption becomes final, with a few exceptions.

- **Domestic adoptions:** with the adoption of a domestic child, qualified expenses paid before the year in which the adoption becomes final may be claimed in the year after the expenses were paid. This is true even if the adoption is unsuccessful.

---

[185] Foreign children, if not a U.S. citizen or U.S. resident, are not considered to have special needs for purposes of the adoption credit.

- **Foreign adoptions:** for a foreign adoption, expenses paid before or during the adoptive process are only deductible once the adoption actually becomes final.
- **Post-adoption expenses:** Any additional expenses paid after an adoption becomes final (for example, additional legal fees related to the adoption), then those expenses would be allowed in the year paid, regardless of whether or not the adoption was foreign or domestic.

Example (domestic adoption): Alicia is attempting to adopt a one-year-old child named Lorena. The child is a U.S. citizen. Alicia's AGI is under the threshold amounts. The adoption process takes several years. Alicia pays qualified legal fees related to the adoption of $3,000 in 2019, $4,200 in 2020, and $5,000 in 2021. On March 5, 2021, Lorena's adoption becomes final. The $3,000 of expenses paid in 2019 is allowable in 2020 (the year *after* the year the costs were incurred) and may be claimed as a credit on Alicia's 2020 tax return. The adoption became final in 2021, so Alicia can claim both the $4,200 paid in 2020 and the $5,000 paid in 2021 as a credit on her 2021 tax return.

Example (foreign adoption): Veronica and Charles are attempting to adopt a foreign child named Manuel, who is 4 years old and a citizen of Colombia. The couple pays qualified adoption expenses of $4,000 in 2019, $6,000 in 2020, and $2,000 in 2021. On February 27, 2021, the adoption becomes final. Veronica and Charles may claim all $12,000 in qualified adoption expenses ($4,000 paid in 2019, $6,000 paid in 2020, and $2,000 in 2021) on their 2021 tax return, because 2021 is the year in which the adoption became final.[186]

Education Credits

Two education credits are available based on qualified expenses a taxpayer pays for post-secondary education:

- **American Opportunity Tax Credit (also called the AOC or AOTC)**
- **Lifetime Learning Credit**

Certain general rules apply to both of these credits, and there are also specific rules for each. A taxpayer may take education credits for himself, his spouse, and his dependents who attended an eligible educational institution during the tax year. Eligible educational institutions include colleges, universities, vocational schools, and community colleges. Taxpayers can claim payments that are prepaid for an academic period that begins in the first three months of the next calendar year.

Example: Fahad is 29 years old and single. On December 28, 2020, he prepaid $1,500 for college tuition for the spring semester that begins on January 9, 2021. Fahad can claim $1,500 of education credits on his 2020 return (in the year he actually paid the costs), even though he will not start college until 2021.

To claim the credit for a dependent's education expenses, the taxpayer must claim the dependent on his return, but he does not necessarily have to pay for all of the dependent's qualified education expenses. If a taxpayer does not claim the eligible student as a dependent,

---

[186] Examples modified from scenarios in IRS Tax Topic 607, Adoption Credit and Adoption Assistance Programs, at: https://www.irs.gov/taxtopics/tc607.

the student may be able to claim an education credit on his own return. A taxpayer *cannot* claim education credits if he or she:

- Can be claimed as a dependent on someone else's tax return,
- Files MFS,
- Has adjusted gross income above the phaseout limit for his filing status,
- Has a spouse who was a nonresident alien for any part of the tax year.[187]

Example: Natalia, age 52, has a 20-year-old son named Raul who is a full-time college student. Natalia and Raul do not have enough money to pay for Raul's college tuition. As a gift, Raul's grandmother pays his tuition directly to the college. For purposes of claiming an education credit, either Natalia or Raul can be treated as receiving the money as a gift and paying for the qualified tuition and related expenses. If Natalia claims Raul as a dependent, she can claim an education credit. Alternatively, if Raul's mother does not claim him as a dependent, he can claim the credit. [188]

If a taxpayer incurs education expenses for more than one student, he may be eligible to take the American Opportunity Credit for one student and the Lifetime Learning Credit for another student on the same tax return.

Example: Armando is 49 and pays college expenses for himself and his dependent daughter, Sarah, age 18. Armando is attending graduate school to earn a doctorate degree. Armando qualifies for the Lifetime Learning Credit. Sarah is an undergraduate student in her first year of college. She qualifies for the American Opportunity Credit. Armando can take both credits on his tax return for each eligible student—Sarah and himself.

Form 8863, *Education Credits,* is used to figure and claim both education credits. Qualified education expenses are tuition and related expenses, such as books and other course materials required as a condition of enrollment. Any course involving sports, games, or hobbies is not a qualifying expense *unless* the course is part of the student's degree program (or if taken to improve job skills, in the case of the Lifetime Learning Credit).

Qualified education expenses must be reduced by the amount of any tax-free educational assistance received, such as Pell grants, tax-free portions of scholarships, and employer-provided educational assistance. Education expenses that do not qualify include:

- Room and board, (even if the housing is on-campus and a condition of enrollment)
- Any medical expenses, including student health fees, even if charged by the college
- Other insurance costs
- Transportation costs
- Personal, living, or family expenses

Tuition expenses are reported to the student on Form 1098-T, *Tuition Statement*, issued by the school.

[187] This rule does not apply if the nonresident spouse elects to be treated as a U.S. resident alien for tax purposes.
[188]Example from Publication 4491, under the section for "education expenses."

Example: Lillian received Form 1098-T, *Tuition Statement,* from the college she attends. It shows that her tuition was $9,500 and that she received a $1,500 tax-free scholarship. Her maximum qualifying expenses for the education credit are $8,000 ($9,500 - $1,500 scholarship).

Example: Arlene is 32 years old and unmarried. She paid $3,000 for tuition and $5,000 for room and board at a state university. She was also awarded a $2,000 tax-free scholarship and a $4,000 student loan. To qualify for an education credit, she must first subtract the tax-free scholarship from her tuition, her only qualified expense. A student loan is not considered tax-free educational assistance because it must be paid back. To calculate her education credit, Arlene has $1,000 of qualified expenses ($3,000 tuition - $2,000 scholarship).

American Opportunity Tax Credit (AOTC)

The American Opportunity Tax Credit (also referred to as the AOTC or AOC) allows taxpayers to claim a maximum credit of up to $2,500 for each eligible student. The credit covers 100% of the first $2,000 and 25% of the second $2,000 of eligible expenses per student. Qualified expenses include tuition and required fees, books, supplies, equipment, and other *required* course materials (but *not* room and board or student health fees).

Example: Bradford is a college senior studying to be a dentist. This year, in addition to tuition, he pays a fee to the university for the rental of the dental equipment he is required to use in the program. Bradford's equipment rental fee is a qualified education expense.

Unlike other education credits and deductions, the American Opportunity Tax Credit is partially refundable. Up to 40% of the credit is refundable, which means the taxpayer can receive up to $1,000 even if no taxes are owed. The credit is not refundable if the student is subject to the "kiddie tax" rules. Requirements for the AOTC are as follows:

- **Degree requirement:** The student must be enrolled in a program that leads to a degree, certificate, or other recognized educational credential. Taking classes merely for fun or recreation does not qualify.
- **Workload:** For at least one academic period of the year, the student must carry at least half of the normal full-time workload for his course of study.
- **No felony drug conviction:** The student must not have any felony convictions for possessing or distributing a controlled substance.
- **Four years of postsecondary education:** The credit can be claimed only for expenses related to a student's post-secondary education and only for a maximum of four years.

Example: Azucena has not yet completed her first bachelor's degree, but it took her five years to get all the credits she needed to graduate. She expects to graduate with her first bachelor's degree in December 2020. Azucena properly claimed the American Opportunity Tax Credit in 2016, 2017, 2018, and 2019. Since the credit has already been claimed for the first four years of her undergraduate education, she cannot claim the credit on any additional returns, including her 2020 return.

For 2020, the AOTC phases for unmarried taxpayers with MAGIs between $80,000 and $90,000 ($160,000 and $180,000 for MFJ). Taxpayers who file MFS cannot claim the credit.

Example: Bella, age 24, and Jonathan, age 33, are married and file jointly. Bella is a full-time student working towards her first bachelor's degree. Bella incurs $15,000 in qualifying tuition expenses during the year. Jonathan works full time and has $220,000 of taxable income. Their joint AGI is over $180,000, so they cannot claim the American Opportunity Credit. They are phased-out because of their income level.

Note: Taxpayers claiming the American Opportunity Credit must have a valid taxpayer identification number by the due date of the tax return (including extensions). Further, the student claimed for the credit must also have a valid identification number by the due date (including extensions). Taxpayers cannot file an amended return to claim the credit for a year that the taxpayer and/or student did not originally have a required identification number by the return due date.

If a student does not meet all of the conditions for the American Opportunity Credit, he may still be able to take the Lifetime Learning Credit.

Lifetime Learning Credit

The Lifetime Learning Credit is a nonrefundable tax credit of 20% of qualified tuition, fees, and any amounts paid directly to the educational institution for required books, supplies and equipment, up to $10,000, paid during the tax year.

The maximum credit is $2,000 per *tax return,* not *per student.* A family's maximum credit is the same regardless of the number of qualified students. The requirements for the Lifetime Learning Credit differ from those for the AOTC as follows:

- **No workload requirement:** A student is eligible no matter how few courses he takes.
- **Non-Degree courses eligible:** A student qualifies if he is simply taking a course to acquire or improve job skills. There is no degree requirement.
- **All levels of postsecondary education:** A student may be an undergraduate, graduate, or professional degree candidate. The courses can also be just for professional development.
- **An unlimited number of years:** There is no limit on the number of years for which the credit can be claimed for each student.
- **Felony drug convictions permissible:** A student can be convicted for a felony drug conviction and still qualify.

Example: Brent attends Creek Community College after spending twelve months in prison for a felony cocaine conviction. He paid $4,400 for the course of study, which included tuition, equipment, and books required for the course. The school requires that students pay for books and equipment when registering for courses. The entire $4,400 is an eligible education expense under the Lifetime Learning Credit. Although he meets all the other requirements for the American Opportunity Credit, Brent does not qualify for the AOC because he has a felony drug conviction. He may claim the Lifetime Learning Credit instead.

Example: Carey works full-time and takes one course a month at night school. Some of the courses are not for credit, but she is taking them to advance her career. She is not pursuing a degree. The education expenses qualify for the Lifetime Learning Credit, but not for the American Opportunity Credit.

In 2020, the Lifetime Learning Credit is phased out at $118,000–138,000 for joint filers and $59,000–69,000 for unmarried filers. Taxpayers who file MFS cannot take the credit.

Earned Income Tax Credit (EITC)

The Earned Income Tax Credit (EITC), also commonly known as the Earned Income Credit (EIC), is a fully refundable federal income tax credit for lower-income people who work and have earned income and adjusted gross income under certain thresholds. This credit is claimed on Schedule EIC, *Earned Income Credit.* There are strict rules[189] and income guidelines for the EITC. To claim the EITC, a taxpayer must meet all of the following tests:

- Have a Social Security number that is valid for employment. Any dependent must also have a valid SSN that is valid for employment.
- Have "earned income" from wages, combat pay, or self-employment,
- Investment income must also be $3,650 or less for the year to be eligible,
- Not file as MFS,
- Not be claimed as a dependent by another taxpayer,
- Be a U.S. citizen or legal resident all year (a nonresident alien married to a U.S. citizen or resident alien filing jointly can still qualify under some circumstances).

Qualifying Income for the EITC: Only earned income, such as: wages, tips, combat pay, union strike benefits, and net earnings from self-employment qualifies for the EITC. For EITC purposes, "earned income" does not include the following income:

- Social Security benefits or welfare payments,
- Alimony (even if taxable to the recipient) or child support,
- Pensions or annuities,[190]
- Unemployment benefits,
- Inmate wages, including work release programs,
- Income from investments, rental activities, or other passive sources.

Note: In 2020, a special temporary rule allows lower-income individuals to use their earned income from the previous tax year (2019) to determine the Earned Income Tax Credit and the Additional Child Tax Credit for the 2020 tax year (the taxpayer can only make this election if their 2019 earned income was higher than their income in 2020).

Income that is excluded from tax is generally not considered earned income for the EITC. Nontaxable combat pay and qualified Medicare waiver payments are the exception. A taxpayer can choose to include this nontaxable pay in their earned income if it gives them a better tax result.

Low-income taxpayers *without children* may qualify for the EITC in certain cases, but the rules are stricter, and the amount of the credit is lower.[191] A taxpayer with a qualifying child can

[189] Among the EITC rules is a requirement that practitioners make reasonable inquiries to determine that the information the taxpayer is giving is correct. We cover the due diligence for the EITC, CTC, and other credits in Book 3, *Representation.*
[190] Although uncommon, some disability retirement benefits qualify as earned income to claim the EITC.
[191] The Congressional Research Service has reported that 97% of all EITC dollars are claimed by families with qualifying children.

claim the EITC without any age limitations, but a taxpayer *without* a child can only claim the EITC if all of the following tests are met:

- Must be at least age 25 but under 65 at the end of the year (if married, either spouse can meet the age test),
- Must not qualify as a dependent of another person,
- Must live in the United States for more than half the year,
- Cannot file Form 2555 (related to foreign earned income exclusion).[192]

Example: Chelsea is single and age 26. She has one 6 year old child. She earns $15,900 in wages during 2020. Her wages would normally qualify her for the Earned Income Tax Credit, but she also has $4,100 of investment income during the year, from a rental property that she inherited from her grandmother. A taxpayer with $3,650 or more of investment income in 2020 does not qualify for the EITC, regardless of her earnings, so Chelsea would not qualify for the EITC due to her investment income.

Qualifying Children for EITC Purposes

The definition of a "qualifying child" for purposes of the EITC is stricter than it is for being able to claim someone as a dependent. The taxpayer's qualifying child must meet all the following tests:

- **Relationship test**
- **Age test**
- **Joint return test**
- **Residency test**

Relationship Test: The child must be related to the taxpayer in one of the following ways:

- Son, daughter, stepchild, eligible foster child, adopted child, or descendant of any of them (for example, a grandchild), or
- Brother, sister, half-brother, half-sister, stepbrother, stepsister, or descendant of any of them (for example, a niece or nephew).

Example: Curtis is 37 and supports his younger sister, Shakira, who is 16. He has taken care of his sister since their parents died five years ago. Shakira is Curtis' qualifying child for purposes of the Earned Income Tax Credit.

Example: Barbara's niece, Aimee, is 23 and attending college full time. Aimee lives with Barbara. Barbara made $31,000 in wages in 2020 and is filing as Head of Household. She is claiming Aimee as her dependent. Aimee meets the rules for a qualifying child. Barbara can claim the EITC.

An adopted child is generally treated as the taxpayer's own child. However, special rules apply for foreign adoptions. Any qualifying child listed on Schedule EIC also must have a valid SSN. Since an ATIN is not sufficient, then a taxpayer with an ATIN is not a qualifying child for EITC purposes. A foster child can also be an eligible child, but they must be placed in the taxpayer's home by an authorized placement agency or by the courts in order to be eligible.

[192] The mere act of *earning* foreign income would not automatically disqualify a taxpayer from claiming EITC. A taxpayer who elects not to exclude foreign income from his gross income may still be eligible for the EITC.

Age Test: To qualify for the EITC, the child must be:

- Age 18 or younger,
- A full-time student, age 23 or younger, or
- Any age, if permanently disabled.

In addition, the qualifying child must be younger than the taxpayer claiming him, *unless* the child (dependent) is permanently disabled.

Example: Caleb, age 45, supports his older brother, Brian, age 56. Brian, who is mentally challenged and permanently disabled, lives with Caleb. Caleb financially supports his disabled brother and also pays for his adult daycare program. In this case, Brian meets the criteria to be Caleb's qualifying child for purposes of the EITC, even though Brian is older than the taxpayer claiming him.

Joint Return Test: The qualifying child (dependent) cannot file a joint return with a spouse, except to claim a refund.

Example: Daniela's 18-year-old son and his 18-year-old wife had $3,010 of wage income and no other income. Neither is required to file a tax return. Taxes were taken out of their wages, so they file a joint return only to get a refund of the income taxes withheld. The exception to the joint return test applies, so Daniela's son and daughter-in-law may still be her qualifying children, if all the other tests are met.

Residency Test: The child must have lived with the taxpayer in the United States for more than half the year.[193] Only a custodial parent can claim the EITC. A child who was born or died during the year would meet the residency test for the entire year if the child lived with the taxpayer the entire time he was alive in 2020.

Example: Catherine gave birth to a baby girl in March. The infant died one month later. The child is still a qualifying child for purposes of the EITC because she meets the other tests for age and relationship.

Earned Income and AGI Limits

The EITC varies based on a taxpayer's earnings. Both the taxpayer's earned income and his AGI must be *less* than the following limits:

Filing Status	2020 Income limits for Qualifying Children Claimed			
	Zero Children	One Child	Two Children	Three or more
Single, HOH, or QW	$15,820	$41,756	$47,440	$50,594
MFJ*	$21,710	$47,646	$53,330	$56,844
*MFS filers do not qualify to take the EITC, so they are not listed in this table.				

193 For purposes of the EITC, U.S. military personnel stationed outside the United States on extended active duty are considered to live in the U.S. during that duty period, so their children meet the residency test.

Example: Barton is unmarried and his AGI is $47,000 in 2020. He has one qualifying child. Barton cannot claim the EITC because his AGI exceeds the income threshold for unmarried filers with one child.

If a taxpayer qualifies for the EITC, the maximum EITC that can potentially be claimed is as follows:

2020 Maximum EITC			
Zero Children	**One Child**	**Two Children**	**Three or more**
$538	$3,584	$5,920	$6,660

EITC Fraud and Penalties: If the IRS audits a taxpayer's return and disallows all or part of the EITC, the taxpayer:

- Must pay back the amount in error with interest,
- May need to file Form 8862, *Information to Claim Earned Income Credit after Disallowance*,
- Cannot claim the EITC for the next two years if the IRS determines the error is because of reckless or intentional disregard of the rules, or
- Cannot claim the EITC for the next ten years if the IRS determines the error is because of fraud.

Retirement Savings Contributions Credit (Saver's Credit)

The credit is 10%–50% of eligible contributions to IRAs and other qualifying retirement plans up to a maximum credit of $1,000 ($2,000 MFJ), depending on a taxpayer's adjusted gross income. Eligible contributions must be made to an IRA or an employer-sponsored retirement plan.[194]

ABLE account designated beneficiaries may now be eligible to claim the Saver's Credit for a percentage of their contributions. The amount of the credit is the eligible contribution multiplied by the applicable credit rate, which is based on filing status and AGI.

Note: On past exams, the IRS has referred to this credit as either the "Retirement Savings Contributions Credit" or the "Saver's Credit." Either term may be used on the EA exam, since both terms are currently used on the IRS website as well as IRS publications. Do not be confused by this—they are the same credit.

The income limitations are as follows:

Credit Rate	MFJ	HOH	Single, QW, MFS
50% of the contribution	AGI not more than $39,000	AGI not more than $29,250	AGI not more than $19,500
20% of the contribution	$39,001 - $42,500	$29,251 - $31,875	$19,501 - $21,250
10% of the contribution	$42,501 - $65,000	$31,876 - $48,750	$21,251 - $32,500

[194] Eligible contributions include those to both traditional IRAs and Roth IRAs, elective deferrals to 401(k) or other qualified employer-sponsored retirement plans, and voluntary employee contributions to other qualified retirement plans.

To be eligible for this credit, the taxpayer must fulfill all the following requirements:

1. Be at least age 18 or older;
2. Not a full-time student; and
3. Not claimed as a dependent on another person's return.

Most workers who contribute to traditional IRAs already deduct all or part of their contributions. The Saver's Credit is *in addition* to these deductions. In essence, a taxpayer could potentially deduct their contribution to a traditional IRA, and then *also* receive the Saver's Credit in the same year.

However, when figuring the credit, a taxpayer generally must subtract the amount of *distributions* received from his retirement plans, in the two years before the year the credit is claimed; the year the credit is claimed; and the period after the end of the credit year but before the due date, including extensions, for filing the return for the credit year. Also, note that foreign income cannot be included in the taxpayer's adjusted gross income for the purposes of calculating this credit.

Example: Alonzo is 24 and earns $41,000 during the year. He is single and contributes $3,000 to his 401(k) plan at work. Alonzo is not eligible for the credit because his income exceeds the threshold limit for single filers.

Example: Karen works at a bank. She is married and earned $36,000 in wages during 2020. Karen's husband is disabled and didn't have any earnings for the year. Karen contributed $1,000 to her traditional IRA in 2020. After deducting her IRA contribution, the adjusted gross income shown on her joint return is $35,000. Karen may claim a 50% Retirement Savings Contribution Credit, or $500, for her $1,000 IRA contribution.

Example: Anthony works as a cashier at a retail store. He is married and earned $31,000 in wages during the year. Anthony's wife, Jillian, has a part time job at a pet food store. She earned $8,000 in wages. Their wage income is $39,000 ($31,000 + $8,000) *before* making any IRA contributions. Anthony contributes $1,000 to his traditional IRA for 2020, and Jillian contributes $1,000 to her IRA. After deducting their IRA contributions, their adjusted gross income is $37,000 ($39,000 wages - $2,000 IRA contributions). Anthony and Jillian may claim a 50% Saver's Credit ($2,000 contributions x 50% = $1,000 credit). Their allowable credit is $1,000 on their jointly-filed return.[195]

This credit is claimed on Form 8880, *Credit for Qualified Retirement Savings Contributions*.

Credit for Excess Social Security and RRTA Tax Withheld

This credit is for workers who overpay their tax for Social Security, which usually happens when an employee is working two jobs, and both employers withhold Social Security tax. Each year, a limit is set as to how much Social Security tax an individual should have withheld from his earnings.

---

[195] To see the income thresholds and similar examples, see the reference page for the Saver's Credit on the IRS website: https://www.irs.gov/retirement-plans/plan-participant-employee/retirement-savings-contributions-savers-credit.

If the taxpayer's withholding for Social Security tax exceeds the annual maximum he can request a refund of the excess amount (the maximum earnings subject to Social Security tax is $137,700 in 2020). This also applies to overpaid Railroad Retirement taxes. This credit is fully refundable. If a single employer overwithheld too much social security (or RRTA tax), this is an error and the employer should adjust the excess for the taxpayer. If a single employer refuses to refund the over-collection, the taxpayer can file a claim for refund using Form 843, *Claim for Refund and Request for Abatement.*

Example: Zachary is a medical doctor. In 2020, he works for two different hospitals as an employee. His first employer pays him $108,000 in wages during the year. The second hospital pays him $50,000. His total wages were $158,000, and the entire amount was subject to Social Security tax, because each of his employers is required by law to withhold Social Security tax from the entire amount. His total wages exceed the 2020 Social Security contribution limit of $137,700. When Zachary files his tax return, his overpayment of Social Security tax is calculated automatically by his software, by adding up the combined Social Security tax withheld from all his wages. He will receive a credit for any overwithheld amounts.

2020 EIP Payments and Recovery Rebate Credits

To help many taxpayers economically through the COVID-19 pandemic, Congress enacted two Economic Impact Payments (EIP-1 and EIP-2) for millions of taxpayers. These are commonly called "stimulus payments."[196] The maximum EIP amounts were as follows:

- **EIP-1:** $1,200 ($2,400 joint) plus $500 for each dependent eligible for the child tax credit
- **EIP-2:** $600 ($1,200 joint) plus $600 for each dependent eligible for the child tax credit

For the first Economic Impact Payment (EIP-1), eligible individuals with adjusted gross income up to $75,000 for single filers, $112,500 for head of household filers and qualifying widows(ers) and $150,000 for married filing jointly were eligible for the full EIP-1 of $1,200 for individuals and $2,400 for those married and filing jointly. In addition, they were eligible for an additional $500 EIP-1 per qualifying child.

For the second Economic Impact Payment (EIP-2), eligible individuals with adjusted gross income up to $75,000 for single filers, $112,500 for head of household filers and $150,000 for married filing jointly and qualifying widows(ers) were are eligible for this second Economic Impact Payment of $600 for individuals and $1,200 for those married and filing jointly. In addition, they were eligible for an additional $600 payment per qualifying child.

Taxpayers over those amounts have their base credit reduced by 5% of the amount their AGI exceeds these thresholds. Congress decided to advance the credit prior to the filing 2020 tax returns. By the end of 2020, most eligible taxpayers had already received their first EIP (EIP-1). For the first credit, the economic impact payment was based on either the taxpayer's 2018 or 2019 tax return.

[196] These advanced payments of the Recovery Rebate Credit are referred to as the "first EIP" and "second EIP." Economic impact payments are not taxable for federal income tax purposes but will reduce a taxpayer's Recovery Rebate Credit. The only offset that applies to the EIP is unpaid child support. Taxpayers must have an SSN that is valid for employment purposes.

For the second credit, the economic impact payment was based on the taxpayer's 2019 tax return. The taxpayer reconciles the economic impact payments on the 2020 tax return; if the taxpayer is entitled to additional amounts based on 2020, the taxpayer gets them as a refundable credit. If the taxpayer received excess economic impact payments, then the difference does not have to be paid back.

EIPs are technically an advance payment of a new temporary tax credit, the Recovery Rebate Credit, that eligible taxpayers can claim on their 2020 tax returns if they did not receive their Recovery Rebate Credit, in full, through EIPs. Eligible individuals for the EIPs and the Recovery Rebate Credit include any individual taxpayer except for:

- Nonresident aliens
- Dependents
- An Estate or Trust
- Deceased taxpayers

A taxpayer must have a Social Security number that is valid for work purposes, although there is an exception for spouses of active military personnel. If either spouse is an active member of the U.S. Armed Forces at any time during the taxable year, only one spouse needs to have a valid SSN for the couple to receive up to $1,200 for themselves

Example: Sanaya is a U.S. citizen living overseas in Greece. She earned $42,000 in self-employment income in 2019, and $40,000 in self-employment income in 2020. She has one dependent son, who is age 10, who lives with her. Her child is also a U.S. citizen. Sanaya files as head of household, claiming her son as a dependent. She is eligible for a stimulus payment for herself, and she will receive stimulus payments for her child, as well.

Example: Azrah is a U.S. resident alien with a green card and an SSN that is valid for work purposes. She made $32,000 in 2019 and $42,000 in 2020. All of her income was from wages. She is eligible for both EIP payments.

Note: A person who is a qualifying resident alien with an SSN valid for employment is eligible for the payment only if he or she is a qualifying resident alien and may not be claimed as a dependent of another taxpayer. A nonresident alien is not eligible for the EIP payment.

As mentioned previously, these EIPs were *advances* of the 2020 Recovery Rebate Credit. If a taxpayer did not receive their full advanced payment of their Recovery Rebate Credit through both EIPs, based on their 2020 adjusted gross income, they can claim the difference on their 2020 tax returns.

- If eligible, taxpayers may claim an additional credit on their 2020 tax return, for example, if a child was born, adopted, or placed into foster care in the taxpayer's home in 2020.
- Any EIP will not reduce a taxpayer's refund or increase the amount they owe when they file a tax return. The EIP itself is not taxable and therefore should not be included in income on a 2020 return as taxable income.

A summary of the two Economic Impact Payments are as follows:

First Economic Impact Payment (EIP-1)				
Filing Status	**Single/MFS**	**HOH**	**QW**	**MFJ**
Stimulus Payment	$1,200/500*	$1,200/$500	$1,200/$500	$2,400/$500
Full Payment (based on AGI)	up to $75,000	up to $112,500	up to $112,500	up to $150,000
Payment disallowed (if no qualifying children)	AGI of $99,000 or more	AGI of $136,500 or more	AGI of $198,000 or more	AGI of $198,000 or more

*An additional $500 is permitted for each qualifying child (the child must be under 17 years old in tax year 2019). If a child turns 17 in 2020 and the parent(s) receive(s) a stimulus for that child, it does not have to be paid back. The payment amount is reduced by 5% that the taxpayer's AGI is above the Full Payment floor. However, each of these adjusted gross income amounts at which the payment is fully reduced to $0 (the payment disallowed section) increases by $10,000 for each additional qualifying child of the taxpayer.

Second Economic Impact Payment (EIP-2)				
Filing Status	**Single/MFS**	**HOH**	**QW**	**MFJ**
Stimulus Payment	$600/600*	$600/$600	$600/600	$1,200/$600
Full Payment (based on AGI)	up to $75,000	up to $112,500	up to $150,000	up to $150,000
Payment disallowed (if no qualifying children)	above $99,000	AGI of $124,500 or more	AGI of $174,000 or more	AGI of $174,000 or more

*An additional $600 is permitted for each qualifying child (the child must be under 17 years old in tax year 2019). If a child turns 17 in 2020 and the parent(s) receive(s) a stimulus for that child, it does not have to be paid back. The payment amount is reduced by 5% that the taxpayer's AGI is above the Full Payment floor. However, each of these adjusted gross income amounts at which the payment is fully reduced to $0 (the payment disallowed section) increases by $12,000 for each additional qualifying child of the taxpayer.

Unit 13: Study Questions

(Test yourself first; then check the correct answers at the end of this quiz.)

1. Orrin was audited in 2020, and the IRS determined that he claimed the Earned Income Tax Credit erroneously due to reckless disregard of the EITC rules. For how many years is Orrin prohibited from claiming the EITC?

A. None.
B. Two years.
C. Five years.
D. Ten years.

2. Which of the following credits are refundable in 2020?

A. Lifetime Learning Credit.
B. Retirement Savings Contribution Credit.
C. The Additional Child Tax Credit.
D. The Child and Dependent Care Credit.

3. Beatrice has three children, ages 11, 16, and 18, who live with her. They are all her qualifying children and full-time students. Assuming she meets the other criteria, what is the maximum Child Tax Credit she can claim on her 2020 tax return?

A. $1,400
B. $2,000
C. $4,000
D. $6,000

4. Which of the following individuals would be a qualifying child for the Child Tax Credit?

A. An 18-year-old dependent who is a full-time student.
B. A six-year-old nephew who lived with the taxpayer for nine months.
C. A step-brother who is 17 years old and disabled.
D. A foster child who has lived with the taxpayer for four months.

5. Which of the following expenses is not a qualified expense for purposes of the Adoption Credit?

A. Court costs.
B. Re-adoption expenses to adopt a foreign child.
C. Attorney fees for a surrogate arrangement.
D. Travel expenses.

6. Danika and Ralph are divorced. They have one child together, Amelie, age 15, who lives with Danika. Amelie is a full-time student at a private high school. All are U.S. citizens and have SSNs. Together, Danika and Ralph provide more than half of Amelie's support, including $10,000 in tuition expenses for Amelie's private high school. Danika's AGI is $31,000, and Ralph's AGI is $39,000. Ralph is the noncustodial parent, but Danika signs Form 8332, giving Ralph the right to claim Amelie on his tax return. Based on this information, which credit might Ralph qualify for if he claims his daughter as a dependent?

A. Earned Income Tax Credit.
B. Adoption Credit.
C. Child Tax Credit.
D. American Opportunity Credit.

7. In 2020, Jonas and Hannah adopt a special-needs child. The child is a U.S. citizen with a valid SSN. Their adoption expenses are $7,000, and their travel expenses related to the adoption are $1,200. What is their maximum Adoption Credit?

A. $0
B. $7,000
C. $8,200
D. $14,300

8. Scott is 43 and unmarried. Scott's half-brother, Jude, turned 16 on December 30, 2020. Jude lived with Scott all year, and he is a U.S. citizen. Scott claimed Jude as a dependent on his return. Which of the following statements is correct?

A. Jude is a qualifying child for the Child Tax Credit.
B. Jude is not a qualifying child for the Child Tax Credit, because he is a sibling.
C. Jude is not a qualifying child for the Child Tax Credit because siblings do not qualify.
D. Jude only qualifies for the Child Tax Credit if he is a full-time student.

9. All of the listed expenses are deductible for the Lifetime Learning Credit except:

A. Required books.
B. Childcare in order to attend class.
C. Tuition.
D. Required fees.

10. The American Opportunity Credit has a maximum credit of up to __________.

A. $2,000 credit per eligible student.
B. $2,500 credit per eligible student.
C. $2,500 credit per tax return.
D. $4,000 credit per eligible student.

11. Rocco has three kids in college. They are all his dependents:

- Cosima, age 21, a college sophomore working on her first bachelor's degree.
- Marico, age 19, a college freshman working on his first bachelor's degree.
- Kasha, age 23, a graduate student, working on her first master's degree. Kasha had a four-year bachelor's degree from the same college.

Based on the above scenario, what is the maximum amount of American Opportunity Tax Credits (AOTC) Rocco can claim on his tax return?

A. $2,500
B. $4,500
C. $5,000
D. $7,500

12. Abigail is 27 and unmarried. Abigail's earned income from wages is $13,900 in 2020. She has qualified dividends of $3,750. She deposits $1,000 into her traditional IRA during the year. She has a valid Social Security number. She does not have any dependents and no other income for the year. Which of the following credits *may* she qualify for in 2020?

A. Earned Income Tax Credit
B. Child Tax Credit
C. Credit for Other Dependents
D. Retirement Savings Contribution Credit

13. Edwin is a professional bookkeeper. He takes an accounting course at the local community college to improve his work-related skills. Edwin is not a degree candidate. Which educational credit does he qualify for?

A. American Opportunity Credit
B. College Saver's Credit
C. Lifetime Learning Credit
D. General Education Credit

14. To qualify for the Earned Income Tax Credit, which of the following statements is correct?

A. The taxpayer must have a dependent child.
B. The taxpayer must be a U.S. citizen or legal U.S. resident all year.
C. The taxpayer's filing status can be MFS or MFJ.
D. The taxpayer's only income can be from Social Security benefits.

15. Aaron pays for daycare costs for the following individuals so he can work. Each is a qualifying individual for purposes of the Child and Dependent Care Credit *except*:

A. Aaron's wife, who is completely disabled.
B. Aaron's son, Cameron, age 15, who is a full-time student, and not disabled.
C. Aaron's nephew, Andy, age 10, who is also his dependent.
D. Aaron's mother, Polly, who is 72, and is permanently disabled.

16. Vincent has two children in graduate school. His wife, Olivia, also attends a graduate program at a local university. Vincent and his wife file jointly. What is the maximum amount of the Lifetime Learning Credit that Vincent and Olivia can claim on their joint return?

A. $2,000
B. $2,500
C. $4,000
D. $6,000

17. Which of the following education tax benefits listed below is partially refundable?

A. Tuition and Fees deduction
B. American Opportunity Credit
C. Lifetime Learning Credit
D. Student Loan Interest Deduction

18. For purposes of the EITC, which of the following types of income is considered earned income?

A. Taxable alimony
B. Interest and dividends
C. Capital gains
D. Household employee income

19. Generally, which is most beneficial to taxpayers when it comes to reducing income tax liability: a nonrefundable credit, a refundable credit, or a deduction?

A. A nonrefundable tax credit.
B. A refundable tax credit.
C. A tax deduction.
D. All are equally beneficial in reducing income tax liability.

20. Zoe attends college full-time, pursuing an undergraduate degree in architecture. Because she changed majors in her junior year, she is now in her fifth year of college. She received a $4,000 Pell grant for 2020, and her parents have claimed the American Opportunity Credit for Zoe the past four years. What amount can they claim for the AOC in 2020 based upon the following expenses for Zoe?

Tuition	$15,000
Room and board	12,000
Required Student Health Fees	1,000

A. $0
B. $2,500
C. $2,000
D. $11,000

21. Which of the following individuals is eligible for the American Opportunity Tax Credit?

A. Garrett, who is enrolled full-time as a graduate student pursuing a master's degree in biology after having completed a four year undergraduate degree.
B. Lucy, who is taking a ceramics class at a community college for fun.
C. Douglas, who is a full-time undergraduate student and was convicted of a felony for distribution of cocaine.
D. Bethany, who is a college freshman pursuing an undergraduate degree in computer science, and who attended classes half-time the entire school year.

22. Which of the following filing conditions would prevent an individual from qualifying for the Earned Income Tax Credit?

A. MFS filing status.
B. A taxpayer with nontaxable combat pay.
C. Investment income of $3,000.
D. A taxpayer who is 68 years old with one qualifying child.

23. All of the following are qualified expenses for purposes of the Child and Dependent Care Credit except:

A. A $500 payment to a grandparent for child care while the taxpayer is employed.
B. A $300 payment to a daycare center while the taxpayer is looking for employment.
C. A $500 child care expense while the taxpayer obtains medical care.
D. A $600 adult daycare expense for a disabled spouse while the taxpayer works.

24. Orlando is a university senior studying to be an optometrist. Which of the following expenses is a qualifying expense for the American Opportunity Tax Credit?

A. Mandatory equipment rental
B. Student health fees
C. Room and board
D. A physical education course unrelated to his program

Unit 13: Quiz Answers

1. The answer is B. Orrin cannot claim the EITC for two tax years. There are restrictions on EITC claims by taxpayers for whom a previous claim was denied or reduced due to any reason other than a math or clerical error. If a taxpayer was determined to have claimed the EITC due to reckless or intentional disregard of the EITC rules, he cannot claim the EITC for two tax years. If the error was due to fraud, the taxpayer cannot claim the EITC for ten tax years.

2. The answer is C. The Additional Child Tax Credit is refundable, meaning it can result in a refund even if a taxpayer does not owe tax.

3. The answer is C. Beatrice can claim $4,000 as a maximum Child Tax Credit, or $2,000 for each qualifying child. For purposes of this credit, she only has two qualifying children, because one of her dependents is already over 17 and, therefore, no longer eligible for the credit.

4. The answer is B. A nephew who lived with the taxpayer for nine months may qualify. In order to qualify for the Child Tax Credit, the taxpayer must have a qualifying child who lived with him for more than six months and who is *under* the age of 17. Answer "A" and "C" are both incorrect because the children are not *under* the age of 17. Answer "D" is incorrect because the foster child only lived with the taxpayer for four months.

5. The answer is C. Expenses related to a surrogate arrangement are not a qualified adoption expense. Qualified adoption expenses are expenses directly related to the legal adoption of an eligible child. These expenses include adoption fees, court costs, attorney fees, travel expenses (including amounts spent for meals and lodging) while away from home, and re-adoption expenses to adopt a foreign child.

6. The answer is C. Ralph, the noncustodial parent, can claim the Child Tax Credit if Danika signs Form 8332. He cannot claim the Earned Income Tax Credit because he is not the custodial parent. He cannot claim the Adoption Credit because the Adoption Credit is only for qualified adoption expenses. He cannot claim the American Opportunity Credit, because the credit only applies to expenses incurred for postsecondary education (i.e., college expenses, not private school tuition for K-12 students, and Amelie is a high school student).

7. The answer is D. Jonas and Hannah can take the full Adoption Credit of $14,300 in 2020 because they adopted a special needs child. Under a special rule for taxpayers who adopt special needs children, the maximum Adoption Credit is allowed, even if the taxpayer has a lesser amount of adoption expenses.

8. The answer is A. Jude is a qualifying child for the Child Tax Credit because he was *under* age 17 at the end of the year. Siblings can be qualifying children for purposes of this credit, and half-siblings are treated the same as full siblings for tax purposes.

9. The answer is B. Childcare is not a qualifying education expense, even if the childcare is offered on-campus. For purposes of the Lifetime Learning Credit, qualified education expenses are tuition

and certain related expenses required for enrollment or attendance at an eligible educational institution.

10. The answer is B. The American Opportunity Tax Credit is worth up to $2,500 per eligible student. The maximum credit equals 100% of the first $2,000 and 25% of the next $2,000 of qualified expenses.

11. The answer is C. The American Opportunity Tax Credit is worth up to $2,500 *per qualifying student.* Rocco can potentially claim $5,000 in AOC credits on his tax return ($2,500 each for Cosima and Marico). Cosima and Marico would be qualifying students for AOC purposes because they are working on their first undergraduate degree. Kasha would not qualify, because she is working on a graduate degree after having completed a four-year undergraduate degree. The American Opportunity Credit is only available for four years of postsecondary school. Kasha's educational expenses may be eligible for the Lifetime Learning Credit, however.

12. The answer is D. She may qualify for the Retirement Savings Contribution Credit (also called the Saver's Credit). Abigail does not qualify for the Earned Income Tax Credit because her investment income (the qualified dividends) exceeds $3,650 in 2020. She does not qualify for the Child Tax Credit or Credit for Other Dependents because she does not have a qualifying child.

13. The answer is C. Edwin qualifies for the Lifetime Learning Credit. He does not qualify for the American Opportunity Credit because he is not a degree candidate and because his course does not meet the requirements. The "College Saver's Credit" and the "General Education Credit" do not exist.

14. The answer is B. The taxpayer must be a U.S. citizen or legal U.S. resident all year. A taxpayer cannot claim the EITC if his filing status is MFS. Taxpayers do not need to have a dependent child to qualify for the Earned Income Tax Credit. However, the amount of the credit is greatly increased if the taxpayer has a qualifying child. A taxpayer must have earned income to qualify for the EITC; Social Security benefits do not qualify.

15. The answer is B. Aaron's son, Cameron, does not qualify because he is over the age limit for the credit. To qualify for the Child and Dependent Care Credit, the dependent must be *under* the age of 13 (or disabled).

16. The answer is A. Vincent and Olivia can claim a maximum credit of $2,000 on their joint tax return. The Lifetime Learning Credit is allowed for 20% of the first $10,000 of qualified tuition and fees paid during the year. The credit is per tax return, not per student, so only a maximum of $2,000 can be claimed each year, no matter how many qualifying students a taxpayer may have.

17. The answer is B. Up to 40% of the American Opportunity Tax Credit is refundable, meaning that the taxpayer can receive a refund even if they have zero tax liability.

18. The answer is D. Household employee income is considered earned income because it is a type of wage. Alimony, workfare payments, and interest and dividends are not considered earned income for purposes of the EITC.

19. The answer is B. A refundable credit, such as the Earned Income Tax Credit, is not limited by an individual's tax liability. The taxpayer can receive a refund even if he has zero tax liability.

20. The answer is A. Zoe does not qualify for the AOC because she is in her fifth year of college, and her parents have already claimed the credit the prior four years. If she had been eligible for the credit, she would have had $11,000 of qualifying expenses. Room and board and student health fees are not qualifying expenses for the AOC, and the qualifying tuition cost must be reduced by any tax-free scholarships, such as the Pell grant. The AOC is a maximum credit of $2,500 per student (100% of the first $2,000 of eligible expenses and 25% of the next $2,000). Zoe qualifies for the Lifetime Learning Credit.

21. The answer is D. Bethany is eligible for the American Opportunity Tax Credit because she is pursuing a degree and is enrolled at least half-time for at least one academic period during the year. Answer "A" is incorrect, because graduate students do not qualify because the AOTC is a credit for qualified education expenses paid for an eligible student only for the first <u>four years</u> of higher education. Answer "B" is incorrect because courses that do not lead to a degree, certificate, or other recognized credential do not qualify for the AOTC. Answer "C" is incorrect because students with felony drug convictions are ineligible for this credit.

22. The answer is A. Taxpayers cannot claim the EITC if they file Married Filing Separately. All the other choices would not disqualify a taxpayer from claiming EITC. Combat pay is considered qualifying income for EITC purposes. The investment income threshold for EITC in 2020 is $3,650. A taxpayer who is 68 years old may be eligible for EITC if they have a qualifying child.

23. The answer is C. Childcare costs to obtain medical care are not a deductible expense. Deductible costs must be "work-related" and for a child under 13, a disabled dependent, or a disabled spouse of any age. Childcare costs incurred so that the taxpayer can volunteer, obtain medical care, run errands, or do other personal businesses do not qualify.

24. The answer is A. Because Orlando's equipment rental fee is mandatory, it is considered a qualified related expense. For AOTC purposes, "qualified education expenses" do not include insurance or medical expenses (such as student health fees), room and board, transportation, or similar personal, living, or family expenses, or any course of instruction or other education involving sports, games, or hobbies, unless the course is part of the student's degree program.

Unit 14: The ACA and the Premium Tax Credit

For additional information, read:
Publication 5187, *Health Care Law: What's New for Individuals & Families*
Publication 974, *Premium Tax Credit (PTC)*

The Affordable Care Act[197] is a comprehensive health care reform law first enacted in March 2010 (it is sometimes also known as the ACA or "Obamacare"). The Affordable Care Act tax provisions are administered by the IRS.

Congress permanently eliminated the penalty under the Affordable Care Act's individual mandate (i.e., the penalty for an individual for failing to maintain minimum essential coverage, or MEC).[198] However, even though the individual healthcare penalty has been reduced to $0, many Marketplace provisions are still active, and taxpayers can still purchase health insurance through the Marketplace and receive the Premium Tax Credit, which is designed to cover a percentage of their health insurance costs.

Also, the two taxes that were instituted to help fund the ACA (the Additional Medicare Tax and the Net Investment Income Tax), were not repealed.

Note: In this book, we will cover the ACA from the individual taxpayer's perspective. The ACA from the *employer's* perspective is covered in detail in Book 2, *Businesses*. All of the employer-shared responsibility provisions remain in place, which means that employers must still offer qualifying health coverage to their employees or face the prospect of severe excise penalties.

Important Forms

In order to simplify employer reporting, the IRS has created a group of forms to help handle some of the requirements of the ACA. If the taxpayer is covered by health insurance, he will most likely receive one of the forms listed below. The taxpayer must use the information from these statements when preparing his taxes. The forms are provided to different groups of people.

- **Form 1095-A**, *Health Insurance Marketplace Statement:* This form is for individuals who enroll in Marketplace[199] coverage. This form reports basic information about the insurance company that issued the taxpayer's policy, the exchange where he enrolled, and it documents the taxpayer's coverage for each month.
- **Form 1095-B,** *Health Coverage:* This is for employees or taxpayers whose insurance comes from a source other than the Marketplace.
- **Form 1095-C,** *Employer-Provided Health Insurance Offer and Coverage*: Individuals who work for applicable large employers will typically get this form (employees will also get this form if they enroll in self-insured coverage provided by an applicable large employer).

[197]Although commonly known as Obamacare, the actual name of the health care law is the "Patient Protection and Affordable Care Act," often shortened to the Affordable Care Act or ACA.

[198] Some states now have their own individual health insurance mandate, requiring taxpayers to have qualifying health coverage or pay a fee with the state for the 2020 plan year.

[199] The "Marketplace," also called the "Health Insurance Marketplace," is an online resource where taxpayers can learn about their health coverage options and sign up for health insurance.

Some taxpayers will receive multiple forms in the same year. For example, if a taxpayer purchased health insurance through the Healthcare Marketplace at the beginning of the year, and then started a new job in the middle of the year that offered health coverage, the taxpayer may receive both Forms 1095-B and 1095-C.

Premium Tax Credit

The Premium Tax Credit is a refundable federal tax credit to help eligible taxpayers pay for health insurance premiums. The credit is based on a taxpayer's income and is only available for taxpayers who purchased their insurance through a federal or state healthcare exchange. There are two ways to get the Premium Tax Credit:

1. If the taxpayer qualifies for *advance* payments of the Premium Tax Credit, they can choose to have the amounts paid directly to the insurance provider to help cover their monthly insurance premiums. This is also called the "Advance Premium Tax Credit" (APTC) because the taxpayers receive the credit in advance in order to lower their monthly health insurance premiums.
2. The taxpayer can also choose to pay full price for their insurance through the Marketplace, then receive the PTC as a refundable credit on their individual tax return.

The amount of the Premium Tax Credit is based on a sliding scale, so the higher the household income, the lower the amount of the credit.

> **Note:** The Premium Tax Credit is *only available* to taxpayers who purchase their insurance from the federal exchange (i.e., the "Marketplace");[200] it is *not* available to taxpayers who obtain insurance through their employer.

To be eligible for a Premium Tax Credit or the Advance Premium Tax Credit, a taxpayer must generally meet all of the following requirements:

- Purchase health insurance through the Marketplace,
- Be a U.S. citizen or legal U.S. resident,
- Be unable to get coverage from an employer or the government (i.e., cannot be enrolled in Medicare, Tricare, Medical, or Medicaid),
- Not be claimed as a dependent on anyone else's tax return,
- If married, the couple must generally file a joint tax return.[201] In general, taxpayers who file separate returns will not qualify for the credit, although there are some exceptions.
- The taxpayer must meet certain household income requirements. Household income must be at least 100%, but not more than 400%, of the federal poverty line for the family size. For purposes of the Premium Tax Credit, a taxpayer's household income is the total of the taxpayer's modified adjusted gross income (MAGI), the taxpayer's spouse's MAGI (if filing jointly), and the MAGI of all dependents required to file a federal income tax return.

---

[200] The Health Insurance Marketplace, also called simply the Marketplace, is the place where you will find information about private health insurance options, purchase health insurance, and obtain help with premiums and out-of-pocket costs if you are eligible. The Department of Health and Human Services (HHS) administers the requirements for the Marketplace and the health plans offered.

[201] In the case of married taxpayers who file separately (MFS), certain eligibility exceptions to the Premium Tax Credit apply, such as for domestic abuse or spousal abandonment.

Example: Hendrik and Vidalia are married and file jointly. They have two dependent children. Vidalia works part-time and does not receive health insurance through her employer. Hendrik was unemployed for several months during 2020 before starting a new job in April. His employer-sponsored health insurance started on May 1, 2020. From January through April, the family purchased health insurance through the federal exchange (the Marketplace). Assuming they meet the income guidelines, Hendrik and Vidalia can claim the Premium Tax Credit for the four months that they had Marketplace coverage.

Advance Premium Tax Credit and Repayments

When a taxpayer first applies for a Marketplace plan, the amount of the credit is estimated using information the taxpayer provides about family size and projected household income. Since it can be difficult to know exactly how much income a taxpayer will earn in a given year and family circumstances can change during the year, the actual amount of the credit can vary from the estimated amount.

Note: A taxpayer who chose Advance Premium Tax Credit (APTC) payments *must* file a tax return, in order to reconcile the advance credit payments with the actual Premium Tax Credit earned. This is called "reconciling" the advance payments of the Premium Tax Credit and the actual Premium Tax Credit the taxpayer actually qualifies for based on their annual income. This reconciliation is calculated on Form 8962, *Premium Tax Credit.*

If at the end of the year, the taxpayer has taken more Premium Tax Credit in advance than they are due based on their final income, the taxpayer will have to pay back the excess when they file their federal tax return. If the taxpayer is under 400% of the federal poverty line, then the amount that must be paid back on the tax return is subject to a maximum cap.

Note: The *American Rescue Plan Act (ARPA)*, passed on March 11, 2021, retroactively waived the payback for the advanced premium tax credit (APTC). In 2020, no repayment is required for taxpayers receiving excess advance PTCs. Since this was a retroactive change passed after December 31, 2020, the APTC repayment is still covered in this book.

If the taxpayer has taken less than they qualify for, they will get the difference back as a refundable credit when they file their tax return.

Changes in family size due to marriage, death, divorce, birth, or adoption can affect the amount of the credit. A taxpayer is supposed to report changes in circumstances to the Marketplace so the amount of the advance credit payments can be recalculated during the year. A taxpayer should also report changes in eligibility for government-sponsored or employer-sponsored health coverage, a move to a new address, an increase or decrease in the number of dependents, and other factors that may affect eligibility for the Premium Tax Credit.

Although the IRS is restricted in its ability to collect the shared responsibility payment, the agency may use full collection actions, including levies and liens, against a taxpayer who does not repay excess advance premium tax credits.

Note: Remember, the Premium Tax Credit is a *refundable credit.* If the amount of the credit is more than the amount of the tax liability of the return, a taxpayer may receive the difference as a refund. If no tax is owed, a taxpayer can receive the full amount of the credit as a refund.

Example: Mariano is self-employed, and his income varies from year to year. When he enrolled in a health insurance plan through his state exchange, he estimated his 2020 earnings based on his prior year income. He learned he was eligible for the Premium Tax Credit, which he chose to take in full as advance credit payments. Mariano's business did better than he expected in 2020, and he made substantially more money than the prior year, and his actual household income did not meet the guidelines for the Premium Tax Credit. He reconciles the advance credit payment amounts on Form 8962 and discovers he received a benefit of $4,000 in payments for which he is no longer eligible. Mariano is not owed a refund, so he must enter $4,000 on the excess advance premium tax credit repayment on Schedule 2 of his Form 1040. The repayment amount is added to his overall tax liability.

Example: Adela was enrolled in a qualified health plan through the Marketplace. She turned 65 on July 1, 2020, and became eligible for Medicare. Adela applied to Medicare in September and became eligible to receive Medicare benefits beginning on December 1, 2020. Adela can get the Premium Tax Credit for her coverage in the qualified health plan for January through November. Beginning in December, Adela cannot get the Premium Tax Credit for her coverage in the qualified health plan because she is eligible for Medicare.

Net Investment Income Tax (NIIT)

The Affordable Care Act imposes a Net Investment Income Tax (also called the "NIIT") on higher-income taxpayers. The tax applies to individuals, estates, and trusts. For individuals, a 3.8% tax is imposed on the lesser of:

- The individual's net investment income for the year, or
- Any excess of the individual's modified adjusted gross income for the tax year over the following thresholds:

Filing Status	Threshold Amounts
MFJ or QW	$250,000
MFS	$125,000
Single or HOH	$200,000

These threshold amounts are not indexed for inflation for each year. The NIIT is imposed only on U.S. citizens and resident aliens; nonresident aliens are not subject to the NIIT. Net investment income that is subject to the tax includes:

- Interest income, unless it is otherwise tax-exempt, (like municipal bonds),
- Dividends and capital gains,
- Rental and royalty income (if passive),
- Nonqualified annuities,
- Income from trading of financial instruments or commodities,
- Income from businesses that are passive activities for the taxpayer (such as a limited partnership).

Net investment income does not include earned income or pension income. The NIIT does not apply to: wages, self-employment income, Social Security benefits, veterans' benefits, unemployment compensation, taxable alimony payments, or distributions from IRAs or certain qualified retirement plans. To the extent that gains are not otherwise offset by capital losses, the following are common examples of items included in computing net investment income:

- Capital gains from the sale of stocks, bonds, and mutual funds,
- Capital gain distributions from mutual funds,
- Gains from the sale of real estate,
- Gains from the sale of interests in partnerships and S corporations, to the extent the partner or shareholder was a passive owner.

Example: Patten is single and earned a salary of $175,000 in 2020. He also had $15,000 of income from dividends and capital gains for a total MAGI of $190,000. This amount is less than the $200,000 threshold for single filers, so Patten is not subject to the Net Investment Income Tax.

Example: Rosalind is single and earned a salary of $175,000 in 2020. She also received $80,000 of dividend income, for a total MAGI of $255,000, which exceeds the threshold for single filers by $55,000. The Net Investment Income Tax is based on the *lesser* of $55,000 (the amount by which her MAGI exceeds the threshold for single filers) or $80,000 (her total "net investment income"). Rosalind owes NIIT of $2,090 ($55,000 × 3.8% = $2,090).

The NIIT does not apply to any gains or investment income that is excluded from gross income for regular income tax purposes. For example, municipal bond interest is exempt from federal tax, so it is not included in the calculation for the NIIT.

Example: Perrin files head of household. In 2020, Perrin has $395,000 of wage income and $40,000 of interest income. All of his interest income is from municipal bonds. Although his total income is $435,000 for the year, he is not subject to the NIIT, because all of his investment income is from tax-exempt municipal bonds.

Additionally, net investment income does not include any gain on the sale of a personal residence that is excluded from gross income (such as the Section 121 exclusion on the sale of a main home).

Example: Deborah is single. She earns $45,000 in wages during the year. In 2020, and sells her main home that she has owned and lived in for the last 10 years. The sale price was $1 million, and Deborah's cost basis in the home was $600,000. She is allowed to exclude $250,000 of the gain under section 121. $1,000,000 sales price - $600,000 basis = $400,000 realized gain

$400,000 - $250,000 section 121 exclusion = $150,000 *recognized* gain

$45,000 wages + $150,000 recognized gain = **$195,000 MAGI**

After subtracting her allowable exclusions, her modified adjusted gross income is $195,000, which is below the threshold amount of $200,000, so she does not owe any Net Investment Income Tax.[202]

---

[202] Based directly on examples from IRS guidance: https://www.irs.gov/newsroom/questions-and-answers-on-the-net-investment-income-tax.

A gain from the sale of a second home or a vacation home would not be eligible for section 121 exclusion and therefore, would be fully subject to the NIIT.

Example: Brandon and Christine are married and file jointly. Brandon earns $75,000 in wages for the year, and Christine does not have any earned income. In 2020, Brandon and Christine also have $225,000 of capital gains from the sale of a vacation home. After adding in the wages from Brandon's job, their joint modified adjusted gross income is $300,000 ($75,000 wages + $225,000 in capital gains). Their MAGI exceeds the threshold amount by $50,000 (the threshold is $250,000 for joint filers). Brandon and Christine are subject to NIIT on the *lesser* of $225,000 (their Net Investment Income) or $50,000 (the amount of their modified adjusted gross income that exceeds the $250,000 MFJ threshold). Brandon and Christine owe Net Investment Income Tax of $1,900 ($50,000 X 3.8%).

Example: Todd is unmarried and earns $180,000 of wages in 2020. He also earned $90,000 in capital gains from the sale of a plot of land. Todd's modified adjusted gross income is $270,000 ($180,000 + $90,000). Todd's modified adjusted gross income exceeds the threshold of $200,000, so he must calculate his Net Investment Income Tax. Todd's investment income is $90,000 for the year (the dividends). His NIIT is based on the *lesser* of $70,000 (the amount that Todd's modified adjusted gross income exceeds the $200,000 threshold) or $90,000 (his investment income). Todd owes NIIT of $2,660 ($70,000 x 3.8%).[203]

Investment interest *expense* can be deducted to determine gross investment income, which is used to arrive at net investment income.

The NIIT is subject to estimated tax provisions, so taxpayers may need to adjust their withholding or estimated payments to avoid underpayment penalties. Employers are not required to withhold the NIIT from an employee's wages, but an employee can choose to increase their annual withholding to cover the NIIT. Individuals, estates, and trusts must compute the tax on Form 8960, *Net Investment Tax.*

Example: Aster, a single filer, typically earns $200,000 in wages during the year. His wages are not subject to the NIIT. However, he has plans to sell a large block of cryptocurrency at the end of the year, and he knows that his normal withholding will not cover the additional tax from the cryptocurrency sale. Aster requests that his employer increase his withholding by filling out a new Form W-4, *Employee's Withholding Certificate.* This way, additional taxes will be taken out with each paycheck. Aster can also choose to make estimated payments directly to the IRS to cover the additional taxes.

Additional Medicare Tax

The Additional Medicare Tax was legislated as part of the Affordable Care Act, and has been in effect since 2013. The tax only applies to *earned* income, like wages. The Additional Medicare Tax is withheld at a rate of 0.9% and computed on Form 8959, *Additional Medicare Tax.*

---

[203] Example modified from the IRS website: "Questions and Answers on the Net Investment Income Tax" https://www.irs.gov/newsroom/questions-and-answers-on-the-net-investment-income-tax.

The tax is assessed only on earned income in excess of the following thresholds:

Filing Status	Threshold Amounts
MFJ	$250,000
MFS	$125,000
Single, HOH, or QW	$200,000

A taxpayer's earned income (including wages, taxable fringe benefits, bonuses, tips, commissions, and self-employment income) that is subject to regular Medicare tax is also subject to the Additional Medicare Tax to the extent it exceeds the applicable threshold amount for his or her filing status.

Unlike regular Medicare taxes, there is no "employer share" of the Additional Medicare Tax. Self-employed taxpayers also cannot deduct one-half of the 0.9% Additional Medicare Tax. It is imposed entirely on the employee (or the self-employed taxpayer).

Example: Sasha is unmarried and files single. She earns $130,000 in self-employment income and $23,000 in wages during the year. Sasha is not liable for the Additional Medicare Tax because her combined self-employment income and wages is less than the $200,000 threshold for single filers.

Filing status determines the threshold amount. For those who are married and file a joint return, they must combine the wages, compensation, or self-employment income of their spouse with their own. These thresholds are not adjusted for inflation.

Extended Example #1: Regan is single and earned $145,000 of salary in 2020. Because his earnings are below the $200,000 threshold for single filers, his company did not withhold any amount for the Additional Medicare Tax. He also had $85,000 of self-employment income from a side job as a web designer. Regan's total earned income is $230,000, so he will be required to pay Additional Medicare Tax on the $30,000 of earned income that exceeds the $200,000 threshold. Regan will owe $270 in Additional Medicare Tax on his 2020 income tax return ($30,000 × 0.9% = $270). He must calculate the tax and attach Form 8959, *Additional Medicare Tax*, to his tax return.

Extended Example #2: Regan gets married on December 31, 2020, to Patty, who earned wages of $7,000 during the year. Because they are married as of the last day of the year and file jointly, their threshold for the Additional Medicare Tax is now $250,000. Their combined earned income is now $237,000, which is below the $250,000 threshold for MFJ. Regan and Patty do not owe the Additional Medicare Tax.

An employer is required to withhold the Additional Medicare Tax if an employee is paid more than $200,000, regardless of an employee's filing status or whether the employee has wages paid by another employer. A taxpayer may be subject to the Additional Medicare Tax even if amounts are not withheld from his wages.

Example: Stanley and Ophelia are married and file jointly. Stanley earned $120,000 of salary in 2020, and Ophelia earned $190,000. Their employers do not withhold amounts for the Additional Medicare Tax because neither earned wages above $200,000. However, their combined earned income is $310,000, which exceeds the $250,000 threshold for joint filers by $60,000. Stanley and Ophelia will owe $540 of Additional Medicare Tax on their income tax return ($60,000 × 0.9% = $540). They must calculate the tax and attach Form 8959, *Additional Medicare Tax*, to their tax return.

Example: Naomi is single. She earns $350,000 in wages during the year. The additional 0.9% tax will be calculated on her earnings above $200,000. This means that $150,000 will be subject to Additional Medicare Tax ($350,000 wages - $200,000 threshold amount). She will pay $1,350 in Additional Medicare Tax on her tax return ($150,000 x 0.9% = $1,350). This additional tax will be withheld from Naomi's wages automatically by her employer.

If an employer withholds amounts for an employee who earns more than $200,000, but the employee and his spouse's combined earnings are *less* than the $250,000 MFJ threshold, they can apply the overpayment against any other type of tax that may be owed on their income tax return.

Example: Herman and Katherine are married and file jointly. Herman makes $225,000 in wages during the year. Herman's employer is required by law to withhold the Additional Medicare Tax on Herman's wages (because he earns more than the $200,000 threshold for when mandatory withholding is necessary). Katherine has a small part-time job at a local church. She only earns $8,000 in wages in 2020. When they file their joint return, their combined wages total $233,000, which is under the threshold amount for joint filers. They do not owe the Additional Medicare Tax. This means that the Additional Medicare Tax that was withheld on Herman's paycheck will be treated as an overpayment on their individual return, and will be applied as a credit against any other taxes they might owe for the year.

Unit 14: Study Questions

(Test yourself first, then check the correct answers at the end of this quiz.)

1. Terry and Myriam are married but choose to file separately because of Terry's past-due child support. Their household income for 2020 is at 200% of the federal poverty line. They enroll in the federal Marketplace for health coverage. Which of the following statements is correct?

A. They are not eligible for the Premium Tax Credit because their income is too high.
B. They are not eligible for the Premium Tax Credit because of their filing status.
C. They will owe a shared responsibility payment.
D. They are eligible for the Advance Premium Tax Credit.

2. Which of the following taxpayers would be subject to the Additional Medicare Tax?

A. Randy, who files as HOH and earned $180,000 of wages and $50,000 of interest income.
B. Kerrie, who is single and earned $196,000 of wages, taxable fringe benefits, and bonuses.
C. Lizzie, who files separately from her husband and earned $140,000 of wages.
D. Adley, who is a qualifying widower and has $200,000 in wages.

3. Which of the following would not be subject to the net investment income tax (NIIT)?

A. An estate of a deceased taxpayer.
B. A nonresident alien.
C. A trust.
D. An individual with only rental income.

4. Which of the following individuals would be eligible for the Premium Tax Credit, assuming they meet the applicable income guidelines?

A. Bowie, who had minimum essential coverage through his employer.
B. Zhavia, who was enrolled for two months through the federal Marketplace.
C. Imran, who received Medicaid coverage for twelve months of the year.
D. Peyton, who is a full-time U.S. military officer.

5. The Additional Medicare Tax is:

A. 0.9% on a taxpayer's earned income above a certain threshold.
B. 3.8% on a taxpayer's earned income above a certain threshold.
C. 0.9% on a taxpayer's investment income above a certain threshold.
D. 3.8% on a taxpayer's investment income above a certain threshold.

6. The Premium Tax Credit is:

A. A nonrefundable credit.
B. A refundable credit.
C. Available to all taxpayers with Marketplace insurance.
D. Available to all taxpayers with any health insurance.

7. Kyong enrolled in the federal Marketplace for 2020 to obtain health insurance. She estimated her household income for the year, qualified for the Premium Tax Credit, and chose to have half of the expected credit paid in advance to her insurance company. What must Kyong do when she files her income tax return?

A. She must repay half of the credit that she received in advance.
B. She will not owe any additional tax but may be eligible for a larger amount of the credit.
C. She must reconcile the advance premium tax credit payments with the actual Premium Tax Credit that she calculates on Form 8962. Any excess amount will be counted as household income and used to project her credit for the next year.
D. She must reconcile the advance premium tax credit payments with the actual Premium Tax Credit she calculates on Form 8962. She may receive a refund, or she may have to repay any excess advance premium tax credit payments, depending on her individual situation.

8. Emilee is single. She has the following income in 2020:

- $50,000 in capital gains from the sale of stock.
- $40,000 in passive royalty income.
- $20,000 in municipal bond interest.
- $170,000 of self-employment income.

Calculate her net investment income tax, if any.

A. $0
B. $2,280
C. $3,420
D. $4,180

9. Adrienne and Konnor are married and file jointly. Adrienne has $133,000 of self-employment income. Konnor earned $184,000 in wages. Compute the amount of their Additional Medicare Tax, if any.

A. $0
B. $603
C. $1,053
D. $2,853

10. If a taxpayer purchases insurance from the Marketplace, and then underestimates their income and receives the Advance Premium Tax Credit, what is the threshold where a full repayment of the excess credit will have to be repaid?

A. 250% or more of the applicable federal poverty line.
B. 300% or more of the applicable federal poverty line.
C. 400% or more of the applicable federal poverty line.
D. There is no threshold where the excess credit has to be repaid.

Unit 14: Quiz Answers

1. The answer is B. Terry and Myriam are not eligible for the Premium Tax Credit because they file separate returns. Unless one of a limited number of exceptions applies,[204] a married couple cannot claim the Premium Tax Credit unless they file jointly.

2. The answer is C. The Additional Medicare Tax is applied to MFS taxpayers whose earned income exceeds $125,000. Lizzie will owe an additional 0.9% tax on the $15,000 of earned income that exceeds the $125,000 threshold ($15,000 × .009 = $135 Additional Medicare Tax).

3. The answer is B. A nonresident alien would not be subject to the net investment income tax (NIIT). The net investment income tax applies to individuals, estates, and trusts. Only U.S. citizens and U.S. residents are subject to the tax.

4. The answer is B. Zhavia would be the only taxpayer who would be eligible, because she is the only one who had coverage from the Marketplace. Answer "A" is incorrect, because a taxpayer enrolled in an employer-sponsored plan is not eligible for the Premium Tax Credit. Answer "C" and "D" are incorrect, because a taxpayer who receives coverage through Medicaid, Medicare, or other government health plans (such as military coverage) *outside* of the Marketplace are not eligible for the PTC.

5. The answer is A. The Additional Medicare Tax applies to 0.9% of a taxpayer's earned income above a threshold based on his filing status. For single, head of household, and qualifying widow(er) filers, the threshold is $200,000. For married couples filing jointly, the amount is $250,000. For married couples filing separately, the amount is $125,000.

6. The answer is B. The Premium Tax Credit is refundable, meaning that a taxpayer may be able to receive the full amount of credit as a refund, assuming he has no other tax liability. The PTC is available only to a taxpayer, his spouse, or his dependents that had health coverage through a federal or state exchange (i.e., the Healthcare Marketplace) for all or part of the year.

7. The answer is D. Kyong must do a monthly calculation to determine the actual amount of her PTC, which must then be reconciled with the advance premium tax credits paid to her insurer to lower her premium payments. Kyong must enter the amount of any excess advance premium tax credit payments made on her behalf on her return and normally repay the excess. Any taxpayer who claims the Premium Tax Credit (whether advance credit payments were made or not) must file a tax return and include Form 8962, *Premium Tax Credit* (PTC). If there were no excess advance premium tax credit payments and the amount of the PTC is more than the amount of her tax liability, she may receive the difference as a refund.

8. The answer is B. Emilee's modified adjusted gross income is $260,000 (170,000 + $50,000 + $40,000). The municipal bond interest is not included in the calculation, because it is tax-exempt.

---

[204] If a taxpayer is MFS and is eligible for relief from the requirement to file MFJ because of spousal abuse or abandonment, there is a special box on Form 8962 that should be checked. See detailed example here: https://apps.irs.gov/app/vita/content/globalmedia/teacher/premium_tax_credit_form_8962_4012.pdf.

Emilee's modified adjusted gross income exceeds the threshold of $200,000 for single taxpayers by $60,000. Her net investment income is $90,000 ($50,000 + $40,000). Her NIIT is based on the *lesser* of $60,000 (the amount that Taxpayer's modified adjusted gross income exceeds the $200,000 threshold) or $90,000 (Taxpayer's Net Investment Income). Taxpayer owes NIIT of $2,280 ($60,000 x 3.8%).

9. The answer is B. Adrienne and Konnor are subject to the Additional Medicare Tax. Their combined compensation is $317,000, which is $67,000 above the applicable threshold of $250,000 for joint filers. Their Additional Medicare Tax is $603 ($67,000 × 0.9%).

10. The answer is C. If a taxpayer's household income is 400 percent or more of the applicable federal poverty line, the taxpayer will have to repay back all of the excess advance credit payments.

Unit 15: Additional Taxes and Credits

More Reading:
Publication 54, *Tax Guide for U.S. Citizens and Resident Aliens Abroad*
Publication 926, *Household Employer's Tax Guide*
Publication 519, *U.S. Tax Guide for Aliens*
Publication 514, *Foreign Tax Credit for Individuals*
Tax Topic 556, *Alternative Minimum Tax*
Form 5405, *Repayment of the First-Time Homebuyer Credit (Instructions)*

In this unit, we cover a variety of other taxes and credits, including the taxation and reporting of foreign income, the "nanny tax," and the "kiddie tax." We start with a look at the Alternative Minimum Tax (AMT).

Note: Under the Tax Cuts and Jobs Act, the *corporate* alternative minimum tax was repealed. The AMT repeal for corporations is permanent. The TCJA does *not* repeal the AMT for individuals, but it does increase the AMT exemption amount through 2025.

Alternative Minimum Tax

The Alternative Minimum Tax (AMT) gives an alternative set of rules to calculate an individual's taxable income. For this reason, the AMT is sometimes called a "parallel tax" system. Congress adopted the AMT in 1969 in an attempt to ensure that individuals and corporations paid at least a minimum amount of tax.

The TCJA made a number of significant changes to the individual AMT. First, the AMT exemption was increased substantially, and is now indexed for inflation every year. The AMT exemption amounts in 2020 are as follows:

Filing Status	Amount
Single or HOH	$72,900
MFJ or QW	$113,400
MFS	$56,700

This means that taxpayers who have Alternative Minimum Taxable Income (AMTI) below this threshold will not be subject to AMT, regardless of how many tax deductions or credits they may have. However, these AMT exemption amounts are reduced 25 cents for every dollar the taxpayer's AMTI exceeds (for 2020):

2020 AMT Exemption Phaseouts	
Single or HOH	$518,400 to $810,000
MFJ or QW	$1,036,800 to $1,499,400
MFS	$518,400 to $745,200

Certain situations may "trigger" the AMT tax. Some scenarios when a taxpayer may have to pay the AMT tax include:

- Having a high amount of household income and a significant amount of itemized deductions,
- The exercise of incentive stock options,

- A large sale of capital assets, including cryptocurrency, that results in long-term capital gains,
- Tax-exempt interest from private activity bonds.

Individuals compute AMT on Form 6251, *Alternative Minimum Tax, Individuals, Estates, and Trusts.* As described in the preceding units, federal tax law provides special treatment for certain types of income and allows deductions and credits for certain types of expenses. These tax benefits can significantly reduce the regular income tax liabilities for some taxpayers.

AMT "Tax Preference" Items

The AMT *limits* the extent to which deductions and credits can be used to reduce the total amount of income tax paid by higher-income taxpayers. These are called "tax preference" items. When calculating the AMT, many common items considered in the computation of the regular income tax liability are either adjusted downward or eliminated entirely.

Because of the Tax Cuts and Jobs Act, fewer AMT adjustments are required (until 2025, when the changes expire). For taxpayers who itemize, only state and local taxes and foreign income taxes need to be adjusted when figuring alternative minimum taxable income. In addition, the benefits of the following tax preference items may also be eliminated when calculating the AMT:

- Depletion
- Excess intangible drilling costs
- Interest on private activity bonds
- Accelerated depreciation on property placed in service before 1987
- Exclusion of gain on qualified small business stock (QSBS)

The AMT is the excess of the tentative minimum tax over the regular income tax. Thus, the AMT is owed only if the tentative minimum tax is greater than the regular tax. In general, the tentative minimum tax is computed by:

1. Starting with AGI minus itemized deductions, if any, for regular tax purposes,
2. Eliminating or reducing certain adjustments and preferences (the exclusions, deductions, and credits that are allowed in computing the regular tax, such as those mentioned above), to derive alternative minimum taxable income (AMTI),
3. Subtracting the AMT exemption amount,
4. Multiplying the amount computed in (3) by the applicable AMT rate, and
5. Subtracting the AMT Foreign Tax Credit.

The AMT exemption in step 3 is an amount that is deducted from alternative minimum taxable income before calculating the tentative minimum tax. Most tax preparation software will automatically compute whether a taxpayer owes the AMT. If a taxpayer received or claimed any of the following items in the tax year, he is required to complete, but may not necessarily need to file, Form 6251, *Alternative Minimum Tax, Individuals, Estates, and Trusts*:

- Accelerated depreciation
- Stock received through incentive stock options that were not sold in the same year
- Tax-exempt interest from private activity bonds
- Intangible drilling, circulation, research, experimental, or mining costs

- Amortization of pollution-control facilities or depletion
- Income (or loss) from tax-shelter farm activities or passive activities
- Interest from long-term contracts not figured using the percentage-of-completion-method
- Mortgage interest that is not used to: buy, build, or substantially improve a home
- Investment interest expense reported on Form 4952
- Net operating loss deduction
- Alternative minimum tax adjustments from an estate, trust, electing large partnership, or cooperative
- Section 1202 exclusion (gains from qualifying small business stock)
- Any general business credit in Part 1 on Form 3800
- Empowerment zone and renewal community employment credit
- Qualified electric vehicle credit
- Alternative fuel vehicle refueling property credit
- Credit for prior year minimum tax

Credit for Prior Year Minimum Tax

A nonrefundable credit may be available to individuals, estates, and trusts for alternative minimum tax paid in prior years to the extent that a taxpayer's regular tax in the current year is greater than his tentative minimum tax. If applicable, the credit is calculated on Form 8801, *Credit for Prior Year Minimum Tax-Individuals, Estates, and Trusts.*

The AMT is caused by two types of adjustments and preferences: "exclusion" items and "deferral" items. Exclusion items are those that affect only a single tax year and therefore cause a permanent difference between regular taxable income and alternative minimum taxable income (AMTI).

For individual taxpayers, an example of an "exclusion item" is the deduction for state and local income taxes. These taxes are never deductible for AMT purposes, and they are added back into AGI in the calculation of AMTI in the year they are paid. Deferral items are adjustment and preference items, such as depreciation, that affect more than one tax year.

Because they affect the difference between regular taxable income and AMTI in multiple tax years, they generally do not cause a permanent difference in taxable income over time. The minimum tax credit is allowed only for the portion of AMT caused by deferral items, which may generate credit for future years.

Example: Tyson and Stacy are married and file jointly. They are high-income earners, but also have high deductions on Schedule A. They had an AMT liability in the previous year after they exercised some incentive stock options. They use Form 8801 to calculate how much of their AMT was related to that and other deferral items and discover they have a $1,500 AMT credit carryforward. Their regular tax in 2020 is $4,000, and their tentative minimum tax is $3,000. They can use $1,000 of the minimum tax credit carryforward to reduce their regular tax, but they cannot reduce it below the tentative minimum tax amount. The credit balance of $500 can be carried forward to be used in a future year.

Kiddie Tax on Investment Income

Years ago, wealthy families could transfer investments to their minor children and save tax dollars because the investment income would be taxed at the children's lower rates. Congress closed this tax loophole, and now investment income earned by dependent children may be taxed at the parent's rate. This law became known as the "Kiddie Tax."

The Tax Cuts and Jobs Act modified the Kiddie tax, making the investment income earned by minor children taxed using the same tax rates applicable to trusts and estates. This provision proved to be extremely unpopular, and Congress repealed the TCJA change to the Kiddie tax as part of the SECURE Act, which was signed into law on December 20, 2019.

Note: The repeal of the TCJA Kiddie tax changes is effective starting in 2020. However, taxpayers who were affected by the prior-year Kiddie tax changes can amend their prior-year returns and *elect* to apply the new rule to both 2018 and 2019 if it gives them a better tax result.

The kiddie tax does not apply to earned income (such as wages); it applies only to unearned income and investment income, such as interest, dividends, and capital gains distributions. The kiddie tax also applies to unemployment income. Part of a child's investment income may be subject to the Kiddie tax if:

- The child's investment income is more than $2,200 (in 2020).
- The child is a dependent under age 18 or a full-time college student under age 24.
- The child is required to file a tax return for the tax year.
- At least one of the child's parents was alive at the end of the year. If both of the child's parents are deceased, then the kiddie tax does not apply, regardless of how much unearned income the child has.

Note: The kiddie tax does not apply to a child who is married and files a joint return with their spouse. This applies whether the child is a minor under age 18 or a full-time college student under age 24.

Remember: the kiddie tax *only* applies when a dependent child's investment income exceeds $2,200 in 2020. The first $1,100 in investment income is tax-free; the second $1,100 is taxed at the child's marginal rate. If this unearned income threshold is not exceeded, then the kiddie tax does not apply. If this threshold is exceeded, only the child's *unearned* income in excess of the threshold is subject to the kiddie tax.

All of the child's investment income in excess of $2,200 is then taxed at the parent's tax rate. There are two ways to report the kiddie tax.

- **Child's return:** The child can file their own return, and report the tax by attaching Form 8615, Tax for Certain Children Who Have Unearned Income, to their Form 1040. This is the most common method.
- **Parent's return:** Or, the parents can report their child's unearned income on Form 8814, Parent's Election to Report Child's Interest and Dividends, on their Form 1040, rather than having the child file a separate return. In order to use this method, the child can only have income from interest, dividends, or capital gain distributions. If the total income is

$11,000 or more in 2020, the Form 8814 cannot be used, and the child must file his or her own return to report the income that way.

A child's investment income may also be subject to the net investment income tax, which is calculated using only the child's income. However, the NIIT applies only if the child's net investment income exceeds the $200,000 threshold for single filers (this scenario would be very rare, and would only apply if a dependent child had *more* than $200,000 in taxable income).

Example: Rochelle is 16 years old. Both of her parents died in a car accident three years ago, and she inherited a number of investments from them. Rochelle lived with her grandmother, Pearl, all year. Pearl has sole custody of her granddaughter and claims her as a dependent. Rochelle has $5,600 in investment income during the year. Rochelle is not subject to the kiddie tax rules because both of her parents are deceased (i.e., she does not have a living parent). In this case, Rochelle's income would not be subject to the kiddie tax, even if Pearl claims her granddaughter as a dependent on her tax return.

Example: Marcus and Renee have an 11-year-old son named Tony. In 2020, Tony has $2,600 of interest income from a CD his grandfather gave him. Tony does not have any other taxable income. The first $1,100 of investment income is not taxable. The next $1,100 is taxed at the 10% income tax rate, (which is the child's marginal rate). The remaining $400, is subject to the kiddie tax. Tony may file his own tax return and attach Form 8615, or Tony's parents can choose to report his income on their joint return by attaching Form 8814.

First-Time Homebuyer Credit Repayment

First-time homebuyers who claimed a special tax credit in 2008 are required to repay a portion of the funds received over a 15-year period. The First-Time Homebuyer Credit took the form of a loan in 2008, and there are still taxpayers who are repaying that loan on their tax returns. For example, a homebuyer who claimed the maximum credit of $7,500 must repay $500 per year as an additional tax. In 2020, the repayment amount is entered on Schedule 2, Form 1040.

Example: Melinda purchased her home in 2008 and claimed the full amount of the First-Time Homebuyer Credit. She still lives in the home and continues to use it as her main residence. She is required to pay back her credit in equal yearly installments of $500 over a period of 15 years. When she files her 2020 tax return, the repayment is listed on her Form 1040 (Schedule 2, Line 7b) as an additional tax.

A taxpayer who claimed the credit and sells the home (or who no longer maintains it as their primary residence, including a conversion to rental property) must complete Form 5405, *Repayment of the First-Time Homebuyer Credit*. In the case of a sale (including through abandonment or foreclosure), the taxpayer must repay the credit with the tax return for the tax year in which the sale is completed. The following are exceptions to the repayment rule:

- **Involuntary conversion:** If the home is destroyed or condemned, and the taxpayer does not acquire a new home within the 2-year replacement period, the repayment owed with the taxpayer's return for the year in which the 2-year period ends is limited to the gain on the disposition. The amount of the credit in excess of the gain doesn't have to be repaid. If the taxpayer does not have a gain on the involuntary conversion, they do not

have to repay any of the credit, unless they sold the home under threat of condemnation to a related party.

- **Transfers Incident to Divorce:** If the home was transferred to a spouse (or ex-spouse as part of a divorce settlement), the spouse who received the home is responsible for repaying the credit (regardless of whether he or she was the purchaser) if none of the other exceptions apply.
- **The person who claimed the credit dies:** If a person who claimed the credit dies, repayment of the remaining balance of the credit is not required unless the credit was claimed on a joint return. If the credit was claimed on a joint return, then the surviving spouse is required to continue repaying his or her half of the credit (regardless of whether he or she was the purchaser) if none of the other exceptions apply.

Example: Giuliana and Arturo purchased a home together in 2008, and claimed the full amount of the First-Time Homebuyer Credit. They use the home as their primary residence. On December 1, 2020, Arturo dies. Giuliana is required to continue repaying her half of the credit, but Arturo's portion of the credit does not have to be repaid (it is considered forgiven).

The repayment is limited to the amount of gain on the sale if the sale is to an unrelated taxpayer. A similar, $8,000 credit was also available in 2009 and 2010 but did not have to be repaid. A taxpayer who purchased his home and received the credit in either 2009 or 2010 did not have to repay the credit unless he sold the home within a three-year period following the purchase.

Nanny Tax (Tax on Household Employees)

A taxpayer who has household employees may need to pay employment taxes. This obligation is commonly referred to as the "nanny tax" or the tax on Household Employees. A worker is the taxpayer's employee if the taxpayer can control not only what work is done, but how it is done, regardless of whether the work is full-time or part-time; the employee is paid on an hourly, daily, weekly, or per-job basis; or the employee is hired through an agency. Examples of household employees include babysitters, housekeepers, private nurses, yard workers, and private chauffeurs.

A self-employed worker, such as a daycare provider who cares for several children from different families in her own home, is not considered a household employee.

Example: Terrance hires Myah to babysit his three children and do housework in his home. Terrance sets Myah's schedule and gives specific directions about household and childcare duties. Terrance also provides all the equipment and supplies Myah needs to do her work. Myah is Terrance's household employee and subject to the nanny tax rules. Terrance must file a Schedule H.

Example: Yelena runs Sunshine Daycare, an in-home day care. Yelena cares for children from multiple families in her home. Brandon brings his 3-year-old son to Yelena's daycare and pays $600 per month for ongoing daycare. Yelena is not considered Brandon's household employee, because she has her own daycare business.

Example: Wagner hires Jorge to do weekly yard maintenance and cut his grass. Jorge runs a lawn care business and provides gardening services to many other clients. Jorge also advertises his business in the local newspaper. Jorge provides his own tools and supplies. Jorge is self-employed and not considered Wagner's household employee.

If a taxpayer pays a household employee cash wages (including amounts paid by check, money order, etc.) of $2,200 or more in 2020, he must normally withhold the employee's share of Social Security and Medicare taxes and remit them along with the employer's matching share, for a total of 15.3%. If the amount of wages paid to an employee during the year is less than this threshold, no Social Security or Medicare taxes are owed.

Example: Randall is a widowed single taxpayer with infant twin boys. Randall hires Hilda to take care of his twin boys while he is at work. Hilda usually works Monday through Friday, 9 AM to 6 PM. She is an experienced nanny, and she also cleans Randall's home during the day. Hilda is a household employee. Randall pays Hilda $33,000 in wages during the year. He is required to file Schedule H with his Form 1040. He must also file a Form W-2 to report the wages he paid to Hilda, and provide her with a copy of her W-2.

Note: An employer is not required to withhold *income* tax from a household employee's wages. However, income tax may be withheld at the employee's request. Even if the employer is not required to pay FICA (Social Security and Medicare) taxes, the employee's wages may be subject to income tax.

A taxpayer who is required to pay Social Security and Medicare taxes or federal unemployment taxes for household employees, or who withholds income tax for them, must file Schedule H, *Household Employment Taxes,* with his Form 1040. The taxpayer will need an employer identification number (EIN) to file Schedule H. He also must file Form W-2, *Wage and Tax Statement,* and furnish a copy of the form to the employee.

Household employees are eligible for certain COVID-19 tax benefits applicable for tax year 2020, including payroll tax deferral and paid sick and family leave tax credits. These benefits are claimed on Schedule H by the employer.

An employer of household employees may need to increase the federal income tax withheld from his pay or pension or make estimated tax payments to avoid an estimated tax penalty resulting from his liability for employment taxes in connection with household employees, (as shown on Schedule H). The taxpayer has several options. He can:

- Increase federal income tax withheld by giving his employer a new Form W-4
- Increase his federal income tax withheld by giving the payor of his pension a new Form W4-P, *Withholding Certificate for Pension or Annuity Payments*
- Make estimated tax payments by filing Form 1040-ES, *Estimated Tax for Individuals*

Estimated taxes must be withheld or paid as the tax liability is incurred, so a taxpayer cannot wait until he files his tax return (and Schedule H) to pay household taxes owed.

Wages paid to a taxpayer's spouse, parent, or child under the age of 21 are exempt from the nanny tax rules. In that case, the taxpayer would not have to withhold FICA tax.

Example: Geraldine hires her mother, Enola, to take care of her children during the week. In this case, since Geraldine has hired her mother, the payments are exempt from the nanny tax rules. No Social Security and Medicare taxes will be owed by either Geraldine or her mother. No Federal Unemployment Tax (FUTA) would be owed. However, Enola would owe income tax on the amounts that she earned, and she would need to report the income on her individual tax return.

A taxpayer cannot claim a household employee as a dependent, even if the employee lives with the taxpayer all year long.

Section 199A Qualified Business Income Deduction

This provision, also known as the "Section 199A Deduction" or the "QBI deduction," allows a deduction of up to 20% of qualified business income for owners of some businesses. The deduction is available, regardless of whether an individual itemizes their deductions on Schedule A or takes the standard deduction. This deduction expires after 2025, unless Congress decides to extend it. The deduction only applies to individuals and estates/trusts who own interests in businesses taxed as sole proprietorships, partnerships, or S corporations. Income earned by a C corporation is not eligible for the 199A deduction for its shareholders. The deduction allows eligible taxpayers to deduct up to 20% of their qualified business income on their own 1040 (or, in the case of an estate or trust, Form 1041), subject to an overall deduction limit of 20% of taxable income (less net long-term capital gains and qualified dividends).

QBI Deduction - Modified Taxable Income Threshold Amounts

For taxpayers with taxable income that exceeds the threshold amounts, the deduction is subject to two limitations: (1) the type of trade or business and (2) the amount of W-2 wages paid by the qualified trade or business and the unadjusted basis immediately after acquisition (UBIA) of qualified property held by the trade or business. The modified taxable income thresholds are indexed for inflation. In 2020, the modified taxable income threshold amounts are as follows:

- **Married filing jointly: $326,600-$426,600**
- **Head of Household/QW/Single: $163,300-$213,300**
- **Married filing Separately: $163,300-$213,300**

Example: Kylie is married and files jointly with her husband, Larry. They take the standard deduction for the year. Kylie operates a medical billing service as a sole proprietor. Her business has one employee, a secretary who is paid $50,000 during 2020. The business has no significant assets. After figuring her allowable deductions, Kylie's business generates $200,000 of net qualified business income. Larry earns $15,000 in wages during the year. Larry and Kylie's modified taxable income (before the QBI deduction) is $190,200 ($215,000 adjusted gross income less the $24,800 standard deduction for joint filers). Kylie is entitled to a QBI deduction of $40,000 ($200,000 net qualified business income x 20% QBI deduction) on their joint tax return. The wage and UBIA limitations do not apply because Kylie and Larry's joint modified taxable income is less than $326,600 in 2020.

The Section 199A deduction only applies to domestic income (U.S. business activities only). Only taxable income is counted. A taxpayer's "QBI component" is generally 20% of the taxpayer's

QBI from qualifying trades or businesses. QBI is the net amount of qualified items of income, gain, deduction and loss from any qualified trade or business. Only items included in taxable income are counted. In addition, the items must be effectively connected with a U.S. trade or business. Items such as capital gains and losses, certain dividends and interest income are excluded.

In other words, the business income must be generated by domestic business activity. "Qualified Business Income," or QBI, does not include:

- Employee wages, (except wages earned by a statutory employee),
- Reasonable compensation of the taxpayer from an S corporation;
- Any guaranteed payment from a partnership for services rendered with respect to the trade or business;
- Investment income; such as capital gains or interest and dividend income,
- Hobby income,
- Non-taxable income, (such as municipal bond interest)
- Rental real estate income where the real estate activity does not rise to the level of a trade/business. This does not mean that the taxpayer has to be a "real estate professional" in order to get the QBI deduction. The rental of real property may constitute a trade or business, even if the rental activity is reported on Schedule E.

The QBI deduction is claimed by individuals, so S corporations and partnerships cannot take the deduction at the entity level. However, all S corporations and partnerships report each shareholder's or partner's share of QBI on Schedule K-1, so the shareholders or partners may potentially claim the 199A deduction on their individual tax returns.[205]

Note: The determination of whether a business qualifies for the 199A QBI deduction occurs at the *entity* level. The deduction then "flows through" to the individual owners in order to be claimed on the taxpayer's individual returns. The QBI deduction is listed on the official Prometric test specs, so you may see a question on this topic on either Part 1 or Part 2 of the exam. See T.D. 9847 (final regulations under section 199A). The QBI deduction is covered in more detail from the business' perspective in Book 2, *Businesses.*

Eligible individuals may also be entitled to a special deduction of up to 20% of their combined qualified real estate investment trust (REIT) dividends and qualified publicly traded partnership (PTP) income. The total Section 199A deduction is the lesser of:

- 20% of qualified business income plus 20% of their qualified real estate investment (REIT) trust dividends and qualified publicly traded partnership (PTP) income, or
- 20% of taxable income minus net capital gains.

An overall qualified business loss results in no QBI deduction for the taxable year. The loss carries over to subsequent years and reduces the section 199A deduction for QBI for those years.

[205] The rules to determine whether or not real estate rental activity rises to the level of a trade/business is complex. However, to help partially alleviate this issue, the IRS issued guidance that provides a safe harbor where a real estate rental activity will be treated as a trade/business. In addition to other requirements, the safe harbor provides for trade/business status when a taxpayer (either themselves, through employees or independent contractors) provides at least 250 hours of qualifying services in the activity for at least three of the past five years (including the current tax year) - or 250 hours every year if the activity has been operated for less than five years. A number of additional rules apply when a taxpayer owns and rents multiple properties.

Foreign Income and Foreign Income Taxes

Generally, all income of U.S. citizens and U.S. resident aliens is subject to tax by the United States, regardless of where the individual lives and even if the income is earned outside the United States.

"Foreign earned income" is income received for services performed in a foreign country while the taxpayer's tax home is also in a foreign country. It does not matter whether the income is paid by a U.S. employer or a foreign employer. The tax home of the taxpayer (where the taxpayer resides) is the main determining factor.

Example: Candice is a U.S. citizen living in Canada. She works online for a U.S. company. She has lived continuously in Canada for the last five years, only coming back to the U.S. on sporadic short visits of less than a few days. Her tax home is in Canada, and therefore, her income is considered "foreign earned income." The *taxpayer's* tax home is what matters, not the physical location of the employer.

Foreign Earned Income Exclusion

If a taxpayer is eligible for the foreign earned income exclusion, his income up to a certain threshold is not taxed. For 2020, the maximum foreign earned income exclusion is $107,600. For married couples, the exclusion is applied on a per spouse basis, whether filing MFS or MFJ. In other words, if married taxpayers file jointly (or separately) and both individuals live and work abroad, each can claim the foreign earned income exclusion, for a total exclusion amount of $215,200 in 2020.

The foreign earned income exclusion is *not* automatic. Eligible taxpayers must file a U.S. income tax return each year with either a Form 2555 attached if they wish to claim the exclusion. All of the normal filing thresholds for U.S. taxpayers apply, regardless of where the taxpayer works or resides.

Example: Sophia and Arron are married and live abroad. In 2020, they were both living and employed in Peru for the entire taxable year. Sophia earned $82,000 and Arron earned $96,000. Each qualifies for the foreign earned income exclusion, whether they file jointly or separately.

Nonresident aliens do not qualify for the foreign earned income exclusion.

A taxpayer must be either a U.S. citizen or a legal resident alien of the United States who has foreign earned income, a foreign tax home, and passes one of two tests to claim the exclusion:

- **Bona Fide Residence Test:** A U.S. citizen or U.S. resident alien who is a bona fide resident of a foreign country for an uninterrupted period that includes an entire tax year.
- **The Physical Presence Test:** A U.S. citizen or U.S. resident alien who is physically present in a foreign country or countries for at least **330 full days** during twelve consecutive months. A taxpayer may qualify under the physical presence test, and the income may span a period of multiple tax years. If so, the taxpayer must prorate the foreign earned income exclusion based on the number of days spent in a foreign country.

Note: The foreign earned income exclusion generally does not apply to the wages and salaries of members of the Armed Forces and government employees of the United States.

Note: IRS now makes an exception for combat-zone contract workers. Citizens or residents of the U.S. working in a combat zone as civilian contract workers may qualify as having a tax home in a foreign country, even if the taxpayer retains a home in the U.S.[206]

The foreign earned income exclusion is calculated using Form 2555, *Foreign Earned Income,* which must be attached to Form 1040. If the election is made to exclude foreign earned income, the election remains in effect for subsequent years, unless it is formally revoked.

2020 COVID-19 Emergency Relief: The COVID-19 pandemic prompted the Department of the Treasury and the Internal Revenue Service to provide a waiver related to the minimum time requirements for the foreign earned income exclusion. If, due to the COVID-19 emergency, the taxpayer was required to leave:

- The People's Republic of China (excluding Hong Kong and Macau) on or after December 1, 2019, but on or before July 15, 2020; or
- Another foreign country on or after February 1, 2020, but on or before July 15, 2020.

Then, the taxpayer may still be able to meet requirements of the bona fide residence test or physical presence test for the purposes of determining the foreign earned income exclusion and housing exclusion or deduction. In order to claim this special waiver, the taxpayer must write **"Revenue Procedure 2020-27"** across the top margin of their Form 2555, and attach it to their Form 1040.

Foreign Housing Exclusion or Deduction

In addition to the foreign earned income exclusion, a taxpayer can claim an exclusion (or a deduction) for foreign housing costs.

The foreign housing *exclusion* applies only to amounts paid by an employer, while the foreign housing *deduction* applies only to amounts paid with self-employment earnings. Qualified housing expenses include reasonable expenses paid for housing in a foreign country. Only housing expenses for the part of the year that the taxpayer actually qualified for the foreign earned income exclusion are considered.

Example: Urbanus is a U.S. citizen who lived in Mexico all of 2020 and was employed by a foreign company as an advertising consultant. He lived rent-free in an apartment provided by his employer. Urbanus received a salary of $95,000, and the fair rental value of his housing was $12,000, for a total of $107,000 of earned income. He qualifies for the foreign earned income exclusion as well as the foreign housing exclusion.

Foreign Income Taxes: Generally, income taxes paid to a foreign country can be deducted as an itemized deduction on Schedule A or as a credit against U.S. income tax. A taxpayer can choose between a deduction or a credit and use whichever one results in the lowest tax.

---

206 The Bipartisan Budget Act changed the tax home requirement for certain eligible taxpayers, specifically contractors or employees of contractors supporting the U.S. Armed Forces in designated combat zones, who may now qualify for the foreign earned income exclusion.

Foreign Tax Credit

U.S. citizens and resident aliens are eligible for the Foreign Tax Credit, which is designed to relieve taxpayers of the double taxation burden that occurs when their foreign source income is taxed by both the U.S. and a foreign country.[207] Nonresident aliens are not eligible for this credit. Four tests must be met to qualify for the credit:

- The tax must be imposed on the taxpayer.
- The taxpayer must have paid the tax.
- The tax must be a legal and actual foreign tax liability.
- The tax must be an income tax (not an excise tax, sales tax, etc.).

Although taxpayers can choose between taking the deduction or the credit for all foreign taxes paid, in most cases, it is to their advantage to take the Foreign Tax Credit, since a credit directly reduces tax liability.

Taxpayers cannot claim the Foreign Tax Credit for taxes paid on any income that has already been excluded using the foreign earned income exclusion or the foreign housing exclusion. Unlike the foreign earned income exclusion, which applies only to income that is earned while a taxpayer is living and working abroad, the Foreign Tax Credit applies to any type of foreign income, including investment income. Foreign tax paid may be reported to the taxpayer by a financial institution on Form 1099-INT or Form 1099-DIV.

If the amount of foreign tax that the taxpayers incur is small, then taxpayers can claim the credit directly on Form 1040 if, among other conditions, all foreign income is specified passive income, reported on an information return (such as a 1099-DIV or 1099-INT) and total taxes paid do not exceed $300 ($600 MFJ).

If the foreign tax paid exceeds $300 ($600 MFJ), the taxpayer must file Form 1116, *Foreign Tax Credit,* in order to claim the credit.

Example: Khadija and Azlan are married and file jointly. They own a number of foreign stocks, and their Form 1099-DIV shows foreign tax paid of $590. The couple is not required to complete Form 1116 because their foreign taxes are less than $600 on their joint return. They can take a foreign tax credit of $590 directly on their Form 1040.

Certain taxes do not qualify for the Foreign Tax Credit, including interest or penalties paid to a foreign country, taxes imposed by countries involved with international terrorism, and taxes on foreign oil or gas extraction income.

Note: Individuals claim the Foreign Tax *deduction* on Schedule A (Form 1040) as an itemized deduction. The Foreign Tax *Credit* is claimed on Form 1116, *Foreign Tax Credit.* A taxpayer cannot claim both—the deduction and the tax credit—on the same return, but may alternate years, taking a credit in one year and a deduction in the next year, choosing whichever one gives them a better tax result.

---

[207] For foreign tax credit purposes, a "foreign country" includes: any foreign country, its political subdivisions, and U.S. possessions. U.S. possessions include Puerto Rico and American Samoa.

Note: Currently, the foreign tax credit does not apply to any tax paid to Iran, North Korea, Sudan, or Syria. These countries are sanctioned by the U.S.

Example: Arshad is a U.S. citizen. He lived and worked in Iran until May 2020, when he was transferred to Greece. Arshad paid taxes to each country on the wages earned in that country. Arshad cannot claim a foreign tax credit for the income taxes he paid in Iran. Because the income he earned in Iran is a disallowed category of foreign income, he must fill out a separate Form 1116 for that income. Further, he cannot take a credit for the taxes paid on the income earned in Iran, but all his worldwide income is taxable by the United States.

A taxpayer is allowed to switch between claiming the Foreign Tax Credit or an itemized deduction for foreign tax paid. If a taxpayer claimed an itemized deduction for a prior year for qualified foreign taxes, the taxpayer can also switch to claiming a credit by filing an amended return within *ten years* from the original due date of the return. This type of amended return has a much longer statute period than normal amended returns.

Fixed, Determinable, Annual, or Periodic (FDAP) Income

Fixed, Determinable, Annual, or Periodic (FDAP) income applies to foreign persons earning income in the U.S. FDAP income consists primarily of passive investment income, but can also include other types of income. The following items are examples of FDAP income:

- Compensation for personal services (such as proceeds from performances by nonresident alien professional athletes, performers, or entertainers),
- Dividends and interest, pensions and annuities,
- Taxable alimony,
- Rents and royalties,
- Taxable scholarships and fellowship grants,
- Other grants, prizes and awards, as well as prizes or purses (such as a "purse" earned by a nonresident alien boxing champion that comes to the U.S. for a boxing match),
- The distributable net income of an estate or trust that is FDAP income, and that must be distributed currently, or has been paid or credited during the tax year, to a nonresident alien beneficiary,
- A distribution from a partnership that is FDAP income, or such an amount that, although not actually distributed, is includible in the gross income of a foreign partner.

Compensation for personal services performed by a nonresident alien in the United States can also be FDAP income. This includes income such as commissions and proceeds from performances. If an individual qualifies as a nonresident alien, then they are taxed only on the income they earn or derive from the US. Deductions are not allowed against FDAP income, and it is taxed at a flat 30% rate (or a lower rate if there is a tax treaty between the U.S. and the taxpayer's country of residency).

This 30% or lower rate only applies if the FDAP income or gains from U.S. sources are not "effectively connected" with a taxpayer's U.S. trade or business. A nonresident alien who receives income that is effectively connected with his trade or business in the United States is taxed at the rates that apply to U.S. citizens and U.S. residents. The IRS definition of FDAP includes all passive investment income except:

- Gains derived from the sale of real or personal property
- Items of income excluded from gross income, regardless of the U.S. or foreign status of the income's owner, such as tax-exempt municipal bond interest and qualified scholarship income

If a nonresident alien receives income for personal services performed partly in the U.S. and partly outside the U.S., he must allocate the income based on the number of days where the services were performed.

Example: Hudielle is a popular Columbian singer that regularly performs all over the world. In 2020, she negotiates a contract for annual performances in Las Vegas. She does not live in Las Vegas, and will only perform for one week every year. The income she receives from the performances will be FDAP income. She must report the income she earns in the U.S. on Form 1040-NR. Her worldwide income is not subject to U.S. tax, only the income derived from her U.S. performances.

Example: Bryce, a citizen and resident of Canada, is employed as a professional hockey player by a U.S. hockey team. He received $200,000 in compensation for 120 days of professional hockey games during 2020: 75 days in the U.S. and 45 days in Canada. The amount of U.S. source income is $125,000 ([75 days of play in the U.S. ÷ 120 total days = .625] × $200,000). Bryce's compensation would be considered FDAP income. Canada has a favorable tax treaty with the U.S., so Bryce should consult with his tax advisor about how best to file his nonresident return.

GILTI Tax

GILTI stands for "Global Intangible Low-Taxed Income." This provision was added into the code by the Tax Cuts and Jobs Act. This provision significantly broadens the scope of foreign earnings that, prior to tax reform, had been subject to U.S. tax. The GILTI tax affects individuals and partnerships that are shareholders of controlled foreign corporations (CFCs).

A "U.S. shareholder" is defined as a U.S. person who owns (directly or indirectly) 10% or more of the total combined voting power of all the classes of voting stock of a CFC or 10% or more of the total value of shares of all classes of stock of a CFC. The GILTI rules requires more-than-10% U.S. shareholders of a foreign corporation to include, as income, a deemed distribution equal to their allocable share of the earnings and profits that are considered GILTI earnings.

Example: Antonin is a legal U.S. resident (green card holder) and a citizen of France. He owns 13% of an industrial plant located in France. The company distributes and sells its products only to foreign consumers. Antonin is subject to the GILTI tax.

The GILTI tax is calculated on Form 8992, *U.S. Shareholder Calculation of Global Intangible Low-Taxed Income.* The rules governing the GILTI are extremely complex. The law is very broad and impacts all companies and all U.S. individuals that have ownership in overseas entities.

Unit 15: Study Questions

(Test yourself first, then check the correct answers at the end of this quiz.)

1. Charlotte is a U.S. citizen who lives and works in France, which is her tax home. She does not maintain a residence in the U.S., although she does own a residential rental property in Florida, which is currently rented and produces rental income. In 2020, she received the following income:

- Rental income earned on the Florida rental: $12,000
- Dividend income earned on investments: $500
- Municipal bond interest: $2,000
- Wages earned in France: $90,000

Charlotte wants to take the foreign earned income exclusion on her individual tax return. What is the total amount of qualifying foreign earned income that Charlotte can report on her Form 2555?

A. $90,000
B. $92,500
C. $99,200
D. $102,100

2. The Foreign Tax Credit applies to:

A. Taxpayers who have paid foreign taxes to a foreign country on foreign-sourced income and are subject to U.S. tax on the same income.
B. Taxpayers who have paid U.S. taxes while living and working abroad.
C. Taxpayers who have paid U.S. taxes while living and working abroad and who are subject to U.S. tax on their worldwide income.
D. Nonresident aliens who have paid foreign taxes to a foreign country on foreign-sourced income and are subject to U.S. tax on the same income.

3. Jabbar is a tax preparer. Upon reviewing a new client's prior-year tax return, Jabbar sees taxes paid for the first-time homebuyer credit repayment. Jabbar should ask the taxpayer all of the following questions *except:*

A. What was the total amount of the original credit received?
B. How much of the original credit was repaid on the prior year's returns?
C. Was the entire credit used towards the purchase of their main home?
D. Are the taxpayers still using the home that generated the credit as their main home?

4. Colton is 22, a full-time college student, and is claimed as a dependent on his parents' tax return. He also has a part-time job at a local mall. Colton has $210 of dividend income in 2020. What is the maximum amount of wages Colton can earn in 2020 without triggering the kiddie tax?

A. $350
B. $2,200
C. $12,200
D. Unlimited - the kiddie tax is not applicable.

5. All of the following statements are correct about the alternative minimum tax *except*:

A. Congress passed the alternative minimum tax to ensure that individuals and corporations that benefit from certain exclusions, deductions, or credits pay at least a minimum amount of tax.
B. The tentative minimum tax is figured in addition to a taxpayer's regular tax.
C. The AMT is the excess of the tentative minimum tax over the regular tax.
D. The AMT is permanently indexed for inflation.

6. In 2020, at which threshold does an employer have to withhold and pay Social Security and Medicare taxes for a household employee?

A. When the taxpayer pays a household employee $400 or more of wage.
B. When the taxpayer pays a household employee $1,050 or more of wages.
C. When the taxpayer pays a household employee $2,200 or more of wages.
D. When the taxpayer pays a household employee $12,200 or more of wages.

7. Which of the following taxpayers would not be eligible for the Credit for the Prior Year Minimum Tax by filing Form 8801?

A. An S corporation.
B. A trust.
C. A decedent's estate.
D. An individual.

8. Which of the following statements is *correct* regarding the Foreign Tax Credit?

A. The Foreign Tax Credit is a refundable credit.
B. The Foreign Tax Credit is available to U.S. citizens and nonresident aliens.
C. Taxpayers may choose to deduct foreign taxes paid, in lieu of the Foreign Tax Credit.
D. Taxpayers can claim both a deduction and a tax credit for foreign taxes paid to different countries.

9. Usman and Alyssa filed their 2008 return as Married Filing Jointly and claimed $7,500 for the first-time homebuyer credit. The couple used their home as a primary residence. In 2020, Usman and Alyssa converted the home into rental property. What, if any, is the tax obligation of the taxpayers regarding the first-time homebuyer credit?

A. Since they used the home at least 2 of the last 5 years, there is no requirement to repay.
B. They must pro-rate the credit received over 15 years and repay 50% of the original credit.
C. They must reduce their basis in the property by 50% of the unpaid balance of the credit.
D. They must repay the entire unpaid balance of the credit in the current year.

10. Abdiel is a citizen and resident of Iran, a country that does not have a tax treaty with the United States. Abdiel is not a U.S. citizen or U.S. resident, but he owns several rental properties in the U.S. that produce passive investment income. His rental income is taxable at a flat _______ rate.

A. 15%
B. 20%
C. 30%
D. 35%

11. Evelyn hired a part-time nanny to work in her home. She paid the nanny $1,900 of wages in 2020 before firing her for being constantly late. Which of the following statements is correct?

A. Evelyn is not required to issue a Form W-2 to the nanny and does not have to report or pay Social Security and Medicare taxes on the nanny's wages.
B. The income is not taxable to the nanny.
C. No reporting is required by either party if the wages are paid in cash.
D. Evelyn can deduct the nanny's wages as a business expense on Schedule C.

Unit 15: Quiz Answers

1. The answer is A. Charlotte has $104,500 of *gross* income, but only her wages ($90,000) would qualify for the foreign earned income exclusion. U.S. citizens and U.S. resident aliens who live abroad are taxed on their worldwide income. However, they may qualify to exclude a portion of their foreign earnings (up to $107,600 for 2020). A qualifying individual with qualifying income may elect to exclude foreign earned income, and this exclusion applies only if a tax return is filed and the income is reported. The municipal bond interest would be nontaxable, so the only income which would potentially be subject to income tax in this scenario would be the $12,000 in rental income and $500 in dividends.

2. The answer is A. The Foreign Tax Credit applies to taxpayers who have paid *foreign income* taxes to a foreign country on foreign-sourced income and are subject to U.S. tax on the same income.

3. The answer is C. Jabbar does not need to ask if the entire credit was used towards the purchase of their main home. From the instructions for Form 5405: To properly complete Form 5405, all of the questions should be asked *except* for the use of the proceeds of the credit. There was no stipulation as to how the credit would be used when the first-time homebuyer received it. (This question is modified from an actual EA exam question that was released by the IRS).

4. The answer is D. Colton's wage income will not be subject to the kiddie tax. The kiddie tax *only* applies to investment income, never to wages or other types of "earned income". Since Colton's dividend income is way below the kiddie tax threshold, he will not be subject to the kiddie tax.

5. The answer is B. The tentative minimum tax is calculated separately from the regular tax (it is *not* figured *in addition* to the taxpayer's regular tax). The AMT is owed only if the tentative minimum tax is *greater* than the regular tax.

6. The answer is C. In 2020, the nanny tax applies when a taxpayer pays a household employee $2,200 or more of wages a year.

7. The answer is A. Only individuals, estates, and trusts are eligible to claim the Credit for the Prior Year Minimum Tax by filing Form 8801. The AMT credit is calculated differently for corporations, which use a different form and set of instructions to determine whether they are eligible for the credit.

8. The answer is C. Taxpayers have the option to claim an itemized deduction for foreign taxes paid on Schedule A. They may choose either the deduction or the credit, whichever gives them the lowest tax. Taxpayers cannot claim both the deduction and a tax credit on the same return.

9. The answer is D. Usman and Alyssa must pay the unpaid balance of the credit in 2020, the year of the rental conversion.

10. The answer is C. Abdiel will be taxed at a flat 30% rate on his FDAP (Fixed, Determinable, Annual, or Periodical) income. A 30% (or lower treaty) tax rate applies to FDAP income or gains from U.S.

sources, but only if they are not effectively connected with a taxpayer's U.S. trade or business. FDAP income consists primarily of passive investment income, including interest, dividends, rents, royalties, pensions, and annuities. FDAP income is all income except:

- Gains derived from the sale of real or personal property.
- Items of income excluded from gross income, without regard to the U.S. or foreign status of the owner of the income, such as tax-exempt municipal bond interest and qualified scholarship income.

11. The answer is A. Evelyn is not required to issue a Form W-2 to her nanny and does not have to report or pay Social Security and Medicare taxes on the nanny's wages. If an employer pays a household employee wages of *less than* $2,200 in 2020, the employer is not required to report or pay Social Security and Medicare taxes on that employee's wages. Regardless of whether Form W-2 is issued, the nanny must report the income on Form 1040.

Unit 16: Individual Retirement Accounts

More Reading:
Publication 590, *Individual Retirement Arrangements (IRAs)*
Publication 575, *Pension and Annuity Income*
Publication 560, *Retirement Plans for Small Business*

There are a variety of retirement accounts individuals can establish for themselves and retirement plans that can be established by employers and self-employed individuals.

In this unit, we primarily cover traditional individual retirement arrangements (traditional IRAs) and Roth IRAs, as they are tested heavily on Part 1 of the EA exam. We will also briefly address other types of retirement plans. Form 1099-R, *Distributions from Pensions, Annuities, Retirement or Profit-Sharing Plans, IRAs, Insurance Contracts, etc.*, is used to report distributions of $10 or more from a retirement plan or an IRA.

Congress passed the SECURE Act on December 20, 2019, which made a significant number of changes to retirement plans. Most of the retirement plan provisions in the SECURE Act did not take effect until January 1, 2020. The Consolidated Appropriations Act of 2021 (CAA 2021) was signed on December 27, 2020, and included several disaster-related provisions that affected the treatment of retirement plan distributions for the 2020 tax year. These changes will be covered in this chapter.

Traditional IRA: Amounts in a traditional IRA, including contributions and earnings, are generally not taxed until they are distributed. Typically, a taxpayer can deduct his traditional IRA contributions as an adjustment to gross income. However, the deduction is phased out at higher income levels, when the taxpayer (or the taxpayer's spouse) is also covered by a workplace retirement plan.

Roth IRA: Contributions to a Roth IRA are paid with after-tax income and are not deductible. In contrast to a traditional IRA, withdrawals from a Roth IRA are generally not taxed. Income limits apply in determining who is eligible to participate in a Roth IRA. However, there is no income limit for taxpayers who wish to convert their traditional IRA to a Roth.

Traditional IRA Rules

To make contributions to a traditional IRA, the taxpayer must have qualifying taxable compensation, such as wages, salaries, commissions, tips, bonuses, or self-employment income. In prior years, there were age limits to contribute to a traditional IRA, but the age limits were abolished by the SECURE Act. Starting in 2020, anyone with qualifying compensation, regardless of age, may contribute to a traditional IRA.

If either the taxpayer or his spouse is covered by an employer plan and his income is too high, his deductible IRA contribution will be phased out. However, as long as a taxpayer has qualifying compensation, he may contribute to a traditional IRA (although he may not be able to *deduct* the contribution).

Note: If the taxpayer (or their spouse) *does not* participate in a retirement plan at work, their traditional IRA contribution is fully deductible up to their allowable contribution limit.

For purposes of making an IRA contribution, *taxable* alimony (but not child support) counts as qualifying compensation. This allows taxpayers to build retirement savings in IRAs even if they rely on alimony income for support. Nontaxable combat pay also qualifies as compensation for this purpose.

In 2020, the SECURE Act allows certain taxable stipends and non-tuition fellowship payments received by graduate students to be treated as "compensation" for IRA purposes. This provision is effective starting in the 2020 tax year.

Also starting in 2020, difficulty-of-care payments (also called "qualified Medicare waiver payments) to home healthcare workers, are considered "qualifying compensation" for IRA contribution purposes. This is true even if the amounts are not subject to income tax; however, the amounts contributed are non-deductible and create basis in the IRA.

Example: Charlton is an Army medic serving in a combat zone for all of 2020. Although none of his combat pay is taxable, it is still considered qualifying compensation for purposes of an IRA contribution. He is allowed to contribute to a Roth or Traditional IRA if he wishes.

Example: Sandra divorced in 2016. She receives $4,000 a month in taxable alimony from her ex-husband. She does not have any other sources of income. Sandra is allowed to contribute to a traditional or Roth IRA if she chooses.

"Compensation" for purposes of contributing to an IRA does *not* include:

- Child support or *nontaxable* alimony,
- Passive rental income,
- Dividend and interest income,
- Pension or annuity income,
- Deferred compensation,
- Prize winnings or gambling income,
- Items that are excluded from income, such as certain foreign earned income and excludable foreign housing costs (except for nontaxable combat pay and qualified Medicare waiver payments).

Example: Leroy is single and 65 years old. He received $14,000 of rental income from a residential rental and $23,000 in pension income during the year. He is not a real estate professional. The passive rental income and the pension income are not qualifying compensation for IRA purposes. Leroy cannot contribute to a Roth IRA or a traditional IRA.

Roth IRA Rules

Roth IRAs and traditional IRAs have many differences, but they are both used for retirement planning. Unlike a traditional IRA, none of the contributions to a Roth IRA are deductible, but qualified distributions are generally tax-free at the time of withdrawal. The major differences between a Roth IRA and a traditional IRA are as follows:

- Contributions to a Roth IRA are not deductible by the taxpayer, and participation in an employer plan has no effect on the taxpayer's contribution limits.
- There are no required minimum distributions from a Roth IRA. No distributions are required until a Roth IRA owner dies.

- Roth IRA contributions can be made at any age.
- Income limits apply, which means high-income earners may be prohibited from contributing to a Roth IRA.

Whether or not a taxpayer can make a Roth IRA contribution depends on his filing status and modified adjusted gross income (MAGI). In 2020, the following income limits apply to Roth IRAs:

Filing Status	2020 Roth IRA Phaseout Ranges
Single, HOH filers	Phaseout begins at $124,000–$139,000
MFJ and QW filers	Phaseout begins at $196,000–$206,000
MFS (lived with spouse)	$0-$10,000
MFS taxpayers who did not live with their spouses at any time during the year may use the "single" phaseout range.	

In general, a taxpayer cannot contribute to a Roth IRA if his income is above the phaseout thresholds. However, a "backdoor" Roth IRA is still possible in 2020. By this method, the taxpayer simply opens a traditional IRA, makes a non-deductible IRA contribution, and then converts the funds to a Roth in the same year. We will cover IRA conversions in more detail later.

IRA Contribution Limits

The limits for contributions to an IRA in 2020 are the lesser of qualifying taxable compensation (as described below) or the following amounts:

- **$6,000** per taxpayer (**$7,000** if age 50 or older)
- Taxpayers filing MFJ: **$12,000** (or **$14,000** if *both* spouses are age 50 or older). Each spouse must have their own IRA account, but in the case of married spouses that file jointly, only one spouse must have qualifying compensation.

This yearly IRA contribution limit does not apply to:

- Rollover contributions[208] (rolling over from one IRA account to another)
- Qualified reservist repayments[209]
- Repayments of qualified disaster distributions (covered later)

Example: Connie is 17 years old and has a part-time job. She is claimed as a dependent on her parent's return. She earns $4,300 in wages during 2020. She also has $3,500 in dividend income. Connie may contribute to an IRA in 2020 because she has qualifying earned income (her wages). Her IRA contribution would be limited to $4,300, the amount of her wages. The investment income is not qualifying compensation for IRA purposes. Connie would be allowed to take a deduction for her IRA contribution on her individual tax return, even if she is claimed as a dependent by her parents.

[208] Trustee-to-trustee rollovers are not limited.

[209] If a taxpayer was a reservist in the Armed Forces and was called to active duty, the taxpayer can contribute (repay) any IRA amounts equal to any qualified reservist distributions received. The taxpayer can make these repayment contributions even if the payments would cause the total yearly contributions to exceed the general limit on IRA contributions.

Example: Dalton is 54 and wants to contribute to his traditional IRA. He received $15,000 of rental income; $8,000 of interest income; and $3,000 of wages from a part-time job. The rental and interest income are not considered for purposes of determining his IRA contribution. Therefore, the maximum he can contribute to his traditional IRA is $3,000, the amount of his wages.

If married taxpayers choose to file separately, they must consider only their own qualifying compensation for IRA contribution purposes.[210]

Example: Falco is 35, works full-time, and earned $55,000 in wages during the year. His wife, Danielle, is 34 and earned $3,600. They choose to file MFS. Therefore, Danielle is limited to a $3,600 IRA contribution, the amount of her qualifying compensation. Falco may contribute the full $6,000 (the limit for his age) to his own IRA account.

IRAs cannot be owned jointly. Therefore, each spouse must have their own IRA account. However, a married couple filing jointly may contribute to each of their IRA accounts, even if only one taxpayer has qualifying compensation. This is called a "spousal IRA contribution."

Example: Derrick, 49, and Elaine, 51, are married and file jointly. Derrick works as a paramedic and makes $76,000 per year. Elaine is a homemaker and has no taxable income. Even though Elaine has no qualifying compensation, they may contribute to her IRA account. Their combined maximum contribution for 2020 is $13,000. Derrick may contribute $6,000 to his IRA, and Elaine may contribute $7,000 to her IRA because she is over 50 years old. This special rule only applies if married taxpayers file jointly.

Contributions can be made to a traditional IRA at any time on or before the due date of the return (*not* including extensions). For the 2020 tax year, a taxpayer may make an IRA contribution up until April 15, 2021.

This makes an IRA contribution a rare opportunity for late-stage tax planning because it can occur after the tax year has already ended. A taxpayer can even file his return claiming a traditional IRA contribution before the contribution is actually made. However, if a contribution is reported on the taxpayer's return, but it is not made by the deadline, the taxpayer must file an amended return.

Example: Felton timely files his 2020 tax return on March 1, 2021, and claims a $4,000 deduction for an IRA contribution on the return. Felton may wait as late as April 15, 2021, the due date of the return, to actually make the IRA contribution.

If a person's only qualifying compensation for the year is from self-employment and the self-employment activity generates a loss for that year, he would not be able to contribute to an IRA. However, if the taxpayer has wages *in addition* to self-employment income, a loss from self-employment would not be subtracted from the wages when figuring total "qualifying" compensation income for purposes of determining his IRA contribution.

[210] Other than the exceptions for MFJ filers, a taxpayer can never contribute more than his earned income for the year. Minors who want to start contributing to an IRA must abide by limits based on their own income, not the income of their parents.

Example: Florence is 41 and earns $10,000 of wages working part-time for a library. She also works as a self-employed photographer, but her photography business has a net loss of ($5,400) for the year. Even though Florence's *net* income for 2020 is only $4,600 ($10,000 wages - $5,400 loss from self-employment), her "qualifying compensation" for purposes of an IRA contribution is still $10,000, the amount of her wages. This means that Florence can make a full IRA contribution of $6,000 in 2020, assuming she has enough available funds to do so.

For married taxpayers filing a joint return, the combined IRA contributions cannot exceed their combined qualifying compensation.

Example: Gilbert and Doreen are both age 49 and married. Gilbert has $43,000 of passive rental income for the year. Doreen has $28,000 of dividend income and $7,000 of wages from a part-time job. Only Doreen's wages count as qualifying compensation for purposes of an IRA contribution. If they file jointly, they can contribute a maximum of $7,000 to their IRAs. One of them can contribute up to the maximum annual amount ($6,000), and the other can contribute up to $1,000 (equal to the remaining amount of Doreen's qualifying compensation), or they could split the $7,000 in another manner, if they wish.

Deductibility of Traditional IRA Contributions

The deductibility of a traditional IRA contribution is based on income, filing status, and whether the taxpayer (or spouse) is covered by an employer retirement plan at work. A taxpayer with qualifying compensation is permitted to contribute to a traditional IRA regardless of whether he or his spouse is covered by an employer retirement plan; however, the *deductibility* of the contribution may be limited. This section only applies to traditional IRA contributions, because Roth IRA contributions are never tax-deductible.

If a taxpayer exceeds the income limits for making a fully deductible contribution to a traditional IRA, the excess portion can still be made as a nondeductible or after-tax contribution. If a taxpayer makes nondeductible contributions to a traditional IRA, he must attach Form 8606, *Nondeductible IRAs.* Form 8606 reflects a taxpayer's cumulative nondeductible contributions, which is his tax basis in the IRA.

If a taxpayer does not report nondeductible contributions properly, all future withdrawals from the IRA will be taxable unless the taxpayer can prove, with satisfactory evidence, that nondeductible contributions were made. Regardless of whether a portion of the contribution is nondeductible, the related earnings will grow on a tax-deferred basis.

Taxpayer (and Spouse) Not Covered by an Employer Plan: If neither the taxpayer nor his spouse is covered by an employer plan, there is *no limitation* on the deductibility of either of their traditional IRA contributions, as long as they have qualifying compensation. Thus, either can deduct the smaller of:

- $6,000 ($7,000 if 50 or older) or $12,000 ($14,000 if 50 or older) if filing MFJ, or
- 100% of qualifying compensation.

Example: Henrietta, age 61, works full-time as a restaurant manager. Her employer does not offer a retirement plan. Henrietta's husband, Kirk, 62, is a welder who is also not covered by a retirement plan at work. Both spouses have a traditional IRA. Their joint AGI in 2020 is $105,000. Since they are over 50 years of age, they can contribute and deduct a traditional IRA contribution up to $7,000 (each) for 2020, no matter how much they earn.

Taxpayer (or Spouse) Covered by an Employer Retirement Plan: If *neither* spouse is a participant in an employer-sponsored retirement plan, their IRA contributions are fully deductible on Form 1040 as an adjustment to income. However, if either a taxpayer or his spouse, (or both,) is covered by (i.e., participates in) an employer retirement plan, the tax-deductible contribution to a traditional IRA may be phased out.

Example: Julie is single and earned $109,000 in 2020. She is covered by a 401(k) retirement plan at work, but she also wants to contribute to a traditional IRA. She is phased out for the deduction because her MAGI exceeds the threshold for single filers covered by an employer plan. If she contributes to a traditional IRA in 2020, she must file Form 8606 to report her nondeductible contribution. She is still allowed to *contribute* to a traditional IRA, but the amounts would not be deductible on her Form 1040.

Taxpayers that are covered by an employer retirement plan are phased out at the following levels of modified adjusted gross income (MAGI):

2020 Phaseouts when Taxpayer (or Spouse) is Covered by an Employer Plan		
Filing Status	**MAGI Range**	**Allowable Deduction**
Single, HOH, or	$65,000 or less	A full deduction
MFS (did not live with spouse*)	more than $65,000 but less than $75,000	A partial deduction
	$75,000 or more	No deduction
MFJ (for the covered spouse*), QW	$104,000 or less	A full deduction
	More than $104,000 but less than $124,000	A partial deduction
	$124,000 or more	No deduction
MFS (lived with spouse*)	less than $10,000	A partial deduction
	$10,000 or more	No deduction
If *neither* spouse is a participant in an employer retirement plan, their traditional IRA contributions are fully deductible.		
*Note #1: If the taxpayer files MFS but did not live with their spouse at all during the year, the IRA deduction is determined under the "Single" filing status.		
*Note #2: If filing as MFJ and only one spouse is covered by a retirement plan, for the non-covered spouse, in 2020, a full deduction is allowed at MAGI of $196,000 or less; a partial deduction for more than $196,000 but less than $206,000; and no deduction at $206,000 or more.		

Remember, taxpayers can have a traditional IRA *whether or not* they are covered by another retirement plan. However, they may not be able to *deduct* all of their traditional IRA contributions if they are also covered by an employer plan.

Example: Leif and Araceli are both age 42, married, and file jointly. Leif is a member of the U.S. House of Representatives and covered by a retirement plan at work. Araceli is not covered by a workplace retirement plan, because she is self-employed. Leif's salary for the year is $210,000. Araceli earned $45,000 in taxable self-employment income. Araceli makes a maximum $6,000 contribution to her traditional IRA during the year. Since Leif is covered by a retirement plan at work, and their joint AGI exceeds the phaseout threshold, (The phaseout is $206,000 or more in 2020 if one spouse is covered by a retirement plan at work) Araceli's IRA contribution is not deductible. She is still allowed to make a nondeductible contribution, and the earnings in her IRA account will grow tax-free.

Married taxpayers who file MFS generally have a much lower phaseout range than those with any other filing status. However, if a taxpayer files a separate return and *did not live* with his spouse at any time during the year, the taxpayer is treated as "single" for IRA contribution purposes.

Example: Stefano, age 43, and his wife are not legally divorced, but they have lived in separate residences for the past two years. In 2020, Stefano earns $48,000 and files MFS. Stefano is covered by a 401(k) at work, but he has a traditional IRA, also. He is nevertheless allowed to deduct his full IRA contribution of $6,000. This is because he did not live with his spouse during the year, and therefore is not subject to the lower IRA phaseout limits that normally apply to MFS filers.

Splitting IRA Contributions Between Multiple Accounts

A person may have IRA accounts with multiple financial institutions and may split his annual contributions between accounts; his aggregate contributions for the year are subject to the limits described above. In other words, a taxpayer can deposit into multiple IRA accounts, as long as he doesn't contribute more than the annual limit. Further, a taxpayer may choose to split his contributions between a traditional IRA and a Roth IRA; again, his combined contributions are subject to the maximum annual contribution limits outlined before.

Example: Bartholomew is 62. He has a traditional IRA through his bank and a Roth IRA through his employer. Bartholomew wants to contribute to both accounts. Bartholomew can contribute to both of his retirement accounts, but the combined contributions for 2020 cannot exceed $7,000, the annual maximum for his age (he is allowed a catch-up contribution because he is over 50). Bartholomew decides to contribute $3,000 to his Roth IRA and $4,000 to his traditional IRA.

Example: In 2020, Gaspar has $3,200 in wages and $45,000 in rental income. He does not have any other earnings during the year. His maximum IRA contribution is limited to $3,200 (the amount of his earned income). Gaspar decides to split his IRA contributions between a traditional IRA and a Roth IRA. He contributes $2,200 to a traditional IRA and $1,000 to a Roth IRA. The most Gaspar will be able to deduct as an adjustment to income is the $2,200 contribution to his traditional IRA. Roth IRA contributions are never deductible.

Example: Inez, 28, has $3,000 of dividend income and no other income in 2020. Inez marries Luiz during the year. Luiz is age 32 and has taxable wages of $64,000. He plans to contribute $6,000 to his traditional IRA. If Luiz and Inez file a joint return, each can contribute $6,000 to a traditional IRA. Inez, who has no qualifying compensation, can use Luiz's compensation, reduced by the amount of his IRA contribution ($64,000 - $6,000 = $58,000), to determine her maximum contribution to a traditional IRA.

Taxability of IRA Distributions

Distributions from a traditional IRA are generally taxable in the year they are received, subject to the following exceptions:

- Rollovers to another retirement plan (other than conversions to a Roth IRA),
- Qualified charitable distributions directly to a qualified charity (must be a trustee-to-trustee transfer),
- Tax-free withdrawal of contributions,
- Distributions of nondeductible contributions.

The rules are different for Roth IRA distributions. A taxpayer can withdraw their regular Roth IRA contributions (their basis, but not the earnings) at any time and at any age with no penalty or tax. However, withdrawing *earnings* before age 59½ may result in a 10% early withdrawal penalty. In order to qualify for completely tax-free and penalty-free withdrawal, Roth IRA distributions generally must meet a five-year holding requirement and occur after age 59½, although there are exceptions for disability or death of the IRA owner.

Disaster Provisions in the CARES Act and CAA-2021

In 2020, the CARES Act provides for special distribution options and favorable tax treatment for up to $100,000 of coronavirus-related distributions from eligible retirement plans (including employer retirement plans and traditional IRAs), as well as special rollover rules with respect to such distributions.[211] These coronavirus-related withdrawals:

- Are included in income ratably over a three-year period, starting with the year in which the taxpayer first receives their distribution, unless the taxpayer elects to include all the income on the 2020 tax return.
- Are not subject to the 10% penalty on early distributions that would otherwise apply to most withdrawals before age 59½,
- Are not subject to mandatory tax withholding, and
- The taxpayer may also choose to repay a coronavirus-related distribution back into their retirement plan, provided that they complete the repayment within three years.

These benefits are claimed on new Form 8915-E, *Qualified 2020 Disaster Retirement Plan Distributions and Repayments.*

---

[211] A "coronavirus-related" distribution is a distribution that is made from an eligible retirement plan to a qualified individual from January 1, 2020, to December 30, 2020, up to an aggregate limit of $100,000 from all plans and IRAs. It is *optional* for employers to adopt the distribution and loan rules of the CARES Act.

Example: Branson is 45 and was diagnosed with coronavirus disease on April 25, 2020. He takes a $9,000 distribution from his traditional IRA on May 1, 2020. The distribution is not subject to an early withdrawal penalty or mandatory withholding. He may reduce the tax impact by "spreading it out" over three years. Branson would report $3,000 in income on his federal income tax return for each of 2020, 2021, and 2022. However, he also has the option of electing to include the entire distribution in his income for the year of the distribution (2020).

The *Consolidated Appropriations Act of 2021* included additional provisions for taxpayers facing economic hardship because of non-COVID-19 disasters. The CAA-2021 offers retirement account holders the ability to take a penalty-free early withdrawal of up to $100,000 from their IRA, 401(k), 403(b), or other qualifying retirement accounts in 2020 and 2021 because of a non-COVID-19-related disaster.

10% Penalty on Early Distributions and Penalty Exceptions

A taxpayer may withdraw funds at any time from a traditional IRA account. However, distributions before age 59½ may be subject to an extra 10% excise tax, in addition to normal income tax on the amount distributed. There are several exceptions to the general rule for early distributions. An individual may not have to pay the additional 10% tax in the following situations:

- To the extent the taxpayer has unreimbursed medical expenses that exceed 7.5% of adjusted gross income,
- The distributions do not exceed the cost of the taxpayer's medical insurance while unemployed,
- The taxpayer becomes disabled or dies,
- The distributions are not more than qualified higher education expenses,
- The distributions are used to buy, build, or rebuild a first home (up to $10,000),
- The distributions are used to pay the IRS due to a levy,
- Made as part of a series of substantially equal periodic payments,
- The distributions are made to a qualified reservist (an individual called up to active duty),
- Qualified disaster distributions (for FEMA disasters other than COVID-19).
- Coronavirus-related distributions up to $100,000 (COVID-related distributions), for the 2020 tax year only.
- Qualified birth and adoption distributions starting in tax year 2020 due to the SECURE Act.

Even though distributions in these situations will not be subject to the additional 10% tax, they will be subject to income tax at the taxpayer's normal rates. Distributions that are properly rolled over into another retirement plan or account (other than conversions to a Roth IRA) are generally not subject to either income tax or the 10% additional penalty.

Example: On January 2, 2020, Oksana, age 39, takes a $5,000 distribution from her traditional IRA account in order to buy a car. She does not meet any of the exceptions to the 10% additional penalty tax, so the $5,000 is an early distribution, and is subject to a penalty. Oksana must include the $5,000 in her gross income and pay income tax on it. In addition, she must pay a 10% penalty tax of $500 (10% × $5,000).

Required Minimum Distributions (RMDs) from Traditional IRAs

A person cannot keep funds in a traditional IRA account indefinitely. However, the SECURE Act raised the required minimum distribution (RMD) age from 70 ½ to 72 for taxpayers turning 70½ *after* December 31, 2019. This is a permanent change.

The *first* RMD payment can be delayed until April 1 of the year *following* the year the taxpayer turns 72. The distribution for each subsequent year must be made by December 31. The amount of each RMD is based on IRS tables.[212]

Example: Gabrielle's 70th birthday was July 1, 2019. She does not have to start taking required minimum distributions until reaching age 72. Her first RMD is not due until April 1 of the year *after* she turns age 72. Gabrielle will turn 72 on July 1, 2021. She must take her *first* RMD (for 2021) by April 1, 2022, and her second RMD (for 2022) by December 31, 2022.[213] Failure to take a required RMD can result in an excise penalty equal to 50% of the amount that Gabrielle *should* have withdrawn but did not. If Gabrielle fails to take her RMD by the deadline, she must file Form 5329, *Additional Taxes on Qualified Plans*, to report the excise tax that applies as a result of her failure to take the RMD.

Note: On March 27, 2020, the CARES Act waived the RMD obligations for the 2020 tax year. This special rule also includes April 1, 2020 RMDs for taxpayers who turned 70½ in 2019. Anyone who took a required minimum distribution (RMD) in 2020 also had the opportunity to recontribute those funds back into their retirement account by August 31, 2020. In addition to IRAs, the CARES Act relief applies to 401(k) plans, 403(b) plans, profit-sharing plans and others. The RMD repayment is also not subject to the one rollover per 12-month period limitation.[214]

Example: Nixon is 76. He has been taking required minimum distributions from his traditional IRA for several years now. He takes out his RMD on March 3, 2020, as he normally does. He then learns that the CARES Act has waived the RMD requirement for 2020. He contacts his IRA trustee and asks to recontribute the amounts back into his IRA. Nixon recontributes the full amount back into his IRA on May 2, 2020. With RMDs suspended for 2020, Nixon can wait until 2021 before he takes his next RMD.

Note that these special rules do not apply to Roth IRAs, because Roth IRAs do not require withdrawals until after the death of the owner.

Qualified Charitable Distributions (QCD)

A taxpayer who is 70½ or older may choose to make a qualified charitable distribution (QCD)[215] of up to $100,000 (and if filing as MFJ, the other spouse can also take a QCD up to $100,000) from his IRA to qualified charitable organizations and exclude that amount from income. QCD amounts count toward a taxpayer's RMD, but cannot be claimed as a charitable

---

212 An RMD is calculated by dividing the balance of the IRA account by a life expectancy factor that the IRS publishes in tables within Publication 590, *Individual Retirement Arrangements (IRAs).*

213 Based on an example from the 2020 IRS VITA training module.

214 You can see the full IRS FAQ regarding the special rules for retirement plan distributions and RMDs here: https://www.irs.gov/newsroom/coronavirus-related-relief-for-retirement-plans-and-iras-questions-and-answers.

215 The PATH Act made the QCD election permanent. Although the SECURE ACT raises the RMD age to age 72, the Act does *not* change the Qualified Charitable Distribution (QCD) rules. This means that a taxpayer who is 70½ may make a QCD in 2020 as well as any future tax years.

deduction. In order to qualify, the funds must come out of the taxpayer's IRA by the deadline for minimum distributions (generally December 31).

Charitable distributions are reported on Form 1099-R for the calendar year the distribution is made. The IRA trustee must make the distribution directly to the qualified charity (the taxpayer cannot request a distribution and then donate the money later). Likewise, any tax withholdings on behalf of the owner from an IRA distribution cannot qualify as QCDs.

Example: Simone is 76. Her required minimum distribution is $9,400 in 2020. Simone does not elect to waive her RMD requirement in 2020. She makes a $15,000 qualified charitable distribution from her traditional IRA account directly to her church on March 31, 2020. She does this by directing her IRA trustee to make the contribution directly to the church. The distribution is not taxable to her, because she never has constructive receipt of the funds.

Note: if a taxpayer over age 70½ makes deductible traditional IRA *contributions*, then that taxpayer must later recapture those deducted amounts by reducing any potential qualified charitable distribution made in later years by including those in the taxpayer's taxable income.

IRA Rollover Rules

A rollover is a transfer from one retirement plan to another retirement plan or account. If executed properly, most rollovers are nontaxable events. A taxpayer can make only one rollover from an IRA to another IRA in any twelve-month period, regardless of the number of IRAs the taxpayer owns. There are two exceptions to this rule:

- Trustee-to-trustee transfers between IRAs are not limited.
- Rollovers from a traditional IRA to a Roth IRA are not limited.

With a *direct* rollover, the funds from the taxpayer's current retirement account are transferred directly to a new retirement plan. This is also called a "trustee-to-trustee" transfer. With an *indirect* rollover, it is up to the employee to redeposit the funds into the new IRA or another qualifying retirement account within the mandatory 60-day period to avoid penalty.[216]

A rollover from a traditional IRA to a Roth IRA is more commonly called a "Roth conversion," but it is still a type of rollover. In this case, the conversion will result in taxation of any previously untaxed amounts in the traditional IRA that were rolled over into a Roth IRA.

If a taxpayer receives an IRA distribution and wishes to make a nontaxable rollover, he must complete the rollover transaction by the 60th day following the day he receives the distribution. The "60-day rollover rule" applies to indirect rollovers of a qualified retirement account, such as an IRA or 401(k). Once a taxpayer takes a distribution from their account, they won't owe any interest or penalties as long as the money is redeposited into another qualified retirement account within 60 days.

It is not uncommon for employees to roll funds from one retirement plan to another, especially after a job change. When employees leave a job that had an existing retirement plan, the employee will often roll over their existing plan (such as an employer's 401k) into a

[216] IRS Revenue Procedure 2016-47 allows eligible taxpayers to qualify for a waiver of the 60-day rollover limit and avoid possible early distribution taxes. Taxpayers will submit the self-certification to their plan administrator or an IRA trustee (NOT to the IRS). In the past, taxpayers who failed to meet the rollover time limit could only obtain a waiver by requesting a private letter ruling from the IRS.

traditional IRA. An "indirect" rollover of a retirement account may be requested when an employee changes jobs or leaves a job to start an independent business, but does not want to share information with his former employer. With an indirect rollover, the employer generally withholds 20% of the amount that is pending transfer in order to pay the taxes due.

This withholding is mandatory, even if the taxpayer intends to roll it over. If the taxpayer does roll it over and wants to defer tax on the entire taxable portion, he will be forced to add funds from other sources equal to the amount of tax withheld. This money is returned as a tax credit for the year when the rollover process is completed.

Example: Sheldon quits his old job on September 1, 2020. On October 14, 2020, Sheldon begins a new job, which happens to be with a competitor of his old employer. He has an existing retirement account at his old employer. He decides to transfer the balance of his traditional IRA account to his new employer's retirement plan. Rather than disclose any information about his new workplace to his former boss, Sheldon decides to receive a direct distribution from his IRA of $60,000 in cash. The IRA custodian is required to apply federal income tax withholding rules to a traditional IRA distribution. Because this was an indirect rollover, Sheldon was forced to replace the amounts that were withheld with his own savings. On October 30, 2020, Sheldon deposits the entire amount of $60,000 into his new employer's retirement plan, making up the difference with his own funds. Because the transaction is completed within 60 days, it is completely non-taxable, and any withheld amounts will be returned as a tax credit when he files his 2020 tax return. The rollover must be reported on Form 1040, by including "Rollover" next to Line 4b.

Example: Johanna, age 32, received a $10,000 distribution from her IRA plan on January 2, 2020. Her IRA trustee withholds $2,000 from her distribution. Thirty days after receiving the money, Johanna regrets the distribution, and wishes to recontribute the amounts. If Jordan decides to rollover the full $10,000, she must contribute $2,000 from her own savings, and she must complete the rollover within 60 days. If she does that, Johanna may report $10,000 as a nontaxable rollover and $2,000 as taxes paid in her 2020 return.

Note: In order to avoid this mandatory 20% withholding, a taxpayer may request a "direct rollover." The distribution is then made directly from the custodian or trustee for the employer-sponsored plan to the custodian for the employee's IRA or his new employer's retirement plan. Under this option, the 20% mandatory withholding does not apply.

If a taxpayer sells the distributed property (such as stocks or bonds distributed from an IRA) and rolls over all the proceeds into another traditional IRA or qualified retirement plan within the required time frame, no gain or loss is recognized. The sale proceeds (including any increase in value) are treated as part of the distribution and are not included in the taxpayer's gross income.

If a taxpayer receives both *property* and *cash* in a rollover distribution, he can roll over part or all of the property, part or all of the cash, or any combination of the two he chooses. He can also sell the property and roll over the proceeds into a traditional IRA. But he cannot *keep* the property and substitute his own funds for property he receives.

Example: Arturo is 60 and has a 401(k) at his current job. At the end of the year, he decides to quit his position and transfer his retirement funds elsewhere. He receives a distribution from his employer's 401(k) plan of $20,000 cash and $30,000 worth of stock. He decides to keep the distributed stock and puts it in a taxable brokerage account. He will owe income tax on this amount, but not a 10% penalty because he is over 59½. He can still roll over the $20,000 cash received into a traditional (rollover) IRA, but he cannot substitute an additional $30,000 in cash in place of the stock and treat this amount as if it had also been rolled over.

Distributions from Inherited IRAs

Inherited IRAs are subject to special rules. Following the death of an IRA owner, the IRA usually passes to a beneficiary. The SECURE Act made major changes to the treatment of inherited retirement plans, starting in 2020. The SECURE Act changes apply to both traditional IRAs and Roth IRAs.

Note: Before the SECURE Act, beneficiaries of inherited IRAs could choose a lump sum withdrawal or stretch the withdrawal of required minimum distributions over their life expectancy. The SECURE Act abolishes "stretch IRAs" for most non-spousal beneficiaries. In most cases, the inherited IRA must now be fully distributed to the beneficiary within 10 years after the original owner passes away.[217] There are no required minimum distributions during the ten years, however, all the amounts must be distributed from the inherited account by the end of the tenth year following the year of the original owner's death. If a beneficiary does not distribute the balance of the account by the end of the tenth year following the year of death, a 50% excise tax will apply to any amount not distributed.

Under the SECURE Act, there are now two classifications of designated beneficiaries for an IRA. The Act distinguishes between an "eligible designated beneficiary" and other beneficiaries who inherit an account or IRA. An "eligible designated beneficiary" includes:

- A surviving spouse,
- A disabled or chronically ill individual,
- A minor child of the IRA owner (but not a grandchild), or
- An individual who is not more than 10 years younger than the account owner.

Spousal Beneficiary: Surviving spouses have the most flexibility. Surviving spouses have the same options they had before the SECURE Act. A surviving spouse can elect to treat the IRA as his own by changing the ownership designation or roll over the IRA balance to his own IRA account or certain other types of retirement plans. The surviving spouse can also choose to take distributions over their own life expectancy.

Example: Tamika, 42, and Onassis, 53, are married. Tamika dies suddenly in 2020, and at the time of her death, she has $83,000 in her traditional IRA account. Onassis chooses to roll over the entire $83,000 into his own IRA account, thereby avoiding taxation on the income until he starts taking distributions.

[217] Beneficiaries who inherited IRAs *before* 2020 are grandfathered, and may still utilize the stretch IRA rules.

Example: Desmond, age 73, and Nanette, age 61, are married. Both spouses have traditional IRA accounts. On February 1, 2020, Desmond dies, and his wife inherits his IRA account. Rather than take a distribution from her late husband's account, Nanette decides to do a spousal rollover of the entire account balance into her own IRA. The rollover is not a taxable event, and Nanette is not required to take any minimum distributions from the account until she reaches age 72 (presuming that she reaches her 72nd birthday).

Other eligible designated beneficiaries (non-spouses): Other eligible designated beneficiaries may take their distributions over their own life expectancy. However, minor children must still take remaining distributions within 10 years of reaching age of majority. In other words, the 10-year payout "clock" will begin to run when the minor reaches the age of 18.

Example: Bruno is 38 and unmarried. On February 1, 2020, Bruno dies. The beneficiary of Bruno's IRA is his disabled sister, Megan, who is 26 at the time of her brother's death. Since Megan is a disabled beneficiary, she is allowed to "stretch" the inherited IRA, taking distributions and stretching the tax liability over her lifetime.

Any other beneficiary: For any other beneficiaries, the account balance must generally be fully distributed by the 10-year period after the death of the IRA owner.

Example: Crystal, who was unmarried and had no children, died on May 30, 2020. At the time of her death, Crystal had a traditional IRA worth $200,000. The beneficiary of her IRA is her step-brother, Rudy, age 42. Rudy is not disabled. Rudy can choose to distribute the IRA as a lump sum, or he has 10 years to distribute the balance and pay the tax. No matter what type of distribution he chooses, the amounts he withdraws from the inherited IRA will be subject to income tax. However, the 10% early withdrawal penalty is waived for a beneficiary of an IRA when the original IRA owner has died, (regardless of how old the beneficiary is).

Conversion of a Traditional IRA to a Roth IRA

In the past, taxpayers in higher income brackets were unable to contribute to a Roth IRA. They were also unable to convert from a traditional IRA to a Roth IRA. The IRS rules changed several years ago, and there is no longer an income threshold on Roth IRA conversions.

High-income taxpayers can convert a traditional IRA to a Roth as long as they pay the appropriate tax on the conversion. This is frequently called a "backdoor Roth" or "backdoor conversion."

There is no 10% early withdrawal penalty if the funds from the traditional IRA are deposited into a Roth IRA within 60 days. If a taxpayer wishes to convert all or a portion of his traditional IRA to a Roth IRA, he is required to pay income taxes on the amount of pre-tax (deductible) contributions converted, as well as the growth in value resulting from earnings on those contributions.

After the funds are converted to a Roth IRA, additional earnings are tax-free, and distributions are generally not subject to tax.

Example: Ruth converted her traditional IRA to a Roth IRA in 2020. The traditional IRA has a balance of $150,000. The entire balance represents deductible contributions and earnings that have not previously been taxed. She reports the amount of the balance that was converted to a Roth IRA as taxable income on her 2020 tax return. The converted amounts are not subject to a penalty, regardless of Ruth's age.

A Roth conversion is reported on Form 8606, *Nondeductible IRAs*. An inherited traditional IRA is generally not eligible to be converted to a Roth IRA unless it is inherited directly from a spouse. Non-spousal beneficiaries (for example, a child who inherits a traditional IRA from a deceased parent) are not allowed to convert a traditional IRA to a Roth IRA.

IRA Recharacterizations

In the past, a taxpayer was able to "undo" or reverse a rollover or conversion of one type of IRA to a different type of IRA through a *recharacterization.* Essentially, by recharacterizing an IRA, it is as if the conversion or rollover never occurred. The Tax Cuts and Jobs Act eliminates the option to recharacterize, or "unwind" an earlier Roth conversion. This means that a Roth IRA conversion made in 2020, cannot be reversed.

Example: On June 1, 2020, Lawrence converts his traditional IRA to a Roth IRA. However, his investments perform poorly, and his account loses value after the conversion. He wants to go back and change his mind. However, since he converted his traditional IRA to a Roth, the conversion is permanent. He cannot undo the conversion.

Some types of recharacterizations are still permitted. For example, a recharacterization is allowed for fixing certain mistakes, or to correct an error in their IRA contributions. A client can use the recharacterization rules to fix an invalid contribution or an invalid rollover, for example. When a taxpayer accidentally makes an overcontribution to a traditional or Roth IRA, they can also choose to either recharacterize the contribution or withdraw it, otherwise a 6% excise tax will apply.

Example: Armin is age 50 and unmarried. He does not have a retirement plan at work. On May 1, 2020, he makes a $7,000 contribution to a Roth IRA for the 2020 tax year. In December, he sells a large block of cryptocurrency at a large gain, which raises his 2020 MAGI is $290,000, which is in excess of the maximum income thresholds to be eligible to contribute to a Roth. By the time he discovers his error, it is February 5, 2021. He moves the entire contribution into a traditional IRA by making a trustee-to-trustee transfer. This is not a "rollover;" it is a *recharacterization.* Armin has recharacterized the prohibited Roth IRA contribution into a traditional IRA, which is allowable. He will avoid the 6% excise tax that would have otherwise applied to his earlier (improper) Roth contribution.

Excise Tax on Excess IRA Contributions

If a taxpayer accidentally contributes more to his IRA than is allowed for the year, the excess contribution is subject to a 6% excise tax. However, the IRS will allow a taxpayer to correct an excess contribution if certain rules are followed.

If he makes a contribution that exceeds the annual maximum or his qualifying compensation, the excess contribution and all related earnings must be withdrawn from the IRA before the due

date (*including* extensions) of the tax return for that year. If a taxpayer corrects the excess contribution within this period, the 6% penalty will apply only to the amounts earned on the excess contribution. The taxpayer must also report the earnings on the excess contribution as taxable income for the year in which the withdrawal is made. For each year that the excess amounts remain in the IRA, the taxpayer must pay the 6% tax. However, this tax can never exceed 6% of the value of the taxpayer's IRA at the end of the tax year.

Note: A taxpayer cannot apply an excess contribution to an earlier year even if the taxpayer contributed less than the maximum amount allowable for an earlier year. However, the taxpayer is allowed to apply an excess contribution to a *later* year if the contributions for that later year are less than the maximum allowable for that year. This is a permitted type of recharacterization.

Prohibited Transactions

Generally, a prohibited transaction is the "improper use" of an IRA by the owner, a beneficiary, or a disqualified person (typically a fiduciary or family member). Prohibited transactions related to an IRA include:

- Using the IRA as security or collateral for a loan,
- Buying property for personal use with IRA funds (for example, using IRA funds to buy a vacation home the IRA owner or his family will use),
- Personally borrowing money from the IRA (i.e., there is no such thing as an "IRA loan," although some types of retirement plans do allow limited borrowing, traditional IRAs do not) [218]
- Selling, leasing, or exchanging property to the IRA account,
- Accepting unreasonable compensation for managing IRA assets,
- Granting account fiduciaries to obtain, use, or borrow against account assets for their own gain,
- Transferring plan assets, lending money, or providing goods and services to "disqualified persons," usually a close family member, or a business that a close family member owns and controls.

For the purposes of the prohibited transaction rules, "family members" includes the taxpayer's spouse, parents, grandparents, children; and grandchildren and spouses of the taxpayer's children and grandchildren. Family members do not include in-laws, cousins, friends, aunts, uncles, siblings, and stepsiblings.

Although occurrences of prohibited transactions are rare, the consequences can be catastrophic. If a prohibited transaction occurs at any time during the year, normally, the account ceases to be treated as an IRA, and its assets are treated as if having been wholly distributed on the first day of the year.

However, in situations where an IRA account, or a portion of an IRA account, is used as security for a loan, only the amount used as security for the loan is treated as a distribution from the IRA as of the first day of the year that the loan was made, but the IRA continues to exist. If the

[218] Do not confuse the borrowing restrictions for traditional IRAs and other types of retirement accounts. Loans are not permitted from IRAs or from other IRA-based plans such as SEP-IRAs and SIMPLE IRA plans. Loans are only possible from qualified plans, such as: 401(k) plans or 403(b) plans, and from governmental plans. Qualified retirement plans are covered in detail in *Book 2, Businesses.*

total fair market value as of that date is more than the taxpayer's basis in the IRA, the excess amount is reportable as taxable income. It may also be subject to the additional 10% penalty on early distributions.

Example: Zamir, age 40, has a self-directed IRA account. The fair market value of Zamir's traditional IRA was $300,000 as of January 1, 2020. He had previously made $200,000 of nondeductible contributions to his IRA, so that was his basis in the account. On January 10, 2020, Zamir borrowed $150,000 from his IRA to purchase a vacation home for himself. This is a prohibited transaction, and Zamir's entire IRA account will no longer be treated as an IRA from the date of the withdrawal. Since the FMV of the IRA on the first day of the year, $300,000, is greater than Zamir's basis, $200,000, the excess amount of $100,000 is reported as taxable income. Zamir would also be subject to the additional 10% penalty on the entire amount, for withdrawing funds before the age of 59½.

Example: Wilbert is 52 and has $180,000 in his traditional IRA. His daughter, Teralynn, wants to buy a home for $140,000 but does not have sufficient funds. As a result, Wilbert lends his daughter $140,000 from his self-directed IRA to buy the home. This is considered "self-dealing" and is a prohibited transaction. For Wilbert, the IRA is deemed immediately disqualified as of January 1, 2020 (the year in which the prohibited transaction occurred). The entire amount of the IRA is deemed distributed in 2020, and an early withdrawal penalty of 10% would also apply to the entire amount of the IRA ($180,000).

Note: Prohibited transactions are rare occurrences, and they generally only occur when a taxpayer has a "self-directed" IRA. A self-directed IRA is a type of account that offers a taxpayer the ability to use his retirement funds to make almost any type of investment without requiring a financial institution or another custodian.

Prohibited IRA Investments

Almost any type of investment is permissible inside an IRA, including stocks, bonds, mutual funds and even real estate. However, there are some investments that are prohibited. For example, the law does not permit IRA funds to be invested in life insurance contracts or collectibles. If the taxpayer invests in any of these prohibited investments using IRA funds, it is treated as a prohibited transaction. The following investments are prohibited:

- Collectibles and jewelry, such as: artwork, antiques, porcelain, baseball cards, uncut gemstones, or comic books,
- Precious metals, coins, and gemstones
- S corporation stock,
- Life insurance contracts,
- Real estate held for personal use (real property can be held in an IRA as long as the investments are not in the taxpayer's personal name, and not used for personal use, such as a vacation home used by the taxpayer).

There is a narrow exception for investments in gold and silver coins minted by the U.S. Treasury Department. Investments in certain gold, silver, palladium, and platinum bullion are also allowable.

Example: Darren has a self-directed traditional IRA. Without consulting his retirement advisor, Darren decides to purchase a piece of artwork as an investment using his IRA funds. Darren has engaged in a prohibited transaction. The IRA is deemed immediately disqualified, and the entire amount in the IRA is deemed distributed in the year that he purchases the collectible with IRA funds.

Retirement Plans for Businesses

Retirement plans for businesses include Simplified Employee Pension (SEP-IRA) plans, Savings Incentive Match Plan for Employees (SIMPLE) plans, and qualified plans. The term "qualified" refers to certain IRS requirements that the employer must adhere to in order to obtain a retirement plan's tax-favored status. SEP and SIMPLE plans must also meet certain requirements but are much less complex than those that apply to qualified plans.

Study Note: Business retirement plans are covered in greater detail, and from the ***employer's*** perspective, in *Book 2: Businesses,* as much of the related information is tested on Part 2 of the EA exam. In Part 1 of the exam, you will need to understand the employee's perspective with regard to retirement plans. For Part 2, you must understand retirement plans from the employer's perspective.

If retirement plans are structured and administered properly, businesses can deduct contributions they make on behalf of their employees or, if self-employed, themselves. Both the contributions and the earnings are generally tax-free until distribution. Further, some plans also allow employees to make contributions, most commonly in pretax dollars (so that a portion of their salaries are not taxed until the amounts are later distributed to them by the plan).

SEP-IRA Plans: SEPs provide a simplified method for employers to make contributions to a retirement plan for themselves and their employees. Instead of setting up a profit-sharing plan with a trust, an employer can adopt a SEP agreement and make contributions directly to individual SEP-IRA accounts (similar to a traditional IRA as described previously) for himself and each eligible employee. A SEP plan is funded exclusively by employer contributions; employee contributions are not permitted. A self-employed taxpayer may set up a SEP and fund it, as long as he has earnings from his business.

SIMPLE Plans: An employer can generally set up a SIMPLE plan if the business has 100 or fewer employees. Under a SIMPLE plan, employees can choose to make salary reduction contributions rather than receiving these amounts as part of their regular pay. An employer is allowed to contribute matching contributions or non-elective contributions.

A SIMPLE plan can be structured in one of two ways: as a SIMPLE IRA (again, similar to traditional IRAs as described previously) or as a SIMPLE 401(k) plan (similar to the qualified 401(k) plans described below).

Qualified Retirement Plans

There are two basic kinds of qualified retirement plans: **defined contribution** plans and **defined benefit** plans, and different rules apply to each. An employer is allowed to have more than one type of qualified plan, but contributions cannot exceed annual limits. All qualified plans are subject to federal regulation under the Employee Retirement Income Security Act (ERISA).

The federal government does not require an employer to establish a retirement plan, but it provides minimum federal standards for qualified plans.

Defined Contribution Plans

A defined contribution plan provides an individual account for each participant in the plan depending upon how the plan is structured. It provides benefits to each participant based on the amounts contributed to the participant's account, along with subsequent investment income or losses, and, in some instances, allocations of forfeitures among participant accounts.

The participants, the employer, or both may contribute to the individual participant accounts. Examples of defined contribution plans include profit-sharing plans, 401(k) plans, 403(b) plans, and 457 plans. Depending upon how a qualified plan is structured, salary reduction/elective deferral contributions are employee contributions based on a percentage of the employee's compensation and are generally made on a pretax basis.

This limitation applies to the aggregate amounts of contributions to any qualified plans, SEPs, and SIMPLE plans in which the individual participates during the year. However, the contribution cannot exceed the amount of the employee's compensation. Depending on the individual plan, the employer may provide matching contributions for employees who make elective deferrals.

Example: Spencer earns $80,000 per year as an insurance executive. He participates in his company's profit-sharing 401(k) plan. He contributes 3% of his pretax wages to the plan in 2020, or $2,400 ($80,000 × .03). Spencer's company contributes a matching 3% to his individual 401(k) account.

Distributions: Distributions to participants may be made either on a periodic basis, such as annuity payments or as a lump sum. As is the case with distributions from traditional IRA accounts (as well as SEP and SIMPLE plans), distributions generally are not permitted prior to when the participant retires or otherwise terminates employment, dies, becomes disabled, or reaches age 59½. Earlier distributions are generally subject to an additional 10% penalty tax.

Note: For purposes of the net investment income tax (NIIT), net investment income does not include distributions from a qualified retirement plan, such as a 401(k), or from traditional or Roth IRAs. However, these distributions are taken into account when determining the modified adjusted gross income threshold.

Required minimum distributions (RMDs) from defined contribution plans[219] must generally begin by April 1 of the year following the calendar year when the taxpayer retires, or the year in which the taxpayer reaches age 72 whichever comes later, although in 2020, taxpayers are allowed to waive their RMD.

Example: In 2020, Norman retires at age 63 after working for three decades at an auto manufacturer. His employer offers a defined benefit plan in which Norman participates. Norman chooses to begin taking distributions from his 401(k) account in the same year he retires. The distributions would be taxed as retirement income on his individual tax return.

[219] Defined contribution plans include 401(k) plans, profit-sharing, and 403(b) plans.

Defined Benefit Plans

A defined benefit plan, often called a traditional pension plan, promises a specified benefit amount or annuity for each participant after retirement. Benefits are typically based on formulas that consider the participant's years of service with the employer and his earnings history. The federal government and most state and local governments provide defined benefit plans for their employees. However, fewer and fewer private businesses offer defined benefit plans because they are costly to administer and inflexible.

The benefits promised by many defined benefit plans are protected by federal insurance. Contributions to a defined benefit plan are not optional. Contributions are typically based on actuarial calculations that estimate the amounts necessary to pay benefits in the future.

Loans and Distributions from Qualified Plans

Unlike traditional IRAs and Roth IRAs, where withdrawals are permitted at any time, distributions from qualified plans are generally restricted. This means that a taxpayer cannot withdraw from the account whenever he chooses, (like he can from a traditional IRA or Roth IRA). Generally, distributions of elective deferrals cannot be made until one of the following occurs:

- The taxpayer dies, becomes disabled, or has a severance from employment.
- The plan terminates, and no successor defined contribution plan is established or maintained by the employer.
- The taxpayer reaches age 59½ or
- The taxpayer incurs significant financial hardship.

Some limited borrowing from qualified plans is allowed. Loans are not dependent upon hardship, but some plans may provide for loans and hardship withdrawals (although the plan is not required to do so).

Note: In 2020, the CARES Act provides special provisions for providing enhanced access to plan distributions and plan loans. In prior years, a plan loan could generally be no more than $50,000, or the greater of $10,000 or 50% of the vested portion of the participant's account balance. But in 2020, participants are allowed to withdraw up to an aggregate limit of $100,000 (or their vested plan balance, whichever is less).

The CARES Act permits an additional year for repayment of loans from eligible retirement plans and relaxes limits on loans.[220]

- **Certain loan repayments may be delayed for one year:** If a loan is outstanding on or after March 27, 2020, and any repayment on the loan is due from March 27, 2020, to December 31, 2020, that due date may be delayed under the plan for up to one year. Any payments after the suspension period will be adjusted to reflect the delay and any interest accruing during the delay.
- **Loan limit may be increased:** The CARES Act also permits employers to increase the maximum loan amount available to qualified individuals. For plan loans made to a qualified individual from March 27, 2020, to September 22, 2020, the limit may be

---

[220] Note that these special rules for the repayment of plan loans do not apply to IRAs, because loans are never permitted from an IRA.

increased up to the lesser of: (1) $100,000 (minus outstanding plan loans of the individual), or (2) the individual's vested benefit under the plan.

Once again, employers are *not required* to adopt the distribution and loan rules of the CARES Act. For example, an employer may choose to provide for coronavirus-related distributions but choose not to change its plan loan provisions or loan repayment schedules.

Even if an employer does not treat a distribution as "coronavirus-related," a qualified individual may treat a distribution that meets the requirements to be a coronavirus-related distribution as coronavirus-related on the individual's federal income tax return.

If a loan is not repaid according to the specified payment terms, it may be considered a taxable distribution. This may apply if a participant terminates employment with the employer that sponsors the plan.[221]

Hardship Distributions

A 401(k) plan may allow participants to receive hardship distributions because of an immediate and heavy financial need, such as sudden medical or funeral expenses. Hardship distributions are limited to the amount of the employee's elective deferrals and generally do not include any income earned on the deferred amounts. The amount of the distribution may include amounts necessary to pay taxes or penalties anticipated to result from the distribution, including the 10% penalty levied on early distributions.

Example: Damara's home is in foreclosure, and she is in immediate danger of being evicted. She requests a hardship distribution from her 401(k), which is granted. Since she is under age 59½, Damara would likely have to pay the 10% early distribution penalty.

Note: Some types of retirement plans provide for hardship distributions. These include 401(k) plans, 403(b) plans, and 457(b) plans, which are common retirement plans that may permit hardship distributions. A "hardship distribution" is not the same as a "disaster distribution." A qualified disaster distribution gets special tax treatment and is only available to taxpayers who have incurred losses or hardship in a presidentially declared disaster area (i.e., a FEMA disaster area).

Qualified Disaster Distributions

On December 20, 2019, extender and disaster tax relief provisions were included in the 2020 *Consolidated Appropriations Act.* The disaster relief provisions are retroactive and cover federally declared disasters that occurred in 2018 and 2019.

The extender provisions allow for an exception to the 10% early withdrawal penalty for taxpayers who are affected by presidentially declared disasters. This is called a "qualified disaster distribution." Amounts distributed can also be *recontributed* over a three-year period, and the taxpayer is allowed to recoup any income tax paid on the distribution.

[221] Most qualified plans offer employees the ability to borrow from their own retirement account and repay that amount with interest to their own retirement account. IRS regulations permit qualified plans to offer loans to plan participants, but the plan is not *required* to.

Note: Other than a participant loan, a retirement plan distribution generally cannot be repaid, unless it qualifies as an eligible rollover distribution. Hardship distributions are also generally not eligible for repayment, but qualified disaster distributions *can* be repaid. Any qualified federal disaster relief withdrawal will *not be taxable* if it is recontributed to the account within three years of the date of distribution.

Example: Dwayne is 32 years old and single. Dwayne's main home was severely damaged by a tornado, which was later declared a presidentially declared disaster. Dwayne takes a $40,000 distribution from his traditional IRA on September 24, 2020, to help him rebuild and also to pay emergency living expenses. This "qualified disaster distribution" is subject to income tax, but not the 10% penalty. If he chooses to do so, Dwayne may repay the distribution within a 3-year period. The amount of the repayment is treated as a trustee-to-trustee transfer and is not included in income.

If a taxpayer's residence is in a qualified disaster area, disaster withdrawals from qualified plans and traditional IRAs are permitted, and not subject to the normal 10% early withdrawal penalty. The law also expands the availability of 401(k) plan loans and extends the normal repayment period for those loans.

With regard to qualified retirement plans (i.e., 401(k), 403(b) and 457(b) plans), the loan limit is increased to $100,000 or 100% for taxpayers in affected presidential disaster areas. Any repayment would be treated as a trustee-to-trustee transfer made within the 60-day time frame under applicable regulations.

Example: Lorelei is 42 and lives in Arkansas. Lorelei's apartment complex was destroyed by severe flooding and storms on May 21, 2020, and she was left homeless. The President officially declared a FEMA disaster on May 27, 2020, and the area became eligible for federal aid. Lorelei withdrew $35,000 from her 401(k) plan on June 1, 2020 to pay emergency expenses and housing costs. Her withdrawal is not subject to a 10% early withdrawal penalty, because it qualifies as a disaster distribution. If she wishes to repay the distribution at a later date, she has three years to do so.

Traditional IRA vs. Roth IRA Comparison		
Issue	**Traditional IRA**	**Roth IRA**
Age limit	No age limit in 2020 for contributions.	No age limit for contributions
2020 Contribution limits	The lesser of $6,000 (or $7,000 if age 50 or older by the end of the year) and qualifying taxable compensation.	Same
Deductibility of contributions	Generally deductible.	No. Contributions to a Roth IRA are never deductible.
Filing requirements	No filing requirement unless nondeductible contributions are made. Nondeductible contributions must be reported on Form 8606.	Filing requirement related to a conversion of a traditional IRA to a Roth IRA. None related to contributions made directly to a Roth IRA.
Mandatory distributions	RMDs by April 1 of the year following the year a taxpayer reaches age 72 (RMD can be waived in 2020).	There are no required distributions unless the IRA owner dies.
How distributions are taxed	Distributions from a traditional IRA are taxed as ordinary income.	Distributions from a Roth IRA are generally not taxed.
Income limits	Anyone with qualifying compensation can contribute. Phaseout of deductibility is based upon AGI if the taxpayer and/or spouse are covered by an employer plan.	There are income limits for contributions, but "backdoor" conversions of a traditional IRA to a Roth IRA are still permissible.

Unit 16: Study Questions

(Test yourself first, then check the correct answers at the end of this quiz.)

1. Joanne e-files her 2020 tax return early, on February 27, 2021. What is the latest date that she can make a traditional IRA contribution for the 2020 tax year?

A. April 15, 2021.
B. February 27, 2021.
C. December 31, 2021.
D. October 15, 2021 (with a valid extension).

2. Alfred is 42 and unmarried. He earned $48,000 in wages during the year. He has a Roth IRA and a traditional IRA with two different financial institutions. In 2020, he contributed $2,500 to his Roth IRA. He also wants to contribute to his traditional IRA account. What is the maximum he can contribute to a traditional IRA in 2020?

A. $0
B. $3,500
C. $4,000
D. $5,000

3. Elizabeth and Aaron are both age 63, married, and lived together all year. They both work, and each has a traditional IRA. Aaron is mostly retired, and Elizabeth still works full-time. In 2020, Aaron earned $4,000 of self-employment income from working for a popular rideshare service on the weekends. He also received $18,000 of annuity income. Elizabeth earned $52,000 in wages. They prefer to file separately. If they file MFS, what is the maximum that Aaron can contribute to his IRA?

A. $1,000
B. $4,000
C. $5,500
D. $6,500

4. When does the IRS require the owner of a Roth IRA to start taking required minimum distributions?

A. After the death of the IRA owner.
B. At age 71½.
C. At age 72.
D. Never required.

5. Shari switched jobs in the middle of the year. She received a distribution in 2020 from her former employer's retirement plan and wanted to roll it over to an IRA with another bank. How long does she have to complete the indirect rollover to avoid income tax and penalties on the distribution?

A. 30 days from distribution.
B. 60 days from distribution.
C. December 31 of that tax year.
D. April 15 of the next tax year.

6. Melissa, age 41, and William, age 47, are married and file jointly. Both are self-employed and report their business income on Schedule C. William's Schedule C business has $9,900 in profits during the year. His wife, Melissa, has a loss of ($5,100) on her Schedule C. Melissa also earned $3,000 in wages from a part-time seasonal job. They also co-own a residential rental property together. The rental earned $58,000 in income during the year. What is their maximum allowable IRA contribution for 2020?

A. William can contribute $6,000, and Melissa can contribute $6,000.
B. William can contribute $6,000, and Melissa can contribute $3,000.
C. William can contribute $6,000, and Melissa cannot contribute.
D. William can contribute $7,000, and Melissa can contribute $3,000.

7. Fyodor, age 25, is an unmarried college student working part-time. He earns $3,500 in wages during 2020. He also receives $500 of interest income and a $9,000 gift from his parents to help pay his college tuition. What is his maximum IRA contribution in 2020?

A. $0
B. $3,500
C. $5,500
D. $6,500

8. Steven, age 36 and single, is in the Marines. He has the following income in 2020:

Nontaxable combat pay	$30,500
Regular wages	$2,100
Interest income	$4,600

What is the maximum amount that Steven can contribute to a traditional IRA?

A. $2,100
B. $4,600
C. $6,000
D. $7,000

9. Kristina, 48, is a full-time graduate student with $1,200 of wages. She marries Ruslan, 50, during the year. Ruslan has taxable compensation of $66,000 in 2020. What is the maximum they can contribute to their traditional IRA accounts in 2020 if they file jointly?

A. $1,200
B. $8,200
C. $12,000
D. $13,000

10. Rafael, 40, earns $26,000 in wages during the year. Although he is allowed to contribute up to $6,000 to his traditional IRA, he only has enough cash to contribute $2,500. On April 30, 2021, Rafael expects to receive a big commission bonus, and he wishes to make a catch-up contribution for 2020. Rafael filed an extension for his tax return, so his federal return isn't due until October 15, 2021. Which of the following statements is correct?

A. Rafael can contribute an additional $3,500 on April 30, 2021, and allocate the contribution for the 2020 tax year as long as he files his tax return by the extended due date.
B. Rafael cannot contribute any additional funds for the 2020 tax year past the normal tax return filing deadline (April 15).
C. Rafael can make a 2020 contribution on April 30, 2021, as long as he files his return on the same day.
D. Rafael cannot make a 2020 contribution to his IRA after December 31.

11. Vadik, age 42, has a traditional IRA account. He wants to convert his traditional IRA to a Roth IRA. Which of the following statements is *correct?*

A. Vadik can convert his traditional IRA to a Roth IRA and the transaction is tax-free.
B. Vadik can convert his traditional IRA to a Roth IRA. Income tax must be paid on the conversion.
C. Vadik can rollover his traditional IRA to a Roth IRA only if his income is under $150,000.
D. Vadik cannot convert his traditional IRA to a Roth IRA because he is under 59½ years of age.

12. Ernesto, age 71, and Susie, age 49, are married and file jointly. In 2020, Ernesto earned wages of $30,000, and Susie earned $5,000. If they file jointly, how much can they contribute to their traditional IRAs?

A. Susie and Ernesto can each contribute $6,000 to their respective IRA accounts.
B. Susie and Ernesto can each contribute $7,000 to their respective IRA accounts.
C. Susie can contribute $6,000. Ernesto can contribute $7,000.
D. Susie can contribute $7,000. Ernesto cannot make an IRA contribution.

13. An "excess" contribution to an IRA is subject to an excise tax. What is the applicable excise tax rate?

A. 3%
B. 6%
C. 10%
D. 50%

14. Nichelle is single, age 63, and has the following taxable income in 2020:

Annuity income	$15,600
W-2 Wages	$5,300
Interest income	$2,800
Passive rental income from a residential rental	$26,000

What is the maximum amount that Nichelle can contribute to her traditional IRA in 2020?

A. $3,000
B. $5,300
C. $6,000
D. $7,000

15. Gwendolyn, age 38, is single and has no dependents. She contributes $6,000 to a traditional IRA, and she also participates in her employer's 401(k) plan. She has a modified adjusted gross income of $239,000 in 2020. Which of the following is correct regarding her IRA contribution?

A. It is fully deductible.
B. It is partially deductible.
C. It is not deductible.
D. It is subject to a 6% excise tax.

16. Which of the following distributions from a traditional IRA is subject to an additional 10% penalty?

A. Distributions made prior to age 59½.
B. Distributions made after age 70½.
C. Distributions made to a beneficiary after the IRA owner's death.
D. Distributions made due to an IRS levy.

Unit 16: Quiz Answers

1. The answer is A. Joanne is allowed to make her retirement contribution at any time during the year up to the due date of her tax return, *not including* extensions. IRA contributions for 2020 must be made by April 15, 2021.

2. The answer is B. Assuming Alfred has sufficient qualifying compensation; he could contribute $3,500 to his traditional IRA ($2,500 + $3,500 = $6,000). The 2020 maximum for contributions to *all types* of IRAs is $6,000 per taxpayer (for taxpayers under the age of 50). Taxpayers are allowed to have different types of IRA accounts, but the maximum contribution limits apply to their total contributions for the year.

3. The answer is B. Since Aaron is married and lived with his wife during the year but is filing separately, he can contribute no more than $4,000, the amount of his qualifying compensation for IRA purposes.

4 The answer is A. Unlike traditional IRAs, Roth IRAs do not require withdrawals until after the death of the owner. This is why Roth IRAs are used as an estate-planning tool. Traditional IRAs require owners to begin taking required minimum distributions (RMDs) at age 72 (but the RMD can be waived in 2020 due to the CARES Act). A Roth IRA does not require any distributions until after the owner's death.

5. The answer is B. Shari has 60 days to complete the rollover. If she does not complete the rollover within 60 days, the entire distribution is subject to income tax in 2020.

6. The answer is A. On a jointly filed return, they are both allowed to contribute and deduct the maximum allowable for their age bracket ($6,000 each in 2020). The rental income is not qualifying compensation for IRA purposes, but William and Melissa may use their combined self-employment income to figure their maximum allowable IRA contribution. Even though Melissa's business had a net operating loss for the year, she is not required to "offset" her Schedule C losses from her wages when determining her "allowable" IRA contribution. The answer is figured as follows:

William: $9,900 self-employment income + Melissa: $3,000 wages
= $12,900 in total "qualifying compensation"

If they file jointly, they can each contribute $6,000 to a traditional IRA for themselves ($6,000 x 2 = $12,000, which is less than the amount of their qualifying compensation).

7. The answer is B. Fyodor's IRA contribution for 2020 is limited to $3,500, the total amount of his wages. The interest income and the gifted money from his parents are not qualifying compensation for IRA purposes.

8. The answer is C. Steven may contribute $6,000 in 2020, the maximum contribution allowed for his age, because a taxpayer may *elect* to treat nontaxable combat pay as qualifying compensation for IRA purposes. The interest income is not considered qualifying compensation, but his wages exceed

the maximum contribution amount, so he is still allowed to make the maximum contribution for the year.

9. The answer is D. They can contribute $13,000 in 2020 if they file jointly. Kristina can contribute $6,000, and Ruslan can contribute $7,000 because he is age 50. Even though Kristina only has $1,200 of qualifying compensation, she can use her husband's compensation to determine her maximum contribution (as long as they file jointly).

10. The answer is B. Rafael cannot contribute any additional funds after April 15, 2021, the due date for filing 2020 tax returns, regardless of whether he files an extension. If contributions to a traditional IRA for the year were less than the limit, a taxpayer cannot contribute more after the original due date of the tax return to make up the difference. If Rafael wants to make an additional contribution for 2020, he must do it by the *normal* filing deadline of April 15, whether he files an extension or not.

11. The answer is B. Vadik may convert his traditional IRA to a Roth IRA, but he will owe income tax on the conversion. If he wishes to convert all or a portion of his traditional IRA to a Roth IRA, he is required to pay income taxes on the amount of pre-tax(deductible) contributions converted, as well as the growth in value resulting from earnings on those contributions. After the funds are converted to a Roth IRA, additional earnings are tax-free, and distributions are generally not subject to tax. However, penalties apply if he withdraws from the Roth IRA within five years of the conversion. The conversion is reported on Form 8606, *Nondeductible IRAs.*

12. The answer is C. If they file jointly, Susie can contribute $6,000 (she is under 50 years of age). Ernesto can contribute $7,000, because he is over the age of 50. The SECURE Act eliminated the age limit for making contributions to a traditional IRA in 2020, so taxpayers of any age can now contribute to a traditional IRA.

13. The answer is B. A 6% excise tax applies to excess contributions. The taxpayer will not have to pay the 6% tax on the excess contribution if the excess contribution and any earnings are withdrawn by the due date of his return, *including* extensions. If a taxpayer corrects the excess contribution in time, the 6% penalty will apply only to the earnings on the excess contribution.

14. The answer is B. Nichelle's maximum contribution for 2020 is $5,300. Only her wage income qualifies as "compensation" for the purposes of an IRA contribution. The annuity income, rental income, and interest income do not qualify.

15. The answer is C. Gwendolyn cannot deduct her IRA contribution. Contributions to a traditional IRA who participates in an employer-sponsored retirement plan are allowed, but their deductibility is phased out at higher income thresholds. When MAGI reaches a certain threshold, the taxpayer's traditional IRA contribution is not deductible. In 2020, unmarried filers who participate in an employer plan and have a MAGI of more than $75,000 are not allowed to make deductible IRA contributions. If Gwendolyn makes *nondeductible* contributions to her traditional IRA, she must attach Form 8606, *Nondeductible IRAs*, to her tax return.

16. The answer is A. Distributions made *prior* to age 59½ are subject to a 10% early withdrawal penalty, (if no exception applies). Some exceptions that allow early distributions from an IRA, as well as from qualified retirement plans, include the following:

- Distributions made to a beneficiary or estate after death.
- Distributions made because of permanent disability.
- Distributions to the extent of medical expenses (medical expenses that exceed 7.5%-of-AGI), whether or not the taxpayer itemizes deductions for the year.
- Distributions made due to an IRS levy.
- Qualified disaster distributions.
- Qualified coronavirus distributions.

The distributions listed above are not subject to the early distribution penalty.

Unit 17: Foreign Financial Reporting

More Reading:
IRS FBAR Reference Guide
Instructions for FinCEN Form 114
Instructions for Form 3520

In this chapter, we will discuss foreign financial reporting requirements for U.S. taxpayers. The *Bank Secrecy Act (BSA)* is the law that imposes reporting requirements on foreign financial accounts. The *Foreign Account Tax Compliance Act (FATCA)* is the law that mandates the reporting of foreign financial assets.

The subject of foreign financial reporting is extremely complex, and the IRS continues to issue guidance on how taxpayers and tax professionals should approach this difficult topic.

A person who holds a foreign financial account may have a reporting obligation even when the account produces no taxable income, and even if the person does not have an individual income tax filing requirement. For the purposes of foreign financial reporting requirements, a "United States person" includes: U.S. citizens, U.S. nationals, U.S. residents, and U.S. entities.[222] It also includes nonresident aliens electing to be treated as U.S. residents in order to file a joint tax return.

There are several different forms[223] used for reporting foreign bank accounts, foreign assets, and foreign gifts. These are:

- **The FBAR** (Form 114, Report of Foreign Bank and Financial Accounts)
- **Form 8938,** Statement of Specified Foreign Financial Assets
- **Schedule B,** Interest and Ordinary Dividends (Part III)
- **Form 3520,** Annual Return to Report Transactions with Foreign Trusts and Receipt of Certain Foreign Gifts
- **Form 5471:** Information Return of U.S. Persons With Respect To Certain Foreign Corporations

Federal law requires that U.S. persons report all worldwide income, including income from foreign trusts and foreign bank accounts. In many cases, these taxpayers need to complete Schedule B and attach it to their tax return. Certain taxpayers may also have to fill out and attach Form 8938, *Statement of Foreign Financial Assets*. Form 3520 is used to report certain foreign gifts and bequests, as well as certain transactions with foreign trusts. Schedule B, Form 3520, and Form 8938 are all filed with the Internal Revenue Service.

The FBAR filing requirement, however, is a separate filing requirement than filing a regular tax return. FBARs are not filed with the IRS. These forms are filed directly with the Financial Crimes Enforcement Network (FinCEN), which is a division of the U.S. Treasury Department. Generally, records of accounts required to be reported on the FBAR should be kept for five years from the due date of the report, which is the year *following* the calendar year being reported.

---

222 See the *IRS Reference Guide on the Report of Foreign Bank and Financial Accounts (FBAR).*

223 This list is not comprehensive; it only includes the most commonly used forms for foreign-financial reporting and those that are listed on the Prometric test specifications for Part 1 of the EA exam. There are additional forms, such as Form 8865, *Return of U.S. Persons with Respect to Certain Foreign Partnerships,* which is used to declare interest in a foreign partnership.

FBARs in General

The term "FBAR" refers to Form 114, *Report of Foreign Bank and Financial Accounts*. The FBAR is a reporting requirement and does not directly impact tax liability. In 2003, the Department of the U.S. Treasury delegated FBAR enforcement authority to the Internal Revenue Service (IRS). This means that the IRS does not process the FBAR filings, but the IRS is responsible for FBAR *enforcement*. With regard to FBAR filings, the IRS is responsible for:

- Investigating possible civil violations,
- Assessing and collecting civil penalties, and
- Issuing administrative rulings.

The FBAR must be filed electronically and is only available online through the BSA E-Filing System.[224] The FBAR is not considered part of the taxpayer's individual tax return. Tax treaties with the United States do not affect FBAR filing obligations. A U.S. taxpayer is required to file an FBAR if:

- The person had a financial interest in, or *signature authority* over, at least one financial account located outside of the United States, and
- The *aggregate* value of all foreign financial accounts exceeded $10,000 (U.S. dollars) at any time during the calendar year reported.[225] This threshold is the same for every filing status. [226]

Example: Gustavo is a U.S. citizen who has a bank account in Mexico. In prior years, the value of his foreign bank account totaled approximately $7,500. Therefore, Gustavo did not have an FBAR requirement. However, in 2020, Gustavo decides that he wants to build a vacation home in Mexico. He transfers $18,000 to his Mexican bank account on January 10, 2020, to begin construction on his new residence. Although he later withdraws all the funds, he is still required to file an FBAR. Gustavo must file his FBAR by October 15, 2021,[227] because the aggregate value of his foreign accounts reached $10,000 in 2020. However, he is not required to file Form 8938 (to be discussed later) because the value of his foreign assets is below the reporting threshold for Form 8938.
Example: Andromeda is a citizen of Spain and a legal U.S. resident (a green-card holder). She frequently travels to her home country and maintains a bank account in Spain with an average balance of $20,000. She is required to file an FBAR to report this foreign account. For tax year 2020, Andromeda must file her FBAR by April 15, 2021, but she is allowed an automatic extension of time to file until October 15, 2021.

[224] The "BSA E-Filing System" is an official U.S. Treasury website and is used for online filing of FBAR returns. The website also supports electronic filing of Bank Secrecy Act (BSA) forms through a secure network.

[225] Accounts are converted to U.S. currency based on the exchange rate as of the end of the calendar year, applied to the highest balance in the account during the year, even if the highest balance in the foreign account (in U.S. dollars) was sometime before the end of the year.

[226] Currently, the Report of Foreign Bank and Financial Accounts (FBAR) regulations do not define a foreign account holding virtual currency as a type of reportable account, but FinCEN intends to propose regulations regarding reports of foreign financial accounts (FBAR) to include virtual currency as a type of reportable account (FinCEN Notice 2020-2).

[227] While the FBAR due date is April 15, an automatic six-month extension is granted without the need to request an extension.

The IRS defines "signature authority" as the authority of an individual or individuals to control the disposition of assets held in a foreign financial account by direct communication with the bank or other financial institution. In other words, FBAR reporting requirements are not determined by ownership of the funds. "Foreign financial accounts" include the following types of accounts:

- Foreign bank accounts, including savings accounts, checking accounts, and time deposits,
- Foreign securities accounts such as brokerage accounts and securities derivatives or other financial instruments accounts, commodity futures or stock options accounts,
- Insurance policies with a cash value (such as a whole life insurance policy),
- Foreign mutual funds or similar pooled funds (i.e., a fund that is available to the general public with a regular net asset value determination and regular redemptions),
- Any other accounts maintained in a foreign financial institution or with a person performing the services of a financial institution.

The FBAR is due by April 15th of the year following the year in which the account holder meets the $10,000 threshold. This threshold is the same for every filing status. Whether or not an account produces income does not affect the requirement to file an FBAR. Also, if the IRS issues a release for extensions of filing due to a disaster situation, do not assume that the FBAR filing deadlines are extended, as well.[228]

Note: U.S. law requires taxpayers to file a Report of Foreign Bank and Financial Accounts (FBAR) if they meet a threshold of $10,000 in a foreign bank account at **<u>any time</u>** during the calendar year. This includes all accounts which the taxpayer may own or have any financial interest in—this includes signature authority, power of attorney, or custodianship.

Note: The due date for FBARs coincides with the tax return due date. The "official" FBAR due date is April 15. However, FinCEN grants filers an automatic extension to October 15 to file the FBAR. There is no requirement or form to request this extra time.

Example: Carlos, a U.S. citizen, co-owns a foreign bank account in Costa Rica with his father, Aquilino, who is a Costa Rican citizen. The highest value in the account was $15,000 USD in 2020. Half of the income in the account belongs to his father, and the account does not produce any interest income. Carlos is required to file an FBAR to report the account.

There is no minimum age requirement for filing an FBAR. The requirement includes minor children, as well. If a child holds $10,000 in a foreign financial account, even if the account is not earning revenues, the child will be required to file their own FBAR.

This is true even if the child would otherwise not have a U.S. filing requirement. If a child cannot file his or her own FBAR for any reason, such as age, the child's parent, guardian, or another legally responsible person must file and sign it for the child.

[228] The IRS coordinated the extension from the usual October 15, 2020 deadline with the Financial Crimes Enforcement Network (FinCEN) for 2020 (for 2019 calendar year FBAR filings). FBAR filers impacted by the California Wildfires, the Iowa Derecho, Hurricane Laura, the Oregon Wildfires and Hurricane Sally had until December 31, 2020, to file their FBARs.

Example: Gideon is six years old. He is a U.S. citizen. Gideon's grandmother, Aurelia, is a citizen of Italy. Aurelia sets up a savings account for her grandson in an Italian bank, and deposits 50,000 Euros into the account. Aurelia then names Gideon as the co-owner of the account. Using current currency conversion rates, the account balance is worth approximately $56,300 U.S. dollars. Gideon is required to file an FBAR to report the existence and value of the account, even if he does not withdraw the funds or personally receive any of the proceeds from the account.

Example: Russell is a U.S. citizen. Russell's parents are citizens of Canada and live in Canada. Russell has signature authority on his elderly parents' accounts in Canada, but he has never written a check or made any withdrawals from his parent's bank account. The bank account balance reaches $10,000 USD for the first time in 2020. Russell is required to file an FBAR by April 15, 2021 (October 15, 2021, with the automatic extension). Whether or not his signature authority is ever exercised is irrelevant to the FBAR filing requirement.

Example: Elizabeth is a legal permanent resident of the United States (i.e., a green card holder). She is a citizen of the United Kingdom. Under a tax treaty, Elizabeth is a tax resident of the United Kingdom and elects to be taxed as a resident of the United Kingdom. Elizabeth is still required to file an FBAR. This is because tax treaties with the United States do not affect FBAR filing obligations.

U.S. partnerships, corporations, estates, and trusts that meet the $10,000 threshold are also required to file an FBAR. The federal tax treatment of an entity does *not* determine whether the entity has an FBAR filing requirement. For example, an entity that is disregarded for purposes of Title 26 of the United States Code must file an FBAR, if otherwise required to do so. Similarly, a trust for which the trust income, deductions, or credits are taken into account by another person for purposes of Title 26 of the United States Code must file an FBAR, if otherwise required to do so.

Spouses and Jointly-Owned Accounts

Spouses do not need to file separate FBARs if they complete and sign Form 114a, *Record of Authorization to Electronically File FBARs*, and:

- All reportable financial accounts of the nonfiling spouse are jointly owned with the filing spouse, and,
- The filing spouse reports all accounts jointly-owned with the nonfiling spouse on a timely-filed FBAR.

Otherwise, both spouses must file separate FBARs, and each spouse must report the entire value of the jointly-owned accounts. The e-filing system will not allow both spouses' signatures on the same electronic form – only the filing spouse signs in the system. Taxpayers don't submit Form 114a with the FBAR, but they must keep it for their records.

Example: Gibson and Lailah are married and file jointly. They are both U.S. citizens, and they live in the United States. Gibson has a foreign bank account in Canada, where his parents live. Lailah has a bank account in Portugal, where she also has family. They each own their foreign bank accounts separately, and both accounts have over $10,000 USD. Since neither account is jointly-owned, each spouse must file their own FBAR.

Penalties for Nonfiling the FBAR

The Treasury Department reports that FBAR filings have surged in recent years, with current filings exceeding one million per year. The consequences of failure to timely file an FBAR can be extremely severe. Both civil penalties and criminal sanctions can be imposed. By law, civil penalties could exceed $10,000 per year (adjusted for inflation) for a "non-willful" failure to file.

A "willful" failure could result in the greater of $100,000 or 50% of the balance in an unreported foreign account per year for up to six years. This is in addition to criminal penalties. Criminal penalties may include a fine of up to $250,000 and five years in prison.[229]

Note: The potential penalties for willful failure to file an FBAR are huge. These penalties can include criminal prosecution as well as severe monetary civil penalties.

The most common FBAR reporting mistake is simply failing to file. The IRS has issued guidance on penalties for failing to file an FBAR that caps the maximum percentage of the penalty.

FBAR penalties for inadvertent or "non-willful" failure to file are limited. In most cases, the total penalty amount for all years under examination will be limited to 50% of the highest aggregate balance of all unreported foreign financial accounts during the years under examination. The guidance also establishes procedures and documentation requirements for IRS examiners conducting examinations related to FBAR penalties.

The IRS will normally not impose a penalty for the failure to file a delinquent FBARs if a taxpayer properly reports on the Federal income tax return, and paid all tax on, the income from the foreign financial accounts reported on the delinquent FBAR, if they have not previously been contacted regarding an income tax audit or a request for delinquent returns for the year for which the delinquent FBAR was submitted.

Foreign Financial Accounts

For FBAR purposes, a "foreign financial account" is a financial account located *outside* of the United States. A foreign financial account also includes a commodity futures or stock options account, an insurance policy with a cash value (such as a whole life insurance policy), an annuity policy with a cash value, and shares in a foreign mutual fund or similar pooled fund (i.e., a fund that is available to the general public with a regular net asset value determination and regular redemptions). The following accounts are not considered "foreign financial accounts":

- Foreign financial accounts owned by a governmental entity,
- Foreign financial accounts owned by an international financial institution,
- Foreign financial accounts maintained on a United States military banking facility (for example, a banking institution on a U.S. military base).

An owner or beneficiary of an IRA or another qualified retirement plan is also not required to report a foreign financial account that is held in the retirement plan.

---

[229] FBAR penalties are adjusted for inflation each year. Here is a list of FBAR penalties with the currently adjusted inflation amounts on the IRS website: https://www.irs.gov/businesses/small-businesses-self-employed/report-of-foreign-bank-and-financial-accounts-fbar.

Example: Grady directly holds shares of a U.S. mutual fund. The mutual fund invests in foreign stocks as well as domestic stocks. Since the foreign stocks are held in a U.S.-based mutual fund, Grady does not need to report his ownership in the mutual fund or the holdings of the mutual fund. The mutual fund itself would be responsible for any foreign financial reporting that was required.

Note: A safe deposit box at a foreign financial institution is not considered a "financial account" for tax reporting purposes. However, under the FBAR rules, if gold, bullion, or foreign currency is held inside a foreign financial institution, it is subject to FBAR reporting. Specified foreign financial assets do not include gold, bullion, or currency *held directly* by the taxpayer.

Example: Ebner is a U.S. citizen who lives in Columbia. Ebner collects gold and silver coins as a hobby. He keeps the coins in a wall safe inside his home. He does not trust banks, so he does not have a foreign bank account. He keeps all his cash inside the wall safe, too. Ebner does not have an FBAR filing requirement.

Form 3520: Reporting Foreign Gifts and Bequests

U.S. individuals who received large gifts or bequests from certain foreign persons may be required to file Form 3520, *Annual Return to Report Transactions with Foreign Trusts and Receipt of Certain Foreign Gifts.* Form 3520 is due at the same time as the U.S. person's income tax return (including extensions) but is filed separately from the income tax return.

A foreign person is defined as a nonresident alien individual or a foreign corporation, partnership, or estate. In 2020, a U.S. person must file Form 3520, *Annual Return to Report Transactions with Foreign Trusts and Receipt of Certain Foreign Gifts,* if he receives gifts or bequests valued at more than $100,000 from a nonresident alien individual or foreign estate. A taxpayer must aggregate gifts received from related parties.

Example: Wendy is a U.S. citizen that has many relatives living in Canada. In 2020, Wendy received $60,000 from her Canadian grandfather and $52,000 from her Canadian brother. Wendy must report the gifts because the total is more than $100,000 in a single year from related parties. She is required to report them in Part IV of Form 3520.

Form 3520 is considered an "information return," not a tax return, and no taxes are assessed on this form, because foreign gifts or bequests are not subject to income tax.

However, failure to file a required Form 3520 can result in steep penalties. The penalty is equal to 5% of the amount of the foreign gift for each month for which the failure to report continues (not to exceed a total of 25%). However, no penalty applies if the failure to report was due to reasonable cause and not willful neglect. The taxpayer is required to report a gift or bequest on Form 3520 when he or she constructively receives it.

Two transferors or grantors of the same foreign trust, or two U.S. beneficiaries of the same foreign trust, may file a joint Form 3520, but only if they file a joint income tax return.

Note: A "foreign gift" to a U.S. person does not include amounts paid for qualified tuition or medical payments made on behalf of the U.S. person.

Example: Jason is a U.S. citizen attending college in the United States. His aunt, Sedona, is a citizen of Australia. Sedona offers to pay her nephew's tuition. She makes a payment directly to Jason's college. There are no filing requirements for this foreign gift.

Example: Daniel is a U.S. citizen who lives and works in the United States. Daniel's grandmother, Claudette, is a French citizen. On January 30, 2020, Claudette dies, and leaves Daniel a large inheritance of $250,000. After his grandmother's estate is settled by the executor, Daniel receives the inheritance via wire transfer on June 10, 2020. Since Daniel constructively received the funds in 2020, his Form 3520 is due on April 15, 2021. The funds are not taxable to Daniel, but the inheritance must be reported, since it is a bequest from a foreign estate over the reporting threshold.

Form 8938: Statement of Specified Foreign Financial Assets

Generally, taxpayers who hold "specified foreign financial assets" must also file Form 8938, *Statement of Specified Foreign Financial Assets,* with their tax returns if the amount of their assets exceeds certain thresholds. This is a separate filing requirement in addition to the FBAR filing requirements. Form 8938 requires the taxpayer to provide detailed financial information about their foreign accounts. Specified foreign assets include:

- Foreign stock or foreign securities (not held in a U.S. brokerage account),
- Financial accounts maintained by a foreign financial institution,
- Foreign pensions or deferred compensation plans,[230]
- Interests in a foreign estate.

Example: Jocelyn has an uncle who is a Greek citizen. In 2020, her uncle died, and Jocelyn inherited $200,000 in foreign bearer bonds from her uncle. The bonds are held outside of a regular bank account. Jocelyn is required to report the value of the bonds on Form 8938, even if she did not cash the bonds out.

Example: Edward, a U.S. citizen, purchased securities of a French corporation through a professional securities brokerage firm located in New York. Edward is not required to report these securities because he purchased the securities through a brokerage institution located in the United States.

Failure to report foreign financial assets on Form 8938 on a timely filed return (including extensions) may result in a penalty of $10,000. If a taxpayer does not file Form 8938 on a timely filed return and receives a written notice from the IRS about the lack of filing, the taxpayer has 90 days after the mailing of the IRS letter to file Form 8938 to avoid additional penalties.

If the taxpayer does not file within that 90 day period, an *additional* $10,000 penalty may apply to each 30-day period (or a portion thereof) that Form 8938 is not filed after the 90-day deadline (up to a maximum of $50,000 of *additional* late filing penalties - resulting in a total late

[230] Payments or the rights to receive the foreign equivalent of social security, social insurance benefits or another similar program of a foreign government are not specified foreign financial assets and do not have to be reported.

filing penalty assessment of $60,000). Further, underpayments of tax attributable to non-disclosed foreign financial assets will be subject to an additional "substantial understatement" penalty of 40%.

If a taxpayer accidentally omits Form 8938 when they file their income tax return, the taxpayer should file Form 1040-X, *Amended U.S. Individual Income Tax Return*, with their Form 8938 attached and attach a statement of reasonable cause to try to avoid any penalties.

Note: If a taxpayer is **not required** to file an income tax return for the year, he does not need to file Form 8938, even if the value of his specified foreign assets is greater than one of the reporting thresholds.

A filing requirement is triggered if the aggregate value of specified foreign financial assets is more than the following **reporting thresholds:**

- **Taxpayers living inside the US:**
  - Unmarried and MFS taxpayers: The total value of specified foreign financial assets is more than $50,000 on the last day of the tax year or more than $75,000 at any time during the tax year.
  - Married taxpayers filing MFJ: The total value of specified foreign financial assets is more than $100,000 on the last day of the tax year or more than $150,000 at any time during the tax year.
- **Taxpayers living abroad:**
  - Unmarried and MFS taxpayers: living abroad must file Form 8938 if the total value of their specified foreign assets is more than $200,000 on the last day of the tax year or more than $300,000 at any time during the year.
  - Married taxpayers filing MFJ: for joint filers, the value of their specified foreign assets is more than $400,000 on the last day of the tax year or more than $600,000 at any time during the year.

The filing of Form 8938 does not relieve a taxpayer of the separate requirement to file the FBAR if they are required to do so, and vice-versa. Depending on the situation, the taxpayer may be required to file both forms, and certain foreign accounts may be required to be reported on both forms.

Example: Demetri is a U.S. citizen who lives in Costa Rica. He does not work or have any taxable income because he inherited a large sum of money from his grandparents 10 years ago, and he lives off of his inheritance. He has $500,000 USD in a checking account at a Costa Rican bank. The bank account does not generate any interest, and he has no other income, so he does not have a U.S. filing requirement. He only needs to file the FBAR, to report the foreign bank account. He does not need to file a Form 1040 or a Form 8938.

This reporting requirement also applies to specified domestic entities, including a domestic trust if one or more of the trust's current beneficiaries is a U.S. citizen or U.S. resident alien and the asset value thresholds are surpassed.

A taxpayer does not need to report a financial account maintained by a U.S. financial institution or U.S. brokerage firm, even if the financial institution or fund invests in foreign stock.

This also includes U.S. affiliates of foreign financial institutions. Examples of financial accounts maintained by U.S. financial institutions include:

- U.S. Mutual fund accounts
- IRAs (traditional or Roth)
- 401 (k) retirement plans
- Qualified U.S. retirement plans
- Brokerage and investing accounts maintained by U.S. financial institutions

Foreign real estate is also not a "specified foreign financial asset." Therefore, a personal residence or a rental property in a foreign country does not have to be reported as a "foreign financial asset," unless the property is held by a foreign entity.[231] Directly-held tangible assets, such as art, gold, antiques, jewelry, cars and other collectibles, are also not specified foreign financial assets.

Foreign currency is not a specified "foreign financial asset" if it is directly-held by the taxpayer and not held in a financial institution.

Example: Inga is a U.S. citizen with funds deposited in three different foreign banks. As of December 31, 2020, bank account #1 had $5,000; bank account #2 had $3,000; and bank account #3 had $2,500. Inga is required to electronically file an FBAR by April 15, 2021 (October 15, 2021 with the automatic extension), because the aggregate value of her accounts is more than $10,000. However, she is not required to file Form 8938, because the value of her offshore assets is below the reporting threshold.

Example: Darius is a U.S. expat living and working in Mexico. At the end of the year, Darius has $385,000 in a Mexican bank account, because he is saving up money to purchase a condo in Cancun. Darius must file an FBAR as well as a Form 8938.

Example: Phineas is a U.S. citizen living and working in Canada. He owns a house in Canada, and also some very valuable artwork. The value of the house is $370,000 USD and the value of the artwork is $125,000. He owns the house and the artwork outright. He is not required to report the value of these assets on Form 8938. He also has a foreign bank account in Canada, with the equivalent of $9,000 USD. His foreign bank account balance has never exceeded $10,000 USD during the year, so he does not have to file an FBAR, either.

Example: Khloe is a U.S. citizen who lives and works in Brazil for an online tutoring company that is based in the United States. Khloe lives with her grandmother, who is a Brazilian citizen. Khloe does not have a bank account in Brazil. Instead, she has a bank account in the U.S. and she uses her ATM card and credit cards to withdraw money and make purchases. She keeps a fairly large amount of Brazilian currency inside her home, in a safe, along with her personal jewelry. Since she does not have a foreign bank account or any other specified foreign assets, she does not have to file Form 8938 or the FBAR.

[231] If the real estate is held through a foreign entity, such as a corporation, partnership, trust or estate, then the interest in the entity is a specified foreign financial asset that is reported on Form 8938, if the total value of all the taxpayer's specified foreign financial assets is greater than the reporting threshold that applies.

Schedule B, Reporting Foreign Accounts and Trusts

Schedule B is used to report interest and dividend income received during the tax year. However, the last part of Schedule B (Part III) is used by taxpayers who have financial accounts in foreign countries. This section of the form is where the taxpayer must disclose any foreign bank or investment accounts and whether or not the taxpayer received any distributions from a foreign trust.

The reporting requirements for these taxpayers have increased significantly in recent years as part of FATCA, which refers to the Foreign Account Tax Compliance Act. The law addresses tax noncompliance by U.S. taxpayers with foreign accounts by focusing on reporting by these taxpayers and by foreign financial institutions.

In general, federal law requires U.S. citizens and resident aliens to report any worldwide income, including income from foreign trusts and foreign bank and securities accounts. In most cases, affected taxpayers need to complete and attach Schedule B to their tax returns. Part III of Schedule B asks about the existence of foreign accounts, such as bank and securities accounts, and generally requires U.S. citizens to report the country in which each account is located.

On Part III, Schedule B, a taxpayer must check "yes" or "no" to the question of whether he had at any time during the year a financial interest in or signature authority over a financial account.

Note: If a taxpayer does not have a filing requirement, they are not required to file a tax return merely to report their foreign financial accounts on Schedule B. However, if a taxpayer is required to file a tax return, he must file Schedule B to report foreign financial accounts even if he would not be otherwise required to file Schedule B.

A taxpayer who had a financial interest in a foreign account during the year should check the "yes" box even if he is not required to file FinCEN Form 114, *Report of Foreign Bank and Financial Accounts* (FBAR). There is no dollar threshold to report foreign accounts on Schedule B. Even if the taxpayer does not have an FBAR reporting requirement, the "yes" box must be checked if the taxpayer has any financial interest in, or signature authority over, a foreign account.

Part III	You must complete this part if you **(a)** had over $1,500 of taxable interest or ordinary dividends; **(b)** had a foreign account; or **(c)** received a distribution from, or were a grantor of, or a transferor to, a foreign trust.	**Yes**	**No**
Foreign Accounts and Trusts	**7a** At any time during 2020, did you have a financial interest in or signature authority over a financial account (such as a bank account, securities account, or brokerage account) located in a foreign country? See instructions		
Caution: If required, failure to file FinCEN Form 114 may result in substantial penalties. See instructions.	If "Yes," are you required to file FinCEN Form 114, Report of Foreign Bank and Financial Accounts (FBAR), to report that financial interest or signature authority? See FinCEN Form 114 and its instructions for filing requirements and exceptions to those requirements		
	b If you are required to file FinCEN Form 114, enter the name of the foreign country where the financial account is located ▶		
	8 During 2020, did you receive a distribution from, or were you the grantor of, or transferor to, a foreign trust? If "Yes," you may have to file Form 3520. See instructions		

For Paperwork Reduction Act Notice, see your tax return instructions. Cat. No. 17146N **Schedule B (Form 1040) 2020**

For reporting purposes on Schedule B, a "foreign financial account" includes securities, brokerage, savings, checking, deposit, time deposit, or other accounts that are maintained within a financial institution.

A financial account also includes a commodity futures or options account, an insurance policy with a cash value (such as a whole life insurance policy), an annuity policy with a cash value, and shares in a foreign mutual fund. A financial account is considered to be located in a foreign country if the account is *physically located outside* of the United States.

This includes accounts maintained with a branch of a U.S. bank if it is physically located outside the United States. However, a branch of a foreign bank is not a foreign account if it is physically located in the United States.

Form 5471: Information Return of U.S. Persons With Respect to Certain Foreign Corporations

When a U.S. taxpayer is an officer, director, or shareholders in a foreign corporation, they may have an IRS reporting requirement. Form 5471 is typically used to report ownership of a foreign corporation that exceeds a **10% threshold.** The categories of U.S. persons potentially liable for filing Form 5471 include:

- U.S. citizen and resident alien individuals,
- U.S. domestic corporations,
- U.S. domestic partnerships, and
- U.S. domestic trusts.

The requirement to file Form 5471 is not based on whether the business generated any income. Form 5471 is an *informational* return, not a tax return. The penalties for nonfiling are severe. Each failure to file a required Form 5471 can result in a $10,000 penalty.

Example: Breanna is a 15% shareholder in three separate foreign corporations. She inherited the stock when her German grandfather died two years ago. Breanna fails to seek proper legal advice and as a result, she doesn't file her returns on time, including the required Forms 5471 for her ownership in the foreign corporations. She later receives a notice from the IRS. Since she did not have any reasonable cause for her failure to file, she is assessed a penalty of $30,000 ($10,000 for each entity that she failed to report on Form 5471).

The Form 5471 is generally filed with a taxpayer's individual return. Even if a person is not required to file a tax return, (for example, their income is below the filing threshold), the Form 5471 may still be required. Exceptions to the filing requirement exist in cases of constructive ownership, or an election to be treated as a domestic corporation.

Differences Between the FBAR vs. Form 8938		
Data	**FBAR**	**Form 8938**
Legal Authority	**Authorized by the Bank Secrecy Act of 1970 (BSA).**	**Authorized by the Foreign Account Tax Compliance Act of 2010 (FATCA).**
Who must file?	U.S. persons, which includes U.S. citizens, U.S. resident aliens, trusts, estates, and other domestic entities.	Specified individuals, which includes U.S. citizens, resident aliens, and nonresident aliens who elect to be treated as resident aliens for purposes of filing a joint income tax return. This form also applies to specified domestic entities.
Reporting thresholds (U.S. tax home)	$10,000 held in any foreign bank at any time during the calendar year. Based on the aggregate value of all reportable accounts.	$50,000 ($100,000 MFJ) on the last day of the tax year or $75,000 ($150,000 MFJ) at any time during the tax year.
Reporting thresholds (foreign tax home)	$10,000 held in any foreign bank at any time during the calendar year. Based on the aggregate value of all reportable accounts	$200,000 ($400,000 MFJ) on the last day of the tax year or $300,000 ($600,000 MFJ) at any time during the tax year.[232]
When does the taxpayer have "an interest" in an account or asset?	Financial interest in an applicable foreign account, or signature authority on an applicable foreign account.	Any income, gains, losses, deductions, credits, gross proceeds, or distributions from holding or disposing of the account or asset that are (or would be required to be) reported, included, or otherwise reflected on the taxpayer's return.
What is reported?	The maximum value of financial accounts.	The maximum value of specified foreign financial assets.
How are values determined and reported?	Converted to U.S. dollars using the end of the calendar year exchange rate and reported in U.S. dollars.	The fair market value of the asset in U.S. dollars.
Due date	Due by April 15 (an extension is allowed to October 15).	The same due date as the taxpayer's individual return, including extensions.
Filing procedures	File electronically through FinCEN's BSA E-Filing System. The FBAR is not filed with a federal tax return.	This form must be filed with the taxpayer's income tax return (Form 1040).
Penalties	Willful non-filing: up to the greater of $100,000 or 50% of account balances; "non-willful" violation civil penalties are up to $10,000 per violation (adjusted for inflation). Criminal penalties may also apply.	Up to $10,000 for failure to disclose, and an additional $10,000 for every 30 days of non-filing after IRS notice of a failure to disclose; up to a $60,000 total maximum penalty. Separate criminal penalties may also apply

232 These thresholds apply even if only one spouse resides abroad. Married individuals who file a joint income tax return for the tax year will file a single Form 8938 that reports all of the specified foreign financial assets in which either spouse has an interest.

Unit 17: Study Questions

(Test yourself first, then check the correct answers at the end of this quiz.)

1. Neema is unmarried and lives in Texas. She is a U.S. citizen and has ownership of specified foreign assets totaling $80,000, (foreign stock held outside of the U.S.) which she inherited when her grandmother died. Which form is Neema required to submit to the IRS?

A. Form 8938
B. Form 1040-X
C. Form 3520
D. FinCEN 114 (FBAR)

2. Part _____ of Schedule B (Form 1040) is completed by taxpayers who have financial accounts in foreign countries.

A. Part I.
B. Part II.
C. Part III.
D. Schedule B is not used for this purpose.

3. Which of the following forms is completed to report foreign bank accounts?

A. Schedule B (Form 1040) and FinCen 114 (FBAR).
B. Form 1116 and FinCen 114 (FBAR).
C. Schedule B (Form 1040) and Form 2555.
D. Only the FinCen 114 (FBAR).

4. When e-filing their federal return, a taxpayer who meets the requirements to file both Form 8938, *Statement of Specified Foreign Financial Assets,* and the FBAR (Form 114, *Report of Foreign Bank and Financial Accounts)* should do which of the following?

A. Attach both forms to their federal return.
B. Attach only Form 8938 to their federal return and file Form 114 through the Financial Crimes Enforcement Network's E-Filing system.
C. Attach only Form 114 to their federal return as it contains the 8938 information.
D. Submit both forms separately to the Internal Revenue Service.

5. As a general rule, how long should taxpayers keep records related to an FBAR filing (from the due date of the FBAR)?

A. 3 years.
B. 5 years.
C. 7 years.
D. 10 years.

6. Noriko is a U.S. citizen who is required to file Form 8938 with her personal income tax return because she has $800,000 in specified foreign assets. Noriko does not include a Form 8938 with her 2020 income tax return, but she later amends her 2020 personal tax return after the due date to include Form 8938. What potential penalty is Noriko subject to regarding the late-filed Form 8938?

A. $2,500
B. $5,000
C. $10,000
D. $60,000

7. Which of the following is NOT considered "U.S. person" for the purposes of filing an FBAR?

A. A U.S. citizen who lives in Israel.
B. A U.S. Resident who lives in Russia.
C. A nonresident alien with $100,000 in U.S. investments that files Form 1040-NR.
D. A U.S. consular officer that lives and works overseas in a U.S. embassy.

8. Duncan, age 65, is a U.S. citizen who lives in Florida, has a bank account located in Austria. He opened the account several years ago to send money to his elderly mother, Ursula, who is a citizen of Austria. He has signature authority on the account but does not withdraw money from it or collect any of the interest income on the account. On December 31, 2020, the account has a balance of $23,000 (which was the highest balance in the account for the year). He receives Social Security and otherwise does not have a U.S. filing requirement or any tax liability for the year. What is Duncan's reporting requirement for this account?

A. Duncan is not required to file any returns.
B. Duncan must file Form 8938, *Statement of Specified Foreign Financial Assets*, with the IRS when he files his tax return.
C. Duncan must file an FBAR, *Report of Foreign Bank and Financial Accounts*.
D. Duncan and Ursula must both file an FBAR, *Report of Foreign Bank and Financial Accounts*, with the Treasury Department, and file Form 8938, *Statement of Specified Foreign Financial Assets*, with the IRS when he files his tax return.

9. A U.S. person who receives a gift or bequest valued at more than _____ from a nonresident alien or foreign estate must file an information return with the IRS.

A. $10,000
B. $25,000
C. $50,000
D. $100,000

10. Which of the following is a "specified foreign asset" for reporting purposes?

A. Artwork displayed in a foreign museum.
B. Jewelry held in a foreign country.
C. Real estate held in a foreign trust.
D. Foreign currency held at a taxpayer's primary residence.

11. Regarding the FBAR reporting requirement, the IRS issued guidance on penalties for failing to file the FBAR that caps the maximum percentage of the penalty. In most cases, the total penalty amount for all years under examination will be limited to ______ of the highest aggregate balance of all unreported foreign financial accounts during the years under investigation.

A. 10%
B. 25%
C. 50%
D. 75%

Unit 17: Quiz Answers

1. The answer is A. Neema must file Form 8938. Generally, U.S.-based taxpayers who hold foreign financial assets with an aggregate value that exceeds $50,000 ($100,000 MFJ) on the last day of the tax year, or that exceeds $75,000 ($150,000 MFJ) at any time during the tax year, must file Form 8938. The thresholds are higher if the taxpayer has a foreign tax home.

2. The answer is C. Part III of Schedule B (Form 1040) is completed by taxpayers who have financial accounts in foreign countries.

3. The answer is A. The FinCen 114 (FBAR) and Schedule B (part III) are both used to report foreign bank accounts and foreign financial accounts. Taxpayers with foreign financial accounts will typically need to complete Part III of Schedule B to indicate that they hold such an account, although they do not need to state the dollar amounts that the account contains. Unlike the FBAR, there is no dollar threshold on the duty to report foreign accounts on Schedule B.

4. The answer is B. The taxpayer must only attach Form 8938 to their federal return. The FBAR, Form 114, is not filed with a federal tax return or with the IRS. It is filed online with the Financial Crimes Enforcement Network e-filing system.

5. The answer is B. Generally, records of accounts required to be reported on the FBAR should be kept for five years from the due date of the report, which is the year *following* the calendar year being reported.

6. The answer is C. Noriko may be subject to a penalty of $10,000 for nonfiling of Form 8938. If a taxpayer is required to file Form 8938, but it is not complete and correctly filed by the due date (including extensions), a taxpayer may be subject to a penalty of $10,000. There would be *additional* penalties if the form is not filed within 90 days from the mailing of a notice from the IRS regarding a notice of a failure to file Form 8938.

7. The answer is C. Nonresident aliens are not subject to the FBAR filing requirement. All of the following are subject to the FBAR filing requirement if they hold foreign bank accounts or applicable foreign assets.

- A U.S. citizen or U.S. resident of the United States, (includes nonresident aliens electing to be treated as residents in order to file a joint tax return).
- A domestic entity, (domestic corporation, domestic estate or trust).

8. The answer is C. Duncan is required to file an FBAR. There are two separate reporting requirements for taxpayers who hold certain types of foreign assets or who have certain amounts of funds in foreign bank accounts. An FBAR generally must be filed with the BSA E-Filing System if a taxpayer has more than $10,000 in offshore bank accounts. Taxpayers also must file a statement with the IRS if they hold foreign financial assets with an aggregate value that exceeds $50,000 ($100,000 MFJ) on the last day of the tax year, or that exceeds $75,000 ($150,000 MFJ) at any time during the tax year. In Duncan's case, since the funds in his foreign account total $23,000, and he does not otherwise have a filing requirement, he is only required to file an FBAR.

9. The answer is D. Form 3520, *Annual Return to Report Transactions with Foreign Trusts and Receipt of Certain Foreign Gifts*, is an information return, not a tax return because foreign gifts or bequests are not subject to income tax. In 2020, a U.S. person must file Form 3520 if he receives gifts or bequests valued at more than $100,000 from a nonresident alien individual or foreign estate.

10. The answer is C. Foreign real estate held in a trust would be a specified foreign asset. If the real estate is held through a foreign entity, such as a corporation, partnership, trust or estate, then the interest in the entity is a specified foreign financial asset that must be reported on Form 8938. Answers "A" and "B" are incorrect, because directly held tangible assets, such as art, antiques, jewelry, cars and other collectibles, are not specified foreign financial assets. Answer "D" is incorrect, because foreign currency is not automatically a specified foreign financial asset, unless it is held in a banking institution.

11. The answer is C. In most cases, the maximum penalty amount for all years under examination will be limited to 50% of the highest aggregate balance of all unreported foreign financial accounts during the years under investigation.

Unit 18: Estate and Gift Taxes for Individuals

More Reading:
Publication 559, *Survivors, Executors, and Administrators*
Publication 950, *Introduction to Estate and Gift Taxes*
Instructions for Form 1041
Instructions for Form 706
Instructions for Form 709

Estates in General

An estate is a separate legal entity created when a taxpayer dies. The estate tax is a tax on the transfer of assets or property from an individual's estate to his beneficiaries after his death. The TCJA made substantial changes to the estate tax exemption.

The TCJA doubled the estate tax exclusion and indexed the amount for inflation for future years. In 2020 the estate tax exemption is $11,580,000 million per decedent.[233] The TCJA will continue to index the exclusion levels for inflation through tax year 2025. The top estate and gift tax rate remains at 40%.

What this means is that most estates of up to $11.58 million in 2020 are free of *estate* tax, and from that point on, anything additional above that is taxable, at progressive rates that start at 18% and rise to 40% at taxable estates that are $1 million above the estate tax exemption (normally $11.58 million).[234]

Note: Sometimes, the estate tax is called a "death tax" or an "inheritance tax." The estate tax is *not* an income tax. It is a tax that is imposed on the transfer of property after someone's death.

A comparable increase applies to the generation-skipping transfer tax exemption (covered later). The portability election remains available in 2020 (also covered later). The 2020 annual gift tax exclusion is $15,000.

Note: For Part 1 of the EA exam, you will be required to understand how estate and gift taxes affect individual taxpayers, especially the surviving spouses and other beneficiaries of those estates. For Part 2 of the exam, you will be tested on the income tax treatment of estates and trusts as legal entities. It is possible that questions will overlap, and therefore we cover the concept of estate taxation from various perspectives.

Personal Representative or Executor

After a person dies, a personal representative (an executor or administrator appointed by a court), will typically manage the estate and settle the decedent's final financial affairs. If there is no executor or administrator, another person with possession of the decedent's property may act as the personal representative. If a probate court proceeding is necessary, the judge will appoint an executor if one is not named in the decedent's will.

---

233 This exemption may be less in situations where the exemption has been reduced due to prior taxable gifts.

234 Be aware that some states have inheritance taxes of their own. Currently, about half of the U.S. states impose some type of inheritance or estate tax. Most states that impose estate taxes match the federal exemption threshold, but some states are much lower. Property left to a surviving spouse is exempt from the tax in all but six states.

Note: Under U.S. law, a "personal representative" is a living person appointed by the courts to administer an estate after a taxpayer has died. *Executors* are appointed when the decedent has a will, and *administrators* are appointed when the decedent dies without a will. The IRS also uses the term "personal representative" to refer to anyone filing a return on behalf of a decedent, regardless if that person has been appointed by the courts or formally named in the taxpayer's will.

Example: Dominik is unmarried. He has one 19-year old son, named Adrian. Dominik dies suddenly on November 3, 2020. Thankfully, Dominik had a will when he died. In the will, Adrian is named as the sole beneficiary and the executor of his late father's estate. Adrian seeks the help of a licensed tax professional as well as an attorney to help him navigate the probate process. The attorney and the accountant will help Adrian file all the necessary paperwork with the court as well as the IRS. Adrian will sign his late father's final return as the executor.

The personal representative is also responsible for determining any estate tax liability before the estate's assets are distributed to beneficiaries. The tax liability for an estate attaches to the assets of the estate itself. If the assets are distributed to the beneficiaries before the taxes are paid, the beneficiaries or the executor may be held liable for the tax debt, up to the value of the assets distributed.

After a taxpayer dies, the following tax returns may need to be filed by the personal representative of the estate:

- **Form 1040:** Final income tax return for the decedent (for income received before death).
- **Form 1041**, *U.S. Income Tax Return for Estates and Trusts*: Fiduciary income tax returns for the estate for the period of its administration
- **Form 706**, *United States Estate (and Generation-Skipping Transfer) Tax Return*: If the gross estate, based on the fair market value of its assets, exceeds the applicable threshold. This return is used to report tax on the taxable estate (the gross estate minus certain deductions).

The personal representative or executor must sign each required return. A personal representative should sign the decedent's final income tax return as "Personal Representative." If the taxpayer's final income tax return is a joint return, then the surviving spouse would sign as a "Surviving Spouse."

The executor or "personal representative" must include fees paid to them from an estate in their gross income. If the executor is not in the trade or business of being an executor (for instance, the executor is a friend or family member of the deceased), these fees are reported on the executor's individual Form 1040, as "other income." If the executor is in the "trade or business" of being an executor, (such as a self-employed estate attorney), the executor would report the fees received from the estate as self-employment income on Schedule C.

Example: Idona is a CPA, but she only does audit work and generally does not prepare tax returns. Her uncle, Durin, dies in 2020. In his final will, Durin names his niece, Idona, as the executor of his estate. Idona has never served as an executor before, but she agrees to be the executor of her uncle's estate as a favor to his family. The fees she receives from the estate would be reported as "other income" on her tax return, because she is not a professional executor.

Note: A personal representative or executor of an estate cannot be held liable if an insolvent estate does not have enough assets to cover any of the income taxes due or debts. *However*, the executor must be sure that any income taxes are paid before any assets are distributed to the beneficiaries of the estate; otherwise, the executor might be held personally liable for the tax debt.

Example: Orion was named the executor of his late mother's estate. Orion has two younger sisters, who are beneficiaries of the estate, but are not executors or personal representatives of the estate. Orion distributes a large amount of stock and cash to both his sisters before he has had his mother's assets properly appraised. After the appraisal is done, Orion realizes that his mother's estate has a filing requirement and an estate tax liability. Since Orion distributed assets to the beneficiaries before determining the correct amount of tax due, he may be held personally responsible for paying the estate tax himself.

Final Income Tax Return (Form 1040)

The taxpayer's final income tax return is filed on the same form that would have been used if the taxpayer were still alive, but "deceased" is written after the taxpayer's name. The filing deadline is April 15 of the year following the taxpayer's death, the same deadline that applies for individual income tax returns.

The personal representative must file the final individual income tax return of the decedent for the year of death and any returns not filed for preceding years. If an individual died after the close of a tax year, but before the return for that year was filed, the return for that year will not be the final return. The return for that year will be a regular return, and the personal representative must file it.

Example: Elaine dies on February 28, 2021. At the time of her death, she had not yet filed her prior-year tax return. She earned $79,000 of wages in 2020. She also earned $16,000 of wages between January 1, 2021, and her death on February 28, 2021. Therefore, Elaine's 2020 and 2021 tax returns must be filed by her representative or executor. The 2021 return will be her final individual tax return.

Example: Huxley was unmarried when he died on April 20, 2020. His only child, Janna, is the executor and sole heir of his estate. Huxley earned wages before his death, so a final tax return is required for 2020. Janna asks her accountant to help prepare her father's final Form 1040, which will include all the taxable income that Huxley received before his death. The accountant also helps Janna with the valuation of her father's estate. After determining the fair market value of all her father's assets, her accountant concludes that Huxley's gross estate is valued at approximately $13 million on the date of his death. As this exceeds the filing threshold for 2020, an estate tax return (Form 706) is also required to be filed, and Janna is responsible for filing both returns and signing them as the official representative of the estate.

On a decedent's final tax return, the rules for deductions are the same as those that apply for any individual taxpayer. The decedent's year of death is *not* treated as a short tax year. In other words, the full amount of the applicable standard deduction or any applicable credits may be claimed on the final tax return, regardless of how long the taxpayer was alive during the year.

For example, a decedent who died in the middle of the year would still be eligible for EITC (the Earned Income Tax Credit), if they otherwise qualified, even though their final return covers less than twelve months.

Example: Tonia, age 62, was unmarried when she passed away on January 30, 2020. Her adult son, Patrick, is named as the sole heir and executor of her estate. Tonia earned a small amount of wages, $5,300 in the month before she died. Her income is below the filing requirement, so a return does not have to be filed. However, taxes were withheld from Tonia's wages, so Patrick files an individual tax return in order to receive a refund. Tonia is allowed the full standard deduction in 2020, even though she was only alive for a single month during the tax year.

Income in Respect of a Decedent (IRD)

Income in respect of a decedent (IRD) is any taxable income that was *earned* but not *received* by the decedent by the time of death. IRD is not taxed on the final return of the deceased taxpayer. IRD is reported on the tax return of the person (or entity) that receives the income.

This could be the estate, in which case it would be reported on Form 1041, as described below. Otherwise, it could be the surviving spouse or another beneficiary, such as a child. If there is no designated beneficiary for the income, then the IRD items are reported on the estate's Form 1041.

IRD retains the same tax nature that would have applied if the deceased taxpayer were still alive. For example, if the income would have been short-term capital gain, it is taxed the same way to the beneficiary. However, wages paid as income in respect of a decedent after the year of death generally are not subject to withholding for any federal taxes. For *self-employment* tax purposes only, the decedent's self-employment income will include the decedent's distributive share of a partnership's income or loss through the end of the month in which death occurred. IRD can come from various sources, including:

- Unpaid salary, wages, or bonuses
- Amounts distributed from retirement plans distributed by payor before the taxpayer's death, but not yet received by the decedent at the time of death.
- Deferred compensation benefits
- Accrued but unpaid interest, dividends, and rent
- Dividends declared *before* the decedent's death, but payable *after* death
- Outstanding income owed to a self-employed decedent (accounts receivable) is considered IRD but is not subject to self-employment tax.

Example: Irving was owed $15,000 of wages when he died on December 27, 2020. The check for these wages was not remitted by his employer until two weeks later (in January 2021, the following year) and was received and cashed by his daughter and sole beneficiary, Jolene. The wages are considered IRD to Jolene, and Jolene must recognize the $15,000 as ordinary income, the same tax treatment that would have applied for Irving. However, the amounts are not subject to FICA taxes.

Example: Kathryn died on April 30, 2020. At the time of her death, she was owed (but had not yet received) $1,500 of interest on bonds and $2,000 of rental income from a residential rental that she owned. Kathryn's beneficiary will include $3,500 of IRD in gross income when the interest and rent are received. The income retains its character as interest income and passive activity rental income.

Example: Freddy is a self-employed architect with many clients. Freddy is married to Polina, who is a homemaker and does not work in his business. Freddy reports his business income on Schedule C. Freddy dies on December 27, 2020, with several unpaid client invoices outstanding at the time of his death. Freddy's surviving spouse, Polina, receives the payments from Freddy's outstanding invoices the following year, in January, 2021. Since the outstanding accounts receivable was *earned* by Freddy while he was alive, but not *received* by Polina until after his death, then it is considered IRD to Polina, and it would be taxed as ordinary income, but not subject to self-employment tax.

Example: Reginald, age 67, decides to cash out his traditional IRA in order to take a nice vacation. He contacts his IRA trustee and requests a distribution of $12,000 on February 1, 2020. The trustee tells Reginald that the check will take 7-10 days to deliver to his home. Two days later, Reginald dies suddenly. The $12,000 check for the IRA distribution is received by Reginald's daughter, Selma, who is the executor of his estate. The distribution is treated as IRD to Selma.

IRD is included in the decedent's estate and may be subject to estate tax. If a beneficiary receives IRD and the income is subject to estate tax, the beneficiary can deduct the tax on Schedule A of their individual income tax return as a miscellaneous itemized deduction. The beneficiary must claim the IRD deduction in the same tax year in which they actually receive the income. The IRD deduction has not been suspended by the Tax Cuts and Jobs Act.

And if the value of the decedent's estate isn't subject to estate tax (because it falls within the estate tax exemption), the IRD deduction is not permitted.

The Estate Tax Return (Form 706)

An estate tax return is filed using Form 706, *United States Estate (and Generation-Skipping Transfer) Tax Return.* This return is due nine months after the death of the decedent. A six-month extension is allowed. After the taxable estate is computed, it is added to the value of lifetime taxable gifts. The applicable estate tax rate is applied to derive a tentative tax, from which any gift taxes paid or payable are subtracted to determine the gross estate tax. The maximum estate tax rate is 40% in 2020.

However, all or a portion of the gross estate tax may be eliminated after applying the Basic Exclusion Amount. The estate tax exclusion is $11.58 million in 2020.[235] Less than 1% of taxpayers are affected by the estate tax.

[235] This threshold is much lower for nonresident aliens at $60,000 in 2020. However, nonresident aliens are only potentially subject to estate tax upon their death for assets located within the United States. Form 706-NA is used for nonresident aliens.

Example: Nelda died in 2020 and left an estate valued at $9 million. She had not previously used any of her basic exclusion amount to avoid paying gift taxes, so the entire exclusion amount of $11.58 million is available to her estate. As this amount exceeds the estate's value, no estate tax is owed, and an estate tax return (Form 706) does not need to be filed.

There is a special rule that applies to widows and widowers. A surviving spouse can add any unused exclusion of his deceased spouse who died most recently to his own estate tax return. This is also known as "portability," or the "DSUE," which we will cover later. The assessment period for estate tax is three years after the due date for a timely filed estate tax return. The assessment period is *four* years for transfers from an estate.

Form 1041, Annual Income Tax Return for Estates and Trusts

An estate is a taxable legal entity that exists from the time of an individual's death until all assets have been distributed to the decedent's beneficiaries. Most estates are administered and distributed within 12-18 months, but sometimes, when the decedent was a very wealthy person, or if the estate is in litigation, the estate may not terminate for years, sometimes, even decades.

Note: "Probate" is the court-supervised process of settling a decedent's estate. It takes longer to probate an estate that owes estate taxes because a taxable estate cannot be closed until a final closing letter is received from the Internal Revenue Service.

As investment assets will usually continue to earn income after a taxpayer has died, this income, such as rents, dividends, and interest, must be reported. Form 1041 is an annual fiduciary return used to report the following items for a domestic decedent's estate, trust, or bankruptcy estate:

- Current income and deductions, including gains and losses from the disposition of the entity's property, and excluding certain items such as tax-exempt interest (collectively, *distributable net income* or DNI),
- A deduction for income either held for future distribution or distributed currently to the beneficiaries (income distribution deduction) that are limited to DNI, and
- Any income tax liability.

"Current income" would include IRD if it was received by the estate, rather than by a specific beneficiary. Expenses of administering the estate can be deducted either from the estate's income on Form 1041 in determining its income tax, or from the gross estate on Form 706 in determining the estate tax liability but cannot be claimed for both purposes. Schedule K-1 is used to report any income that is distributed or distributable to each beneficiary and is filed with Form 1041, with a copy also given to the beneficiary.

Example: Matthew owned three rental properties before his death on June 1, 2020. The gross value of his assets on the date of Matthew's death was $2 million, so an estate tax return (Form 706) does not have to be filed. The income from the rental properties that was received while he was alive would be reported on his final Form 1040, Schedule E. The rental income that was received by his estate *after* his death would be reportable on Form 1041, *Annual Tax Return for Estates and Trusts.*

Estates and trusts are allowed some of the same tax credits that are allowed to individuals. The credits are generally allocated between the estate and the beneficiaries. However, estates are not allowed the Child Tax Credit, or the Earned Income Tax Credit. However, the Earned Income Tax Credit, Child Tax Credit, and any other applicable credits can be claimed on the decedent's final return even if the return covers less than 12 months.

Note: Just like individual taxpayers, estates and certain trusts are subject to the Net Investment Income Tax (an additional tax of 3.8% on net investment income). The provisions for this tax are generally similar to those for individuals, and it must be reported on Form 8960, *Net Investment Tax: Individuals, Estates, and Trusts.*

The due date for Form 1041 is the fifteenth day of the fourth month following the end of the entity's tax year but is subject to an automatic extension of five-and-one-half months if Form 7004 is filed by the original due date. The tax year may be either a calendar or a fiscal year for an estate, subject to the election made at the time the first return is filed. An election will be made on the first return as to the accounting method (cash, accrual, or other) of reporting the estate's income.

Form 1041 is required to be filed for any domestic estate that has (1) gross income for the tax year of $600 or more or (2) a beneficiary who is a nonresident alien (with any amount of income).

The Gross Estate

The gross estate is based upon the fair market value of the decedent's property, which is not necessarily equal to his cost, and includes:

- The FMV of all tangible and intangible property owned partially or outright by the decedent at the time of death,
- Life insurance proceeds payable to the estate or, for policies owned by the decedent, payable to the heirs,
- The value of certain annuities or survivor benefits payable to the heirs, and
- The value of certain property that was transferred within three years before the decedent's death.

The gross estate does not include property owned solely by the decedent's spouse or other individuals. Lifetime gifts that are complete (so that no control over the gifts was retained) are not included in the gross estate.

Deductions from the Gross Estate

Once the gross estate has been calculated, certain deductions (and in special circumstances, reductions to value) are allowed to determine the taxable estate. Deductions may include:

- Funeral expenses paid out of the estate,
- Estate administrative expenses, if not deducted on Form 1041,
- Debts owed at the time of death,
- The marital deduction (generally, the value of property that passes from the estate to a surviving spouse),

- The charitable deduction (generally, the value of property that passes from the estate to qualifying charities),
- The state death tax deduction (generally, any inheritance or estate taxes paid to any state).

The following items are *not* deductible from the gross estate:

- Federal estate taxes paid,
- Alimony paid after the taxpayer's death; these payments are treated as distributions to a beneficiary.

Property taxes are deductible only if they accrue under state law *prior* to the decedent's death.

Special Rule for Medical Expenses

Debts not paid before death, including medical expenses subsequently paid on behalf of the decedent, are liabilities that can be deducted from the gross estate on the estate tax return. Medical expenses outstanding at the time of death are liabilities of the estate.

However, if medical expenses for the decedent are paid out of the estate during the one-year period beginning with the day after death, the personal representative can alternatively *elect* to treat all or part of the expenses as paid by the decedent at the time they were *incurred*, and deduct them on the decedent's final tax return (1040), if that gives the taxpayer a better tax result. This special election can be made on an amended return, as well.

Example: Lauretta, age 76, died on March 30, 2020, after a long battle with cancer. She incurred $42,000 of medical expenses, half during 2019 (the prior tax year) and half during 2020. When she died in March, all of her medical bills remained unpaid. The estate's executor is her adult son, Ralph. After consulting with an accountant, Ralph paid the entire outstanding $42,000 bill on December 10, 2020. The executor elects to file an amended return (Form 1040-X) for Lauretta for 2019, claiming $21,000 as a medical expense deduction on Schedule A (the year the medical expenses were incurred). The remaining $21,000 will be deducted on Lauretta's final income tax return (her 2020 Form 1040).

The Marital Deduction

Transfers from one spouse to the other are typically tax-free. The marital deduction allows spouses to transfer an unlimited amount of property to one another during their lifetimes or at death without being subject to estate or gift taxes.

Note: The marital deduction is NOT the same thing as the Deceased Spousal Unused Exclusion, or DSUE, which is covered in the next section. The DSUE is an *election* that is only available to U.S. citizen spouses.

To receive an unlimited marital deduction, the spouse receiving the assets must be a U.S. citizen and a legal spouse and must have outright ownership of the assets. The unlimited marital deduction is generally not allowed if the transferee spouse is not a U.S. citizen (even if the spouse is a legal resident of the United States).

Example: Lorenzo and Margie are married, and both are U.S. citizens. Lorenzo dies and leaves his wife, Margie, all his assets, which total $15 million on the date of his death. The transfer is tax-free to Margie because of the unlimited marital deduction. Margie's estate may or may not owe tax when she dies, but the transfer of assets to a surviving spouse is generally a nontaxable event, provided that the surviving spouse is a U.S. citizen.

Note: If the receiving spouse is not a U.S. citizen, assets transferred tax-free are limited to an annual exclusion amount. Noncitizen spouses can only receive $157,000 in 2020. This is true even if the spouse is a legal U.S. resident (a green card holder). This is one of the rare instances where U.S. citizens are taxed differently than legal U.S. residents.

Deceased Spousal Unused Exclusion (DSUE)

This is the unused portion of the decedent's predeceased spouse's basic exclusion (the amount that was not used to offset gift or estate tax liabilities). A "portability" election must be made to claim the DSUE on behalf of the surviving spouse's estate. This election can be made automatically by timely completion and filing of Form 706 for the estate of the predeceased spouse. Portability is *not* automatic: Form 706 must be filed in order to make the election.

This means that the executor, (usually, this is the surviving spouse), will need to transfer the unused exclusion to the surviving spouse. This is done by filing an estate tax return. In order to make the election, an estate tax return is required when the first spouse dies, even if no tax is owed. This return is due nine months after the death of the first spouse. A six-month extension is allowed.[236] The DSUE is not available to nonresident alien spouses.

Example: Myron died on January 4, 2020, and left a gross estate valued at $19 million. All of his assets were transferred to his wife, Polly (who is a U.S. citizen) under his will. As a result, none of his estate was taxed because of the unlimited marital deduction. None of the $11.58 million basic exclusion amount available to Myron's estate was used (and none had been used to offset gift tax liabilities during his lifetime). Polly then died later in the same year, on December 20, 2020. Assuming Form 706 was timely filed for Myron's estate, electing the DSUE, and Polly had not used any of her basic exclusion amount, Myron's unused basic exclusion is added to Polly's basic exclusion, for a total exclusion amount of $23.16 million between their two estates. If Polly's estate is valued at less than $23.16 million at her death, the full amount can be excluded, and no estate tax will be owed by Polly's heirs.

Inheritances

For federal income tax purposes, cash inheritances are generally not taxable to the beneficiary, although the beneficiary may be responsible if there is a related estate tax liability that has not been satisfied.

Example: Caruso's aunt, Georgina, died and left him $175,000 cash in her will. Georgina's estate did not have a filing requirement, and no estate tax return was required. Caruso is a U.S. citizen. He does not owe any federal tax on this inheritance.

[236] Revenue Procedure 2017-34 allows an executor up to two years to elect portability provided that no estate tax return is otherwise due.

Example: Raquel dies and leaves her entire estate to her son, Atticus. At the time of her death, she had a significant cash balance in her personal bank account as well as several valuable rental properties in New York. Raquel's estate is worth over $12 million, so it has a filing requirement, but Atticus ignores his accountant's advice and simply withdraws all the money from his late mother's bank account. He also sells all the rental properties and uses the money to take several lavish trips. Although inheritances are generally not taxable to the beneficiary, the fact that Atticus took possession of his mother's assets without filing her required estate tax return or satisfying the estate tax liability would make him directly responsible for the tax. The IRS can come after Atticus in order to satisfy the estate's tax liability.

Inherited retirement accounts are treated a bit differently. Distributions of retirement plan benefits or distributions from taxable IRA accounts to the decedent's beneficiaries are generally subject to income tax when received, although inherited IRAs are not subject to an early-withdrawal penalty, regardless of the beneficiary's age. Qualified distributions from a Roth IRA[237] or of previously nondeductible contributions to a traditional IRA are generally not taxable.

The decedent's surviving spouse may be able to defer taxation by rolling over the assets of a taxable IRA to another IRA or to a qualified plan.

Example: Benjamin, age 55, dies on September 1, 2020. He was unmarried at the time of his death and did not have any children. His sister, Chanel, age 43, is named as the beneficiary of his estate, which consists entirely of a $150,000 traditional IRA account. There are no other assets. Since Chanel is a non-spousal beneficiary, she is not allowed to transfer the funds from her deceased brother's IRA into her own retirement account. Instead, she is required to either distribute the funds as a lump-sum, or make a new inherited IRA account in her name and transfer the funds to this account. When Chanel starts withdrawing the money from the inherited IRA, she will not be charged a 10% early withdrawal penalty, even though she is under age 59½. She will only have to pay income tax on the withdrawals.[238]

Basis of Estate Property

Although cash inheritances are not subject to federal income tax, money received from the sale of inherited property may be taxable. The basis of property inherited from a decedent is generally one of the following:

- The FMV of the property on the date of death,
- The FMV on an alternate valuation date, if elected by the personal representative,
- The value under a special-use valuation method for real property used in farming or another closely held business, if elected by the personal representative,
- The decedent's adjusted basis in land to the extent of the value excluded from the taxable estate as a qualified conservation easement.

---

[237] Inherited Roth IRAs are subject to a 5-year "inheritance" rule. Inherited Roth IRAs have a series of rules that mandate a five-year waiting period. As long as the Roth was held for more than 5 years by the decedent, the full ROTH IRA inheritance is tax-free - including any earnings generated by the ROTH.

[238] Starting January 1, 2020, the SECURE Act made several changes to IRAs and inherited IRAs. In previous tax years, a non-spousal beneficiary of an inherited IRA or 401(k) was allowed to take required annual distributions over their lifetime in order to minimize the tax impact. Starting in 2020, most non-spousal beneficiaries need to ensure all of the money is withdrawn within 10 years (with some exceptions, which are covered more extensively in Chapter 16).

Example: Easton is the executor of his late father's estate. His father owned a large collection of collectible figurines and rare comic books. His father's will directs that the estate be split equally between Easton and his four siblings. Their father died on February 1, 2020, and Easton does not elect the alternate valuation date. The fair market value of his father's collectibles on the date of his father's death is $500,000. The collectibles are the only valuable asset that the estate owns. On December 15, 2020, the siblings all agree to sell their late father's collection. The entire collection sells at auction for $552,000. Collectively, they must report a capital gain of $52,000 ($552,000 sale price minus $500,000 inherited basis).

Alternate Valuation Date: If elected, the alternate valuation date is six months after the date of death. The estate value and related estate tax must be less than they would have been on the date of the taxpayer's death. However, for any assets distributed to a beneficiary after death, but prior to six months after death, the basis for these assets is the fair market value as of the date of distribution.

Jointly Owned Property: Property that is jointly owned by a decedent and another person will be included in full in the decedent's gross estate unless it can be shown that the other person originally owned or otherwise contributed to the purchase price. The surviving owner's new basis of property that was jointly owned must be calculated. To do so, the surviving owner's original basis in the property is added to the value of the part of the property included in the decedent's estate. Any deductions for depreciation allowed to the surviving owner for his portion of the property are subtracted from the sum.

If a property is jointly held between a husband and wife as tenants by the entirety, or as joint tenants with the right of survivorship, one-half of the property's value is included in the gross estate, and there is a step-up in basis for that one-half. The other half is stated at the surviving spouse's cost basis, net of any deductions for depreciation allowed to the surviving spouse on that half. If the decedent holds property in a community property state, half of the value of the community property will be included in the gross estate of the decedent, but the entire value of the community property will receive a step-up in basis.

Example: Bong-Cha and Hyun-Shik are married and live in Texas, which is a community property state. They hold their personal residence as community property. They purchased it for $450,000 five years ago. Bong-Cha dies on December 15, 2020, and the house is valued at $630,000 on the date of her death. Hyun-Shik's basis in the house is now $630,000. The entire house gets a step-up in basis to the FMV on the date of one spouse's death because it was held as community property. If Hyun-Shik sells the home at a later date, he would use $630,000 as his basis for determining whether or not he has any gain on the sale.

The Estate Tax

The estate tax may apply to the decedent's taxable estate, which is the gross estate minus any allowable deductions. In 2020, an estate valued at less than $11.58 million would generally not be taxable or have an estate tax return filing requirement. However, this threshold is much lower for nonresident aliens at $60,000.

Example: Fabio is a U.S. citizen who dies on April 3, 2020. The FMV of all his assets on the date of his death totals 8 million dollars, therefore, his estate is not subject to estate tax. Form 706 does not need to be filed. His executor may be required to file a final Form 1040 for the income that Fabio earned while he was alive (from January 1 to April 3, 2020). A Form 1041 may need to be filed if the estate earns gross income of $600 or more in 2020.

Example: Daeshim is a citizen and resident of South Korea. Daeshim is a popular Korean recording artist, and his travels bring him to the U.S. quite frequently. Daeshim owns a vacation home in Hollywood, CA, which he uses at least once a year to entertain his celebrity guests. When he is not in the U.S., he uses a management company to rent out the home to short-term tenants. Daeshim dies on November 15, 2020. The Hollywood vacation home is the only U.S. asset that Daeshim owned. The house's FMV on the date of his death was approximately $450,000. Since Daeshim is a nonresident for U.S. tax purposes, his estate has a filing requirement. His executor must file Form 706-NA and report the value of the asset and pay any estate taxes owed.

Generation-Skipping Transfer Tax (GST)

In the past, wealthy families used various strategies to transfer wealth and assets to their grandchildren and other descendants. In response to this, Congress created the generation-skipping transfer tax, also known as the GST, to close this tax loophole.

The generation-skipping transfer tax (GST) may apply to gifts during a taxpayer's lifetime or transfers occurring after his death, called bequests, made to "skip persons." A skip person is usually a grandchild, but it also applies to those who are more than 37½ years younger than the person making the gift or bequest. The most common scenario is when a taxpayer makes a gift to a grandchild.

The GST is assessed when the property transfer is made, including instances in which property is transferred from a trust. The GST is based on the amounts transferred to skip persons, after subtracting the allocated portions of the donor's available GST exemption. The GST exemption is the same as the estate tax basic exclusion amount, and the GST tax rate is set at the estate tax rates, with a maximum of 40%. The GST is imposed separately and in *addition* to the estate and gift taxes.

Example: Roosevelt sets up a trust that names his adult daughter, Nannette, as the sole beneficiary of the trust. On January 10, 2020, Roosevelt dies, and the trust passes to Nannette. However, on June 1, 2020, Nannette also dies, and the trust passes to her children (Roosevelt's grandchildren). Roosevelt's grandchildren are skip persons for purposes of the GST, and the trust's property may now be subject to the GST.

Any payments for tuition or medical expenses on behalf of a skip person that are made directly to an educational or medical institution are exempt from gift tax and GST. There is no reporting requirement for this type of gift, regardless of the dollar amount.

Example: Melton wants to help support his grandchildren, but he tries to make sure that his gifts are not subject to gift tax, GST, or estate tax. In 2020, he pays his grandchild's college tuition in full and writes a check directly to the college for $25,000. Since the amounts were paid directly to the college, there is no tax consequence for this gift, and no additional reporting is required.

The Gift Tax

The gift tax may apply to the transfer of property by one individual to another, whether the donor intends the transfer to be a gift or not. Gift tax is imposed on the *donor*, not the *receiver*, of the property. The recipient of a gift typically owes no taxes and does have to report the gift unless it comes from a foreign donor. However, under special arrangements, the donee may *agree* to pay the tax instead of the donor.

As discussed previously, an individual taxpayer's liability for estate tax and gift tax is subject to a combined basic exclusion amount ($11.58 million in 2020), and the use of any portion of this exclusion amount to reduce payment of gift taxes during the taxpayer's lifetime will reduce the amount available upon death to reduce applicable estate taxes. The following gifts are not taxable:

- Gifts to an individual that do not exceed the annual exclusion amount. In 2020, the gift exclusion amount is $15,000 per donee.
- Tuition or medical expenses paid directly to the educational or medical institution for someone else.
- Unlimited gifts to a spouse, as long as the spouse is a U.S. citizen.
- Gifts to a political organization for its use.
- Gifts to a qualifying charity.
- A parent's support for a minor child. This may include support required as part of a legal obligation, such as by a divorce decree.

Example: Mack is 26, and Lynette is his mother. Lynette gives her son, Mack, a gift of $15,000 of cash during the year. She also pays his college tuition, totaling $21,000, and writes the check directly to the college. Lynette also pays for Mack's medical bills by issuing an $18,000 check directly to his doctor's office. None of these gifts are taxable, and no gift tax return is required.

Example: Andrew is single. In 2020, Andrew gives his nephew, Jimmy, $39,000 to help start his first business. The money is intended as a gift, not a loan, so Andrew is required to file a gift tax return (Form 709) since the amount exceeds the annual exclusion amount.

Gift taxes are reported on Form 709, *United States Gift (and Generation-Skipping Transfer) Tax Return*. Form 709 must be filed if:

- A taxpayer gives more than the annual exclusion amount to at least one individual (except to a U.S. citizen spouse),
- A taxpayer "splits gifts" with a spouse,
- A taxpayer gives a future interest to anyone other than a U.S. citizen spouse.

If a gift tax return is required to be filed, Form 709 is generally due by April 15 of the following year. However, if the donor dies during the year, the filing deadline may be the due date (with extensions) for his estate tax return, if earlier than April 15 of the following year. Taxpayers who extend the filing of Form 1040 for six months using Form 4868 are deemed to have extended their gift tax returns, if no gift tax is due with the extension.

If the taxpayer does not extend their individual return, the gift tax return can be extended separately by using Form 8892, *Application for Automatic Extension of Time to File Form 709 and/or Payment of Gift/Generation-Skipping Transfer Tax.*

Note: A gift is considered a **present interest** if the donee has all immediate rights to the use, possession, and enjoyment of the property or income from the property, with no strings attached. A gift is considered a **future interest** if the donee's rights to the use, possession, and enjoyment of the property or income from the property will not begin until some future date. A gift of a future interest cannot be excluded under the annual exclusion ($15,000 per donee in 2020). With a "future interest" the beneficiary typically does not become the owner of the property until the donor's death.

Example: Shepard creates an irrevocable trust for the beneficial enjoyment of Bethany, who is his girlfriend. Shepard transfers an office building to the trust. The office building is currently rented to business tenants and is subject to a mortgage. The terms of the trust provides that the rental income from the property will first be used to pay off the mortgage. After the mortgage is paid in full, the net rental income is then to be paid to Bethany. Since Bethany's right to receive the rental income will not begin until *after* the mortgage is paid in full, the transfer in trust represents a gift of a future interest.

Applying the Applicable Credit to Gift Tax: After a taxpayer determines which of his gifts are taxable, he must calculate the amount of gift tax on the total taxable gifts and apply the applicable credit for the year.

Gift Splitting by Married Couples

Both the basic exclusion amount and the annual exclusion amount apply separately to each spouse, and each spouse must separately file a gift tax return if he or she made reportable gifts during the year. However, if either spouse makes a gift to another person, the gift can be considered as being one-half from one spouse and one-half from the other spouse. This concept is known as *gift splitting.*

Gift splitting allows a married couple to give up to $30,000 (in 2020) to a single individual without making a taxable gift. Both spouses must consent to split the gift.

Example: Ignacio and his wife, Elinda, agree to split gifts of cash. Ignacio gives his friend a check for $21,000, and Elinda gives her niece a check for $18,000. Although each gift is more than the annual exclusion amount of $15,000, they can use gift splitting to avoid making a taxable gift to each donee. In each case, because one-half of the split gift is not more than the annual exclusion amount, it is not taxable. A gift tax return is required.

Example: Gertrude gives her favorite cousin, Freddie, $25,000. Gertrude elects to split the gift with her husband, Maurizio, and Maurizio is treated as if he gave Freddie half the amount, or $12,500. Assuming they make no other gifts to Freddie during the year, the entire $25,000 gift is tax-free. However, a gift tax return is required in order to report the "split gift."

Note: A married couple can avoid filing a gift tax return if they each make a gift separately, such as by writing separate checks or giving separate property. In the example above, if each spouse had written separate checks for less than $15,000 each, then a gift tax return would not be required.

If a married couple splits a gift, each spouse must generally file his or her own individual gift tax return. However, certain exceptions may apply that allow for only one spouse to file a return if the other spouse signifies consent on the donor spouse's Form 709. Note that if gifts are made by a spouse from community property funds, the gift is deemed to have been made 50% by each spouse.

Basis of Property Received as a Gift

For purposes of determining gain or loss on a subsequent disposition of property received as a gift, a taxpayer must consider:

- The gift's adjusted basis to the donor just before it was given to the taxpayer,
- The gift's FMV at the time it was given to the taxpayer, and
- Any gift tax actually paid on the appreciation of the property's value while held by the donor (as opposed to gift tax offset by the donor's applicable credit amount).

If the FMV of the gift was equal to or greater than the donor's adjusted basis in the gift right before the transfer, the donee's basis will be the donor's basis (transferred basis), adjusted for any gift tax paid on the donor's appreciation. If the FMV of the gift was less than the donor's adjusted basis in the gift right before the transfer:

- When the donee sells the property received as a gift, he calculates gain based upon the donor's adjusted basis.
- If the donee sells the property at a loss, the taxpayer's basis would be the FMV at the time of the gift.
- If the donee sells the property at a price higher than the FMV at the time of the gift, but lower than the donor's adjusted basis at the time of the gift, the basis at the time of the sale will be the sales price, resulting in no gain or loss on the sale.

Example: Donovan gives his son, Maurice, 20 shares of stock on January 20, 2020. Donovan's basis in the stock is $500. Maurice's basis in the stock is also $500. This is called a "transferred basis."

Example: Manuela receives an acre of land as a gift from her brother. Her brother's adjusted basis in the land is $50,000, and its FMV on the date of the gift is $40,000 (it has dropped in value since he bought it). A year later, Manuela sells the gifted land for $35,000. Since she sold the property at a loss, her basis in the land is $40,000, because it is *lower* than her brother's adjusted basis and the FMV at the date of the gift.

Generally, the value of a gift is its fair market value on the date of the gift. However, the value of the gift may be less than its fair market value to the extent that the donee gives the donor something in return.

Example: Albus sells his son, Tanner, a house well below market value. Tanner only pays $10,000 for the house. In 2020, the fair market value of the house is $90,000. Therefore, Albus has made a gift to his son of $80,000 ($90,000 - $10,000 = $80,000). Albus is required to file a gift tax return because the gift exceeds the $15,000 threshold for 2020.

The Unified Credit (the Applicable Credit)

A taxpayer's gross estate tax is reduced by the *applicable credit*, also referred to as the *unified credit*. The unified credit is the combination of the lifetime gift tax exclusion and estate tax exclusion. For the 2020 tax year, the estate tax exclusion is $11.58 million for single filers. The basic credit amount for 2020 is $4,577,800.

Note: For taxable gifts, each taxpayer has an aggregate lifetime exemption before any out-of-pocket gift tax is due. For example, a taxpayer can give away up to $11.58 million during their lifetime *above* the annual $15,000 exclusion and still avoid paying any gift tax.

Just as with the basic exclusion amount, any portion of the applicable credit amount used to avoid payment of gift taxes reduces the amount of credit available in later years that can be used to offset gift or estate taxes.

For example, if a taxpayer exceeds the annual gift tax exclusion amount in any year, the taxpayer can choose to either pay the gift tax on the excess or take advantage of the unified credit to avoid paying the tax in the current year.

Example: Adelle, who was single, died in 2020 and left an estate valued at $20 million. During her lifetime, she had used $1 million of her basic exclusion to offset payments of gift tax. That reduces the amount her estate may exclude to $10.58 million, which is then subtracted from her $20 million taxable estate, to determine that amount of her estate subject to the estate tax.

Unit 18: Study Questions

(Test yourself first, then check the correct answers at the end of this quiz.)

1. Maximo is a legal U.S. resident (a green card holder). He dies on May 1, 2020, and leaves his entire estate to his wife, Jeanne, who is a U.S. citizen. Maximo's estate is valued at $50 million on the date of his death. What amount of tax must Jeanne pay on her late husband's estate in 2020?

A. $0
B. $15.52 million.
C. $20.4 million.
D. $38.82 million.

2. Claude dies on May 4, 2020. His assets are valued at $40 million on the date of his death, so a Form 706 needs to be filed for his estate. When is the estate tax return due?

A. November 4, 2021.
B. November 5, 2021.
C. February 4, 2021.
D. April 15, 2021.

3. Eileen's aunt gives her a gift of a "future interest" on her estate. Eileen will have full use of the estate after her aunt dies. Which is the correct statement about this gift?

A. Eileen's aunt can use the annual gift tax exclusion for this gift.
B. The gift is considered a present interest.
C. Eileen must pay estate tax on the gift.
D. Eileen's aunt cannot use the annual gift tax exclusion for this gift.

4. Shawn, a single taxpayer, has never been required to file a gift tax return. In 2020, Shawn gave the following gifts:

- Tuition paid directly to a state university for his nephew: $18,000.
- Payment to General Hospital for his brother's medical bills: $15,500.
- Cash donation to a homeless shelter, a qualified 501(c)(3) organization: $50,000.
- Gift paid to the Libertarian Party (not a qualified charity): $25,000.

Is Shawn required to file a gift tax return for 2020?

A. No
B. Yes, because the donation to the political party is not an excludable gift.
C. Yes, because each of the gifts exceeded $15,000.
D. Yes, because the political gift is a reportable transaction.

5. All of the following tax returns may include income in respect of a decedent (IRD) *except*:

A. The final Form 1040 for the decedent.
B. The decedent's estate, Form 1041, if the decedent's estate receives right to the income.
C. The Form 1040 of any person to whom the estate properly distributes the income.
D. A beneficiary's Form 1040, if the right to income arising out of the decedent's death is passed directly to the beneficiary and is never acquired by the decedent's estate.

6. Cash inheritances are generally:

A. Taxable to the beneficiary for any amount
B. Taxable to the beneficiary for amounts over $15,000
C. Taxable to the beneficiary for amounts over $5 million
D. Not taxable to the beneficiary for any amount

7. When is an estate tax return (Form 706) due?

A. Four months after the close of the taxable year.
B. Six months after the close of the calendar year.
C. Nine months after the date of death.
D. Twelve months after the date of death.

8. Ahmed, age 73, died in 2020, after a long battle with Alzheimer's disease. At the time of his death, he had assets of $14 million and owed a mortgage totaling $2,500,000. He also had outstanding medical debts of $300,000 that were unpaid at the time of his death. He had not used any of his basic exclusion amount during his lifetime. Based upon the information provided, what is the *taxable* amount of Ahmed's estate that must be reported on Form 706?

A. $0
B. $4 million.
C. $4.5 million.
D. $5 million.

9. Delia's estate has funeral expenses for the cost of her burial. How should the executor deduct these costs?

A. Funeral expenses are an itemized deduction on Form 1040.
B. Funeral expenses are deducted on Form 1041.
C. Funeral expenses are deducted on Form 706.
D. Funeral expenses are a non-deductible expense.

10. In general, who is responsible for paying gift tax?

A. The estate.
B. The donor.
C. The gift recipient.
D. The executor.

11. Cullen died in 2020. Following his death, the executor of his estate paid the following bills. Which of these is not an allowable deduction in determining Cullen's taxable estate?

A. Estate administration expenses, including lawyer's fees.
B. State inheritance taxes.
C. Charitable contributions.
D. Alimony paid after the taxpayer's death.

12. Alana had gifts totaling $48,000 in 2020 that were subject to gift tax. Assuming no extensions are filed, when is her gift tax return due?

A. March 15, 2021.
B. April 15, 2021.
C. October 15, 2021.
D. December 15, 2021.

13. Which of the following statements concerning the deceased spousal unused exclusion (DSUE) is correct?

A. The DSUE allows an unlimited estate tax deduction for a surviving spouse.
B. The predeceased spouse must have died from natural causes.
C. The maximum DSUE available for a spouse who dies in 2020 is $15,000.
D. A portability election can only be made by filing Form 706.

14. Leighton received 100 shares of stock as an inheritance from her brother, who died on January 6, 2020. Her brother's adjusted basis in the stock was $10,750. The stock's fair market value on the date of her brother's death was $26,200. The executor of the estate elects the alternate valuation date for valuing the gross estate. Six months later, on July 6, 2020, the stock's fair market value had dropped to $23,100. Leighton finally received the stock on August 26, 2020, when its fair market value was $23,500. She sold the stock a week later for $23,450. What is Leighton's basis in the inherited stock, in order to determine her taxable gain on the sale?

A. $10,750
B. $22,200
C. $23,100
D. $23,450

15. The executor of Ophelia's estate is her sister, Elise. Elise decides to make a distribution of 100% of the estate's assets before paying the estate's income tax liability. Which of the following statements is correct?

A. The beneficiaries of the estate can be held liable for the payment of the liability, even if the liability exceeds the value of the estate assets.
B. No one can be held liable for the tax if the assets have been distributed.
C. Elise and the beneficiaries can be held liable for the tax debt, up to the value of the assets distributed.
D. None of the above.

16. Sandy and Matthew are married and have combined assets of $15 million. They are both U.S. citizens. On May 10, 2020, Sandy dies. The FMV of Sandy's estate is $5 million on the date of her death. Matthew is the executor of his wife's estate and her sole beneficiary. Since the value of Sandy's estate was below the $11.58 million threshold, Matthew decides not to file an estate tax return, and he declines to take the portability election. What future impact does this have on Matthew, the surviving spouse?

A. There is no taxable effect on Matthew in this scenario.
B. Since Matthew declined to file an estate tax return, he did not elect portability. There will be estate tax due upon Matthew's death, assuming that the value of his assets does not decline, and there will be no deductions for estate tax purposes.
C. Matthew will owe estate tax in 2020 on his inheritance.
D. Sandy's estate will owe estate tax in 2020. Her estate tax return must be filed by the executor.

17. Emma's father dies during the year. Emma is the sole beneficiary of her father's traditional IRA. Emma is 46 years old when she takes possession of her father's IRA. Which of the following statements is correct about the distributions from the inherited IRA account?

A. Emma can avoid taxation by rolling over the IRA to her own IRA account.
B. Any distributions are taxable to Emma but not subject to an early withdrawal penalty.
C. Any tax on the distributions must be paid from her father's estate.
D. The distributions are taxable to Emma, and also subject to an early withdrawal penalty because Emma is younger than 59½.

18. Bruno pays $19,000 of college tuition for his granddaughter, Margaret, directly to her college. Which of the following statements is correct?

A. The gift is taxable, and Margaret must report the gift tax on her individual tax return.
B. The gift is not taxable, but Bruno must file a gift tax return.
C. The gift is taxable, and Bruno must file a gift tax return.
D. The gift is not taxable, and no gift tax return is required.

19. Which of the following items is not an allowable deduction from the gross estate?

A. Debts owed at the time of death.
B. Medical expenses of the decedent.
C. Funeral expenses of the decedent.
D. Federal estate tax.

20. Which of the following is *not* income in respect of a decedent (IRD)?

A. Wages earned before death but still unpaid at the time of death.
B. Vacation time paid after death.
C. IRA funds that were distributed before the taxpayer's death, but not received until after death.
D. A royalty check that was received before death but not cashed.

21. In which case must a gift tax return be filed?

A. A married couple gives a gift of $15,000 to an unrelated person.
B. A married couple gives a gift of $35,000 to a related person with a single check.
C. A single individual gives a gift of $14,000 to an unrelated person.
D. A wife gives a gift of $20,000 to her husband who is a U.S. citizen.

22. All of the following gifts are excluded from the determination of the gift tax except:

A. A gift made to a political organization.
B. A cash gift given to a nonresident alien spouse of a U.S. citizen.
C. A medical bill paid directly to a hospital on behalf of a relative.
D. A gift made to a qualifying charity.

23. Esther is the executor for her father's estate. He died on November 5, 2020. Which of the following dates may she elect to use as an alternate valuation date for his estate?

A. December 31, 2020.
B. April 15, 2021.
C. May 5, 2021.
D. October 15, 2021.

24. Jeffrey gives $26,000 to his friend, Rachel. Which of the following statements is correct?

A. The first $15,000 of the gift is not subject to the gift tax, but the remainder is subject to gift tax, and Rachel is responsible for paying it.
B. Rachel is required to file a gift tax return and pay tax on the entire gift.
C. Jeffrey is required to file a gift tax return, Form 709.
D. Jeffrey may choose to report the gift on his individual Form 1040, Schedule A.

25. Mildred died on February 20, 2020. Her estate is valued at $24 million, so an estate tax return must be filed. Which of the following assets would *not* be included in the calculation of her gross estate?

A. Life insurance proceeds payable to Mildred's children.
B. The value of real property transferred to Mildred's son five years before her death.
C. The value of property owned jointly by Mildred and her spouse.
D. The value of Mildred's traditional IRA.

Unit 18: Quiz Answers

1. The answer is A. Jeanne will owe no estate taxes related to the value of Maximo's estate. The marital deduction allows for the transfer of an unlimited value of property from one spouse to another during his lifetime or from his estate after death without being subject to gift or estate taxes. To qualify for this unlimited deduction, the spouse receiving the assets must be a U.S. citizen and a legal spouse and must have outright ownership of the assets.

2. The answer is C. The estate tax return for Claude's estate is due on February 4, 2021. If required to be filed, Form 706, *United States Estate (and Generation-Skipping Transfer) Tax Return,* must be filed nine months *after* the date of a decedent's death. Any estate tax would be owed at this time. An executor may request a six-month extension to file Form 706, but the tax would still be owed on the earlier date.

3. The answer is D. A gift of a future interest cannot be excluded under the annual exclusion ($15,000 per person in 2020). A gift is considered a present interest if the donee has all immediate rights to the use, possession, and enjoyment of the property or income from the property. A gift is considered a future interest if the donee's rights to the use, possession, and enjoyment of the property or income from the property will not begin until some future date. "Future interests" include: reversions, remainders, and other similar interests or estates.

4. The answer is A. Shawn is not required to file a gift tax return. None of the gifts are taxable gifts, and therefore, no reporting is required. Tuition or medical expenses paid for someone directly to an educational or medical institution are not counted as taxable gifts. Nor are gifts to a political organization or gifts to a qualified charity.

5. The answer is A. The final Form 1040 for the decedent would not include IRD.

6. The answer is D. For federal income tax purposes, cash inheritances are generally not taxable to the beneficiary, although the beneficiary may be responsible for a related estate tax liability that has not been satisfied.

7. The answer is C. Estate tax returns are due nine months from the date of death, although the executor may request an extension of time to file.

8. The answer is A. After calculating allowable deductions from the gross estate, Ahmed's net estate is valued at $11.2 million. This amount is less than the basic exclusion amount of $11.58 million for 2020, so no estate tax is applicable in this case. However, because the gross value of the estate is more than 11.58 million, an estate tax return (Form 706) is required to be filed.

FMV of Assets	$14,000,000
Mortgage debt	($2,500,000)
Medical debt	($300,000)
Net Estate	$11,200,000

9. The answer is C. No deduction for Delia's funeral expenses can be taken on Form 1041 or Form 1040. Funeral expenses may be claimed only as a deduction from the gross estate on Form 706. If an estate tax return is not filed, then the funeral expenses are not deductible.

10. The answer is B. The donor is generally responsible for paying gift tax. Under special arrangements the donee may *agree* to pay the tax instead.

11. The answer is D. Alimony paid after a taxpayer's death is never deductible from the gross estate. It is merely considered a distribution to a beneficiary. Deductions from the gross estate are allowed for:

- Funeral expenses paid out of the estate and administration expenses for the estate.
- Debts owed at the time of death.
- Estate administration expenses.
- The marital deduction, charitable deduction, and state death tax deduction.

12. The answer is B. Alana would be required to file her gift tax return by April 15, 2021, the filing deadline for individual returns. Gift tax returns are typically due on April 15 of the following calendar year (the individual filing deadline), and payment of the tax is also due then, although the filing may be subject to a six-month extension. If the donor died during the year, the filing deadline is the earlier of (1) the due date for his estate tax return (with extensions) or (2) April 15, 2021 (with a six-month extension available via a personal income tax return extension or by Form 8892).

13. The answer is D. The portability election allows a surviving spouse's estate the right to use a deceased spousal unused exclusion (DSUE), which is the remaining unused portion of the previously deceased spouse's basic exclusion amount. The portability election must be made by filing an estate tax return for the deceased spouse, even if no estate tax is owed.

14. The answer is C. Since the alternate valuation date was elected by the executor, Leighton's basis is the fair market value on the alternate valuation date, or $23,100. This is the basis that she must use in order to calculate her gain or loss on the sale of the stock. The basis of property received from a decedent is generally the fair market value of the property on the date of the decedent's death. However, an executor has the option of choosing an alternate valuation date, which is six months after the date of death for valuing the gross estate.

15. The answer is C. Elise and the beneficiaries can be held liable for the tax debt, up to the value of the assets distributed. The tax liability for an estate attaches to the assets of the estate itself. If the assets are distributed to the beneficiaries before the taxes are paid, the executor and the beneficiaries can be held liable for the tax debt, up to the value of the assets distributed.

16. The answer is B. Since Matthew declined to file an estate tax return, he did not elect portability. No estate tax is due after Sandy's death because the value of her estate is below the exclusion amount. However, all her assets passed to her surviving spouse. Matthew's estate is now in excess of the annual exclusion amount. Assuming there is no change in the value of Matthew's assets and no applicable deductions upon his passing, there will be estate tax due upon his death. He could have avoided this scenario if he had filed an estate tax return and elected portability.

17. The answer is B. Any IRA distributions from an inherited IRA are taxable to Emma, but not subject to an early withdrawal penalty. Distributions of retirement plan benefits or distributions from taxable IRA accounts to a decedent's beneficiaries are generally subject to income tax when received. The decedent's surviving spouse may be able to defer taxation by rolling over the assets of a taxable IRA to another IRA or to a qualified plan. However, a child or other beneficiary is not allowed this same treatment. Qualified distributions from a Roth IRA or of previously nondeductible contributions to a traditional IRA are generally not taxable.

18. The answer is D. Bruno does not have a gift tax return requirement. Tuition or medical expenses paid directly to a medical or educational institution for someone else are not included in the calculation of taxable gifts, and there is no reporting requirement.

19. The answer is D. Federal estate tax is not deductible from the gross estate. The other items listed are allowable deductions from the gross estate. The decedent's unpaid medical expenses represent liabilities that can be deducted from the gross estate. Alternatively, if the expenses are paid by the estate during the one-year period beginning with the day after death, the personal representative can elect to treat all or part of the expenses as paid by the decedent at the time they were incurred and deduct them on the decedent's final tax return (1040).

20. The answer is D. Since the royalty check was received before the taxpayer died, it is not considered IRD income. Income in respect of a decedent is taxable income earned but not received by the decedent by the time of death. The fact that the royalty check was not cashed has no bearing on the nature of the income, and it should be reported as taxable income on the decedent's final income tax return (Form 1040).

21. The answer is B. In order to make a gift to one individual in excess of the annual exclusion of $15,000 and avoid using any of their basic exclusion amounts; a married couple can use gift splitting. Gift splitting allows married couples to give up to $30,000 to a single person in 2020 without making a taxable gift, but they each must consent to the gift, and each may be required to file a gift tax return. Gifts to a spouse generally do not require a return to be filed, unless the spouse is not a U.S. citizen.

22. The answer is B. Although a full marital deduction is allowed for a spouse who is a U.S. citizen, a transfer of property to a noncitizen spouse is limited, and the excess amount would be subject to gift tax. Noncitizen spouses can only receive $157,000 in 2020. This is true even if the spouse is a legal U.S. resident (a green card holder).

23. The answer is C. Esther can choose an alternate valuation date of May 5, 2021. An estate is normally valued on the date of the decedent's death. However, an executor may elect, under certain requirements, an alternate valuation date for an estate, which would be six months after the date of death.

24. The answer is C. Jeffrey is required to file a gift tax return. Gift tax reporting must be done by the donor, not the recipient, of the gift. The first $15,000 of the gift is not subject to gift tax because of the annual exclusion. The remaining $11,000 will be shown as a net taxable gift on Form 709.

25. The answer is B. The value of property transferred to Mildred's son five years before her death would not be included in her gross estate. A taxpayer's gross estate includes the following:

- The FMV of all tangible and intangible property owned partially or outright by the decedent at the time of death.
- Life insurance proceeds payable to the estate or, for policies owned by the decedent, payable to the heirs or beneficiaries.
- The value of certain annuities or survivor benefits payable to the heirs or beneficiaries.
- The value of certain property transferred within three years before the taxpayer's death (not five years, as stated in answer B).

This page intentionally left blank.

Index

D

E

F

G

H

I

J

K

L

M

N

O

P

Q

R

S

T

U

V

W

About the Authors

Joel Busch, CPA, JD

Joel Busch is a tax professor at San Jose State University, where he teaches courses at both the graduate and undergraduate levels. Previously, he was in charge of tax audits, research, and planning for one of the largest civil construction and mining companies in the United States. He received both a BS in Accounting and a MS in Taxation from SJSU and he has a JD from the Monterey College of Law. He is licensed in California as both a CPA and an attorney.

Christy Pinheiro, EA, ABA®

Christy Pinheiro is an Enrolled Agent and an Accredited Business Accountant. Christy was an accountant for two private CPA firms and for the State of California before going into private practice.

Kolleen Wells, EA

Kolleen Wells is an Enrolled Agent and a Certified Bookkeeper who specializes in tax preparation for individuals and small businesses. She has worked in the accounting field for many years, including positions at a CPA office and at the county assessor's office.

Thomas A. Gorczynski, EA, USTCP

Thomas A. Gorczynski is an Enrolled Agent, a Certified Tax Planner, and admitted to the bar of the United States Tax Court. Tom is also a nationally known tax educator and currently serves as editor-in-chief of EA Journal. He received the 2019 Excellence in Education Award from the National Association of Enrolled Agents. He earned a Master of Science in Taxation from Golden Gate University and a Certificate in Finance and Accounting from the Wharton School at the University of Pennsylvania.

Made in the USA
Columbia, SC
16 May 2021

38028773R00248

Printed in the United States of America